Atlas content

GW00705992

Scale 1:250,000 or 3.95 miles to 1

Distances and journey times	inside front cover

Route planning	**2–24**
Route planner	2–7
Road safety and fixed speed cameras	8–9
Channel hopping	10–11
Ferries to Ireland and the Isle of Man	12–13
Caravan and camping sites in Britain	14–17
Tourist sites with satnav friendly postcodes	18–19
Traffic signs and road markings	20–23
Map pages	24

Road map symbols	**1**

Road maps	**2–115**
Britain 1:250,000 scale	**2–111**
Some islands are shown at slightly smaller scales.	
Ireland 1:1,000,000 scale	112–115

Motorways	**116–121**
Restricted junctions	116–119
M25 London orbital	120
M6 Toll motorway	121

Street map symbols	**122**

Towns and ports	**123–135**

District maps	**136–147**
Birmingham	136–137
Glasgow	138–139
Manchester	140–141
Newcastle	142–143
London	144–147

Central London	**148–165**
Central London street map	148–157
Central London index	158–165

Index to place names	**166–200**
County, administrative area map	166
Place name index	167–200

AA promotions	inside back cover

33rd edition June 2010

© AA Media Limited 2010

Revised version of the atlas formerly known as *Complete Atlas of Britain*. Original edition printed 1979.

Cartography:
All cartography in this atlas edited, designed and produced by the Mapping Services Department of AA Publishing (A04366).

 This product includes mapping data licensed from Ordnance Survey® with the permission of the Controller of Her Majesty's Stationery Office. © Crown copyright 2010. All rights reserved. Licence number 100021153.

 Land & Property Services. This is based upon Crown Copyright and is reproduced with the permission of Land and Property Services under delegated authority from the Controller of Her Majesty's Stationery Office, © Crown copyright and database rights 2010. Licence No. 100363. Permit No. 90174.

 Ordnance Survey *Ireland's National Mapping Agency* © Ordnance Survey Ireland/ Government of Ireland Copyright Permit No. MP000110.

This product includes map data from Mountain High Maps® Copyright© 1993 Digital Wisdom Inc.

Publisher's Notes:
Published by AA Publishing (a trading name of AA Media Limited, whose registered office is Fanum House, Basing View, Basingstoke, Hampshire RG21 4EA, UK. Registered number 06112600).

All rights reserved. No part of this publication may be reproduced, stored in a retrieval system, or transmitted in any form or by any means – electronic, mechanical, photocopying, recording or otherwise – unless the permission of the publisher has been given beforehand.

ISBN: 978 0 7495 6621 0

A CIP catalogue record for this book is available from The British Library.

Disclaimer:
The contents of this atlas are believed to be correct at the time of the latest revision, it will not contain any subsequent amended, new or temporary information including diversions and traffic control or enforcement systems. The publishers cannot be held responsible or liable for any loss or damage occasioned to any person acting or refraining from action as a result of any use or reliance on material in this atlas, nor for any errors, omissions or changes in such material. This does not affect your statutory rights.

The publishers would welcome information to correct any errors or omissions and to keep this atlas up to date.

Please write to the Atlas Editor, AA Publishing, The Automobile Association, Fanum House, Basing View, Basingstoke, Hampshire RG21 4EA, UK.
E-mail: *roadatlasfeedback@theaa.com*

Acknowledgements:
AA Publishing would like to thank the following for their assistance in producing this atlas:

RoadPilot® Information on fixed speed camera locations provided by RoadPilot © 2010 RoadPilot® Driving Technology. Information on truckstops and transport cafés kindly provided by John Eden (*www.transportcafe.co.uk*). Crematoria data provided by the Cremation Society of Great Britain. Cadw, English Heritage, English Nature, Forestry Commission, Historic Scotland, Johnsons, National Trust and National Trust for Scotland, RSPB, Scottish Natural Heritage, The Countryside Agency, The Countryside Council for Wales (road maps).

Crown copyright material (pages 8, 20–23) reproduced under licence from the Controller of HMSO and the Driving Standards Agency.

Education Direct, Johnsons, The Post Office, Transport for London (Central London Map).

Nexus (Newcastle district map).

Printer:
 **Mixed Sources** Product group from well-managed forests, controlled sources and recycled wood or fiber www.fsc.org Cert no. INV-COC-070402 © 1996 Forest Stewardship Council Printed in Italy by Canale & C. S.p.A., Torino, on F.S.C. accredited paper. Paper: 90gsm Matt Coated.

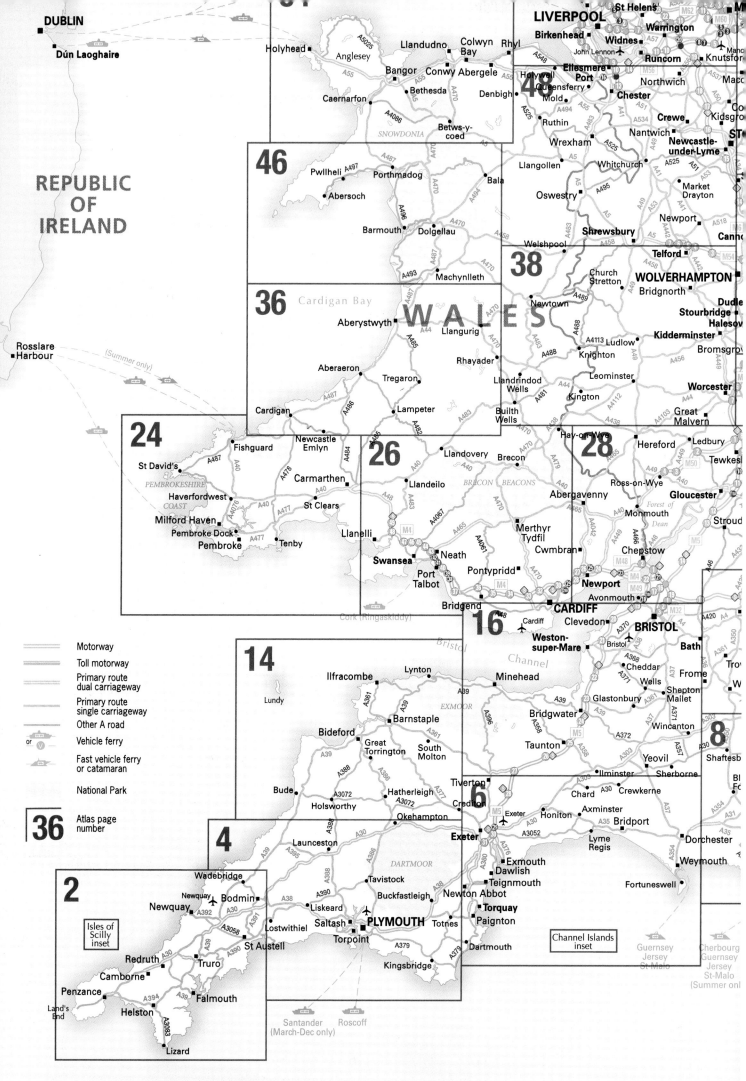

Motorway

Toll motorway

Primary route dual carriageway

Primary route single carriageway

Other A road

Vehicle ferry

Fast vehicle ferry or catamaran

National Park

36 Atlas page number

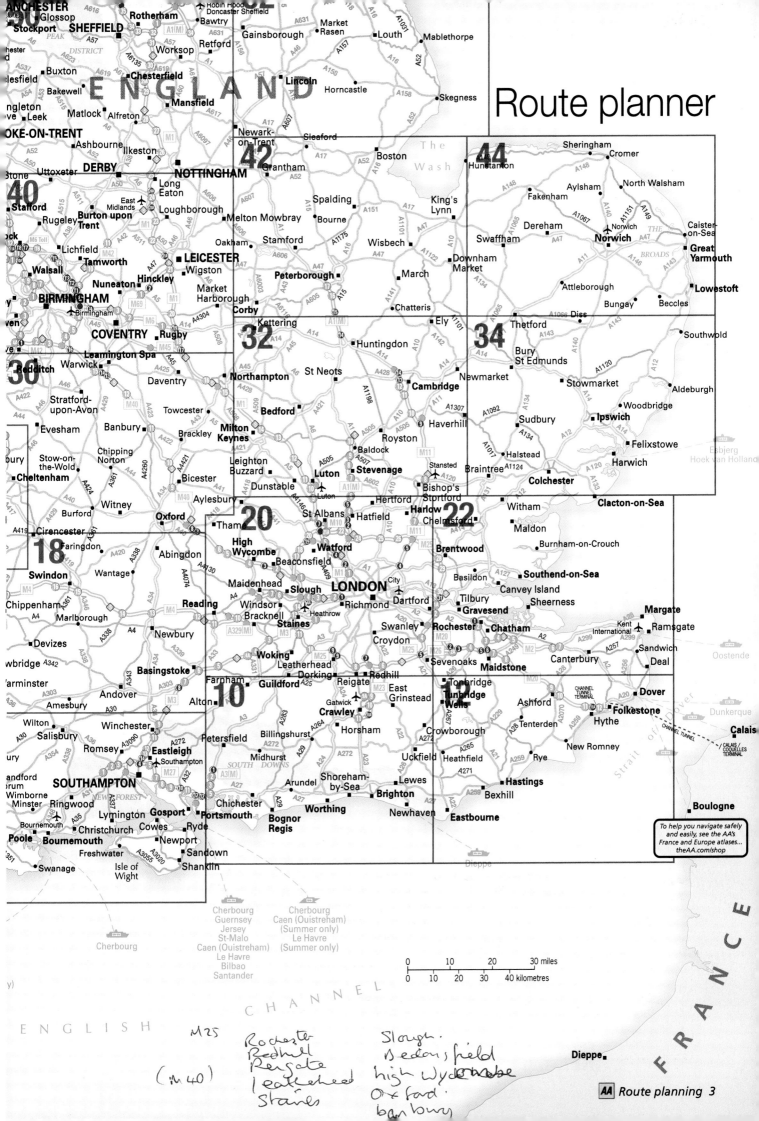

Route planner

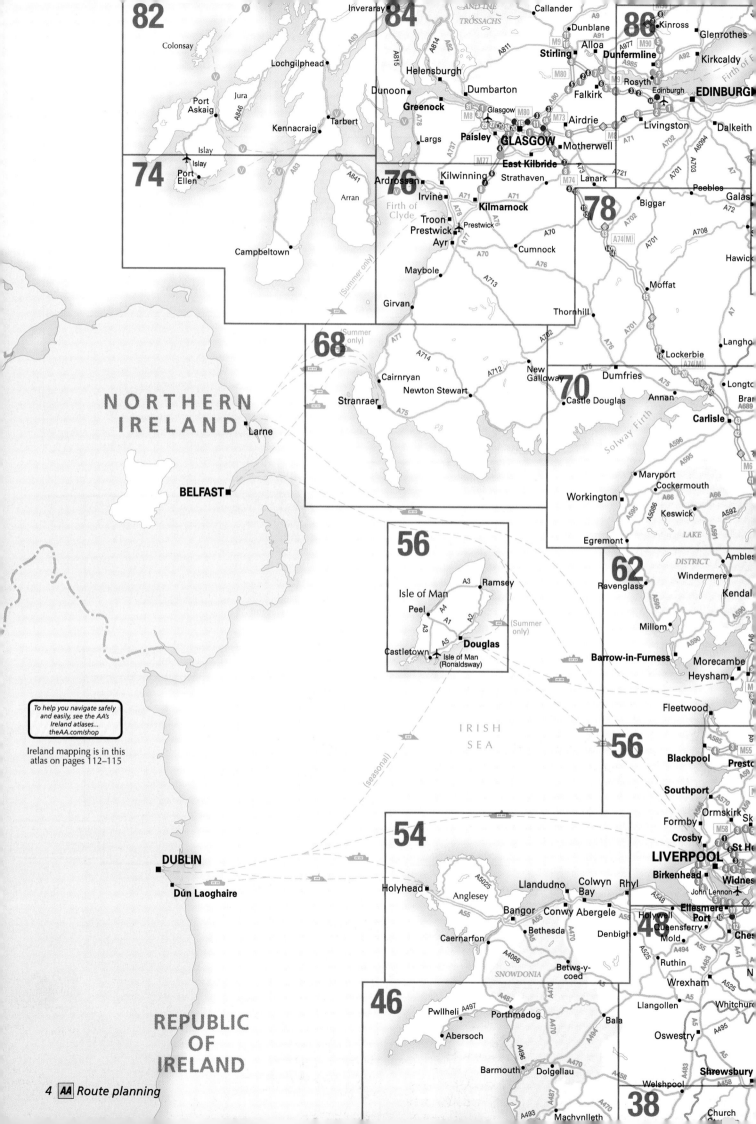

82

Colonsay

Lochgilphead

Port Askaig

Jura

A846

Kennacraig

Tarbert

Islay

Islay

Port Ellen

74

Campbeltown

Arran

NORTHERN IRELAND

Larne

BELFAST

To help you navigate safely and easily, see the AA's Ireland atlases...
theAA.com/shop

Ireland mapping is in this atlas on pages 112–115

DUBLIN

Dún Laoghaire

REPUBLIC OF IRELAND

Inveraray

84

Helensburgh

Dunoon

Greenock

Largs

Paisley

GLASGOW

East Kilbride

Dumbarton

A811

Callander

Dunblane

Stirling

Alloa

M9

Dunfermline

Falkirk

Airdrie

Motherwell

86

Kinross

Glenrothes

Kirkcaldy

Rosyth

Edinburgh

EDINBURGH

Livingston

Dalkeith

76

Ardrossan

Kilwinning

Irvine

Kilmarnock

Troon

Prestwick

Prestwick

Ayr

Maybole

Girvan

Strathaven

Lanark

A71

A70

Cumnock

A76

A713

Thornhill

78

A74(M)

Biggar

Peebles

Galas

A72

Hawick

Langho

Moffat

68

(Summer only)

A77

Cairnryan

Newton Stewart

Stranraer

A75

A714

A712

New Galloway

70

Dumfries

Castle Douglas

A75

Annan

Lockerbie

A74(M)

Longto

Bran

Carlisle

Solway Firth

Maryport

Cockermouth

Workington

Keswick

Egremont

LAKE

56

Isle of Man

Peel

A4

A3

Ramsey

A1

A2

Castletown

A5

Douglas

Isle of Man (Ronaldsway)

62

Ravenglass

Windermere

Kendal

Millom

DISTRICT

Ambles

A6

Barrow-in-Furness

Morecambe

Heysham

Fleetwood

IRISH SEA

(seasonal)

54

Holyhead

Anglesey

Bangor

Caernarfon

Llandudno

Conwy

Abergele

Bethesda

Betws-y-coed

SNOWDONIA

46

Pwllheli

A497

Abersoch

Porthmadog

Barmouth

Dolgellau

A470

Machynlleth

56

Blackpool

Southport

Formby

Crosby

LIVERPOOL

Birkenhead

Widnes

John Lennon

Ormskirk

M58

St He

Colwyn Bay

Rhyl

Denbigh

Holywell

Queensferry

Mold

Ruthin

Wrexham

Llangollen

Oswestry

Ellesmere Port

Ches

A494

Shrewsbury

Welshpool

Whitchur

Church

38

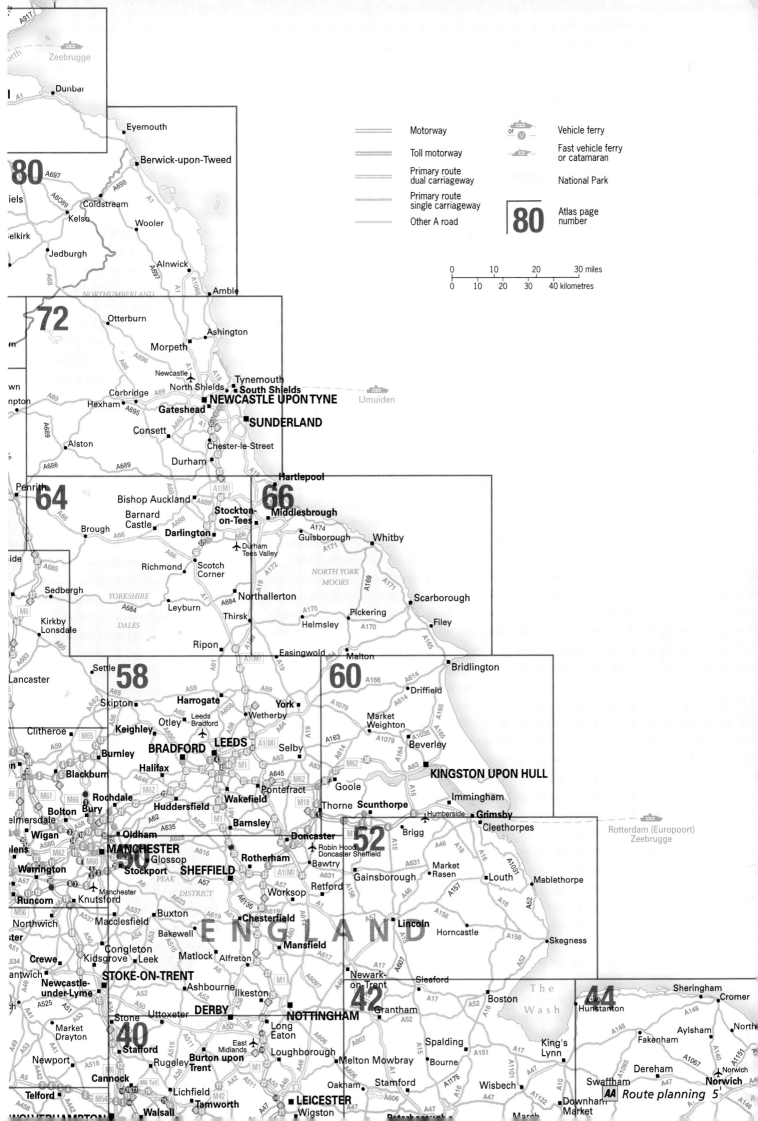

Legend

Motorway

Toll motorway

Primary route dual carriageway

Primary route single carriageway

Other A road

Vehicle ferry

Fast vehicle ferry or catamaran

National Park

80 Atlas page number

Scale: 0 10 20 30 miles / 0 10 20 30 40 kilometres

Zeebrugge
Dunbar
Eyemouth
Berwick-upon-Tweed
80 A697
Coldstream
Kelso
elkirk
Jedburgh
Wooler
Alnwick
A1068
Amble
NORTHUMBERLAND
72 Otterburn
Ashington
Morpeth
Newcastle
Tynemouth
North Shields
South Shields
Corbridge
Hexham
Gateshead
NEWCASTLE UPON TYNE
IJmuiden
Alston
Consett
SUNDERLAND
Chester-le-Street
Durham
Hartlepool
Penrith
64 Bishop Auckland
66
Middlesbrough
Barnard Castle
Stockton-on-Tees
Brough
Darlington
A174
Guisborough
Whitby
Durham Tees Valley
A171
Richmond
Scotch Corner
NORTH YORK MOORS
Sedbergh
YORKSHIRE
Northallerton
Scarborough
Kirkby Lonsdale
DALES
Leyburn
Thirsk
Pickering
Filey
Helmsley
A170
Ripon
Easingwold
Malton
Settle
58
60 A166
Bridlington
Lancaster
Skipton
Driffield
Harrogate
Wetherby
Market Weighton
Keighley
Otley
Leeds Bradford
York
Beverley
Clitheroe
BRADFORD
LEEDS
Selby
Burnley
Halifax
A1079
Blackburn
KINGSTON UPON HULL
Pontefract
Rochdale
Huddersfield
Wakefield
Goole
Immingham
Bury
Thorne
Humberside
Grimsby
Wigan
Oldham
Barnsley
Scunthorpe
Rotterdam (Europoort) Zeebrugge
MANCHESTER
Glossop
Doncaster
Robin Hood Doncaster Sheffield
52 Brigg
Cleethorpes
Stockport
PEAK
SHEFFIELD
Rotherham
Bawtry
Market Rasen
Louth
Warrington
Knutsford
Manchester
DISTRICT
Worksop
Retford
Mablethorpe
Runcorn
ENGLAND
Gainsborough
Northwich
Macclesfield
Buxton
Chesterfield
Lincoln
Horncastle
Skegness
Crewe
Congleton
Bakewell
Matlock
Alfreton
Mansfield
Kidsgrove
Leek
Newcastle-under-Lyme
STOKE-ON-TRENT
Newark-on-Trent
Sleaford
Boston
The Wash
44 Sheringham
Cromer
Market Drayton
Ashbourne
Ilkeston
DERBY
42
Grantham
Hunstanton
Aylsham
Newport
40
East Midlands
NOTTINGHAM
Spalding
King's Lynn
Fakenham
Dereham
Stafford
Long Eaton
Loughborough
Bourne
Stamford
Swaffham
Norwich
Cannock
Rugeley
Burton upon Trent
Melton Mowbray
Wisbech
Downham Market
Telford
Lichfield
Oakham
Stamford
WOLVERHAMPTON
Walsall
Tamworth
LEICESTER
Wigston
Peterborough
March

AA *Route planning 5*

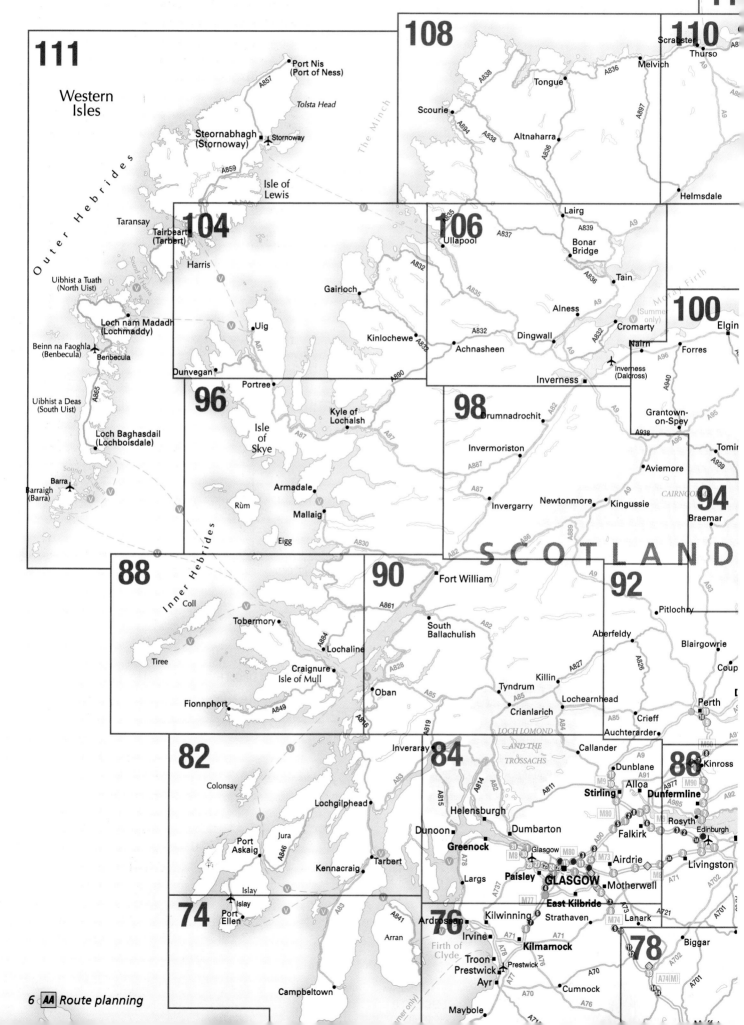

111

Western
Isles

Port Nis
(Port of Ness)

Tolsta Head

Steornabhagh
(Stornoway) ✈ Stornoway

Isle of
Lewis

Taransay

Tairbeart
(Tarbert)

Harris

Uibhist a Tuath
(North Uist)

Loch nam Madadh
(Lochmaddy)

Beinn na Faoghla
(Benbecula)
Benbecula

Uibhist a Deas
(South Uist)

Loch Baghasdail
(Lochboisdale)

Barra
Barraigh
(Barra) ✈

108

Scrabster
Thurso
Melvich

Tongue

Scourie

Altnaharra

The Minch

Helmsdale

110

11

104

Uig

Dunvegan

Portree

Gairloch

Kinlochewe

96

Isle
of
Skye

Armadale

Mallaig

Rùm

Eigg

Kyle of
Lochalsh

106

Ullapool

Achnasheen

Lairg
A839

Bonar
Bridge

Tain

Alness

Dingwall

Cromarty

Inverness

Nairn
Inverness
(Dalcross)

100

Elgin

Forres

Grantown-
on-Spey

Tomin

Moray Firth

98

Drumnadrochit

Invermoriston

Invergarry

Newtonmore

Kingussie

Aviemore

CAIRNGOR

94

Braemar

S C O T L A N D

88

Inner Hebrides

Coll

Tobermory

Lochaline

Tiree

Craignure
Isle of Mull

Fionnphort

90

Fort William

South
Ballachulish

Tyndrum

Crianlarich

Oban

92

Pitlochry

Aberfeldy

Blairgowrie

Killin

Lochearnhead

Crieff

Coup

Perth

82

Colonsay

Lochgilphead

Port
Askaig

Jura

Kennacraig

Islay

74

Islay
Port
Ellen

Arran

84

Inveraray

Helensburgh

Dunoon

Dumbarton

Greenock

Largs

Paisley

*LOCH LOMOND
AND THE
TROSSACHS*

Callander

Dunblane

Alloa

Stirling

Glasgow

Airdrie

GLASGOW

Motherwell

East Kilbride

86

Kinross

Dunfermline

Rosyth

Edinburgh

Falkirk

Livingston

Lanark

78

Biggar

76

Ardrossan

Kilwinning

Strathaven

Irvine

Kilmarnock

Troon
Prestwick ✈ Prestwick

Ayr

Cumnock

Maybole

Campbeltown

Tarbert

*Firth of
Clyde*

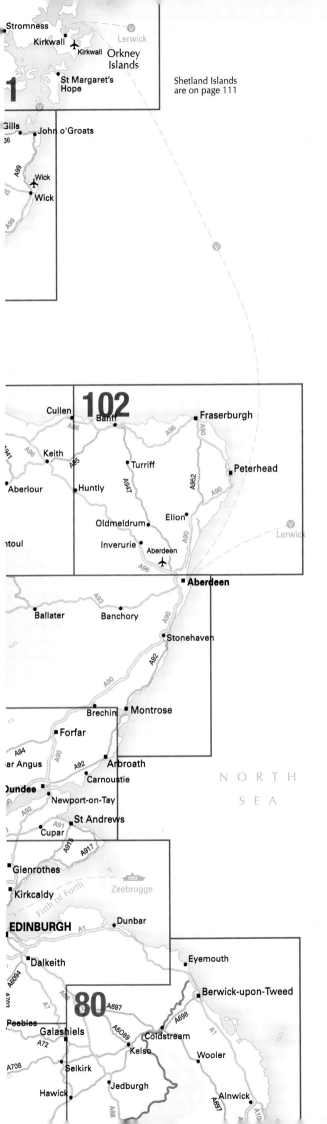

1

Stromness
Kirkwall
Kirkwall ✈
St Margaret's Hope

Orkney Islands

Shetland Islands are on page 111

Gills
John o'Groats
Wick ✈
Wick

102

Cullen
Banff
Fraserburgh
Keith
Turriff
Peterhead
Aberlour
Huntly
Oldmeldrum
Ellon
Inverurie
Aberdeen ✈
Lerwick

■ Aberdeen

Ballater
Banchory
Stonehaven

Brechin
Montrose
Forfar
ar Angus
Arbroath
Carnoustie
Dundee
Newport-on-Tay
St Andrews
Cupar

Glenrothes
Zeebrugge
Kirkcaldy
Firth of Forth

EDINBURGH
Dunbar
Dalkeith
Eyemouth

80
Berwick-upon-Tweed

Peebles
Galashiels
Coldstream
Kelso
Wooler
Selkirk
Hawick
Jedburgh
Alnwick

NORTH SEA

FERRY INFORMATION

Hebrides and west coast Scotland
calmac.co.uk	0800 066 5000
skyeferry.co.uk	01599 522 756
western-ferries.co.uk	01369 704 452

Orkney and Shetland
jogferry.co.uk	01955 611353
northlinkferries.co.uk	0845 6000 449
pentlandferries.co.uk	01856 831 226
orkneyferries.co.uk	01856 872 044
shetland.gov.uk/ferries	01595 693 535

Isle of Man
steam-packet.com	08722 992 992

Ireland
fastnetline.com	0844 576 8831
irishferries.com	08705 17 17 17
norfolkline.com	0844 499 0007
poirishsea.com	0871 664 4999
stenaline.co.uk	08705 70 70 70

North Sea (Scandinavia and Benelux)
dfdsseaways.co.uk	0871 522 9955
poferries.com	08716 645 645
norfolkline.com	0844 847 5042
stenaline.co.uk	08705 70 70 70

Isle of Wight
wightlink.co.uk	0871 376 1000
redfunnel.co.uk	0844 844 9988

Channel Islands
condorferries.co.uk	0845 609 1024

Channel hopping (France and Belgium)
brittany-ferries.co.uk	0871 244 0744
condorferries.co.uk	0845 609 1024
eurotunnel.com	08443 35 35 35
ldlines.co.uk	0844 576 8836
norfolkline.com	0844 847 5042
poferries.com	08716 645 645
seafrance.com	0871 423 7119
transeuropaferries.com	01843 595 522
transmancheferries.co.uk	0844 576 8836

Northern Spain
brittany-ferries.co.uk	0871 244 0744
poferries.com	08716 645 645

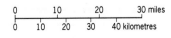

═══	Motorway	🚢 or Ⓥ	Vehicle ferry
═══	Toll motorway	🚤	Fast vehicle ferry or catamaran
═══	Primary route dual carriageway		National Park
═══	Primary route single carriageway	**92**	Atlas page number
═══	Other A road		

0   10   20   30 miles
0   10   20   30   40 kilometres

Road safety and fixed speed cameras

First, the advice you would expect from the AA - we advise drivers to always follow the signed speed limits – breaking the speed limit is illegal and can cost lives.

Both the AA and the Government believe that speed cameras should be operated within a transparent system. By providing information relating to road safety and speed hotspots, the AA believes that the driver is better placed to be aware of speed limits and can ensure adherence to them, thus making the roads safer for all users.

Most fixed speed cameras are installed at accident 'black spots' where four or more fatal or serious road collisions have occurred over the previous three years. It is the policy of both the police and the Department for Transport to make the location of cameras as well known as possible. By showing speed camera locations in this atlas the AA is identifying the places where extra care should be taken while driving. Speeding is illegal and dangerous and you MUST keep within the speed limit at all times.

Gatso™

Truvelo™

SPECS™

Traffipax™

There are currently more than 4,000 fixed speed cameras in Britain and the road mapping in this atlas identifies their on-the-road locations.

This symbol is used on the mapping to identify **individual** camera locations - with speed limits (mph)

This symbol is used on the mapping to identify **multiple** cameras on the same stretch of road - with speed limits (mph)

This symbol is used on the mapping to highlight SPECS™ camera systems which calculate your **average speed** along a stretch of road between two or more sets of cameras - with speed limits (mph)

Mobile cameras are also deployed at other sites where speed is perceived to be a problem and mobile enforcement often takes place at the fixed camera sites shown on the maps in this atlas. Additionally, regular police enforcement can take place on any road.

Speed Limits

Types of vehicle	Built up areas* MPH (km/h)	Single carriageways MPH (km/h)	Dual carriageways MPH (km/h)	Motorways MPH (km/h)
Cars & motorcycles (including car derived vans up to 2 tonnes maximum laden weight)	30 (48)	60 (96)	70 (112)	70 (112)
Cars towing caravans or trailers (including car derived vans and motorcycles)	30 (48)	50 (80)	60 (96)	60 (96)
Buses, coaches and minibuses (not exceeding 12 metres (39 feet) in overall length)	30 (48)	50 (80)	60 (96)	70 (112)
Goods vehicles (not exceeding 7.5 tonnes maximum laden weight)	30 (48)	50 (80)	60 (96)	70† (112)
Goods vehicles (exceeding 7.5 tonnes maximum laden weight)	30 (48)	40 (64)	50 (80)	60 (96)

* The 30mph (48km/h) limit usually applies to all traffic on all roads with street lighting unless signs show otherwise.
† 60mph (96km/h) if articulated or towing a trailer.

Camera locations – read this before you use the atlas

1 The speed camera locations were correct at the time of finalising the information to go to press.

2 Camera locations are approximate due to limitations in the scale of road mapping used in this atlas.

3 In towns and urban areas speed camera locations are shown only on roads that appear on the road maps in this atlas.

4 Where two or more cameras occur close together, a special symbol is used to indicate multiple cameras on the same stretch of road.

5 Our symbols do not indicate the direction in which speed cameras point.

6 On the mapping we symbolise more than 4,000 fixed camera locations. Mobile laser device locations and fixed 'red light' speed cameras cannot be shown.

*RoadPilot*mobile®

RoadPilot is the UK's pioneer and market leader in GPS (Global Positioning System) road safety technologies and the developer of one of the largest and most accurate databases of speed camera locations in the UK and Europe. It has provided the speed camera information in this atlas.

RoadPilot's latest speed camera location system is now available on your mobile phone. It improves road safety by alerting you to the location of accident black spots and fixed and mobile camera sites, and is completely legal.

RoadPilot **mobile** enables you to always have the very latest data of fixed and mobile sites on your mobile phone without having to connect it to your computer. Updates are available automatically.

There is also the facility to report new data that will be shared with the RoadPilot community.

Global Positioning System (GPS)

Relaying information from a constellation of satellites orbiting the earth, a GPS enabled phone listens for the signals of four or more satellites at a time in order to calculate your position, speed and direction of travel.

Available Now
Austria, Belgium, Finland, France, Germany, Italy, Netherlands, Norway, Poland, Portugal, Romania, Spain, Sweden

Available Q1 2009
Denmark

Available Q2 2009
Czech Republic, Hungary

Available Q3 2009
Croatia, Slovenia

Not Planned

| Camera Warning | GPS Information | Congestion Charge |

RoadPilot is dedicated to creating and maintaining the most accurate database of safety cameras in Europe.

A team of surveyors visit and accurately record the exact position and attributes of each and every camera in the RoadPilot database. More than 400 new safety cameras are added every month.

RoadPilot's latest mobile speed camera location system is now available on your mobile phone.

Visual Countdown
To camera location

Speed Limit at Camera
Dial turns red as an additional visual alert

Your Speed
The speed you are travelling when approaching a camera

Camera Types Located
Gatso, Specs, Truvelo, TSS/DSS, Taffipax, mobile camera sites, accident black spots, Congestion Charging Zones

RoadPilot Surveyors add more than **400** new safety cameras every month

For more information on RoadPilot's GPS road safety products and a list of compatible phones, please visit **www.roadpilot.com** or telephone 0870 240 1701.

RoadPilot®
DRIVING TECHNOLOGY

Channel Hopping

For business or pleasure, hopping on a ferry across to France, Belgium or the Channel Islands has never been easier.

The vehicle ferry routes shown on this map give you all the options, together with detailed port plans to help you navigate to and from the ferry terminals. Simply choose your preferred route, not forgetting the fast sailings; then check the colour-coded table for ferry operators, crossing times and contact details.

Bon voyage!

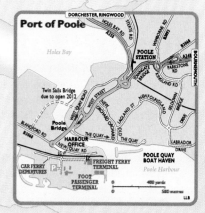

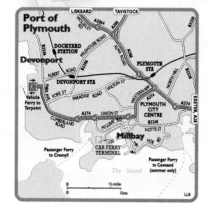

ENGLISH CHANNEL FERRY CROSSINGS AND OPERATORS

To	From	Journey Time	Operator	Telephone	Website
Boulogne	Dover	1 hr 45 mins	LD Lines	0844 576 8836	ldlines.co.uk
Caen (Ouistreham)	Portsmouth	6 - 7 hrs	Brittany Ferries	0871 244 0744	brittany-ferries.co.uk
Caen (Ouistreham)	Portsmouth	3 hrs 30 mins - Mar-Oct	Brittany Ferries	0871 244 0744	brittany-ferries.co.uk
Calais (Coquelles)	Channel Tunnel	35 mins	Eurotunnel	08443 35 35 35	eurotunnel.com
Calais	Dover	1 hr 30 mins	Sea France	0871 423 7119	seafrance.com
Calais	Dover	1 hr 30 mins	P&O	08716 645 645	poferries.com
Cherbourg	Poole	4 hrs 30 mins - 6 hrs 30 mins	Brittany Ferries	0871 244 0744	brittany-ferries.co.uk
Cherbourg	Poole	2 hrs 15 mins - May-Sept	Brittany Ferries	0871 244 0744	brittany-ferries.co.uk
Cherbourg	Portsmouth	3 hrs - Mar-Oct	Brittany Ferries	0871 244 0744	brittany-ferries.co.uk
Cherbourg	Portsmouth	4 hrs 30 mins(day) 8 hrs(o/night)	Brittany Ferries	0871 244 0744	brittany-ferries.co.uk
Cherbourg	Portsmouth	5 hrs 30 mins - May-Sept	Condor	0845 609 1024	condorferries.co.uk
Dieppe	Newhaven	4 hrs	Transmanche Ferries	0844 576 8836	transmancheferries.co.uk
Dunkerque	Dover	2 hrs	Norfolkline	0844 847 5042	norfolkline.com
Guernsey	Poole	2 hrs 30 mins - April-Oct	Condor	0845 609 1024	condorferries.co.uk
Guernsey	Portsmouth	7 hrs	Condor	0845 609 1024	condorferries.co.uk
Guernsey	Weymouth	2 hrs 10 mins	Condor	0845 609 1024	condorferries.co.uk
Jersey	Poole	3 hrs - April-Oct	Condor	0845 609 1024	condorferries.co.uk
Jersey	Portsmouth	10 hrs 30 mins	Condor	0845 609 1024	condorferries.co.uk
Jersey	Weymouth	3 hrs 25 mins	Condor	0845 609 1024	condorferries.co.uk
Le Havre	Portsmouth	5 hrs 30 mins - 8 hrs	LD Lines	0844 576 8836	ldlines.co.uk
Le Havre	Portsmouth	3 hrs 15 mins - Mar-Sept	LD Lines	0844 576 8836	ldlines.co.uk
Oostende	Ramsgate	4 hrs	Transeuropa	01843 595 522	transeuropaferries.com
Roscoff	Plymouth	6 - 8 hrs	Brittany Ferries	0871 244 0744	brittany-ferries.co.uk
St-Malo	Poole	4 hrs 35 mins - May-Sept	Condor	0845 609 1024	condorferries.co.uk
St-Malo	Portsmouth	9 - 10 hrs 45 mins	Brittany Ferries	0871 244 0744	brittany-ferries.co.uk
St-Malo	Weymouth	5 hrs 15 mins	Condor	0845 609 1024	condorferries.co.uk

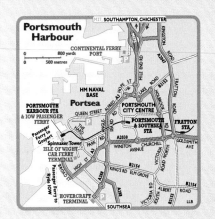

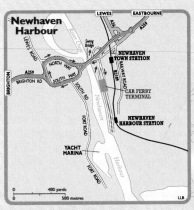

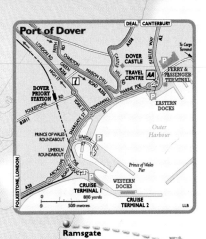

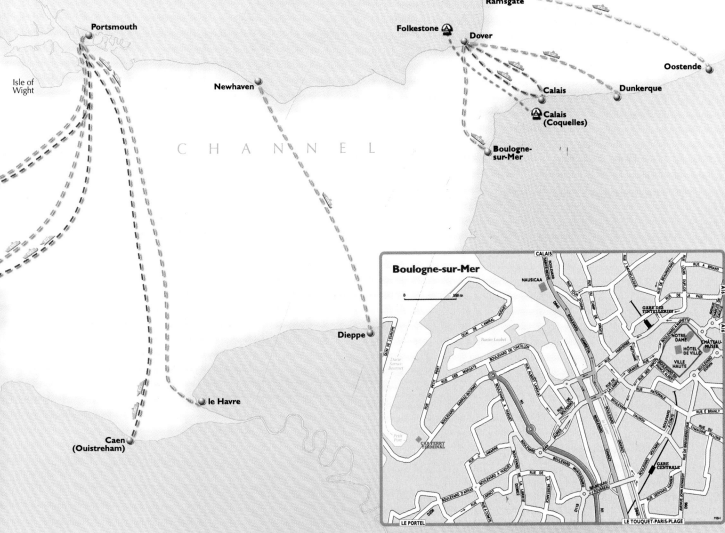

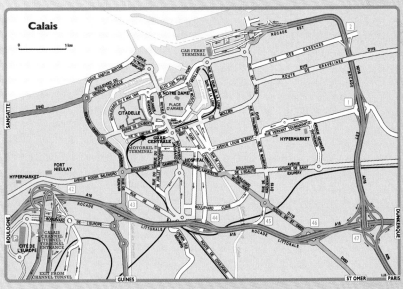

Ferries to Ireland and the Isle of Man

With so many sea crossings to Ireland and the Isle of Man this map will help you make the right choice.

The vehicle ferry routes shown on this map give you all the options, together with detailed port plans to help you navigate to and from the ferry terminals. Simply choose your preferred route, not forgetting the fast sailings; then check the colour-coded table for ferry operators, crossing times and contact details.

Fast ferry   Conventional ferry

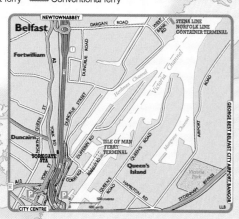

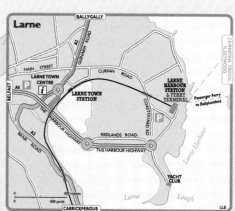

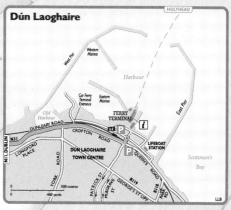

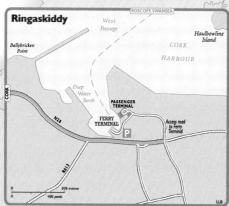

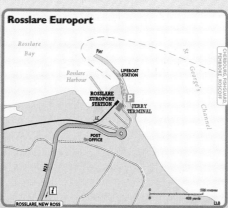

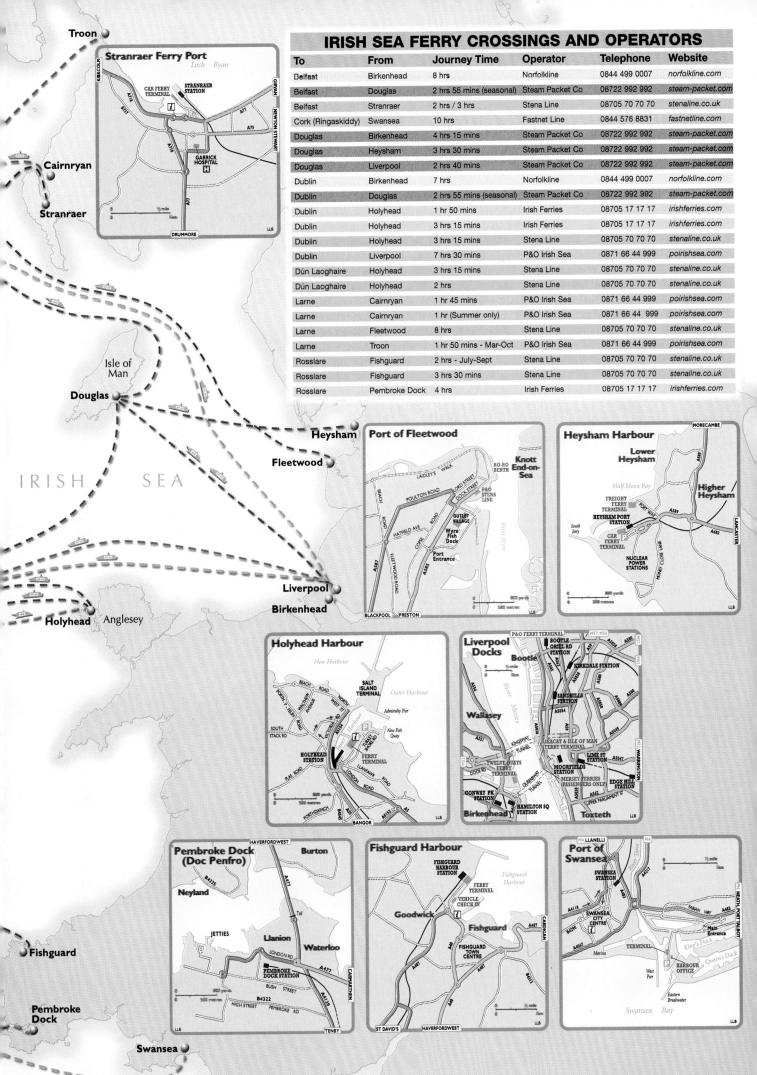

IRISH SEA FERRY CROSSINGS AND OPERATORS

To	From	Journey Time	Operator	Telephone	Website
Belfast	Birkenhead	8 hrs	Norfolkline	0844 499 0007	norfolkline.com
Belfast	Douglas	2 hrs 55 mins (seasonal)	Steam Packet Co	08722 992 992	steam-packet.com
Belfast	Stranraer	2 hrs / 3 hrs	Stena Line	08705 70 70 70	stenaline.co.uk
Cork (Ringaskiddy)	Swansea	10 hrs	Fastnet Line	0844 576 8831	fastnetline.com
Douglas	Birkenhead	4 hrs 15 mins	Steam Packet Co	08722 992 992	steam-packet.com
Douglas	Heysham	3 hrs 30 mins	Steam Packet Co	08722 992 992	steam-packet.com
Douglas	Liverpool	2 hrs 40 mins	Steam Packet Co	08722 992 992	steam-packet.com
Dublin	Birkenhead	7 hrs	Norfolkline	0844 499 0007	norfolkline.com
Dublin	Douglas	2 hrs 55 mins (seasonal)	Steam Packet Co	08722 992 992	steam-packet.com
Dublin	Holyhead	1 hr 50 mins	Irish Ferries	08705 17 17 17	irishferries.com
Dublin	Holyhead	3 hrs 15 mins	Irish Ferries	08705 17 17 17	irishferries.com
Dublin	Holyhead	3 hrs 15 mins	Stena Line	08705 70 70 70	stenaline.co.uk
Dublin	Liverpool	7 hrs 30 mins	P&O Irish Sea	0871 66 44 999	poirishsea.com
Dún Laoghaire	Holyhead	3 hrs 15 mins	Stena Line	08705 70 70 70	stenaline.co.uk
Dún Laoghaire	Holyhead	2 hrs	Stena Line	08705 70 70 70	stenaline.co.uk
Larne	Cairnryan	1 hr 45 mins	P&O Irish Sea	0871 66 44 999	poirishsea.com
Larne	Cairnryan	1 hr (Summer only)	P&O Irish Sea	0871 66 44 999	poirishsea.com
Larne	Fleetwood	8 hrs	Stena Line	08705 70 70 70	stenaline.co.uk
Larne	Troon	1 hr 50 mins - Mar-Oct	P&O Irish Sea	0871 66 44 999	poirishsea.com
Rosslare	Fishguard	2 hrs - July-Sept	Stena Line	08705 70 70 70	stenaline.co.uk
Rosslare	Fishguard	3 hrs 30 mins	Stena Line	08705 70 70 70	stenaline.co.uk
Rosslare	Pembroke Dock	4 hrs	Irish Ferries	08705 17 17 17	irishferries.com

Caravan and Camping Sites in Britain

These pages list the top 300 AA-inspected Caravan and Camping (C & C) sites in the Pennant rating scheme. Listings include addresses, websites and telephone numbers together with page and grid references to locate the sites in the atlas.

Available touring pitches are also included, abbreviated as follows: C = Caravan   CV = Campervan   T = Tent

To find out more about the AA's Pennant rating scheme and other rated caravan and camping sites visit *theAA.com*

ENGLAND

Abbey Farm Caravan Park
Dark Lane, Ormskirk,
L40 5TX
Tel: 01695 572686 **56 H6**
abbeyfarmcaravanpark.co.uk
Pitches: C 46, CV 46, T 10

Adgestone C & C Club Site
Lower Adgestone Road,
Adgestone, Nr Sandown,
PO36 0HL
Tel: 01983 403432 **9 P9**
thefriendlyclub.co.uk
Pitches: C 270, CV 270, T 270

Alders Caravan Park
Home Farm, Alne, York,
YO61 1RY
Tel: 01347 838722 **59 L2**
alderscaravanpark.co.uk
Pitches: C 87, CV 6, T 5

Andrewshayes Caravan Park
Dalwood, Axminster,
EX13 7DY
Tel: 01404 831225 **6 H3**
andrewshayes.co.uk
Pitches: C 25, CV 5, T 15

Ayr Holiday Park
St Ives, Cornwall, TR26 1EJ
Tel: 01736 795855 **2 D7**
ayrholidaypark.co.uk
Pitches: C 40, CV 40, T 40

Back of Beyond Touring Park
234 Ringwood Rd, St Leonards,
Dorset, BH24 2SB
Tel: 01202 876968 **8 G7**
backofbeyondtouringpark.co.uk
Pitches: C 80, CV 80, T 80

Bagwell Farm Touring Park
Knights in the Bottom,
Chickerell, Weymouth,
DT3 4EA
Tel: 01305 782575 **7 P6**
bagwellfarm.co.uk
Pitches: C 320, CV 320, T 170

Bardsea Leisure Park
Priory Road, Ulverston,
LA12 9QE
Tel: 01229 584712 **62 F6**
bardsealeisure.co.uk
Pitches: C 83, CV 83, T 0

Barnard Castle C & C Club Site
Dockenflatts Lane, Lartington,
Barnard Castle, DL12 9DG
Tel: 01833 630228 **64 H4**
thefriendlyclub.co.uk
Pitches: C 90, CV 90, T 90

Barnstones C & C Site
Great Bourton, Banbury,
OX17 1QU
Tel: 01295 750289 **31 L5**
Pitches: C 49, CV 49, T 49

Beaconsfield Farm Caravan Park
Battlefield, Shrewsbury,
SY4 4AA
Tel: 01939 210370 **49 K10**
beaconsfield-farm.co.uk
Pitches: C 60, CV 50, T 0

Bellingham Brown Rigg C & C Club Site
Brown Rigg, Bellingham,
NE48 2JY
Tel: 01434 220175 **72 E4**
thefriendlyclub.co.uk
Pitches: C 64, CV 64, T 64

Bingham Grange Touring & Camping Park
Melplash, Bridport,
DT6 3TT
Tel: 01308 488234 **7 L4**
binghamgrange.co.uk
Pitches: C 111, CV 111, T 111

Blackmore C & C Club Site
Blackmore Camp Site No 2,
Hanley Swan, WR8 0EE
Tel: 01684 310280 **39 P12**
thefriendlyclub.co.uk
Pitches: C 200, CV 200, T 200

Bo Peep Farm Caravan Park
Bo Peep Farm, Aynho Road,
Banbury, OX17 3NP
Tel: 01295 810605 **31 L7**
bo-peep.demon.co.uk
Pitches: C 104, CV 104, T 40

Boroughbridge C & C Club Site
Bar Lane, Roecliffe,
Boroughbridge, YO51 9LS
Tel: 01423 322683 **59 J2**
thefriendlyclub.co.uk
Pitches: C 85, CV 85, T 85

Broad Hembury C & C Park
Steeds Lane, Kingsnorth,
Ashford, TN26 1NQ
Tel: 01233 620859 **13 J3**
broadhembury.co.uk
Pitches: C 60, CV 60, T 60

Brokerswood Country Park
Brokerswood, Westbury,
BA13 4EH
Tel: 01373 822238 **18 C9**
brokerswood.co.uk
Pitches: C 69, CV 69, T 16

Brompton Caravan Park
Brompton-on-Swale,
Richmond,
DL10 7EZ
Tel: 01748 824629 **65 L7**
bromptoncaravanpark.co.uk
Pitches: C 177, CV 177, T 35

Budemeadows Touring Park
Widemouth Bay, Bude,
EX23 0NA
Tel: 01288 361646 **14 D11**
budemeadows.com
Pitches: C 145, CV 100, T 145

Burrowhayes Farm C & C Site
West Luccombe, Porlock,
Minehead, TA24 8HT
Tel: 01643 862463 **16 B6**
burrowhayes.co.uk
Pitches: C 54, CV 54, T 66

Cakes & Ale, Abbey Lane
Theberton, Leiston,
IP16 4TE
Tel: 01728 831655 **35 N4**
cakesandale.net
Pitches: C 50, CV 50, T 50

Calloose C & C Park
Leedstown, Hayle,
TR27 5ET
Tel: 01736 850431 **2 E8**
calloose.co.uk
Pitches: C 109, CV 20, T 80

Carlton Meres Country Park
Rendham Road, Carlton,
Saxmundham,
IP17 2QP
Tel: 01728 603344 **35 M4**
carlton-meres.co.uk
Pitches: C 96, CV 96, T 0

Carlyon Bay C & C Park
Bethesda, Cypress Avenue,
Carlyon Bay,
PL25 3RE
Tel: 01726 812735 **3 M5**
carlyonbay.net
Pitches: C 180, CV 180, T 180

Carnevas Holiday Park & Farm Cottages
Carnevas Farm, St Merryn,
PL28 8PN
Tel: 01841 520230 **3 J2**
carnevasholidaypark.co.uk
Pitches: C 195, CV 195, T 195

Carnon Downs C & C Park
Carnon Downs, Truro,
TR3 6JJ
Tel: 01872 862283 **3 J7**
carnon-downs-caravanpark.co.uk
Pitches: C 120, CV 20, T 10

Carvynick Country Club
Summercourt, Newquay,
TR8 5AF
Tel: 01872 510716 **3 K5**
carvynick.co.uk
Pitches: C 0, CV 47, T 0

Castlerigg Hall C & C Park
Castlerigg Hall, Keswick,
CA12 4TE
Tel: 017687 74499 **71 L10**
castlerigg.co.uk
Pitches: C 48, CV 48, T 120

Cawood Park, Ryther Road
Vale of York, YO8 3TT
Tel: 01757 268450 **59 M6**
cawoodpark.com
Pitches: C 40, CV 10, T 0

Channel View C & C Park
Manor Farm, Lynton,
EX35 6LD
Tel: 01598 753349 **15 M3**
channel-view.co.uk
Pitches: C 76, CV 76, T 76

Charmouth C & C Club Site
Monkton Wylde Farm,
Charmouth,
DT6 6DB
Tel: 01297 32965 **7 J4**
thefriendlyclub.co.uk
Pitches: C 150, CV 150, T 150

Cheddar Bridge Touring Park
Draycott Rd, Cheddar,
BS27 3RJ
Tel: 01934 743048 **17 L5**
cheddarbridge.co.uk
Pitches: C 45, CV 45, T 45

Cheddar, Mendip Heights C & C Club Site
Townsend, Priddy, Wells,
BA5 3BP
Tel: 01749 870241 **17 M6**
thefriendlyclub.co.uk
Pitches: C 90, CV 90, T 90

Chertsey C & C Club Site
Bridge Road, Chertsey,
KT16 8JX
Tel: 01932 562405 **20 G9**
thefriendlyclub.co.uk
Pitches: C 200, CV 200, T 200

Church Farm C & C Park
The Bungalow, Church Farm
High Street, Sixpenny Handley,
Salisbury,
SP5 5ND
Tel: 01725 553005 **8 E4**
churchfarmcandcpark.co.uk
Pitches: C 35, CV 35, T 35

Claylands Caravan Park
Cabus, Garstang,
PR3 1AJ
Tel: 01524 791242 **63 J11**
claylands.com
Pitches: C 30, CV 30, T 10

Clent Hills C & C Club Site
Fieldhouse Lane, Romsley,
Halesowen,
B62 0NH
Tel: 01562 710015 **40 C10**
thefriendlyclub.co.uk
Pitches: C 95, CV 95, T 95

Clippesby Hall, Hall Lane
Clippesby, Great Yarmouth,
NR29 3BL
Tel: 01493 367800 **45 N7**
clippesby.com
Pitches: C 70, CV 10, T 20

Clitheroe C & C Club Site
Edisford Road, Clitheroe,
BB7 3LA
Tel: 01200 425294 **57 N1**
thefriendlyclub.co.uk
Pitches: C 80, CV 80, T 80

Cofton Country Holidays
Starcross, Dawlish,
EX6 8RP
Tel: 01626 890111 **6 C6**
coftonholidays.co.uk
Pitches: C 450, CV 450, T 450

Colchester Holiday Park
Cymbeline Way, Lexden,
Colchester,
CO3 4AG
Tel: 01206 545551 **34 F10**
colchestercamping.co.uk
Pitches: C 168, CV 168, T 168

Coombe Touring Park
Race Plain, Netherhampton,
Salisbury,
SP2 8PN
Tel: 01722 328451 **8 G2**
coombecaravanpark.co.uk
Pitches: C 50, CV 50, T 20

Cornish Farm Touring Park
Shoreditch, Taunton,
TA3 7BS
Tel: 01823 327746 **16 H10**
cornishfarm.com
Pitches: C 50, CV 50, T 25

Cosawes Park
Perranarworthal, Truro,
TR3 7QS
Tel: 01872 863724 **2 H8**
cosawestouringandcamping.co.uk
Pitches: C 20, CV 20, T 30

Cote Ghyll C & C Park
Osmotherley, Northallerton,
DL6 3AH
Tel: 01609 883425 **66 C7**
coteghyll.com
Pitches: C 77, CV 77, T 77

Cotswold View Touring Park
Enstone Road, Charlbury,
OX7 3JH
Tel: 01608 810314 **31 J9**
cotswoldview.co.uk
Pitches: C 90, CV 90, T 35

Dartmoor Barley Meadow C & C Club Site
Crockernwell, Exeter,
EX6 6NR
Tel: 01647 281629 **5 P2**
barleymeadow.com
Pitches: C 40, CV 35, T 35

Dell Touring Park
Beyton Road, Thurston,
Bury St Edmunds,
IP31 3RB
Tel: 01359 270121 **34 F4**
thedellcaravanpark.co.uk
Pitches: C 60, CV 15, T 15

Devizes C & C Club Site
Spout Lane, Nr Seend, Devizes,
SN12 6RN
Tel: 01380 828839 **18 D8**
thefriendlyclub.co.uk
Pitches: C 90, CV 90, T 90

Diamond Farm C & C Park
Islip Road, Bletchingdon,
OX5 3DR
Tel: 01869 350909 **31 L10**
diamondpark.co.uk
Pitches: C 37, CV 37, T 25

Dolbeare Park C & C
St Ive Road, Landrake, Saltash,
PL12 5AF
Tel: 01752 851332 **4 H7**
dolbeare.co.uk
Pitches: C 60, CV 60, T 30

Dornafield
Dornafield Farm, Two Mile Oak,
Newton Abbot,
TQ12 6DD
Tel: 01803 812732 **5 Q6**
dornafield.com
Pitches: C 135, CV 135, T 135

East Fleet Farm Touring Park
Chickerell, Weymouth,
DT3 4DW
Tel: 01305 785768 **7 P6**
eastfleet.co.uk
Pitches: C 400, CV 400, T 400

Eden Valley Holiday Park
Lanlivery, Nr Lostwithiel,
PL30 5BU
Tel: 01208 872277 **3 N4**
edenvalleyholidaypark.co.uk
Pitches: C 56, CV 12, T 56

Eskdale C & C Club Site
Boot, Holmrook,
CA19 1TH
Tel: 019467 23253 **62 D3**
thefriendlyclub.co.uk
Pitches: C 80, CV 80, T 80

Exe Valley Caravan Site
Mill House, Bridgetown,
Dulverton,
TA22 9JR
Tel: 01643 851432 **16 C9**
exevalleycamping.co.uk
Pitches: C 41, CV 41, T 9

Fallbarrow Park
Rayrigg Road, Windermere,
LA23 3DL
Tel: 015394 44422 **62 H3**
slholidays.co.uk
Pitches: C 38, CV 38, T 0

Fernwood Caravan Park
Lyneal, Ellesmere,
SY12 0QF
Tel: 01948 710221 **49 J8**
fernwoodpark.co.uk
Pitches: C 60, CV 60, T 0

Flusco Wood Caravan Park
Flusco, Penrith,
CA11 0JB
Tel: 017684 80020 **71 P9**
fluscowood.co.uk
Pitches: C 12, CV 12, T 0

Folkestone C & C Club Site
The Warren, Folkestone,
CT19 6NQ
Tel: 01303 255093 **13 N3**
thefriendlyclub.co.uk
Pitches: C 0, CV 80, T 80

Forest Glade Holiday Park
Cullompton, Kentisbeare,
EX15 2DT
Tel: 01404 841381 **6 E2**
forest-glade.co.uk
Pitches: C 80, CV 80, T 80

Gelderwood Country Park
Ashworth Road,
Rochdale,
OL11 5UP
Tel: 01706 364858 **57 Q6**
ukparks.co.uk/gelderwood
Pitches: C 34, CV 34, T 0

Gill Head Farm C & C Park
Troutbeck, Penrith,
CA11 0ST
Tel: 017687 79652 **71 N9**
gillheadfarm.co.uk
Pitches: C 25, CV 17, T 42

Globe Vale Holiday Park
Radnor, Redruth,
TR16 4BH
Tel: 01209 891183 **2 G6**
globevale.co.uk
Pitches: C 77, CV 19, T 58

Golden Cap Holiday Park
Seatown, Chideock,
Bridport,
DT6 6JX
Tel: 01308 422139 **7 K4**
wdlh.co.uk
Pitches: C 55, CV 53, T 159

Golden Square Touring Caravan Park
Oswaldkirk, Helmsley,
YO62 5YQ
Tel: 01439 788269 **66 E10**
goldensquarecaravanpark.com
Pitches: C 129, CV 129, T 129

Golden Valley C & C Park
Coach Road, Ripley,
DE55 4ES
Tel: 01773 513881 **51 K9**
goldenvalleycaravanpark.co.uk
Pitches: C 45, CV 45, T 120

Goosewood Caravan Park
Sutton-on-the-Forest,
YO61 1ET
Tel: 01347 810829 **59 N2**
goosewood.co.uk
Pitches: C 75, CV 75, T 0

Greenacres Touring Park, Haywards Lane
Chelston, Wellington,
TA21 9PH
Tel: 01823 652844 **16 F11**
greenacres-wellington.co.uk
Pitches: C 20, CV 20, T 20

Grove Farm Meadow Holiday Caravan Park
Stour Way, Christchurch,
BH23 2PQ
Tel: 01202 483597 **8 G8**
meadowbank-holidays.co.uk
Pitches: C 41, CV 41, T 0

Gunvenna Caravan Park
St Minver, Wadebridge,
PL27 6QN
Tel: 01208 862405 **4 B5**
gunvenna.co.uk
Pitches: C 75, CV 75, T 25

Harbury Fields
Harbury Fields Farm, Harbury,
Nr Leamington Spa,
CV33 9JN
Tel: 01926 612457 **31 J3**
harburyfields.co.uk
Pitches: C 30, CV 30, T 0

Hawthorn Farm Caravan Park
Station Road, Martin Mill,
Dover,
CT15 5LA
Tel: 01304 852658 **13 Q2**
keatfarm.co.uk
Pitches: C 147, CV 147, T 100

Heathfield Farm Camping
Heathfield Road, Freshwater,
PO40 9SH
Tel: 01983 407822 **9 K9**
heathfieldcamping.co.uk
Pitches: C 60, CV 60, T 60

Heathland Beach Caravan Park
London Road, Kessingland,
NR33 7PJ
Tel: 01502 740337 **45 Q11**
heathlandbeach.co.uk
Pitches: C 63, CV 63, T 63

Hele Valley Holiday Park
Hele Bay, Ilfracombe, North
Devon, EX34 9RD
Tel: 01271 862460 **15 J3**
helevalley.co.uk
Pitches: C 4, CV 8, T 38

Hereford C & C Club Site
The Millpond, Little Tarrington,
HR1 4JA
Tel: 01432 890243 **28 H1**
thefriendlyclub.co.uk
Pitches: C 55, CV 55, T 55

Hertford C & C Club Site
Mangrove Road, Hertford,
SG13 8QF
Tel: 01992 586696 **21 M2**
thefriendlyclub.co.uk
Pitches: C 250, CV 250, T 250

Hidden Valley Park
West Down, Ilfracombe,
EX34 8NU
Tel: 01271 813837 **15 J4**
hiddenvalleypark.com
Pitches: C 115, CV 65, T 55

High Moor Farm Park
Skipton Road, Harrogate,
HG3 2LT
Tel: 01423 563637 **58 G3**
highmoorfarmpark.co.uk
Pitches: C 145, CV 15, T 0

Higher Chellew Holiday Park
Higher Trenowin, Nancledra,
Penzance,
TR20 8BD
Tel: 01736 364532 **2 D8**
higherchellewcamping.co.uk
Pitches: C 5, CV 5, T 25

Highfield Farm Touring Park
Long Road, Comberton,
Cambridge, CB23 7DG
Tel: 01223 262308 **33 L5**
highfieldfarmtouringpark.co.uk
Pitches: C 60, CV 60, T 60

Highlands End Holiday Park
Eype, Bridport, Dorset,
DT6 6AR
Tel: 01308 422139 **7 L5**
wdlh.co.uk
Pitches: C 60, CV 60, T 75

Hill Cottage Farm C & C Park
Sandleheath Road, Alderholt,
Fordingbridge,
SP6 3EG
Tel: 01425 650513 **8 G5**
hillcottagefarmcampingand
caravanpark.co.uk
Pitches: C 35, CV 35, T 60

Hill Farm Caravan Park
Branches Lane, Sherfield English,
Romsey, SO51 6FH
Tel: 01794 340402 **9 K3**
hillfarmpark.com
Pitches: C 70, CV 30, T 50

Hillside Caravan Park
Canvas Farm, Moor Road,
Thirsk, YO7 4BR
Tel: 01845 537349 **66 C9**
hillsidecaravanpark.co.uk
Pitches: C 35, CV 35, T 0

Holgate's Caravan Park
Middlebarrow Plain, Cove Road,
Silverdale, Nr Carnforth,
LA5 0SH
Tel: 01524 701508 **63 J7**
holgates.co.uk
Pitches: C 80, CV 80, T 5

Homing Park
Church Lane, Seasalter,
Whitstable, CT5 4BU
Tel: 01227 771777 **23 L9**
homingpark.co.uk
Pitches: C 43, CV 43, T 43

Honeybridge Park
Honeybridge Lane, Dial Post,
Horsham, RH13 8NX
Tel: 01403 710923 **11 J6**
honeybridgepark.co.uk
Pitches: C 112, CV 112, T 90

Hurley Riverside Park
Park Office, Hurley, Nr
Maidenhead, SL6 5NE
Tel: 01628 824493 **20 D6**
hurleyriversidepark.co.uk
Pitches: C 138, CV 138, T 62

Hutton-le-Hole Caravan Park
Westfield Lodge,
Hutton-le-Hole, YO62 6UG
Tel: 01751 417261 **66 G9**
westfieldlodge.co.uk
Pitches: C 38, CV 38, T 4

Hylton Caravan Park
Eden Street, Silloth,
CA7 4AY
Tel: 016973 31707 **70 H5**
stanwix.com
Pitches: C 90, CV 90, T 90

Island Meadow Caravan Park
The Mill House, Aston Cantlow,
B95 6JP
Tel: 01789 488273 **30 F3**
islandmeadowcaravanpark.co.uk
Pitches: C 24, CV 24, T 10

Isle of Avalon Touring Caravan Park
Godney Road, Glastonbury,
BA6 9AF
Tel: 01458 833618 **17 L8**
Pitches: C 70, CV 70, T 50

Jacobs Mount Caravan Park
Jacobs Mount, Stepney Road,
Scarborough, YO12 5NL
Tel: 01723 361178 **67 L9**
jacobsmount.com
Pitches: C 144, CV 156, T 16

Jasmine Caravan Park
Cross Lane, Snainton,
Scarborough, YO13 9BE
Tel: 01723 859240 **67 K10**
jasminepark.co.uk
Pitches: C 94, CV 94, T 20

Juliot's Well Holiday Park
Camelford, PL32 9RF
Tel: 01840 213302 **4 D4**
juliotswell.com
Pitches: C 39, CV 39, T 39

Kendal C & C Club Site
Millcrest, Kendal, LA9 6NY
Tel: 01539 741363 **63 K4**
thefriendlyclub.co.uk
Pitches: C 50, CV 50, T 50

Kennford International Caravan Park
Kennford, Exeter, EX6 7YN
Tel: 01392 833046 **6 B5**
kennfordinternational.co.uk
Pitches: C 96, CV 96, T 96

Kessingland C & C Club Site
Suffolk Wildlife Park, Whites
Lane, Kessingland, Nr Lowestoft,
NR33 7TF
Tel: 01502 742040 **45 Q11**
thefriendlyclub.co.uk
Pitches: C 90, CV 90, T 90

Kingsbury Water Park C & C Club Site
Kingsbury Water Park, Bodymoor,
Sutton Coldfield, B76 0DY
Tel: 01827 874101 **40 G7**
thefriendlyclub.co.uk
Pitches: C 150, CV 150, T 150

Kneps Farm Holiday Park
River Road, Stanah, Thornton-
Cleveleys, Blackpool, FY5 5LR
Tel: 01253 823632 **62 G12**
knepsfarm.co.uk
Pitches: C 40, CV 5, T 15

Knight Stainforth Hall Caravan & Campsite
Stainforth, Settle, BD24 0DP
Tel: 01729 822200 **63 P8**
knightstainforth.co.uk
Pitches: C 50, CV 50, T 50

Ladycross Plantation Caravan Park
Egton, Whitby, YO21 1UA
Tel: 01947 895502 **66 H6**
ladycrossplantation.co.uk
Pitches: C 120, CV 10, T 0

Lamb Cottage Caravan Park
Dalefords Lane, Whitegate,
Northwich, CW8 2BN
Tel: 01606 882302 **49 L2**
lambcottage.co.uk
Pitches: C 45, CV 28, T 0

Larches Caravan Park
Mealsgate, Wigton, CA7 1LQ
Tel: 016973 71379 **71 K7**
larchescaravanpark.co.uk
Pitches: C 73, CV 73, T 73

Lebberston Touring Park
Filey Road, Lebberston,
Scarborough, YO11 3PE
Tel: 01723 585723 **67 M10**
lebberstontouring.co.uk
Pitches: C 125, CV 50, T 0

Lemonford Caravan Park
Bickington (near Ashburton),
Newton Abbot, TQ12 6JR
Tel: 01626 821242 **5 Q6**
lemonford.co.uk
Pitches: C 82, CV 82, T 35

Lickpenny Caravan Site
Lickpenny Lane, Tansley,
Matlock, DE4 5GF
Tel: 01629 583040 **51 J8**
lickpennycaravanpark.co.uk
Pitches: C 80, CV 80, T 0

Lime Tree Park
Dukes Drive, Buxton,
SK17 9RP
Tel: 01298 22988 **50 E6**
limetreeparkbuxton.co.uk
Pitches: C 71, CV 22, T 35

Limefitt Park
Patterdale Road, Troutbeck,
Windermere, LA23 1PA
Tel: 015394 32300 **62 H2**
southlakelandparks.co.uk/
holidays
Pitches: C 35, CV 35, T 0

Lincoln Farm Park Oxfordshire
High Street, Standlake,
OX29 7RH
Tel: 01865 300239 **31 K12**
lincolnfarmpark.co.uk
Pitches: C 75, CV 36, T 16

Little Cotton Caravan Park
Little Cotton, Dartmouth,
TQ6 0LB
Tel: 01803 832558 **6 B11**
littlecotton.co.uk
Pitches: C 95, CV 15, T 20

Little Lakeland Caravan Park
Wortwell, Harleston,
IP20 0EL
Tel: 01986 788646 **45 L12**
littlelakeland.co.uk
Pitches: C 38, CV 38, T 32

Lizard Lane C & C Site
Lizard Lane, South Shields,
NE34 7AB
Tel: 0191 454 4982 **73 P7**
Pitches: C 45, CV 45, T 45

Longnor Wood Holiday Park
Longnor, Nr Buxton,
SK17 0NG
Tel: 01298 83648 **50 E7**
longnorwood.co.uk
Pitches: C 47, CV 47, T 47

Lowther Holiday Park
Eamont Bridge, Penrith,
CA10 2JB
Tel: 01768 863631 **71 Q9**
lowther-holidaypark.co.uk
Pitches: C 144, CV 50, T 36

Lytton Lawn Touring Park
Lymore Lane, Milford on Sea,
SO41 0TX
Tel: 01590 648331 **9 K8**
shorefield.co.uk
Pitches: C 136, CV 136, T 83

Manor Wood Country Caravan Park
Manor Wood, Coddington,
Chester, CH3 9EN
Tel: 01829 782990 **49 J4**
cheshire-caravan-sites.co.uk
Pitches: C 45, CV 45, T 45

Maustin Caravan Park
Kearby with Netherby,
Netherby,
LS22 4DA
Tel: 0113 288 6234 **59 J5**
maustin.co.uk
Pitches: C 25, CV 25, T 25

Mayfield Touring Park
Cheltenham Road, Cirencester,
GL7 7BH
Tel: 01285 831301 **30 D11**
mayfieldpark.co.uk
Pitches: C 36, CV 36, T 36

Merley Court
Merley, Wimbourne Minster,
BH21 3AA
Tel: 01590 648331 **8 E7**
shorefield.co.uk
Pitches: C 160, CV 160, T 80

Middlewood Farm Holiday Park
Middlewood Lane,
Fylingthorpe,
Robin Hood's Bay, Whitby,
YO22 4UF
Tel: 01947 880414 **67 K6**
middlewoodfarm.com
Pitches: C 20, CV 20, T 80

Minnows Touring Park
Holbrook Lane, Sampford
Peverell,
EX16 7EN
Tel: 01884 821770 **16 E11**
ukparks.co.uk/minnows
Pitches: C 45, CV 45, T 5

Monkton Wyld Farm Caravan Park
Scotts Lane, Charmouth,
DT6 6DB
Tel: 01297 631131 **7 J4**
monktonwyld.co.uk
Pitches: C 150, CV 150, T 150

Moon & Sixpence
Newbourn Road, Waldringfield,
Woodbridge,
IP12 4PP
Tel: 01473 736650 **35 L7**
moonandsixpence.eu
Pitches: C 65, CV 65, T 65

Mosswood Caravan Park
Crimbles Lane, Cockerham,
LA2 0ES
Tel: 01524 791041 **63 J11**
mosswood.co.uk
Pitches: C 25, CV 25, T 25

New House Caravan Park
Kirkby Lonsdale,
LA6 2HR
Tel: 01524 271590 **63 L6**
Pitches: C 50, CV 50, T 0

Newlands C & C Park
Charmouth, Bridport,
DT6 6RB
Tel: 01297 560259 **7 K4**
newlandsholidays.co.uk
Pitches: C 140, CV 140, T 100

Newperran Holiday Park
Rejerrah, Newquay,
TR8 5QJ
Tel: 01872 572407 **2 H5**
newperran.co.uk
Pitches: C 357, CV 357, T 357

Newton Mill Holiday Park
Newton Road, Bath,
BA2 9JF
Tel: 01225 333909 **17 Q3**
newtonmillpark.co.uk
Pitches: C 85, CV 66, T 116

Northam Farm Caravan & Touring Park
Brean, Burnham on Sea,
TA8 2SE
Tel: 01278 751244 **17 J5**
northamfarm.co.uk
Pitches: C 350, CV 350, T 350

Oakdown Holiday Park
Gatedown Lane, Sidmouth,
EX10 0PT
Tel: 01297 680387 **6 G5**
oakdown.co.uk
Pitches: C 150, CV 150, T 150

Old Barn Touring Park
Cheverton Farm, Newport Road,
Sandown, PO36 9PJ
Tel: 01983 866414 **9 P10**
oldbarntouring.co.uk
Pitches: C 60, CV 60, T 60

Orchard Park
Frampton Lane,
Hubbert's Bridge, Boston,
PE20 3QU
Tel: 01205 290328 **43 J2**
orchardpark.co.uk
Pitches: C 87, CV 87, T 87

Orchards Holiday Caravan Park
Main Road, Newbridge,
Yarmouth, PO41 0TS
Tel: 01983 531331 **9 M9**
orchards-holiday-park.co.uk
Pitches: C 171, CV 171, T 171

Ord House Country Park
East Ord, Berwick-upon-Tweed,
TD15 2NS
Tel: 01289 305288 **81 K4**
ordhouse.co.uk
Pitches: C 70, CV 35, T 9

Otterington Park
Station Farm,
South Otterington,
Northallerton,
DL7 9JB
Tel: 01609 780656 **65 P9**
otteringtonpark.com
Pitches: C 40, CV 40, T 0

Oxon Hall Touring Park
Welshpool Road, Shrewsbury,
SY3 5FB
Tel: 01743 340868 **49 J11**
morris-leisure.co.uk
Pitches: C 124, CV 124, T 124

Padstow Touring Park
Padstow, PL28 8LE
Tel: 01841 532061 **3 K2**
padstowtouringpark.co.uk
Pitches: C 100, CV 100, T 100

Park Cliffe Camping & Caravan Estate
Birks Road, Tower Wood,
Windermere, LA23 3PG
Tel: 01539 531344 **62 H4**
parkcliffe.co.uk
Pitches: C 60, CV 60, T 100

Parkers Farm Holiday Park
Higher Mead Farm, Ashburton,
Devon, TQ13 7LJ
Tel: 01364 654869 **5 Q6**
parkersfarm.co.uk
Pitches: C 100, CV 100, T 100

Pear Tree Holiday Park
Organford Road, Holton Heath,
Organford, Poole,
BH16 6LA
Tel: 01202 622434 **8 D8**
peartreepark.co.uk
Pitches: C 145, CV 145, T 72

Penrose Farm Touring Park
Goonhavern, Truro,
TR4 9QF
Tel: 01872 573185 **2 H5**
penrosefarmtouringpark.com
Pitches: C 100, CV 100, T 100

Pilgrims Way C & C Park
Church Green Road, Fishtoft,
Boston, PE21 0QY
Tel: 01205 366646 **43 K2**
pilgrimsway-caravanand
camping.com
Pitches: C 17, CV 13, T 22

Polmanter Tourist Park
Halsetown, St Ives,
TR26 3LX
Tel: 01736 795640 **2 D7**
polmanter.com
Pitches: C 240, CV 240, T 240

Porlock Caravan Park
Porlock, Minehead,
TA24 8ND
Tel: 01643 862269 **15 Q3**
porlockcaravanpark.co.uk
Pitches: C 40, CV 40, T 40

Portesham Dairy Farm Campsite
Portesham, Weymouth,
DT3 4HG
Tel: 01305 871297 **7 N6**
porteshamdairyfarm.co.uk
Pitches: C 90, CV 90, T 31

Porthtowan Tourist Park
Mile Hill, Porthtowan, Truro,
TR4 8TY
Tel: 01209 890256 **2 G6**
porthtowantouristpark.co.uk
Pitches: C 80, CV 80, T 80

Quantock Orchard Caravan Park
Flaxpool, Crowcombe, Taunton,
TA4 4AW
Tel: 01984 618618 **16 F8**
quantock-orchard.co.uk
Pitches: C 31, CV 19, T 19

Quiet Waters Caravan Park
Hemingford Abbots,
Huntingdon, PE28 9AJ
Tel: 01480 463405 **33 J3**
quietwaterscaravanpark.co.uk
Pitches: C 20, CV 20, T 20

Ranch Caravan Park
Station Road, Honeybourne,
Evesham,
WR11 7PR
Tel: 01386 830744 **30 E5**
ranch.co.uk
Pitches: C 120, CV 120, T 0

Ripley Caravan Park
Knaresborough Road, Ripley,
Harrogate,
HG3 3AU
Tel: 01423 770050 **58 H3**
ripleycaravanpark.com
Pitches: C 75, CV 75, T 25

River Dart Country Park
Holne Park, Ashburton,
TQ13 7NP
Tel: 01364 652511 **5 P6**
riverdart.co.uk
Pitches: C 50, CV 67, T 67

River Valley Holiday Park
London Apprentice, St Austell,
PL26 7AP
Tel: 01726 73533 **3 M6**
cornwall-holidays.co.uk
Pitches: C 45, CV 45, T 45

Riverside C & C Park
Marsh Lane, North Molton Road,
South Molton,
EX36 3HQ
Tel: 01769 579269 **15 M6**
exmoorriverside.co.uk
Pitches: C 42, CV 42, T 42

Riverside Caravan Park
High Bentham, Lancaster,
LA2 7FJ
Tel: 015242 61272 **5 L8**
riversidecaravanpark.co.uk
Pitches: C 61, CV 61, T 0

Riverside Caravan Park
Longbridge Road, Plymouth,
PL6 8LL
Tel: 01752 344122 **63 M8**
riversidecaravanpark.com
Pitches: C 236, CV 236, T 60

Robin Hood C & C Park
Green Dyke Lane, Slingsby,
YO62 4AP
Tel: 01653 628391 **66 F11**
robinhoodcaravanpark.co.uk
Pitches: C 32, CV 32, T 32

Rose Farm Touring & Camping Park
Stepshort, Belton,
Nr Great Yarmouth,
NR31 9JS
Tel: 01493 780896 **45 P9**
rosefarmtouringpark.co.uk
Pitches: C 80, CV 80, T 40

Rosedale C & C Park
Rosedale Abbey, Pickering,
YO18 8SA
Tel: 01751 417272 **66 G8**
flowerofmay.com
Pitches: C 30, CV 30, T 70

Ross Park, Park Hill Farm
Ipplepen, Newton Abbot,
TQ12 5TT
Tel: 01803 812983 **5 R6**
rossparkcaravanpark.co.uk
Pitches: C 110, CV 82, T 110

Rudding Holiday Park
Follifoot, Harrogate,
HG3 1JH
Tel: 01423 870439 **59 J4**
ruddingpark.co.uk
Pitches: C 141, CV 141, T 141

Salisbury C & C Club Site
Hudsons Field, Castle Road,
Salisbury,
SP1 3RR
Tel: 01722 320713 **8 G2**
thefriendlyclub.co.uk
Pitches: C 150, CV 150, T 150

Sandringham C & C Club Site
The Sandringham Estate,
Double Lodges, Sandringham,
PE35 6EA
Tel: 01485 542555 **44 B5**
thefriendlyclub.co.uk
Pitches: C 275, CV 275, T 275

Scarborough C & C Club Site
Field Lane, Burniston Road,
Scarborough,
YO13 0DA
Tel: 01723 366212 **67 L8**
thefriendlyclub.co.uk
Pitches: C 300, CV 300, T 300

Seaview International Holiday Park
Boswinger, Mevagissey,
PL26 6LL
Tel: 01726 843425 **3 L7**
seaviewinternational.com
Pitches: C 189, CV 189, T 189

Severn Gorge Park
Bridgnorth Road, Tweedale,
Telford,
TF7 4JB
Tel: 01952 684789 **39 N2**
severngorgepark.co.uk
Pitches: C 10, CV 10, T 0

Shamba Holidays
230 Ringwood Road,
St Leonards, Ringwood,
BH24 2SB
Tel: 01202 873302 **8 G7**
shambaholidays.co.uk
Pitches: C 150, CV 150, T 150

Shrubbery Touring Park
Rousdon, Lyme Regis,
DT7 3XW
Tel: 01297 442227 **6 H5**
shrubberypark.co.uk
Pitches: C 90, CV 10, T 20

Silverbow Park
Perranwell, Goonhavern,
TR4 9NX
Tel: 01872 572347 **2 H5**
chycor.co.uk/parks/silverbow
Pitches: C 100, CV 100, T 100

Skelwith Fold Caravan Park
Ambleside, Cumbria,
LA22 0HX
Tel: 015394 32277 **62 G2**
skelwith.com
Pitches: C 75, CV 75, T 0

Somers Wood Caravan Park
Somers Road, Meriden,
CV7 7PL
Tel: 01676 522978 **40 G10**
somerswood.co.uk
Pitches: C 48, CV 48, T 0

South Lytchett Manor
Dorchester Road,
Lytchett Minster, Poole,
BH16 6JB
Tel: 01202 622577 **8 E8**
southlytchettmanor.co.uk
Pitches: C 120, CV 120, T 30

Southfork Caravan Park
Parrett Works, Martock,
TA12 6AE
Tel: 01935 825661 **17 L11**
southforkcaravans.co.uk
Pitches: C 27, CV 27, T 5

Springfield Holiday Park
Tedburn St Mary, Exeter,
EX6 6EW
Tel: 01647 24242 **5 Q2**
springfieldholidaypark.co.uk
Pitches: C 11, CV 3, T 11

St Helens Caravan Park
Wykeham, Scarborough,
YO13 9QD
Tel: 01723 862771 **67 L10**
sthelenscaravanpark.co.uk
Pitches: C 210, CV 210, T 40

Stanmore Hall Touring Park
Stourbridge Road, Bridgnorth,
WV15 6DT
Tel: 01746 761761 **39 N4**
morris-leisure.co.uk
Pitches: C 131, CV 53, T 10

Stowford Farm Meadows
Berry Down, Combe Martin,
EX34 0PW
Tel: 01271 882476 **15 K4**
stowford.co.uk
Pitches: C 600, CV 50, T 50

Strawberry Hill Farm C & C Park
Old Cassop, Durham,
DH6 4QA
Tel: 0191 372 3457 **73 N11**
strawberry-hill-farm.co.uk
Pitches: C 35, CV 35, T 10

Stroud Hill Park
Fen Road, Pidley,
PE28 3DE
Tel: 01487 741333 **33 K2**
stroudhillpark.co.uk
Pitches: C 60, CV 60, T 6

Sun Haven Valley Holiday Park
Mawgan Porth, Newquay,
TR8 4BQ
Tel: 01637 860373 **3 J3**
sunhavenvalley.com
Pitches: C 38, CV 38, T 61

Sun Valley Holiday Park
Pentewan Road, St Austell,
PL26 6DJ
Tel: 01726 843266 **3 M6**
sunvalleyholidays.co.uk
Pitches: C 28, CV 28, T 29

Swiss Farm Touring & Camping
Marlow Road,
Henley-on-Thames,
RG9 2HY
Tel: 01491 573419 **20 C6**
swissfarmcamping.co.uk
Pitches: C 140, CV 140, T 100

Teversal C & C Club Site
Silverhill Lane, Teversal,
NG17 3JJ
Tel: 01623 551838 **51 L8**
thefriendlyclub.co.uk
Pitches: C 126, CV 126, T 126

The Inside Park
Down House Estate,
Blandford Forum,
DT11 9AD
Tel: 01258 453719 **8 C6**
theinsidepark.co.uk
Pitches: C 125, CV 125, T 125

The Old Brick Kilns
Little Barney Lane, Barney,
Fakenham,
NR21 0NL
Tel: 01328 878305 **44 G4**
old-brick-kilns.co.uk
Pitches: C 65, CV 65, T 60

The Old Oaks Touring Park
Wick Farm, Wick, Glastonbury,
BA6 8JS
Tel: 01458 831437 **17 M8**
theoldoaks.co.uk
Pitches: C 60, CV 20, T 20

The Quiet Site
Ullswater, Watermillock,
CA11 0LS
Tel: 07768 727016 **71 N10**
thequietsite.co.uk
Pitches: C 100, CV 100, T 100

The Star C & C Park
Star Road, Cotton, Oakamoor,
Near Alton Towers,
ST10 3DW
Tel: 01538 702219 **50 E10**
starcaravanpark.co.uk
Pitches: C 30, CV 30, T 60

Townsend Touring Park
Townsend Farm, Pembridge,
Leominster, HR6 9HB
Tel: 01544 388527 **38 H9**
townsendfarm.co.uk
Pitches: C 60, CV 60, T 60

Tregoad Park
St Martin, Looe, PL13 1PB
Tel: 01503 262718 **4 G8**
tregoadpark.co.uk
Pitches: C 150, CV 150, T 50

Trencreek Holiday Park
Hillcrest, Higher Trencreek,
Newquay, TR8 4NS
Tel: 01637 874210 **3 J4**
trencreekholidaypark.co.uk
Pitches: C 194, CV 194, T 194

Trethem Mill Touring Park
St Just-in-Roseland,
Nr St Mawes, TR2 5JF
Tel: 01872 580504 **3 J8**
trethem.com
Pitches: C 84, CV 84, T 35

Trevella Tourist Park
Crantock, Newquay,
TR8 5EW
Tel: 01637 830308 **3 J4**
trevella.co.uk
Pitches: C 313, CV 313, T 313

Troutbeck C & C Club Site
Hutton Moor End, Troutbeck,
Penrith, CA11 0SX
Tel: 01768 779615 **71 M9**
thefriendlyclub.co.uk
Pitches: C 54, CV 54, T 24

Truro C & C Park
Truro, TR4 8QN
Tel: 01872 560274 **2 H6**
liskey.co.uk
Pitches: C 51, CV 51, T 28

Tudor C & C
Shepherds Patch, Slimbridge,
Gloucester, GL2 7BP
Tel: 01453 890483 **29 K7**
tudorcaravanpark.com
Pitches: C 75, CV 75, T 30

Two Mills Touring Park
Yarmouth Road, North Walsham,
NR28 9NA
Tel: 01692 405829 **45 L4**
twomills.co.uk
Pitches: C 81, CV 81, T 70

Vale of Pickering Caravan Park
Carr House Farm, Allerston,
Pickering,
YO18 7PQ
Tel: 01723 859280 **67 J10**
valeofpickering.co.uk
Pitches: C 120, CV 120, T 120

Virginia Lake Caravan Park
Smeeth Road, St John's Fen End,
Wisbech, PE14 8JF
Tel: 01945 430332 **43 N7**
virginialake.co.uk
Pitches: C 50, CV 50, T 50

Warcombe Farm C & C Park
Station Road, Mortehoe,
EX34 7EJ
Tel: 01271 870690 **14 H3**
warcombefarm.co.uk
Pitches: C 250, CV 250, T 250

Wareham Forest Tourist Park
North Trigon, Wareham,
BH20 7NZ
Tel: 01929 551393 **8 D8**
warehamforest.co.uk
Pitches: C 200, CV 200, T 200

Waren Caravan Park
Waren Mill, Bamburgh,
NE70 7EE
Tel: 01668 214366 **81 N7**
meadowhead.co.uk
Pitches: C 120, CV 120, T 60

Watergate Bay Touring Park
Watergate Bay, Tregurrian,
TR8 4AD
Tel: 01637 860387 **3 J3**
watergatebaytouringpark.co.uk
Pitches: C 171, CV 171, T 171

Waterrow Touring Park
Wiveliscombe, Taunton,
TA4 2AZ
Tel: 01984 623464 **16 E10**
waterrowpark.co.uk
Pitches: C 38, CV 38, T 7

Wayfarers C & C Park
Relubbus Lane, St Hilary,
Penzance,
TR20 9EF
Tel: 01736 763326 **2 E9**
wayfarerspark.co.uk
Pitches: C 45, CV 5, T 15

Wells Holiday Park
Haybridge, Wells,
BA5 1AJ
Tel: 01749 676869 **17 M7**
wellsholidaypark.co.uk
Pitches: C 72, CV 54, T 30

West Runton C & C Club Site
Holgate Lane, West Runton,
Cromer,
NR27 9NW
Tel: 01263 837544 **45 K2**
thefriendlyclub.co.uk
Pitches: C 200, CV 200, T 200

Westwood Caravan Park
Old Felixstowe Road,
Bucklesham, Ipswich,
IP10 0BN
Tel: 01473 659637 **35 L8**
westwoodcaravanpark.co.uk
Pitches: C 100, CV 100, T 100

Whitefield Forest Touring Park
Brading Road, Ryde,
Isle of Wight,
PO33 1QL
Tel: 01983 617069 **9 Q9**
whitefieldforest.co.uk
Pitches: C 80, CV 80, T 80

Whitemead Caravan Park
East Burton Road, Wool,
BH20 6HG
Tel: 01929 462241 **8 C9**
whitemeadcaravanpark.co.uk
Pitches: C 95, CV 95, T 95

Whitsand Bay Lodge & Touring Park
Millbrook, Torpoint,
PL10 1JZ
Tel: 01752 822597 **5 J9**
whitsandbayholidays.co.uk
Pitches: C 49, CV 49, T 0

Wicks Farm Camping Park
Redlands Lane, West Wittering,
Chichester, PO20 8QE
Tel: 01243 513116 **10 C9**
wicksfarm.co.uk
Pitches: C 0, CV 40, T 40

Widdicombe Farm Touring Park
Marldon, Paignton,
TQ3 1ST
Tel: 01803 558325 **6 B9**
widdicombefarm.co.uk
Pitches: C 180, CV 180, T 20

Widemouth Fields C & C Park
Park Farm, Poundstock, Bude,
EX23 0NA
Tel: 01288 361351 **14 D11**
widemouthbaytouring.co.uk
Pitches: C 156, CV 156, T 120

Widend Touring Park
Berry Pomeroy Road, Marldon,
Paignton, TQ3 1RT
Tel: 01803 550116 **6 B9**
Pitches: C 207, CV 207, T 207

Wild Rose Park
Ormside,
Appleby-in-Westmorland,
CA16 6EJ
Tel: 017683 51077 **64 C4**
wildrose.co.uk
Pitches: C 240, CV 100, T 20

Wilksworth Farm Caravan Park
Cranborne Road,
Wimborne Minster,
BH21 4HW
Tel: 01202 885467 **8 E7**
wilksworthfarmcaravanpark.co.uk
Pitches: C 60, CV 60, T 25

Willow Valley Holiday Park
Bush, Bude, EX23 9LB
Tel: 01288 353104 **14 E9**
willowvalley.co.uk
Pitches: C 41, CV 41, T 41

Windermere C & C Club Site
Ashes Lane, Staveley, Kendal,
LA8 9JS
Tel: 01539 821119 **63 J3**
thefriendlyclub.co.uk
Pitches: C 250, CV 250, T 250

Wood Farm C & C Park
Axminster Road, Charmouth,
DT6 6BT
Tel: 01297 560697 **7 J4**
woodfarm.co.uk
Pitches: C 175, CV 175, T 35

Wooda Farm Holiday Park
Poughill, Bude,
EX23 9HJ
Tel: 01288 352069 **14 D9**
wooda.co.uk
Pitches: C 100, CV 50, T 50

Woodclose Caravan Park
High Casterton, Kirkby Lonsdale,
LA6 2SE
Tel: 01524 271597 **63 L6**
woodclosepark.com
Pitches: C 17, CV 17, T 12

Woodland Springs Adult Touring Park
Venton, Drewsteignton,
EX6 6PG
Tel: 01647 231695 **5 N2**
woodlandsprings.co.uk
Pitches: C 85, CV 39, T 38

Woodlands Leisure Park
Blackawton, Dartmouth,
TQ9 7DQ
Tel: 01803 712598 **5 Q9**
woodlands-caravanpark.com
Pitches: C 170, CV 25, T 30

Woodlands Park
Wash Lane, Allostock,
Knutsford, WA16 9LG
Tel: 01565 723429 **49 N2**
Pitches: C 30, CV 10, T 10

Woodovis Park
Gulworthy, Tavistock,
PL19 8NY
Tel: 01822 832968 **5 J5**
woodovis.com
Pitches: C 50, CV 50, T 50

Yeatheridge Farm Caravan Park
East Worlington, Crediton,
EX17 4TN
Tel: 01884 860330 **15 N9**
yeatheridge.co.uk
Pitches: C 85, CV 85, T 85

York Touring Caravan Site
Greystones Farm, Towthorpe
Moor Lane, Towthorpe, York,
YO32 9ST
Tel: 01904 499275 **59 P3**
yorkcaravansite.co.uk
Pitches: C 20, CV 20, T 20

Zeacombe House Caravan Park
Blackerton Cross, East Anstey,
Tiverton, EX16 9JU
Tel: 01398 341279 **15 P7**
zeacombeadultretreat.co.uk
Pitches: C 50, CV 50, T 50

SCOTLAND

Aird Donald Caravan Park
London Road, Stranraer,
DG9 8RN
Tel: 01776 702025 **68 E7**
aird-donald.co.uk
Pitches: C 50, CV 15, T 35

Anwoth Caravan Site
Gatehouse of Fleet,
Castle Douglas, DG7 2JU
Tel: 01557 814333 **69 N7**
auchenlarie.co.uk
Pitches: C 28, CV 28, T 28

Barrhill Holiday Park
Barrhill, Girvan,
KA26 0PZ
Tel: 01465 821355 **68 G3**
barrhillholidaypark.com
Pitches: C 20, CV 20, T 10

Beecraigs C & C Site
Beecraigs Country Park,
The Park Centre, Linlithgow,
EH49 6PL
Tel: 01506 844516 **86 B7**
beecraigs.com
Pitches: C 36, CV 36, T 14

Blair Castle Caravan Park
Blair Atholl, Pitlochry,
PH18 5SR
Tel: 01796 481263 **92 C3**
blaircastlecaravanpark.co.uk
Pitches: C 190, CV 27, T 63

Braids Caravan Park
Annan Road, Gretna,
DG16 5DQ
Tel: 01461 337409 **71 M3**
thebraidscaravanpark.co.uk
Pitches: C 93, CV 93, T 0

Brighouse Bay Holiday Park
Brighouse Bay, Borgue,
DG6 4TS
Tel: 01557 870267 **69 P9**
gillespie-leisure.co.uk
Pitches: C 120, CV 120, T 70

Camusdarach Campsite
Arisaig,
PH39 4NT
Tel: 01687 450221 **97 J10**
camusdarach.com
Pitches: C 42, CV 42, T 42

Castle Cary Holiday Park
Creetown, Newton Stewart,
DG8 7DQ
Tel: 01671 820264 **69 L7**
castlecary-caravans.com
Pitches: C 50, CV 50, T 50

Craigtoun Meadows Holiday Park
Mount Melville, St Andrews,
KY16 8PQ
Tel: 01334 475959 **93 N11**
craigtounmeadows.co.uk
Pitches: C 55, CV 55, T 2

Crossburn Caravan Park
Edinburgh Road, Peebles,
EH45 8ED
Tel: 01721 720501 **79 L1**
crossburncaravans.co.uk
Pitches: C 45, CV 45, T 45

Drum Mohr Caravan Park
Levenhall, Musselburgh,
EH21 8JS
Tel: 0131 665 6867 **86 H7**
drummohr.org
Pitches: C 45, CV 45, T 30

Dunbar C & C Club Site
Oxwellmains, Dunbar,
EH42 1WG
Tel: 01368 866881 **87 N6**
thefriendlyclub.co.uk
Pitches: C 90, CV 90, T 90

East Bowstrips Caravan Park
St Cyrus, Nr Montrose,
DD10 0DE
Tel: 01674 850328 **95 M8**
caravancampingsites.co.uk
Pitches: C 27, CV 27, T 5

Faskally Caravan Park
Pitlochry, Perthshire,
PH16 5LA
Tel: 01796 472007 **92 D4**
faskally.co.uk
Pitches: C 300, CV 300, T 100

Glen Nevis C & C Park
Glen Nevis, Fort William,
PH33 6SX
Tel: 01397 702191 **90 F2**
glen-nevis.co.uk
Pitches: C 250, CV 250, T 130

Glencoe C & C Club Site
Glencoe, PH49 4LA
Tel: 01855 811397 **90 F5**
thefriendlyclub.co.uk
Pitches: C 120, CV 120, T 120

Glendochart Holiday Park
Luib, Crianlarich,
FK20 8QT
Tel: 01567 820637 **91 L10**
glendochart-caravanpark.co.uk
Pitches: C 28, CV 28, T 7

Glenearly Caravan Park
Dalbeattie,
DG5 4NE
Tel: 01556 611393 **70 D3**
glenearlycaravanpark.co.uk
Pitches: C 39, CV 39, T 39

Hoddom Castle Caravan Park
Hoddom, Lockerbie,
DG11 1AS
Tel: 01576 300251 **71 J2**
hoddomcastle.co.uk
Pitches: C 170, CV 170, T 40

Huntly Castle Caravan Park
The Meadow, Huntly,
AB54 4UJ
Tel: 01466 794999 **102 C7**
huntlycastle.co.uk
Pitches: C 66, CV 66, T 24

Invercoe C & C Park
Glencoe, Ballachulish,
PH49 4HP
Tel: 01855 811210 **90 F5**
invercoe.co.uk
Pitches: C 60, CV 60, T 60

King Robert the Bruce's Cave
Cove Estate,
Kirkpatrick Fleming, Gretna,
DG11 3AT
Tel: 01461 800285 **71 L2**
brucescave.co.uk
Pitches: C 50, CV 10, T 15

Linnhe Lochside Holidays
Corpach, Fort William,
PH33 7NL
Tel: 01397 772376 **90 E2**
linnhe-lochside-holidays.co.uk
Pitches: C 63, CV 63, T 22

Lomond Woods Holiday Park
Old Luss Road, Balloch,
Loch Lomond,
G83 8QP
Tel: 01389 755000 **84 G6**
holiday-parks.co.uk
Pitches: C 100, CV 10, T 0

Machrihanish Caravan Park
East Trodigal, Machrihanish,
Mull of Kintyre,
PA28 6PT
Tel: 01586 810366 **75 J8**
campkintyre.co.uk
Pitches: C 32, CV 25, T 50

Milarrochy Bay C & C Club Site
Milarrochy Bay, Balmaha,
Drymen,
G63 0AL
Tel: 01360 870236 **84 G5**
thefriendlyclub.co.uk
Pitches: C 150, CV 150, T 150

Milton of Fonab Caravan Site
Bridge Road, Pitlochry,
PH16 5NA
Tel: 01796 472882 **92 E4**
fonab.co.uk
Pitches: C 114, CV 15, T 25

River Tilt Caravan Park
Blair Atholl, Pitlochry,
PH18 5TE
Tel: 01796 481467 **92 D3**
rivertilt.co.uk
Pitches: C 37, CV 37, T 37

Riverview Caravan Park
Marine Drive, Monifieth,
DD5 4NN
Tel: 01382 535471 **93 N8**
riverview.co.uk
Pitches: C 40, CV 40, T 0

Sands of Luce Holiday Park
Sands of Luce, Sandhead,
Stranraer,
DG9 9JN
Tel: 01776 830456 **68 E8**
sandsofluceholidaypark.co.uk
Pitches: C 25, CV 10, T 15

Seaward Caravan Park
Dhoon Bay, Kirkudbright,
DG6 4TJ
Tel: 01557 870267 **69 P8**
gillespie-leisure.co.uk
Pitches: C 20, CV 20, T 12

Shieling Holidays
Craignure, Isle of Mull,
PA65 6AY
Tel: 01680 812496 **89 P8**
shielingholidays.co.uk
Pitches: C 30, CV 30, T 60

Silver Sands Leisure Park
Covesea, West Beach,
Lossiemouth,
IV31 6SP
Tel: 01343 813262 **101 J2**
travel.to/silversands
Pitches: C 140, CV 140, T 140

Springwood Caravan Park
Kelso, TD5 8LS
Tel: 01573 224596 **80 F7**
springwood.biz
Pitches: C 20, CV 20, T 0

The Park of Brandedleys
Crocketford, Dumfries,
DG2 8RG
Tel: 01387 266700 **70 D2**
holgates.com
Pitches: C 80, CV 40, T 40

Thurston Manor Holiday Home Park
Innerwick, Dunbar,
EH42 1SA
Tel: 01368 840643 **87 N7**
thurstonmanor.co.uk
Pitches: C 100, CV 10, T 20

Trossachs Holiday Park
Aberfoyle, FK8 3SA
Tel: 01877 382614 **85 J4**
trossachsholiday.co.uk
Pitches: C 46, CV 46, T 20

Witches Craig C & C Park
Blairlogie, Stirling,
FK9 5PX
Tel: 01786 474947 **85 N4**
witchescraig.co.uk
Pitches: C 60, CV 60, T 60

WALES

Barcdy Touring C & C Park
Talsarnau, LL47 6YG
Tel: 01766 770736 **47 K4**
barcdy.co.uk
Pitches: C 35, CV 5, T 40

Bishops Meadow Caravan Park
Bishops Meadow, Hay Road,
Brecon, LD3 9SW
Tel: 01874 610000 **27 M3**
bishops-meadow.co.uk
Pitches: C 25, CV 25, T 32

Bodnant Caravan Park
Nebo Road, Llanrwst,
Conwy Valley,
LL26 0SD
Tel: 01492 640248 **55 L9**
bodnant-caravan-park.co.uk
Pitches: C 38, CV 54, T 16

Bron Derw Touring Caravan Park
Llanrwst, LL26 0YT
Tel: 01492 640494 **55 L8**
bronderw-wales.co.uk
Pitches: C 20, CV 20, T 0

Bron-Y-Wendon Caravan Park
Wern Road, Llanddulas,
Colwyn Bay, LL22 8HG
Tel: 01492 512903 **55 N6**
northwales-holidays.co.uk
Pitches: C 120, CV 10, T 0

Bryn Gloch C & C Park
Betws Garmon, Caernarfon,
LL54 7YY
Tel: 01286 650216 **54 G9**
bryngloch.co.uk
Pitches: C 80, CV 80, T 80

Caerfai Bay Caravan & Tent Park
Caerfai Bay, St David's,
Haverfordwest,
SA62 6QT
Tel: 01437 720274 **24 D4**
caerfaibay.co.uk
Pitches: C 26, CV 18, T 78

Cenarth Falls Holiday Park
Cenarth, Newcastle Emlyn,
SA38 9JS
Tel: 01239 710345 **36 D11**
cenarth-holipark.co.uk
Pitches: C 30, CV 30, T 30

Creampots Touring C & C Park
Broadway, Broad Haven,
Haverfordwest,
SA62 3TU
Tel: 01437 781776 **24 F6**
creampots.co.uk
Pitches: C 56, CV 9, T 40

Dinlle Caravan Park
Dinas Dinlle, Caernarfon,
LL54 5TW
Tel: 01286 830324 **54 F9**
thornleyleisure.co.uk
Pitches: C 100, CV 20, T 50

Eisteddfa, Eisteddfa Lodge
Pentrefelin, Criccieth,
LL52 0PT
Tel: 01766 522696 **46 H4**
eisteddfapark.co.uk
Pitches: C 6, CV 27, T 70

Erwlon C & C Park
Brecon Road, Llandovery,
SA20 0RD
Tel: 01550 721021 **26 G2**
erwlon.co.uk
Pitches: C 40, CV 10, T 20

Hendre Mynach Touring C & C Park
Llanaber Road, Barmouth,
LL42 1YR
Tel: 01341 280262 **47 K7**
hendremynach.co.uk
Pitches: C 60, CV 60, T 120

Home Farm Caravan Park
Marian-Glas, Isle of Anglesey,
LL73 8PH
Tel: 01248 410614 **54 G5**
homefarm-anglesey.co.uk
Pitches: C 98, CV 10, T 20

Hunters Hamlet Caravan Park
Sirior Goch Farm, Betws-yn-Rhos,
Abergele, LL22 8PL
Tel: 01745 832237 **55 N7**
huntershamlet.co.uk
Pitches: C 23, CV 23, T 0

Pencelli Castle C & C Park
Pencelli, Brecon, LD3 7LX
Tel: 01874 665451 **27 M4**
pencelli-castle.com
Pitches: C 40, CV 40, T 60

Pen-Y-Bont
Llangynog Road, Bala,
LL23 7PH
Tel: 01678 520549 **47 Q4**
penybont-bala.co.uk
Pitches: C 59, CV 35, T 36

Pont Kemys C & C Park
Chainbridge, Abergavenny,
NP7 9DS
Tel: 01873 880688 **28 D7**
pontkemys.com
Pitches: C 45, CV 45, T 20

River View Touring Park
The Dingle, Llanedi,
Pontarddulais, SA4 0FH
Tel: 01269 844876 **26 D7**
riverviewtouringpark.com
Pitches: C 60, CV 10, T 30

The Plassey Leisure Park
The Plassey, Eyton, Wrexham,
LL13 0SP
Tel: 01978 780277 **48 G6**
plassey.com
Pitches: C 30, CV 45, T 15

Trawsdir Touring C & C Park
Llanaber, Barmouth,
LL42 1RR
Tel: 01341 280999 **47 K7**
barmouthholidays.co.uk
Pitches: C 70, CV 70, T 30

Trefalun Park
Devonshire Drive, St Florence,
Tenby, SA70 8RD
Tel: 01646 651514 **25 J7**
trefalunpark.co.uk
Pitches: C 55, CV 5, T 30

Tyddyn Isaf Caravan Park
Lligwy Bay, Dulas, Anglesey,
LL70 9PQ
Tel: 01248 410203 **54 G4**
tyddynisaf.co.uk
Pitches: C 6, CV 4, T 20

Well Park C & C Site
Tenby, SA70 8TL
Tel: 01834 842179 **25 K8**
wellparkcaravans.co.uk
Pitches: C 40, CV 10, T 50

White Tower Caravan Park
Llandwrog, Caernarfon,
LL54 5UH
Tel: 01286 830649 **54 F9**
whitetower.supanet.com
Pitches: C 70, CV 29, T 5

CHANNEL ISLANDS

Beuvelande Camp Site
Beuvelande, St Martin, Jersey,
JE3 6EZ
Tel: 01534 853575 **7 c1**
campingjersey.com
Pitches: C 0, CV 0, T 150

Bleu Soleil Campsite
La Route de Vinchelez, Leoville,
St Ouen, JE3 2DB
Tel: 01534 481007 **7 a1**
bleusoleilcamping.com
Pitches: C 0, CV 55, T 55

Fauxquets Valley Campsite
Castel, Guernsey, GY5 7QL
Tel: 01481 236951 **6 b2**
fauxquets.co.uk
Pitches: C 0, CV 0, T 120

Rozel Camping Park
Summerville Farm, St Martin,
Jersey, JE3 6AX
Tel: 01534 855200 **7 c1**
rozelcamping.com
Pitches: C 15, CV 15, T 100

Tourist sites with satnav friendly postcodes

ENGLAND

- Acorn Bank Garden
  CA10 1SP Cumb 64 B2
- Aldborough Roman Site
  YO51 9ES N York 59 K2
- Alfriston Clergy House
  BN26 5TL E Susx 11 Q9
- Alton Towers
  ST10 4DB Staffs 50 E11
- Anglesey Abbey
  CB25 9EJ Cambs 33 N4
- Anne Hathaway's Cottage
  CV37 9HH Warwks 30 F3
- Antony House
  PL11 2QA Cnwll 5 J8
- Appuldurcombe House
  PO38 3EW IoW 9 P10
- Apsley House
  W1J 7NT Gt Lon 21 L7
- Arlington Court
  EX31 4LP Devon 15 K4
- Ascott
  LU7 0PS Bucks 32 C11
- Ashton Court Estate
  BS41 9JN N Som 17 M2
- Athelhampton House & Gardens
  DT2 7LG Dorset 8 B8
- Attingham Park
  SY4 4TP Shrops 49 K12
- Audley End House & Gardens
  CB11 4JF Essex 33 N8
- Avebury Manor & Garden
  SN8 1RF Wilts 18 G6
- Baconsthorpe Castle
  NR25 6LN Norfk 45 J3
- Baddesley Clinton Hall
  B93 0DQ Warwks 40 G11
- Bamburgh Castle
  NE69 7DF Nthumb 81 N7
- Barnard Castle
  DL12 8PW Dur 65 J4
- Barrington Court
  TA19 0NQ Somset 17 K11
- Basildon Park
  RG8 9NR W Berk 19 Q5
- Bateman's
  TN19 7DS E Susx 12 D5
- Battle of Britain Memorial Flight
  LN4 4SY Lincs 52 H11
- Beamish Open Air Museum
  DH9 0RG Dur 73 L9
- Beatrix Potter Gallery
  LA22 0NS Cumb 62 G3
- Beaulieu House
  SO42 7ZN Hants 9 L6
- Belton House
  NG32 2LS Lincs 42 D3
- Belvoir Castle
  NG32 1PD Leics 42 B4
- Bembridge Windmill
  PO35 5SQ IoW 9 Q9
- Beningbrough Hall & Gardens
  YO30 1DD N York 59 M3
- Benthall Hall
  TF12 5RX Shrops 39 M2
- Berkeley Castle
  GL13 9BQ Gloucs 29 J8
- Berrington Hall
  HR6 0DW Herefs 39 K9
- Berry Pomeroy Castle
  TQ9 6NJ Devon 6 B9
- Beth Chatto Gardens
  CO7 7DB Essex 34 H11
- Biddulph Grange Garden
  ST8 7SD Staffs 50 B8
- Bishop's Waltham Palace
  SO32 1DH Hants 9 P4
- Blackpool Pleasure Beach
  FY4 1EZ Bpool 56 F3
- Blenheim Palace
  OX20 1PX Oxon 31 K10
- Blickling Hall
  NR11 6NF Norfk 45 K4
- Blue John Cavern
  S33 8WP Derbys 50 F4
- Bodiam Castle
  TN32 5UA E Susx 12 F5
- Bolsover Castle
  S44 6PR Derbys 51 L6
- Boscobel House
  ST19 9AR Staffs 39 Q1
- Bovington Tank Museum
  BH20 6JG Dorset 8 C9
- Bowes Castle
  DL12 9LD Dur 64 H5

- Bradgate Country Park
  LE6 0HE Leics 41 M5
- Bradley Manor
  TQ12 6BN Devon 6 B8
- Bramber Castle
  BN44 3WW W Susx 11 J7
- Brinkburn Priory
  NE65 8AP Nthumb 73 K2
- Bristol Zoo
  BS8 3HA Bristl 17 N2
- British Library
  NW1 2DB Gt Lon 21 L6
- British Museum
  WC1B 3DG Gt Lon 21 L7
- Brockhampton Estate
  WR6 5TB Herefs 39 M10
- Brough Castle
  CA17 4EJ Cumb 64 E5
- Buckfast Abbey
  TQ11 0EE Devon 5 P6
- Buckingham Palace
  SW1A 1AA Gt Lon 21 L7
- Buckland Abbey
  PL20 6EY Devon 5 K6
- Buscot Park
  SN7 8BU Oxon 19 J2
- Byland Abbey
  YO61 4BD N York 66 D10
- Caldicot Castle & Country Park
  NP26 4HU Mons 28 F10
- Calke Abbey
  DE73 7LE Derbys 41 J3
- Canons Ashby House
  NN11 3SD Nhants 31 M4
- Canterbury Cathedral
  CT1 2EH Kent 23 M10
- Carisbrooke Castle
  PO30 1XY IoW 9 N9
- Carlyle's House
  SW3 5HL Gt Lon 21 L7
- Castle Drogo
  EX6 6PB Devon 5 P3
- Castle Howard
  YO60 7DA N York 66 G12
- Castle Rising Castle
  PE31 6AH Norfk 43 Q5
- Charlecote Park
  CV35 9ER Warwks 30 H3
- Chartwell
  TN16 1PS Kent 21 N12
- Chastleton House
  GL56 0SU Oxon 30 G8
- Chatsworth
  DE45 1PP Derbys 50 H6
- Chedworth Roman Villa
  GL54 3LJ Gloucs 30 D10
- Chessington World of Adventures
  KT9 2NE Gt Lon 21 J10
- Chester Cathedral
  CH1 2HU Ches 48 H3
- Chester Zoo
  CH2 1LH Ches 48 H2
- Chesters Roman Fort
  NE46 4EP Nthumb 72 G6
- Chiswick House
  W4 2RP Gt Lon 21 K7
- Chysauster Ancient Village
  TR20 8XA Cnwll 2 C8
- Clandon Park
  GU4 7RQ Surrey 20 G12
- Claremont Landscape Garden
  KT10 9JG Surrey 20 H10
- Claydon House
  MK18 2EY Bucks 31 Q8
- Cleeve Abbey
  TA23 0PS Somset 16 E7
- Clevedon Court
  BS21 6QU N Som 17 K2
- Cliveden
  SL6 0JA Bucks 20 E6
- Clouds Hill
  BH20 7NQ Dorset 8 B8
- Clumber Park
  S80 3AZ Notts 51 N6
- Colchester Zoo
  CO3 0SL Essex 34 F11
- Coleridge Cottage
  TA5 1NQ Somset 16 G8
- Coleton Fishacre
  TQ6 0EQ Devon 6 B11
- Compton Castle
  TQ3 1TA Devon 6 B9
- Conisbrough Castle
  DN12 3HH Donc 51 L2
- Corbridge Roman Site
  NE45 5NT Nthumb 72 H7
- Corfe Castle
  BH20 5EZ Dorset 8 E10
- Cornish Mines & Engines
  TR15 3NP Cnwll 2 G7
- Cotehele
  PL12 6TA Cnwll 5 J6

- Coughton Court
  B49 5JA Warwks 30 E3
- Courts Garden
  BA14 6RR Wilts 18 C8
- Cragside
  NE65 7PX Nthumb 73 J1
- Crealy Adventure Park
  EX5 1DR Devon 6 D5
- Crich Tramway Village
  DE4 5DP Derbys 51 J9
- Croft Castle
  HR6 9PW Herefs 39 J8
- Croome Park
  WR8 9JS Worcs 30 B5
- Deddington Castle
  OX15 0TE Oxon 31 L7
- Didcot Railway Centre
  OX11 7NJ Oxon 19 N3
- Dover Castle
  CT16 1HU Kent 13 P2
- Drayton Manor Theme Park
  B78 3TW Staffs 40 G7
- Dudmaston
  WV15 6QN Shrops 39 N4
- Dunham Massey
  WA14 4SJ Traffd 57 N10
- Dunstanburgh Castle
  NE66 3TT Nthumb 81 Q9
- Dunster Castle
  TA24 6SL Somset 16 D7
- Durham Cathedral
  DH1 3EH Dur 73 M11
- Dyrham Park
  SN14 8ER S Glos 17 Q2
- East Riddlesden Hall
  BD20 5EL Brad 58 E6
- Eden Project
  PL24 2SG Cnwll 3 M5
- Eltham Palace
  SE9 5QE Gt Lon 21 N8
- Emmetts Garden
  TN14 6AY Kent 21 P11
- Fairlands Valley Park
  SG2 0BL Herts 33 J11
- Farleigh Hungerford Castle
  BA2 7RS Somset 18 B8
- Farnborough Hall
  OX17 1DU Warwks 31 K4
- Felbrigg Hall
  NR11 8PR Norfk 45 K3
- Fenton House
  NW3 6RT Gt Lon 21 L6
- Finch Foundry
  EX20 2NW Devon 5 M2
- Finchale Priory
  DH1 5SH Dur 73 N10
- Fishbourne Roman Palace
  PO19 3QR W Susx 10 D8
- Flamingo Family Fun Park
  TN34 3AR E Susx 12 G8
- Flamingo Land
  YO17 6UX N York 66 H10
- Forde Abbey
  TA20 4LU Dorset 7 J2
- Fountains Abbey & Studley Royal
  HG4 3DY N York 58 H1
- Gawthorpe Hall
  BB12 8UA Lancs 57 P3
- Gisborough Priory
  TS14 6HG R & Cl 66 E4
- Glendurgan
  TR11 5JZ Cnwll 2 H9
- Goodrich Castle
  HR9 6HY Herefs 28 G5
- Great Chalfield Manor
  SN12 8NH Wilts 18 C7
- Great Yarmouth Pleasure Beach
  NR30 3EH Norfk 45 Q8
- Greenway
  TQ5 0ES Devon 6 B10
- Greyfriars
  WR1 2LZ Worcs 39 Q10
- Hailes Abbey
  GL54 5PB Gloucs 30 D7
- Ham House
  TW10 7RS Gt Lon 21 J8
- Hampton Court Palace
  KT8 9AU Gt Lon 21 J9
- Hanbury Hall
  WR9 7EA Worcs 30 C2
- Hardwick Hall
  S44 5QJ Derbys 51 L7
- Hardy's Cottage
  DT2 8QJ Dorset 7 Q4
- Hare Hill
  SK10 4QB Ches 57 Q12
- Hatchlands Park
  GU4 7RT Surrey 20 H11
- Heale Gardens
  SP4 6NT Wilts 18 G12
- Helmsley Castle
  YO62 5AB N York 66 E10

- Hereford Cathedral
  HR1 2NG Herefs 28 F2
- Hergest Croft Gardens
  HR5 3EG Herefs 38 F10
- Hever Castle & Gardens
  TN8 7NG Kent 11 P2
- Hidcote Manor Garden
  GL55 6LR Gloucs 30 F5
- Hill Top
  LA22 0LF Cumb 62 G3
- Hinton Ampner
  SO24 0LA Hants 9 P2
- Holkham Hall
  NR23 1AB Norfk 44 E2
- Housesteads Roman Fort
  NE47 6NN Nthumb 72 E7
- Howletts Wild Animal Park
  CT4 5EL Kent 23 M11
- Hughenden Manor
  HP14 4LA Bucks 20 D4
- Hurst Castle
  SO41 0TR Hants 9 K9
- Ickworth House & Gardens
  IP29 5QE Suffk 34 D5
- Ightham Mote
  TN15 0NT Kent 22 C11
- Ironbridge Gorge Museums
  TF8 7DQ Wrekin 39 M2
- Kedleston Hall
  DE22 5JH Derbys 50 H11
- Kenilworth Castle
  CV8 1NE Warwks 40 H11
- Kenwood House
  NW3 7JR Gt Lon 21 L6
- Kew Gardens
  TW9 3AB Gt Lon 21 J7
- Killerton House & Garden
  EX5 3LE Devon 6 D3
- King John's Hunting Lodge
  BS26 2AP Somset 17 L5
- Kingston Lacy
  BH21 4EA Dorset 8 E7
- Kirby Hall
  NN17 3EN Nhants 42 D10
- Knightshayes Court
  EX16 7RQ Devon 16 C12
- Knole
  TN15 0RP Kent 22 B11
- Knowsley Safari Park
  L34 4AN Knows 57 J9
- Lacock Abbey
  SN15 2LG Wilts 18 D7
- Lamb House
  TN31 7ES E Susx 12 H6
- Lanhydrock
  PL30 5AD Cnwll 3 N3
- Launceston Castle
  PL15 7DR Cnwll 4 H4
- Leeds Castle
  ME17 1PL Kent 22 G11
- Lindisfarne Castle
  TD15 2SH Nthumb 81 N6
- Lindisfarne Priory
  TD15 2RX Nthumb 81 N6
- Little Moreton Hall
  CW12 4SD Ches 49 P4
- Liverpool Cathedral
  L1 7AZ Lpool 56 G10
- London Zoo
  NW1 4RY Gt Lon 21 L6
- Long Crendon Courthouse
  HP18 9AN Bucks 20 B2
- Longleat
  BA12 7NW Wilts 18 B11
- Lost Gardens of Heligan
  PL26 6EN Cnwll 3 M6
- Ludgershall Castle
  SP11 9QR Wilts 19 J9
- Lydford Castle
  EX20 4BH Devon 5 K4
- Lyme Park
  SK12 2NX Ches 50 C4
- Lytes Cary Manor
  TA11 7HU Somset 17 M10
- Lyveden New Bield
  PE8 5AH Nhants 42 E11
- Maiden Castle
  DT2 9PP Dorset 7 P5
- Mapledurham House
  RG4 7TR Oxon 19 R5
- Marble Hill House
  TW1 2NL Gt Lon 21 J8
- Marwell Zoological Park
  SO21 1JH Hants 9 N3
- Melford Hall
  CO10 9AA Suffk 34 E7
- Merseyside Maritime Museum
  L3 4AQ Lpool 56 G10
- Minster Lovell Hall
  OX29 0RN Oxon 30 H10
- Mompesson House
  SP1 2EL Wilts 8 G2

- Monk Bretton Priory
  S71 5QD Barns 59 J11
- Montacute House
  TA15 6XP Somset 17 M11
- Morwellham Quay
  PL19 8JL Devon 5 J6
- Moseley Old Hall
  WV10 7HY Staffs 40 B6
- Mottisfont Abbey & Garden
  SO51 0LP Hants 9 K3
- Mottistone Manor Garden
  PO30 4ED IoW 9 L10
- Mount Grace Priory
  DL6 3JG N York 66 C7
- National Gallery
  WC2N 5DN Gt Lon 21 L7
- National Maritime Museum
  SE10 9NF Gt Lon 21 M7
- National Motorcycle Museum
  B92 0EJ Solhll 40 G10
- National Portrait Gallery
  WC2H 0HE Gt Lon 21 L7
- National Railway Museum
  YO26 4XJ York 59 N4
- National Space Centre
  LE4 5NS C Leic 41 N6
- Natural History Museum
  SW7 5BD Gt Lon 21 L7
- Needles Old Battery
  PO39 0JH IoW 9 K9
- Nether Alderley Mill
  SK10 4TW Ches 49 Q1
- Netley Abbey
  SO31 5FB Hants 9 M5
- Newark Air Museum
  NG24 2NY Notts 52 B11
- Newtown Old Town Hall
  PO30 4PA IoW 9 N8
- North Leigh Roman Villa
  OX29 6QB Oxon 31 K10
- Norwich Cathedral
  NR1 4DH Norfk 45 K8
- Nostell Priory
  WF4 1QE Wakefd 59 K10
- Nunnington Hall
  YO62 5UY N York 66 F10
- Nymans
  RH17 6EB W Susx 11 L4
- Old Royal Naval College
  SE10 9LW Gt Lon 21 M7
- Old Sarum
  SP1 3SD Wilts 8 G2
- Old Wardour Castle
  SP3 6RR Wilts 8 D3
- Oldway Mansion
  TQ3 2TE Torbay 6 B9
- Orford Castle
  IP12 2ND Suffk 35 N6
- Ormesby Hall
  TS7 9AS R & Cl 66 D4
- Osborne House
  PO32 6JY IoW 9 N8
- Osterley Park & House
  TW7 4RB Gt Lon 21 J7
- Overbeck's
  TQ8 8LW Devon 5 P11
- Oxburgh Hall
  PE33 9PS Norfk 44 C9
- Packwood House
  B94 6AT Warwks 40 F11
- Paignton Zoo
  TQ4 7EU Torbay 6 B10
- Paycocke's
  CO6 1NS Essex 34 D11
- Peckover House & Garden
  PE13 1JR Cambs 43 M8
- Pendennis Castle
  TR11 4LP Cnwll 3 J8
- Petworth House & Park
  GU28 0AE W Susx 10 F6
- Pevensey Castle
  BN24 5LE E Susx 12 D8
- Peveril Castle
  S33 8WQ Derbys 50 F4
- Polesden Lacey
  RH5 6BD Surrey 21 J11
- Portland Castle
  DT5 1AZ Dorset 7 P7
- Portsmouth Historic Dockyard
  PO1 3LJ C Port 9 Q7
- Powderham Castle
  EX6 8JQ Devon 6 C6
- Prior Park Landscape Garden
  BA2 5AH BaNES 18 B8
- Prudhoe Castle
  NE42 6NA Nthumb 73 J8
- Quarry Bank Mill
  SK9 4LA Ches 57 Q11
- Quebec House
  TN16 1TD Kent 21 N11
- Ramsey Abbey Gatehouse
  PE26 1BX Cambs 43 J11

- Reculver Towers
CT6 6SU Kent 23 N9
- Red House
DA6 8JF Gt Lon 21 P8
- Restormel Castle
PL22 0HN Cnwll 4 D7
- Richborough Roman Fort
CT13 9JW Kent 23 P10
- Richmond Castle
DL10 4QW N York 65 L7
- Roche Abbey
S66 8NW Rothm 51 M3
- Rochester Castle
ME1 1SX Medway 22 E9
- Rockbourne Roman Villa
SP6 3PG Hants 8 G4
- Roman Baths & Pump Room
BA1 1LZ BaNES 17 Q4
- Royal Observatory Greenwich
SE10 9NF Gt Lon 21 M7
- Rufford Old Hall
L40 1SG Lancs 57 J5
- Runnymede
SL4 2JJ W & M 20 F8
- Rushton Triangular Lodge
NN14 1RP Nhants 42 B12
- Rycote Chapel
OX9 2PA Oxon 31 P12
- Salisbury Cathedral
SP1 2EJ Wilts 8 G2
- Saltram
PL7 1UH C Plym 5 L8
- Sandham Memorial Chapel
RG20 9JT Hants 19 M8
- Sandringham House & Grounds
PE35 6EN Norfk 44 B4
- Saxtead Green Post Mill
IP13 9QQ Suffk 35 L4
- Scarborough Castle
YO11 1HY N York 67 M9
- Science Museum
SW7 2DD Gt Lon 21 L7
- Scotney Castle
TN3 8JN Kent 12 D3
- Shaw's Corner
AL6 9BX Herts 32 H12
- Sheffield Park Garden
TN22 3QX E Susx 11 N5
- Sherborne Old Castle
DT9 3SA Dorset 17 P11
- Sissinghurst Castle Garden
TN17 2AB Kent 12 F3
- Sizergh Castle & Garden
LA8 8AE Cumb 63 J5
- Smallhythe Place
TN30 7NG Kent 12 H4
- Snowshill Manor
WR12 7JU Gloucs 30 E7
- Souter Lighthouse
SR6 7NH S Tyne 73 P7
- Speke Hall
L24 1XD Lpool 56 H11
- Spinnaker Tower
PO1 3TT C Port 9 Q7
- SS Great Britain
BS1 6TY Bristl 17 N2
- St Michael's Mount
TR17 0HT Cnwll 2 D9
- St Paul's Cathedral
EC4M 8AD Gt Lon 21 L7
- Stokesay Castle
SY7 9AH Shrops 38 H6
- Stonehenge
SP4 7DE Wilts 18 G11
- Stourhead
BA12 6QD Wilts 8 B1
- Stowe Landscape Gardens
MK18 5EH Bucks 31 P6
- Sudbury Hall
DE6 5HT Derbys 40 F2
- Sulgrave Manor
OX17 2SD Nhants 31 M5
- Sunnycroft
TF1 2DR Wrekin 49 M12
- Sutton Hoo
IP12 3DJ Suffk 35 L7
- Sutton House
E9 6JQ Gt Lon 21 M6
- Tate Britain
SW1P 4RG Gt Lon 21 L7
- Tate Liverpool
L3 4BB Lpool 56 G10
- Tate Modern
SE1 9TG Gt Lon 21 L7
- Tattershall Castle
LN4 4LR Lincs 52 H11
- Tatton Park
WA16 6QN Ches 57 N11
- The Lowry
M50 3AZ Salfd 57 P9
- The Vyne
RG24 9HL Hants 19 Q9
- Thornton Abbey
DN39 6TU N Linc 61 J9
- Thorpe Park
KT16 8PN Surrey 20 G9

- Tilbury Fort
RM18 7NR Thurr 22 D8
- Tintagel Castle
PL34 0HE Cnwll 4 C3
- Tintinhull Garden
BA22 8PZ Somset 17 M11
- Totnes Castle
TQ9 5NU Devon 5 Q7
- Tower of London
EC3N 4AB Gt Lon 21 M7
- Townend
LA23 1LB Cumb 62 H2
- Treasurer's House
YO1 7JL York 59 N4
- Trelissick Garden
TR3 6QL Cnwll 3 J7
- Trengwainton Garden
TR20 8RZ Cnwll 2 C9
- Trerice
TR8 4PG Cnwll 3 J4
- Twycross Zoo
CV9 3PX Leics 40 H6
- Upnor Castle
ME2 4XG Medway 22 F8
- Uppark
GU31 5QR W Susx 10 C6
- Upton House & Garden
OX15 6HT Warwks 31 J5
- Victoria & Albert Museum
SW7 2RL Gt Lon 21 L7
- Waddesdon Manor
HP18 0JH Bucks 31 Q10
- Wakehurst Place
RH17 6TN W Susx 11 M4
- Wall Roman Site
WS14 0AW Staffs 40 E6
- Wallington House
NE61 4AR Nthumb 72 H4
- Walmer Castle & Gardens
CT14 7LJ Kent 23 Q12
- Warkworth Castle
NE65 0UJ Nthumb 81 P11
- Warwick Castle
CV34 4QU Warwks 30 H2
- Washington Old Hall
NE38 7LE Sundld 73 N9
- Waterperry Gardens
OX33 1JZ Oxon 31 N11
- Weeting Castle
IP27 0RQ Norfk 44 C11
- Weir Gardens
HR4 7QF Herefs 28 E1
- Wenlock Priory
TF13 6HS Shrops 39 L3
- West Midland Safari Park
DY12 1LF Worcs 39 P7
- West Wycombe Park
HP14 3AJ Bucks 20 D5
- Westbury Court Garden
GL14 1PD Gloucs 29 J6
- Westminster Abbey
SW1P 3PA Gt Lon 21 L7
- Westonbirt Arboretum
GL8 8QS Gloucs 29 L10
- Westwood Manor
BA15 2AF Wilts 18 B8
- Whipsnade Wild
Animal Park
LU6 2LF Beds 32 E12
- Whitby Abbey
YO22 4JT N York 67 K5
- Wightwick Manor
WV6 8EE Wolves 39 Q3
- Wimpole Hall & Home Farm
SG8 0BW Cambs 33 K6
- Winchester City Mill
SO23 0EJ Hants 9 N2
- Windermere Lake Cruises
LA23 3HE Cumb 62 H3
- Windsor Castle
SL4 1NJ W & M 20 F7
- Winkworth Arboretum
GU8 4AD Surrey 10 F2
- Wisley Garden
GU23 6QB Surrey 20 H10
- Woburn Safari Park
MK17 9QN Beds 32 D9
- Wookey Hole Caves
BA5 1BB Somset 17 M6
- Woolsthorpe Manor
NG33 5NR Lincs 42 D5
- Wordsworth House
CA13 9RX Cumb 71 J9
- Wrest Park Gardens
MK45 4HS Beds 32 F9
- Wroxeter Roman City
SY5 6PR Shrops 39 L2
- Xscape Castleford
WF10 4TA Wakefd 59 K8
- Yarmouth Castle
PO41 0PB IoW 9 L9
- York Minster
YO1 7JF York 59 N4

SCOTLAND

- Aberdour Castle
KY3 0SL Fife 86 E5
- Alloa Tower
FK10 1PP Clacks 85 P5
- Angus Folk Museum
DD8 1RT Angus 93 L6
- Arbroath Abbey
DD11 1EG Angus 93 Q7
- Arduaine Garden
PA34 4XQ Ag & B 83 M2
- Bachelors' Club
KA5 5RB S Ayrs 76 G6
- Balmoral Castle Grounds
AB35 5TB Abers 94 D3
- Balvenie Castle
AB55 4DH Moray 101 L7
- Bannockburn Heritage Centre
FK7 0LJ Stirlg 85 N5
- Blackness Castle
EH49 7NH Falk 86 C6
- Blair Castle
PH18 5TL P & K 92 C3
- Bothwell Castle
G71 8BL S Lans 85 L10
- Branklyn Garden
PH2 7BB P & K 92 G10
- Brodick Castle
KA27 8HY N Ayrs 75 Q5
- Brodie Castle
IV36 2TE Moray 100 F4
- Broughton House & Garden
DG6 4JX D & G 69 P8
- Burleigh Castle
KY13 9GG P & K 86 D2
- Burrell Collection
G43 1AT C Glas 85 J10
- Caerlaverock Castle
DG1 4RU D & G 70 G3
- Cardoness Castle
DG7 2EH D & G 69 N7
- Carnassarie Castle
PA31 8RQ Ag & B 83 M3
- Castle Campbell
FK14 7PP Clacks 85 Q3
- Castle Fraser
AB51 7LD Abers 102 F11
- Castle Kennedy & Gardens
DG9 8BX D & G 68 F7
- Castle Menzies
PH15 2JD P & K 92 C6
- Corgarff Castle
AB36 8YL Abers 94 E1
- Craigievar Castle
AB33 8JF Abers 102 D12
- Craigmillar Castle
EH16 4SY C Edin 86 F7
- Crarae Garden
PA32 8YA Ag & B 83 Q4
- Crathes Castle & Garden
AB31 5QJ Abers 95 M3
- Crichton Castle
EH37 5QH Mdloth 86 H9
- Crossraguel Abbey
KA19 8HQ S Ayrs 76 E9
- Culloden Battlefield
IV2 5EU Highld 107 M12
- Culross Palace
KY12 8JH Fife 86 B5
- Culzean Castle & Country Park
KA19 8LE S Ayrs 76 D8
- Dallas Dhu Distillery
IV36 2RR Moray 100 G4
- David Livingstone Centre
G72 9BT S Lans 85 L10
- Dirleton Castle
EH39 5ER E Loth 87 K5
- Doune Castle
FK16 6EA Stirlg 85 M3
- Drum Castle
AB31 5EY Abers 95 N2
- Dryburgh Abbey
TD6 0RQ Border 80 D7
- Duff House
AB45 3SX Abers 102 F3
- Dumbarton Castle
G82 1JJ W Duns 84 G7
- Dundrennan Abbey
DG6 4QH D & G 70 C6
- Dunnottar Castle
AB39 2TL Abers 95 P5
- Dunstaffnage Castle
PA37 1PZ Ag & B 90 B9
- Edinburgh Castle
EH1 2NG C Edin 86 F7
- Edinburgh Zoo
EH12 6TS C Edin 86 E7

- Edzell Castle
DD9 7UE Angus 95 K8
- Elgin Cathedral
IV30 1EL Moray 101 J3
- Falkland Palace & Garden
KY15 7BU Fife 86 F2
- Fort George
IV2 7TE Highld 107 M10
- Fyvie Castle
AB53 8JS Abers 102 G7
- Georgian House
EH2 4DR C Edin 86 F7
- Gladstone's Land
EH1 2NT C Edin 86 F7
- Glamis Castle
DD8 1RJ Angus 93 L6
- Glasgow Botanic Gardens
G12 0UE C Glas 85 J9
- Glasgow Cathedral
G4 0QZ C Glas 85 K9
- Glasgow Museum of Transport
G3 8DP C Glas 85 J9
- Glasgow Science Centre
G51 1EA C Glas 85 J9
- Glenluce Abbey
DG8 0AF D & G 68 G7
- Greenbank Garden
G76 8RB E Rens 85 J10
- Haddo House
AB41 7EQ Abers 102 H8
- Harmony Garden
TD6 9LJ Border 80 D7
- Hermitage Castle
TD9 0LU Border 79 P9
- Highland Wildlife Park
PH21 1NL Highld 99 M8
- Hill House
G84 9AJ Ag & B 84 E6
- Hill of Tarvit Mansionhouse
& Garden
KY15 5PB Fife 93 L12
- Holmwood House
G44 3YG C Glas 85 K10
- House of Dun
DD10 9LQ Angus 93 R4
- House of The Binns
EH49 7NA W Loth 86 C6
- Hunterian Museum
G12 8QQ C Glas 85 J9
- Huntingtower Castle
PH1 3JL P & K 92 G9
- Huntly Castle
AB54 4SH Abers 102 C7
- Hutchesons' Hall
G1 1EJ C Glas 85 K9
- Inchmahome Priory
FK8 3RA Stirlg 85 K3
- Inveresk Lodge Garden
EH21 7TE E Loth 86 G7
- Inverewe Garden
IV22 2LG Highld 105 M6
- Inverlochy Castle
PH33 7NR Highld 90 F2
- Kellie Castle & Garden
KY10 2RF Fife 87 K2
- Kildrummy Castle
AB33 8RA Abers 101 N11
- Killiecrankie Visitor Centre
PH16 5LG P & K 92 D3
- Leith Hall & Garden
AB54 4NQ Abers 102 C8
- Linlithgow Palace
EH49 7AL W Loth 86 B6
- Loch Leven Castle
KY13 8AS P & K 86 D2
- Logan Botanic Garden
DG9 9ND D & G 68 E9
- Malleny Garden
EH14 7AF C Edin 86 E8
- Melrose Abbey
TD6 9LG Border 80 D7
- National Museum
of Scotland
EH1 1JF C Edin 86 F7
- Newark Castle
PA14 5NH Inver 84 F7
- Palace of Holyroodhouse
EH8 8DX C Edin 86 F7
- Pitmedden Garden
AB41 7PD Abers 103 J9
- Preston Mill
EH40 3DS E Loth 87 L6
- Priorwood Garden
TD6 9PX Border 80 D7
- Robert Smail's Printing Works
EH44 6HA Border 79 M2
- Rothesay Castle
PA20 0DA Ag & B 84 B9
- Royal Botanic Garden
Edinburgh
EH3 5LR C Edin 86 F7
- Royal Yacht Britannia
EH6 6JJ C Edin 86 F6

- Scone Palace
PH2 6BD P & K 92 G9
- Smailholm Tower
TD5 7PG Border 80 E7
- Souter Johnnie's Cottage
KA19 8HY S Ayrs 76 D9
- St Andrew's Cathedral
KY16 9QU Fife 93 N11
- Stirling Castle
FK8 1EJ Stirlg 85 N4
- Sweetheart Abbey
DG2 8BU D & G 70 F3
- Tantallon Castle
EH39 5PN E Loth 87 L5
- Tenement House
G3 6QN C Glas 85 K9
- The Lighthouse
G1 3NU C Glas 85 K9
- Threave Castle
DG7 1RX D & G 70 C3
- Threave Garden
DG7 1RX D & G 70 C4
- Tolquhon Castle
AB41 7LP Abers 102 H9
- Traquair House
EH44 6PW Border 79 M2
- Urquhart Castle
IV63 6XJ Highld 98 G4
- Weaver's Cottage
PA10 2JG Rens 84 G9
- Whithorn Priory
DG8 8PY D & G 69 L10

WALES

- Aberconwy House
LL32 8AY Conwy 55 L6
- Aberdulais Falls
SA10 8EU Neath 26 G8
- Beaumaris Castle
LL58 8AP IoA 54 H6
- Big Pit National Coal Museum
NP4 9XP Torfn 27 P7
- Bodnant Garden
LL28 5RE Conwy 55 L7
- Caerleon Roman Amphitheatre
NP18 1AE Newpt 28 D10
- Caernarfon Castle
LL55 2AY Gwynd 54 F8
- Cardiff Castle
CF10 3RB Cardif 16 G2
- Castell Coch
CF15 7JS Cardif 27 N11
- Chirk Castle
LL14 5AF Wrexhm 48 F7
- Colby Woodland Garden
SA67 8PP Pembks 25 K7
- Conwy Castle
LL32 8AY Conwy 55 L6
- Criccieth Castle
LL52 0DP Gwynd 46 H4
- Dan-yr-Ogof Showcaves
SA9 1GJ Powys 26 H5
- Dinefwr Park
SA19 6RT Carmth 26 E4
- Dolaucothi Gold Mines
SA19 8RR Carmth 37 L11
- Erddig
LL13 0YT Wrexhm 48 G6
- Ffestiniog Railway
LL49 9NF Gwynd 47 J4
- Harlech Castle
LL46 2YH Gwynd 47 J5
- Llanerchaeron
SA48 8DG Cerdgn 36 H8
- Penrhyn Castle
LL57 4HN Gwynd 54 H7
- Plas Newydd
LL61 6DQ IoA 54 G7
- Plas Yn Rhiw
LL53 8AB Gwynd 46 D5
- Portmeirion
LL48 6ET Gwynd 47 J4
- Powis Castle & Garden
SY21 8RF Powys 38 E2
- Raglan Castle
NP15 2BT Mons 28 E7
- Sygun Copper Mine
LL55 4NE Gwynd 54 H10
- Tintern Abbey
NP16 6SE Mons 28 F8
- Tudor Merchant's House
SA70 7BX Pembks 25 K8
- Tŷ Mawr Wybrnant
LL25 0HJ Conwy 55 L10
- Valle Crucis Abbey
LL20 8DD Denbgs 48 E6

Traffic signs and road markings

Traffic signs

Signs giving orders

Signs with red circles are mostly prohibitive. Plates below signs qualify their message.

Entry to 20mph zone

End of 20mph zone

Maximum speed

National speed limit applies

School crossing patrol

Stop and give way

Give way to traffic on major road

Manually operated temporary STOP and GO signs

No entry for vehicular traffic

No vehicles except bicycles being pushed

No cycling

No motor vehicles

No buses (over 8 passenger seats)

No overtaking

No towed caravans

No vehicles carrying explosives

No vehicle or combination of vehicles over length shown

No vehicles over height shown

No vehicles over width shown

Give priority to vehicles from opposite direction

No right turn

No left turn

No U-turns

No goods vehicles over maximum gross weight shown (in tonnes) except for loading and unloading

WEAK BRIDGE
No vehicles over maximum gross weight shown (in tonnes)

Parking restricted to permit holders

No waiting

RED ROUTE
No stopping during period indicated except for buses

No stopping (Clearway)

URBAN CLEARWAY Monday to Friday
No stopping during times shown except for as long as necessary to set down or pick up passengers

Signs with blue circles but no red border mostly give positive instruction.

Ahead only

Turn left ahead (right if symbol reversed)

Turn left (right if symbol reversed)

Keep left (right if symbol reversed)

Vehicles may pass either side to reach same destination

Mini-roundabout (roundabout circulation – give way to vehicles from the immediate right)

Route to be used by pedal cycles only

Segregated pedal cycle and pedestrian route

Minimum speed

End of minimum speed

Buses and cycles only

Trams only

Pedestrian crossing point over tramway

One-way traffic (note: compare circular 'Ahead only' sign)

With-flow bus and cycle lane

Contraflow bus lane

With-flow pedal cycle lane

Warning signs

Mostly triangular

STOP 100 yds
Distance to 'STOP' line ahead

Dual carriageway ends

Road narrows on right (left if symbol reversed)

Road narrows on both sides

GIVE WAY 50 yds
Distance to 'Give Way' line ahead

Crossroads

Junction on bend ahead

T-junction with priority over vehicles from the right

Staggered junction

Traffic merging from left ahead

The priority through route is indicated by the broader line.

Double bend first to left (symbol may be reversed)

Bend to right (or left if symbol reversed)

Roundabout

Uneven road

REDUCE SPEED NOW
Plate below some signs

Two-way traffic crosses one-way road

Two-way traffic straight ahead

Opening or swing bridge ahead

Low-flying aircraft or sudden aircraft noise

Falling or fallen rocks

Traffic signals not in use

Traffic signals

Slippery road

Steep hill downwards

Steep hill upwards

Gradients may be shown as a ratio i.e. 20% = 1:5

Tunnel ahead

Trams crossing ahead

Level crossing with barrier or gate ahead

Level crossing without barrier or gate ahead

Level crossing without barrier

Patrol

School crossing patrol ahead (some signs have amber lights which flash when crossings are in use)

Frail (or blind or disabled if shown) pedestrians likely to cross road ahead

No footway for 400 yds

Pedestrians in road ahead

Zebra crossing

Safe height 16'-6"

Overhead electric cable; plate indicates maximum height of vehicles which can pass safely

Available width of headroom indicated

Sharp deviation of route to left (or right if chevrons reversed)

STOP when lights show

Light signals ahead at level crossing, airfield or bridge

Red STOP
Green Clear
IF NO LIGHT - PHONE CROSSING OPERATOR

Miniature warning lights at level crossings

Cattle

Wild animals

Wild horses or ponies

Accompanied horses or ponies

Cycle route ahead

Ice
Risk of ice

Queues likely
Traffic queues likely ahead

Humps for ½ mile
Distance over which road humps extend

Hidden dip
Other danger; plate indicates nature of danger

Soft verges for 2 miles
Soft verges

Side winds

Hump bridge

Ford
Worded warning sign

Quayside or river bank

Risk of grounding

Direction signs

Mostly rectangular

Signs on motorways – blue backgrounds

At a junction leading directly into a motorway (junction number may be shown on a black background)

On approaches to junctions (junction number on black background)

Route confirmatory sign after junction

Downward pointing arrows mean 'Get in lane'
The left-hand lane leads to a different destination from the other lanes.

The panel with the inclined arrow indicates the destinations which can be reached by leaving the motorway at the next junction

Signs on primary routes - green backgrounds

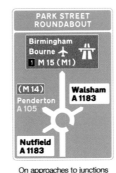
On approaches to junctions

At the junction

A 46
The SOUTH
Nottingham 17
Leicester 32
(M1 South) 35

Route confirmatory sign after junction

On approaches to junctions

On approach to a junction in Wales (bilingual)

Blue panels indicate that the motorway starts at the junction ahead.
Motorways shown in brackets can also be reached along the route indicated.
White panels indicate local or non-primary routes leading from the junction ahead.
Brown panels show the route to tourist attractions.
The name of the junction may be shown at the top of the sign.
The aircraft symbol indicates the route to an airport.
A symbol may be included to warn of a hazard or restriction along that route.

Primary route forming part of a ring road

R

Signs on non-primary and local routes - black borders

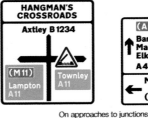
On approaches to junctions

(A1(M)) 8
Barnes 10
Mackstone 2½
Elkington 1
A404 (A41)
Millington Green 3
(A4011)

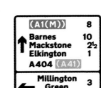
Market Walborough B 486 7
At the junction

Direction to toilets with access for the disabled

Green panels indicate that the primary route starts at the junction ahead.
Route numbers on a blue background show the direction to a motorway.
Route numbers on a green background show the direction to a primary route.

Note: Although this road atlas shows many of the signs commonly in use, a comprehensive explanation of the signing system is given in the AA's handbook *Know Your Road Signs*, which is on sale at booksellers. The booklet also illustrates and explains the vast majority of signs the road user is likely to encounter. The signs illustrated in this road atlas are not all drawn to the same scale. In Wales, bilingual versions of some signs are used including Welsh and English versions of place names. Some older designs of signs may still be seen on the roads.

Traffic signs and road markings

Other direction signs

Picnic site

Ancient monument in the care of English Heritage

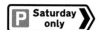
Direction to a car park

'Countdown' markers at exit from motorway (each bar represents 100 yards to the exit). Green-backed markers may be used on primary routes and white-backed markers with black bars on other routes. At approaches to concealed level crossings white-backed markers with red bars may be used. Although these will be erected at equal distances the bars do not represent 100 yard intervals.

Motorway service area sign showing the operator's name

Direction to camping and caravan site

Advisory route for lorries

Route for pedal cycles forming part of a network

Recommended route for pedal cycles to place shown

Route for pedestrians

Traffic has priority over oncoming vehicles

Hospital ahead with Accident and Emergency facilities

Tourist information point

No through road for vehicles

Symbols showing emergency diversion route for motorway and other main road traffic

Diversion route

Recommended route for pedal cycles

Home Zone Entry*

Area in which cameras are used to enforce traffic regulations

Bus lane on road at junction ahead

*Home Zone Entry – You are entering an area where people could be using the whole street for a range of activities. You should drive slowly and carefully and be prepared to stop to allow people time to move out of the way.

Information signs

All rectangular

Entrance to controlled parking zone

Entrance to congestion charging zone

Greater London Low Emission Zone (LEZ)

Advance warning of restriction or prohibition ahead

Parking place for solo motorcycles

With-flow bus lane ahead which pedal cycles and taxis may also use

Lane designated for use by high occupancy vehicles (HOV) - see rule 142

Vehicles permitted to use an HOV lane ahead

End of motorway

Start of motorway and point from which motorway regulations apply

Appropriate traffic lanes at junction ahead

Traffic on the main carriageway coming from right has priority over joining traffic

Additional traffic joining from left ahead. Traffic on main carriageway has priority over joining traffic from right hand side of slip road

Traffic in right hand lane of slip road joining the main carriageway has priority over left hand lane

Roadworks signs

Road works

Loose chippings

Temporary hazard at roadworks

Temporary lane closure (the number and position of arrows and red bars may be varied according to lanes open and closed)

Slow-moving or stationary works vehicle blocking a traffic lane. Pass in the direction shown by the arrow.

Mandatory speed limit ahead

Roadworks 1 mile ahead

End of roadworks and any temporary restrictions including speed limits

Signs used on the back of slow-moving or stationary vehicles warning of a lane closed ahead by a works vehicle. There are no cones on the road.

Lane restrictions at roadworks ahead

One lane crossover at contraflow roadworks

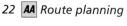

Road markings

Across the carriageway

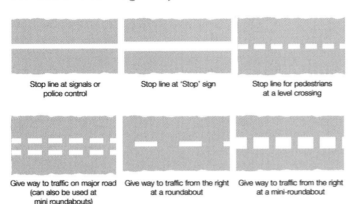

Stop line at signals or police control

Stop line at "Stop" sign

Stop line for pedestrians at a level crossing

Give way to traffic on major road (can also be used at mini roundabouts)

Give way to traffic from the right at a roundabout

Give way to traffic from the right at a mini-roundabout

Along the carriageway

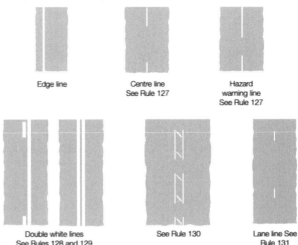

Edge line

Centre line See Rule 127

Hazard warning line See Rule 127

Double white lines See Rules 128 and 129

See Rule 130

Lane line See Rule 131

Along the edge of the carriageway

Waiting restrictions

Waiting restrictions indicated by yellow lines apply to the carriageway, pavement and verge. You may stop to load or unload (unless there are also loading restrictions as described below) or while passengers board or alight. Double yellow lines mean no waiting at any time, unless there are signs that specifically indicate seasonal restrictions. The times at which the restrictions apply for other road markings are shown on nearby plates or on entry signs to controlled parking zones. If no days are shown on the signs, the restrictions are in force every day including Sundays and Bank Holidays. White bay markings and upright signs (see below) indicate where parking is allowed.

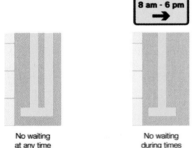

No waiting at any time

No waiting during times shown on sign

Waiting is limited to the duration specified during the days and times shown

Red Route stopping controls

Red lines are used on some roads instead of yellow lines. In London the double and single red lines used on Red Routes indicate that stopping to park, load/unload or to board and alight from a vehicle (except for a licensed taxi or if you hold a Blue Badge) is prohibited. The red lines apply to the carriageway, pavement and verge. The times that the red line prohibitions apply are shown on nearby signs, but the double red line ALWAYS means no stopping at any time. On Red Routes you may stop to park, load/unload in specially marked boxes and adjacent signs specify the times and purposes and duration allowed. A box MARKED IN RED indicates that it may only be available for the purpose specified for part of the day (e.g. between busy peak periods). A box MARKED IN WHITE means that it is available throughout the day.

RED AND SINGLE YELLOW LINES CAN ONLY GIVE A GUIDE TO THE RESTRICTIONS AND CONTROLS IN FORCE AND SIGNS, NEARBY OR AT A ZONE ENTRY, MUST BE CONSULTED.

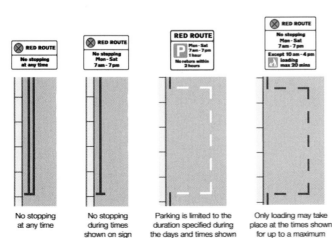

No stopping at any time

No stopping during times shown on sign

Parking is limited to the duration specified during the days and times shown

Only loading may take place at the times shown for up to a maximum duration of 20 mins

On the kerb or at the edge of the carriageway

Loading restrictions on roads other than Red Routes

Yellow marks on the kerb or at the edge of the carriageway indicate that loading or unloading is prohibited at the times shown on the nearby black and white plates. You may stop while passengers board or alight. If no days are indicated on the signs the restrictions are in force every day including Sundays and Bank Holidays.

ALWAYS CHECK THE TIMES SHOWN ON THE PLATES.

Lengths of road reserved for vehicles loading and unloading are indicated by a white 'bay' marking with the words 'Loading Only' and a sign with the white on blue 'trolley' symbol. This sign also shows whether loading and unloading is restricted to goods vehicles and the times at which the bay can be used. If no times or days are shown it may be used at any time. Vehicles may not park here if they are not loading or unloading.

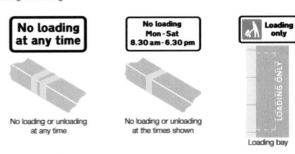

No loading or unloading at any time

No loading or unloading at the times shown

Loading bay

Other road markings

Keep entrance clear of stationary vehicles, even if picking up or setting down children

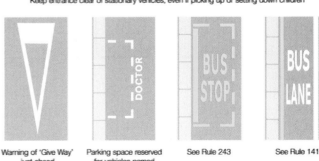

Warning of "Give Way" just ahead

Parking space reserved for vehicles named

See Rule 243

See Rule 141

Box junction - See Rule 174

Do not block that part of the carriageway indicated

Indication of traffic lanes

Map pages

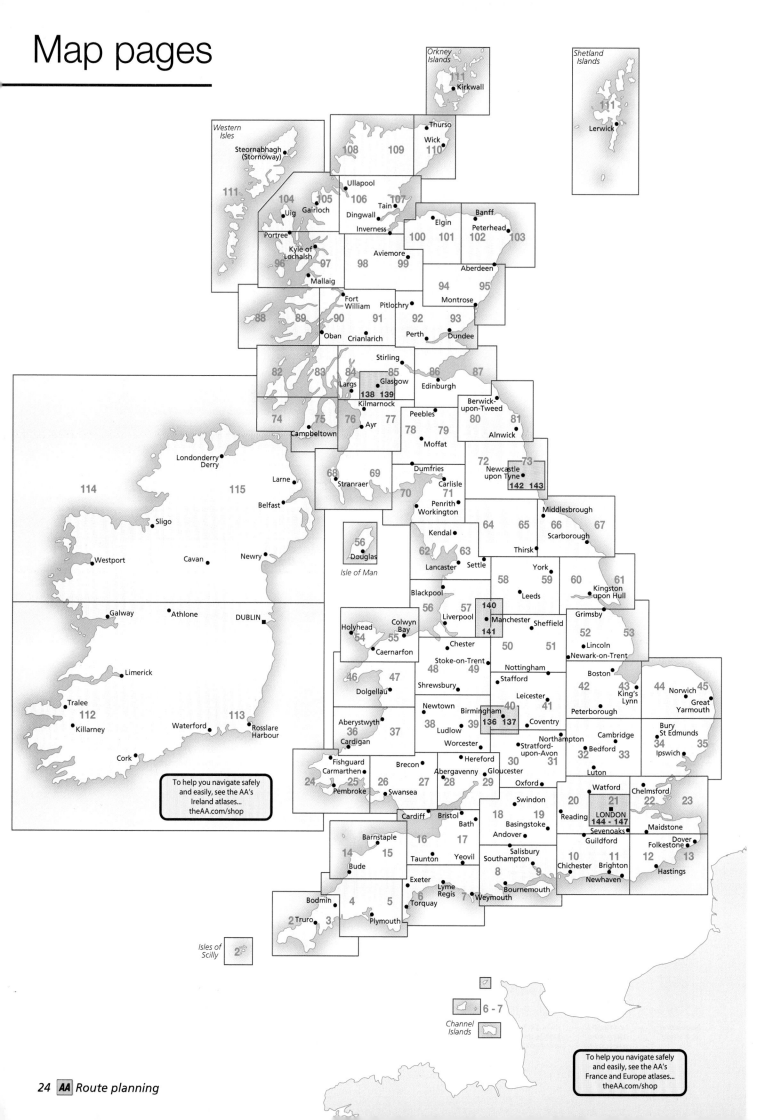

Orkney Islands

111
Kirkwall

Shetland Islands

111
Lerwick

Western Isles

Steornabhagh (Stornoway)

111

108
109
Thurso
Wick
110

104
105
Uig
Gairloch
106
Ullapool
107
Tain
Dingwall
Inverness

Elgin
Banff
Peterhead
100
101
102
103

Portree
96
Kyle of Lochalsh
97
98
Aviemore
99
94
Aberdeen
95
Montrose

Mallaig
88
89
90
Fort William
Pitlochry
91
92
93
Oban
Crianlarich
Perth
Dundee

82
83
84
Stirling
85
Glasgow
86
Edinburgh
87
Largs
138 139
Kilmarnock

Londonderry Derry

114

Larne

Belfast

Sligo

115

Westport

Cavan

Newry

DUBLIN

Galway
Athlone

74
75
76
Ayr
77
78
79
Moffat
80
Berwick-upon-Tweed
81
Alnwick

Campbeltown
68
Stranraer
69
Dumfries
Carlisle
72
Newcastle upon Tyne
73
142 143

70
71
Penrith
Workington
64
65
66
Middlesbrough
67
Scarborough

56
Douglas
Isle of Man
Kendal
62
63
Thirsk

Lancaster
Settle
58
59
York
60
61
Kingston upon Hull

Blackpool
57
Leeds

Holyhead
54
Colwyn Bay
55
56
Liverpool
140
Manchester
141
Sheffield
52
Grimsby
53
Lincoln
Newark-on-Trent

Caernarfon
Chester
50
51
Boston
44
Norwich
45

46
47
Stoke-on-Trent
48
49
Nottingham
Stafford
Leicester
41
42
Peterborough
King's Lynn
Great Yarmouth

Dolgellau
Shrewsbury
Birmingham
40
136 137
Coventry
Northampton
32
Bedford
33
Cambridge
34
Bury St Edmunds
35
Ipswich

Aberystwyth
36
37
Newtown
38
Ludlow
39
Worcester
Hereford
Stratford-upon-Avon
31
Luton

Cardigan
30
Gloucester
Oxford
20
Watford
21
Chelmsford
22
23

Fishguard
Carmarthen
24
25
Pembroke
26
Brecon
27
Abergavenny
28
29
Swindon
19
Reading
LONDON
144 - 147
Sevenoaks
Maidstone

Swansea
Cardiff
Bristol
Bath
18
Basingstoke
Andover
Guildford
10
Chichester
11
Brighton
Newhaven
Dover
Folkestone
12
Hastings
13

Barnstaple
16
17
Salisbury
Southampton
8
Bournemouth
9

14
15
Taunton
Yeovil
Weymouth

Limerick
Tralee
112
Killarney
Waterford
113
Rosslare Harbour
Cork

Bude
Exeter
Lyme Regis
7

Bodmin
4
5
Torquay
6

Truro
2
3
Plymouth

Isles of Scilly
2

6 - 7

Channel Islands

To help you navigate safely and easily, see the AA's Ireland atlases... theAA.com/shop

To help you navigate safely and easily, see the AA's France and Europe atlases... theAA.com/shop

Road map symbols

Motoring information

M4	Motorway with number		Transport café	Toll →	Road toll, steep gradient (arrows point downhill)	50	Speed camera site (fixed location) with speed limit in mph
Toll	Toll motorway with toll station	BATH	Primary route destination	5	Distance in miles between symbols	60	Section of road with two or more fixed speed cameras, with speed limit in mph
	Motorway junction with and without number	A1123	Other A road single/dual carriageway	or	Vehicle ferry	50 50	Average speed (SPECS™) camera system with speed limit in mph
3	Restricted motorway junctions	B2070	B road single/dual carriageway		Fast vehicle ferry or catamaran	V	Fixed speed camera site with variable speed limit
S Fleet	Motorway service area		Minor road more than 4 metres wide, less than 4 metres wide		Railway line, in tunnel	P·R	Park and Ride (at least 6 days per week)
	Motorway and junction under construction		Roundabout	—○—✕—	Railway station and level crossing		City, town, village or other built-up area
A3	Primary route single/dual carriageway		Interchange/junction	+++++++	Tourist railway	628 ▲ 637 Lecht Summit	Height in metres, mountain pass
1	Primary route junction with and without number		Narrow primary/other A/B road with passing places (Scotland)	✈ Ⓗ Ⓕ	Airport, heliport, international freight terminal		Sandy beach
3	Restricted primary route junctions		Road under construction	Ⓗ	24-hour Accident & Emergency hospital		National boundary
S Grantham North	Primary route service area	╞═════╡	Road tunnel	Ⓒ	Crematorium		County, administrative boundary

Touring information

Places of interest are also shown on town plans. Before visiting, check opening times to avoid disappointment.

	Scenic route	⅏	Aqueduct or viaduct	– – – –	National trail		Horse racing, show jumping
ℹ	Tourist Information Centre	❀ ♣	Garden, arboretum	☀	Viewpoint		Air show venue, motor-racing circuit
ℹ	Tourist Information Centre (seasonal)	♣	Vineyard		Hill-fort		Ski slope (natural, artificial)
ℹ	Visitor or heritage centre	♈	Country park		Roman antiquity		National Trust property (England & Wales, Scotland)
	Picnic site		Agricultural showground	▮▮	Prehistoric monument	✠	English Heritage site
	Caravan site		Theme park	✕ 1066	Battle site with year		Historic Scotland site
▲	Camping site		Farm or animal centre		Steam railway centre		Cadw (Welsh heritage) site
▲	Caravan & camping site		Zoological or wildlife collection	⌒	Cave	★	Other place of interest
	Abbey, cathedral or priory		Bird collection	✗	Windmill	☐	Boxed symbols indicate attractions within urban areas
	Ruined abbey, cathedral or priory		Aquarium	⊥	Monument	◉	World Heritage Site (UNESCO)
✗	Castle	RSPB	RSPB site		Golf course		National Park and National Scenic Area (Scotland)
	Historic house or building		National Nature Reserve (England, Scotland, Wales)		County cricket ground		Forest Park
	Museum or art gallery		Local nature reserve		Rugby Union national stadium		Heritage coast
	Industrial interest	··········	Forest drive		International athletics stadium		Major shopping centre

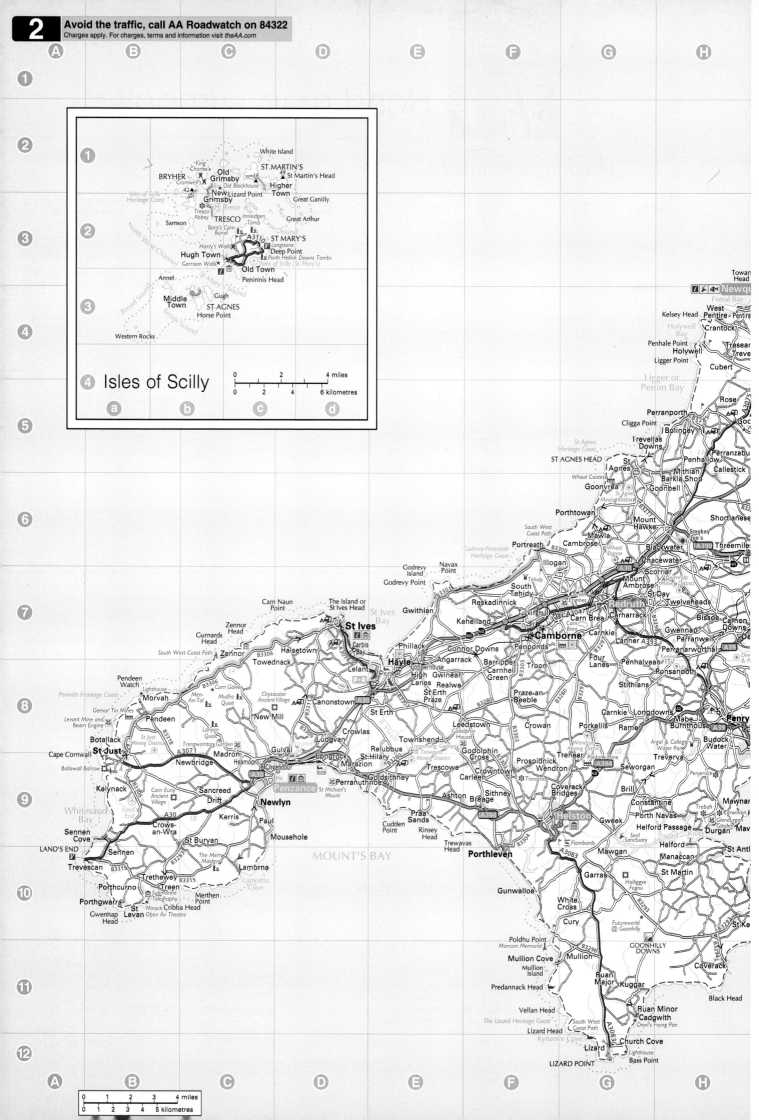

Isles of Scilly

White Island

ST MARTIN'S
King Charles's
Castle
BRYHER
Cromwell's
Castle
42
New Grimsby
Old Grimsby
Old Blockhouse
St Martin's Head
Higher Town
Lizard Point
Great Ganilly
Tresco Abbey
TRESCO
Tresco
Innisidgen Tomb
Great Arthur
Samson
Bant's Carn Burial
A3110
Harry's Walls
ST MARY'S
Longstone
Deep Point
Hugh Town
Garrison Walls
Old Town
Porth Hellick Downs Tombs
Isles of Scilly (St Mary's)
Annet
Peninnis Head
St Mary's Sound
Middle Town
Gugh
ST AGNES
Horse Point
Western Rocks

North West Channel
Isles of Scilly Heritage Coast
Broad Sound
Smith Sound

0 — 2 — 4 miles
0 — 2 — 4 — 6 kilometres

Towan Head
Newquay
Fistral Bay
West Pentire — Pentire
Kelsey Head
Holywell Bay
Crantock
Penhale Point
Holywell
Ligger Point
Tresearn
Treve
Cubert
Ligger or Perran Bay
Rose
Perranporth
Cligga Point
Bolingey
Trevellas Downs
Perranzabu
Penhallow
St Agnes Heritage Coast
ST AGNES HEAD
St Agnes
Mithian
Barkla Shop
Callestick
Goonvrea
Goonbell
Wheal Coates
St Agnes Mining District
Porthtowan
Mount Hawke
Smokey Joe's
Mawla
Blackwater
Threemile
South West Coast Path
Godrevy-Portreath Heritage Coast
Portreath
B3300
Cambrose
Wheal
Chacewater
A390
A30
Scorrier
Mount Ambrose
St-Day
Twelveheads
Navax Point
Godrevy Island
Illogan
Tehidy
South Tehidy
Gwennap Mining District
Redruth
A3047
Carharrack
Bissoe
Carnon Downs
Godrevy Point
Reskadinnick
Tuckingmill
Carn Brea
Gwennap
Perranwell
Gwithian
Kehelland
POOL
Carn Brea
Lanner A393
De
Carn Naun Point
The Island or St Ives Head
Phillack
Connor Downs
Camborne
Penhalvean
A39
Zennor Head
St Ives Head
St Ives Bay
Angarrack
Copperhouse
Penponds
Carnkie
Four Lanes
Perranarworthal
Gurnards Head
St Ives
Carbis Bay
Hayle
High Gwinear
Barripper
Carnhell Green
Troon
Ponsanooth
South West Coast Path
Zennor
Halsetown
Lelant
Realwa
St Erth Praze
Praze-an-Beeble
Stithians
Towednack
B3306
Carn Galver
P+R
Penwith Heritage Coast
Pendeen Watch
Lighthouse
B3306
Mulfra Quoit
Chysauster Ancient Village
Canonstown
St Erth
Leedstown
Crowan
Porkellis
Carnkie
Longdowns
Mabe Burnthouse
Penry
Morvah
Men-An-Tol
New Mill
Townshend
Godolphin House
Rame
Geevor Tin Mines
Pendeen
Lanyon Quoit
Trengwainton Garden
Crowlas
Ludgvan
B3280
Godolphin Cross
Wendron
Trenear
A394
Treverva
Budock Water
Levant Mine and Beam Engine
St Just Mining District
Gulval
Longrock
Crowntown
Prospidnick
Argal & College Water Park
Penjerrick
Botallack
Cape Cornwall
St Just
A3071
Madron
Heamoor
Chyandour
Marazion
St Hilary
Trescowe
Carleen
Sithney
Coverack Bridges
Brill
Penzance
St Michael's Mount
Ashton
Breage
Helston
Gweek
Porth Navas
Constantine
Trebah
Mawnan
Ballowall Barrow
Newbridge
Perranuthnoe
Goldsithney
Helford Passage
Glendurgan Garden
Durgan
Mav
Kelynack
Carn Euny Ancient Village
Sancreed
Drift
Newlyn
Cudden Point
Praa Sands
Rinsey Head
Trewavas Head
A3083
Mawgan
Helford
Manaccan
St Anth
Whitesand Bay
A30
Kerris
Paul
Garras
St Martin
Sennen Cove
Crows-an-Wra
Mousehole
MOUNT'S BAY
Porthleven
Halliggye Fogou
LAND'S END
Sennen
St Buryan
The Merry Maidens
Lamorna
Gunwalloe
White Cross
Trevescan
Trethewey
Treen
B3315
Lamorna Cove
Cury
Futureworld @ Goonhilly
St Ke
Porthcurno
Merthen Point
Poldhu Point
Marconi Memorial
GOONHILLY DOWNS
Porthgwarra
Minack Open Air Theatre
Cribba Head
B3296
Mullion Cove
Mullion
Coverack
Gwennap Head
St Levan
Submarine Telegraphy
Mullion Island
Ruan Major
Kuggar
Predannack Head
Ruan Minor
Cadgwith
Black Head
Vellan Head
The Lizard Heritage Coast
Devil's Frying Pan
Lizard Head
South West Coast Path
A3083
Lizard
Church Cove
Kynance Cove
Lighthouse
Bass Point
LIZARD POINT

0 — 1 — 2 — 3 — 4 miles
0 — 1 — 2 — 3 — 4 — 5 kilometres

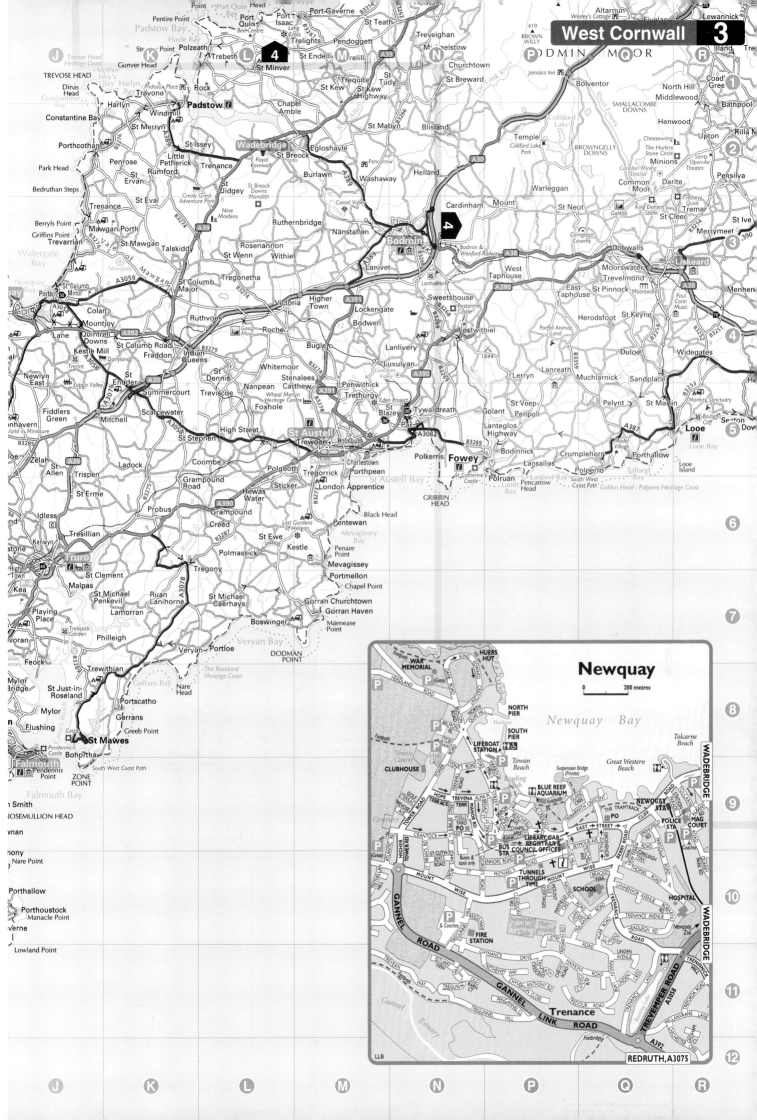

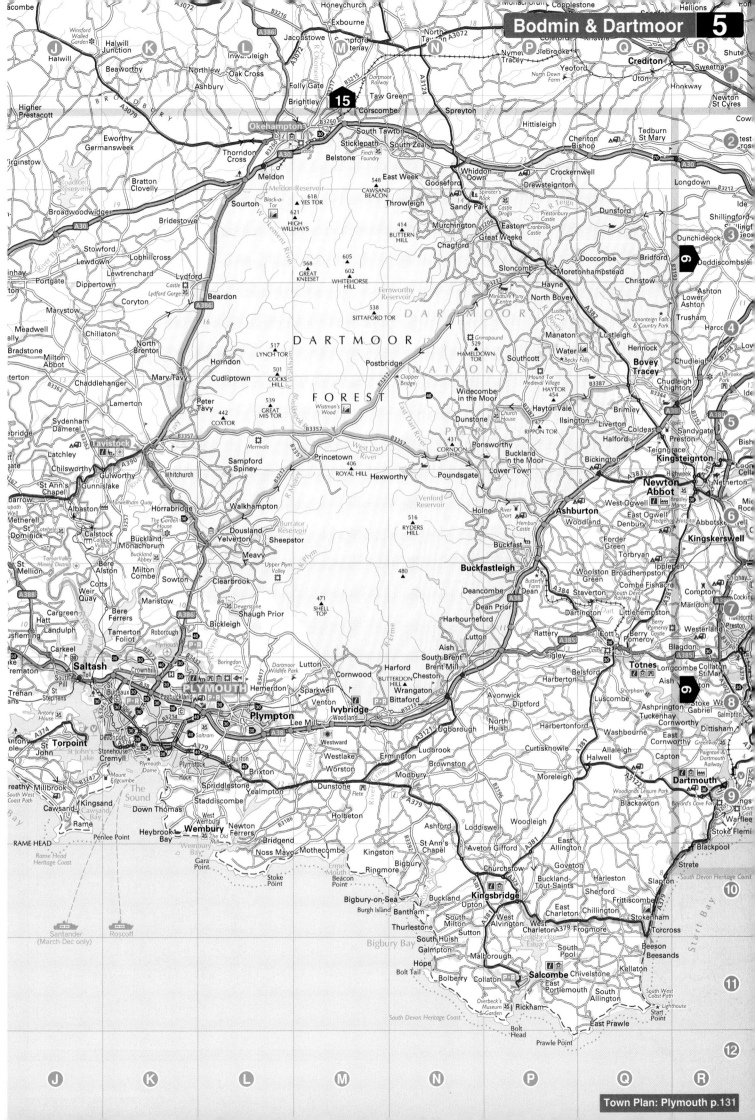

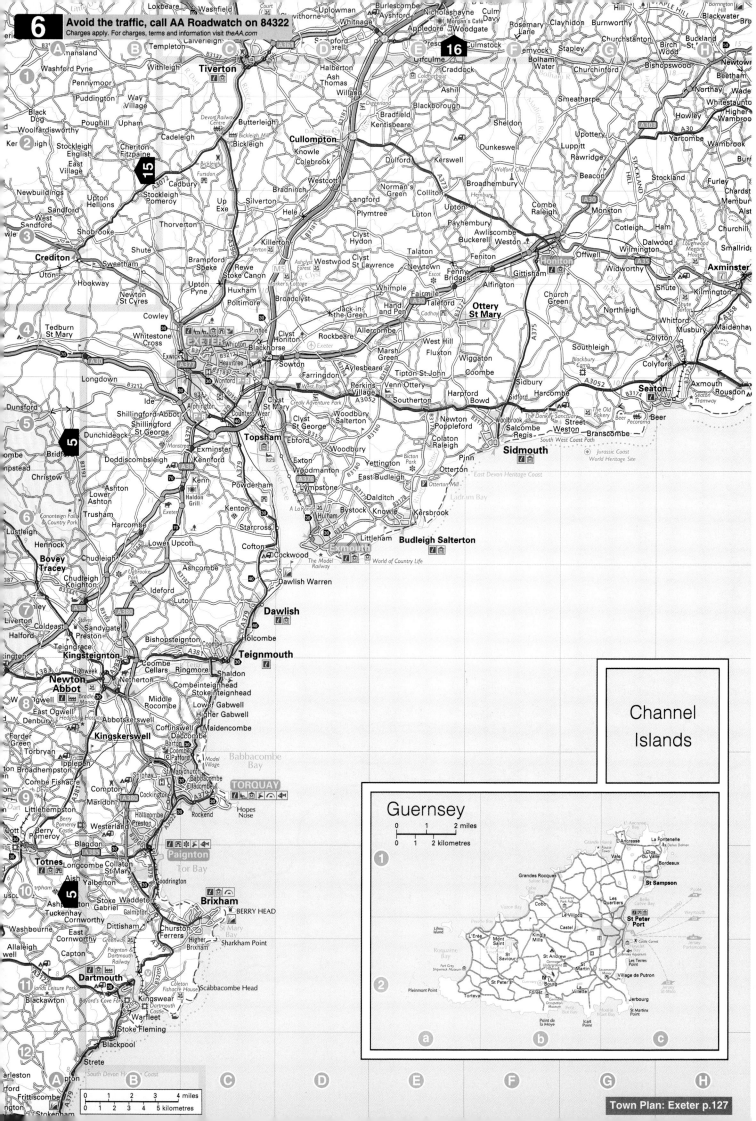

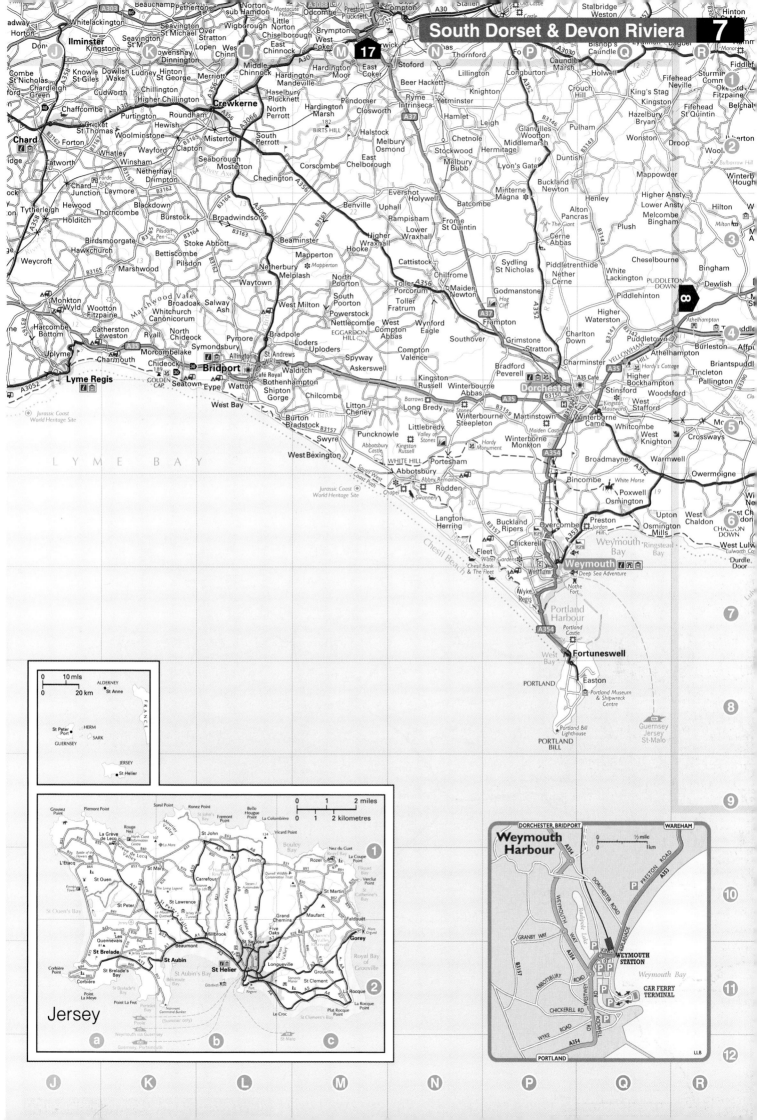

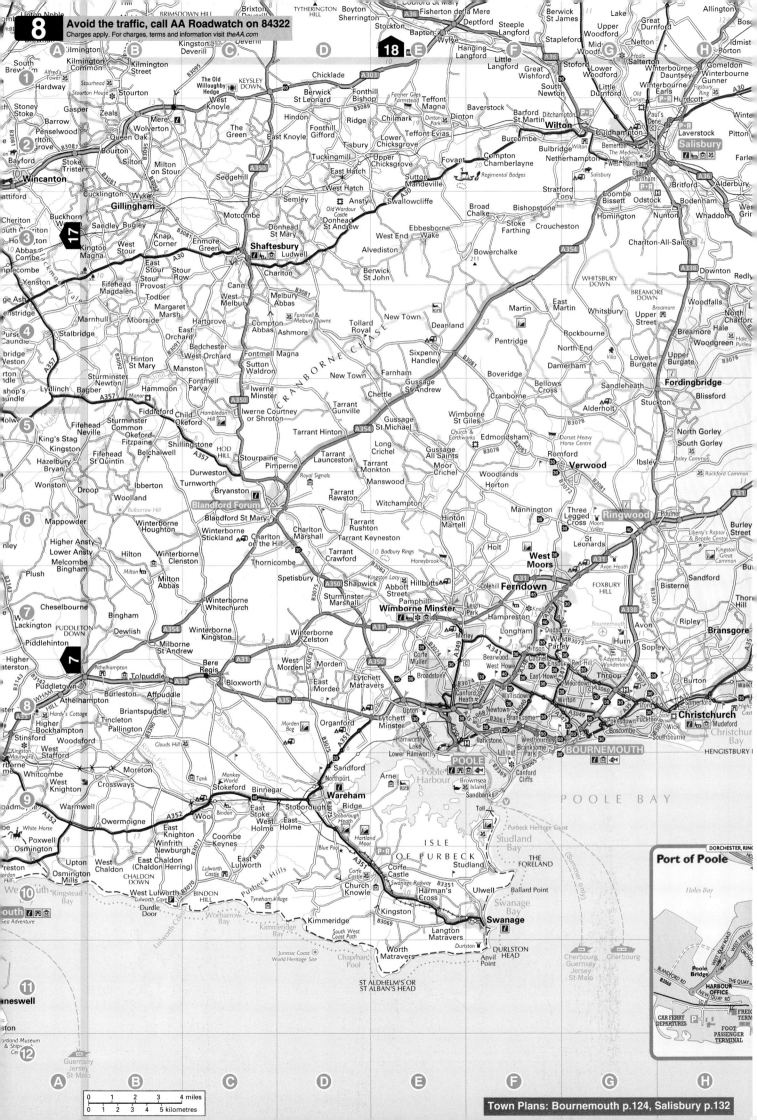

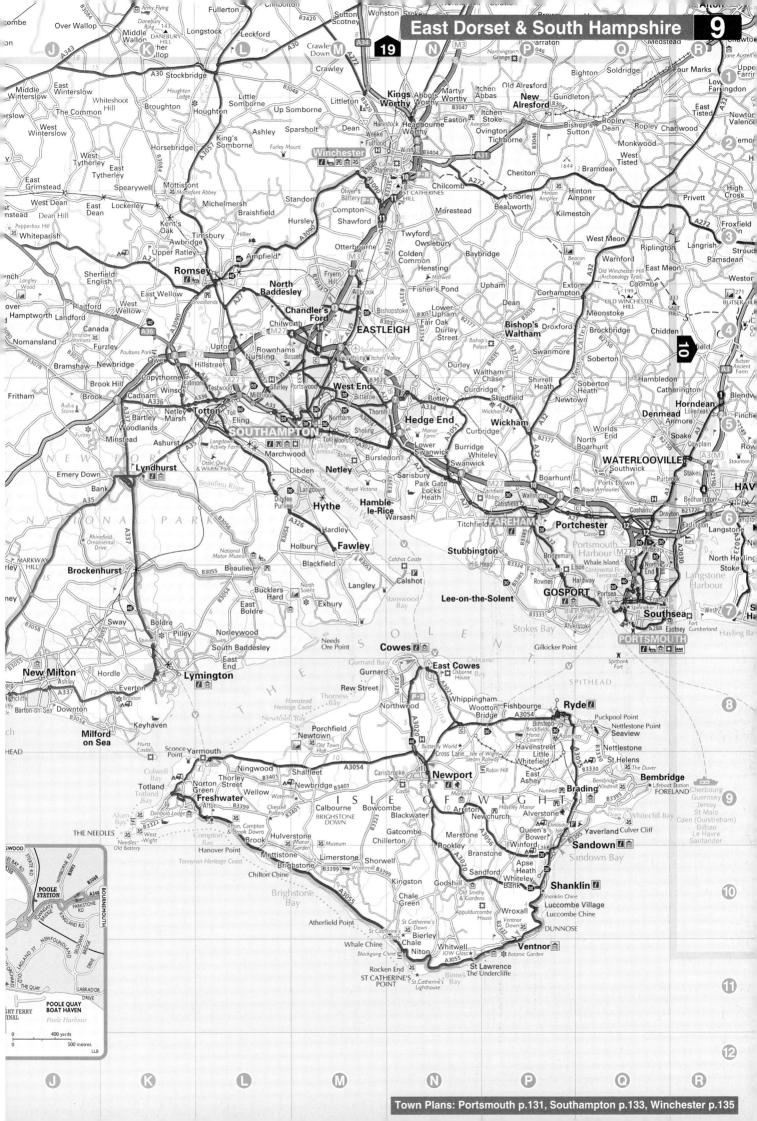

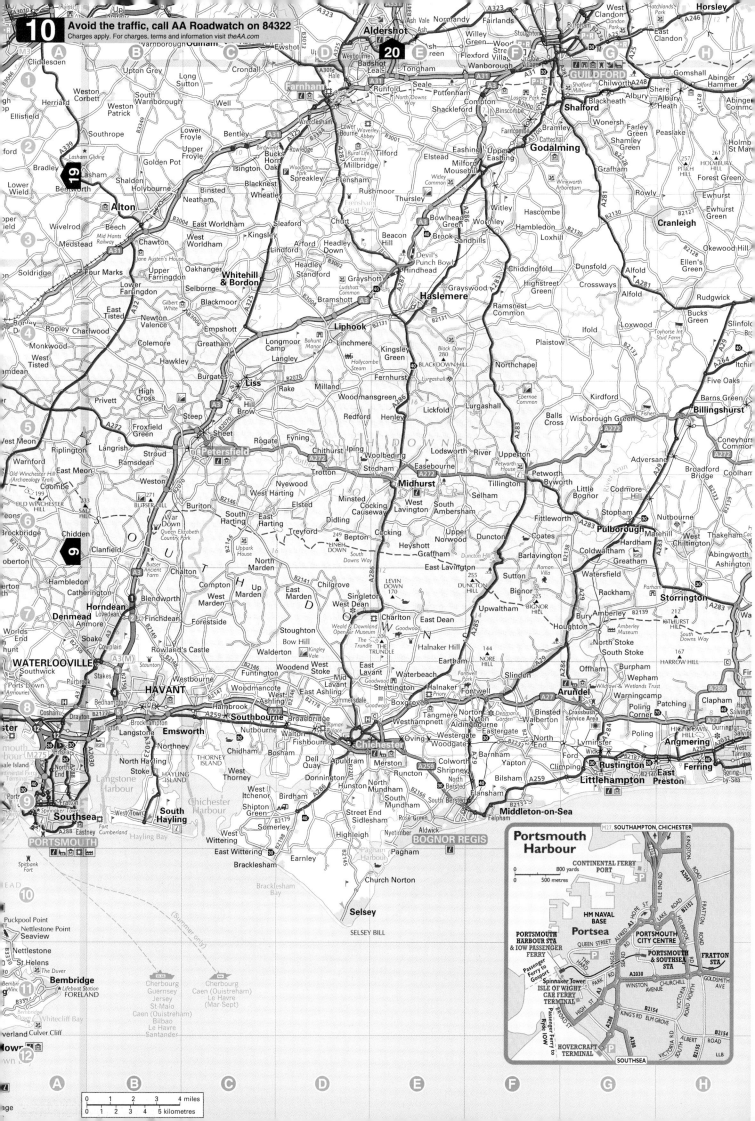

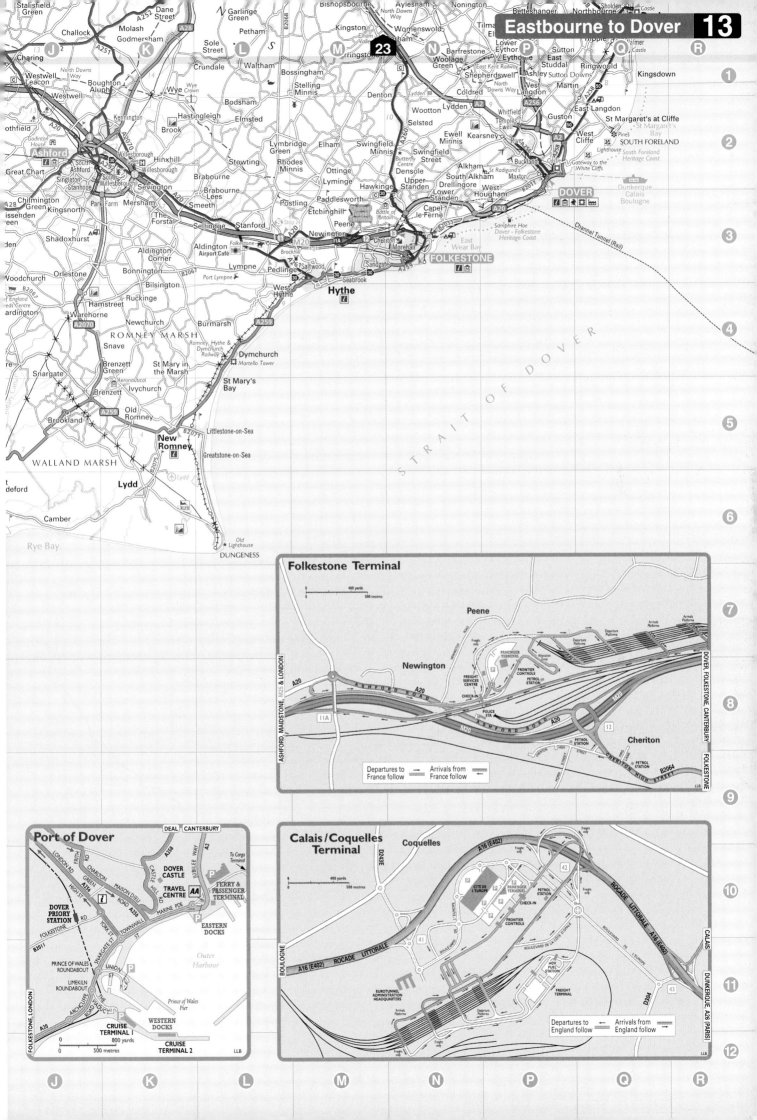

14

Avoid the traffic, call AA Roadwatch on 84322

Charges apply. For charges, terms and information visit *theAA.com*

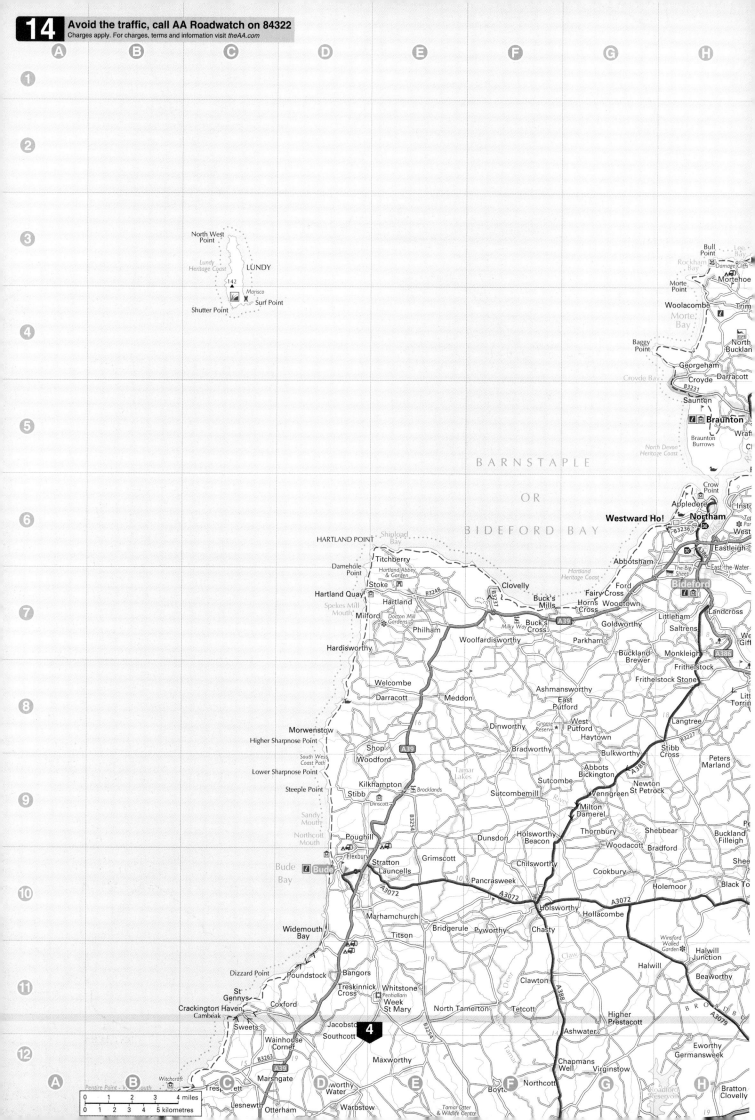

North West
Point

*Lundy
Heritage Coast*   LUNDY

▲142

Marisco

Shutter Point   *Surf Point*

Bull
Point   Lee
Bay
Rockham   Damage Cliffs
Bay   Mortehoe
Morte
Point   Trim

Woolacombe   *Morte
Bay*

Baggy
Point   North
Bucklan
Croyde   Darracott
Croyde Bay   B3231
Saunton

Braunton

Braunton
Burrows
*North Devon
Heritage Coast*

B A R N S T A P L E   Crow
Point
Appledore
O R   **Northam**
Westward Ho!   B3236
B I D E F O R D   B A Y   Eastleigh
Abbotsham   East-the-Water
HARTLAND POINT   *Shipload
Bay*   Ford   *The Big
Sheep*
Titchberry   Clovelly   Fairy Cross   **Bideford**
Damehole   Hartland Abbey   *Hartland   Horns   Woodtown
Point   & Garden   Buck's   Heritage Coast*   Cross
Stoke   B3248   Clovelly   Buck's   Cross
Hartland Quay   Hartland   Mills   Goldworthy   Littleham
*Spekes Mill
Mouth*   Milford   Docton Mill   *Milky Way*   Buck's   Parkham   Saltrens
Gardens   Cross   A386
Philham   Woolfardisworthy   Buckland
Hardisworthy   Brewer   Monkleigh
Frithelstock
Frithelstock Stone
Welcombe   Ashmansworthy
Darracott   Meddon   East   Langtree
Dinworthy   Gnome   Putford
Morwenstow   Reserve   West   Haytown
Higher Sharpnose Point   Putford   Stibb
Bradworthy   Cross
*South West
Coast Path*   Shop   A39   Sutcombe   Abbots
Woodford   Bickington   Newton
Lower Sharpnose Point   Tamar   St Petrock
Lakes   Sutcombemill
Steeple Point   Kilkhampton   Brocklands   Venngreen
Stibb   Milton
*Sandy
Mouth*   Dinscott   B3254   *River*   Damerel   Shebbear
Holsworthy   Thornbury   Buckland
*Northcott
Mouth*   Poughill   Dunsdon   Beacon   Woodacott   Filleigh
Bradford
Flexbury   Grimscott   Chilsworthy
Bude   Stratton   Cookbury
*Bude
Bay*   Launcells   Pancrasweek   Holemoor
A3072   Holsworthy
Marhamchurch   A3072   A3072   Black To
Hollacombe
Widemouth   Titson   Bridgerule   Pyworthy   Chasty   Winsford
Bay   Walled
Garden   Halwill
Junction
Dizzard Point   Poundstock   Bangors   Clawton   Beaworthy
Treskinnick   Whitstone
St   Cross   Penhallam   North Tamerton   Tetcott   Higher   B R O A D
Gennys   Week   Prestacott
Crackington Haven   Coxford   St Mary   A3079
Cambeak   Jacobstow   Ashwater   Eworthy
Sweets   Southcott   **4**   Germansweek
Wainhouse   Chapmans
Corner   Maxworthy   Well   Virginstow
B3263
Witchcroft   A39   Boyt   Northcott   Bratton
Pentire Point   Marshate   D.worthy   Clovelly
Tresp.ett   Water   Warbstow
Lesnewth   Otterham   *Tamar Otter
& Wildlife Centre*

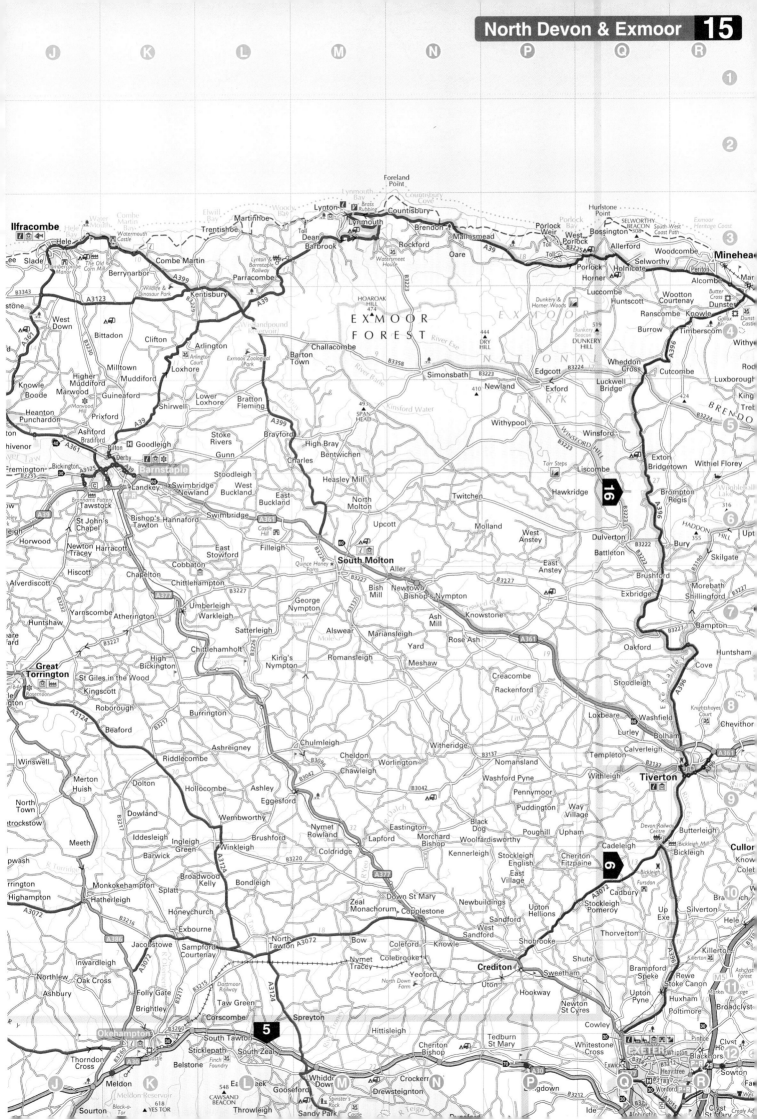

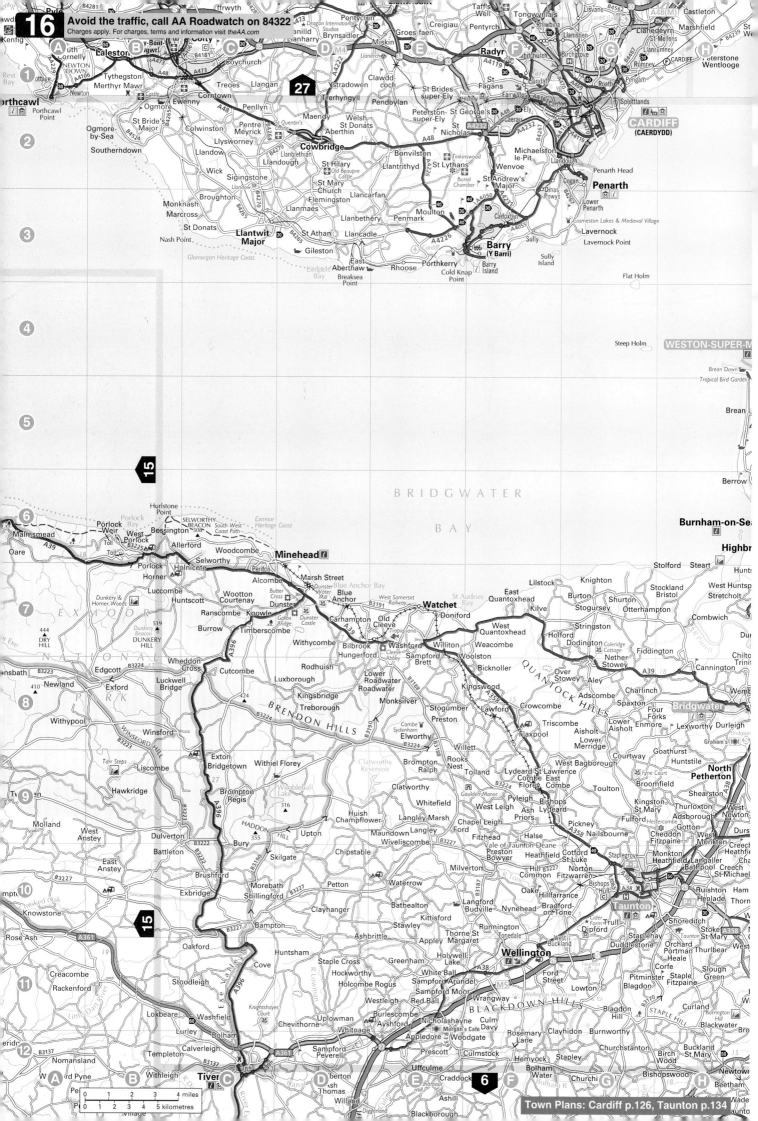

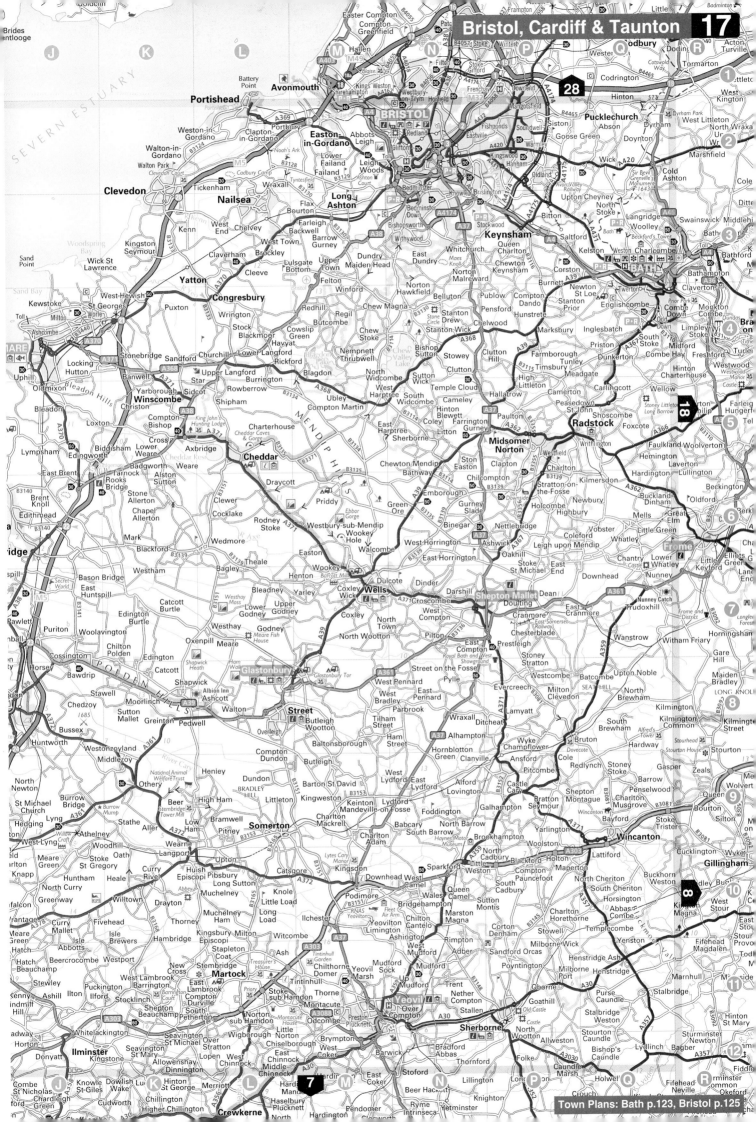

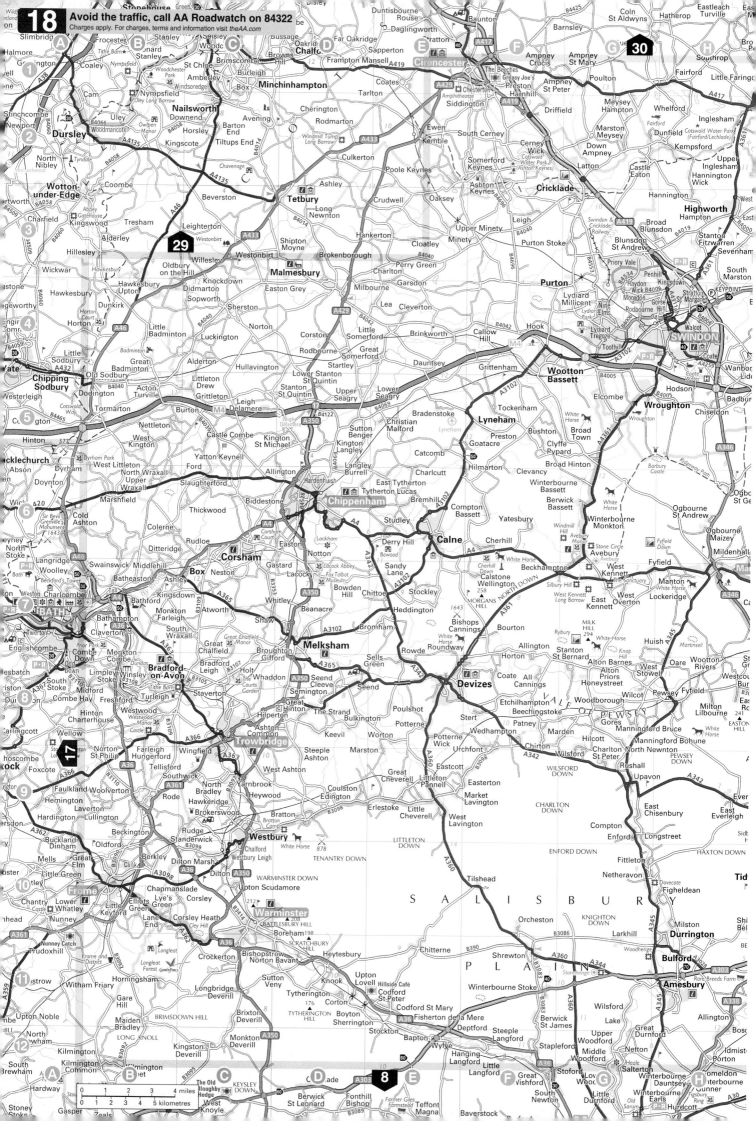

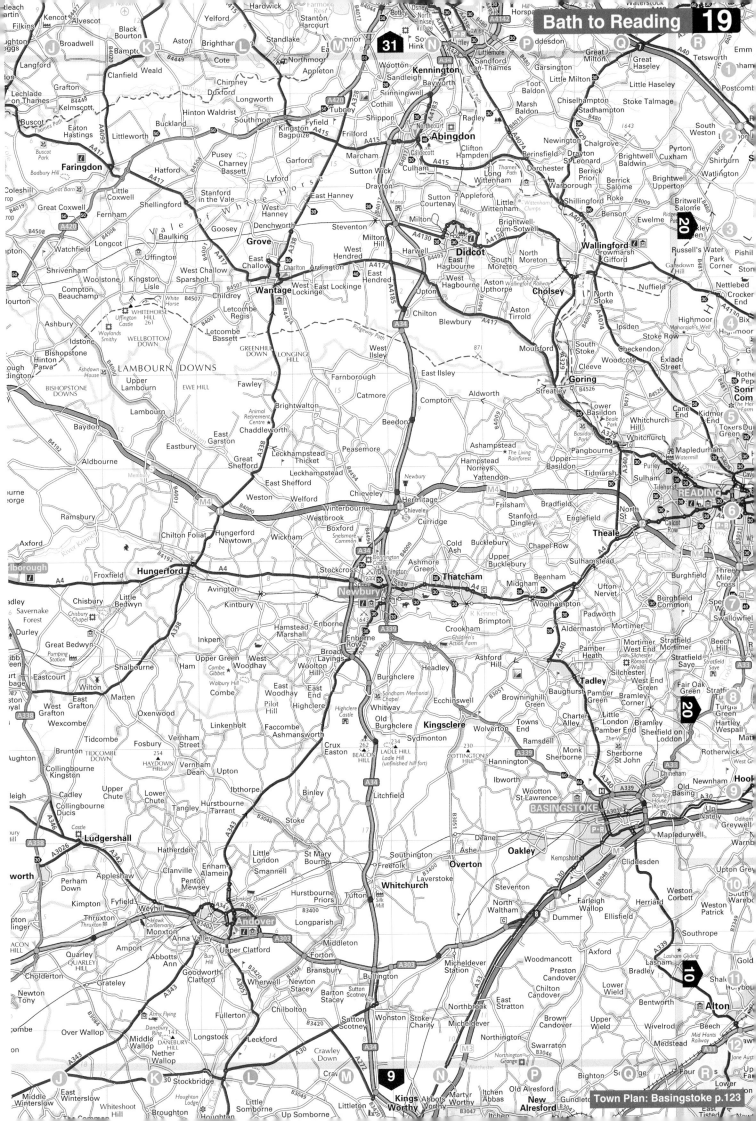

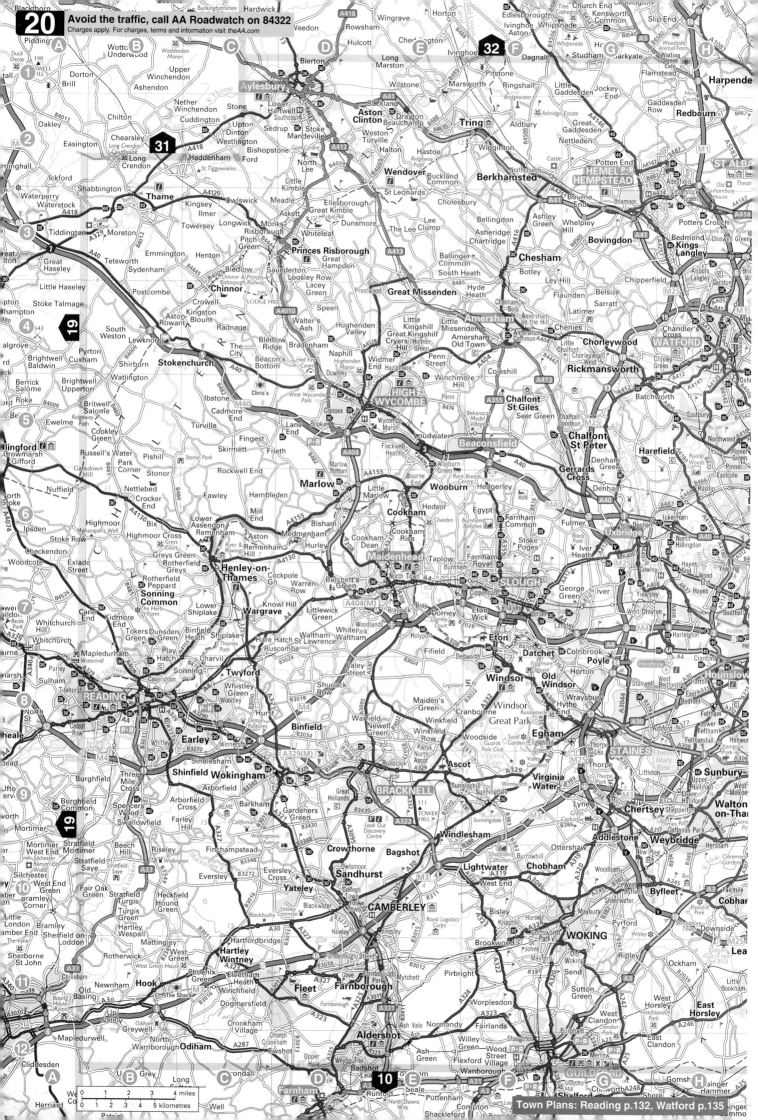

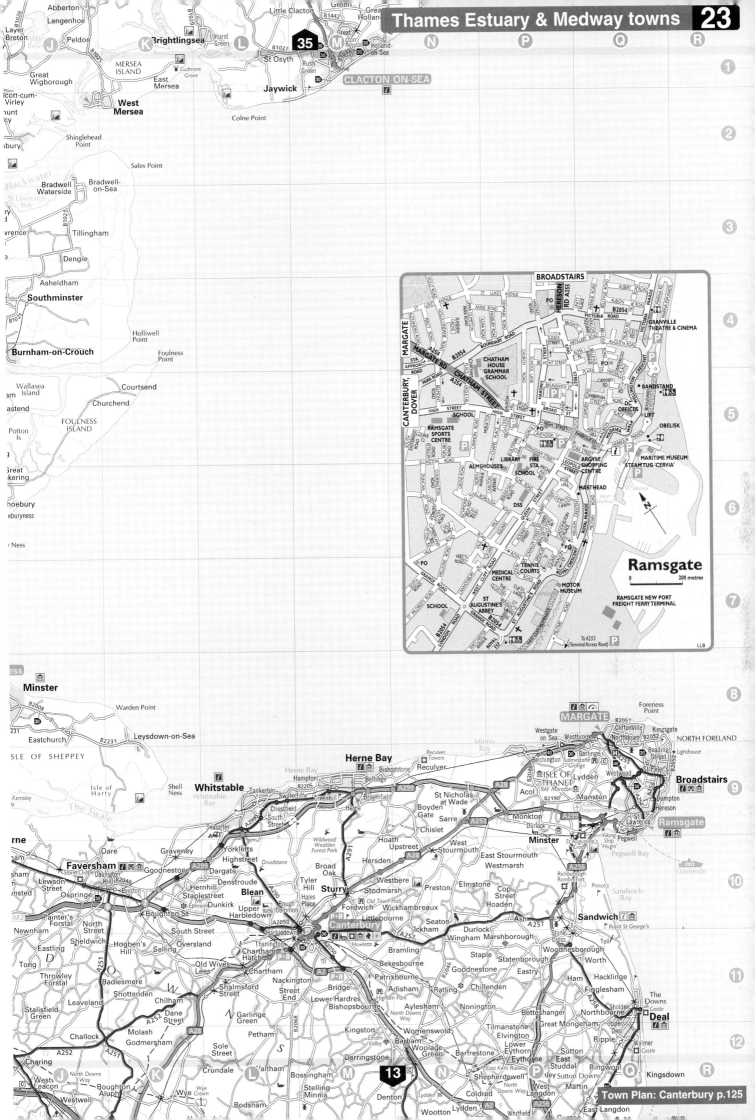

Ramsgate

BROADSTAIRS

CHATHAM HOUSE GRAMMAR SCHOOL

RAMSGATE SPORTS CENTRE

LIBRARY

ALMSHOUSES

FIRE STA.

SCHOOL

DSS

LEOPOLD STREET

ARGYLE SHOPPING CENTRE

MASTHEAD

GRANVILLE THEATRE & CINEMA

DC OFFICES

LIFT

OBELISK

BANDSTAND

MARITIME MUSEUM
STEAM TUG 'CERVIA'

TENNIS COURTS

MEDICAL CENTRE

MOTOR MUSEUM

ST AUGUSTINE'S ABBEY

SCHOOL

RAMSGATE NEW PORT
FREIGHT FERRY TERMINAL

To A253
(Terminal Access Road)

0   200 metres

LLB

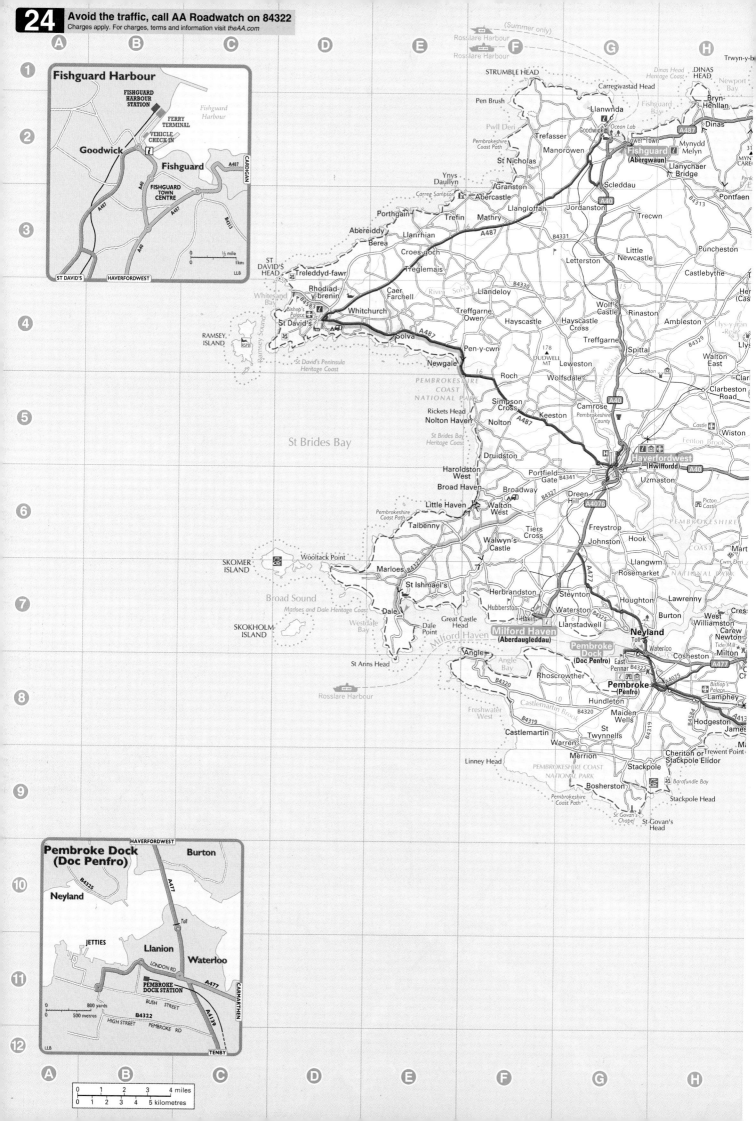

Fishguard Harbour

FISHGUARD HARBOUR STATION
FERRY TERMINAL
VEHICLE CHECK IN
Goodwick
Fishguard
FISHGUARD TOWN CENTRE
A487
CARDIGAN
B4313
A40
A487
A40
ST DAVID'S
HAVERFORDWEST
0 ½ mile
0 1km
LLB

Pembroke Dock (Doc Penfro)

HAVERFORDWEST
Burton
Neyland
B4325
A477
Toll
JETTIES
Llanion
Waterloo
LONDON RD
PEMBROKE DOCK STATION
A477
CARMARTHEN
BUSH STREET
B4322
HIGH STREET   PEMBROKE RD
A4139
TENBY
LLB
0   1   2   3   800 yards
0 1 2 3 4 500 metres

Trwyn-y-b
(Summer only)
Rosslare Harbour
Rosslare Harbour
STRUMBLE HEAD
DINAS HEAD
Dinas Head Heritage Coast
Newport Bay
Bryn-Henllan
Pen Brush
Carregwastad Head
Llanwnda
Goodwick
Dinas
Ocean Lab
Lower Town
Mynydd Melyn
Trefasser
Fishguard Bay
MYN CAE
Manorowen
Fishguard (Abergwaun)
Pembrokeshire Coast Path
St Nicholas
Llanychaer Bridge
Granston
Scleddau
Pontfaen
Ynys Daullyn
Abercastle
Jordanston
A40
Trecwn
B4313
Carreg Sampson
Llangloffan
Mathry
A487
Porthgain
Trefin
Little Newcastle
Castlebythe
Abereiddy
Llanrhian
B4331
Letterston
Berea
Croes-goch
A487
Wolf's Castle
Rinaston
Puncheston
Treglemais
Ambleston
Llys-y-fran Resr
St DAVID'S HEAD
Treleddyd-fawr
Treffgarne Owen
Hayscastle
Hayscastle Cross
Treffgarne
Whitesand Bay
Rhodiad-y-brenin
Caer Farchell
Spittal
Walton East
Lli
Bishop's Palace
Whitchurch
Llandeloy
B4330
River Solva
A40
Scolton
RAMSEY ISLAND
St David's
A487
Pen-y-cwn
178 DUDWELL MT
Leweston
Wolfsdale
Clarbeston Road
RSPB
Solva
Roch
Her (Cas
Ramsey Sound
St David's Peninsula Heritage Coast
Newgale
16
Camrose
Castle
Wiston
PEMBROKESHIRE COAST NATIONAL PARK
Simpson Cross
A487
Keeston
Pembrokeshire County
Fenton Brook
Rickets Head
Nolton Haven
Nolton
Druidston
H
Haverfordwest (Hwlffordd)
A40
St Brides Bay
St Brides Bay Heritage Coast
Haroldston West
Portfield Gate
B4341
Uzmaston
PEMBROKESHIRE
Broad Haven
Broadway
B4327
Dreen Hill
A4076
Picton Castle
Little Haven
Walton West
Freystrop
COAST
Pembrokeshire Coast Path
Talbenny
Tiers Cross
Johnston
Hook
Llangwm
NATIONAL PARK
SKOMER ISLAND
Wooltack Point
Marloes
Walwyn's Castle
Rosemarket
Mar
B4327
Herbrandston
Steynton
A477
Lawrenny
West Williamston
Broad Sound
St Ishmael's
Houghton
Burton
Carew Newton
Marloes and Dale Heritage Coast
Hubberston
Waterston
B4325
Cres
SKOKHOLM ISLAND
Dale
Hakin
Llanstadwell
Neyland
Milton
Westdale Bay
Great Castle Head
Milford Haven (Aberdaugleddau)
Llanreath
Waterloo
Coshelston
Ch
Dale Point
Pembroke Dock (Doc Penfro)
Tide Mill
A477
St Anns Head
Milford Haven
Angle
Bishop's Palace
Lamphey
Angle Bay
East Pennar
B4322
Pembroke (Penfro)
A4075
Rosslare Harbour
Rhoscrowther
10
Hundleton
A4584
Hodgeston
A413
Freshwater West
Castlemartin Brook
Maiden Wells
St Twynnells
B4319
James
Castlemartin
B4320
B4319
Merrion
M
Warren
Cheriton or Trewent Point
Stackpole Elidor
Linney Head
PEMBROKESHIRE COAST NATIONAL PARK
Stackpole
Barafundle Bay
Bosherston
Pembrokeshire Coast Path
Stackpole Head
St Govan's Chapel
St Govan's Head

0   1   2   3   4 miles
0 1 2 3 4 5 kilometres

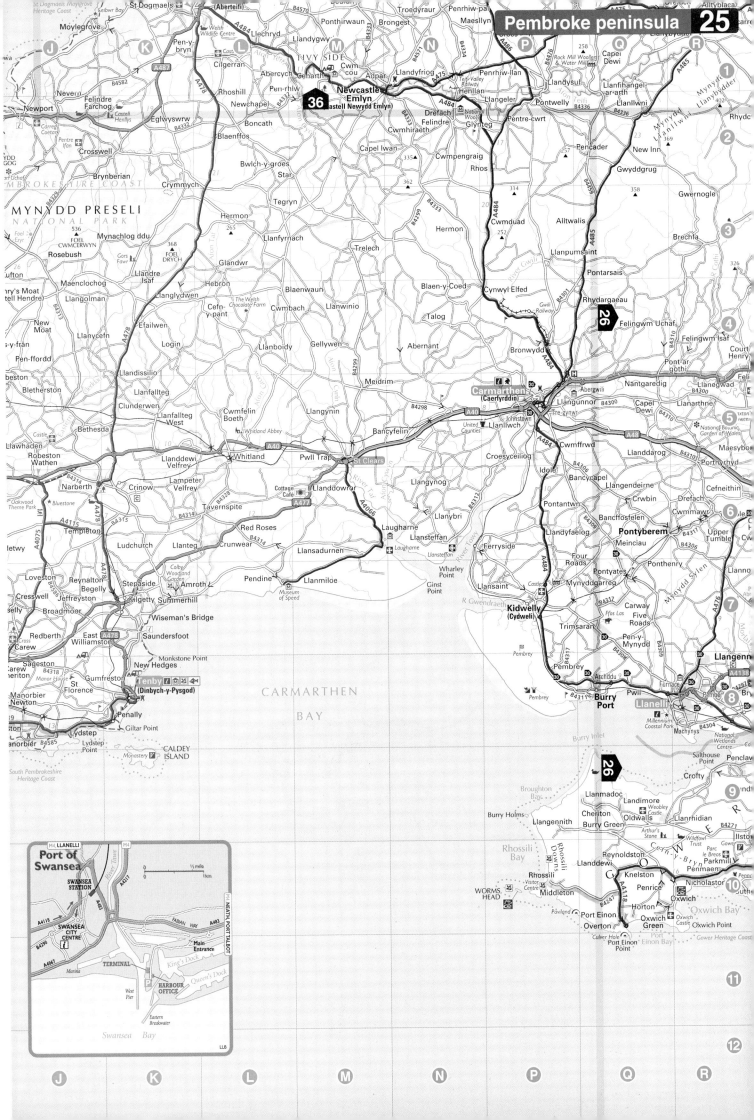

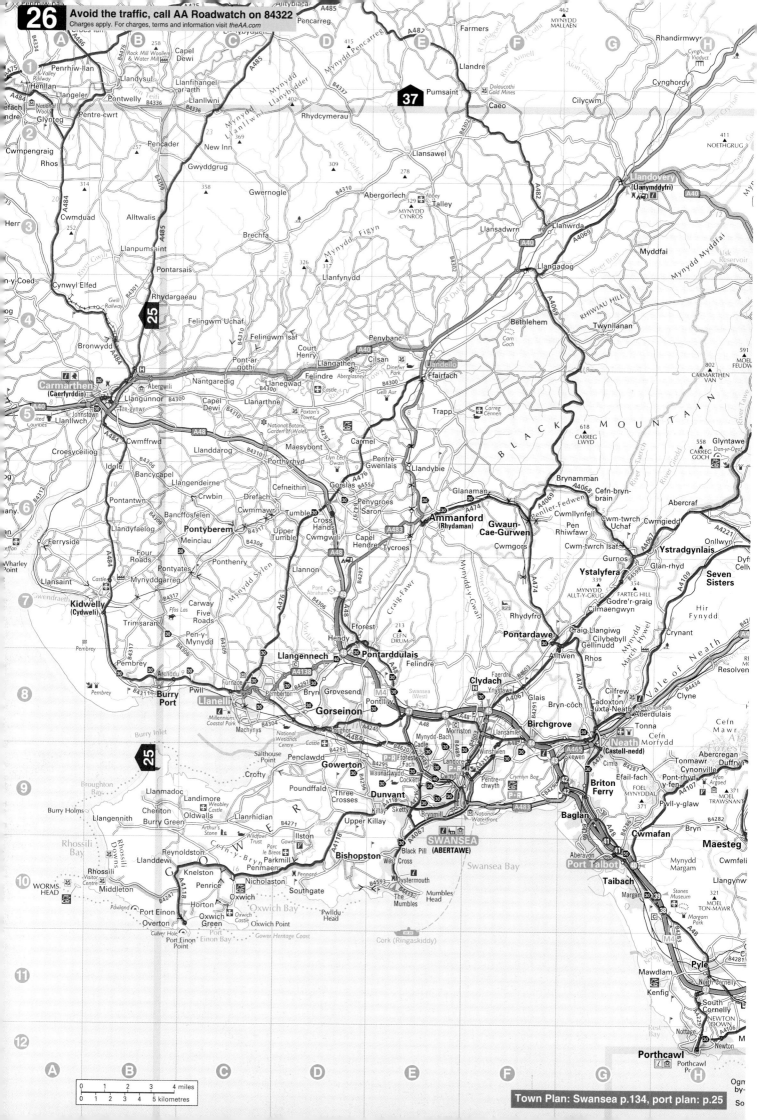

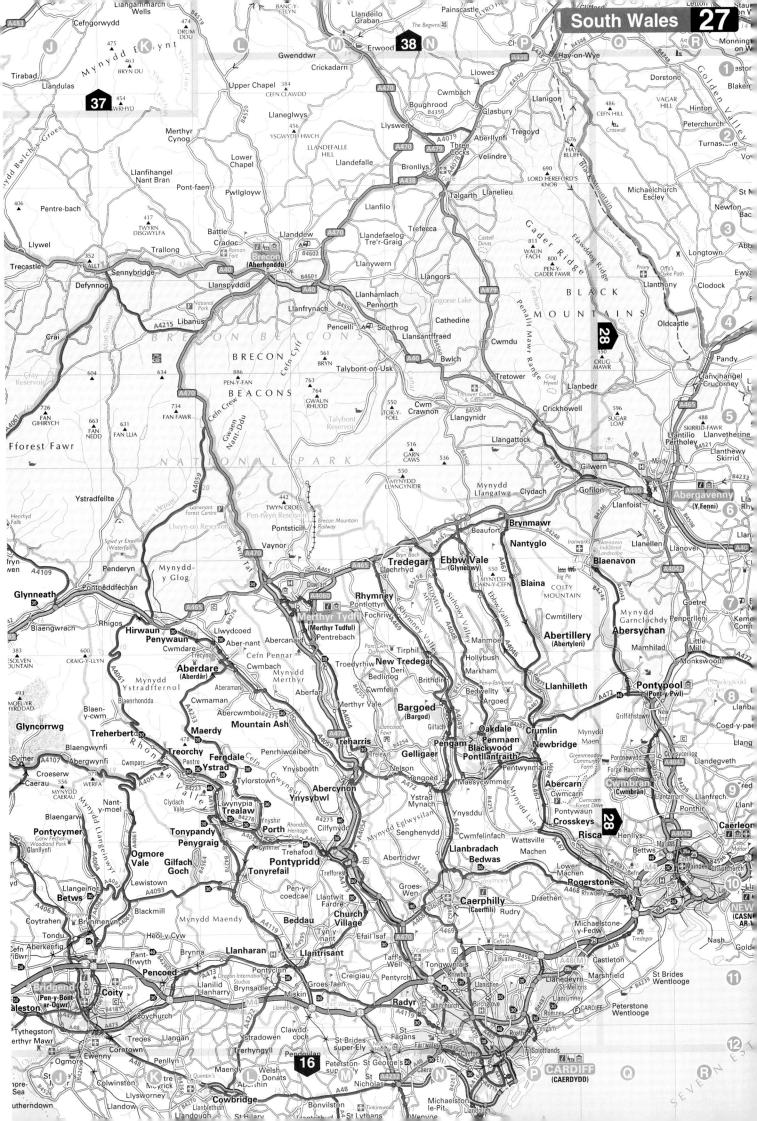

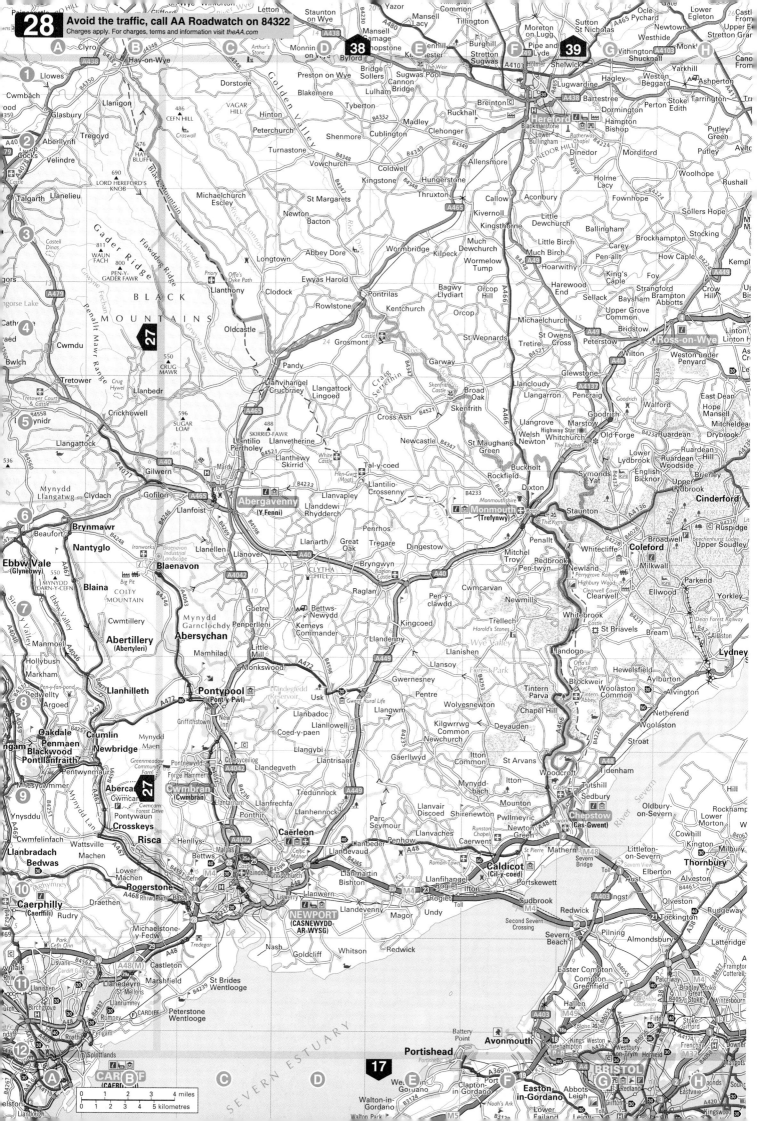

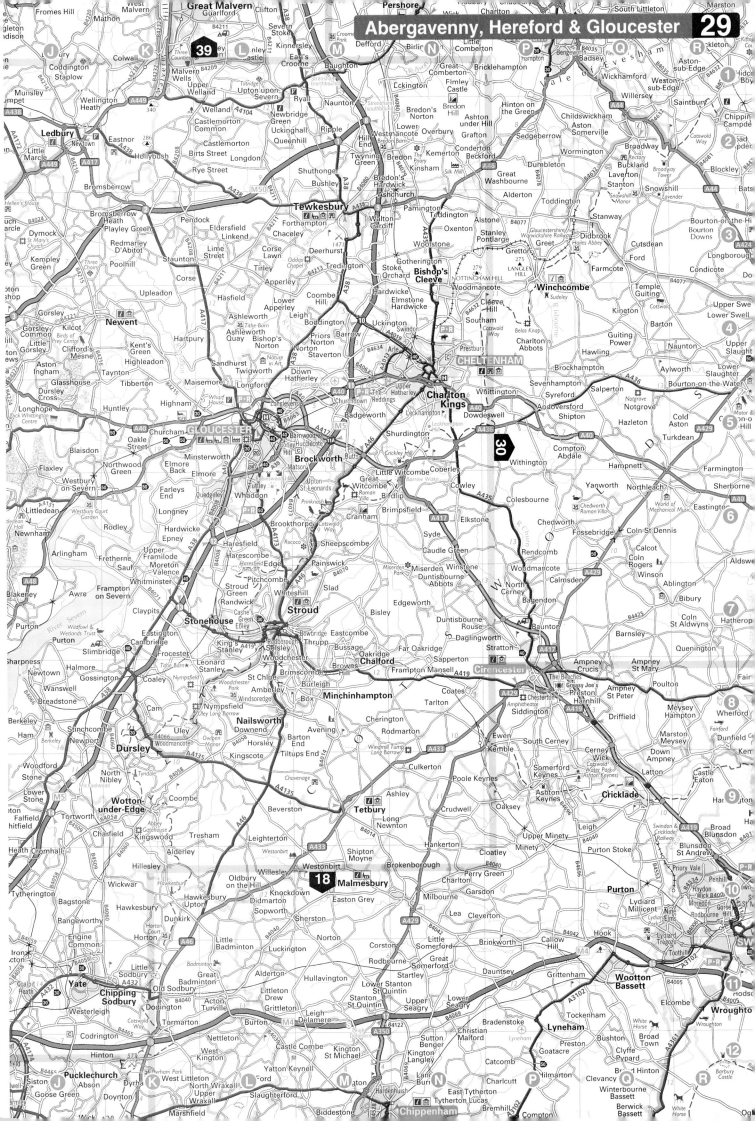

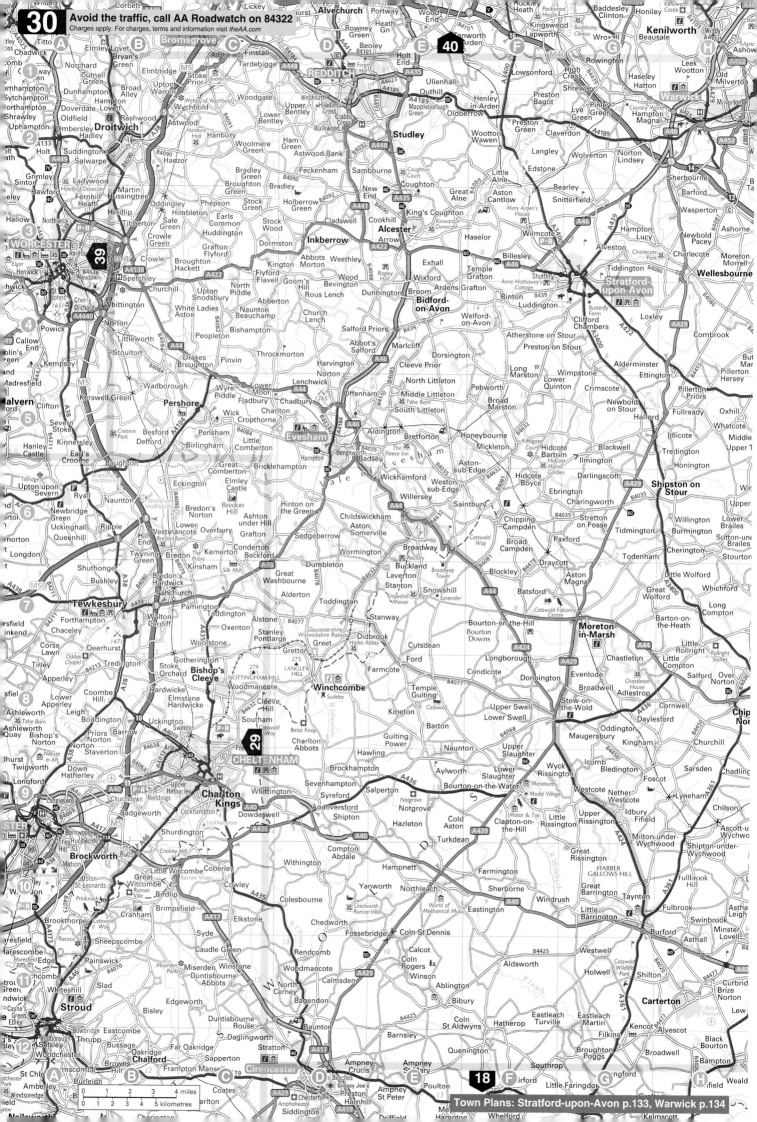

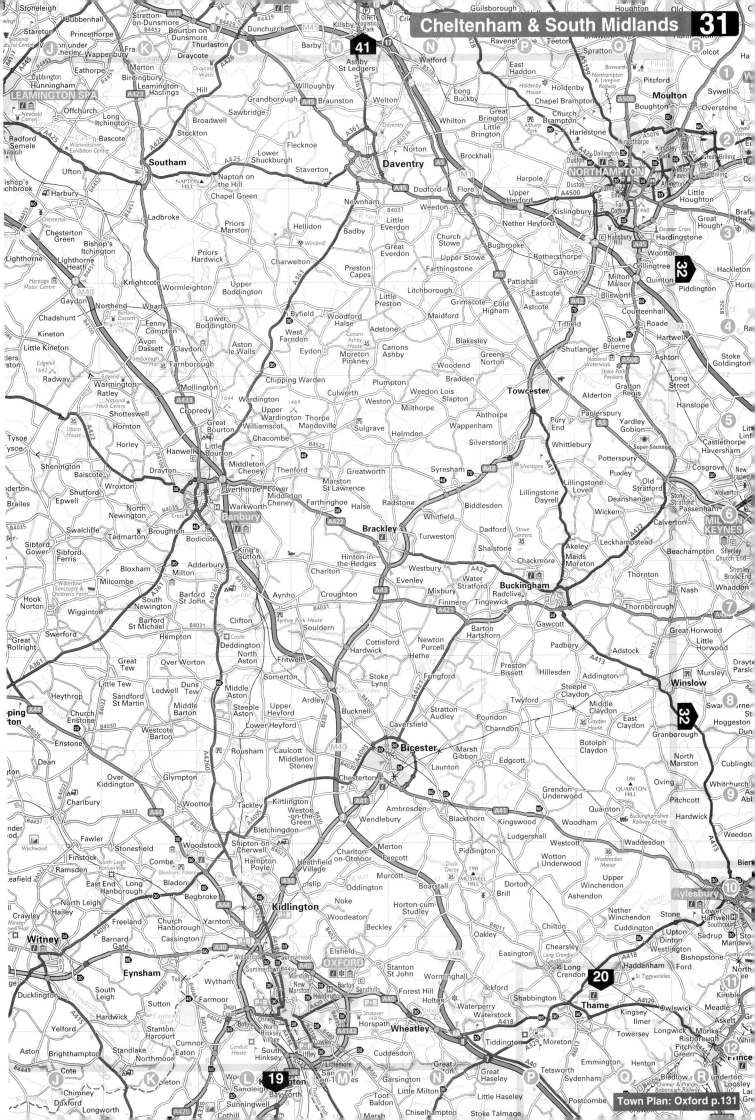

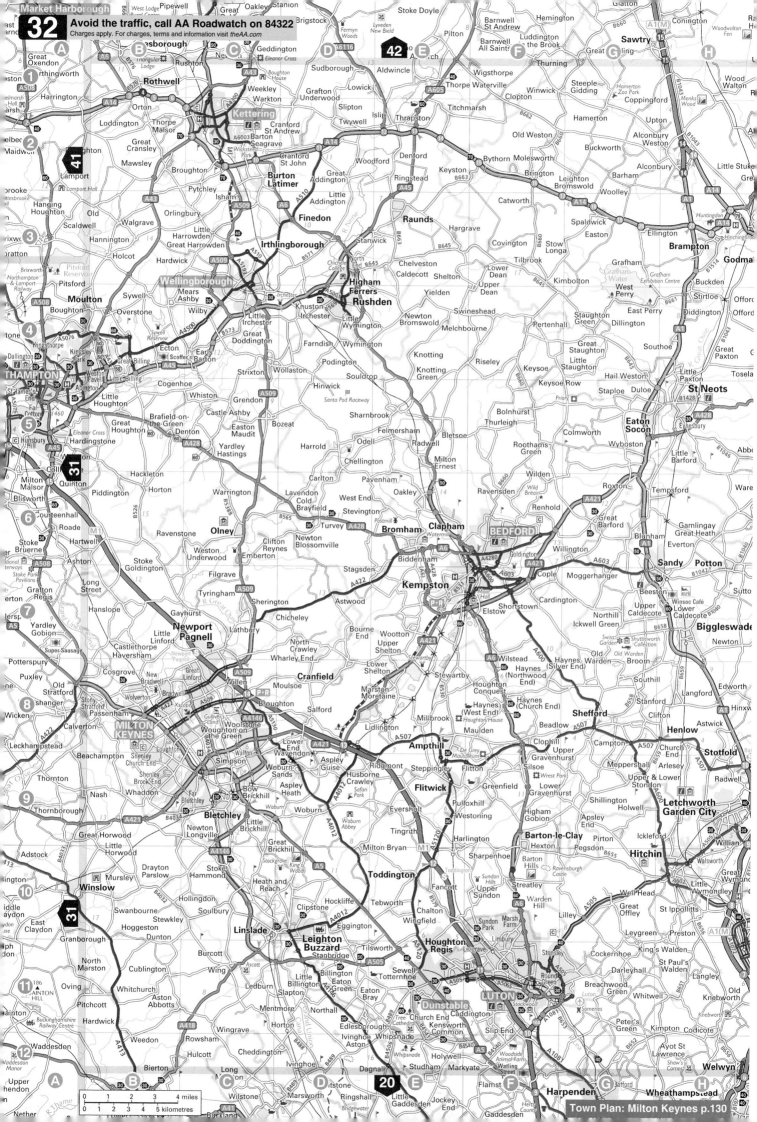

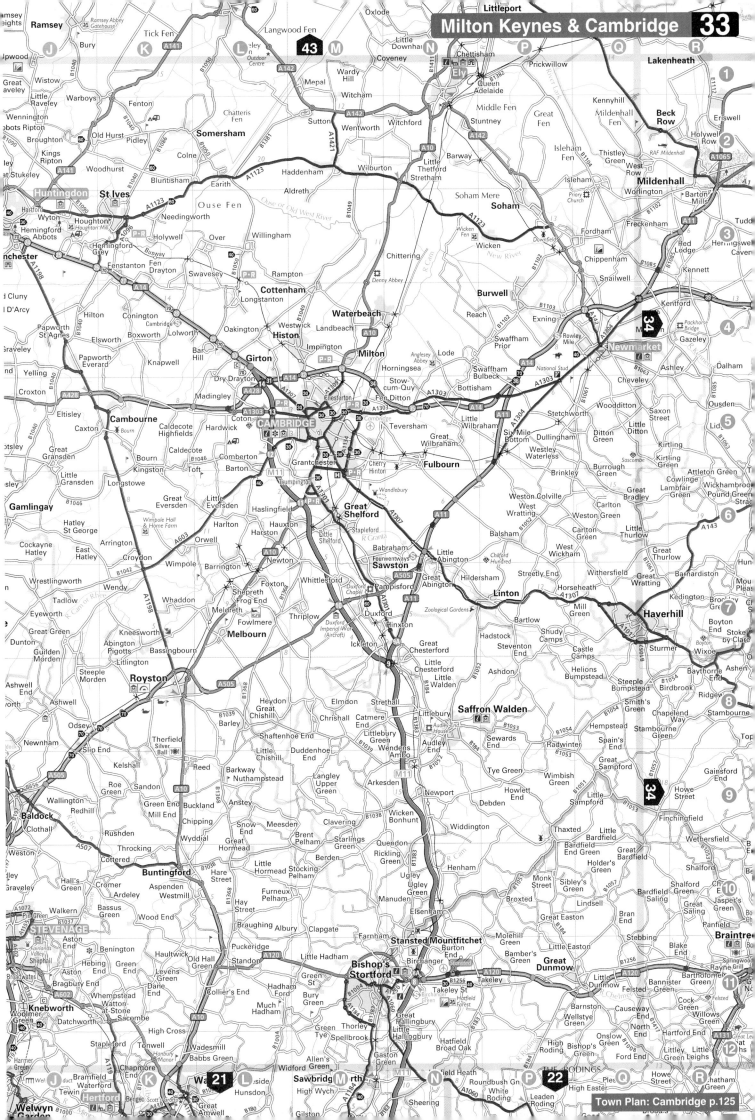

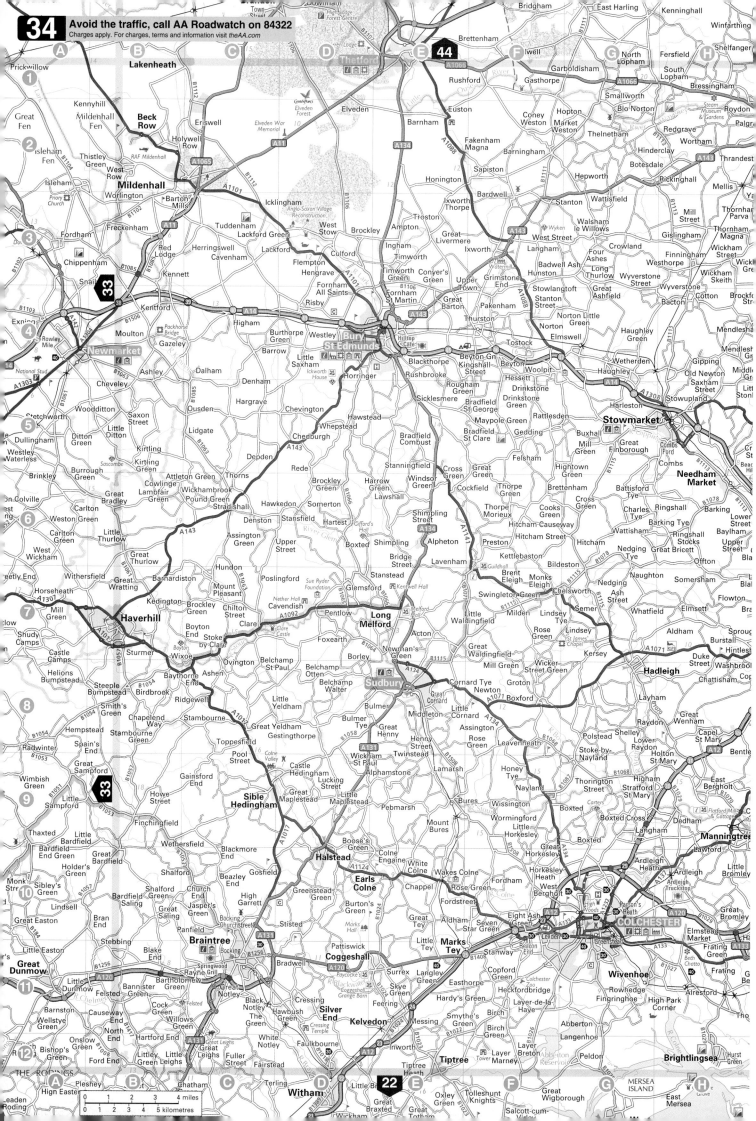

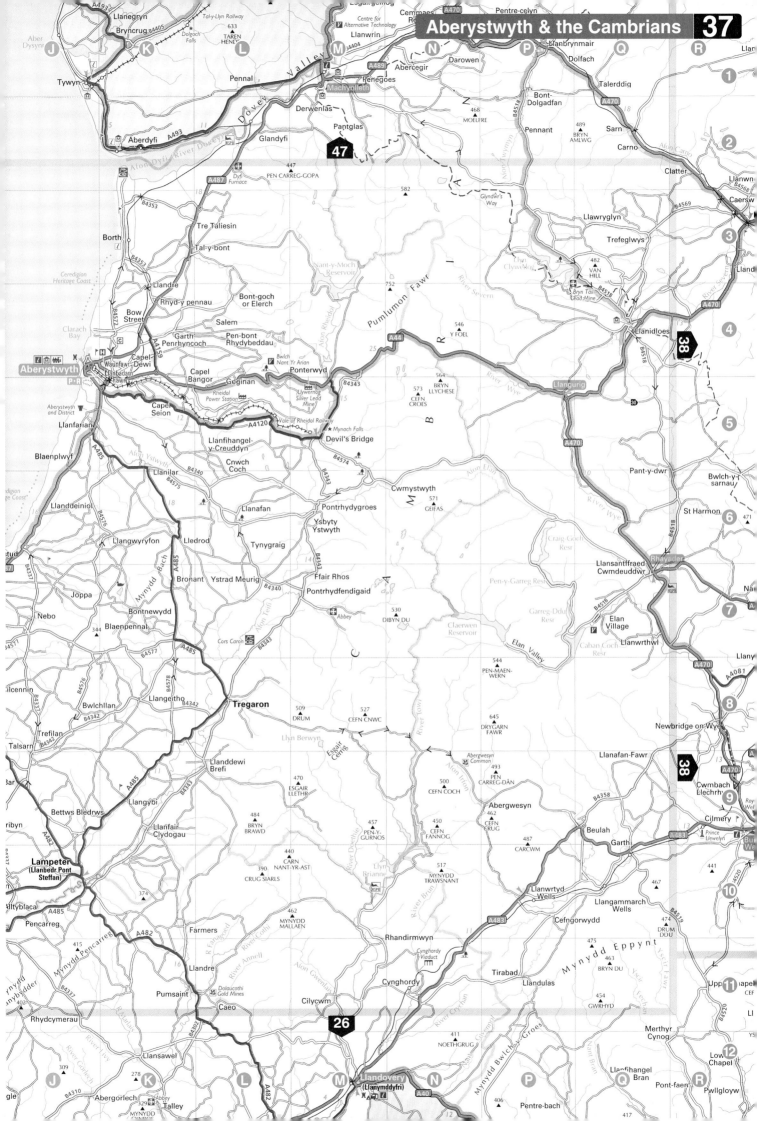

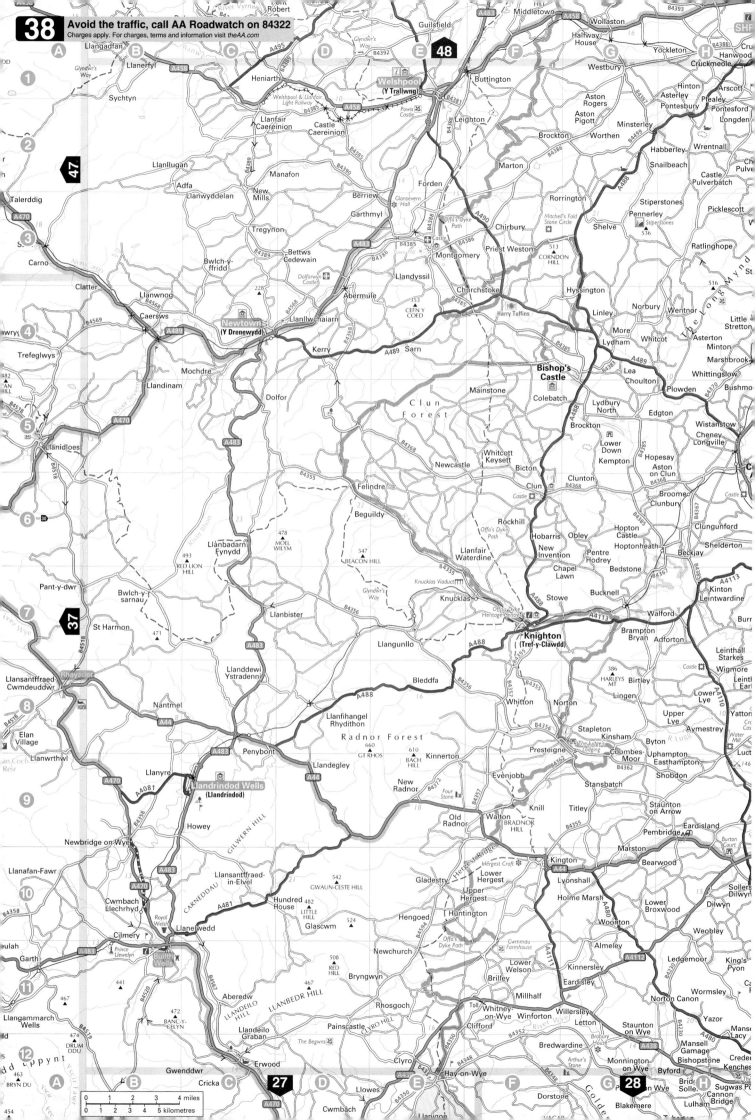

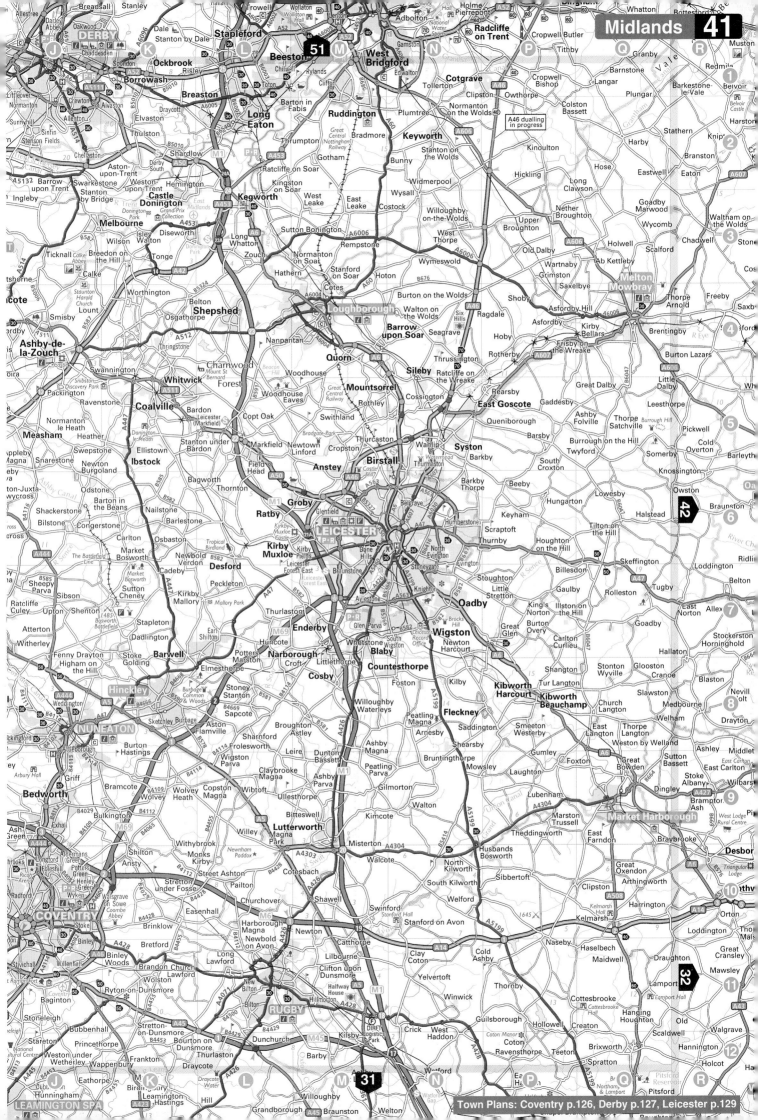

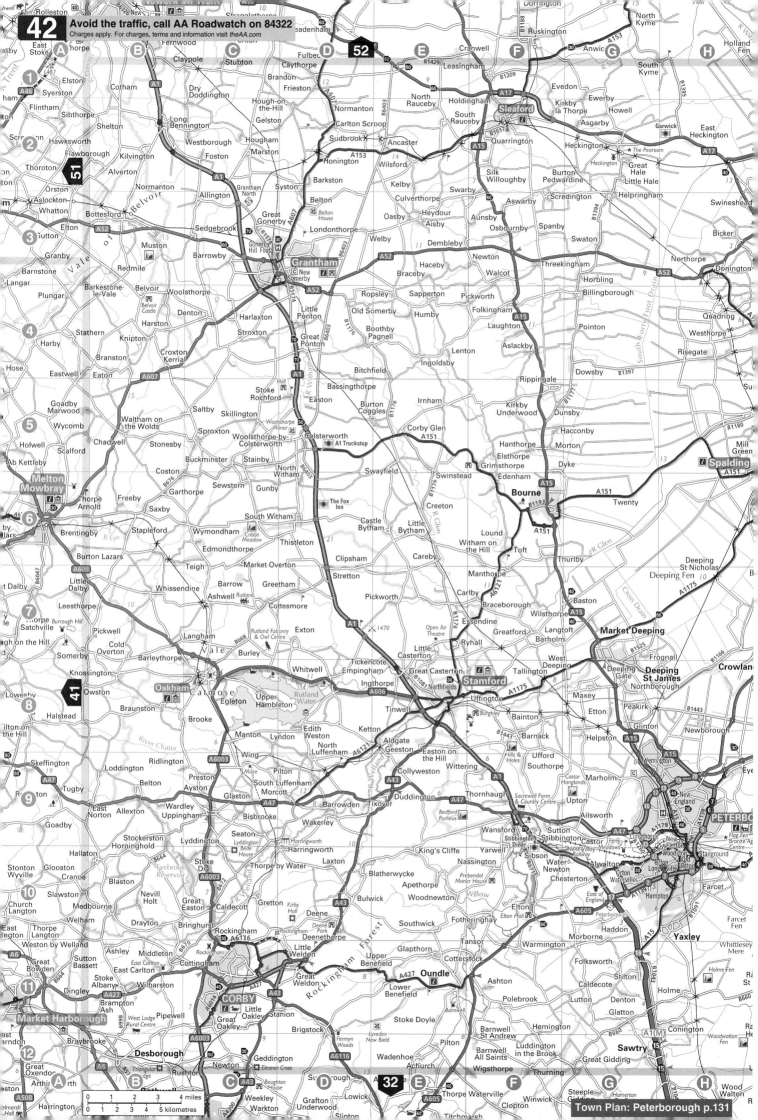

A B C D E F G H

1
2
3
4
5
6
7
8
9
10
11
12

North Norfolk Heritage Coast
Holkham Bay
Blakeney Point
Blakeney Point
North Norfolk Heritage Coast
Brancaster Bay
Scolt Head Island
Peddars Way & Norfolk Coast Path
Morston Marshes
Blakeney
Guildhall
Cley next the Sea
Holme next the Sea
Holme Dunes
Brancaster
Brancaster Staithe
Burnham Norton
Burnham Overy Staithe
Holkham
Wells-next-the-sea
Morston
Wiveton
Salthouse
Old Hunstanton
Thornham
Titchwell
Branodonum Roman Fort
Burnham Deepdale
Burnham Market
Burnham Overy
Warham St Mary
Stiffkey
Cockthorpe
Langham
Glandford
Holt
Hunstanton
Ringstead
Burnham Thorpe
Holkham Hall
Warham All Saints
Wighton
Warham
Binham
Saxlingham
North Norfolk Railway
Heacham
Norfolk Lavender
Summerfield
Peddars Way & Norfolk Coast Path
North Creake
Creake Abbey
Wells & Walsingham Light Railway
The Shrine of Our Lady
Little Walsingham
Great Walsingham
Binham Priory & Market Cross
Field Dalling
Letheringsett
Holt Lowes
Hempstead
Thornage
Hunworth
Edg
Sedgeford
Docking
Stanhoe
South Creake
North Barsham
Houghton St Giles
Hindringham
Great Snoring
Thursford
Bale
Brinton
Sharrington
Stody
Briningham
Edgefield
Snettisham
Fring
Bircham Newton
Syderstone
West Barsham
East Barsham
Little Snoring
Croxton
Barney
Gunthorpe
Melton Constable
Swanton Novers
Briston
Ingoldisthorpe
Park Farm
Shernborne
Great Bircham
Bircham Tofts
Wicken Green Village
Sculthorpe
Dunton
Coxford
Shereford
Hempton
Tatterford
Toftrees
Colkirk
Kettlestone
Fakenham
Stibbard
Wood Norton
Hindolveston
Thurning
Corpu
Dersingham
Wolferton
Sandringham
West Newton
Flitcham
Anmer
New Houghton
Houghton Hall
West Rudham
East Rudham
Helhoughton
East Raynham
West Raynham
South Raynham
Great Ryburgh
Little Ryburgh
Guist
Foulsham
Guestwick
Themelthorpe
Wood Dalling
Wood Dalling
Castle Rising
North Wootton
Congham
Roydon
Grimston
Hillington
Little Massingham
Great Massingham
Weasenham St Peter
Weasenham All Saints
Wellingham
Tittleshall
Stanfield
Brisley
North Elmham
North Elmham Chapel
Billingford
Bawdeswell
Sparham
Foxley
Twyford
Bintree
Reepham
Salle
South Wootton
Gaywood
Fairstead
King's Lynn
Gayton
Ashwicken
Gayton Thorpe
Rougham
Whissonsett
Horningtoft
Gateley
Brandon Parva
West Lynn
Fair Green
East Winch
East Walton
West Acre
Castle Acre
Newton
Litcham
East Bilney
Old Beetley
Beetley
Worthing
Swanton Morley
Lyng
Elsing
Lenwade
Mort the N
Saddle Bow
West Winch
Middleton
Blackborough End
Pentney
West Bilney
West Lexham
East Lexham
Beeston
Mileham
Longham
Gressenhall
Gressenhall Green
Hoe
Wiggenhall St Germans
Setchey
Wormegay
Narborough
South Acre
Priory
South Acre
Little Dunham
Great Dunham
Dereham
Dereham
Hockering
North Tuddenham
Mattishall Burgh
East Tuddenham
Welborne
Watlington
Tottenhill
Marham
Sporle
Necton
Little Fransham
Great Fransham
Scarning
Westfield
Yaxham
Mattishall
Clint Green
South Green
Whinburgh
Colton
North Runcton
South Runcton
Shouldham
Swaffham
Ecotech Discovery Centre
North Pickenham
Holme Hale
West Bradenham
East Bradenham
Shipdham
Garveston
Reymerston
Thuxton
Coston
Runhall
Barnham Broom
Barfor
Stow Bardolph
Stradsett
Fincham
Barton Bendish
Beachamwell
South Pickenham
Ashill
Saham Hills
Cranworth
Woodrising
Southburgh
Hardingham
Hingham
Kimberley
Hackford
Wicklewood
Crownth
Downham Market
Bexwell
Crimplesham
Boughton
Wereham
Oxborough
Gooderstone
Hilborough
Great Cressingham
Saham Toney
Ovington
Carbrooke
Watton
Deopham
Morley St Botolph
Denver
West Dereham
Wretton
Stoke Ferry
Whittington
Foulden
Little Cressingham
Merton
Griston
Scoulton
Little Ellingham
Deopham Green
Fora
Hilgay
Oxburgh Hall
Northwold
Thompson
Gaston
Rockland St Peter
Rockland All Saints
Fen Street
Great Ellingham
Southery
Methwold Hythe
Methwold
Cranwich
Ickburgh
Stow Bedon
Lower Stow Bedon
Breckles
Shropham
Besthorpe
Attleborough
Methwold Fens
Queens Ground
Feltwell
Mundford
Peddars Way & Norfolk Coast Path
Great Hockham
Snetterton
Eccles Road
Wilby
Carleton Rode
Burnt Fen
Hockwold Fens
Hockwold cum Wilton
Weeting
Castle
Grime's Graves
East Wretham
Snetterton
Larling
Quidenham
Banham
Kenninghall
New Buckenh
Brandon
Town Street
Santon Downham
High Lodge Forest Centre
Croxton
Bridgham
East Harling
North Lopham
South Lopham
Winfarthing
Banham
Lakenheath
Warren Lodge
Thetford
Brettenham
Shadwell
Gasthorpe
Garboldisham
Fersfield
Prickwillow
Ashford
Kenninghall
Smallworth
Bressingham
Winfarthing

0 1 2 3 4 miles
0 1 2 3 4 5 kilometres

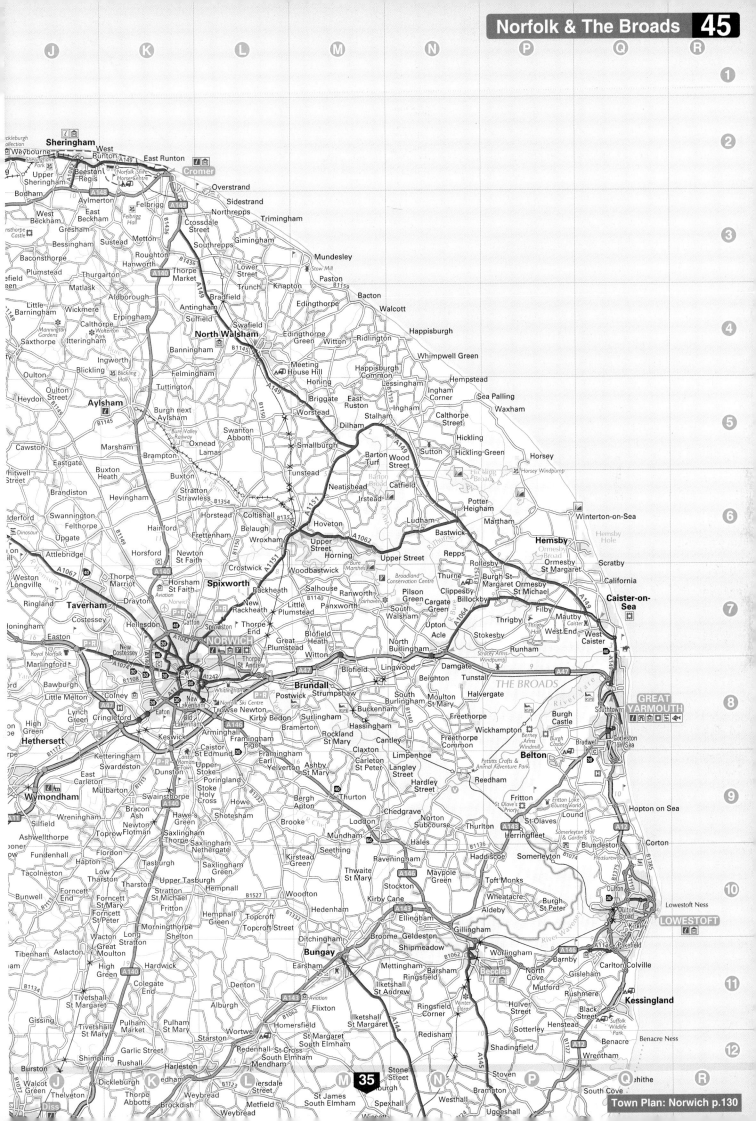

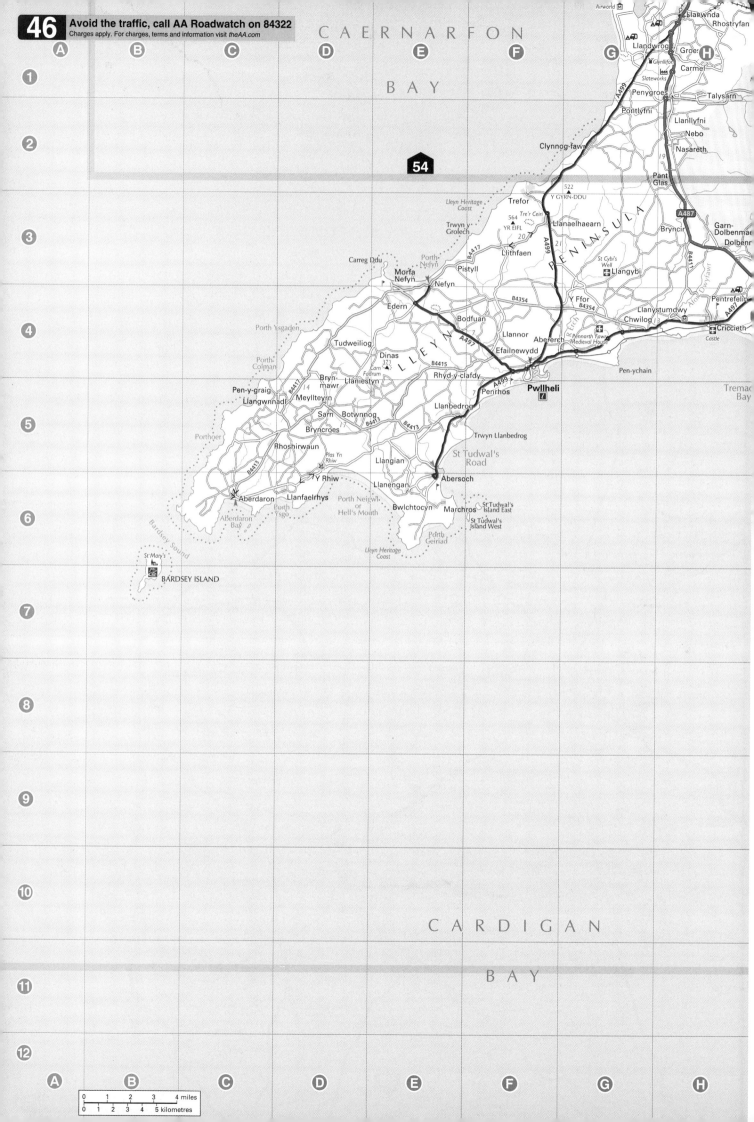

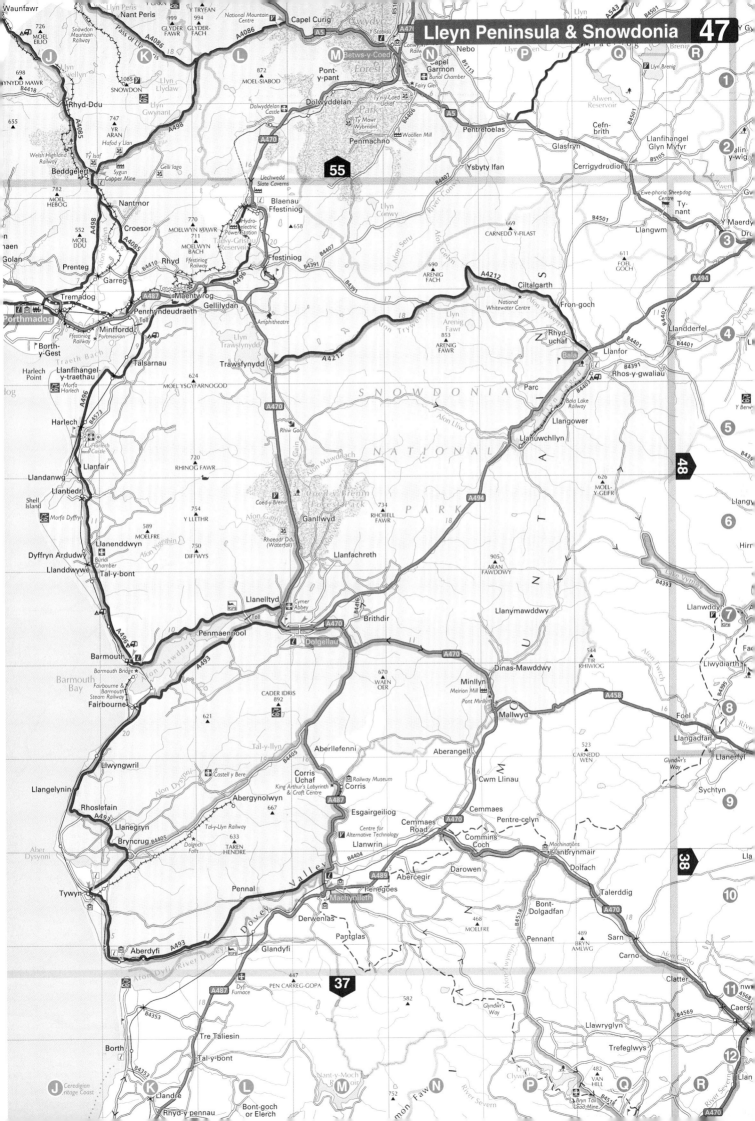

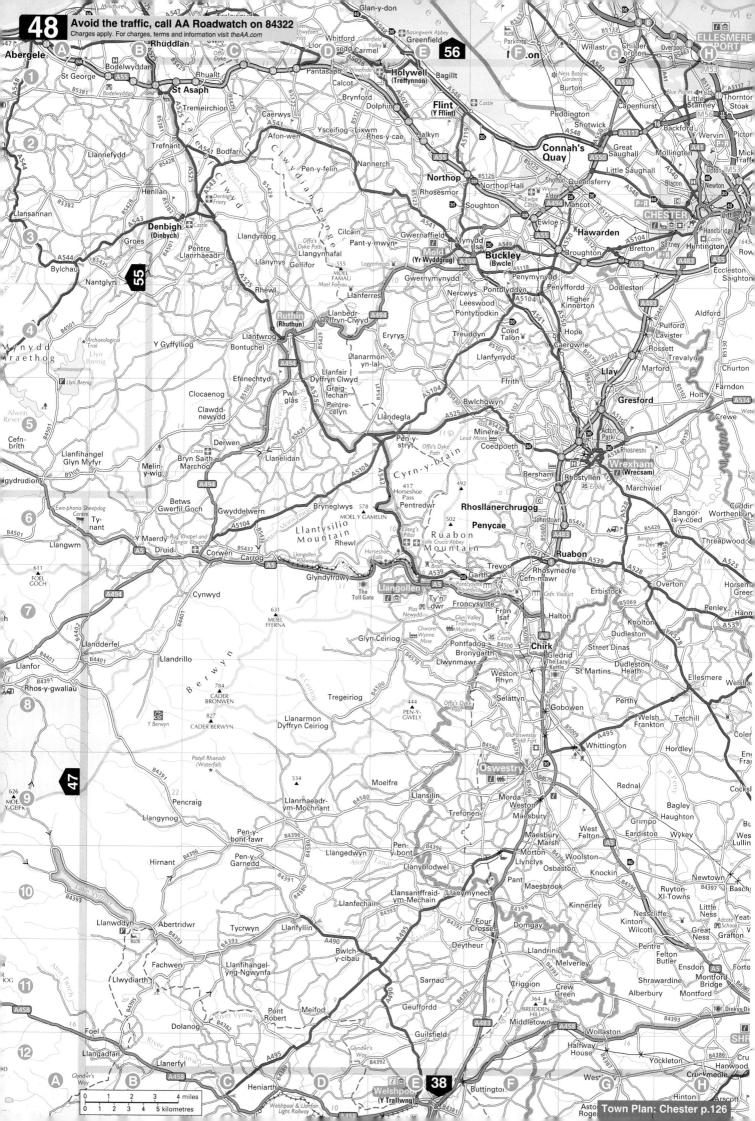

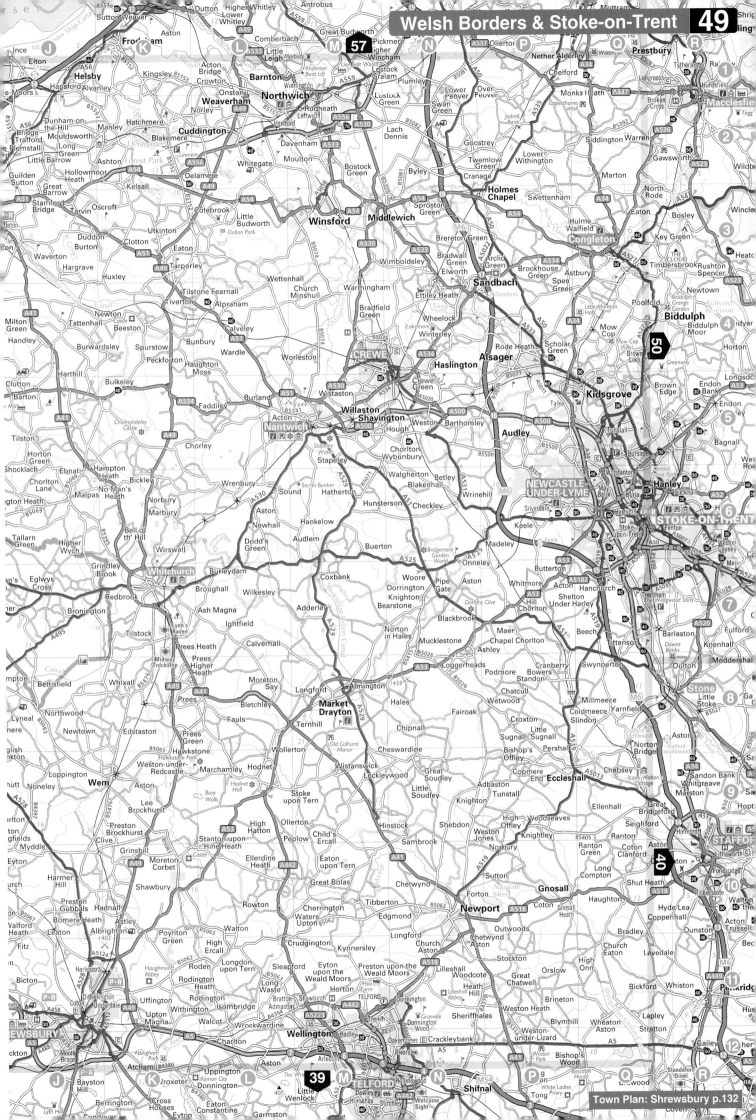

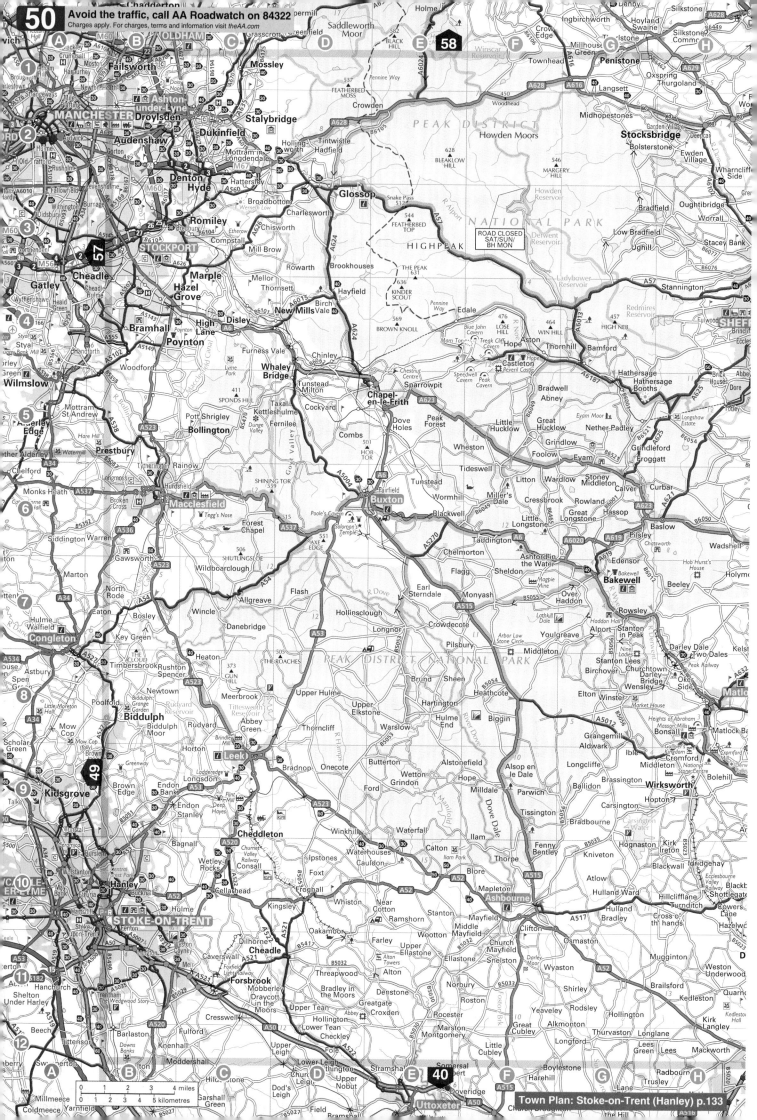

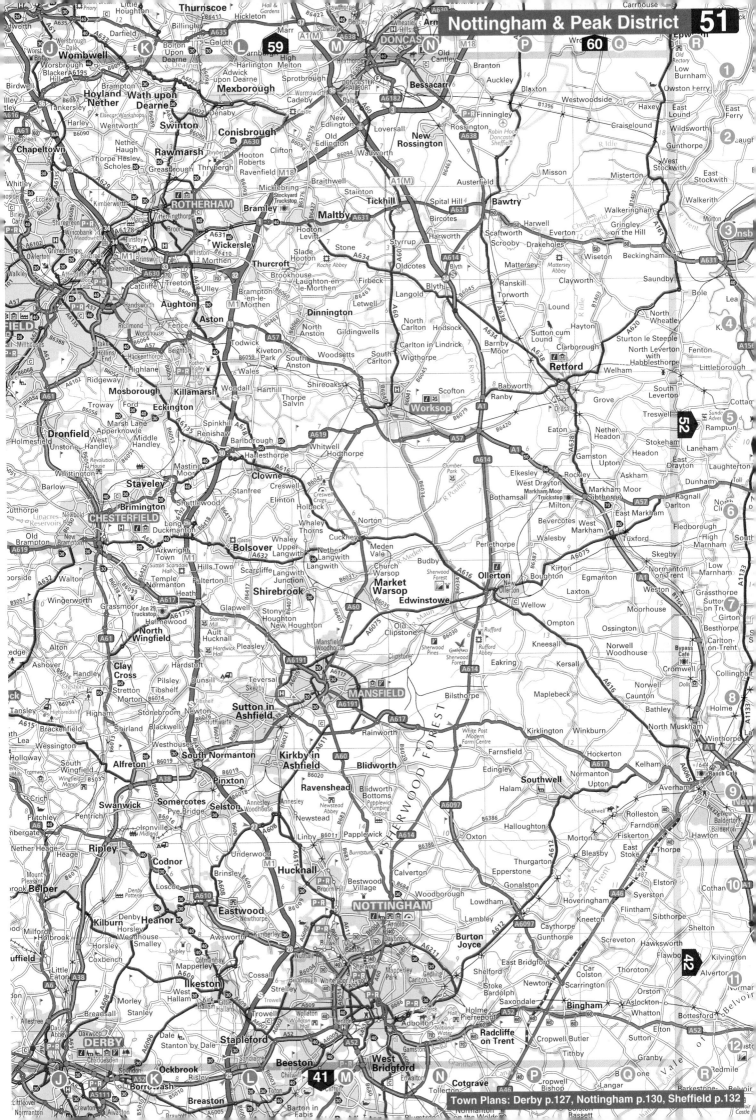

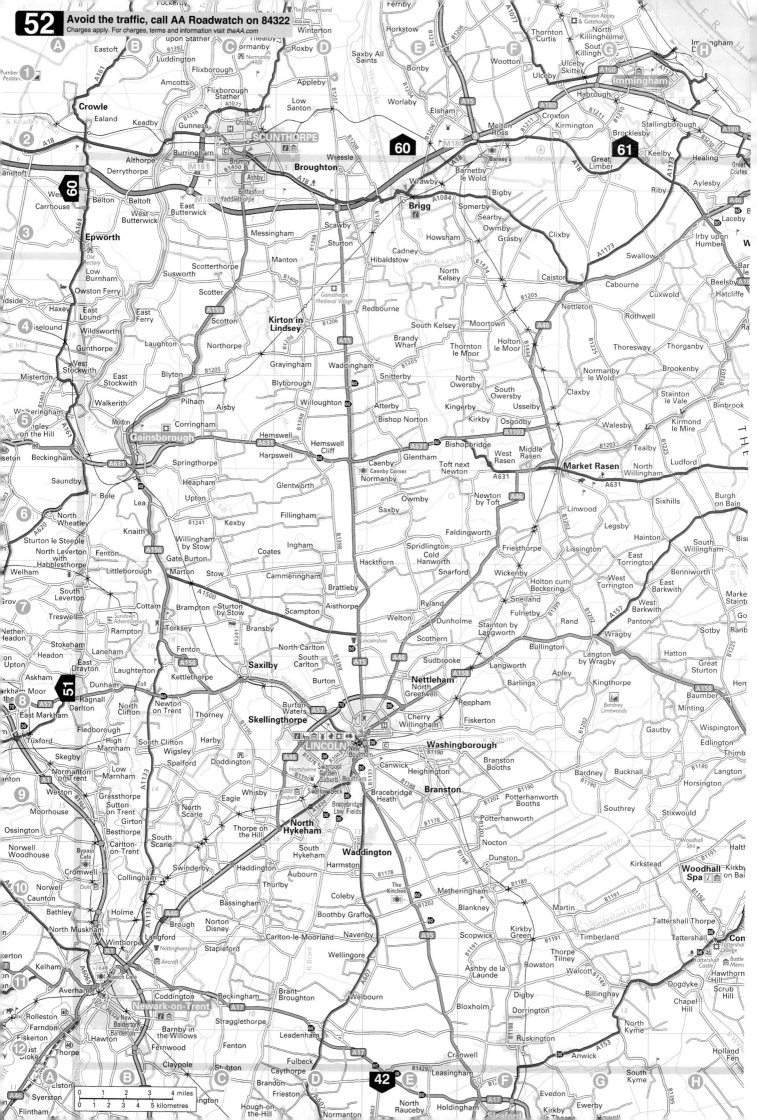

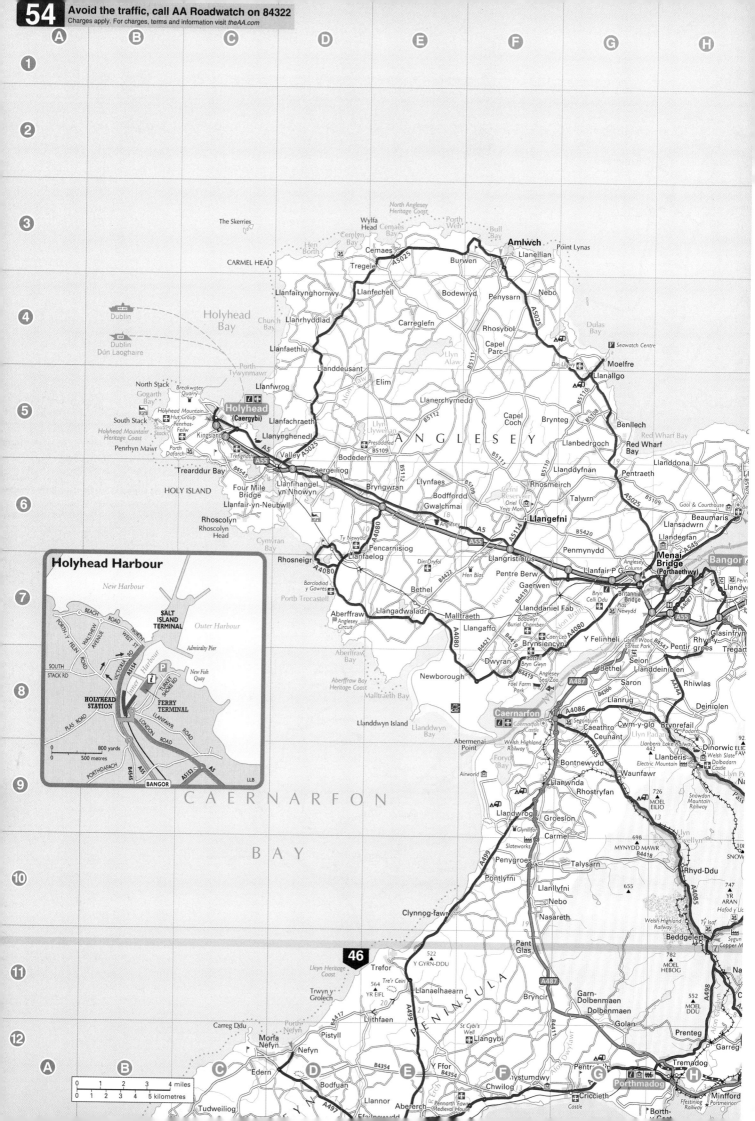

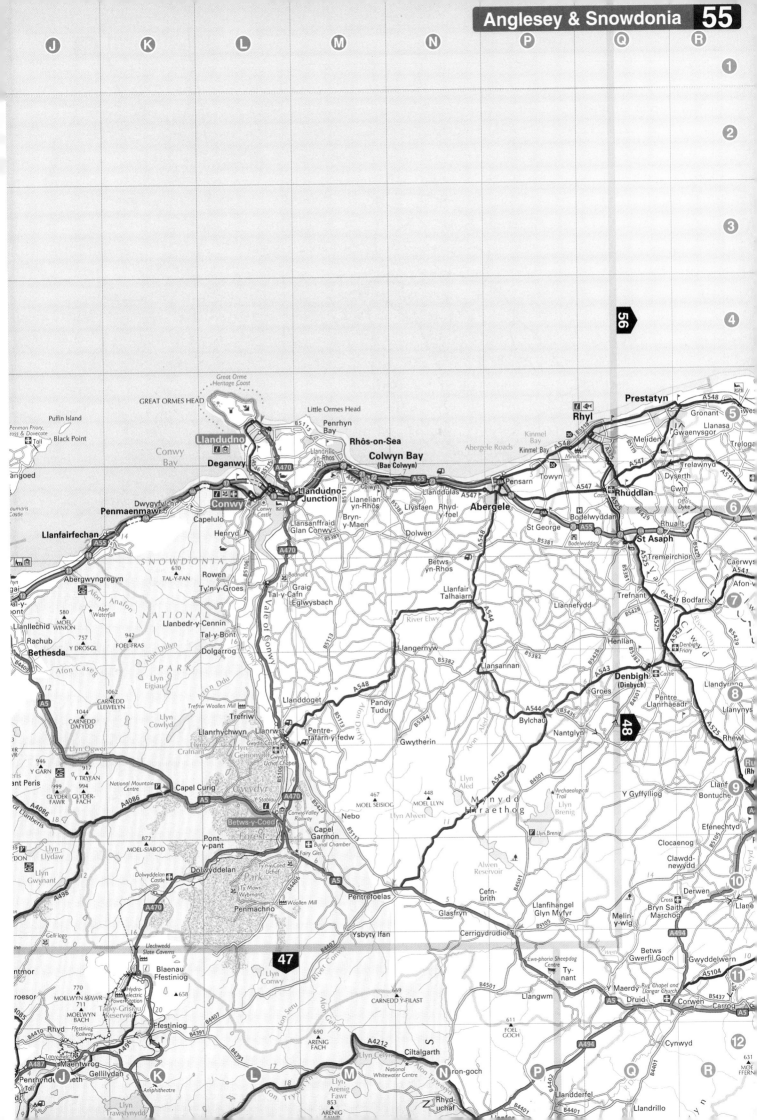

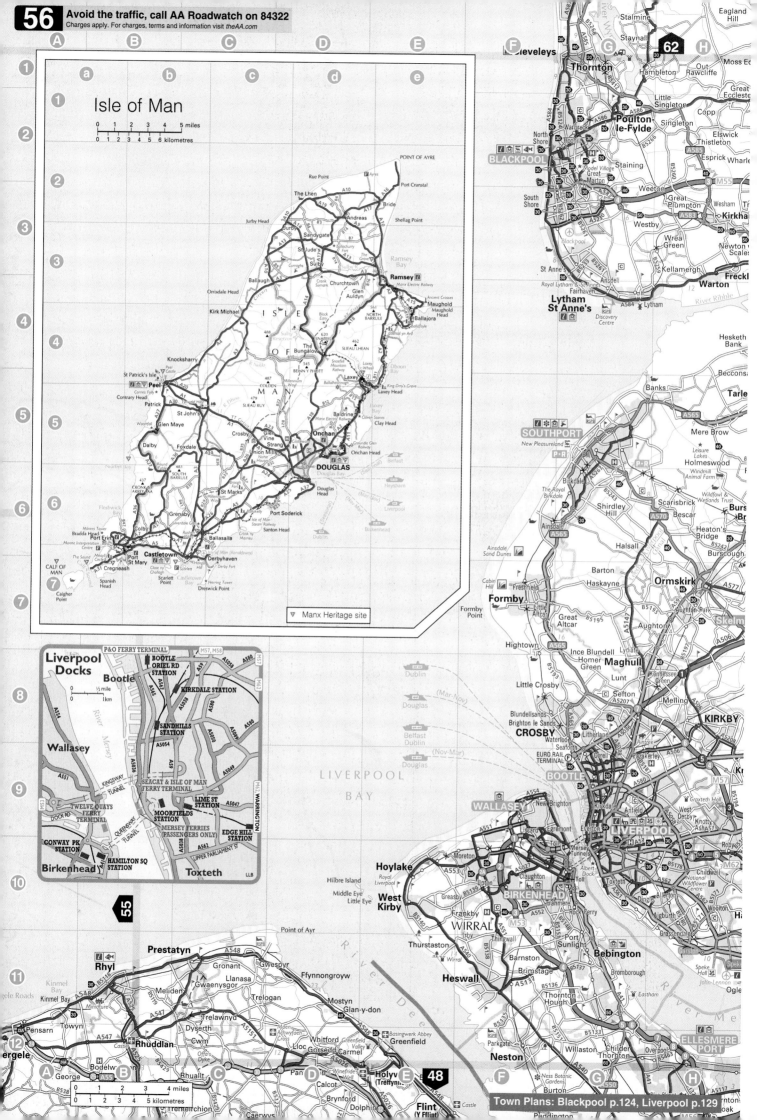

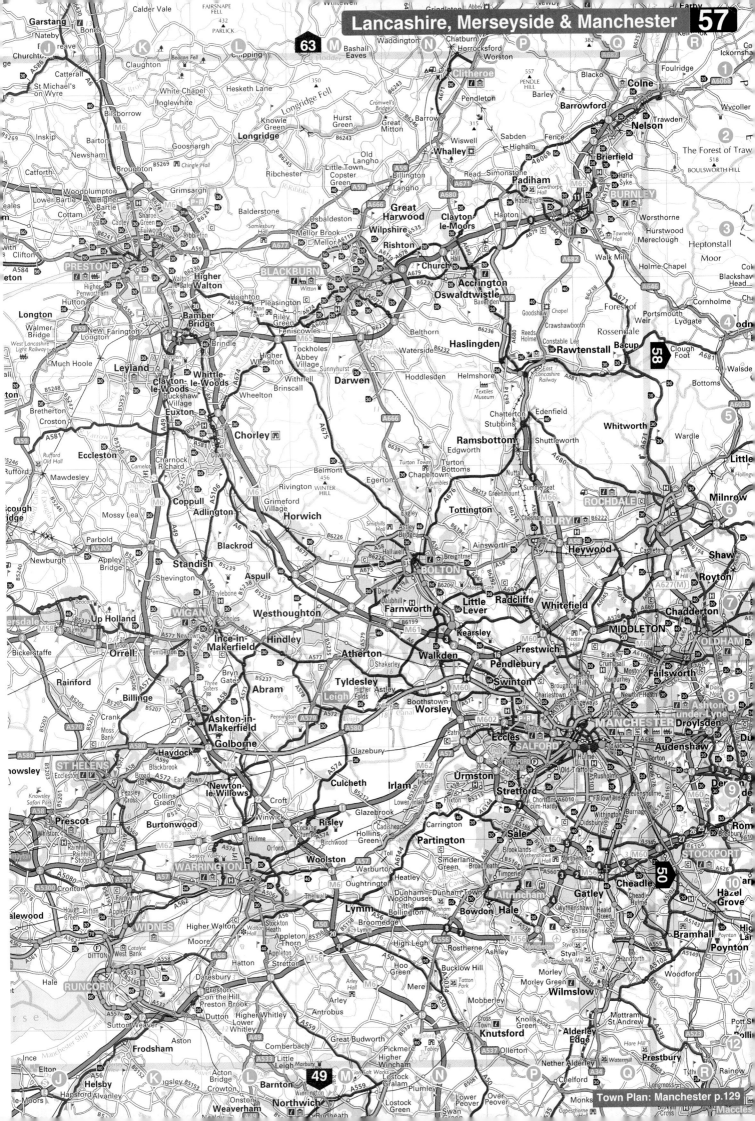

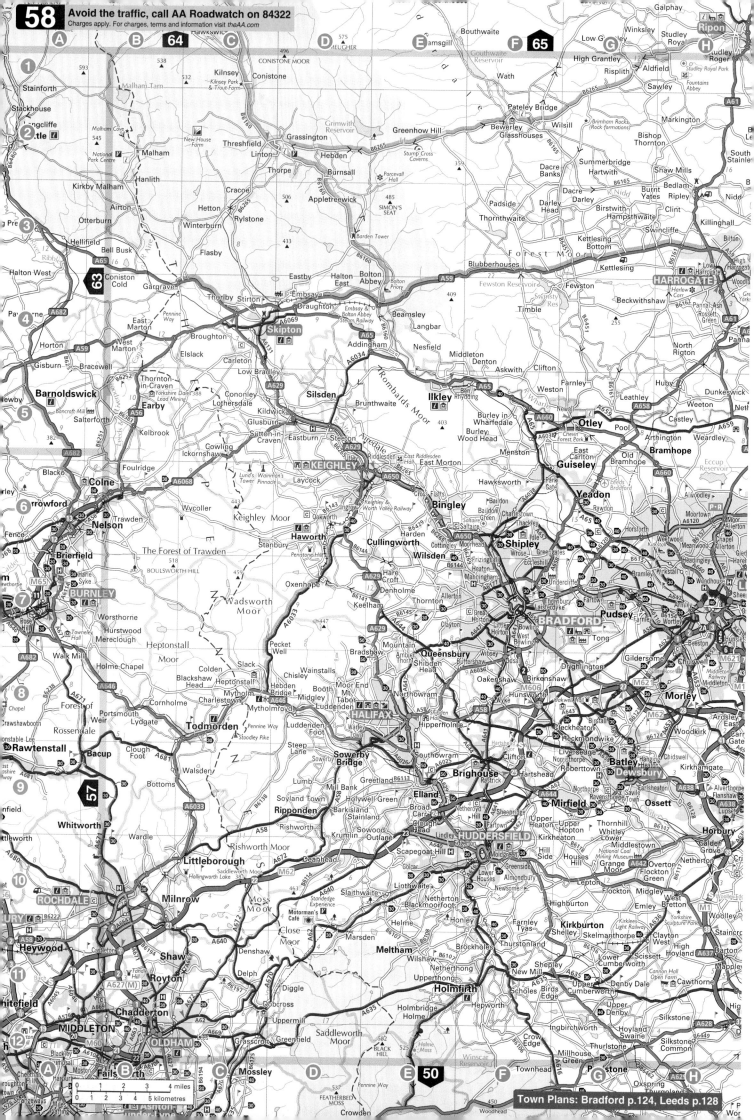

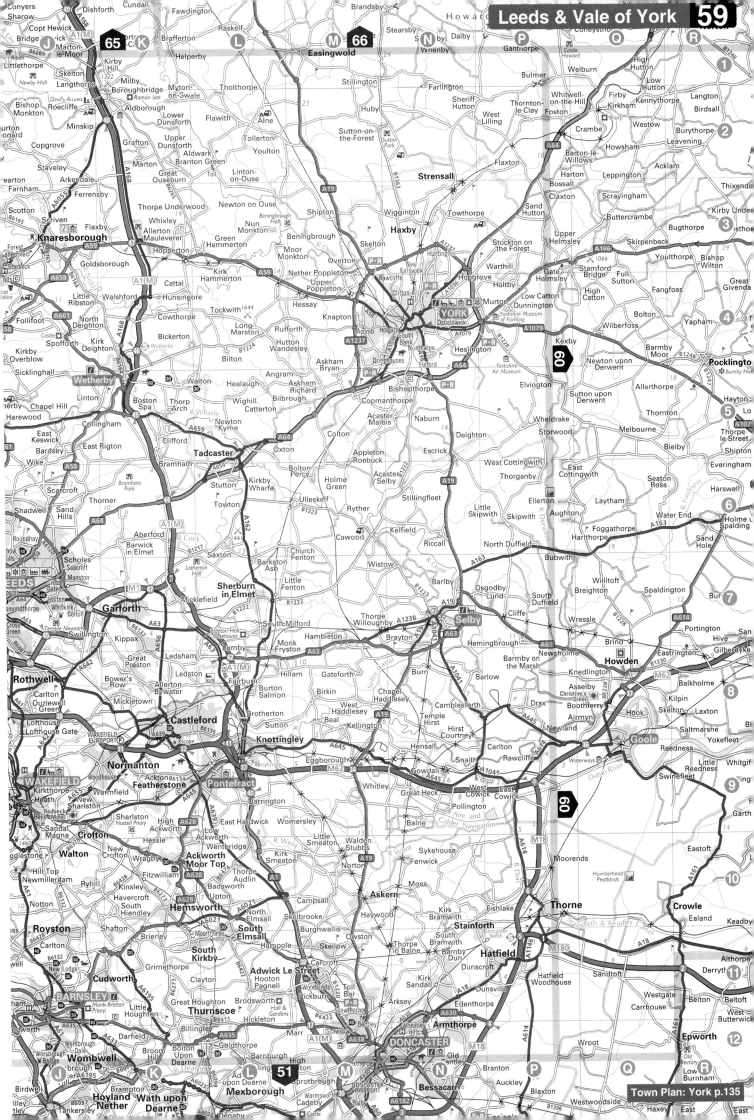

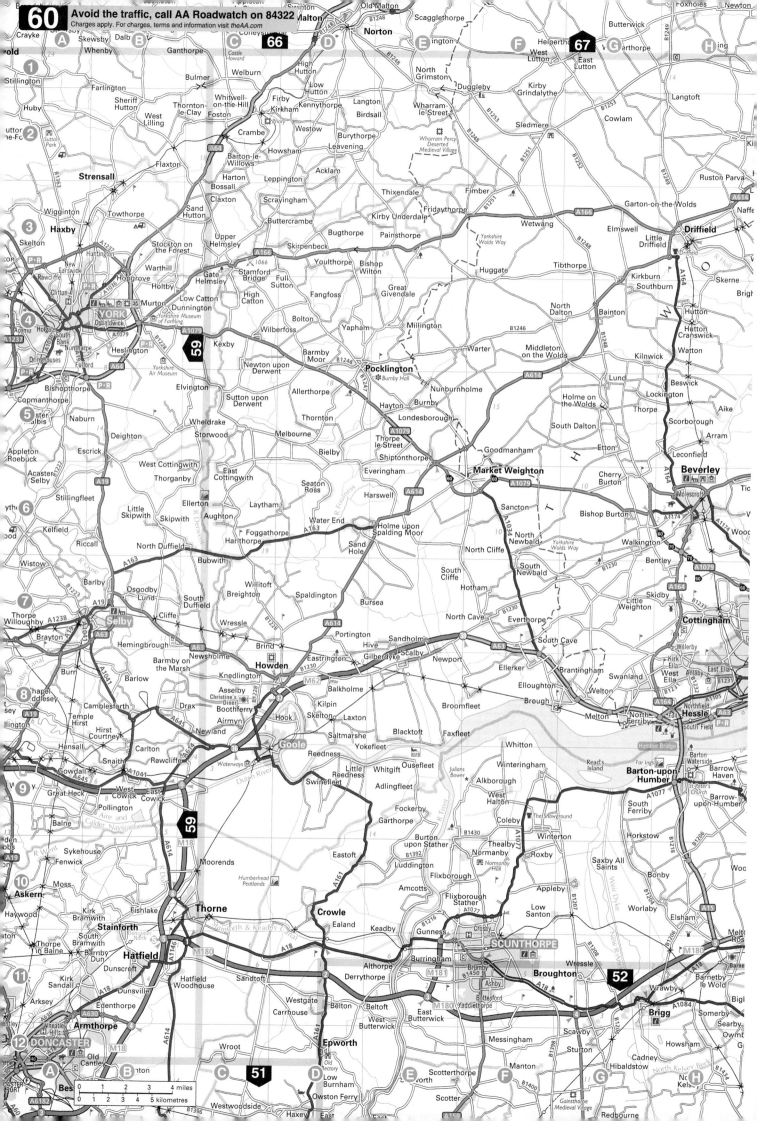

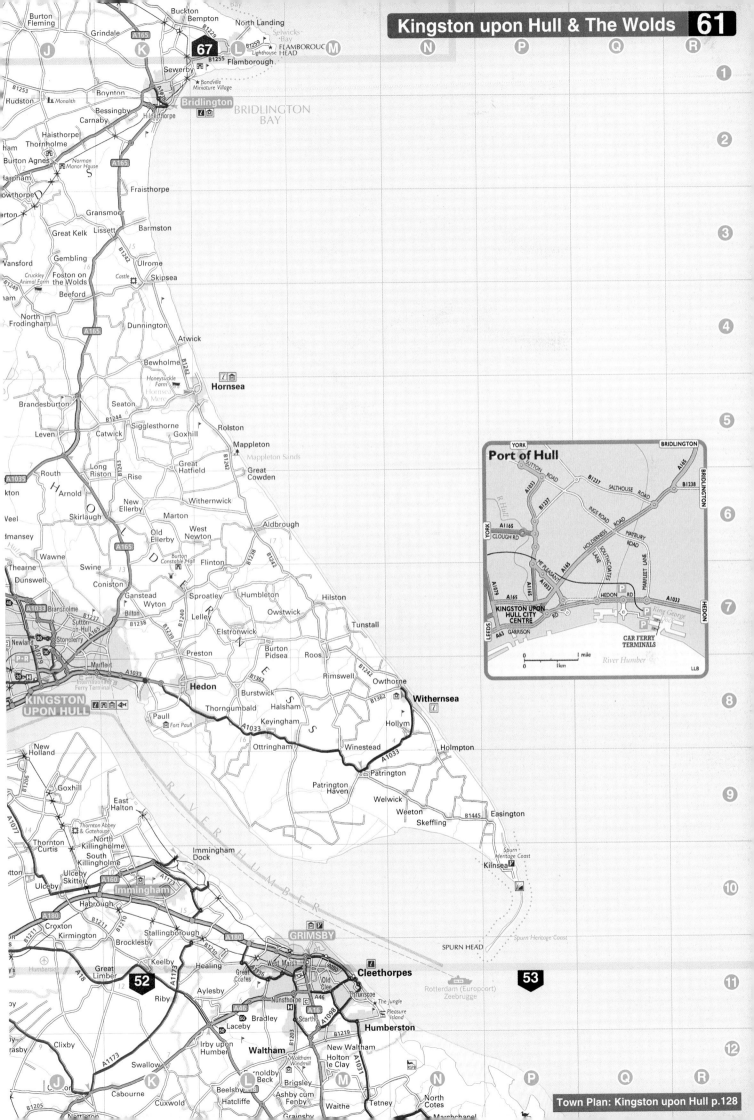

J K 67 L M N P Q R

Burton
Fleming
Grindale
A165
Rudston
Boynton
Bessingby
Carnaby
Haisthorpe
Thornholme
Burton Agnes
Harpham
Lowthorpe
Gransmoor
Great Kelk
Lissett
Gembling
Vansford
Foston on
the Wolds
B1249
Beeford
North
Frodingham
Brandesburton
Seaton
Leven
Catwick
Sigglesthorne
Goxhill
B1244
Long
Riston
Rise
Routh
A1035
Arnold
Skirlaugh
New
Ellerby
Marton
West
Newton
Wawne
Swine
Coniston
Dunswell
Ganstead
Wyton
Sproatley
Bilton
Lelley
Preston
Burton
Pidsea

North Landing
Bempton
Buckton
B1229
67
Selwicks
Bay
Lighthouse
Flamborough
B1255
Sewerby
Bondville
Miniature Village
Bridlington
BRIDLINGTON
BAY

Fraisthorpe

Barmston

Ulrome
Skipsea
Castle

Atwick

Bewholme
B1242
Hornsea
Hornsea
Mere

Rolston
Mappleton
Mappleton Sands
Great
Hatfield
Great
Cowden
Withernwick
Aldbrough
Flinton
Burton
Constable Hall
B1238
B1242
Humbleton
Owstwick
Hilston
Tunstall
Roos
Elstronwick
Rimswell
B1362
Owthorne
Withernsea
Hollym

Hedon
Burstwick
Thorngumbald
Halsham
Keyingham
Paull
Fort Paull
A1033
Ottringham
Winestead
A1033
Holmpton
Patrington
Patrington
Haven
Welwick
Weeton
Skeffling
B1445
Easington
Spurn
Heritage Coast
Kilnsea

KINGSTON
UPON HULL
A1033
Marfleet
Stonferry
Sutton-
on-Hull
A165
B1237
B1238
Bransholme
Newland
A1079
A1033
40

New
Holland
B1206
Goxhill
East
Halton
Thornton Abbey
& Gatehouse
North
Killingholme
South
Killingholme
Immingham
Dock
Thornton
Curtis
Ulceby
Skitter
A1077
Ulceby
A160
Immingham
A1173
Habrough
Croxton
Kirmington
Brocklesby
A180
B1211
Keelby
Great
Limber
52
Riby
Aylesby
Healing
West Marsh
Great
Coates
A180
GRIMSBY
B1210
Stallingborough
Clixby
Cabourne
Swallow
Waltham
Irby upon
Humber
Bradley
Laceby
Scartho
Nunsthorpe
Old
Clee
A46
A16
Cleethorpes
Humberston
New Waltham
Holton
le Clay
A1031
Waltham
Windmill
Arnoldby
le Beck
Beelsby
Ashby cum
Fenby
Brigsley
Hatcliffe
Cuxwold
Waithe
Tetney
North Cotes
B1205
Grainsby
Marshchapel

The Jungle
Pleasure
Island
B1219
B1203
B1098
Thrunscoe

Rotterdam (Europoort)
Zeebrugge
53
SPURN HEAD
Spurn Heritage Coast

RIVER HUMBER

Port of Hull

YORK
BRIDLINGTON
SUTTON ROAD
A1033
B1237
SALTHOUSE ROAD
A165
BRIDLINGTON
B1238
INGS ROAD
A1165
CLOUGH RD
YORK
HOLDERNESS ROAD
SOUTHCOATES LANE
MAYBURY ROAD
MARFLEET LANE
A1033
MT PLEASANT
A1033
A1165
A1079
A165
HEDON RD
RD
KINGSTON UPON
HULL CITY CENTRE
LEEDS
A63
GARRISON
King George
Dock
CAR FERRY
TERMINALS
HEDON
0   1 mile
0   1 km
River Humber
LLB

1 2 3 4 5 6 7 8 9 10 11 12

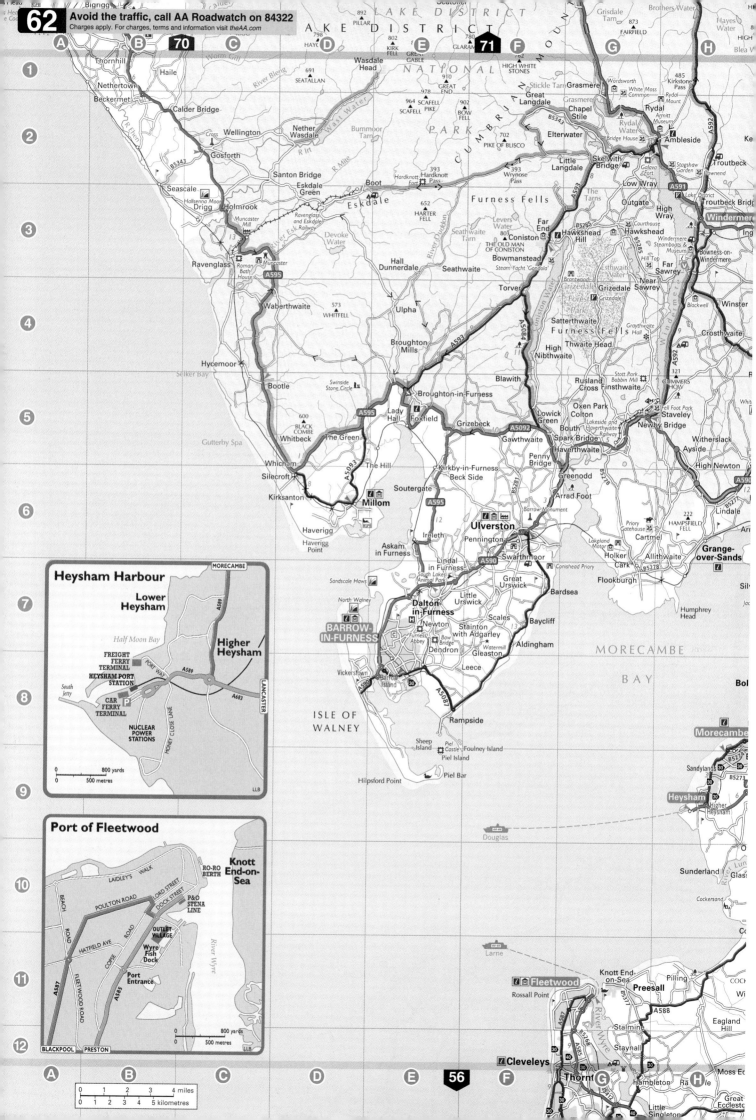

Heysham Harbour

Lower
Heysham

Higher Heysham

MORECAMBE

Half Moon Bay

FREIGHT
FERRY
TERMINAL
HEYSHAM PORT
STATION

CAR
FERRY
TERMINAL

NUCLEAR
POWER
STATIONS

South
jetty

PORT WAY

MONEY CLOSE LANE

A589

A589

A683

LANCASTER

0   800 yards
0   500 metres
LLB

Port of Fleetwood

RO-RO
BERTH

Knott
End-on-
Sea

LAIDLEY'S WALK

POULTON ROAD

LORD STREET

DOCK STREET

P&O
STENA
LINE

OUTLET
VILLAGE

Wyre
Fish
Dock

Port
Entrance

BEACH
ROAD

COPSE ROAD

HATFIELD AVE

FLEETWOOD ROAD

A587

A585

River Wyre

0   800 yards
0   500 metres
LLB

BLACKPOOL   PRESTON

0   1   2   3   4 miles
0   1   2   3   4   5 kilometres

56

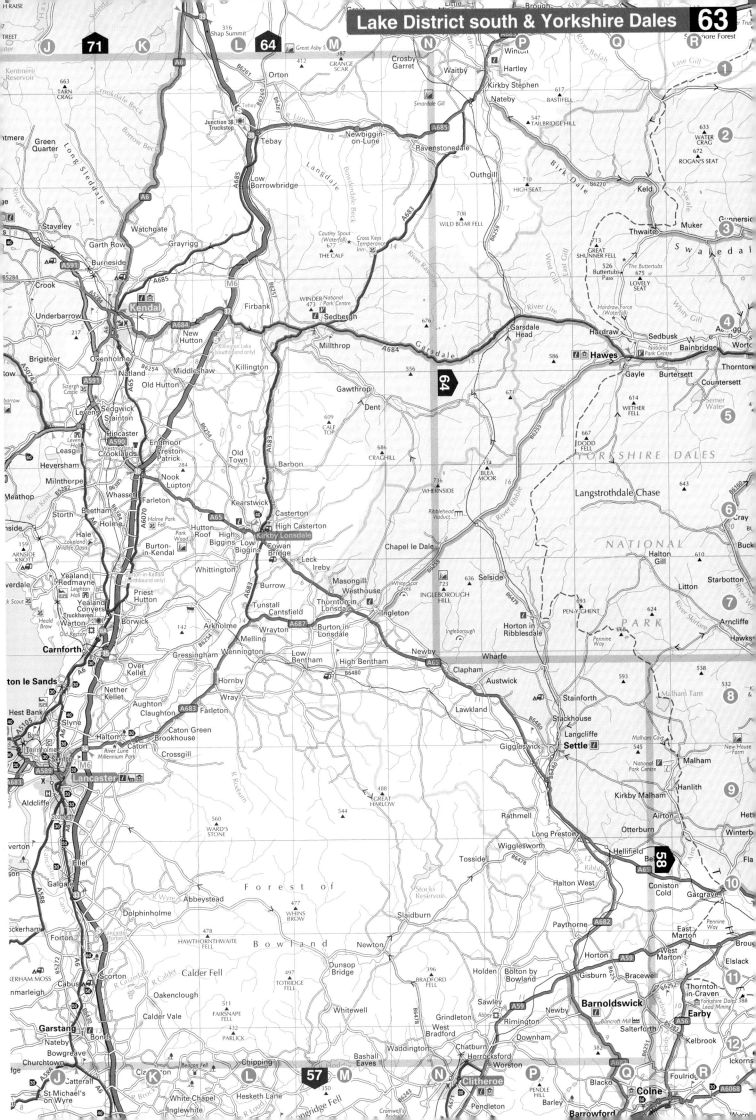

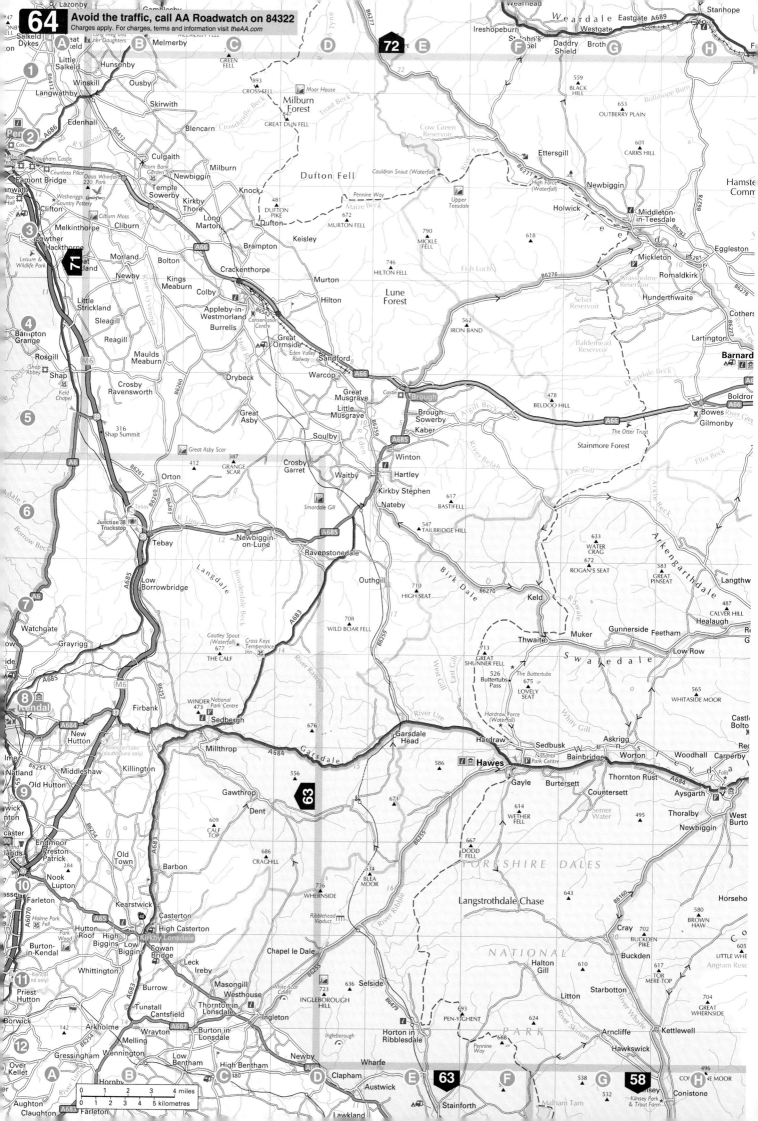

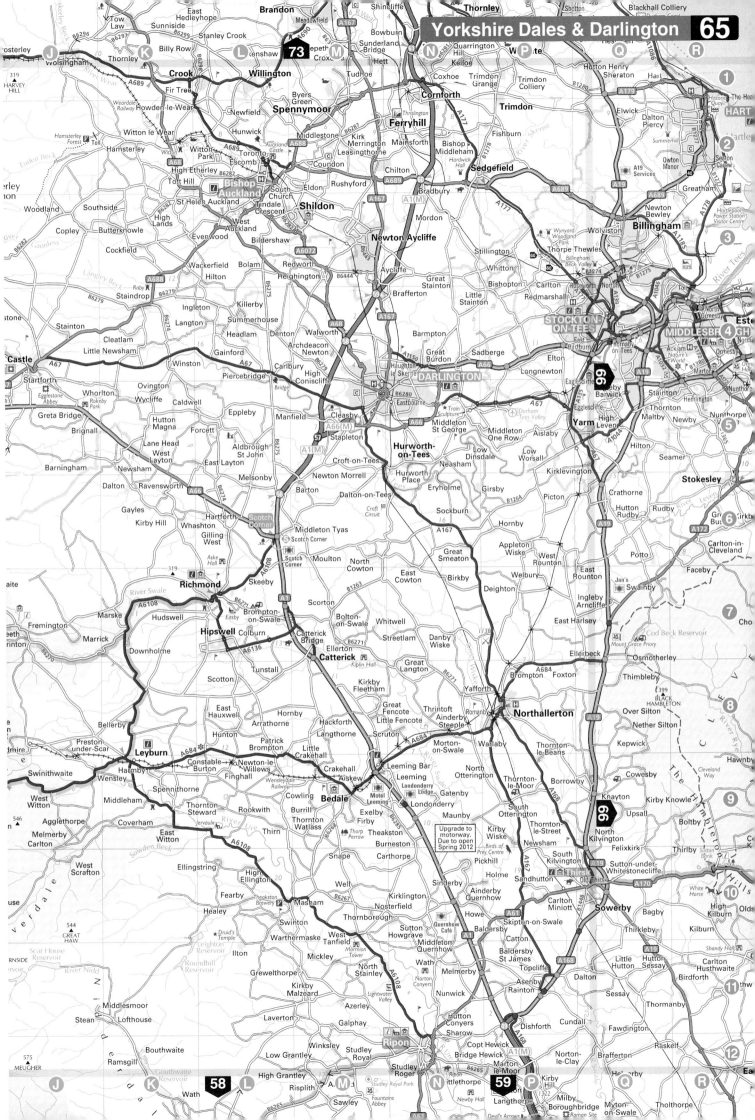

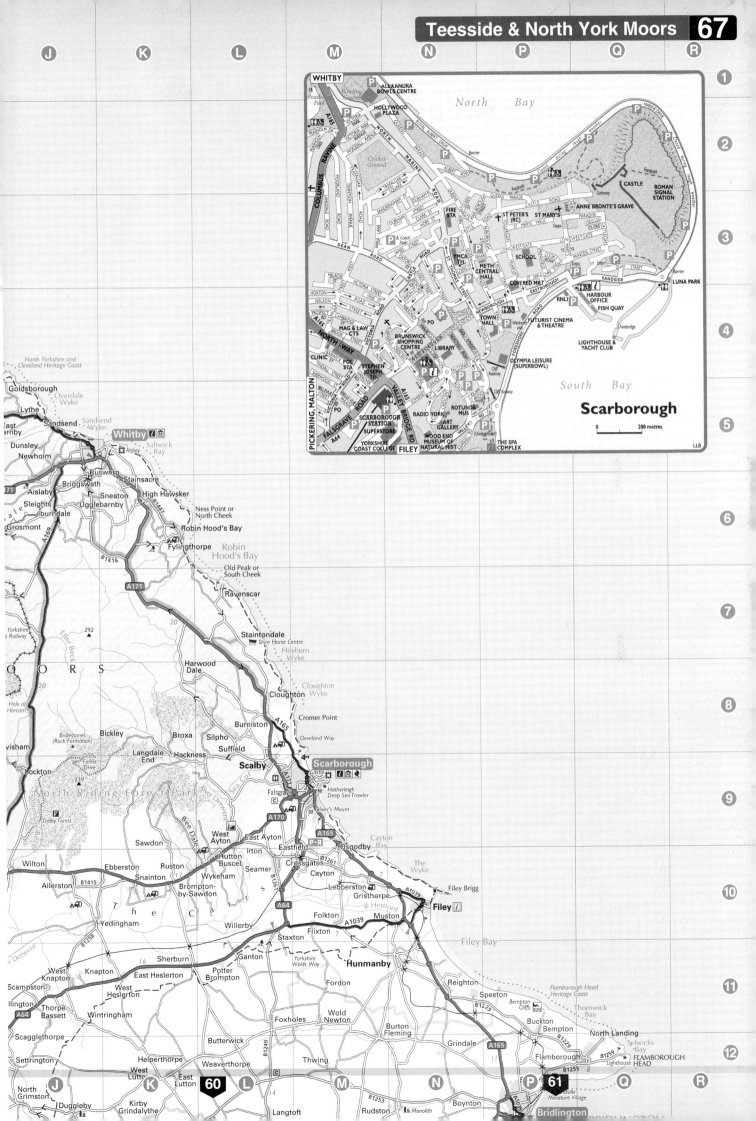

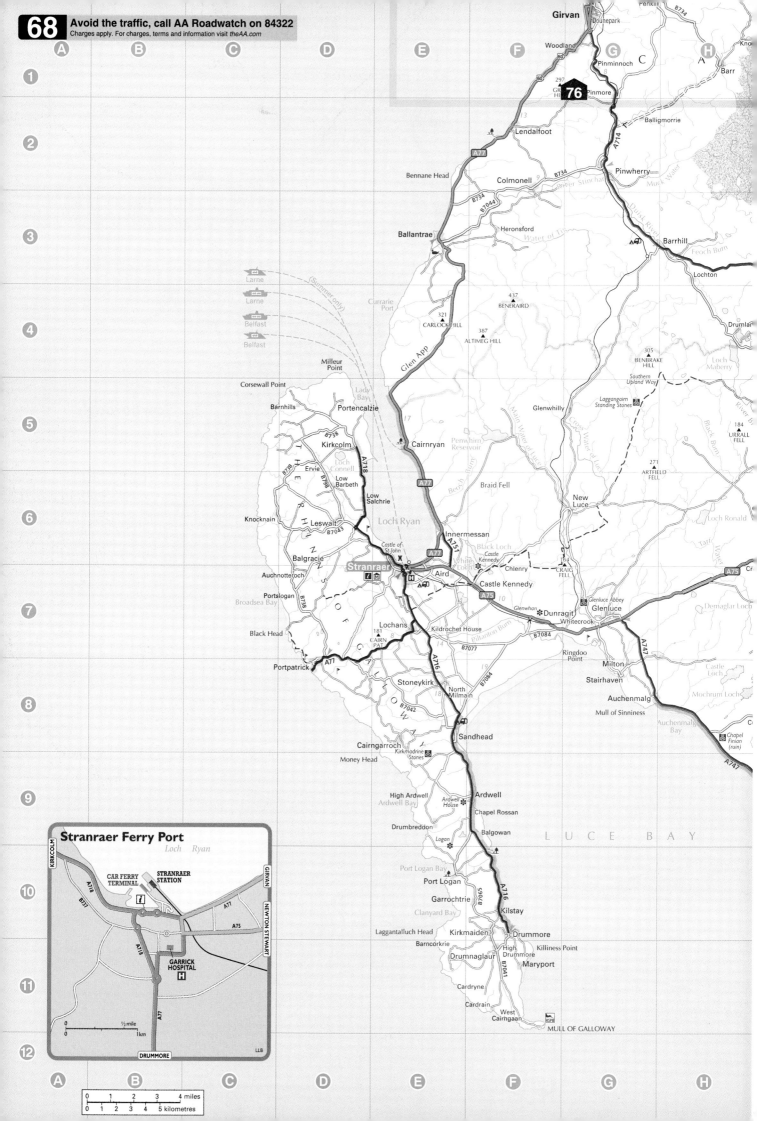

Girvan
Dounepark
Penkill
B734

Woodland

Pinminnoch
C
A
Barr

297
GRI
HILL
76
Pinmore
Knoi

B734

A714
Balligmorrie

Lendalfoot

A77

Colmonell
B734

Pinwherry

Bennane Head
B734
B7044
River Stinchar
Muck Water

Heronsford

Barrhill

Ballantrae
Water of Tig
Lochton

Currarie Port

437
BENERAIRD
Drumlan

Milleur Point

Glen App
321
CARLOCK HILL

387
ALTIMEG HILL

305
BENBRAKE HILL
Loch Maberry

Corsewall Point
Lady Bay

Southern Upland Way

Barnhills
Portencalzie

Larne
Larne
Belfast
Belfast
(Summer only)

A718

Cairnryan
Glenwhilly
Laggangairn Standing Stones
River by

Kirkcolm
Loch Connell

A77
Penwhirn Reservoir

Glenwhilly

184
URRALL FELL

Ervie
B798
Low Barbeth
B738

Braid Fell

271
ARTFIELD FELL

Low Salchrie

New Luce

Knocknain
Leswalt
B7043

Loch Ryan

Innermessan
A751

Black Loch
Castle Kennedy

Loch Ronald

Balgracie
Castle of St John

A77
White Loch
Chlenry
164
CRAIG FELL

Stranraer
H
Aird
Castle Kennedy

A75

Auchnotteroch

Glenluce Abbey
Glenluce

A75

Portslogan
B738
Broadsea Bay

A75
10

Glenwhan
Dunragit
Whitecrook
B7084

Dernaglar Loch

Lochans
181
CAIRN PAT
Kildrochet House

Pilanton Burn

Ringdoo Point
Milton

Black Head
A77
14
B7077

Stairhaven

Portpatrick
A716

Stoneykirk
North Milmain

B7084
18

Auchenmalg
Mull of Sinniness
Mochrum Loch

Castle Loch

A747

Sandhead

A716
18
B7042

B7084

Auchenmalg Bay

Cairngarroch
Kirkmadrine Stones

Chapel Finian (ruin)
Co

Money Head

High Ardwell
Ardwell House
Ardwell Bay

Ardwell
Chapel Rossan

L U C E   B A Y

Drumbreddon

Balgowan

Logan

Port Logan Bay

A716

Port Logan
Garrochtrie
B7065

Kilstay

Clanyard Bay

Laggantalluch Head

Kirkmaiden
Drummore

Barncorkrie
High Drummore
Killiness Point

Drumnaglaur
Maryport

B7041

Cardryne

Cardrain

West Cairngaan
RSPB

MULL OF GALLOWAY

Stranraer Ferry Port
Loch   Ryan

KIRKCOLM
A718
B757

CAR FERRY TERMINAL
STRANRAER STATION

i

GIRVAN
NEWTON STEWART

A77
A75

A718
A77

GARRICK HOSPITAL
H

0   ½ mile
0   1km

DRUMMORE
LLB

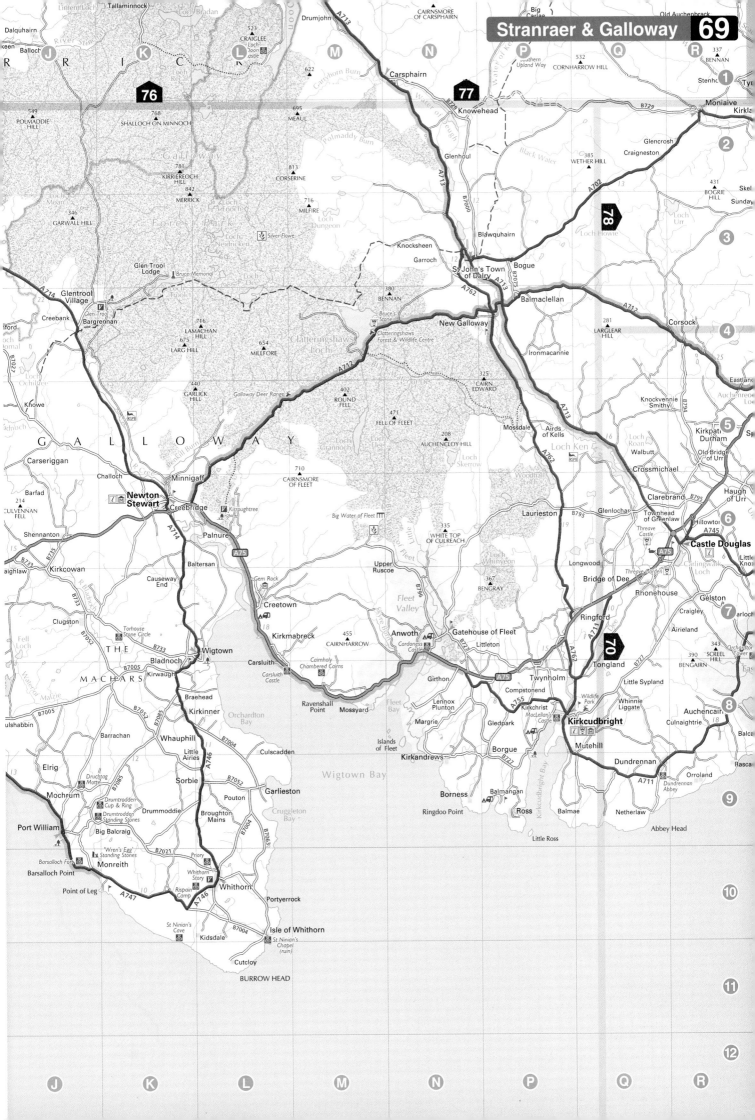

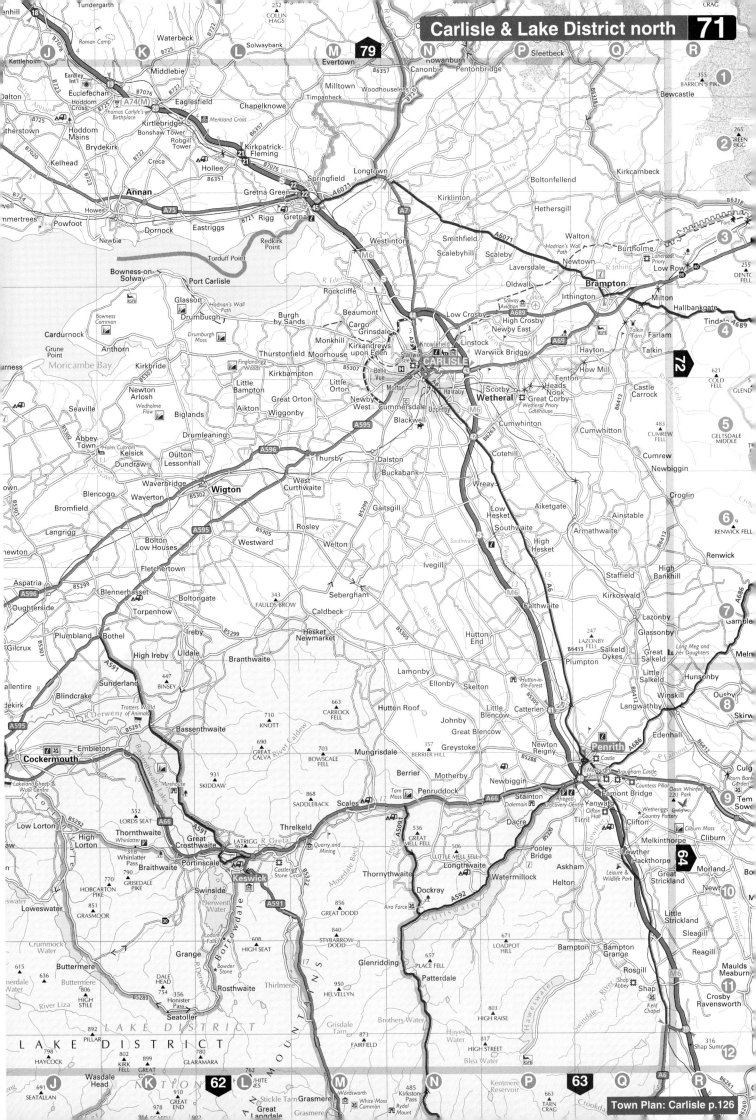

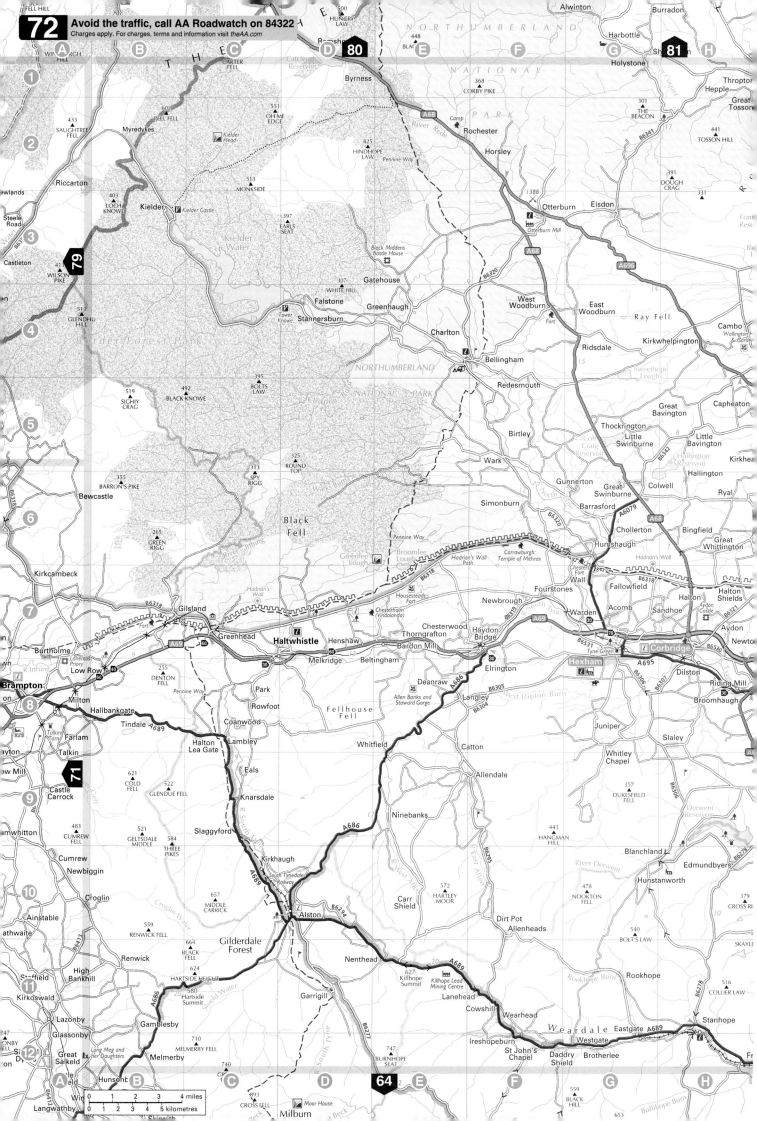

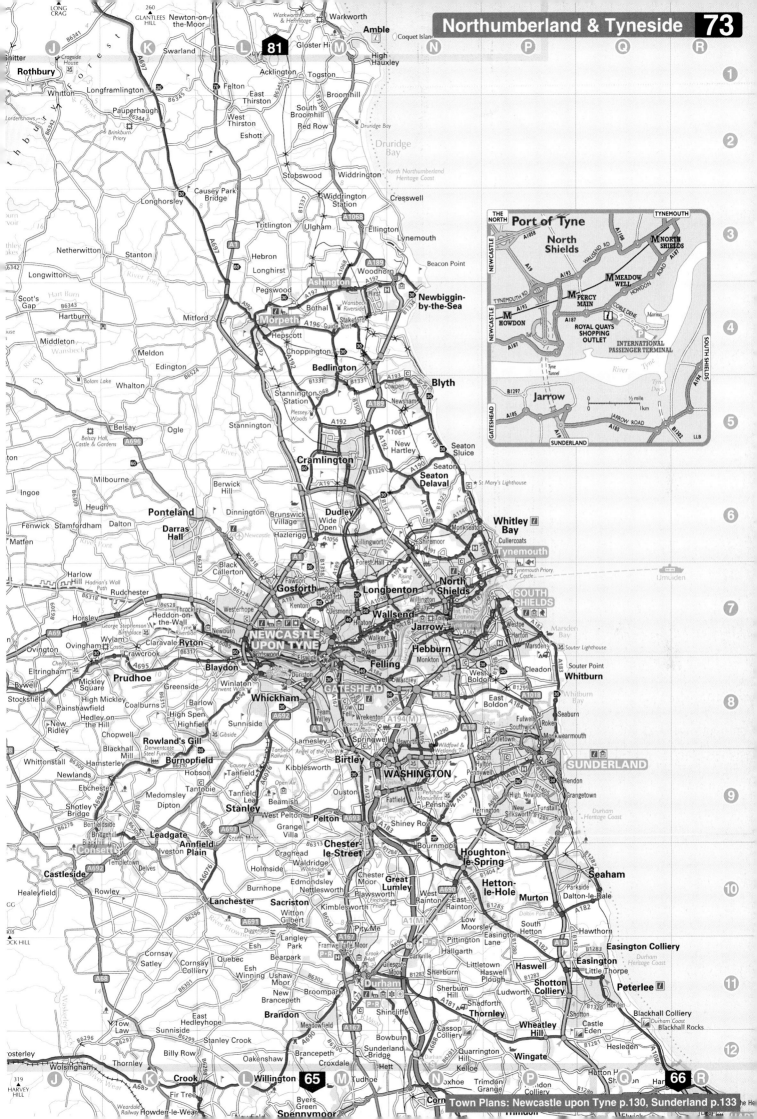

Port of Tyne

THE NORTH

TYNEMOUTH

North Shields

NEWCASTLE

North Shields

Meadow Well

Percy Main

Howdon

Royal Quays Shopping Outlet

International Passenger Terminal

Jarrow

GATESHEAD

River Tyne

Tyne Tunnel

Tyne Dock

SOUTH SHIELDS

SUNDERLAND

½ mile / 1km

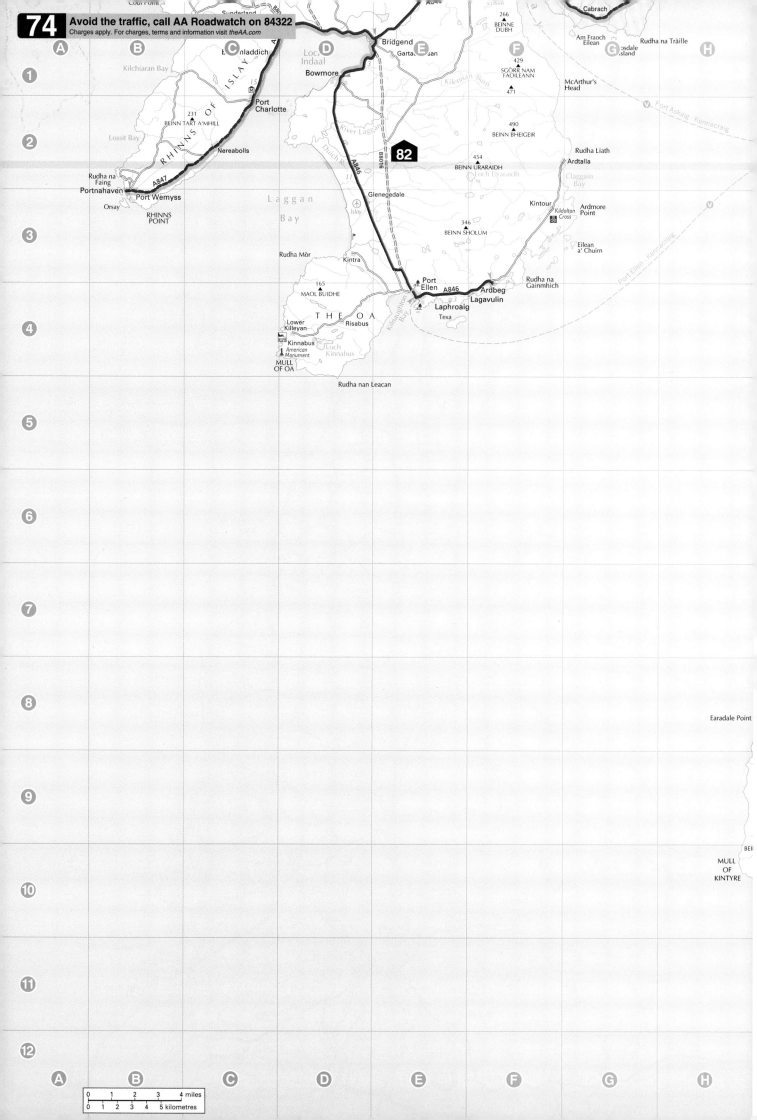

Sunderland

A B C D E F G H

1

Kilchiaran Bay
Bowmore
Loch Indaal
Bridgend
Gartachossan
266
BEINNE DUBH
Am Fraoch Eilean
Rudha na Tràille
Rosdale Island
Cabrach

429
SGÒRR NAM FAOILEANN
McArthur's Head
Port Askaig - Kennacraig

Port Charlotte
15
BEINN TART A'MHILL
231
RHINNS OF ISLAY

2

Lossit Bay
Nereabolls
471
490
BEINN BHEIGEIR
Rudha Liath
Ardtalla

Rudha na Faing
Portnahaven
A847
Port Wemyss
Dutch R
River Laggan
B8016
A846
82
454
BEINN URARAIDH
Loch Uraraidh
Claggain Bay

3

Orsay
RHINNS POINT
Laggan Bay
Islay
Glenegedale
346
BEINN SHOLUM
Kintour
Kildalton Cross
Ardmore Point

Rudha Mòr
Kintra
Eilean a' Chuirn

Port Ellen
A846
Ardbeg
Lagavulin
Rudha na Gainmhich
Port Ellen - Kennacraig

4

165
MAOL BUIDHE
THE OA
Lower Killeyan
Risabus
Laphroaig
Texa

Kinnabus
RSPB
American Monument
Loch Kinnabus
Kilnaughton Bay

MULL OF OA
Rudha nan Leacan

5

6

7

8

Earadale Point

9

10

MULL OF KINTYRE
BEI

11

12

A B C D E F G H

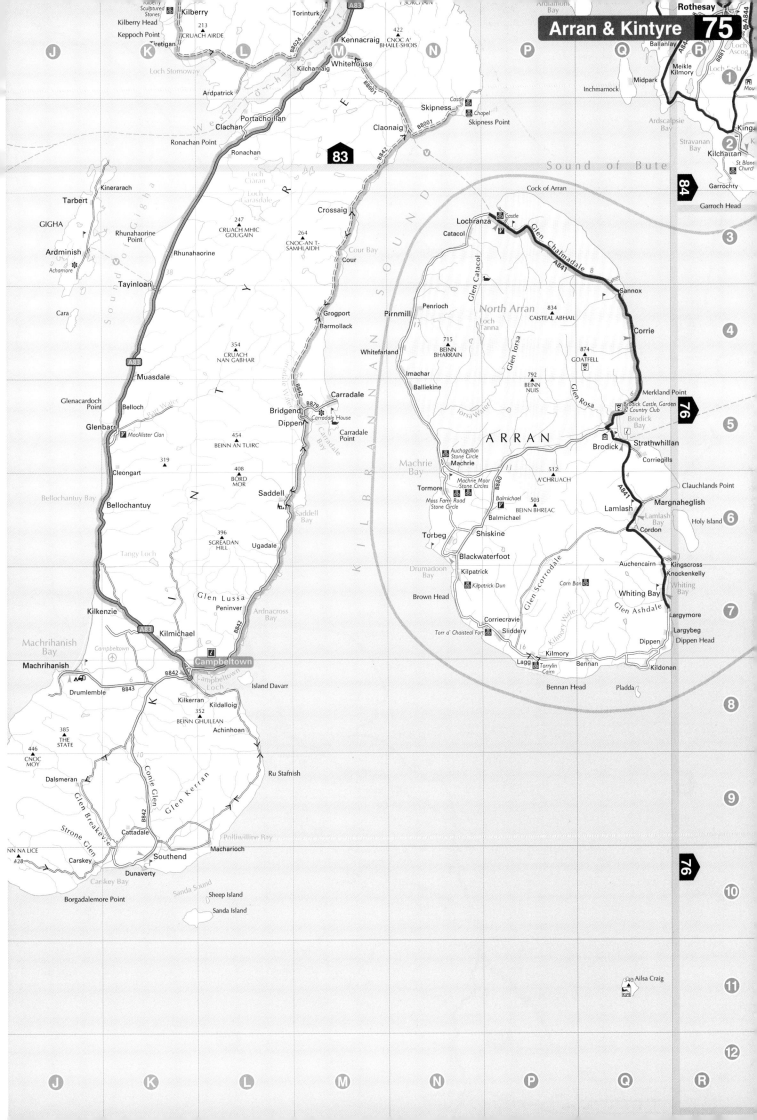

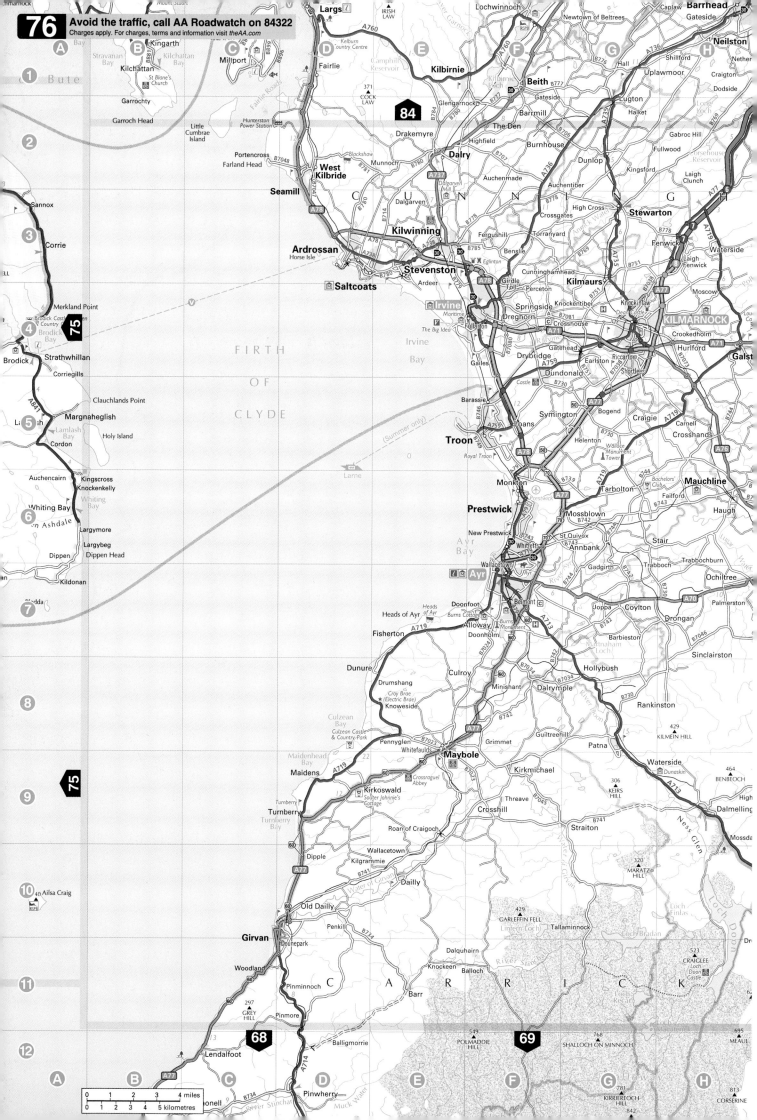

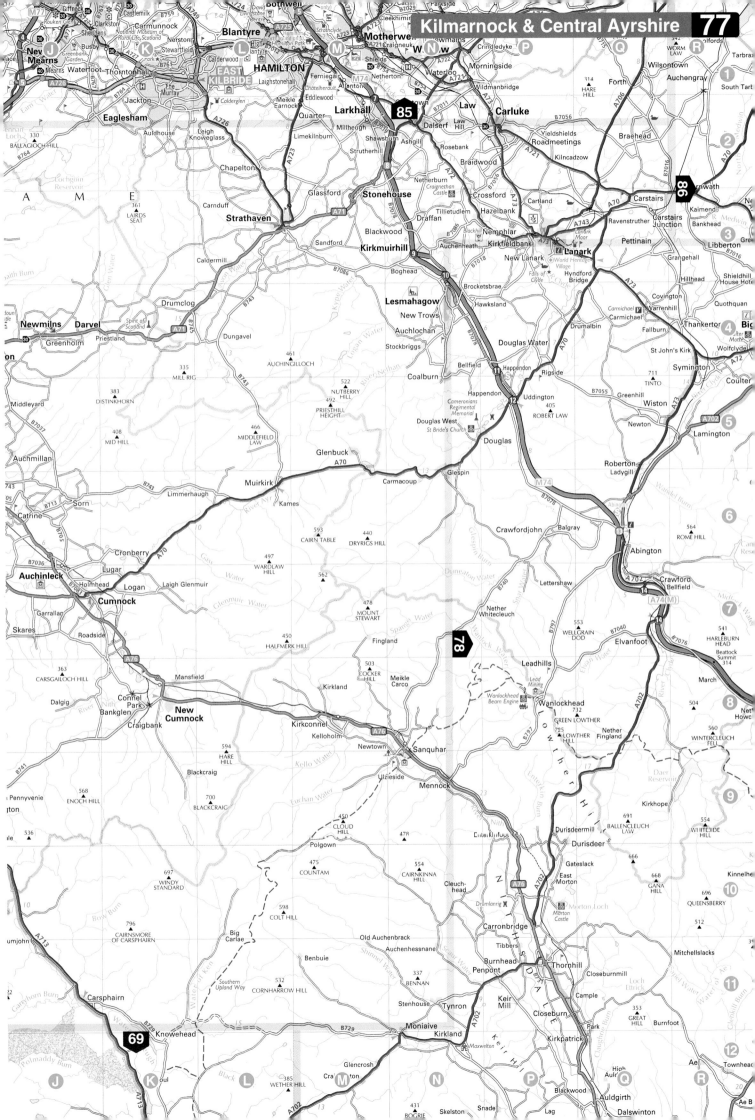

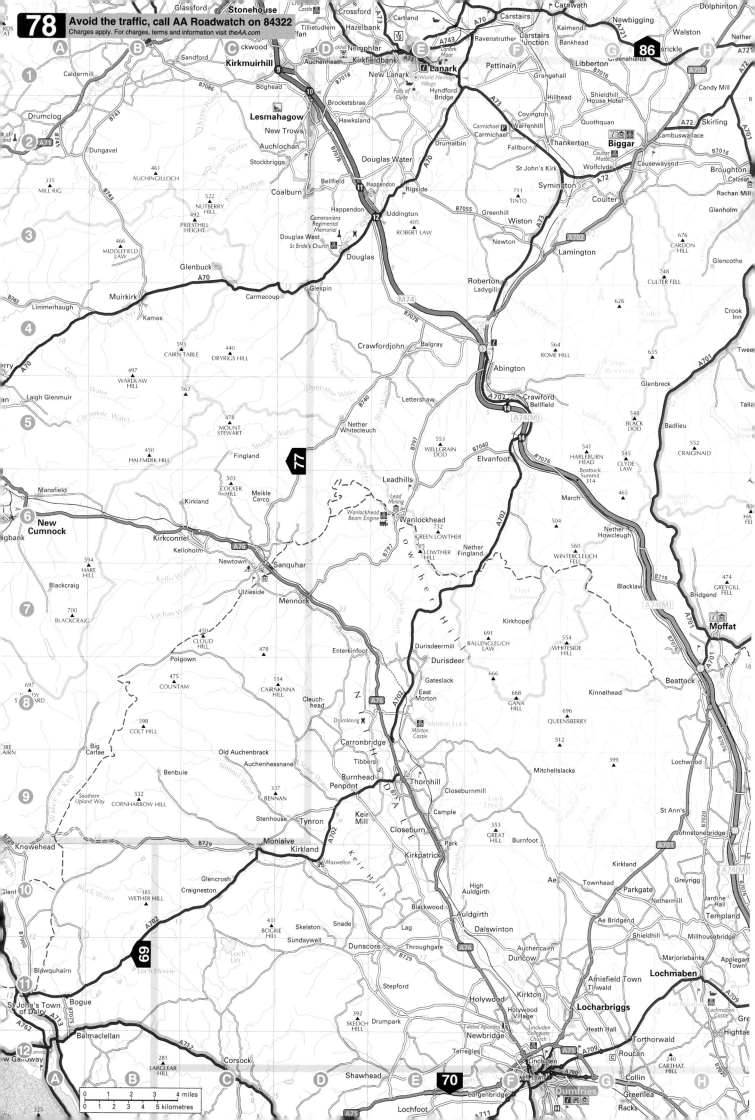

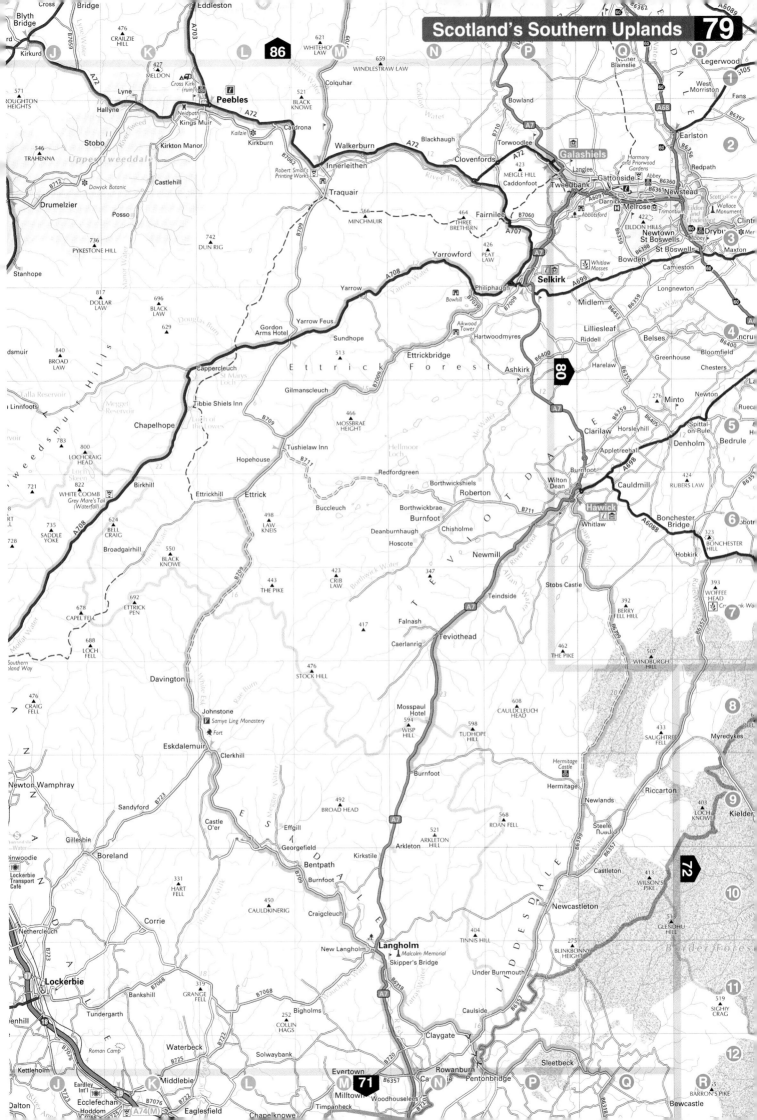

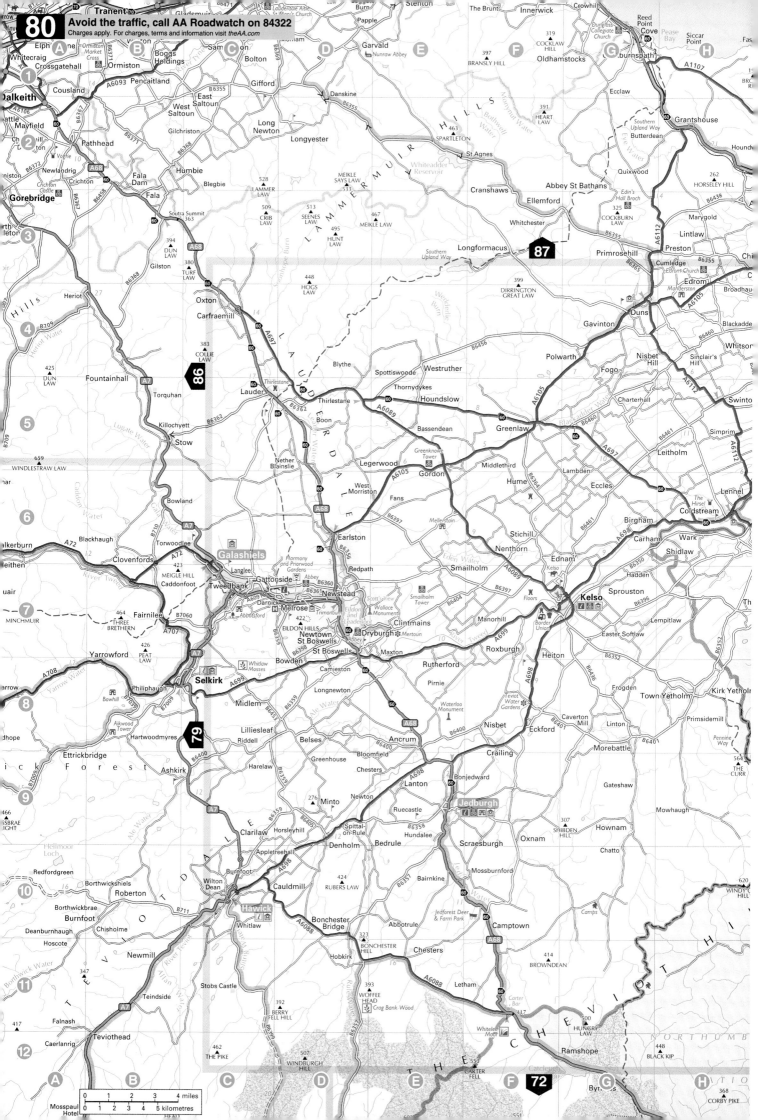

J K L M N P Q R

Castle Head
St ABB'S HEAD
Coldingham
Loch
St Abbs
Coldingham
Coldingham Bay
wood
Heugh Head 60
Cairncross
Eyemouth
Reston
A1
Ayton 80
Burnmouth
Auchencrow
B6355
60
Lamberton
irnside
B6437
70
Marshall Meadows Bay
Foulden
B6437
North Northumberland Heritage Coast
Foulden Tithe Barn
1333
hirnsidebridge
Edington
Whiteadder Water
Berwick-upon-Tweed Barracks
Allanton
Hutton
A6105
Castle
Paxton
70 Town Ramparts Tweedmouth
B6460
Paxton
B6461
Spittal
Hilton
Huds Head
Horndean
Horncliffe
Scremerston
Ladykirk
Murton
Thornton
A1
B6470
Norham
A698
Cheswick
Upsettlington
River Tweed
Ancroft
CAUSEWAY FLOODED AT HIGH TIDE
HOLY ISLAND
B6354
Haggerston
Holy Island
Duddo
Bowsden
Beal
Lindisfarne Castle
B6525
Lindisfarne Priory
Castle Point
Cornhill-on-Tweed
Castle
Etal
B6353
Lowick
Guile Point
Heatherslaw Light Railway
Fenwick
Branxton
Crookham
Heatherslaw Corn Mill
Buckton
Longstone Lighthouse
The Lady Waterford Hall
1513
Ford
B6525
St Cuthbert's Cave
FARNE ISLANDS
14
ornington
Howtel
B6352
Fenton
Belford
Budle Bay
Bamburgh
Staple Sound
Milfield
Nesbit
B6349
Inner Sound
North Northumberland Heritage Coast
Lanton
Doddington
B1342
Bamburgh
Yeavering
Coupland
B6351
Lucker
Seahouses
Kirknewton
362
B6348
A1
Warenford
North Sunderland
YEAVERING BELL
Akeld
Chatton
B6348
Chathill
Swinhoe
Wooler
Ros Castle
Newstead
Tughall
Beadnell
525
Chillingham
Preston
Beadnell Bay
PRESTON HILL
NORTHUMBERLAND
Newtown
Wild Cattle Park
Ellingham
Newton-by-the-Sea
816
267
North Charlton
Preston Pele Tower
Embleton & Newton Links
THE CHEVIOT
CATERAN HILL
Falloden
Christon Bank
Embleton
NATIONAL PARK
Ilderton
Old Bewick
B6341
Embleton Bay
605
South Charlton
Dunstanburgh Castle
THE SCHIL
B6346
Rock
Dunstan
567
New Bewick
Eglingham
Rennington
Craster
DUNMOOR HILL
Stamford
A697
Beanley
60
Howick Hall
Branton
Powburn
B6347
Howick
YLE
Ingram
River Breamish
B6341
Cullernose Point
616
CUSHAT LAW
Glanton
River Aln
Denwick
Longhoughton
500
334
Bolton
Boulmer
SHILLHOPE LAW
COCHRANE PIKE
Alnwick
Seaton Point
Alnham
Whittingham
B6341
Lesbury
RLAND
Netherton
A1
Alnmouth
Burradon
319
Shilbottle
Alnmouth Bay
Alwinton
LONG CRAG
260
A1068
Harbottle
GLANTLEES HILL
Newton-on-the-Moor
Warkworth Castle & Hermitage
NAL
Holystone
Sharperton
Snitter
Rothbury
Swarland
Warkworth
Hepple
Thropton
73
Cragside House
Guyzance
Gloster Hill
Coquet Island
Amble
Great Tosson
Longframlington
80
Felton
East Thirston
High Buxley
301
B6341
70
Togston
Broomhill

J K L M N P Q R

1 2 3 4 5 6 7 8 9 10 11 12

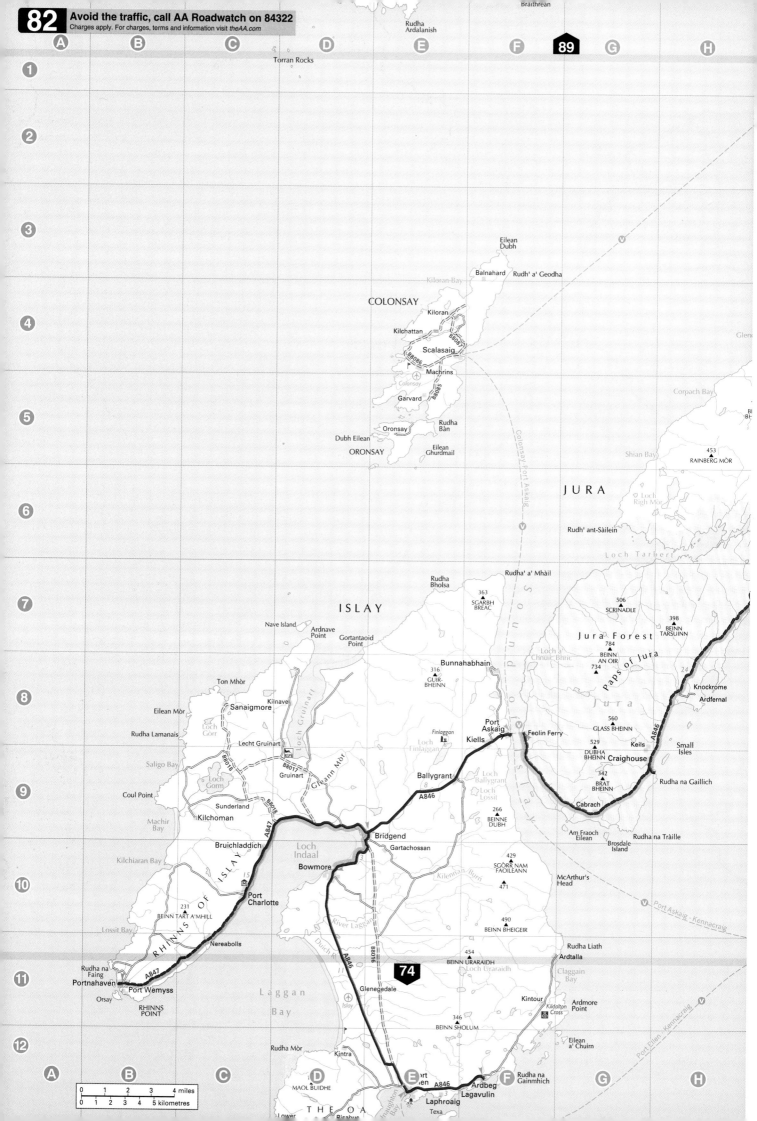

89

74

Braithrean

Rudha
Ardalanish

Torran Rocks

COLONSAY

Eilean
Dubh

Balnahard   Rudh' a' Geodha

Kiloran Bay

Kiloran

Kilchattan

Scalasaig

B8086

B8087

Machrins

Colonsay

B8085

Garvard

Oronsay

Rudha
Bàn

Dubh Eilean

Eilean
Ghurdmail

ORONSAY

Corpach Bay

J U R A

Loch
Righ Mòr

Shian Bay

453
RAINBERG MÒR

Rudh' ant-Sàilein

Loch Tarbert

Rudha
Bholsa

363
SCARBH
BREAC

Rudha' a' Mhàil

I S L A Y

Nave Island

Ardnave
Point

Gortantaoid
Point

Bunnahabhain

316
GUIR-
BHEINN

Loch a
Chnuic Bhric

Jura   Forest

506
SCRINADLE

398
BEINN
TARSUINN

784
BEINN
AN OIR

Paps of Jura

734

24

Knockrome

Ardfernal

Ton Mhòr

Kilnave

Sanaigmore

Eilean Mòr

Loch
Gorr

Rudha Lamanais

Lecht Gruinart

Loch Gruinart

Finlaggan

Port
Askaig

Kiells

Feolin Ferry

560
GLASS BHEINN

Keils

A846

Small
Isles

Saligo Bay

B8018

B8017

Gruinart

Gleann Mòr

Loch
Finlaggan

529
DUBHA
BHEINN

Craighouse

Coul Point

Loch
Gorm

Ballygrant

Loch
Ballygrant

A846

342
BRAT
BHEINN

Rudha na Gaillich

Machir
Bay

Sunderland

Kilchoman

B8018

Loch
Lossit

Cabrach

Am Fraoch
Eilean

Rudha na Tràille

Kilchiaran Bay

Bruichladdich

A847

Loch
Indaal

Bridgend

Gartachossan

266
BEINNE
DUBH

Brosdale
Island

Bowmore

429
SGÒRR NAM
FAOILEANN

McArthur's
Head

231
BEINN TART A'MHILL

Port
Charlotte

15

471

Kilennan Burn

490
BEINN BHEIGEIR

Port Askaig - Kennacraig

Lossit Bay

RHINNS

OF

ISLAY

Nereabolls

River Laggan

B8016

A846

Rudha Liath

Ardtalla

454
BEINN URARAIDH

Loch Uraraidh

Claggain
Bay

Rudha na
Faing

A847

Portnahaven

Port Wemyss

Laggan

Glenegedale

Kintour

Ardmore
Point

Orsay

RHINNS
POINT

Islay

Bay

Kildalton
Cross

Eilean
a' Chuirn

Rudha Mòr

Kintra

346
BEINN SHOLUM

Port Ellen - Kennacraig

Port
Ellen

A846

Ardbeg
Lagavulin

Rudha na
Gainmhich

MAOL BUIDHE

Laphroaig

Texa

THE   OA

Lower

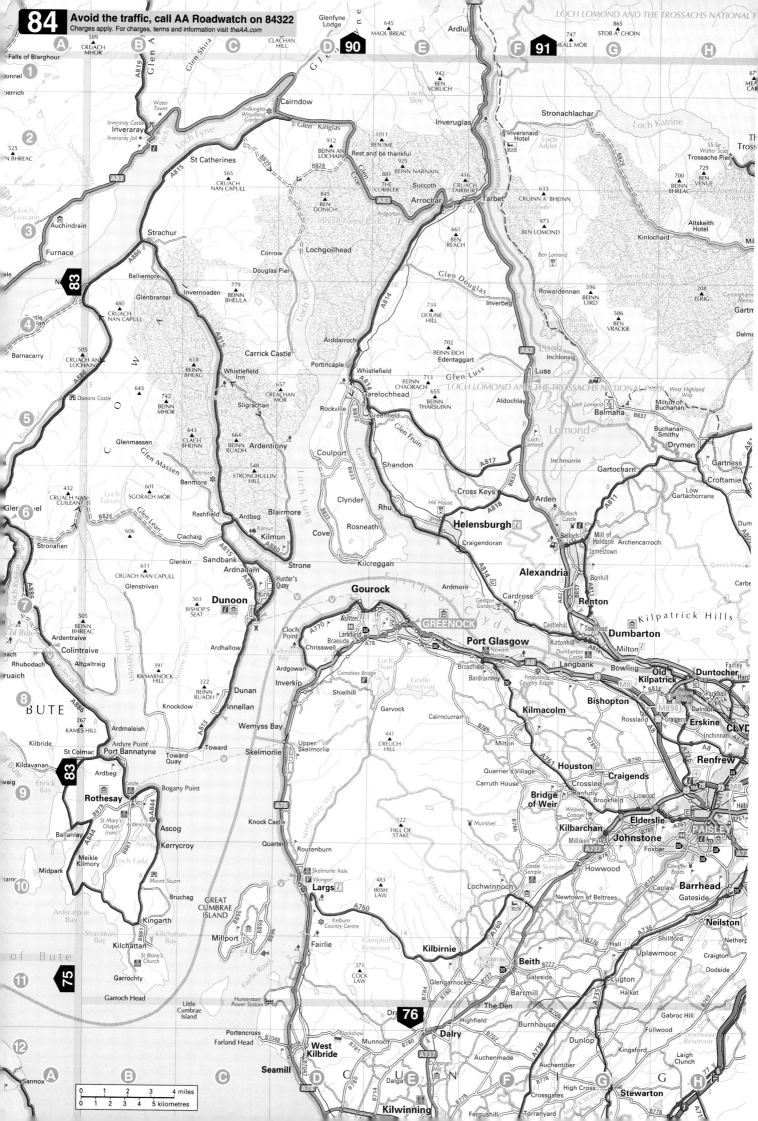

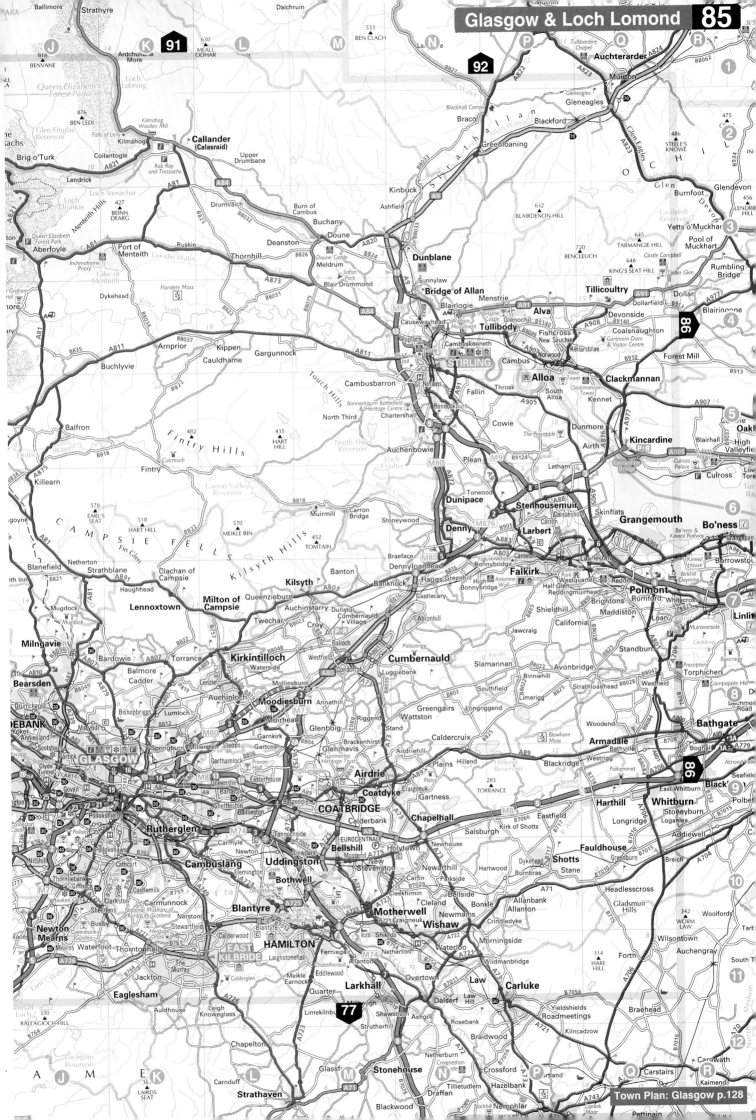

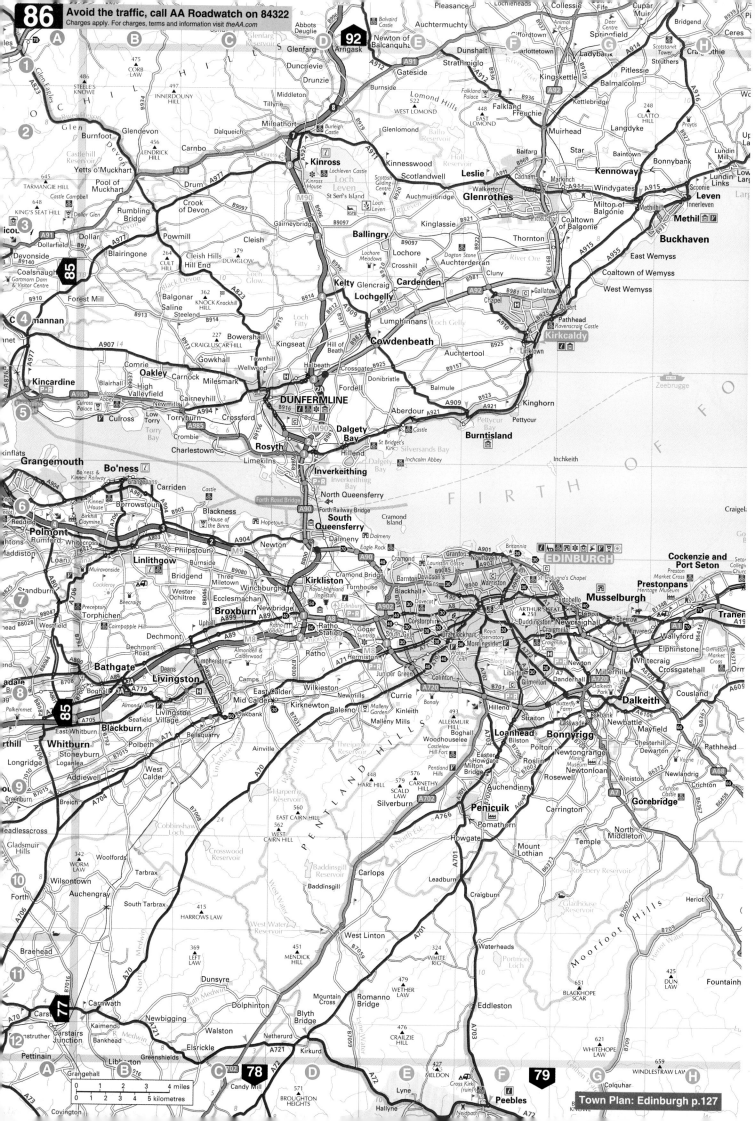

Denhead
A915
Cameron Reservoir
Scottie
Baldinnie
B940
Dunino
93
Kingsbarns
J
K
L
Balcomie Links
M
N
P
Q
R
Peat Inn
Radernie
Kingsmuir
FIFE NESS
1
New Gilston
Lathones
B940
Lochty
Scotland's Secret Bunker
Crail
odside
Largoward
B941
Carnbee
Kellie Castle
Easter Pitkierie
B9171
Wester Pitkierie
A917
B9131
2
A915
Arncroach
B9171
Newton of Balcormo
Kilrenny
Cellardyke
per
Colinsburgh
B942
Fisheries
Anstruther
rgo
B941
B942
Kilconquhar
Pittenweem
A917
St Monans
Isle of May
3
Earlsferry
Elie
go Bay

DUNFERMLINE

Rosyth Harbour
A823(M)
M90
PERTH
0   ½ mile
ROSYTH STATION
KINCARDINE BRIDGE
0   1 km
B980
A921
4
A985
Rosyth
INVERKEITHING STATION
LC
PORT OF ROSYTH
ROSYTH EUROPARC
B980
HM NAVAL BASE
FERRY TERMINAL
Inverkeithing
5
River Forth
B981
A90
NORTH QUEENSFERRY STATION
LLB
EDINBURGH

Fidra
Craigleith
Bass Rock
Eyebroughy
North Berwick
Scottish Seabird
Tantallon Castle
Dirleton Castle & Gardens
A198
187
Muirfield
NORTH BERWICK LAW
Cleghornie
Gullane Bay
Dirleton
Whitekirk
6
Gullane Point
Gullane
Fenton Barns
Kingston
A198
St Baldred's Cradle
Aberlady Bay
B1345
Prora
B1377
East Fortune
B1347
Tyne Mouth
Belhaven Bay
aw Point
B1377
Drem
B1347
Preston Mill & Phantassie Doocot
Tyninghame
Belhaven
Dunbar
Aberlady
Luffness
Chesters Hill Fort
B1343
Markle
John Muir
West Barns
Broxburn
Barns Ness
ford ay
A198
Motors
B1371
Ballencrieff
Museum of Flight
B1407
Spittal
East Linton
A1087
A1
East Barns
Seton Mains
A6137
Athelstaneford
B1347
A199
Hailes Castle
B6370
Chapel Point
Longniddry
Huntington
Haddington
Traprain
Spott
Doonhill Homestead
1650
Skateraw
7
Elvingston
St Martin's Kirk (ruin)
Pitcox
70
Thorntonloch
Gladsmuir
B6471
Lauderdale Aisle St Mary's Church
Traprain Law
Luggate Burn
Stenton
The Brunt
Innerwick
Dry Burn
A1
Macmerry
A6093
Lennoxlove
Morham
Papple
319 COCKLAW HILL
Crowhill
Reed Point
Cove
Pease Bay
Fast Castle Head
New Winton
B6368
Bolton
B6370
Garvald
Nunraw Abbey
Dunglass Collegiate Church
A1107
196 BROWN RIG
Coldingham Loch
ST ABB'S
Boggs Holdings
Samuelston
B6369
397 BRANSLY HILL
Oldhamstocks
Cockburnspath
8
niston
Pencaitland
B6355
Gifford
Danskine
B6355
Ecclaw
Grantshouse
Coldingham
A1107
.bb
East Saltoun
West Saltoun
Long Newton
391 HEART LAW
Quixwood
Houndwood
Heugh Head
60
Cairncross
Gilchriston
B6371
B6368
Longyester
463 SPARTLETON
Bothwell Water
Butterdean
Southern Upland Way
21
262 HORSELEY HILL
Reston
A1
Ayto
9
Fala Dam
Humbie
Blegbie
528 LAMMER LAW
Meikle Says Law
St Agnes
Abbey St Bathans
Edin's Hall Broch
B6438
Auchencrow
Fala
533
Whiteadder Reservoir
Cranshaws
Ellemford
325 COCKBURN LAW
Marygold
Soutra Summit 363
509 CRIB LAW
513 SEENES LAW
467 MEIKLE LAW
Whitchester
Lintlaw
Chirnside
B6437
60
394 DUN LAW
A68
HUNT LAW
Longformacus
Southern Upland Way
Primrosehill
Preston
B6355
Chirnsidebridge
10
Gilston
380 TURF LAW
A6112
Cumledge
Edrom Church
Edrom
Broadhaugh
Allanton
Hutton
Oxton
448 HOGS LAW
399 **80** DIRRINGTON GREAT LAW
Manderston
A6105
Edington
Whit
Carfraemill
Duns
Blackadder
Hilton
B6456
Gavinton
Foulder
60
383 COLLIE LAW
Polwarth
Nisbet Hill
Sinclair's Hill
Whitsome
11
A7
Blythe
Spottiswoode
Westruther
Fogo
A6112
Swinton
Ladykirk
Norham
Torquhan
Thirlestane
Thornydykes
Houndslow
Charterhall
A697
Horndean
Lauder
B6362
Thirlestane
Bassendean
A6089
Leitholm
Simprim
Killochyett
Boon
Greenlaw
B6461
Upsettlington
12
Stow
Legerwood
Greenknowe Tower
Middlethird
Hume
Lambden
Eccles
Lennel
J
K
L
M
N
P
Q
R
Bowland
Nether Blainslie
West Morriston
Fans
A68
Gordon
A6105
Coldstream
River TILL
Castle
Cornhill-on-Tweed

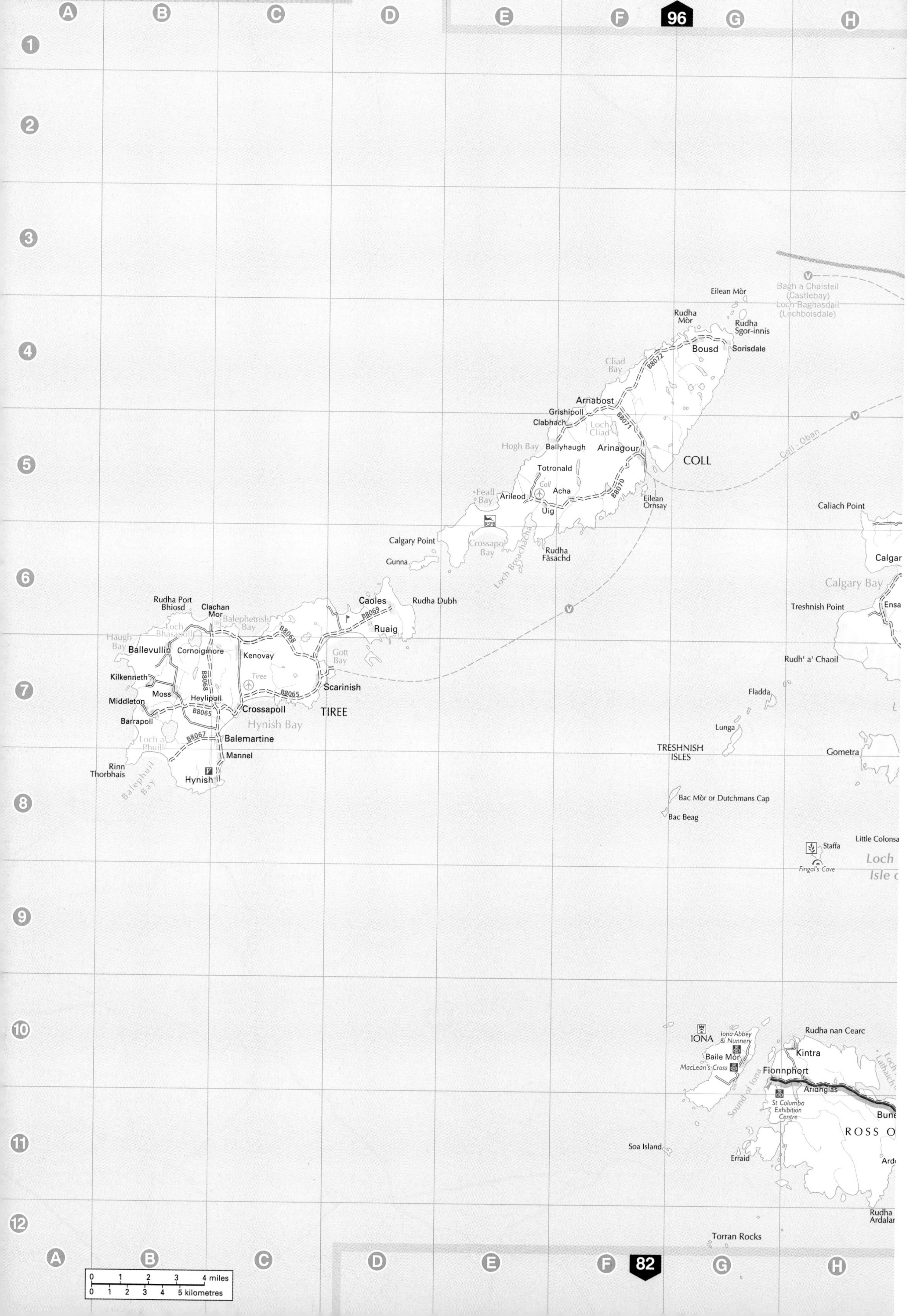

A   B   C   D   E   F **96** G   H

1
2
3

Eilean Mòr

Bagh a Chaisteil
(Castlebay)
Loch Baghasdail
(Lochboisdale)

Rudha
Mòr

Rudha
Sgor-innis

4

Cliad
Bay

B8072

Bousd

Sorisdale

Coll Oban

Arnabost

Grishipoll

Clabhach

B8071

Loch
Cliad

Hogh Bay

Ballyhaugh

Arinagour

COLL

5

Totronald

Coll

Acha

Caliach Point

Feall
Bay

Arileod

B8070

Uig

Eilean
Ornsay

Crossapol
Bay

Calgar

Calgary Point

Loch Breachacha

Rudha
Fàsachd

Gunna

6

Calgary Bay

Rudha Port
Bhiosd

Clachan
Mor

Caoles

Rudha Dubh

Treshnish Point

Ensa

Balephetrish
Bay

B8069

Ruaig

Loch
Bhasapoll

B8068

Haugh
Bay

Ballevullin

Cornoigmore

Kenovay

Gott
Bay

Rudh' a' Chaoil

Tiree

Kilkenneth

B8068

Fladda

7

Moss

Heylipoll

B8065

Scarinish

Middleton

Crossapoll

Lunga

Barrapoll

B8065

TIREE

Hynish Bay

TRESHNISH
ISLES

Gometra

B8067

Balemartine

Loch a'
Phuill

Mannel

Rinn
Thorbhais

Hynish

Bac Mòr or Dutchmans Cap

8

Balephuill
Bay

Bac Beag

Staffa

Little Colonsa

Fingal's Cave

Loch
Isle o

9
10

Rudha nan Cearc

IONA

Iona Abbey
& Nunnery

Kintra

Baile Mòr

Fionnphort

MacLean's Cross

Aridhglas

Sound of Iona

St Columba
Exhibition
Centre

Bune

ROSS O

11

Soa Island

Erraid

Ard

Rudha
Ardalar

12

Torran Rocks

A   B   C   D   E   F **82** G   H

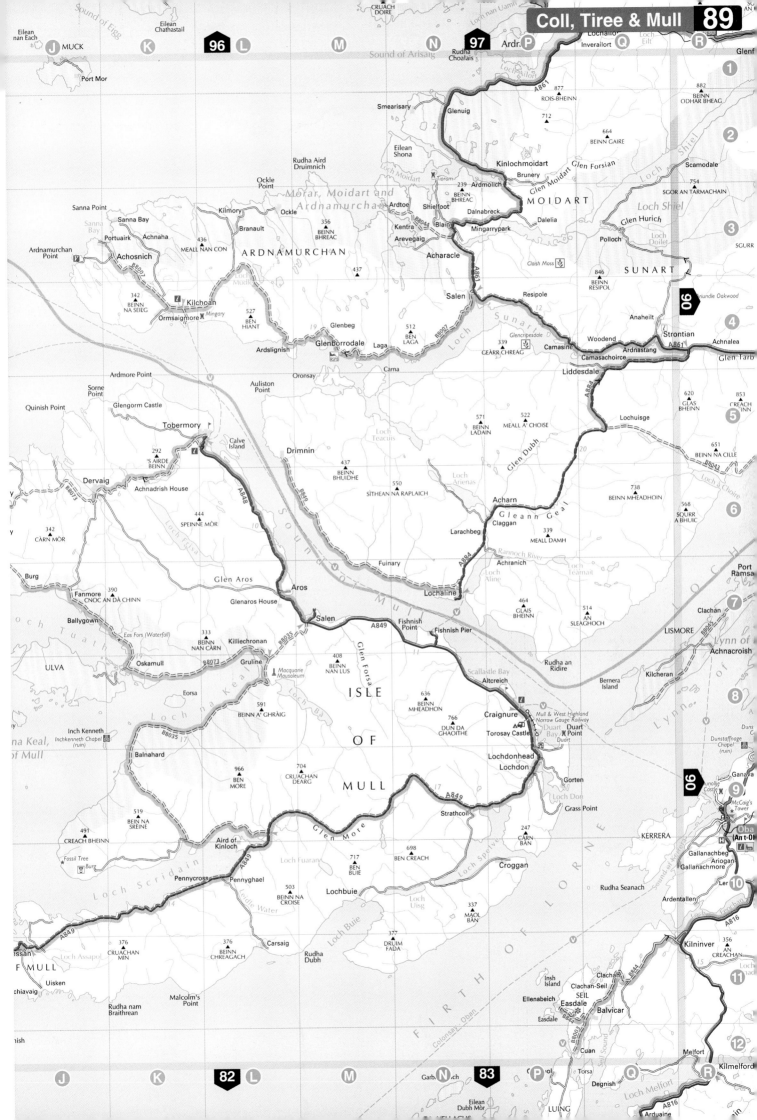

J MUCK
Port Mor
Eilean nan Each
Sound of Eigg
Eilean Chathastail

K

L **96**

M

N

97 Ardr
Rudha Choalais
Loch nan Uamh
Sound of Arisaig

P Lochailort
Inverailort
Loch Eilt
Loch
Q
Glenf
R

89

Sanna Point
Ockle Point
Rudha Aird Druimnich
Smearisary
Glenuig
A861
ROIS-BHEINN 877
BEINN ODHAR BHEAG 882

Kilmory
Branault
Ockle
Eilean Shona
Loch Moidart
Tioram
Kinlochmoidart
Brunery
712
BEINN GAIRE 664
Glen Forsian
Scamodale
754
SGOR AN TARMACHAIN
Loch Shiel

Sanna Bay
Achnaha
BEINN BHREAC 356
Ardmolich
239 BEINN BHREAC
MOIDART
Glen Moidart
Sanna Bay
MEALL NAN CON 436
ARDNAMURCHAN
Ardtoe
Shielfoot
Dalnabreck
Dalelia
Polloch
Glen Hurich
Loch Doilet
SGURR

Portuairk
Achosnich
Ardnamurchan Point
Kentra
Blain
B8044
Mingarrypark
Dalelia

Kilchoan
BEINN NA SEILG 342
537
BEN HIANT 527
Glenbeg
Acharacle
A861
Claish Moss
BEINN RESIPOL 846
SUNART
Triundle Oakwood
06

Ormsaigmore
Mingary
Ardslignish
Glenborrodale
Laga
BEN LAGA 512
Salen
Resipole
12
Woodend
Anaheilt
Strontian
A861
Achnalea

Ardmore Point
Carna
Oronsay
Glencripesdale
GEARR CHREAG 339
Camasine
Camasachoirce
Ardnastang
Liddesdale
A884
Glen Tarb
Glen Tarb
ACHNALEA

Sorne Point
Quinish Point
Glengorm Castle
Auliston Point
BEINN LADAIN 571
MEALL A' CHOISE 522
Glen Dubh
Lochuisge
GLAS BHEINN 620
CREACH 853

Tobermory
Calve Island
Drimnin
BEINN BHUIDHE 437
Loch Teacuis
20
BEINN NA CILLE 651
Loch a' Choire

Dervaig
'S AIRDE BEINN 292
Achnadrish House
BEINN BHUIDHE 437
SITHEAN NA RAPLAICH 550
Loch Arienas
Acharn
BEINN MHEADHOIN 738
SQURR A BHUIC 568

CÀRN MÒR 342
SPEINNE MÒR 444
A848
Claggan
Gleann Geal
Larachbeg
MEALL DAMH 339
Port Ramsa

Burg
CNOC AN DÀ CHINN 390
Fanmore
Glen Aros
Aros
Fuinary
Achranich
Loch Aline
Rannoch River
Loch Teamait
Clachan
7
LISMORE
Lynn of

Ballygown
Eas Fors (Waterfall)
BEINN NAN CÀRN 333
Glenaros House
Salen
A849
Fishnish Point
Lochaline
GLAIS BHEINN 464
AN SLEAGHOCH 514
Achnacroish

ULVA
Oskamull
Killiechronan
Gruline
B8073
BEINN NAN LUS 408
Glen Forsa
Fishnish Pier
Scallastle Bay
Rudha an Ridire
Bernera Island
Kilcheran
8

Inch Kenneth
Inchkenneth Chapel (ruin)
Eorsa
Macquarie Mausoleum
BEINN A' GHRÀIG 591
ISLE
BEINN MHEADHON 636
Altcreich
Mull & West Highland Narrow Gauge Railway
Craignure
Duart Bay
Duart Point
Dunstaffnage Chapel (ruin)

Balnahard
B8035
OF
DUN DA GHAOITHE 766
Torosay Castle
Duart
06

na Keal
of Mull
BEN MORE 966
CRUACHAN DEARG 704
MULL
A849
Lochdonhead
Lochdon
Loch Don
Gorten
Dunollie Castle
McCaig's Tower
Oba (An t-O
9

BEIN NA SREINE 519
Aird of Kinloch
Strathcoil
Grass Point
KERRERA
Gallanachbeg
Ariogan
Gallanachmore

CREACH BHEINN 491
Fossil Tree
Burg
A849
Glen More
CÀRN BÀN 247
Ardentallen
10
Ler

Pennycross
Pennyghael
BEN BUIE 717
BEN CREACH 698
Croggan
Rudha Seanach
A816

Balnahard
Loch Fuaran
Lochbuie
Loch Uisg
Loch Spelve
MAOL BÀN 337
Kilninver
AN CREACHAN 356

BEINN NA CROISE 503
Leidle Water

Uisken
CRUACHAN MIN 376
BEINN CHREAGACH 376
Carsaig
Rudha Dubh
DRUIM FADA 377
Insh Island
Clachan
Clachan-Seil
SEIL
Easdale
Balvicar
11

chiavaig
Malcolm's Point
Ellenabeich
Easdale
B8003
12

Rudha nam Braithrean

J

K

82 L

M

83 N

P
Garb
N
Loch
Cuan
Torsa
Degnish
Q
Melfort
R
Kilmelford

Eilean Dubh Mòr
Loch Melfort
LUING
Arduaine
A816

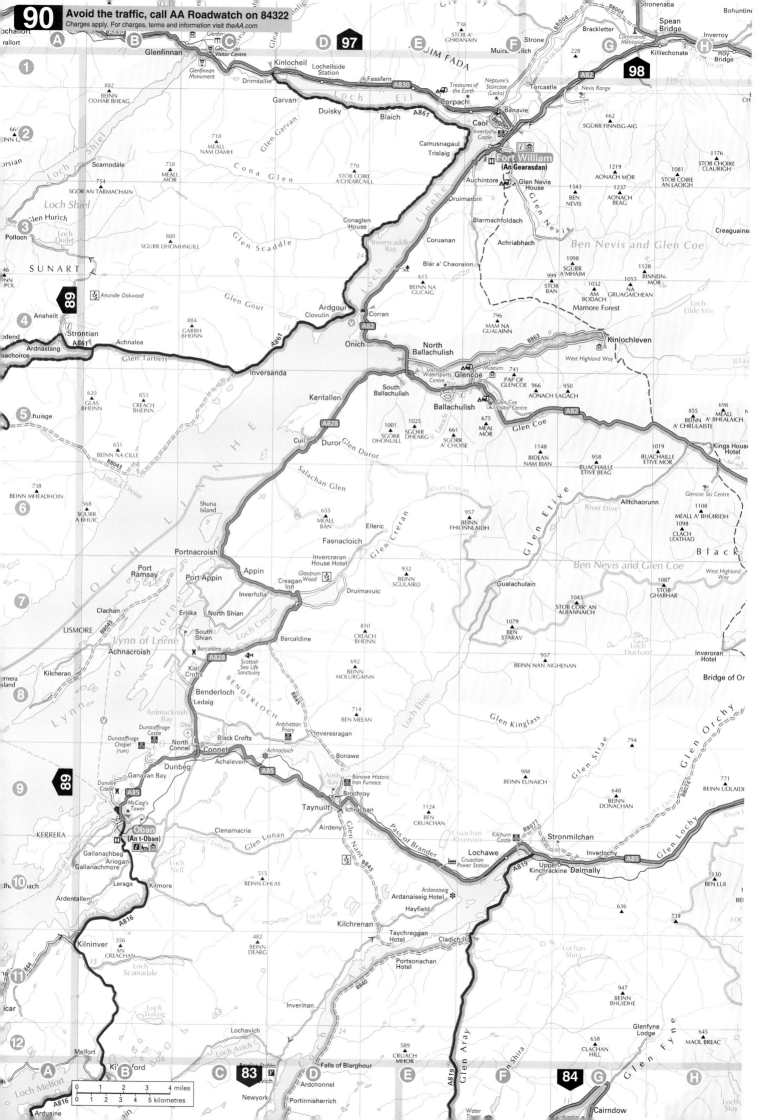

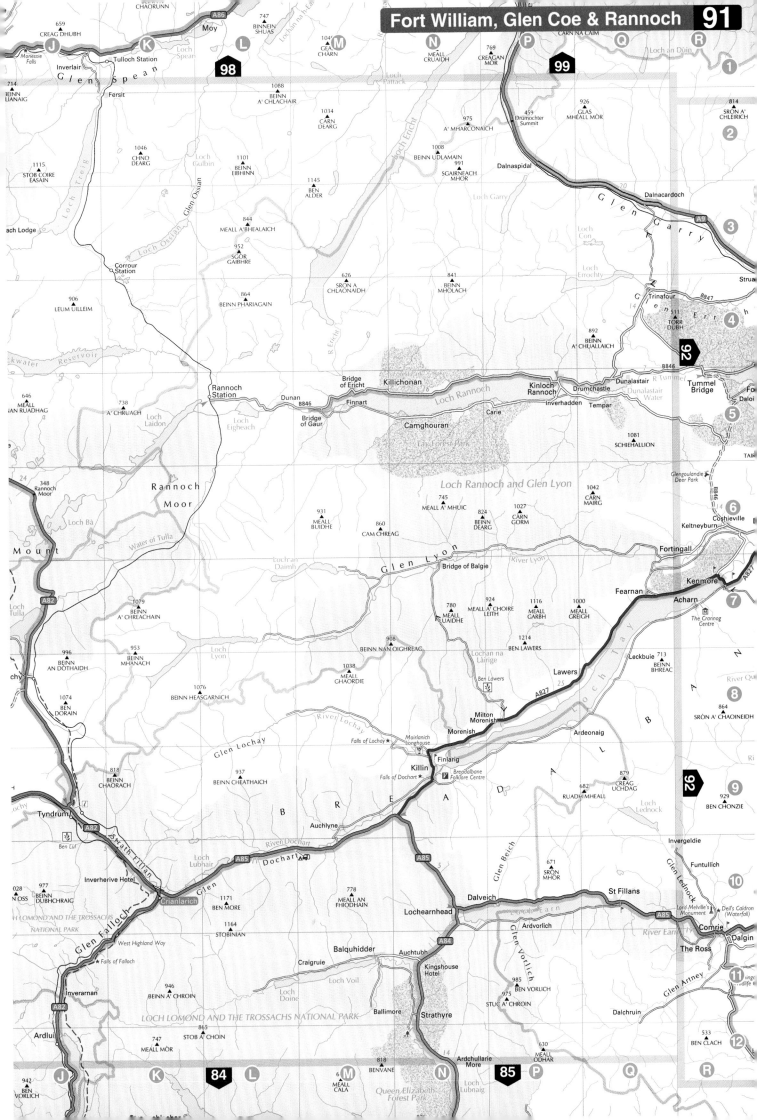

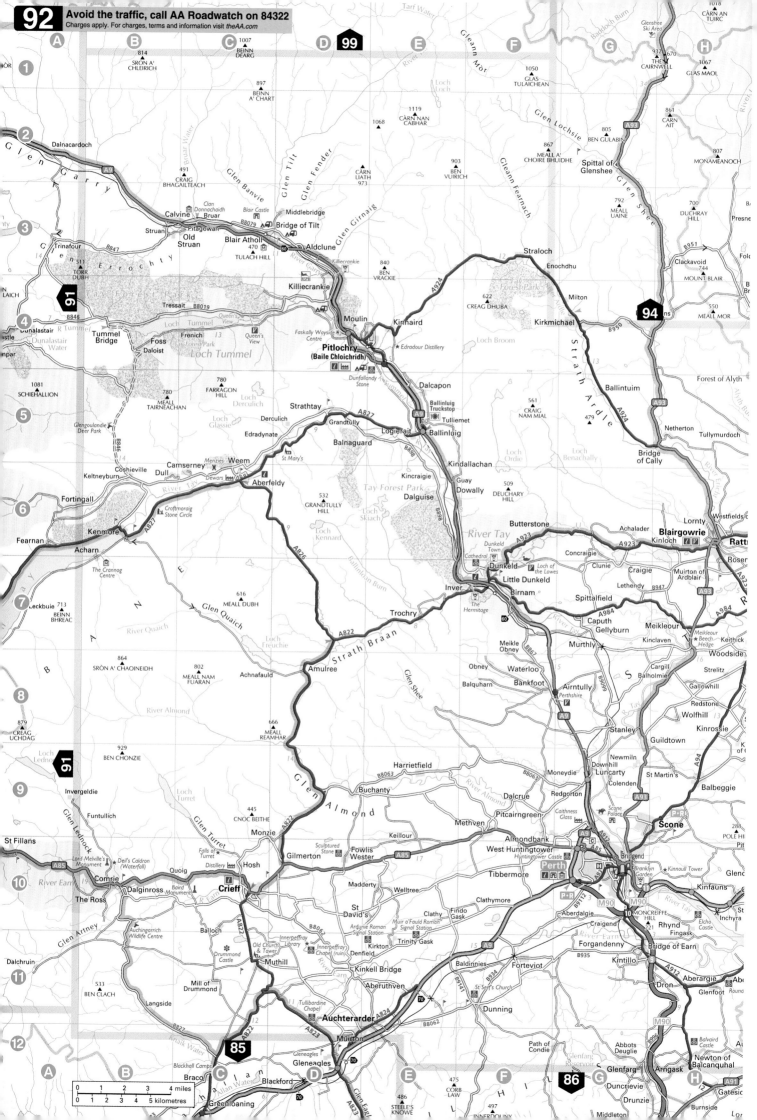

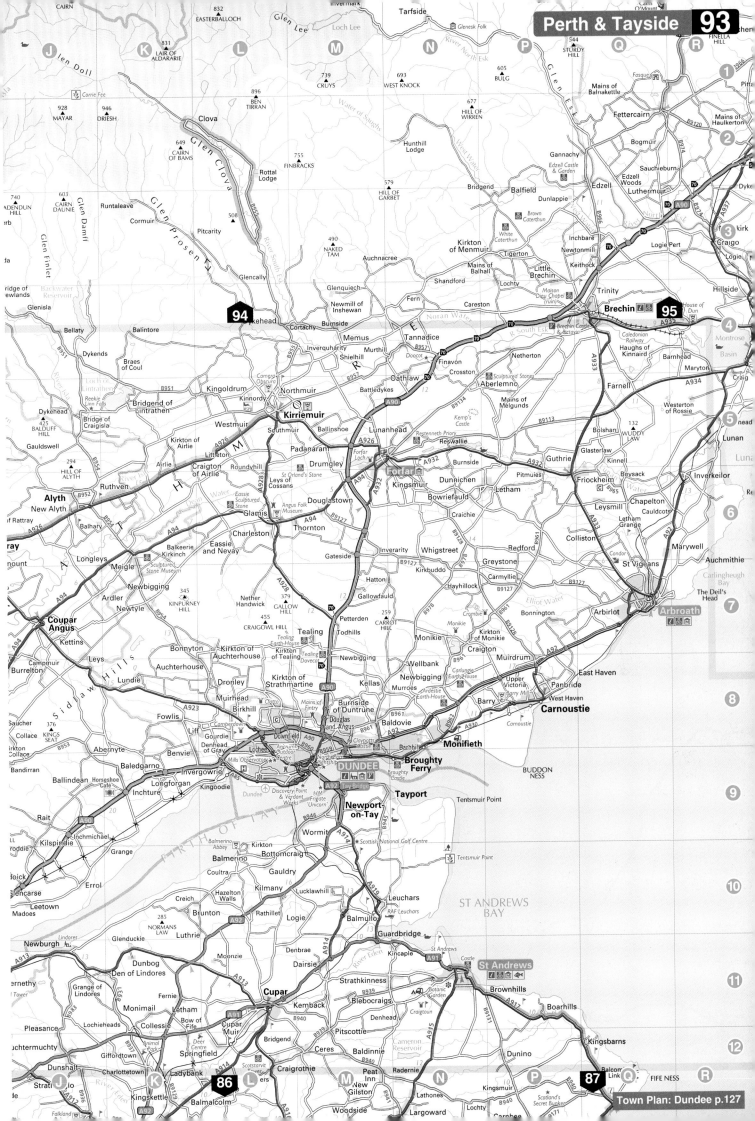

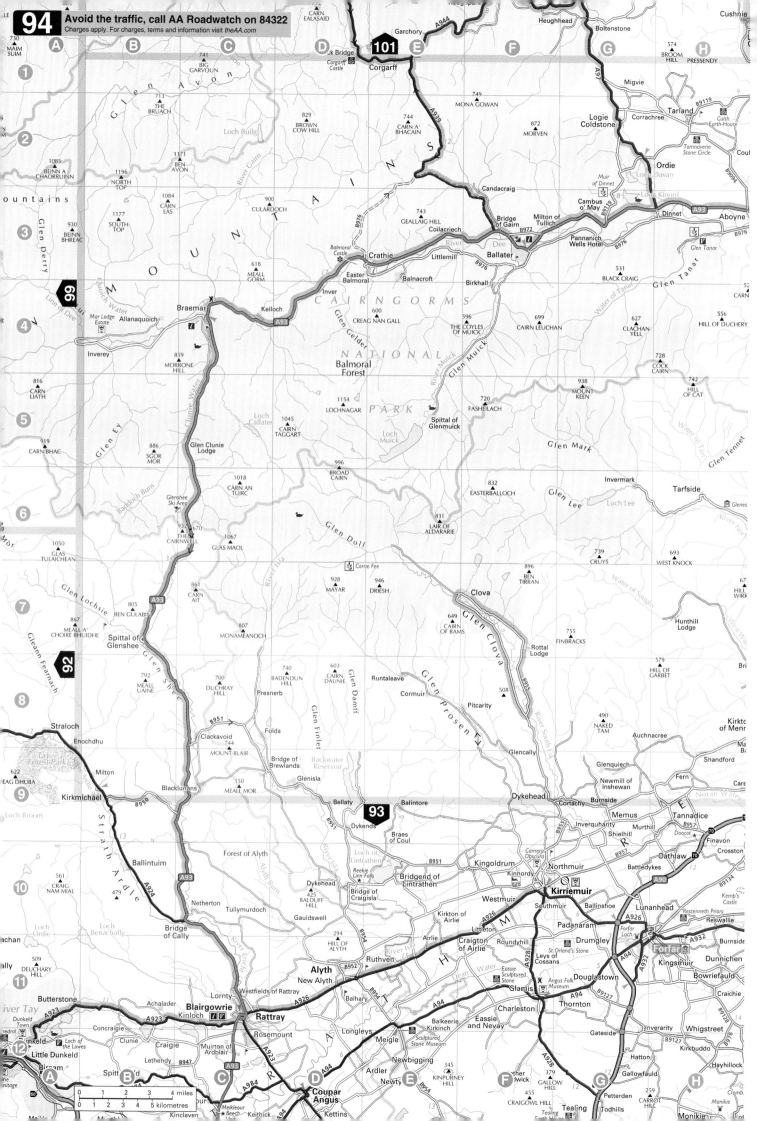

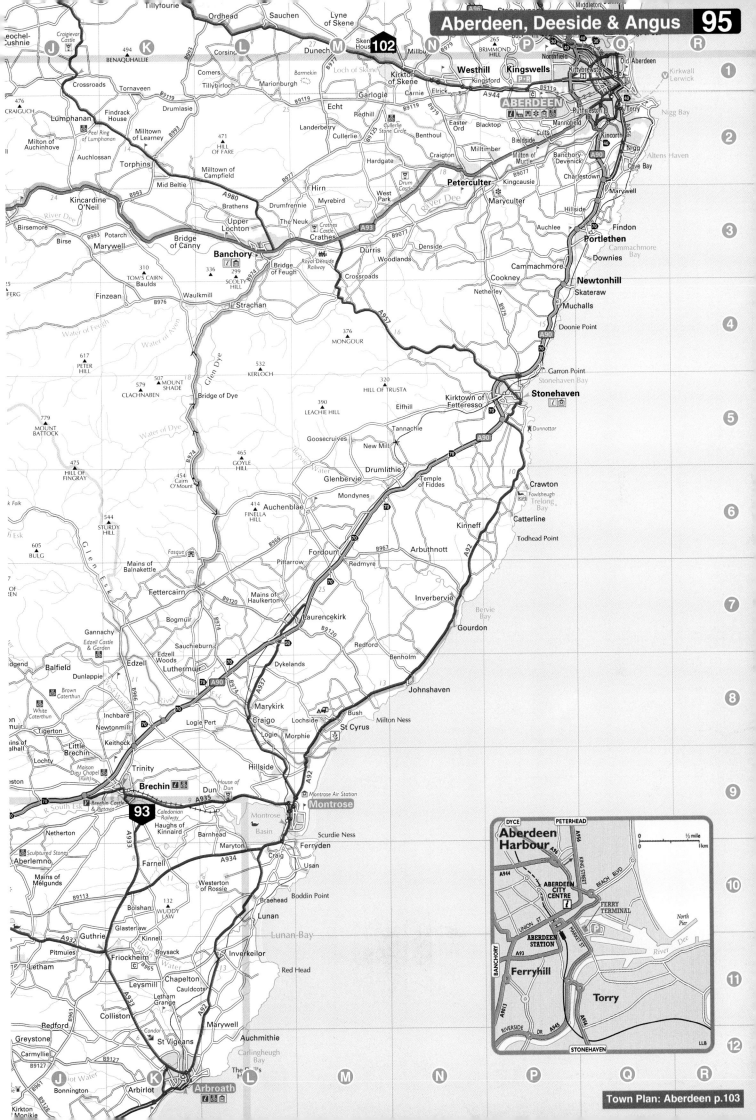

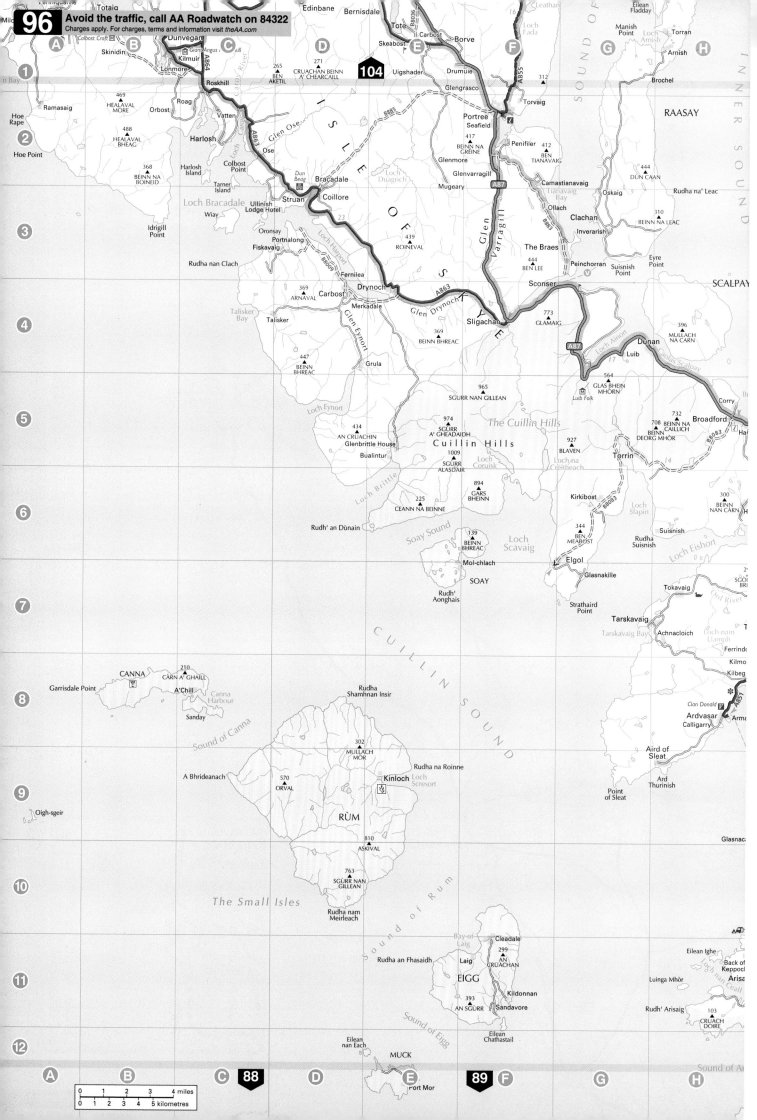

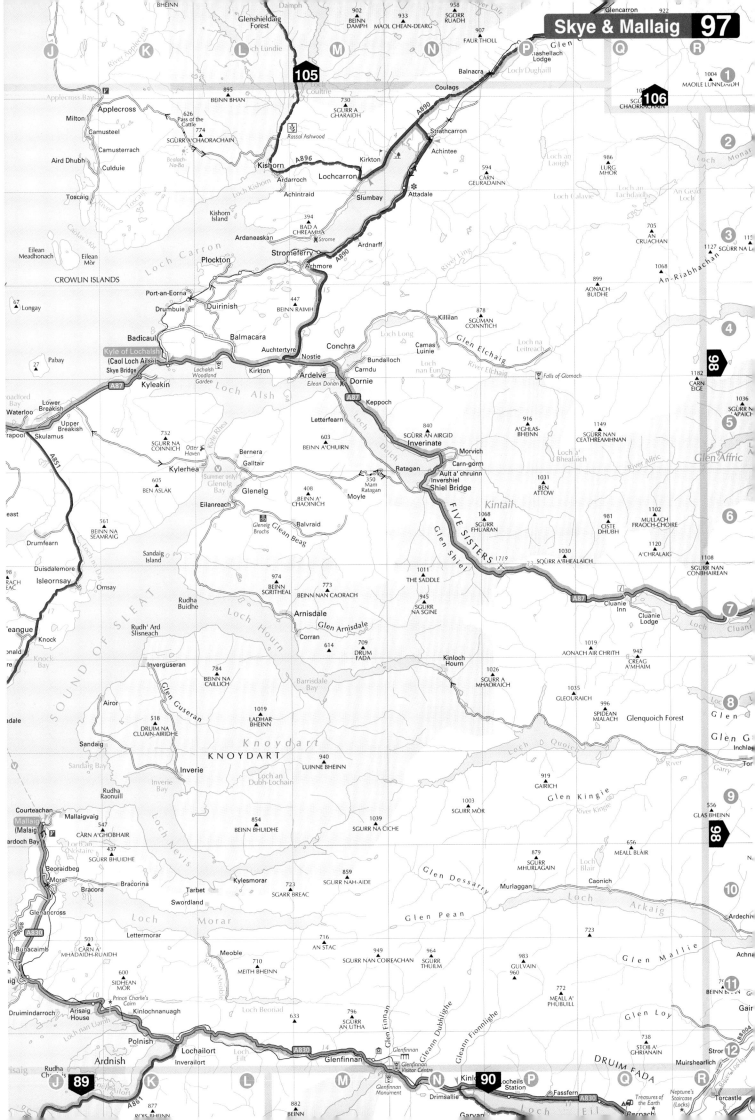

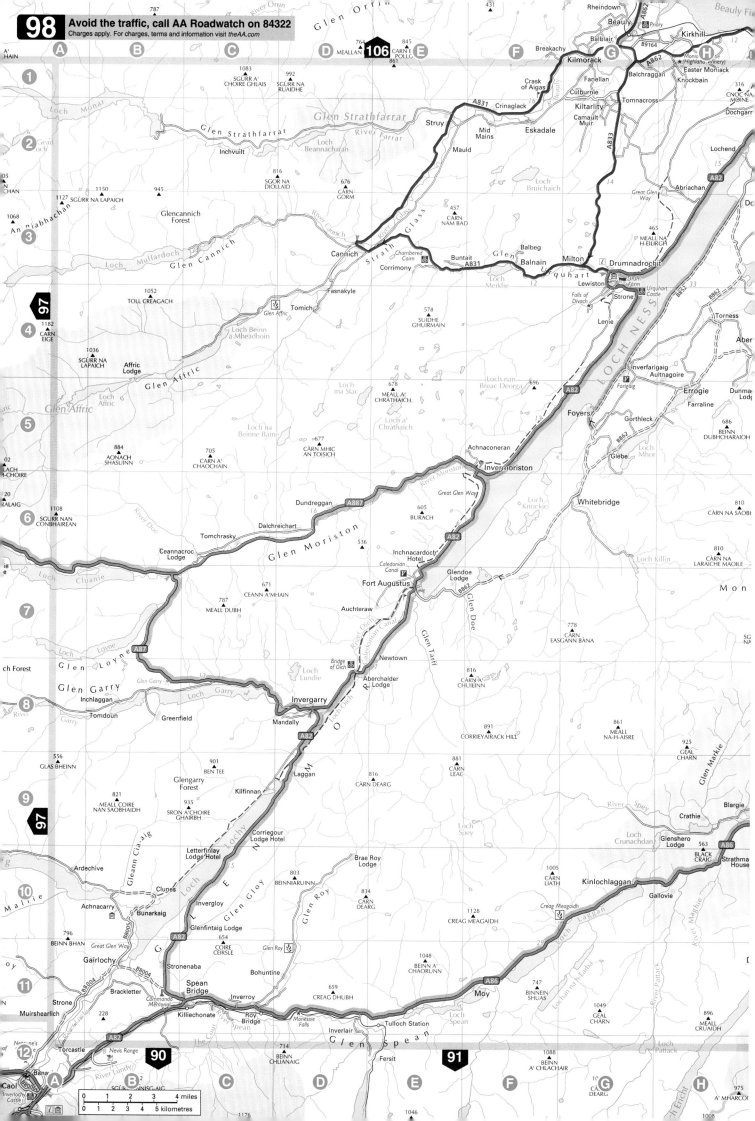

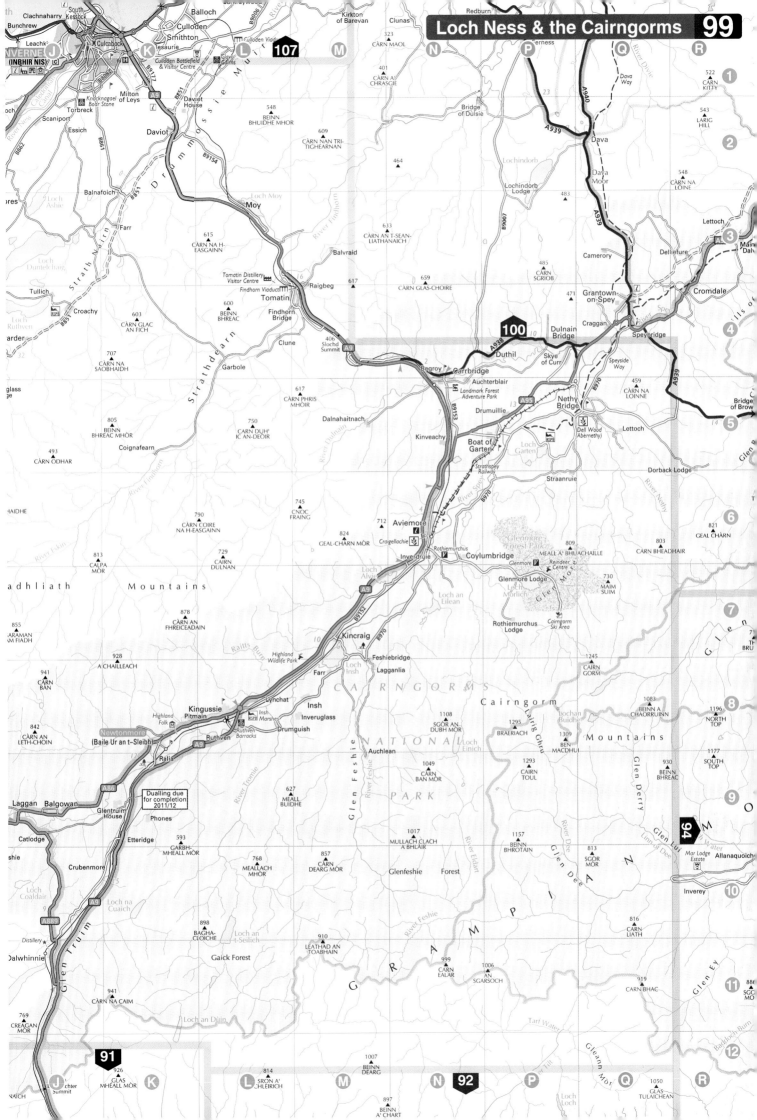

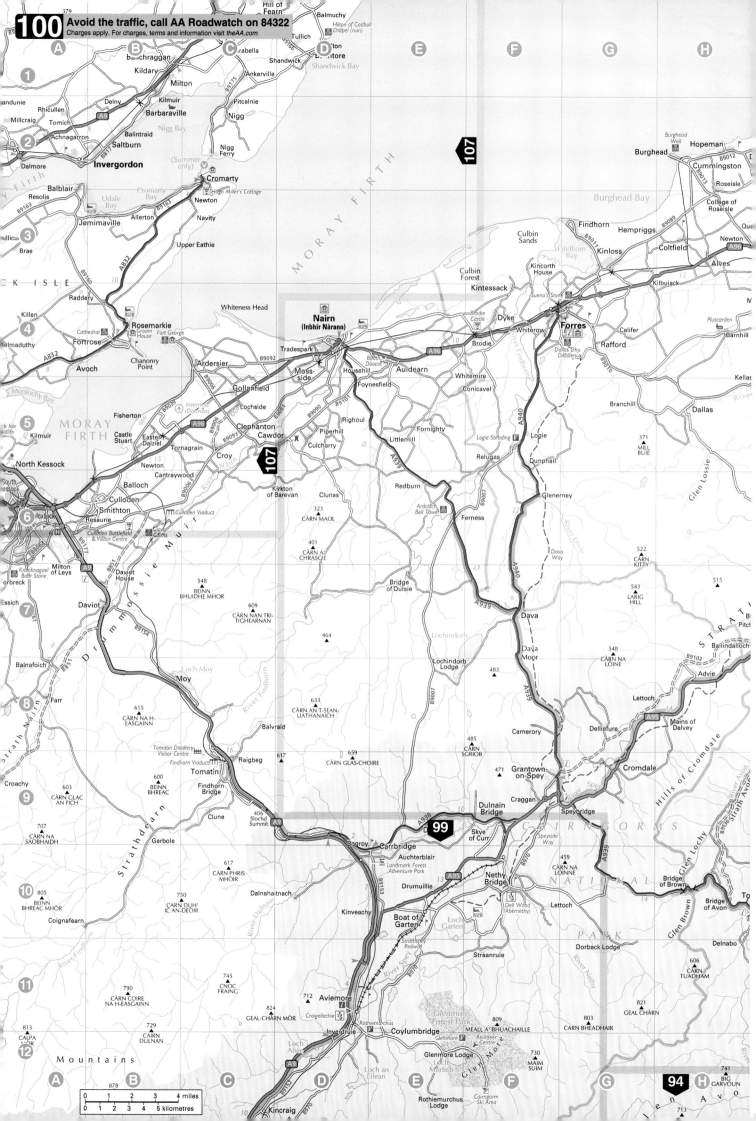

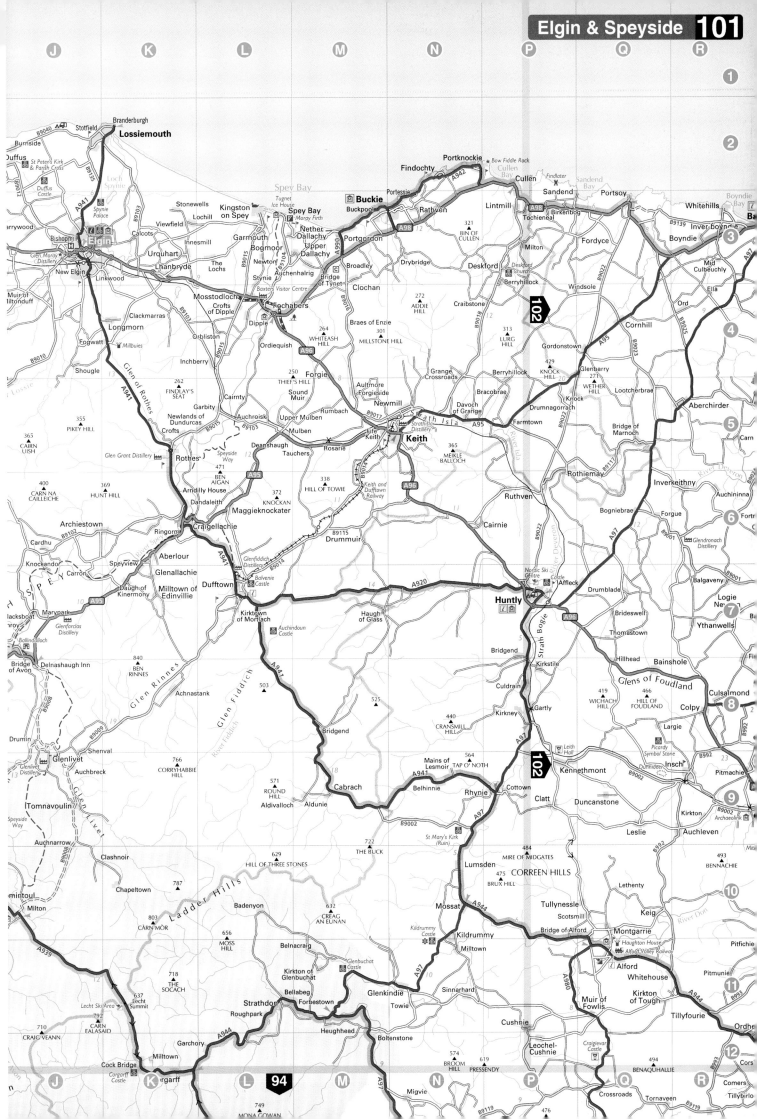

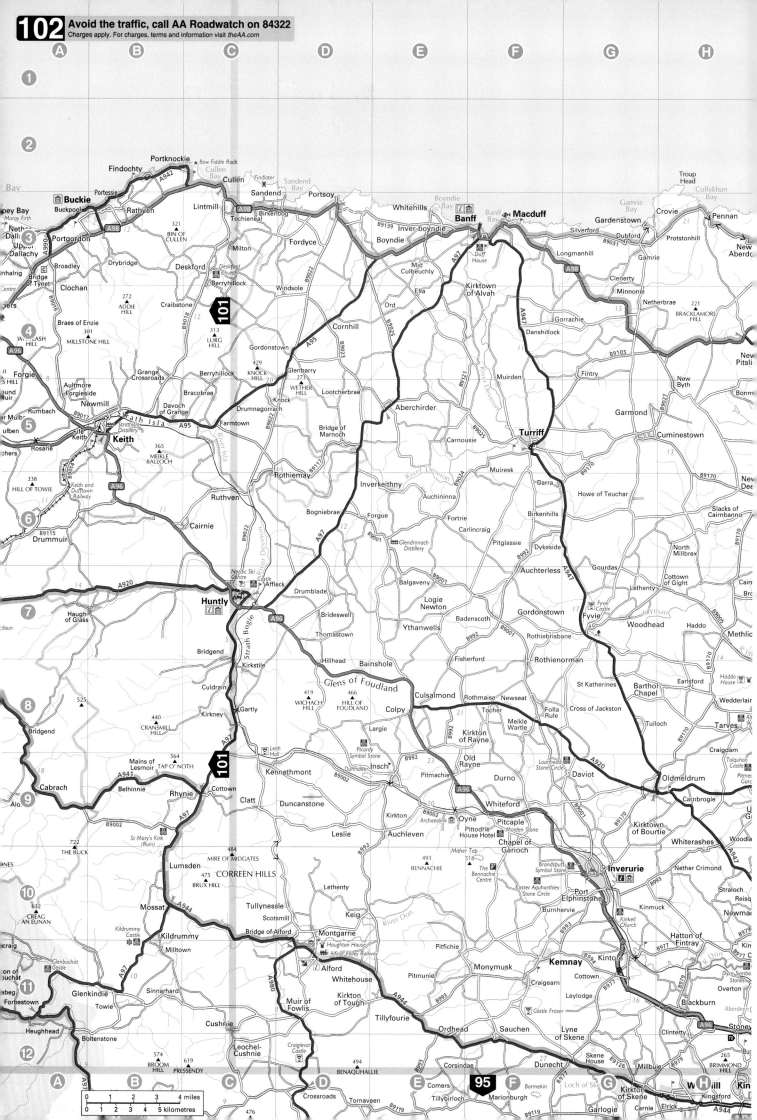

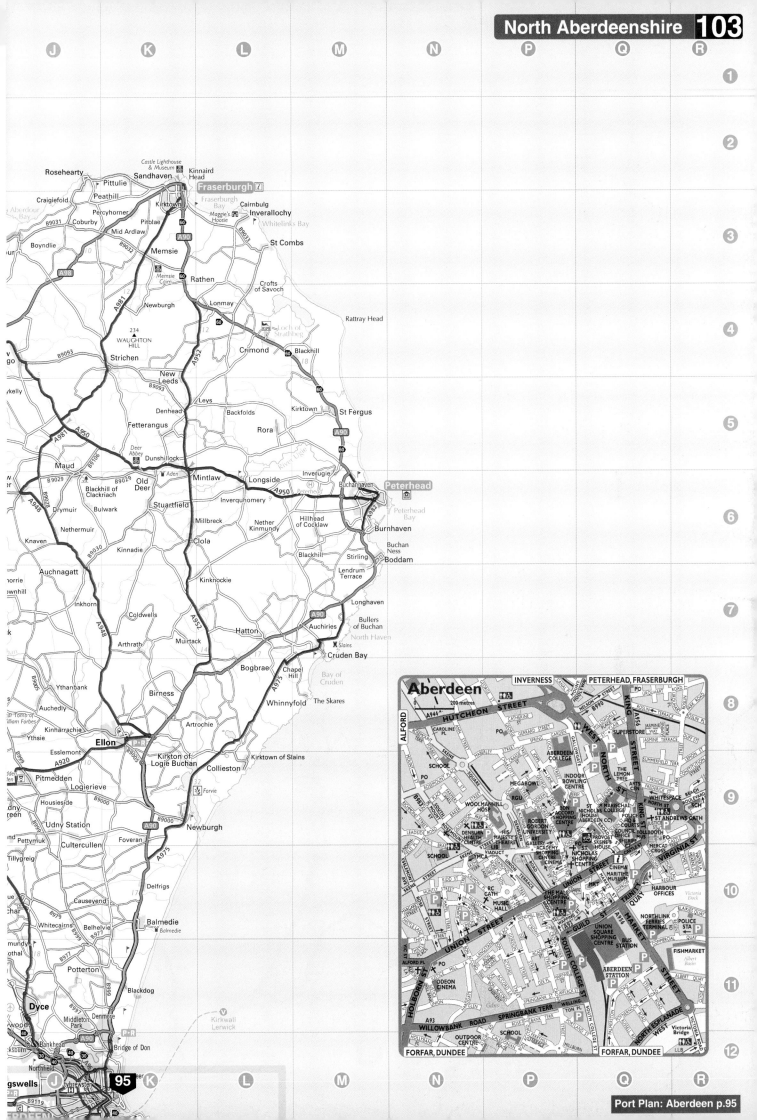

Port Plan: Aberdeen p.95

see page 111
for Western Isles

A   B   C   D   E   F   G   H

1

2

3

4

5

6

Fladda-chùain

Eilean Trodday

7

Rudha Hunish

Tairbeart
(Tarbert)

North
Duntulm   Kilmaluag
Duntulm   Flodigarry
Lùb Score   Skye Museum   Eilean Flodigarry
                   of Island Life
Borneskitaig   Staffin
Kilmuir   Heribusta   Digg   Bay
           Kilvaxter   542   Staffin Island
Balgown   MEAL NA Digg
8   SUIREAMACH
Loch nam Madadh   Linicro   Brogaig
(Lochmaddy)   Stenscholl   Staffin
Waternish Point   Totscore   Kilt Rock Waterfall
                              464   Ellishader
                              BIODA
Ascrib   Idrigill   BUIDHE   Trotternish Valtos
Islands   Uig   Maligar
                          (Uige)   611   Marishader   Rudha nam Brathairean
9   Uig Bay   BEINN   Garros Culnaknock
283   Geary   EDRA
BEN   Earlish   Lealt
GEARY   Tote
Trumpan   Gillen   Peinlich   608
Ardmore   Hallin   Loch Snizort   CREAG A' LAIN
Point   A855

DUNVEGAN   Isay Mingay   A87   River Hinnisdal
HEAD   Stein Lusta   451
10   214 Greshornish BEINN
                    Claigan   BEN House Hotel A' SGA   Old Man
           Boreraig   DIUBAIG   Kingsburgh   719 of Storr
                        Bay 327   Romesdal THE   Eilean
           Uig   BEINN   Flashader   Eyre   STORR   Tigh
Loch   BHREAC   Treaslane
Pooltiel   Feriniquarrie   Upperglen   Kensaleyre   Eilean
11 Milovaig Glendale   Edinbane Bernisdale   Fladday
    Lephin Colbost Totaig   Tote   Manish
Waterstein   Colbost Croft   Skeabost Carbost Point Loch
              Dunvegan   Borve   Arnish
Neist   Giant Angus MacAskill   Loch
Point   Kilmuir   265   271   Uigshader Drumuie Fada
Moonen Bay Lonmore   BEN CRUACHAN BEINN   312
12   Roskhill   AKETIL A' CHEARCAILL   Glengrasco
           Ramasaig   469   96   A855 Torvaig
    oe Rape   Roag HEALAVAL   Vatten   Portree
                    MORE   Orbost   Glen Ose   S   Seafield
A   B   Harlosh C   D   E   F   Penifiler G   H

0   1   2   3   4 miles
0   1   2   3   4   5 kilometres

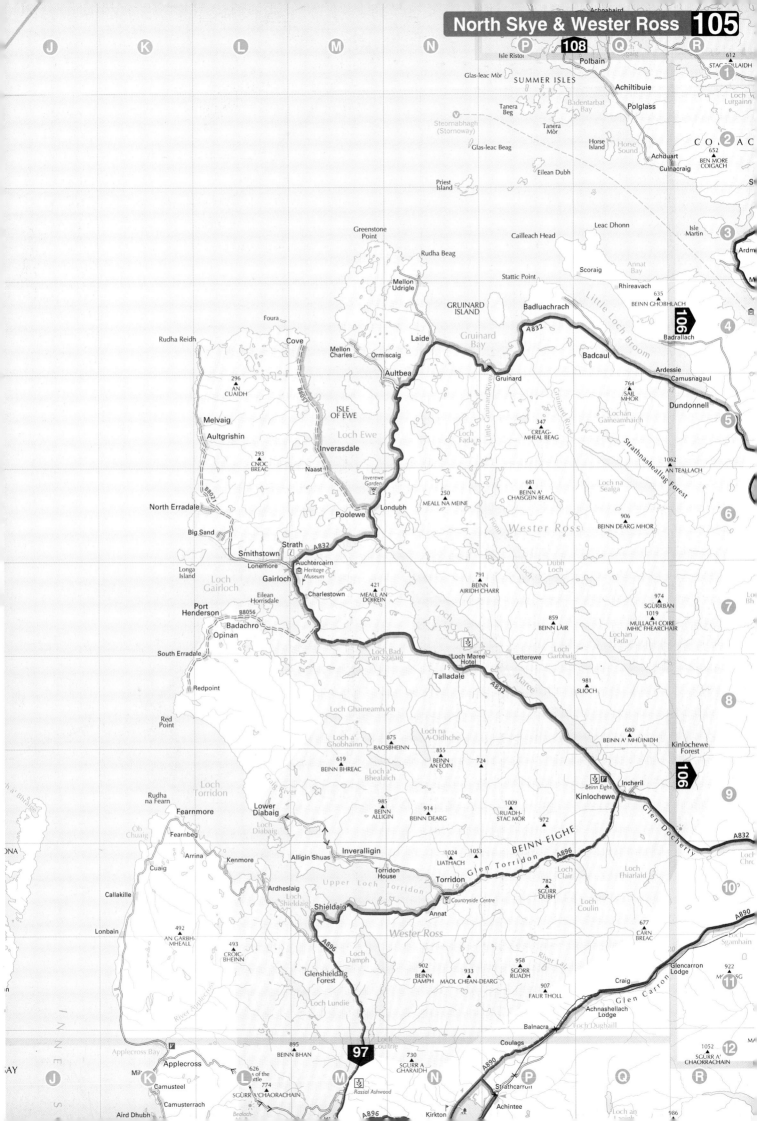

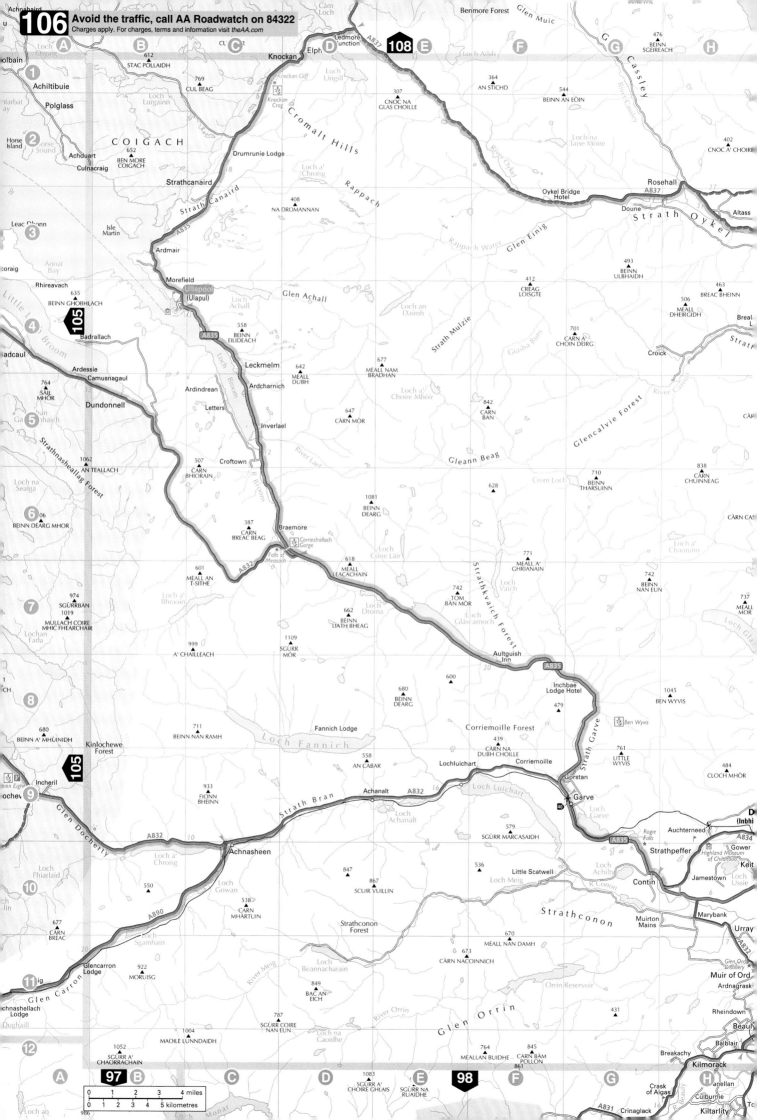

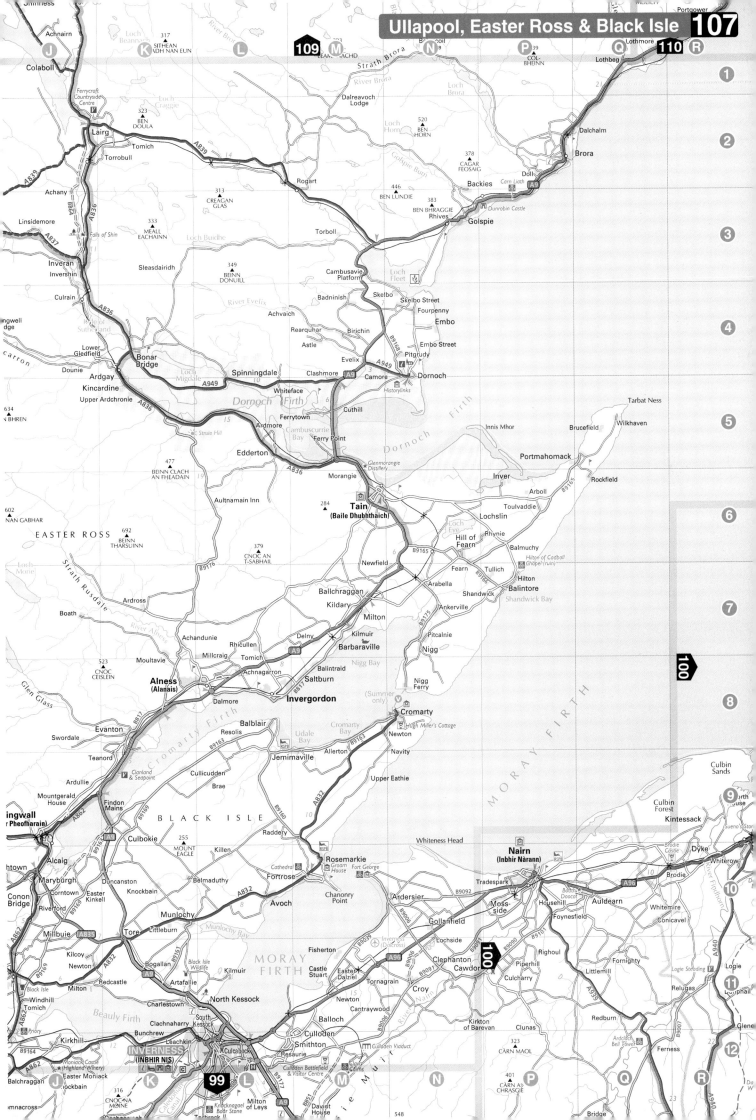

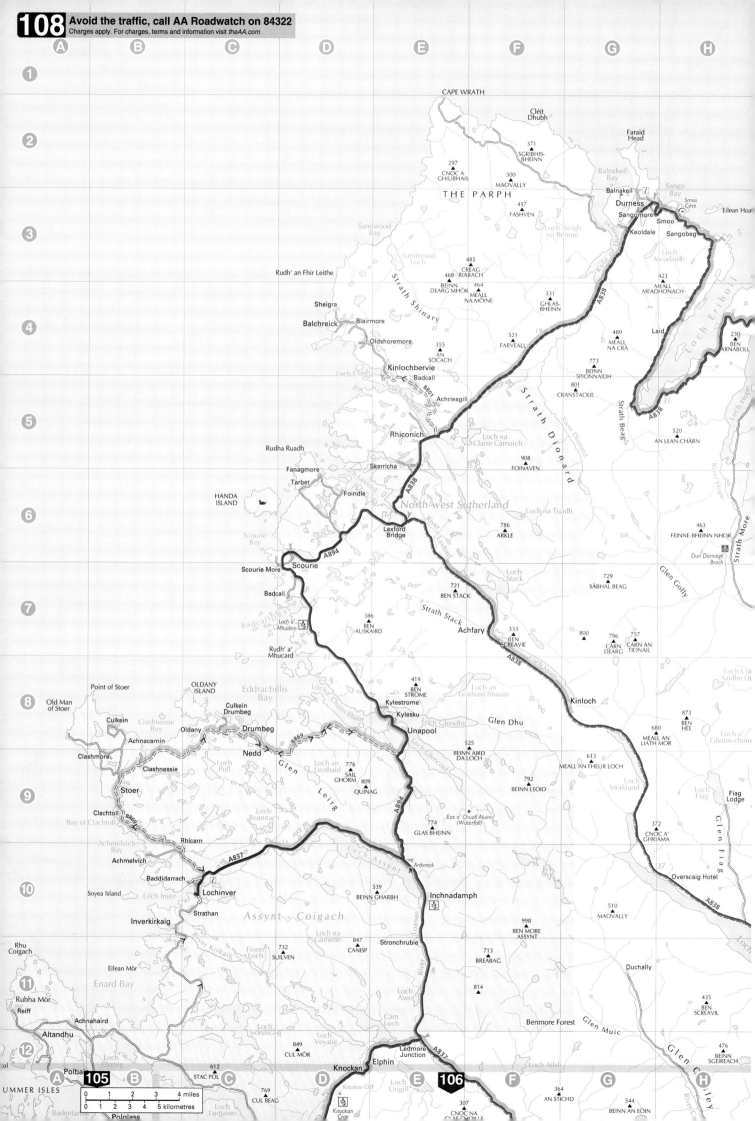

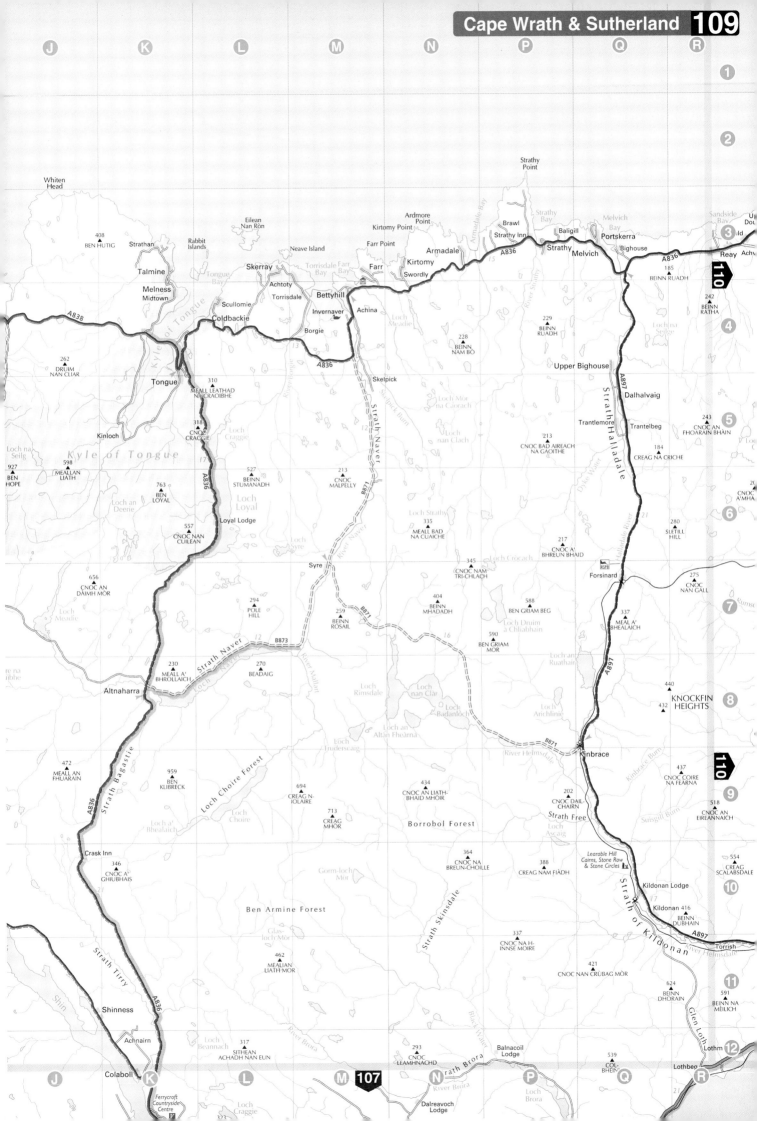

J K L M N P Q R

1
2
3
4
5
6
7
8
9
10
11
12

Whiten Head

408
BEN HUTIG

Strathan

Eilean Nan Ròn

Rabbit Islands

Neave Island

Ardmore Point

Kirtomy Point

Farr Point

Strathy Point

Strathy Bay

Melvich Bay

Sandside Bay

Ud Dou

Armadale Bay

Brawl

Baligill

Melvich

Portskerra

Bighouse

Reay

Achv

185
BEINN RUADH

242
BEINN RATHA

Talmine

Skerray

Achtoty

Torrisdale

Torrisdale Bay

Farr Bay

Farr

Swordly

Kirtomy

Armadale

Strathy Inn

Strathy

Strathy

A836

A836

Melness
Midtown

Scullomie

Bettyhill

Invernaver

Borgie

Achina

Loch Meadie

229
BEINN RUADH

Upper Bighouse

Loch na Seilge

Coldbackie

A838

Kyle of Tongue

Tongue

Skelpick

228
BEINN NAM BÒ

A836

Dalhalvaig

Trantlemore

Trantelbeg

243
CNOC AN FHOARAIN BHÀIN

262
DRUIM NAN CLIAR

310
MEALL LEATHAD NA CRAOIBHE

Loch Mòr na Caorach

Strath Halladale

184
CREAG NA CRICHE

Kinloch

318
CNOC CRAGGIE

Loch Craggie

Skelpick Burn

Loch nan Clach

213
CNOC BAD AIREACH NA GAOITHE

A897

Loch na Seilg

927
BEN HOPE

598
MEALLAN LIATH

763
BEN LOYAL

A836

527
BEINN STUMANADH

Strath Naver

213
CNOC MALPELLY

B871

Strathy Water

Loch Strathy

280
SLETILL HILL

20
CNOC A'MHA

Loch an Deserie

Kyle of Tongue

Loch Loyal

Loyal Lodge

River Naver

335
MEALL BAD NA CUAICHE

217
CNOC A' BHREUN BHAID

Halladale River

557
CNOC NAN CUILEAN

Loch Syre

Syre

345
Loch Cròcach

CNOC NAM TRI-CHLACH

RSPB

Forsinard

275
CNOC NAN GALL

656
CNOC AN DÀIMH MÒR

294
POLE HILL

259
BEINN ROSAIL

B871

404
BEINN MHADADH

588
Ben Griam Beg

337
MEALL A' BHEALAICH

Loch Meadie

Strath Naver

Loch Naver

B873

B871

River Mallart

590
BEN GRIAM MÒR

Loch an Ruathair

440
432

KNOCKFIN HEIGHTS

230
MEALL A' BHROLLAICH

270
BEADAIG

Loch Rinsdale

Loch nan Clàr

Loch Badanloch

Loch Arichlinie

B871

Altnaharra

Strath Bagastie

Loch Choire Forest

Loch an Altan Fhearna

River Helmsdale

Kinbrace

437
CNOC COIRE NA FEARNA

472
MEALL AN FHUARAIN

959
BEN KLIBRECK

694
CREAG N-IOLAIRE

434
CNOC AN LIATH-BHAID MHÒIR

202
CNOC DAIL-CHAIRN

Strath Free

518
CNOC AN EIREANNAICH

A836

Crask Inn

713
CREAG MHÒR

Loch Choire

Borrobol Forest

Loch Ascaig

Learable Hill Cairns, Stone Row & Stone Circles

554
CREAG SCALABSDALE

346
CNOC A' GHIUBHAIS

Loch a' Bhealaich

364
CNOC NA BREUN-CHOILLE

388
CREAG NAM FIÀDH

Kildonan Lodge

Strath of Kildonan

Ben Armine Forest

Glas-loch Mòr

462
MEALLAN LIATH MÒR

Gorm-loch Mòr

Strath Skinsdale

337
CNOC NA H-INNSE MOIRE

Kildonan

416
BEINN DUBHAIN

A897

Torrish

River Helmsdale

Strath Tirry

Shin

421
CNOC NAN CRÙBAG MÒR

624
BEINN DHORAIN

591
BEINN NA MEILICH

Shinness

A836

Achnairn

Loch Beannach

317
SITHEAN ACHADH NAN EUN

River Brora

293
CNOC LEAMHNACHD

Balnacoil Lodge

539
COL-BHEIN

Glen Loth

Lothm

Colaboll

Ferrycroft Countryside Centre

Loch Craggie

Strath Brora

Dalreavoch Lodge

Loch Brora

Lothbeg

110
110

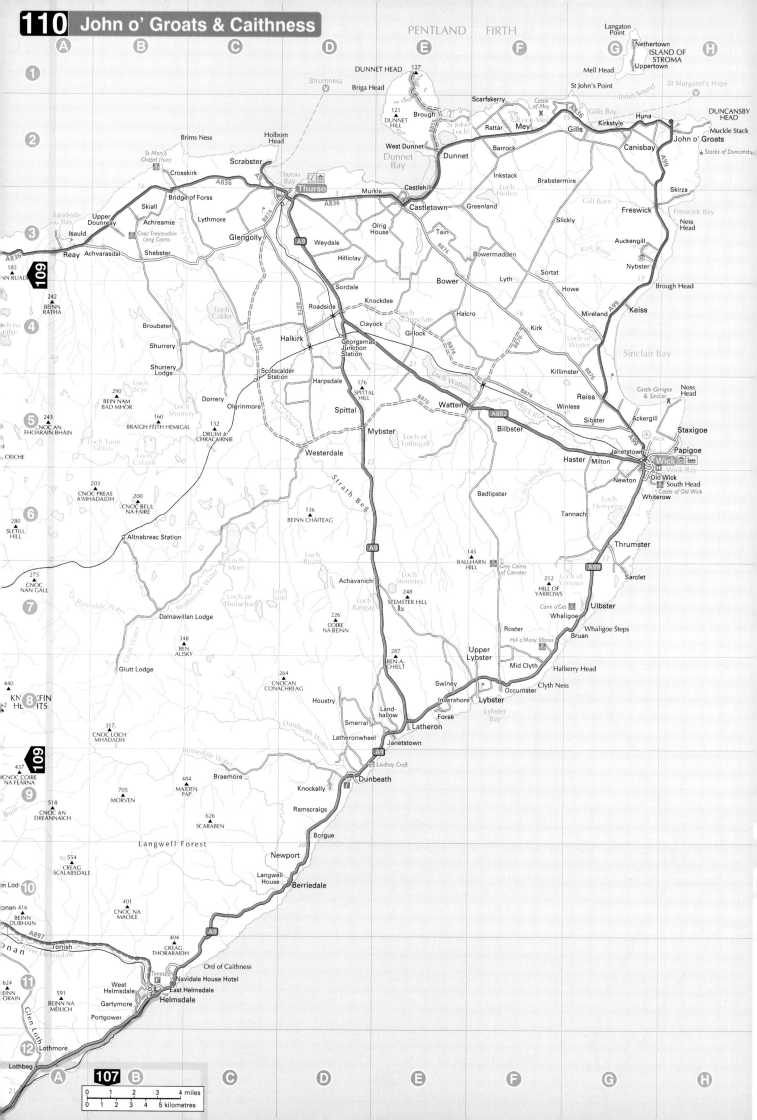

Western Isles

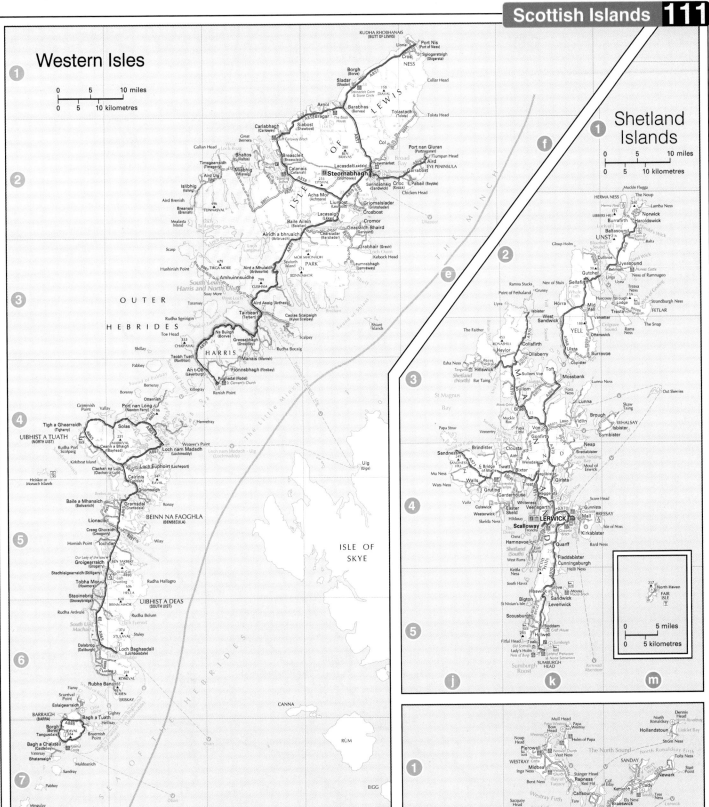

0   5   10 miles
0   5   10 kilometres

FERRY SERVICES

Western Isles

Lewis is linked by ferry to the mainland at Ullapool, with daily sailings. There are ferry services from Harris (Tairbeart) and North Uist (Loch nam Madadh) to Uig on Skye. Harris and North Uist are connected by a ferry service between An t-Ob (Leverburgh) and Berneray, and then causeway to Otternish. South Uist and Barra are served by ferry services from Oban, and a ferry service operates between Eriskay and Barra, and another causeway links South Uist to Eriskay. Berneray, North Uist, Benbecula, South Uist and Eriskay are all connected by causeways.

Shetland Islands

The main service is from Aberdeen on the mainland to the island port of Lerwick. A service from Kirkwall (Orkney) to Lerwick is also available. Shetland Islands Council operates an inter-island car ferry service.

Orkney Islands

The main service is from Scrabster on the Caithness coast to the island port of Stromness and there is a further service from Gills (Caithness) to St Margaret's Hope on South Ronaldsay. A service from Aberdeen to Kirkwall provides a link to Shetland at Lerwick. Inter-island car ferry services are also operated (advance reservations recommended).

Shetland Islands

0   5   10 miles
0   5   10 kilometres

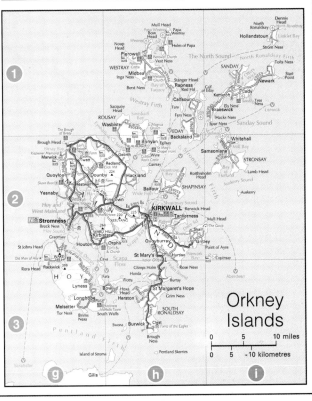

Orkney Islands

0   5   10 miles
0   5   10 kilometres

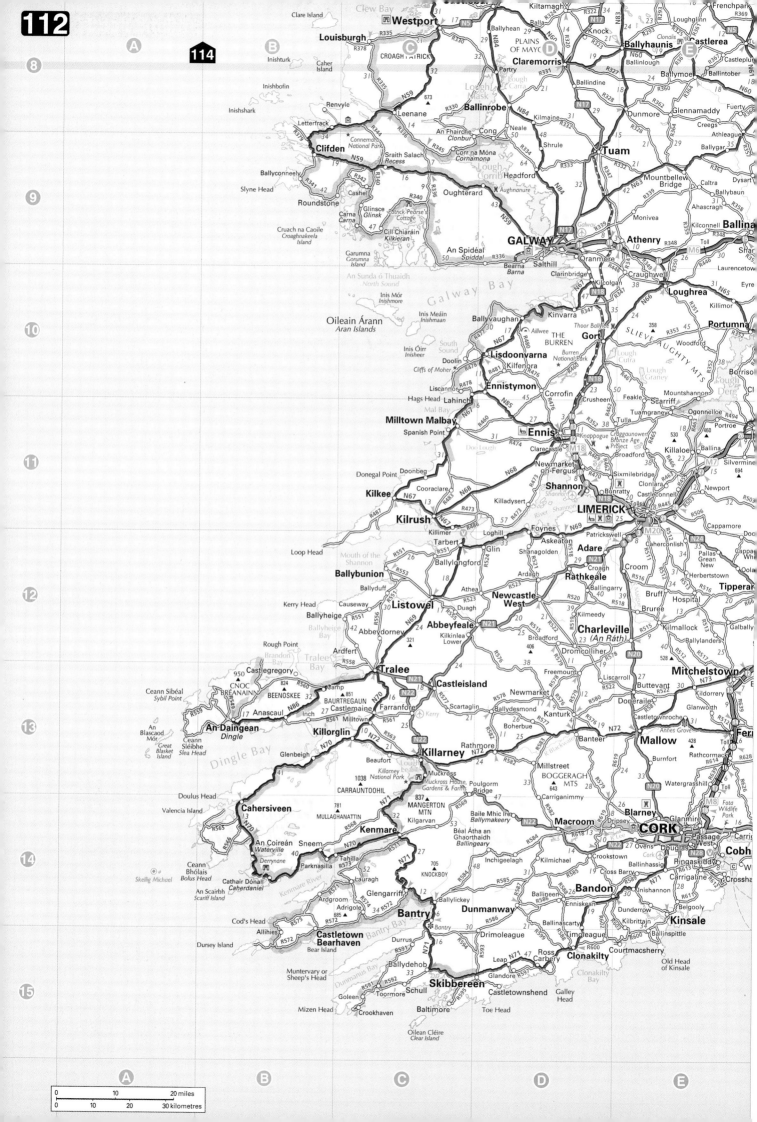

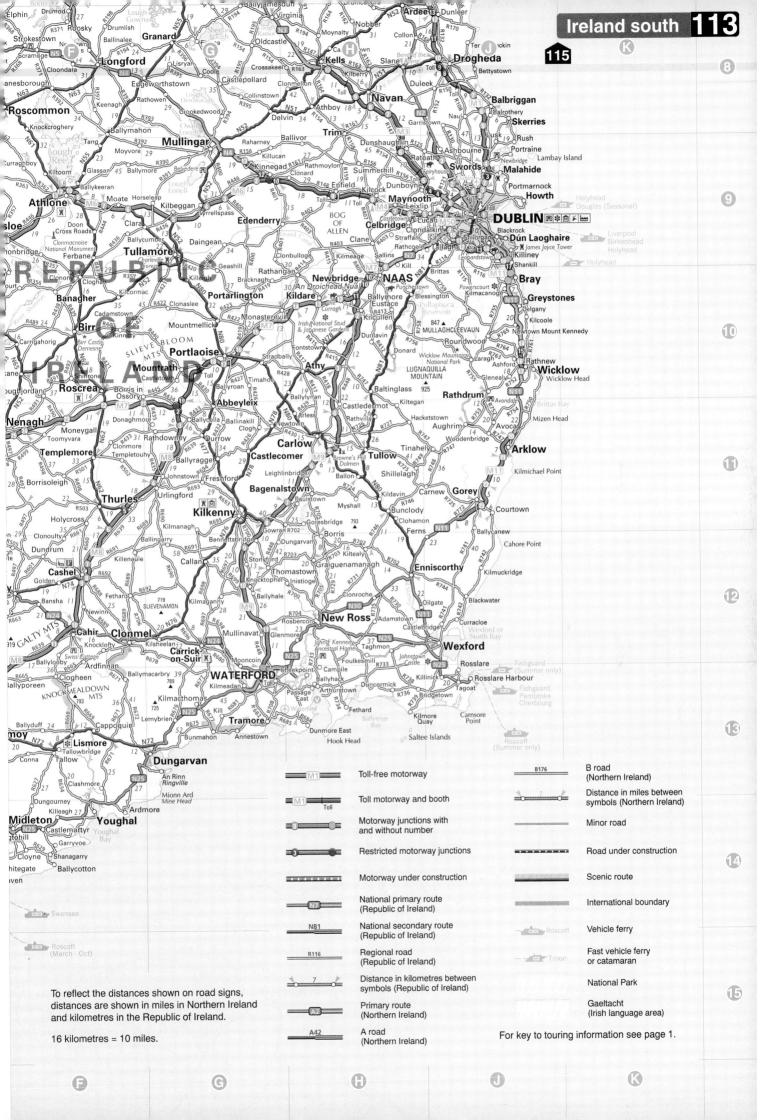

Legend:

═══M1═══	Toll-free motorway
═══M1═══ Toll	Toll motorway and booth
═══①═══	Motorway junctions with and without number
═══③═══	Restricted motorway junctions
▭▭▭▭▭	Motorway under construction
═══N7═══	National primary route (Republic of Ireland)
N81	National secondary route (Republic of Ireland)
R116	Regional road (Republic of Ireland)
▷ 7	Distance in kilometres between symbols (Republic of Ireland)
A7	Primary route (Northern Ireland)
A42	A road (Northern Ireland)

B176	B road (Northern Ireland)
▷ 7	Distance in miles between symbols (Northern Ireland)
───────	Minor road
▬▬▬▬▬	Road under construction
━━━━━━	Scenic route
───────	International boundary
Roscoff	Vehicle ferry
Troon	Fast vehicle ferry or catamaran
	National Park
	Gaeltacht (Irish language area)

To reflect the distances shown on road signs, distances are shown in miles in Northern Ireland and kilometres in the Republic of Ireland.

16 kilometres = 10 miles.

For key to touring information see page 1.

Ireland index

C12 Abbeydorney
D12 Abbeyfeale
G11 Abbeyleix
H12 Adamstown
D12 Adare
C14 Adrigole
H4 Aghadowey
E9 Ahascragh
J4 Ahoghill
B15 Allihies
B13 Anascaul
E4 An Bun Beag
E5 An Charraig
E4 An Clochán Liath
B14 An Coireán
B13 An Daingean
C9 An Fhairche
J7 Annalong
G13 Annestown
G13 An Rinn
D9 An Spidéal
J5 Antrim
D12 Ardagh
E5 Ardara
H8 Ardee
C12 Ardfert
F12 Ardfinnan
K6 Ardglass
B14 Ardgroom
F14 Ardmore
J11 Arklow
H11 Arless
H6 Armagh
J3 Armoy
H13 Arthurstown
G7 Arvagh
J9 Ashbourne
J10 Ashford
D12 Askeaton
H8 Athboy
D12 Athea
E9 Athenry
E8 Athleague
F9 Athlone
H10 Athy
G6 Augher
H6 Aughnacloy
J11 Aughrim
J11 Avoca

H11 Bagenalstown
D14 Baile Mhic Íre
H7 Bailieborough
J8 Balbriggan
D8 Balla
E7 Ballaghaderreen
D7 Ballina
E11 Ballina
E7 Ballinafad
G7 Ballinagh
G11 Ballinakill
F8 Ballinalee
G6 Ballinamallard
F7 Ballinamore
D14 Ballinascarty
E9 Ballinasloe
D8 Ballindine
D14 Ballineen
D12 Ballingarry
G12 Ballingarry
D14 Ballingeary
E14 Ballinhassig
E8 Ballinlough
D8 Ballinrobe
E15 Ballinspittle
E8 Ballintober
F5 Ballintra
H9 Ballivor
H11 Ballon
E9 Ballybaun
H7 Ballybay
F5 Ballybofey
C12 Ballybunion
J11 Ballycanew
K5 Ballycarry
J3 Ballycastle
C6 Ballycastle
J5 Ballyclare
G11 Ballycolla
B9 Ballyconneely
G7 Ballyconnell
F14 Ballycotton
F9 Ballycumber
C15 Ballydehob
D13 Ballydesmond
C12 Ballyduff
F13 Ballyduff
E7 Ballyfarnan
J4 Ballygalley
E9 Ballygar
E6 Ballygawley
H6 Ballygawley
K5 Ballygowan
H13 Ballyhack
G7 Ballyhaise
G12 Ballyhale
E8 Ballyhaunis
D8 Ballyhean
C12 Ballyheige
G8 Ballyjamesduff
F9 Ballykeeran
E12 Ballylanders
C14 Ballylickey
G3 Ballyliffin
C12 Ballylongford
F12 Ballylooby
H10 Ballylynan
F13 Ballymacarbry
F8 Ballymahon
D14 Ballymakeery
J4 Ballymena
E8 Ballymoe
H4 Ballymoney
F9 Ballymore
H10 Ballymore Eustace
E7 Ballymote
J6 Ballynahinch
J5 Ballynure

F13 Ballyporeen
G11 Ballyragget
G10 Ballyroan
H5 Ballyronan
E6 Ballysadare
F5 Ballyshannon
D10 Ballyvaughan
K5 Ballywalter
J8 Balrothery
C15 Baltimore
H10 Baltinglass
F10 Banagher
J6 Banbridge
E14 Bandon
K5 Bangor
C7 Bangor Erris
F12 Bansha
D13 Banteer
C14 Bantry
D9 Barna
B6 Béal an Mhuirhead
D14 Béal Átha an Ghaorthaidh
D9 Bearna
C13 Beaufort
F6 Belcoo
J5 Belfast
E14 Belgooly
H4 Bellaghy
F6 Belleek
B6 Belmullet
G7 Belturbet
H6 Benburb
G12 Bennettsbridge
G5 Beragh
J8 Bettystown
F10 Birr
F6 Blacklion
J9 Blackrock
J12 Blackwater
E14 Blarney
H10 Blessington
D13 Boherbue
H12 Borris
F10 Borris in Ossory
F10 Borrisokane
F11 Borrisoleigh
E7 Boyle
G10 Bracknagh
J10 Bray
H13 Bridgetown
J9 Brittas
E11 Broadford
D12 Broadford
J4 Broughshane
E12 Bruff
E12 Bruree
E4 Bunbeg
H11 Bunclody
G3 Buncrana
E6 Bundoran
G13 Bunmahon
C6 Bun na hAbhna
C6 Bunnahowen
D7 Bunnyconnellan
D11 Bunratty
E13 Burnfort
H3 Bushmills
E13 Buttevant

F10 Cadamstown
E12 Caherconlish
B14 Caherdaniel
B14 Cahersiveen
F12 Cahir
H6 Caledon
G12 Callan
E9 Caltra
B13 Camp
H13 Campile
F12 Cappagh White
E11 Cappamore
F13 Cappoquin
H8 Carlanstown
J7 Carlingford
H11 Carlow
C9 Carna
G3 Carndonagh
J11 Carnew
J4 Carnlough
E7 Carracastle
F3 Carraig Airt
E5 Carrick
F3 Carrickart
K5 Carrickfergus
H7 Carrickmacross
G5 Carrickmore or Termon Rock
F7 Carrick-on-Shannon
G12 Carrick-on-Suir
F10 Carrigahorig
E14 Carrigaline
F7 Carrigallen
D14 Carriganimmy
G4 Carrigans
E14 Carrigtohill
J5 Carryduff
C9 Cashel
F12 Cashel
D8 Castlebar
J7 Castlebellingham
H7 Castleblaney
J12 Castlebridge
G11 Castlecomer
E11 Castleconnell
G5 Castlederg
H11 Castledermot
B13 Castlegregory
C13 Castleisland
C13 Castlemaine
F14 Castlemartyr
E8 Castleplunket
G8 Castlepollard
E8 Castlerea
H3 Castlerock
H6 Castleshane
G10 Castletown

B15 Castletown Bearhaven
E13 Castletownroche
D15 Castletownshend
J6 Castlewellan
B14 Cathair Dónall
C12 Causeway
G7 Cavan
H9 Celbridge
D7 Charlestown
E12 Charleville
H13 Cheekpoint
E5 Cill Charthaigh
C9 Cill Chiaráin
G5 Clady
H9 Clane
G9 Clara
D11 Clarecastle
D8 Claremorris
D10 Clarinbridge
F13 Clashmore
G4 Claudy
B9 Clifden
E6 Cliffony
G11 Clogh
F10 Cloghan
F13 Clogheen
G6 Clogher
H11 Clohamon
D15 Clonakilty
H9 Clonard
G10 Clonaslee
G9 Clonbulloge
C9 Clonbur
J9 Clondalkin
G7 Clones
E11 Clonlara
G3 Clonmany
F12 Clonmel
H8 Clonmellon
F11 Clonmore
F10 Clonony
F12 Clonoulty
H12 Clonroche
H6 Clontibret
F8 Cloondara
K6 Clough
F10 Cloughjordan
F14 Cloyne
H5 Coagh
H5 Coalisland
E14 Cobh
G8 Coleraine
G8 Collinstown
H8 Collon
E6 Collooney
K5 Comber
D9 Cong
F13 Conna
H5 Cookstown
G8 Coole
C11 Cooraclare
G7 Cootehill
E14 Cork
C9 Cornamona
C9 Corr na Móna
D10 Corrofin
E15 Courtmacsherry
J11 Courtown
J6 Craigavon
E10 Craughwell
K5 Crawfordsburn
E8 Creegs
F4 Creeslough
D12 Croagh
E4 Croithlí
E4 Crolly
G8 Crookedwood
C15 Crookhaven
D14 Crookstown
E12 Croom
H8 Crossakeel
E14 Cross Barry
E14 Crosshaven
H7 Crossmaglen

D7 Crossmolina
J5 Crumlin
D10 Crusheen
G3 Culdaff
J4 Cullybackey
J12 Curracloe
F9 Curraghboy
E7 Curry
J4 Cushendall
J3 Cushendun

G9 Daingean
J10 Delgany
G8 Delvin
G4 Derry
F6 Derrygonnelly
G6 Derrylin
H3 Dervock
B13 Dingle
J5 Doagh
K5 Donaghadee
G11 Donaghmore
H10 Donard
F5 Donegal
E13 Doneraile
C10 Doolin
E12 Doon
C11 Doonbeg
F9 Doon Cross Roads
E14 Douglas
K6 Downpatrick
F6 Dowra
H5 Draperstown
D15 Drimoleague
E14 Dripsey
J8 Drogheda
E6 Dromahair
D12 Dromcolliher
J6 Dromore
G5 Dromore
D6 Dromore West
E6 Drumcliff
H8 Drumcondra
F7 Drumkeeran
F8 Drumlish
F8 Drumod
G5 Drumquin
F7 Drumshanbo
F7 Drumsna
C12 Duagh
J9 Dublin
J8 Duleek
J9 Dunboyne
H13 Duncormick
J7 Dundalk
K5 Dunderrow
K6 Dundonald
F12 Dundrum
J6 Dundrum
F3 Dunfanaghy
H5 Dungannon
G12 Dungarvan
G13 Dungarvan
H4 Dungiven
E4 Dunglow
F14 Dungourney
E5 Dunkineely
J9 Dún Laoghaire
H10 Dunlavin
J8 Dunleer
J4 Dunloy
D14 Dunmanway
E8 Dunmore
H13 Dunmore East
J5 Dunmurry
H9 Dunshaughlin
G11 Durrow
C15 Durrus
E9 Dysart

D6 Easky
H9 Edenderry
G8 Edgeworthstown
G4 Eglinton
F8 Elphin

H6 Emyvale
H9 Enfield
D11 Ennis
H12 Enniscorthy
D14 Enniskean
F6 Enniskillen
D10 Ennistymon
F10 Eyrecourt

G4 Fahan
C13 Farranfore
E10 Feakle
F7 Fenagh
F9 Ferbane
E13 Fermoy
J12 Ferns
F12 Fethard
H13 Fethard
G8 Finnea
G6 Fintona
G6 Fivemiletown
H10 Fontstown
H12 Foulkesmill
D7 Foxford
D11 Foynes
E13 Freemount
E8 Frenchpark
G11 Freshford
E8 Fuerty

E12 Galbally
D9 Galway
F6 Garrison
J8 Garristown
F14 Garryvoe
H4 Garvagh
G10 Geashill
J6 Gilford
D15 Glandore
E14 Glanmire
E13 Glanworth
H6 Glaslough
F9 Glassan
E5 Gleann Cholm Cille
J4 Glenarm
J5 Glenavy
B13 Glenbeigh
E5 Glencolumbkille
J10 Glenealy
C14 Glengarriff
H12 Glenmore
E8 Glennamaddy
E5 Glenties
D12 Glin
C9 Glinsce
C9 Glinsk
F12 Golden
C15 Goleen
H11 Goresbridge
J11 Gorey
D10 Gort
G5 Gortin
H11 Gowran
H12 Graiguenamanagh
G8 Granard
E6 Grange
J7 Greenore
K5 Greyabbey
J10 Greystones
H4 Gulladuff

H11 Hacketstown
D9 Headford
E12 Herbertstown
J6 Hillsborough
J6 Hilltown
F11 Holycross
G9 Holywood
G9 Horseleap
E12 Hospital
J9 Howth

B13 Inch
D14 Inchigeelagh

E14 Inishannon
D6 Inishcrone
H12 Inistioge
F6 Irvinestown

G11 Johnstown

D13 Kanturk
F7 Keadew
H6 Keady
B7 Keel
F8 Keenagh
J4 Kells
H8 Kells
C14 Kenmare
F5 Kesh
G9 Kilbeggan
H8 Kilberry
E14 Kilbrittan
E5 Kilcar
H9 Kilcock
D10 Kilcolgan
E9 Kilconnell
J10 Kilcoole
F10 Kilcormac
H10 Kilcullen
J7 Kilcurry
H10 Kildare
H11 Kildavin
E13 Kildorrery
D10 Kilfenora
C14 Kilgarvan
C11 Kilkee
J7 Kilkeel
D7 Kilkelly
G11 Kilkenny
C9 Kilkieran
C12 Kilkinlea Lower
H9 Kill
G13 Kill
D11 Killadysert
D6 Killala
E11 Killaloe
C13 Killarney
G7 Killashandra
F14 Killeagh
G10 Killeigh
F12 Killenaule
C11 Killimer
E10 Killimor
J9 Killiney
J13 Killinick
C13 Killorglin
K6 Killough
G9 Killucan
K6 Killyleagh
J10 Kilmacanoge
F4 Kilmacrenan
G13 Kilmacthomas
G12 Kilmaganny
D8 Kilmaine
E12 Kilmallock
G11 Kilmanagh
G13 Kilmeaden
H9 Kilmeage
D12 Kilmeedy
D14 Kilmichael
H13 Kilmore Quay
J12 Kilmuckridge
G8 Kilnaleck
H4 Kilrea
C11 Kilrush
G12 Kilsheelan
D8 Kiltamagh
H12 Kiltealy
H11 Kiltegan
F9 Kiltoom
E6 Kinlough
G9 Kinnegad
F10 Kinnitty
E14 Kinsale
D10 Kinvarra
K5 Kircubbin

D8 Knock
F8 Knockcroghery
F12 Knocklofty
G12 Knocktopher

C10 Lahinch
C8 Lanesborough
J10 Laragh
K4 Larne
C14 Lauragh
F10 Laurencetown
D15 Leap
C8 Leenane
H11 Leighlinbridge
F7 Leitrim
H9 Leixlip
G13 Lemybrien
B8 Letterfrack
F4 Letterkenny
G4 Lifford
H4 Limavady
E11 Limerick
G6 Lisbellaw
J5 Lisburn
C10 Liscannor
D13 Liscarroll
D10 Lisdoonvarna
F13 Lismore
G6 Lisnaskea
G8 Lisryan
C12 Listowel
D12 Loghill
G4 Londonderry
F8 Longford
J6 Loughbrickland
H6 Loughgall

E8 Loughglinn
E10 Loughrea
C8 Louisburgh
J9 Lucan
J6 Lurgan
J9 Lusk

F3 Machair Loiscthe
D14 Macroom
J6 Maghera
H4 Maghera
H5 Magherafelt
G6 Maguiresbridge
J9 Malahide
E5 Málainn Mhóir
G3 Malin
E5 Malin More
E13 Mallow
F6 Manorhamilton
G4 Markethill
H6 Martinstown
H9 Maynooth
J5 Mazetown
H6 Middletown
F14 Midleton
F4 Milford
D13 Millstreet
C13 Milltown
C11 Milltown Malbay
E13 Mitchelstown
F9 Moate
F7 Mohill
H6 Monaghan
G10 Monasterevin
F11 Moneygall
H5 Moneymore

0   10   20 miles
0   10   20   30 kilometres

E9 Monivea	G7 Newbliss	G5 Omagh	G4 Ray	E11 Scarriff
G13 Mooncoin	H10 Newbridge	J7 Omeath	C9 Recess	C13 Scartaglin
J4 Moorfields	J6 Newcastle	E12 Oola	B8 Renvyle	J6 Scarva
E9 Mountbellew Bridge	D12 Newcastle West	D9 Oranmore	E14 Ringaskiddy	C15 Schull
F5 Mountcharles	F12 Newinn	D9 Oughterard	G13 Ringville	F8 Scramoge
G10 Mountmellick	D13 Newmarket	E14 Ovens	H7 Rockcorry	G5 Seskinore
G10 Mountrath	D11 Newmarket-on-Fergus	J9 Portraine	F8 Roosky	F14 Shanagarry
E10 Mountshannon	C7 Newport	E11 Portroe	H12 Rosbercon	D12 Shanagolden
G3 Moville	E11 Newport	H3 Portrush	F8 Roscommon	J9 Shankill
H6 Moy	H12 New Ross	H3 Portstewart	F10 Roscrea	D11 Shannon
H8 Moynalty	J6 Newry	E10 Portumna	F3 Rosepenna	F9 Shannonbridge
F9 Moyvore	G11 Newtown	C13 Poulgorm Bridge	D15 Ross Carbery	H7 Shercock
C13 Muckross	J5 Newtownabbey	J6 Poyntz Pass	E6 Rosses Point	H11 Shillelagh
G4 Muff	K5 Newtownards	G9 Raharney	J13 Rosslare	F10 Shinrone
E6 Mullaghmore	G7 Newtownbutler	J5 Randalstown	J13 Rosslare Harbour	D9 Shrule
G12 Mullinavat	F8 Newtown Forbes	H4 Rasharkin	G6 Rosslea	E11 Silvermines
G9 Mullingar	H6 Newtownhamilton	H10 Rathangan	F5 Rossnowlagh	G5 Sion Mills
C7 Mulrany	J10 Newtown Mount Kennedy	J9 Rathcoole	J7 Rostrevor	D11 Sixmilebridge
H11 Myshall	G5 Newtownstewart	E13 Rathcormack	B9 Roundstone	J8 Skerries
H10 Naas	H8 Nobber	G11 Rathdowney	J10 Roundwood	D15 Skibbereen
J8 Naul		J10 Rathdrum	J9 Rush	H8 Slane
H8 Navan	E11 Ogonnelloe	J6 Rathfriland		E6 Sligo
D8 Neale	H12 Oilgate	D12 Rathkeale	K6 Saintfield	G6 Smithborough
E11 Nenagh	G8 Oldcastle	F4 Rathmelton	G4 St Johnston	B14 Sneem
		D13 Rathmore	H9 Sallins	C11 Spanish Point
		H9 Rathmoylon	D9 Salthill	D9 Spiddal
		G4 Rathmullan		
		J10 Rathnew		
		G8 Rathowen		
		H11 Rathvilly		
		J9 Ratoath		

C9 Sraith Salach	F12 Tipperary
H5 Stewartstown	E7 Tobercurry
J9 Stillorgan	H4 Tobermore
G12 Stonyford	F11 Toomyvara
G4 Strabane	C15 Toormore
G10 Stradbally	C13 Tralee
G7 Stradone	G13 Tramore
H9 Straffan	H8 Trim
E6 Strandhill	D9 Tuam
K6 Strangford	E11 Tuamgraney
F5 Stranorlar	D11 Tulla
F8 Strokestown	G9 Tullamore
H9 Summerhill	H11 Tullow
F6 Swanlinbar	E8 Tulsk
H4 Swatragh	D7 Turlough
D7 Swinford	G9 Tyrrellspass
J9 Swords	
H12 Taghmon	G11 Urlingford
J13 Tagoat	
C14 Tahilla	G8 Virginia
J9 Tallaght	
F13 Tallow	J7 Warrenpoint
F13 Tallowbridge	G13 Waterford
J6 Tandragee	E13 Watergrasshill
F9 Tang	B14 Waterville
C12 Tarbert	C8 Westport
F11 Templemore	J12 Wexford
F11 Templetouhy	E14 Whitegate
J8 Termonfeckin	K5 Whitehead
G12 Thomastown	J10 Wicklow
F11 Thurles	J11 Woodenbridge
G10 Timahoe	E10 Woodford
D15 Timoleague	
J11 Tinahely	F14 Youghal

Restricted junctions

Motorway and Primary Route junctions which have access or exit restrictions are shown thus ⬦3⬦ , ⬦56⬦ on the map pages.

M1 London - Leeds

Northbound
Access only from A1 (northbound)

Southbound
Exit only to A1 (southbound)

Northbound
Access only from A41 (northbound)

Southbound
Exit only to A41 (southbound)

Northbound
Access only from M25 (no link from A405)

Southbound
Exit only to M25 (no link from A405)

Northbound
Access only from A414

Southbound
Exit only to A414

Northbound
Exit only to M45

Southbound
Access only from M45

Northbound
Exit only to M6 (northbound)

Southbound
Access only from M6

Northbound
Exit only, no access

Southbound
Access only, no exit

Northbound
Access only from A42

Southbound
No Restriction

Northbound
No exit, access only

Southbound
Exit only, no access

Northbound
Exit only, no access

Southbound
Access only, no exit

Northbound
Exit only to M621

Southbound
Access only from M621

Northbound
Exit only to A1(M) (northbound)

Southbound
Access only from A1(M) (southbound)

M2 Rochester - Faversham

Westbound
No exit to A2 (eastbound)

Eastbound
No access from A2 (westbound)

M3 Sunbury - Southampton

Northeastbound
Access only from A303, no exit

Southwestbound
Exit only to A303, no access

Northbound
Exit only, no access

Southbound
Access only, no exit

Northeastbound
Access from M27 only. No exit

Southwestbound
No access to M27 (westbound)

M4 London - South Wales

Westbound
Access only from A4 (westbound)

Eastbound
Exit only to A4 (eastbound)

Westbound
No exit to A4 (westbound)

Eastbound
No restriction

Westbound
Exit only to M48

Eastbound
Access only from M48

Westbound
Access only from M48

Eastbound
Exit only to M48

Westbound
Exit only, no access

Eastbound
Access only, no exit

Westbound
Exit only, no access

Eastbound
Access only, no exit

Westbound
Exit only to A48(M)

Eastbound
Access only from A48(M)

Westbound
Exit only, no access

Eastbound
No restriction

Westbound
Access only, no exit

Eastbound
No access or exit

M5 Birmingham - Exeter

Northeastbound
Access only, no exit

Southwestbound
Exit only, no access

Northeastbound
Access only from A417 (westbound)

Southwestbound
Exit only to A417 (eastbound)

Northeastbound
No access, exit only

Southwestbound
No exit, access only

Northeastbound
Exit only to M49

Southwestbound
Access only from M49

Northeastbound
No restriction

Southwestbound
Access only from A30 (westbound)

M6 Toll Motorway

See M6 Toll Motorway map on page 121

M6 Rugby - Carlisle

Northbound
Exit only to M6 Toll

Southbound
Access only from M6 Toll

Northbound
Access only from M42 (southbound)

Southbound
Exit only to M42

Northbound
Exit only, no access

Southbound
Access only, no exit

Northbound
Exit only to M54

Southbound
Access only from M54

Northbound
Access only from M6 Toll

Southbound
Exit only to M6 Toll

Northbound
No restriction

Southbound
Access only from M56 (eastbound)

Northbound
Access only, no exit

Southbound
No restriction

Northbound
Access only, no exit

Southbound
Exit only, no access

Northbound
No direct access, use adjacent slip road to jct 29A

Southbound
No direct exit, use adjacent slip road from jct 29A

Northbound
Access only, no exit

Southbound
Exit only, no access

Northbound
Access only from M61

Southbound
Exit only to M61

Northbound
Exit only, no access

Southbound
Access only, no exit

Northbound
Exit only, no access

Southbound
Access only, no exit

M8 Edinburgh - Bishopton

See Glasgow District map on pages 138-139

M9 Edinburgh - Dunblane

Northwestbound
Exit only to M9 spur

Southeastbound
Access only from M9 spur

Northwestbound
Access only, no exit

Southeastbound
Exit only, no access

Northwestbound
Exit only, no access

Southeastbound
Access only, no exit

Northwestbound
Access only, no exit

Southeastbound
Exit only to A905

Northwestbound
Exit only to M876 (southwestbound)

Southeastbound
Access only from M876 (northeastbound)

M11 London - Cambridge

Northbound
Access only from A406 (eastbound)

Southbound
Exit only to A406

Northbound
Exit only, no access

Southbound
Access only, no exit

Northbound
Exit only to A11

Southbound
Access only from A11

Northbound
Exit only, no access

Southbound
Access only, no exit

Northbound
Exit only, no access

Southbound
Access only, no exit

M20 Swanley - Folkestone

Northwestbound
Staggered junction; follow signs - access only

Southeastbound
Staggered junction; follow signs - exit only

Northwestbound
Exit only to M26 (westbound)

Southeastbound
Access only from M26 (eastbound)

Northwestbound
Access only from A20

Southeastbound
For access follow signs - exit only to A20

Northwestbound
No restriction

Southeastbound
For exit follow signs

Northwestbound
Access only, no exit

Southeastbound
Exit only, no access

M23 Hooley - Crawley

Northbound
Exit only to A23 (northbound)

Southbound
Access only from A23 (southbound)

Northbound
Access only, no exit

Southbound
Exit only, no access

M25 London Orbital Motorway

See M25 London Orbital Motorway map on page 120

M26 Sevenoaks - Wrotham

Westbound
Exit only to clockwise M25 (westbound)

Eastbound
Access only from anti-clockwise M25 (eastbound)

Westbound
Access only from M20 (northwestbound)

Eastbound
Exit only to M20 (southeastbound)

M27 Cadnam - Portsmouth

Westbound
Staggered junction; follow signs - access only from M3 (southbound). Exit only to M3 (northbound)

Eastbound
Staggered junction; follow signs - access only from M3 (southbound). Exit only to M3 (northbound)

Westbound
Exit only, no access

Eastbound
Access only, no exit

Westbound
Staggered junction; follow signs - exit only to M275 (southbound)

Eastbound
Staggered junction; follow signs - access only from M275 (northbound)

M40 London - Birmingham

Northwestbound
Exit only, no access

Southeastbound
Access only, no exit

Northwestbound
Exit only, no access

Southeastbound
Access only, no exit

Northwestbound
Exit only to M40/A40

Southeastbound
Access only from M40/A40

Northwestbound
Exit only, no access

Southeastbound
Access only, no exit

Northwestbound
Access only, no exit

Southeastbound
Exit only, no access

Northwestbound
Access only, no exit

Southeastbound
Exit only, no access

M42 Bromsgrove - Measham

See Birmingham District map on pages 136-137

M45 Coventry - M1

Westbound
Access only from A45 (northbound)

Eastbound
Exit only, no access

Westbound
Access only from M1 (northbound)

Eastbound
Exit only to M1 (southbound)

M53 Mersey Tunnel - Chester

Northbound
Access only from M56 (westbound). Exit only to M56 (eastbound)

Southbound
Access only from M56 (westbound). Exit only to M56 (westbound)

M54 Telford

Westbound
Access only from M6 (northbound)

Eastbound
Exit only to M6 (southbound)

M56 North Cheshire

For junctions 1,2,3,4 & 7 see Manchester District map on pages 140-141

Westbound
Access only, no exit

Eastbound
No access or exit

Westbound
Exit only to M53

Eastbound
Access only from M53

M57 Liverpool Outer Ring Road

Northwestbound
Access only, no exit

Southeastbound
Exit only, no access

Northwestbound
Access only from A580 (westbound)

Southeastbound
Exit only, no access

M58 Liverpool - Wigan

Westbound
Exit only, no access

Eastbound
Access only, no exit

M60 Manchester Orbital

See Manchester District map on pages 140-141

M61 Manchester - Preston

Northwestbound
No access or exit

Southeastbound
Exit only

Northwestbound
Exit only to M6 (northbound)

Southeastbound
Access only from M6 (southbound)

M62 Liverpool - Kingston upon Hull

Westbound
Access only, no exit

Eastbound
Exit only, no access

M65 Preston - Colne

Northeastbound
Exit only, no access

Southwestbound
Access only, no exit

Northeastbound
Access only, no exit

Southwestbound
Exit only, no access

M66 Bury

Northbound
Exit only to A56 (northbound)

Southbound
Access only from A56 (southbound)

Northbound
Exit only, no access

Southbound
Access only, no exit

M67 Hyde Bypass

Westbound
Access only, no exit

Eastbound
Exit only, no access

Westbound
Exit only, no access

Eastbound
Access only, no exit

Westbound
Exit only, no access

Eastbound
No restriction

M69 Coventry - Leicester

Northbound
Access only, no exit

Southbound
Exit only, no access

M73 East of Glasgow

Northbound
No access from or exit to A89. No access from M8 (eastbound)

Southbound
No access from or exit to A89. No exit to M8 (westbound)

Northbound
Exit only to A80 (northeastbound)

Southbound
Access only from A80 (southwestbound)

M74 and A74(M) Glasgow - Gretna

Northbound
Exit only, no access

Southbound
Access only, no exit

Northbound
Access only, no exit

Southbound
Exit only, no access

(M74 continued)

Northbound
Access only, no exit

Southbound
Exit only, no access

Northbound
No access or exit

Southbound
Exit only, no access

Northbound
No restriction

Southbound
Access only, no exit

Northbound
Access only, no exit

Southbound
Exit only, no access

Northbound
Exit only, no access

Southbound
Access only, no exit

Northbound
Exit only, no access

Southbound
Access only, no exit

M77 South of Glasgow

Northbound
No exit to M8 (westbound)

Southbound
No access from M8 (eastbound)

Northbound
Access only, no exit

Southbound
Exit only, no access

Northbound
Access only, no exit

Southbound
Exit only, no access

Northbound
Access only, no exit

Southbound
No restriction

M80 Stepps Bypass

See Glasgow District map on pages 138-139

M80 Bonnybridge - Stirling

Northbound
Exit only, no access

Southbound
Access only, no exit

Northbound
Exit only to M876 (northeastbound)

Southbound
Access only from M876 (southwestbound)

M90 Forth Road Bridge - Perth

Northbound
Exit only to A92 (eastbound)

Southbound
Access only from A92 (westbound)

Northbound
Access only, no exit

Southbound
Exit only, no access

Northbound
Access only, no exit

Southbound
Access only, no exit

Northbound
No access from A912. No exit to A912

Southbound
No access from A912 (northbound). No exit to A912

M180 Doncaster - Grimsby

Westbound
Access only, no exit

Eastbound
Exit only, no access

M606 Bradford Spur

Northbound
Exit only, no access

Southbound
No restriction

M621 Leeds - M1

Clockwise
Access only, no exit

Anticlockwise
Exit only, no access

Clockwise
No exit or access

Anticlockwise
No restriction

Clockwise
Access only, no exit

Anticlockwise
Exit only, no access

Clockwise
Exit only, no access

Anticlockwise
Access only, no exit

Northbound
No access. Exit only to A194(M) & A1 (northbound)

Southbound
No exit. Access only from A194(M) & A1 (southbound)

Northeastbound
Access only, no exit

Southwestbound
Exit only, no access

Westbound
Access only, no exit

Eastbound
Exit only, no access

Clockwise
Exit only to M1 (southbound)

Anticlockwise
Access only from M1 (northbound)

A3(M) Horndean - Havant

Northbound
Access only from A3

Southbound
Exit only to A3

Northeastbound
No restriction

Southwestbound
Access only, no exit

Westbound
Exit only to A11

Eastbound
Access only from A11

M876 Bonnybridge - Kincardine Bridge

Northeastbound
Access only from M80 (northbound)

Southwestbound
Exit only to M80 (southbound)

Northbound
Exit only, no access

Southbound
Access only, no exit

Northeastbound
Exit only, no access

Southwestbound
Access only, no exit

Westbound
Access only from A11

Eastbound
Exit only to A11

Northeastbound
Exit only to M9 (eastbound)

Southwestbound
Access only from M9 (westbound)

A48(M) Cardiff Spur

Westbound
Access only from M4 (westbound)

Eastbound
Exit only to M4 (eastbound)

Northeastbound
Access only, no exit

Southwestbound
Exit only, no access

Westbound
Exit only, no access

Eastbound
Access only, no exit

A1(M) South Mimms - Baldock

Northbound
Exit only, no access

Southbound
Access only, no exit

Westbound
Exit only to A48 (westbound)

Eastbound
Access only from A48 (eastbound)

Northeastbound
Exit only, no access

Southwestbound
Access only, no exit

Westbound
Access only, no exit

Eastbound
Exit only, no access

A66(M) Darlington Spur

Northbound
No restriction

Southbound
Exit only, no access

Westbound
Exit only to A1(M) (southbound)

Eastbound
Access only from A1(M) (northbound)

With A120
Northeastbound
Exit only, no access

Southwestbound
Access only, no exit

A55 Holyhead - Chester

Westbound
Exit only, no access

Eastbound
Access only, no exit

Northbound
Access only, no exit

Southbound
No access or exit

A194(M) Newcastle upon Tyne

Northbound
Access only from A1(M) (northbound)

Southbound
Exit only to A1(M) (southbound)

Northeastbound
Access only, no exit

Southwestbound
Exit only, no access

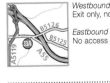
Westbound
Access only, no exit

Eastbound
Exit only, no access

A1(M) East of Leeds

Northbound
Access only from M1 (northbound)

Southbound
Exit only to M1 (southbound)

Northeastbound
Exit only (for Stratford St Mary and Dedham)

Southwestbound
Access only

A14 M1 Felixstowe

Westbound
Exit only, no access

Eastbound
No access or exit.

A12 M25 - Ipswich

Northeastbound
Access only, no exit

Southwestbound
No restriction

Westbound
Exit only to M6 & M1 (northbound)

Eastbound
Access only from M6 & M1 (southbound)

Westbound
Exit only, no access

Eastbound
No access or exit

A1(M) Scotch Corner - Newcastle upon Tyne

Northeastbound
Exit only, no access

Southwestbound
Access only, no exit

Westbound
Exit only, no access

Eastbound
Access only, no exit

Westbound
Exit only, no access

Eastbound
Access only, no exit

Northbound
Exit only to A66(M) (eastbound)

Southbound
Access only from A66(M) (westbound)

Northeastbound
Exit only, no access

Southwestbound
Access only, no exit

Westbound
Access only from A1307

Eastbound
Exit only to A1307

Westbound
Exit only to A5104

Eastbound
Access only from A5104

M25 London Orbital motorway

Refer also to atlas pages 20–21

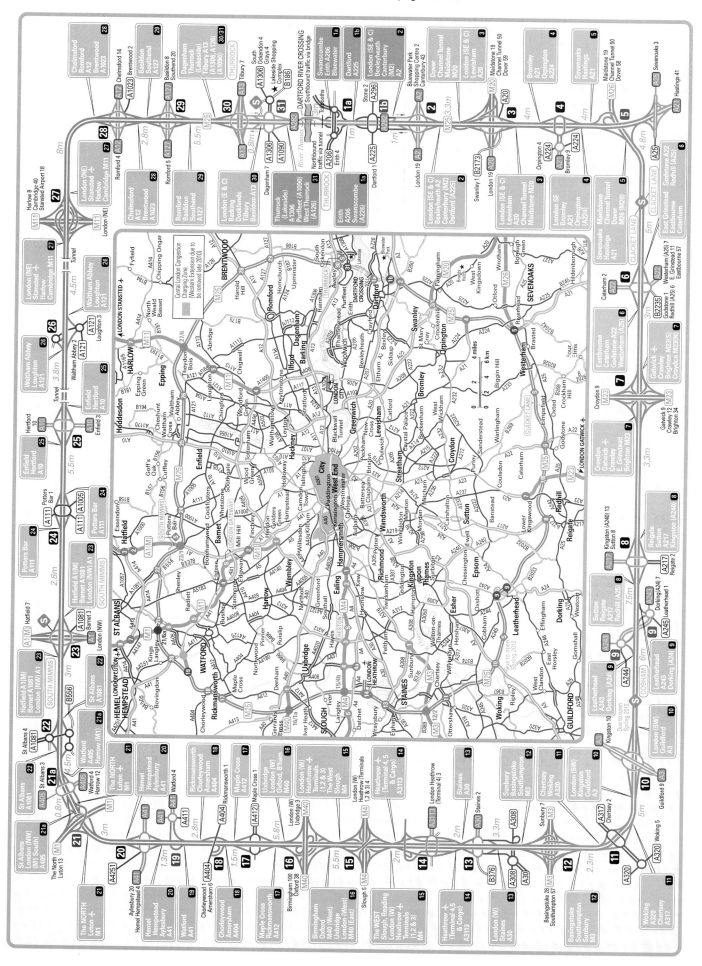

M6 Toll motorway

Refer also to atlas page 40

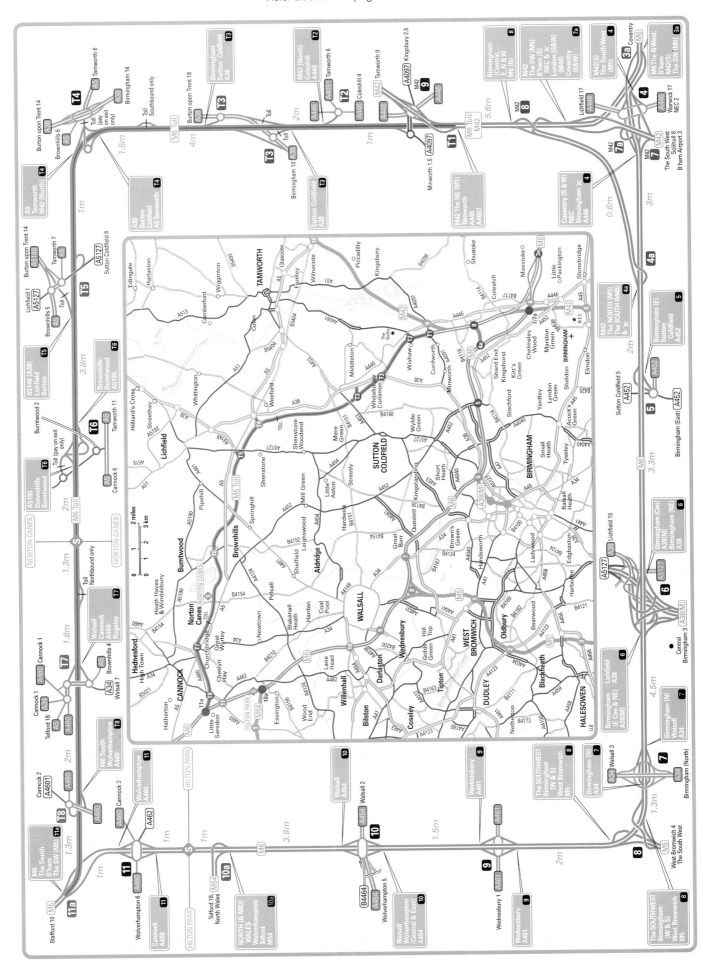

Street map symbols

Town plans   For key to touring information see page 1

M8 Motorway with number	B road	Restricted road/ pedestrians only	← One-way street
Primary road	Other road	**COLLEGE** Building of interest	**P** Car park
A road	6 3 Numbered junction	⊙ World Heritage Site (UNESCO)	**P+** Park and Ride (at least 6 days per week)
H 24-hour Accident & Emergency hospital	*i* Tourist Information Centre		
Toilet, with facilities for the less able	⊶ Light rapid transit system (with station)		
Shopmobility	✝ Church/chapel		

District maps (see pages 136–147)   For key to touring information see page 1

M42 Motorway with number	Unclassified road single/dual	● Railway station	⊖ Docklands Light Railway (DLR) station
M6 Toll M6 Toll motorway (Birmingham district)	Road under construction	○ Light rapid transit system station	**H** **N** 24-hour Accident & Emergency, hospital
Primary route single/dual	Restricted road	⊖ London Underground station (TfL)	**C** Crematorium
Other A road single/dual	Railway line/in tunnel	⊖ London Overground station (TfL)	Central London Congestion Charging Zone
B road single/dual	┼┼┼┼┼ Tourist railway	⬮ Railway station/TfL interchange	Charge free route through the Charging Zone

Central London street map (see pages 148–157)

Primary route single/dual	Minor/private road (access may be restricted)	**P** Car park	Cathedral, church/chapel ✝
Other A road single/dual	Track or footpath	Filling station open 24-hours/not 24-hour (main suppliers only)	**M** Museum or art gallery
B road single/dual	Pedestrian street	Toilet, with facilities for the less able	Theatre or performing arts centre, cinema
Unclassified road single/dual	Railway line	**PO** Post Office, public library	AA inspected restaurant
Road under construction	← One-way street	**H** 24-hour Accident & Emergency hospital	*i* Tourist Information Centre (open all year)
Road tunnel	⇄ Railway station	Historic house or building, National Trust property	Park or open space, woodland
30 Speed camera site (fixed location) with speed limit in mph	*LC* Level crossing	Building of interest	Cemetery
40 Section of road with two or more fixed camera sites; speed limit in mph	⊖ ⊖ London Underground/ Overground station (TfL)	⊙ World Heritage Site (UNESCO)	Central London Congestion Charging Zone boundary
50→ ←50 Average speed (SPECS™) camera system with speed limit in mph	⊖ Docklands Light Railway (DLR) station	⧉ English Heritage site	Charge free route through the Charging Zone

Royal Parks (opening and closing times for traffic)
Green Park   Constitution Hill: closed Sundays, 8 am–dusk
Hyde Park   Open 5 am–midnight
Regent's Park   Open 5 am–midnight
St James's Park   The Mall: closed Sundays, 8 am–dusk

Traffic regulations in the City of London include security checkpoints and restrict the number of entry and exit points.

Note: Oxford Street is closed to through-traffic (except buses & taxis) 7 am–7 pm Monday-Saturday. Restricted parts of Frith Street/Old Compton Street are closed to vehicles 12 noon–1 am daily.

Central London Congestion Charging Zone
The charge for driving or parking on public roads in the Congestion Charging Zone (CCZ) is £8 per vehicle per day. Payment permits entry, travel within and exit from the CCZ by the vehicle as often as required on that day. A higher charge (£25) applies to certain vehicles, including some older vehicles that produce high levels of CO_2. The CCZ operates between 7am and 6pm, Mon–Fri only. There is no charge at weekends, public holidays or betwen 25th Dec and 1st Jan inclusive.

For up to date information on the CCZ, exemptions, discounts or ways to pay, telephone 0845 900 1234, visit www.cclondon.com or write to Congestion Charging, P.O. Box 4782, Worthing BN11 9PS.

Western Extension
Following informal consultation in 2008 with the public, businesses and other organisations, Transport for London submitted recommendations to the Mayor of London for the removal of the Western extension from the CCZ as part of a broader revision of the Mayor's Transport Strategy. Together with changes to the Congestion Charging scheme covering the original zone, the earliest that this would take effect would be late 2010.

Town and port plans

Town plan contents

Page	
103	Aberdeen
36	Aberystwyth
123	Basingstoke
123	Bath
124	Birmingham
124	Blackpool
124	Bournemouth
124	Bradford
125	Brighton
125	Bristol
125	Cambridge
125	Canterbury
126	Cardiff
126	Carlisle
126	Chester
126	Coventry
127	Derby
127	Dundee
127	Edinburgh
127	Exeter
128	Glasgow
128	Ipswich
128	Kingston upon Hull
128	Leeds
129	Leicester
129	Liverpool
148–157	LONDON
129	Manchester
129	Middlesbrough
130	Milton Keynes
130	Newcastle upon Tyne
3	Newquay

Page	
130	Norwich
130	Nottingham
131	Oxford
131	Peterborough
131	Plymouth
131	Portsmouth
23	Ramsgate
132	Reading
132	Salisbury
67	Scarborough
132	Sheffield
132	Shrewsbury
133	Southampton
133	Stoke-on-Trent (Hanley)
133	Stratford-upon-Avon
133	Sunderland
134	Swansea
134	Taunton
134	Tunbridge Wells
134	Warwick
135	Watford
135	Winchester
135	Worcester
135	York

Ferry Ports

Page	
95	Aberdeen Harbour
11	Boulogne
11	Calais
11	Dover Port
13	Fishguard Harbour
13	Fleetwood, Port of
35	Harwich International Port
13	Heysham Harbour
13	Holyhead Harbour
61	Hull Port
13	Liverpool Docks
11	Newhaven Harbour
11	Pembroke Dock
10	Plymouth Ferry Port
10	Poole Harbour
73	Port of Tyne
11	Portsmouth Harbour
87	Rosyth Harbour
13	Stranraer Ferry Port
13	Swansea, Port of
10	Weymouth Harbour

Channel Tunnel

Page	
13	Folkestone Terminal
13	Calais / Coquelles Terminal

Central London

Basingstoke Bath

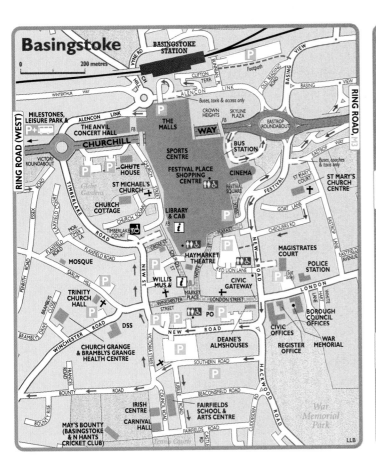

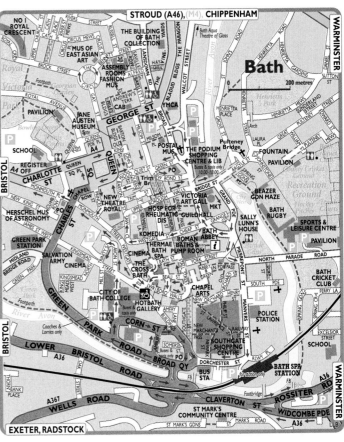

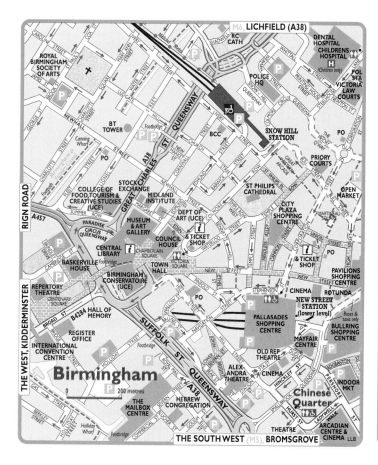

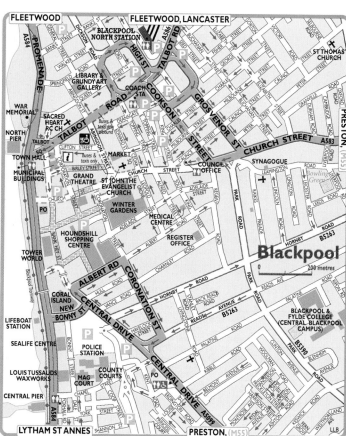

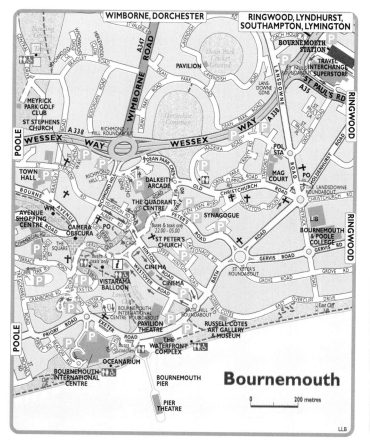

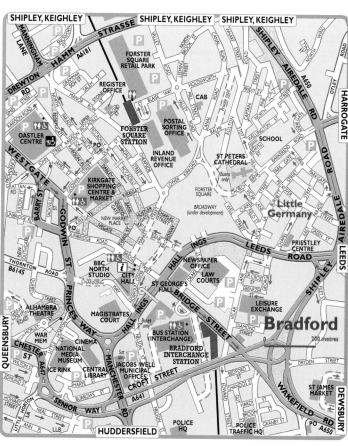

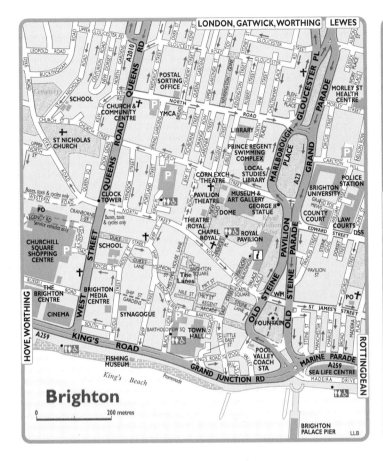

Brighton

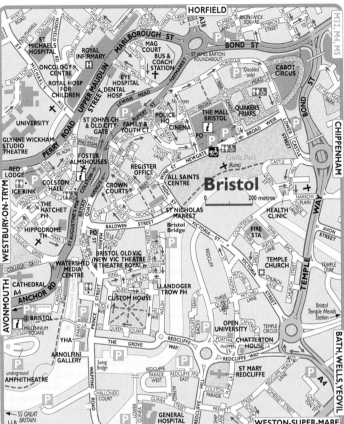

Bristol

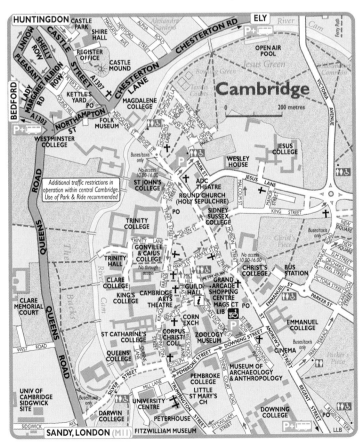

Cambridge

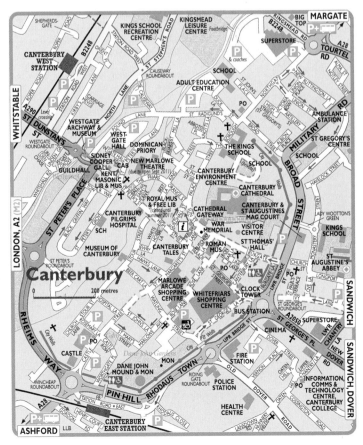

Canterbury

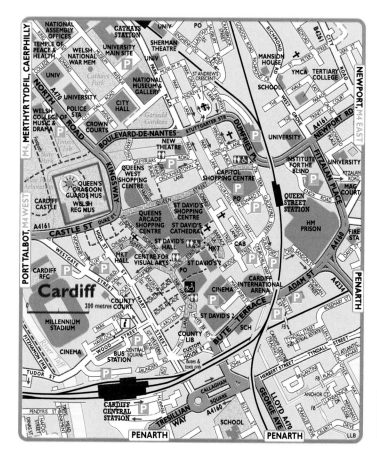

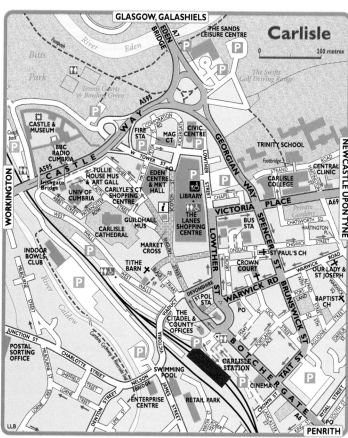

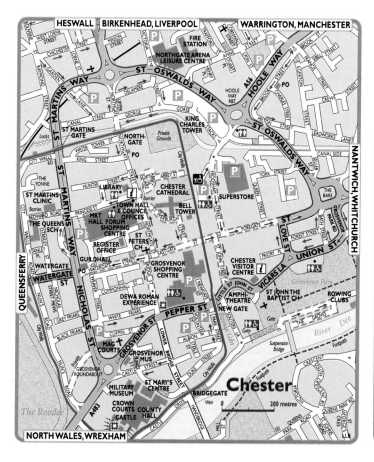

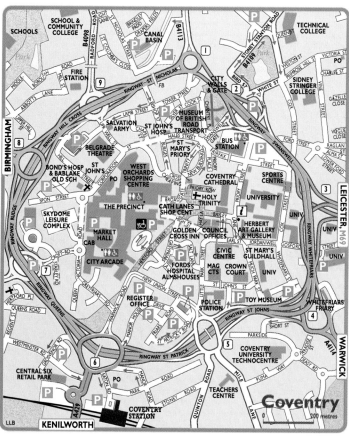

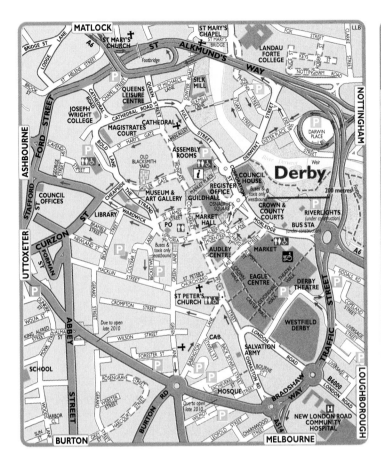

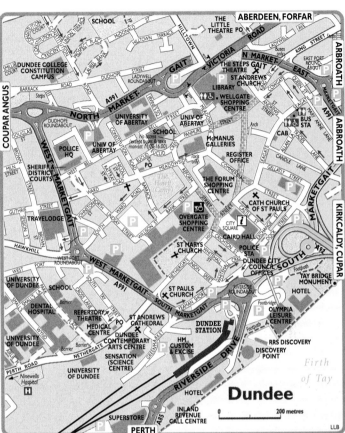

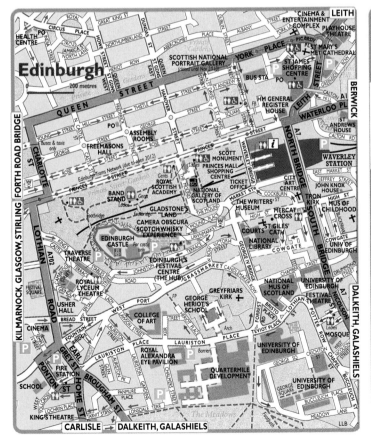

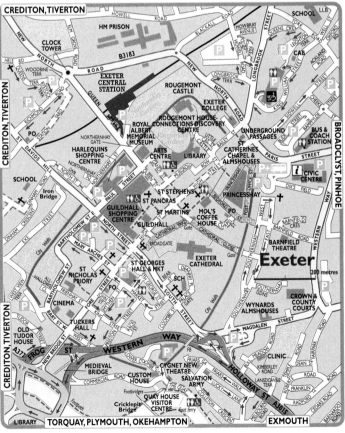

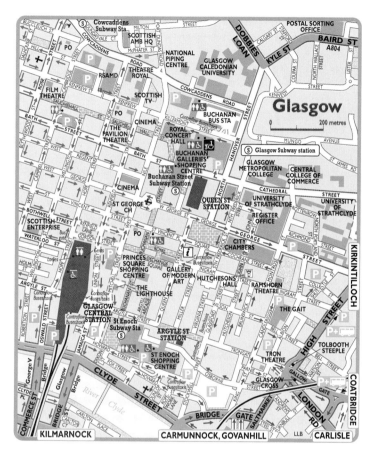

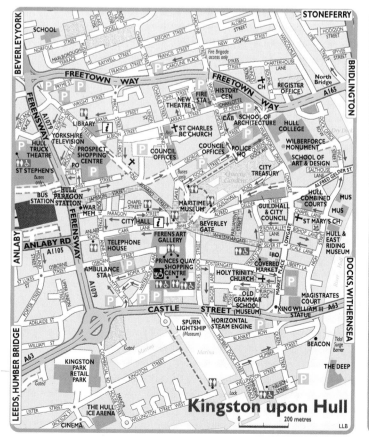

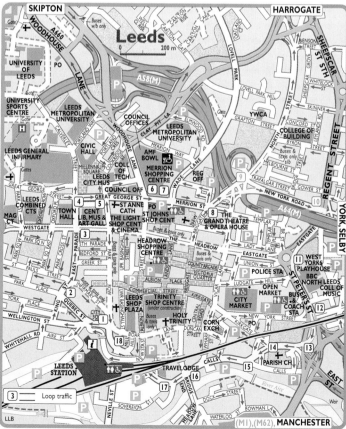

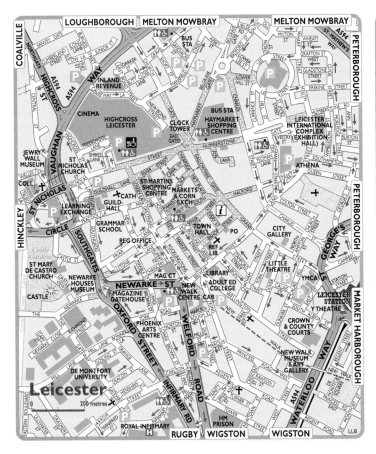

Leicester

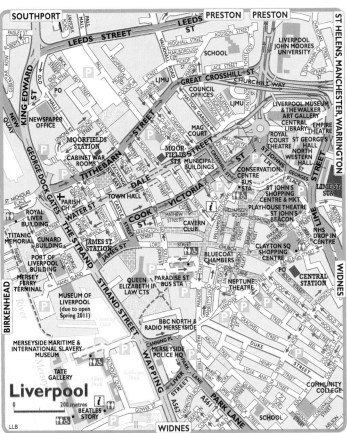

Liverpool

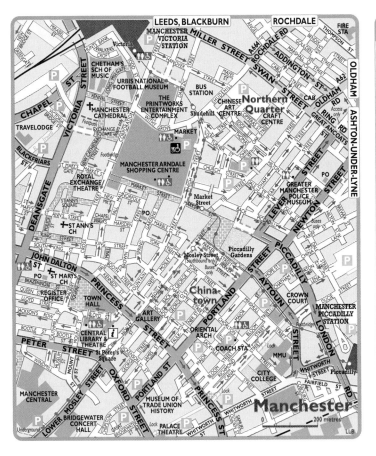

Manchester

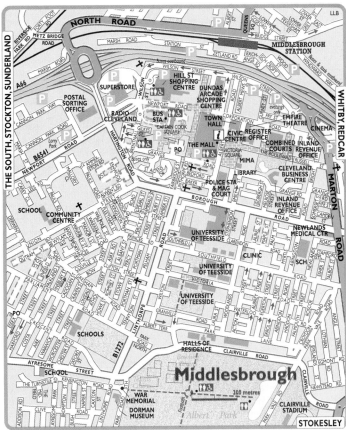

Middlesbrough

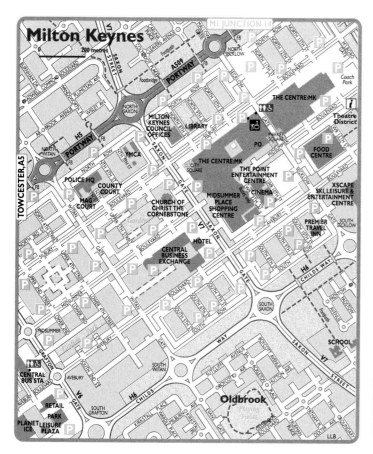

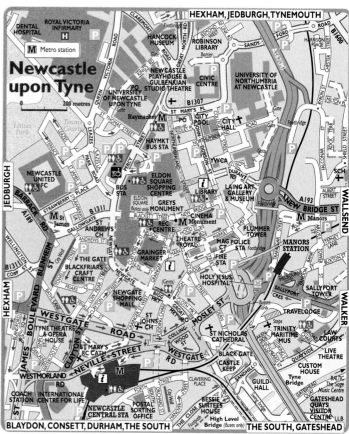

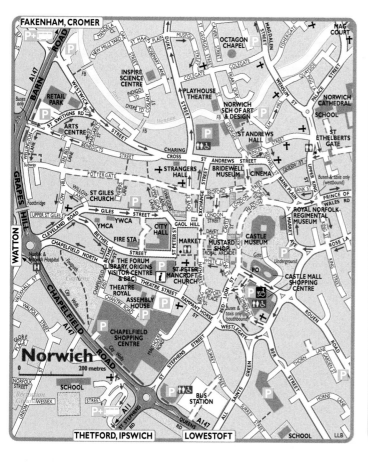

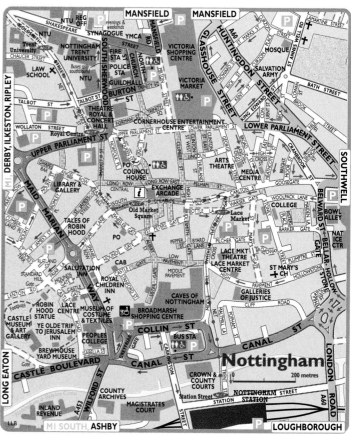

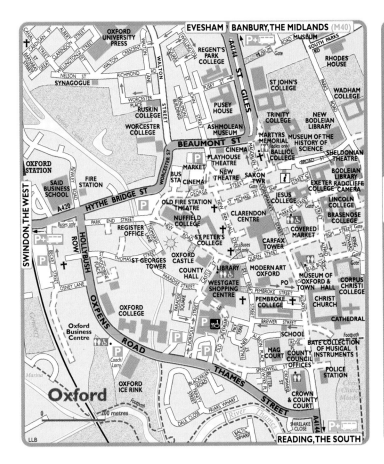

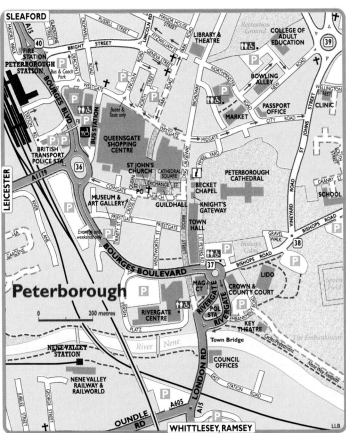

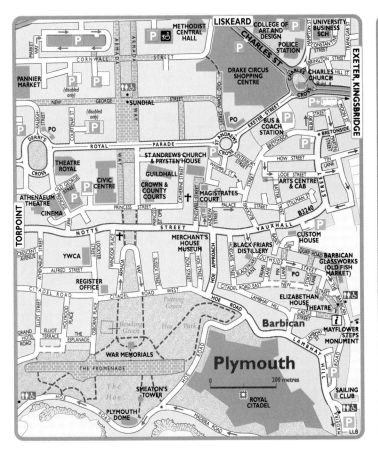

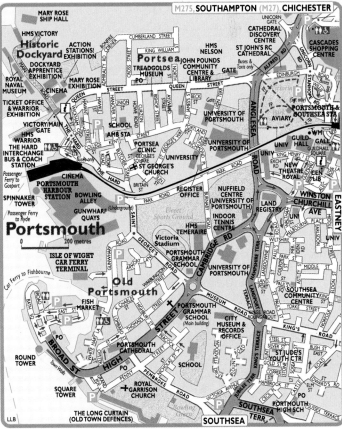

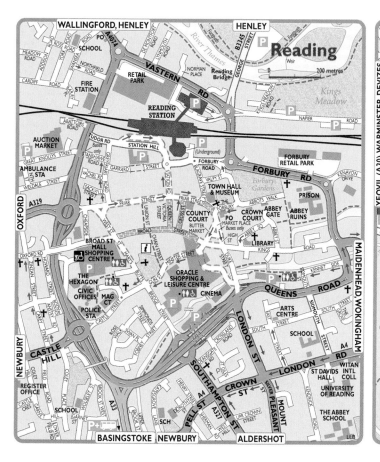

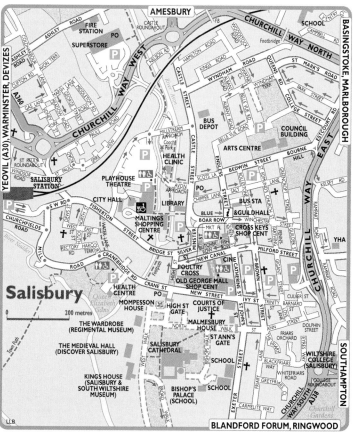

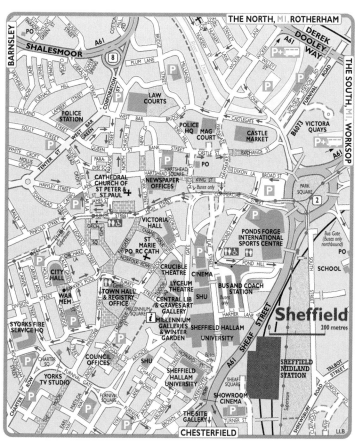

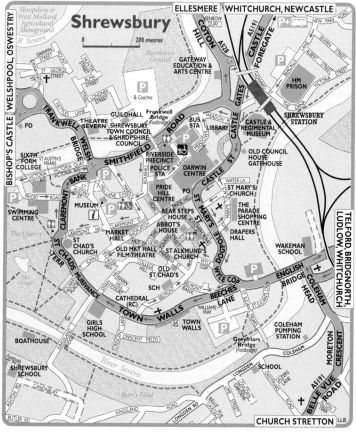

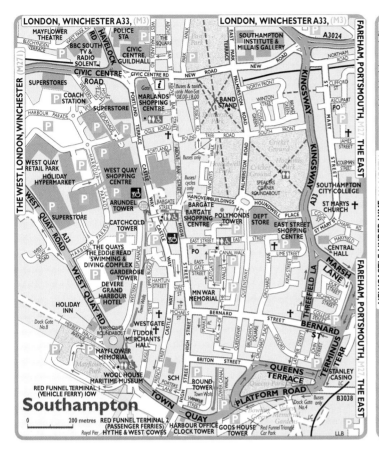

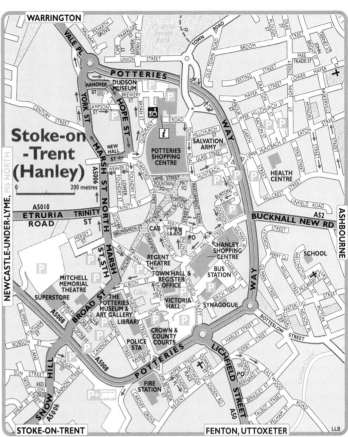

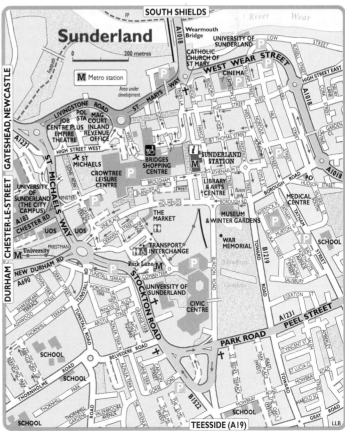

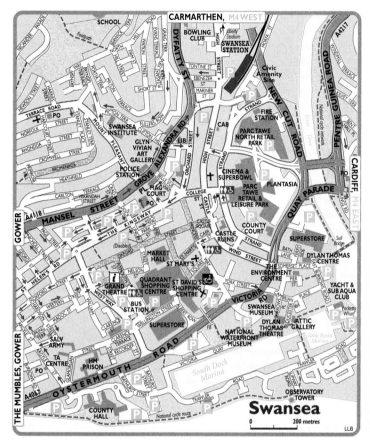

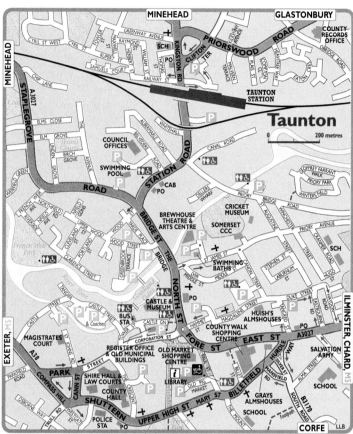

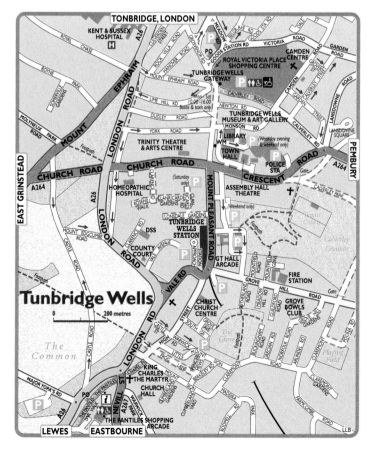

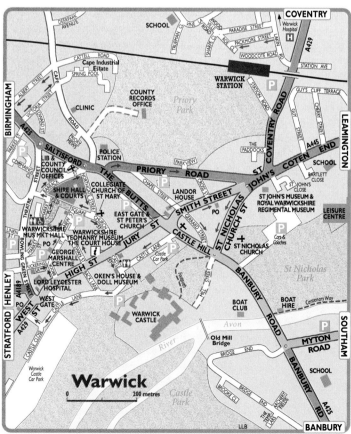

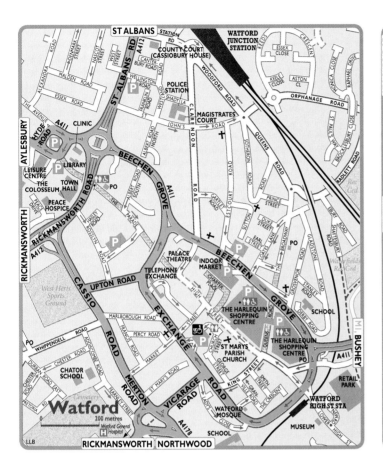

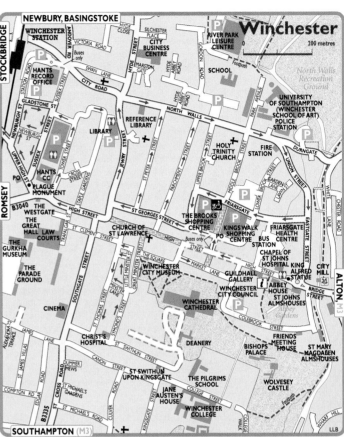

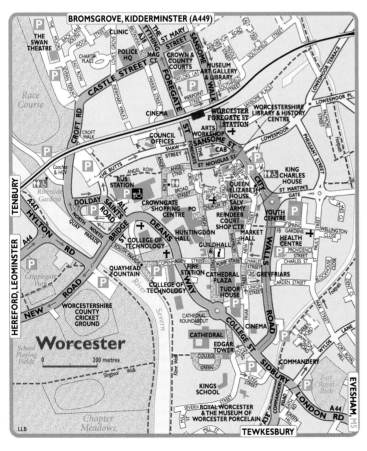

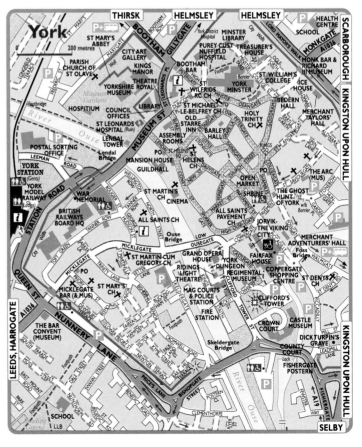

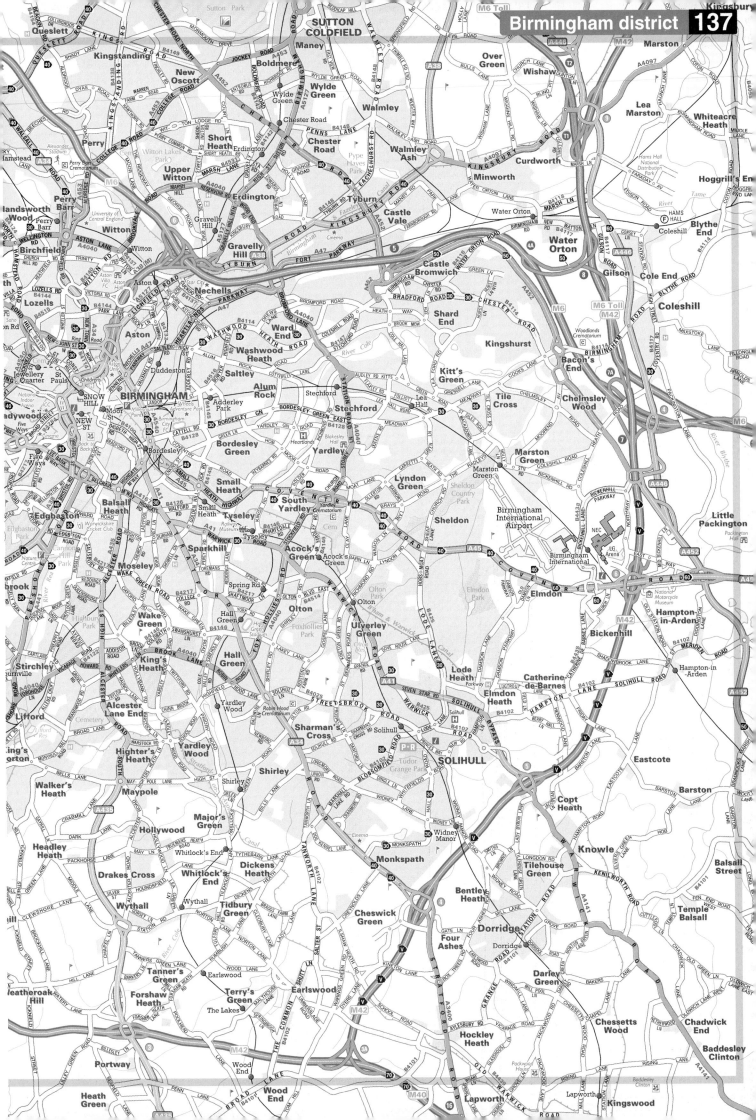

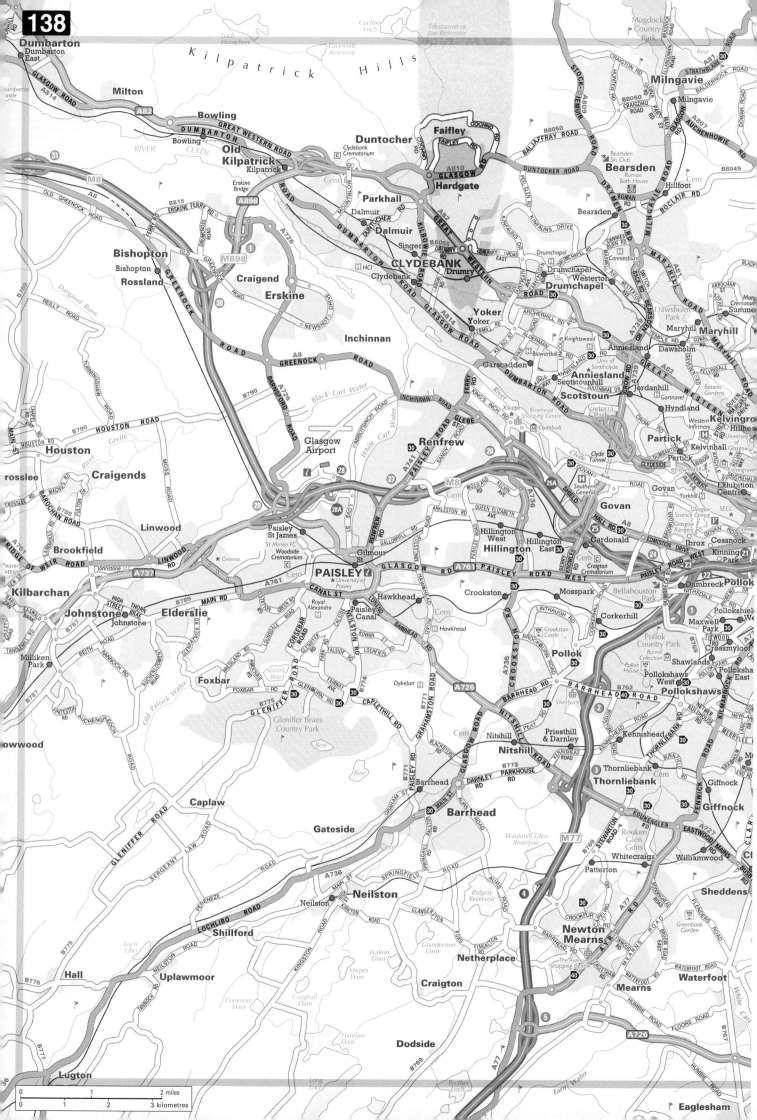

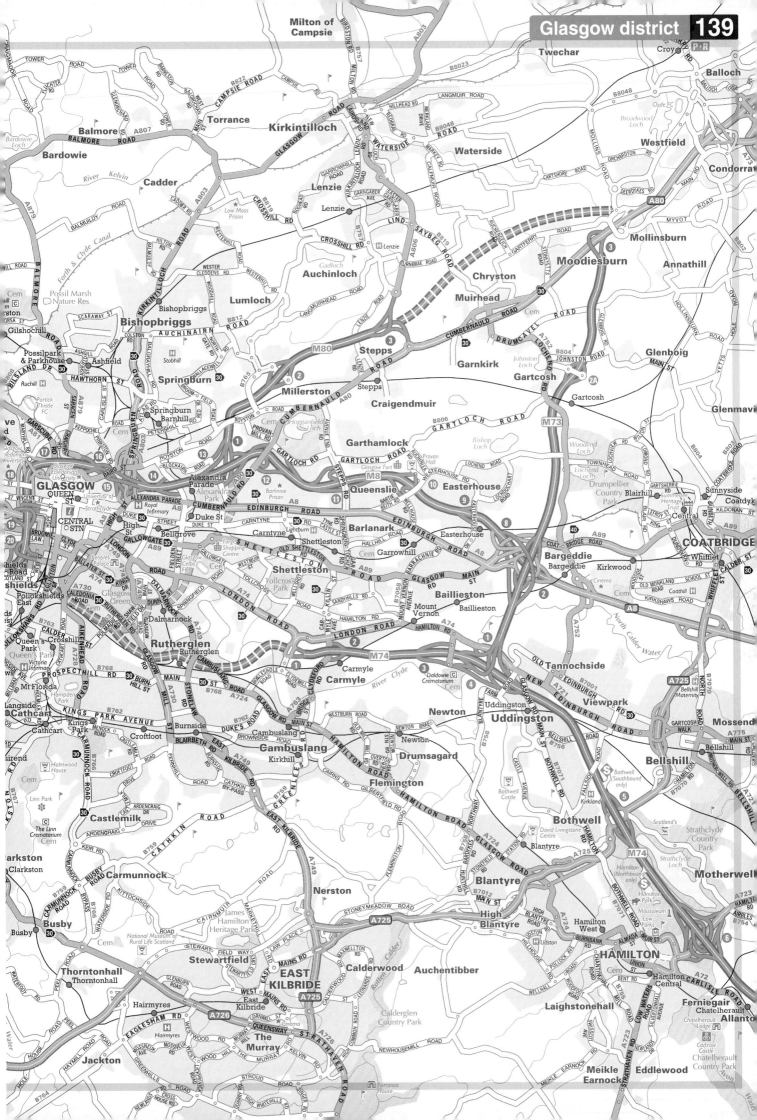

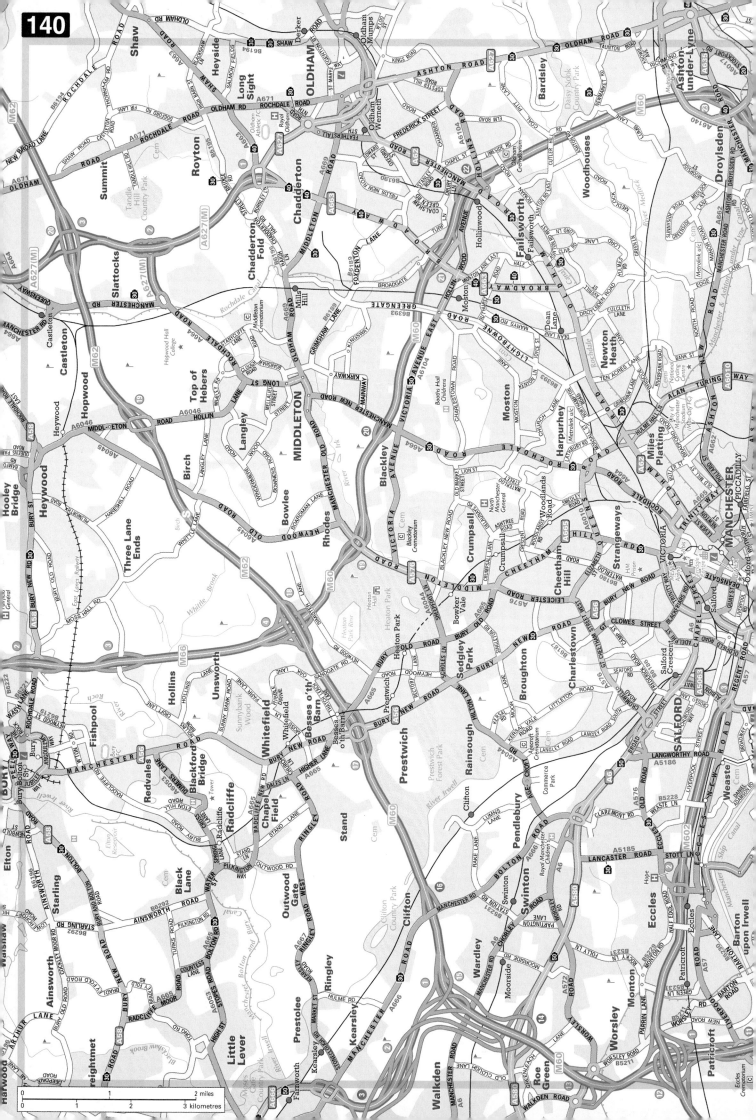

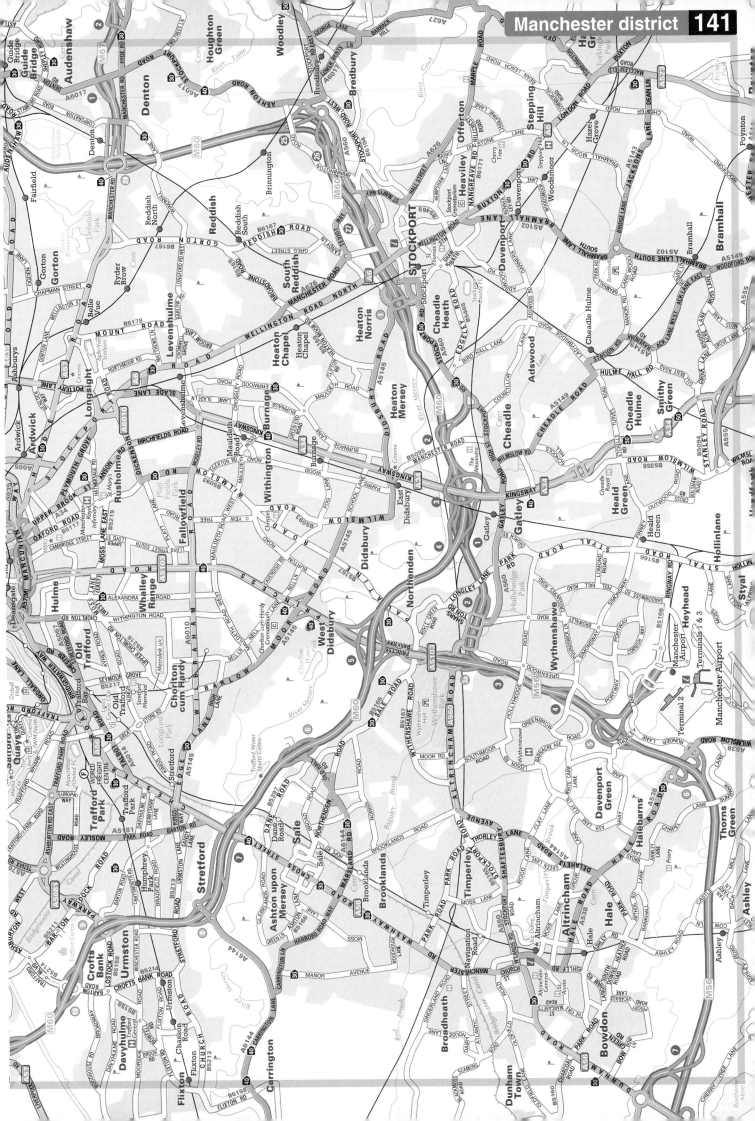

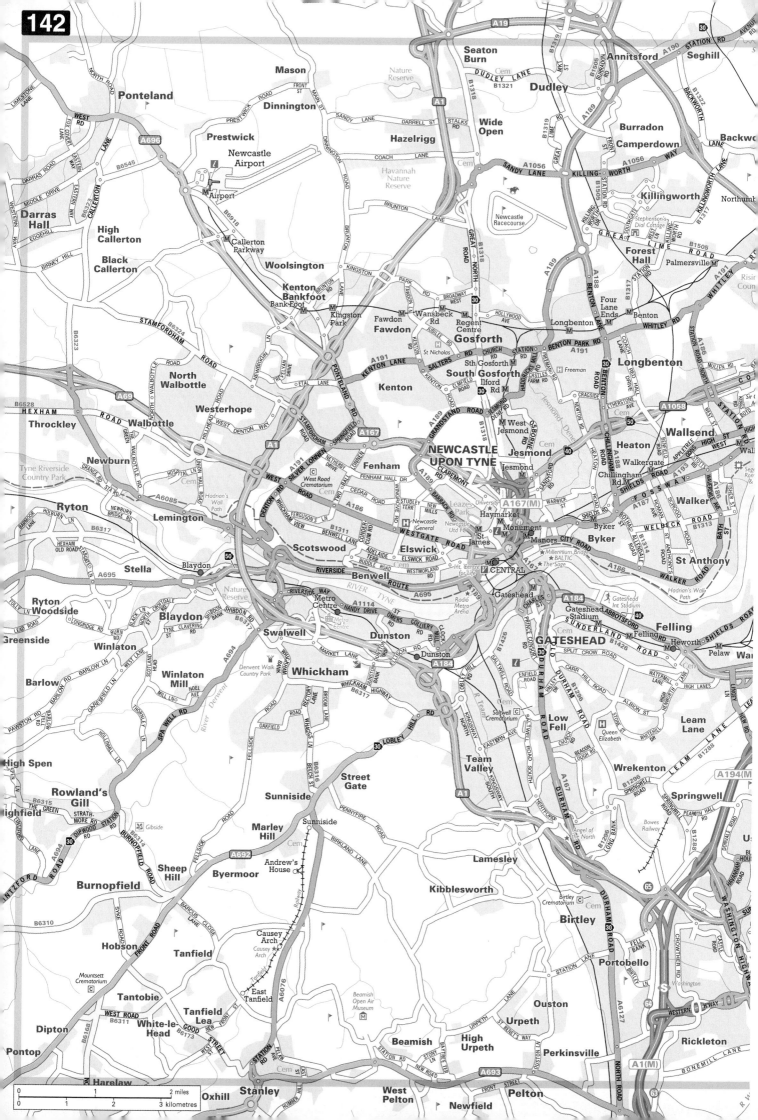

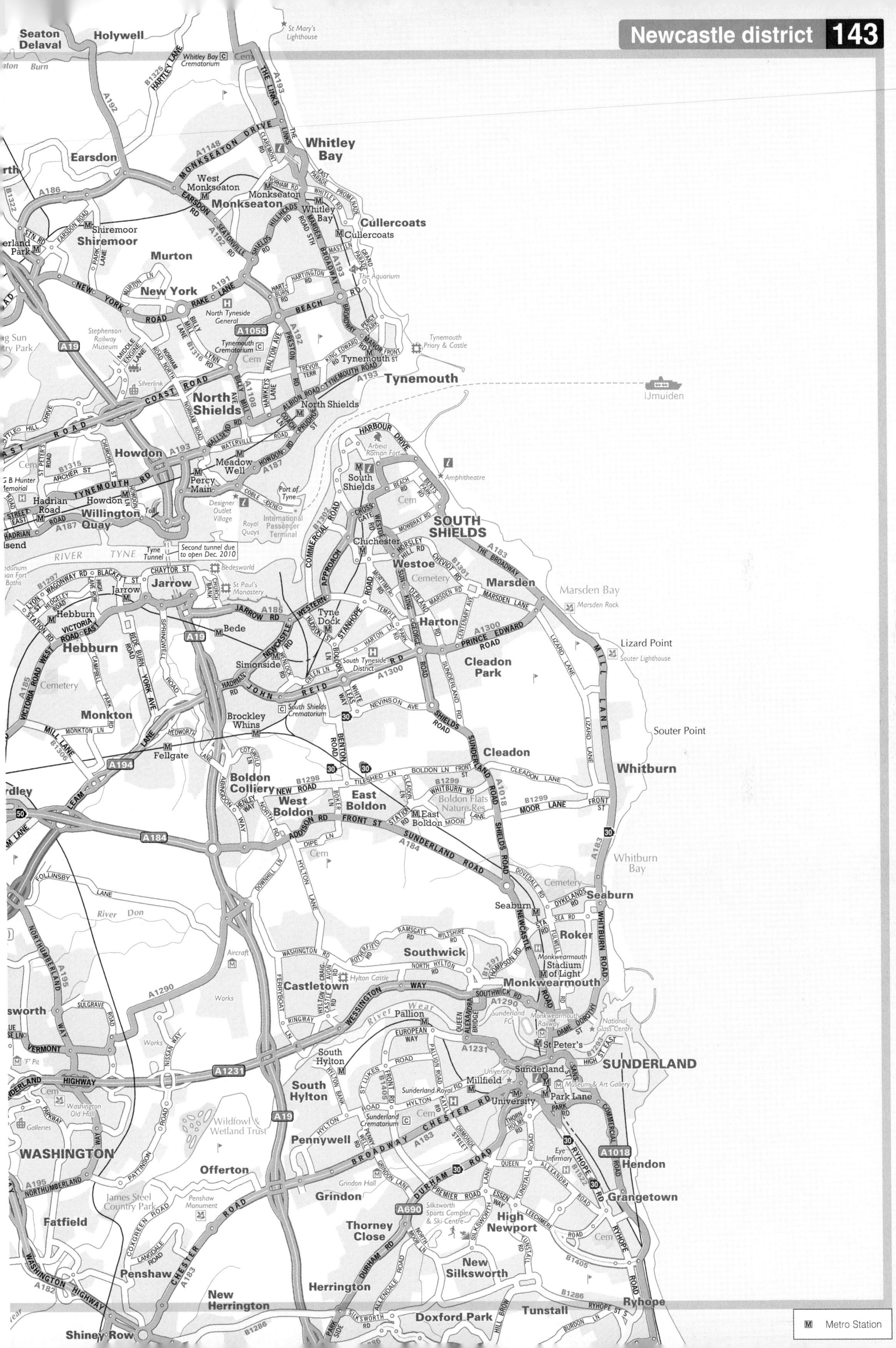

Seaton Delaval Holywell St Mary's Lighthouse

Earsdon West Monkseaton Monkseaton Whitley Bay Cullercoats

Shiremoor Murton New York Whitley Bay Cullercoats The Aquarium

Stephenson Railway Museum North Tyneside General Tynemouth Tynemouth Priory & Castle

Silverlink Coast Road North Shields Tynemouth IJmuiden

Howdon Meadow Well Percy Main Arbeia Roman Fort South Shields Amphitheatre

Hadrian Road Willington Quay Designer Outlet Village Port of Tyne International Passenger Terminal Royal Quays

Chichester Westoe Marsden Marsden Bay Marsden Rock

River Tyne Tyne Tunnel Second tunnel due to open Dec. 2010 Bedesworld St Paul's Monastery

Jarrow Tyne Dock Harton Cleadon Park Lizard Point Souter Lighthouse

Hebburn Bede Simonside South Tyneside District Cleadon Souter Point

Monkton Brockley Whins South Shields Crematorium Cleadon Whitburn

Fellgate Boldon Colliery West Boldon East Boldon Boldon Flats Nature Res. East Boldon Moor Whitburn Bay

Seaburn Seaburn Roker Washington Southwick Castletown Hylton Castle Monkwearmouth Stadium of Light Monkwearmouth National Glass Centre

Pallion River Wear Sunderland AFC St Peter's Sunderland Museum & Art Gallery

South Hylton University Millfield Sunderland Park Lane

Washington Old Hall Galleries Pennywell Sunderland Royal Hospital Sunderland Crematorium University Eye Infirmary Hendon

Offerton Grindon Grindon Hall Penshaw Monument Silksworth Sports Complex & Ski-Centre High Newport Grangetown

Fatfield Penshaw Thorney Close New Silksworth Ryhope

New Herrington Herrington Doxford Park Tunstall

Shiney Row

M Metro Station

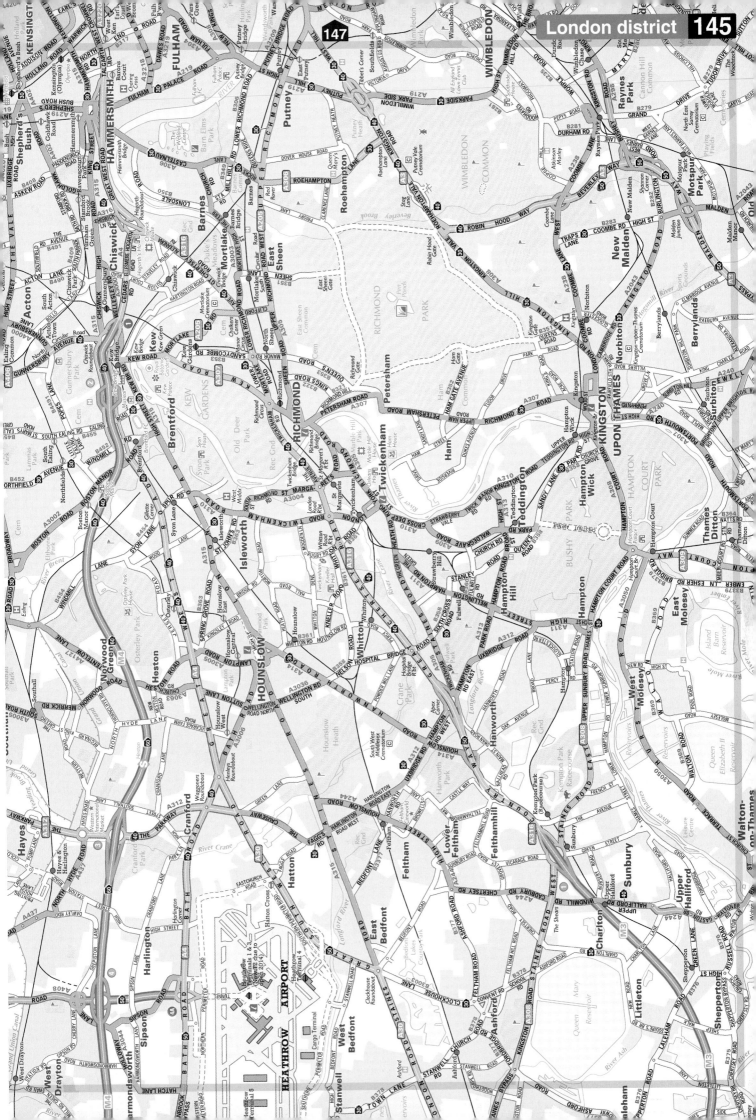

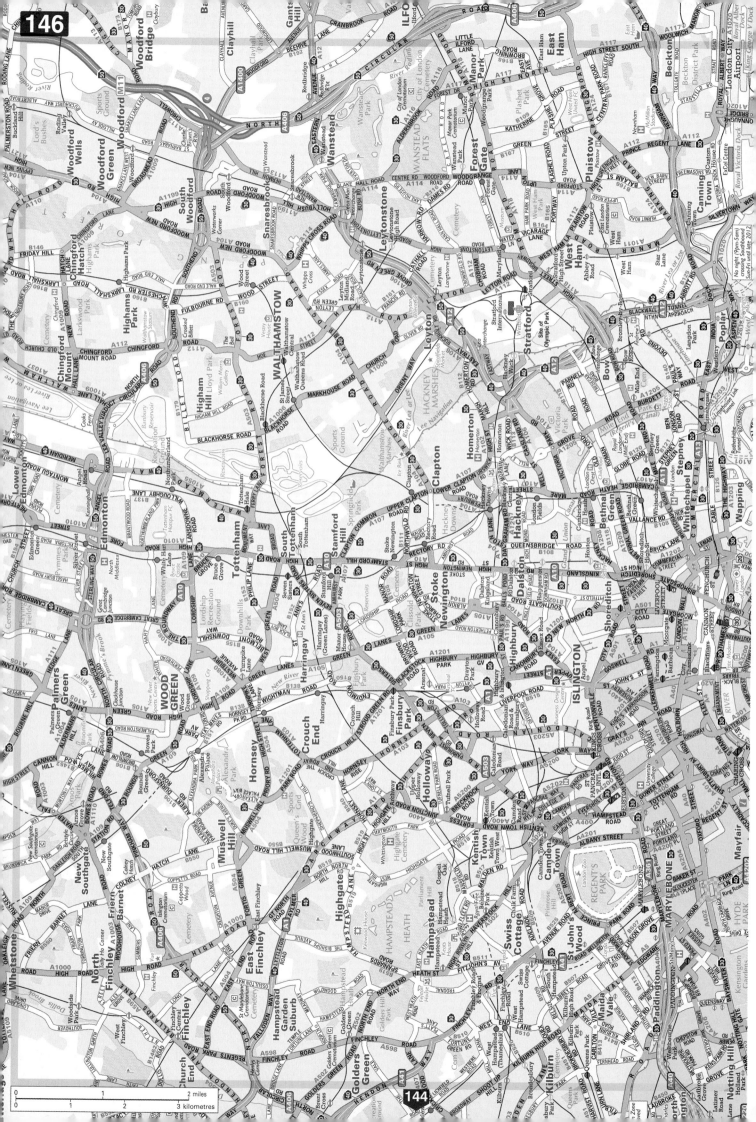

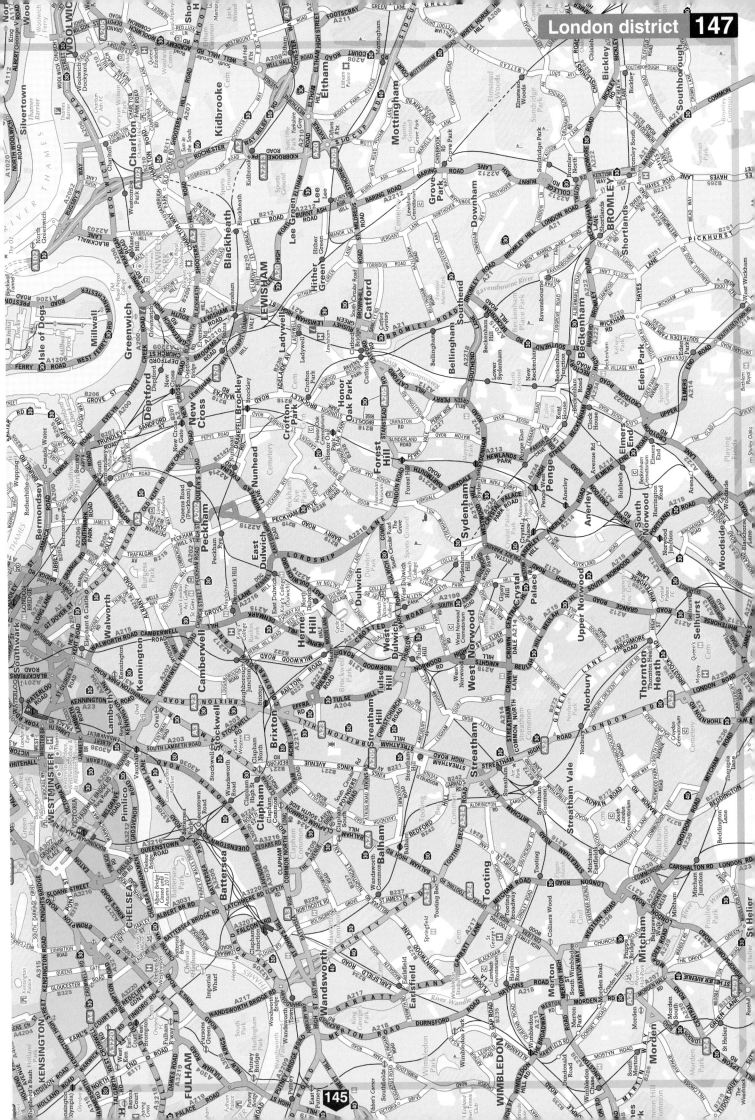

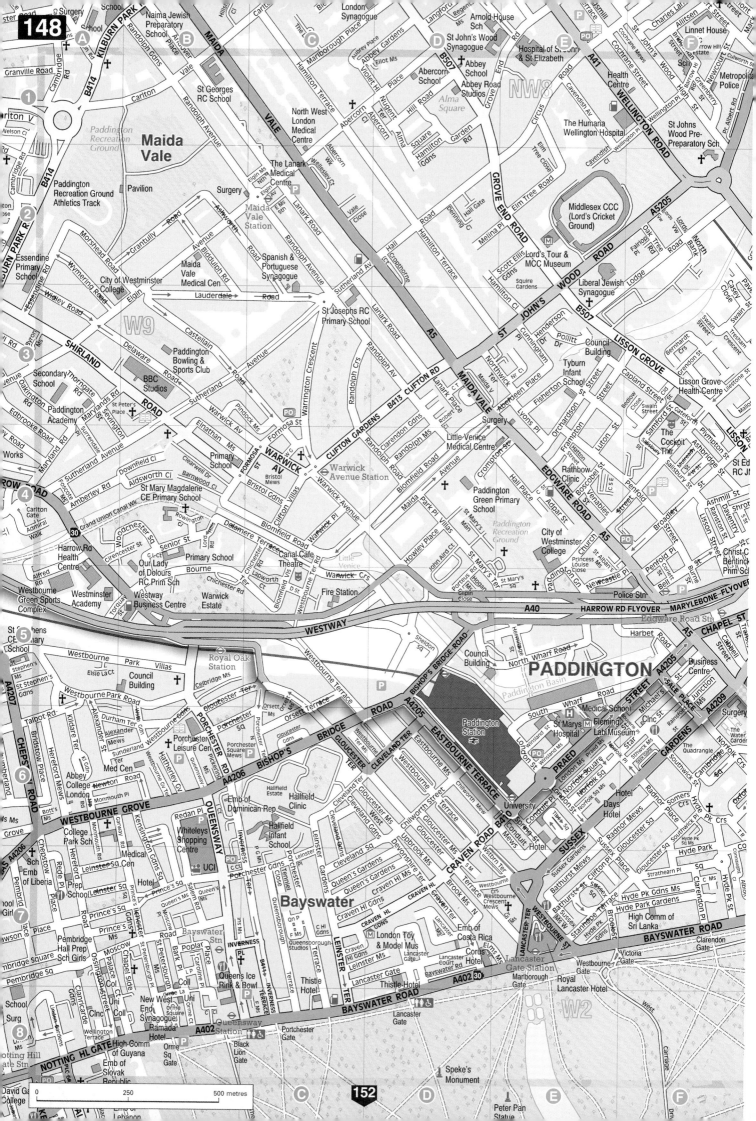

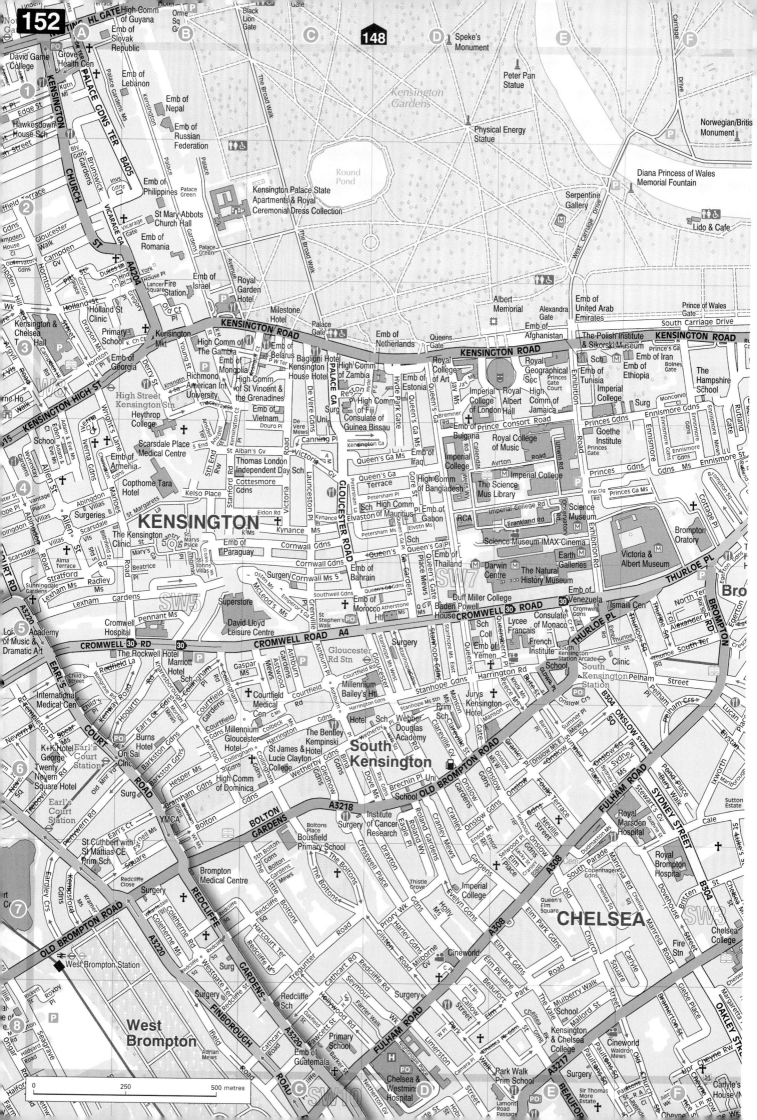

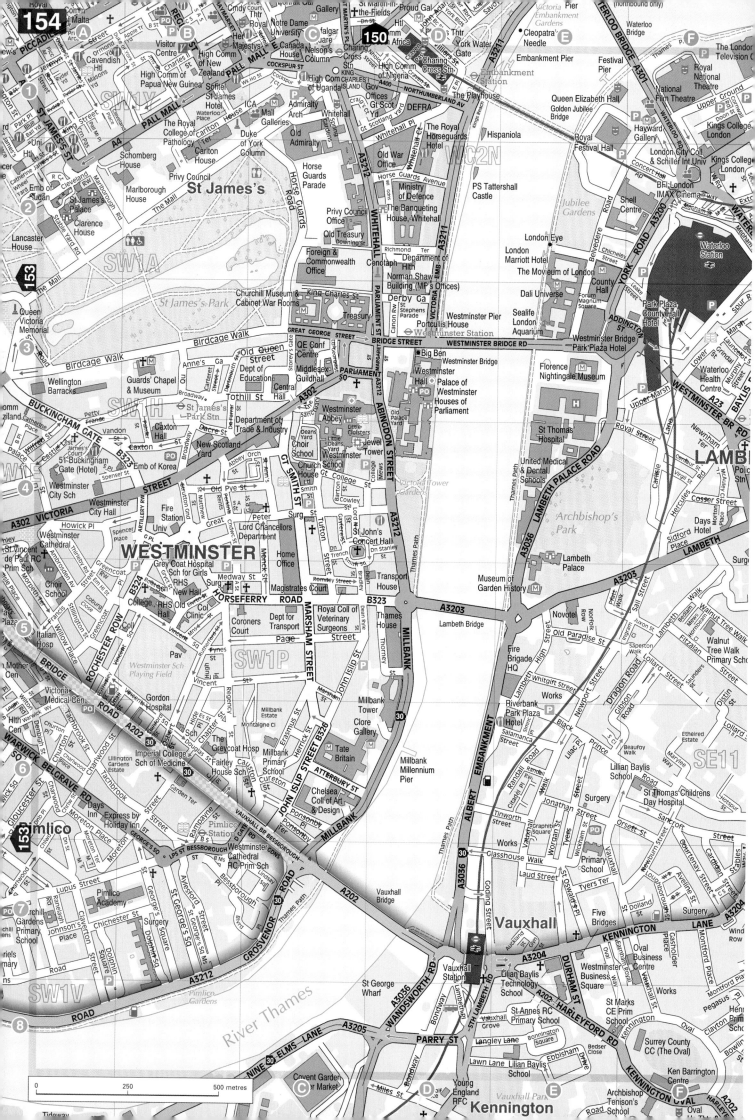

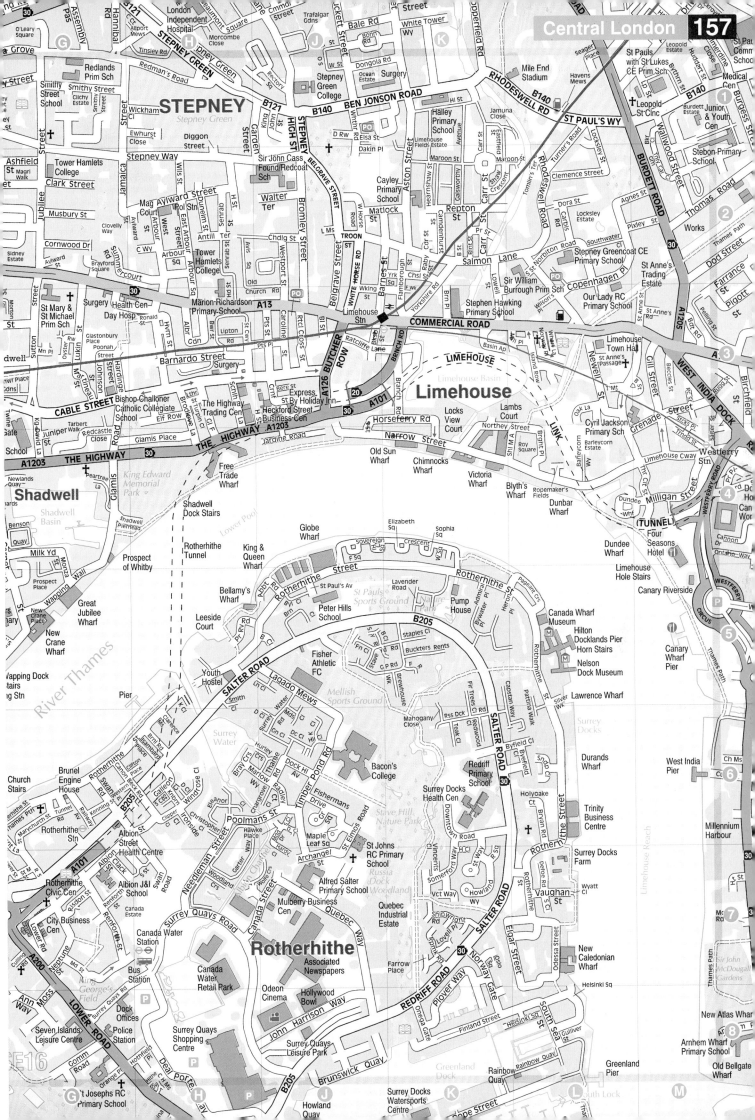

Central London street index

In the index, street and station names are listed in alphabetical order and written in full, but may be abbreviated on the map. Each entry is followed by its Postcode District and each street name is preceded by the page number and the grid reference to the square in which the name is found. Names are asterisked (*) in the index where there is insufficient space to show them on the map.

A

148 C1 Abbey Gardens NW8
154 B4 Abbey Orchard Street SW1P
156 B7 Abbey Street SE1
157 J5 Abbotshade Road SE16
153 L6 Abbots Manor SW1V
153 L6 Abbots Manor Estate SW1V
152 B4 Abbots Walk * W8
151 L7 Abchurch Lane EC4N
148 C1 Abercorn Close NW8
148 C1 Abercorn Place NW8
148 C1 Abercorn Walk NW8
148 E3 Aberdeen Place W2
155 M5 Aberdour Street SE1
152 A4 Abingdon Road W8
154 D3 Abingdon Street SW1P
152 A4 Abingdon Villas W8
157 M1 Ackroyd Drive E3
150 E2 Acton Street WC1X
152 A4 Adam & Eve Mews W8
151 M6 Adams Court EC2N
149 K8 Adam's Row W1K
150 D8 Adam Street WC2N
154 E3 Addington Street SE1
151 J7 Addle Hill EC4V
151 K5 Addle Street * EC2V
150 D8 Adelaide Street * WC2N
156 F1 Adelina Grove E1
150 B5 Adeline Place WC1B
150 D8 Adelphi Terrace WC2N
156 D2 Adler Street E1
157 K5 Admiral Place SE16
148 A4 Admiral Walk W9
148 E4 Adpar Street W2
152 B8 Adrian Mews SW10
150 E1 Affleck Street * N1
150 D8 Agar Street WC2N
156 F4 Agatha Close E1W
151 H3 Agdon Street EC1V
157 L2 Agnes Street E14
157 G6 Ainsty Street * SE16
150 A7 Air Street W1B
155 G2 Alaska Street SE1
150 A8 Albany Courtyard W1J
155 K8 Albany Mews SE5
155 L8 Albany Road SE17
149 L1 Albany Street NW1
149 M8 Albemarle Street W1S
151 H4 Albemarle Way EC1V
155 H6 Alberta Estate SE17
155 H7 Alberta Street SE17
156 D1 Albert Cottages * E1
154 D6 Albert Embankment SE1
157 H3 Albert Gardens E1
153 H2 Albert Gate SW1X
152 C4 Albert Mews W8
157 K4 Albert Mews * E14
152 C3 Albert Place * W8
148 F7 Albion Close W2
149 G7 Albion Gate W2
149 G7 Albion Mews W2
151 H4 Albion Place EC1M
149 G7 Albion Street W2
157 G7 Albion Street SE16
150 D1 Albion Walk N1
151 J5 Albion Way EC1A
150 D1 Albion Yard N1
149 K6 Aldburgh Mews W1U
150 B1 Aldenham Street NW1
151 K6 Aldermanbury * EC2V
151 K5 Aldermanbury Square EC2V
155 K4 Alderney Mews SE1
153 L6 Alderney Street SW1V
151 J4 Aldersgate Street EC1A
149 J8 Aldford Street W1K
156 B3 Aldgate EC3M
156 B3 Aldgate EC3N ⊖
156 C2 Aldgate Barrs * E1
156 C2 Aldgate East E1 ⊖
156 B3 Aldgate High Street EC3N
148 B4 Aldsworth Close W9
150 E7 Aldwych WC2B
148 A6 Alexander Mews W2
152 F5 Alexander Place SW7
152 F5 Alexander Square SW3
148 A6 Alexander Street W2
152 E3 Alexandra Gate SW7
151 K1 Alford Place * N1
150 B4 Alfred Mews WC1E
150 B5 Alfred Place WC1E
148 A5 Alfred Road W2
156 A8 Alice Street SE1
156 C3 Alie Street E1
152 A4 Allen Street W8
151 L1 Allerton Street N1
151 L8 Allhallows Lane EC4R
153 L4 Allington Street SW1W
148 F1 Allitsen Road NW8
157 H1 Allport Mews E1
149 H4 Allsop Place NW1
149 L5 All Souls' Place W1B
148 D1 Alma Square NW8
152 A5 Alma Terrace W8
149 G3 Alpha Close NW1
153 G8 Alpha Place SW3
155 M7 Alsace Road SE17
156 C8 Alscot Road SE1
155 M6 Alvey Street SE17
156 E2 Amazon Street * E1
155 H7 Ambergate Street SE17
148 A4 Amberley Road W9
154 A4 Ambrosden Avenue SW1P
155 J6 Amelia Street SE17
151 H6 Amen Corner EC4M
151 H6 Amen Court EC4M
156 B3 America Square EC3N
155 J2 America Street SE1
157 K2 Ames Cottages * E14
156 D8 Amina Way SE16
149 M1 Ampthill Estate NW1
150 A1 Ampthill Square NW1
150 E2 Ampton Street WC1X
150 F2 Amwell Street EC1R
151 K3 Anchor Yard * EC1V
153 H6 Anderson Street SW3
148 B1 Andover Place NW6
150 C6 Andrew Borde Street * WC2H
151 G1 Angel N1 ⊖
156 C2 Angel Alley E1
151 L6 Angel Court EC2R
156 F3 Angel Mews E1
151 L8 Angel Passage EC4R
151 G1 Angel Square * EC1V
151 J6 Angel Street EC1A
156 B1 Annexe Market * E1
157 G8 Ann Moss Way SE16
153 J3 Ann's Close SW1X
152 B4 Ansdell Street W8
152 B4 Ansdell Terrace W8
156 D5 Anthony's Close E1W
156 F2 Anthony Street * E1
157 H2 Antill Terrace E1
151 H7 Apothecary Street * EC4V
150 B8 Apple Tree Yard SW1Y
156 A1 Appold Street EC2A
153 K2 Apsley Way * W1J
155 G1 Aquinas Street SE1
157 H2 Arbour Square E1
157 J7 Archangel Street SE16
150 B7 Archer Street W1D
149 G6 Archery Close W2
155 J4 Arch Street SE1
151 M1 Arden Estate N1
150 D2 Argyle Square WC1H
150 D2 Argyle Street NW1
150 D2 Argyle Walk * WC1H
152 A3 Argyll Road W8
149 M6 Argyll Street W1D
156 B7 Arhchie Street SE1
153 M1 Arlington Street W1J
151 G2 Arlington Way EC1R
150 D6 Arne Street WC2H
154 B5 Arneway Street SW1P
157 M8 Arnheim Place E14
156 C7 Arnold Estate SE1
155 K8 Arnside Street SE17
151 L7 Arthur Street EC4R
156 E4 Artichoke Hill E1W
156 A1 Artillery Lane EC2M
156 B1 Artillery Passage * E1
154 B4 Artillery Row SW1P
156 B2 Artizan Street E1
150 F7 Arundel Street WC2R
148 F4 Ashbridge Street NW8
152 C5 Ashburn Gardens SW7
152 C6 Ashburn Place SW7
151 H2 Ashby Street EC1V
156 D4 Asher Way E1W
156 F2 Ashfield Street E1
157 G2 Ashfield Yard * E1
151 M2 Ashford Street N1
149 J5 Ashland Place W1U
153 M4 Ashley Place SW1E
148 F4 Ashmill Street NW8
148 B2 Ashworth Road W9
151 M1 Aske Street N1
155 K6 Asolando Drive SE17
156 D2 Assam Street E1
153 G6 Astell Street SW3
157 K2 Aston Street E14
152 C5 Astwood Mews SW7
152 D5 Atherstone Mews SW7
154 C6 Atterbury Street SW1P
150 F3 Attneave Street WC1X
148 C1 Aubrey Place NW8
154 E7 Auckland Street SE11
153 K1 Audley Square * W1K
153 K1 Audley Street W1K
149 L1 Augustus Street NW1
155 G7 Aulton Place SE11
151 M6 Austin Friars EC2N
151 M6 Austin Friars Square * EC2N
155 H5 Austral Street SE11
154 F7 Aveline Street SE11
151 J6 Ave Marie Lane EC4M
153 K6 Avery Farm Row * SW1W
149 L7 Avery Row W1K
157 H2 Avis Square E1
155 J4 Avonmouth Street SE1
149 J5 Aybrook Street W1U
155 M7 Aylesbury Estate SE17
155 L7 Aylesbury Road SE17
151 H4 Aylesbury Street EC1R
154 B7 Aylesford Street SW1V
157 H2 Aylward Street E1
155 K2 Ayres Street SE1
152 D4 Ayrton Road SW7

B

150 B8 Babmaes Street SW1Y
151 L2 Bache's Street N1
156 D3 Back Church Lane E1
151 G4 Back Hill EC1R
155 L3 Baden Place SE1
157 K2 Bailey Cottages * E14
150 C6 Bainbridge Street WC1A
151 K3 Baird Street EC1Y
149 J6 Baker's Mews W1U
151 G3 Baker's Row EC1R
149 H4 Baker Street NW1
149 H4 Baker Street NW1 ⊖
151 G3 Bakers Yard EC1R
150 F3 Baker's Yard EC1R
149 H4 Balcombe Street NW1
149 J7 Balderton Street W1C
150 F5 Baldwin's Gardens WC1X
151 L2 Baldwin Street EC1V
157 J1 Bale Road E1
150 D1 Balfe Street N1
149 K8 Balfour Mews W1K
149 J8 Balfour Place W1K
155 L5 Balfour Street SE1
156 E4 Balkan Walk E1W
151 J3 Baltic Street East EC1Y
151 J4 Baltic Street West EC1M
154 B7 Balvaird Place SW1V
150 C7 Banbury Court * WC2E
151 L6 Bank EC2R ⊖⊖
155 K1 Bank End SE1
151 J8 Bankside SE1
151 K3 Banner Street EC1Y
156 F8 Banyard Road SE16
151 J4 Barbican EC1M ⊖
156 A2 Barbon Alley EC2M
150 D4 Barbon Close WC1N
151 G8 Barge House Street SE1
152 C8 Barker Street SW10
148 B7 Bark Place W2
152 B6 Barkston Gardens SW5
157 L4 Barleycorn Estate E14
157 L4 Barleycorn Way E14
149 L7 Barlow Place W1J
155 L5 Barlow Street SE17
152 E6 Barnaby Place SW7
157 H3 Barnardo Gardens * E1
157 H3 Barnardo Street E1
150 A1 Barnby Street NW1
157 K3 Barnes Street E14
156 E2 Barnett Street * E1
156 A6 Barnham Street SE1
148 B4 Barnwood Close W9
151 G1 Barons Close * N1
155 G3 Baron's Place SE1
151 G1 Baron Street N1
149 K6 Barrett Street W1U
148 F1 Barrow Hill Estate NW8
148 F1 Barrow Hill Road NW8
150 D5 Barter Street WC1A
151 J5 Bartholomew Close EC1A
151 L6 Bartholomew Lane EC2N
151 K3 Bartholomew Square EC1V
155 L5 Bartholomew Street SE1
151 G6 Bartlett Court * EC4A
154 C4 Barton Street SW1P
153 H4 Basil Street SW3
157 K3 Basin Approach E14
151 K5 Basinghall Avenue EC2V
151 K6 Basinghall Street EC2V
151 J3 Bastwick Street EC1V
150 B6 Bateman's Buildings W1D
150 B6 Bateman Street W1D
157 M3 Bate Street E14
151 M2 Bath Place * EC2A
151 K2 Bath Street EC1V
155 K4 Bath Terrace SE1
148 E7 Bathurst Mews W2
148 E7 Bathurst Street W2
157 K2 Batten Cottages * E14
155 M1 Battle Bridge Lane SE1
156 D2 Batty Street E1
150 B5 Bayley Street W1T
154 F3 Baylis Road SE1
148 B7 Bayswater W2 ⊖
148 C8 Bayswater Road W2
157 L1 Baythorne Street E3
155 M7 Beaconsfield Road SE17
150 A7 Beak Street W1B
155 K1 Bear Gardens SE1
155 H1 Bear Lane SE1
150 C7 Bear Street WC2H
152 B5 Beatrice Place W8
153 G4 Beauchamp Place SW3
151 G5 Beauchamp Street EC1N
153 G4 Beaufort Gardens SW3
152 E8 Beaufort Street SW3
154 F6 Beaufoy Walk SE11
149 K4 Beaumont Mews * W1U
150 A3 Beaumont Place W1T
149 K4 Beaumont Street W1G
157 M3 Beccles Street E14
155 L4 Becket Street SE1
155 K7 Beckford Place * SE17
155 M5 Beckway Street SE17
155 L1 Bedale Street * SE1
150 B5 Bedford Avenue WC1B
150 D7 Bedfordbury WC2N
150 D7 Bedford Court WC2N
150 D4 Bedford Place WC1B
150 E4 Bedford Row WC1R
150 B5 Bedford Square WC1B
150 D7 Bedford Street WC2E
150 C4 Bedford Way WC1H
154 F5 Bedlam Mews SE11
148 F3 Bedlow Close NW8
154 E8 Bedser Close SE11
151 J4 Beech Street (Below) EC2Y
153 L4 Beeston Place SW1W
157 K3 Bekesbourne Street E14
153 K4 Belgrave Mews South SW1X
153 J4 Belgrave Mews West SW1X
153 K4 Belgrave Place SW1X
154 A6 Belgrave Road SW1V
153 J4 Belgrave Square SW1X
157 J2 Belgrave Street E1
150 D2 Belgrove Street NW1
157 M6 Bellamy Close E14
156 B1 Bell Lane E1
148 F5 Bell Street W2
151 K7 Bell Wharf Lane EC4R
150 F6 Bell Yard WC2A
156 A7 Bell Yard Mews SE1
155 J3 Belvedere Buildings SE1
154 E2 Belvedere Road SE1
149 G4 Bendall Mews NW1
151 H4 Benjamin Street EC1M
157 J1 Ben Jonson Road E1
151 J7 Bennet's Hill EC4V
153 M1 Bennett Street SW1A
156 D7 Ben Smith Way SE16
157 G4 Benson Quay E1W
149 K5 Bentinck Mews W1U
149 K6 Bentinck Street W1U
157 J3 Bere Street E1W
152 A2 Berkeley Gardens W8
149 H6 Berkeley Mews W1H
149 L8 Berkeley Square W1J
149 L8 Berkeley Street W1J
156 D7 Bermondsey SE16 ⊖
156 A6 Bermondsey Street SE1
156 D7 Bermondsey Wall East SE16
156 C6 Bermondsey Wall West SE1
150 D4 Bernard Street WC1N
150 A5 Berners Mews W1T
150 A5 Berners Place W1T
150 A5 Berners Street W1T
156 D3 Berner Terrace * E1
148 F3 Bernhardt Crescent NW8
157 K2 Berry Cottages * E14
155 J7 Berryfield Road SE17
151 H2 Berry Place EC1V
151 H3 Berry Street EC1V
150 B7 Berwick Street W1F
154 C6 Bessborough Gardens SW1V
154 B7 Bessborough Place SW1V
154 B7 Bessborough Street SW1V
150 D6 Betterton Street WC2H
156 E4 Betts Street E1W
151 L2 Bevenden Street N1
149 H5 Beverston Mews W1H
157 J5 Bevin Close SE16
156 D7 Bevington Street SE16
150 F1 Bevin Way WC1X
156 B2 Bevis Marks EC3A
156 F3 Bewley Street E1
149 H4 Bickenhall Street W1U
156 A7 Bickles Yard SE1
150 C2 Bidborough Street WC1H
148 B2 Biddulph Road W9
156 E3 Bigland Street E1
156 A3 Billiter Square * EC3M
156 A3 Billiter Street EC3M
152 C6 Bina Gardens SW5
149 J4 Bingham Place NW1
149 K7 Binney Street W1K
157 M3 Birchfield Street E14
151 L7 Birchin Lane EC3V
154 A3 Birdcage Walk SW1E
149 K6 Bird Street W1U
150 D1 Birkenhead Street NW1
148 C6 Bishop's Bridge Road W2
151 H6 Bishop's Court EC4M
156 A2 Bishopsgate EC2M
156 A1 Bishopsgate Arcade EC2M
155 G5 Bishops Terrace SE11
155 G5 Bishop's Terrace SE11
155 J3 Bittern Street SE1
151 M3 Blackall Street EC2A
149 J7 Blackburne's Mews W1K
151 H7 Blackfriars EC4Y ⇌
151 H8 Blackfriars Bridge SE1
151 H7 Black Friars Lane EC4V
151 H7 Blackfriars Passage EC4V
155 H1 Blackfriars Road SE1
151 H7 Blackfriars Underpass EC4V
155 L4 Black Horse Court * SE1
153 H6 Blacklands Terrace SW3
148 B8 Black Lion Gate W2
154 F6 Black Prince Road SE11
156 A6 Black Swan Yard SE1
155 K6 Blackwood Street SE17
149 G4 Blandford Square NW1
149 J5 Blandford Street W1U
151 G5 Bleeding Heart Yard * EC1N
149 L7 Blenheim Street W1S
148 C1 Blenheim Terrace NW8
151 K1 Bletchley Street N1
152 A4 Blithfield Street W8
148 D4 Blomfield Road W9
151 M5 Blomfield Street EC2M
148 C5 Blomfield Villas W2
149 L7 Bloomfield Place W1K
153 J6 Bloomfield Terrace SW1W
150 D5 Bloomsbury Place WC1A
150 D5 Bloomsbury Square WC1A
150 B4 Bloomsbury Street WC1E
150 D5 Bloomsbury Way WC1A
157 K2 Blount Street E14
156 C4 Blue Anchor Yard E1
153 M1 Blue Ball Yard SW1A
156 A7 Blue Lion Place SE1
157 K4 Blyth's Wharf * E14
157 J1 Bohn Road E1
148 F3 Boldero Place * NW8
152 F3 Bolney Gate SW7
149 L4 Bolsover Street W1W
151 G6 Bolt Court EC4A
152 C6 Bolton Gardens SW5
152 C7 Bolton Gardens Mews SW10
152 C6 Boltons Place SW5
153 L1 Bolton Street W1J
154 B7 Bonaparte Mews SW1V
149 K6 Bond Street W1C ⊖
154 D8 Bondway SW8
151 L4 Bonhill Street EC2A
154 E8 Bonnington Square SW8
157 M1 Booker Close E14
151 J7 Booth Lane EC4V
151 M2 Boot Street EC1V
151 H1 Boreas Walk N1
155 K3 Borough SE1 ⊖
155 K3 Borough High Street SE1
155 L1 Borough High Street SE1
155 H3 Borough Road SE1
155 J3 Borough Square SE1
155 J7 Borrett Close SE17
153 K5 Boscobel Place SW1W
148 E4 Boscobel Street W2
156 B6 Boss Street SE1
149 G3 Boston Place NW1
150 E4 Boswell Court WC1N
150 D4 Boswell Street WC1N
151 M7 Botolph Alley EC3R
151 M7 Botolph Lane EC3R
148 A6 Bott's Mews W2
157 J3 Boulcott Street E1
155 K8 Boundary Lane SE5
155 H2 Boundary Row SE1
150 B7 Bourchier Street W1D
149 L7 Bourdon Place W1K
149 L7 Bourdon Street W1K
149 M5 Bourlet Close W1W
150 F4 Bourne Estate * EC1N
153 J6 Bourne Street SW1W
148 B5 Bourne Terrace W2
148 E6 Bouverie Place W2
151 G6 Bouverie Street EC4Y
151 K6 Bow Churchyard * EC4M
155 G7 Bowden Street SE11
157 H3 Bower Street E1
153 H3 Bowland Yard * SW1X
151 K6 Bow Lane EC4M
151 G3 Bowling Green Lane EC1R
155 L2 Bowling Green Place * SE1
154 F8 Bowling Green Street SE11
151 M2 Bowling Green Walk N1
156 D3 Bowmans Mews E1
150 D7 Bow Street WC2E
156 D3 Boyd Street E1
155 H3 Boyfield Street SE1
155 K8 Boyson Road SE17
151 K4 Brackley Street EC2Y
155 L8 Bradenham Close SE17
148 B4 Braden Street * W9
151 G1 Bradley's Close N1
157 K2 Bradshaw Cottages * E14
155 G2 Brad Street SE1
155 H7 Braganza Street SE17
156 C3 Braham Street E1
156 A5 Braidwood Street SE1
152 F8 Bramerton Street SW3
152 B6 Bramham Gardens SW5
157 K3 Branch Road E14
155 H8 Brandon Estate SE17
151 K5 Brandon Mews * EC2Y
155 K5 Brandon Street SE17
154 F7 Brangton Road SE11
150 D1 Bravingtons Walk N1
157 H6 Bray Crescent SE16
157 G2 Brayford Square E1
153 H6 Bray Place SW3
151 K7 Bread Street EC4M
150 F6 Bream's Buildings WC2A
152 D6 Brechin Place SW7
156 E4 Breezer's Hill E1W
152 D4 Bremner Road SW7
149 G5 Brendon Street W1H
157 K2 Brenton Street E14
153 L4 Bressenden Place SW1E
155 L7 Brettell Street SE17
150 A7 Brewer Street W1B
151 H3 Brewery Square EC1V
156 B6 Brewery Square SE1
156 F5 Brewhouse Lane E1W
157 K5 Brewhouse Walk SE16
151 H3 Brewhouse Yard EC1V
150 F7 Brick Court * EC4Y
153 K2 Brick Street W1K
151 H6 Bride Court EC4Y
151 H6 Bride Lane EC4Y
151 H1 Bridel Mews EC1V
156 C7 Bridewain Street SE1
151 H7 Bridewell Place EC4V
156 F5 Bridewell Place E1W
149 L4 Bridford Mews W1W
148 F1 Bridgeman Street NW8
153 L5 Bridge Place SW1V
156 D5 Bridgeport Place * E1W
154 C3 Bridge Street SW1A
151 J4 Bridgewater Square * EC2Y
151 K4 Bridgewater Street EC2Y
150 B1 Bridgeway Street NW1
150 A7 Bridle Lane W1F
148 A6 Bridstow Place W2
157 L4 Brightlingsea Place E14
150 C1 Brill Place NW1
156 F3 Brinsley Street E1

155 H2 Brinton Walk SE1
151 H4 Briset Street EC1M
148 C4 Bristol Gardens W9
148 C4 Bristol Mews W9
150 E2 Britannia Street WC1X
151 L1 Britannia Walk N1
152 F7 Britten Street SW3
151 H4 Britton Street EC1M
155 G8 Brixton Road SE11
149 L7 Broadbent Street * W1K
150 D6 Broad Court * WC2E
148 F4 Broadley Street NW8
149 G3 Broadley Terrace NW1
149 J5 Broadstone Place W1U
151 M5 Broad Street Avenue EC2M
151 M5 Broad Street Place EC2M
155 G1 Broadwall SE1
154 B3 Broadway SW1H
150 A7 Broadwick Street W1F
151 G4 Broad Yard EC1M
155 K4 Brockham Street SE1
157 H3 Brodlove Lane E1W
151 J7 Broken Wharf EC4V
156 F2 Bromehead Street * E1
157 J2 Bromley Street E1
153 H3 Brompton Arcade * SW3
152 A8 Brompton Park Crescent SW6
153 G4 Brompton Place SW3
153 G4 Brompton Road SW3
152 F4 Brompton Square SW3
155 K7 Bronti Close SE17
155 H5 Brook Drive SE11
151 G5 Brooke's Market EC1N
151 G5 Brooke Street EC1N
149 H7 Brook Gate W1K
148 D7 Brook Mews North W2
149 L7 Brook's Mews W1K
148 E7 Brook Street W2
149 K7 Brook Street W1K
149 L7 Brown Hart Gardens W1K
148 D3 Browning Close * W9
149 K5 Browning Mews W1G
155 K6 Browning Street SE17
150 F4 Brownlow Mews WC1N
150 F5 Brownlow Street WC1V
149 G5 Brown Street W1H
148 A5 Brunel Estate * W2
157 H6 Brunel Road SE16
156 B1 Brune Street E1
156 B6 Brunswick Court SE1
152 A2 Brunswick Gardens W8
149 H6 Brunswick Mews W1H
149 K4 Brunswick Place NW1
151 L2 Brunswick Place N1
157 J8 Brunswick Quay SE16
150 D3 Brunswick Square WC1N
157 K3 Brunton Place E14
156 B1 Brushfield Street E1
149 L7 Bruton Lane W1J
149 L7 Bruton Place W1J
149 L7 Bruton Street W1J
157 L6 Bryan Road SE16
149 H5 Bryanston Mews East W1H
149 G5 Bryanston Mews West W1H
149 G5 Bryanston Place W1H
149 H5 Bryanston Square W1H
149 H7 Bryanston Street W1H
150 C8 Brydges Place WC2N
153 M4 Buckingham Gate SW1E
153 M3 Buckingham Mews * SW1E
153 L5 Buckingham Palace Road SW1W
153 M4 Buckingham Place SW1E
150 D8 Buckingham Street WC2N
151 M1 Buckland Street N1
151 L7 Bucklersbury * EC4N
156 C2 Buckle Street E1
150 C6 Bucknall Street WC1A
157 K5 Buckters Rents SE16
151 K7 Budge Row EC4N
154 C6 Bulinca Street * SW1P
153 L5 Bulleid Way SW1W
153 G5 Bull's Gardens SW3
149 K5 Bulstrode Place W1U
149 K5 Bulstrode Street W1U
151 L3 Bunhill Row EC1Y
153 J6 Bunhouse Place SW1W
155 L4 Burbage Close SE1
157 M1 Burdett Estate E14
157 M3 Burdett Road E14
157 M1 Burgess Street E14
155 L4 Burge Street SE1
151 H7 Burgon Street EC4V
150 D7 Burleigh Street WC2E
149 M8 Burlington Arcade W1S
149 M8 Burlington Gardens W1S
148 F5 Burne Street NW1
153 G7 Burnsall Street SW3
157 J5 Burnside Close SE16
156 F2 Buross Street * E1
156 D5 Burr Close E1W
155 H1 Burrell Street SE1
157 K1 Burroughs Cottages * E14
155 H2 Burrows Mews SE1
156 A6 Bursar Street * SE1
156 E3 Burslem Street E1
155 L7 Burton Grove SE17
153 K5 Burton Mews SW1W
150 C3 Burton Place WC1H
150 C3 Burton Street WC1H
156 F3 Burwell Close E1
149 G6 Burwood Place W2
157 J5 Bury Close SE16
156 A2 Bury Court EC3A
150 D5 Bury Place WC1A
156 A3 Bury Street EC3A
154 A1 Bury Street SW1Y
152 F6 Bury Walk SW3
156 A8 Bushbaby Close SE1
151 L7 Bush Lane EC4R
157 J3 Butcher Row E1W
152 E5 Bute Street SW7
156 C6 Butlers & Colonial Wharf SE1
156 E7 Butterfield Close SE16
151 M2 Buttesland Street N1
157 L6 Byefield Close SE16
157 J5 Byelands Close SE16
157 K6 Byfield Close SE16
150 B4 Byng Place WC1E
148 A3 Byron Mews W9
156 B4 Byward Street EC3R
157 K5 Bywater Place SE16
153 G6 Bywater Street SW3
149 M5 Bywell Place * W1W

C

148 F5 Cabbell Street NW1
157 G3 Cable Street E1
156 D3 Cable Street E1
156 C8 Cadbury Way SE16
155 K7 Cadiz Street SE17
153 H5 Cadogan Gardens SW3
153 H5 Cadogan Gate SW1X
153 J4 Cadogan Lane SW1X
153 H5 Cadogan Place SW1X
153 H4 Cadogan Square SW1X
153 G6 Cadogan Street SW3
151 K3 Cahill Street * EC1Y
150 D1 Caledonia Street N1
152 F6 Cale Street SW3
156 F1 Callaghan Cottages * E1
152 D4 Callendar Road SW7
157 M2 Callingham Close E14
152 D8 Callow Street SW3
150 E3 Calthorpe Street WC1X
157 L8 Calypso Way SE16
150 C7 Cambridge Circus W1D
148 A1 Cambridge Gardens NW6
149 L3 Cambridge Gate NW1
149 L3 Cambridge Gate Mews NW1
152 C3 Cambridge Place * W8
148 A2 Cambridge Road NW6
148 F6 Cambridge Square W2
153 L6 Cambridge Street SW1V
149 L2 Cambridge Terrace NW1
149 L2 Cambridge Terrace Mews * NW1
157 K2 Camdenhurst Street E14
152 D8 Camera Place SW10
156 F2 Cameron Place E1
156 A2 Camomile Street EC3A
152 A2 Campden Grove W8
152 A3 Campden Hill Road W8
152 A2 Campden House Close W8
152 A2 Campden House Terrace * W8
156 C3 Camperdown Street E1
157 G7 Canada Estate SE16
157 H7 Canada Street SE16
157 G7 Canada Water SE16 ⊖ ⊖
155 L8 Canal Street SE5
149 M5 Candover Street * W1W
152 C4 Canning Passage * W8
152 C4 Canning Place W8
152 C3 Canning Place Mews * W8
157 M4 Cannon Drive E14
151 J6 Cannon Street EC4V
151 K7 Cannon Street EC4R ⇌ ⊖
156 E3 Cannon Street Road E1
157 G6 Canon Beck Road SE16
154 D3 Canon Row SW1A
155 J6 Canterbury Place SE17
155 J1 Canvey Street SE1
153 J3 Capeners Close SW1X
156 E5 Cape Yard E1W
148 F3 Capland Street NW8
157 K5 Capstan Way SE16
157 L2 Carbis Road E14
149 L4 Carburton Street W1W
154 F7 Cardigan Street SE11
155 L4 Cardinal Bourne Street * SE1
150 A2 Cardington Street NW1
151 J6 Carey Lane EC2V
154 B6 Carey Place SW1V
150 F6 Carey Street WC2A
156 B3 Carlisle Avenue EC3N
154 F4 Carlisle Lane SE1
153 M5 Carlisle Place SW1P
150 B6 Carlisle Street W1D
149 K7 Carlos Place W1K
148 A4 Carlton Gate W9
148 C1 Carlton Hill NW8
154 B1 Carlton House Terrace SW1Y
150 B8 Carlton Street SW1Y
153 H4 Carlton Tower Place SW1X
148 B1 Carlton Vale NW6
152 E7 Carlyle Square SW3
152 A3 Carmel Court W8
151 G7 Carmelite Street EC4Y
149 M7 Carnaby Street W1F
148 B8 Caroline Close W2
148 B7 Caroline Place W2
148 B8 Caroline Place Mews * W2
157 J3 Caroline Street E1
153 J6 Caroline Terrace SW1W
149 K7 Carpenter Street W1K
153 L2 Carrington Street W1J
157 K2 Carr Street E14
154 B3 Carteret Street SW1H
151 H6 Carter Lane EC4V
155 K7 Carter Place SE17
155 J7 Carter Street SE17
151 J4 Carthusian Street EC1M
150 D8 Carting Lane WC2R
150 C3 Cartwright Gardens WC1H
156 C4 Cartwright Street E1
148 F2 Casey Close NW8
156 D1 Casson Street E1
148 B3 Castellain Road W9
151 J7 Castle Baynard Street EC4V
155 H5 Castlebrook Close SE11
151 L6 Castle Court * EC3V
154 A4 Castle Lane SW1E
156 E1 Castlemaine Street E1
149 G6 Castlereagh Street W1H
155 H1 Castle Yard * SE1
155 L6 Catesby Street SE17
156 F7 Cathay Street SE16
152 C8 Cathcart Road SW10
155 L1 Cathedral Street SE1
151 G3 Catherine Griffiths Court EC1R
153 M4 Catherine Place SW1E
150 E7 Catherine Street * WC2B
156 A1 Catherine Wheel Alley EC2M
153 M2 Catherine Wheel Yard SW1A
149 G5 Cato Street W1H
150 E5 Catton Street WC1B
157 K2 Causton Cottages * E14
154 B6 Causton Street SW1P
152 D7 Cavaye Place SW10
156 F1 Cavell Street E1
148 E1 Cavendish Avenue NW8
148 E2 Cavendish Close NW8
149 L5 Cavendish Mews North W1W
149 L5 Cavendish Mews South * W1W
149 L6 Cavendish Place W1G
149 L6 Cavendish Square W1G
151 L1 Cavendish Street N1
153 G8 Caversham Street SW3
154 B4 Caxton Street SW1H
156 A6 Cayenne Court SE1
151 K2 Cayton Street EC1V
150 C7 Cecil Court WC2H
148 B5 Celbridge Mews W2
154 F4 Centaur Street SE1
151 J2 Central Street EC1V
148 E7 Cerney Mews W2
148 B7 Cervantes Court W2
151 G1 Chadwell Street EC1R
154 B4 Chadwick Street SW1P
149 H3 Chagford Street NW1
150 B1 Chalton Street NW1
156 D6 Chambers Street SE16
156 C3 Chamber Street E1
155 H1 Chancel Street SE1
150 F5 Chancery Lane WC1X ⊖
150 F5 Chancery Lane WC2A
157 M6 Chandlers Mews E14
156 F5 Chandler Street E1W
150 D8 Chandos Place WC2N
149 L5 Chandos Street W1G
152 B4 Chantry Square W8
155 K2 Chapel Court SE1
149 L6 Chapel Place W1G
148 B7 Chapel Side W2
148 F5 Chapel Street W2
153 K3 Chapel Street SW1X
155 G3 Chaplin Close SE1
156 E3 Chapman Street E1
155 H7 Chapter Road SE17
154 B6 Chapter Street SW1P
157 H6 Chargrove Close SE16
154 C1 Charing Cross * WC2N
154 C1 Charing Cross WC2N ⇌ ⊖
150 C6 Charing Cross Road WC2H
153 G7 Charles II Place SW3
154 B1 Charles II Street SW1Y
148 F1 Charles Lane NW8
150 A2 Charles Place * NW1
151 M2 Charles Square N1
151 M2 Charles Square Estate N1
153 L1 Charles Street W1J
155 K6 Charleston Street SE17
150 A4 Charlotte Mews W1T
150 A5 Charlotte Place W1T
153 M5 Charlotte Place SW1V
151 M2 Charlotte Road EC2A
150 B5 Charlotte Street W1T
154 A6 Charlwood Place SW1V
154 A6 Charlwood Street SW1V
151 J4 Charterhouse Buildings EC1M
151 H4 Charterhouse Mews EC1M
151 G5 Charterhouse Street EC1N
151 L2 Chart Street N1
157 K2 Chaseley Street E14
155 L5 Chatham Street SE17
151 K6 Cheapside EC2V
153 K8 Chelsea Bridge SW1W
153 J6 Chelsea Bridge Road SW1W
153 G8 Chelsea Embankment SW3
152 F7 Chelsea Manor Gardens SW3
152 F7 Chelsea Manor Street SW3
152 D8 Chelsea Park Gardens SW3
152 F7 Chelsea Square SW3
153 H6 Cheltenham Terrace SW3
150 B4 Chenies Mews WC1E
150 B4 Chenies Street WC1E
152 A4 Cheniston Gardens W8
148 A6 Chepstow Corner * W2
148 A6 Chepstow Place W2
148 A6 Chepstow Road W2
151 L3 Chequer Street EC1Y
151 L1 Cherbury Street N1
156 E7 Cherry Garden Street SE16
151 K4 Cherry Tree Walk EC1Y
153 J4 Chesham Close * SW1X
153 J4 Chesham Mews SW1X
153 J4 Chesham Place SW1X
153 J4 Chesham Street SW1X
153 K3 Chester Close SW1X
149 L2 Chester Close North NW1
149 L2 Chester Close South NW1
153 K1 Chesterfield Gardens * W1J
149 K8 Chesterfield Hill W1K
153 K1 Chesterfield Street W1J
149 L2 Chester Gate NW1
153 K4 Chester Mews SW1X
149 L1 Chester Place NW1
149 K2 Chester Road NW1
153 J6 Chester Row SW1W
153 K5 Chester Square SW1W
153 K4 Chester Square Mews * SW1W
153 K4 Chester Street SW1X
149 L2 Chester Terrace NW1
155 G6 Chester Way SE11
155 L4 Chettle Close SE1
152 F4 Cheval Place SW7
153 G8 Cheyne Gardens SW3
153 G8 Cheyne Mews SW3
153 G8 Cheyne Place SW3
152 F8 Cheyne Row SW3
152 F8 Cheyne Walk SW3
154 E2 Chicheley Street SE1
148 C5 Chichester Road W2
154 A7 Chichester Street SW1V
156 D1 Chicksand Estate E1
156 C1 Chicksand Street E1
156 E4 Chigwell Hill E1W
152 A6 Child's Mews * SW5
152 A6 Child's Place SW5
152 A5 Child's Street SW5
152 A5 Child's Walk * SW5
149 J4 Chiltern Street W1U
148 D6 Chilworth Mews W2
148 D6 Chilworth Street W2
157 H8 China Hall Mews SE16
151 L4 Chiswell Street EC1Y
150 A4 Chitty Street W1T
153 H7 Christchurch Street SW3
153 H8 Christchurch Terrace * SW3
156 E2 Christian Street E1
151 M3 Christina Street EC2A
157 H6 Christopher Close SE16
150 F2 Christopher Place * NW1
151 M4 Christopher Street EC2A
157 J2 Chudleigh Street E1
155 M8 Chumleigh Street SE5
153 M7 Churchill Gardens SW1V
153 L7 Churchill Gardens Road SW1V
148 E4 Church Street W2
148 E4 Church Street Estate NW8
150 B2 Churchway NW1
155 H5 Churchyard Row SE11
154 A6 Churton Place SW1V
154 A6 Churton Street SW1V
156 F5 Cinnamon Street E1W
149 G5 Circus Mews * W1H
151 L5 Circus Place * EC2M
148 E1 Circus Road NW8
148 A4 Cirencester Street W2
154 E6 Citadel Place SE11
151 J1 City Garden Row N1
151 H1 City Road EC1V
151 L4 City Road EC1Y
151 H6 City Thameslink EC4A ⇌
155 M3 City Walk SE1
153 H5 Clabon Mews SW1X
157 G7 Clack Street SE16
148 A8 Clanricarde Gardens W2
151 G1 Claremont Close N1
151 G1 Claremont Square N1
149 L2 Clarence Gardens NW1
149 H3 Clarence Gate NW1
157 H6 Clarence Mews SE16
150 C1 Clarence Passage * NW1
149 H3 Clarence Terrace NW1
148 F7 Clarendon Close * W2
148 D3 Clarendon Gardens W9
148 F7 Clarendon Gate W2
148 F7 Clarendon Mews W2
148 F7 Clarendon Place W2
153 L7 Clarendon Street SW1V
148 D3 Clarendon Terrace W9
152 D6 Clareville Grove SW7
152 D6 Clareville Street SW7
153 L1 Clarges Mews W1J
153 L1 Clarges Street W1J
149 K5 Clarkes Mews W1G
149 M1 Clarkson Row NW1
157 G2 Clark Street E1
154 A7 Claverton Street SW1V
156 F5 Clave Street E1W
154 E8 Claylands Road SW8
149 H5 Clay Street W1U
154 F8 Clayton Street SE11
157 H2 Clearbrook Way E1
148 B4 Clearwell Drive W9
155 G7 Cleaver Square SE11
155 G7 Cleaver Street SE11
156 F5 Clegg Street E1W
157 L2 Clemence Street E3
150 F6 Clements Inn WC2A
151 L7 Clement's Lane EC4N
156 E8 Clement's Road SE16
155 K2 Clennam Street * SE1
149 H6 Clenston Mews W1H
151 M3 Clere Place EC2A
151 M3 Clere Street EC2A
151 G3 Clerkenwell Close EC1R
151 G4 Clerkenwell Green EC1R
150 F4 Clerkenwell Road EC1R
148 C6 Cleveland Gardens W2
149 M4 Cleveland Mews W1T
154 A1 Cleveland Place SW1Y
154 A2 Cleveland Row SW1A
148 C7 Cleveland Square W2
149 L3 Cleveland Street NW1
148 D6 Cleveland Terrace W2
157 G1 Clichy Estate E1
149 M7 Clifford Street W1S
148 C4 Clifton Gardens W9
148 E7 Clifton Place W2
157 G6 Clifton Place SE16
148 D3 Clifton Road W9
151 M3 Clifton Street EC2A
148 C4 Clifton Villas W9
155 L1 Clink Street SE1
157 H6 Clipper Close SE16
149 M4 Clipstone Mews W1T
149 L4 Clipstone Street W1W
153 J5 Cliveden Place SW1W
151 K7 Cloak Lane EC4R
151 J5 Cloth Court EC1A
151 J5 Cloth Fair EC1A
156 B2 Clothier Street EC3A
151 J4 Cloth Street EC1A
157 G2 Clovelly Way E1
153 H8 Clover Mews SW3
151 M1 Clunbury Street N1
155 M4 Cluny Estate SE1
156 A8 Cluny Place SE1
150 B1 Clyde Court NW1
149 L7 Coach & Horses Yard W1S
156 B2 Cobb Street E1
150 A2 Cobourg Street NW1
154 A5 Coburg Close SW1P
157 G3 Coburg Dwellings * E1
148 E1 Cochrane Mews NW8
148 E1 Cochrane Street NW8
151 H5 Cock Lane EC1A
154 C1 Cockspur Court SW1Y
154 C1 Cockspur Street SW1Y
156 E5 Codling Close * E1W
155 G1 Coin Street SE1
156 D2 Coke Street E1
152 C6 Colbeck Mews SW7
150 F3 Coldbath Square EC1R
151 H1 Colebrooke Row N1
152 B7 Coleherne Mews SW10
152 B7 Coleherne Road SW10
151 L6 Coleman Street EC2V
155 K3 Cole Street SE1
150 F3 Coley Street WC1X
156 C2 College East * E1
151 K7 College Hill * EC4R
154 D4 College Mews SW1P
151 K7 College Street * EC4R
156 E8 Collett Road SE16
150 E1 Collier Street N1
152 C6 Collingham Gardens SW5
152 B5 Collingham Place SW5
152 B5 Collingham Road SW5
155 J3 Collinson Street SE1
155 J3 Collinson Walk SE1
155 H4 Colnbrook Street SE1
155 H1 Colombo Street SE1
150 D4 Colonnade WC1N
149 L3 Colosseum Terrace NW1
150 B5 Colville Place W1T
155 K6 Colworth Grove SE17
157 K3 Commercial Road E14
156 C2 Commercial Road E1
156 B1 Commercial Street E1
157 J1 Commodore Street E1
149 L2 Compton Close NW1
151 H3 Compton Passage EC1V
150 D3 Compton Place WC1H
151 H3 Compton Street EC1V
155 M6 Comus Place SE17
156 D3 Conant Mews E1
154 F2 Concert Hall Approach SE1
157 K2 Conder Street E14
150 C7 Conduit Court * WC2E
148 E6 Conduit Mews W2
148 E6 Conduit Place W2
149 L7 Conduit Street W1S
155 M5 Congreve Street SE17
149 G6 Coniston Court * W2
148 F7 Connaught Close W2
149 G6 Connaught Square W2
148 F6 Connaught Street W2
155 G2 Cons Street * SE1
153 L3 Constitution Hill W1J
155 K6 Content Street SE17
149 M4 Conway Mews W1T
149 M4 Conway Street W1T
155 H8 Cook's Road SE17
151 J1 Coombs Street N1
155 G3 Cooper Close SE1
150 C1 Coopers Lane NW1
156 B3 Cooper's Row EC3N
152 E7 Copenhagen Gardens SW3
157 L3 Copenhagen Place E14
152 A4 Cope Place W8
155 J8 Copley Close SE5
155 J2 Copperfield Street SE1
156 B6 Copper Row SE1
151 L6 Copthall Avenue EC2R
150 C5 Coptic Street WC1A
155 G3 Coral Street SE1
150 C3 Coram Street WC1H
156 C1 Corbet Place E1
149 M8 Cork St Mews W1S
156 E5 Cork Square E1W
149 M7 Cork Street W1S
148 F4 Corlett Street NW1
151 M6 Cornhill EC3V
152 C4 Cornwall Gardens SW7
152 B5 Cornwall Gardens Walk SW7
152 C5 Cornwall Mews South SW7
152 B4 Cornwall Mews West * SW7
154 F1 Cornwall Road SE1
156 E3 Cornwall Street E1
149 H3 Cornwall Terrace NW1
149 H3 Cornwall Terrace Mews NW1
157 G2 Cornwood Drive E1
151 M2 Coronet Street N1
151 G3 Corporation Row EC1R
151 L2 Corsham Street N1
150 D4 Cosmo Place WC1B
154 F4 Cosser Street SE1
149 G4 Cosway Street NW1
155 K6 Cotham Street SE17
152 F4 Cottage Place SW3
155 G4 Cottesloe Mews SE1
152 B4 Cottesmore Gardens W8
155 G6 Cottington Street SE11
155 G6 Cotton Gardens Estate SE11
155 M1 Cottons Centre * SE1
153 H6 Coulson Street SW3
155 M1 Counter Street SE1
155 K5 County Street SE1
154 F7 Courtenay Square SE11
154 F6 Courtenay Street SE11
152 B6 Courtfield Gardens SW5
152 C6 Courtfield Mews SW5
152 C5 Courtfield Road SW7
156 E1 Court Street E1
151 K7 Cousin Lane EC4R
150 D7 Covent Garden WC2E
150 C7 Covent Garden WC2E ⊖
150 D7 Covent Garden Piazza WC2E
150 B8 Coventry Street W1D
156 D1 Coverley Close * E1
151 H4 Cowcross Street EC1M
154 C4 Cowley Street SW1P
151 L3 Cowper Street EC1Y
156 B7 Coxson Way SE1
154 C1 Craig's Court SW1A
155 L5 Crail Row SE17
149 J5 Cramer Street W1U
155 J6 Crampton Street SE17
150 C7 Cranbourn Street WC2H
151 G6 Crane Court EC4A
157 J3 Cranford Cottages * E1W
157 J3 Cranford Street E1W
150 A1 Cranleigh Street NW1
152 E7 Cranley Gardens SW7
152 D6 Cranley Mews SW7
152 E6 Cranley Place SW7
151 L1 Cranston Estate N1
151 L2 Cranwood Street EC1V
148 D7 Craven Hill W2
148 C7 Craven Hill Gardens W2
148 D7 Craven Hill Mews W2
154 D1 Craven Passage WC2N
148 D7 Craven Road W2
154 D1 Craven Street WC2N
148 D7 Craven Terrace W2
149 H5 Crawford Mews * W1H
151 G3 Crawford Passage EC1R
149 G5 Crawford Place W1H
149 G5 Crawford Street W1H
156 B2 Creechurch Lane EC3A
156 B3 Creechurch Place * EC3A
151 H6 Creed Lane EC4V
156 B3 Crescent EC3N
152 F5 Crescent Place SW3
151 J3 Crescent Row EC1Y
152 C6 Cresswell Gardens * SW5
152 C6 Cresswell Place SW10
157 G1 Cressy Court E1
157 G1 Cressy Houses * E1
150 D2 Crestfield Street NW1
156 B8 Crimscott Street SE1
151 K4 Cripplegate Street * EC2Y
156 B1 Crispin Street E1
156 C4 Crofts Street E1
148 C7 Cromarty Villas * W2
150 D2 Cromer Street WC1H
148 D4 Crompton Street W2
152 E5 Cromwell Gardens SW7
152 E5 Cromwell Mews * SW7
152 E5 Cromwell Place SW7
152 A5 Cromwell Road SW5
151 M1 Crondall Street N1
148 D2 Cropthorne Court W9
155 L3 Crosby Row SE1
156 A2 Crosby Square EC3A
149 K5 Cross Keys Close W1U

156 A4 Cross Lane EC3R
155 M5 Crosslet Street SE17
156 B3 Crosswall EC3N
156 E3 Crowder Street E1
150 D6 Crown Court WC2B
151 G7 Crown Office Row EC4Y
154 A1 Crown Passage SW1Y
151 M4 Crown Place EC2A
156 A5 Crucifix Lane SE1
150 F1 Cruickshank Street WC1X
156 B3 Crutched Friars EC3N
157 M6 Cuba Street E14
150 E2 Cubitt Street WC1X
153 H6 Culford Gardens SW3
157 G7 Culling Road SE16
156 A3 Cullum Street EC3M
149 J8 Culross Street W1K
148 F1 Culworth Street NW8
150 F2 Cumberland Gardens WC1X
149 H7 Cumberland Gate W2
149 K1 Cumberland Gate NW1
149 L2 Cumberland Market NW1
155 G7 Cumberland Mews SE11
149 L2 Cumberland Place NW1
153 L6 Cumberland Street SW1V
149 K1 Cumberland Terrace NW1
149 L1 Cumberland Terrace Mews NW1
150 E1 Cumming Street N1
153 K6 Cundy Street SW1W
148 E3 Cunningham Place NW8
154 C6 Cureton Street SW1P
156 C6 Curlew Street SE1
150 F6 Cursitor Street EC4A
151 M4 Curtain Road EC2A
153 K1 Curzon Street W1J
157 L7 Custom House Reach * SE16
148 E4 Cuthbert Street W2
156 B2 Cutlers Gardens Arcade EC2M
156 B2 Cutler Street EC3A
150 F1 Cynthia Street N1
150 A4 Cypress Place W1T
151 H3 Cyrus Street EC1V

D

154 B4 Dacre Street SW1H
157 J2 Dakin Place E1
151 H3 Dallington Square EC1V
151 H3 Dallington Street EC1V
156 F2 Damien Street E1
156 D7 Damsel Court * SE16
150 E5 Dane Street WC1R
150 B7 Dansey Place W1D
155 H5 Dante Road SE11
153 G6 Danube Street SW3
152 F8 Danvers Street SW3
156 D1 Daplyn Street E1
150 A6 D'Arblay Street W1F
155 K8 Dartford Street SE17
154 B3 Dartmouth Street SW1H
155 L5 Darwin Street SE17
155 K7 Date Street SE17
156 D1 Davenant Street E1
148 F4 Daventry Street NW1
155 H3 Davidge Street SE1
149 J4 David Mews W1U
149 K7 Davies Mews W1K
149 K7 Davies Street W1K
155 L6 Dawes Street SE17
148 A7 Dawson Place W2
155 K5 Deacon Way SE17
157 H8 Deal Porters Way SE16
156 D1 Deal Street E1
154 C5 Dean Bradley Street SW1P
157 H6 Dean Close SE16
156 F3 Deancross Street E1
153 K1 Deanery Mews * W1K
153 K1 Deanery Street W1K
154 B3 Dean Farrar Street SW1H
154 C5 Dean Ryle Street SW1P
155 L6 Dean's Buildings SE17
151 J6 Dean's Court EC4M
149 L5 Dean's Mews * W1G
154 D4 Dean Stanley Street SW1P
150 B6 Dean Street W1D
154 C4 Deans Yard SW1P
154 C4 Dean Trench Street SW1P
155 M4 Decima Street SE1
157 J6 Deck Close SE16
157 L7 Defoe Road SE16
148 C5 Delamere Street W2
148 B4 Delamere Terrace W2
155 H7 De Laune Street SE17
148 B3 Delaware Road W9
156 F3 Dellow Street E1
154 A6 Dell's Mews * SW1V
155 H7 Delverton Road SE17
154 A6 Denbigh Place SW1V
154 A6 Denbigh Street SW1V
150 B7 Denman Street W1D
150 C6 Denmark Street WC2H
148 D2 Denning Close NW8
155 G6 Denny Crescent SE11
155 G6 Denny Street SE11
153 G5 Denyer Street SW3
154 D3 Derby Gate SW1A
153 K1 Derby Street W1J
149 L6 Dering Street W1C
152 B3 Derry Street W8
152 C3 De Vere Gardens W8
155 L4 Deverell Street SE1
152 C4 De Vere Mews W8
150 F7 Devereux Court WC2R
149 K4 Devonshire Close W1G
149 K4 Devonshire Mews South W1G
149 K4 Devonshire Mews West W1G
149 K4 Devonshire Place W1G
152 B5 Devonshire Place * W8
149 K4 Devonshire Place Mews W1G
156 A2 Devonshire Row EC2M
149 L4 Devonshire Row Mews W1W
156 A2 Devonshire Square EC2M
149 K4 Devonshire Street W1G
148 D6 Devonshire Terrace W2
149 K5 De Walden Street W1G
150 B6 Diadem Court W1F
156 C7 Dickens Estate SE1
151 H4 Dickens Mews EC1M
155 K4 Dickens Square SE1
157 H1 Diggon Street E1
153 H8 Dilke Street SW3
151 K2 Dingley Place EC1V
151 J2 Dingley Road EC1V
156 E4 Discovery Walk E1W
155 K3 Disney Place SE1
155 K2 Disney Street SE1
151 J7 Distaff Lane EC4V
154 F6 Distin Street SE11
156 C7 Dockhead SE1
157 J6 Dock Hill Avenue SE16
156 D8 Dockley Road SE16
156 D4 Dock Street E1
155 H7 Doddington Grove SE17
155 H8 Doddington Place SE17
155 G3 Dodson Street SE1
157 M2 Dod Street E14
155 H2 Dolben Street * SE1
154 F7 Dolland Street SE11
157 H6 Dolphin Close SE16
154 A7 Dolphin Square SW1V
150 E4 Dombey Street WC1N
151 J3 Domingo Street EC1V
151 L5 Dominion Street EC2M
150 F1 Donegal Street N1
157 J1 Dongola Road E1
153 G5 Donne Place SW3
157 K2 Donoghue Cottages * E14
154 F1 Doon Street SE1
157 J2 Dora Street E14
156 F2 Dorian Estate E1
150 B2 Doric Way NW1
151 G5 Dorrington Street EC1N
155 K2 Dorrit Street * SE1
151 H6 Dorset Buildings * EC4Y
149 H4 Dorset Close NW1
153 K4 Dorset Mews SW1X
151 G6 Dorset Rise EC4Y
149 H4 Dorset Square NW1
149 J5 Dorset Street W1U
150 E3 Doughty Mews WC1N
150 E3 Doughty Street WC1N
154 B6 Douglas Street SW1P
152 C4 Douro Place W8
156 E5 Douthwaite Square E1W
151 L6 Dove Court * EC2R
152 F7 Dovehouse Street SW3
152 C6 Dove Mews SW5
149 L8 Dover Street W1S
153 L1 Dover Yard W1J
151 L7 Dowgate Hill EC4R
148 B4 Downfield Close W9
154 C2 Downing Street SW1A
153 K1 Down Street W1J
157 K6 Downtown Road SE16
155 J2 Doyce Street * SE1
153 J5 D'Oyley Street SW1W
155 J8 Draco Street SE17
154 E6 Dragon Road SE11
157 J6 Drake Close SE16
150 E5 Drake Street WC1X
155 J5 Draper Estate SE1
153 G5 Draycott Avenue SW3
153 H6 Draycott Place SW3
153 H5 Draycott Terrace SW3
152 A3 Drayson Mews W8
152 D7 Drayton Gardens SW10
156 B6 Druid Street SE1
150 B2 Drummond Crescent NW1
154 B7 Drummond Gate SW1V
156 E8 Drummond Road SE16
149 M3 Drummond Street NW1
156 C2 Drum Street E1
150 D6 Drury Lane WC2E
150 D6 Dryden Street WC2E
149 L5 Duchess Mews W1G
149 L5 Duchess Street W1B
155 G1 Duchy Street SE1
150 B6 Duck Lane W1F
148 D5 Dudley Street * W2
152 E7 Dudmaston Mews SW3
151 K3 Dufferin Avenue EC1Y
151 K4 Dufferin Street EC1Y
150 A7 Dufour's Place W1F
155 H6 Dugard Way SE11
153 K3 Duke of Wellington Place SW1X
153 H6 Duke of York Square SW3
150 A8 Duke of York Street SW1Y
152 A2 Dukes Lane W8
149 J6 Duke's Mews W1U
156 B3 Duke's Place EC3A
150 C2 Duke's Road NW1
149 K6 Duke Street W1U
155 L1 Duke Street Hill SE1
150 A8 Duke Street St James's W1J
149 K7 Duke's Yard W1K
150 C8 Duncannon Street WC2N
151 H1 Duncan Terrace N1
156 F6 Dundee Street E1W
157 L4 Dundee Wharf E14
157 H2 Dunelm Street E1
156 C8 Dunlop Place SE16
149 H7 Dunraven Street W1K
149 K4 Dunstable Mews W1G
157 H1 Dunstan Houses * E1
156 A3 Dunster Court EC3R
155 L3 Dunsterville Way SE1
153 H3 Duplex Ride SW1X
150 D8 Durham House Street * WC2N
153 H7 Durham Place SW3
157 J1 Durham Row E1
154 E7 Durham Street SE11
148 A6 Durham Terrace W2
156 E1 Durward Street E1
149 H5 Durweston Mews * W1U
149 H5 Durweston Street W1H
151 G5 Dyer's Buildings EC4A
150 C5 Dyott Street WC1B
151 M4 Dysart Street EC2A

E

151 H4 Eagle Court EC1M
152 D6 Eagle Place SW7
150 E5 Eagle Street WC1V
152 A7 Eardley Crescent SW5
150 C7 Earlham Street WC2H
152 A6 Earl's Court SW5 ⊖
152 B6 Earl's Court Gardens SW5
152 A5 Earl's Court Road SW5
152 B7 Earl's Court Square SW5
151 H2 Earlstoke Estate EC1V
151 H2 Earlstoke Street EC1V
151 M4 Earl Street EC2A
150 C6 Earnshaw Street WC1A
157 H2 East Arbour Street E1
148 D6 Eastbourne Mews W2
148 D6 Eastbourne Terrace W2
149 M6 Eastcastle Street W1W
151 L7 Eastcheap EC4N
157 K1 Eastfield Street E14
151 G6 East Harding Street EC4A
157 M3 East India Dock Road E14
156 F3 East Mount Street * E1
150 F3 Easton Street WC1X
151 J4 East Passage EC1A
151 H5 East Poultry Avenue EC1M
153 J7 East Road SW3
151 L2 East Road N1
156 C4 East Smithfield E1W
155 K7 East Street SE17
156 C3 East Tenter Street E1
153 J5 Eaton Close SW1W
153 J5 Eaton Gate SW1W
153 L4 Eaton Lane SW1W
153 J5 Eaton Mews North SW1X
153 K5 Eaton Mews South SW1W
153 K5 Eaton Mews West SW1W
153 K5 Eaton Place SW1X
153 K4 Eaton Row SW1W
153 K4 Eaton Square SW1W
153 J5 Eaton Terrace SW1W
153 J5 Eaton Terrace Mews SW1W
154 E8 Ebbisham Drive SW8
151 L2 Ebenezer Street N1
153 K6 Ebury Bridge SW1W
153 K7 Ebury Bridge Road SW1W
153 K5 Ebury Mews SW1W
153 K5 Ebury Mews East SW1W
153 K6 Ebury Square SW1W
153 K5 Ebury Street SW1W
153 K4 Eccleston Mews SW1X
153 L5 Eccleston Place SW1W
153 L6 Eccleston Square SW1V
153 L6 Eccleston Square Mews SW1V
153 K4 Eccleston Street SW1W
148 A3 Edbrooke Road W9
152 A4 Eden Close W8
152 A1 Edge Street W8
148 E4 Edgware Road W2
148 F5 Edgware Road NW1 ⊖
153 G3 Edinburgh Gate SW1X
150 B2 Edith Neville Cottages NW1
157 J3 Edward Mann Close East * E1
157 J3 Edward Mann Close West * E1
149 L1 Edward Mews * NW1
149 J6 Edwards Mews W1U
152 F5 Egerton Crescent SW3
153 G5 Egerton Gardens SW3
153 G4 Egerton Gardens Mews SW3
153 G4 Egerton Place * SW3
153 G5 Egerton Terrace SW3
155 K5 Elba Place * SE17
152 C4 Eldon Road W8
151 L5 Eldon Street EC2M
157 H6 Eleanor Close SE16
155 J5 Elephant & Castle SE1 ⇌ ⊖
155 J5 Elephant & Castle SE1
156 F6 Elephant Lane SE16
155 J5 Elephant Road SE17
157 H3 Elf Row E1W
157 K7 Elgar Street SE16
148 C2 Elgin Avenue W9
148 C2 Elgin Mews North W9
148 C2 Elgin Mews South W9
151 H1 Elia Mews N1
151 H1 Elia Street N1
155 M4 Elim Street SE1
148 D1 Eliot Mews NW8
153 L6 Elizabeth Bridge SW1W
148 D3 Elizabeth Close * W9
157 K4 Elizabeth Square SE16
153 K5 Elizabeth Street SW1W
156 D3 Ellen Street E1
155 H5 Elliott's Row SE11
153 J5 Ellis Street SW1X
152 E7 Elm Park Gardens SW10
152 D7 Elm Park Lane SW10
152 D8 Elm Park Road SW3
152 E7 Elm Place SW7
148 D7 Elms Mews W2
150 F4 Elm Street WC1X
148 E1 Elm Tree Close NW8
148 E2 Elm Tree Road NW8
148 B4 Elnathan Mews W9
157 K1 Elsa Cottages * E14
157 J1 Elsa Street E1
148 A5 Elsie Lane Court W2
155 M6 Elsted Street SE17
152 D4 Elvaston Mews SW7
152 C4 Elvaston Place SW7
154 B5 Elverton Street SW1P
151 G5 Ely Place EC1N
153 G6 Elystan Place SW3
152 F6 Elystan Street SW3
154 D1 Embankment WC2N ⊖
153 H8 Embankment Gardens SW3
154 D1 Embankment Place WC2N
156 E7 Emba Street SE16
150 E4 Emerald Street WC1N
155 J1 Emerson Street SE1
154 A5 Emery Hill Street SW1P
155 G3 Emery Street SE1
152 C5 Emperor's Gate SW7
155 L3 Empire Square SE1
152 A7 Empress Place SW6
155 K8 Empress Street SE17
151 H3 Enclave Court EC1V
150 C6 Endell Street WC2H
150 B3 Endsleigh Gardens WC1H
150 B3 Endsleigh Place WC1H
150 B3 Endsleigh Street WC1H
149 G4 Enford Street NW1
156 C7 Enid Street SE16
152 F4 Ennismore Gardens SW7
152 F4 Ennismore Gardens Mews SW7
152 F4 Ennismore Mews SW7
152 F4 Ennismore Street SW7
156 D3 Ensign Street E1
152 D6 Ensor Mews SW7
151 L3 Epworth Street EC2A
154 C6 Erasmus Street SW1P
156 F1 Erlich Cottages * E1
151 K4 Errol Street EC1Y
148 A3 Essendine Road W9
150 F7 Essex Court * EC4Y
150 F7 Essex Street WC2R
157 K1 Essian Street E1
154 B6 Esterbrooke Street SW1P
154 F6 Ethelred Estate SE11
155 K6 Ethel Street * SE17
151 J2 Europa Place EC1V
150 B2 Euston NW1 ⇌ ⊖ ⊖
149 M3 Euston Centre NW1
149 M3 Euston Road NW1
150 C2 Euston Road WC1H
150 B2 Euston Square NW1
150 A3 Euston Square NW1 ⊖
150 A3 Euston Street NW1
156 D8 Eveline Lowe Estate SE16
152 D7 Evelyn Gardens SW7
151 L1 Evelyn Walk N1
150 A1 Eversholt Street NW1
149 M2 Everton Buildings NW1
155 J2 Ewer Street SE1
157 H1 Ewhurst Close E1
150 B8 Excel Court WC2H
151 M5 Exchange Arcade EC2M
150 D7 Exchange Court * WC2E
156 A1 Exchange Square * EC2A
150 D7 Exeter Street WC2E
152 E3 Exhibition Road SW7
151 G3 Exmouth Market EC1R
151 G3 Exmouth Mews * NW1
157 G2 Exmouth Street * E1
155 M6 Exon Street SE17
154 F2 Exton Street SE1
151 G4 Eyre Street Hill EC1R

F

151 L1 Fairbank Estate N1
156 D3 Fairclough Street E1
153 G4 Fairholt Street SW7
148 F2 Fairlop Place NW8
156 B6 Fair Street SE1
150 B6 Falconberg Court * W1D
151 J1 Falcon Court N1
155 K4 Falmouth Road SE1
151 J4 Fann Street EC1M
151 M1 Fanshaw Street N1
150 B6 Fareham Street * W1F
152 A1 Farmer Street W8
152 A8 Farm Lane SW6
149 K8 Farm Street W1J
156 E7 Farncombe Street SE16
152 B7 Farnell Mews SW5
155 J1 Farnham Place SE1
154 E7 Farnham Royal SE11
157 M3 Farrance Street E14
152 C8 Farrier Walk SW10
151 G4 Farringdon EC1M ⇌ ⊖
151 G3 Farringdon Lane EC1R
150 F3 Farringdon Road EC1R
151 H5 Farringdon Road EC1N
151 H5 Farringdon Street EC4A
157 K5 Farrins Rents SE16
157 J7 Farrow Place SE16
156 C7 Farthing Alley SE1
156 F5 Farthing Fields E1W
156 C1 Fashion Street E1
155 H7 Faunce Street SE17
152 C8 Fawcett Street SW10
151 L3 Featherstone Street EC1Y
156 A3 Fenchurch Avenue EC3M
156 A3 Fenchurch Buildings EC3M
156 B3 Fenchurch Place * EC3M
151 M7 Fenchurch Street EC3M
156 B3 Fenchurch Street EC3M ⇌
156 B8 Fendall Street SE1
155 M2 Fenning Street SE1
156 F2 Fenton Street E1
150 F2 Fernsbury Street WC1X
151 G6 Fetter Lane EC4A
150 F5 Field Court WC1R
156 D2 Fieldgate Street E1
155 J7 Fielding Street SE17
150 E1 Field Street WC1X
152 B8 Finborough Road SW10
151 M6 Finch Lane EC3V
157 K8 Finland Street SE16
151 M5 Finsbury Avenue * EC2M
151 L5 Finsbury Circus EC2M
151 G3 Finsbury Estate EC1R
151 M4 Finsbury Market EC2A
151 L5 Finsbury Pavement EC2M
151 L4 Finsbury Square EC2A
151 L4 Finsbury Street EC1Y
153 G5 First Street SW3
157 K5 Fir Trees Close SE16
157 J6 Fishermans Drive SE16
150 E5 Fisher Street WC1B
148 E3 Fisherton Street NW8
151 L7 Fish Street Hill EC3R
154 F5 Fitzalan Street SE11
149 J6 Fitzhardinge Street W1H
149 L8 Fitzmaurice Place * W1J
149 M4 Fitzroy Mews W1T
149 M4 Fitzroy Square W1T
149 M3 Fitzroy Street NW1
150 A4 Fitzroy Street W1T
157 K2 Flamborough Street E14
157 K3 Flamborough Walk E14
156 D4 Flank Street E1
150 C2 Flaxman Terrace WC1H
151 H6 Fleet Place EC4A
150 E2 Fleet Square WC1X
150 F6 Fleet Street EC4Y
155 H8 Fleming Road SE17
156 D3 Fletcher Street E1
155 L6 Flint Street SE17
150 C6 Flitcroft Street WC2H
156 D6 Flockton Street SE16
153 G7 Flood Street SW3
153 G7 Flood Walk SW3
150 D7 Floral Street WC2E
156 C1 Flower & Dean Walk E1
149 M5 Foley Street W1W
156 D3 Forbes Street E1
156 E2 Fordham Street E1
156 F2 Ford Square E1
151 L5 Fore Street EC2Y
148 B4 Formosa Street W9
149 G6 Forset Street W1H
155 H8 Forsyth Gardens SE17
156 B1 Fort Street * E1
151 K4 Fortune Street EC1Y
154 E3 Forum Magnum Square SE1
148 C8 Fosbury Mews W2
148 A4 Foscote Mews W9
151 J6 Foster Lane EC2V
149 M7 Foubert's Place W1F
152 E6 Foulis Terrace SW7
157 J5 Foundry Close SE16
150 A3 Foundry Mews NW1
156 E7 Fountain Green Square SE16
156 C1 Fournier Street E1
156 E5 Fowey Close E1W
151 J4 Fox & Knot Street * EC1M
148 E4 Frampton Street NW8
154 A5 Francis Street SW1P
152 E4 Frankland Road SW7
153 H7 Franklins Row * SW3
153 H6 Franklin's Row SW3
155 G3 Frazier Street SE1
156 D8 Frean Street SE16
149 G7 Frederick Close W2
155 H7 Frederick Road * SE17
151 K6 Frederick's Place * EC2R
157 J4 Frederick Square SE16
151 H1 Frederick's Row EC1V
150 E2 Frederick Street WC1X
153 J3 Frederic Mews * SW1X
155 M6 Freemantle Street SE17
155 H1 Friars Close * SE1
151 K7 Friday Street EC4M
151 H2 Friend Street EC1V
150 B6 Frith Street W1D
151 K4 Frobisher Crescent * EC2Y
156 C1 Frostic Walk E1
156 B1 Frying Pan Alley E1
156 E1 Fulbourne Street E1
156 F7 Fulford Street SE16
152 D8 Fulham Road SW10
150 F5 Fullwood Place WC1R
151 L1 Fullwood's Mews N1
148 C7 Fulton Mews W2
151 G5 Furnival Street EC4A
151 J7 Fye Foot Lane EC4V
154 B5 Fynes Street SW1P

G

151 G8 Gabriel's Wharf SE1
150 D4 Gage Street WC1N
156 B6 Gainsford Street SE1
155 K3 Gaitskell Way SE1
157 H6 Galleon Close SE16
157 K1 Galsworthy Avenue E14
151 K2 Galway Street EC1V
155 H2 Gambia Street SE1
149 M7 Ganton Street W1B
149 J5 Garbutt Place * W1U
150 F7 Garden Court * EC4Y
148 D1 Garden Road NW8
155 H4 Garden Row SE1
157 H1 Garden Street E1
148 C5 Garden Studios * W2
154 B6 Garden Terrace SW1V
151 M3 Garden Walk EC2A
151 J7 Gardners Lane EC4V
151 J2 Gard Street EC1V
157 M4 Garford Street E14
151 K7 Garlick Hill EC4V
151 G2 Garnault Mews EC1R
151 G2 Garnault Place EC1R
156 F4 Garnet Street E1W
151 K3 Garrett Street EC1Y
150 C7 Garrick Street WC2E
150 C7 Garrick Yard WC2N
157 H7 Garter Way SE16
148 B6 Garway Road W2
154 F7 Gasholder Place SE11
152 C5 Gaspar Close * SW5
152 B5 Gaspar Mews SW5
156 F8 Gataker Street * SE16
148 F3 Gateforth Street NW8
155 K1 Gatehouse Square SE1
153 G3 Gate Mews SW7
150 E5 Gate Street WC2A
155 K8 Gateway SE17
153 K7 Gatliff Road SW1W
155 J4 Gaunt Street SE1
155 M5 Gavel Street * SE17
154 C4 Gayfere Street SW1P
155 H4 Gaywood Street SE1
155 H7 Gaza Street SE17
156 C7 Gedling Place SE1
149 K6 Gees Court W1U
151 J3 Gee Street EC1V
148 B4 George Lowe Court W2
155 H5 George Mathers Road * SE11
150 A2 George Mews NW1
156 D7 George Row SE16
149 G6 George Street W1H
151 L7 George Yard EC3V
149 K7 George Yard W1K
155 H4 Geraldine Street SE11
153 K5 Gerald Road SW1W
150 C7 Gerrard Place * W1D
150 B7 Gerrard Street W1D
155 G3 Gerridge Street SE1
154 E6 Gibson Road SE11
150 D5 Gilbert Place WC1A
155 G5 Gilbert Road SE11
149 K7 Gilbert Street W1K
149 L5 Gildea Street W1W
153 M5 Gillingham Row SW1V
153 M5 Gillingham Street SW1V
156 E8 Gillison Walk SE16
157 M3 Gill Street E14
148 D5 Gilpin Close W2
152 D7 Gilston Road SW10
151 H5 Giltspur Street EC1A
155 H4 Gladstone Street SE1
157 H4 Glamis Place E1W
157 G4 Glamis Road E1W
153 M7 Glasgow Terrace SW1V
155 H2 Glasshill Street SE1
157 H3 Glasshouse Fields E1W
150 A7 Glasshouse Street W1B
154 D7 Glasshouse Walk SE11
151 J4 Glasshouse Yard EC1M
157 G3 Glastonbury Place E1
152 F7 Glebe Place SW3
152 C6 Gledhow Gardens SW5
152 E5 Glendower Place SW7
149 H3 Glentworth Street NW1
157 J5 Globe Pond Road SE16
155 L3 Globe Street SE1
148 C6 Gloucester Gardens W2
148 D6 Gloucester Mews W2
148 D6 Gloucester Mews West W2
149 H3 Gloucester Place NW1
149 H5 Gloucester Place Mews W1H
152 C4 Gloucester Road SW7
152 C5 Gloucester Road SW7 ⊖

148 F7 Gloucester Square W2
153 M6 Gloucester Street SW1V
148 C6 Gloucester Terrace W2
152 A2 Gloucester Walk W8
151 G2 Gloucester Way EC1R
153 G5 Glynde Mews SW3
154 E7 Glyn Street SE11
153 G6 Godfrey Street SW3
154 D7 Goding Street SE11
151 J7 Godliman Street EC4V
150 F1 Godson Street N1
151 K1 Godwin Close N1
154 E1 Golden Jubilee Bridge SE1
151 K3 Golden Lane EC1Y
151 J4 Golden Lane Estate EC1Y
150 A7 Golden Square W1F
156 E3 Golding Street E1
151 K6 Goldsmith Street EC2V
157 G8 Gomm Road SE16
150 A5 Goodge Place W1T
150 B4 Goodge Street W1T ⊖
150 A5 Goodge Street W1T
156 B3 Goodman's Yard EC3N
156 C8 Goodwin Close SE16
150 C7 Goodwins Court WC2N
151 L7 Gophir Lane * EC4R
152 A3 Gordon Place W8
150 B3 Gordon Square WC1H
150 B3 Gordon Street WC1H
152 D4 Gore Street SW7
156 B2 Goring Street EC3A
149 L5 Gosfield Street W1W
150 B6 Goslett Yard W1D
151 H2 Goswell Place EC1V
151 H2 Goswell Road EC1V
151 G6 Gough Square EC4A
150 F3 Gough Street WC1X
156 B2 Goulston Street E1
150 B5 Gower Mews WC1E
150 B3 Gower Place WC1E
150 B4 Gower Street WC1E
156 D2 Gower's Walk E1
151 M7 Gracechurch Street EC3V
156 D4 Grace's Alley E1
148 D1 Graces Mews * NW8
155 M3 Graduate Place SE1
149 M3 Grafton Mews W1T
150 B2 Grafton Place NW1
149 L8 Grafton Street W1S
150 A4 Grafton Way W1T
151 J1 Graham Street N1
153 J6 Graham Terrace SW1W
149 M1 Granby Terrace NW1
151 H5 Grand Avenue EC1M
151 J1 Grand Junction Wharf * N1
148 A4 Grand Union Canal Walk W9
156 A8 Grange Road SE1
156 B8 Grange Walk SE1
156 B8 Grange Walk Mews SE1
156 B8 Grange Yard SE1
153 K2 Grantham Place W1K
148 B2 Grantully Road W9
149 J6 Granville Place W1H
148 A1 Granville Road NW6
150 F2 Granville Street WC1X
150 C6 Grape Street WC2H
154 E6 Graphite Square SE11
156 B2 Gravel Lane E1
150 D1 Gray's Inn Road WC1X
150 F5 Gray's Inn Square WC1R
149 K6 Gray's Yard * W1U
149 M6 Great Castle Street W1B
149 G4 Great Central Street NW1
150 B6 Great Chapel Street W1D
154 C4 Great College Street SW1P
149 H6 Great Cumberland Mews W1H
149 H6 Great Cumberland Place W1H
155 L4 Great Dover Street SE1
151 M3 Great Eastern Street EC2A
154 C3 Great George Street SW1H
155 J2 Great Guildford Street SE1
150 E4 Great James Street WC1N
149 M6 Great Marlborough Street W1B
155 L2 Great Maze Pond SE1
151 G6 Great New Street * EC4A
156 D1 Greatorex Street E1
150 D4 Great Ormond Street WC1N
150 F2 Great Percy Street WC1X
154 B4 Great Peter Street SW1P
149 L4 Great Portland Street W1W
149 L4 Great Portland Street W1W ⊖
150 A7 Great Pulteney Street W1F
150 D6 Great Queen Street WC2B
150 C5 Great Russell Street WC1B
151 K7 Great St Thomas Apostle EC4V
154 C1 Great Scotland Yard SW1A
154 C4 Great Smith Street SW1P
155 H2 Great Suffolk Street SE1
151 H4 Great Sutton Street EC1V
151 L6 Great Swan Alley EC2R
149 M4 Great Titchfield Street W1W
156 A4 Great Tower Street EC3R
151 K7 Great Trinity Lane EC4V
150 E5 Great Turnstile * WC1V
151 M5 Great Winchester Street EC2N
150 B7 Great Windmill Street W1D
157 K2 Greaves Cottages * E14
150 B6 Greek Street W1D
157 J6 Greenacre Square SE16
151 H6 Green Arbour Court * EC1A
156 F5 Green Bank E1W
148 F1 Greenberry Street NW8
154 A5 Greencoat Place SW1P
154 A5 Greencoat Row SW1P
156 C2 Green Dragon Yard E1
156 D2 Greenfield Road E1
155 G3 Greenham Close SE1
151 H4 Greenhill's Rents * EC1M
153 L1 Green Park W1J ⊖
150 B7 Green's Court W1F
149 J7 Green Street W1K
151 G2 Green Terrace EC1R
155 M2 Green Walk SE1
149 L4 Greenwell Street W1W
150 E3 Green Yard WC1X
155 G2 Greet Street SE1
152 B3 Gregory Place W8
155 J8 Greig Terrace SE17
157 L4 Grenade Street E14
148 F3 Grendon Street NW8
152 C5 Grenville Place SW7
150 D3 Grenville Street WC1N
151 J6 Gresham Street EC2V
150 B5 Gresse Street W1T
151 G5 Greville Street EC1N
154 B4 Greycoat Place SW1P
154 B5 Greycoat Street SW1P
156 B8 Grigg's Place SE1
154 F3 Grindal Street SE1
151 L6 Grocers' Hall Court * EC2R
153 K4 Groom Place SW1X
153 L8 Grosvenor Bridge SW1V
153 J5 Grosvenor Cottages SW1X
153 J3 Grosvenor Crescent SW1X
153 J3 Grosvenor Crescent Mews SW1X
153 L4 Grosvenor Gardens SW1W
153 L4 Grosvenor Gardens Mews East * SW1W
153 L4 Grosvenor Gardens Mews North SW1W
149 H8 Grosvenor Gate W1K
149 L7 Grosvenor Hill W1K
153 K2 Grosvenor Place SW1X
153 L8 Grosvenor Road SW1V
149 K7 Grosvenor Square W1K
149 K7 Grosvenor Street W1K
155 J3 Grotto Court * SE1
149 J5 Grotto Passage W1U
153 G8 Grove Cottages SW3
157 G1 Grove Dwellings * E1
148 D2 Grove End Road NW8
148 F2 Grove Gardens NW8
151 K6 Groveland Court EC4M
151 K6 Guildhall Buildings EC2V
151 K6 Guildhall Yard EC2V
153 M5 Guildhouse Street SW1V
150 E4 Guilford Place WC1N
150 E3 Guilford Street WC1N
156 A8 Guinness Square SE1
153 H6 Guinness Trust Estate SW3
157 L8 Gulliver Street SE16
156 B1 Gun Street E1
156 C2 Gunthorpe Street E1
157 G3 Gunwhale Close SE16
152 F6 Guthrie Street SW3
151 K6 Gutter Lane EC2V
155 L3 Guy Street SE1
150 F2 Gywnne Place WC1X

H

151 M2 Haberdasher Place N1
151 L2 Haberdasher Street N1
156 F5 Hainton Close E1
156 F1 Halcrow Street * E1
156 C2 Half Moon Passage E1
153 L1 Half Moon Street W1J
152 A8 Halford Road SW6
153 J4 Halkin Arcade SW1X
153 J4 Halkin Mews * SW1X
153 J4 Halkin Place SW1X
153 J3 Halkin Street SW1X
149 L4 Hallam Mews W1W
149 L4 Hallam Street W1W
157 K1 Halley Street E14
148 C6 Hallfield Estate W2
148 D2 Hall Gate NW8
148 E4 Hall Place W2
148 D2 Hall Road W9
151 H2 Hall Street EC1V
155 M6 Halpin Place SE17
153 G5 Halsey Street SW3
157 K7 Hamilton Close SE16
148 D2 Hamilton Close NW8
148 D2 Hamilton Gardens NW8
153 K2 Hamilton Mews W1J
153 K2 Hamilton Place W1K
148 C1 Hamilton Terrace NW8
155 L3 Hamlet Way SE1
156 B4 Hammett Street EC3N
150 C1 Hampden Close NW1
149 H6 Hampden Gurney Street W1H
149 M1 Hampstead Road NW1
155 J8 Hampton Street SE17
150 B7 Ham Yard * W1D
156 D1 Hanbury Street E1
150 E5 Hand Court WC1V
150 D3 Handel Street WC1N
155 L3 Hankey Place SE1
150 D7 Hanover Place WC2E
149 L6 Hanover Square W1S
149 G7 Hanover Steps * W2
149 L7 Hanover Street W1S
149 G2 Hanover Terrace NW1
149 G3 Hanover Terrace Mews NW1
153 H3 Hans Crescent SW1X
149 M4 Hanson Street W1W
153 H4 Hans Place SW1X
153 G4 Hans Road SW3
153 H4 Hans Street SW1X
150 B5 Hanway Place W1T
150 B6 Hanway Street W1T
148 F5 Harbet Road W2
151 G7 Harcourt Buildings * EC4Y
149 G5 Harcourt Street W1H
152 C7 Harcourt Terrace SW10
155 J8 Harding Close SE17
157 G3 Hardinge Street E1
150 F2 Hardwick Mews * WC1X
151 G2 Hardwick Street EC1R
155 M2 Hardwidge Street SE1
157 J6 Hardy Close SE16
151 G7 Hare Court * EC4Y
149 G3 Harewood Avenue NW8
149 L6 Harewood Place W1S
149 G4 Harewood Row NW1
154 E8 Harleyford Road SE11
154 F8 Harleyford Street SE11
152 D7 Harley Gardens SW10
149 K5 Harley Place W1G
149 K5 Harley Street W1G
155 G5 Harmsworth Mews SE1
155 H7 Harmsworth Street SE17
155 K4 Harper Road SE1
156 A4 Harp Lane EC3R
150 E4 Harpur Mews WC1N
150 E4 Harpur Street WC1N
153 H3 Harriet Street SW1X
153 H3 Harriet Walk SW1X
152 C6 Harrington Gardens SW7
152 D5 Harrington Road SW7
149 M1 Harrington Square NW1
149 M1 Harrington Street NW1
150 D2 Harrison Street WC1H
149 G6 Harrowby Street W1H
156 B2 Harrow Place E1
148 E5 Harrow Road Flyover W2
148 F4 Harrow Street * NW1
156 A3 Hart Street EC3R
153 G5 Hasker Street SW3
150 C2 Hastings Street WC1H
156 A7 Hatchers Mews SE1
155 G1 Hatfields SE1
148 B6 Hatherley Grove W2
154 A6 Hatherley Street SW1P
151 H4 Hat & Mitre Court EC1M
157 G6 Hatteraick Street * SE16
151 G4 Hatton Garden EC1N
151 G4 Hatton Place EC1N
148 E4 Hatton Row * NW8
148 E4 Hatton Street NW8
151 G4 Hatton Wall EC1N
149 L7 Haunch of Venison Yard * W1C
157 L1 Havens Mews E3
157 H3 Havering Street E1
151 G1 Haverstock Place EC1V
151 J1 Haverstock Street N1
157 H6 Hawke Place SE16
156 E3 Hawksmoor Mews * E1
156 B3 Haydon Street EC3N
156 C3 Haydon Walk E1
149 G4 Hayes Place NW1
149 L8 Hay Hill W1J
155 H5 Hayles Street SE11
150 B8 Haymarket SW1Y
151 J4 Hayne Street EC1A
155 M1 Hay's Lane SE1
149 L8 Hay's Mews W1J
151 H3 Hayward's Place * EC1R
153 K3 Headfort Place SW1X
157 H2 Head Street E1
155 M6 Hearn's Buildings SE17
157 K2 Hearnshaw Street E14
150 E3 Heathcote Street WC1N
157 H3 Heckford Street E1W
149 M7 Heddon Street W1S
155 H5 Hedger Street SE11
155 J8 Heiron Street SE17
157 J4 Helena Square SE16
156 D5 Hellings Street E1W
151 K3 Helmet Row EC1V
157 K8 Helsinki Square SE16
155 L5 Hemp Walk SE17
148 E3 Henderson Drive NW8
156 B2 Heneage Lane EC3A
156 C1 Heneage Street E1
152 D8 Henniker Mews SW3
150 D3 Henrietta Mews WC1N
149 K6 Henrietta Place W1G
150 D7 Henrietta Street WC2E
156 D3 Henriques Street E1
155 L5 Henshaw Street SE17
155 H5 Heralds Place SE11
151 G4 Herbal Hill EC1R
153 H4 Herbert Crescent SW1X
150 D4 Herbrand Street WC1N
154 F4 Hercules Road SE1
148 A6 Hereford Mews W2
148 A7 Hereford Road W2
152 D6 Hereford Square SW7
150 F1 Hermes Street N1
148 E5 Hermitage Street W2
156 D5 Hermitage Wall E1W
151 H2 Hermit Street EC1V
157 K5 Heron Place SE16
154 C6 Herrick Street SW1P
150 A4 Hertford Place W1T
153 K1 Hertford Street W1J
157 M5 Hertsmere Road E14
152 B6 Hesper Mews SW5
156 E3 Hessel Street E1
155 K5 Heygate Estate SE17
155 J5 Heygate Street SE17
154 B6 Hide Place SW1P
150 D5 High Holborn WC1V
152 A3 High Street Kensington W8 ⊖
151 J7 High Timber Street EC4V
149 G4 Highworth Street * NW1
152 A8 Hildyard Road SW6
155 L6 Hillery Close SE17
148 C7 Hill Gardens Craven * W2
156 F5 Hilliard's Court E1W
148 D1 Hill Road NW8
148 B1 Hillside Close NW8
149 M6 Hills Place W1D
153 K1 Hill Street W1J
151 G6 Hind Court EC4A
149 K6 Hinde Mews * W1U
149 K6 Hinde Street W1U
156 D4 Hindmarsh Close E1
157 H8 Hithe Grove SE16
153 K4 Hobart Place SW1W
156 D1 Hobsons Place E1
152 D8 Hobury Street SW10
151 L2 Hoffman Square * N1
148 D5 Hogan Mews W2
152 A6 Hogarth Place * SW5
152 B6 Hogarth Road SW5
156 F4 Hogshead Passage * E1W
153 J6 Holbein Mews SW1W
153 J6 Holbein Place SW1W
150 D5 Holborn WC1V ⊖
151 G5 Holborn EC4A
151 G5 Holborn Circus EC1N
150 E5 Holborn Place WC1V
151 H5 Holborn Viaduct EC1A
150 F5 Holburn WC1R
150 E2 Holford Mews * WC1X
150 F2 Holford Street WC1X
150 F1 Holford Yard * WC1X
152 A3 Holland Place W8
152 A3 Holland Street W8
151 H8 Holland Street SE1
150 B6 Hollen Street W1F
149 L6 Holles Street W1G
152 D7 Holly Mews SW10
152 C8 Hollywood Mews SW10
152 C8 Hollywood Road SW10
155 G3 Holmes Terrace SE1
150 F4 Holsworthy Square WC1X
157 L6 Holyoake Court SE16
155 H5 Holyoak Road SE11
156 A4 Holyrood Street SE1
151 M4 Holywell Row EC2A
151 M1 Homefield Street * N1
149 G5 Homer Row NW1
149 G5 Homer Street W1H
151 J3 Honduras Street EC1V
156 D3 Hooper Street E1
156 A2 Hope Square EC2M
156 C1 Hopetown Street E1
150 C7 Hop Gardens WC2N
150 B7 Hopkins Street W1F
155 H1 Hoptons Gardens * SE1
151 J8 Hopton Street SE1
155 L8 Hopwood Road SE17
154 F5 Hornbeam Close SE11
152 A3 Hornton Place W8
152 A3 Hornton Street W8
157 J3 Horseferry Road E14
154 B5 Horseferry Road SW1P
154 D2 Horse Guards Avenue SW1A
154 C2 Horse Guards Road SW1A
156 B6 Horselydown Lane SE1
155 K8 Horsley Street SE17
155 K8 Horsman Street SE5
151 H5 Hosier Lane EC1A
157 G8 Hothfield Place SE16
154 F6 Hotspur Street SE11
150 E6 Houghton Street * WC2A
156 B2 Houndsditch EC3A
155 J6 Howell Walk SE1
154 A4 Howick Place SW1E
150 A4 Howland Mews East W1T
150 A4 Howland Street W1T
157 K7 Howland Way SE16
148 D4 Howley Place W2
151 M2 Hoxton Market N1
151 M2 Hoxton Square N1
157 M1 Huddart Street E3
151 K7 Huggin Hill EC4V
153 L6 Hugh Mews SW1V
154 B5 Hugh Place SW1P
153 L6 Hugh Street SW1V
156 C1 Huguenot Place E1
157 J6 Hull Close SE16
151 J2 Hull Street EC1V
155 K3 Hulme Place SE1
156 F2 Hungerford Street * E1
155 M4 Hunter Close SE1
150 D3 Hunter Street WC1N
150 B4 Huntley Street WC1E
156 D1 Hunton Street E1
155 M6 Huntsman Street SE17
149 G3 Huntsworth Mews NW1
157 H6 Hurley Crescent SE16
157 M7 Hutching's Street E14
151 G7 Hutton Street EC4Y
153 J2 Hyde Park Corner SW1X ⊖
153 K2 Hyde Park Corner W1J
148 F6 Hyde Park Crescent W2
148 E7 Hyde Park Gardens W2
148 F7 Hyde Park Gardens Mews W2
152 D3 Hyde Park Gate SW7
152 D3 Hyde Park Gate Mews * SW7
149 G7 Hyde Park Place W2
148 F7 Hyde Park Square W2
148 F6 Hyde Park Square Mews W2
148 F7 Hyde Park Street W2

I

156 A4 Idol Lane EC3R
152 B8 Ifield Road SW10
148 B7 Ilchester Gardens W2
155 J6 Iliffe Street SE17
155 J6 Iliffe Yard SE17
152 E4 Imperial College Road SW7
156 B3 India Street EC3N
150 A7 Ingestre Place W1F
150 F2 Inglebert Street EC1R
156 F5 Inglefield Square * E1W
154 F5 Ingram Close SE11
149 J3 Inner Circle NW1
148 B6 Inver Court W2
152 A2 Inverness Gardens W8
148 B7 Inverness Mews W2
148 B7 Inverness Place W2
148 B6 Inverness Terrace W2
155 H1 Invicta Plaza SE1
155 L7 Inville Road SE17
151 K6 Ironmonger Lane EC2V
151 K2 Ironmonger Row EC1V
157 H6 Ironside Close SE16
150 C8 Irving Street WC2H
155 K3 Isaac Way SE1
155 H2 Isabella Street SE1
157 H6 Isambard Place SE16
157 L3 Island Row E14
152 A4 Iverna Court W8
152 A4 Iverna Gardens W8
153 G5 Ives Street SW3
149 G4 Ivor Place NW1
152 F6 Ixworth Place SW3

J

156 D6 Jacob Street SE1
149 K5 Jacob's Well Mews W1U
156 C7 Jamaica Road SE1
157 G2 Jamaica Street E1
152 A1 Jameson Street W8
150 D7 James Street WC2E
149 K6 James Street W1U
156 F3 James Voller Way E1
157 K1 Jamuna Close E14
156 E2 Jane Street E1
156 E7 Janeway Place SE16
156 E7 Janeway Street SE16
157 J4 Jardine Road E1W
152 D3 Jay Mews SW7
150 B8 Jermyn Street SW1Y
156 B1 Jerome Street E1
151 H3 Jerusalem Passage EC1R
156 B3 Jewry Street EC3N
155 H2 Joan Street SE1
150 E4 Jockey's Fields WC1X
154 F3 Johanna Street * SE1
150 D8 John Adam Street WC2N
148 D5 John Aird Court W2
151 G7 John Carpenter Street EC4Y
156 D7 John Felton Road SE16
156 D4 John Fisher Street E1
157 J8 John Harrison Way SE16
154 C6 John Islip Street SW1P
155 L5 John Maurice Close SE17
156 E8 John McKenna Walk SE16
149 L6 John Prince's Street W1G
156 F5 John Rennie Walk E1W
156 D7 John Roll Way SE16
155 J8 John Ruskin Street SE5
150 E4 John's Mews WC1N
151 G6 Johnson's Court EC4A
154 A7 Johnson's Place SW1V
157 G3 Johnson Street E1
156 F2 Johns Place E1
150 E4 John Street WC1N
151 J5 John Trundle Highwalk * EC2Y
155 L2 Joiner Street SE1
154 E6 Jonathan Street SE11
151 G2 Joseph Trotter Close EC1R
154 E2 Jubilee Gardens * SE1
150 D7 Jubilee Market * WC2E
153 G6 Jubilee Place SW3
157 G2 Jubilee Street E1
150 D2 Judd Street WC1H
148 F5 Junction Mews W2
148 F5 Junction Place * W2
157 G4 Juniper Street E1
152 F8 Justice Walk SW3
154 F5 Juxon Street SE11

K

157 H5 Katherine Close SE16
150 E6 Kean Street WC2B
157 J6 Keel Close SE16
150 E6 Keeley Street WC2B
155 L8 Keesey Street SE17
156 E8 Keeton's Road SE16
155 H4 Kell Street SE1
152 B4 Kelso Place W8
150 E6 Kemble Street WC2B
152 A7 Kempsford Gardens SW5
155 G6 Kempsford Road SE11
149 J5 Kendall Place W1U
149 G7 Kendal Steps * W2
149 G6 Kendal Street W2
152 E5 Kendrick Mews SW7
152 E6 Kendrick Place * SW7
155 L6 Kennedy Walk SE17
156 D5 Kennet Street E1W
151 K7 Kennett Wharf Lane EC4V
157 G6 Kenning Street SE16
155 G7 Kennings Way SE11
155 H7 Kennington SE11 ⊖
154 E7 Kennington Lane SE11
154 F8 Kennington Oval SE11
155 H8 Kennington Park Gardens SE11
155 G7 Kennington Park Place SE11
155 H6 Kennington Park Road SE11
155 G5 Kennington Road SE11
149 J5 Kenrick Place W1U
152 B3 Kensington Church Court W8
152 A1 Kensington Church Street W8
152 A3 Kensington Church Walk * W8
152 C3 Kensington Court W8
152 B4 Kensington Court Gardens * W8
152 B3 Kensington Court Mews * W8
152 B4 Kensington Court Place W8
148 B6 Kensington Gardens Square W2
152 C4 Kensington Gate W8
152 A4 Kensington High Street W8
152 A1 Kensington Mall W8
152 B2 Kensington Palace * W8
152 B2 Kensington Palace Gardens W8
152 B3 Kensington Road W8
152 D3 Kensington Road SW7
152 B3 Kensington Square W8
150 D3 Kenton Street WC1H
149 G3 Kent Passage NW1
149 G2 Kent Terrace NW1
153 G3 Kent Yard SW7
152 A6 Kenway Road SW5
150 C4 Keppel Street WC1E
150 D1 Keystone Crescent N1
155 H4 Keyworth Street SE1
151 M3 Kiffen Street EC2A
148 A1 Kilburn Park Road NW6
148 A6 Kildare Gardens W2
148 A6 Kildare Terrace W2
150 E1 Killick Street N1
157 H6 Kinburn Street SE16
156 E3 Kinder Street E1
155 K6 King & Queen Street SE17
154 C1 King Charles I Island SW1A
154 C3 King Charles Street SW1A
156 F4 King Charles Terrace * E1W
157 G3 King David Lane E1
151 J6 King Edward Street EC1A
156 F7 King Edward III Mews SE16
155 G4 King Edward Walk SE1
156 F4 King Henry Terrace * E1W
151 J5 Kinghorn Street EC1A
155 J3 King James Court SE1
155 H3 King James Street SE1
157 J1 King John Street E1
155 M7 Kinglake Estate * SE17
155 M7 Kinglake Street SE17
150 A7 Kingly Court * W1B
149 M7 Kingly Street W1B
155 K6 King & Queen Street * SE17
157 J5 King & Queen Wharf * SE16
151 L6 King's Arms Yard EC2R
155 H3 King's Bench Street SE1
151 G7 King's Bench Walk * EC4Y
151 H7 Kingscote Street EC4V
155 J3 King's Court * SE1 ⊖
150 D1 King's Cross N1 ⇌
150 D1 King's Cross Bridge * N1
150 E1 King's Cross Road WC1X
150 D1 King's Cross St Pancras N1 ⊖
152 B4 Kingsley Mews W8
156 F4 Kingsley Mews E1W
150 F4 King's Mews WC1N
155 K3 King's Place SE1
151 J2 King Square EC1V
151 G7 Kings Reach * EC4Y
154 D1 Kings Reach SW1A
153 G7 King's Road SW3
153 M5 King's Scholars' Passage SW1V
156 F6 King Stairs Close SE16
151 K6 King Street EC2V
150 D7 King Street WC2E
154 A1 King Street SW1A

150 E6 Kingsway WC2B
151 G3 Kingsway Place * EC1R
151 L7 King William Street EC4R
153 H3 Kinnerton Place North * SW1X
153 J3 Kinnerton Place South * SW1X
153 J3 Kinnerton Street SW1X
153 J3 Kinnerton Yard * SW1X
155 L3 Kipling Estate SE1
155 L3 Kipling Street SE1
156 F7 Kirby Estate SE16
155 M3 Kirby Grove SE1
151 G4 Kirby Street EC1N
152 B5 Knaresborough Place SW5
156 E6 Knighten Street E1W
151 J7 Knightrider Court * EC4V
151 J7 Knightrider Street EC4V
153 G4 Knightsbridge SW1X ⊖
153 G3 Knightsbridge SW7
153 H3 Knightsbridge Green * SW1X
155 H6 Knights Walk SE11
149 H4 Knox Street NW1
152 A7 Kramer Mews SW5
152 C4 Kynance Mews SW7
152 C4 Kynance Place W8

L

151 L4 Lackington Street EC2A
156 B6 Lafone Street SE1
157 J5 Lagado Mews SE16
151 J4 Lambert Jones Mews * EC2Y
154 D5 Lambeth Bridge SW1P
155 G5 Lambeth High Street SE1
151 J7 Lambeth Hill EC4V
154 F3 Lambeth North SE1 ⊖
154 E4 Lambeth Palace Road SE1
154 F4 Lambeth Road SE1
155 G4 Lambeth Walk SE11
150 E4 Lamb's Conduit Passage WC1X
150 E4 Lamb's Conduit Street WC1N
151 K4 Lamb's Passage EC1Y
156 B1 Lamb Street E1
156 A7 Lamb Walk SE1
155 H5 Lamlash Street SE11
152 E8 Lamont Road Passage SW10
148 D3 Lanark Place W9
148 C3 Lanark Road W9
149 L7 Lancashire Court W1K
148 D7 Lancaster Court W2
148 D8 Lancaster Gate W2
148 E7 Lancaster Gate W2 ⊖
148 D7 Lancaster Mews W2
150 E7 Lancaster Place WC2R
155 H3 Lancaster Street SE1
148 E7 Lancaster Terrace W2
153 G3 Lancelot Place SW7
152 B3 Lancer Square W8
150 B2 Lancing Street NW1
153 H4 Landon Place SW1X
155 J8 Langdale Close SE17
156 E3 Langdale Street * E1
148 D1 Langford Place NW8
149 L5 Langham Place W1B
149 L5 Langham Street W1B
150 D7 Langley Court WC2E
154 D8 Langley Lane SW8
150 D7 Langley Street WC2H
151 L5 Langthorn Court * EC2R
150 E3 Langton Close WC1X
155 L4 Lansdowne Place SE1
150 D3 Lansdowne Terrace WC1N
155 J3 Lant Street SE1
148 C5 Lapworth Court W2
155 K6 Larcom Street SE17
155 M6 Larissa Street * SE17
148 B3 Lauderdale Parade * W9
151 K5 Lauderdale Place * EC2Y
148 B3 Lauderdale Road W9
154 E7 Laud Street SE11
154 F3 Launcelot Street SE1
152 C4 Launceston Place W8
151 L7 Laurence Pountney Hill EC4R
151 L7 Laurence Pountney Lane EC4R
152 F8 Lavender Close SW3
157 K5 Lavender Road SE16
152 B6 Laverton Mews * SW5
152 B6 Laverton Place SW5
155 J2 Lavington Street SE1
154 D8 Lawn Lane SW8
151 K6 Lawrence Lane EC2V
152 F8 Lawrence Street SW3
155 L4 Law Street SE1
149 L3 Laxton Place NW1
150 F4 Laystall Street WC1X
150 D7 Lazenby Court * WC2E
156 A3 Leadenhall Place EC3V
151 M6 Leadenhall Street EC3V
154 E3 Leake Street SE1
151 G4 Leather Lane EC1R
155 M3 Leathermarket Court SE1
155 M3 Leathermarket Street SE1
157 H3 Leather Street E1W
152 E7 Lecky Street SW7
150 E2 Leeke Street WC1X
149 J7 Lees Place W1K
150 C7 Leicester Place * WC2H
150 C7 Leicester Square WC2H
150 C7 Leicester Square WC2H ⊖
150 B7 Leicester Street WC2H
150 C3 Leigh Street WC1H
148 C6 Leinster Gardens W2
148 C7 Leinster Mews W2
148 C7 Leinster Place W2
148 A7 Leinster Square W2
148 C7 Leinster Terrace W2
156 C3 Leman Street E1
153 G5 Lennox Gardens SW1X
153 G5 Lennox Gardens Mews SW1X
151 M3 Leonard Street EC2A
157 M1 Leopold Estate E3
157 M1 Leopold Street E3
155 M5 Leroy Street SE1
153 G5 Leverett Street SW3
151 J2 Lever Street EC1V
152 A5 Lexham Gardens W8
152 A5 Lexham Mews W8
150 A7 Lexington Street W1F
156 B2 Leyden Street E1
157 H5 Leydon Close SE16
155 H3 Library Street SE1
150 A1 Lidlington Place NW1
157 J2 Lighterman Mews E1
154 E6 Lilac Place SE11
148 F3 Lilestone Street NW8
156 F5 Lilley Close E1W
152 A8 Lillie Yard SW6
154 A6 Lillington Gardens Estate SW1V
151 G4 Lily Place EC1M
151 H6 Limeburner Lane EC4M
156 D5 Lime Close E1W
157 M4 Limehouse * E14
157 J3 Limehouse E1 ⇌ ⊖
157 M4 Limehouse Causeway E14
157 K1 Limehouse Fields Estate E14
157 K3 Limehouse Link E14
152 D8 Limerston Street SW10
151 M7 Lime Street EC3M
151 M7 Lime Street Passage * EC3V
150 E6 Lincoln's Inn Fields WC2A
153 H6 Lincoln Street SW3
148 A8 Linden Gardens W2
148 A8 Linden Mews W2
156 F2 Lindley Street E1
154 C7 Lindsay Square SW1V
151 J4 Lindsey Street EC1M
149 G3 Linhope Street NW1
156 C1 Links Yard E1
156 D8 Linsey Street SE16
157 H3 Lipton Road E1
150 B7 Lisle Street WC2H
148 F3 Lisson Grove NW8
148 F4 Lisson Street NW1
150 C7 Litchfield Street WC2H
149 L3 Little Albany Street NW1
149 M6 Little Argyll Street * W1B
151 J5 Little Britain EC1A
153 K4 Little Chester Street SW1X
154 C4 Little Cloisters SW1P
154 C4 Little Deans Yard SW1P
155 K2 Little Dorrit Court SE1
149 L2 Little Edward Street * NW1
150 F7 Little Essex Street * WC2R
154 C3 Little George Street SW1P
149 M7 Little Marlborough Street * W1B
150 C7 Little Newport Street WC2H
151 G6 Little New Street EC4A
149 L6 Little Portland Street W1B
150 D5 Little Russell Street WC1A
153 M2 Little St James's Street SW1A
154 C4 Little Smith Street SW1P
156 B3 Little Somerset Street EC3N
149 M5 Little Titchfield Street W1W
151 K7 Little Trinity Lane EC4V
150 E5 Little Turnstile WC1V
155 K7 Liverpool Grove SE17
151 M5 Liverpool Street EC2M
156 A1 Liverpool Street EC2M ⇌ ⊖
151 K2 Lizard Street EC1V
156 D7 Llewellyn Street SE16
150 F2 Lloyd Baker Street WC1X
156 B3 Lloyd's Avenue EC3M
150 F2 Lloyd Square WC1X
151 G2 Lloyd's Row EC1R
150 F2 Lloyd Street WC1X
157 L2 Locksley Estate E14
157 L1 Locksley Street E14
156 E8 Lockwood Square SE16
155 L3 Lockyer Street SE1
148 F2 Lodge Road NW8
156 D7 Loftie Street SE16
156 C1 Lolesworth Close E1
154 F5 Lollard Street SE11
155 J2 Loman Street SE1
156 E1 Lomas Street E1
151 G6 Lombard Lane EC4Y
151 L7 Lombard Street EC3V
148 B7 Lombardy Place W2
151 L8 London Bridge EC4R
155 M2 London Bridge SE1 ⇌ ⊖
155 L1 London Bridge Street SE1
155 L1 London Bridge Walk * SE1
156 B1 London Fruit Exchange * E1
148 E6 London Mews W2
155 H4 London Road SE1
148 E6 London Street W2
156 A3 London Street * EC3M
151 K5 London Wall EC2V
151 L5 London Wall Buildings EC2M
150 C7 Long Acre WC2H
149 L3 Longford Street NW1
151 J5 Long Lane EC1A
155 M4 Long Lane SE1
153 M6 Longmoore Street SW1V
155 H5 Longville Road SE11
156 B8 Long Walk SE1
150 E4 Long Yard WC1N
148 B4 Lord Hills Road W2
154 C4 Lord North Street SW1P
152 F8 Lordship Place SW3
148 F2 Lords View NW8
150 E1 Lorenzo Street WC1X
149 G2 Lorne Close NW8
155 J8 Lorrimore Road SE17
155 J8 Lorrimore Square SE17
151 L6 Lothbury EC2R
154 F7 Loughborough Street SE11
151 M7 Lovat Lane EC3M
151 K6 Love Lane EC2V
157 K7 Lovell Place SE16
157 K2 Lowell Street E14
153 K4 Lower Belgrave Street SW1W
153 L4 Lower Grosvenor Place SW1W
150 A7 Lower James Street * W1F
150 A7 Lower John Street W1F
154 F3 Lower Marsh SE1
157 G8 Lower Road SE16
150 D8 Lower Robert Street WC2N
153 J6 Lower Sloane Street SW1W
156 A4 Lower Thames Street EC3R
153 J4 Lowndes Close SW1X
149 M7 Lowndes Court * W1F
153 J4 Lowndes Place * SW1X
153 H3 Lowndes Square SW1X
153 J4 Lowndes Street SW1X
156 F4 Lowood Street E1
150 D2 Loxham Street * WC1H
152 F6 Lucan Place SW3
152 A1 Lucerne Mews * W8
156 D8 Lucey Road SE16
156 E8 Lucey Way SE16
151 H6 Ludgate Broadway * EC4V
151 H6 Ludgate Circus EC4M
151 H6 Ludgate Hill EC4M
151 H6 Ludgate Square * EC4M
151 J3 Ludlow Street * EC1V
151 M3 Luke Street EC2A
157 G3 Lukin Street E1
149 K7 Lumley Street W1C
153 L7 Lupus Street SW1V
148 E4 Luton Street NW8
149 J4 Luxborough Street NW1
153 J4 Lyall Mews SW1X
153 J5 Lyall Mews West * SW1X
153 J5 Lyall Street SW1X
153 L4 Lygon Place * SW1W
148 E3 Lyons Place NW8
155 L7 Lytham Street SE17

M

150 C2 Mabledon Place NW1
151 J2 Macclesfield Road EC1V
150 B7 Macclesfield Street * W1D
156 E5 Mace Close E1W
149 K4 Mac Farren Place NW1
148 F1 Mackennal Street NW8
150 D6 Macklin Street * WC2B
149 M2 Mackworth Street NW1
155 K7 Macleod Street SE17
155 H8 Maddock Way SE17
149 L7 Maddox Street W1S
153 G1 Magazine Gate * W2
156 A6 Magdalen Street SE1
154 F8 Magee Street SE11
157 G2 Magri Walk E1
156 C6 Maguire Street SE1
157 K6 Mahogany Close SE16
148 D4 Maida Avenue W2
148 B1 Maida Vale W9
148 D3 Maida Vale NW8
148 C2 Maida Vale W9 ⊖
150 D7 Maiden Lane WC2E
155 K1 Maiden Lane SE1
155 K2 Maidstone Buildings Mews SE1
156 E7 Major Road SE16
153 G6 Makins Street SW3
150 B4 Malet Street WC1E
152 A1 Mall Chambers * W8
152 E8 Mallord Street SW3
148 F3 Mallory Street NW8
151 L3 Mallow Street EC1V
151 H3 Malta Street EC1V
156 B7 Maltby Street SE1
156 B6 Maltings Place SE1
150 F7 Maltravers Street WC2R
149 J5 Manchester Mews W1U
149 J6 Manchester Square W1H
149 J5 Manchester Street W1U
155 L3 Manciple Street SE1
149 K6 Mandeville Place W1U
150 B6 Manette Street W1D
157 M6 Manilla Street E14
151 H2 Manningford Close * EC1V
156 C2 Manningtree Street E1
155 J7 Manor Place SE17
152 E7 Manresa Road SW3
156 C3 Mansell Street E1
149 L5 Mansfield Mews W1G
149 L5 Mansfield Street W1G
151 K7 Mansion House EC4M ⊖
151 L7 Mansion House Place * EC4N
151 L6 Mansion House Street EC4N
152 D5 Manson Mews SW7
152 E6 Manson Place SW7
157 J6 Maple Leaf Square SE16
150 A4 Maple Place W1T
156 F1 Maples Place E1
149 M4 Maple Street W1T
149 H7 Marble Arch W1C ⊖
156 C5 Marble Quay E1W
150 C3 Marchmont Street WC1H
156 E8 Marden Square SE16
149 L6 Margaret Street W1B
152 F8 Margaretta Terrace SW3
150 F3 Margery Street EC1R
151 G8 Marigold Alley SE1
156 E7 Marigold Street SE16
156 D8 Marine Street SE16
153 K2 Market Mews W1J
149 M6 Market Place W1W
156 A7 Market Yard Mews SE1
153 G6 Markham Place * SW3
153 G6 Markham Square SW3
153 G6 Markham Street SW3
156 A4 Mark Lane EC3R
151 M3 Mark Street EC2A
155 J6 Marlborough Close SE17
149 M7 Marlborough Court * W1B
148 E7 Marlborough Gate W2
148 C1 Marlborough Place NW8
154 A2 Marlborough Road SW1A
152 F6 Marlborough Street SW3
152 A4 Marloes Road W8
157 H6 Marlow Way SE16
157 K2 Maroon Street E14
156 C8 Marshall's Place SE16
150 A7 Marshall Street W1F
155 K2 Marshalsea Road SE1
154 C5 Marsham Street SW1P
155 J7 Marsland Close SE17
151 L3 Martha's Buildings EC1V
156 F3 Martha Street E1
157 G3 Martineau Street E1
151 L7 Martin Lane EC4R
150 D6 Martlett Court WC2B
148 A4 Maryland Road W9
148 A3 Marylands Road W9
149 G4 Marylebone NW1 ⇌ ⊖
148 F5 Marylebone Flyover W2
149 K4 Marylebone High Street W1U
149 K6 Marylebone Lane W1U
149 K5 Marylebone Mews W1G
150 A6 Marylebone Passage W1W
149 G4 Marylebone Road W1H
149 K5 Marylebone Street W1G
154 F6 Marylee Way SE11
149 L7 Mason's Arms Mews * W1S
151 L6 Mason's Avenue EC2V
151 H2 Mason's Place EC1V
155 M5 Mason Street SE17
151 J3 Masons Yard EC1V
154 A1 Masons Yard SW1Y
155 M6 Massinger Street SE17
157 J1 Master's Street E1
155 J7 Matara Mews SE17
150 C6 Mathews Yard * WC2H
155 H3 Mathieson Court SE1
157 J2 Matlock Street E14
154 B5 Maunsel Street SW1P
155 K3 Mayall Close SE1
153 L1 Mayfair Place W1J
156 F7 Mayflower Street SE16
156 F4 Maynards Quay E1W
150 C7 Mays Court WC2N
154 F4 McAuley Close SE1
155 J3 McCoid Way SE1
152 C5 McLeod's Mews SW7
155 H8 Meadcroft Road SE11
155 J5 Meadow Row SE1
155 G4 Mead Row SE1
150 B7 Meard Street W1F
150 E3 Mecklenburgh Place WC1N
150 E3 Mecklenburgh Square WC1N
150 E3 Mecklenburgh Street WC1N
154 B5 Medway Street SW1P
156 F5 Meeting House Alley * E1W
150 E6 Melbourne Place WC2B
149 G4 Melbury Terrace NW1
149 G4 Melcombe Place NW1
149 H4 Melcombe Street NW1
148 D2 Melina Place NW8
155 M2 Melior Place * SE1
155 M2 Melior Street SE1
152 A2 Melon Place * W8
150 B2 Melton Street NW1
151 J3 Memel Street EC1Y
154 F2 Mepham Street SE1
157 J2 Mercers Cottages * E1
150 C6 Mercer Street WC2H
151 H2 Meredith Street EC1R
151 G2 Merlin Street WC1X
155 L2 Mermaid Court SE1
155 K4 Merrick Square SE1
152 A8 Merrington Road SW6
155 L7 Merrow Street SE17
155 L6 Merrow Walk SE17
149 G5 Mertoun Terrace * W1H
155 G7 Methley Street SE11
157 G5 Metropolitan Wharf * E1W
153 L4 Mews North SW1W
156 C5 Mews Street E1W
155 G2 Meymott Street SE1
156 D5 Miah Terrace * E1W
151 K1 Micawber Street N1
152 A8 Micklethwaite Road SW6
156 B1 Middlesex Street E1
151 J5 Middle Street EC1A
150 F6 Middle Temple Lane EC4Y
157 J6 Middleton Drive SE16
149 M5 Middleton Place W1W
155 M1 Middle Yard SE1
150 A4 Midford Place * W1T
150 D2 Midhope Street WC1H
150 C1 Midland Road NW1
157 J6 Midship Close SE16
152 D7 Milborne Grove SW10
155 H3 Milcote Street SE1
156 F1 Mile End Road E1
154 D8 Miles Street SW8
150 F7 Milford Lane WC2R
151 K6 Milk Street EC2V
157 G4 Milk Yard E1W
154 D5 Millbank SW1P
154 C6 Millbank Estate SW1P
151 J8 Millennium Bridge SE1
156 C6 Millennium Square SE1
155 G1 Miller Walk SE1
157 M4 Milligan Street E14
150 E4 Millman Mews * WC1N
150 E4 Millman Place WC1N
150 E3 Millman Street WC1N
157 L3 Mill Place E14
154 C1 Millshott Close * SW1A
156 B7 Millstream Road SE1
149 L7 Mill Street W1S
156 C7 Mill Street SE1
156 D3 Mill Yard E1
152 E8 Milman's Street SW10
153 G5 Milner Street SW3
151 G8 Milroy Walk SE1
151 L4 Milton Court EC2Y
151 K4 Milton Street EC2Y
155 G7 Milverton Street SE11
156 E2 Milward Street E1
156 A4 Mincing Lane EC3R
153 J5 Minera Mews SW1W
156 B3 Minories EC3N
156 A4 Minster Court * EC3R
155 J2 Mint Street SE1
156 F2 Miranda Close * E1
156 D3 Mitali Passage E1
151 J3 Mitchell Street EC1V
155 G3 Mitre Road SE1
156 B3 Mitre Square EC3A
156 B3 Mitre Street EC3A
157 M7 Moiety Road E14
149 G5 Molyneux Street W1H
154 C4 Monck Street SW1P
152 F3 Moncorvo Close SW7
155 G5 Monkton Street SE11
151 K5 Monkwell Square EC2Y
148 A6 Monmouth Place W2
148 A6 Monmouth Road W2
150 C6 Monmouth Street WC2H
155 L1 Montague Close SE1
150 C5 Montague Place WC1E
150 D5 Montague Street WC1B
151 J5 Montague Street EC1A
149 H5 Montagu Mansions W1U
149 H5 Montagu Mews North W1H
149 H6 Montagu Mews South W1H
149 H5 Montagu Mews West W1H
149 H5 Montagu Place W1H
149 H5 Montagu Row W1U
149 H5 Montagu Square W1H
149 H6 Montagu Street W1H
154 C6 Montaigne Close SW1P
154 F7 Montford Place SE11
156 D1 Monthope Road E1
153 G4 Montpelier Mews SW7
157 G3 Montpelier Place E1
153 G3 Montpelier Square SW7
153 G3 Montpelier Street SW7
152 F3 Montpelier Terrace SW7
152 F3 Montpelier Walk SW7
150 E7 Montreal Place WC2B
153 K3 Montrose Place SW1X
151 L7 Monument EC4N ⊖
157 G4 Monza Street E1W
157 G7 Moodkee Street SE16
153 H5 Moore Street SW3
151 L5 Moorfields EC2M
151 L5 Moorfields Highwalk EC2Y
151 L5 Moorgate EC2M
151 L5 Moorgate Place * EC2R
151 K5 Moorgate EC2Y ⇌ ⊖
151 L5 Moor Lane EC2Y
150 C7 Moor Street W1D
151 K2 Mora Street EC1V
155 K6 Morecambe Street SE17
157 H1 Morecambe Close E1
155 M7 Morecambe Street SE17
151 H2 Moreland Street EC1V
156 A5 More London Riverside SE1
154 A6 Moreton Place SW1V
154 A7 Moreton Street SW1V
154 A6 Moreton Terrace SW1V
154 A7 Moreton Terrace Mews South SW1V
155 G3 Morley Street SE1
149 M1 Mornington Crescent NW1
149 L1 Mornington Place NW1
156 A7 Morocco Street SE1
153 M5 Morpeth Terrace SW1P
155 G7 Morrells Yard SE11
156 F3 Morris Street E1
148 A2 Morshead Road W9
149 L5 Mortimer Street W1W
156 F3 Morton Close E1
152 B6 Morton Mews SW5
154 F4 Morton Place SE1
150 B5 Morwell Street WC1B
148 B7 Moscow Place W2
148 A7 Moscow Road W2
156 D1 Moss Close E1
153 G5 Mossop Street SW3
153 J4 Motcomb Street SW1X
156 D2 Mountford Street E1
151 J3 Mount Mills EC1V
150 F4 Mount Pleasant WC1X
149 K8 Mount Row W1K
149 K8 Mount Street W1K
156 E1 Mount Terrace E1
149 J5 Moxon Street W1U
156 D2 Mulberry Street E1
152 E8 Mulberry Walk SW3
148 F4 Mulready Street NW8
151 K6 Mumford Court EC2V
151 M2 Mundy Street N1
149 L3 Munster Square NW1
155 K5 Munton Road SE17
154 F3 Murphy Street SE1
151 K1 Murray Grove N1
157 G2 Musbury Street E1
156 B4 Muscovy Street EC3R
150 C5 Museum Street WC1A
151 G2 Myddelton Passage EC1R
151 G2 Myddelton Square EC1R
151 G2 Myddelton Street EC1R
151 G1 Mylne Street N1
156 E2 Myrdle Street E1
151 M1 Myrtle Street N1
151 M1 Myrtle Walk N1

N

150 F2 Naoroji Street WC1X
151 K1 Napier Grove N1
157 K4 Narrow Street E14
149 L2 Nash Street NW1
149 M5 Nassau Street W1W
156 C2 Nathaniel Close E1
150 C6 Neal Street WC2H
150 C6 Neal Yard WC2H
153 M5 Neathouse Place SW1V
156 C7 Neckinger SE16
156 C8 Neckinger Estate SE16
156 C7 Neckinger Street SE1
157 H7 Needleman Street SE16
150 C6 Neils Yard * WC2H
148 A1 Nelson Close NW6
151 H1 Nelson Place N1
155 H2 Nelson Square SE1
156 F2 Nelson Street E1
151 H1 Nelson Terrace EC1V
157 G7 Neptune Street SE16
156 D4 Nesham Street E1W
156 D8 Ness Street SE16
152 D8 Netherton Grove SW10
149 M2 Netley Street NW1
152 A6 Nevern Place SW5
152 A6 Nevern Square SW5
150 C1 Neville Close NW1
152 E6 Neville Street SW7
152 E6 Neville Terrace * SW7
156 F1 Newark Street E1
156 F2 Newbold Cottages * E1
149 L7 New Bond Street W1S
151 H6 New Bridge Street EC4Y
151 M5 New Broad Street EC2M
150 A7 Newburgh Street W1F
149 M7 New Burlington Mews W1S
149 M7 New Burlington Place W1S
149 M7 New Burlington Street W1S
154 F7 Newburn Street SE11
151 J5 Newbury Street EC1A
151 H6 Newcastle Close EC4A
148 E5 Newcastle Place W2
151 G3 Newcastle Row EC1R
149 K5 New Cavendish Street W1G
151 J6 New Change EC4M
151 H2 New Charles Street EC1V
155 M8 New Church Road SE5
152 A1 Newcombe Street * W8
155 L2 Newcomen Street SE1
150 C6 New Compton Street * WC2H
150 F7 New Court * EC4Y
148 F1 Newcourt Street NW8
157 G5 New Crane Place E1W
157 L3 Newell Street E14
151 G6 New Fetter Lane EC4A
151 H6 Newgate Street EC1A
151 K8 New Globe Walk SE1
156 B2 New Goulston Street E1
156 A7 Newham's Row SE1
155 H6 Newington Butts SE17
155 J4 Newington Causeway SE1
155 K5 New Kent Road SE17
157 G4 Newlands Quay E1W
156 B3 New London Street * EC3R
150 F5 Newman's Row WC2A
150 A5 Newman Street W1T
154 F4 Newnham Terrace SE1
151 M3 New North Place EC2A

151 L1 New North Road N1
150 E4 New North Street WC1N
150 C6 New Oxford Street WC1A
156 E7 New Place Square SE16
150 C7 Newport Court WC2H
150 C7 Newport Place * W1D
152 E6 Newport Street SE11
149 H6 New Quebec Street W1H
156 E2 New Road E1
150 C7 New Row WC2N
154 D7 New Spring Gardens Walk * SE1
150 F6 New Square WC2A
156 A2 New Street EC2M
151 G6 New Street Square EC4A
148 A6 Newton Road W2
150 D5 Newton Street WC2B
156 F6 New Tower Buildings * E1W
151 L5 New Union Street EC2Y
151 L7 Nicholas Lane EC4N
155 H2 Nicholson Street SE1
155 G5 Nightingale Mews SE11
152 D8 Nightingale Place SW10
151 K2 Nile Street N1
154 C8 Nine Elms Lane SW8
151 K6 Noble Street EC2V
150 A6 Noel Street W1F
157 L2 Norbiton Road E14
148 F6 Norfolk Crescent W2
148 E6 Norfolk Place W2
154 E5 Norfolk Row SE1
148 E6 Norfolk Square W2
148 E6 Norfolk Square Mews W2
151 J3 Norman Street EC1V
150 B8 Norris Street SW1Y
151 G3 Northampton Road EC1R
151 G3 Northampton Row * EC1R
151 H2 Northampton Square EC1V
149 J7 North Audley Street W1K
148 F2 North Bank NW8
151 H3 Northburgh Street EC1V
149 G7 North Carriage Drive W2
150 A4 Northcourt W1T
150 B4 North Crescent WC1E
150 E1 Northdown Street N1
157 K4 Northey Street E14
150 A2 North Gower Street NW1
150 E4 Northington Street WC1N
150 F4 North Mews WC1N
149 G6 North Rise * W2
149 J7 North Row W1K
156 C3 North Tenter Street E1
152 F5 North Terrace SW7
156 B3 Northumberland Alley * EC3M
154 D1 Northumberland Avenue WC2N
148 A6 Northumberland Place W2
154 C1 Northumberland Street WC2N
148 E5 North Wharf Road W2
148 E3 Northwick Close NW8
148 D3 Northwick Terrace NW8
157 K7 Norway Gate SE16
157 L3 Norway Place E14
151 G5 Norwich Street EC4A
150 D6 Nottingham Court WC2H
149 J4 Nottingham Place NW1
149 J4 Nottingham Street W1U
149 J4 Nottingham Terrace NW1
148 A8 Notting Hill Gate W2 ⊖
148 A8 Notting Hill Gate W11
148 D1 Nugent Terrace NW8
155 L6 Nursery Row SE17
149 G6 Nutford Place W1H

O

155 G5 Oakden Street SE11
155 G4 Oakey Lane SE1
152 C8 Oakfield Street SW10
148 A3 Oakington Road W9
157 L3 Oak Lane E14
151 H1 Oakley Crescent * EC1V
153 G8 Oakley Gardens SW3
150 A1 Oakley Square NW1
152 F8 Oakley Street SW3
148 F2 Oak Tree Road NW8
151 K5 Oat Lane EC2V
152 A2 Observatory Gardens W8
152 E4 Observatory Road SW7
155 J6 Occupation Road SE17
157 J1 Ocean Estate E1
157 J1 Ocean Street E1
151 M5 Octagon Arcade * EC2M
157 L7 Odessa Street SE16
150 D6 Odhams Walk * WC2H
149 M5 Ogle Street W1W
151 H6 Old Bailey EC4M
153 J3 Old Barrack Yard SW1X
157 M8 Old Bellgate Wharf E14
149 M8 Old Bond Street W1S
151 M5 Old Broad Street EC2M
152 A7 Old Brompton Road SW5
152 D6 Old Brompton Road SW7
150 F6 Old Buildings WC2A
149 M7 Old Burlington Street W1S
149 J4 Oldbury Place W1U
156 C2 Old Castle Street E1
149 L6 Old Cavendish Street W1G
157 H2 Old Church Road E1
152 E7 Old Church Street SW3
150 B7 Old Compton Street W1D
152 B3 Old Court Place W8
151 J7 Old Fish Street Hill * EC4V
151 H6 Old Fleet Lane EC4A
150 D4 Old Gloucester Street WC1N
156 C7 Old Jamaica Road SE16
151 L6 Old Jewry * EC2R
155 M5 Old Kent Road SE1
152 A6 Old Manor Yard SW5
149 G5 Old Marylebone Road NW1
151 G6 Old Mitre Court * EC4Y
156 D1 Old Montague Street E1
150 E5 Old North Street * WC1X
154 D3 Old Palace Yard SW1A
154 E5 Old Paradise Street SE11
153 K2 Old Park Lane W1K
154 B4 Old Pye Street SW1P
149 H6 Old Quebec Street W1H
154 B3 Old Queen Street SW1H
151 H6 Old Seacoal Lane EC4M
150 F5 Old Square WC2A
151 J3 Old Street EC1V
151 L3 Old Street EC1V ⇌ ⊖
157 G1 O'Leary Square E1
151 L3 Oliver's Yard EC1Y
155 J8 Olney Road SE17
155 K2 O'Meara Street SE1
150 D1 Omega Place N1
157 K8 Onega Gate SE16
152 A8 Ongar Road SW6
152 E5 Onslow Crescent SW7
152 D6 Onslow Gardens SW7
152 E6 Onslow Mews East SW7
152 E6 Onslow Mews West SW7
152 E6 Onslow Square SW7
151 G4 Onslow Street EC1R
155 J4 Ontario Street SE1
157 M4 Ontario Way E14
155 H6 Opal Street SE11
157 G8 Orange Place SE16
150 C8 Orange Street WC2H
156 D5 Orange Street E1W
152 F6 Oratory Lane * SW3
155 L6 Orb Street SE17
148 E4 Orchardson Street NW8
149 J6 Orchard Street W1H
150 E4 Orde Hall Street * WC1N
155 H5 Orient Street SE11
148 B8 Orme Court W2
148 B8 Orme Court Mews * W2
148 B8 Orme Lane W2
148 B8 Orme Square W2
148 B8 Orme Square Gate W2
150 D4 Ormond Close WC1N
153 H7 Ormonde Gate SW3
153 J6 Ormonde Place SW1W
154 A1 Ormond Yard SW1Y
148 C6 Orsett Mews W2
154 E6 Orsett Street SE11
148 C6 Orsett Terrace W2
156 D5 Orton Street E1W
154 B6 Osbert Street SW1P
156 C2 Osborn Street E1
157 K7 Oslo Square SE16
149 L3 Osnaburgh Street NW1
149 L3 Osnaburgh Terrace NW1
149 J5 Ossington Buildings * W1U
148 A7 Ossington Close * W2
148 A7 Ossington Street W2
150 B1 Ossulston Street NW1
152 D5 Osten Mews SW7
155 H5 Oswin Street SE11
155 H6 Othello Close SE11
155 H8 Otto Street SE17
149 H3 Outer Circle NW1
156 A2 Outwich Street * EC3A
154 E7 Oval Way SE11
153 G4 Ovington Gardens SW3
153 G4 Ovington Mews SW3
153 G4 Ovington Square SW3
153 G5 Ovington Street SW3
151 H1 Owen's Row EC1V
151 G1 Owen Street EC1V
150 B8 Oxendon Street * W1D
149 L6 Oxford Circus W1B ⊖
151 L7 Oxford Court EC4N
149 G6 Oxford Square W2
149 J7 Oxford Street W1C
150 A6 Oxford Street W1D
157 G3 Oyster Row E1

P

156 F3 Pace Place E1
148 D6 Paddington W2 ⇌ ⊖
148 E5 Paddington Green W2
149 J5 Paddington Street W1U
157 L5 Pageant Crescent SE16
154 C5 Page Street SW1P
156 A8 Pages Walk SE1
155 M5 Page's Walk SE1
151 H1 Paget Street EC1V
150 F3 Pakenham Street WC1X
152 B2 Palace Avenue W8
148 A7 Palace Court W2
152 A1 Palace Gardens Mews W8
152 A1 Palace Gardens Terrace W8
148 A8 Palace Gardens Terrace W11
152 C3 Palace Gate W8
152 B2 Palace Green W8
153 M4 Palace Place SW1W
153 L4 Palace Street SW1E
149 G3 Palgrave Gardens NW1
154 B1 Pall Mall SW1Y
154 B1 Pall Mall East SW1Y
154 A1 Pall Mall Place SW1Y
154 B4 Palmer Street SW1H
151 K6 Pancras Lane EC4N
150 C1 Pancras Road NW1
150 B8 Panton Street SW1Y
151 G7 Paper Buildings * EC4Y
156 E7 Paradise Street SE16
153 H8 Paradise Walk SW3
155 M5 Paragon Mews SE1
155 L4 Pardoner Street SE1
151 J3 Pardon Street EC1V
156 E2 Parfett Street E1
155 G1 Paris Garden SE1
156 F8 Park Approach SE16
153 G3 Park Close * SW7
149 L4 Park Crescent W1B
149 L4 Park Crescent Mews East W1W
149 K4 Park Crescent Mews West W1G
150 D6 Parker Mews * WC2B
156 C7 Parkers Row SE1
156 C7 Parker's Row SE1
150 D6 Parker Street WC2B
153 K2 Park Lane W1J
149 J8 Park Lane W1K
157 M5 Park Place E14
153 M1 Park Place SW1A
148 D4 Park Place Villas W2
149 G2 Park Road NW8
149 L3 Park Square East NW1
149 K3 Park Square Mews NW1
149 K3 Park Square West NW1
149 G7 Park Steps * W2
149 J8 Park Street W1K
155 J1 Park Street SE1
152 D8 Park Walk SW10
149 G6 Park West Place W2
156 B1 Parliament Court * E1
154 C3 Parliament Square SW1P
154 D3 Parliament Street SW1A
157 K2 Parnham Street E14
154 D8 Parry Street SW8
155 J7 Pasley Close SE17
153 J6 Passmore Street SW1W
155 H5 Pastor Street SE11
151 J6 Paternoster Square EC4M
152 A4 Pater Street W8
157 L5 Pattina Walk SE16
151 M3 Paul Street EC2A
152 E8 Paultons Square SW3
152 F8 Paultons Street SW3
148 F2 Paveley Street NW8
153 H4 Pavilion Road SW1X
153 H4 Pavilion Street SW1X
153 L8 Paxton Terrace SW1V
153 L7 Peabody Avenue SW1V
153 L7 Peabody Close SW1V
151 G3 Peabody Estate * EC1R
155 G1 Peabody Estate * SE1
155 K1 Peabody Estate * SE1
151 K3 Peabody Estate * EC1Y
151 G4 Peabody Terrace * EC1R
155 J6 Peacock Street SE17
155 J6 Peacock Yard SE17
156 F5 Pearl Street E1W
155 G3 Pearman Street SE1
155 G3 Pear Place SE1
151 G3 Pear Tree Court EC1R
157 G4 Peartree Lane E1W
151 J3 Pear Tree Street EC1V
156 C1 Pecks Yard * E1
152 A2 Peel Passage * W8
152 A2 Peel Street W8
151 K2 Peerless Street EC1V
154 F8 Pegasus Place SE11
152 F6 Pelham Crescent SW7
152 F5 Pelham Place SW7
152 F5 Pelham Street SW7
155 K8 Pelier Street SE17
157 M3 Pelling Street E14
151 G6 Pemberton Row EC4A
148 A8 Pembridge Gardens W2
148 A7 Pembridge Place W11
148 A7 Pembridge Square W2
153 J3 Pembroke Close SW1X
156 F5 Penang Street E1W
148 F5 Penfold Place W2
148 F4 Penfold Street NW8
152 B5 Pennant Mews W8
156 E4 Pennington Street E1W
155 J7 Penrose Grove SE17
155 J7 Penrose Street SE17
150 F1 Penton Grove N1
155 H6 Penton Place SE17
150 E2 Penton Rise WC1X
150 F1 Penton Street N1
150 E1 Pentonville Road N1
152 A7 Penywern Road SW5
155 J2 Pepper Street SE1
156 B4 Pepys Street EC3N
151 H3 Percival Street EC1V
150 B5 Percy Mews W1T
150 B5 Percy Street W1T
154 B4 Perkin's Rents SW1P
155 K1 Perkins Square SE1
156 E7 Perryn Road SE16
152 C4 Petersham Lane SW7
152 C4 Petersham Mews SW7
152 C4 Petersham Place SW7
151 J7 Peter's Hill EC4V
150 B7 Peter Street W1F
149 L3 Peto Place NW1
156 B2 Petticoat Lane E1
156 B2 Petticoat Square E1
156 B2 Petticoat Tower * E1
154 A3 Petty France SW1E
156 B4 Petty Wales EC3R
153 G6 Petyward SW3
155 L7 Phelp Street SE17
153 G8 Phene Street SW3
156 D3 Philchurch Place E1
151 M7 Philpot Lane EC3M
156 F2 Philpot Street E1
153 L5 Phipp's Mews SW1W
151 M3 Phipp Street EC2A
150 F3 Phoenix Place WC1X
150 B2 Phoenix Road NW1
150 C6 Phoenix Street WC2H
156 C7 Phoenix Wharf Road SE1
153 M1 Piccadilly W1J
154 A1 Piccadilly Arcade SW1Y
150 B8 Piccadilly Circus W1J ⊖
150 B8 Piccadilly Circus W1B
151 J2 Pickard Street EC1V
148 B6 Pickering Mews W2
154 A2 Pickering Place * SW1A
151 J1 Pickfords Wharf * N1
155 J3 Pickwick Street SE1
149 K6 Picton Place W1U
153 J8 Pier SW3
156 E6 Pier Head E1W
157 M3 Pigott Street E14
155 L3 Pilgrimage Street SE1
151 H6 Pilgrim Street * EC4V
155 K6 Pilton Place SE17
154 B6 Pimlico SW1V ⊖
153 K6 Pimlico Road SW1W
156 E3 Pinchin & Johnsons Yard E1
156 D3 Pinchin Street E1
151 M4 Pindar Street EC2A
148 C3 Pindock Mews W9
154 A4 Pine Apple Court * SW1E
157 M3 Pinefield Close E14
151 G3 Pine Street EC1R
151 M2 Pitfield Street N1
157 J3 Pitsea Place E1
157 J3 Pitsea Street E1
153 K2 Pitts Head Mews W1J
152 A3 Pitt Street W8
157 M2 Pixley Street E14
155 L3 Plantain Place SE1
156 A4 Plantation Lane EC3M
151 L3 Platina Street EC2A
150 B1 Platt Street NW1
155 K2 Playhouse Court SE1
151 H7 Playhouse Yard EC4V
151 K2 Pleydell Estate * EC1V
151 G6 Pleydell Street EC4Y
151 G6 Plough Place EC4A
156 C2 Plough Street * E1
157 K8 Plover Way SE16
150 F7 Plowden Buildings * EC4Y
156 D2 Plumbers Row E1
151 G5 Plumtree Court EC4A
148 F4 Plympton Place * NW8
148 F4 Plympton Street NW8
155 H3 Pocock Street SE1
150 A6 Poland Street W1D
149 L7 Pollen Street W1S
148 E3 Pollitt Drive NW8
155 G5 Polperro Mews SE11
150 B1 Polygon Road NW1
156 C2 Pomell Way E1
152 F6 Pond Place SW3
156 E3 Ponler Street E1
154 C6 Ponsonby Place SW1P
154 C6 Ponsonby Terrace SW1P
153 H4 Pont Street SW1X
153 H4 Pont Street Mews SW1X
150 F4 Pooles Buildings WC1X
157 H6 Poolmans Street SE16
157 G3 Poonah Street E1
156 B7 Pope Street SE1
148 B7 Poplar Place W2
151 H6 Poppins Court EC4A
148 C6 Porchester Garden Mews W2
148 B7 Porchester Gardens W2
148 C8 Porchester Gate * W2
149 G6 Porchester Place W2
148 B6 Porchester Road W2
148 B6 Porchester Square W2
148 B6 Porchester Square Mews W2
148 C7 Porchester Terrace W2
148 C6 Porchester Terrace North W2
155 L3 Porlock Street SE1
148 C8 Portchester Gate W2
149 H4 Porter Street W1U
155 K1 Porter Street SE1
156 F4 Porters Walk * E1W
148 D5 Porteus Road W2
150 A6 Portland Mews W1F
149 L4 Portland Place W1B
156 E5 Portland Square E1W
155 L7 Portland Street SE17
149 J6 Portman Close W1H
149 G4 Portman Gate NW1
149 J6 Portman Mews South W1H
149 J6 Portman Square W1H
149 J6 Portman Street W1H
150 F4 Portpool Lane WC1X
149 G6 Portsea Mews W2
149 G6 Portsea Place W2
150 E6 Portsmouth Street WC2A
156 B3 Portsoken Street EC3N
150 E6 Portugal Street WC2A
155 M4 Potier Street SE1
156 B6 Potters Fields SE1
156 E7 Pottery Street SE16
151 K6 Poultry EC2R
150 D4 Powis Place WC1N
148 E6 Praed Mews W2
148 F5 Praed Street W2
154 E5 Pratt Walk SE11
157 M4 Premiere Place E14
156 C3 Prescot Street E1
156 E5 President Drive E1W
151 J2 President Street * EC1V
155 M5 Preston Close SE1
151 K1 Prestwood Street * N1
155 H1 Price's Street SE1
150 F2 Prideaux Place WC1X
151 G7 Primrose Hill EC4Y
156 A1 Primrose Street EC2A
149 G1 Prince Albert Road NW8
152 D4 Prince Consort Road SW7
156 C1 Princelet Street E1
152 F3 Prince of Wales Gate SW7
149 M2 Prince of Wales Passage * NW1
152 C3 Prince of Wales Terrace W8
149 M2 Prince Regent Mews NW1
150 A8 Princes Arcade W1J
156 F4 Princes Court E1W
152 E4 Princes Gardens SW7
152 E4 Princes Gate SW7
152 F3 Prince's Gate SW7
152 E3 Princes Gate Court SW7
152 E4 Princes Gate Mews SW7
148 A7 Prince's Mews W2
157 H5 Princes Riverside Road SE16
148 E4 Princess Louise Close W2
148 B7 Prince's Square W2
155 H4 Princess Street SE1
149 L6 Princes Street W1B
151 L6 Prince's Street EC2R
150 E5 Princeton Street WC1R
150 F5 Printers Inn Court EC4A
155 M4 Prioress Street SE1
151 H6 Priory Court * EC4V
152 D7 Priory Walk SW10
156 D8 Priter Road SE16
150 E5 Procter Street WC1R
157 G5 Prospect Place E1W
156 F7 Prospect Street SE16
149 J7 Providence Court W1K
155 M2 Providence Square SE1
151 L1 Provost Estate N1
151 L1 Provost Street N1
156 F5 Prusom Street E1W
151 M7 Pudding Lane EC3R
151 H7 Puddle Dock EC4V
156 C1 Puma Court E1
150 F7 Pump Court * EC4Y
156 D3 Pump House Mews E1
156 B7 Purbrook Street SE1
151 M1 Purcell Street N1

Q

150 A8 Quadrant Arcade W1B
150 F5 Quality Court WC2A
149 H6 Quebec Mews W1H
157 J7 Quebec Way SE16
149 L5 Queen Anne Mews W1G
154 B3 Queen Anne's Gate SW1H
149 K5 Queen Anne Street W1G
156 F4 Queen Anne Terrace * E1W
150 F7 Queen Elizabeth Buildings * EC4Y
156 B6 Queen Elizabeth Street SE1
151 K7 Queenhithe EC4V
151 J6 Queen Isabella Way EC1A
153 J2 Queen Mother Gate W1J
152 D5 Queensberry Mews West * SW7
152 E5 Queensberry Place SW7
152 E5 Queensberry Way * SW7
148 C7 Queensborough Mews * W2
148 C7 Queensborough Passage W2
148 C7 Queensborough Studios W2
148 C7 Queensborough Terrace W2
152 E7 Queen's Elm Square SW3
148 C7 Queen's Gardens W2
152 D3 Queens Gate SW7
152 D3 Queen's Gate SW7
152 C5 Queen's Gate Gardens SW7
152 C4 Queen's Gate Mews SW7
152 D4 Queen's Gate Place SW7
152 D4 Queen's Gate Place Mews SW7
152 C4 Queen's Gate Terrace SW7
148 B7 Queen's Mews W2
150 D4 Queen Square WC1N
155 K8 Queens Row * SE17
155 K7 Queen's Row SE17
153 L1 Queen Street W1J
151 K7 Queen Street EC4M
151 K8 Queen Street Place EC4R
148 B6 Queensway W2
148 B8 Queensway W2 ⊖
150 A4 Queen's Yard W1T
151 H7 Queen Victoria Street EC4V
156 F4 Queen Victoria Terrace * E1W
151 H1 Quick Street N1
155 J2 Quilp Street SE1

R

152 A1 Rabbit Row * W8
157 K2 Raby Street E14
156 B8 Radcliffe Road SE1
155 G7 Radcot Street SE11
157 J6 Radley Court SE16
152 A5 Radley Mews W8
148 E6 Radnor Mews W2
148 F6 Radnor Place W2
151 K3 Radnor Street EC1V
153 G7 Radnor Walk SW3
155 L1 Railway Approach SE1
157 G6 Railway Avenue SE16
150 D1 Railway Street N1
157 L8 Rainbow Quay SE16
156 F5 Raine Street E1W
148 F6 Rainsford Street W2
153 H7 Ralston Street SW3
149 M6 Ramillies Place W1F
149 M6 Ramillies Street W1D
156 E2 Rampart Street * E1
154 B6 Rampayne Street SW1V
154 E6 Randall Road SE11
154 E6 Randall Row SE11
148 C3 Randolph Avenue W9
148 C3 Randolph Crescent W9
148 B1 Randolph Gardens NW6
148 D4 Randolph Mews W9
148 C4 Randolph Road W9
153 K7 Ranelagh Grove SW1W
154 A7 Ranelagh Road SW1V
156 B3 Rangoon Street * EC3N
148 F4 Ranston Street NW1
153 G3 Raphael Street SW7
157 J3 Ratcliffe Cross Street E1
157 J3 Ratcliffe Lane E14
150 B5 Rathbone Place W1T
150 A5 Rathbone Street W1T
156 F1 Raven Row E1
155 G7 Ravensdon Street SE11
151 M3 Ravey Street EC2A
153 G5 Rawlings Street SW3
151 H2 Rawstorne Place * EC1V
151 H2 Rawstorne Street EC1V
150 F4 Raymond Buildings * WC1R
151 G4 Ray Street EC1R
151 G4 Ray Street Bridge * EC1R
156 F5 Reardon Path E1W
156 F5 Reardon Street E1W
157 J1 Rectory Square E1
152 F8 Red Anchor Close SW3
148 B6 Redan Place W2
153 G8 Redburn Street SW3
157 G4 Redcastle Close E1
152 B7 Redcliffe Close SW5
152 B7 Redcliffe Gardens SW10
152 C7 Redcliffe Mews SW10
152 C8 Redcliffe Place SW10
152 C7 Redcliffe Road SW10
152 B7 Redcliffe Square SW10
152 B8 Redcliffe Street SW10
155 K2 Redcross Way SE1
148 A7 Rede Place W2
153 G8 Redesdale Street SW3
152 A5 Redfield Lane SW5
149 L2 Redhill Street NW1
155 K8 Red Lion Close SE17
151 G6 Red Lion Court EC4A
155 K8 Red Lion Row SE5
150 E5 Red Lion Square WC1R
150 E5 Red Lion Street WC1R
153 K1 Red Lion Yard * W1K
157 H1 Redman's Road E1
156 D5 Redmead Lane * E1W
149 J7 Red Place W1K
157 K8 Redriff Road SE16
157 K6 Redwood Close SE16
152 E5 Reece Mews SW7
155 G6 Reedworth Street SE11
149 J8 Reeves Mews W1K
156 E1 Regal Close E1
151 M1 Regan Way N1
154 B5 Regency Place * SW1P
154 B5 Regency Street SW1P
152 E7 Regency Terrace * SW7
148 D1 Regents Mews NW8
149 L4 Regent's Park NW1 ⊖
150 D2 Regent Square WC1H
149 L6 Regent Street W1B
150 B8 Regent Street SW1Y
150 A3 Regnart Buildings NW1
153 G4 Relton Mews SW7
153 J6 Rembrandt Close SW1W
151 J1 Remington Street N1
150 E6 Remnant Street WC2B
157 G7 Renforth Street SE16
155 H5 Renfrew Road SE11
151 H8 Rennie Street SE1
155 M5 Rephidim Street SE1
157 K2 Repton Street E14
152 C3 Reston Place W8
156 F4 Reunion Row E1W
157 K7 Reveley Square SE16
149 J8 Rex Place W1K
157 K1 Rhodeswell Road E14
149 M4 Richardson's Mews W1T

153 G5 Richard's Place SW3
156 E2 Richard Street E1
150 E4 Richbell Place WC1X
150 B6 Richmond Buildings W1D
150 B6 Richmond Mews W1D
154 D2 Richmond Terrace SW1A
157 M3 Rich Street E14
152 A8 Rickett Street SW6
150 B4 Ridgmount Gardens WC1E
150 B4 Ridgmount Street WC1E
149 L5 Riding House Street W1B
156 B7 Riley Road SE1
155 J2 Risborough Street SE1
157 G7 Risdon Street SE16
150 F1 Risinghill Street N1
151 G2 River Street EC1R
149 J6 Robert Adam Street W1U
148 D3 Robert Close W9
155 J6 Robert Dashwood Way SE17
153 J4 Roberts Mews * SW1X
151 G3 Robert's Place * EC1R
149 L2 Robert Street NW1
150 D8 Robert Street WC2N
153 G8 Robinson Street SW3
154 A8 Rochester Row SW1P
154 B5 Rochester Street SW1P
155 L1 Rochester Walk * SE1
155 J4 Rockingham Street SE1
151 H1 Rocliffe Street N1
156 E5 Roding Mews E1W
149 H5 Rodmarton Street W1U
155 K5 Rodney Place SE1
155 K5 Rodney Road SE17
150 E4 Roger Street WC1N
152 D6 Roland Gardens SW7
157 H1 Roland Mews * E1
152 D6 Roland Way SW7
155 L7 Roland Way SE17
151 G6 Rolls Buildings EC4A
156 E2 Romford Street E1
150 B7 Romilly Street W1D
154 C5 Romney Street SW1P
157 H3 Ronald Street E1
151 M7 Rood Lane EC3M
156 D7 Ropemaker Road SE16
157 L4 Ropemaker's Fields E14
151 L4 Ropemaker Street EC2Y
156 B7 Roper Lane SE1
157 K8 Rope Street SE16
156 E2 Ropewalk Gardens * E1
152 D6 Rosary Gardens SW7
151 K3 Roscoe Street EC1Y
156 A1 Rose Alley EC2M
155 K1 Rose Alley SE1
154 A1 Rose & Crown Yard * SW1Y
150 F4 Rosebery Avenue EC1R
150 F3 Rosebery Court EC1R
156 C2 Rose Court E1
153 G6 Rosemoor Street SW3
150 C7 Rose Street WC2E
151 G3 Rosoman Place EC1R
151 G3 Rosoman Street EC1R
149 G4 Rossmore Close * NW1
149 G3 Rossmore Road NW1
155 H4 Rotary Street SE1
155 H2 Rotherham Walk * SE1
157 G6 Rotherhithe SE16 ⊖
157 J5 Rotherhithe Street SE16
157 G6 Rotherhithe Street SE16
155 M4 Rothsay Street SE1
153 G2 Rotten Row SW1X
156 D8 Rouel Road SE16
155 G2 Roupell Street SE1
148 B4 Rowington Close W2
152 A8 Roxby Place SW6
149 M8 Royal Arcade W1S
153 H6 Royal Avenue SW3
151 L6 Royal Court EC3V
153 H8 Royal Hospital Road SW3
156 C4 Royal Mint Place E1
156 C4 Royal Mint Street E1
148 B5 Royal Oak W2 ⊖
156 A7 Royal Oak Yard SE1
154 B1 Royal Opera Arcade * SW1Y
155 H8 Royal Road SE11
154 E4 Royal Street SE1
157 L4 Roy Square E14
154 D8 Rudolf Place SW8
148 A1 Rudolph Road NW6
151 M2 Rufus Street EC1V
150 E4 Rugby Street WC1N
157 M3 Rugg Street E14
156 F4 Rum Close E1W
157 G7 Rupack Street SE16
150 B7 Rupert Court W1D
150 B7 Rupert Street W1D
155 H3 Rushworth Street SE1
154 A2 Russell Court SW1A
150 D4 Russell Square WC1B
150 C4 Russell Square WC1H ⊖
150 D7 Russell Street WC2B
157 K6 Russia Dock Road SE16
151 K6 Russia Row EC2V
154 B5 Rutherford Street SW1P
152 F3 Rutland Court SW7
153 G3 Rutland Gardens SW7
153 G3 Rutland Gardens Mews SW7
152 F3 Rutland Gate SW7
152 F3 Rutland Gate Mews * SW7
152 F4 Rutland Mews South * SW7
151 J4 Rutland Place * EC1M
152 F4 Rutland Street SW7
155 H8 Rutley Close SE17
154 A1 Ryder Street SW1Y
154 A1 Ryder Yard SW1Y
153 H3 Rysbrack Street SW3

S

150 A8 Sackville Street W1S
151 G5 Saffron Hill EC1N
151 G4 Saffron Street EC1N
156 F3 Sage Street E1
150 E2 Sage Way WC1X
154 F5 Sail Street SE11
151 L3 St Agnes Well EC1Y
152 B4 St Alban's Grove W8
148 E4 St Alban's Mews W2
150 B8 St Alban's Street SW1Y
151 K5 St Alphage Gardens EC2Y
151 K5 St Alphage Highwalk EC2Y
151 K6 St Andrew's Hill EC4V
149 L3 St Andrew's Place NW1
151 G5 St Andrew Street EC1N
150 B6 St Annes Court W1F
157 L3 St Anne's Passage E14
157 M3 St Anne's Row E14
157 M3 St Anne Street E14
154 C4 St Ann's Street SW1P
156 D5 St Anthony's Close E1W
153 K6 St Barnabas Street SW1W
156 B2 St Botolph Street EC3N
151 H6 St Bride Street EC4A
153 G5 St Catherines Mews SW3
150 E1 St Chad's Place WC1X
150 D2 St Chad's Street WC1H
149 K6 St Christopher's Place W1U
156 B3 St Clare Street EC3N
150 E6 St Clement's Lane WC2A
151 G4 St Cross Street EC1N
156 A4 St Dunstan's Hill * EC3R
151 M7 St Dunstan's Lane * EC3R
157 J7 St Elmos Road SE16
155 H3 St George's Circus SE1
153 L6 St George's Drive SW1V
156 D4 St George's Estate E1
149 G7 St Georges Fields W2
151 M7 St George's Lane * EC3R
155 H4 St George's Road SE1
151 H6 St Georges's Court * EC4M
154 B6 St George's Square SW1V
154 B7 St George's Square Mews SW1V
149 L7 St George Street W1S
151 K5 St Giles Churchyard * EC2Y
150 C6 St Giles Circus W1D
150 C6 St Giles Court WC2H
150 C6 St Giles High Street WC2H
150 C6 St Giles Passage WC2H
150 F2 St Helena Street * WC1X
156 A2 St Helen's Place EC3A
154 A1 St James's Chambers * SW1Y
154 A4 St James's Court SW1E
149 M2 St James's Gardens * NW1
150 B8 St James's Market * SW1Y
154 B3 St James's Park SW1H ⊖
153 M2 St James's Place SW1A
156 D7 St James's Road SE16
154 B1 St James's Square SW1Y
153 M1 St James's Street SW1A
151 H3 St James Walk EC1R
151 M1 St John's Estate N1
156 B6 St John's Estate SE1
151 H4 St John's Lane EC1M
151 H4 St John's Place EC1M
151 H4 St John's Square EC1M
151 G1 St John Street EC1V
152 B5 St Johns Villas W8
148 F1 St John's Wood High Street NW8
148 E3 St John's Wood Road NW8
149 K1 St Katharine's Precinct * NW1
156 C5 St Katharine's Way E1W
153 H7 St Leonard's Terrace SW3
153 G8 St Loo Avenue SW3
151 L2 St Luke's Estate EC1V
151 K3 St Lukes's Close EC1V
152 F5 St Luke's Street SW3
152 B4 St Margarets Lane W8
154 C3 St Margaret Street SW1P
156 C3 St Mark Street E1
150 C8 St Martin-in-the-Fields * WC2N
150 C7 St Martins Court WC2N
150 C7 St Martin's Lane WC2N
151 J6 St Martin's le Grand EC1A
150 C8 St Martin's Place WC2N
150 C8 St Martin's Street * WC2H
151 M7 St Mary at Hill EC3R
151 M7 St Mary Axe EC3A
157 G7 St Marychurch Street SE16
156 C4 St Mary Graces Court * E1
155 G5 St Mary's Gardens SE11
152 B4 St Mary's Gate W8
148 D4 St Mary's Mansions W2
156 D2 St Mary's Path E1
152 B4 St Marys Place W8
148 E5 St Mary's Square W2
148 D4 St Mary's Terrace W2
155 G5 St Mary's Walk SE11
154 B4 St Matthew Street SW1P
151 M6 St Michael's Alley EC3V
153 J6 St Michael's Mews SW1W
148 F6 St Michael's Street W2
151 L6 St Mildred's Court * EC2R
154 E7 St Oswald's Place SE11
154 C6 St Oswulf Street * SW1P
150 C1 St Pancras International NW1 ≠ ⊖
151 J6 St Paul's EC4M ⊖
157 J5 St Paul's Avenue SE16
151 J6 St Paul's Church Yard EC4M
155 H7 St Pauls Terrace SE17
157 L3 St Paul's Way E3
148 B7 St Petersburgh Mews W2
148 B7 St Petersburgh Place W2
148 A3 St Peter's Place W9
156 B7 St Saviour's Estate SE1
148 A5 St Stephen's Crescent * W2
148 A5 St Stephen's Gardens W2
148 A5 St Stephen's Mews W2
154 D3 St Stephens Parade SW1A
152 C5 St Stephen's Walk SW7
151 L7 St Swithin's Lane EC4N
155 L2 St Thomas Street SE1
149 J5 St Vincent Street W1U
154 E6 Salamanca Place SE1
154 E6 Salamanca Street SE1
148 B7 Salem Road W2
148 F5 Sale Place W2
155 L5 Salisbury Close SE17
151 G6 Salisbury Court EC4Y
149 H4 Salisbury Place W1H
151 G6 Salisbury Square * EC4Y
148 F4 Salisbury Street NW8
157 K2 Salmon Lane E14
157 L2 Salmon Street E14
157 H5 Salter Road SE16
151 L7 Salters' Hall Court * EC4N
157 M4 Salter Street E14
155 L7 Saltwood Grove SE17
148 F4 Samford Street NW8
156 E5 Sampson Street E1W
154 F6 Sancroft Street SE11
155 K5 Sanctuary Street SE1
155 G2 Sandell Street SE1
155 K7 Sandford Row SE17
150 E5 Sandland Street WC1R
157 L6 Sandpiper Close SE16
150 C2 Sandwich Street WC1H
156 B1 Sandy's Row E1
151 H3 Sans Walk EC1R
154 F5 Saperton Walk SE11
156 B3 Saracen's Head Yard EC3M
150 E6 Sardinia Street WC2B
157 M4 Saunders Close * E14
154 F5 Saunders Street SE11
156 B3 Savage Gardens EC3N
149 M7 Savile Row W1S
150 D7 Savoy Court * WC2R
150 E8 Savoy Hill WC2R
150 D8 Savoy Place WC2N
150 E7 Savoy Row WC2R
150 E7 Savoy Steps * WC2R
150 E7 Savoy Street WC2R
150 E8 Savoy Way WC2R
155 J2 Sawyer Street SE1
150 A5 Scala Street W1T
156 E6 Scandrett Street E1W
156 C3 Scarborough Street E1
152 B4 Scarsdale Place * W8
152 A4 Scarsdale Villas W8
157 H3 Schoolhouse Lane E1W
157 H6 Schooner Close SE16
155 H2 Scoresby Street SE1
151 G3 Scotswood Street * EC1R
148 E2 Scott Ellis Gardens NW8
156 D7 Scott Lidgett Crescent SE16
151 L7 Scott's Yard EC4N
155 J3 Scovell Crescent * SE1
155 J3 Scovell Road SE1
151 M3 Scrutton Street EC2A
150 D2 Seaford Street WC1H
154 A4 Seaforth Place SW1E
157 L1 Seager Place E3
157 H2 Seagrave Close * E1
152 A8 Seagrave Road SW6
155 L5 Searles Road SE1
155 G6 Seaton Close SE11
151 H2 Sebastian Street EC1V
154 F2 Secker Street SE1
155 M6 Sedan Way SE17
153 J5 Sedding Street SW1X
150 E3 Seddon Street WC1X
149 M6 Sedley Place W1C
156 B4 Seething Lane EC3N
151 H3 Sekforde Street EC1R
157 M1 Selsey Street E3
152 E7 Selwood Place SW7
152 E6 Selwood Terrace SW7
153 K6 Semley Place SW1W
148 B4 Senior Street W2
157 H2 Senrab Street E1
151 G6 Serjeant's Inn * EC4Y
150 F6 Serle Street WC2A
151 J7 Sermon Lane EC4V
153 G2 Serpentine Road W2
157 H7 Seth Street SE16
156 D2 Settles Street E1
150 C6 Seven Dials WC2H
156 C1 Seven Stars Yard E1
153 H3 Seville Street SW1X
148 A3 Sevington Street W9
151 J3 Seward Street EC1V
149 J6 Seymour Mews W1H
149 G5 Seymour Place W1H
149 G7 Seymour Street W2
152 D8 Seymour Walk SW10
156 B6 Shad Thames SE1
156 F3 Shadwell E1 ⊖ ⊖
156 F3 Shadwell Gardens E1
157 G4 Shadwell Pierhead E1W
156 F3 Shadwell Place E1
150 B7 Shaftesbury Avenue W1D
152 A5 Shaftesbury Mews * W8
151 J5 Shaftesbury Place * EC2Y
151 K1 Shaftesbury Street N1
153 H4 Shafto Mews SW1X
152 D8 Shalcomb Street SW10
156 A6 Shand Street SE1
155 H7 Sharsted Street SE17
150 B8 Shavers Place W1J
157 K2 Shaw Crescent E14
153 G7 Shawfield Street SW3
150 E6 Sheffield Street * WC2A
148 D5 Sheldon Square W2
157 M1 Shelmerdine Close E3
150 D6 Shelton Street * WC2H
151 K2 Shepherdess Place EC1V
151 K1 Shepherdess Walk N1
153 L1 Shepherd Market W1J
149 J7 Shepherds Place W1K
153 K2 Shepherd Street W1J
150 B6 Sheraton Street * W1F
151 L7 Sherborne Lane EC4N
156 F3 Sheridan Street * E1
149 J4 Sherlock Mews W1U
149 G5 Sherwood Court * W1H
150 A7 Sherwood Street W1F
149 G5 Shillibeer Place W1H
155 M3 Ship & Mermaid Row SE1
151 M7 Ship Tavern Passage EC3V
157 K7 Shipwright Road SE16
155 M2 Shipwright Yard * SE1
148 A3 Shirland Road W9
151 G5 Shoe Lane EC4A
156 B1 Shoreditch High Street E1
156 C4 Shorter Street EC3N
150 D6 Shorts Gardens * WC2H
155 G2 Short Street SE1
157 L4 Shoulder of Mutton Alley E14
149 G5 Shouldham Street W1H
148 F4 Shroton Street NW1
150 D5 Sicilian Avenue * WC1A
149 H4 Siddons Lane NW1
154 F4 Sidford Place SE1
150 D3 Sidmouth Street WC1H
157 G2 Sidney Estate E1
151 H1 Sidney Grove EC1V
156 F2 Sidney Square E1
156 F1 Sidney Street E1
156 F1 Sidney Street Estate E1
151 L2 Silbury Street * N1
155 H3 Silex Street SE1
151 K4 Silk Street EC2Y
150 A7 Silver Place W1F
157 L5 Silver Walk SE16
155 K3 Silvester Street SE1
151 M3 Singer Street EC1V
152 E8 Sir Thomas More Estate SW3
151 K6 Sise Lane * EC4N
153 J6 Skinner Place * SW1W
151 K7 Skinners Lane EC4V
151 G3 Skinner Street EC1R
155 J8 Slade Walk SE17
150 C7 Slingsby Place WC2H
156 F8 Slippers Place SE16
153 G6 Sloane Avenue SW3
153 J6 Sloane Court East SW3
153 J7 Sloane Court West SW3
153 J6 Sloane Gardens SW1W
153 J5 Sloane Square SW1W
153 J6 Sloane Square SW1W ⊖
153 H3 Sloane Street SW1X
153 J5 Sloane Terrace SW1X
156 E2 Sly Street E1
148 D7 Smallbrook Mews W2
150 D6 Smart's Place WC1A
156 E5 Smeaton Street E1W
157 H6 Smith Close SE16
151 H5 Smithfield Street EC1A
150 B7 Smith's Court * W1D
154 C4 Smith Square SW1P
153 G7 Smith Street SW3
153 G7 Smith Terrace SW3
157 G1 Smithy Street E1
151 H5 Snow Hill EC1A
155 L2 Snowsfields SE1
150 B6 Soho Square W1D
150 B6 Soho Street W1D
156 F4 Solander Gardens E1
157 K7 Somerford Way SE16
150 B1 Somers Close NW1
148 F6 Somers Crescent W2
155 L8 Sondes Street SE17
157 K4 Sophia Square SE16
155 L3 Southall Place SE1
150 F5 Southampton Buildings * WC2A
150 D5 Southampton Place WC1A
150 D4 Southampton Row WC1B
150 D7 Southampton Street WC2E
149 K8 South Audley Street W1K
151 G8 South Bank SE1
152 C7 South Bolton Gardens SW10
153 H3 South Carriage Drive SW1X
152 F3 South Carriage Drive SW7
153 K5 South Eaton Place SW1W
152 B4 South End W8
152 B4 South End Row W8
150 E1 Southern Street N1
152 E5 South Kensington SW7 ⊖
152 E5 South Kensington Station Arcade SW7
154 D7 South Lambeth Place SW8
154 D8 South Lambeth Road SW8
149 K7 South Molton Lane W1K
149 K6 South Molton Street W1K
152 E7 South Parade SW3
151 L5 South Place EC2M
151 L5 South Place Mews EC2M
149 G7 South Rise * W2
157 L8 South Sea Street SE16
150 F5 South Square WC1R
153 J1 South Street W1K
156 C3 South Tenter Street E1
152 F5 South Terrace SW7
155 H2 Southwark SE1 ⊖
151 K8 Southwark Bridge EC4R
155 J4 Southwark Bridge Road SE1
156 F7 Southwark Park Road SE16
155 H1 Southwark Street SE1
157 L2 Southwater Close E14
152 C5 Southwell Gardens SW7
148 E6 South Wharf Road W2
148 F6 Southwick Mews W2
148 F6 Southwick Place W2
148 F6 Southwick Street W2
148 F6 Southwick Yard * W2
156 F4 Sovereign Close E1W
156 F4 Sovereign Court E1W
157 K4 Sovereign Crescent SE16
151 G3 Spafield Street EC1R
151 G2 Spa Green Estate * EC1R
149 J5 Spanish Place * W1U
156 D8 Spa Road SE16
152 A6 Spear Mews SW5
155 L7 Spectrum Place SE17
150 D2 Speedy Place WC1H
156 C1 Spelman Street E1
157 L7 Spence Close SE16
154 A4 Spencer Place SW1P
151 H2 Spencer Street EC1V
156 F3 Spencer Way E1
154 A4 Spenser Street SW1E
157 J3 Spert Street E14
156 E5 Spirit Quay E1W
156 B1 Spital Square E1
156 C1 Spital Street E1
156 B1 Spital Yard * E1
153 G6 Sprimont Place SW3
154 C1 Spring Gardens SW1A
149 H5 Spring Mews * W1U
148 E6 Spring Street W2
156 D1 Spring Walk E1
155 L4 Spurgeon Street SE1
154 F3 Spur Road SE1
153 M3 Spur Road SW1A
148 E2 Squire Gardens NW8
154 F7 Stables Way SE11
150 D1 Stable Walk N1
154 A2 Stable Yard Road SW1A
150 C6 Stacey Street WC2H
153 H3 Stackhouse Street SW1X
153 M3 Stafford Place SW1E
149 M8 Stafford Street W1S
153 M4 Stag Place SW1E
155 M2 Stainer Street SE1
151 K6 Staining Lane EC2V
148 F4 Stalbridge Street NW1
156 F8 Stalham Street SE16
155 G1 Stamford Street SE1
155 M6 Stanford Place SE17
152 B4 Stanford Road W8
154 B6 Stanford Street SW1V
157 J6 Stanhope Close SE16
152 D5 Stanhope Gardens SW7
149 G7 Stanhope Gate W2
153 J1 Stanhope Gate W1K
152 D5 Stanhope Mews East SW7
152 D6 Stanhope Mews South SW7
152 D5 Stanhope Mews West SW7
149 L2 Stanhope Parade NW1
149 G7 Stanhope Place W2
153 K2 Stanhope Row * W1J
149 M2 Stanhope Street NW1
148 E7 Stanhope Terrace W2
150 C1 Stanley Passage NW1
155 G7 Stannary Place SE11
155 G8 Stannary Street SE11
156 C7 Stanworth Street SE1
150 F5 Staple Inn WC1V
157 K5 Staples Close SE16
155 L3 Staple Street SE1
150 A2 Starcross Street NW1
156 C4 Star Place E1W
148 F6 Star Street W2
150 F6 Star Yard WC2A
149 J4 Station Approach * NW1
149 L4 Station Arcade * W1W
151 H6 Stationers Hall Court * EC4M
157 J5 Stave Yard Road SE16
155 K6 Stead Street SE17
155 J6 Steedman Street SE17
157 K7 Steers Way SE16
150 B5 Stephen Mews W1T
150 A3 Stephenson Way NW1
150 B5 Stephen Street W1T
157 H3 Stepney Causeway E1
157 H1 Stepney Green E1
157 J1 Stepney High Street E1
156 E1 Stepney Way E1
153 G3 Sterling Street SW7
155 L3 Sterry Street SE1
156 E5 Stevedore Street E1W
156 B7 Stevens Street SE1
152 F6 Stewart's Grove SW3
151 K7 Stew Lane EC4V
154 A5 Stillington Street SW1P
156 D5 Stockholm Way E1W
157 M3 Stocks Place E14
150 F5 Stone Buildings WC2A
151 H6 Stonecutter Street EC4A
152 B4 Stone Hall Gardens * W8
152 B4 Stone Hall Place * W8
156 A2 Stone House Court EC2M
155 J3 Stones End Street SE1
156 B2 Stoney Lane EC3A
155 K1 Stoney Street SE1
155 J7 Stopford Road * SE17
150 B5 Store Street WC1E
154 C3 Storey's Gate SW1H
156 E8 Storks Road SE16
154 E6 Stoughton Close SE11
149 G6 Stourcliffe Street W1H
157 M6 Strafford Street E14
150 D8 Strand WC2N
149 K6 Stratford Place W1C
152 A5 Stratford Road W8
152 A4 Stratford Studios W8
148 F7 Strathearn Place W2
153 L1 Stratton Street W1J
150 C5 Streatham Street WC1A
154 B4 Strutton Ground SW1H
156 B2 Strype Street E1
153 J3 Studio Place SW1X
150 D6 Stukeley Street WC2B
155 J7 Sturgeon Road SE17
155 J3 Sturge Street SE1
151 K1 Sturt Street N1
156 D3 Stutfield Street E1
151 H1 Sudeley Street N1
155 J3 Sudrey Street SE1
151 L7 Suffolk Lane EC4R
150 C8 Suffolk Street SW1Y
155 G5 Sullivan Road SE11
157 G2 Summercourt Road E1
151 G4 Summers Street EC1R
152 E6 Sumner Place SW7
152 E6 Sumner Place Mews SW7
155 J1 Sumner Street SE1
148 A6 Sunderland Terrace W2
152 A5 Sunningdale Gardens W8
156 D8 Sun Passage SE16
151 M4 Sun Street EC2A
156 A1 Sun Street Passage EC2M
148 A4 Surrendale Place W9
155 M7 Surrey Grove SE17
157 H8 Surrey Quays SE16 ⊖
157 H7 Surrey Quays Road SE16
155 H2 Surrey Row SE1
155 M6 Surrey Square SE17
150 F7 Surrey Street WC2R
157 J6 Surrey Water Road SE16
148 E7 Sussex Gardens W2
148 E7 Sussex Mews East * W2
148 E7 Sussex Mews West W2
148 E6 Sussex Place W2
149 H3 Sussex Place NW1
148 E7 Sussex Square W2
153 L7 Sussex Street SW1V
148 B3 Sutherland Avenue W9
153 L7 Sutherland Row SW1V
155 K7 Sutherland Square SE17
153 L7 Sutherland Street SW1V
155 K7 Sutherland Walk SE17
152 F6 Sutton Dwelling Estate SW3
151 H4 Sutton Lane EC1M
150 B6 Sutton Row W1D
157 G3 Sutton Street E1
151 K4 Sutton Way EC1Y
148 F3 Swain Street NW8
149 L6 Swallow Place W1B
150 A8 Swallow Street W1B
151 L8 Swan Lane EC4R
156 A8 Swan Mead SE1
156 C4 Swan Passage E1
157 H7 Swan Road SE16
155 K3 Swan Street SE1
153 H8 Swan Walk SW3
156 E4 Swedenborg Gardens E1
157 K8 Sweden Gate SE16
156 C7 Sweeney Crescent SE1
150 E2 Swinton Place WC1X
150 E2 Swinton Street WC1X
151 J3 Sycamore Street EC1V
152 E6 Sydney Close SW7
152 E6 Sydney Mews SW3
152 F6 Sydney Place SW7
152 F6 Sydney Street SW3
151 M2 Symister Mews N1
153 H6 Symons Street SW3

T

155 L3 Tabard Garden Estate SE1
155 K3 Tabard Street SE1
151 L4 Tabernacle Street EC2A
154 A6 Tachbrook Street SW1V
156 E3 Tait Street E1
151 M7 Talbot Court EC3V
148 A6 Talbot Road W2
148 E6 Talbot Square W2

155 L2 Talbot Yard SE1
151 G7 Tallis Street EC4Y
156 D5 Tamarind Yard E1W
150 D2 Tankerton Houses * WC1H
150 D2 Tankerton Street WC1H
156 D7 Tanner Street SE1
155 G3 Tanswell Street * SE1
151 K1 Taplow Street N1
157 G3 Tarbert Walk E1
156 F3 Tarling Street E1
155 J4 Tarn Street SE1
149 G5 Tarrant Place W1H
155 J7 Tarver Road SE17
155 M6 Tatum Street SE17
149 H4 Taunton Mews NW1
149 G3 Taunton Place NW1
150 D7 Tavistock Court * WC2E
150 D3 Tavistock Place WC1H
150 C3 Tavistock Square WC1H
150 D7 Tavistock Street WC2E
150 B3 Taviton Street WC1H
155 G6 Tavy Close SE11
157 K6 Teak Close SE16
153 G7 Tedworth Gardens SW3
153 H7 Tedworth Square SW3
151 L6 Telegraph Street EC2R
156 D4 Telfords Yard E1W
153 M8 Telford Terrace SW1V
150 F7 Temple WC2R ⊖
151 G7 Temple Avenue EC4Y
151 G7 Temple Gardens * EC4Y
151 G7 Temple Lane EC4Y
150 F7 Temple Place WC2R
152 A6 Templeton Place SW5
156 E5 Tench Street E1W
154 F2 Tenison Way SE1
148 C7 Tenniel Close W2
155 L3 Tennis Street SE1
149 L6 Tenterden Street W1S
156 B1 Tenter Ground E1
153 L5 Terminus Place SW1W
152 B3 Thackeray Street W8
157 J6 Thame Road SE16
157 M2 Thames Path E14
157 M8 Thames Path E14
154 E4 Thames Path SE1
154 F1 Thames Path SE1
156 C6 Thames Path SE1
150 F7 Thames Path WC2R
156 B4 Thames Path EC3N
154 C7 Thames Path SW1P
150 C2 Thanet Street WC1H
151 G6 Thavies Inn EC4A
149 K5 Thayer Street W1U
151 M5 The Arcade * EC2M
150 D8 The Arches * WC2N
152 C7 The Boltons SW10
152 C1 The Broad Walk W2
151 H4 The Charterhouse * EC1M
155 G2 The Cut SE1
155 G2 Theed Street SE1
156 B8 The Grange SE1
156 E4 The Highway E1W
148 C1 The Lane NW8
152 C7 The Little Boltons SW10
154 B2 The Mall SW1A
150 D7 The Market * WC2E
157 L3 The Mitre E14
150 E4 Theobald's Road WC1R
155 L5 Theobald Street SE1
156 B1 The Postern * EC2Y
148 F6 The Quadrangle W2
156 B5 The Queens Walk SE1
154 C3 The Sanctuary SW1P
151 J1 Theseus Walk N1
154 F1 The South Bank Centre * SE1
152 E8 The Vale SW3
148 F6 The Water Gardens W2
154 A4 Thirleby Road SW1P
152 D7 Thistle Grove SW10
155 H4 Thomas Doyle Street SE1
156 D4 Thomas More Square E1W
156 D4 Thomas More Street E1W
152 B4 Thomas Place W8
157 M2 Thomas Road E14
151 K1 Thoresby Street N1
154 B6 Thorndike Street * SW1V
154 D5 Thorney Street SW1P
148 A3 Thorngate Road W9
150 C4 Thornhaugh Street WC1H
149 H4 Thornton Place W1H
155 K2 Thrale Street SE1
156 C1 Thrawl Street E1
151 L6 Threadneedle Street EC2R
157 M4 Three Colt Street E14
149 K7 Three Kings Yard W1K
156 B6 Three Oak Lane SE1
151 L6 Throgmorton Avenue EC2N
151 L6 Throgmorton Street EC2N
155 J6 Thrush Street SE17
156 D8 Thurland Road SE16
152 F5 Thurloe Close SW7
152 F5 Thurloe Place SW7
152 E5 Thurloe Place Mews * SW7
152 F5 Thurloe Square SW7
152 E5 Thurloe Street SW7
155 M7 Thurlow Street SE17
155 M7 Thurlow Walk SE17
156 F3 Tillman Street E1
153 K1 Tilney Street W1K
156 F3 Timberland Road E1
157 J6 Timber Pond Road SE16
151 J3 Timber Street * EC1V
157 H1 Tinsley Road E1
154 E6 Tinworth Street SE11
155 L6 Tisdall Place SE17
148 F6 Titchborne Row W2
153 H7 Tite Street SW3
155 J4 Tiverton Street SE1
151 L6 Tokenhouse Yard EC2R
150 A3 Tolmer's Square NW1
157 L2 Tomlin's Terrace E14
151 H2 Tompion Street EC1V
150 D2 Tonbridge Street WC1H
150 F5 Took's Court EC4A
155 M2 Tooley Street SE1
151 G3 Topham Street * EC1R
148 A5 Torquay Street W2
151 G1 Torrens Street EC1V
150 B4 Torrington Place W1T
156 E5 Torrington Place E1W
150 B4 Torrington Square WC1H
154 B3 Tothill Street SW1H
157 J2 Tottan Terrace * E1
150 A4 Tottenham Court Road W1T
150 B6 Tottenham Court Road W1D ⊖
150 A5 Tottenham Mews * W1T
150 A5 Tottenham Street W1T
155 J3 Toulmin Street SE1
156 D8 Toussaint Walk SE16
156 C5 Tower Bridge E1W
156 C5 Tower Bridge Approach EC3N
156 A8 Tower Bridge Road SE1
156 F5 Tower Buildings * E1W
150 C7 Tower Court * WC2H
156 B4 Tower Gateway EC3N ⊖
156 B4 Tower Hill EC3N
156 B4 Tower Hill EC3N ⊖
156 B4 Tower Hill Terrace EC3R
156 A4 Tower Place EC3R
151 K7 Tower Royal * EC4N
150 C7 Tower Street WC2H
155 K6 Townley Street SE17
155 M5 Townsend Street SE17
156 B1 Toynbee Street E1
157 J1 Trafalgar Gardens E1
150 C8 Trafalgar Square * SW1Y
155 L7 Trafalgar Street SE17
148 F5 Transept Street NW1
156 E8 Tranton Road SE16
153 L1 Trebeck Street W1J
152 A6 Trebovir Road SW5
152 C7 Tregunter Road SW10
148 F3 Tresham Crescent NW8
155 H1 Treveris Street SE1
153 G3 Trevor Place SW7
153 G3 Trevor Square SW7
153 G3 Trevor Street SW7
157 M4 Trinidad Street E14
155 K3 Trinity Church Square SE1
156 F1 Trinity Green * E1
156 B4 Trinity Square EC3N
155 K3 Trinity Street SE1
155 K3 Trio Place SE1
157 J2 Troon Street E1
151 K6 Trump Street EC2V
155 J3 Trundle Street SE1
153 G6 Tryon Street SW3
151 G7 Tudor Street EC4Y
154 C4 Tufton Street SW1P
157 M2 Tunley Green E14
157 G6 Tunnel Road SE16
153 H7 Turks Row SW3
151 H5 Turnagain Lane * EC4A
157 L5 Turner's Road E3
156 E2 Turner Street E1
151 G4 Turnmill Street EC1M
153 L7 Turpentine Lane SW1V
157 H3 Turpin Close E1W
155 K6 Turquand Street SE17
157 G3 Twine Court E1
149 H7 Tyburn Way W1H
156 A7 Tyers Gate SE1
154 E7 Tyers Street SE11
154 E7 Tyers Terrace SE11
156 C2 Tyne Street E1
151 G3 Tysoe Street EC1R

U

154 A6 Udall Street SW1P
155 G3 Ufford Street SE1
149 K4 Ulster Place NW1
156 E2 Umberston Street * E1
156 A3 Undershaft EC3A
151 K2 Underwood Row N1
151 K1 Underwood Street N1
151 M6 Union Court EC2N
155 H2 Union Street SE1
150 A4 University Street W1T
152 E4 Unwin Road SW7
148 D6 Upbrook Mews W2
153 K4 Upper Belgrave Street SW1X
149 H6 Upper Berkeley Street W1H
149 J7 Upper Brook Street W1K
152 F8 Upper Cheyne Row SW3
149 J8 Upper Grosvenor Street W1K
154 F1 Upper Ground SE1
149 K3 Upper Harley Street NW1
150 A7 Upper John Street W1F
152 B2 Upper Lodge * W8
154 F3 Upper Marsh SE1
149 H4 Upper Montagu Street W1H
150 C7 Upper St Martin's Lane WC2H
151 G1 Upper Street N1
154 A5 Upper Tachbrook Street SW1V
151 J7 Upper Thames Street EC4V
149 K4 Upper Wimpole Street W1G
150 B2 Upper Woburn Place NW1
152 A1 Uxbridge Street * W11

V

148 C2 Vale Close W9
155 H3 Valentine Place SE1
154 A4 Vandon Street SW1H
151 M4 Vandy Street EC2A
152 A4 Vantage Place W8
156 E2 Varden Street E1
149 M2 Varndell Street NW1
156 C8 Vauban Estate SE16
156 C8 Vauban Street SE16
157 L7 Vaughan Street SE16
156 D4 Vaughan Way E1W
154 D7 Vauxhall SW8 ⇌ ⊖
154 D7 Vauxhall Bridge SE1
153 M5 Vauxhall Bridge Road SW1V
154 D8 Vauxhall Grove SW8
154 E7 Vauxhall Street SE11
154 E7 Vauxhall Walk SE11
148 E4 Venables Street NW8
149 K6 Vere Street W1G
150 D5 Vernon Place WC1X
150 E2 Vernon Rise WC1X
150 F2 Vernon Square WC1X
150 F4 Verulam Street WC1X
151 L2 Vestry Street N1
152 A2 Vicarage Gardens * W8
152 A2 Vicarage Gate W8
153 L5 Victoria SW1V ⇌ ⊖
153 L4 Victoria Arcade SW1E
156 D1 Victoria Cottages * E1
151 G7 Victoria Embankment EC4Y
150 E8 Victoria Embankment WC2R
154 D3 Victoria Embankment SW1A
150 D8 Victoria Embankment Gardens * WC2N
148 F7 Victoria Gate W2
152 C4 Victoria Grove W8
148 A8 Victoria Grove Mews * W2
152 C4 Victoria Road W8
153 L4 Victoria Square SW1W
153 L4 Victoria Street SW1E
156 D3 Victoria Yard * E1
155 K5 Victory Place SE17
157 K7 Victory Way SE16
150 A8 Vigo Street W1S
155 L7 Villa Street SE17
154 D1 Villiers Street WC2N
157 K6 Vincents Close SE16
154 B5 Vincent Square SW1P
154 B5 Vincent Street SW1P
151 H1 Vincent Terrace N1
151 L2 Vince Street EC1V
157 G2 Vine Cottages * E1
156 E1 Vine Court E1
156 E5 Vinegar Street E1W
155 M2 Vinegar Yard SE1
150 F4 Vine Hill EC1R
156 A6 Vine Lane SE1
150 A8 Vine Street W1J
156 B3 Vine Street EC3N
151 G4 Vine Street Bridge EC1M
155 K3 Vine Yard SE1
151 G3 Vineyard Mews * EC1R
151 G3 Vineyard Walk EC1R
148 C1 Violet Hill NW8
154 F4 Virgil Street SE1
156 D4 Virginia Street E1
151 K4 Viscount Street EC2Y

W

155 K6 Wadding Street SE17
151 H6 Waithman Street EC4M
150 D3 Wakefield Mews WC1H
150 D3 Wakefield Street WC1N
157 J3 Wakeling Street E1
151 H1 Wakley Street EC1V
151 L7 Walbrook EC4N
156 E3 Walburgh Street E1
155 K6 Walcorde Avenue SE17
155 G5 Walcot Square SE11
154 A5 Walcott Street * SW1P
156 E2 Walden Street E1
152 E8 Waldron Mews SW3
157 J1 Waley Street E1
150 B7 Walker's Court W1F
152 A5 Wallgrave Road SW5
151 K5 Wallside * EC2Y
157 M1 Wallwood Street E14
149 G5 Walmer Place * W1H
154 F5 Walnut Tree Walk SE11
153 H6 Walpole Street SW3
157 J2 Walter Terrace E1
153 H4 Walton Place SW3
153 G5 Walton Street SW3
155 K7 Walworth Place SE17
155 J5 Walworth Road SE1
154 D8 Wandsworth Road SW8
155 K6 Wansey Street SE17
156 F5 Wapping E1W ⊖
156 F5 Wapping Dock Street * E1W
156 D5 Wapping High Street E1W
156 F5 Wapping Lane E1W
156 F4 Wapping Walk E1W
157 G5 Wapping Wall E1W
155 J2 Wardens Grove SE1
150 B6 Wardour Mews W1F
150 A6 Wardour Street W1F
151 H7 Wardrobe Place * EC4V
150 F3 Warner Street EC1R
150 F4 Warner Yard EC1R
149 M4 Warren Mews W1T
150 A3 Warren Street NW1 ⊖
149 M4 Warren Street W1T
148 C3 Warrington Crescent W9
148 C4 Warrington Gardens W9
148 C4 Warwick Avenue W9
148 C4 Warwick Avenue W9 ⊖
150 F5 Warwick Court WC1V
148 C5 Warwick Crescent W2
154 B1 Warwick House Street SW1Y
151 J6 Warwick Lane EC4M
148 C4 Warwick Place W9
153 M6 Warwick Place North * SW1V
153 L4 Warwick Row SW1E
153 M6 Warwick Square SW1V
151 H6 Warwick Square * EC4M
153 M6 Warwick Square Mews SW1V
150 A7 Warwick Street W1B
153 M6 Warwick Way SW1V
151 K3 Warwick Yard * EC1Y
151 H7 Watergate EC4Y
157 M8 Wateridge Close E14
154 F2 Waterloo SE1 ⇌ ⊖
150 E8 Waterloo Bridge SE1
155 G2 Waterloo East SE1 ⇌
154 B1 Waterloo Place SW1Y
154 F1 Waterloo Road SE1
156 E5 Waterman Way E1W
156 D7 Waterside Close * SE16
150 F7 Water Street WC2R
151 K6 Watling Court EC4M
151 K6 Watling Street EC4M
156 F3 Watney Market E1
156 F3 Watney Street E1
149 G5 Watson's Mews NW1
156 F5 Watts Street E1W
156 D5 Waveney Close E1W
153 K1 Waverton Street W1J
149 K8 Waverton Street W1K
157 M1 Weatherley Close E3
156 B6 Weaver's Lane SE1
155 G3 Webber Row SE1
155 G3 Webber Street SE1
156 A8 Webb Street SE1
156 E8 Webster Road SE16
149 K7 Weighhouse Street W1K
150 C2 Weirs Passage NW1
149 K6 Welbeck Street W1G
149 K6 Welbeck Way W1G
156 E5 Welland Mews E1W
156 D4 Wellclose Square E1
156 D4 Wellclose Street E1
151 K6 Well Court EC4M
155 K3 Weller Street SE1
148 C2 Wellesley Court W9
150 B2 Wellesley Place * NW1
157 H2 Wellesley Street E1
151 K2 Wellesley Terrace N1
148 F1 Wellington Place NW8
148 E1 Wellington Road NW8
153 H7 Wellington Square SW3
150 D7 Wellington Street WC2E
148 A8 Wellington Terrace W2
156 E5 Wellington Terrace E1W
150 A5 Wells Mews * W1T
150 E2 Wells Square WC1X
150 A5 Wells Street W1T
149 M5 Wells Street W1W
155 M8 Wells Way SE5
152 D4 Wells Way SW7
151 K1 Wenlock Road N1
151 K1 Wenlock Street N1
156 C2 Wentworth Street E1
150 A1 Werrington Street NW1
155 H6 Wesley Close SE17
149 K5 Wesley Street W1G
157 H2 West Arbour Street E1
148 D7 Westbourne Crescent W2
148 D7 Westbourne Crescent Mews W2
148 B6 Westbourne Gardens W2
148 E7 Westbourne Gate W2
148 A6 Westbourne Grove W2
148 B6 Westbourne Grove Terrace W2
148 A5 Westbourne Park Road W2
148 A5 Westbourne Park Villas W2
148 E7 Westbourne Street W2
148 C5 Westbourne Terrace W2
148 C6 Westbourne Terrace Mews W2
148 C5 Westbourne Terrace Road W2
152 A7 West Brompton SW5 ⇌ ⊖ ⊖
152 E2 West Carriage Drive W2
150 C5 West Central Street WC2H
155 H8 Westcott Road SE17
153 J5 West Eaton Place SW1W
153 J5 West Eaton Place Mews SW1X
157 G6 Western Place SE16
157 M4 Westferry E14 ⊖
157 M5 Westferry Circle E14
157 M5 Westferry Circus E14
157 M4 Westferry Road E14
156 F4 West Gardens E1W
152 B7 Westgate Terrace SW10
153 J4 West Halkin Street SW1X
151 G6 West Harding Street * EC4A
157 M5 West India Avenue E14
157 M3 West India Dock Road E14
151 K2 Westland Place EC1V
156 F7 West Lane SE16
153 L6 West Mews SW1V
154 D3 Westminster SW1A ⊖
154 D3 Westminster Bridge SW1A
154 D3 Westminster Bridge Road SW1A
153 L7 Westmoreland Place SW1V
155 K8 Westmoreland Road SE5
149 K5 Westmoreland Street W1G
153 L7 Westmoreland Terrace SW1V
150 E1 Weston Rise WC1X
155 M2 Weston Street SE1
157 J2 Westport Street E1
151 H5 West Poultry Avenue EC1M
149 G7 West Rise * W2
153 H7 West Road SW3
151 H5 West Smithfield EC1A
155 H4 West Square SE11
150 C7 West Street WC2H
156 C3 West Tenter Street E1
153 M6 West Warwick Place * SW1V
148 C5 Westway W2
152 C6 Wetherby Gardens SW5
152 B6 Wetherby Mews SW5
152 C6 Wetherby Place SW7
156 D2 Weyhill Road E1
149 L5 Weymouth Mews W1G
149 K5 Weymouth Street W1G
152 B7 Wharfedale Street SW10
157 L3 Wharf Lane E14
151 J1 Wharf Road N1
150 F2 Wharton Cottages * WC1X
150 F2 Wharton Street WC1X
149 K5 Wheatley Street W1G
156 B1 Wheeler Lane E1
150 E5 Whetstone Park WC2A
154 F2 Whichcote Street * SE1
150 D2 Whidborne Street WC1H
151 G2 Whiskin Street EC1R
155 G7 Whitacre Mews SE11
150 B7 Whitcomb Street W1D
151 G4 White Bear Yard * EC1R
156 E1 Whitechapel E1 ⊖ ⊖
156 C2 Whitechapel High Street EC3N
156 D2 Whitechapel Road E1
156 D2 White Church Lane E1
151 K3 Whitecross Street EC1Y
151 G6 Whitefriars Street EC4Y
154 C2 Whitehall SW1A
154 D2 Whitehall Court SW1A
154 D2 Whitehall Gardens SW1A
154 D2 Whitehall Place SW1A
155 G6 White Hart Street SE11
155 L2 White Hart Yard SE1
148 F4 Whitehaven Street NW8
153 G6 Whiteheads Grove SW3
153 G6 Whitehead's Grove SW3
157 J1 Whitehorse Road E1
157 J3 White Horse Road E1
153 L2 White Horse Street W1J
156 B2 White Kennett Street EC3A
151 M6 White Lion Court EC2R
151 J7 White Lion Hill EC4V
150 F1 White Lion Street N1
151 J4 White Lyon Court EC1A
156 A6 White's Grounds SE1
156 A6 Whites Grounds Estate SE1
156 B1 White's Row E1
157 K1 White Tower Way E1
149 M3 Whitfield Place W1T
150 A4 Whitfield Street W1T
154 E5 Whitgift Street SE11
153 J6 Whittaker Street SW1W
151 M6 Whittington Avenue EC3V
155 G2 Whittlesey Street SE1
156 E3 Wicker Street E1
157 H1 Wickham Close E1
154 E6 Wickham Street SE11
150 E1 Wicklow Street WC1X
156 B1 Widegate Street E1
148 A3 Widley Road W9
149 K5 Wigmore Place * W1U
149 K6 Wigmore Street W1U
155 G7 Wigton Place SE11
153 J5 Wilbraham Place SW1X
150 E6 Wild Court WC2B
155 M4 Wild's Rents SE1
150 D6 Wild Street WC2B
153 M4 Wilfred Street SW1E
156 C1 Wilkes Street E1
156 D8 William Ellis Way * SE16
150 C8 William IV Street WC2N
153 H3 William Mews SW1X
149 M3 William Road NW1
157 K4 William Square SE16
153 H3 William Street SW1X
154 A5 Willow Place SW1P
151 M3 Willow Street EC2A
150 F3 Wilmington Square WC1X
150 F2 Wilmington Street WC1X
156 E7 Wilson Grove SE16
157 L3 Wilson's Place E14
151 M5 Wilson Street EC2M
153 J3 Wilton Crescent SW1X
153 K4 Wilton Mews SW1X
153 J3 Wilton Place SW1X
153 L5 Wilton Road SW1V
153 J3 Wilton Row SW1X
153 K4 Wilton Street SW1X
153 J4 Wilton Terrace SW1X
153 G6 Wiltshire Close SW3
149 K5 Wimpole Mews W1G
149 K6 Wimpole Street W1G
155 H5 Winchester Close * SE11
155 L1 Winchester Square SE1
153 L7 Winchester Street SW1V
155 K1 Winchester Walk SE1
155 G5 Wincott Street SE11
154 F7 Windmill Row SE11
150 B5 Windmill Street W1T
155 G2 Windmill Walk * SE1
157 H6 Windrose Close SE16
151 K1 Windsor Terrace N1
157 L8 Windstock Close SE16
156 F5 Wine Close E1W
151 G6 Wine Office Court EC4A
150 B7 Winnett Street W1D
148 E6 Winsland Mews W2
148 E6 Winsland Street W2
150 A6 Winsley Street W1W
152 D8 Winterton Place SW10
150 C3 Woburn Place WC1H
150 C3 Woburn Square WC1H
150 C3 Woburn Walk * WC1H
156 E1 Wodeham Gardens E1
157 H7 Wolfe Crescent SE16
155 J5 Wollaston Close SE1
156 C7 Wolseley Street SE1
157 G1 Wolsey Street E1
151 H3 Woodbridge Street EC1R
148 B4 Woodchester Square W2
153 H7 Woodfall Street SW3
157 H7 Woodland Crescent SE16
156 C1 Woodseer Street E1
149 H7 Wood's Mews W1K
156 A8 Wood's Place SE1
149 K5 Woodstock Mews W1G
149 K6 Woodstock Street W1C
151 K5 Wood Street EC2Y
155 L7 Wooler Street SE17
150 C3 Woolf Mews WC1H
156 D8 Woolstaplers Way SE16
155 G2 Wootton Street SE1
157 J8 Worgan Street SE16
154 E7 Worgan Street SE11
151 M5 Wormwood Street EC2N
151 M4 Worship Street EC2A
155 L7 Worth Grove SE17
150 F3 Wren Street WC1X
152 A4 Wrights Lane * W8
152 A3 Wright's Lane W8
157 L7 Wyatt Close SE16
149 L3 Wybert Street NW1
151 H2 Wyclif Street EC1V
148 A2 Wymering Road W9
149 H5 Wyndham Mews W1H
149 H5 Wyndham Place W1H
149 G4 Wyndham Street NW1
149 H5 Wyndham Yard * W1H
152 A4 Wynnstay Gardens W8
154 F7 Wynyard Terrace SE11
151 H2 Wynyatt Street EC1V
149 H6 Wythburn Place W1H

Y

156 D8 Yalding Road SE16
150 F3 Yardley Street WC1X
153 L2 Yarmouth Place W1J
153 G4 Yeoman's Row SW3
156 C4 Yeoman's Yard E1
149 J3 York Bridge NW1
150 D8 York Buildings WC2N
149 J3 York Gate NW1
152 B2 York House Place W8
154 E3 York Road SE1
150 E5 Yorkshire Grey Yard * WC1R
157 K3 Yorkshire Road E14
157 K2 York Square E14
149 G5 York Street W1H
149 H4 York Street Chambers * W1U
149 K4 York Terrace East NW1
149 J4 York Terrace West NW1
152 B3 Young Street W8

Z

155 J1 Zoar Street SE1

Index to place names

This index lists places appearing in the main-map section of the atlas in alphabetical order. The reference before each name gives the atlas page number and grid reference of the square in which the place appears. The map shows counties, unitary authorities and administrative areas, together with a list of the abbreviated name forms used in the index.

The top 100 places of tourist interest are indexed in **red** (or **green** if a World Heritage site), motorway service areas in **blue** and airports in blue *italic*.

Scotland

Abers	**Aberdeenshire**
Ag & B	**Argyll and Bute**
Angus	**Angus**
Border	**Scottish Borders**
C Aber	**City of Aberdeen**
C Dund	**City of Dundee**
C Edin	**City of Edinburgh**
C Glas	**City of Glasgow**
Clacks	**Clackmannanshire (1)**
D & G	**Dumfries & Galloway**
E Ayrs	**East Ayrshire**
E Duns	**East Dunbartonshire (2)**
E Loth	**East Lothian**
E Rens	**East Renfrewshire (3)**
Falk	**Falkirk**
Fife	**Fife**
Highld	**Highland**
Inver	**Inverclyde (4)**
Mdloth	**Midlothian (5)**
Moray	**Moray**
N Ayrs	**North Ayrshire**
N Lans	**North Lanarkshire (6)**
Ork	**Orkney Islands**
P & K	**Perth & Kinross**
Rens	**Renfrewshire (7)**
S Ayrs	**South Ayrshire**
Shet	**Shetland Islands**
S Lans	**South Lanarkshire**
Stirlg	**Stirling**
W Duns	**West Dunbartonshire (8)**
W Isls	**Western Isles (Na h-Eileanan an Iar)**
W Loth	**West Lothian**

Wales

Blae G	**Blaenau Gwent (9)**
Brdgnd	**Bridgend (10)**
Caerph	**Caerphilly (11)**
Cardif	**Cardiff**
Carmth	**Carmarthenshire**
Cerdgn	**Ceredigion**
Conwy	**Conwy**
Denbgs	**Denbighshire**
Flints	**Flintshire**
Gwynd	**Gwynedd**
IoA	**Isle of Anglesey**
Mons	**Monmouthshire**
Myr Td	**Merthyr Tydfil (12)**
Neath	**Neath Port Talbot (13)**
Newpt	**Newport (14)**
Pembks	**Pembrokeshire**
Powys	**Powys**
Rhondd	**Rhondda Cynon Taff (15)**
Swans	**Swansea**
Torfn	**Torfaen (16)**
V Glam	**Vale of Glamorgan (17)**
Wrexhm	**Wrexham**

Channel Islands & Isle of Man

Guern	**Guernsey**
Jersey	**Jersey**
IoM	**Isle of Man**

England

BaNES	**Bath & N E Somerset (18)**
Barns	**Barnsley (19)**
Bed	**Bedford**
Birm	**Birmingham**
Bl w D	**Blackburn with Darwen (20)**
Bmouth	**Bournemouth**
Bolton	**Bolton (21)**
Bpool	**Blackpool**
Br & H	**Brighton & Hove (22)**
Br For	**Bracknell Forest (23)**
Bristl	**City of Bristol**
Bucks	**Buckinghamshire**
Bury	**Bury (24)**
C Beds	**Central Bedfordshire**
C Brad	**City of Bradford**
C Derb	**City of Derby**
C KuH	**City of Kingston upon Hull**
C Leic	**City of Leicester**
C Nott	**City of Nottingham**
C Pete	**City of Peterborough**
C Plym	**City of Plymouth**
C Port	**City of Portsmouth**
C Sotn	**City of Southampton**
C York	**City of York**
C Stke	**City of Stoke-on-Trent**
Calder	**Calderdale (25)**
Cambs	**Cambridgeshire**
Ches E	**Cheshire East**
Ches W	**Cheshire West and Chester**
Cnwll	**Cornwall**
Covtry	**Coventry**
Cumb	**Cumbria**
Darltn	**Darlington (26)**
Derbys	**Derbyshire**
Devon	**Devon**
Donc	**Doncaster (27)**
Dorset	**Dorset**
Dudley	**Dudley (28)**
Dur	**Durham**

E R Yk	**East Riding of Yorkshire**
E Susx	**East Sussex**
Essex	**Essex**
Gatesd	**Gateshead (29)**
Gloucs	**Gloucestershire**
Gt Lon	**Greater London**
Halton	**Halton (30)**
Hants	**Hampshire**
Hartpl	**Hartlepool (31)**
Herefs	**Herefordshire**
Herts	**Hertfordshire**
IoS	**Isles of Scilly**
IoW	**Isle of Wight**
Kent	**Kent**
Kirk	**Kirklees (32)**
Knows	**Knowsley (33)**
Lancs	**Lancashire**
Leeds	**Leeds**
Leics	**Leicestershire**
Lincs	**Lincolnshire**
Lpool	**Liverpool**
Luton	**Luton**
M Keyn	**Milton Keynes**
Manch	**Manchester**
Medway	**Medway**
Middsb	**Middlesbrough**
NE Lin	**North East Lincolnshire**
N Linc	**North Lincolnshire**
N Som	**North Somerset (34)**
N Tyne	**North Tyneside (35)**
N u Ty	**Newcastle upon Tyne**
N York	**North Yorkshire**
Nhants	**Northamptonshire**
Norfk	**Norfolk**
Notts	**Nottinghamshire**
Nthumb	**Northumberland**
Oldham	**Oldham (36)**
Oxon	**Oxfordshire**
Poole	**Poole**
R & Cl	**Redcar & Cleveland**
Readg	**Reading**
Rochdl	**Rochdale (37)**
Rothm	**Rotherham (38)**
Rutlnd	**Rutland**
S Glos	**South Gloucestershire (39)**
S on T	**Stockton-on-Tees (40)**
S Tyne	**South Tyneside (41)**
Salfd	**Salford (42)**
Sandw	**Sandwell (43)**
Sefton	**Sefton (44)**
Sheff	**Sheffield**
Shrops	**Shropshire**
Slough	**Slough (45)**
Solhll	**Solihull (46)**
Somset	**Somerset**
St Hel	**St Helens (47)**
Staffs	**Staffordshire**
Sthend	**Southend-on-Sea**
Stockp	**Stockport (48)**
Suffk	**Suffolk**
Sundld	**Sunderland**
Surrey	**Surrey**
Swindn	**Swindon**
Tamesd	**Tameside (49)**
Thurr	**Thurrock (50)**
Torbay	**Torbay**
Traffd	**Trafford (51)**
W & M	**Windsor and Maidenhead (52)**
W Berk	**West Berkshire**
W Susx	**West Sussex**
Wakefd	**Wakefield (53)**
Warrtn	**Warrington (54)**
Warwks	**Warwickshire**
Wigan	**Wigan (55)**
Wilts	**Wiltshire**
Wirral	**Wirral (56)**
Wokham	**Wokingham (57)**
Wolves	**Wolverhampton (58)**
Worcs	**Worcestershire**
Wrekin	**Telford & Wrekin (59)**
Wsall	**Walsall (60)**

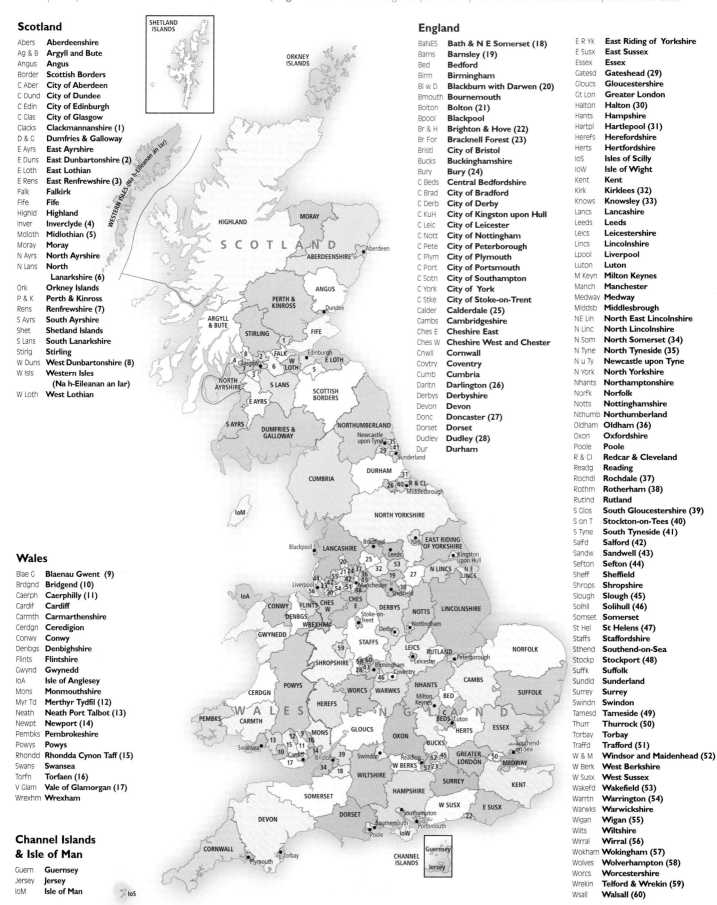

A

17 Q10 **Abbas Combe** Somset
39 N8 **Abberley** Worcs
39 N8 **Abberley Common** Worcs
34 G11 **Abberton** Essex
30 C4 **Abberton** Worcs
22 C2 **Abbess Roding** Essex
50 H4 **Abbeydale** Sheff
28 D3 **Abbey Dore** Herefs
50 C8 **Abbey Green** Staffs
87 P9 **Abbey St Bathans** Border
63 K10 **Abbeystead** Lancs
71 J5 **Abbey Town** Cumb
57 M4 **Abbey Village** Lancs
21 P7 **Abbey Wood** Gt Lon
80 E10 **Abbotrule** Border
14 G9 **Abbots Bickington** Devon
40 E3 **Abbots Bromley** Staffs
7 N6 **Abbotsbury** Dorset
92 G12 **Abbots Deuglie** P & K
14 H6 **Abbotsham** Devon
6 B8 **Abbotskerswell** Devon
20 H3 **Abbots Langley** Herts
17 M2 **Abbots Leigh** N Som
32 H5 **Abbotsley** Cambs
30 D3 **Abbots Morton** Worcs
32 H2 **Abbots Ripton** Cambs
30 E4 **Abbot's Salford** Warwks
9 N2 **Abbots Worthy** Hants
19 K11 **Abbotts Ann** Hants
8 E7 **Abbott Street** Dorset
39 L5 **Abdon** Shrops
36 G7 **Aberaeron** Cerdgn
27 L8 **Aberaman** Rhondd
47 N8 **Aberangell** Gwynd
99 J4 **Aberarder** Highld
92 H11 **Aberargie** P & K
36 H7 **Aberarth** Cerdgn
26 G10 **Aberavon** Neath
27 M7 **Abercanaid** Myr Td
27 P9 **Abercarn** Caerph
24 F3 **Abercastle** Pembks
47 N10 **Abercegir** Powys
98 D8 **Aberchalder Lodge** Highld
102 E5 **Aberchirder** Abers
26 H6 **Abercraf** Powys
26 H9 **Abercregan** Neath
27 L8 **Abercwmboi** Rhondd
36 D11 **Abercych** Pembks
27 M9 **Abercynon** Rhondd
92 G10 **Aberdalgie** P & K
27 L8 **Aberdare** Rhondd
46 C6 **Aberdaron** Gwynd
95 Q1 **Aberdeen** C Aber
103 J11 **Aberdeen Airport** C Aber
86 E5 **Aberdour** Fife
26 G8 **Aberdulais** Neath
47 K11 **Aberdyfi** Gwynd
38 C11 **Aberedw** Powys
24 E3 **Abereiddy** Pembks
46 G4 **Abererch** Gwynd
27 M8 **Aberfan** Myr Td
92 C6 **Aberfeldy** P & K
54 E7 **Aberffraw** IoA
59 K6 **Aberford** Leeds
85 J3 **Aberfoyle** Stirlg
28 C6 **Abergavenny** Mons
55 P6 **Abergele** Conwy
26 D3 **Abergorlech** Carmth
37 P9 **Abergwesyn** Powys
25 Q5 **Abergwili** Carmth
27 J9 **Abergwynfi** Neath
55 J7 **Abergwyngregyn** Gwynd
47 L9 **Abergynolwyn** Gwynd
27 J11 **Aberkenfig** Brdgnd
87 J6 **Aberlady** E Loth
93 N5 **Aberlemno** Angus
47 M8 **Aberllefenni** Gwynd
27 N2 **Aberllynfi** Powys
101 K6 **Aberlour** Moray
38 D4 **Abermule** Powys
25 N4 **Abernant** Carmth
27 L7 **Aber-nant** Rhondd
92 H11 **Abernethy** P & K
93 J8 **Abernyte** P & K
36 D9 **Aberporth** Cerdgn
46 E6 **Abersoch** Gwynd
28 B7 **Abersychan** Torfn
16 D2 **Aberthin** V Glam
27 P7 **Abertillery** Blae G
27 N10 **Abertridwr** Caerph
48 B10 **Abertridwr** Powys
92 E11 **Aberuthven** P & K
37 J4 **Aberystwyth** Cerdgn
37 K4 **Aberystwyth Crematorium** Cerdgn
19 N2 **Abingdon** Oxon
10 H2 **Abinger Common** Surrey
10 H1 **Abinger Hammer** Surrey
32 A5 **Abington** Nhants
78 F4 **Abington** S Lans
33 K7 **Abington Pigotts** Cambs
78 F4 **Abington Services** S Lans
10 H6 **Abingworth** W Susx
41 Q3 **Ab Kettleby** Leics
30 E11 **Ablington** Gloucs
50 G5 **Abney** Derbys
95 J3 **Aboyne** Abers
57 L8 **Abram** Wigan
98 H2 **Abriachan** Highld
21 P4 **Abridge** Essex
85 N7 **Abronhill** N Lans
17 Q2 **Abson** S Glos
31 N5 **Abthorpe** Nhants
53 L7 **Aby** Lincs
59 N5 **Acaster Malbis** C York
59 M6 **Acaster Selby** N York
57 N3 **Accrington** Lancs
57 N3 **Accrington Crematorium** Lancs
88 F5 **Acha** Ag & B
83 L7 **Achahoish** Ag & B
92 G6 **Achalader** P & K
90 C9 **Achaleven** Ag & B
111 d2 **Acha Mor** W Isls
106 D9 **Achanalt** Highld
107 K7 **Achandunie** Highld
107 J3 **Achany** Highld
89 N3 **Acharacle** Highld
89 P6 **Acharn** Highld
92 B6 **Acharn** P & K
110 E7 **Achavanich** Highld
105 Q2 **Achduart** Highld
108 F7 **Achfary** Highld
96 C8 **A'Chill** Highld
105 Q1 **Achiltibuie** Highld
109 M4 **Achina** Highld
75 L8 **Achinhoan** Ag & B
97 N2 **Achintee** Highld
97 L2 **Achintraid** Highld
108 B10 **Achmelvich** Highld
97 M3 **Achmore** Highld
111 d2 **Achmore** W Isls
108 B8 **Achnacarnin** Highld
98 B10 **Achnacarry** Highld
96 H7 **Achnacloich** Highld
98 F5 **Achnaconeran** Highld
90 B7 **Achnacroish** Ag & B
89 K6 **Achnadrish House** Ag & B
92 D8 **Achnafauld** P & K
107 L8 **Achnagarron** Highld
89 K3 **Achnaha** Highld
108 A11 **Achnahaird** Highld
109 K12 **Achnairn** Highld
90 B4 **Achnalea** Highld
83 L5 **Achnamara** Ag & B
106 C10 **Achnasheen** Highld
105 Q11 **Achnashellach Lodge** Highld
101 K8 **Achnastank** Moray
89 K3 **Achosnich** Highld
89 P6 **Achranich** Highld
110 B3 **Achreamie** Highld
90 F3 **Achriabhach** Highld
108 E5 **Achriesgill** Highld
109 M3 **Achtoty** Highld
42 E12 **Achurch** Nhants
107 L4 **Achvaich** Highld
110 B3 **Achvarasdal** Highld
110 G5 **Ackergill** Highld
66 C4 **Acklam** Middsb
60 D2 **Acklam** N York
39 P3 **Ackleton** Shrops
73 M1 **Acklington** Nthumb
59 K9 **Ackton** Wakefd
59 K10 **Ackworth Moor Top** Wakefd
45 N7 **Acle** Norfk
40 E10 **Acock's Green** Birm
23 P9 **Acol** Kent
59 M4 **Acomb** C York
72 G7 **Acomb** Nthumb
28 F3 **Aconbury** Herefs
49 L5 **Acton** Ches E
21 K7 **Acton** Gt Lon
49 P7 **Acton** Staffs
34 E7 **Acton** Suffk
39 M11 **Acton Beauchamp** Herefs
49 L1 **Acton Bridge** Ches W
39 K2 **Acton Burnell** Shrops
39 M11 **Acton Green** Herefs
48 G5 **Acton Park** Wrexhm
39 L3 **Acton Round** Shrops
39 J4 **Acton Scott** Shrops
40 C4 **Acton Trussell** Staffs
18 B5 **Acton Turville** S Glos
49 N9 **Adbaston** Staffs
17 N11 **Adber** Dorset
51 N12 **Adbolton** Notts
31 L7 **Adderbury** Oxon
49 M7 **Adderley** Shrops
86 B9 **Addiewell** W Loth
58 E4 **Addingham** C Brad
31 Q8 **Addington** Bucks
21 M9 **Addington** Gt Lon
22 D10 **Addington** Kent
21 M9 **Addiscombe** Gt Lon
20 G9 **Addlestone** Surrey
53 N9 **Addlethorpe** Lincs
20 H2 **Adeyfield** Herts
38 C2 **Adfa** Powys
38 H7 **Adforton** Herefs
23 N11 **Adisham** Kent
30 G8 **Adlestrop** Gloucs
60 E9 **Adlingfleet** E R Yk
57 L6 **Adlington** Lancs
40 D3 **Admaston** Staffs
49 L11 **Admaston** Wrekin
36 E11 **Adpar** Cerdgn
16 H9 **Adsborough** Somset
16 G8 **Adscombe** Somset
31 Q7 **Adstock** Bucks
31 N4 **Adstone** Nhants
10 H5 **Adversane** W Susx
100 H8 **Advie** Highld
59 M11 **Adwick Le Street** Donc
51 L1 **Adwick upon Dearne** Donc
78 G10 **Ae** D & G
78 G10 **Ae Bridgend** D & G
26 H8 **Afan Forest Park** Neath
102 D7 **Affleck** Abers
8 B8 **Affpuddle** Dorset
98 B5 **Affric Lodge** Highld
48 D2 **Afon-wen** Flints
9 L9 **Afton** IoW
57 P8 **Agecroft Crematorium** Salfd
65 J9 **Agglethorpe** N York
56 H10 **Aigburth** Lpool
60 H5 **Aike** E R Yk
71 P6 **Aiketgate** Cumb
71 L5 **Aikton** Cumb
42 G9 **Ailsworth** C Pete
65 N10 **Ainderby Quernhow** N York
65 N8 **Ainderby Steeple** N York
35 J11 **Aingers Green** Essex
56 F6 **Ainsdale** Sefton
71 Q6 **Ainstable** Cumb
57 N6 **Ainsworth** Bury
66 G6 **Ainthorpe** N York
86 D9 **Ainville** W Loth
83 L3 **Aird** Ag & B
68 E7 **Aird** D & G
111 e2 **Aird** W Isls
111 c3 **Aird a Mhulaidh** W Isls
111 c3 **Aird Asaig** W Isls
97 J2 **Aird Dhubh** Highld
90 D9 **Airdeny** Ag & B
89 L9 **Aird of Kinloch** Ag & B
96 H9 **Aird of Sleat** Highld
85 M9 **Airdrie** N Lans
85 N9 **Airdriehill** N Lans
69 P5 **Airds of Kells** D & G
111 c2 **Aird Uig** W Isls
111 c3 **Airidh a bhruaich** W Isls
70 C4 **Airieland** D & G
93 K5 **Airlie** Angus
60 C8 **Airmyn** E R Yk
92 G8 **Airntully** P & K
97 J8 **Airor** Highld
85 Q5 **Airth** Falk
58 B3 **Airton** N York
42 E3 **Aisby** Lincs
52 C5 **Aisby** Lincs
5 N7 **Aish** Devon
6 A10 **Aish** Devon
16 G8 **Aisholt** Somset
65 M9 **Aiskew** N York
66 H9 **Aislaby** N York
67 J6 **Aislaby** N York
65 P5 **Aislaby** S on T
52 D7 **Aisthorpe** Lincs
111 k4 **Aith** Shet
81 K8 **Akeld** Nthumb
31 P6 **Akeley** Bucks
5 J6 **Albaston** Cnwll
48 G11 **Alberbury** Shrops
11 K6 **Albourne** W Susx
39 P2 **Albrighton** Shrops
49 J10 **Albrighton** Shrops
45 L11 **Alburgh** Norfk
33 M10 **Albury** Herts
10 G1 **Albury** Surrey
10 G2 **Albury Heath** Surrey
107 J10 **Alcaig** Highld
39 J5 **Alcaston** Shrops
30 E3 **Alcester** Warwks
11 P8 **Alciston** E Susx
16 C7 **Alcombe** Somset
32 H2 **Alconbury** Cambs
32 H2 **Alconbury Weston** Cambs
59 K2 **Aldborough** N York
45 K4 **Aldborough** Norfk
19 J5 **Aldbourne** Wilts
61 L6 **Aldbrough** E R Yk
65 L5 **Aldbrough St John** N York
20 F2 **Aldbury** Herts
63 J9 **Aldcliffe** Lancs
92 D3 **Aldclune** P & K
35 P5 **Aldeburgh** Suffk
45 P10 **Aldeby** Norfk
21 J4 **Aldenham** Herts
8 H2 **Alderbury** Wilts
45 J6 **Alderford** Norfk
8 G5 **Alderholt** Dorset
29 K10 **Alderley** Gloucs
57 Q12 **Alderley Edge** Ches E
41 J10 **Aldermans Green** Covtry
19 P7 **Aldermaston** W Berk
30 G4 **Alderminster** Warwks
20 D12 **Aldershot** Hants
30 D7 **Alderton** Gloucs
31 Q5 **Alderton** Nhants
35 M8 **Alderton** Suffk
18 C4 **Alderton** Wilts
58 H1 **Aldfield** N York
48 H4 **Aldford** Ches W
42 E8 **Aldgate** Rutlnd
34 F10 **Aldham** Essex
34 H7 **Aldham** Suffk
10 E8 **Aldingbourne** W Susx
62 F7 **Aldingham** Cumb
13 K3 **Aldington** Kent
30 E5 **Aldington** Worcs
13 K3 **Aldington Corner** Kent
101 M9 **Aldivalloch** Moray
84 F5 **Aldochlay** Ag & B
33 M3 **Aldreth** Cambs
40 D7 **Aldridge** Wsall
35 P5 **Aldringham** Suffk
30 F11 **Aldsworth** Gloucs
101 M9 **Aldunie** Moray
50 G8 **Aldwark** Derbys
59 L2 **Aldwark** N York
10 E9 **Aldwick** W Susx
32 E1 **Aldwincle** Nhants
19 P5 **Aldworth** W Berk
84 G7 **Alexandria** W Duns
16 G8 **Aley** Somset
6 F4 **Alfington** Devon
10 G4 **Alfold** Surrey
10 G3 **Alfold Crossways** Surrey
102 D11 **Alford** Abers
53 M8 **Alford** Lincs
17 N9 **Alford** Somset
53 M8 **Alford Crematorium** Lincs
51 K9 **Alfreton** Derbys
39 N10 **Alfrick** Worcs
39 N10 **Alfrick Pound** Worcs
11 P9 **Alfriston** E Susx
43 J3 **Algarkirk** Lincs
17 P8 **Alhampton** Somset
60 F9 **Alkborough** N Linc
13 N2 **Alkham** Kent
50 F12 **Alkmonton** Derbys
5 Q9 **Allaleigh** Devon
94 B4 **Allanaquoich** Abers
85 P10 **Allanbank** N Lans
81 J4 **Allanton** Border
85 P10 **Allanton** N Lans
85 M11 **Allanton** S Lans
28 H7 **Allaston** Gloucs
9 M4 **Allbrook** Hants
18 F8 **All Cannings** Wilts
72 F9 **Allendale** Nthumb
40 F7 **Allen End** Warwks
72 F10 **Allenheads** Nthumb
33 M12 **Allen's Green** Herts
28 F2 **Allensmore** Herefs
41 J2 **Allenton** C Derb
15 N7 **Aller** Devon
17 K9 **Aller** Somset
70 H7 **Allerby** Cumb
6 E4 **Allercombe** Devon
16 B6 **Allerford** Somset
67 J10 **Allerston** N York
60 D5 **Allerthorpe** E R Yk
58 E7 **Allerton** C Brad
107 M8 **Allerton** Highld
56 H10 **Allerton** Lpool
59 K8 **Allerton Bywater** Leeds
59 K3 **Allerton Mauleverer** N York
40 H10 **Allesley** Covtry
51 J11 **Allestree** C Derb
42 B9 **Allexton** Leics
50 C7 **Allgreave** Ches E
22 G7 **Allhallows** Medway
105 M10 **Alligin Shuas** Highld
7 L4 **Allington** Dorset
42 C3 **Allington** Lincs
18 D5 **Allington** Wilts
18 F8 **Allington** Wilts
18 H11 **Allington** Wilts
62 H6 **Allithwaite** Cumb
85 P4 **Alloa** Clacks
70 H7 **Allonby** Cumb
76 F7 **Alloway** S Ayrs
17 K12 **Allowenshay** Somset
39 J3 **All Stretton** Shrops
90 G6 **Alltchaorunn** Highld
25 Q3 **Alltwalis** Carmth
26 G7 **Alltwen** Neath
36 H10 **Alltyblaca** Cerdgn
17 P12 **Allweston** Dorset
38 G11 **Almeley** Herefs
49 N8 **Almington** Staffs
92 F9 **Almondbank** P & K
58 F10 **Almondbury** Kirk
28 H11 **Almondsbury** S Glos
59 L2 **Alne** N York
107 L8 **Alness** Highld
81 L11 **Alnham** Nthumb
81 P11 **Alnmouth** Nthumb
81 P10 **Alnwick** Nthumb
21 J6 **Alperton** Gt Lon
34 E9 **Alphamstone** Essex
34 E6 **Alpheton** Suffk
6 C5 **Alphington** Devon
50 G7 **Alport** Derbys
49 L4 **Alpraham** Ches E
34 H11 **Alresford** Essex
40 F5 **Alrewas** Staffs
49 P4 **Alsager** Ches E
50 F9 **Alsop en le Dale** Derbys
72 D10 **Alston** Cumb
7 J3 **Alston** Devon
29 N3 **Alstone** Gloucs
50 F9 **Alstonefield** Staffs
17 K6 **Alston Sutton** Somset
15 M7 **Alswear** Devon
108 A12 **Altandhu** Highld
4 F4 **Altarnun** Cnwll
106 H3 **Altass** Highld
89 N8 **Altcreich** Ag & B
83 Q8 **Altgaltraig** Ag & B
22 H4 **Althorne** Essex
60 E11 **Althorpe** N Linc
110 B6 **Altnabreac Station** Highld
109 K8 **Altnaharra** Highld
51 J7 **Alton** Derbys
10 B3 **Alton** Hants
50 E11 **Alton** Staffs
18 G8 **Alton Barnes** Wilts
7 Q3 **Alton Pancras** Dorset
18 G8 **Alton Priors** Wilts
50 E11 **Alton Towers** Staffs
57 P10 **Altrincham** Traffd
57 N10 **Altrincham Crematorium** Traffd
84 H3 **Altskeith Hotel** Stirlg
85 P4 **Alva** Clacks
49 J1 **Alvanley** Ches W
41 K2 **Alvaston** C Derb
40 D11 **Alvechurch** Worcs
40 G6 **Alvecote** Warwks
8 E3 **Alvediston** Wilts
39 N5 **Alveley** Shrops
15 J7 **Alverdiscott** Devon
9 P7 **Alverstoke** Hants
9 P9 **Alverstone** IoW
58 H9 **Alverthorpe** Wakefd
42 B2 **Alverton** Notts
100 H3 **Alves** Moray
30 H12 **Alvescot** Oxon
28 H10 **Alveston** S Glos
30 G3 **Alveston** Warwks
53 K5 **Alvingham** Lincs
28 H8 **Alvington** Gloucs
42 G10 **Alwalton** C Pete
81 J11 **Alwinton** Nthumb
58 H6 **Alwoodley** Leeds
93 J6 **Alyth** P & K
51 J9 **Ambergate** Derbys
29 L8 **Amberley** Gloucs
10 G7 **Amberley** W Susx
81 Q12 **Amble** Nthumb
40 B9 **Amblecote** Dudley
58 E8 **Ambler Thorn** C Brad
62 G2 **Ambleside** Cumb
24 H4 **Ambleston** Pembks
31 N9 **Ambrosden** Oxon
60 E10 **Amcotts** N Linc
20 F4 **Amersham** Bucks
20 F4 **Amersham Common** Bucks
20 F4 **Amersham Old Town** Bucks
20 F4 **Amersham on the Hill** Bucks
18 H11 **Amesbury** Wilts
111 c3 **Amhuinnsuidhe** W Isls
40 G6 **Amington** Staffs
78 G11 **Amisfield Town** D & G
54 F3 **Amlwch** IoA
26 E6 **Ammanford** Carmth
66 G11 **Amotherby** N York
9 L3 **Ampfield** Hants
66 E10 **Ampleforth** N York
18 F1 **Ampney Crucis** Gloucs
18 G1 **Ampney St Mary** Gloucs
18 F1 **Ampney St Peter** Gloucs
19 K11 **Amport** Hants
32 E8 **Ampthill** C Beds
34 E3 **Ampton** Suffk
25 K7 **Amroth** Pembks
92 D8 **Amulree** P & K
21 J2 **Amwell** Herts
89 Q4 **Anaheilt** Highld
42 E2 **Ancaster** Lincs
81 L5 **Ancroft** Nthumb
80 E8 **Ancrum** Border
53 N8 **Anderby** Lincs
19 L10 **Andover** Hants
30 D9 **Andoversford** Gloucs
56 d2 **Andreas** IoM
21 M9 **Anerley** Gt Lon
56 G9 **Anfield** Lpool
56 G9 **Anfield Crematorium** Lpool
2 E7 **Angarrack** Cnwll
39 L7 **Angelbank** Shrops
24 F8 **Angle** Pembks
54 F5 **Anglesey** IoA
10 H8 **Angmering** W Susx
59 M5 **Angram** N York
107 N7 **Ankerville** Highld
60 H8 **Anlaby** E R Yk
44 C4 **Anmer** Norfk
9 Q5 **Anmore** Hants
71 K3 **Annan** D & G
78 H9 **Annandale Water Services** D & G
105 N10 **Annat** Highld
85 M8 **Annathill** N Lans
19 L11 **Anna Valley** Hants
76 G6 **Annbank** S Ayrs
30 F3 **Anne Hathaway's Cottage** Warwks
51 L9 **Annesley** Notts
51 L9 **Annesley Woodhouse** Notts
73 L9 **Annfield Plain** Dur
85 J8 **Anniesland** C Glas
56 G3 **Ansdell** Lancs
17 P9 **Ansford** Somset
40 H8 **Ansley** Warwks
40 G3 **Anslow** Staffs
40 G3 **Anslow Gate** Staffs
33 L9 **Anstey** Herts
41 M6 **Anstey** Leics
87 L2 **Anstruther** Fife
11 L5 **Ansty** W Susx
41 K10 **Ansty** Warwks
8 E3 **Ansty** Wilts
71 K4 **Anthorn** Cumb
45 L4 **Antingham** Norfk
111 c4 **An t-Ob** W Isls
43 J1 **Anton's Gowt** Lincs
5 J8 **Antony** Cnwll
57 M11 **Antrobus** Ches W
52 G12 **Anwick** Lincs
69 N7 **Anwoth** D & G
21 N10 **Aperfield** Gt Lon
42 E10 **Apethorpe** Nhants
52 G8 **Apley** Lincs
51 J5 **Apperknowle** Derbys
29 M3 **Apperley** Gloucs
90 C7 **Appin** Ag & B
60 G10 **Appleby** N Linc
64 C4 **Appleby-in-Westmorland** Cumb
40 H5 **Appleby Magna** Leics
40 H6 **Appleby Parva** Leics
97 J2 **Applecross** Highld
14 H6 **Appledore** Devon
16 E12 **Appledore** Devon
13 J4 **Appledore** Kent
19 N3 **Appleford** Oxon
78 H11 **Applegarth Town** D & G
19 K10 **Appleshaw** Hants
57 K10 **Appleton** Halton
19 M1 **Appleton** Oxon
57 L11 **Appleton** Warrtn
66 G9 **Appleton-le-Moors** N York
66 G11 **Appleton-le-Street** N York
59 M6 **Appleton Roebuck** N York
57 M11 **Appleton Thorn** Warrtn
65 P6 **Appleton Wiske** N York
80 C10 **Appletreehall** Border
58 D3 **Appletreewick** N York
16 E10 **Appley** Somset
57 K7 **Appley Bridge** Lancs
9 P10 **Apse Heath** IoW
32 G9 **Apsley End** C Beds
10 D9 **Apuldram** W Susx
107 N7 **Arabella** Highld
93 Q7 **Arbirlot** Angus
107 P6 **Arboll** Highld
20 C9 **Arborfield** Wokham
20 C9 **Arborfield Cross** Wokham
93 Q7 **Arbroath** Angus
95 N6 **Arbuthnott** Abers
25 Q8 **Archddu** Carmth
65 M4 **Archdeacon Newton** Darltn
84 G6 **Archencarroch** W Duns
101 J6 **Archiestown** Moray
49 P3 **Arclid Green** Ches E
103 L7 **Ardallie** Abers
90 E10 **Ardanaiseig Hotel** Ag & B
97 L3 **Ardaneaskan** Highld
97 L2 **Ardarroch** Highld
74 F4 **Ardbeg** Ag & B
84 B9 **Ardbeg** Ag & B
84 C6 **Ardbeg** Ag & B
106 C5 **Ardcharnich** Highld
89 J11 **Ardchiavaig** Ag & B
83 P1 **Ardchonnel** Ag & B
85 K1 **Ardchullarie More** Stirlg
84 D4 **Arddarroch** Ag & B
98 A10 **Ardechive** Highld
76 E4 **Ardeer** N Ayrs
33 K10 **Ardeley** Herts
97 M4 **Ardelve** Highld
84 F6 **Arden** Ag & B
30 E4 **Ardens Grafton** Warwks
90 B10 **Ardentallen** Ag & B
84 D5 **Ardentinny** Ag & B
83 Q7 **Ardentraive** Ag & B
91 P8 **Ardeonaig** Stirlg
107 N10 **Ardersier** Highld
105 Q5 **Ardessie** Highld
83 M3 **Ardfern** Ag & B
82 H8 **Ardfernal** Ag & B
107 K4 **Ardgay** Highld
90 D4 **Ardgour** Highld
84 D8 **Ardgowan** Inver
84 C7 **Ardhallow** Ag & B
111 c3 **Ardhasig** W Isls
105 L10 **Ardheslaig** Highld
106 C5 **Ardindrean** Highld
11 M4 **Ardingly** W Susx
19 M3 **Ardington** Oxon
83 P9 **Ardlamont** Ag & B
34 H10 **Ardleigh** Essex
34 H10 **Ardleigh Heath** Essex
93 J7 **Ardler** P & K
31 M8 **Ardley** Oxon
91 J12 **Ardlui** Ag & B
83 J5 **Ardlussa** Ag & B
106 B3 **Ardmair** Highld
84 B8 **Ardmaleish** Ag & B
75 J3 **Ardminish** Ag & B
89 P2 **Ardmolich** Highld
84 F7 **Ardmore** Ag & B
107 L5 **Ardmore** Highld
84 C7 **Ardnadam** Ag & B
106 H11 **Ardnagrask** Highld
97 M3 **Ardnarff** Highld
89 Q4 **Ardnastang** Highld
83 L10 **Ardpatrick** Ag & B
83 M6 **Ardrishaig** Ag & B
107 K7 **Ardross** Highld
76 D3 **Ardrossan** N Ayrs
58 H8 **Ardsley East** Leeds
89 L4 **Ardslignish** Highld
82 G11 **Ardtalla** Ag & B
89 M3 **Ardtoe** Highld
83 M2 **Arduaine** Ag & B
107 J9 **Ardullie** Highld
96 H8 **Ardvasar** Highld
91 P10 **Ardvorlich** P & K
111 c3 **Ardvourlie** W Isls
68 F9 **Ardwell** D & G
57 Q9 **Ardwick** Manch
39 P7 **Areley Kings** Worcs
89 N3 **Arevegaig** Highld
10 D3 **Arford** Hants
27 N8 **Argoed** Caerph
84 D3 **Argyll Forest Park** Ag & B
111 c3 **Aribruach** W Isls
88 H10 **Aridhglas** Ag & B
88 E5 **Arileod** Ag & B
88 F5 **Arinagour** Ag & B
90 B10 **Ariogan** Ag & B
97 J11 **Arisaig** Highld
97 J11 **Arisaig House** Highld
59 K2 **Arkendale** N York
33 M9 **Arkesden** Essex
63 L7 **Arkholme** Lancs
79 N10 **Arkleton** D & G
21 K4 **Arkley** Gt Lon
59 M11 **Arksey** Donc
51 K6 **Arkwright Town** Derbys
29 N4 **Arle** Gloucs
70 G10 **Arlecdon** Cumb
32 H9 **Arlesey** C Beds
49 M12 **Arleston** Wrekin
57 M11 **Arley** Ches E
40 H8 **Arley** Warwks
29 J6 **Arlingham** Gloucs
15 K4 **Arlington** Devon
12 B8 **Arlington** E Susx
96 H8 **Armadale** Highld
109 N3 **Armadale** Highld
85 Q8 **Armadale** W Loth
71 Q6 **Armathwaite** Cumb
45 L8 **Arminghall** Norfk
40 E4 **Armitage** Staffs

58 H7 **Armley** Leeds
59 N12 **Armthorpe** Donc
88 F4 **Arnabost** Ag & B
64 G12 **Arncliffe** N York
87 K2 **Arncroach** Fife
101 K6 **Arndilly House** Moray
8 E9 **Arne** Dorset
41 N8 **Arnesby** Leics
92 H12 **Arngask** P & K
97 L7 **Arnisdale** Highld
104 H11 **Arnish** Highld
86 G9 **Arniston** Mdloth
111 d1 **Arnol** W Isls
61 J6 **Arnold** E R Yk
51 N10 **Arnold** Notts
85 K4 **Arnprior** Stirlg
63 J6 **Arnside** Cumb
89 L7 **Aros** Ag & B
62 F6 **Arrad Foot** Cumb
60 H5 **Arram** E R Yk
75 P5 **Arran** N Ayrs
65 L8 **Arrathorne** N York
9 N9 **Arreton** IoW
105 L10 **Arrina** Highld
33 K6 **Arrington** Cambs
84 E3 **Arrochar** Ag & B
30 E3 **Arrow** Warwks
38 H1 **Arscott** Shrops
107 K11 **Artafallie** Highld
58 H5 **Arthington** Leeds
41 Q10 **Arthingworth** Nhants
103 K7 **Arthrath** Abers
103 L8 **Artrochie** Abers
10 G8 **Arundel** W Susx
70 H10 **Asby** Cumb
84 B9 **Ascog** Ag & B
20 E9 **Ascot** W & M
30 H9 **Ascott-under-Wychwood** Oxon
65 P11 **Asenby** N York
41 P4 **Asfordby** Leics
41 Q4 **Asfordby Hill** Leics
42 G2 **Asgarby** Lincs
22 C9 **Ash** Kent
23 P10 **Ash** Kent
17 L11 **Ash** Somset
20 E12 **Ash** Surrey
19 P5 **Ashampstead** W Berk
35 K6 **Ashbocking** Suffk
50 F10 **Ashbourne** Derbys
16 E11 **Ashbrittle** Somset
5 P6 **Ashburton** Devon
15 J11 **Ashbury** Devon
19 J4 **Ashbury** Oxon
52 C2 **Ashby** N Linc
53 L9 **Ashby by Partney** Lincs
53 J4 **Ashby cum Fenby** NE Lin
52 F11 **Ashby de la Launde** Lincs
41 J4 **Ashby-de-la-Zouch** Leics
41 P5 **Ashby Folville** Leics
41 M9 **Ashby Magna** Leics
41 M9 **Ashby Parva** Leics
53 K8 **Ashby Puerorum** Lincs
31 M1 **Ashby St Ledgers** Nhants
45 M9 **Ashby St Mary** Norfk
29 N3 **Ashchurch** Gloucs
6 C6 **Ashcombe** Devon
17 J4 **Ashcombe** N Som
17 L8 **Ashcott** Somset
33 P8 **Ashdon** Essex
19 N10 **Ashe** Hants
23 J3 **Asheldham** Essex
34 C8 **Ashen** Essex
31 P10 **Ashendon** Bucks
20 F3 **Asheridge** Bucks
85 N3 **Ashfield** Stirlg
35 K4 **Ashfield cum Thorpe** Suffk
35 L3 **Ashfield Green** Suffk
5 N9 **Ashford** Devon
15 J5 **Ashford** Devon
13 J2 **Ashford** Kent
20 H8 **Ashford** Surrey
39 K7 **Ashford Bowdler** Shrops
39 K7 **Ashford Carbonell** Shrops
19 P8 **Ashford Hill** Hants
50 G6 **Ashford in the Water** Derbys
77 N2 **Ashgill** S Lans
20 E12 **Ash Green** Surrey
41 J9 **Ash Green** Warwks
6 E1 **Ashill** Devon
44 E8 **Ashill** Norfk
17 J11 **Ashill** Somset
22 G5 **Ashingdon** Essex
73 M4 **Ashington** Nthumb
17 N11 **Ashington** Somset
11 J7 **Ashington** W Susx
79 P4 **Ashkirk** Border
29 L4 **Ashleworth** Gloucs
29 L4 **Ashleworth Quay** Gloucs
34 B5 **Ashley** Cambs
57 P11 **Ashley** Ches E
15 L9 **Ashley** Devon
29 N9 **Ashley** Gloucs
9 J8 **Ashley** Hants
9 L2 **Ashley** Hants
13 P1 **Ashley** Kent
42 B11 **Ashley** Nhants
49 N7 **Ashley** Staffs
18 B7 **Ashley** Wilts
20 F3 **Ashley Green** Bucks
49 K7 **Ash Magna** Shrops
19 M8 **Ashmansworth** Hants
14 F8 **Ashmansworthy** Devon
15 N7 **Ash Mill** Devon
8 D4 **Ashmore** Dorset
19 N6 **Ashmore Green** W Berk
30 H3 **Ashorne** Warwks
51 J8 **Ashover** Derbys
40 H12 **Ashow** Warwks
28 H1 **Ashperton** Herefs
5 Q8 **Ashprington** Devon
16 F9 **Ash Priors** Somset
15 L9 **Ashreigney** Devon
34 G7 **Ash Street** Suffk
21 J10 **Ashtead** Surrey
6 D1 **Ash Thomas** Devon
49 J2 **Ashton** Ches W
2 F9 **Ashton** Cnwll
6 B6 **Ashton** Devon
39 K8 **Ashton** Herefs
84 D7 **Ashton** Inver
31 Q4 **Ashton** Nhants
42 F11 **Ashton** Nhants
18 D8 **Ashton Common** Wilts
57 L8 **Ashton-in-Makerfield** Wigan
18 F2 **Ashton Keynes** Wilts
30 C6 **Ashton under Hill** Worcs
50 C2 **Ashton-under-Lyne** Tamesd
9 K5 **Ashurst** Hants
11 P3 **Ashurst** Kent
11 J6 **Ashurst** W Susx
11 N3 **Ashurstwood** W Susx
20 E11 **Ash Vale** Surrey
5 J2 **Ashwater** Devon
33 J8 **Ashwell** Herts
42 C7 **Ashwell** Rutlnd
33 J8 **Ashwell End** Herts
45 J9 **Ashwellthorpe** Norfk
17 P6 **Ashwick** Somset
44 B6 **Ashwicken** Norfk
62 E6 **Askam in Furness** Cumb
59 M10 **Askern** Donc
7 M4 **Askerswell** Dorset
20 D3 **Askett** Bucks
71 Q10 **Askham** Cumb
51 Q6 **Askham** Notts
59 M5 **Askham Bryan** C York
59 M5 **Askham Richard** C York
83 P5 **Asknish** Ag & B
64 G8 **Askrigg** N York
58 F5 **Askwith** N York
42 F4 **Aslackby** Lincs
45 J11 **Aslacton** Norfk
51 Q11 **Aslockton** Notts
71 J7 **Aspatria** Cumb
33 K10 **Aspenden** Herts
32 D9 **Aspley Guise** C Beds
32 D9 **Aspley Heath** C Beds
57 L7 **Aspull** Wigan
60 C8 **Asselby** E R Yk
34 F8 **Assington** Suffk
34 C6 **Assington Green** Suffk
49 Q3 **Astbury** Ches E
31 P4 **Astcote** Nhants
53 J7 **Asterby** Lincs
38 G1 **Asterley** Shrops
38 H4 **Asterton** Shrops
30 H10 **Asthall** Oxon
30 H10 **Asthall Leigh** Oxon
107 M4 **Astle** Highld
49 K10 **Astley** Shrops
40 H9 **Astley** Warwks
57 M8 **Astley** Wigan
39 P8 **Astley** Worcs
39 N3 **Astley Abbots** Shrops
57 N6 **Astley Bridge** Bolton
39 P8 **Astley Cross** Worcs
49 L6 **Aston** Ches E
57 K12 **Aston** Ches W
50 F4 **Aston** Derbys
48 F3 **Aston** Flints
33 J11 **Aston** Herts
31 J12 **Aston** Oxon
51 L4 **Aston** Rothm
39 P4 **Aston** Shrops
49 K9 **Aston** Shrops
40 B2 **Aston** Staffs
40 B3 **Aston** Staffs
49 N7 **Aston** Staffs
20 C6 **Aston** Wokham
49 L12 **Aston** Wrekin
32 C11 **Aston Abbotts** Bucks
39 L5 **Aston Botterell** Shrops
30 F3 **Aston Cantlow** Warwks
20 E2 **Aston Clinton** Bucks
29 J4 **Aston Crews** Herefs
33 J11 **Aston End** Herts
40 C12 **Aston Fields** Worcs
41 L8 **Aston Flamville** Leics
29 J4 **Aston Ingham** Herefs
31 L4 **Aston le Walls** Nhants
30 G7 **Aston Magna** Gloucs
39 K5 **Aston Munslow** Shrops
38 H6 **Aston on Clun** Shrops
38 G2 **Aston Pigott** Shrops
38 G2 **Aston Rogers** Shrops
20 B4 **Aston Rowant** Oxon
30 D6 **Aston Somerville** Worcs
30 F6 **Aston-sub-Edge** Gloucs
19 P4 **Aston Tirrold** Oxon
41 K2 **Aston-upon-Trent** Derbys
19 P4 **Aston Upthorpe** Oxon
32 H8 **Astwick** C Beds
32 D7 **Astwood** M Keyn
30 C2 **Astwood** Worcs
30 D2 **Astwood Bank** Worcs
39 Q10 **Astwood Crematorium** Worcs
42 F3 **Aswarby** Lincs
53 L9 **Aswardby** Lincs
39 K1 **Atcham** Shrops
8 B8 **Athelhampton** Dorset
35 K3 **Athelington** Suffk
17 J9 **Athelney** Somset
87 K6 **Athelstaneford** E Loth
15 K7 **Atherington** Devon
40 H7 **Atherstone** Warwks
30 G4 **Atherstone on Stour** Warwks
57 M8 **Atherton** Wigan
50 G10 **Atlow** Derbys
97 N3 **Attadale** Highld
52 E5 **Atterby** Lincs
51 J3 **Attercliffe** Sheff
41 J7 **Atterton** Leics
44 H10 **Attleborough** Norfk
41 J8 **Attleborough** Warwks
45 J6 **Attlebridge** Norfk
34 C6 **Attleton Green** Suffk
61 K4 **Atwick** E R Yk
18 C7 **Atworth** Wilts
52 D10 **Aubourn** Lincs
101 J9 **Auchbreck** Moray
103 J8 **Auchedly** Abers
95 M6 **Auchenblae** Abers
85 N5 **Auchenbowie** Stirlg
70 D5 **Auchencairn** D & G
78 F11 **Auchencairn** D & G
75 Q6 **Auchencairn** N Ayrs
87 Q9 **Auchencrow** Border
86 F9 **Auchendinny** Mdloth
86 B10 **Auchengray** S Lans
101 M3 **Auchenhalrig** Moray
77 N3 **Auchenheath** S Lans
77 N11 **Auchenhessnane** D & G
83 P8 **Auchenlochan** Ag & B
76 F2 **Auchenmade** N Ayrs
68 G8 **Auchenmalg** D & G
76 F2 **Auchentiber** N Ayrs
83 Q3 **Auchindrain** Ag & B
106 C6 **Auchindrean** Highld
102 E6 **Auchininna** Abers
77 J7 **Auchinleck** E Ayrs
85 L8 **Auchinloch** N Lans
85 M7 **Auchinstarry** N Lans
90 F2 **Auchintore** Highld
103 M7 **Auchiries** Abers
99 M9 **Auchlean** Highld
95 P3 **Auchlee** Abers
102 E9 **Auchleven** Abers
77 N4 **Auchlochan** S Lans
95 J2 **Auchlossan** Abers
91 M9 **Auchlyne** Stirlg
77 J5 **Auchmillan** E Ayrs
93 R6 **Auchmithie** Angus
86 E3 **Auchmuirbridge** Fife
94 H8 **Auchnacree** Angus
103 J7 **Auchnagatt** Abers
101 J9 **Auchnarrow** Moray
68 D7 **Auchnotteroch** D & G
101 L5 **Auchroisk** Moray
92 E12 **Auchterarder** P & K
98 E7 **Auchteraw** Highld
99 N5 **Auchterblair** Highld
105 M7 **Auchtercairn** Highld
86 E3 **Auchterderran** Fife
93 L8 **Auchterhouse** Angus
102 F7 **Auchterless** Abers
93 J12 **Auchtermuchty** Fife
106 H9 **Auchterneed** Highld
86 E4 **Auchtertool** Fife
97 L4 **Auchtertyre** Highld
91 N11 **Auchtubh** Stirlg
110 G3 **Auckengill** Highld
51 P1 **Auckley** Donc
50 B2 **Audenshaw** Tamesd
49 M6 **Audlem** Ches E
49 P5 **Audley** Staffs
33 N8 **Audley End** Essex
33 N8 **Audley End House** Essex
60 C6 **Aughton** E R Yk
56 H7 **Aughton** Lancs
63 K8 **Aughton** Lancs
51 L4 **Aughton** Rothm
19 J9 **Aughton** Wilts
56 H7 **Aughton Park** Lancs
100 E4 **Auldearn** Highld
39 J10 **Aulden** Herefs
78 E10 **Auldgirth** D & G
77 K2 **Auldhouse** S Lans
97 N5 **Ault a' chruinn** Highld
105 N5 **Aultbea** Highld
105 L5 **Aultgrishin** Highld
106 F8 **Aultguish Inn** Highld
51 L7 **Ault Hucknall** Derbys
101 M5 **Aultmore** Moray
98 H4 **Aultnagoire** Highld
107 L6 **Aultnamain Inn** Highld
42 F3 **Aunsby** Lincs
28 G10 **Aust** S Glos
51 P2 **Austerfield** Donc
40 H6 **Austrey** Warwks
63 N8 **Austwick** N York
53 L7 **Authorpe** Lincs
18 G6 **Avebury** Wilts
22 C7 **Aveley** Thurr
29 M8 **Avening** Gloucs
51 Q9 **Averham** Notts
5 N10 **Aveton Gifford** Devon
99 N6 **Aviemore** Highld
19 L7 **Avington** W Berk
107 L10 **Avoch** Highld
8 G7 **Avon** Hants
85 Q8 **Avonbridge** Falk
31 K4 **Avon Dassett** Warwks
28 F12 **Avonmouth** Bristl
5 P8 **Avonwick** Devon
9 K3 **Awbridge** Hants
6 F3 **Awliscombe** Devon
29 J7 **Awre** Gloucs
51 L11 **Awsworth** Notts
17 L5 **Axbridge** Somset
19 Q11 **Axford** Hants
19 J6 **Axford** Wilts
6 H3 **Axminster** Devon
6 H5 **Axmouth** Devon
65 M3 **Aycliffe** Dur
72 H7 **Aydon** Nthumb
28 H8 **Aylburton** Gloucs
6 D4 **Aylesbeare** Devon
20 D1 **Aylesbury** Bucks
52 H3 **Aylesby** NE Lin
22 E10 **Aylesford** Kent
23 N11 **Aylesham** Kent
41 M7 **Aylestone** C Leic
45 K3 **Aylmerton** Norfk
45 K5 **Aylsham** Norfk
28 H2 **Aylton** Herefs
30 E9 **Aylworth** Gloucs
38 H8 **Aymestrey** Herefs
31 L7 **Aynho** Nhants
32 H12 **Ayot St Lawrence** Herts
76 F7 **Ayr** S Ayrs
64 H9 **Aysgarth** N York
16 E11 **Ayshford** Devon
62 H5 **Ayside** Cumb
42 C9 **Ayston** Rutlnd
81 J3 **Ayton** Border
65 M11 **Azerley** N York

B

6 C9 **Babbacombe** Torbay
33 L12 **Babbs Green** Herts
17 N9 **Babcary** Somset
33 N6 **Babraham** Cambs
51 P5 **Babworth** Notts
111 h1 **Backaland** Ork
103 L5 **Backfolds** Abers
48 H2 **Backford** Ches W
107 N3 **Backies** Highld
97 J11 **Back of Keppoch** Highld
17 L3 **Backwell** N Som
45 J3 **Baconsthorpe** Norfk
28 D3 **Bacton** Herefs
45 M4 **Bacton** Norfk
34 H4 **Bacton** Suffk
57 Q4 **Bacup** Lancs
105 L7 **Badachro** Highld
18 H5 **Badbury** Swindn
31 M3 **Badby** Nhants
108 D7 **Badcall** Highld
108 E5 **Badcall** Highld
105 Q4 **Badcaul** Highld
40 G11 **Baddesley Clinton** Warwks
40 H7 **Baddesley Ensor** Warwks
108 C10 **Baddidarrach** Highld
86 D10 **Baddinsgill** Border
102 F7 **Badenscoth** Abers
101 L10 **Badenyon** Abers
39 N3 **Badger** Shrops
29 M5 **Badgeworth** Gloucs
17 K5 **Badgworth** Somset
97 K4 **Badicaul** Highld
35 M3 **Badingham** Suffk
23 J11 **Badlesmere** Kent
78 H5 **Badlieu** Border
110 F6 **Badlipster** Highld
105 P4 **Badluachrach** Highld
107 M4 **Badninish** Highld
105 Q4 **Badrallach** Highld
30 E5 **Badsey** Worcs
10 D1 **Badshot Lea** Surrey
59 L10 **Badsworth** Wakefd
34 G3 **Badwell Ash** Suffk
17 Q12 **Bagber** Dorset
66 C10 **Bagby** N York
53 K8 **Bag Enderby** Lincs
30 D11 **Bagendon** Gloucs
111 a7 **Bagh a Chaisteil** W Isls
111 a7 **Bagh a Tuath** W Isls
48 E1 **Bagillt** Flints
41 J11 **Baginton** Warwks
26 G9 **Baglan** Neath
48 H9 **Bagley** Shrops
17 L7 **Bagley** Somset
50 B10 **Bagnall** Staffs
39 L7 **Bagot** Shrops
20 E10 **Bagshot** Surrey
29 J10 **Bagstone** S Glos
41 K6 **Bagworth** Leics
28 E4 **Bagwy Llydiart** Herefs
58 F6 **Baildon** C Brad
58 F6 **Baildon Green** C Brad
111 d2 **Baile Ailein** W Isls
111 b5 **Baile a Mhanaich** W Isls
88 G10 **Baile Mor** Ag & B
85 L9 **Baillieston** C Glas
64 G9 **Bainbridge** N York
102 D8 **Bainshole** Abers
42 F8 **Bainton** C Pete
60 G4 **Bainton** E R Yk
86 G2 **Baintown** Fife
80 E10 **Bairnkine** Border
50 G7 **Bakewell** Derbys
47 Q4 **Bala** Gwynd
111 d2 **Balallan** W Isls
98 F3 **Balbeg** Highld
92 H9 **Balbeggie** P & K
106 H12 **Balblair** Highld
107 L8 **Balblair** Highld
51 M1 **Balby** Donc
70 D5 **Balcary** D & G
98 G1 **Balchraggan** Highld
108 D4 **Balchreick** Highld
11 L4 **Balcombe** W Susx
87 M1 **Balcomie Links** Fife
65 N10 **Baldersby** N York
65 P11 **Baldersby St James** N York
57 L3 **Balderstone** Lancs
52 B12 **Balderton** Notts
93 M12 **Baldinnie** Fife
92 F11 **Baldinnies** P & K
33 J9 **Baldock** Herts
32 H9 **Baldock Services** Herts
93 M8 **Baldovie** C Dund
56 d5 **Baldrine** IoM
12 F7 **Baldslow** E Susx
44 G3 **Bale** Norfk
93 K9 **Baledgarno** P & K
88 C7 **Balemartine** Ag & B
86 D8 **Balerno** C Edin
86 F2 **Balfarg** Fife
95 J8 **Balfield** Angus
111 h2 **Balfour** Ork
85 J5 **Balfron** Stirlg
102 E7 **Balgaveny** Abers
86 B4 **Balgonar** Fife
68 F9 **Balgowan** D & G
99 J9 **Balgowan** Highld
104 E8 **Balgown** Highld
68 D7 **Balgracie** D & G
78 E4 **Balgray** S Lans
21 L8 **Balham** Gt Lon
93 J6 **Balhary** P & K
92 H8 **Balholmie** P & K
109 P3 **Baligill** Highld
93 K4 **Balintore** Angus
107 P7 **Balintore** Highld
107 M8 **Balintraid** Highld
111 b5 **Balivanich** W Isls
93 K6 **Balkeerie** Angus
60 D8 **Balkholme** E R Yk
90 E5 **Ballachulish** Highld
56 e4 **Ballajora** IoM
83 Q9 **Ballanlay** Ag & B
68 E3 **Ballantrae** S Ayrs
56 b6 **Ballasalla** IoM
94 F3 **Ballater** Abers
56 c3 **Ballaugh** IoM
107 M7 **Ballchraggan** Highld
87 J6 **Ballencrieff** E Loth
88 B7 **Ballevullin** Ag & B
50 G9 **Ballidon** Derbys
75 N5 **Balliekine** N Ayrs
84 B3 **Balliemore** Ag & B
68 G2 **Balligmorrie** S Ayrs
91 M11 **Ballimore** Stirlg
101 J7 **Ballindalloch** Moray
93 J9 **Ballindean** P & K
20 E3 **Ballinger Common** Bucks
28 G3 **Ballingham** Herefs
86 E3 **Ballingry** Fife
92 E5 **Ballinluig** P & K
93 M5 **Ballinshoe** Angus
92 G5 **Ballintuim** P & K
107 M11 **Balloch** Highld
85 M7 **Balloch** N Lans
92 C10 **Balloch** P & K
76 F11 **Balloch** S Ayrs
84 G6 **Balloch** W Duns
10 F5 **Balls Cross** W Susx
11 P3 **Balls Green** E Susx
89 J7 **Ballygown** Ag & B
82 E9 **Ballygrant** Ag & B
88 E5 **Ballyhaugh** Ag & B
69 P4 **Balmaclellan** D & G
69 P9 **Balmae** D & G
84 G5 **Balmaha** Stirlg
86 G1 **Balmalcolm** Fife
69 P9 **Balmangan** D & G
103 K10 **Balmedie** Abers
93 L10 **Balmerino** Fife
75 P6 **Balmichael** N Ayrs
94 D3 **Balmoral Castle Grounds** Abers
85 K8 **Balmore** E Duns
107 P6 **Balmuchy** Highld
86 E5 **Balmule** Fife
93 M10 **Balmullo** Fife
109 P12 **Balnacoil Lodge** Highld
105 P12 **Balnacra** Highld
94 E3 **Balnacroft** Abers
99 K2 **Balnafoich** Highld
92 E5 **Balnaguard** P & K
82 F3 **Balnahard** Ag & B
89 K9 **Balnahard** Ag & B
98 F3 **Balnain** Highld
108 G3 **Balnakeil** Highld
59 N9 **Balne** N York
92 F8 **Balquharn** P & K
91 M11 **Balquhidder** Stirlg
40 G11 **Balsall Common** Solhll
40 E9 **Balsall Heath** Birm
31 K6 **Balscote** Oxon
33 P6 **Balsham** Cambs
111 m2 **Baltasound** Shet
69 K6 **Baltersan** D & G
17 M8 **Baltonsborough** Somset
89 Q11 **Balvicar** Ag & B
97 M6 **Balvraid** Highld
99 M3 **Balvraid** Highld
57 K4 **Bamber Bridge** Lancs
33 P11 **Bamber's Green** Essex
81 N7 **Bamburgh** Nthumb
81 N7 **Bamburgh Castle** Nthumb
50 G4 **Bamford** Derbys
71 Q11 **Bampton** Cumb
16 C10 **Bampton** Devon
30 H12 **Bampton** Oxon
71 Q11 **Bampton Grange** Cumb
90 F2 **Banavie** Highld
31 L6 **Banbury** Oxon
31 L5 **Banbury Crematorium** Oxon
26 C6 **Bancffosfelen** Carmth
95 L3 **Banchory** Abers
95 P2 **Banchory-Devenick** Abers
25 P6 **Bancycapel** Carmth
25 N5 **Bancyfelin** Carmth
93 J9 **Bandirran** P & K
102 F3 **Banff** Abers
54 H7 **Bangor** Gwynd
54 H7 **Bangor Crematorium** Gwynd
48 H6 **Bangor-is-y-coed** Wrexhm
14 D11 **Bangors** Cnwll
44 H11 **Banham** Norfk
9 K6 **Bank** Hants
70 G2 **Bankend** D & G
92 F8 **Bankfoot** P & K
77 K8 **Bankglen** E Ayrs
103 J12 **Bankhead** C Aber
86 B12 **Bankhead** S Lans
85 N7 **Banknock** Falk
56 H5 **Banks** Lancs
79 K11 **Bankshill** D & G
45 K4 **Banningham** Norfk
34 B11 **Bannister Green** Essex
85 N5 **Bannockburn** Stirlg
21 K10 **Banstead** Surrey
5 N10 **Bantham** Devon
85 M7 **Banton** N Lans
17 K4 **Banwell** N Som
22 H10 **Bapchild** Kent
18 E12 **Bapton** Wilts
111 d1 **Barabhas** W Isls
76 F5 **Barassie** S Ayrs
107 M7 **Barbaraville** Highld
76 G7 **Barbieston** S Ayrs
63 L6 **Barbon** Cumb
15 M3 **Barbrook** Devon
41 M12 **Barby** Nhants
90 D7 **Barcaldine** Ag & B
11 N7 **Barcombe** E Susx
11 N6 **Barcombe Cross** E Susx
12 C2 **Barden Park** Kent
33 Q9 **Bardfield End Green** Essex
34 B10 **Bardfield Saling** Essex
52 G9 **Bardney** Lincs
41 K5 **Bardon** Leics
72 E7 **Bardon Mill** Nthumb
85 K8 **Bardowie** E Duns
84 F8 **Bardrainney** Inver
62 F7 **Bardsea** Cumb
59 J5 **Bardsey** Leeds
46 B7 **Bardsey Island** Gwynd
34 F3 **Bardwell** Suffk
63 J8 **Bare** Lancs
69 J6 **Barfad** D & G
45 J8 **Barford** Norfk
30 H2 **Barford** Warwks
31 K7 **Barford St John** Oxon
8 F2 **Barford St Martin** Wilts
31 K7 **Barford St Michael** Oxon
23 N12 **Barfrestone** Kent
85 L9 **Bargeddie** N Lans
27 N8 **Bargoed** Caerph
69 J4 **Bargrennan** D & G
32 G2 **Barham** Cambs
23 N12 **Barham** Kent
35 J6 **Barham** Suffk
13 N1 **Barham Crematorium** Kent
33 L4 **Bar Hill** Cambs
42 F7 **Barholm** Lincs
41 N5 **Barkby** Leics
41 N5 **Barkby Thorpe** Leics
41 R1 **Barkestone-le-Vale** Leics
20 C9 **Barkham** Wokham
21 N6 **Barking** Gt Lon
34 H6 **Barking** Suffk
21 N5 **Barkingside** Gt Lon
34 H6 **Barking Tye** Suffk
58 D9 **Barkisland** Calder
2 H5 **Barkla Shop** Cnwll
42 D2 **Barkston** Lincs
59 L7 **Barkston Ash** N York
33 L9 **Barkway** Herts
85 L9 **Barlanark** C Glas
50 B11 **Barlaston** Staffs
10 F6 **Barlavington** W Susx
51 L5 **Barlborough** Derbys
59 N7 **Barlby** N York
41 K6 **Barlestone** Leics
33 L8 **Barley** Herts
57 P1 **Barley** Lancs
42 C8 **Barleythorpe** Rutlnd
22 H5 **Barling** Essex
52 F8 **Barlings** Lincs
70 D4 **Barlochan** D & G
51 J6 **Barlow** Derbys
73 K8 **Barlow** Gatesd
59 N8 **Barlow** N York
60 D4 **Barmby Moor** E R Yk
59 P8 **Barmby on the Marsh** E R Yk
75 M4 **Barmollack** Ag & B
47 K7 **Barmouth** Gwynd
65 N4 **Barmpton** Darltn
61 K3 **Barmston** E R Yk
83 Q4 **Barnacarry** Ag & B
42 F8 **Barnack** C Pete
65 J4 **Barnard Castle** Dur
31 K11 **Barnard Gate** Oxon
34 B7 **Barnardiston** Suffk
70 D4 **Barnbarroch** D & G
59 L12 **Barnburgh** Donc
45 P11 **Barnby** Suffk
59 N11 **Barnby Dun** Donc
52 C11 **Barnby in the Willows** Notts
51 P4 **Barnby Moor** Notts
68 E11 **Barncorkrie** D & G
21 K7 **Barnes** Gt Lon
12 D1 **Barnes Street** Kent
21 K4 **Barnet** Gt Lon
52 F2 **Barnetby le Wold** N Linc
44 G4 **Barney** Norfk
34 E2 **Barnham** Suffk
10 F8 **Barnham** W Susx
44 H8 **Barnham Broom** Norfk
93 R4 **Barnhead** Angus

93 N8 **Barnhill** C Dund
100 H4 **Barnhill** Moray
68 D5 **Barnhills** D & G
65 J5 **Barningham** Dur
34 F2 **Barningham** Suffk
52 H3 **Barnoldby le Beck** NE Lin
63 Q11 **Barnoldswick** Lancs
10 H5 **Barns Green** W Susx
59 J11 **Barnsley** Barns
30 E12 **Barnsley** Gloucs
59 J12 **Barnsley Crematorium** Barns
15 K5 **Barnstaple** Devon
33 Q11 **Barnston** Essex
56 F11 **Barnston** Wirral
41 Q1 **Barnstone** Notts
40 D11 **Barnt Green** Worcs
86 E7 **Barnton** C Edin
49 L1 **Barnton** Ches W
42 F12 **Barnwell All Saints** Nhants
42 F12 **Barnwell St Andrew** Nhants
29 M5 **Barnwood** Gloucs
76 E11 **Barr** S Ayrs
111 a7 **Barra** W Isls
111 a6 *Barra Airport* W Isls
69 J8 **Barrachan** D & G
111 a7 **Barraigh** W Isls
88 B7 **Barrapoll** Ag & B
72 G6 **Barrasford** Nthumb
84 H10 **Barrhead** E Rens
68 H3 **Barrhill** S Ayrs
33 L6 **Barrington** Cambs
17 K11 **Barrington** Somset
2 F7 **Barripper** Cnwll
84 F11 **Barrmill** N Ayrs
110 F2 **Barrock** Highld
29 M4 **Barrow** Gloucs
57 N2 **Barrow** Lancs
42 C7 **Barrow** Rutlnd
17 Q9 **Barrow** Somset
34 C4 **Barrow** Suffk
42 C3 **Barrowby** Lincs
42 D9 **Barrowden** Rutlnd
57 Q2 **Barrowford** Lancs
17 M3 **Barrow Gurney** N Som
60 H9 **Barrow Haven** N Linc
62 E8 **Barrow-in-Furness** Cumb
62 E8 **Barrow Island** Cumb
60 H9 **Barrow-upon-Humber** N Linc
41 M4 **Barrow upon Soar** Leics
41 J2 **Barrow upon Trent** Derbys
93 P8 **Barry** Angus
16 F3 **Barry** V Glam
16 F3 **Barry Island** V Glam
41 P5 **Barsby** Leics
45 N11 **Barsham** Suffk
40 G10 **Barston** Solhll
28 G1 **Bartestree** Herefs
102 H8 **Barthol Chapel** Abers
34 C11 **Bartholomew Green** Essex
49 N5 **Barthomley** Ches E
9 K5 **Bartley** Hants
40 D10 **Bartley Green** Birm
33 P7 **Bartlow** Cambs
33 L5 **Barton** Cambs
49 J5 **Barton** Ches W
30 E8 **Barton** Gloucs
56 G7 **Barton** Lancs
57 K2 **Barton** Lancs
65 M6 **Barton** N York
31 M1 **Barton** Oxon
6 C8 **Barton** Torbay
44 B8 **Barton Bendish** Norfk
29 L8 **Barton End** Gloucs
31 N7 **Barton Hartshorn** Bucks
41 M2 **Barton in Fabis** Notts
41 K6 **Barton in the Beans** Leics
32 F9 **Barton-le-Clay** C Beds
66 G11 **Barton-le-Street** N York
60 C2 **Barton-le-Willows** N York
34 C3 **Barton Mills** Suffk
9 J8 **Barton-on-Sea** Hants
30 G7 **Barton-on-the-Heath** Warwks
17 M9 **Barton St David** Somset
32 C2 **Barton Seagrave** Nhants
19 M11 **Barton Stacey** Hants
15 L4 **Barton Town** Devon
45 M5 **Barton Turf** Norfk
40 F4 **Barton-under-Needwood** Staffs
60 H9 **Barton-upon-Humber** N Linc
60 H9 **Barton Waterside** N Linc
111 d1 **Barvas** W Isls
33 N2 **Barway** Cambs
41 K8 **Barwell** Leics
15 K10 **Barwick** Devon
17 M12 **Barwick** Somset
59 K6 **Barwick in Elmet** Leeds
48 H10 **Baschurch** Shrops
31 K2 **Bascote** Warwks
63 M4 **Bashall Eaves** Lancs
22 E5 **Basildon** Essex
22 E6 **Basildon & District Crematorium** Essex
19 Q9 **Basingstoke** Hants
19 P10 **Basingstoke Crematorium** Hants
50 G6 **Baslow** Derbys
17 J7 **Bason Bridge** Somset
28 C10 **Bassaleg** Newpt
80 E5 **Bassendean** Border
71 K8 **Bassenthwaite** Cumb
9 M4 **Bassett** C Sotn
33 K7 **Bassingbourn** Cambs
52 C11 **Bassingham** Lincs
42 D5 **Bassingthorpe** Lincs
33 K10 **Bassus Green** Herts
42 G7 **Baston** Lincs
45 N6 **Bastwick** Norfk
20 G5 **Batchworth** Herts
7 N3 **Batcombe** Dorset
17 Q8 **Batcombe** Somset
21 J1 **Batford** Herts
17 Q4 **Bath** BaNES
18 B7 **Bathampton** BaNES
16 E10 **Bathealton** Somset
18 B7 **Batheaston** BaNES
18 B7 **Bathford** BaNES
86 B8 **Bathgate** W Loth
51 Q8 **Bathley** Notts
4 G5 **Bathpool** Cnwll
16 H10 **Bathpool** Somset
35 L9 **Bath Side** Cumb
85 Q9 **Bathville** W Loth
17 N6 **Bathway** Somset
58 G8 **Batley** Kirk
30 F7 **Batsford** Gloucs
66 E6 **Battersby** N York

21 L7 **Battersea** Gt Lon
34 G6 **Battisford Tye** Suffk
12 E7 **Battle** E Susx
27 L3 **Battle** Powys
93 M5 **Battledykes** Angus
52 H11 **Battle of Britain Memorial Flight** Lincs
22 F5 **Battlesbridge** Essex
16 C10 **Battleton** Somset
29 M1 **Baughton** Worcs
19 P8 **Baughurst** Hants
95 K4 **Baulds** Abers
19 K3 **Baulking** Oxon
52 H8 **Baumber** Lincs
30 D12 **Baunton** Gloucs
8 F2 **Baverstock** Wilts
45 J8 **Bawburgh** Norfk
44 H6 **Bawdeswell** Norfk
17 J8 **Bawdrip** Somset
35 M8 **Bawdsey** Suffk
51 P3 **Bawtry** Donc
57 P4 **Baxenden** Lancs
40 H7 **Baxterley** Warwks
104 C10 **Bay** Highld
111 e2 **Bayble** W Isls
9 N3 **Baybridge** Hants
62 F7 **Baycliff** Cumb
19 K5 **Baydon** Wilts
21 L2 **Bayford** Herts
17 Q9 **Bayford** Somset
111 a4 **Bayhead** W Isls
34 H6 **Bayham** Suffk
28 G4 **Baysham** Herefs
39 J1 **Bayston Hill** Shrops
34 C8 **Baythorne End** Essex
39 M7 **Bayton** Worcs
19 N1 **Bayworth** Oxon
31 Q6 **Beachampton** Bucks
44 C8 **Beachamwell** Norfk
12 C10 **Beachy Head** E Susx
6 G2 **Beacon** Devon
34 F10 **Beacon End** Essex
10 E3 **Beacon Hill** Surrey
35 J6 **Beacon Hill Services** Suffk
20 C4 **Beacon's Bottom** Bucks
20 F5 **Beaconsfield** Bucks
20 F5 *Beaconsfield Services* Bucks
66 F9 **Beadlam** N York
32 F8 **Beadlow** C Beds
81 P8 **Beadnell** Nthumb
15 K8 **Beaford** Devon
59 M8 **Beal** N York
81 M6 **Beal** Nthumb
4 H5 **Bealsmill** Cnwll
7 L3 **Beaminster** Dorset
73 L9 **Beamish** Dur
58 E4 **Beamsley** N York
18 D7 **Beanacre** Wilts
81 M9 **Beanley** Nthumb
5 L4 **Beardon** Devon
11 J2 **Beare Green** Surrey
30 F3 **Bearley** Warwks
73 M11 **Bearpark** Dur
85 J8 **Bearsden** E Duns
22 F11 **Bearsted** Kent
49 N7 **Bearstone** Shrops
40 D9 **Bearwood** Birm
38 H10 **Bearwood** Herefs
8 F7 **Bearwood** Poole
78 H8 **Beattock** D & G
22 C2 **Beauchamp Roding** Essex
27 N6 **Beaufort** Blae G
9 L7 **Beaulieu** Hants
9 L6 **Beaulieu House** Hants
107 J11 **Beauly** Highld
54 H6 **Beaumaris** IoA
71 M4 **Beaumont** Cumb
35 J10 **Beaumont** Essex
7 b2 **Beaumont** Jersey
40 G12 **Beausale** Warwks
9 P3 **Beauworth** Hants
14 H11 **Beaworthy** Devon
34 C10 **Beazley End** Essex
56 G11 **Bebington** Wirral
45 N11 **Beccles** Suffk
57 J4 **Becconsall** Lancs
39 N2 **Beckbury** Shrops
21 M9 **Beckenham** Gt Lon
21 M9 **Beckenham Crematorium** Gt Lon
62 B2 **Beckermet** Cumb
70 H5 **Beckfoot** Cumb
29 N2 **Beckford** Worcs
18 D7 **Beckhampton** Wilts
52 C11 **Beckingham** Lincs
51 R3 **Beckingham** Notts
18 B9 **Beckington** Somset
38 H6 **Beckjay** Shrops
12 G5 **Beckley** E Susx
31 M10 **Beckley** Oxon
34 B2 **Beck Row** Suffk
62 E6 **Beck Side** Cumb
21 N7 **Beckton** Gt Lon
58 H4 **Beckwithshaw** N York
21 P6 **Becontree** Gt Lon
65 M9 **Bedale** N York
8 C4 **Bedchester** Dorset
27 M10 **Beddau** Rhondd
54 H11 **Beddgelert** Gwynd
11 N8 **Beddingham** E Susx
21 L9 **Beddington** Gt Lon
21 L9 **Beddington Corner** Gt Lon
35 K4 **Bedfield** Suffk
32 F6 **Bedford** Bed
32 F6 **Bedford Crematorium** Bed
10 B8 **Bedhampton** Hants
35 K3 **Bedingfield** Suffk
58 H2 **Bedlam** N York
73 M5 **Bedlington** Nthumb
27 M8 **Bedlinog** Myr Td
17 N2 **Bedminster** Bristl
17 N3 **Bedminster Down** Bristl
20 H3 **Bedmond** Herts
40 C4 **Bednall** Staffs
80 E10 **Bedrule** Border
38 G7 **Bedstone** Shrops
27 N10 **Bedwas** Caerph
27 N8 **Bedwellty** Caerph
41 J9 **Bedworth** Warwks
41 P6 **Beeby** Leics
10 B3 **Beech** Hants
49 Q7 **Beech** Staffs
20 B9 **Beech Hill** W Berk
18 G8 **Beechingstoke** Wilts
19 N5 **Beedon** W Berk
61 J4 **Beeford** E R Yk
50 H7 **Beeley** Derbys
52 H3 **Beelsby** NE Lin
19 P7 **Beenham** W Berk
6 G5 **Beer** Devon
17 K9 **Beer** Somset
17 J11 **Beercrocombe** Somset

7 N1 **Beer Hackett** Dorset
5 Q11 **Beesands** Devon
53 M7 **Beesby** Lincs
5 Q11 **Beeson** Devon
32 G7 **Beeston** C Beds
25 K4 **Beeston** Ches W
58 H7 **Beeston** Leeds
44 E7 **Beeston** Norfk
51 M12 **Beeston** Notts
45 J2 **Beeston Regis** Norfk
70 E2 **Beeswing** D & G
63 J6 **Beetham** Cumb
6 H1 **Beetham** Somset
44 F6 **Beetley** Norfk
31 L10 **Begbroke** Oxon
25 K7 **Begelly** Pembks
38 E6 **Beguildy** Powys
45 N8 **Beighton** Norfk
51 K4 **Beighton** Sheff
111 b5 **Beinn Na Faoghla** W Isls
84 F11 **Beith** N Ayrs
23 M11 **Bekesbourne** Kent
45 L6 **Belaugh** Norfk
40 B11 **Belbroughton** Worcs
8 B5 **Belchalwell** Dorset
34 D8 **Belchamp Otten** Essex
34 D8 **Belchamp St Paul** Essex
34 D8 **Belchamp Walter** Essex
53 J8 **Belchford** Lincs
81 M7 **Belford** Nthumb
41 N6 **Belgrave** C Leic
87 M6 **Belhaven** E Loth
103 K10 **Belhelvie** Abers
101 N9 **Belhinnie** Abers
101 L11 **Bellabeg** Abers
83 M5 **Bellanoch** Ag & B
93 J4 **Bellaty** Angus
58 B3 **Bell Busk** N York
53 L7 **Belleau** Lincs
40 C11 **Bell End** Worcs
65 K8 **Bellerby** N York
71 M4 **Belle Vue** Cumb
59 J9 **Belle Vue** Wakefd
78 D2 **Bellfield** S Lans
78 F5 **Bellfield** S Lans
20 F3 **Bellingdon** Bucks
72 F4 **Bellingham** Nthumb
75 K5 **Belloch** Ag & B
75 K6 **Bellochantuy** Ag & B
49 K6 **Bell o' th' Hill** Ches W
85 M10 **Bellshill** N Lans
85 N10 **Bellside** N Lans
86 C8 **Bellsquarry** W Loth
12 C3 **Bells Yew Green** E Susx
17 N4 **Belluton** BaNES
107 K10 **Belmaduthy** Highld
57 M6 **Belmont** Bl w D
21 K10 **Belmont** Gt Lon
76 F7 **Belmont** S Ayrs
111 m2 **Belmont** Shet
101 M11 **Belnacraig** Abers
51 J10 **Belper** Derbys
73 K5 **Belsay** Nthumb
80 D8 **Belses** Border
5 P8 **Belsford** Devon
20 G4 **Belsize** Herts
35 J8 **Belstead** Suffk
5 M2 **Belstone** Devon
57 N4 **Belthorn** Lancs
23 M9 **Beltinge** Kent
72 E7 **Beltingham** Nthumb
52 B3 **Beltoft** N Linc
41 K4 **Belton** Leics
42 D3 **Belton** Lincs
52 B3 **Belton** N Linc
45 P9 **Belton** Norfk
42 B9 **Belton** Rutlnd
21 P7 **Belvedere** Gt Lon
42 B4 **Belvoir** Leics
42 B4 **Belvoir Castle** Leics
9 Q9 **Bembridge** IoW
8 G2 **Bemerton** Wilts
67 P12 **Bempton** E R Yk
45 Q12 **Benacre** Suffk
111 b5 **Benbecula** W Isls
111 b5 *Benbecula Airport* W Isls
77 M11 **Benbuie** D & G
90 C8 **Benderloch** Ag & B
12 F4 **Benenden** Kent
73 J9 **Benfieldside** Dur
21 L1 **Bengeo** Herts
30 D5 **Bengeworth** Worcs
35 N5 **Benhall Green** Suffk
35 M5 **Benhall Street** Suffk
95 M1 **Benholm** Abers
59 M3 **Beningbrough** N York
33 J11 **Benington** Herts
43 L2 **Benington** Lincs
54 G5 **Benllech** IoA
84 C6 **Benmore** Ag & B
75 Q8 **Bennan** N Ayrs
90 G3 **Ben Nevis** Highld
52 H7 **Benniworth** Lincs
12 E1 **Benover** Kent
58 F5 **Ben Rhydding** C Brad
76 F3 **Benslie** N Ayrs
19 Q3 **Benson** Oxon
95 N2 **Benthoul** C Aber
59 M11 **Bentley** Donc
60 H7 **Bentley** E R Yk
10 C2 **Bentley** Hants
35 J8 **Bentley** Suffk
40 H8 **Bentley** Warwks
79 M10 **Bentpath** D & G
15 M5 **Bentwichen** Devon
19 Q11 **Bentworth** Hants
93 K8 **Benvie** Angus
7 M3 **Benville** Dorset
43 K11 **Benwick** Cambs
40 E12 **Beoley** Worcs
97 J10 **Beoraidbeg** Highld
10 D6 **Bepton** W Susx
33 N10 **Berea** Pembks
5 J6 **Bere Alston** Devon
5 K7 **Bere Ferrers** Devon
8 C8 **Bere Regis** Dorset
45 M9 **Bergh Apton** Norfk
19 P2 **Berinsfield** Oxon
29 J8 **Berkeley** Gloucs
20 F2 **Berkhamsted** Herts
18 B10 **Berkley** Somset
40 G10 **Berkswell** Solhll
21 M7 **Bermondsey** Gt Lon
97 L5 **Bernera** Highld
104 E11 **Bernisdale** Highld
19 Q2 **Berrick Prior** Oxon
19 Q3 **Berrick Salome** Oxon
110 D10 **Berriedale** Highld
71 N9 **Berrier** Cumb
38 E2 **Berriew** Powys
39 K2 **Berrington** Shrops
39 L8 **Berrington** Worcs
39 L8 **Berrington Green** Worcs
16 H6 **Berrow** Somset

86 F8 **Bilston** Mdloth
40 C8 **Bilston** Wolves
41 J6 **Bilstone** Leics
61 K7 **Bilton** E R Yk
58 H3 **Bilton** N York
59 L4 **Bilton** N York
41 L11 **Bilton** Warwks
52 H5 **Binbrook** Lincs
7 P6 **Bincombe** Dorset
17 N6 **Binegar** Somset
20 D8 **Binfield** Br For
20 C7 **Binfield Heath** Oxon
72 H6 **Bingfield** Nthumb
51 P11 **Bingham** Notts
58 E6 **Bingley** C Brad
44 G3 **Binham** Norfk
41 J10 **Binley** Covtry
19 M9 **Binley** Hants
41 K11 **Binley Woods** Warwks
8 C9 **Binnegar** Dorset
85 P8 **Binniehill** Falk
10 F2 **Binscombe** Surrey
9 P8 **Binstead** IoW
10 C2 **Binsted** Hants
10 F8 **Binsted** W Susx
30 F4 **Binton** Warwks
44 G5 **Bintree** Norfk
34 F11 **Birch** Essex
44 C4 **Bircham Newton** Norfk
44 C4 **Bircham Tofts** Norfk
33 N11 **Birchanger** Essex
33 N11 *Birchanger Green Services* Essex
40 E2 **Birch Cross** Staffs
39 J8 **Bircher** Herefs
34 F11 **Birch Green** Essex
27 N11 **Birchgrove** Cardif
26 F8 **Birchgrove** Swans
11 N4 **Birchgrove** W Susx
23 P9 **Birchington** Kent
40 H8 **Birchley Heath** Warwks
50 G8 **Birchover** Derbys
57 Q7 *Birch Services* Rochdl
50 D4 **Birch Vale** Derbys
16 H12 **Birch Wood** Somset
57 M9 **Birchwood** Warrtn
51 N3 **Bircotes** Notts
34 B8 **Birdbrook** Essex
66 C11 **Birdforth** N York
10 D9 **Birdham** W Susx
31 K1 **Birdingbury** Warwks
29 N6 **Birdlip** Gloucs
60 E2 **Birdsall** N York
58 G11 **Birds Edge** Kirk
22 C2 **Birds Green** Essex
39 P5 **Birdsgreen** Shrops
7 K3 **Birdsmoorgate** Dorset
51 J1 **Birdwell** Barns
80 G6 **Birgham** Border
107 M4 **Birichin** Highld
65 N7 **Birkby** N York
56 G6 **Birkdale** Sefton
102 C3 **Birkenbog** Abers
56 G10 **Birkenhead** Wirral
102 F6 **Birkenhills** Abers
58 G8 **Birkenshaw** Kirk
94 F4 **Birkhall** Abers
93 L8 **Birkhill** Angus
79 K6 **Birkhill** D & G
59 M8 **Birkin** N York
39 J10 **Birley** Herefs
51 J3 **Birley Carr** Sheff
22 D10 **Birling** Kent
30 C5 **Birlingham** Worcs
40 E9 **Birmingham** Birm
40 F10 *Birmingham Airport* Solhll
92 F7 **Birnam** P & K
103 K8 **Birness** Abers
95 J3 **Birse** Abers
95 J3 **Birsemore** Abers
58 G8 **Birstall** Kirk
41 N5 **Birstall** Leics
58 G3 **Birstwith** N York
73 M9 **Birtley** Gatesd
38 G8 **Birtley** Herefs
72 F5 **Birtley** Nthumb
73 M9 **Birtley Crematorium** Gatesd
29 K2 **Birts Street** Worcs
42 C9 **Bisbrooke** Rutlnd
52 H6 **Biscathorpe** Lincs
20 D6 **Bisham** W & M
30 C4 **Bishampton** Worcs
15 M7 **Bish Mill** Devon
65 L2 **Bishop Auckland** Dur
52 E5 **Bishopbridge** Lincs
85 K8 **Bishopbriggs** E Duns
60 G8 **Bishop Burton** E R Yk
65 N2 **Bishop Middleham** Dur
101 J3 **Bishopmill** Moray
59 J2 **Bishop Monkton** N York
52 E5 **Bishop Norton** Lincs
23 M11 **Bishopsbourne** Kent
18 F7 **Bishops Cannings** Wilts
38 G4 **Bishop's Castle** Shrops
7 Q12 **Bishop's Caundle** Dorset
29 N4 **Bishop's Cleeve** Gloucs
39 M11 **Bishop's Frome** Herefs
33 Q12 **Bishop's Green** Essex
16 G10 **Bishops Hull** Somset
31 K3 **Bishop's Itchington** Warwks
16 G9 **Bishops Lydeard** Somset
29 L4 **Bishop's Norton** Gloucs
15 N7 **Bishop's Nympton** Devon
49 P9 **Bishop's Offley** Staffs
33 M11 **Bishop's Stortford** Herts
9 Q2 **Bishop's Sutton** Hants
30 H2 **Bishop's Tachbrook** Warwks
15 K6 **Bishop's Tawton** Devon
6 B7 **Bishopsteignton** Devon
9 M4 **Bishopstoke** Hants
26 D10 **Bishopston** Swans
20 C2 **Bishopstone** Bucks
11 P9 **Bishopstone** E Susx
38 H12 **Bishopstone** Herefs
23 N9 **Bishopstone** Kent
8 F3 **Bishopstone** Swindn
8 D11 **Bishopstone** Wilts
17 N4 **Bishop Sutton** BaNES
9 P4 **Bishop's Waltham** Hants
6 H1 **Bishopswood** Somset
49 Q12 **Bishop's Wood** Staffs
17 N3 **Bishopsworth** Bristl
58 H2 **Bishop Thornton** N York
59 N5 **Bishopthorpe** York
65 P4 **Bishopton** Darltn
84 G8 **Bishopton** Rens
60 D3 **Bishop Wilton** E R Yk
28 D5 **Bishton** Newpt
40 D4 **Bishton** Staffs
30 F9 **Bisley** Gloucs
20 F10 **Bisley** Surrey

2 H7	Bissoe Cnwll	
8 G7	Bisterne Hants	
42 E4	Bitchfield Lincs	
15 J4	Bittadon Devon	
5 N8	Bittaford Devon	
39 K6	Bitterley Shrops	
9 M5	Bitterne C Sotn	
41 M9	Bitteswell Leics	
17 P3	Bitton S Glos	
20 B6	Bix Oxon	
111 k4	Bixter Shet	
41 M7	Blaby Leics	
80 H4	Blackadder Border	
5 Q9	Blackawton Devon	
6 E2	Blackborough Devon	
43 Q7	Blackborough End Norfk	
30 H12	Black Bourton Oxon	
11 Q6	Blackboys E Susx	
51 J10	Blackbrook Derbys	
57 K9	Blackbrook St Hel	
49 N7	Blackbrook Staffs	
102 H11	Blackburn Abers	
57 M4	Blackburn Bl w D	
86 B8	Blackburn W Loth	
57 M4	Blackburn with Darwen Services Bl w D	
73 L7	Black Callerton N u Ty	
77 K9	Blackcraig E Ayrs	
90 C8	Black Crofts Ag & B	
103 K11	Blackdog Abers	
15 N9	Black Dog Devon	
7 K3	Blackdown Dorset	
51 J1	Blacker Hill Barns	
21 P8	Blackfen Gt Lon	
9 M7	Blackfield Hants	
85 P2	Blackford P & K	
17 K6	Blackford Somset	
17 P10	Blackford Somset	
41 J4	Blackfordby Leics	
86 E7	Blackhall C Edin	
73 Q11	Blackhall Colliery Dur	
73 K9	Blackhall Mill Gatesd	
79 N2	Blackhaugh Border	
21 M7	Blackheath Gt Lon	
40 C9	Blackheath Sandw	
35 N2	Blackheath Suffk	
10 G2	Blackheath Surrey	
103 M4	Blackhill Abers	
103 M6	Blackhill Abers	
73 J9	Blackhill Dur	
103 J6	Blackhill of Clackriach Abers	
6 D4	Blackhorse Devon	
78 G7	Blacklaw D & G	
57 Q8	Blackley Manch	
57 Q7	Blackley Crematorium Manch	
94 C9	Blacklunans P & K	
28 F2	Blackmarstone Herefs	
27 K10	Blackmill Brdgnd	
10 C4	Blackmoor Hants	
17 L4	Blackmoor N Som	
58 E10	Blackmoorfoot Kirk	
22 C3	Blackmore Essex	
34 C9	Blackmore End Essex	
86 C6	Blackness Falk	
10 C2	Blacknest Hants	
34 C11	Black Notley Essex	
57 Q1	Blacko Lancs	
26 E10	Black Pill Swans	
56 F2	Blackpool Bpool	
6 B12	Blackpool Devon	
56 G3	Blackpool Airport Lancs	
85 P9	Blackridge W Loth	
57 L6	Blackrod Bolton	
101 J7	Blacksboat Moray	
70 G3	Blackshaw D & G	
58 C8	Blackshaw Head Calder	
11 K6	Blackstone W Susx	
45 Q11	Black Street Suffk	
31 N9	Blackthorn Oxon	
34 E4	Blackthorpe Suffk	
60 E8	Blacktoft E R Yk	
95 P2	Blacktop C Aber	
14 H10	Black Torrington Devon	
50 G10	Blackwall Derbys	
2 H6	Blackwater Cnwll	
20 D10	Blackwater Hants	
9 N9	Blackwater IoW	
16 H11	Blackwater Somset	
75 N6	Blackwaterfoot N Ayrs	
71 N5	Blackwell Cumb	
50 E6	Blackwell Derbys	
51 K8	Blackwell Derbys	
30 G5	Blackwell Warwks	
40 C11	Blackwell Worcs	
27 N8	Blackwood Caerph	
78 E10	Blackwood D & G	
77 N3	Blackwood S Lans	
48 H2	Blacon Ches W	
69 K8	Bladnoch D & G	
31 K10	Bladon Oxon	
36 D10	Blaenannerch Cerdgn	
47 L3	Blaenau Ffestiniog Gwynd	
27 Q7	Blaenavon Torfn	
25 L2	Blaenffos Pembks	
27 J9	Blaengarw Brdgnd	
27 J9	Blaengwrach Neath	
27 J9	Blaengwynfi Neath	
37 K7	Blaenpennal Cerdgn	
37 J5	Blaenplwyf Cerdgn	
36 D10	Blaenporth Cerdgn	
27 K8	Blaenrhondda Rhondd	
25 L4	Blaenwaun Carmth	
25 N4	Blaen-y-Coed Carmth	
27 K8	Blaen-y-cwm Rhondd	
17 M4	Blagdon N Som	
16 G11	Blagdon Somset	
6 B9	Blagdon Torbay	
16 G11	Blagdon Hill Somset	
90 E2	Blaich Highld	
89 N3	Blain Highld	
27 P7	Blaina Blae G	
92 C3	Blair Atholl P & K	
85 M3	Blair Drummond Stirlg	
92 H6	Blairgowrie P & K	
86 B5	Blairhall Fife	
86 B3	Blairingone P & K	
85 N4	Blairlogie Stirlg	
84 D6	Blairmore Ag & B	
108 D4	Blairmore Highld	
83 P8	Blair's Ferry Ag & B	
29 J5	Blaisdon Gloucs	
39 P6	Blakebrook Worcs	
39 Q6	Blakedown Worcs	
34 B11	Blake End Essex	
49 K2	Blakemere Ches W	
28 D1	Blakemere Herefs	
40 D7	Blakenall Heath Wsall	
29 J7	Blakeney Gloucs	
44 G2	Blakeney Norfk	
49 N6	Blakenhall Ches E	
40 B7	Blakenhall Wolves	
31 N4	Blakesley Nhants	
72 H10	Blanchland Nthumb	
8 C6	Blandford Forum Dorset	
8 C6	Blandford St Mary Dorset	
85 J7	Blanefield Stirlg	
52 F10	Blankney Lincs	
85 L10	Blantyre S Lans	
90 F3	Blar a' Chaorainn Highld	
98 H9	Blargie Highld	
90 F3	Blarmachfoldach Highld	
42 B10	Blaston Leics	
42 D10	Blatherwycke Nhants	
62 F5	Blawith Cumb	
69 P3	Blawquhairn D & G	
35 M5	Blaxhall Suffk	
51 P2	Blaxton Donc	
73 L8	Blaydon Gatesd	
17 L7	Bleadney Somset	
17 J5	Bleadon N Som	
23 L10	Blean Kent	
51 Q10	Bleasby Notts	
93 M11	Bleasdale Lancs	
38 E8	Bleddfa Powys	
30 G9	Bledington Gloucs	
20 C3	Bledlow Bucks	
20 C4	Bledlow Ridge Bucks	
87 J9	Blegbie E Loth	
64 B2	Blencarn Cumb	
71 K6	Blencogo Cumb	
10 B7	Blendworth Hants	
71 J7	Blennerhasset Cumb	
31 L9	Bletchingdon Oxon	
21 M12	Bletchingley Surrey	
32 C3	Bletchley M Keyn	
49 L8	Bletchley Shrops	
25 J5	Bletherston Pembks	
32 E5	Bletsoe Bed	
19 N4	Blewbury Oxon	
45 K4	Blickling Norfk	
51 N9	Blidworth Notts	
51 N9	Blidworth Bottoms Notts	
71 J8	Blindcrake Cumb	
11 M2	Blindley Heath Surrey	
4 D5	Blisland Cnwll	
8 H5	Blissford Hants	
39 N7	Bliss Gate Worcs	
31 Q4	Blisworth Nhants	
40 E4	Blithbury Staffs	
30 F7	Blockley Gloucs	
45 M8	Blofield Norfk	
45 M7	Blofield Heath Norfk	
34 G2	Blo Norton Norfk	
80 D8	Bloomfield Border	
50 F10	Blore Staffs	
31 K7	Bloxham Oxon	
52 F11	Bloxholm Lincs	
40 D7	Bloxwich Wsall	
4 C8	Bloxworth Dorset	
58 F3	Blubberhouses N York	
16 D7	Blue Anchor Somset	
22 E10	Blue Bell Hill Kent	
50 F4	Blue John Cavern Derbys	
56 F8	Blundellsands Sefton	
45 Q10	Blundeston Suffk	
32 G6	Blunham C Beds	
18 G3	Blunsdon St Andrew Swindn	
40 B11	Bluntington Worcs	
33 K2	Bluntisham Cambs	
52 D5	Blyborough Lincs	
35 N2	Blyford Suffk	
49 P11	Blymhill Staffs	
51 N4	Blyth Notts	
73 N5	Blyth Nthumb	
86 D12	Blyth Bridge Border	
35 P2	Blythburgh Suffk	
73 N5	Blyth Crematorium Nthumb	
80 D7	Blythe Border	
51 N3	Blyth Services Notts	
52 C5	Blyton Lincs	
93 P11	Boarhills Fife	
9 P6	Boarhunt Hants	
31 N10	Boarstall Bucks	
107 J7	Boath Highld	
99 P5	Boat of Garten Highld	
22 H9	Bobbing Kent	
39 P4	Bobbington Staffs	
34 C11	Bocking Essex	
34 C10	Bocking Churchstreet Essex	
103 M6	Boddam Abers	
111 k5	Boddam Shet	
29 M4	Boddington Gloucs	
54 D5	Bodedern IoA	
56 Q6	Bodelwyddan Denbgs	
39 K11	Bodenham Herefs	
8 H3	Bodenham Wilts	
39 K11	Bodenham Moor Herefs	
54 E4	Bodewryd IoA	
48 C2	Bodfari Denbgs	
54 F6	Bodffordd IoA	
46 E4	Bodfuan Gwynd	
45 J3	Bodham Norfk	
12 F5	Bodiam E Susx	
12 F5	Bodiam Castle E Susx	
31 L6	Bodicote Oxon	
4 E9	Bodinnick Cnwll	
12 D7	Bodle Street Green E Susx	
3 N3	Bodmin Cnwll	
4 F5	Bodmin Moor Cnwll	
55 L7	Bodnant Garden Conwy	
13 L2	Bodsham Kent	
3 M4	Bodwen Cnwll	
107 K11	Bogallan Highld	
103 L8	Bogbrae Abers	
76 G5	Bogend S Ayrs	
87 J7	Boggs Holdings E Loth	
86 F8	Boghall Mdloth	
86 B8	Boghall W Loth	
77 N3	Boghead S Lans	
101 L3	Bogmoor Moray	
95 K7	Bogmuir Abers	
102 D6	Bogniebrae Abers	
10 E9	Bognor Regis W Susx	
99 N4	Bogroy Highld	
69 P3	Bogue D & G	
3 J8	Bohortha Cnwll	
98 D11	Bohuntine Highld	
65 L3	Bolam Dur	
5 N11	Bolberry Devon	
40 E8	Boldmere Birm	
9 K7	Boldre Hants	
65 J5	Boldron Dur	
52 B6	Bole Notts	
50 H9	Bolehill Derbys	
16 C12	Bolham Devon	
6 F1	Bolham Water Devon	
2 H5	Bolingey Cnwll	
50 C5	Bollington Ches E	
11 L5	Bolney W Susx	
32 F5	Bolnhurst Bed	
93 Q5	Bolshan Angus	
51 L6	Bolsover Derbys	
50 H2	Bolsterstone Sheff	
66 C9	Boltby N York	
101 M12	Boltenstone Abers	
57 N7	Bolton Bolton	
64 B3	Bolton Cumb	
87 K8	Bolton E Loth	
60 D4	Bolton E R Yk	
81 M10	Bolton Nthumb	
58 E4	Bolton Abbey N York	
63 P11	Bolton by Bowland Lancs	
71 P2	Boltonfellend Cumb	
71 K7	Boltongate Cumb	
63 J8	Bolton le Sands Lancs	
71 K6	Bolton Low Houses Cumb	
65 M7	Bolton-on-Swale N York	
59 M6	Bolton Percy N York	
51 L1	Bolton Upon Dearne Barns	
57 L6	Bolton West Services Lancs	
4 E5	Bolventor Cnwll	
49 N10	Bomere Heath Shrops	
107 K4	Bonar Bridge Highld	
90 D9	Bonawe Ag & B	
60 G10	Bonby N Linc	
25 L2	Boncath Pembks	
80 D10	Bonchester Bridge Border	
15 L10	Bondleigh Devon	
63 J12	Bonds Lancs	
86 B6	Bo'ness Falk	
40 D5	Boney Hay Staffs	
84 G7	Bonhill W Duns	
39 P2	Boningale Shrops	
80 E9	Bonjedward Border	
85 P10	Bonkle N Lans	
93 P7	Bonnington Angus	
13 K3	Bonnington Kent	
86 G2	Bonnybank Fife	
85 N7	Bonnybridge Falk	
102 H5	Bonnykelly Abers	
86 G8	Bonnyrigg Mdloth	
93 M11	Bonnyton Angus	
50 H8	Bonsall Derbys	
71 K2	Bonshaw Tower D & G	
47 P10	Bont-Dolgadfan Powys	
37 L4	Bont-goch or Elerch Cerdgn	
37 K7	Bontnewydd Cerdgn	
54 G9	Bontnewydd Gwynd	
48 C4	Bontuchel Denbgs	
16 E2	Bonvilston V Glam	
15 J5	Boode Devon	
20 D5	Booker Bucks	
80 D5	Boon Border	
66 F4	Boosbeck R & Cl	
34 E9	Boose's Green Essex	
62 D3	Boot Cumb	
58 D8	Booth Calder	
52 E10	Boothby Graffoe Lincs	
42 D4	Boothby Pagnell Lincs	
60 C8	Boothferry E R Yk	
57 N8	Boothstown Salfd	
62 C5	Bootle Cumb	
56 G9	Bootle Sefton	
39 L8	Boraston Shrops	
6 C1	Bordeaux Guern	
22 G10	Borden Kent	
72 B4	Border Forest Park	
22 F2	Boreham Essex	
18 D11	Boreham Wilts	
12 D7	Boreham Street E Susx	
21 J4	Borehamwood Herts	
79 J10	Boreland D & G	
104 B10	Boreraig Highld	
111 a7	Borgh W Isls	
111 d1	Borgh W Isls	
109 M4	Borgie Highld	
69 P9	Borgue D & G	
110 D9	Borgue Highld	
34 E7	Borley Essex	
104 E7	Borneskitaig Highld	
69 N9	Borness D & G	
59 K2	Boroughbridge N York	
22 C11	Borough Green Kent	
41 K1	Borrowash Derbys	
65 Q9	Borrowby N York	
86 B6	Borrowstoun Falk	
22 E9	Borstal Medway	
37 K3	Borth Cerdgn	
79 N6	Borthwickbrae Border	
79 N6	Borthwickshiels Border	
47 J4	Borth-y-Gest Gwynd	
104 F11	Borve Highld	
69 N9	Borve W Isls	
111 a7	Borve W Isls	
111 c3	Borve W Isls	
111 d1	Borve W Isls	
63 K7	Borwick Lancs	
39 M12	Bosbury Herefs	
4 D3	Boscastle Cnwll	
8 G8	Boscombe Bmouth	
18 H11	Boscombe Wilts	
10 D8	Bosham W Susx	
24 G9	Bosherston Pembks	
50 B7	Bosley Ches E	
60 C3	Bossall N York	
4 D3	Bossiney Cnwll	
13 M1	Bossingham Kent	
16 B6	Bossington Somset	
49 M2	Bostock Green Ches W	
43 K2	Boston Lincs	
43 K2	Boston Crematorium Lincs	
59 K5	Boston Spa Leeds	
3 L7	Boswinger Cnwll	
2 B8	Botallack Cnwll	
21 L4	Botany Bay Gt Lon	
34 H2	Botesdale Suffk	
73 M4	Bothal Nthumb	
51 P6	Bothamsall Notts	
71 K7	Bothel Cumb	
7 L5	Bothenhampton Dorset	
85 L10	Bothwell S Lans	
85 M10	Bothwell Services S Lans	
20 F3	Botley Bucks	
9 N5	Botley Hants	
31 L11	Botley Oxon	
31 Q8	Botolph Claydon Bucks	
11 J8	Botolphs W Susx	
42 B3	Bottesford Leics	
52 C3	Bottesford N Linc	
33 N5	Bottisham Cambs	
93 L10	Bottomcraig Fife	
58 B9	Bottoms Calder	
5 J7	Botusfleming Cnwll	
46 D5	Botwnnog Gwynd	
11 P1	Bough Beech Kent	
38 H3	Boughrood Powys	
31 Q2	Boughton Nhants	
44 B9	Boughton Norfk	
51 P7	Boughton Notts	
13 K1	Boughton Aluph Kent	
22 F11	Boughton Green Kent	
22 F12	Boughton Monchelsea Kent	
23 K10	Boughton Street Kent	
39 K5	Bouldon Shrops	
81 Q10	Boulmer Nthumb	
52 D9	Boultham Lincs	
33 K5	Bourn Cambs	
42 F6	Bourne Lincs	
21 P5	Bournebridge Essex	
40 D10	Bournebrook Birm	
20 E6	Bourne End Bucks	
32 D7	Bourne End C Beds	
20 G3	Bourne End Herts	
8 G7	Bournemouth Bmouth	
8 G7	Bournemouth Airport Dorset	
8 G8	Bournemouth Crematorium Bmouth	
22 H6	Bournes Green Sthend	
40 C11	Bournheath Worcs	
73 N9	Bournmoor Dur	
40 D10	Bournville Birm	
8 B2	Bourton Dorset	
19 J4	Bourton Oxon	
39 L3	Bourton Shrops	
18 F7	Bourton Wilts	
41 K12	Bourton on Dunsmore Warwks	
30 F7	Bourton-on-the-Hill Gloucs	
30 F9	Bourton-on-the-Water Gloucs	
88 G4	Bousd Ag & B	
62 G5	Bouth Cumb	
65 K12	Bouthwaite N York	
8 F4	Boveridge Dorset	
5 Q5	Bovey Tracey Devon	
20 G3	Bovingdon Herts	
8 C9	Bovington Tank Museum Dorset	
15 M10	Bow Devon	
21 M6	Bow Gt Lon	
111 h3	Bow Ork	
31 N12	Bow Brickhill M Keyn	
29 M7	Bowbridge Gloucs	
73 N12	Bowburn Dur	
9 M9	Bowcombe IoW	
6 F5	Bowd Devon	
80 D7	Bowden Border	
18 D7	Bowden Hill Wilts	
57 N10	Bowdon Traffd	
110 E3	Bower Highld	
8 F3	Bowerchalke Wilts	
110 F3	Bowermadden Highld	
49 P8	Bowers Staffs	
22 E6	Bowers Gifford Essex	
86 C4	Bowershall Fife	
59 K8	Bower's Row Leeds	
64 H5	Bowes Dur	
63 J12	Bowgreave Lancs	
70 G3	Bowhouse D & G	
79 P2	Bowland Border	
39 K10	Bowley Herefs	
10 E3	Bowlhead Green Surrey	
58 F7	Bowling C Brad	
84 G8	Bowling W Duns	
62 F3	Bowmanstead Cumb	
82 D10	Bowmore Ag & B	
71 K3	Bowness-on-Solway Cumb	
62 H3	Bowness-on-Windermere Cumb	
93 K12	Bow of Fife Fife	
93 N6	Bowriefauld Angus	
81 L6	Bowsden Nthumb	
37 K4	Bow Street Cerdgn	
29 M8	Box Gloucs	
18 C7	Box Wilts	
34 F8	Boxford Suffk	
19 M6	Boxford W Berk	
10 E8	Boxgrove W Susx	
22 F10	Boxley Kent	
20 G3	Boxmoor Herts	
34 G9	Boxted Essex	
34 G9	Boxted Suffk	
34 D6	Boxted Suffk	
34 G9	Boxted Cross Essex	
33 K4	Boxworth Cambs	
23 N9	Boyden Gate Kent	
40 F1	Boylestone Derbys	
102 E3	Boyndie Abers	
103 J3	Boyndlie Abers	
61 K1	Boynton E R Yk	
93 Q6	Boysack Angus	
4 H2	Boyton Cnwll	
35 N7	Boyton Suffk	
18 D11	Boyton Wilts	
22 D2	Boyton Cross Essex	
34 C7	Boyton End Suffk	
32 C5	Bozeat Nhants	
13 L2	Brabourne Kent	
13 L2	Brabourne Lees Kent	
110 G2	Brabstermire Highld	
96 D2	Bracadale Highld	
42 F7	Braceborough Lincs	
52 D9	Bracebridge Heath Lincs	
52 D9	Bracebridge Low Fields Lincs	
42 E3	Braceby Lincs	
63 Q11	Bracewell Lancs	
51 J8	Brackenfield Derbys	
85 M8	Brackenhirst N Lans	
10 D10	Bracklesham W Susx	
98 B11	Brackletter Highld	
31 N6	Brackley Nhants	
20 E9	Bracknell Br For	
85 N2	Braco P & K	
101 P5	Bracobrae Moray	
45 K9	Bracon Ash Norfk	
97 K10	Bracora Highld	
97 K10	Bracorina Highld	
50 G9	Bradbourne Derbys	
65 M2	Bradbury Dur	
20 D4	Bradenham Bucks	
18 E5	Bradenstoke Wilts	
6 E2	Bradfield Devon	
33 J9	Bradfield Essex	
45 L4	Bradfield Norfk	
50 H3	Bradfield Sheff	
19 P6	Bradfield W Berk	
34 E5	Bradfield Combust Suffk	
49 M4	Bradfield Green Ches E	
35 J10	Bradfield Heath Essex	
34 E5	Bradfield St Clare Suffk	
34 E5	Bradfield St George Suffk	
58 F7	Bradford C Brad	
4 G10	Bradford Devon	
17 N12	Bradford Abbas Dorset	
18 C8	Bradford Leigh Wilts	
18 C8	Bradford-on-Avon Wilts	
16 G10	Bradford-on-Tone Somset	
7 P4	Bradford Peverell Dorset	
15 K5	Bradiford Devon	
9 Q9	Brading IoW	
50 G10	Bradley Derbys	
19 Q11	Bradley Hants	
53 J3	Bradley NE Lin	
49 Q11	Bradley Staffs	
40 C8	Bradley Wolves	
30 C2	Bradley Worcs	
50 D11	Bradley Green Worcs	
50 D11	Bradley in the Moors Staffs	
28 H11	Bradley Stoke S Glos	
41 N2	Bradmore Notts	
6 D3	Bradninch Devon	
50 D9	Bradnop Staffs	
7 L4	Bradpole Dorset	
58 E8	Bradshaw Calder	
4 H4	Bradstone Devon	
49 N3	Bradwall Green Ches E	
50 F5	Bradwell Derbys	
34 D11	Bradwell Essex	
32 B8	Bradwell M Keyn	
45 Q8	Bradwell Norfk	
49 Q5	Bradwell Crematorium Staffs	
23 J3	Bradwell-on-Sea Essex	
23 J2	Bradwell Waterside Essex	
14 F8	Bradworthy Devon	
107 L9	Brae Highld	
111 k3	Brae Shet	
85 N7	Braeface Falk	
95 L10	Braehead Angus	
69 K8	Braehead D & G	
77 Q2	Braehead S Lans	
94 C4	Braemar Abers	
106 C6	Braemore Highld	
110 C9	Braemore Highld	
98 D10	Brae Roy Lodge Highld	
84 D7	Braeside Inver	
93 K4	Braes of Coul Angus	
101 M4	Braes of Enzie Moray	
111 i1	Braeswick Ork	
83 P2	Braevallich Ag & B	
65 N4	Brafferton Darltn	
66 B12	Brafferton N York	
32 B5	Brafield-on-the-Green Nhants	
111 d1	Bragar W Isls	
33 J11	Bragbury End Herts	
77 P2	Braidwood S Lans	
50 G11	Brailsford Derbys	
34 C11	Braintree Essex	
35 J3	Braiseworth Suffk	
9 L3	Braishfield Hants	
71 K10	Braithwaite Cumb	
51 M2	Braithwell Donc	
11 J7	Bramber W Susx	
41 K9	Bramcote Warwks	
51 L11	Bramcote Crematorium Notts	
9 Q2	Bramdean Hants	
45 L8	Bramerton Norfk	
33 J12	Bramfield Herts	
35 N3	Bramfield Suffk	
35 J7	Bramford Suffk	
50 B4	Bramhall Stockp	
59 K5	Bramham Leeds	
58 G5	Bramhope Leeds	
19 Q8	Bramley Hants	
58 G7	Bramley Leeds	
51 L3	Bramley Rothm	
10 G2	Bramley Surrey	
19 Q8	Bramley Corner Hants	
23 N11	Bramling Kent	
6 C3	Brampford Speke Devon	
32 H3	Brampton Cambs	
64 C3	Brampton Cumb	
71 Q4	Brampton Cumb	
52 B7	Brampton Lincs	
45 K5	Brampton Norfk	
51 K1	Brampton Rothm	
35 P1	Brampton Suffk	
28 H4	Brampton Abbotts Herefs	
42 B11	Brampton Ash Nhants	
38 G7	Brampton Bryan Herefs	
51 L4	Brampton-en-le-Morthen Rothm	
40 D2	Bramshall Staffs	
9 J4	Bramshaw Hants	
10 D4	Bramshott Hants	
17 L9	Bramwell Somset	
89 L3	Branault Highld	
44 C1	Brancaster Norfk	
44 D2	Brancaster Staithe Norfk	
73 L12	Brancepeth Dur	
100 G5	Branchill Moray	
101 K2	Branderburgh Moray	
61 J5	Brandesburton E R Yk	
35 L5	Brandeston Suffk	
45 J6	Brandiston Norfk	
73 M11	Brandon Dur	
42 C1	Brandon Lincs	
44 D11	Brandon Suffk	
41 K11	Brandon Warwks	
44 H8	Brandon Parva Norfk	
66 E11	Brandsby N York	
52 D11	Brandy Wharf Lincs	
33 Q10	Bran End Essex	
8 F8	Branksome Poole	
8 F8	Branksome Park Poole	
19 M11	Bransbury Hants	
52 C7	Bransby Lincs	
6 G5	Branscombe Devon	
39 P10	Bransford Worcs	
8 H7	Bransgore Hants	
61 J7	Bransholme C KuH	
39 M7	Bransley Shrops	
42 B4	Branston Leics	
52 E10	Branston Lincs	
40 G4	Branston Staffs	
52 F9	Branston Booths Lincs	
9 P10	Branstone IoW	
52 D11	Brant Broughton Lincs	
35 J9	Brantham Suffk	
70 H9	Branthwaite Cumb	
71 L7	Branthwaite Cumb	
60 E7	Brantingham E R Yk	
51 N1	Branton Donc	
81 L10	Branton Nthumb	
59 J2	Branton Green N York	
81 J6	Branxton Nthumb	
50 G9	Brassington Derbys	
21 P11	Brasted Kent	
21 P11	Brasted Chart Kent	
95 L3	Brathens Abers	
53 M9	Bratoft Lincs	
52 D7	Brattleby Lincs	
18 D7	Bratton Wilts	
39 L2	Bratton Wrekin	
5 K2	Bratton Clovelly Devon	
73 J5	Bratton Fleming Devon	
17 P9	Bratton Seymour Somset	
33 L10	Braughing Herts	
31 M2	Braunston Nhants	
42 B8	Braunston Rutlnd	
41 M7	Braunstone Leics	
15 J4	Braunton Devon	
66 G11	Brawby N York	

93 N8 Barnhill C Dund
100 H4 Barnhill Moray
68 D5 Barnhills D & G
65 J5 Barningham Dur
34 F2 Barningham Suffk
52 H3 Barnoldby le Beck NE Lin
63 Q11 Barnoldswick Lancs
10 H5 Barns Green W Susx
59 J11 Barnsley Barns
30 E12 Barnsley Gloucs
59 J12 Barnsley Crematorium Barns
15 K5 Barnstaple Devon
33 Q11 Barnston Essex
56 F11 Barnston Wirral
41 Q1 Barnstone Notts
40 D11 Barnt Green Worcs
86 E7 Barnton C Edin
49 L1 Barnton Ches W
42 F12 Barnwell All Saints Nhants
42 F12 Barnwell St Andrew Nhants
29 M5 Barnwood Gloucs
76 E11 Barr S Ayrs
111 a7 Barra W Isls
111 a6 Barra Airport W Isls
69 J8 Barrachan D & G
111 a7 Barraigh W Isls
88 B7 Barrapoll Ag & B
72 G6 Barrasford Nthumb
84 H10 Barrhead E Rens
68 H3 Barrhill S Ayrs
33 L6 Barrington Cambs
17 K11 Barrington Somset
2 F7 Barripper Cnwll
84 F11 Barrmill N Ayrs
110 F2 Barrock Highld
29 M4 Barrow Gloucs
57 N2 Barrow Lancs
42 C7 Barrow Rutlnd
17 Q9 Barrow Somset
34 C4 Barrow Suffk
42 C3 Barrowby Lincs
42 D9 Barrowden Rutlnd
57 Q2 Barrowford Lancs
17 M3 Barrow Gurney N Som
60 H9 Barrow Haven N Linc
62 E8 Barrow-in-Furness Cumb
62 E8 Barrow Island Cumb
60 H9 Barrow-upon-Humber N Linc
41 M4 Barrow upon Soar Leics
41 J2 Barrow upon Trent Derbys
93 P8 Barry Angus
16 F3 Barry V Glam
16 F3 Barry Island V Glam
41 P5 Barsby Leics
45 N11 Barsham Suffk
40 G10 Barston Solhll
28 G1 Bartestree Herefs
102 H8 Barthol Chapel Abers
34 C11 Bartholomew Green Essex
49 N5 Barthomley Ches E
9 K5 Bartley Hants
40 D10 Bartley Green Birm
33 P7 Bartlow Cambs
33 L5 Barton Cambs
49 J5 Barton Ches W
30 E8 Barton Gloucs
56 G7 Barton Lancs
57 K2 Barton Lancs
65 M6 Barton N York
31 M11 Barton Oxon
6 C8 Barton Torbay
44 B8 Barton Bendish Norfk
29 L8 Barton End Gloucs
31 N7 Barton Hartshorn Bucks
41 M2 Barton in Fabis Notts
41 K6 Barton in the Beans Leics
32 F9 Barton-le-Clay C Beds
66 G11 Barton-le-Street N York
60 C2 Barton-le-Willows N York
34 C3 Barton Mills Suffk
9 J8 Barton-on-Sea Hants
30 G7 Barton-on-the-Heath Warwks
17 M9 Barton St David Somset
32 C2 Barton Seagrave Nhants
19 M11 Barton Stacey Hants
15 L4 Barton Town Devon
45 M5 Barton Turf Norfk
40 F4 Barton-under-Needwood Staffs
60 H9 Barton-upon-Humber N Linc
60 H9 Barton Waterside N Linc
111 a1 Barvas W Isls
33 N2 Barway Cambs
41 K8 Barwell Leics
15 K10 Barwick Devon
17 M12 Barwick Somset
59 K6 Barwick in Elmet Leeds
48 H10 Baschurch Shrops
31 K2 Bascote Warwks
63 M12 Bashall Eaves Lancs
22 E5 Basildon Essex
22 E6 Basildon & District Crematorium Essex
19 Q9 Basingstoke Hants
19 P10 Basingstoke Crematorium Hants
50 G6 Baslow Derbys
17 J7 Bason Bridge Somset
28 C10 Bassaleg Newpt
80 E5 Bassendean Border
71 K8 Bassenthwaite Cumb
9 M4 Bassett C Sotn
33 K7 Bassingbourn Cambs
52 C10 Bassingham Lincs
42 D5 Bassingthorpe Lincs
33 K10 Bassus Green Herts
42 G7 Baston Lincs
45 N6 Bastwick Norfk
20 G5 Batchworth Herts
7 N3 Batcombe Dorset
17 Q8 Batcombe Somset
21 J1 Batford Herts
17 Q4 Bath BaNES
18 B7 Bathampton BaNES
16 E10 Bathealton Somset
18 B7 Batheaston BaNES
18 B7 Bathford BaNES
86 B8 Bathgate W Loth
51 Q8 Bathley Notts
4 G5 Bathpool Cnwll
16 H10 Bathpool Somset
35 L9 Bath Side Essex
85 Q9 Bathville W Loth
17 N6 Bathway Somset
58 G8 Batley Kirk
30 F7 Batsford Gloucs
66 E6 Battersby N York

21 L7 Battersea Gt Lon
34 G6 Battisford Tye Suffk
12 E7 Battle E Susx
27 L3 Battle Powys
93 M5 Battledykes Angus
52 H11 Battle of Britain Memorial Flight Lincs
22 F5 Battlesbridge Essex
16 C10 Battleton Somset
29 M1 Baughton Worcs
19 P8 Baughurst Hants
95 K4 Baulds Abers
19 K3 Baulking Oxon
52 H8 Baumber Lincs
30 D12 Baunton Gloucs
8 F2 Baverstock Wilts
45 J8 Bawburgh Norfk
44 H6 Bawdeswell Norfk
17 J8 Bawdrip Somset
35 M8 Bawdsey Suffk
51 P3 Bawtry Donc
57 P4 Baxenden Lancs
40 H7 Baxterley Warwks
104 C10 Bay Highld
111 e2 Bayble W Isls
9 N3 Baybridge Hants
62 F7 Baycliff Cumb
19 K5 Baydon Wilts
21 L2 Bayford Herts
17 Q9 Bayford Somset
111 a4 Bayhead W Isls
34 H6 Bayham Abbey E Susx
28 G4 Baysham Herefs
39 J1 Bayston Hill Shrops
34 C8 Baythorne End Essex
39 M7 Bayton Worcs
19 N1 Bayworth Oxon
31 Q6 Beachampton Bucks
44 C8 Beachamwell Norfk
12 C10 Beachy Head E Susx
6 G2 Beacon Devon
34 F10 Beacon End Essex
10 E3 Beacon Hill Surrey
35 J6 Beacon Hill Services Suffk
20 C4 Beacon's Bottom Bucks
20 F5 Beaconsfield Bucks
20 F5 Beaconsfield Services Bucks
66 F9 Beadlam N York
32 F8 Beadlow C Beds
81 P8 Beadnell Nthumb
15 K8 Beaford Devon
59 M8 Beal N York
81 M6 Beal Nthumb
4 H5 Bealsmill Cnwll
7 L3 Beaminster Dorset
73 L9 Beamish Dur
58 E4 Beamsley N York
18 D7 Beanacre Wilts
81 M9 Beanley Nthumb
5 L4 Beardon Devon
11 J2 Beare Green Surrey
30 F3 Bearley Warwks
73 M11 Bearpark Dur
85 J8 Bearsden E Duns
22 F11 Bearsted Kent
49 N7 Bearstone Shrops
40 D9 Bearwood Birm
38 H10 Bearwood Herefs
8 F7 Bearwood Poole
78 H8 Beattock D & G
22 C2 Beauchamp Roding Essex
27 N6 Beaufort Blae G
9 L7 Beaulieu Hants
9 L6 Beaulieu House Hants
107 J11 Beauly Highld
54 H6 Beaumaris IoA
71 M4 Beaumont Cumb
35 J10 Beaumont Essex
7 b2 Beaumont Jersey
40 G12 Beausale Warwks
9 P3 Beauworth Hants
14 H11 Beaworthy Devon
34 C10 Beazley End Essex
56 G11 Bebington Wirral
45 N11 Beccles Suffk
57 J4 Becconsall Lancs
39 N2 Beckbury Shrops
21 M9 Beckenham Gt Lon
21 M9 Beckenham Crematorium Gt Lon
62 B2 Beckermet Cumb
70 H5 Beckfoot Cumb
29 N2 Beckford Worcs
18 D7 Beckhampton Wilts
52 C11 Beckingham Lincs
51 R3 Beckingham Notts
18 B9 Beckington Somset
38 H6 Beckjay Shrops
12 G5 Beckley E Susx
31 M10 Beckley Oxon
34 B2 Beck Row Suffk
62 E6 Beck Side Cumb
21 N7 Beckton Gt Lon
58 H4 Beckwithshaw N York
21 P6 Becontree Gt Lon
65 M9 Bedale N York
8 C4 Bedchester Dorset
27 M10 Beddau Rhondd
54 H11 Beddgelert Gwynd
11 N8 Beddingham E Susx
21 L9 Beddington Gt Lon
21 L9 Beddington Corner Gt Lon
35 K4 Bedfield Suffk
32 F6 Bedford Bed
32 F6 Bedford Crematorium Bed
10 B8 Bedhampton Hants
35 K3 Bedingfield Suffk
58 H2 Bedlam N York
73 M5 Bedlington Nthumb
27 M8 Bedlinog Myr Td
17 N2 Bedminster Bristl
17 N3 Bedminster Down Bristl
20 H3 Bedmond Herts
40 C4 Bednall Staffs
80 E10 Bedrule Border
38 G7 Bedstone Shrops
27 N10 Bedwas Caerph
27 N8 Bedwellty Caerph
41 J9 Bedworth Warwks
41 P6 Beeby Leics
10 B3 Beech Hants
49 Q7 Beech Staffs
20 B9 Beech Hill W Berk
18 G8 Beechingstoke Wilts
19 N5 Beedon W Berk
61 J4 Beeford E R Yk
50 H7 Beeley Derbys
52 H3 Beelsby NE Lin
19 P7 Beenham W Berk
6 G5 Beer Devon
17 K9 Beer Somset
17 J11 Beercrocombe Somset

7 N1 Beer Hackett Dorset
5 Q11 Beesands Devon
53 M7 Beesby Lincs
5 Q11 Beeson Devon
32 G7 Beeston C Beds
49 K4 Beeston Ches W
41 M12 Beeston Leeds
44 E7 Beeston Norfk
51 M12 Beeston Notts
45 J2 Beeston Regis Norfk
70 E2 Beeswing D & G
63 J6 Beetham Cumb
6 H1 Beetham Somset
44 F6 Beetley Norfk
31 L10 Begbroke Oxon
25 K7 Begelly Pembks
38 E6 Beguildy Powys
45 N8 Beighton Norfk
51 K4 Beighton Sheff
111 b5 Beinn Na Faoghla W Isls
84 F11 Beith N Ayrs
23 M11 Bekesbourne Kent
45 L6 Belaugh Norfk
40 B11 Belbroughton Worcs
8 B5 Belchalwell Dorset
34 D8 Belchamp Otten Essex
34 D8 Belchamp St Paul Essex
34 D8 Belchamp Walter Essex
53 J8 Belchford Lincs
81 M7 Belford Nthumb
41 N6 Belgrave C Leic
87 M6 Belhaven E Loth
103 K10 Belhelvie Abers
101 N9 Belhinnie Abers
101 L11 Bellabeg Abers
85 M5 Bellanoch Ag & B
93 J4 Bellaty Angus
58 B3 Bell Busk N York
53 L7 Belleau Lincs
40 C11 Bell End Worcs
65 K8 Bellerby N York
71 M4 Belle Vue Cumb
59 J9 Belle Vue Wakefd
78 D2 Bellfield S Lans
78 F5 Bellfield S Lans
20 F3 Bellingdon Bucks
72 F4 Bellingham Nthumb
75 K5 Belloch Ag & B
75 K6 Bellochantuy Ag & B
49 K6 Bell o' th' Hill Ches W
85 M10 Bellshill N Lans
85 N10 Bellside N Lans
86 C8 Bellsquarry W Loth
12 C3 Bells Yew Green E Susx
17 N4 Belluton BaNES
107 K10 Belmaduthy Highld
57 M6 Belmont Bl w D
21 K10 Belmont Gt Lon
76 F7 Belmont S Ayrs
111 m2 Belmont Shet
101 M11 Belnacraig Abers
51 J10 Belper Derbys
73 K5 Belsay Nthumb
80 D8 Belses Border
5 P8 Belsford Devon
20 G4 Belsize Herts
35 J8 Belstead Suffk
5 M2 Belstone Devon
57 N4 Belthorn Lancs
23 M9 Beltinge Kent
72 E7 Beltingham Nthumb
52 B3 Beltoft N Linc
41 K4 Belton Leics
42 D3 Belton Lincs
52 B3 Belton N Linc
45 P9 Belton Norfk
42 B9 Belton Rutlnd
21 P7 Belvedere Gt Lon
42 B4 Belvoir Leics
42 B4 Belvoir Castle Leics
9 Q9 Bembridge IoW
8 G2 Bemerton Wilts
67 P12 Bempton E R Yk
45 Q12 Benacre Suffk
111 b5 Benbecula W Isls
111 b5 Benbecula Airport W Isls
77 M11 Benbuie D & G
90 C8 Benderloch Ag & B
12 F4 Benenden Kent
73 J9 Benfieldside Dur
21 L1 Bengeo Herts
30 D5 Bengeworth Worcs
35 N5 Benhall Green Suffk
35 M5 Benhall Street Suffk
95 N1 Benholm Abers
59 M3 Beningbrough N York
33 J11 Benington Herts
43 L2 Benington Lincs
54 G5 Benllech IoA
84 C6 Benmore Ag & B
75 Q8 Bennan N Ayrs
52 H7 Benniworth Lincs
12 E1 Benover Kent
58 F5 Ben Rhydding C Brad
76 F3 Benslie N Ayrs
19 Q3 Benson Oxon
95 N2 Benthoul C Aber
59 M11 Bentley Donc
60 H7 Bentley E R Yk
10 C2 Bentley Hants
35 J8 Bentley Suffk
40 H8 Bentley Warwks
79 M10 Bentpath D & G
15 M5 Bentwichen Devon
19 Q11 Bentworth Hants
93 M3 Benvie Angus
7 M3 Benville Dorset
43 M11 Benwick Cambs
40 E12 Beoley Worcs
97 M10 Beoraidbeg Highld
10 D6 Bepton W Susx
24 E3 Berea Pembks
5 J6 Bere Alston Devon
5 K7 Bere Ferrers Devon
8 C8 Bere Regis Dorset
45 M9 Bergh Apton Norfk
19 P2 Berinsfield Oxon
29 J8 Berkeley Gloucs
20 F2 Berkhamsted Herts
18 B10 Berkley Somset
40 G10 Berkswell Solhll
21 M7 Bermondsey Gt Lon
97 L5 Bernera Highld
104 E11 Bernisdale Highld
19 Q2 Berrick Prior Oxon
19 Q3 Berrick Salome Oxon
110 D10 Berriedale Highld
71 N9 Berrier Cumb
38 E2 Berriew Powys
39 K2 Berrington Shrops
39 L8 Berrington Worcs
39 L8 Berrington Green Worcs
16 H6 Berrow Somset

39 N9 Berrow Green Worcs
101 P3 Berryhillock Moray
101 P5 Berryhillock Moray
15 K3 Berrynarbor Devon
5 Q7 Berry Pomeroy Devon
39 F6 Bersham Wrexhm
11 P8 Berwick E Susx
18 G6 Berwick Bassett Wilts
73 L6 Berwick Hill Nthumb
18 F11 Berwick St James Wilts
8 D3 Berwick St John Wilts
8 D2 Berwick St Leonard Wilts
81 L4 Berwick-upon-Tweed Nthumb
56 H6 Bescar Lancs
30 B5 Besford Worcs
51 N1 Bessacarr Donc
61 K2 Bessingby E R Yk
45 J3 Bessingham Norfk
44 H10 Besthorpe Norfk
52 B9 Besthorpe Notts
51 M10 Bestwood Village Notts
60 H5 Beswick E R Yk
21 K12 Betchworth Surrey
34 H11 Beth Chatto Garden Essex
54 G8 Bethel Gwynd
54 E7 Bethel IoA
12 H3 Bethersden Kent
55 J8 Bethesda Gwynd
25 J5 Bethesda Pembks
26 F4 Bethlehem Carmth
21 M6 Bethnal Green Gt Lon
49 N6 Betley Staffs
22 C8 Betsham Kent
23 P11 Betteshanger Kent
7 K3 Bettiscombe Dorset
49 J8 Bettisfield Wrexhm
28 C10 Bettws Newpt
37 K9 Bettws Bledrws Cerdgn
38 D3 Bettws Cedewain Powys
36 E10 Bettws Evan Cerdgn
28 D7 Bettws-Newydd Mons
109 M4 Bettyhill Highld
27 J10 Betws Brdgnd
48 B6 Betws Gwerfil Goch Denbgs
55 L9 Betws-y-Coed Conwy
55 N6 Betws-yn-Rhos Conwy
36 E10 Beulah Cerdgn
37 Q9 Beulah Powys
29 H6 Bevercotes Notts
60 H6 Beverley E R Yk
18 C11 Beverston Gloucs
71 Q1 Bewcastle Cumb
39 P7 Bewdley Worcs
58 F2 Bewerley N York
61 K4 Bewholme E R Yk
12 E8 Bexhill E Susx
21 P8 Bexley Gt Lon
21 P8 Bexleyheath Gt Lon
43 Q9 Bexwell Norfk
34 F4 Beyton Suffk
34 F4 Beyton Green Suffk
111 c2 Bhaltos W Isls
111 a7 Bhatarsaigh W Isls
30 E11 Bibury Gloucs
31 N9 Bicester Oxon
40 F10 Bickenhill Solhll
42 H3 Bicker Lincs
57 J7 Bickerstaffe Lancs
59 K4 Bickerton N York
40 B5 Bickford Staffs
5 Q6 Bickington Devon
15 J6 Bickington Devon
5 L7 Bickleigh Devon
6 C2 Bickleigh Devon
49 K6 Bickley Ches W
21 N9 Bickley Gt Lon
67 K8 Bickley N York
22 F3 Bicknacre Essex
16 F8 Bicknoller Somset
22 G10 Bicknor Kent
38 F5 Bicton Shrops
39 J11 Bicton Shrops
12 C2 Bidborough Kent
12 G3 Biddenden Kent
32 E6 Biddenham Bed
18 C7 Biddestone Wilts
17 K5 Biddisham Somset
31 N6 Biddlesden Bucks
50 B8 Biddulph Staffs
50 B8 Biddulph Moor Staffs
14 H6 Bideford Devon
30 E4 Bidford-on-Avon Warwks
60 D5 Bielby E R Yk
95 P2 Bieldside C Aber
9 N10 Bierley IoW
20 D1 Bierton Bucks
69 K9 Big Balcraig D & G
5 N10 Bigbury Devon
5 N10 Bigbury-on-Sea Devon
52 F3 Bigby Lincs
77 L10 Big Carlae S Lans
78 G2 Biggar S Lans
57 F8 Biggin Derbys
21 N10 Biggin Hill Gt Lon
21 N10 Biggin Hill Airport Gt Lon
32 H7 Biggleswade C Beds
79 M11 Bigholms D & G
109 Q3 Bighouse Highld
9 Q1 Bighton Hants
71 L5 Biglands Cumb
10 F7 Bignor W Susx
71 H9 Bigrigg Cumb
105 L6 Big Sand Highld
111 k5 Bigton Shet
51 M11 Bilborough C Nott
16 D7 Bilbrook Somset
59 M5 Bilbrough N York
110 F5 Bilbster Highld
65 L3 Bildershaw Dur
34 G6 Bildeston Suffk
22 D5 Billericay Essex
41 Q7 Billesdon Leics
30 F3 Billesley Warwks
42 G4 Billingborough Lincs
57 K8 Billinge St Hel
45 J7 Billingford Norfk
44 G6 Billingford Norfk
66 C3 Billingham S on T
52 G11 Billinghay Lincs
59 K12 Billingley Barns
10 H5 Billingshurst W Susx
39 N5 Billingsley Shrops
32 D11 Billington C Beds
57 N2 Billington Lancs
45 N7 Billockby Norfk
73 L12 Billy Row Dur
57 K2 Bilsborrow Lancs
53 M8 Bilsby Lincs
10 F9 Bilsham W Susx
13 K3 Bilsington Kent
51 N8 Bilsthorpe Notts

86 F8 Bilston Mdloth
40 C8 Bilston Wolves
41 J6 Bilstone Leics
61 K7 Bilton E R Yk
58 H3 Bilton N York
59 L4 Bilton N York
41 L11 Bilton Warwks
52 H5 Binbrook Lincs
7 P6 Bincombe Dorset
17 N6 Binegar Somset
20 B8 Binfield Br For
20 C7 Binfield Heath Oxon
72 H6 Bingfield Nthumb
51 P11 Bingham Notts
58 E6 Bingley C Brad
44 G3 Binham Norfk
41 J10 Binley Covtry
19 M9 Binley Hants
41 K11 Binley Woods Warwks
8 C9 Binnegar Dorset
85 P8 Binniehill Falk
10 F2 Binscombe Surrey
9 P8 Binstead IoW
10 C2 Binsted Hants
11 E8 Binsted W Susx
30 F4 Binton Warwks
44 G5 Bintree Norfk
34 F11 Birch Essex
44 C4 Bircham Newton Norfk
44 C4 Bircham Tofts Norfk
33 N11 Birchanger Essex
33 N11 Birchanger Green Services Essex
40 E2 Birch Cross Staffs
39 J8 Bircher Herefs
34 F11 Birch Green Essex
27 N11 Birchgrove Cardif
26 F8 Birchgrove Swans
11 N4 Birchgrove W Susx
23 P9 Birchington Kent
40 H8 Birchley Heath Warwks
50 G8 Birchover Derbys
57 Q7 Birch Services Rochdl
50 D4 Birch Vale Derbys
16 H12 Birch Wood Somset
57 M9 Birchwood Warrtn
51 N3 Bircotes Notts
34 B8 Birdbrook Essex
66 C11 Birdforth N York
10 D9 Birdham W Susx
31 K1 Birdingbury Warwks
29 N6 Birdlip Gloucs
60 E2 Birdsall N York
58 G11 Birds Edge Kirk
22 C2 Birds Green Essex
39 P5 Birdsgreen Shrops
7 K3 Birdsmoorgate Dorset
51 J1 Birdwell Barns
80 G6 Birgham Border
107 M4 Birichin Highld
65 N7 Birkby N York
56 G6 Birkdale Sefton
102 C3 Birkenbog Abers
56 G10 Birkenhead Wirral
102 F6 Birkenhills Abers
58 G8 Birkenshaw Kirk
94 F4 Birkhall Abers
93 L8 Birkhill Angus
79 K6 Birkhill D & G
59 M8 Birkin N York
39 J10 Birley Herefs
51 J3 Birley Carr Sheff
22 D10 Birling Kent
30 C5 Birlingham Worcs
40 E9 Birmingham Birm
40 F10 Birmingham Airport Solhll
92 F7 Birnam P & K
103 K8 Birness Abers
95 J3 Birse Abers
95 J3 Birsemore Abers
58 G8 Birstall Kirk
41 N5 Birstall Leics
58 G3 Birstwith N York
73 M9 Birtley Gatesd
38 G8 Birtley Herefs
72 F5 Birtley Nthumb
73 M9 Birtley Crematorium Gatesd
29 K2 Birts Street Worcs
42 C9 Bisbrooke Rutlnd
52 H6 Biscathorpe Lincs
20 D6 Bisham W & M
30 C4 Bishampton Worcs
15 M7 Bish Mill Devon
65 L2 Bishop Auckland Dur
52 E5 Bishopbridge Lincs
85 K8 Bishopbriggs E Duns
60 G8 Bishop Burton E R Yk
65 N2 Bishop Middleham Dur
101 J3 Bishopmill Moray
59 J2 Bishop Monkton N York
52 E5 Bishop Norton Lincs
23 M11 Bishopsbourne Kent
18 F7 Bishops Cannings Wilts
38 G4 Bishop's Castle Shrops
17 Q12 Bishop's Caundle Dorset
29 M4 Bishop's Cleeve Gloucs
39 M11 Bishop's Frome Herefs
33 Q12 Bishop's Green Essex
16 G10 Bishops Hull Somset
31 K3 Bishop's Itchington Warwks
16 G9 Bishops Lydeard Somset
29 L4 Bishop's Norton Gloucs
15 N7 Bishop's Nympton Devon
49 P9 Bishop's Offley Staffs
33 M11 Bishop's Stortford Herts
9 Q2 Bishop's Sutton Hants
30 H2 Bishop's Tachbrook Warwks
15 K6 Bishop's Tawton Devon
6 B7 Bishopsteignton Devon
9 M4 Bishopstoke Hants
26 D10 Bishopston Swans
20 C2 Bishopstone Bucks
11 P9 Bishopstone E Susx
38 H12 Bishopstone Herefs
23 N9 Bishopstone Kent
19 J4 Bishopstone Swindn
8 F3 Bishopstone Wilts
18 D11 Bishopstrow Wilts
17 N4 Bishop Sutton BaNES
9 P4 Bishop's Waltham Hants
6 H1 Bishopswood Somset
49 Q12 Bishop's Wood Staffs
17 N3 Bishopsworth Bristl
58 H2 Bishop Thornton N York
59 N5 Bishopthorpe C York
65 P4 Bishopton Darltn
80 F3 Bishopton Rens
60 D3 Bishop Wilton E R Yk
28 B10 Bishton Newpt
30 D4 Bishton Staffs
29 M7 Bisley Gloucs
20 F10 Bisley Surrey

2 H7	**Bissoe** Cnwll
8 G7	**Bisterne** Hants
42 E4	**Bitchfield** Lincs
15 J4	**Bittadon** Devon
5 N8	**Bittaford** Devon
39 K6	**Bitterley** Shrops
9 M5	**Bitterne** C Sotn
41 M9	**Bitteswell** Leics
17 P3	**Bitton** S Glos
20 B6	**Bix** Oxon
111 k4	**Bixter** Shet
41 M7	**Blaby** Leics
80 H4	**Blackadder** Border
5 Q9	**Blackawton** Devon
6 E2	**Blackborough** Devon
43 Q7	**Blackborough End** Norfk
30 H12	**Black Bourton** Oxon
11 Q6	**Blackboys** E Susx
51 J10	**Blackbrook** Derbys
57 K9	**Blackbrook** St Hel
49 N7	**Blackbrook** Staffs
102 H11	**Blackburn** Abers
57 M4	**Blackburn** Bl w D
86 B8	**Blackburn** W Loth
57 M4	*Blackburn with Darwen Services* Bl w D
73 L7	**Black Callerton** N u Ty
77 K9	**Blackcraig** E Ayrs
90 C8	**Black Crofts** Ag & B
103 K11	**Blackdog** Abers
15 N9	**Black Dog** Devon
7 K3	**Blackdown** Dorset
51 J1	**Blacker Hill** Barns
21 P8	**Blackfen** Gt Lon
9 M7	**Blackfield** Hants
85 P2	**Blackford** P & K
17 K6	**Blackford** Somset
17 P10	**Blackford** Somset
41 J4	**Blackfordby** Leics
86 E7	**Blackhall** C Edin
73 Q11	**Blackhall Colliery** Dur
73 K9	**Blackhall Mill** Gatesd
79 N2	**Blackhaugh** Border
21 M7	**Blackheath** Gt Lon
40 C9	**Blackheath** Sandw
35 N2	**Blackheath** Suffk
10 G2	**Blackheath** Surrey
103 M4	**Blackhill** Abers
103 M6	**Blackhill** Abers
73 J9	**Blackhill** Dur
103 J6	**Blackhill of Clackriach** Abers
6 D4	**Blackhorse** Devon
78 G7	**Blacklaw** D & G
57 Q8	**Blackley** Manch
57 Q7	**Blackley Crematorium** Manch
94 C9	**Blacklunans** P & K
28 F2	**Blackmarstone** Herefs
27 K10	**Blackmill** Brdgnd
10 C4	**Blackmoor** Hants
17 L4	**Blackmoor** N Som
58 E10	**Blackmoorfoot** Kirk
22 C3	**Blackmore** Essex
34 C9	**Blackmore End** Essex
86 C6	**Blackness** Falk
10 C2	**Blacknest** Hants
34 C11	**Black Notley** Essex
57 Q1	**Blacko** Lancs
26 E10	**Black Pill** Swans
56 F2	**Blackpool** Bpool
6 B12	**Blackpool** Devon
56 G3	*Blackpool Airport* Lancs
85 P9	**Blackridge** W Loth
57 L6	**Blackrod** Bolton
101 J7	**Blacksboat** Moray
70 G3	**Blackshaw** D & G
58 C8	**Blackshaw Head** Calder
11 K6	**Blackstone** W Susx
45 Q11	**Black Street** Suffk
31 N9	**Blackthorn** Oxon
34 E4	**Blackthorpe** Suffk
60 E8	**Blacktoft** E R Yk
95 P2	**Blacktop** C Aber
14 H10	**Black Torrington** Devon
50 G10	**Blackwall** Derbys
2 H6	**Blackwater** Cnwll
20 D10	**Blackwater** Hants
9 N9	**Blackwater** IoW
16 H11	**Blackwater** Somset
75 N6	**Blackwaterfoot** N Ayrs
71 N5	**Blackwell** Cumb
50 E6	**Blackwell** Derbys
51 K8	**Blackwell** Derbys
30 G5	**Blackwell** Warwks
40 C11	**Blackwell** Worcs
27 N8	**Blackwood** Caerph
78 E10	**Blackwood** D & G
77 N3	**Blackwood** S Lans
48 H2	**Blacon** Ches W
69 K8	**Bladnoch** D & G
31 K10	**Bladon** Oxon
36 D10	**Blaenannerch** Cerdgn
47 L3	**Blaenau Ffestiniog** Gwynd
27 Q7	**Blaenavon** Torfn
25 L2	**Blaenffos** Pembks
27 J9	**Blaengarw** Brdgnd
27 J7	**Blaengwrach** Neath
27 J9	**Blaengwynfi** Neath
37 K7	**Blaenpennal** Cerdgn
37 J5	**Blaenplwyf** Cerdgn
36 D10	**Blaenporth** Cerdgn
27 K8	**Blaenrhondda** Rhondd
25 L4	**Blaenwaun** Carmth
25 N4	**Blaen-y-Coed** Carmth
27 K8	**Blaen-y-cwm** Rhondd
17 M4	**Blagdon** N Som
16 G11	**Blagdon** Somset
6 B9	**Blagdon** Torbay
16 G11	**Blagdon Hill** Somset
90 E2	**Blaich** Highld
89 N3	**Blain** Highld
27 P7	**Blaina** Blae G
92 C3	**Blair Atholl** P & K
85 M3	**Blair Drummond** Stirlg
92 H6	**Blairgowrie** P & K
86 B5	**Blairhall** Fife
86 B3	**Blairingone** P & K
85 N4	**Blairlogie** Stirlg
84 D6	**Blairmore** Ag & B
108 D4	**Blairmore** Highld
83 P8	**Blair's Ferry** Ag & B
29 J5	**Blaisdon** Gloucs
39 P6	**Blakebrook** Worcs
39 Q6	**Blakedown** Worcs
34 B11	**Blake End** Essex
49 K2	**Blakemere** Ches W
28 D1	**Blakemere** Herefs
40 D7	**Blakenall Heath** Wsall
29 J7	**Blakeney** Gloucs
44 G2	**Blakeney** Norfk
49 N6	**Blakenhall** Ches E
40 B7	**Blakenhall** Wolves
31 N4	**Blakesley** Nhants

72 H10	**Blanchland** Nthumb
8 C6	**Blandford Forum** Dorset
8 C6	**Blandford St Mary** Dorset
85 J7	**Blanefield** Stirlg
52 F10	**Blankney** Lincs
85 L10	**Blantyre** S Lans
90 F3	**Blar a' Chaorainn** Highld
98 H9	**Blargie** Highld
90 F3	**Blarmachfoldach** Highld
42 B10	**Blaston** Leics
42 D10	**Blatherwycke** Nhants
62 F5	**Blawith** Cumb
69 P3	**Blawquhairn** D & G
35 M5	**Blaxhall** Suffk
51 P2	**Blaxton** Donc
73 L8	**Blaydon** Gatesd
17 L7	**Bleadney** Somset
17 J5	**Bleadon** N Som
23 L10	**Blean** Kent
51 Q10	**Bleasby** Notts
93 M11	**Blebocraigs** Fife
38 E8	**Bleddfa** Powys
30 G9	**Bledington** Gloucs
20 C3	**Bledlow** Bucks
20 C4	**Bledlow Ridge** Bucks
87 J9	**Blegbie** E Loth
64 B2	**Blencarn** Cumb
71 K6	**Blencogo** Cumb
10 B7	**Blendworth** Hants
71 J7	**Blennerhasset** Cumb
31 L9	**Bletchingdon** Oxon
21 M12	**Bletchingley** Surrey
32 C9	**Bletchley** M Keyn
49 L8	**Bletchley** Shrops
25 J5	**Bletherston** Pembks
32 E5	**Bletsoe** Bed
19 N4	**Blewbury** Oxon
45 K4	**Blickling** Norfk
51 N9	**Blidworth** Notts
51 N9	**Blidworth Bottoms** Notts
71 J8	**Blindcrake** Cumb
11 M2	**Blindley Heath** Surrey
4 D5	**Blisland** Cnwll
8 H5	**Blissford** Hants
39 N7	**Bliss Gate** Worcs
31 Q4	**Blisworth** Nhants
40 E4	**Blithbury** Staffs
30 F7	**Blockley** Gloucs
45 M8	**Blofield** Norfk
45 M7	**Blofield Heath** Norfk
34 G2	**Blo Norton** Norfk
80 D8	**Bloomfield** Border
50 F10	**Blore** Staffs
31 K7	**Bloxham** Oxon
52 F11	**Bloxholm** Lincs
40 D7	**Bloxwich** Wsall
8 C8	**Bloxworth** Dorset
58 F3	**Blubberhouses** N York
16 D7	**Blue Anchor** Somset
22 E10	**Blue Bell Hill** Kent
50 F4	*Blue John Cavern* Derbys
56 F8	**Blundellsands** Sefton
45 Q10	**Blundeston** Suffk
32 G6	**Blunham** C Beds
18 G3	**Blunsdon St Andrew** Swindn
40 B11	**Bluntington** Worcs
33 K2	**Bluntisham** Cambs
52 D5	**Blyborough** Lincs
35 N2	**Blyford** Suffk
49 P11	**Blymhill** Staffs
51 N4	**Blyth** Notts
73 N5	**Blyth** Nthumb
86 D12	**Blyth Bridge** Border
35 P2	**Blythburgh** Suffk
73 N5	**Blyth Crematorium** Nthumb
80 D7	**Blythe** Border
51 N3	**Blyth Services** Notts
52 C5	**Blyton** Lincs
93 P11	**Boarhills** Fife
9 P6	**Boarhunt** Hants
31 N10	**Boarstall** Bucks
107 J7	**Boath** Highld
99 P5	**Boat of Garten** Highld
22 H9	**Bobbing** Kent
39 P4	**Bobbington** Staffs
34 C11	**Bocking** Essex
34 C10	**Bocking Churchstreet** Essex
103 M6	**Boddam** Abers
111 k5	**Boddam** Shet
29 M4	**Boddington** Gloucs
54 D5	**Bodedern** IoA
55 Q6	**Bodelwyddan** Denbgs
39 K11	**Bodenham** Herefs
8 H3	**Bodenham** Wilts
39 K11	**Bodenham Moor** Herefs
54 E4	**Bodewryd** IoA
48 C2	**Bodfari** Denbgs
54 F6	**Bodffordd** IoA
46 E4	**Bodfuan** Gwynd
45 J3	**Bodham** Norfk
12 F5	**Bodiam** E Susx
12 F5	*Bodiam Castle* E Susx
31 L6	**Bodicote** Oxon
4 E9	**Bodinnick** Cnwll
12 D7	**Bodle Street Green** E Susx
3 N3	**Bodmin** Cnwll
4 F5	**Bodmin Moor** Cnwll
55 L7	*Bodnant Garden* Conwy
13 L2	**Bodsham** Kent
3 M4	**Bodwen** Cnwll
107 K11	**Bogallan** Highld
103 L8	**Bogbrae** Abers
76 G5	**Bogend** S Ayrs
87 J7	**Boggs Holdings** E Loth
86 F8	**Boghall** Mdloth
86 B8	**Boghall** W Loth
77 N3	**Boghead** S Lans
101 L3	**Bogmoor** Moray
95 K7	**Bogmuir** Abers
102 D6	**Bogniebrae** Abers
10 E9	**Bognor Regis** W Susx
99 N4	**Bogroy** Highld
69 P3	**Bogue** D & G
3 J8	**Bohortha** Cnwll
98 D11	**Bohuntine** Highld
65 L3	**Bolam** Dur
5 N11	**Bolberry** Devon
40 E8	**Boldmere** Birm
9 K7	**Boldre** Hants
65 J5	**Boldron** Dur
52 B6	**Bole** Notts
50 H9	**Bolehill** Derbys
15 K10	**Bolham** Devon
16 C12	**Bolham Water** Devon
6 F1	**Bolingey** Cnwll
50 C5	**Bollington** Ches E
11 L5	**Bolney** W Susx
32 F5	**Bolnhurst** Bed
93 Q5	**Bolshan** Angus
51 L6	**Bolsover** Derbys
50 H2	**Bolsterstone** Sheff
66 C9	**Boltby** N York

101 M12	**Boltenstone** Abers
57 N7	**Bolton** Bolton
64 B3	**Bolton** Cumb
87 K8	**Bolton** E Loth
60 D4	**Bolton** E R Yk
81 M10	**Bolton** Nthumb
58 E4	**Bolton Abbey** N York
63 P11	**Bolton by Bowland** Lancs
71 P2	**Boltonfellend** Cumb
71 K7	**Boltongate** Cumb
63 J8	**Bolton le Sands** Lancs
71 K6	**Bolton Low Houses** Cumb
65 M7	**Bolton-on-Swale** N York
59 M6	**Bolton Percy** N York
51 L1	**Bolton Upon Dearne** Barns
57 L6	*Bolton West Services* Lancs
4 E5	**Bolventor** Cnwll
49 J10	**Bomere Heath** Shrops
107 K4	**Bonar Bridge** Highld
90 D9	**Bonawe** Ag & B
60 G10	**Bonby** N Linc
25 L2	**Boncath** Pembks
80 D10	**Bonchester Bridge** Border
15 L10	**Bondleigh** Devon
63 J12	**Bonds** Lancs
86 B6	**Bo'ness** Falk
40 D5	**Boney Hay** Staffs
84 G7	**Bonhill** W Duns
39 P2	**Boningale** Shrops
80 E9	**Bonjedward** Border
85 P10	**Bonkle** N Lans
93 P7	**Bonnington** Angus
13 K3	**Bonnington** Kent
86 G2	**Bonnybank** Fife
85 N7	**Bonnybridge** Falk
102 H5	**Bonnykelly** Abers
86 G8	**Bonnyrigg** Mdloth
93 L7	**Bonnyton** Angus
50 H8	**Bonsall** Derbys
71 K2	**Bonshaw Tower** D & G
47 P10	**Bont-Dolgadfan** Powys
37 L4	**Bont-goch or Elerch** Cerdgn
37 K7	**Bontnewydd** Cerdgn
54 G9	**Bontnewydd** Gwynd
48 C4	**Bontuchel** Denbgs
16 E2	**Bonvilston** V Glam
15 J5	**Boode** Devon
20 D5	**Booker** Bucks
80 D5	**Boon** Border
66 F4	**Boosbeck** R & Cl
34 E9	**Boose's Green** Essex
62 D3	**Boot** Cumb
58 D8	**Booth** Calder
52 E10	**Boothby Graffoe** Lincs
42 D4	**Boothby Pagnell** Lincs
60 C8	**Boothferry** E R Yk
57 N8	**Boothstown** Salfd
62 C5	**Bootle** Cumb
56 G9	**Bootle** Sefton
39 L8	**Boraston** Shrops
6 C1	**Bordeaux** Guern
22 G10	**Borden** Kent
72 B4	**Border Forest Park**
22 F2	**Boreham** Essex
18 D11	**Boreham** Wilts
12 D7	**Boreham Street** E Susx
21 J4	**Borehamwood** Herts
79 J10	**Boreland** D & G
104 B10	**Boreraig** Highld
111 a7	**Borgh** W Isls
111 d1	**Borgh** W Isls
109 M4	**Borgie** Highld
69 P9	**Borgue** D & G
110 D9	**Borgue** Highld
34 E7	**Borley** Essex
104 E7	**Borneskitaig** Highld
69 N9	**Borness** D & G
59 K2	**Boroughbridge** N York
22 C11	**Borough Green** Kent
41 K1	**Borrowash** Derbys
65 Q9	**Borrowby** N York
86 B6	**Borrowstoun** Falk
22 E9	**Borstal** Medway
37 K3	**Borth** Cerdgn
79 N6	**Borthwickbrae** Border
79 N6	**Borthwickshiels** Border
47 J4	**Borth-y-Gest** Gwynd
104 F11	**Borve** Highld
111 a7	**Borve** W Isls
111 c3	**Borve** W Isls
111 d1	**Borve** W Isls
63 K7	**Borwick** Lancs
39 M12	**Bosbury** Herefs
4 D3	**Boscastle** Cnwll
8 G8	**Boscombe** Bmouth
18 H11	**Boscombe** Wilts
10 D8	**Bosham** W Susx
24 G9	**Bosherston** Pembks
50 B7	**Bosley** Ches E
60 C3	**Bossall** N York
4 D3	**Bossiney** Cnwll
13 M1	**Bossingham** Kent
16 B6	**Bossington** Somset
49 M2	**Bostock Green** Ches W
43 K2	**Boston** Lincs
43 K2	**Boston Crematorium** Lincs
59 K5	**Boston Spa** Leeds
3 L7	**Boswinger** Cnwll
2 B8	**Botallack** Cnwll
21 L4	**Botany Bay** Gt Lon
34 H2	**Botesdale** Suffk
73 M4	**Bothal** Nthumb
51 P6	**Bothamsall** Notts
71 K7	**Bothel** Cumb
7 L5	**Bothenhampton** Dorset
85 L10	**Bothwell** S Lans
85 M10	**Bothwell Services** S Lans
20 F3	**Botley** Bucks
9 N5	**Botley** Hants
31 L11	**Botley** Oxon
31 Q8	**Botolph Claydon** Bucks
11 J8	**Botolphs** W Susx
42 B3	**Bottesford** Leics
52 C3	**Bottesford** N Linc
33 N5	**Bottisham** Cambs
93 L10	**Bottomcraig** Fife
58 B9	**Bottoms** Calder
5 J7	**Botusfleming** Cnwll
46 D5	**Botwnnog** Gwynd
11 P1	**Bough Beech** Kent
27 N2	**Boughrood** Powys
31 Q2	**Boughton** Nhants
44 B9	**Boughton** Norfk
51 P7	**Boughton** Notts
13 K1	**Boughton Aluph** Kent
22 F12	**Boughton Green** Kent
22 F12	**Boughton Monchelsea** Kent
23 K10	**Boughton Street** Kent

39 K5	**Bouldon** Shrops
81 Q10	**Boulmer** Nthumb
52 D9	**Boultham** Lincs
33 K5	**Bourn** Cambs
42 F6	**Bourne** Lincs
21 P5	**Bournebridge** Essex
40 D10	**Bournebrook** Birm
20 E6	**Bourne End** Bucks
32 D7	**Bourne End** C Beds
20 G3	**Bourne End** Herts
8 G8	**Bournemouth** Bmouth
8 G7	*Bournemouth Airport* Dorset
8 G8	**Bournemouth Crematorium** Bmouth
22 H6	**Bournes Green** Sthend
40 C11	**Bournheath** Worcs
73 N9	**Bournmoor** Dur
40 D10	**Bournville** Birm
8 B2	**Bourton** Dorset
19 J4	**Bourton** Oxon
39 L3	**Bourton** Shrops
18 F7	**Bourton** Wilts
41 K12	**Bourton on Dunsmore** Warwks
30 F7	**Bourton-on-the-Hill** Gloucs
30 F9	**Bourton-on-the-Water** Gloucs
88 G4	**Bousd** Ag & B
62 G5	**Bouth** Cumb
65 K12	**Bouthwaite** N York
8 F4	**Boveridge** Dorset
5 Q5	**Bovey Tracey** Devon
20 G3	**Bovingdon** Herts
8 C9	**Bovington Tank Museum** Dorset
15 M10	**Bow** Devon
21 M6	**Bow** Gt Lon
111 h3	**Bow** Ork
32 C9	**Bow Brickhill** M Keyn
29 M7	**Bowbridge** Gloucs
73 N12	**Bowburn** Dur
9 M9	**Bowcombe** IoW
6 F5	**Bowd** Devon
20 D7	**Bowden** Border
18 D7	**Bowden Hill** Wilts
57 N10	**Bowdon** Traffd
110 E3	**Bower** Highld
8 F3	**Bowerchalke** Wilts
110 F3	**Bowermadden** Highld
49 P8	**Bowers** Staffs
22 E6	**Bowers Gifford** Essex
86 C4	**Bowershall** Fife
59 K8	**Bower's Row** Leeds
64 H5	**Bowes** Dur
63 J12	**Bowgreave** Lancs
70 G3	**Bowhouse** D & G
79 P2	**Bowland** Border
39 K10	**Bowley** Herefs
10 E3	**Bowlhead Green** Surrey
58 F7	**Bowling** C Brad
84 G8	**Bowling** W Duns
62 F3	**Bowmanstead** Cumb
82 D10	**Bowmore** Ag & B
71 K3	**Bowness-on-Solway** Cumb
62 H3	**Bowness-on-Windermere** Cumb
93 K12	**Bow of Fife** Fife
93 N6	**Bowriefauld** Angus
81 L6	**Bowsden** Nthumb
37 K4	**Bow Street** Cerdgn
29 M8	**Box** Gloucs
18 C7	**Box** Wilts
34 F8	**Boxford** Suffk
19 M6	**Boxford** W Berk
10 E8	**Boxgrove** W Susx
22 F10	**Boxley** Kent
20 G3	**Boxmoor** Herts
34 G9	**Boxted** Essex
34 G9	**Boxted** Essex
34 D6	**Boxted** Suffk
34 G9	**Boxted Cross** Essex
33 K4	**Boxworth** Cambs
23 N9	**Boyden Gate** Kent
40 F1	**Boylestone** Derbys
102 E3	**Boyndie** Abers
103 J3	**Boyndlie** Abers
61 K1	**Boynton** E R Yk
93 Q6	**Boysack** Angus
4 H2	**Boyton** Cnwll
35 N7	**Boyton** Suffk
18 D11	**Boyton** Wilts
22 D2	**Boyton Cross** Essex
34 C7	**Boyton End** Suffk
32 C5	**Bozeat** Nhants
13 L2	**Brabourne** Kent
13 L3	**Brabourne Lees** Kent
110 G2	**Brabstermire** Highld
96 D2	**Bracadale** Highld
42 F7	**Braceborough** Lincs
52 E8	**Bracebridge Heath** Lincs
52 D9	**Bracebridge Low Fields** Lincs
42 E3	**Braceby** Lincs
63 Q11	**Bracewell** Lancs
51 J8	**Brackenfield** Derbys
85 M8	**Brackenhirst** N Lans
10 D10	**Brackenhurst** W Susx
98 B11	**Brackletter** Highld
31 N6	**Brackley** Nhants
20 E9	**Bracknell** Br For
85 N2	**Braco** P & K
101 P5	**Bracobrae** Moray
45 K9	**Bracon Ash** Norfk
97 K10	**Bracora** Highld
97 K10	**Bracorina** Highld
50 G9	**Bradbourne** Derbys
65 N2	**Bradbury** Dur
31 N5	**Bradden** Nhants
20 C4	**Bradenham** Bucks
18 E5	**Bradenstoke** Wilts
6 E2	**Bradfield** Devon
35 J9	**Bradfield** Essex
45 L4	**Bradfield** Norfk
50 H3	**Bradfield** Sheff
19 P6	**Bradfield** W Berk
34 E5	**Bradfield Combust** Suffk
49 M4	**Bradfield Green** Ches E
35 J10	**Bradfield Heath** Essex
34 E5	**Bradfield St Clare** Suffk
34 E5	**Bradfield St George** Suffk
58 F7	**Bradford** C Brad
14 G10	**Bradford** Devon
17 N12	**Bradford Abbas** Dorset
18 C8	**Bradford Leigh** Wilts
18 C8	**Bradford-on-Avon** Wilts
16 G10	**Bradford-on-Tone** Somset
7 P4	**Bradford Peverell** Dorset
5 K5	**Bradiford** Devon
9 Q9	**Brading** IoW
50 G10	**Bradley** Derbys
19 Q11	**Bradley** Hants

53 J3	**Bradley** NE Lin
49 Q11	**Bradley** Staffs
40 C8	**Bradley** Wolves
30 C2	**Bradley** Worcs
30 C2	**Bradley Green** Worcs
50 D11	**Bradley in the Moors** Staffs
28 H11	**Bradley Stoke** S Glos
41 N2	**Bradmore** Notts
6 D3	**Bradninch** Devon
50 D9	**Bradnop** Staffs
7 L4	**Bradpole** Dorset
58 E8	**Bradshaw** Calder
4 H4	**Bradstone** Devon
49 N3	**Bradwall Green** Ches E
50 F5	**Bradwell** Derbys
34 D11	**Bradwell** Essex
32 B8	**Bradwell** M Keyn
45 Q8	**Bradwell** Norfk
49 Q5	**Bradwell Crematorium** Staffs
23 J3	**Bradwell-on-Sea** Essex
23 J2	**Bradwell Waterside** Essex
14 F8	**Bradworthy** Devon
107 L9	**Brae** Highld
111 k3	**Brae** Shet
85 N7	**Braeface** Falk
95 L10	**Braehead** Angus
69 K8	**Braehead** D & G
77 Q2	**Braehead** S Lans
94 C3	**Braemar** Abers
106 C6	**Braemore** Highld
110 C6	**Braemore** Highld
98 D10	**Brae Roy Lodge** Highld
84 D7	**Braeside** Inver
93 K4	**Braes of Coul** Angus
101 M4	**Braes of Enzie** Moray
111 i1	**Braeswick** Ork
83 P2	**Braevallich** Ag & B
65 N4	**Brafferton** Darltn
66 B12	**Brafferton** N York
32 B5	**Brafield-on-the-Green** Nhants
111 d1	**Bragar** W Isls
33 J11	**Bragbury End** Herts
77 P2	**Braidwood** S Lans
50 G11	**Brailsford** Derbys
34 C11	**Braintree** Essex
35 J3	**Braiseworth** Suffk
9 L3	**Braishfield** Hants
71 K10	**Braithwaite** Cumb
51 M2	**Braithwell** Donc
11 J7	**Bramber** W Susx
41 K9	**Bramcote** Warwks
51 L11	**Bramcote Crematorium** Notts
9 Q2	**Bramdean** Hants
45 L8	**Bramerton** Norfk
33 J12	**Bramfield** Herts
35 N3	**Bramfield** Suffk
35 J7	**Bramford** Suffk
50 B4	**Bramhall** Stockp
59 K5	**Bramham** Leeds
58 G5	**Bramhope** Leeds
19 Q8	**Bramley** Hants
58 G7	**Bramley** Leeds
51 L3	**Bramley** Rothm
10 G2	**Bramley** Surrey
19 Q8	**Bramley Corner** Hants
23 N11	**Bramling** Kent
6 C3	**Brampford Speke** Devon
32 H3	**Brampton** Cambs
64 C3	**Brampton** Cumb
71 Q4	**Brampton** Cumb
52 B7	**Brampton** Lincs
45 K5	**Brampton** Norfk
51 K1	**Brampton** Rothm
35 P1	**Brampton** Suffk
28 H4	**Brampton Abbotts** Herefs
42 B11	**Brampton Ash** Nhants
38 G7	**Brampton Bryan** Herefs
51 L4	**Brampton-en-le-Morthen** Rothm
40 D2	**Bramshall** Staffs
9 J4	**Bramshaw** Hants
10 D4	**Bramshott** Hants
17 L9	**Bramwell** Somset
89 L3	**Branault** Highld
44 C2	**Brancaster** Norfk
44 D2	**Brancaster Staithe** Norfk
73 L12	**Brancepeth** Dur
100 G5	**Branchill** Moray
101 K2	**Branderburgh** Moray
61 J5	**Brandesburton** E R Yk
35 L5	**Brandeston** Suffk
45 J6	**Brandiston** Norfk
73 M11	**Brandon** Dur
42 C11	**Brandon** Lincs
44 D11	**Brandon** Suffk
41 K11	**Brandon** Warwks
44 H8	**Brandon Parva** Norfk
66 E11	**Brandsby** N York
52 E4	**Brandy Wharf** Lincs
33 Q10	**Bran End** Essex
8 F8	**Branksome** Poole
8 F8	**Branksome Park** Poole
19 M11	**Bransbury** Hants
52 C7	**Bransby** Lincs
6 G5	**Branscombe** Devon
39 P10	**Bransford** Worcs
8 H7	**Bransgore** Hants
61 J7	**Bransholme** C KuH
39 M7	**Bransley** Shrops
42 B4	**Branston** Leics
52 E9	**Branston** Lincs
40 G4	**Branston** Staffs
52 F9	**Branston Booths** Lincs
9 P10	**Branstone** IoW
52 D11	**Brant Broughton** Lincs
35 J9	**Brantham** Suffk
70 H9	**Branthwaite** Cumb
71 L7	**Branthwaite** Cumb
60 E7	**Brantingham** E R Yk
51 N10	**Branton** Donc
81 L10	**Branton** Nthumb
59 K2	**Branton Green** N York
81 N6	**Branxton** Nthumb
50 G9	**Brassington** Derbys
21 P11	**Brasted** Kent
21 P11	**Brasted Chart** Kent
95 L3	**Brathens** Abers
53 M9	**Bratoft** Lincs
52 D7	**Brattleby** Lincs
18 D9	**Bratton** Wilts
49 L11	**Bratton** Wrekin
5 K2	**Bratton Clovelly** Devon
15 L5	**Bratton Fleming** Devon
17 P9	**Bratton Seymour** Somset
33 M2	**Braughing** Herts
31 M2	**Braunston** Nhants
41 M7	**Braunstone** Leics
15 J4	**Braunton** Devon
66 G11	**Brawby** N York

109 P3 Brawl Highld
20 E7 Bray W & M
41 Q9 Braybrooke Nhants
15 M5 Brayford Devon
4 H5 Bray Shop Cnwll
59 N7 Brayton N York
20 E7 Braywick W & M
32 G11 Breachwood Green Herts
51 J11 Breadsall Derbys
29 J8 Breadstone Gloucs
2 F9 Breage Cnwll
106 H12 Breakachy Highld
20 H5 Breakspear Crematorium Gt Lon
106 H4 Brealangwell Lodge Highld
28 H7 Bream Gloucs
8 H4 Breamore Hants
16 H5 Brean Somset
111 b2 Breanais W Isls
58 H3 Brearton N York
111 c2 Breascleit W Isls
111 c2 Breasclete W Isls
41 L2 Breaston Derbys
26 C3 Brechfa Carmth
95 K9 Brechin Angus
44 F10 Breckles Norfk
27 L3 Brecon Powys
27 L4 Brecon Beacons National Park
50 B3 Bredbury Stockp
12 G6 Brede E Susx
39 L10 Bredenbury Herefs
35 L6 Bredfield Suffk
22 G10 Bredgar Kent
22 F10 Bredhurst Kent
29 N2 Bredon Worcs
29 M2 Bredon's Hardwick Worcs
29 N2 Bredon's Norton Worcs
38 G12 Bredwardine Herefs
41 K3 Breedon on the Hill Leics
85 Q10 Breich W Loth
57 N7 Breightmet Bolton
60 C7 Breighton E R Yk
28 F2 Breinton Herefs
18 E6 Bremhill Wilts
12 D2 Brenchley Kent
15 N3 Brendon Devon
83 M6 Brenfield Ag & B
111 b2 Brenish W Isls
34 F7 Brent Eleigh Suffk
21 J7 Brentford Gt Lon
42 B6 Brentingby Leics
17 J6 Brent Knoll Somset
5 N8 Brent Mill Devon
33 M10 Brent Pelham Herts
22 C5 Brentwood Essex
13 J5 Brenzett Kent
13 J4 Brenzett Green Kent
40 D4 Brereton Staffs
49 P3 Brereton Green Ches E
111 k4 Bressay Shet
34 H1 Bressingham Norfk
40 H3 Bretby Derbys
40 H3 Bretby Crematorium Derbys
41 K11 Bretford Warwks
30 E5 Bretforton Worcs
57 J5 Bretherton Lancs
111 k4 Brettabister Shet
44 F12 Brettenham Norfk
34 F6 Brettenham Suffk
48 G3 Bretton Flints
40 B6 Brewood Staffs
8 B8 Briantspuddle Dorset
21 L2 Brickendon Herts
20 H3 Bricket Wood Herts
50 H5 Brick Houses Sheff
29 N1 Bricklehampton Worcs
56 e2 Bride IoM
71 J8 Bridekirk Cumb
5 L3 Bridestowe Devon
102 D7 Brideswell Abers
5 Q3 Bridford Devon
23 M11 Bridge Kent
17 N10 Bridgehampton Somset
65 N12 Bridge Hewick N York
73 K9 Bridgehill Dur
9 P6 Bridgemary Hants
101 P7 Bridgend Abers
82 E9 Bridgend Ag & B
95 J8 Bridgend Angus
27 J11 Bridgend Brdgnd
78 H7 Bridgend D & G
5 L9 Bridgend Devon
93 L12 Bridgend Fife
101 M8 Bridgend Moray
92 G10 Bridgend P & K
86 C7 Bridgend W Loth
93 K5 Bridgend of Lintrathen Angus
102 D10 Bridge of Alford Abers
85 N4 Bridge of Allan Stirlg
100 H10 Bridge of Avon Moray
101 J7 Bridge of Avon Moray
91 N7 Bridge of Balgie P & K
94 C9 Bridge of Brewlands Angus
100 H10 Bridge of Brown Highld
92 H5 Bridge of Cally P & K
95 K3 Bridge of Canny Abers
93 J5 Bridge of Craigisla Angus
70 C4 Bridge of Dee D & G
103 K12 Bridge of Don C Aber
100 E7 Bridge of Dulsie Highld
95 K5 Bridge of Dye Abers
92 G11 Bridge of Earn P & K
91 M5 Bridge of Ericht P & K
95 L3 Bridge of Feugh Abers
110 B3 Bridge of Forss Highld
94 F3 Bridge of Gairn Abers
91 M5 Bridge of Gaur P & K
102 D5 Bridge of Marnoch Abers
91 J8 Bridge of Orchy Ag & B
92 D3 Bridge of Tilt P & K
101 M3 Bridge of Tynet Moray
111 j4 Bridge of Walls Shet
84 G9 Bridge of Weir Rens
14 E10 Bridgerule Devon
28 E1 Bridge Sollers Herefs
34 E6 Bridge Street Suffk
16 C9 Bridgetown Somset
49 J2 Bridge Trafford Ches W
44 F11 Bridgham Norfk
39 N4 Bridgnorth Shrops
16 H8 Bridgwater Somset
17 J8 Bridgwater Services Somset
61 K2 Bridlington E R Yk
7 L4 Bridport Dorset
28 G4 Bridstow Herefs
57 Q2 Brierfield Lancs
59 K11 Brierley Barns
28 H6 Brierley Gloucs
40 B9 Brierley Hill Dudley
52 E3 Brigg N Linc
45 M5 Briggate Norfk
67 J6 Briggswath N York
70 H9 Brigham Cumb
61 J4 Brigham E R Yk
58 F9 Brighouse Calder
9 M10 Brighstone IoW
31 K12 Brighthampton Oxon
15 K11 Brightley Devon
12 D6 Brightling E Susx
34 H12 Brightlingsea Essex
11 L8 Brighton Br & H
56 F8 Brighton le Sands Sefton
85 Q7 Brightons Falk
19 M5 Brightwalton W Berk
35 L7 Brightwell Suffk
19 Q2 Brightwell Baldwin Oxon
19 P3 Brightwell-cum-Sotwell Oxon
19 Q2 Brightwell Upperton Oxon
65 J5 Brignall Dur
85 J2 Brig o'Turk Stirlg
53 J3 Brigsley NE Lin
63 J4 Brigsteer Cumb
42 D11 Brigstock Nhants
31 P10 Brill Bucks
2 G9 Brill Cnwll
38 F11 Brilley Herefs
39 K8 Brimfield Herefs
39 K8 Brimfield Cross Herefs
51 K6 Brimington Derbys
5 Q5 Brimley Devon
29 N6 Brimpsfield Gloucs
19 P7 Brimpton W Berk
29 M8 Brimscombe Gloucs
56 F11 Brimstage Wirral
51 J4 Brincliffe Sheff
60 C7 Brind E R Yk
111 j4 Brindister Shet
57 L4 Brindle Lancs
49 P11 Brineton Staffs
42 B10 Bringhurst Leics
39 M10 Bringsty Herefs
32 F2 Brington Cambs
44 G4 Briningham Norfk
53 L8 Brinkhill Lincs
33 Q6 Brinkley Cambs
41 K10 Brinklow Warwks
18 E4 Brinkworth Wilts
57 L5 Brinscall Lancs
51 L10 Brinsley Notts
51 K3 Brinsworth Rothm
44 G3 Brinton Norfk
111 h2 Brinyan Ork
44 F6 Brisley Norfk
17 N3 Brislington Bristl
12 H3 Brissenden Green Kent
17 N2 Bristol Bristl
17 M3 Bristol Airport N Som
17 N2 Bristol Zoo Bristl
44 H4 Briston Norfk
8 H2 Britford Wilts
27 N8 Brithdir Caerph
47 M7 Brithdir Gwynd
22 E11 British Legion Village Kent
26 G9 Briton Ferry Neath
19 R3 Britwell Salome Oxon
6 C10 Brixham Torbay
5 L9 Brixton Devon
21 L8 Brixton Gt Lon
18 C11 Brixton Deverill Wilts
41 Q12 Brixworth Nhants
30 H11 Brize Norton Oxon
30 H11 Brize Norton Airport Oxon
30 B1 Broad Alley Worcs
18 G3 Broad Blunsdon Swindn
50 C3 Broadbottom Tamesd
10 D8 Broadbridge W Susx
11 J4 Broadbridge Heath W Susx
30 F6 Broad Campden Gloucs
58 E9 Broad Carr Calder
8 F3 Broad Chalke Wilts
6 D4 Broadclyst Devon
84 F8 Broadfield Inver
96 H5 Broadford Highld
10 H6 Broadford Bridge W Susx
79 K6 Broadgairhill Border
39 P10 Broad Green Worcs
81 J4 Broadhaugh Border
24 F6 Broad Haven Pembks
57 N10 Broadheath Traffd
6 E2 Broadhembury Devon
5 Q7 Broadhempston Devon
18 G5 Broad Hinton Wilts
12 G6 Broadland Row E Susx
19 M8 Broad Layings Hants
101 M3 Broadley Moray
30 F5 Broad Marston Worcs
7 Q5 Broadmayne Dorset
25 J7 Broadmoor Pembks
7 L4 Broadoak Dorset
12 C5 Broad Oak E Susx
12 G6 Broad Oak E Susx
28 F5 Broad Oak Herefs
23 M10 Broad Oak Kent
57 K9 Broad Oak St Hel
22 E2 Broad's Green Essex
23 Q9 Broadstairs Kent
8 E8 Broadstone Poole
39 K4 Broadstone Shrops
12 G6 Broad Street E Susx
22 G11 Broad Street Kent
18 G5 Broad Town Wilts
39 N10 Broadwas Worcs
33 J11 Broadwater Herts
11 J8 Broadwater W Susx
39 Q6 Broadwaters Worcs
24 F6 Broadway Pembks
17 J11 Broadway Somset
30 E6 Broadway Worcs
28 G6 Broadwell Gloucs
30 G8 Broadwell Gloucs
30 G12 Broadwell Oxon
31 L2 Broadwell Warwks
7 L3 Broadwindsor Dorset
15 K10 Broadwood Kelly Devon
5 J3 Broadwoodwidger Devon
104 H12 Brochel Highld
90 D9 Brochroy Ag & B
39 P10 Brockamin Worcs
9 Q4 Brockbridge Hants
35 K2 Brockdish Norfk
9 K7 Brockenhurst Hants
78 D2 Brocketsbrae S Lans
35 J4 Brockford Street Suffk
31 N2 Brockhall Nhants
21 K12 Brockham Surrey
30 D9 Brockhampton Gloucs
10 B8 Brockhampton Hants
28 H3 Brockhampton Herefs
39 M10 Brockhampton Estate Herefs
58 F11 Brockholes Kirk
61 K11 Brocklesby Lincs
17 L3 Brockley N Som
34 D3 Brockley Suffk
34 C7 Brockley Green Suffk
34 D6 Brockley Green Suffk
38 G2 Brockton Shrops
38 G5 Brockton Shrops
39 L4 Brockton Shrops
28 G8 Brockweir Gloucs
29 M5 Brockworth Gloucs
40 C4 Brocton Staffs
75 Q5 Brodick N Ayrs
100 F4 Brodie Moray
59 L11 Brodsworth Donc
104 F8 Brogaig Highld
18 D3 Brokenborough Wilts
50 B6 Broken Cross Ches E
18 C9 Brokerswood Wilts
56 G11 Bromborough Wirral
35 J2 Brome Suffk
35 J2 Brome Street Suffk
35 M6 Bromeswell Suffk
71 J6 Bromfield Cumb
39 J6 Bromfield Shrops
32 E6 Bromham Bed
18 E7 Bromham Wilts
21 N9 Bromley Gt Lon
39 N3 Bromley Shrops
22 F9 Brompton Medway
65 P8 Brompton N York
67 K10 Brompton-by-Sawdon N York
65 L7 Brompton-on-Swale N York
16 E9 Brompton Ralph Somset
16 C9 Brompton Regis Somset
29 K3 Bromsberrow Gloucs
29 K3 Bromsberrow Heath Gloucs
40 C12 Bromsgrove Worcs
39 M10 Bromyard Herefs
37 K7 Bronant Cerdgn
36 E10 Brongest Cerdgn
49 J7 Bronington Wrexhm
27 N2 Bronllys Powys
25 P4 Bronwydd Carmth
48 F7 Bronygarth Shrops
55 M6 Bron-y-Nant Crematorium Conwy
9 J5 Brook Hants
9 L9 Brook IoW
13 K2 Brook Kent
10 E3 Brook Surrey
45 L9 Brooke Norfk
42 C8 Brooke Rutlnd
52 H4 Brookenby Lincs
84 G9 Brookfield Rens
17 P9 Brookhampton Somset
9 J5 Brook Hill Hants
63 K8 Brookhouse Lancs
51 L3 Brookhouse Rothm
49 P4 Brookhouse Green Ches E
50 D3 Brookhouses Derbys
13 J5 Brookland Kent
57 P10 Brooklands Traffd
21 K3 Brookmans Park Herts
22 C5 Brook Street Essex
12 H4 Brook Street Kent
29 L6 Brookthorpe Gloucs
20 F11 Brookwood Surrey
32 G8 Broom C Beds
51 K3 Broom Rothm
30 E4 Broom Warwks
45 M10 Broome Norfk
38 H6 Broome Shrops
40 B10 Broome Worcs
57 N10 Broomedge Warrtn
22 E2 Broomfield Essex
22 G11 Broomfield Kent
23 M9 Broomfield Kent
16 G9 Broomfield Somset
60 F8 Broomfleet E R Yk
72 H8 Broomhaugh Nthumb
59 K12 Broom Hill Barns
51 M10 Broom Hill Notts
73 M1 Broomhill Nthumb
73 M11 Broompark Dur
107 P2 Brora Highld
39 M2 Broseley Shrops
72 G12 Brotherlee Dur
59 L8 Brotherton N York
66 F4 Brotton R & Cl
110 B4 Broubster Highld
64 E5 Brough Cumb
60 F8 Brough E R Yk
110 E2 Brough Highld
52 B10 Brough Notts
111 m3 Brough Shet
49 K7 Broughall Shrops
111 m2 Brough Lodge Shet
64 E5 Brough Sowerby Cumb
78 H2 Broughton Border
33 J2 Broughton Cambs
48 G3 Broughton Flints
9 K2 Broughton Hants
57 K2 Broughton Lancs
32 C8 Broughton M Keyn
52 D2 Broughton N Linc
58 C4 Broughton N York
66 H11 Broughton N York
32 B2 Broughton Nhants
31 K6 Broughton Oxon
57 P8 Broughton Salfd
16 C3 Broughton V Glam
41 M8 Broughton Astley Leics
18 C7 Broughton Gifford Wilts
30 C2 Broughton Green Worcs
30 B3 Broughton Hackett Worcs
62 E5 Broughton-in-Furness Cumb
69 L9 Broughton Mains D & G
62 E4 Broughton Mills Cumb
70 H8 Broughton Moor Cumb
30 G12 Broughton Poggs Oxon
93 N9 Broughty Ferry C Dund
19 P11 Brown Candover Hants
50 B9 Brown Edge Staffs
102 H7 Brownhill Abers
93 P11 Brownhills Fife
40 D6 Brownhills Wsall
19 P8 Browninghill Green Hants
49 Q4 Brown Lees Staffs
8 F9 Brownsea Island Dorset
29 M8 Browns Hill Gloucs
5 N9 Brownston Devon
67 K8 Broxa N York
21 M3 Broxbourne Herts
87 N6 Broxburn E Loth
86 C7 Broxburn W Loth
33 P10 Broxted Essex
110 G7 Bruan Highld
92 C3 Bruar P & K
107 Q5 Brucefield Highld
84 B10 Bruchag Ag & B
82 C10 Bruichladdich Ag & B
35 M4 Bruisyard Suffk
35 M4 Bruisyard Street Suffk
52 C2 Brumby N Linc
50 E8 Brund Staffs
45 M8 Brundall Norfk
35 L3 Brundish Suffk
35 L3 Brundish Street Suffk
89 P2 Brunery Highld
73 M6 Brunswick Village N u Ty
58 D5 Brunthwaite C Brad
41 N9 Bruntingthorpe Leics
93 K10 Brunton Fife
19 J9 Brunton Wilts
15 L9 Brushford Devon
16 C10 Brushford Somset
17 P8 Bruton Somset
30 B1 Bryan's Green Worcs
8 C6 Bryanston Dorset
71 K2 Brydekirk D & G
2 b2 Bryher IoS
17 M11 Brympton Somset
26 D8 Bryn Carmth
26 H9 Bryn Neath
26 F6 Brynamman Carmth
25 J2 Brynberian Pembks
46 H3 Bryncir Gwynd
26 G8 Bryn-coch Neath
46 D5 Bryncroes Gwynd
47 K9 Bryncrug Gwynd
48 D6 Bryneglwys Denbgs
48 D1 Brynford Flints
57 L8 Bryn Gates Wigan
54 D6 Bryngwran IoA
28 D7 Bryngwyn Mons
38 E11 Bryngwyn Powys
24 H2 Bryn-Henllan Pembks
36 E9 Brynhoffnant Cerdgn
27 P6 Brynmawr Blae G
46 D5 Bryn-mawr Gwynd
27 J10 Brynmenyn Brdgnd
26 E9 Brynmill Swans
27 L11 Brynna Rhondd
54 H8 Brynrefail Gwynd
27 L11 Brynsadler Rhondd
48 C5 Bryn Saith Marchog Denbgs
54 F7 Brynsiencyn IoA
54 G5 Brynteg IoA
55 M6 Bryn-y-Maen Conwy
96 E5 Bualintur Highld
41 J11 Bubbenhall Warwks
60 C7 Bubwith E R Yk
79 M6 Buccleuch Border
84 H5 Buchanan Smithy Stirlg
103 M6 Buchanhaven Abers
92 D9 Buchanty P & K
85 M3 Buchany Stirlg
85 J4 Buchlyvie Stirlg
71 M6 Buckabank Cumb
32 H4 Buckden Cambs
64 G11 Buckden N York
45 M8 Buckenham Norfk
6 F3 Buckerell Devon
5 P6 Buckfast Devon
5 P7 Buckfastleigh Devon
86 G3 Buckhaven Fife
28 F5 Buckholt Mons
17 R10 Buckhorn Weston Dorset
21 N5 Buckhurst Hill Essex
101 M3 Buckie Moray
31 P7 Buckingham Bucks
20 E2 Buckland Bucks
5 N10 Buckland Devon
30 E7 Buckland Gloucs
33 K9 Buckland Herts
13 P2 Buckland Kent
19 K2 Buckland Oxon
21 K12 Buckland Surrey
14 G7 Buckland Brewer Devon
20 E3 Buckland Common Bucks
17 R6 Buckland Dinham Somset
14 H9 Buckland Filleigh Devon
5 P5 Buckland in the Moor Devon
5 K6 Buckland Monachorum Devon
7 P2 Buckland Newton Dorset
7 P6 Buckland Ripers Dorset
16 H12 Buckland St Mary Somset
5 P10 Buckland-Tout-Saints Devon
19 P6 Bucklebury W Berk
9 L7 Bucklers Hard Hants
35 L8 Bucklesham Suffk
48 F3 Buckley Flints
57 N11 Bucklow Hill Ches E
42 C5 Buckminster Leics
50 B10 Bucknall C Stke
52 G9 Bucknall Lincs
31 M8 Bucknell Oxon
38 G7 Bucknell Shrops
101 M3 Buckpool Moray
103 J12 Bucksburn C Aber
14 F7 Buck's Cross Devon
10 H4 Bucks Green W Susx
57 K5 Buckshaw Village Lancs
10 D2 Bucks Horn Oak Hants
14 F7 Buck's Mills Devon
67 P11 Buckton E R Yk
81 M6 Buckton Nthumb
32 G2 Buckworth Cambs
51 N6 Budby Notts
14 D10 Bude Cnwll
4 H8 Budge's Shop Cnwll
6 E6 Budleigh Salterton Devon
2 H9 Budock Water Cnwll
49 M6 Buerton Ches E
31 P3 Bugbrooke Nhants
3 M4 Bugle Cnwll
8 B3 Bugley Dorset
60 D3 Bugthorpe E R Yk
39 L2 Buildwas Shrops
38 B11 Builth Wells Powys
19 J9 Bulbridge Wilts
18 H11 Bulford Wilts
49 K5 Bulkeley Ches E
41 K9 Bulkington Warwks
18 D8 Bulkington Wilts
14 G8 Bulkworthy Devon
20 E9 Bullbrook Br For
19 M11 Bullington Hants
52 F7 Bullington Lincs
34 D8 Bulmer Essex
60 C1 Bulmer N York
34 D8 Bulmer Tye Essex
22 D6 Bulphan Thurr
103 J6 Bulwark Abers
51 M11 Bulwell C Nott
42 D10 Bulwick Nhants
21 N3 Bumble's Green Essex
97 J11 Bunacaimb Highld
98 B10 Bunarkaig Highld
49 K4 Bunbury Ches E
107 K12 Bunchrew Highld
97 M4 Bundalloch Highld
89 J11 Bunessan Ag & B
45 M11 Bungay Suffk
82 F8 Bunnahabhain Ag & B
41 N2 Bunny Notts
98 E3 Buntait Highld
33 K10 Buntingford Herts
45 J10 Bunwell Norfk
41 K8 Burbage Leics
19 J8 Burbage Wilts
20 D7 Burchett's Green W & M
8 F2 Burcombe Wilts
32 C11 Burcott Bucks
34 E9 Bures Essex
30 G10 Burford Oxon
39 L8 Burford Shrops
89 J7 Burg Ag & B
10 C4 Burgates Hants
11 L6 Burgess Hill W Susx
35 K6 Burgh Suffk
71 M4 Burgh by Sands Cumb
45 P8 Burgh Castle Norfk
19 M8 Burghclere Hants
100 H2 Burghead Moray
19 Q7 Burghfield W Berk
19 Q7 Burghfield Common W Berk
21 K10 Burgh Heath Surrey
39 J12 Burghill Herefs
5 M10 Burgh Island Devon
53 N9 Burgh le Marsh Lincs
45 K5 Burgh next Aylsham Norfk
52 H6 Burgh on Bain Lincs
45 P7 Burgh St Margaret Norfk
45 P10 Burgh St Peter Norfk
59 M10 Burghwallis Donc
22 E10 Burham Kent
10 C6 Buriton Hants
49 L5 Burland Ches E
3 M2 Burlawn Cnwll
29 M8 Burleigh Gloucs
16 E11 Burlescombe Devon
8 B8 Burleston Dorset
8 H6 Burley Hants
42 C7 Burley Rutlnd
49 L7 Burleydam Ches E
39 L11 Burley Gate Herefs
58 F5 Burley in Wharfedale C Brad
8 H6 Burley Street Hants
58 F5 Burley Wood Head C Brad
49 J9 Burlton Shrops
13 L4 Burmarsh Kent
30 H6 Burmington Warwks
59 N8 Burn N York
57 Q9 Burnage Manch
40 H2 Burnaston Derbys
85 P10 Burnbrae N Lans
60 E5 Burnby E R Yk
63 J3 Burneside Cumb
65 N9 Burneston N York
17 P3 Burnett BaNES
79 N6 Burnfoot Border
80 C10 Burnfoot Border
78 F9 Burnfoot D & G
79 M10 Burnfoot D & G
79 N9 Burnfoot D & G
86 B2 Burnfoot P & K
20 E7 Burnham Bucks
44 D2 Burnham Deepdale Norfk
44 D2 Burnham Market Norfk
44 D2 Burnham Norton Norfk
23 J4 Burnham-on-Crouch Essex
17 J6 Burnham-on-Sea Somset
44 D2 Burnham Overy Norfk
44 D2 Burnham Overy Staithe Norfk
44 E2 Burnham Thorpe Norfk
103 M6 Burnhaven Abers
78 E9 Burnhead D & G
102 F10 Burnhervie Abers
39 P3 Burnhill Green Staffs
73 L10 Burnhope Dur
76 G2 Burnhouse N Ayrs
67 L8 Burniston N York
57 Q3 Burnley Lancs
57 P3 Burnley Crematorium Lancs
81 K3 Burnmouth Border
85 M3 Burn of Cambus Stirlg
73 L9 Burnopfield Dur
58 D2 Burnsall N York
93 M4 Burnside Angus
93 N5 Burnside Angus
86 D1 Burnside Fife
101 J2 Burnside Moray
86 C7 Burnside W Loth
93 M8 Burnside of Duntrune Angus
86 F5 Burntisland Fife
40 D5 Burntwood Staffs
40 E6 Burntwood Green Staffs
58 G2 Burnt Yates N York
16 G11 Burnworthy Somset
20 G11 Burpham Surrey
10 G8 Burpham W Susx
81 K11 Burradon Nthumb
111 m2 Burrafirth Shet
111 k3 Burravoe Shet
64 C4 Burrells Cumb
92 H8 Burrelton P & K
7 J2 Burridge Devon
9 N5 Burridge Hants
65 M9 Burrill N York
52 B2 Burringham N Linc
15 L8 Burrington Devon
38 H7 Burrington Herefs
17 L4 Burrington N Som
33 Q6 Burrough Green Cambs
41 Q5 Burrough on the Hill Leics
63 L7 Burrow Lancs
16 C7 Burrow Somset
17 J9 Burrow Bridge Somset
20 F10 Burrowhill Surrey
26 B9 Burry Green Swans
25 Q8 Burry Port Carmth
56 H6 Burscough Lancs
57 J6 Burscough Bridge Lancs
60 D7 Bursea E R Yk
9 N5 Bursledon Hants
49 Q5 Burslem C Stke
34 H7 Burstall Suffk
7 K3 Burstock Dorset
45 J12 Burston Norfk
11 L2 Burstow Surrey
61 L8 Burstwick E R Yk
64 F9 Burtersett N York
71 Q3 Burtholme Cumb

34 C4 Burthorpe Green Suffk
43 J3 Burtoft Lincs
48 G1 Burton Ches W
49 K3 Burton Ches W
8 H8 Burton Dorset
52 D8 Burton Lincs
24 H7 Burton Pembks
16 G7 Burton Somset
18 B5 Burton Wilts
61 J2 Burton Agnes E R Yk
7 L5 Burton Bradstock Dorset
42 E5 Burton Coggles Lincs
61 K7 Burton Constable Hall E R Yk
33 N11 Burton End Essex
67 M12 Burton Fleming E R Yk
41 K9 Burton Hastings Warwks
63 K7 Burton-in-Kendal Cumb
63 K7 Burton-in-Kendal Services Cumb
63 M7 Burton in Lonsdale N York
51 N11 Burton Joyce Notts
32 C2 Burton Latimer Nhants
41 Q4 Burton Lazars Leics
59 J2 Burton Leonard N York
41 N4 Burton on the Wolds Leics
41 P7 Burton Overy Leics
42 G2 Burton Pedwardine Lincs
61 L7 Burton Pidsea E R Yk
59 L8 Burton Salmon N York
34 D10 Burton's Green Essex
60 E10 Burton upon Stather N Linc
40 G3 Burton upon Trent Staffs
52 D8 Burton Waters Lincs
57 K9 Burtonwood Warrtn
57 L9 Burtonwood Services Warrtn
49 K4 Burwardsley Ches W
39 L5 Burwarton Shrops
12 D5 Burwash E Susx
12 D5 Burwash Common E Susx
12 D5 Burwash Weald E Susx
33 P4 Burwell Cambs
53 K7 Burwell Lincs
54 F3 Burwen IoA
111 h3 Burwick Ork
57 P6 Bury Bury
43 J12 Bury Cambs
16 C10 Bury Somset
10 G7 Bury W Susx
33 M11 Bury Green Herts
34 E4 Bury St Edmunds Suffk
60 D2 Burythorpe N York
85 K10 Busby E Rens
19 J2 Buscot Oxon
95 M8 Bush Abers
39 J10 Bush Bank Herefs
40 B7 Bushbury Wolves
40 B6 Bushbury Crematorium Wolves
21 J4 Bushey Herts
21 J5 Bushey Heath Herts
21 M4 Bush Hill Park Gt Lon
29 M2 Bushley Worcs
38 H5 Bushmoor Shrops
18 F5 Bushton Wilts
29 M7 Bussage Gloucs
17 J8 Bussex Somset
17 M4 Butcombe N Som
83 Q8 Bute Ag & B
17 M9 Butleigh Somset
17 M8 Butleigh Wootton Somset
30 H4 Butlers Marston Warwks
35 N6 Butley Suffk
60 C3 Buttercrambe N York
87 P8 Butterdean Border
65 K3 Butterknowle Dur
6 D2 Butterleigh Devon
71 J11 Buttermere Cumb
58 F8 Buttershaw C Brad
92 F6 Butterstone P & K
49 P7 Butterton Staffs
50 E9 Butterton Staffs
43 L2 Butterwick Lincs
66 G11 Butterwick N York
67 L12 Butterwick N York
38 F1 Buttington Powys
39 N6 Buttonoak Shrops
34 G5 Buxhall Suffk
11 P5 Buxted E Susx
50 D6 Buxton Derbys
45 K5 Buxton Norfk
45 K6 Buxton Heath Norfk
27 N4 Bwlch Powys
48 F5 Bwlchgwyn Wrexhm
37 J8 Bwlchllan Cerdgn
46 E6 Bwlchtocyn Gwynd
48 D11 Bwlch-y-cibau Powys
38 C3 Bwlch-y-ffridd Powys
25 M2 Bwlch-y-groes Pembks
38 B7 Bwlch-y-sarnau Powys
65 L2 Byers Green Dur
31 M4 Byfield Nhants
20 G10 Byfleet Surrey
38 H12 Byford Herefs
73 M7 Byker N u Ty
55 P8 Bylchau Conwy
49 N2 Byley Ches W
72 D1 Byrness Nthumb
6 D6 Bystock Devon
32 F2 Bythorn Cambs
38 G8 Byton Herefs
73 J8 Bywell Nthumb
10 F6 Byworth W Susx

C

52 G3 Cabourne Lincs
82 G9 Cabrach Ag & B
101 M9 Cabrach Moray
63 J11 Cabus Lancs
6 C2 Cadbury Devon
85 K8 Cadder E Duns
32 F11 Caddington C Beds
79 P2 Caddonfoot Border
51 L1 Cadeby Donc
41 K7 Cadeby Leics
6 C2 Cadeleigh Devon
12 C6 Cade Street E Susx
2 G11 Cadgwith Cnwll
86 F2 Cadham Fife
57 N9 Cadishead Salfd
26 E9 Cadle Swans
57 K3 Cadley Lancs
18 H7 Cadley Wilts
19 J9 Cadley Wilts
20 C5 Cadmore End Bucks
9 K5 Cadnam Hants
52 E3 Cadney N Linc
16 F3 Cadoxton V Glam
26 G8 Cadoxton Juxta-Neath Neath
54 G8 Caeathro Gwynd
52 E5 Caenby Lincs
37 L11 Caeo Carmth
27 J9 Caerau Brdgnd
16 F2 Caerau Cardif
24 E4 Caer Farchell Pembks
54 D6 Caergeiliog IoA
48 F4 Caergwrle Flints
79 N7 Caerlanrig Border
28 D10 Caerleon Newpt
28 D10 Caerleon Roman Amphitheatre Newpt
54 F8 Caernarfon Gwynd
54 F8 Caernarfon Castle Gwynd
27 N10 Caerphilly Caerph
38 B4 Caersws Powys
36 F9 Caerwedros Cerdgn
28 F10 Caerwent Mons
48 D2 Caerwys Flints
111 b5 Cairinis W Isls
83 M5 Cairnbaan Ag & B
103 L3 Cairnbulg Abers
81 J2 Cairncross Border
84 F8 Cairncurran Inver
84 C2 Cairndow Ag & B
86 C5 Cairneyhill Fife
68 E8 Cairngarroch D & G
99 Q8 Cairngorm Mountains
101 N6 Cairnie Abers
102 H7 Cairnorrie Abers
68 E5 Cairnryan D & G
101 L5 Cairnty Moray
45 Q7 Caister-on-Sea Norfk
52 G3 Caistor Lincs
45 K8 Caistor St Edmund Norfk
111 c2 Calanais W Isls
9 M9 Calbourne IoW
48 D1 Calcot Flints
30 E11 Calcot Gloucs
19 R6 Calcot Row W Berk
101 K3 Calcots Moray
71 M7 Caldbeck Cumb
33 K5 Caldecote Cambs
42 G11 Caldecote Cambs
33 K5 Caldecote Highfields Cambs
32 E3 Caldecott Nhants
19 N2 Caldecott Oxon
42 C10 Caldecott Rutlnd
85 M9 Calderbank N Lans
62 B2 Calder Bridge Cumb
85 N9 Caldercruix N Lans
58 H10 Calder Grove Wakefd
77 L3 Caldermill S Lans
63 K11 Calder Vale Lancs
85 L11 Calderwood S Lans
25 K9 Caldey Island Pembks
28 F10 Caldicot Mons
40 D7 Caldmore Wsall
65 L5 Caldwell N York
56 a7 Calf of Man IoM
111 h1 Calfsound Ork
89 J6 Calgary Ag & B
100 G4 Califer Moray
85 P7 California Falk
45 Q7 California Norfk
41 J3 Calke Derbys
105 K10 Callakille Highld
85 K2 Callander Stirlg
111 c2 Callanish W Isls
2 H6 Callestick Cnwll
96 H8 Calligarry Highld
4 H6 Callington Cnwll
28 F2 Callow Herefs
39 Q11 Callow End Worcs
18 F4 Callow Hill Wilts
9 K5 Calmore Hants
30 D11 Calmsden Gloucs
18 E6 Calne Wilts
9 N7 Calshot Hants
5 J6 Calstock Cnwll
18 F7 Calstone Wellington Wilts
45 K4 Calthorpe Norfk
45 N5 Calthorpe Street Norfk
71 P7 Calthwaite Cumb
50 E10 Calton Staffs
49 L4 Calveley Ches E
50 G6 Calver Derbys
39 L7 Calverhall Shrops
16 C12 Calverleigh Devon
32 B8 Calverton M Keyn
51 N10 Calverton Notts
92 B3 Calvine P & K
78 H2 Calzeat Border
29 K8 Cam Gloucs
89 Q4 Camasachoirce Highld
89 P4 Camasine Highld
97 N4 Camas Luinie Highld
96 F2 Camastianavaig Highld
98 G2 Camault Muir Highld
13 J6 Camber E Susx
20 E10 Camberley Surrey
21 L7 Camberwell Gt Lon
59 N8 Camblesforth N York
72 H4 Cambo Nthumb
2 F7 Camborne Cnwll
33 K5 Cambourne Cambs
33 M5 Cambridge Cambs
29 K7 Cambridge Gloucs
33 M5 Cambridge Airport Cambs
33 L4 Cambridge City Crematorium Cambs
33 K4 Cambridge Services Cambs
2 G6 Cambrose Cnwll
85 P4 Cambus Clacks
107 M3 Cambusavie Platform Highld
85 N5 Cambusbarron Stirlg
85 N4 Cambuskenneth Stirlg
85 L10 Cambuslang S Lans
94 G3 Cambus o' May Abers
78 G2 Cambuswallace S Lans
21 L6 Camden Town Gt Lon
17 N5 Cameley BaNES
4 D4 Camelford Cnwll
85 P6 Camelon Falk
100 F8 Camerory Highld
17 P5 Camerton BaNES
70 G8 Camerton Cumb
91 N5 Camghouran P & K
80 D8 Camieston Border
95 P3 Cammachmore Abers
52 D7 Cammeringham Lincs
107 N4 Camore Highld
75 K8 Campbeltown Ag & B
75 K7 Campbeltown Airport Ag & B
78 E9 Cample D & G
93 J7 Campmuir P & K
86 C8 Camps W Loth
59 M10 Campsall Donc
35 M5 Campsea Ash Suffk
32 G8 Campton C Beds
80 F10 Camptown Border
24 G5 Camrose Pembks
92 C6 Camserney P & K
90 E2 Camusnagaul Highld
105 Q5 Camusnagaul Highld
97 J2 Camusteel Highld
97 J2 Camusterrach Highld
9 K4 Canada Hants
94 F3 Candacraig Abers
53 M9 Candlesby Lincs
78 H1 Candy Mill Border
20 B7 Cane End Oxon
22 H5 Canewdon Essex
8 F9 Canford Cliffs Poole
28 G12 Canford Crematorium Bristl
8 F8 Canford Heath Poole
110 G2 Canisbay Highld
40 H11 Canley Covtry
40 H11 Canley Crematorium Covtry
8 C3 Cann Dorset
96 B8 Canna Highld
98 D3 Cannich Highld
16 H8 Cannington Somset
21 N7 Canning Town Gt Lon
40 C5 Cannock Staffs
40 C4 Cannock Chase Staffs
28 E1 Cannon Bridge Herefs
71 N1 Canonbie D & G
39 M12 Canon Frome Herefs
39 J11 Canon Pyon Herefs
31 M4 Canons Ashby Nhants
2 D8 Canonstown Cnwll
23 M10 Canterbury Kent
23 M10 Canterbury Cathedral Kent
45 N8 Cantley Norfk
16 F2 Canton Cardif
107 N11 Cantraywood Highld
63 L7 Cantsfield Lancs
22 F6 Canvey Island Essex
52 E9 Canwick Lincs
4 F2 Canworthy Water Cnwll
90 F2 Caol Highld
111 c3 Caolas Scalpaigh W Isls
88 D6 Caoles Ag & B
97 Q10 Caonich Highld
12 D2 Capel Kent
11 J2 Capel Surrey
37 K5 Capel Bangor Cerdgn
54 F5 Capel Coch IoA
55 K9 Capel Curig Conwy
26 C5 Capel Dewi Carmth
36 G11 Capel Dewi Cerdgn
37 K4 Capel-Dewi Cerdgn
55 M9 Capel Garmon Conwy
26 E6 Capel Hendre Carmth
25 M2 Capel Iwan Carmth
13 N3 Capel le Ferne Kent
54 F4 Capel Parc IoA
35 N7 Capel St Andrew Suffk
34 H8 Capel St Mary Suffk
37 K5 Capel Seion Cerdgn
55 L6 Capelulo Conwy
48 G2 Capenhurst Ches W
73 J5 Capheaton Nthumb
84 G10 Caplaw E Rens
79 K4 Cappercleuch Border
5 Q9 Capton Devon
92 G7 Caputh P & K
85 J7 Carbeth Inn Stirlg
2 D7 Carbis Bay Cnwll
96 D4 Carbost Highld
104 F11 Carbost Highld
51 J3 Carbrook Sheff
44 F9 Carbrooke Norfk
51 Q11 Car Colston Notts
59 M11 Carcroft Donc
86 E4 Cardenden Fife
101 J6 Cardhu Moray
16 G2 Cardiff Cardif
16 E3 Cardiff Airport V Glam
27 P11 Cardiff Gate Services Cardif
27 M11 Cardiff West Services Cardif
36 C10 Cardigan Cerdgn
32 F7 Cardington Bed
39 J3 Cardington Shrops
4 D6 Cardinham Cnwll
68 F11 Cardrain D & G
79 L2 Cardrona Border
84 F7 Cardross Ag & B
68 F11 Cardryne D & G
71 J4 Cardurnock Cumb
42 E6 Careby Lincs
95 J9 Careston Angus
24 H7 Carew Pembks
24 H8 Carew Cheriton Pembks
24 H7 Carew Newton Pembks
28 G3 Carey Herefs
85 N10 Carfin N Lans
80 C4 Carfraemill Border
45 N7 Cargate Green Norfk
78 F11 Cargenbridge D & G
92 H8 Cargill P & K
71 M4 Cargo Cumb
5 J7 Cargreen Cnwll
80 H6 Carham Nthumb
16 D7 Carhampton Somset
2 G7 Carharrack Cnwll
91 P5 Carie P & K
111 b5 Carinish W Isls
9 N9 Carisbrooke IoW
62 G6 Cark Cumb
5 J7 Carkeel Cnwll
111 c2 Carlabhagh W Isls
65 L4 Carlbury Darltn
42 F7 Carlby Lincs
2 F9 Carleen Cnwll
58 C4 Carleton N York
56 G2 Carleton Crematorium Bpool
44 H8 Carleton Forehoe Norfk
44 H10 Carleton Rode Norfk
45 M9 Carleton St Peter Norfk
102 E6 Carlincraig Abers
17 Q5 Carlingcott BaNES
71 N4 Carlisle Cumb
71 P4 Carlisle Airport Cumb
71 N5 Carlisle Crematorium Cumb
86 D10 Carlops Border
111 c2 Carloway W Isls
59 J11 Carlton Barns
32 D6 Carlton Bed
33 Q6 Carlton Cambs
59 J8 Carlton Leeds
41 K6 Carlton Leics
59 N9 Carlton N York
65 J9 Carlton N York
66 E9 Carlton N York
51 N11 Carlton Notts
65 P3 Carlton S on T
35 N4 Carlton Suffk
45 Q11 Carlton Colville Suffk
41 P7 Carlton Curlieu Leics
33 Q6 Carlton Green Cambs
66 C11 Carlton Husthwaite N York
66 C6 Carlton-in-Cleveland N York
51 N4 Carlton in Lindrick Notts
52 C10 Carlton-le-Moorland Lincs
65 P10 Carlton Miniott N York
52 B10 Carlton-on-Trent Notts
42 D2 Carlton Scroop Lincs
77 P2 Carluke S Lans
77 N6 Carmacoup S Lans
25 P5 Carmarthen Carmth
26 D5 Carmel Carmth
56 D12 Carmel Flints
54 G9 Carmel Gwynd
78 F2 Carmichael S Lans
50 B10 Carmountside Crematorium C Stke
85 K10 Carmunnock C Glas
85 L9 Carmyle C Glas
93 P7 Carmyllie Angus
61 K2 Carnaby E R Yk
87 K2 Carnbee Fife
86 C2 Carnbo P & K
2 G7 Carn Brea Cnwll
102 H9 Carnbrogie Abers
97 M4 Carndu Highld
77 L3 Carnduff S Lans
76 H5 Carnell E Ayrs
63 J7 Carnforth Lancs
97 N5 Carn-gorm Highld
2 F8 Carnhell Green Cnwll
95 N2 Carnie Abers
2 G7 Carnkie Cnwll
2 G8 Carnkie Cnwll
47 Q11 Carno Powys
86 C4 Carnock Fife
3 J7 Carnon Downs Cnwll
102 E5 Carnousie Abers
93 P8 Carnoustie Angus
86 B11 Carnwath S Lans
40 H11 Carol Green Solhll
64 H9 Carperby N York
75 M5 Carradale Ag & B
99 N4 Carrbridge Highld
7 b1 Carrefour Jersey
54 E4 Carreglefn IoA
58 H8 Carr Gate Wakefd
60 D11 Carrhouse N Linc
83 N5 Carrick Ag & B
84 D4 Carrick Castle Ag & B
86 B6 Carriden Falk
86 G9 Carrington Mdloth
57 N9 Carrington Traffd
48 C6 Carrog Denbgs
85 P6 Carron Falk
101 J7 Carron Moray
78 E8 Carronbridge D & G
85 M6 Carron Bridge Stirlg
85 P6 Carronshore Falk
72 E10 Carr Shield Nthumb
70 H2 Carrutherstown D & G
84 F9 Carruth House Inver
73 N11 Carrville Dur
89 L11 Carsaig Ag & B
69 J5 Carseriggan D & G
70 G4 Carsethorn D & G
21 L9 Carshalton Gt Lon
50 G9 Carsington Derbys
75 J10 Carskey Ag & B
69 L8 Carsluith D & G
77 J11 Carsphairn D & G
77 Q3 Carstairs S Lans
77 Q3 Carstairs Junction S Lans
30 H11 Carterton Oxon
3 M5 Carthew Cnwll
65 N10 Carthorpe N York
77 P3 Cartland S Lans
62 H6 Cartmel Cumb
26 C7 Carway Carmth
29 L7 Cashe's Green Gloucs
31 L11 Cassington Oxon
73 N12 Cassop Colliery Dur
6 b2 Castel Guern
63 L6 Casterton Cumb
44 D7 Castle Acre Norfk
32 C5 Castle Ashby Nhants
111 a7 Castlebay W Isls
65 J8 Castle Bolton N York
40 F9 Castle Bromwich Solhll
42 E6 Castle Bytham Lincs
24 H3 Castlebythe Pembks
38 D2 Castle Caereinion Powys
33 P8 Castle Camps Cambs
71 Q5 Castle Carrock Cumb
85 N7 Castlecary Falk
17 P9 Castle Cary Somset
18 C5 Castle Combe Wilts
41 K3 Castle Donington Leics
70 C3 Castle Douglas D & G
18 G2 Castle Eaton Swindn
73 Q12 Castle Eden Dur
59 K8 Castleford Wakefd
39 M11 Castle Frome Herefs
40 H4 Castle Gresley Derbys
34 D9 Castle Hedingham Essex
79 K2 Castlehill Border
110 E3 Castlehill Highld
35 J7 Castle Hill Suffk
84 G7 Castlehill W Duns
68 F7 Castle Kennedy D & G
83 Q4 Castle Lachlan Ag & B
24 F8 Castlemartin Pembks
85 K10 Castlemilk C Glas
29 L2 Castlemorton Worcs
29 K2 Castlemorton Common Worcs
79 L9 Castle O'er D & G
38 H2 Castle Pulverbatch Shrops
71 L10 Castlerigg Stone Circle Cumb
43 Q5 Castle Rising Norfk
73 J10 Castleside Dur
107 M11 Castle Stuart Highld
32 B7 Castlethorpe M Keyn
79 Q10 Castleton Border
50 F4 Castleton Derbys
66 F6 Castleton N York
27 Q11 Castleton Newpt
58 B11 Castleton Rochdl
110 E3 Castletown Highld
56 b7 Castletown IoM
73 P8 Castletown Sundld
58 H5 Castley N York
44 F9 Caston Norfk
42 G9 Castor C Pete
75 N3 Catacol N Ayrs
51 K3 Catcliffe Rothm
18 E5 Catcomb Wilts
17 K8 Catcott Somset
17 K7 Catcott Burtle Somset
21 M11 Caterham Surrey
45 N6 Catfield Norfk
21 M8 Catford Gt Lon
57 J2 Catforth Lancs
85 K10 Cathcart C Glas
27 N4 Cathedine Powys
10 B7 Catherington Hants
7 K4 Catherston Leweston Dorset
9 P6 Catisfield Hants
99 J9 Catlodge Highld
33 M8 Catmere End Essex
19 M5 Catmore W Berk
63 K8 Caton Lancs
63 K8 Caton Green Lancs
77 J6 Catrine E Ayrs
12 E7 Catsfield E Susx
17 M10 Catsgore Somset
40 C11 Catshill Worcs
75 K9 Cattadale Ag & B
59 K4 Cattal N York
34 H9 Cattawade Suffk
57 J1 Catterall Lancs
65 M7 Catterick N York
65 M7 Catterick Bridge N York
71 P8 Catterlen Cumb
95 P6 Catterline Abers
59 L5 Catterton N York
10 F2 Catteshall Surrey
41 M10 Catthorpe Leics
7 N3 Cattistock Dorset
65 P11 Catton N York
72 E8 Catton Nthumb
61 J5 Catwick E R Yk
32 F3 Catworth Cambs
29 N6 Caudle Green Gloucs
31 L8 Caulcott Oxon
93 Q6 Cauldcots Angus
85 L4 Cauldhame Stirlg
80 C10 Cauldmill Border
50 E10 Cauldon Staffs
40 G4 Cauldwell Derbys
70 F4 Caulkerbush D & G
79 P11 Caulside D & G
17 P12 Caundle Marsh Dorset
51 Q8 Caunton Notts
69 K7 Causeway End D & G
34 B11 Causeway End Essex
78 G2 Causewayend S Lans
85 N4 Causewayhead Stirlg
103 K10 Causeyend Abers
73 L2 Causey Park Bridge Nthumb
34 D7 Cavendish Suffk
34 C3 Cavenham Suffk
31 M8 Caversfield Oxon
20 B8 Caversham Readg
50 C11 Caverswall Staffs
80 G8 Caverton Mill Border
100 D5 Cawdor Highld
59 M6 Cawood N York
5 J9 Cawsand Cnwll
45 J5 Cawston Norfk
58 H11 Cawthorne Barns
33 K5 Caxton Cambs
39 K7 Caynham Shrops
42 D1 Caythorpe Lincs
51 P10 Caythorpe Notts
67 M10 Cayton N York
111 a4 Ceann a Bhaigh W Isls
98 C6 Ceannacroc Lodge Highld
111 d2 Cearsiadar W Isls
28 C10 Cefn Newpt
55 N10 Cefn-brith Conwy
26 G6 Cefn-bryn-brain Carmth
27 J11 Cefn Cribwr Brdgnd
26 D6 Cefneithin Carmth
37 P10 Cefngorwydd Powys
48 F7 Cefn-mawr Wrexhm
25 L4 Cefn-y-pant Carmth
87 L2 Cellardyke Fife
50 C10 Cellarhead Staffs
54 E3 Cemaes IoA
47 N9 Cemmaes Powys
47 N9 Cemmaes Road Powys
36 E11 Cenarth Cerdgn
93 M12 Ceres Fife
7 P3 Cerne Abbas Dorset
18 F2 Cerney Wick Gloucs
55 P11 Cerrigydrudion Conwy
54 G8 Ceunant Gwynd
29 M3 Chaceley Gloucs
2 H6 Chacewater Cnwll
31 P7 Chackmore Bucks
31 L5 Chacombe Nhants
30 D5 Chadbury Worcs
58 B12 Chadderton Oldham
51 J12 Chaddesden C Derb
40 B11 Chaddesley Corbett Worcs
5 K5 Chaddlehanger Devon
19 M5 Chaddleworth W Berk
31 J9 Chadlington Oxon
31 J4 Chadshunt Warwks
42 B5 Chadwell Leics
21 P6 Chadwell Heath Gt Lon
22 D7 Chadwell St Mary Thurr
39 Q8 Chadwick Worcs
40 G11 Chadwick End Solhll
7 J2 Chaffcombe Somset
5 N3 Chagford Devon
11 N6 Chailey E Susx
12 E1 Chainhurst Kent
21 L11 Chaldon Surrey
9 N11 Chale IoW
9 N10 Chale Green IoW
20 G5 Chalfont Common Bucks
20 F5 Chalfont St Giles Bucks
20 G5 Chalfont St Peter Bucks
29 M8 Chalford Gloucs
18 C10 Chalford Wilts
19 Q2 Chalgrove Oxon
22 D8 Chalk Kent
22 H10 Chalkwell Kent
15 M4 Challacombe Devon
69 K5 Challoch D & G
23 J12 Challock Kent
32 E10 Chalton C Beds
10 B6 Chalton Hants
20 F7 Chalvey Slough
11 P8 Chalvington E Susx
20 H4 Chandler's Cross Herts
9 M4 Chandler's Ford Hants
61 J7 Chanterlands Crematorium C KuH
17 Q6 Chantry Somset
35 J7 Chantry Suffk
86 F4 Chapel Fife
58 H6 Chapel Allerton Leeds
17 K6 Chapel Allerton Somset
3 M1 Chapel Amble Cnwll

31 Q2 Chapel Brampton Nhants
49 P7 Chapel Chorlton Staffs
34 B8 Chapelend Way Essex
50 D5 Chapel-en-le-Frith Derbys
51 L3 Chapel Green Warwks
59 M8 Chapel Haddlesey N York
85 N9 Chapelhall N Lans
103 L8 Chapel Hill Abers
52 H11 Chapel Hill Lincs
28 G8 Chapel Hill Mons
59 J5 Chapel Hill N York
79 K5 Chapelhope Border
71 M2 Chapelknowe D & G
38 G6 Chapel Lawn Shrops
64 D11 Chapel le Dale N York
16 F9 Chapel Leigh Somset
102 F9 Chapel of Garioch Abers
68 F9 Chapel Rossan D & G
19 P6 Chapel Row W Berk
53 N8 Chapel St Leonards Lincs
62 G2 Chapel Stile Cumb
93 Q6 Chapelton Angus
15 K6 Chapelton Devon
77 L2 Chapelton S Lans
57 N6 Chapeltown Bl w D
101 K10 Chapeltown Moray
51 J2 Chapeltown Sheff
18 C10 Chapmanslade Wilts
4 H2 Chapmans Well Devon
33 K12 Chapmore End Herts
34 E10 Chappel Essex
7 J2 Chard Somset
7 J2 Chard Junction Somset
7 J1 Chardleigh Green Somset
7 J2 Chardstock Devon
29 J9 Charfield S Glos
23 J12 Charing Kent
13 J1 Charing Crematorium Kent
30 G6 Charingworth Gloucs
31 J9 Charlbury Oxon
17 Q3 Charlcombe BaNES
18 E5 Charlcutt Wilts
30 H3 Charlecote Warwks
40 D8 Charlemont Sandw
15 M5 Charles Devon
93 L6 Charleston Angus
95 Q2 Charlestown C Aber
58 F6 Charlestown C Brad
58 C8 Charlestown Calder
3 M5 Charlestown Cnwll
86 C5 Charlestown Fife
105 M7 Charlestown Highld
107 K11 Charlestown Highld
57 P8 Charlestown Salfd
34 G6 Charles Tye Suffk
50 D3 Charlesworth Derbys
16 H8 Charlinch Somset
93 K12 Charlottetown Fife
21 N7 Charlton Gt Lon
31 M7 Charlton Nhants
72 E4 Charlton Nthumb
19 L3 Charlton Oxon
16 H10 Charlton Somset
17 P6 Charlton Somset
10 E7 Charlton W Susx
8 D3 Charlton Wilts
18 E3 Charlton Wilts
30 D5 Charlton Worcs
49 L12 Charlton Wrekin
30 D8 Charlton Abbots Gloucs
17 M9 Charlton Adam Somset
18 G3 Charlton-All-Saints Wilts
7 P4 Charlton Down Dorset
17 P10 Charlton Horethorne Somset
29 N5 Charlton Kings Gloucs
17 M9 Charlton Mackrell Somset
8 D6 Charlton Marshall Dorset
17 Q9 Charlton Musgrove Somset
31 M10 Charlton-on-Otmoor Oxon
8 D6 Charlton on the Hill Dorset
18 G9 Charlton St Peter Wilts
10 A4 Charlwood Hants
11 K2 Charlwood Surrey
7 P4 Charminster Dorset
7 J4 Charmouth Dorset
31 P8 Charndon Bucks
19 L2 Charney Bassett Oxon
57 K6 Charnock Richard Lancs
57 K5 Charnock Richard Crematorium Lancs
57 K6 Charnock Richard Services Lancs
35 L5 Charsfield Suffk
19 P8 Charter Alley Hants
80 G5 Charterhall Border
17 M5 Charterhouse Somset
85 N5 Chartershall Stirlg
23 L11 Chartham Kent
23 L11 Chartham Hatch Kent
20 E3 Chartridge Bucks
22 F12 Chart Sutton Kent
20 C8 Charvil Wokham
31 M3 Charwelton Nhants
40 D5 Chase Terrace Staffs
40 D6 Chasetown Staffs
30 G8 Chastleton Oxon
14 F10 Chasty Devon
63 P12 Chatburn Lancs
49 P8 Chatcull Staffs
22 F9 Chatham Medway
22 E1 Chatham Green Essex
81 P8 Chathill Nthumb
50 H6 Chatsworth House Derbys
22 F8 Chattenden Medway
43 L11 Chatteris Cambs
57 P5 Chatterton Lancs
34 H8 Chattisham Suffk
80 G10 Chatto Border
81 M8 Chatton Nthumb
15 M9 Chawleigh Devon
10 B3 Chawton Hants
50 D11 Cheadle Staffs
57 Q10 Cheadle Stockp
57 Q10 Cheadle Hulme Stockp
21 K10 Cheam Gt Lon
31 Q11 Chearsley Bucks
49 Q9 Chebsey Staffs
19 Q4 Checkendon Oxon
49 N6 Checkley Ches E
50 D12 Checkley Staffs
34 D5 Chedburgh Suffk
17 L5 Cheddar Somset
32 D12 Cheddington Bucks
50 C9 Cheddleton Staffs
16 H9 Cheddon Fitzpaine Somset
45 M9 Chedgrave Norfk
7 L2 Chedington Dorset
35 M2 Chediston Suffk
30 D10 Chedworth Gloucs
17 J8 Chedzoy Somset
57 Q8 Cheetham Hill Manch
15 M9 Cheldon Devon
49 P1 Chelford Ches E
41 J2 Chellaston C Derb
32 D5 Chellington Bed
39 N5 Chelmarsh Shrops
35 K8 Chelmondiston Suffk
50 E6 Chelmorton Derbys
22 E3 Chelmsford Essex
22 E3 Chelmsford Crematorium Essex
40 F9 Chelmsley Wood Solhll
21 L7 Chelsea Gt Lon
21 P9 Chelsfield Gt Lon
34 G7 Chelsworth Suffk
29 N4 Cheltenham Gloucs
29 N4 Cheltenham Crematorium Gloucs
32 E3 Chelveston Nhants
17 L3 Chelvey N Som
17 P4 Chelwood BaNES
11 N4 Chelwood Gate E Susx
38 H5 Cheney Longville Shrops
20 G4 Chenies Bucks
28 G9 Chepstow Mons
18 F6 Cherhill Wilts
29 M8 Cherington Gloucs
30 H6 Cherington Warwks
9 P2 Cheriton Hants
13 M3 Cheriton Kent
26 B9 Cheriton Swans
5 P2 Cheriton Bishop Devon
15 P10 Cheriton Fitzpaine Devon
24 H8 Cheriton or Stackpole Elidor Pembks
49 M10 Cherrington Wrekin
60 G6 Cherry Burton E R Yk
33 M5 Cherry Hinton Cambs
39 Q10 Cherry Orchard Worcs
52 E8 Cherry Willingham Lincs
20 G9 Chertsey Surrey
31 M8 Cherwell Valley Services Oxon
8 B7 Cheselbourne Dorset
20 F3 Chesham Bucks
57 P6 Chesham Bury
20 F4 Chesham Bois Bucks
21 M3 Cheshunt Herts
7 N6 Chesil Beach Dorset
40 C6 Cheslyn Hay Staffs
40 F11 Chessetts Wood Warwks
21 J10 Chessington Gt Lon
21 J10 Chessington World of Adventures Gt Lon
48 H3 Chester Ches W
17 P7 Chesterblade Somset
48 H3 Chester Cathedral Ches W
48 H2 Chester Crematorium Ches W
51 J6 Chesterfield Derbys
51 K6 Chesterfield Crematorium Derbys
51 K8 Chesterfield Services Derbys
86 H8 Chesterhill Mdloth
73 M9 Chester-le-Street Dur
73 M10 Chester Moor Dur
80 E11 Chesters Border
80 E9 Chesters Border
49 J1 Chester Services Ches W
33 M5 Chesterton Cambs
42 G10 Chesterton Cambs
18 E1 Chesterton Gloucs
31 M9 Chesterton Oxon
39 P3 Chesterton Shrops
31 J3 Chesterton Green Warwks
72 F7 Chesterwood Nthumb
48 H2 Chester Zoo Ches W
23 L9 Chestfield Kent
5 N8 Cheston Devon
49 N9 Cheswardine Shrops
81 L5 Cheswick Nthumb
7 N2 Chetnole Dorset
43 N12 Chettisham Cambs
8 D5 Chettle Dorset
39 M4 Chetton Shrops
49 N10 Chetwynd Wrekin
49 N11 Chetwynd Aston Wrekin
34 B5 Cheveley Cambs
21 P11 Chevening Kent
34 D5 Chevington Suffk
80 G11 Cheviot Hills
16 D11 Chevithorne Devon
17 N4 Chew Magna BaNES
17 M4 Chew Stoke BaNES
17 P3 Chewton Keynsham BaNES
17 N5 Chewton Mendip Somset
32 C7 Chicheley M Keyn
10 D8 Chichester W Susx
10 E8 Chichester Crematorium W Susx
7 P6 Chickerell Dorset
8 D1 Chicklade Wilts
9 Q4 Chidden Hants
10 F3 Chiddingfold Surrey
12 B7 Chiddingly E Susx
11 P2 Chiddingstone Kent
11 Q1 Chiddingstone Causeway Kent
7 K4 Chideock Dorset
10 C8 Chidham W Susx
58 H9 Chidswell Kirk
19 M6 Chieveley W Berk
19 N6 Chieveley Services W Berk
22 D2 Chignall St James Essex
22 D2 Chignall Smealy Essex
21 N5 Chigwell Essex
21 P5 Chigwell Row Essex
19 L11 Chilbolton Hants
9 N2 Chilcomb Hants
7 M5 Chilcombe Dorset
17 P6 Chilcompton Somset
40 H5 Chilcote Leics
56 G12 Childer Thornton Ches W
8 C5 Child Okeford Dorset
19 L3 Childrey Oxon
49 M9 Child's Ercall Shrops
30 E6 Childswickham Worcs
56 H10 Childwall Lpool
7 N3 Chilfrome Dorset
10 D7 Chilgrove W Susx
23 K11 Chilham Kent
5 J4 Chillaton Devon
23 N11 Chillenden Kent
9 N10 Chillerton IoW
35 N6 Chillesford Suffk
81 M8 Chillingham Nthumb
5 Q10 Chillington Devon
7 K1 Chillington Somset
8 E2 Chilmark Wilts
13 J3 Chilmington Green Kent
30 H9 Chilson Oxon
5 J6 Chilsworthy Cnwll
14 F10 Chilsworthy Devon
20 C4 Chiltern Hills
20 F4 Chilterns Crematorium Bucks
17 M11 Chilthorne Domer Somset
31 P10 Chilton Bucks
65 M2 Chilton Dur
19 N4 Chilton Oxon
19 P11 Chilton Candover Hants
17 N10 Chilton Cantelo Somset
19 K6 Chilton Foliat Wilts
17 K7 Chilton Polden Somset
34 C7 Chilton Street Suffk
16 H8 Chilton Trinity Somset
41 L1 Chilwell Notts
9 L4 Chilworth Hants
10 G1 Chilworth Surrey
19 L1 Chimney Oxon
19 Q9 Chineham Hants
21 M5 Chingford Gt Lon
50 D4 Chinley Derbys
20 C3 Chinnor Oxon
49 N8 Chipnall Shrops
33 Q3 Chippenham Cambs
18 D6 Chippenham Wilts
20 G3 Chipperfield Herts
33 K9 Chipping Herts
63 L12 Chipping Lancs
30 F6 Chipping Campden Gloucs
30 H8 Chipping Norton Oxon
22 B3 Chipping Ongar Essex
29 K11 Chipping Sodbury S Glos
31 L5 Chipping Warden Nhants
16 E10 Chipstable Somset
21 P11 Chipstead Kent
21 L11 Chipstead Surrey
38 F3 Chirbury Shrops
48 F7 Chirk Wrexhm
81 J3 Chirnside Border
80 H3 Chirnsidebridge Border
18 F8 Chirton Wilts
19 J7 Chisbury Wilts
17 L12 Chiselborough Somset
18 H5 Chiseldon Swindn
19 P2 Chiselhampton Oxon
79 N6 Chisholme Border
21 N9 Chislehurst Gt Lon
23 N9 Chislet Kent
58 D8 Chisley Calder
21 J3 Chiswell Green Herts
21 K7 Chiswick Gt Lon
50 C3 Chisworth Derbys
10 D5 Chithurst W Susx
33 M3 Chittering Cambs
18 E11 Chitterne Wilts
15 L7 Chittlehamholt Devon
15 L7 Chittlehampton Devon
18 E7 Chittoe Wilts
5 Q11 Chivelstone Devon
15 J5 Chivenor Devon
68 F6 Chlenry D & G
20 F10 Chobham Surrey
19 J11 Cholderton Wilts
20 E3 Cholesbury Bucks
72 G6 Chollerton Nthumb
19 P4 Cholsey Oxon
39 J9 Cholstrey Herefs
66 D7 Chop Gate N York
73 M4 Choppington Nthumb
73 K8 Chopwell Gatesd
49 K5 Chorley Ches E
57 L5 Chorley Lancs
39 M5 Chorley Shrops
20 G4 Chorleywood Herts
20 G4 Chorleywood West Herts
49 N5 Chorlton Ches E
57 P9 Chorlton-cum-Hardy Manch
49 J6 Chorlton Lane Ches W
38 H5 Choulton Shrops
33 M8 Chrishall Essex
84 D7 Chrisswell Inver
43 M10 Christchurch Cambs
8 H8 Christchurch Dorset
28 D10 Christchurch Newpt
18 E5 Christian Malford Wilts
49 J3 Christleton Ches W
17 K5 Christon N Som
81 P9 Christon Bank Nthumb
5 Q4 Christow Devon
6 B6 Chudleigh Devon
6 B7 Chudleigh Knighton Devon
15 M8 Chulmleigh Devon
57 N3 Church Lancs
29 K5 Churcham Gloucs
49 N11 Church Aston Wrekin
31 Q2 Church Brampton Nhants
40 G2 Church Broughton Derbys
2 G12 Church Cove Cnwll
20 D12 Church Crookham Hants
29 M5 Churchdown Gloucs
49 Q11 Church Eaton Staffs
32 E11 Church End C Beds
32 H8 Church End C Beds
23 J5 Churchend Essex
34 C10 Church End Essex
21 K5 Church End Gt Lon
31 J8 Church Enstone Oxon
59 L6 Church Fenton N York
40 D8 Churchfield Sandw
6 G4 Church Green Devon
31 K10 Church Hanborough Oxon
66 F7 Church Houses N York
6 H3 Churchill Devon
17 L4 Churchill N Som
30 H8 Churchill Oxon
30 B4 Churchill Worcs
39 Q6 Churchill Worcs
6 G1 Churchinford Somset
8 D10 Church Knowle Dorset
41 Q8 Church Langton Leics
41 L11 Church Lawford Warwks
40 D1 Church Leigh Staffs
30 D4 Church Lench Worcs
50 F11 Church Mayfield Staffs
49 M4 Church Minshull Ches E
10 E10 Church Norton W Susx
41 L10 Churchover Warwks
39 K3 Church Preen Shrops
38 H2 Church Pulverbatch Shrops
16 G12 Churchstanton Somset
38 F4 Churchstoke Powys
5 P10 Churchstow Devon
31 N3 Church Stowe Nhants
22 E8 Church Street Kent
39 J4 Church Stretton Shrops
4 D5 Churchtown Cnwll
50 H8 Churchtown Derbys
56 d3 Churchtown IoM
63 J12 Churchtown Lancs
27 M10 Church Village Rhondd
51 M7 Church Warsop Notts
6 B10 Churston Ferrers Torbay
10 D3 Churt Surrey
48 H3 Churton Ches W
58 H8 Churwell Leeds
46 G4 Chwilog Gwynd
2 D9 Chyandour Cnwll
2 D8 Chysauster Cnwll
48 D3 Cilcain Flints
36 H8 Cilcennin Cerdgn
26 G8 Cilfrew Neath
27 M9 Cilfynydd Rhondd
36 C11 Cilgerran Pembks
26 G7 Cilmaengwyn Neath
38 B11 Cilmery Powys
26 E4 Cilsan Carmth
47 P4 Ciltalgarth Gwynd
37 M11 Cilycwm Carmth
26 G9 Cimla Neath
28 H6 Cinderford Gloucs
20 F7 Cippenham Slough
18 F1 Cirencester Gloucs
21 M7 City Gt Lon
21 N7 City Airport Gt Lon
21 N6 City of London Crematorium Gt Lon
88 F5 Clabhach Ag & B
84 B6 Clachaig Ag & B
83 L10 Clachan Ag & B
89 Q11 Clachan Ag & B
90 B7 Clachan Ag & B
96 G3 Clachan Highld
111 b4 Clachan-a-Luib W Isls
88 C6 Clachan Mor Ag & B
111 b4 Clachan na Luib W Isls
85 K7 Clachan of Campsie E Duns
89 Q11 Clachan-Seil Ag & B
107 K11 Clachnaharry Highld
108 B9 Clachtoll Highld
94 C8 Clackavoid P & K
21 N11 Clacket Lane Services Surrey
85 Q5 Clackmannan Clacks
101 K4 Clackmarras Moray
23 M1 Clacton-on-Sea Essex
90 F11 Cladich Ag & B
30 D3 Cladswell Worcs
89 P6 Claggan Highld
104 C10 Claigan Highld
10 B6 Clanfield Hants
19 K1 Clanfield Oxon
19 K10 Clanville Hants
17 P9 Clanville Somset
83 N10 Claonaig Ag & B
33 M10 Clapgate Herts
32 E6 Clapham Bed
21 L8 Clapham Gt Lon
63 N8 Clapham N York
10 H8 Clapham W Susx
7 K2 Clapton Somset
17 P5 Clapton Somset
17 L2 Clapton-in-Gordano N Som
30 F9 Clapton-on-the-Hill Gloucs
73 K7 Claravale Gatesd
25 J5 Clarbeston Pembks
24 H5 Clarbeston Road Pembks
51 Q4 Clarborough Notts
34 C7 Clare Suffk
70 C3 Clarebrand D & G
70 H2 Clarencefield D & G
80 C9 Clarilaw Border
85 J10 Clarkston E Rens
107 M5 Clashmore Highld
108 B9 Clashmore Highld
108 B9 Clashnessie Highld
101 J10 Clashnoir Moray
92 E10 Clathy P & K
92 F10 Clathymore P & K
102 C9 Clatt Abers
38 B4 Clatter Powys
16 E9 Clatworthy Somset
57 K1 Claughton Lancs
63 K8 Claughton Lancs
56 F10 Claughton Wirral
30 G2 Claverdon Warwks
17 L3 Claverham N Som
33 M9 Clavering Essex
39 P4 Claverley Shrops
18 B7 Claverton BaNES
27 M12 Clawdd-coch V Glam
48 C5 Clawdd-newydd Denbgs
14 F11 Clawton Devon
52 G5 Claxby Lincs
59 P3 Claxton N York
45 M9 Claxton Norfk
41 L9 Claybrooke Magna Leics
41 N11 Clay Coton Nhants
51 K8 Clay Cross Derbys
31 L4 Claydon Oxon
35 J6 Claydon Suffk
79 N11 Claygate D & G
12 E2 Claygate Kent
21 J10 Claygate Surrey
21 N5 Clayhall Gt Lon
16 D10 Clayhanger Devon
16 F11 Clayhidon Devon
12 G5 Clayhill E Susx
110 D4 Clayock Highld
29 K7 Claypits Gloucs
42 C1 Claypole Lincs
58 E7 Clayton C Brad
59 L11 Clayton Donc
11 L7 Clayton W Susx
57 N3 Clayton-le-Moors Lancs
57 K4 Clayton-le-Woods Lancs
58 H11 Clayton West Kirk
51 Q4 Clayworth Notts
96 F11 Cleadale Highld
73 P8 Cleadon S Tyne
5 L7 Clearbrook Devon
28 G7 Clearwell Gloucs
65 M5 Cleasby N York
111 h3 Cleat Ork
65 K4 Cleatlam Dur
70 G11 Cleator Cumb
70 G11 Cleator Moor Cumb
58 F8 Cleckheaton Kirk
39 L7 Cleehill Shrops
85 M10 Cleekhimin N Lans
39 K5 Clee St Margaret Shrops
53 K2 Cleethorpes NE Lin
39 L6 Cleeton St Mary Shrops
17 L3 Cleeve N Som
19 Q5 Cleeve Oxon
29 N4 Cleeve Hill Gloucs
30 E4 Cleeve Prior Worcs
87 L5 Cleghornie E Loth
28 E2 Clehonger Herefs
86 C3 Cleish P & K
85 N10 Cleland N Lans
90 C9 Clenamacrie Ag & B
43 P6 Clenchwarton Norfk
102 G3 Clenerty Abers
40 B10 Clent Worcs
39 M7 Cleobury Mortimer Shrops
39 L5 Cleobury North Shrops
75 K5 Cleongart Ag & B
107 N11 Clephanton Highld
79 L8 Clerkhill D & G
78 D8 Cleuch-head D & G
18 F6 Clevancy Wilts
17 K2 Clevedon N Som
62 G12 Cleveleys Lancs
18 E4 Cleverton Wilts
17 L6 Clewer Somset
44 H2 Cley next the Sea Norfk
64 B3 Cliburn Cumb
19 Q10 Cliddesden Hants
22 E7 Cliffe Medway
59 P7 Cliffe N York
12 H7 Cliff End E Susx
22 E8 Cliffe Woods Medway
38 E11 Clifford Herefs
59 K5 Clifford Leeds
30 G4 Clifford Chambers Warwks
29 J4 Clifford's Mesne Gloucs
17 N2 Clifton Bristl
32 G8 Clifton C Beds
41 M1 Clifton C Nott
59 N4 Clifton C York
58 F9 Clifton Calder
71 Q9 Clifton Cumb
50 F11 Clifton Derbys
15 K4 Clifton Devon
51 M2 Clifton Donc
57 J3 Clifton Lancs
58 F5 Clifton N York
31 L7 Clifton Oxon
39 Q11 Clifton Worcs
40 G5 Clifton Campville Staffs
19 P2 Clifton Hampden Oxon
32 C6 Clifton Reynes M Keyn
41 M11 Clifton upon Dunsmore Warwks
39 N9 Clifton upon Teme Worcs
23 Q8 Cliftonville Kent
10 F9 Climping W Susx
18 B10 Clink Somset
58 H3 Clint N York
102 H11 Clinterty C Aber
44 G7 Clint Green Norfk
80 E7 Clintmains Border
45 N7 Clippesby Norfk
42 D6 Clipsham Rutlnd
41 Q10 Clipston Nhants
41 N1 Clipston Notts
32 D10 Clipstone C Beds
51 N8 Clipstone Notts
57 N1 Clitheroe Lancs
49 K9 Clive Shrops
52 F3 Clixby Lincs
29 N10 Cloatley Wilts
48 C5 Clocaenog Denbgs
101 M3 Clochan Moray
28 C4 Clodock Herefs
103 K6 Clola Abers
32 F8 Clophill C Beds
32 F1 Clopton Nhants
35 K6 Clopton Suffk
35 K6 Clopton Corner Suffk
6 c1 Clos du Valle Guern
78 E9 Closeburn D & G
78 E9 Closeburnmill D & G
7 N2 Closworth Somset
33 J9 Clothall Herts
49 K3 Clotton Ches W
58 B9 Clough Foot Calder
58 E9 Clough Head Calder
67 L8 Cloughton N York
111 k4 Clousta Shet
94 F7 Clova Angus
14 F7 Clovelly Devon
79 P2 Clovenfords Border
90 D4 Clovulin Highld
51 L6 Clowne Derbys
39 N7 Clows Top Worcs
97 Q7 Cluanie Inn Highld
97 Q7 Cluanie Lodge Highld
69 J7 Clugston D & G
38 F6 Clun Shrops
100 D6 Clunas Highld
38 G6 Clunbury Shrops
25 K5 Clunderwen Carmth
99 L4 Clune Highld
98 B10 Clunes Highld
38 H6 Clungunford Shrops
92 G6 Clunie P & K
38 G6 Clunton Shrops
86 F3 Cluny Fife
17 N4 Clutton BaNES
49 J5 Clutton Ches W
17 P4 Clutton Hill BaNES
27 P6 Clydach Mons
26 F8 Clydach Swans
27 K9 Clydach Vale Rhondd
84 H8 Clydebank W Duns
18 F5 Clyffe Pypard Wilts
84 D6 Clynder Ag & B
26 H8 Clyne Neath
54 E10 Clynnog-fawr Gwynd
38 E12 Clyro Powys
6 D4 Clyst Honiton Devon
6 D3 Clyst Hydon Devon
6 D5 Clyst St George Devon
6 D3 Clyst St Lawrence Devon
6 C5 Clyst St Mary Devon
111 d2 Cnoc W Isls
37 L5 Cnwch Coch Cerdgn
4 G5 Coad's Green Cnwll
78 D2 Coalburn S Lans
73 K8 Coalburns Gatesd
29 K8 Coaley Gloucs
22 F4 Coalhill Essex
29 J11 Coalpit Heath S Glos
39 M2 Coalport Wrekin
85 Q4 Coalsnaughton Clacks
86 G3 Coaltown of Balgonie Fife
86 G3 Coaltown of Wemyss Fife
41 K5 Coalville Leics
72 C8 Coanwood Nthumb
17 L11 Coat Somset
85 M9 Coatbridge N Lans
85 M9 Coatdyke N Lans
18 H4 Coate Swindn
18 F8 Coate Wilts
43 K9 Coates Cambs
29 N8 Coates Gloucs
52 C6 Coates Lincs
10 F6 Coates W Susx

15 K6 Cobbaton Devon
29 N5 Coberley Gloucs
22 D9 Cobham Kent
20 H10 Cobham Surrey
20 H11 Cobham Services Surrey
39 J9 Cobnash Herefs
6 b1 Cobo Guern
103 J3 Coburby Abers
33 J6 Cockayne Hatley C Beds
101 K12 Cock Bridge Abers
87 P7 Cockburnspath Border
22 F3 Cock Clarks Essex
86 H7 Cockenzie and Port Seton E Loth
63 J10 Cockerham Lancs
71 J9 Cockermouth Cumb
32 G11 Cockernhoe Herts
26 E9 Cockett Swans
65 K3 Cockfield Dur
34 E6 Cockfield Suffk
21 L4 Cockfosters Gt Lon
34 B11 Cock Green Essex
10 E6 Cocking W Susx
10 E6 Cocking Causeway W Susx
6 B9 Cockington Torbay
17 L6 Cocklake Somset
44 D8 Cockley Cley Norfk
12 G6 Cock Marling E Susx
20 C7 Cockpole Green Wokham
48 H9 Cockshutt Shrops
44 G2 Cockthorpe Norfk
6 D6 Cockwood Devon
50 D5 Cockyard Derbys
35 J6 Coddenham Suffk
29 J1 Coddington Herefs
52 B11 Coddington Notts
18 E11 Codford St Mary Wilts
18 E11 Codford St Peter Wilts
32 H11 Codicote Herts
10 G6 Codmore Hill W Susx
51 K10 Codnor Derbys
29 K11 Codrington S Glos
39 Q2 Codsall Staffs
39 Q2 Codsall Wood Staffs
48 F5 Coedpoeth Wrexhm
48 F4 Coed Talon Flints
28 D8 Coed-y-paen Mons
6 B8 Coffinswell Devon
6 C6 Cofton Devon
40 D11 Cofton Hackett Worcs
16 G2 Cogan V Glam
32 B5 Cogenhoe Nhants
34 E11 Coggeshall Essex
99 K5 Coignafearn Highld
94 E3 Coilacriech Abers
85 K2 Coilantogle Stirlg
96 D3 Coillore Highld
27 K11 Coity Brdgnd
111 d2 Col W Isls
107 J1 Colaboll Highld
3 K4 Colan Cnwll
6 E5 Colaton Raleigh Devon
104 B11 Colbost Highld
65 L7 Colburn N York
64 C4 Colby Cumb
56 b6 Colby IoM
34 G10 Colchester Essex
34 G11 Colchester Crematorium Essex
19 N6 Cold Ash W Berk
41 P11 Cold Ashby Nhants
17 Q2 Cold Ashton S Glos
30 F9 Cold Aston Gloucs
109 L4 Coldbackie Highld
32 D6 Cold Brayfield M Keyn
11 M8 Coldean Br & H
5 Q5 Coldeast Devon
58 C8 Colden Calder
9 N3 Colden Common Hants
52 E6 Cold Hanworth Lincs
11 J2 Coldharbour Surrey
31 P4 Cold Higham Nhants
81 J2 Coldingham Border
66 D10 Cold Kirby N York
49 Q8 Coldmeece Staffs
22 G4 Cold Norton Essex
42 B7 Cold Overton Leics
13 P1 Coldred Kent
15 M10 Coldridge Devon
80 H6 Coldstream Border
10 G6 Coldwaltham W Susx
28 E2 Coldwell Herefs
103 K7 Coldwells Abers
17 P9 Cole Somset
38 G5 Colebatch Shrops
6 D2 Colebrook Devon
15 N11 Colebrooke Devon
52 D10 Coleby Lincs
60 F9 Coleby N Linc
15 N11 Coleford Devon
28 G6 Coleford Gloucs
17 P6 Coleford Somset
45 K11 Colegate End Norfk
8 F7 Colehill Dorset
11 N4 Coleman's Hatch E Susx
48 H8 Colemere Shrops
10 B4 Colemore Hants
92 G9 Colenden P & K
18 B6 Colerne Wilts
30 D10 Colesbourne Gloucs
20 F4 Coleshill Bucks
19 J3 Coleshill Oxon
40 G9 Coleshill Warwks
17 N5 Coley BaNES
11 K4 Colgate W Susx
87 J2 Colinsburgh Fife
86 E8 Colinton C Edin
83 Q7 Colintraive Ag & B
44 F5 Colkirk Norfk
88 F5 Coll Ag & B
93 J8 Collace P & K
111 k3 Collafirth Shet
88 E5 Coll Airport Ag & B
5 P11 Collaton Devon
6 B10 Collaton St Mary Torbay
100 H3 College of Roseisle Moray
20 D10 College Town Br For
93 K11 Collessie Fife
21 P5 Collier Row Gt Lon
33 L11 Collier's End Herts
12 E2 Collier Street Kent
103 L9 Collieston Abers
70 G1 Collin D & G
19 J9 Collingbourne Ducis Wilts
19 J9 Collingbourne Kingston Wilts
59 K5 Collingham Leeds
52 B10 Collingham Notts
39 M9 Collington Herefs
31 Q3 Collingtree Nhants
57 K9 Collins Green Warrtn
93 Q6 Colliston Angus
6 E2 Colliton Devon
42 E9 Collyweston Nhants
68 F2 Colmonell S Ayrs
32 F5 Colmworth Bed
20 G7 Colnbrook Slough
33 L2 Colne Cambs
58 B6 Colne Lancs
34 E10 Colne Engaine Essex
45 K8 Colney Norfk
21 K3 Colney Heath Herts
30 E11 Coln Rogers Gloucs
30 F12 Coln St Aldwyns Gloucs
30 E11 Coln St Dennis Gloucs
82 E4 Colonsay Ag & B
82 E5 Colonsay Airport Ag & B
102 E8 Colpy Abers
79 M1 Colquhar Border
42 D5 Colsterworth Lincs
41 P2 Colston Bassett Notts
100 H3 Coltfield Moray
45 L6 Coltishall Norfk
62 G5 Colton Cumb
59 J7 Colton Leeds
59 M5 Colton N York
44 H7 Colton Norfk
40 D4 Colton Staffs
12 D2 Colt's Hill Kent
70 E5 Colvend D & G
29 K1 Colwall Herefs
72 G6 Colwell Nthumb
40 D4 Colwich Staffs
16 C2 Colwinston V Glam
10 E9 Colworth W Susx
55 M6 Colwyn Bay Conwy
6 H4 Colyford Devon
6 H4 Colyton Devon
31 K10 Combe Oxon
19 L8 Combe W Berk
18 B8 Combe Down BaNES
6 A9 Combe Fishacre Devon
16 F9 Combe Florey Somset
17 Q4 Combe Hay BaNES
6 B8 Combeinteignhead Devon
15 K3 Combe Martin Devon
6 F3 Combe Raleigh Devon
57 M12 Comberbach Ches W
40 F6 Comberford Staffs
33 L5 Comberton Cambs
39 J8 Comberton Herefs
7 J1 Combe St Nicholas Somset
30 H4 Combrook Warwks
50 D5 Combs Derbys
34 H5 Combs Suffk
34 H5 Combs Ford Suffk
16 H7 Combwich Somset
95 L1 Comers Abers
39 Q8 Comhampton Worcs
47 N10 Commins Coch Powys
66 F5 Commondale N York
70 G10 Common End Cumb
4 F6 Common Moor Cnwll
50 C3 Compstall Stockp
69 P8 Compstonend D & G
6 B9 Compton Devon
9 M3 Compton Hants
39 P5 Compton Staffs
10 F1 Compton Surrey
19 N5 Compton W Berk
10 C7 Compton W Susx
18 G9 Compton Wilts
8 C4 Compton Abbas Dorset
30 D10 Compton Abdale Gloucs
18 F6 Compton Bassett Wilts
19 J4 Compton Beauchamp Oxon
17 K5 Compton Bishop Somset
8 F2 Compton Chamberlayne Wilts
17 P4 Compton Dando BaNES
17 L9 Compton Dundon Somset
17 K11 Compton Durville Somset
28 G11 Compton Greenfield S Glos
17 M5 Compton Martin BaNES
17 P10 Compton Pauncefoot Somset
7 N4 Compton Valence Dorset
86 B4 Comrie Fife
92 B10 Comrie P & K
90 E3 Conaglen House Highld
97 M4 Conchra Highld
92 G6 Concraigie P & K
29 N2 Conderton Worcs
30 F8 Condicote Gloucs
85 M8 Condorrat N Lans
39 J2 Condover Shrops
29 L5 Coney Hill Gloucs
10 H5 Coneyhurst Common W Susx
66 G12 Coneysthorpe N York
34 F2 Coney Weston Suffk
41 J6 Congerstone Leics
44 B5 Congham Norfk
49 Q3 Congleton Ches E
17 L4 Congresbury N Som
70 G2 Conheath D & G
100 F5 Conicavel Moray
52 H11 Coningsby Lincs
33 K4 Conington Cambs
42 H11 Conington Cambs
51 L2 Conisbrough Donc
53 L4 Conisholme Lincs
62 F3 Coniston Cumb
61 K7 Coniston E R Yk
58 B3 Coniston Cold N York
58 C1 Conistone N York
48 F2 Connah's Quay Flints
90 C9 Connel Ag & B
77 K8 Connel Park E Ayrs
2 E7 Connor Downs Cnwll
107 J10 Conon Bridge Highld
58 C5 Cononley N York
50 C10 Consall Staffs
73 K10 Consett Dur
65 L8 Constable Burton N York
57 P4 Constable Lee Lancs
2 G9 Constantine Cnwll
3 K2 Constantine Bay Cnwll
106 G10 Contin Highld
55 L6 Conwy Conwy
33 K3 Conyer's Green Suffk
12 E8 Cooden E Susx
14 G10 Cookbury Devon
20 E6 Cookham W & M
20 D6 Cookham Dean W & M
20 E6 Cookham Rise W & M
30 D3 Cookhill Worcs
35 M2 Cookley Suffk
39 Q6 Cookley Worcs
20 B5 Cookley Green Oxon
95 P4 Cookney Abers
35 K11 Cook's Green Essex
34 G6 Cooks Green Suffk
22 D3 Cooksmill Green Essex
10 H5 Coolham W Susx
22 F8 Cooling Medway
3 L5 Coombe Cnwll
6 C7 Coombe Devon
6 E4 Coombe Devon
29 K9 Coombe Gloucs
9 Q4 Coombe Hants
8 G3 Coombe Bissett Wilts
6 B8 Coombe Cellars Devon
29 M4 Coombe Hill Gloucs
8 C9 Coombe Keynes Dorset
6 C9 Coombe Pafford Torbay
11 J8 Coombes W Susx
38 G9 Coombes-Moor Herefs
21 P3 Coopersale Common Essex
35 J8 Copdock Suffk
34 F11 Copford Green Essex
59 J2 Copgrove N York
111 k3 Copister Shet
32 F7 Cople Bed
65 J3 Copley Dur
59 M5 Copmanthorpe C York
49 P9 Copmere End Staffs
56 H2 Copp Lancs
40 B4 Coppenhall Staffs
2 E8 Copperhouse Cnwll
32 G2 Coppingford Cambs
15 N10 Copplestone Devon
57 K6 Coppull Lancs
11 J5 Copsale W Susx
57 M3 Copster Green Lancs
41 L9 Copston Magna Warwks
23 P10 Cop Street Kent
65 N12 Copt Hewick N York
11 L3 Copthorne W Susx
41 L5 Copt Oak Leics
9 K5 Copythorne Hants
22 C6 Corbets Tey Gt Lon
7 a2 Corbiere Jersey
72 H7 Corbridge Nthumb
42 C11 Corby Nhants
42 E5 Corby Glen Lincs
75 Q6 Cordon N Ayrs
39 L7 Coreley Shrops
16 G11 Corfe Somset
8 E10 Corfe Castle Dorset
8 E8 Corfe Mullen Dorset
39 J5 Corfton Shrops
94 E1 Corgarff Abers
9 Q4 Corhampton Hants
40 H9 Corley Warwks
40 H9 Corley Services Warwks
94 E8 Cormuir Angus
34 E8 Cornard Tye Suffk
65 N1 Cornforth Dur
102 D4 Cornhill Abers
81 J6 Cornhill-on-Tweed Nthumb
58 B8 Cornholme Calder
88 C7 Cornoigmore Ag & B
73 K11 Cornsay Dur
73 L11 Cornsay Colliery Dur
107 J10 Corntown Highld
27 J12 Corntown V Glam
30 H8 Cornwell Oxon
5 M8 Cornwood Devon
5 Q8 Cornworthy Devon
90 F2 Corpach Highld
45 J4 Corpusty Norfk
94 H2 Corrachree Abers
90 D4 Corran Highld
97 M7 Corran Highld
79 K10 Corrie D & G
75 Q4 Corrie N Ayrs
75 P7 Corriecravie N Ayrs
75 Q5 Corriegills N Ayrs
98 C9 Corriegour Lodge Hotel Highld
106 F9 Corriemoille Highld
98 E3 Corrimony Highld
52 C5 Corringham Lincs
22 E6 Corringham Thurr
47 M9 Corris Gwynd
47 M9 Corris Uchaf Gwynd
84 D3 Corrow Ag & B
96 H5 Corry Highld
15 L11 Corscombe Devon
7 M2 Corscombe Dorset
29 K3 Corse Gloucs
29 L3 Corse Lawn Gloucs
18 C6 Corsham Wilts
102 F12 Corsindae Abers
18 C10 Corsley Wilts
18 B10 Corsley Heath Wilts
78 C12 Corsock D & G
17 Q3 Corston BaNES
18 D4 Corston Wilts
86 E7 Corstorphine C Edin
94 F9 Cortachy Angus
45 Q10 Corton Suffk
18 D11 Corton Wilts
17 P10 Corton Denham Somset
90 E3 Coruanan Highld
48 C6 Corwen Denbgs
5 K4 Coryton Devon
22 E6 Coryton Thurr
41 M8 Cosby Leics
40 C8 Coseley Dudley
32 B8 Cosgrove Nhants
9 Q6 Cosham C Port
24 H7 Cosheston Pembks
92 B6 Coshieville P & K
51 L11 Cossall Notts
41 N5 Cossington Leics
17 J7 Cossington Somset
45 K7 Costessey Norfk
41 M3 Costock Notts
42 B6 Coston Leics
44 H8 Coston Norfk
19 L1 Cote Oxon
49 L3 Cotebrook Ches W
71 P5 Cotehill Cumb
41 M4 Cotes Leics
41 M10 Cotesbach Leics
16 G9 Cotford St Luke Somset
41 N1 Cotgrave Notts
102 H11 Cothal Abers
42 B1 Cotham Notts
64 H4 Cotherstone Dur
19 M2 Cothill Oxon
6 G3 Cotleigh Devon
51 L11 Cotmanhay Derbys
33 L5 Coton Cambs
41 P12 Coton Nhants
49 P10 Coton Staffs
49 Q10 Coton Clanford Staffs
49 J11 Coton Hill Shrops
40 G4 Coton in the Elms Derbys
30 C11 Cotswolds
5 Q7 Cott Devon
57 J3 Cottam Lancs
52 B7 Cottam Notts
33 M4 Cottenham Cambs
33 K10 Cottered Herts
42 F11 Cotterstock Nhants
41 P11 Cottesbrooke Nhants
42 C7 Cottesmore Rutlnd
60 H7 Cottingham E R Yk
42 B11 Cottingham Nhants
58 E6 Cottingley C Brad
58 H7 Cottingley Hall Crematorium Leeds
31 N7 Cottisford Oxon
34 H4 Cotton Suffk
101 P9 Cottown Abers
102 G11 Cottown Abers
102 H7 Cottown of Gight Abers
5 J7 Cotts Devon
30 E3 Coughton Warwks
83 K9 Coulaghailtro Ag & B
97 N1 Coulags Highld
94 H2 Coull Abers
84 D5 Coulport Ag & B
21 L10 Coulsdon Gt Lon
18 D9 Coulston Wilts
78 G3 Coulter S Lans
66 E11 Coulton N York
93 L10 Coultra Fife
39 K2 Cound Shrops
65 M2 Coundon Dur
64 G9 Countersett N York
6 C5 Countess Wear Devon
41 N8 Countesthorpe Leics
15 M3 Countisbury Devon
93 J7 Coupar Angus P & K
81 K7 Coupland Nthumb
75 M3 Cour Ag & B
97 J9 Courteachan Highld
31 Q4 Courteenhall Nhants
26 D4 Court Henry Carmth
23 K5 Courtsend Essex
16 G8 Courtway Somset
86 H8 Cousland Mdloth
12 D4 Cousley Wood E Susx
84 D6 Cove Ag & B
87 P7 Cove Border
16 C11 Cove Devon
20 D11 Cove Hants
105 M4 Cove Highld
95 Q2 Cove Bay C Aber
35 Q1 Covehithe Suffk
40 B6 Coven Staffs
33 M1 Coveney Cambs
53 K5 Covenham St Bartholomew Lincs
53 K5 Covenham St Mary Lincs
41 J10 Coventry Covtry
41 J11 Coventry Airport Warwks
2 H11 Coverack Cnwll
2 G9 Coverack Bridges Cnwll
65 K9 Coverham N York
32 F3 Covington Cambs
78 F2 Covington S Lans
63 L7 Cowan Bridge Lancs
12 C7 Cowbeech E Susx
43 J6 Cowbit Lincs
16 D2 Cowbridge V Glam
11 P3 Cowden Kent
86 D4 Cowdenbeath Fife
50 H10 Cowers Lane Derbys
9 N8 Cowes IoW
66 C9 Cowesby N York
11 K5 Cowfold W Susx
28 H9 Cowhill S Glos
85 P5 Cowie Stirlg
60 G2 Cowlam E R Yk
6 B4 Cowley Devon
29 N6 Cowley Gloucs
20 G7 Cowley Gt Lon
31 M12 Cowley Oxon
57 L5 Cowling Lancs
58 C5 Cowling N York
65 M9 Cowling N York
34 B6 Cowlinge Suffk
73 N5 Cowpen Nthumb
10 B7 Cowplain Hants
72 F11 Cowshill Dur
17 L4 Cowslip Green N Som
59 K4 Cowthorpe N York
49 M7 Coxbank Ches E
51 J11 Coxbench Derbys
14 C11 Coxford Cnwll
44 E4 Coxford Norfk
22 E12 Coxheath Kent
65 N1 Coxhoe Dur
17 M7 Coxley Somset
17 M7 Coxley Wick Somset
22 C4 Coxtie Green Essex
66 D11 Coxwold N York
27 K11 Coychurch Brdgnd
27 K11 Coychurch Crematorium Brdgnd
76 G7 Coylton S Ayrs
99 N6 Coylumbridge Highld
27 J10 Coytrahen Brdgnd
30 D2 Crabbs Cross Worcs
11 K5 Crabtree W Susx
64 C3 Crackenthorpe Cumb
14 C11 Crackington Haven Cnwll
49 N12 Crackleybank Shrops
58 C3 Cracoe N York
6 E1 Craddock Devon
40 C9 Cradley Dudley
39 N11 Cradley Herefs
40 C9 Cradley Heath Sandw
27 L3 Cradoc Powys
4 H9 Crafthole Cnwll
100 F9 Craggan Highld
73 L10 Craghead Dur
27 J4 Crai Powys
101 P4 Craibstone Moray
93 N6 Craichie Angus
95 L10 Craig Angus
105 Q11 Craig Highld
77 K8 Craigbank E Ayrs
86 F10 Craigburn Border
79 M10 Craigcleuch D & G
102 H8 Craigdam Abers
83 M2 Craigdhu Ag & B
102 F11 Craigearn Abers
101 K6 Craigellachie Moray
92 G10 Craigend P & K
84 H8 Craigend Rens
84 E6 Craigendoran Ag & B
84 G9 Craigends Rens
69 J6 Craighlaw D & G
82 G9 Craighouse Ag & B
92 G7 Craigie P & K
76 G5 Craigie S Ayrs
103 J3 Craigiefold Abers
70 C4 Craigley D & G
26 G7 Craig Llangiwg Neath
86 E7 Craiglockhart C Edin
86 G7 Craigmillar C Edin
78 C10 Craigneston D & G
85 N10 Craigneuk N Lans
85 N9 Craigneuk N Lans
89 P8 Craignure Ag & B
95 L8 Craigo Angus
93 L12 Craigrothie Fife
91 M11 Craigruie Stirlg
93 N7 Craigton Angus
95 N2 Craigton C Aber
84 H11 Craigton E Rens
93 K5 Craigton of Airlie Angus
87 L1 Crail Fife
80 F8 Crailing Border
51 Q2 Craiselound N Linc
65 M9 Crakehall N York
60 C2 Crambe N York
73 M5 Cramlington Nthumb
86 E7 Cramond C Edin
86 E7 Cramond Bridge C Edin
49 N2 Cranage Ches E
49 P8 Cranberry Staffs
8 F5 Cranborne Dorset
20 E8 Cranbourne Br For
12 F3 Cranbrook Kent
32 D8 Cranfield C Beds
20 H7 Cranford Gt Lon
32 D2 Cranford St Andrew Nhants
32 D2 Cranford St John Nhants
29 M6 Cranham Gloucs
57 J8 Crank St Hel
10 G3 Cranleigh Surrey
17 P7 Cranmore Somset
41 Q8 Cranoe Leics
35 M4 Cransford Suffk
87 N9 Cranshaws Border
2 H4 Crantock Cnwll
52 E12 Cranwell Lincs
44 C10 Cranwich Norfk
44 G8 Cranworth Norfk
83 M2 Craobh Haven Ag & B
83 Q4 Crarae Ag & B
109 J10 Crask Inn Highld
98 F1 Crask of Aigas Highld
81 Q9 Craster Nthumb
35 M2 Cratfield Suffk
95 M3 Crathes Abers
95 M3 Crathes Castle Abers
94 E3 Crathie Abers
98 H9 Crathie Highld
66 B6 Crathorne N York
38 H5 Craven Arms Shrops
73 K8 Crawcrook Gatesd
78 F5 Crawford S Lans
78 E4 Crawfordjohn S Lans
9 M1 Crawley Hants
31 J10 Crawley Oxon
11 L3 Crawley W Susx
11 M3 Crawley Down W Susx
57 P4 Crawshawbooth Lancs
95 P6 Crawton Abers
64 G10 Cray N York
21 P8 Crayford Gt Lon
66 D12 Crayke N York
22 E5 Crays Hill Essex
15 P8 Creacombe Devon
90 D7 Creagan Inn Ag & B
111 b5 Creag Ghoraidh W Isls
111 b5 Creagorry W Isls
91 J3 Creaguaineach Lodge Highld
41 P12 Creaton Nhants
71 K2 Creca D & G
39 J12 Credenhill Herefs
15 P11 Crediton Devon
69 J4 Creebank D & G
69 K6 Creebridge D & G
16 H10 Creech Heathfield Somset
16 H10 Creech St Michael Somset
3 L6 Creed Cnwll
21 P7 Creekmouth Gt Lon
34 H5 Creeting St Mary Suffk
42 E6 Creeton Lincs
69 L7 Creetown D & G
56 a7 Cregneash IoM
93 K10 Creich Fife
27 M11 Creigiau Cardif
5 K9 Cremyll Cnwll
39 L2 Cressage Shrops
50 F6 Cressbrook Derbys
25 J7 Cresselly Pembks
20 D5 Cressex Bucks
34 D11 Cressing Essex
73 N3 Cresswell Nthumb
25 J7 Cresswell Pembks
50 C11 Cresswell Staffs
51 M6 Creswell Derbys
35 K5 Cretingham Suffk
83 K9 Cretshengan Ag & B
49 N4 Crewe Ches E
48 H5 Crewe Ches W
49 N4 Crewe Crematorium Ches E
49 N5 Crewe Green Ches E
48 G11 Crew Green Powys
7 L2 Crewkerne Somset
41 J2 Crewton C Derb
91 K10 Crianlarich Stirlg
36 H9 Cribyn Cerdgn
46 H4 Criccieth Gwynd
51 J9 Crich Derbys
86 H9 Crichton Mdloth
41 N11 Crick Nhants
27 M1 Crickadarn Powys
7 K2 Cricket St Thomas Somset
27 P5 Crickhowell Powys
18 G3 Cricklade Wilts
21 K6 Cricklewood Gt Lon
92 C10 Crieff P & K
48 F11 Criggion Powys
58 H10 Crigglestone Wakefd
103 L4 Crimond Abers
43 Q8 Crimplesham Norfk
30 G5 Crimscote Warwks
98 F2 Crinaglack Highld
83 L4 Crinan Ag & B
85 N10 Crindledyke N Lans
45 K8 Cringleford Norfk
25 K6 Crinow Pembks
99 J4 Croachy Highld
21 P9 Crockenhill Kent
20 B6 Crocker End Oxon
5 P2 Crockernwell Devon
18 C11 Crockerton Wilts
70 D2 Crocketford D & G
21 N12 Crockham Hill Kent
27 J9 Croeserw Neath
24 E3 Croes-goch Pembks
36 F10 Croes-lan Cerdgn
47 K3 Croesor Gwynd
25 P5 Croesyceiliog Carmth
28 C9 Croesyceiliog Torfn
41 L8 Croft Leics
53 N10 Croft Lincs
57 L9 Croft Warrtn
84 H6 Croftamie Stirlg
59 J9 Crofton Wakefd
65 M5 Croft-on-Tees N York

106 C5 Croftown Highld
101 K5 Crofts Moray
101 L4 Crofts of Dipple Moray
103 L4 Crofts of Savoch Abers
26 C9 Crofty Swans
89 P10 Croggan Ag & B
71 R6 Croglin Cumb
106 H4 Croick Highld
107 N8 Cromarty Highld
86 C5 Crombie Fife
100 G9 Cromdale Highld
33 J10 Cromer Herts
45 K2 Cromer Norfk
50 H9 Cromford Derbys
29 J10 Cromhall S Glos
111 d2 Cromor W Isls
52 B10 Cromwell Notts
77 K6 Cronberry E Ayrs
10 C1 Crondall Hants
57 J10 Cronton Knows
63 J3 Crook Cumb
65 L1 Crook Dur
76 H4 Crookedholm E Ayrs
81 J6 Crookham Nthumb
19 P7 Crookham W Berk
20 C11 Crookham Village Hants
78 H4 Crook Inn Border
63 K5 Crooklands Cumb
86 C3 Crook of Devon P & K
31 L5 Cropredy Oxon
41 M5 Cropston Leics
30 D5 Cropthorne Worcs
66 G9 Cropton N York
41 P1 Cropwell Bishop Notts
51 P12 Cropwell Butler Notts
111 e1 Cros W Isls
111 d2 Crosbost W Isls
70 H7 Crosby Cumb
56 c5 Crosby IoM
60 F10 Crosby N Linc
56 G8 Crosby Sefton
63 N1 Crosby Garret Cumb
64 B5 Crosby Ravensworth Cumb
17 N7 Croscombe Somset
17 K5 Cross Somset
75 M3 Crossaig Ag & B
88 C7 Crossapoll Ag & B
28 E5 Cross Ash Mons
12 F2 Cross-at-Hand Kent
70 H7 Crosscanonby Cumb
45 K3 Crossdale Street Norfk
58 E6 Cross Flatts C Brad
86 C5 Crossford Fife
77 N3 Crossford S Lans
86 H8 Crossgatehall E Loth
76 F3 Crossgates E Ayrs
86 D5 Crossgates Fife
59 J7 Cross Gates Leeds
67 M10 Crossgates N York
63 K9 Crossgill Lancs
59 J7 Cross Green Leeds
34 E5 Cross Green Suffk
34 G6 Cross Green Suffk
26 D6 Cross Hands Carmth
76 H5 Crosshands E Ayrs
86 E3 Crosshill Fife
76 F9 Crosshill S Ayrs
76 G4 Crosshouse E Ayrs
39 K1 Cross Houses Shrops
12 C6 Cross in Hand E Susx
36 F8 Cross Inn Cerdgn
84 F6 Cross Keys Ag & B
27 P9 Crosskeys Caerph
110 B2 Crosskirk Highld
9 N9 Cross Lane IoW
39 N3 Cross Lane Head Shrops
84 G9 Crosslee Rens
70 C3 Crossmichael D & G
102 G8 Cross of Jackston Abers
50 H10 Cross o' th' hands Derbys
95 J1 Crossroads Abers
95 M3 Crossroads Abers
35 K2 Cross Street Suffk
93 N5 Crosston Angus
57 N12 Cross Town Ches E
39 Q8 Crossway Green Worcs
8 B9 Crossways Dorset
25 K2 Crosswell Pembks
62 H4 Crosthwaite Cumb
57 J5 Croston Lancs
45 L7 Crostwick Norfk
21 L6 Crouch End Gt Lon
8 F3 Croucheston Wilts
7 Q1 Crouch Hill Dorset
31 M7 Croughton Nhants
102 G3 Crovie Abers
2 F8 Crowan Cnwll
11 P4 Crowborough E Susx
16 F8 Crowcombe Somset
50 E7 Crowdecote Derbys
50 E2 Crowden Derbys
58 F12 Crow Edge Barns
20 C4 Crowell Oxon
35 J5 Crowfield Suffk
87 N7 Crowhill E Loth
28 H4 Crow Hill Herefs
12 F7 Crowhurst E Susx
11 M1 Crowhurst Surrey
43 J7 Crowland Lincs
34 G3 Crowland Suffk
2 D8 Crowlas Cnwll
60 D10 Crowle N Linc
30 B3 Crowle Worcs
30 B3 Crowle Green Worcs
19 Q3 Crowmarsh Gifford Oxon
35 L3 Crown Corner Suffk
5 K8 Crownhill C Plym
32 B8 Crownhill Crematorium M Keyn
44 H9 Crownthorpe Norfk
2 F9 Crowntown Cnwll
2 B9 Crows-an-Wra Cnwll
20 D9 Crowthorne Wokham
49 L1 Crowton Ches W
73 M12 Croxdale Dur
50 E11 Croxden Staffs
20 H4 Croxley Green Herts
33 J5 Croxton Cambs
61 J10 Croxton N Linc
44 E11 Croxton Norfk
44 G4 Croxton Norfk
49 P8 Croxton Staffs
42 B4 Croxton Kerrial Leics
107 N11 Croy Highld
85 M7 Croy N Lans
14 H4 Croyde Devon
33 K6 Croydon Cambs
21 L9 Croydon Gt Lon
21 L9 Croydon Crematorium Gt Lon
99 K10 Crubenmore Highld
38 H1 Cruckmeole Shrops
48 H12 Cruckton Shrops
103 M7 Cruden Bay Abers
49 L11 Crudgington Wrekin
29 N9 Crudwell Wilts
27 P8 Crumlin Caerph
4 F9 Crumplehorn Cnwll
57 Q8 Crumpsall Manch
13 K1 Crundale Kent
25 L6 Crunwear Pembks
19 M9 Crux Easton Hants
26 C6 Crwbin Carmth
20 E4 Cryers Hill Bucks
25 L2 Crymmych Pembks
26 H7 Crynant Neath
21 M8 Crystal Palace Gt Lon
105 K10 Cuaig Highld
89 P12 Cuan Ag & B
31 J1 Cubbington Warwks
2 H4 Cubert Cnwll
32 B11 Cublington Bucks
28 E2 Cublington Herefs
11 L5 Cuckfield W Susx
17 R10 Cucklington Somset
51 M6 Cuckney Notts
31 N12 Cuddesdon Oxon
31 Q11 Cuddington Bucks
49 L2 Cuddington Ches W
49 J6 Cuddington Heath Ches W
21 N10 Cudham Gt Lon
5 L4 Cudliptown Devon
8 F7 Cudnell Bmouth
59 K11 Cudworth Barns
7 K1 Cudworth Somset
21 L3 Cuffley Herts
90 D5 Cuil Highld
107 K9 Culbokie Highld
98 G1 Culburnie Highld
107 L12 Culcabock Highld
100 D5 Culcharry Highld
57 M9 Culcheth Warrtn
101 P8 Culdrain Abers
97 K2 Culduie Highld
34 D3 Culford Suffk
64 B2 Culgaith Cumb
19 N2 Culham Oxon
108 B8 Culkein Highld
108 C8 Culkein Drumbeg Highld
29 N9 Culkerton Gloucs
101 P2 Cullen Moray
73 P6 Cullercoats N Tyne
95 M2 Cullerlie Abers
107 K9 Cullicudden Highld
58 E6 Cullingworth C Brad
96 F5 Cuillin Hills Highld
83 L1 Cullipool Ag & B
111 k2 Cullivoe Shet
107 M12 Culloden Highld
6 D2 Cullompton Devon
6 D2 Cullompton Services Devon
16 F12 Culm Davy Devon
39 J6 Culmington Shrops
16 E12 Culmstock Devon
106 A2 Culnacraig Highld
70 C5 Culnaightrie D & G
104 G9 Culnaknock Highld
107 J4 Culrain Highld
86 B5 Culross Fife
76 F8 Culroy S Ayrs
102 E8 Culsalmond Abers
69 L8 Culscadden D & G
69 J8 Culshabbin D & G
111 j4 Culswick Shet
103 J9 Cultercullen Abers
95 P2 Cults C Aber
22 D10 Culverstone Green Kent
42 E3 Culverthorpe Lincs
31 M5 Culworth Nhants
76 D8 Culzean Castle & Country Park S Ayrs
85 M7 Cumbernauld N Lans
85 M7 Cumbernauld Village N Lans
53 N8 Cumberworth Lincs
102 G5 Cuminestown Abers
80 G3 Cumledge Border
71 N5 Cummersdale Cumb
71 J3 Cummertrees D & G
100 H2 Cummingston Moray
77 J7 Cumnock E Ayrs
31 L12 Cumnor Oxon
71 Q5 Cumrew Cumb
78 H10 Cumrue D & G
71 P5 Cumwhinton Cumb
71 Q5 Cumwhitton Cumb
65 Q11 Cundall N York
76 F3 Cunninghamhead N Ayrs
111 k4 Cunningsburgh Shet
93 L11 Cupar Fife
93 L11 Cupar Muir Fife
50 G6 Curbar Derbys
9 N5 Curbridge Hants
31 J11 Curbridge Oxon
9 N5 Curdridge Hants
40 F8 Curdworth Warwks
16 H11 Curland Somset
19 N6 Curridge W Berk
86 E8 Currie C Edin
17 J10 Curry Mallet Somset
17 K10 Curry Rivel Somset
12 E3 Curtisden Green Kent
5 P9 Curtisknowle Devon
2 G10 Cury Cnwll
102 C11 Cushnie Abers
69 L11 Cutcloy D & G
16 C8 Cutcombe Somset
107 M5 Cuthill Highld
39 Q8 Cutnall Green Worcs
30 E7 Cutsdean Gloucs
51 J6 Cutthorpe Derbys
19 Q2 Cuxham Oxon
22 E9 Cuxton Medway
52 G4 Cuxwold Lincs
56 C12 Cwm Denbgs
26 G9 Cwmafan Neath
27 L8 Cwmaman Rhondd
25 M4 Cwmbach Carmth
27 N2 Cwmbach Powys
27 L8 Cwmbach Rhondd
38 B10 Cwmbach Llechrhyd Powys
28 C9 Cwmbran Torfn
27 P9 Cwmcarn Caerph
28 F7 Cwmcarvan Mons
36 E11 Cwm-cou Cerdgn
27 N5 Cwm Crawnon Powys
27 L7 Cwmdare Rhondd
27 P4 Cwmdu Powys
26 E9 Cwmdu Swans
25 P3 Cwmduad Carmth
27 J10 Cwmfelin Brdgnd
27 M8 Cwmfelin Myr Td
25 L5 Cwmfelin Boeth Carmth
27 P9 Cwmfelinfach Caerph
25 P5 Cwmffrwd Carmth
26 H6 Cwmgiedd Powys
26 F6 Cwmgorse Carmth
26 D6 Cwmgwili Carmth
25 N2 Cwmhiraeth Carmth
47 N9 Cwm Llinau Powys
26 G6 Cwmllynfell Neath
26 D6 Cwmmawr Carmth
27 K9 Cwmparc Rhondd
25 N2 Cwmpengraig Carmth
27 P7 Cwmtillery Blae G
26 G6 Cwm-twrch Isaf Powys
26 G6 Cwm-twrch Uchaf Powys
54 H8 Cwm-y-glo Gwynd
37 N6 Cwmystwyth Cerdgn
36 H10 Cwrt-newydd Cerdgn
26 G7 Cylibebyll Neath
27 J9 Cymer Neath
27 L10 Cymmer Rhondd
37 N11 Cynghordy Carmth
26 H9 Cynonville Neath
48 C7 Cynwyd Denbgs
25 P4 Cynwyl Elfed Carmth

D

6 B8 Daccombe Devon
71 P9 Dacre Cumb
58 F3 Dacre N York
58 G2 Dacre Banks N York
72 F12 Daddry Shield Dur
31 P6 Dadford Bucks
41 K7 Dadlington Leics
21 P6 Dagenham Gt Lon
30 C12 Daglingworth Gloucs
32 E12 Dagnall Bucks
76 E10 Dailly S Ayrs
93 M11 Dairsie Fife
111 a6 Dalabrog W Isls
83 P1 Dalavich Ag & B
70 D4 Dalbeattie D & G
56 b5 Dalby IoM
66 F12 Dalby N York
92 E5 Dalcapon P & K
107 Q2 Dalchalm Highld
98 D6 Dalchreichart Highld
91 Q11 Dalchruin P & K
92 F9 Dalcrue P & K
6 E6 Dalditch Devon
51 K12 Dale Derbys
24 E7 Dale Pembks
89 P3 Dalelia Highld
76 E3 Dalgarven N Ayrs
86 E5 Dalgety Bay Fife
77 J8 Dalgig E Ayrs
92 B10 Dalginross P & K
92 E6 Dalguise P & K
109 Q5 Dalhalvaig Highld
34 C4 Dalham Suffk
111 a6 Daliburgh W Isls
86 G8 Dalkeith Mdloth
100 H5 Dallas Moray
35 L6 Dallinghoo Suffk
12 D6 Dallington E Susx
31 Q2 Dallington Nhants
90 G10 Dalmally Ag & B
85 J4 Dalmary Stirlg
76 H9 Dalmellington E Ayrs
86 D6 Dalmeny C Edin
107 L8 Dalmore Highld
84 H8 Dalmuir W Duns
89 P3 Dalnabreck Highld
91 Q3 Dalnacardoch P & K
99 M5 Dalnahaitnach Highld
91 P2 Dalnaspidal P & K
110 B7 Dalnawillan Lodge Highld
92 B4 Daloist P & K
86 C2 Dalqueich P & K
76 F11 Dalquhairn S Ayrs
107 M1 Dalreavoch Lodge Highld
76 E2 Dalry N Ayrs
76 F8 Dalrymple E Ayrs
77 N2 Dalserf S Lans
75 J9 Dalsmeran Ag & B
71 M5 Dalston Cumb
21 M6 Dalston Gt Lon
78 F10 Dalswinton D & G
70 H2 Dalton D & G
65 K6 Dalton N York
66 B11 Dalton N York
73 K6 Dalton Nthumb
62 E7 Dalton-in-Furness Cumb
73 P10 Dalton-le-Dale Dur
65 N6 Dalton-on-Tees N York
66 C2 Dalton Piercy Hartpl
91 P10 Dalveich Stirlg
99 J11 Dalwhinnie Highld
6 H3 Dalwood Devon
8 G4 Damerham Hants
45 N8 Damgate Norfk
22 F3 Danbury Essex
66 G6 Danby N York
65 N7 Danby Wiske N York
101 K6 Dandaleith Moray
86 G8 Danderhall Mdloth
50 C7 Danebridge Ches E
33 K11 Dane End Herts
11 N5 Danehill E Susx
41 M6 Dane Hills C Leic
23 K11 Dane Street Kent
102 F4 Danshillock Abers
87 L8 Danskine E Loth
22 C8 Darenth Kent
57 L11 Daresbury Halton
59 K12 Darfield Barns
23 L10 Dargate Kent
4 G6 Darite Cnwll
40 C7 Darlaston Wsall
40 C7 Darlaston Green Wsall
58 G3 Darley N York
51 J12 Darley Abbey C Derb
50 H8 Darley Bridge Derbys
50 H7 Darley Dale Derbys
40 F11 Darley Green Solhll
32 G11 Darleyhall Herts
58 G3 Darley Head N York
30 G6 Darlingscott Warwks
65 M5 Darlington Darltn
65 M5 Darlington Crematorium Darltn
51 Q6 Darlton Notts
80 D7 Darnick Border
47 N10 Darowen Powys
102 F6 Darra Abers
14 E8 Darracott Devon
14 H4 Darracott Devon
73 K6 Darras Hall Nthumb
59 L9 Darrington Wakefd
35 N3 Darsham Suffk
17 N7 Darshill Somset
22 B8 Dartford Kent
5 Q7 Dartington Devon
5 N4 Dartmoor National Park Devon
6 B11 Dartmouth Devon
58 H11 Darton Barns
77 J4 Darvel E Ayrs
57 M4 Darwen Bl w D
20 F7 Datchet W & M
33 J11 Datchworth Herts
57 M7 Daubhill Bolton
101 K7 Daugh of Kinermony Moray
18 E4 Dauntsey Wilts
100 F7 Dava Highld
49 M2 Davenham Ches W
31 M2 Daventry Nhants
86 E7 Davidson's Mains C Edin
4 E3 Davidstow Cnwll
79 K8 Davington D & G
23 J10 Davington Hill Kent
102 G9 Daviot Abers
99 K2 Daviot Highld
99 K2 Daviot House Highld
101 N5 Davoch of Grange Moray
11 K1 Dawesgreen Surrey
39 M1 Dawley Wrekin
6 C7 Dawlish Devon
6 D7 Dawlish Warren Devon
51 M10 Daybrook Notts
30 G8 Daylesford Gloucs
23 Q11 Deal Kent
70 H9 Dean Cumb
5 P7 Dean Devon
15 M3 Dean Devon
9 P4 Dean Hants
31 J9 Dean Oxon
17 P7 Dean Somset
22 C9 Dean Bottom Kent
79 N6 Deanburnhaugh Border
5 P7 Deancombe Devon
31 L11 Dean Court Oxon
57 M7 Deane Bolton
19 P10 Deane Hants
58 D10 Deanhead Kirk
8 E4 Deanland Dorset
5 P7 Dean Prior Devon
72 E8 Deanraw Nthumb
86 B8 Deans W Loth
70 H9 Deanscales Cumb
31 Q6 Deanshanger Nhants
101 L5 Deanshaugh Moray
85 M3 Deanston Stirlg
70 H8 Dearham Cumb
35 L6 Debach Suffk
21 N4 Debden Essex
33 N9 Debden Essex
35 K4 Debenham Suffk
39 P11 Deblin's Green Worcs
86 C7 Dechmont W Loth
86 B8 Dechmont Road W Loth
31 L7 Deddington Oxon
34 H9 Dedham Essex
20 F8 Dedworth W & M
42 D10 Deene Nhants
42 D10 Deenethorpe Nhants
50 H2 Deepcar Sheff
42 G8 Deeping Gate C Pete
42 G8 Deeping St James Lincs
42 H7 Deeping St Nicholas Lincs
29 M3 Deerhurst Gloucs
30 B5 Defford Worcs
27 K4 Defynnog Powys
55 L6 Deganwy Conwy
83 L1 Degnish Ag & B
59 N5 Deighton C York
65 P7 Deighton N York
54 H8 Deiniolen Gwynd
4 D4 Delabole Cnwll
49 K2 Delamere Ches W
103 K10 Delfrigs Abers
100 G8 Dellefure Highld
10 D9 Dell Quay W Susx
100 H11 Delnabo Moray
101 J8 Delnashaugh Inn Moray
107 M7 Delny Highld
58 C11 Delph Oldham
73 K10 Delves Dur
42 E3 Dembleby Lincs
51 L2 Denaby Donc
48 C3 Denbigh Denbgs
93 L11 Denbrae Fife
5 Q6 Denbury Devon
51 K10 Denby Derbys
58 G11 Denby Dale Kirk
19 L3 Denchworth Oxon
62 E7 Dendron Cumb
92 E11 Denfield P & K
32 E2 Denford Nhants
23 J3 Dengie Essex
20 G6 Denham Bucks
34 C5 Denham Suffk
35 K2 Denham Suffk
20 G6 Denham Green Bucks
103 K5 Denhead Abers
93 N11 Denhead Fife
93 L8 Denhead of Gray C Dund
80 D9 Denholm Border
58 E7 Denholme C Brad
9 Q5 Denmead Hants
103 K11 Denmore C Aber
35 L4 Dennington Suffk
85 N6 Denny Falk
85 N7 Dennyloanhead Falk
93 K11 Den of Lindores Fife
58 C11 Denshaw Oldham
95 N3 Denside Abers
13 N2 Densole Kent
34 C6 Denston Suffk
50 E11 Denstone Staffs
23 L10 Denstroude Kent
63 N5 Dent Cumb
42 G11 Denton Cambs
65 L4 Denton Darltn
11 P9 Denton E Susx
13 N1 Denton Kent
42 C4 Denton Lincs
58 F4 Denton N York
32 B5 Denton Nhants
45 L11 Denton Norfk
50 B2 Denton Tamesd
43 P9 Denver Norfk
81 P10 Denwick Nthumb
44 H9 Deopham Norfk
44 H9 Deopham Green Norfk
34 C5 Depden Suffk
21 M7 Deptford Gt Lon
18 E12 Deptford Wilts
41 J1 Derby C Derb
15 K5 Derby Devon
56 b7 Derbyhaven IoM
41 K2 Derby Services Derbys
41 K2 Derby South Services Derbys
92 D5 Derculich P & K
44 G7 Dereham Norfk
27 N8 Deri Caerph
23 M12 Derringstone Kent
40 B3 Derrington Staffs
18 E6 Derry Hill Wilts
52 B2 Derrythorpe N Linc
44 B4 Dersingham Norfk
89 J6 Dervaig Ag & B
48 C5 Derwen Denbgs
47 L10 Derwenlas Powys
71 L10 Derwent Water Cumb
42 B12 Desborough Nhants
41 L6 Desford Leics
101 P3 Deskford Moray
22 F10 Detling Kent
28 F8 Devauden Mons
37 M5 Devil's Bridge Cerdgn
18 E8 Devizes Wilts
5 K8 Devonport C Plym
85 Q4 Devonside Clacks
2 H7 Devoran Cnwll
86 H9 Dewarton Mdloth
8 B7 Dewlish Dorset
58 G9 Dewsbury Kirk
58 G9 Dewsbury Moor Crematorium Kirk
48 E11 Deytheur Powys
11 J6 Dial Post W Susx
9 L6 Dibden Hants
9 M6 Dibden Purlieu Hants
35 J1 Dickleburgh Norfk
30 D7 Didbrook Gloucs
19 N3 Didcot Oxon
19 N3 Didcot Railway Centre Oxon
32 H4 Diddington Cambs
39 K5 Diddlebury Shrops
10 D6 Didling W Susx
18 B4 Didmarton Gloucs
57 Q9 Didsbury Manch
52 F11 Digby Lincs
104 F8 Digg Highld
58 D11 Diggle Oldham
57 J7 Digmoor Lancs
36 H9 Dihewyd Cerdgn
45 M5 Dilham Norfk
50 C11 Dilhorne Staffs
57 N3 Dill Hall Lancs
32 G4 Dillington Cambs
72 H8 Dilston Nthumb
18 C10 Dilton Wilts
18 C10 Dilton Marsh Wilts
38 H10 Dilwyn Herefs
46 E4 Dinas Gwynd
24 H2 Dinas Pembks
47 P8 Dinas-Mawddwy Gwynd
16 F2 Dinas Powys V Glam
17 N7 Dinder Somset
28 G2 Dinedor Herefs
28 E6 Dingestow Mons
56 G10 Dingle Lpool
41 Q9 Dingley Nhants
107 J9 Dingwall Highld
94 H3 Dinnet Abers
73 L6 Dinnington N u Ty
51 M4 Dinnington Rothm
17 K12 Dinnington Somset
54 H8 Dinorwic Gwynd
31 Q11 Dinton Bucks
8 E2 Dinton Wilts
78 H10 Dinwoodie D & G
14 F8 Dinworthy Devon
16 G10 Dipford Somset
75 M5 Dippen Ag & B
75 Q7 Dippen N Ayrs
5 J4 Dippertown Devon
101 L4 Dipple Moray
76 D10 Dipple S Ayrs
5 P8 Diptford Devon
73 K9 Dipton Dur
87 K5 Dirleton E Loth
72 F10 Dirt Pot Nthumb
41 L3 Diseworth Leics
65 P11 Dishforth N York
50 C4 Disley Ches E
35 J1 Diss Norfk
70 G10 Distington Cumb
70 G10 Distington Hall Crematorium Cumb
8 G2 Ditchampton Wilts
17 P8 Ditcheat Somset
45 M11 Ditchingham Norfk
11 M7 Ditchling E Susx
49 J11 Ditherington Shrops
18 B6 Ditteridge Wilts
6 B10 Dittisham Devon
57 J10 Ditton Halton
22 E10 Ditton Kent
33 Q5 Ditton Green Cambs
39 L4 Ditton Priors Shrops
28 F6 Dixton Mons
58 C11 Dobcross Oldham
4 F7 Dobwalls Cnwll
5 Q3 Doccombe Devon
99 J2 Dochgarroch Highld
44 C3 Docking Norfk
39 K10 Docklow Herefs
71 N10 Dockray Cumb
22 C4 Doddinghurst Essex
43 L11 Doddington Cambs
22 H11 Doddington Kent
52 C9 Doddington Lincs
81 L7 Doddington Nthumb
39 L6 Doddington Shrops
6 B5 Doddiscombsleigh Devon
49 L6 Dodd's Green Ches E
31 N3 Dodford Nhants
40 C11 Dodford Worcs
29 K11 Dodington S Glos
16 G7 Dodington Somset
48 G4 Dodleston Ches W
84 H11 Dodside E Rens
40 D1 Dod's Leigh Staffs
58 H12 Dodworth Barns
52 H11 Dogdyke Lincs
20 C11 Dogmersfield Hants
48 C11 Dolanog Powys
46 H3 Dolbenmaen Gwynd
47 P10 Dolfach Powys
38 C5 Dolfor Powys
55 L7 Dolgarrog Conwy
47 M7 Dolgellau Gwynd
107 P2 Doll Highld
85 Q4 Dollar Clacks
85 Q4 Dollarfield Clacks
48 E2 Dolphin Flints
63 K10 Dolphinholme Lancs
86 D11 Dolphinton S Lans
15 K9 Dolton Devon
55 N6 Dolwen Conwy
55 K10 Dolwyddelan Conwy
48 F10 Domgay Powys
59 M12 Doncaster Donc
59 P11 Doncaster North Services Donc
8 D3 Donhead St Andrew Wilts
8 D3 Donhead St Mary Wilts
86 E5 Donibristle Fife
16 E7 Doniford Somset
42 H3 Donington Lincs

52 H7 Donington on Bain Lincs
41 L3 Donington Park Services Leics
40 H5 Donisthorpe Leics
30 F8 Donnington Gloucs
39 L1 Donnington Shrops
19 M7 Donnington W Berk
10 D9 Donnington W Susx
49 N11 Donnington Wrekin
49 N11 Donnington Wood Wrekin
17 J12 Donyatt Somset
76 F7 Doonfoot S Ayrs
76 F7 Doonholm S Ayrs
100 G11 Dorback Lodge Highld
7 Q5 Dorchester Dorset
19 P2 Dorchester Oxon
40 H7 Dordon Warwks
50 H5 Dore Sheff
98 H3 Dores Highld
21 J12 Dorking Surrey
11 N2 Dormans Land Surrey
28 G2 Dormington Herefs
30 C3 Dormston Worcs
20 E7 Dorney Bucks
97 M5 Dornie Highld
107 N4 Dornoch Highld
71 K3 Dornock D & G
110 C5 Dorrery Highld
40 F11 Dorridge Solhll
52 F11 Dorrington Lincs
39 J2 Dorrington Shrops
49 N7 Dorrington Shrops
30 F4 Dorsington Warwks
28 C1 Dorstone Herefs
31 P10 Dorton Bucks
56 d6 Douglas IoM
78 D3 Douglas S Lans
93 M8 Douglas and Angus C Dund
56 d5 Douglas Borough Crematorium IoM
84 D3 Douglas Pier Ag & B
93 M6 Douglastown Angus
78 E2 Douglas Water S Lans
78 D3 Douglas West S Lans
17 P7 Doulting Somset
111 g2 Dounby Ork
106 G3 Doune Highld
85 M3 Doune Stirlg
76 D11 Dounepark S Ayrs
107 J4 Dounie Highld
5 L6 Dousland Devon
50 E5 Dove Holes Derbys
70 H8 Dovenby Cumb
13 P2 Dover Kent
13 P2 Dover Castle Kent
35 L9 Dovercourt Essex
39 Q8 Doverdale Worcs
40 E1 Doveridge Derbys
11 K1 Doversgreen Surrey
92 E6 Dowally P & K
30 D9 Dowdeswell Gloucs
27 M7 Dowlais Myr Td
15 K9 Dowland Devon
7 K1 Dowlish Wake Somset
18 G2 Down Ampney Gloucs
4 G9 Downderry Cnwll
21 N10 Downe Gt Lon
29 L8 Downend Gloucs
28 H12 Downend S Glos
93 L8 Downfield C Dund
4 H5 Downgate Cnwll
22 E4 Downham Essex
21 M8 Downham Gt Lon
63 P12 Downham Lancs
43 P9 Downham Market Norfk
29 M4 Down Hatherley Gloucs
17 N10 Downhead Somset
17 Q7 Downhead Somset
92 G9 Downhill P & K
65 K7 Downholme N York
95 Q3 Downies Abers
20 D4 Downley Bucks
15 M10 Down St Mary Devon
11 M8 Downs Crematorium Br & H
20 H10 Downside Surrey
5 K9 Down Thomas Devon
9 J8 Downton Hants
8 H3 Downton Wilts
42 G4 Dowsby Lincs
17 Q2 Doynton S Glos
27 P10 Draethen Caerph
77 N3 Draffan S Lans
51 P3 Drakeholes Notts
76 E2 Drakemyre N Ayrs
30 B4 Drakes Broughton Worcs
58 D4 Draughton N York
41 Q11 Draughton Nhants
59 P8 Drax N York
41 K12 Draycote Warwks
41 K2 Draycott Derbys
30 F7 Draycott Gloucs
17 L6 Draycott Somset
40 F2 Draycott in the Clay Staffs
50 C11 Draycott in the Moors Staffs
9 R6 Drayton C Port
42 B10 Drayton Leics
45 K7 Drayton Norfk
19 N2 Drayton Oxon
31 K6 Drayton Oxon
17 K10 Drayton Somset
40 B11 Drayton Worcs
40 G7 Drayton Bassett Staffs
20 E2 Drayton Beauchamp Bucks
40 G7 Drayton Manor Park Staffs
32 B10 Drayton Parslow Bucks
19 P2 Drayton St Leonard Oxon
24 G6 Dreen Hill Pembks
25 N2 Drefach Carmth
26 D6 Drefach Carmth
36 H10 Drefach Cerdgn
76 F4 Dreghorn N Ayrs
13 N2 Drellingore Kent
87 K6 Drem E Loth
5 P2 Drewsteignton Devon
60 H3 Driffield E R Yk
18 F2 Driffield Gloucs
2 C9 Drift Cnwll
62 C3 Drigg Cumb
58 G8 Drighlington Leeds
89 L5 Drimnin Highld
7 K2 Drimpton Dorset
90 C1 Drimsallie Highld
59 N4 Dringhouses C York
34 F5 Drinkstone Suffk
34 F5 Drinkstone Green Suffk
40 D3 Drointon Staffs
30 B2 Droitwich Worcs
92 H11 Dron P & K
51 J5 Dronfield Derbys
76 H7 Drongan E Ayrs
93 L8 Dronley Angus
7 Q2 Droop Dorset
9 Q4 Droxford Hants
50 B2 Droylsden Tamesd
48 B6 Druid Denbgs
24 F5 Druidston Pembks
90 E3 Druimarbin Highld
90 D7 Druimavuic Ag & B
83 L8 Druimdrishaig Ag & B
97 J11 Druimindarroch Highld
83 P7 Drum Ag & B
86 C3 Drum P & K
78 E2 Drumalbin S Lans
108 C8 Drumbeg Highld
102 D7 Drumblade Abers
68 E9 Drumbreddon D & G
97 K4 Drumbuie Highld
71 L4 Drumburgh Cumb
70 E5 Drumburn D & G
85 J8 Drumchapel C Glas
91 Q5 Drumchastle P & K
77 L4 Drumclog S Lans
87 J2 Drumeldrie Fife
79 J3 Drumelzier Border
97 J6 Drumfearn Highld
95 M3 Drumfrennie Abers
93 M5 Drumgley Angus
99 L8 Drumguish Highld
101 J8 Drumin Moray
77 J10 Drumjohn D & G
68 H4 Drumlamford S Ayrs
95 K2 Drumlasie Abers
71 L5 Drumleaning Cumb
75 K8 Drumlemble Ag & B
95 N6 Drumlithie Abers
69 K9 Drummoddie D & G
68 F10 Drummore D & G
101 M6 Drummuir Moray
98 G3 Drumnadrochit Highld
68 F11 Drumnaglaur D & G
102 C5 Drumnagorrach Moray
78 E11 Drumpark D & G
106 C2 Drumrunie Lodge Highld
76 E8 Drumshang S Ayrs
104 F11 Drumuie Highld
99 P5 Drumuillie Highld
85 L3 Drumvaich Stirlg
86 D1 Drunzie P & K
64 C5 Drybeck Cumb
101 N3 Drybridge Moray
76 F4 Drybridge N Ayrs
28 H5 Drybrook Gloucs
80 D7 Dryburgh Border
42 C2 Dry Doddington Lincs
33 L4 Dry Drayton Cambs
84 H5 Drymen Stirlg
103 J6 Drymuir Abers
96 E4 Drynoch Highld
102 G3 Dubford Abers
108 G11 Duchally Highld
31 J11 Ducklington Oxon
33 M9 Duddenhoe End Essex
86 F7 Duddingston C Edin
42 E9 Duddington Nhants
16 H11 Duddlestone Somset
81 K6 Duddo Nthumb
49 K3 Duddon Ches W
48 G7 Dudleston Shrops
48 G8 Dudleston Heath Shrops
40 C9 Dudley Dudley
73 M6 Dudley N Tyne
40 C8 Dudley Port Sandw
8 F7 Dudsbury Dorset
51 J11 Duffield Derbys
26 H9 Duffryn Neath
101 L7 Dufftown Moray
101 J2 Duffus Moray
64 C3 Dufton Cumb
60 F2 Duggleby N York
96 H3 Duirinish Highld
97 L4 Duisdalemore Highld
90 D2 Duisky Highld
34 H8 Duke Street Suffk
50 C2 Dukinfield Tamesd
50 C2 Dukinfield Crematorium Tamesd
17 N7 Dulcote Somset
6 E2 Dulford Devon
92 B6 Dull P & K
85 M7 Dullatur N Lans
33 Q5 Dullingham Cambs
99 P4 Dulnain Bridge Highld
32 G5 Duloe Bed
4 F8 Duloe Cnwll
16 C9 Dulverton Somset
21 M8 Dulwich Gt Lon
84 G7 Dumbarton W Duns
30 D7 Dumbleton Gloucs
70 F1 Dumfries D & G
85 J6 Dumgoyne Stirlg
19 P10 Dummer Hants
23 Q9 Dumpton Kent
95 L9 Dun Angus
91 Q5 Dunalastair P & K
84 C8 Dunan Ag & B
96 G4 Dunan Highld
91 L5 Dunan P & K
75 K10 Dunaverty Ag & B
17 J7 Dunball Somset
87 M6 Dunbar E Loth
110 D9 Dunbeath Highld
90 B9 Dunbeg Ag & B
85 N3 Dunblane Stirlg
93 K11 Dunbog Fife
107 J10 Duncanston Highld
102 D9 Duncanstone Abers
6 B5 Dunchideock Devon
41 L12 Dunchurch Warwks
78 F11 Duncow D & G
86 D1 Duncrievie P & K
10 F6 Duncton W Susx
93 M9 Dundee C Dund
93 L9 Dundee Airport C Dund
93 L8 Dundee Crematorium C Dund
17 L9 Dundon Somset
76 F5 Dundonald S Ayrs
106 B5 Dundonnell Highld
71 K5 Dundraw Cumb
98 D6 Dundreggan Highld
70 C6 Dundrennan D & G
17 N3 Dundry N Som
102 G12 Dunecht Abers
86 C5 Dunfermline Fife
86 D5 Dunfermline Crematorium Fife
18 G2 Dunfield Gloucs
77 L4 Dungavel S Lans
13 L6 Dungeness Kent
52 B8 Dunham Notts
49 J2 Dunham-on-the-Hill Ches W
39 Q8 Dunhampton Worcs
57 N10 Dunham Town Traffd
57 N10 Dunham Woodhouses Traffd
52 E7 Dunholme Lincs
93 P12 Dunino Fife
85 N6 Dunipace Falk
92 F7 Dunkeld P & K
17 Q4 Dunkerton BaNES
6 F2 Dunkeswell Devon
58 H5 Dunkeswick N York
23 L10 Dunkirk Kent
18 B4 Dunkirk S Glos
22 C11 Dunk's Green Kent
95 K8 Dunlappie Angus
39 P8 Dunley Worcs
76 G2 Dunlop E Ayrs
98 H5 Dunmaglass Highld
85 P5 Dunmore Falk
110 E2 Dunnet Highld
93 N6 Dunnichen Angus
92 F11 Dunning P & K
59 P4 Dunnington C York
61 K4 Dunnington E R Yk
30 E4 Dunnington Warwks
84 C7 Dunoon Ag & B
100 F5 Dunphail Moray
68 F7 Dunragit D & G
80 G4 Duns Border
42 F5 Dunsby Lincs
78 E11 Dunscore D & G
59 P11 Dunscroft Donc
66 E4 Dunsdale R & Cl
20 B7 Dunsden Green Oxon
14 F9 Dunsdon Devon
10 G3 Dunsfold Surrey
5 Q3 Dunsford Devon
93 J12 Dunshalt Fife
103 K5 Dunshillock Abers
51 L8 Dunsill Notts
67 J5 Dunsley N York
39 Q5 Dunsley Staffs
20 D3 Dunsmore Bucks
63 M11 Dunsop Bridge Lancs
32 E11 Dunstable C Beds
40 F4 Dunstall Staffs
81 Q9 Dunstan Nthumb
16 D7 Dunster Somset
31 L8 Duns Tew Oxon
73 M8 Dunston Gatesd
52 F10 Dunston Lincs
45 K9 Dunston Norfk
40 B4 Dunston Staffs
5 M9 Dunstone Devon
5 P5 Dunstone Devon
59 N11 Dunsville Donc
61 J7 Dunswell E R Yk
86 C11 Dunsyre S Lans
4 H4 Dunterton Devon
29 N7 Duntisbourne Abbots Gloucs
29 P7 Duntisbourne Rouse Gloucs
7 Q2 Duntish Dorset
84 H8 Duntocher W Duns
32 B11 Dunton Bucks
33 J7 Dunton C Beds
44 E4 Dunton Norfk
41 M8 Dunton Bassett Leics
21 P11 Dunton Green Kent
104 F7 Duntulm Highld
76 E8 Dunure S Ayrs
26 D9 Dunvant Swans
104 C11 Dunvegan Highld
35 P3 Dunwich Suffk
2 H9 Durgan Cnwll
73 M11 Durham Dur
73 M11 Durham Cathedral Dur
73 M11 Durham Crematorium Dur
73 N12 Durham Services Dur
65 P5 Durham Tees Valley Airport S on T
78 E8 Durisdeer D & G
78 E7 Durisdeermill D & G
16 H8 Durleigh Somset
9 N4 Durley Hants
19 J7 Durley Wilts
9 N4 Durley Street Hants
23 P10 Durlock Kent
23 P9 Durlock Kent
108 G3 Durness Highld
102 F9 Durno Abers
90 D5 Duror Highld
83 P2 Durran Ag & B
10 H8 Durrington W Susx
18 H10 Durrington Wilts
95 M3 Durris Abers
29 K8 Dursley Gloucs
29 J5 Dursley Cross Gloucs
16 H9 Durston Somset
8 C6 Durweston Dorset
31 Q2 Duston Nhants
99 P4 Duthil Highld
57 L11 Dutton Ches W
33 M7 Duxford Cambs
19 L2 Duxford Oxon
33 M7 Duxford Aircraft Museum Cambs
55 K6 Dwygyfylchi Conwy
54 F8 Dwyran IoA
103 J11 Dyce C Aber
47 J6 Dyffryn Ardudwy Gwynd
27 J6 Dyffryn Cellwen Neath
42 F5 Dyke Lincs
100 F4 Dyke Moray
93 J5 Dykehead Angus
94 F9 Dykehead Angus
85 P10 Dykehead N Lans
85 K4 Dykehead Stirlg
95 L8 Dykelands Abers
93 J4 Dykends Angus
102 F6 Dykeside Abers
13 L4 Dymchurch Kent
29 J3 Dymock Gloucs
17 Q2 Dyrham S Glos
86 G4 Dysart Fife
56 C11 Dyserth Denbgs

E

62 H12 Eagland Hill Lancs
52 C9 Eagle Lincs
65 Q5 Eaglescliffe S on T
70 H9 Eaglesfield Cumb
71 K1 Eaglesfield D & G
85 J11 Eaglesham E Rens
57 N6 Eagley Bolton
51 P8 Eakring Notts
60 D10 Ealand N Linc
21 J7 Ealing Gt Lon
72 C9 Eals Nthumb
71 Q9 Eamont Bridge Cumb
58 B5 Earby Lancs
39 N4 Eardington Shrops
38 H9 Eardisland Herefs
38 F11 Eardisley Herefs
48 G9 Eardiston Shrops
39 M8 Eardiston Worcs
33 L2 Earith Cambs
57 L9 Earlestown St Hel
20 C8 Earley Wokham
45 K8 Earlham Crematorium Norfk
104 E9 Earlish Highld
32 C4 Earls Barton Nhants
34 E10 Earls Colne Essex
30 C3 Earls Common Worcs
29 M1 Earl's Croome Worcs
40 H10 Earlsdon Covtry
87 J3 Earlsferry Fife
21 K8 Earlsfield Gt Lon
102 H8 Earlsford Abers
58 H9 Earlsheaton Kirk
41 L7 Earl Shilton Leics
35 K4 Earl Soham Suffk
50 E7 Earl Sterndale Derbys
80 D6 Earlston Border
76 G4 Earlston E Ayrs
21 L12 Earlswood Surrey
40 E11 Earlswood Warwks
10 D10 Earnley W Susx
73 N6 Earsdon N Tyne
45 M11 Earsham Norfk
10 F8 Eartham W Susx
66 E6 Easby N York
89 P11 Easdale Ag & B
10 E5 Easebourne W Susx
41 L10 Easenhall Warwks
10 F2 Eashing Surrey
31 P11 Easington Bucks
73 P11 Easington Dur
61 P9 Easington E R Yk
66 G4 Easington R & Cl
73 Q11 Easington Colliery Dur
73 P10 Easington Lane Sundld
66 D12 Easingwold N York
93 L6 Eassie and Nevay Angus
16 D3 East Aberthaw V Glam
5 P9 East Allington Devon
15 P6 East Anstey Devon
9 P9 East Ashey IoW
10 D8 East Ashling W Susx
67 L9 East Ayton N York
52 G7 East Barkwith Lincs
22 E11 East Barming Kent
66 H5 East Barnby N York
21 L4 East Barnet Gt Lon
87 N7 East Barns E Loth
44 F4 East Barsham Norfk
45 J3 East Beckham Norfk
20 H8 East Bedfont Gt Lon
34 H9 East Bergholt Suffk
44 F6 East Bilney Norfk
11 P9 East Blatchington E Susx
73 P8 East Boldon S Tyne
9 L7 East Boldre Hants
65 N5 Eastbourne Darltn
12 C9 Eastbourne E Susx
12 D9 Eastbourne Crematorium E Susx
44 F8 East Bradenham Norfk
17 J6 East Brent Somset
35 P4 Eastbridge Suffk
51 P11 East Bridgford Notts
15 L6 East Buckland Devon
6 E6 East Budleigh Devon
58 D5 Eastburn C Brad
20 H5 Eastbury Herts
19 K5 Eastbury W Berk
52 B3 East Butterwick N Linc
58 D4 Eastby N York
86 C8 East Calder W Loth
45 K9 East Carleton Norfk
58 G5 East Carlton Leeds
42 B11 East Carlton Nhants
8 B10 East Chaldon (Chaldon Herring) Dorset
19 L3 East Challow Oxon
5 P10 East Charleton Devon
7 M2 East Chelborough Dorset
11 M7 East Chiltington E Susx
17 L12 East Chinnock Somset
18 G9 East Chisenbury Wilts
23 J8 Eastchurch Kent
20 G11 East Clandon Surrey
31 Q8 East Claydon Bucks
7 M1 East Coker Somset
29 M7 Eastcombe Gloucs
16 F9 East Combe Somset
17 N7 East Compton Somset
6 B10 East Cornworthy Devon
20 H6 Eastcote Gt Lon
31 P4 Eastcote Nhants
40 G10 Eastcote Solhll
18 F9 Eastcott Wilts
60 C6 East Cottingwith E R Yk
19 J8 Eastcourt Wilts
9 N8 East Cowes IoW
59 P9 East Cowick E R Yk
65 N6 East Cowton N York
17 P7 East Cranmore Somset
12 C9 East Dean E Susx
28 H5 East Dean Gloucs
9 J3 East Dean Hants
10 E7 East Dean W Susx
51 Q6 East Drayton Notts
21 M8 East Dulwich Gt Lon
17 N3 East Dundry N Som
60 H8 East Ella C KuH
22 H5 Eastend Essex
9 L7 East End Hants
19 M8 East End Hants
12 G3 East End Kent
31 K10 East End Oxon
17 P6 East End Somset
94 E3 Easter Balmoral Abers
28 G11 Easter Compton S Glos
107 M11 Easter Dalziel Highld
10 F8 Eastergate W Susx
85 L9 Easterhouse C Glas
86 F9 Easter Howgate Mdloth
107 J10 Easter Kinkell Highld
98 H1 Easter Moniack Highld
40 H10 Eastern Green Covtry
95 N2 Easter Ord Abers
87 L2 Easter Pitkierie Fife
111 k4 Easter Skeld Shet
80 G7 Easter Softlaw Border
18 F9 Easterton Wilts
18 H9 East Everleigh Wilts
22 E11 East Farleigh Kent
41 Q9 East Farndon Nhants
52 B4 East Ferry Lincs
85 P9 Eastfield N Lans
67 M10 Eastfield N York
87 K6 East Fortune E Loth
19 L5 East Garston W Berk
72 G12 Eastgate Dur
45 J5 Eastgate Norfk
41 N5 East Goscote Leics
19 J8 East Grafton Wilts
9 J2 East Grimstead Wilts
11 N3 East Grinstead W Susx
12 H6 East Guldeford E Susx
31 P1 East Haddon Nhants
19 N3 East Hagbourne Oxon
61 K9 East Halton N Linc
21 N6 East Ham Gt Lon
20 D9 Easthampstead Park Crematorium Br For
38 H9 Easthampton Herefs
19 M3 East Hanney Oxon
22 F3 East Hanningfield Essex
59 L9 East Hardwick Wakefd
44 G11 East Harling Norfk
65 Q7 East Harlsey N York
8 G2 East Harnham Wilts
17 N5 East Harptree BaNES
65 Q4 East Hartburn S on T
10 C6 East Harting W Susx
8 D2 East Hatch Wilts
33 J6 East Hatley Cambs
65 L8 East Hauxwell N York
93 P8 East Haven Angus
42 H2 East Heckington Lincs
73 K11 East Hedleyhope Dur
110 B11 East Helmsdale Highld
19 M3 East Hendred Oxon
67 K11 East Heslerton N York
11 Q6 East Hoathly E Susx
8 D9 East Holme Dorset
39 K3 Easthope Shrops
34 F11 Easthorpe Essex
17 N6 East Horrington Somset
20 H11 East Horsley Surrey
8 F8 East Howe Bmouth
17 J7 East Huntspill Somset
19 N5 East Ilsley W Berk
15 M9 Eastington Devon
29 K7 Eastington Gloucs
30 F10 Eastington Gloucs
53 L10 East Keal Lincs
18 G7 East Kennett Wilts
59 J5 East Keswick Leeds
85 K11 East Kilbride S Lans
53 K10 East Kirkby Lincs
8 B9 East Knighton Dorset
8 C2 East Knoyle Wilts
17 L11 East Lambrook Somset
57 P7 East Lancashire Crematorium Bury
70 D2 Eastlands D & G
13 P2 East Langdon Kent
41 Q8 East Langton Leics
10 D8 East Lavant W Susx
10 F6 East Lavington W Susx
65 L5 East Layton N York
30 G12 Eastleach Martin Gloucs
30 G11 Eastleach Turville Gloucs
41 M3 East Leake Notts
14 H6 Eastleigh Devon
9 M4 Eastleigh Hants
44 E6 East Lexham Norfk
23 J11 Eastling Kent
87 L6 East Linton E Loth
19 M4 East Lockinge Oxon
21 N6 East London Crematorium Gt Lon
52 B4 East Lound N Linc
8 C10 East Lulworth Dorset
60 G1 East Lutton N York
17 N9 East Lydford Somset
22 E11 East Malling Kent
10 D7 East Marden W Susx
51 Q6 East Markham Notts
8 F4 East Martin Hants
58 B4 East Marton N York
10 B5 East Meon Hants
23 K1 East Mersea Essex
41 K3 East Midlands Airport Leics
21 J9 East Molesey Surrey
8 D8 East Morden Dorset
58 E6 East Morton C Brad
78 E8 East Morton D & G
66 F10 East Ness N York
9 Q7 Eastney C Port
29 K2 Eastnor Herefs
42 B9 East Norton Leics
60 D10 Eastoft N Linc
5 Q6 East Ogwell Devon
32 G3 Easton Cambs
5 P3 Easton Devon
7 Q8 Easton Dorset
9 N2 Easton Hants
42 D5 Easton Lincs
45 J7 Easton Norfk
17 M6 Easton Somset
35 L5 Easton Suffk
18 D6 Easton Wilts
18 C4 Easton Grey Wilts
17 M2 Easton-in-Gordano N Som
32 C5 Easton Maudit Nhants
42 E8 Easton on the Hill Nhants
18 H8 Easton Royal Wilts
8 C4 East Orchard Dorset
12 D1 East Peckham Kent
24 G8 East Pennar Pembks
17 N8 East Pennard Somset
32 G4 East Perry Cambs
5 P11 East Portlemouth Devon
5 Q11 East Prawle Devon
10 H9 East Preston W Susx
14 G8 East Putford Devon
16 F7 East Quantoxhead Somset
73 N10 East Rainton Sundld
52 H4 East Ravendale NE Lin
44 E5 East Raynham Norfk
43 J10 Eastrea Cambs
60 H1 East Riding Crematorium E R Yk
71 L3 Eastriggs D & G
59 J5 East Rigton Leeds
60 D8 Eastrington E R Yk
18 H3 Eastrop Swindn
65 Q6 East Rounton N York
44 D5 East Rudham Norfk
45 K2 East Runton Norfk
45 M5 East Ruston Norfk
23 P11 Eastry Kent
87 J8 East Saltoun E Loth
21 K8 East Sheen Gt Lon
19 L6 East Shefford W Berk
52 B5 East Stockwith Lincs
8 C9 East Stoke Dorset
51 Q10 East Stoke Notts
8 B3 East Stour Dorset
23 N10 East Stourmouth Kent
15 L6 East Stowford Devon
19 P11 East Stratton Hants
23 P12 East Studdal Kent

4 E7 East Taphouse Cnwll
14 H6 East-the-Water Devon
73 L2 East Thirston Nthumb
22 D7 East Tilbury Thurr
10 B4 East Tisted Hants
52 G6 East Torrington Lincs
44 H7 East Tuddenham Norfk
9 K2 East Tytherley Hants
18 E6 East Tytherton Wilts
15 P10 East Village Devon
17 N2 Eastville Bristl
53 L11 Eastville Lincs
44 C6 East Walton Norfk
5 N2 East Week Devon
41 Q2 Eastwell Leics
9 K4 East Wellow Hants
86 G3 East Wemyss Fife
85 Q9 East Whitburn W Loth
21 N2 Eastwick Herts
21 P7 East Wickham Gt Lon
25 J7 East Williamston Pembks
44 B6 East Winch Norfk
9 J1 East Winterslow Wilts
10 C9 East Wittering W Susx
65 K9 East Witton N York
51 L10 Eastwood Notts
22 G6 Eastwood Sthend
72 G4 East Woodburn Nthumb
19 L8 East Woodhay Hants
10 C3 East Worldham Hants
44 F11 East Wretham Norfk
14 E8 East Youlstone Devon
31 K1 Eathorpe Warwks
49 Q3 Eaton Ches E
49 L3 Eaton Ches W
42 B4 Eaton Leics
45 K8 Eaton Norfk
51 P5 Eaton Notts
31 K12 Eaton Oxon
39 J4 Eaton Shrops
32 D11 Eaton Bray C Beds
39 L2 Eaton Constantine Shrops
32 D11 Eaton Green C Beds
19 J2 Eaton Hastings Oxon
39 K2 Eaton Mascott Shrops
32 G5 Eaton Socon Cambs
49 M10 Eaton upon Tern Shrops
67 K10 Ebberston N York
8 E3 Ebbesborne Wake Wilts
27 N6 Ebbw Vale Blae G
73 K9 Ebchester Dur
6 D5 Ebford Devon
29 L7 Ebley Gloucs
49 J6 Ebnal Ches W
30 F6 Ebrington Gloucs
19 N8 Ecchinswell Hants
87 P8 Ecclaw Border
71 K1 Ecclefechan D & G
80 G6 Eccles Border
22 E10 Eccles Kent
57 P8 Eccles Salfd
50 H4 Ecclesall Sheff
57 N8 Eccles Crematorium Salfd
51 J3 Ecclesfield Sheff
49 P9 Eccleshall Staffs
58 F6 Eccleshill C Brad
86 C7 Ecclesmachan W Loth
44 G11 Eccles Road Norfk
48 H3 Eccleston Ches W
57 K5 Eccleston Lancs
57 J9 Eccleston St Hel
95 M2 Echt Abers
80 F8 Eckford Border
51 K5 Eckington Derbys
29 N1 Eckington Worcs
32 B4 Ecton Nhants
50 E4 Edale Derbys
111 h1 Eday Ork
111 h1 Eday Airport Ork
11 K7 Edburton W Susx
107 L5 Edderton Highld
86 F11 Eddleston Border
85 M11 Eddlewood S Lans
11 N2 Edenbridge Kent
57 P5 Edenfield Lancs
71 Q8 Edenhall Cumb
42 F6 Edenham Lincs
21 M9 Eden Park Gt Lon
3 M5 Eden Project Cnwll
50 G6 Edensor Derbys
84 F4 Edentaggart Ag & B
59 N11 Edenthorpe Donc
46 E4 Edern Gwynd
40 D9 Edgbaston Birm
31 P9 Edgcott Bucks
15 P4 Edgcott Somset
29 L6 Edge Gloucs
44 H4 Edgefield Norfk
44 H4 Edgefield Green Norfk
58 F10 Edgerton Kirk
29 N7 Edgeworth Gloucs
49 N10 Edgmond Wrekin
38 H5 Edgton Shrops
21 J5 Edgware Gt Lon
57 N5 Edgworth Bl w D
104 D11 Edinbane Highld
86 F7 Edinburgh C Edin
86 D7 Edinburgh Airport C Edin
86 F7 Edinburgh Castle C Edin
86 F7 Edinburgh Royal Botanic Gardens C Edin
86 E7 Edinburgh Zoo C Edin
40 G5 Edingale Staffs
70 D3 Edingham D & G
51 P9 Edingley Notts
45 M4 Edingthorpe Norfk
45 M4 Edingthorpe Green Norfk
81 J3 Edington Border
73 K4 Edington Nthumb
17 K8 Edington Somset
18 D9 Edington Wilts
17 K7 Edington Burtle Somset
17 J5 Edingworth Somset
17 J6 Edithmead Somset
42 D8 Edith Weston Rutlnd
32 D11 Edlesborough Bucks
81 M11 Edlingham Nthumb
52 H8 Edlington Lincs
8 F5 Edmondsham Dorset
73 M10 Edmondsley Dur
42 C6 Edmondthorpe Leics
21 M5 Edmonton Gt Lon
72 H10 Edmundbyers Dur
80 G6 Ednam Border
92 D5 Edradynate P & K
80 H3 Edrom Border
49 K8 Edstaston Shrops
30 F2 Edstone Warwks
41 N1 Edwalton Notts
51 N7 Edwinstowe Notts
32 H8 Edworth C Beds
39 M9 Edwyn Ralph Herefs
95 K8 Edzell Angus
95 K7 Edzell Woods Abers
26 G9 Efail-fach Neath
27 M11 Efail Isaf Rhondd
46 F4 Efailnewydd Gwynd
25 K4 Efailwen Carmth
48 C4 Efenechtyd Denbgs
79 L9 Effgill D & G
20 H11 Effingham Surrey
5 K8 Efford Crematorium C Plym
57 N6 Egerton Bolton
12 H1 Egerton Kent
59 M9 Eggborough N York
5 K8 Eggbuckland C Plym
15 M9 Eggesford Devon
32 D10 Eggington C Beds
40 H2 Egginton Derbys
65 P5 Egglescliffe S on T
64 H3 Eggleston Dur
20 G8 Egham Surrey
42 C8 Egleton Rutlnd
81 M9 Eglingham Nthumb
3 M2 Egloshayle Cnwll
4 G3 Egloskerry Cnwll
55 L7 Eglwysbach Conwy
49 J7 Eglwys Cross Wrexhm
25 K2 Eglwyswrw Pembks
51 Q7 Egmanton Notts
70 G12 Egremont Cumb
56 G9 Egremont Wirral
66 H6 Egton N York
66 H6 Egton Bridge N York
20 F6 Egypt Bucks
96 F11 Eigg Highld
34 F10 Eight Ash Green Essex
97 L6 Eilanreach Highld
37 P7 Elan Valley Powys
37 Q7 Elan Village Powys
28 H10 Elberton S Glos
5 L9 Elburton C Plym
18 G5 Elcombe Swindn
29 L3 Eldersfield Worcs
84 H9 Elderslie Rens
65 M2 Eldon Dur
95 N5 Elfhill Abers
40 F5 Elford Staffs
101 J3 Elgin Moray
96 G6 Elgol Highld
13 M2 Elham Kent
87 K3 Elie Fife
54 E5 Elim IoA
9 L5 Eling Hants
51 P6 Elkesley Notts
29 N6 Elkstone Gloucs
102 E4 Ella Abers
6 C9 Ellacombe Torbay
58 E9 Elland Calder
83 L7 Ellary Ag & B
50 E11 Ellastone Staffs
63 J10 Ellel Lancs
87 N9 Ellemford Border
89 P11 Ellenabeich Ag & B
49 Q9 Ellenhall Staffs
10 H3 Ellen's Green Surrey
66 B8 Ellerbeck N York
66 H5 Ellerby N York
49 L10 Ellerdine Heath Wrekin
90 E6 Elleric Ag & B
60 F8 Ellerker E R Yk
60 C6 Ellerton E R Yk
65 M7 Ellerton N York
20 D3 Ellesborough Bucks
48 H8 Ellesmere Shrops
56 H12 Ellesmere Port Ches W
45 N10 Ellingham Norfk
81 N8 Ellingham Nthumb
65 L10 Ellingstring N York
32 G3 Ellington Cambs
73 M3 Ellington Nthumb
18 B10 Elliots Green Somset
19 Q10 Ellisfield Hants
104 G8 Ellishader Highld
41 K5 Ellistown Leics
103 K8 Ellon Abers
71 N8 Ellonby Cumb
60 G8 Elloughton E R Yk
28 G7 Ellwood Gloucs
43 M8 Elm Cambs
30 B1 Elmbridge Worcs
33 M8 Elmdon Essex
40 F10 Elmdon Solhll
21 M9 Elmers End Gt Lon
41 L8 Elmesthorpe Leics
40 E5 Elmhurst Staffs
29 N1 Elmley Castle Worcs
39 Q8 Elmley Lovett Worcs
29 K6 Elmore Gloucs
29 K5 Elmore Back Gloucs
21 Q6 Elm Park Gt Lon
34 H7 Elmsett Suffk
34 H10 Elmstead Market Essex
13 L2 Elmsted Kent
23 N10 Elmstone Kent
29 M4 Elmstone Hardwicke Gloucs
60 G3 Elmswell E R Yk
34 G4 Elmswell Suffk
51 L6 Elmton Derbys
108 E12 Elphin Highld
86 H8 Elphinstone E Loth
95 N1 Elrick Abers
69 J9 Elrig D & G
72 F8 Elrington Nthumb
72 G3 Elsdon Nthumb
33 N10 Elsenham Essex
31 M11 Elsfield Oxon
60 H10 Elsham N Linc
44 H6 Elsing Norfk
58 B4 Elslack N York
9 P7 Elson Hants
86 C12 Elsrickle S Lans
10 E2 Elstead Surrey
10 D6 Elsted W Susx
42 F5 Elsthorpe Lincs
51 Q10 Elston Notts
32 F7 Elstow Bed
21 J4 Elstree Herts
61 L7 Elstronwick E R Yk
56 H2 Elswick Lancs
73 M7 Elswick N u Ty
33 K4 Elsworth Cambs
62 G2 Elterwater Cumb
21 N8 Eltham Gt Lon
21 N8 Eltham Crematorium Gt Lon
33 J5 Eltisley Cambs
42 F10 Elton Cambs
49 J1 Elton Ches W
50 G8 Elton Derbys
39 J7 Elton Herefs
51 Q11 Elton Notts
65 P4 Elton S on T
73 J8 Eltringham Nthumb
78 F5 Elvanfoot S Lans
41 K2 Elvaston Derbys
34 D2 Elveden Suffk
20 C11 Elvetham Heath Hants
87 J7 Elvingston E Loth
60 C5 Elvington C York
23 P12 Elvington Kent
66 C2 Elwick Hartpl
49 N3 Elworth Ches E
16 E8 Elworthy Somset
33 N1 Ely Cambs
16 F2 Ely Cardif
32 C6 Emberton M Keyn
71 J9 Embleton Cumb
81 P9 Embleton Nthumb
107 N4 Embo Highld
17 N6 Emborough Somset
107 N4 Embo Street Highld
58 D4 Embsay N York
9 K6 Emery Down Hants
58 G10 Emley Kirk
20 C3 Emmington Oxon
43 M8 Emneth Norfk
43 N8 Emneth Hungate Norfk
42 D8 Empingham Rutlnd
10 C4 Empshott Hants
49 K12 Emstrey Crematorium Shrops
10 C8 Emsworth Hants
19 M7 Enborne W Berk
19 M7 Enborne Row W Berk
41 M7 Enderby Leics
63 K5 Endmoor Cumb
50 B9 Endon Staffs
50 B9 Endon Bank Staffs
21 M4 Enfield Gt Lon
21 M4 Enfield Crematorium Gt Lon
21 M4 Enfield Lock Gt Lon
21 M4 Enfield Wash Gt Lon
18 G9 Enford Wilts
29 J11 Engine Common S Glos
19 Q6 Englefield W Berk
20 F8 Englefield Green Surrey
28 G5 English Bicknor Gloucs
17 Q4 Englishcombe BaNES
49 J9 English Frankton Shrops
19 L10 Enham-Alamein Hants
16 H8 Enmore Somset
8 C3 Enmore Green Dorset
70 H11 Ennerdale Bridge Cumb
92 F3 Enochdhu P & K
88 H6 Ensay Ag & B
8 F8 Ensbury Bmouth
48 H11 Ensdon Shrops
31 J8 Enstone Oxon
78 E7 Enterkinfoot D & G
39 P5 Enville Staffs
111 a6 Eolaigearraidh W Isls
29 K6 Epney Gloucs
51 P10 Epperstone Notts
21 P3 Epping Essex
21 N3 Epping Green Essex
21 N3 Epping Upland Essex
65 L5 Eppleby N York
21 K10 Epsom Surrey
31 J6 Epwell Oxon
52 A3 Epworth N Linc
48 G7 Erbistock Wrexhm
40 E8 Erdington Birm
12 B3 Eridge Green E Susx
83 N7 Erines Ag & B
90 C7 Eriska Ag & B
111 b6 Eriskay W Isls
34 C2 Eriswell Suffk
21 P7 Erith Gt Lon
18 E9 Erlestoke Wilts
5 M9 Ermington Devon
45 K4 Erpingham Norfk
98 H5 Errogie Highld
93 J10 Errol P & K
84 H8 Erskine Rens
68 D5 Ervie D & G
35 K9 Erwarton Suffk
38 C12 Erwood Powys
65 N6 Eryholme N York
48 E4 Eryrys Denbgs
65 L2 Escomb Dur
59 N5 Escrick N York
47 M9 Esgairgeiliog Powys
73 L11 Esh Dur
21 J9 Esher Surrey
73 L2 Eshott Nthumb
73 L11 Esh Winning Dur
98 F2 Eskadale Highld
86 G8 Eskbank Mdloth
62 D3 Eskdale Green Cumb
79 L8 Eskdalemuir D & G
56 H2 Esprick Lancs
42 F7 Essendine Rutlnd
21 L2 Essendon Herts
99 J2 Essich Highld
40 C6 Essington Staffs
103 J8 Esslemont Abers
66 D4 Eston R & Cl
81 K6 Etal Nthumb
18 F8 Etchilhampton Wilts
12 E5 Etchingham E Susx
13 M3 Etchinghill Kent
40 D4 Etchinghill Staffs
20 F7 Eton W & M
20 F7 Eton Wick W & M
49 Q6 Etruria C Stke
99 K8 Etteridge Highld
64 F2 Ettersgill Dur
49 N4 Ettiley Heath Ches E
40 B8 Ettingshall Wolves
30 H4 Ettington Warwks
42 G9 Etton C Pete
60 G5 Etton E R Yk
79 L6 Ettrick Border
79 N4 Ettrickbridge Border
79 L6 Ettrickhill Border
40 H2 Etwall Derbys
34 E2 Euston Suffk
57 K5 Euxton Lancs
107 K8 Evanton Highld
42 F1 Evedon Lincs
107 M4 Evelix Highld
38 F9 Evenjobb Powys
31 N7 Evenley Nhants
30 G8 Evenlode Gloucs
65 K3 Evenwood Dur
17 P8 Evercreech Somset
60 D6 Everingham E R Yk
18 H9 Everleigh Wilts
32 E9 Eversholt C Beds
7 N2 Evershot Dorset
20 C10 Eversley Hants
20 C10 Eversley Cross Hants
60 F7 Everthorpe E R Yk
32 H6 Everton C Beds
9 K8 Everton Hants
56 G9 Everton Lpool
51 P3 Everton Notts
71 M1 Evertown D & G
39 M11 Evesbatch Herefs
30 D5 Evesham Worcs
41 N6 Evington C Leic
50 H2 Ewden Village Sheff
21 K10 Ewell Surrey
13 N2 Ewell Minnis Kent
19 Q3 Ewelme Oxon
18 E2 Ewen Gloucs
27 J12 Ewenny V Glam
42 G1 Ewerby Lincs
10 H3 Ewhurst Surrey
12 F5 Ewhurst Green E Susx
10 H3 Ewhurst Green Surrey
48 F3 Ewloe Flints
5 J2 Eworthy Devon
20 D12 Ewshot Hants
28 D3 Ewyas Harold Herefs
15 K10 Exbourne Devon
16 C10 Exbridge Somset
9 M7 Exbury Hants
65 N9 Exelby N York
6 C4 Exeter Devon
6 D4 Exeter Airport Devon
6 C5 Exeter & Devon Crematorium Devon
6 C4 Exeter Services Devon
15 P5 Exford Somset
39 J2 Exfordsgreen Shrops
30 E3 Exhall Warwks
41 J9 Exhall Warwks
19 Q4 Exlade Street Oxon
6 C5 Exminster Devon
15 P4 Exmoor National Park
6 D6 Exmouth Devon
33 P4 Exning Suffk
6 D5 Exton Devon
9 Q4 Exton Hants
42 D7 Exton Rutlnd
16 C9 Exton Somset
6 B4 Exwick Devon
50 G5 Eyam Derbys
31 M4 Eydon Nhants
42 H9 Eye C Pete
39 J8 Eye Herefs
35 J3 Eye Suffk
81 K2 Eyemouth Border
33 J7 Eyeworth C Beds
22 G11 Eyhorne Street Kent
35 M6 Eyke Suffk
32 H5 Eynesbury Cambs
22 B9 Eynsford Kent
31 K11 Eynsham Oxon
7 L5 Eype Dorset
104 F10 Eyre Highld
23 P12 Eythorne Kent
39 J9 Eyton Herefs
48 H10 Eyton Shrops
39 L2 Eyton on Severn Shrops
49 M11 Eyton upon the Weald Moors Wrekin

F

19 L8 Faccombe Hants
66 C7 Faceby N York
48 B11 Fachwen Powys
49 L5 Faddiley Ches E
66 F9 Fadmoor N York
26 F8 Faerdre Swans
84 H8 Faifley W Duns
17 M2 Failand N Som
76 H6 Failford S Ayrs
50 B1 Failsworth Oldham
47 K8 Fairbourne Gwynd
59 L8 Fairburn N York
50 E6 Fairfield Derbys
40 C11 Fairfield Worcs
18 H1 Fairford Gloucs
70 F4 Fairgirth D & G
43 Q6 Fair Green Norfk
56 G4 Fairhaven Lancs
111 m5 Fair Isle Shet
20 F11 Fairlands Surrey
84 D11 Fairlie N Ayrs
12 G7 Fairlight E Susx
6 E4 Fairmile Devon
20 H10 Fairmile Surrey
79 P3 Fairnilee Border
9 N4 Fair Oak Hants
49 N8 Fairoak Staffs
19 Q8 Fair Oak Green Hants
22 D10 Fairseat Kent
34 C12 Fairstead Essex
43 Q6 Fairstead Norfk
11 P5 Fairwarp E Susx
27 N12 Fairwater Cardif
14 G7 Fairy Cross Devon
44 F4 Fakenham Norfk
34 E2 Fakenham Magna Suffk
87 J9 Fala Mdloth
87 J9 Fala Dam Mdloth
52 F6 Faldingworth Lincs
7 c2 Faldouet Jersey
29 J9 Falfield S Glos
35 L8 Falkenham Suffk
85 P7 Falkirk Falk
86 F2 Falkland Fife
78 F2 Fallburn S Lans
85 N5 Fallin Stirlg
81 P9 Falloden Nthumb
57 Q9 Fallowfield Manch
72 G7 Fallowfield Nthumb
83 Q1 Falls of Blarghour Ag & B
11 M8 Falmer E Susx
3 J8 Falmouth Cnwll
79 N7 Falnash Border
67 M9 Falsgrave N York
72 D4 Falstone Nthumb
108 D6 Fanagmore Highld
32 E10 Fancott C Beds
98 G1 Fanellan Highld
66 D8 Fangdale Beck N York
60 D4 Fangfoss E R Yk
89 J7 Fanmore Ag & B
106 D8 Fannich Lodge Highld
80 E6 Fans Border
32 C9 Far Bletchley M Keyn
42 H10 Farcet Cambs
31 Q3 Far Cotton Nhants
9 P6 Fareham Hants
62 F3 Far End Cumb
40 E5 Farewell Staffs
19 K2 Faringdon Oxon
57 K4 Farington Lancs
71 Q4 Farlam Cumb
17 M3 Farleigh N Som
21 M10 Farleigh Surrey
18 B8 Farleigh Hungerford Somset
19 Q10 Farleigh Wallop Hants
53 M8 Farlesthorpe Lincs
63 K6 Farleton Cumb
63 L8 Farleton Lancs
50 E11 Farley Staffs
9 J2 Farley Wilts
10 G2 Farley Green Surrey
20 C9 Farley Hill Wokham
29 K6 Farleys End Gloucs
10 B8 Farlington C Port
59 N1 Farlington N York
39 L6 Farlow Shrops
17 P4 Farmborough BaNES
30 D8 Farmcote Gloucs
37 K10 Farmers Carmth
30 F10 Farmington Gloucs
31 L11 Farmoor Oxon
57 K7 Far Moor Wigan
101 P5 Farmtown Moray
21 N9 Farnborough Gt Lon
20 E11 Farnborough Hants
19 M4 Farnborough W Berk
31 K4 Farnborough Warwks
20 E11 Farnborough Park Hants
20 E11 Farnborough Street Hants
10 F2 Farncombe Surrey
32 D4 Farndish Bed
48 H5 Farndon Ches W
51 Q9 Farndon Notts
81 Q6 Farne Islands Nthumb
93 Q5 Farnell Angus
8 E4 Farnham Dorset
33 M10 Farnham Essex
59 J3 Farnham N York
35 M5 Farnham Suffk
10 D1 Farnham Surrey
20 F6 Farnham Common Bucks
20 F6 Farnham Royal Bucks
22 B9 Farningham Kent
58 G7 Farnley Leeds
58 G5 Farnley N York
58 F10 Farnley Tyas Kirk
51 P9 Farnsfield Notts
57 N7 Farnworth Bolton
57 K10 Farnworth Halton
29 N7 Far Oakridge Gloucs
99 K3 Farr Highld
99 M8 Farr Highld
109 M3 Farr Highld
98 H5 Farraline Highld
6 D5 Farringdon Devon
17 P5 Farrington Gurney BaNES
62 H3 Far Sawrey Cumb
31 M6 Farthinghoe Nhants
31 N3 Farthingstone Nhants
58 F9 Fartown Kirk
58 G7 Fartown Leeds
90 D6 Fasnacloich Ag & B
98 D4 Fasnakyle Highld
90 D1 Fassfern Highld
73 N9 Fatfield Sundld
85 Q10 Fauldhouse W Loth
34 D12 Faulkbourne Essex
17 Q5 Faulkland Somset
49 L8 Fauls Shrops
23 K10 Faversham Kent
66 B11 Fawdington N York
73 M7 Fawdon N u Ty
22 C9 Fawkham Green Kent
31 J10 Fawler Oxon
20 C6 Fawley Bucks
9 M6 Fawley Hants
19 L5 Fawley W Berk
60 E8 Faxfleet E R Yk
11 K4 Faygate W Susx
56 G9 Fazakerley Lpool
40 G7 Fazeley Staffs
65 L10 Fearby N York
107 N7 Fearn Highld
91 Q7 Fearnan P & K
105 L9 Fearnbeg Highld
105 K9 Fearnmore Highld
83 P7 Fearnoch Ag & B
40 C6 Featherstone Staffs
59 K9 Featherstone Wakefd
30 D2 Feckenham Worcs
34 E11 Feering Essex
64 H7 Feetham N York
11 M3 Felbridge Surrey
45 K3 Felbrigg Norfk
11 M2 Felcourt Surrey
25 N2 Felindre Carmth
26 D5 Felindre Carmth
38 D6 Felindre Powys
26 E8 Felindre Swans
36 B11 Felindre Farchog Pembks
26 C4 Felingwm Isaf Carmth
26 C4 Felingwm Uchaf Carmth
66 C9 Felixkirk N York
35 L9 Felixstowe Suffk
73 M8 Felling Gatesd
32 E5 Felmersham Bed
45 L4 Felmingham Norfk
10 F9 Felpham W Susx
34 F5 Felsham Suffk
34 B11 Felsted Essex
20 H8 Feltham Gt Lon
20 H8 Felthamhill Surrey
45 J6 Felthorpe Norfk
39 L11 Felton Herefs
17 M3 Felton N Som
73 L2 Felton Nthumb
48 H11 Felton Butler Shrops
44 B11 Feltwell Norfk
57 P2 Fence Lancs
51 K4 Fence Rothm
31 M10 Fencott Oxon
53 M10 Fendike Corner Lincs
33 M5 Fen Ditton Cambs
33 K3 Fen Drayton Cambs
57 M4 Feniscowles Bl w D
6 F3 Feniton Devon
39 P5 Fenn Green Shrops
22 F8 Fenn Street Medway
50 F10 Fenny Bentley Derbys
6 F3 Fenny Bridges Devon
31 K4 Fenny Compton Warwks
41 J7 Fenny Drayton Leics
33 K3 Fenstanton Cambs
44 G10 Fen Street Norfk
50 B11 Fenton C Stke
33 K2 Fenton Cambs
71 Q4 Fenton Cumb
52 B8 Fenton Lincs
52 C12 Fenton Lincs
52 B6 Fenton Notts
81 K7 Fenton Nthumb
87 K6 Fenton Barns E Loth
59 N10 Fenwick Donc
76 H3 Fenwick E Ayrs
73 J6 Fenwick Nthumb
81 M6 Fenwick Nthumb
3 J7 Feock Cnwll
82 F8 Feolin Ferry Ag & B
76 F3 Fergushill N Ayrs
104 B11 Feriniquarrie Highld
94 H9 Fern Angus
27 L9 Ferndale Rhondd
8 F7 Ferndown Dorset
100 E6 Ferness Highld

19 K3 Fernham Oxon
39 Q9 Fernhill Heath Worcs
10 E4 Fernhurst W Susx
93 K11 Fernie Fife
85 M11 Ferniegair S Lans
96 D3 Fernilea Highld
50 D5 Fernilee Derbys
52 B12 Fernwood Notts
59 J3 Ferrensby N York
97 J7 Ferrindonald Highld
10 H9 Ferring W Susx
59 L9 Ferrybridge Services Wakefd
95 M9 Ferryden Angus
65 M2 Ferryhill Dur
107 M5 Ferry Point Highld
25 N6 Ferryside Carmth
107 M5 Ferrytown Highld
44 H12 Fersfield Norfk
91 K2 Fersit Highld
99 M8 Feshiebridge Highld
21 J11 Fetcham Surrey
111 m2 Fetlar Shet
103 K5 Fetterangus Abers
95 K7 Fettercairn Abers
58 G4 Fewston N York
26 E5 Ffairfach Carmth
37 M7 Ffair Rhos Cerdgn
47 L3 Ffestiniog Gwynd
47 K3 Ffestiniog Railway Gwynd
26 D7 Fforest Carmth
26 E9 Fforest Fach Swans
36 F10 Ffostrasol Cerdgn
48 F4 Ffrith Flints
56 D11 Ffynnongroyw Flints
108 H9 Fiag Lodge Highld
21 M10 Fickleshole Surrey
16 G7 Fiddington Somset
8 B5 Fiddleford Dorset
3 J5 Fiddlers Green Cnwll
40 D2 Field Staffs
44 G3 Field Dalling Norfk
41 L5 Field Head Leics
8 B3 Fifehead Magdalen Dorset
8 B5 Fifehead Neville Dorset
8 B5 Fifehead St Quintin Dorset
101 M5 Fife Keith Moray
30 G9 Fifield Oxon
20 E7 Fifield W & M
18 H10 Figheldean Wilts
45 P7 Filby Norfk
67 N10 Filey N York
32 C7 Filgrave M Keyn
30 G12 Filkins Oxon
15 L6 Filleigh Devon
52 D6 Fillingham Lincs
40 H9 Fillongley Warwks
28 H11 Filton S Glos
60 F3 Fimber E R Yk
93 N4 Finavon Angus
44 B8 Fincham Norfk
20 C10 Finchampstead Wokham
83 N3 Fincharn Ag & B
10 B7 Finchdean Hants
34 B9 Finchingfield Essex
21 L5 Finchley Gt Lon
40 H2 Findern Derbys
100 G3 Findhorn Moray
99 M4 Findhorn Bridge Highld
101 N2 Findochty Moray
92 E10 Findo Gask P & K
95 Q3 Findon Abers
10 H8 Findon W Susx
107 K9 Findon Mains Highld
95 K2 Findrack House Abers
32 D3 Finedon Nhants
92 H10 Fingask P & K
20 C5 Fingest Bucks
65 L9 Finghall N York
77 M7 Fingland D & G
23 P11 Finglesham Kent
34 G11 Fingringhoe Essex
91 N9 Finlarig Stirlg
31 N7 Finmere Oxon
91 M5 Finnart P & K
34 H3 Finningham Suffk
51 P2 Finningley Donc
111 c4 Finsbay W Isls
40 C12 Finstall Worcs
62 G5 Finsthwaite Cumb
31 J10 Finstock Oxon
111 h2 Finstown Ork
102 G4 Fintry Abers
85 K5 Fintry Stirlg
95 K4 Finzean Abers
88 G10 Fionnphort Ag & B
111 c4 Fionnsbhagh W Isls
63 L4 Firbank Cumb
51 M3 Firbeck Rothm
60 C2 Firby N York
65 M9 Firby N York
11 P8 Firle E Susx
53 M10 Firsby Lincs
65 K1 Fir Tree Dur
9 P8 Fishbourne IoW
10 D8 Fishbourne W Susx
10 D8 Fishbourne Roman Palace W Susx
65 P2 Fishburn Dur
85 P4 Fishcross Clacks
102 E8 Fisherford Abers
86 G7 Fisherrow E Loth
9 N4 Fisher's Pond Hants
107 M11 Fisherton Highld
76 E7 Fisherton S Ayrs
18 E11 Fisherton de la Mere Wilts
24 G2 Fishguard Pembks
59 P10 Fishlake Donc
89 N7 Fishnish Pier Ag & B
17 P2 Fishponds Bristl
43 K2 Fishtoft Lincs
43 K1 Fishtoft Drove Lincs
96 D3 Fiskavaig Highld
52 F8 Fiskerton Lincs
51 Q9 Fiskerton Notts
18 G10 Fittleton Wilts
10 G6 Fittleworth W Susx
49 J11 Fitz Shrops
16 F9 Fitzhead Somset
59 K10 Fitzwilliam Wakefd
11 P5 Five Ash Down E Susx
12 B5 Five Ashes E Susx
17 J10 Fivehead Somset
4 F4 Fivelanes Cnwll
12 D2 Five Oak Green Kent
7 c2 Five Oaks Jersey
10 H4 Five Oaks W Susx
26 C7 Five Roads Carmth
20 E5 Flackwell Heath Bucks
30 C5 Fladbury Worcs
111 k4 Fladdabister Shet
50 F7 Flagg Derbys
67 Q12 Flamborough E R Yk
67 Q12 Flamborough Head E R Yk
66 H10 Flamingo Land Theme Park N York
20 H1 Flamstead Herts
10 F9 Flansham W Susx
58 H9 Flanshaw Wakefd
58 C3 Flasby N York
50 D7 Flash Staffs
104 D10 Flashader Highld
20 G4 Flaunden Herts
42 B2 Flawborough Notts
59 L2 Flawith N York
17 M3 Flax Bourton N Som
59 K3 Flaxby N York
29 J6 Flaxley Gloucs
16 F8 Flaxpool Somset
59 P2 Flaxton N York
41 P8 Fleckney Leics
31 L2 Flecknoe Warwks
52 B8 Fledborough Notts
7 P6 Fleet Dorset
20 D11 Fleet Hants
43 L5 Fleet Lincs
43 L5 Fleet Hargate Lincs
20 C11 Fleet Services Hants
62 G11 Fleetwood Lancs
16 D3 Flemingston V Glam
85 L10 Flemington S Lans
34 D3 Flempton Suffk
71 K7 Fletchertown Cumb
11 N5 Fletching E Susx
14 D10 Flexbury Cnwll
20 E12 Flexford Surrey
70 G8 Flimby Cumb
12 E4 Flimwell E Susx
48 E2 Flint Flints
51 Q10 Flintham Notts
61 L7 Flinton E R Yk
44 C5 Flitcham Norfk
32 F9 Flitton C Beds
32 E9 Flitwick C Beds
60 E10 Flixborough N Linc
60 E10 Flixborough Stather N Linc
67 M10 Flixton N York
45 M11 Flixton Suffk
57 N9 Flixton Traffd
58 G10 Flockton Kirk
58 G10 Flockton Green Kirk
104 F7 Flodigarry Highld
62 G7 Flookburgh Cumb
45 K10 Flordon Norfk
31 N3 Flore Nhants
34 H7 Flowton Suffk
3 J8 Flushing Cnwll
6 E4 Fluxton Devon
30 C3 Flyford Flavell Worcs
22 E6 Fobbing Thurr
101 L4 Fochabers Moray
27 M7 Fochriw Caerph
60 E9 Fockerby N Linc
17 N9 Foddington Somset
48 B12 Foel Powys
60 D6 Foggathorpe E R Yk
80 G4 Fogo Border
101 K4 Fogwatt Moray
108 D6 Foindle Highld
94 C8 Folda Angus
50 D12 Fole Staffs
41 J10 Foleshill Covtry
17 P12 Folke Dorset
13 N3 Folkestone Kent
42 F4 Folkingham Lincs
12 C8 Folkington E Susx
42 G11 Folksworth Cambs
67 M10 Folkton N York
102 F8 Folla Rule Abers
59 J4 Follifoot N York
15 K11 Folly Gate Devon
8 D2 Fonthill Bishop Wilts
8 D2 Fonthill Gifford Wilts
8 C4 Fontmell Magna Dorset
8 C5 Fontmell Parva Dorset
10 F8 Fontwell W Susx
50 F5 Foolow Derbys
101 M11 Forbestown Abers
65 L5 Forcett N York
83 N3 Ford Ag & B
31 Q11 Ford Bucks
51 K5 Ford Derbys
14 G7 Ford Devon
30 E8 Ford Gloucs
81 K6 Ford Nthumb
16 E9 Ford Somset
50 E9 Ford Staffs
10 F8 Ford W Susx
18 C6 Ford Wilts
11 Q3 Fordcombe Kent
86 D5 Fordell Fife
38 E2 Forden Powys
34 B12 Ford End Essex
5 Q6 Forder Green Devon
33 Q3 Fordham Cambs
34 F10 Fordham Essex
43 P9 Fordham Norfk
8 G5 Fordingbridge Hants
67 M11 Fordon E R Yk
95 M6 Fordoun Abers
34 F10 Fordstreet Essex
16 F11 Ford Street Somset
23 M10 Fordwich Kent
102 D3 Fordyce Abers
40 B3 Forebridge Staffs
6 b2 Forest Guern
50 C6 Forest Chapel Ches E
21 N6 Forest Gate Gt Lon
10 H2 Forest Green Surrey
73 M6 Forest Hall N Tyne
21 M8 Forest Hill Gt Lon
31 N11 Forest Hill Oxon
59 J3 Forest Lane Head N York
85 Q4 Forest Mill Clacks
28 H6 Forest of Dean Gloucs
21 P5 Forest Park Crematorium Gt Lon
11 N3 Forest Row E Susx
10 C7 Forestside W Susx
93 M5 Forfar Angus
92 G11 Forgandenny P & K
28 C9 Forge Hammer Torfn
101 M4 Forgie Moray
101 M5 Forgieside Moray
102 D6 Forgue Abers
56 F7 Formby Sefton
45 J10 Forncett End Norfk
45 J10 Forncett St Mary Norfk
45 J10 Forncett St Peter Norfk
34 D4 Fornham All Saints Suffk
34 E4 Fornham St Martin Suffk
100 E5 Fornighty Highld
100 F4 Forres Moray
50 C11 Forsbrook Staffs
110 E8 Forse Highld
109 Q7 Forsinard Highld
98 E7 Fort Augustus Highld
92 F11 Forteviot P & K
85 Q11 Forth S Lans
29 M3 Forthampton Gloucs
91 Q6 Fortingall P & K
19 M11 Forton Hants
63 J11 Forton Lancs
48 H11 Forton Shrops
7 J2 Forton Somset
49 N10 Forton Staffs
102 E6 Fortrie Abers
107 M10 Fortrose Highld
7 P7 Fortuneswell Dorset
90 F2 Fort William Highld
21 M4 Forty Hill Gt Lon
19 K8 Fosbury Wilts
30 G9 Foscot Oxon
43 K4 Fosdyke Lincs
92 B4 Foss P & K
30 E11 Fossebridge Gloucs
21 P2 Foster Street Essex
40 F2 Foston Derbys
41 N8 Foston Leics
42 C2 Foston Lincs
59 P2 Foston N York
61 J3 Foston on the Wolds E R Yk
53 K5 Fotherby Lincs
42 F10 Fotheringhay Nhants
81 K3 Foulden Border
44 C9 Foulden Norfk
40 G8 Foul End Warwks
23 J5 Foulness Island Essex
6 b2 Foulon Vale Crematorium Guern
58 B6 Foulridge Lancs
44 G5 Foulsham Norfk
87 J11 Fountainhall Border
34 G3 Four Ashes Suffk
48 F10 Four Crosses Powys
11 P1 Four Elms Kent
16 G8 Four Forks Somset
43 M6 Four Gotes Cambs
2 G7 Four Lanes Cnwll
9 R1 Four Marks Hants
54 C6 Four Mile Bridge IoA
40 G10 Four Oaks Solhll
107 N4 Fourpenny Highld
25 Q7 Four Roads Carmth
72 F7 Fourstones Nthumb
12 F4 Four Throws Kent
33 N6 Fourwentways Services Cambs
8 E2 Fovant Wilts
103 K9 Foveran Abers
4 D9 Fowey Cnwll
12 E2 Fowlhall Kent
93 K8 Fowlis Angus
92 D10 Fowlis Wester P & K
33 L7 Fowlmere Cambs
28 G3 Fownhope Herefs
84 H10 Foxbar Rens
17 Q5 Foxcote Somset
56 b5 Foxdale IoM
34 D7 Foxearth Essex
62 E5 Foxfield Cumb
3 L5 Foxhole Cnwll
67 L11 Foxholes N York
44 H6 Foxley Norfk
50 D10 Foxt Staffs
33 L7 Foxton Cambs
41 P9 Foxton Leics
65 Q8 Foxton N York
39 L6 Foxwood Shrops
28 H3 Foy Herefs
98 G5 Foyers Highld
100 D5 Foynesfield Highld
3 K4 Fraddon Cnwll
40 F5 Fradley Staffs
40 C2 Fradswell Staffs
61 K2 Fraisthorpe E R Yk
11 P6 Framfield E Susx
45 K9 Framingham Earl Norfk
45 L9 Framingham Pigot Norfk
35 L4 Framlingham Suffk
7 P4 Frampton Dorset
43 K3 Frampton Lincs
29 J11 Frampton Cotterell S Glos
29 N8 Frampton Mansell Gloucs
29 K7 Frampton on Severn Gloucs
35 K5 Framsden Suffk
73 M11 Framwellgate Moor Dur
39 P6 Franche Worcs
56 E10 Frankby Wirral
40 C10 Frankley Worcs
40 C10 Frankley Services Worcs
41 K12 Frankton Warwks
12 C3 Frant E Susx
103 K2 Fraserburgh Abers
34 H11 Frating Essex
34 H11 Frating Green Essex
9 Q7 Fratton C Port
5 J9 Freathy Cnwll
33 Q3 Freckenham Suffk
56 H3 Freckleton Lancs
42 B6 Freeby Leics
19 N10 Freefolk Hants
31 K10 Freeland Oxon
45 N8 Freethorpe Norfk
45 N8 Freethorpe Common Norfk
43 L2 Freiston Lincs
15 J6 Fremington Devon
65 J7 Fremington N York
28 H12 Frenchay S Glos
92 C4 Frenich P & K
10 D2 Frensham Surrey
56 F7 Freshfield Sefton
18 B8 Freshford Wilts
9 K9 Freshwater IoW
35 L2 Fressingfield Suffk
35 J8 Freston Suffk
110 G3 Freswick Highld
29 K6 Fretherne Gloucs
45 L6 Frettenham Norfk
86 F2 Freuchie Fife
24 G6 Freystrop Pembks
40 D8 Friar Park Sandw
43 M8 Friday Bridge Cambs
35 N5 Friday Street Suffk
60 E3 Fridaythorpe E R Yk
21 L5 Friern Barnet Gt Lon
52 F6 Friesthorpe Lincs
42 D1 Frieston Lincs
20 C5 Frieth Bucks
19 M2 Frilford Oxon
19 P6 Frilsham W Berk
20 E10 Frimley Surrey
22 E9 Frindsbury Medway
44 C3 Fring Norfk
31 N8 Fringford Oxon
22 H11 Frinsted Kent
35 K11 Frinton-on-Sea Essex
93 Q6 Friockheim Angus
41 P4 Frisby on the Wreake Leics
53 M11 Friskney Lincs
12 B9 Friston E Susx
35 N5 Friston Suffk
51 J9 Fritchley Derbys
9 J5 Fritham Hants
14 H8 Frithelstock Devon
14 H8 Frithelstock Stone Devon
53 K12 Frithville Lincs
12 F2 Frittenden Kent
5 Q10 Frittiscombe Devon
45 K10 Fritton Norfk
45 P9 Fritton Norfk
31 M8 Fritwell Oxon
58 F7 Frizinghall C Brad
70 G11 Frizington Cumb
29 K8 Frocester Gloucs
39 K2 Frodesley Shrops
57 K12 Frodsham Ches W
80 G8 Frogden Border
33 L7 Frog End Cambs
50 G5 Froggatt Derbys
50 D10 Froghall Staffs
5 P10 Frogmore Devon
42 G7 Frognall Lincs
39 P8 Frog Pool Worcs
4 H6 Frogwell Cnwll
41 L8 Frolesworth Leics
18 B10 Frome Somset
7 N3 Frome St Quintin Dorset
39 M11 Fromes Hill Herefs
48 F7 Froncysyllte Denbgs
47 P6 Fron-goch Gwynd
48 F7 Fron Isaf Wrexhm
72 H12 Frosterley Dur
19 K7 Froxfield Wilts
10 B5 Froxfield Green Hants
9 M4 Fryern Hill Hants
22 D4 Fryerning Essex
89 M7 Fuinary Highld
52 D12 Fulbeck Lincs
33 N5 Fulbourn Cambs
30 H10 Fulbrook Oxon
9 M2 Fulflood Hants
59 N4 Fulford C York
16 G9 Fulford Somset
50 C12 Fulford Staffs
21 K8 Fulham Gt Lon
11 K7 Fulking W Susx
76 F4 Fullarton N Ayrs
34 C12 Fuller Street Essex
19 L11 Fullerton Hants
53 J8 Fulletby Lincs
30 H5 Fullready Warwks
60 D3 Full Sutton E R Yk
76 G2 Fullwood E Ayrs
20 F6 Fulmer Bucks
44 G4 Fulmodeston Norfk
52 F7 Fulnetby Lincs
43 J5 Fulney Lincs
53 K4 Fulstow Lincs
73 P8 Fulwell Sundld
57 K3 Fulwood Lancs
50 H4 Fulwood Sheff
45 J10 Fundenhall Norfk
10 C8 Funtington W Susx
92 B9 Funtullich P & K
6 H2 Furley Devon
83 Q3 Furnace Ag & B
26 C8 Furnace Carmth
50 D4 Furness Vale Derbys
33 L10 Furneux Pelham Herts
9 K4 Furzley Hants
22 C3 Fyfield Essex
19 K10 Fyfield Hants
19 M2 Fyfield Oxon
18 G7 Fyfield Wilts
18 H8 Fyfield Wilts
67 K6 Fylingthorpe N York
10 D5 Fyning W Susx
102 G7 Fyvie Abers

G

76 H2 Gabroc Hill E Ayrs
41 P5 Gaddesby Leics
20 G2 Gaddesden Row Herts
76 G6 Gadgirth S Ayrs
28 E9 Gaer-llwyd Mons
54 F7 Gaerwen IoA
76 F4 Gailes N Ayrs
40 B5 Gailey Staffs
65 L4 Gainford Dur
52 B5 Gainsborough Lincs
34 C9 Gainsford End Essex
105 M7 Gairloch Highld
98 B11 Gairlochy Highld
86 D3 Gairneybridge P & K
71 N6 Gaitsgill Cumb
80 C7 Galashiels Border
63 J10 Galgate Lancs
17 P9 Galhampton Somset
90 B10 Gallanachbeg Ag & B
89 R10 Gallanachmore Ag & B
86 G4 Gallatown Fife
22 E3 Galleywood Essex
98 H10 Gallovie Highld
69 L3 Galloway Forest Park
93 M7 Gallowfauld Angus
92 H8 Gallowhill P & K
97 L5 Galltair Highld
5 N11 Galmpton Devon
6 B10 Galmpton Torbay
65 M11 Galphay N York
76 H4 Galston E Ayrs
72 B11 Gamblesby Cumb
33 J6 Gamlingay Cambs
32 H6 Gamlingay Great Heath Cambs
102 G3 Gamrie Abers
51 N12 Gamston Notts
51 P5 Gamston Notts
90 B9 Ganavan Bay Ag & B
47 M6 Ganllwyd Gwynd
95 K7 Gannachy Angus
61 K7 Ganstead E R Yk
66 F12 Ganthorpe N York
67 L11 Ganton N York
101 L5 Garbity Moray
34 G1 Garboldisham Norfk
99 L4 Garbole Highld
101 L12 Garchory Abers
20 D9 Gardeners Green Wokham
102 G3 Gardenstown Abers
50 H2 Garden Village Sheff
111 k4 Garderhouse Shet
18 B11 Gare Hill Somset
84 D5 Garelochhead Ag & B
19 M2 Garford Oxon
59 K7 Garforth Leeds
58 B4 Gargrave N York
85 M4 Gargunnock Stirlg
45 K12 Garlic Street Norfk
69 L9 Garlieston D & G
23 P9 Garlinge Kent
23 L11 Garlinge Green Kent
95 M2 Garlogie Abers
102 G5 Garmond Abers
101 L3 Garmouth Moray
39 L2 Garmston Shrops
46 H3 Garn-Dolbenmaen Gwynd
85 L8 Garnkirk N Lans
111 e2 Garrabost W Isls
77 J7 Garrallan E Ayrs
2 G10 Garras Cnwll
47 K3 Garreg Gwynd
72 D11 Garrigill Cumb
69 N3 Garroch D & G
68 F10 Garrochtrie D & G
84 B11 Garrochty Ag & B
104 G9 Garros Highld
64 E8 Garsdale Head Cumb
18 E4 Garsdon Wilts
40 C1 Garshall Green Staffs
31 M12 Garsington Oxon
63 J12 Garstang Lancs
20 H4 Garston Herts
56 H11 Garston Lpool
82 E10 Gartachossan Ag & B
85 L9 Gartcosh N Lans
37 Q10 Garth Powys
48 F7 Garth Wrexhm
85 L9 Garthamlock C Glas
38 E3 Garthmyl Powys
42 B6 Garthorpe Leics
60 E9 Garthorpe N Linc
37 K4 Garth Penrhyncoch Cerdgn
63 K3 Garth Row Cumb
102 C8 Gartly Abers
85 J4 Gartmore Stirlg
85 N9 Gartness N Lans
84 H5 Gartness Stirlg
84 G6 Gartocharn W Duns
60 G3 Garton-on-the-Wolds E R Yk
110 B11 Gartymore Highld
87 L7 Garvald E Loth
90 D2 Garvan Highld
82 E5 Garvard Ag & B
106 G9 Garve Highld
83 K2 Garvellachs Ag & B
44 G8 Garvestone Norfk
84 E8 Garvock Inver
28 E4 Garway Herefs
111 d2 Garyvard W Isls
8 B2 Gasper Wilts
18 C7 Gastard Wilts
34 F1 Gasthorpe Norfk
33 N12 Gaston Green Essex
9 N9 Gatcombe IoW
52 B7 Gate Burton Lincs
59 M8 Gateforth N York
76 G4 Gatehead E Ayrs
59 P3 Gate Helmsley N York
72 E3 Gatehouse Nthumb
69 N7 Gatehouse of Fleet D & G
44 F5 Gateley Norfk
65 N9 Gatenby N York
80 G9 Gateshaw Border
73 M8 Gateshead Gatesd
93 M6 Gateside Angus
84 H10 Gateside E Rens
86 E1 Gateside Fife
84 F11 Gateside N Ayrs
78 E8 Gateslack D & G
57 Q10 Gatley Stockp
80 D7 Gattonside Border
11 L2 Gatwick Airport W Susx
41 P7 Gaulby Leics
93 L10 Gauldry Fife
93 J5 Gauldswell P & K
52 H8 Gautby Lincs
80 G4 Gavinton Border
31 P7 Gawcott Bucks
50 B6 Gawsworth Ches E
63 M5 Gawthrop Cumb
62 F5 Gawthwaite Cumb
31 J4 Gaydon Warwks
32 C7 Gayhurst M Keyn
64 F9 Gayle N York
65 K6 Gayles N York
31 P4 Gayton Nhants
44 C6 Gayton Norfk
40 C2 Gayton Staffs
53 L6 Gayton le Marsh Lincs
44 C6 Gayton Thorpe Norfk
43 Q6 Gaywood Norfk
34 C4 Gazeley Suffk
111 d2 Gearraidh Bhaird W Isls
104 C9 Geary Highld
34 F5 Gedding Suffk
42 C12 Geddington Nhants
51 N11 Gedling Notts
43 L5 Gedney Lincs
43 L5 Gedney Broadgate Lincs
43 M4 Gedney Drove End Lincs
43 L5 Gedney Dyke Lincs
43 K7 Gedney Hill Lincs
42 E8 Geeston Rutlnd
45 N10 Geldeston Norfk
48 D3 Gellifor Denbgs
27 N9 Gelligaer Caerph
47 L4 Gellilydan Gwynd
26 G7 Gellinudd Neath
92 G7 Gellyburn P & K
25 M4 Gellywen Carmth
70 C4 Gelston D & G
42 C2 Gelston Lincs
61 J3 Gembling E R Yk
40 D5 Gentleshaw Staffs
79 L9 Georgefield D & G
20 F7 George Green Bucks
14 H4 Georgeham Devon
110 D4 Georgemas Junction Station Highld
15 M7 George Nympton Devon
111 h2 Georth Ork
5 J2 Germansweek Devon
3 K8 Gerrans Cnwll
20 G6 Gerrards Cross Bucks
66 G5 Gerrick R & Cl
34 D8 Gestingthorpe Essex
48 E11 Geuffordd Powys
21 Q5 Gidea Park Gt Lon
85 J10 Giffnock E Rens
87 K8 Gifford E Loth
93 K12 Giffordtown Fife
63 P9 Giggleswick N York
75 J3 Gigha Ag & B
60 E8 Gilberdyke E R Yk
87 J8 Gilchriston E Loth
70 H7 Gilcrux Cumb
58 G8 Gildersome Leeds

51 M4 Gildingwells Rothm
73 N11 Gilesgate Moor Dur
16 D3 Gileston V Glam
27 N8 Gilfach Caerph
27 K10 Gilfach Goch Brdgnd
36 G8 Gilfachrheda Cerdgn
70 G10 Gilgarran Cumb
66 F9 Gillamoor N York
104 C9 Gillen Highld
79 J9 Gillesbie D & G
66 E11 Gilling East N York
8 B3 Gillingham Dorset
22 F9 Gillingham Medway
45 N10 Gillingham Norfk
65 L6 Gilling West N York
110 E4 Gillock Highld
110 G2 Gills Highld
79 M5 Gilmanscleuch Border
86 F8 Gilmerton C Edin
92 D10 Gilmerton P & K
64 H5 Gilmonby Dur
41 M9 Gilmorton Leics
41 M6 Gilroes Crematorium C Leic
72 B7 Gilsland Nthumb
87 J10 Gilston Border
21 N2 Gilston Herts
27 Q6 Gilwern Mons
45 L3 Gimingham Norfk
34 H4 Gipping Suffk
53 J12 Gipsey Bridge Lincs
76 F3 Girdle Toll N Ayrs
111 k4 Girlsta Shet
65 N6 Girsby N York
69 N8 Girthon D & G
33 L4 Girton Cambs
52 B9 Girton Notts
76 D10 Girvan S Ayrs
63 P11 Gisburn Lancs
45 Q11 Gisleham Suffk
34 H3 Gislingham Suffk
45 J11 Gissing Norfk
6 F3 Gittisham Devon
38 E10 Gladestry Powys
87 J7 Gladsmuir E Loth
26 F8 Glais Swans
66 H6 Glaisdale N York
93 L6 Glamis Angus
26 F6 Glanaman Carmth
44 H2 Glandford Norfk
25 L3 Glandwr Pembks
47 L11 Glandyfi Cerdgn
27 J10 Glanllynfi Brdgnd
26 G7 Glan-rhyd Powys
81 M10 Glanton Nthumb
7 P2 Glanvilles Wootton Dorset
56 D11 Glan-y-don Flints
42 E11 Glapthorn Nhants
51 L7 Glapwell Derbys
27 P2 Glasbury Powys
38 D10 Glascwm Powys
55 N10 Glasfryn Conwy
85 K9 Glasgow C Glas
84 H9 Glasgow Airport Rens
85 J9 Glasgow Science Centre C Glas
54 H7 Glasinfryn Gwynd
97 J9 Glasnacardoch Bay Highld
96 G7 Glasnakille Highld
77 M2 Glassford S Lans
29 J5 Glasshouse Gloucs
58 F2 Glasshouses N York
71 L4 Glasson Cumb
63 J10 Glasson Lancs
72 B12 Glassonby Cumb
93 Q5 Glasterlaw Angus
42 C9 Glaston Rutlnd
17 M8 Glastonbury Somset
42 G11 Glatton Cambs
57 M9 Glazebrook Warrtn
57 M9 Glazebury Warrtn
39 N5 Glazeley Shrops
62 F7 Gleaston Cumb
98 G5 Glebe Highld
58 H6 Gledhow Leeds
69 P8 Gledpark D & G
48 F7 Gledrid Shrops
34 D7 Glemsford Suffk
101 K7 Glenallachie Moray
97 J10 Glenancross Highld
89 L7 Glenaros House Ag & B
56 d3 Glen Auldyn IoM
75 K5 Glenbarr Ag & B
102 D4 Glenbarry Abers
89 M4 Glenbeg Highld
95 M6 Glenbervie Abers
85 M8 Glenboig N Lans
89 M4 Glenborrodale Highld
84 B4 Glenbranter Ag & B
78 H5 Glenbreck Border
96 E5 Glenbrittle House Highld
77 M5 Glenbuck E Ayrs
94 F8 Glencally Angus
70 G2 Glencaple D & G
105 R11 Glencarron Lodge Highld
92 H10 Glencarse P & K
94 C5 Glen Clunie Lodge Abers
90 F5 Glencoe Highld
78 H3 Glencothe Border
86 E4 Glencraig Fife
78 C10 Glencrosh D & G
104 B11 Glendale Highld
83 Q6 Glendaruel Ag & B
86 B2 Glendevon P & K
98 E7 Glendoe Lodge Highld
93 J10 Glendoick P & K
93 K11 Glenduckie Fife
85 Q2 Gleneagles P & K
74 D3 Glenegedale Ag & B
97 L6 Glenelg Highld
100 F6 Glenerney Moray
92 G12 Glenfarg P & K
41 M6 Glenfield Leics
97 M12 Glenfinnan Highld
98 C10 Glenfintaig Lodge Highld
92 H11 Glenfoot P & K
90 H12 Glenfyne Lodge Ag & B
84 F11 Glengarnock N Ayrs
110 C3 Glengolly Highld
89 K5 Glengorm Castle Ag & B
96 E1 Glengrasco Highld
78 H3 Glenholm Border
69 N2 Glenhoul D & G
94 D9 Glenisla Angus
84 C7 Glenkin Ag & B
101 N11 Glenkindie Abers
101 J9 Glenlivet Moray
70 C3 Glenlochar D & G
86 E2 Glenlomond P & K
68 G7 Glenluce D & G
84 B5 Glenmassen Ag & B
85 M9 Glenmavis N Lans
56 b5 Glen Maye IoM
96 E2 Glenmore Highld
99 P7 Glenmore Lodge Highld
90 F2 Glen Nevis House Highld
85 P4 Glenochil Clacks
41 M7 Glen Parva Leics
94 G9 Glenquiech Angus
83 M8 Glenralloch Ag & B
71 N11 Glenridding Cumb
86 F3 Glenrothes Fife
98 H9 Glenshero Lodge Highld
84 B7 Glenstriven Ag & B
52 E5 Glentham Lincs
69 K3 Glen Trool Lodge D & G
69 J4 Glentrool Village D & G
99 K9 Glentruim House Highld
52 D6 Glentworth Lincs
89 N2 Glenuig Highld
96 F2 Glenvarragill Highld
56 c5 Glen Vine IoM
68 G5 Glenwhilly D & G
78 D4 Glespin S Lans
28 G4 Glewstone Herefs
42 G8 Glinton C Pete
41 Q8 Glooston Leics
50 D3 Glossop Derbys
81 Q12 Gloster Hill Nthumb
29 L5 Gloucester Gloucs
29 L5 Gloucester Crematorium Gloucs
29 M5 Gloucestershire Airport Gloucs
58 D5 Glusburn N York
110 B8 Glutt Lodge Highld
31 K9 Glympton Oxon
36 E10 Glynarthen Cerdgn
48 E7 Glyn Ceiriog Wrexhm
27 J8 Glyncorrwg Neath
11 P8 Glynde E Susx
48 D7 Glyndyfrdwy Denbgs
27 J7 Glynneath Neath
3 N3 Glynn Valley Crematorium Cnwll
27 M10 Glyntaff Crematorium Rhondd
26 H5 Glyntawe Powys
25 N2 Glynteg Carmth
49 P10 Gnosall Staffs
49 P10 Gnosall Heath Staffs
41 Q7 Goadby Leics
41 R3 Goadby Marwood Leics
18 F5 Goatacre Wilts
17 P11 Goathill Dorset
67 J7 Goathland N York
16 H8 Goathurst Somset
48 F8 Gobowen Shrops
10 F2 Godalming Surrey
12 G3 Goddard's Green Kent
33 J3 Godmanchester Cambs
7 P4 Godmanstone Dorset
23 K12 Godmersham Kent
17 L7 Godney Somset
2 F9 Godolphin Cross Cnwll
26 G7 Godre'r-graig Neath
9 N10 Godshill IoW
21 M11 Godstone Surrey
28 C7 Goetre Mons
21 M3 Goff's Oak Herts
28 B6 Gofilon Mons
86 E7 Gogar C Edin
37 L4 Goginan Cerdgn
46 H3 Golan Gwynd
4 D8 Golant Cnwll
4 H6 Golberdon Cnwll
57 L8 Golborne Wigan
58 E10 Golcar Kirk
28 D11 Goldcliff Newpt
12 D1 Golden Green Kent
10 B2 Golden Pot Hants
21 K6 Golders Green Gt Lon
21 K6 Golders Green Crematorium Gt Lon
22 H2 Goldhanger Essex
32 F6 Goldington Bed
59 J3 Goldsborough N York
67 J5 Goldsborough N York
2 E9 Goldsithney Cnwll
20 F10 Goldsworth Park Surrey
59 L12 Goldthorpe Barns
14 G7 Goldworthy Devon
107 N10 Gollanfield Highld
107 N3 Golspie Highld
8 H1 Gomeldon Wilts
10 H1 Gomshall Surrey
51 P10 Gonalston Notts
42 C3 Gonerby Hill Foot Lincs
111 k3 Gonfirth Shet
22 D2 Good Easter Essex
44 C9 Gooderstone Norfk
15 K5 Goodleigh Devon
60 F5 Goodmanham E R Yk
21 P6 Goodmayes Gt Lon
23 K10 Goodnestone Kent
23 N11 Goodnestone Kent
28 G5 Goodrich Herefs
28 G5 Goodrich Castle Herefs
6 B10 Goodrington Torbay
57 P4 Goodshaw Lancs
24 G2 Goodwick Pembks
19 L11 Goodworth Clatford Hants
60 C9 Goole E R Yk
30 D3 Goom's Hill Worcs
2 G6 Goonbell Cnwll
2 H5 Goonhavern Cnwll
2 G6 Goonvrea Cnwll
95 M5 Goosecruives Abers
5 N2 Gooseford Devon
35 J10 Goose Green Essex
17 P2 Goose Green S Glos
19 L3 Goosey Oxon
57 K2 Goosnargh Lancs
49 P2 Goostrey Ches E
17 M2 Gordano Services N Som
80 E5 Gordon Border
79 L4 Gordon Arms Hotel Border
102 D4 Gordonstown Abers
102 F7 Gordonstown Abers
86 G9 Gorebridge Mdloth
43 L7 Gorefield Cambs
18 G8 Gores Wilts
7 c2 Gorey Jersey
19 P5 Goring Oxon
10 H9 Goring-by-Sea W Susx
45 Q8 Gorleston on Sea Norfk
40 B8 Gornal Wood Crematorium Dudley
102 F4 Gorrachie Abers
3 M7 Gorran Churchtown Cnwll
3 M7 Gorran Haven Cnwll
56 D12 Gorsedd Flints
18 H4 Gorse Hill Swindn
26 D8 Gorseinon Swans
36 H9 Gorsgoch Cerdgn
26 D6 Gorslas Carmth
29 J4 Gorsley Gloucs
29 J4 Gorsley Common Herefs
106 F9 Gorstan Highld
40 E2 Gorsty Hill Staffs
89 P9 Gorten Ag & B
98 G5 Gorthleck Highld
50 B2 Gorton Manch
35 J5 Gosbeck Suffk
43 J4 Gosberton Lincs
34 D10 Gosfield Essex
62 C2 Gosforth Cumb
73 M7 Gosforth N u Ty
40 B8 Gospel End Staffs
9 Q7 Gosport Hants
29 K8 Gossington Gloucs
41 M2 Gotham Notts
29 N3 Gotherington Gloucs
16 H9 Gotton Somset
12 E3 Goudhurst Kent
53 J7 Goulceby Lincs
102 G7 Gourdas Abers
93 L8 Gourdie C Dund
95 N7 Gourdon Abers
84 D7 Gourock Inver
85 J9 Govan C Glas
5 P10 Goveton Devon
59 N9 Gowdall E R Yk
106 H10 Gower Highld
26 C10 Gower Swans
26 D9 Gowerton Swans
86 C5 Gowkhall Fife
61 K5 Goxhill E R Yk
61 J9 Goxhill N Linc
111 d3 Grabhair W Isls
10 E6 Graffham W Susx
32 G3 Grafham Cambs
10 G2 Grafham Surrey
59 K2 Grafton N York
19 J1 Grafton Oxon
48 H10 Grafton Shrops
29 N2 Grafton Worcs
30 C3 Grafton Flyford Worcs
31 Q5 Grafton Regis Nhants
32 D2 Grafton Underwood Nhants
12 G1 Grafty Green Kent
55 L7 Graig Conwy
48 D5 Graig-fechan Denbgs
22 H7 Grain Medway
53 J4 Grainsby Lincs
53 L4 Grainthorpe Lincs
3 L6 Grampound Cnwll
3 K5 Grampound Road Cnwll
111 b5 Gramsdal W Isls
111 b5 Gramsdale W Isls
31 Q8 Granborough Bucks
41 Q1 Granby Notts
31 L2 Grandborough Warwks
7 c2 Grand Chemins Jersey
6 b1 Grandes Rocques Guern
41 K3 Grand Prix Collection Donington Leics
92 D5 Grandtully P & K
71 L11 Grange Cumb
22 F9 Grange Medway
93 K10 Grange P & K
101 N4 Grange Crossroads Moray
100 G3 Grange Hall Moray
78 F1 Grangehall S Lans
21 N5 Grange Hill Essex
50 G8 Grangemill Derbys
58 G10 Grange Moor Kirk
85 Q6 Grangemouth Falk
93 J11 Grange of Lindores Fife
62 H6 Grange-over-Sands Cumb
86 B6 Grangepans Falk
66 D4 Grangetown R & Cl
73 P9 Grangetown Sundld
73 M9 Grange Villa Dur
61 J3 Gransmoor E R Yk
24 F2 Granston Pembks
33 M6 Grantchester Cambs
42 D3 Grantham Lincs
42 D3 Grantham Crematorium Lincs
42 C3 Grantham North Services Lincs
86 F6 Granton C Edin
100 F9 Grantown-on-Spey Highld
87 P8 Grantshouse Border
52 F3 Grasby Lincs
62 G1 Grasmere Cumb
58 C12 Grasscroft Oldham
56 H10 Grassendale Lpool
58 D2 Grassington N York
51 K7 Grassmoor Derbys
52 B9 Grassthorpe Notts
19 J11 Grateley Hants
33 J4 Graveley Cambs
32 H10 Graveley Herts
23 K10 Graveney Kent
22 D8 Gravesend Kent
111 d3 Gravir W Isls
52 D4 Grayingham Lincs
63 L3 Grayrigg Cumb
22 C7 Grays Thurr
10 E3 Grayshott Hants
10 E3 Grayswood Surrey
51 K2 Greasbrough Rothm
56 F10 Greasby Wirral
33 N7 Great Abington Cambs
32 D2 Great Addington Nhants
30 E3 Great Alne Warwks
56 G7 Great Altcar Lancs
21 M2 Great Amwell Herts
64 C5 Great Asby Cumb
34 G4 Great Ashfield Suffk
66 D5 Great Ayton N York
22 E3 Great Baddow Essex
18 B4 Great Badminton S Glos
34 B10 Great Bardfield Essex
32 G6 Great Barford Bed
40 D8 Great Barr Sandw
30 G10 Great Barrington Gloucs
49 J2 Great Barrow Ches W
34 E4 Great Barton Suffk
66 G10 Great Barugh N York
72 H5 Great Bavington Nthumb
35 K7 Great Bealings Suffk
19 J7 Great Bedwyn Wilts
35 J11 Great Bentley Essex
32 B4 Great Billing Nhants
44 C4 Great Bircham Norfk
35 J6 Great Blakenham Suffk
71 P8 Great Blencow Cumb
49 M10 Great Bolas Wrekin
21 J11 Great Bookham Surrey
31 L5 Great Bourton Oxon
41 Q9 Great Bowden Leics
34 B6 Great Bradley Suffk
22 G1 Great Braxted Essex
34 G6 Great Bricett Suffk
32 C10 Great Brickhill Bucks
40 B3 Great Bridgeford Staffs
31 P2 Great Brington Nhants
34 H10 Great Bromley Essex
70 H8 Great Broughton Cumb
66 D6 Great Broughton N York
57 M12 Great Budworth Ches W
65 N4 Great Burdon Darltn
22 D5 Great Burstead Essex
66 D6 Great Busby N York
53 L6 Great Carlton Lincs
42 E8 Great Casterton Rutlnd
18 C7 Great Chalfield Wilts
13 J2 Great Chart Kent
49 P11 Great Chatwell Staffs
33 N8 Great Chesterford Essex
18 E9 Great Cheverell Wilts
33 L8 Great Chishill Cambs
35 K12 Great Clacton Essex
70 G9 Great Clifton Cumb
61 L11 Great Coates NE Lin
29 N1 Great Comberton Worcs
71 P5 Great Corby Cumb
34 E8 Great Cornard Suffk
61 L6 Great Cowden E R Yk
19 J3 Great Coxwell Oxon
32 B2 Great Cransley Nhants
44 E9 Great Cressingham Norfk
71 L10 Great Crosthwaite Cumb
50 F12 Great Cubley Derbys
84 C10 Great Cumbrae Island N Ayrs
41 Q5 Great Dalby Leics
32 C4 Great Doddington Nhants
44 E7 Great Dunham Norfk
33 Q11 Great Dunmow Essex
18 G12 Great Durnford Wilts
33 P10 Great Easton Essex
42 C10 Great Easton Leics
56 H2 Great Eccleston Lancs
44 G10 Great Ellingham Norfk
17 Q6 Great Elm Somset
31 N3 Great Everdon Nhants
33 K6 Great Eversden Cambs
65 M8 Great Fencote N York
34 G5 Great Finborough Suffk
42 F7 Greatford Lincs
44 E7 Great Fransham Norfk
20 G2 Great Gaddesden Herts
50 D11 Greatgate Staffs
42 G12 Great Gidding Cambs
60 E4 Great Givendale E R Yk
35 M4 Great Glemham Suffk
41 P7 Great Glen Leics
42 C3 Great Gonerby Lincs
33 J5 Great Gransden Cambs
33 J7 Great Green Cambs
34 F5 Great Green Suffk
66 G11 Great Habton N York
42 G2 Great Hale Lincs
33 N11 Great Hallingbury Essex
10 C4 Greatham Hants
66 C3 Greatham Hartpl
10 G6 Greatham W Susx
20 D3 Great Hampden Bucks
32 C3 Great Harrowden Nhants
57 N3 Great Harwood Lancs
19 Q1 Great Haseley Oxon
61 K5 Great Hatfield E R Yk
40 D3 Great Haywood Staffs
59 N9 Great Heck N York
34 E8 Great Henny Essex
18 D8 Great Hinton Wilts
44 F10 Great Hockham Norfk
35 K11 Great Holland Essex
20 D9 Great Hollands Br For
34 F9 Great Horkesley Essex
33 L10 Great Hormead Herts
58 F7 Great Horton C Brad
31 Q7 Great Horwood Bucks
59 K11 Great Houghton Barns
32 B5 Great Houghton Nhants
50 F5 Great Hucklow Derbys
61 J3 Great Kelk E R Yk
20 D3 Great Kimble Bucks
20 E4 Great Kingshill Bucks
62 F2 Great Langdale Cumb
65 N8 Great Langton N York
34 C12 Great Leighs Essex
52 G2 Great Limber Lincs
32 C8 Great Linford M Keyn
34 E3 Great Livermere Suffk
50 G6 Great Longstone Derbys
73 N10 Great Lumley Dur
39 P11 Great Malvern Worcs
34 D9 Great Maplestead Essex
56 G2 Great Marton Bpool
44 D5 Great Massingham Norfk
19 Q1 Great Milton Oxon
20 E3 Great Missenden Bucks
57 N2 Great Mitton Lancs
23 Q12 Great Mongeham Kent
45 J11 Great Moulton Norfk
64 D5 Great Musgrave Cumb
48 H10 Great Ness Shrops
34 C11 Great Notley Essex
28 D6 Great Oak Mons
35 K10 Great Oakley Essex
42 C11 Great Oakley Nhants
32 G10 Great Offley Herts
64 C4 Great Ormside Cumb
71 M5 Great Orton Cumb
59 K2 Great Ouseburn N York
41 Q10 Great Oxendon Nhants
22 D3 Great Oxney Green Essex
32 H4 Great Paxton Cambs
56 H3 Great Plumpton Lancs
45 L7 Great Plumstead Norfk
42 D4 Great Ponton Lincs
59 K8 Great Preston Leeds
33 J1 Great Raveley Cambs
30 G10 Great Rissington Gloucs
31 J7 Great Rollright Oxon
44 F5 Great Ryburgh Norfk
39 J2 Great Ryton Shrops
34 B10 Great Saling Essex
71 Q8 Great Salkeld Cumb
33 Q9 Great Sampford Essex
48 G2 Great Saughall Ches W
19 L6 Great Shefford W Berk
33 M6 Great Shelford Cambs
65 N6 Great Smeaton N York
44 F4 Great Snoring Norfk
18 E4 Great Somerford Wilts
49 N9 Great Soudley Shrops
65 N3 Great Stainton Darltn
22 H5 Great Stambridge Essex
32 G4 Great Staughton Cambs
53 M9 Great Steeping Lincs
28 H11 Great Stoke S Glos
13 L5 Greatstone-on-Sea Kent
71 Q10 Great Strickland Cumb
32 H2 Great Stukeley Cambs
52 H7 Great Sturton Lincs
72 G6 Great Swinburne Nthumb
31 K8 Great Tew Oxon
34 E10 Great Tey Essex
34 B6 Great Thurlow Suffk
15 J8 Great Torrington Devon
72 H2 Great Tosson Nthumb
22 G2 Great Totham Essex
22 G2 Great Totham Essex
62 F7 Great Urswick Cumb
22 H6 Great Wakering Essex
34 E7 Great Waldingfield Suffk
44 F3 Great Walsingham Norfk
22 E2 Great Waltham Essex
22 C5 Great Warley Essex
29 N2 Great Washbourne Gloucs
5 P3 Great Weeke Devon
42 D11 Great Weldon Nhants
34 H8 Great Wenham Suffk
72 H6 Great Whittington Nthumb
23 J1 Great Wigborough Essex
33 N5 Great Wilbraham Cambs
8 F1 Great Wishford Wilts
29 M6 Great Witcombe Gloucs
39 N8 Great Witley Worcs
30 G7 Great Wolford Warwks
31 M6 Greatworth Nhants
34 B7 Great Wratting Suffk
32 H10 Great Wymondley Herts
40 C6 Great Wyrley Staffs
45 Q8 Great Yarmouth Norfk
45 Q9 Great Yarmouth Crematorium Norfk
34 C8 Great Yeldham Essex
85 Q10 Greenburn W Loth
33 K11 Green End Herts
33 K9 Green End Herts
84 D5 Greenfield Ag & B
32 F9 Greenfield C Beds
56 E12 Greenfield Flints
98 B8 Greenfield Highld
58 C12 Greenfield Oldham
21 J7 Greenford Gt Lon
85 N8 Greengairs N Lans
58 G6 Greengates C Brad
16 E11 Greenham Somset
59 L3 Green Hammerton N York
72 E4 Greenhaugh Nthumb
72 C7 Greenhead Nthumb
40 C5 Green Heath Staffs
78 H11 Greenhill D & G
85 N7 Greenhill Falk
23 M9 Greenhill Kent
78 F3 Greenhill S Lans
22 C8 Greenhithe Kent
77 J4 Greenholm E Ayrs
80 D9 Greenhouse Border
58 E2 Greenhow Hill N York
110 E3 Greenland Highld
51 K3 Greenland Sheff
80 F5 Greenlaw Border
70 G1 Greenlea D & G
85 N2 Greenloaning P & K
57 P6 Greenmount Bury
84 E7 Greenock Inver
62 G6 Greenodd Cumb
17 N6 Green Ore Somset
63 J2 Green Quarter Cumb
86 B12 Greenshields S Lans
73 K8 Greenside Gatesd
58 F10 Greenside Kirk
31 P4 Greens Norton Nhants
34 G10 Greenstead Essex
34 D10 Greenstead Green Essex
21 J4 Green Street Herts
33 M11 Green Street Herts
22 C8 Green Street Green Kent
33 M11 Green Tye Herts
17 J10 Greenway Somset
21 M7 Greenwich Gt Lon
30 D7 Greet Gloucs
39 L7 Greete Shrops
53 K8 Greetham Lincs
42 D7 Greetham Rutlnd
58 E9 Greetland Calder
17 K8 Greinton Somset
56 b6 Grenaby IoM
32 C5 Grendon Nhants
40 H7 Grendon Warwks
31 P9 Grendon Underwood Bucks
51 J3 Grenoside Sheff
51 J3 Grenoside Crematorium Sheff
111 c3 Greosabhagh W Isls
48 G5 Gresford Wrexhm
45 J3 Gresham Norfk
104 D10 Greshornish House Hotel Highld
44 F7 Gressenhall Norfk
44 F6 Gressenhall Green Norfk
63 K8 Gressingham Lancs
65 J5 Greta Bridge Dur
71 M3 Gretna D & G
71 M2 Gretna Green D & G
71 L2 Gretna Services D & G
30 D7 Gretton Gloucs
42 C10 Gretton Nhants
39 K3 Gretton Shrops
65 M11 Grewelthorpe N York
78 H10 Greyrigg D & G
20 B6 Greys Green Oxon
70 H9 Greysouthen Cumb
71 P8 Greystoke Cumb
93 P7 Greystone Angus
20 B12 Greywell Hants
41 J9 Griff Warwks
28 C8 Griffithstown Torfn
57 L6 Grimeford Village Lancs
51 J3 Grimesthorpe Sheff
59 K11 Grimethorpe Barns
39 Q9 Grimley Worcs
76 F8 Grimmet S Ayrs
53 L6 Grimoldby Lincs
48 G9 Grimpo Shrops
57 L3 Grimsargh Lancs
61 M11 Grimsby NE Lin
53 J3 Grimsby Crematorium NE Lin
31 P4 Grimscote Nhants
14 E10 Grimscott Cnwll
111 d2 Grimshader W Isls
42 F5 Grimsthorpe Lincs
41 P3 Grimston Leics
44 C5 Grimston Norfk
7 P4 Grimstone Dorset
34 F3 Grimstone End Suffk
67 N12 Grindale E R Yk
50 G5 Grindleford Derbys
63 N11 Grindleton Lancs
49 K7 Grindley Brook Shrops
50 F5 Grindlow Derbys
50 E9 Grindon Staffs
51 Q3 Gringley on the Hill Notts
71 M4 Grinsdale Cumb
49 K10 Grinshill Shrops

65 J7 Grinton N York
111 d2 Griomaisiader W Isls
111 b5 Griomsaigh W Isls
88 F5 Grishipoll Ag & B
67 M10 Gristhorpe N York
44 F9 Griston Norfk
111 h2 Gritley Ork
18 F4 Grittenham Wilts
18 C5 Grittleton Wilts
62 E5 Grizebeck Cumb
62 G4 Grizedale Cumb
41 M6 Groby Leics
55 Q8 Groes Conwy
27 M11 Groes-faen Rhondd
54 F9 Groeslon Gwynd
27 N10 Groes-Wen Caerph
111 a5 Grogarry W Isls
75 M4 Grogport Ag & B
111 a5 Groigearraidh W Isls
56 C11 Gronant Flints
11 Q3 Groombridge E Susx
111 c3 Grosebay W Isls
28 E4 Grosmont Mons
67 J6 Grosmont N York
34 F8 Groton Suffk
7 c2 Grouville Jersey
51 Q5 Grove Notts
19 L3 Grove Oxon
22 F11 Grove Green Kent
21 N8 Grove Park Gt Lon
26 D8 Grovesend Swans
105 P4 Gruinard Highld
82 D9 Gruinart Ag & B
96 D4 Grula Highld
89 L8 Gruline Ag & B
35 K6 Grundisburgh Suffk
111 j4 Gruting Shet
90 F7 Gualachulain Highld
93 M11 Guardbridge Fife
39 P11 Guarlford Worcs
92 E6 Guay P & K
6 b2 Guernsey Airport Guern
12 G7 Guestling Green E Susx
12 G6 Guestling Thorn E Susx
44 H5 Guestwick Norfk
73 M4 Guide Post Nthumb
33 J7 Guilden Morden Cambs
49 J2 Guilden Sutton Ches W
20 F12 Guildford Surrey
10 F2 Guildford Crematorium Surrey
92 G8 Guildtown P & K
41 P11 Guilsborough Nhants
48 E12 Guilsfield Powys
76 F8 Guiltreehill S Ayrs
15 J5 Guineaford Devon
66 E4 Guisborough R & Cl
58 G6 Guiseley Leeds
44 G5 Guist Norfk
30 E8 Guiting Power Gloucs
87 J5 Gullane E Loth
2 D9 Gulval Cnwll
5 K5 Gulworthy Devon
25 J8 Gumfreston Pembks
41 P9 Gumley Leics
42 D6 Gunby Lincs
53 M9 Gunby Lincs
9 Q2 Gundleton Hants
12 C7 Gun Hill E Susx
15 L5 Gunn Devon
64 G7 Gunnerside N York
72 G6 Gunnerton Nthumb
60 E11 Gunness N Linc
5 J6 Gunnislake Cnwll
111 k4 Gunnista Shet
52 B4 Gunthorpe N Linc
44 G3 Gunthorpe Norfk
51 P11 Gunthorpe Notts
2 F10 Gunwalloe Cnwll
9 N8 Gurnard IoW
17 N6 Gurney Slade Somset
26 G7 Gurnos Powys
8 E5 Gussage All Saints Dorset
8 E5 Gussage St Andrew Dorset
8 E5 Gussage St Michael Dorset
13 P2 Guston Kent
111 k2 Gutcher Shet
93 P5 Guthrie Angus
43 L8 Guyhirn Cambs
81 P12 Guyzance Nthumb
56 C11 Gwaenysgor Flints
54 E6 Gwalchmai IoA
26 F6 Gwaun-Cae-Gurwen Carmth
2 G9 Gweek Cnwll
38 C12 Gwenddwr Powys
2 H7 Gwennap Cnwll
28 C8 Gwent Crematorium Mons
48 E3 Gwernaffield Flints
28 E8 Gwernesney Mons
26 D3 Gwernogle Carmth
48 E3 Gwernymynydd Flints
56 C11 Gwespyr Flints
2 E8 Gwinear Cnwll
2 E7 Gwithian Cnwll
48 C6 Gwyddelwern Denbgs
26 C2 Gwyddgrug Carmth
55 N8 Gwytherin Conwy

H

38 H2 Habberley Shrops
39 P6 Habberley Worcs
57 P3 Habergham Lancs
53 N9 Habertoft Lincs
61 K10 Habrough NE Lin
42 F5 Hacconby Lincs
42 E3 Haceby Lincs
35 M5 Hacheston Suffk
21 L9 Hackbridge Gt Lon
51 K4 Hackenthorpe Sheff
44 H9 Hackford Norfk
65 M8 Hackforth N York
111 h2 Hackland Ork
32 B6 Hackleton Nhants
23 Q11 Hacklinge Kent
67 L9 Hackness N York
21 M6 Hackney Gt Lon
52 E7 Hackthorn Lincs
71 Q10 Hackthorpe Cumb
80 G7 Hadden Border
20 B2 Haddenham Bucks
33 M2 Haddenham Cambs
87 K7 Haddington E Loth
52 D10 Haddington Lincs
45 P10 Haddiscoe Norfk
102 H7 Haddo Abers
42 G10 Haddon Cambs
50 D2 Hadfield Derbys
33 M11 Hadham Ford Herts
22 F6 Hadleigh Essex
34 G8 Hadleigh Suffk
39 Q8 Hadley Worcs
49 M12 Hadley Wrekin
40 F4 Hadley End Staffs
21 L4 Hadley Wood Gt Lon
22 D12 Hadlow Kent
11 Q5 Hadlow Down E Susx
49 K10 Hadnall Shrops
72 G6 Hadrian's Wall Nthumb
33 N7 Hadstock Essex
30 B2 Hadzor Worcs
111 k4 Haggersta Shet
81 L5 Haggerston Nthumb
85 N7 Haggs Falk
28 G1 Hagley Herefs
40 B10 Hagley Worcs
53 K9 Hagworthingham Lincs
62 B1 Haile Cumb
31 J10 Hailey Oxon
12 C8 Hailsham E Susx
32 G4 Hail Weston Cambs
21 P5 Hainault Gt Lon
45 K6 Hainford Norfk
52 H6 Hainton Lincs
61 J2 Haisthorpe E R Yk
24 F7 Hakin Pembks
51 P9 Halam Notts
86 D5 Halbeath Fife
6 D1 Halberton Devon
110 E4 Halcro Highld
63 J6 Hale Cumb
57 J11 Hale Halton
8 H4 Hale Hants
10 D1 Hale Surrey
57 P10 Hale Traffd
45 N10 Hales Norfk
49 N8 Hales Staffs
40 C10 Halesowen Dudley
23 M10 Hales Place Kent
22 D12 Hale Street Kent
35 N2 Halesworth Suffk
57 J10 Halewood Knows
5 Q5 Halford Devon
30 H5 Halford Warwks
39 P4 Halfpenny Green Staffs
48 G12 Halfway House Shrops
22 H8 Halfway Houses Kent
58 E8 Halifax Calder
110 D4 Halkirk Highld
48 E2 Halkyn Flints
84 G11 Hall E Rens
11 P6 Halland E Susx
42 B10 Hallaton Leics
17 P5 Hallatrow BaNES
72 B8 Hallbankgate Cumb
62 E3 Hall Dunnerdale Cumb
28 G11 Hallen S Glos
73 N11 Hallgarth Dur
85 P7 Hall Glen Falk
40 E10 Hall Green Birm
104 C9 Hallin Highld
22 E10 Halling Medway
53 K6 Hallington Lincs
72 H6 Hallington Nthumb
57 M6 Halliwell Bolton
51 P9 Halloughton Notts
39 P9 Hallow Worcs
5 Q11 Hallsands Devon
33 J10 Hall's Green Herts
79 K2 Hallyne Border
29 J8 Halmore Gloucs
10 E8 Halnaker W Susx
56 G6 Halsall Lancs
31 M6 Halse Nhants
16 F9 Halse Somset
2 D7 Halsetown Cnwll
61 M8 Halsham E R Yk
34 D10 Halstead Essex
21 P10 Halstead Kent
41 Q6 Halstead Leics
7 M2 Halstock Dorset
60 H7 Haltemprice Crematorium E R Yk
53 J10 Haltham Lincs
20 E2 Halton Bucks
63 J8 Halton Lancs
59 J7 Halton Leeds
72 H7 Halton Nthumb
48 F7 Halton Wrexhm
58 D4 Halton East N York
64 F11 Halton Gill N York
53 L9 Halton Holegate Lincs
72 C8 Halton Lea Gate Nthumb
72 H7 Halton Shields Nthumb
63 Q10 Halton West N York
72 D7 Haltwhistle Nthumb
45 N8 Halvergate Norfk
5 Q9 Halwell Devon
14 H11 Halwill Devon
14 H11 Halwill Junction Devon
6 H3 Ham Devon
29 J8 Ham Gloucs
21 J8 Ham Gt Lon
23 P11 Ham Kent
16 H10 Ham Somset
19 K8 Ham Wilts
20 C6 Hambleden Bucks
9 Q4 Hambledon Hants
10 F3 Hambledon Surrey
9 N6 Hamble-le-Rice Hants
56 G1 Hambleton Lancs
59 M7 Hambleton N York
17 K10 Hambridge Somset
10 C8 Hambrook W Susx
53 K9 Hameringham Lincs
32 G2 Hamerton Cambs
30 D2 Ham Green Worcs
85 M11 Hamilton S Lans
85 M10 Hamilton Services S Lans
7 N2 Hamlet Dorset
21 K7 Hammersmith Gt Lon
40 E6 Hammerwich Staffs
8 B5 Hammoon Dorset
111 k4 Hamnavoe Shet
12 C9 Hampden Park E Susx
30 E10 Hampnett Gloucs
59 L11 Hampole Donc
8 F7 Hampreston Dorset
21 L6 Hampstead Gt Lon
19 N5 Hampstead Norreys W Berk
58 H3 Hampsthwaite N York
42 G10 Hampton C Pete
21 J9 Hampton Gt Lon
23 M9 Hampton Kent
39 N5 Hampton Shrops
18 H3 Hampton Swindn
30 D5 Hampton Worcs
28 G2 Hampton Bishop Herefs
21 J9 Hampton Court Palace & Gardens Gt Lon
49 J5 Hampton Heath Ches W
40 G10 Hampton in Arden Solhll
30 B2 Hampton Lovett Worcs
30 G3 Hampton Lucy Warwks
30 H2 Hampton Magna Warwks
31 L10 Hampton Poyle Oxon
21 J9 Hampton Wick Gt Lon
9 J4 Hamptworth Wilts
11 N7 Hamsey E Susx
40 E4 Hamstall Ridware Staffs
19 M7 Hamstead Marshall W Berk
65 K2 Hamsterley Dur
73 K9 Hamsterley Dur
13 J4 Hamstreet Kent
17 M8 Ham Street Somset
8 E8 Hamworthy Poole
40 F2 Hanbury Staffs
30 C2 Hanbury Worcs
49 Q7 Hanchurch Staffs
108 C6 Handa Island Highld
6 E4 Hand and Pen Devon
48 H3 Handbridge Ches W
11 L4 Handcross W Susx
57 Q11 Handforth Ches E
49 J4 Handley Ches W
51 J8 Handley Derbys
40 D9 Handsworth Birm
51 K4 Handsworth Sheff
58 G9 Hanging Heaton Kirk
41 Q11 Hanging Houghton Nhants
18 F12 Hanging Langford Wilts
11 L8 Hangleton Br & H
17 P2 Hanham S Glos
49 M6 Hankelow Ches E
29 N9 Hankerton Wilts
50 B10 Hanley C Stke
50 B10 Hanley C Stke
39 Q12 Hanley Castle Worcs
39 M8 Hanley Child Worcs
39 P12 Hanley Swan Worcs
39 M8 Hanley William Worcs
58 B2 Hanlith N York
49 J7 Hanmer Wrexhm
15 K6 Hannaford Devon
19 N9 Hannington Hants
32 B3 Hannington Nhants
18 H3 Hannington Swindn
18 H2 Hannington Wick Swindn
32 B7 Hanslope M Keyn
42 F5 Hanthorpe Lincs
21 J7 Hanwell Gt Lon
31 K5 Hanwell Oxon
49 J12 Hanwood Shrops
20 H8 Hanworth Gt Lon
45 K3 Hanworth Norfk
78 E3 Happendon S Lans
78 D3 Happendon Services S Lans
45 N4 Happisburgh Norfk
45 N4 Happisburgh Common Norfk
49 J1 Hapsford Ches W
57 P3 Hapton Lancs
45 K10 Hapton Norfk
5 Q8 Harberton Devon
5 Q8 Harbertonford Devon
23 L10 Harbledown Kent
40 D10 Harborne Birm
41 L10 Harborough Magna Warwks
81 K12 Harbottle Nthumb
5 P7 Harbourneford Devon
31 J3 Harbury Warwks
41 Q2 Harby Leics
52 C8 Harby Notts
6 B6 Harcombe Devon
6 F5 Harcombe Devon
7 J4 Harcombe Bottom Devon
58 E6 Harden C Brad
40 D7 Harden Wsall
18 D6 Hardenhuish Wilts
95 N2 Hardgate Abers
70 D3 Hardgate D & G
84 H8 Hardgate W Duns
10 G6 Hardham W Susx
44 H8 Hardingham Norfk
31 Q3 Hardingstone Nhants
17 Q5 Hardington Somset
7 M1 Hardington Mandeville Somset
7 M2 Hardington Marsh Somset
7 M1 Hardington Moor Somset
14 E7 Hardisworthy Devon
9 M6 Hardley Hants
45 N9 Hardley Street Norfk
64 F8 Hardraw N York
51 K8 Hardstoft Derbys
9 Q7 Hardway Hants
17 Q8 Hardway Somset
32 B11 Hardwick Bucks
33 L5 Hardwick Cambs
32 C3 Hardwick Nhants
45 K11 Hardwick Norfk
31 J11 Hardwick Oxon
31 M7 Hardwick Oxon
29 L6 Hardwicke Gloucs
29 M4 Hardwicke Gloucs
34 F11 Hardy's Green Essex
58 E7 Hare Croft C Brad
20 G5 Harefield Gt Lon
34 H10 Hare Green Essex
20 C7 Hare Hatch Wokham
40 F1 Harehill Derbys
59 J7 Harehills Leeds
80 C9 Harelaw Border
79 N12 Harelaw D & G
29 L6 Harescombe Gloucs
29 L6 Haresfield Gloucs
9 M2 Harestock Hants
21 N2 Hare Street Essex
33 L10 Hare Street Herts
58 H5 Harewood Leeds
28 F4 Harewood End Herefs
5 M8 Harford Devon
49 J3 Hargrave Ches W
32 E3 Hargrave Nhants
34 C5 Hargrave Suffk
35 K9 Harkstead Suffk
40 G5 Harlaston Staffs
42 C4 Harlaxton Lincs
47 J5 Harlech Gwynd
49 J11 Harlescott Shrops
21 K6 Harlesden Gt Lon
51 L5 Harlesthorpe Derbys
5 Q10 Harleston Devon
45 L12 Harleston Norfk
34 G5 Harleston Suffk
31 P2 Harlestone Nhants
57 Q2 Harle Syke Lancs
51 J2 Harley Rothm
39 L2 Harley Shrops
32 E10 Harlington C Beds
51 L1 Harlington Donc
20 H7 Harlington Gt Lon
96 C2 Harlosh Highld
21 N2 Harlow Essex
73 J7 Harlow Hill Nthumb
60 C6 Harlthorpe E R Yk
33 L6 Harlton Cambs
3 K1 Harlyn Cnwll
8 E10 Harman's Cross Dorset
65 K9 Harmby N York
33 J12 Harmer Green Herts
49 J10 Harmer Hill Shrops
52 D10 Harmston Lincs
39 K2 Harnage Shrops
18 F1 Harnhill Gloucs
21 Q5 Harold Hill Gt Lon
24 F6 Haroldston West Pembks
111 m2 Haroldswick Shet
22 B5 Harold Wood Gt Lon
66 F10 Harome N York
21 J1 Harpenden Herts
6 E5 Harpford Devon
61 J2 Harpham E R Yk
44 D5 Harpley Norfk
39 M9 Harpley Worcs
31 P2 Harpole Nhants
110 D5 Harpsdale Highld
52 D5 Harpswell Lincs
57 Q8 Harpurhey Manch
71 N5 Harraby Cumb
15 K6 Harracott Devon
97 J5 Harrapool Highld
92 E9 Harrietfield P & K
22 G11 Harrietsham Kent
21 L6 Harringay Gt Lon
70 G9 Harrington Cumb
53 L8 Harrington Lincs
41 Q10 Harrington Nhants
42 D10 Harringworth Nhants
111 c3 Harris W Isls
58 H3 Harrogate N York
59 J4 Harrogate Crematorium N York
32 D5 Harrold Bed
21 J6 Harrow Gt Lon
5 J6 Harrowbarrow Cnwll
34 E6 Harrow Green Suffk
21 J6 Harrow on the Hill Gt Lon
21 J5 Harrow Weald Gt Lon
33 L6 Harston Cambs
42 B4 Harston Leics
60 E6 Harswell E R Yk
66 C1 Hart Hartpl
73 J4 Hartburn Nthumb
34 D6 Hartest Suffk
11 P3 Hartfield E Susx
33 J3 Hartford Cambs
49 L2 Hartford Ches W
20 C10 Hartfordbridge Hants
34 B12 Hartford End Essex
65 L6 Hartforth N York
8 C4 Hartgrove Dorset
49 J4 Harthill Ches W
85 Q9 Harthill N Lans
51 L5 Harthill Rothm
50 F8 Hartington Derbys
14 E7 Hartland Devon
14 D7 Hartland Quay Devon
39 Q7 Hartlebury Worcs
66 C2 Hartlepool Hartpl
66 C2 Hartlepool Crematorium Hartpl
64 E6 Hartley Cumb
12 F3 Hartley Kent
22 C9 Hartley Kent
20 B10 Hartley Wespall Hants
20 C11 Hartley Wintney Hants
22 G9 Hartlip Kent
60 C2 Harton N York
73 P7 Harton S Tyne
29 L4 Hartpury Gloucs
58 F9 Hartshead Kirk
58 F8 Hartshead Moor Services Calder
49 Q6 Hartshill C Stke
41 J8 Hartshill Warwks
41 J4 Hartshorne Derbys
32 B6 Hartwell Nhants
58 G2 Hartwith N York
85 P10 Hartwood N Lans
79 N4 Hartwoodmyres Border
22 D10 Harvel Kent
30 D4 Harvington Worcs
39 Q7 Harvington Worcs
51 P3 Harwell Notts
19 N3 Harwell Oxon
35 L9 Harwich Essex
67 L8 Harwood Dale N York
33 J11 Harwood Park Crematorium Herts
51 N3 Harworth Notts
40 C10 Hasbury Dudley
10 G3 Hascombe Surrey
41 P11 Haselbech Nhants
7 L1 Haselbury Plucknett Somset
30 G1 Haseley Warwks
30 E3 Haselor Warwks
29 L4 Hasfield Gloucs
56 G7 Haskayne Lancs
35 L6 Hasketon Suffk
10 E4 Haslemere Surrey
57 P4 Haslingden Lancs
33 L6 Haslingfield Cambs
49 N4 Haslington Ches E
45 N8 Hassingham Norfk
11 L7 Hassocks W Susx
50 G6 Hassop Derbys
110 G5 Haster Highld
13 L2 Hastingleigh Kent
12 G7 Hastings E Susx
12 G7 Hastings Borough Crematorium E Susx
21 P2 Hastingwood Essex
20 E2 Hastoe Herts
73 P11 Haswell Dur
73 P11 Haswell Plough Dur
17 J11 Hatch Beauchamp Somset
21 J5 Hatch End Gt Lon
49 K2 Hatchmere Ches W
52 H4 Hatcliffe NE Lin
59 P11 Hatfield Donc
39 L9 Hatfield Herefs
21 K2 Hatfield Herts
33 N12 Hatfield Broad Oak Essex
21 Q1 Hatfield Heath Essex
22 F2 Hatfield Peverel Essex
59 P11 Hatfield Woodhouse Donc
19 K2 Hatford Oxon
19 K10 Hatherden Hants
15 J10 Hatherleigh Devon
41 L3 Hathern Leics
30 F11 Hatherop Gloucs
50 G5 Hathersage Derbys
50 G5 Hathersage Booths Derbys
49 M6 Hatherton Ches E
40 C5 Hatherton Staffs
33 J6 Hatley St George Cambs
5 J7 Hatt Cnwll
50 C2 Hattersley Tamesd
103 L7 Hatton Abers
93 N7 Hatton Angus
40 G2 Hatton Derbys
20 H8 Hatton Gt Lon
52 H7 Hatton Lincs
39 J4 Hatton Shrops
57 L11 Hatton Warrtn
30 G1 Hatton Warwks
102 H11 Hatton of Fintray Abers
76 H6 Haugh E Ayrs
53 K7 Haugham Lincs
85 K7 Haughhead E Duns
34 G4 Haughley Suffk
34 G4 Haughley Green Suffk
101 M7 Haugh of Glass Moray
70 D3 Haugh of Urr D & G
93 Q4 Haughs of Kinnaird Angus
48 H9 Haughton Shrops
49 Q10 Haughton Staffs
65 N4 Haughton le Skerne Darltn
49 L4 Haughton Moss Ches E
33 K11 Haultwick Herts
40 G5 Haunton Staffs
33 M6 Hauxton Cambs
10 B8 Havant Hants
9 P8 Havenstreet IoW
59 K10 Havercroft Wakefd
24 G6 Haverfordwest Pembks
33 Q7 Haverhill Suffk
62 D6 Haverigg Cumb
21 P5 Havering-atte-Bower Gt Lon
32 B8 Haversham M Keyn
62 G5 Haverthwaite Cumb
17 L4 Havyat N Som
48 G3 Hawarden Flints
34 D11 Hawbush Green Essex
36 F10 Hawen Cerdgn
64 F9 Hawes N York
45 L9 Hawe's Green Norfk
39 Q9 Hawford Worcs
80 C10 Hawick Border
7 J3 Hawkchurch Devon
34 D6 Hawkedon Suffk
18 C9 Hawkeridge Wilts
18 B4 Hawkesbury S Glos
18 B4 Hawkesbury Upton S Glos
12 F4 Hawkhurst Kent
13 N3 Hawkinge Kent
13 M3 Hawkinge Crematorium Kent
10 C4 Hawkley Hants
15 P6 Hawkridge Somset
62 G3 Hawkshead Cumb
62 G3 Hawkshead Hill Cumb
78 D2 Hawksland S Lans
49 L9 Hawkstone Shrops
64 G12 Hawkswick N York
58 F6 Hawksworth Leeds
51 Q11 Hawksworth Notts
22 G5 Hawkwell Essex
20 D10 Hawley Hants
30 E9 Hawling Gloucs
66 D9 Hawnby N York
58 D6 Haworth C Brad
34 E5 Hawstead Suffk
73 P10 Hawthorn Dur
52 H11 Hawthorn Hill Lincs
52 B12 Hawton Notts
59 N3 Haxby C York
51 Q2 Haxey N Linc
17 Q4 Haycombe Crematorium BaNES
57 K9 Haydock St Hel
72 F7 Haydon Bridge Nthumb
18 G4 Haydon Wick Swindn
20 H7 Hayes Gt Lon
21 N9 Hayes Gt Lon
20 H7 Hayes End Gt Lon
90 E10 Hayfield Ag & B
50 D4 Hayfield Derbys
93 N7 Hayhillock Angus
2 E8 Hayle Cnwll
40 C10 Hayley Green Dudley
10 B9 Hayling Island Hants
5 P3 Hayne Devon
32 F8 Haynes (Church End) C Beds
32 F8 Haynes (Northwood End) C Beds
32 F8 Haynes (Silver End) C Beds
32 F8 Haynes (West End) C Beds
27 P1 Hay-on-Wye Powys
24 F4 Hayscastle Pembks
24 F4 Hayscastle Cross Pembks
33 L10 Hay Street Herts
70 H7 Hayton Cumb
71 Q4 Hayton Cumb
60 E5 Hayton E R Yk
51 Q4 Hayton Notts
5 P5 Haytor Vale Devon
14 G8 Haytown Devon
11 M5 Haywards Heath W Susx
59 N10 Haywood Donc
77 P3 Hazelbank S Lans
7 Q2 Hazelbury Bryan Dorset
22 G3 Hazeleigh Essex
50 B4 Hazel Grove Stockp
93 L10 Hazelton Walls Fife
51 J10 Hazelwood Derbys
20 E4 Hazlemere Bucks
73 M6 Hazlerigg N u Ty
30 E9 Hazleton Gloucs
44 B3 Heacham Norfk
9 N2 Headbourne Worthy Hants
12 G2 Headcorn Kent
58 H7 Headingley Leeds
31 M11 Headington Oxon
65 L4 Headlam Dur
85 Q10 Headlesscross N Lans
30 D2 Headless Cross Worcs
10 D3 Headley Hants
19 N8 Headley Hants
21 K11 Headley Surrey
10 D3 Headley Down Hants
51 Q5 Headon Notts
71 P5 Heads Nook Cumb
51 J10 Heage Derbys
59 L5 Healaugh N York
64 H7 Healaugh N York
57 Q10 Heald Green Stockp
16 H11 Heale Somset
17 K10 Heale Somset
65 L10 Healey N York

73 J10 Healeyfield Dur
61 L11 Healing NE Lin
2 C9 Heamoor Cnwll
51 K10 Heanor Derbys
15 J5 Heanton Punchardon Devon
52 C6 Heapham Lincs
41 J8 Heart of England Crematorium Warwks
85 Q9 Heart of Scotland Services N Lans
15 M6 Heasley Mill Devon
96 H6 Heast Highld
51 K7 Heath Derbys
59 J9 Heath Wakefd
32 D10 Heath and Reach C Beds
50 F8 Heathcote Derbys
41 K5 Heather Leics
12 C6 Heathfield E Susx
16 F10 Heathfield Somset
40 E12 Heath Green Worcs
78 G11 Heath Hall D & G
40 D5 Heath Hayes & Wimblebury Staffs
49 N11 Heath Hill Shrops
20 H8 Heathrow Airport Gt Lon
39 P4 Heathton Shrops
40 B7 Heath Town Wolves
57 N10 Heatley Warrtn
58 F7 Heaton C Brad
73 M7 Heaton N u Ty
50 C8 Heaton Staffs
56 H6 Heaton's Bridge Lancs
22 C10 Heaverham Kent
6 C4 Heavitree Devon
73 N7 Hebburn S Tyne
58 D2 Hebden N York
58 C8 Hebden Bridge Calder
33 K11 Hebing End Herts
25 L4 Hebron Carmth
73 L3 Hebron Nthumb
20 B10 Heckfield Hants
35 K2 Heckfield Green Suffk
34 F11 Heckfordbridge Essex
42 G2 Heckington Lincs
58 G9 Heckmondwike Kirk
18 E7 Heddington Wilts
73 K7 Heddon-on-the-Wall Nthumb
45 M10 Hedenham Norfk
9 N5 Hedge End Hants
20 F6 Hedgerley Bucks
17 J9 Hedging Somset
73 J8 Hedley on the Hill Nthumb
40 D5 Hednesford Staffs
61 K8 Hedon E R Yk
20 E6 Hedsor Bucks
111 k4 Heglibister Shet
65 M3 Heighington Darltn
52 E9 Heighington Lincs
39 N7 Heightington Worcs
80 F7 Heiton Border
6 D3 Hele Devon
15 J3 Hele Devon
84 E6 Helensburgh Ag & B
76 G5 Helenton S Ayrs
2 H9 Helford Cnwll
2 H9 Helford Passage Cnwll
44 E5 Helhoughton Norfk
33 Q8 Helions Bumpstead Essex
3 N2 Helland Cnwll
4 G3 Hellescott Cnwll
45 K7 Hellesdon Norfk
31 M3 Hellidon Nhants
63 Q10 Hellifield N York
12 C7 Hellingly E Susx
31 N5 Helmdon Nhants
58 E10 Helme Kirk
35 K5 Helmingham Suffk
110 B11 Helmsdale Highld
57 P5 Helmshore Lancs
66 E10 Helmsley N York
59 K1 Helperby N York
67 K12 Helperthorpe N York
42 G3 Helpringham Lincs
42 G8 Helpston C Pete
49 J1 Helsby Ches W
2 F9 Helston Cnwll
4 D4 Helstone Cnwll
71 Q10 Helton Cumb
20 G2 Hemel Hempstead Herts
5 L8 Hemerdon Devon
59 P7 Hemingbrough N York
53 J8 Hemingby Lincs
33 J3 Hemingford Abbots Cambs
33 J3 Hemingford Grey Cambs
35 J6 Hemingstone Suffk
41 L2 Hemington Leics
42 F12 Hemington Nhants
17 Q5 Hemington Somset
35 L8 Hemley Suffk
66 C5 Hemlington Middsb
45 L10 Hempnall Norfk
45 L10 Hempnall Green Norfk
100 H3 Hempriggs Moray
33 Q8 Hempstead Essex
44 H3 Hempstead Norfk
45 N5 Hempstead Norfk
44 E4 Hempton Norfk
31 K7 Hempton Oxon
45 P6 Hemsby Norfk
52 D5 Hemswell Lincs
52 D5 Hemswell Cliff Lincs
59 K10 Hemsworth Wakefd
16 F12 Hemyock Devon
21 K5 Hendon Gt Lon
73 P9 Hendon Sundld
21 K5 Hendon Crematorium Gt Lon
26 D7 Hendy Carmth
11 K6 Henfield W Susx
27 N9 Hengoed Caerph
38 E10 Hengoed Powys
34 D3 Hengrave Suffk
33 N10 Henham Essex
38 D1 Heniarth Powys
16 H10 Henlade Somset
7 Q2 Henley Dorset
17 L9 Henley Somset
35 J6 Henley Suffk
10 E5 Henley W Susx
30 F2 Henley-in-Arden Warwks
20 C6 Henley-on-Thames Oxon
12 E7 Henley's Down E Susx
36 F11 Henllan Cerdgn
55 Q7 Henllan Denbgs
28 B9 Henllys Torfn
32 H8 Henlow C Beds
5 Q4 Hennock Devon
34 E8 Henny Street Essex
55 L6 Henryd Conwy
24 H4 Henry's Moat (Castell Hendre) Pembks
59 N9 Hensall N York
72 D7 Henshaw Nthumb
70 G11 Hensingham Cumb
45 P11 Henstead Suffk
9 N3 Hensting Hants
17 Q11 Henstridge Somset
17 Q11 Henstridge Ash Somset
20 C3 Henton Oxon
17 L7 Henton Somset
39 Q10 Henwick Worcs
4 G5 Henwood Cnwll
27 K11 Heol-y-Cyw Brdgnd
72 H1 Hepple Nthumb
73 L4 Hepscott Nthumb
58 C8 Heptonstall Calder
58 F11 Hepworth Kirk
34 G2 Hepworth Suffk
24 F7 Herbrandston Pembks
28 F2 Hereford Herefs
28 F2 Hereford Crematorium Herefs
23 Q9 Hereson Kent
104 E8 Heribusta Highld
86 H10 Heriot Border
86 E8 Hermiston C Edin
79 P9 Hermitage Border
7 P2 Hermitage Dorset
19 N6 Hermitage W Berk
25 N3 Hermon Carmth
25 L3 Hermon Pembks
23 M9 Herne Kent
23 M9 Herne Bay Kent
21 L8 Herne Hill Gt Lon
22 D11 Herne Pound Kent
23 K10 Hernhill Kent
4 F7 Herodsfoot Cnwll
68 F3 Heronsford S Ayrs
19 Q10 Herriard Hants
45 P9 Herringfleet Suffk
34 C3 Herringswell Suffk
51 K3 Herringthorpe Rothm
73 P9 Herrington Sundld
23 M10 Hersden Kent
20 H9 Hersham Surrey
12 D7 Herstmonceux E Susx
111 h3 Herston Ork
21 M2 Hertford Herts
21 M2 Hertford Heath Herts
21 L2 Hertingfordbury Herts
57 J4 Hesketh Bank Lancs
57 L1 Hesketh Lane Lancs
71 M7 Hesket Newmarket Cumb
73 Q12 Hesleden Dur
59 N4 Heslington C York
59 M4 Hessay C York
4 G8 Hessenford Cnwll
34 F4 Hessett Suffk
60 H8 Hessle E R Yk
59 K10 Hessle Wakefd
63 J8 Hest Bank Lancs
20 H7 Heston Gt Lon
20 H7 Heston Services Gt Lon
111 g2 Hestwall Ork
56 F11 Heswall Wirral
31 N8 Hethe Oxon
45 J8 Hethersett Norfk
71 P3 Hethersgill Cumb
73 M12 Hett Dur
58 C3 Hetton N York
73 N10 Hetton-le-Hole Sundld
73 J6 Heugh Nthumb
101 M11 Heughhead Abers
87 Q9 Heugh Head Border
35 M3 Heveningham Suffk
11 P2 Hever Kent
63 J5 Heversham Cumb
45 K6 Hevingham Norfk
3 L6 Hewas Water Cnwll
28 G8 Hewelsfield Gloucs
7 K2 Hewish Somset
7 J3 Hewood Dorset
72 G7 Hexham Nthumb
21 P8 Hextable Kent
51 M1 Hexthorpe Donc
32 F10 Hexton Herts
4 H4 Hexworthy Cnwll
5 N6 Hexworthy Devon
22 D4 Heybridge Essex
22 G2 Heybridge Essex
5 K9 Heybrook Bay Devon
33 M8 Heydon Cambs
45 J5 Heydon Norfk
42 E3 Heydour Lincs
88 B7 Heylipoll Ag & B
111 j3 Heylor Shet
62 H9 Heysham Lancs
10 E6 Heyshott W Susx
18 D11 Heytesbury Wilts
31 J8 Heythrop Oxon
57 Q6 Heywood Rochdl
18 C9 Heywood Wilts
52 D3 Hibaldstow N Linc
59 L12 Hickleton Donc
45 N5 Hickling Norfk
41 P2 Hickling Notts
45 N5 Hickling Green Norfk
11 L6 Hickstead W Susx
30 F5 Hidcote Bartrim Gloucs
30 F6 Hidcote Boyce Gloucs
59 K9 High Ackworth Wakefd
58 H11 Higham Barns
51 K8 Higham Derbys
12 C1 Higham Kent
22 E8 Higham Kent
57 P2 Higham Lancs
34 C4 Higham Suffk
34 G9 Higham Suffk
32 D3 Higham Ferrers Nhants
32 F9 Higham Gobion C Beds
21 M5 Higham Hill Gt Lon
41 J8 Higham on the Hill Leics
14 H10 Highampton Devon
21 M5 Highams Park Gt Lon
68 E9 High Ardwell D & G
78 E10 High Auldgirth D & G
71 Q7 High Bankhill Cumb
21 N4 High Beach Essex
63 M8 High Bentham N York
15 K7 High Bickington Devon
63 L6 High Biggins Cumb
85 L10 High Blantyre S Lans
85 N7 High Bonnybridge Falk
15 M5 High Bray Devon
17 J6 Highbridge Somset
11 M4 Highbrook W Susx
12 C2 High Brooms Kent
58 F10 Highburton Kirk
21 L6 Highbury Gt Lon
17 Q6 Highbury Somset
63 L6 High Casterton Cumb
60 C4 High Catton E R Yk
19 M8 Highclere Hants
8 H8 Highcliffe Dorset
65 M5 High Coniscliffe Darltn
71 P4 High Crosby Cumb
76 G3 High Cross E Ayrs
10 B5 High Cross Hants
33 K11 High Cross Herts
30 G1 High Cross Warwks
68 F11 High Drummore D & G
22 C1 High Easter Essex
65 L10 High Ellington N York
8 B6 Higher Ansty Dorset
57 J3 Higher Bartle Lancs
7 Q4 Higher Bockhampton Dorset
6 C10 Higher Brixham Torbay
49 L11 High Ercall Wrekin
7 K2 Higher Chillington Somset
57 M8 Higher Folds Wigan
6 C8 Higher Gabwell Devon
62 H9 Higher Heysham Lancs
57 N9 Higher Irlam Salfd
48 G4 Higher Kinnerton Flints
15 K5 Higher Muddiford Devon
57 K3 Higher Penwortham Lancs
14 G11 Higher Prestacott Devon
3 J6 Higher Town Cnwll
3 M4 Higher Town Cnwll
2 c1 Higher Town IoS
57 L4 Higher Walton Lancs
57 L10 Higher Walton Warrtn
6 H2 Higher Wambrook Somset
7 Q4 Higher Waterston Dorset
57 L4 Higher Wheelton Lancs
57 L11 Higher Whitley Ches W
57 M12 Higher Wincham Ches W
7 N3 Higher Wraxhall Dorset
49 J6 Higher Wych Ches W
65 L2 High Etherley Dur
73 K8 Highfield Gatesd
76 E2 Highfield N Ayrs
34 C10 High Garrett Essex
21 L6 Highgate Gt Lon
65 M12 High Grantley N York
45 J11 High Green Norfk
45 J8 High Green Norfk
51 J2 High Green Sheff
12 H3 High Halden Kent
22 F8 High Halstow Medway
17 K9 High Ham Somset
58 H3 High Harrogate N York
49 L9 High Hatton Shrops
73 M1 High Hauxley Nthumb
67 K6 High Hawsker N York
71 P6 High Hesket Cumb
58 H11 High Hoyland Barns
11 P5 High Hurstwood E Susx
60 D1 High Hutton N York
71 K7 High Ireby Cumb
66 D10 High Kilburn N York
65 K3 High Lands Dur
99 M7 Highland Wildlife Park Highld
51 K4 Highlane Derbys
50 C4 High Lane Stockp
2 E8 High Lanes Cnwll
29 K4 Highleadon Gloucs
57 M11 High Legh Ches E
10 D9 Highleigh W Susx
66 C5 High Leven S on T
39 N5 Highley Shrops
17 P5 High Littleton BaNES
71 J9 High Lorton Cumb
52 B9 High Marnham Notts
51 L1 High Melton Donc
73 J8 High Mickley Nthumb
20 B6 Highmoor Oxon
20 B6 Highmoor Cross Oxon
29 K5 Highnam Gloucs
73 P9 High Newport Sundld
62 H5 High Newton Cumb
62 F4 High Nibthwaite Cumb
49 P9 High Offley Staffs
22 C3 High Ongar Essex
49 P11 High Onn Staffs
34 G11 High Park Corner Essex
76 H9 High Pennyvenie E Ayrs
33 P12 High Roding Essex
10 H8 High Salvington W Susx
73 K8 High Spen Gatesd
22 H10 Highsted Kent
3 L5 High Street Cnwll
23 L10 Highstreet Kent
10 F3 Highstreet Green Surrey
78 H11 Hightae D & G
56 F7 Hightown Sefton
34 F5 Hightown Green Suffk
53 J9 High Toynton Lincs
86 B5 High Valleyfield Fife
6 B8 Highweek Devon
21 K5 Highwood Hill Gt Lon
18 H3 Highworth Swindn
62 G3 High Wray Cumb
21 P1 High Wych Herts
20 D5 High Wycombe Bucks
44 D9 Hilborough Norfk
18 G8 Hilcott Wilts
12 C1 Hildenborough Kent
12 C1 Hilden Park Kent
33 N7 Hildersham Cambs
40 C1 Hilderstone Staffs
61 K2 Hilderthorpe E R Yk
43 P9 Hilgay Norfk
28 H9 Hill S Glos
31 L2 Hill Warwks
59 L8 Hillam N York
10 C5 Hill Brow Hants
8 E7 Hillbutts Dorset
49 P7 Hill Chorlton Staffs
50 H10 Hillcliffane Derbys
16 F10 Hill Common Somset
43 K1 Hilldyke Lincs
86 C3 Hill End Fife
86 D5 Hillend Fife
29 M2 Hill End Gloucs
86 F8 Hillend Mdloth
85 N9 Hillend N Lans
31 P8 Hillesden Bucks
29 K10 Hillesley Gloucs
16 F10 Hillfarrance Somset
22 G10 Hill Green Kent
102 D8 Hillhead Abers
9 P6 Hill Head Hants
78 F2 Hillhead S Lans
103 M6 Hillhead of Cocklaw Abers
110 D3 Hilliclay Highld
20 H6 Hillingdon Gt Lon
85 J9 Hillington C Glas
44 C5 Hillington Norfk
41 M11 Hillmorton Warwks
86 D4 Hill of Beath Fife
107 N6 Hill of Fearn Highld
70 C3 Hillowton D & G
40 E4 Hill Ridware Staffs
95 Q3 Hillside Abers
95 L9 Hillside Angus
58 F10 Hill Side Kirk
51 L6 Hills Town Derbys
9 K4 Hillstreet Hants
111 j3 Hillswick Shet
59 J10 Hill Top Wakefd
111 k5 Hillwell Shet
18 E6 Hilmarton Wilts
18 C8 Hilperton Wilts
9 Q6 Hilsea C Port
61 M7 Hilston E R Yk
81 J4 Hilton Border
33 J4 Hilton Cambs
64 D4 Hilton Cumb
40 G2 Hilton Derbys
8 B6 Hilton Dorset
65 L3 Hilton Dur
107 P7 Hilton Highld
66 C5 Hilton S on T
39 P3 Hilton Shrops
40 C6 Hilton Park Services Staffs
30 C3 Himbleton Worcs
39 Q4 Himley Staffs
63 K5 Hincaster Cumb
21 J9 Hinchley Wood Surrey
41 K8 Hinckley Leics
34 G2 Hinderclay Suffk
66 H4 Hinderwell N York
10 E3 Hindhead Surrey
57 L7 Hindley Wigan
39 Q9 Hindlip Worcs
44 G4 Hindolveston Norfk
8 D2 Hindon Wilts
44 G3 Hindringham Norfk
44 H9 Hingham Norfk
49 M9 Hinstock Shrops
34 H7 Hintlesham Suffk
28 D2 Hinton Herefs
17 Q2 Hinton S Glos
38 H1 Hinton Shrops
9 P2 Hinton Ampner Hants
17 N5 Hinton Blewett BaNES
18 B8 Hinton Charterhouse BaNES
31 M6 Hinton-in-the-Hedges Nhants
8 E6 Hinton Martell Dorset
30 D6 Hinton on the Green Worcs
19 J4 Hinton Parva Swindn
7 K1 Hinton St George Somset
8 B4 Hinton St Mary Dorset
19 L2 Hinton Waldrist Oxon
40 F6 Hints Staffs
32 D5 Hinwick Bed
13 K2 Hinxhill Kent
33 M7 Hinxton Cambs
32 H8 Hinxworth Herts
58 E8 Hipperholme Calder
65 L7 Hipswell N York
95 M2 Hirn Abers
48 B10 Hirnant Powys
73 M4 Hirst Nthumb
59 N8 Hirst Courtney N York
27 K7 Hirwaun Rhondd
15 J7 Hiscott Devon
33 M4 Histon Cambs
34 G6 Hitcham Suffk
34 G6 Hitcham Causeway Suffk
34 G6 Hitcham Street Suffk
32 H10 Hitchin Herts
21 M8 Hither Green Gt Lon
5 P2 Hittisleigh Devon
60 E7 Hive E R Yk
40 D3 Hixon Staffs
23 N10 Hoaden Kent
40 F3 Hoar Cross Staffs
28 G3 Hoarwithy Herefs
23 M9 Hoath Kent
38 F6 Hobarris Shrops
80 D11 Hobkirk Border
73 L9 Hobson Dur
41 P4 Hoby Leics
44 H7 Hockering Norfk
51 Q9 Hockerton Notts
22 G5 Hockley Essex
40 F11 Hockley Heath Solhll
32 D10 Hockliffe C Beds
44 C11 Hockwold cum Wilton Norfk
16 D11 Hockworthy Devon
21 M2 Hoddesdon Herts
57 N4 Hoddlesden Bl w D
71 J2 Hoddom Cross D & G
71 J2 Hoddom Mains D & G
24 H8 Hodgeston Pembks
49 L9 Hodnet Shrops
51 N4 Hodsock Notts
22 D10 Hodsoll Street Kent
18 H5 Hodson Swindn
51 M5 Hodthorpe Derbys
44 G6 Hoe Norfk
23 K11 Hogben's Hill Kent
32 B10 Hoggeston Bucks
40 G8 Hoggrill's End Warwks
57 L4 Hoghton Lancs
50 G10 Hognaston Derbys
53 N8 Hogsthorpe Lincs
43 K5 Holbeach Lincs
43 K5 Holbeach Bank Lincs
43 K5 Holbeach Clough Lincs
43 K7 Holbeach Drove Lincs
43 L5 Holbeach Hurn Lincs
43 K6 Holbeach St Johns Lincs
43 L4 Holbeach St Mark's Lincs
43 L4 Holbeach St Matthew Lincs
51 M6 Holbeck Notts
30 D3 Holberrow Green Worcs
5 M9 Holbeton Devon
21 L7 Holborn Gt Lon
51 J11 Holbrook Derbys
35 J9 Holbrook Suffk
41 J10 Holbrooks Covtry
9 M6 Holbury Hants
6 C7 Holcombe Devon
17 P6 Holcombe Somset
16 E11 Holcombe Rogus Devon
32 B3 Holcot Nhants
63 P11 Holden Lancs
31 P1 Holdenby Nhants
33 Q10 Holder's Green Essex
39 K4 Holdgate Shrops
42 F1 Holdingham Lincs
7 J3 Holditch Dorset
14 H10 Holemoor Devon
16 F7 Holford Somset
59 N4 Holgate C York
62 G6 Holker Cumb
44 E2 Holkham Norfk
44 E2 Holkham Hall Norfk
14 G10 Hollacombe Devon
52 H12 Holland Fen Lincs
35 K12 Holland-on-Sea Essex
111 i1 Hollandstoun Ork
71 L2 Hollee D & G
35 M7 Hollesley Suffk
6 B9 Hollicombe Torbay
22 G11 Hollingbourne Kent
11 L8 Hollingbury Br & H
32 C10 Hollingdon Bucks
50 G11 Hollington Derbys
50 D11 Hollington Staffs
50 D2 Hollingworth Tamesd
50 E7 Hollinsclough Staffs
51 J4 Hollins End Sheff
57 M10 Hollins Green Warrtn
39 N1 Hollinswood Wrekin
50 B1 Hollinwood Crematorium Oldham
15 L9 Hollocombe Devon
51 J9 Holloway Derbys
21 L6 Holloway Gt Lon
41 P11 Hollowell Nhants
49 J2 Hollowmoor Heath Ches W
79 N12 Hollows D & G
27 N7 Hollybush Caerph
76 G8 Hollybush E Ayrs
29 K2 Hollybush Herefs
61 N8 Hollym E R Yk
58 E11 Holmbridge Kirk
10 H2 Holmbury St Mary Surrey
3 M5 Holmbush Cnwll
40 B3 Holmcroft Staffs
42 H11 Holme Cambs
63 K6 Holme Cumb
58 E11 Holme Kirk
65 P10 Holme N York
52 B10 Holme Notts
57 Q3 Holme Chapel Lancs
59 M6 Holme Green N York
44 E8 Holme Hale Norfk
28 G2 Holme Lacy Herefs
38 G10 Holme Marsh Herefs
44 B2 Holme next the Sea Norfk
60 G5 Holme on the Wolds E R Yk
51 N11 Holme Pierrepont Notts
28 F1 Holmer Herefs
20 E4 Holmer Green Bucks
70 H6 Holme St Cuthbert Cumb
49 N3 Holmes Chapel Ches E
50 H5 Holmesfield Derbys
56 H5 Holmeswood Lancs
21 L12 Holmethorpe Surrey
60 D6 Holme upon Spalding Moor E R Yk
51 K7 Holmewood Derbys
58 F11 Holmfirth Kirk
77 J7 Holmhead E Ayrs
61 N9 Holmpton E R Yk
62 C3 Holmrook Cumb
76 F4 Holmsford Bridge Crematorium N Ayrs
73 L10 Holmside Dur
5 N6 Holne Devon
16 C6 Holnicote Somset
14 F10 Holsworthy Devon
14 G9 Holsworthy Beacon Devon
8 F6 Holt Dorset
44 H3 Holt Norfk
18 C8 Holt Wilts
39 P9 Holt Worcs
48 H5 Holt Wrexhm
59 P4 Holtby C York
40 E12 Holt End Worcs
39 P9 Holt Heath Worcs
31 N11 Holton Oxon
17 P10 Holton Somset
35 N2 Holton Suffk
52 G7 Holton cum Beckering Lincs
53 J3 Holton le Clay Lincs
52 F4 Holton le Moor Lincs
34 H8 Holton St Mary Suffk
7 Q1 Holwell Dorset
32 G9 Holwell Herts
41 Q3 Holwell Leics
30 G11 Holwell Oxon
64 G3 Holwick Dur
10 B2 Holybourne Hants
54 C5 Holyhead IoA
54 C5 Holy Island IoA
81 N5 Holy Island Nthumb
81 N6 Holy Island Nthumb
51 J7 Holymoorside Derbys
20 E7 Holyport W & M
72 G1 Holystone Nthumb
85 M10 Holytown N Lans
32 E12 Holywell C Beds
33 K3 Holywell Cambs
2 H4 Holywell Cnwll
7 N2 Holywell Dorset
48 E1 Holywell Flints
58 E9 Holywell Green Calder
16 F11 Holywell Lake Somset
34 B2 Holywell Row Suffk
78 F11 Holywood D & G
78 F11 Holywood Village D & G
39 L2 Homer Shrops
56 G8 Homer Green Sefton
45 L11 Homersfield Suffk
8 G3 Homington Wilts
30 E5 Honeybourne Worcs
15 L10 Honeychurch Devon
18 G8 Honeystreet Wilts
34 F9 Honey Tye Suffk
40 G11 Honiley Warwks
45 M5 Honing Norfk
44 H7 Honingham Norfk
42 D2 Honington Lincs
34 E2 Honington Suffk
30 H5 Honington Warwks
6 F3 Honiton Devon
58 F10 Honley Kirk
21 M8 Honor Oak Crematorium Gt Lon
5 K9 Hooe C Plym
12 E7 Hooe E Susx
57 N11 Hoo Green Ches E
56 G2 Hoohill Bpool
60 D8 Hook E R Yk
21 J9 Hook Gt Lon
20 B11 Hook Hants
24 G6 Hook Pembks
18 F4 Hook Wilts
7 M3 Hooke Dorset
12 D3 Hook Green Kent
22 C8 Hook Green Kent
31 J7 Hook Norton Oxon
15 P11 Hookway Devon
21 L11 Hooley Surrey
22 F8 Hoo St Werburgh Medway
51 M3 Hooton Levitt Rothm

59 L11 Hooton Pagnell Donc
51 L2 Hooton Roberts Rothm
50 F4 Hope Derbys
5 N11 Hope Devon
48 F4 Hope Flints
39 L7 Hope Shrops
50 E9 Hope Staffs
39 J4 Hope Bowdler Shrops
79 L5 Hopehouse Border
100 H2 Hopeman Moray
28 H5 Hope Mansell Herefs
38 H5 Hopesay Shrops
39 K10 Hope under Dinmore Herefs
59 N3 Hopgrove C York
59 K3 Hopperton N York
39 P4 Hopstone Shrops
50 H9 Hopton Derbys
40 C3 Hopton Staffs
34 G2 Hopton Suffk
39 K6 Hopton Cangeford Shrops
38 G6 Hopton Castle Shrops
38 H6 Hoptonheath Shrops
45 Q9 Hopton on Sea Norfk
39 M6 Hopton Wafers Shrops
40 F6 Hopwas Staffs
40 D11 Hopwood Worcs
40 D11 Hopwood Park Services Worcs
12 C6 Horam E Susx
42 G3 Horbling Lincs
58 H9 Horbury Wakefd
73 Q11 Horden Dur
9 J8 Hordle Hants
48 H8 Hordley Shrops
17 N2 Horfield Bristl
35 K3 Horham Suffk
34 G10 Horkesley Heath Essex
60 G9 Horkstow N Linc
31 K5 Horley Oxon
11 L2 Horley Surrey
17 N9 Hornblotton Green Somset
63 L8 Hornby Lancs
65 L8 Hornby N York
65 P6 Hornby N York
53 J9 Horncastle Lincs
21 Q6 Hornchurch Gt Lon
81 K4 Horncliffe Nthumb
81 J4 Horndean Border
10 B7 Horndean Hants
5 L4 Horndon Devon
22 D6 Horndon on the Hill Thurr
11 M2 Horne Surrey
16 B7 Horner Somset
45 M6 Horning Norfk
42 B10 Horninghold Leics
40 G3 Horninglow Staffs
33 M4 Horningsea Cambs
18 B11 Horningsham Wilts
44 F5 Horningtoft Norfk
14 G7 Horns Cross Devon
61 K5 Hornsea E R Yk
21 L5 Hornsey Gt Lon
31 K5 Hornton Oxon
111 k2 Horra Shet
5 K6 Horrabridge Devon
34 D4 Horringer Suffk
63 N12 Horrocksford Lancs
5 J5 Horsebridge Devon
12 C7 Horsebridge E Susx
9 L2 Horsebridge Hants
39 M1 Horsehay Wrekin
33 P7 Horseheath Cambs
65 J10 Horsehouse N York
20 F10 Horsell Surrey
49 J7 Horseman's Green Wrexhm
45 P5 Horsey Norfk
17 J8 Horsey Somset
45 K6 Horsford Norfk
58 G6 Horsforth Leeds
11 J4 Horsham W Susx
39 N9 Horsham Worcs
45 K7 Horsham St Faith Norfk
52 H9 Horsington Lincs
17 Q10 Horsington Somset
51 J11 Horsley Derbys
29 L8 Horsley Gloucs
72 F2 Horsley Nthumb
73 J7 Horsley Nthumb
35 J10 Horsleycross Street Essex
80 C9 Horsleyhill Border
51 K11 Horsley Woodhouse Derbys
12 E2 Horsmonden Kent
31 M12 Horspath Oxon
45 L6 Horstead Norfk
11 M5 Horsted Keynes W Susx
32 D11 Horton Bucks
8 F6 Horton Dorset
63 Q11 Horton Lancs
32 B6 Horton Nhants
18 A4 Horton S Glos
17 J12 Horton Somset
50 C8 Horton Staffs
26 C10 Horton Swans
20 G8 Horton W & M
18 F7 Horton Wilts
49 M11 Horton Wrekin
31 N10 Horton-cum-Studley Oxon
49 J5 Horton Green Ches W
64 E12 Horton in Ribblesdale N York
22 C9 Horton Kirby Kent
57 M6 Horwich Bolton
15 J6 Horwood Devon
79 N6 Hoscote Border
41 Q2 Hose Leics
92 C10 Hosh P & K
111 k5 Hoswick Shet
60 F7 Hotham E R Yk
13 J2 Hothfield Kent
41 M3 Hoton Leics
49 N5 Hough Ches E
43 L4 Hougham Lincs
57 J10 Hough Green Halton
42 D2 Hough-on-the-Hill Lincs
33 J3 Houghton Cambs
9 K2 Houghton Hants
24 H7 Houghton Pembks
10 G7 Houghton W Susx
32 F8 Houghton Conquest C Beds
12 H5 Houghton Green E Susx
73 N10 Houghton-le-Spring Sundld
41 P6 Houghton on the Hill Leics
32 E11 Houghton Regis C Beds
44 F3 Houghton St Giles Norfk
20 B10 Hound Green Hants
80 E5 Houndslow Border
87 Q9 Houndwood Border
21 J8 Hounslow Gt Lon
100 D4 Househill Highld
58 G10 Houses Hill Kirk
103 J9 Housieside Abers
84 G9 Houston Rens
110 D8 Houstry Highld
111 g2 Houton Ork
11 L8 Hove Br & H
51 P10 Hoveringham Notts
45 M6 Hoveton Norfk
66 F11 Hovingham N York
28 H3 How Caple Herefs
60 D8 Howden E R Yk
65 L2 Howden-le-Wear Dur
110 F4 Howe Highld
65 P10 Howe N York
45 L9 Howe Norfk
57 M8 Howe Bridge Crematorium Wigan
22 E3 Howe Green Essex
22 G3 Howegreen Essex
42 G2 Howell Lincs
102 G6 Howe of Teuchar Abers
71 K3 Howes D & G
22 E1 Howe Street Essex
34 B9 Howe Street Essex
38 C9 Howey Powys
70 G10 Howgate Cumb
86 F10 Howgate Mdloth
81 Q10 Howick Nthumb
33 P9 Howlett End Essex
6 H2 Howley Somset
71 Q4 How Mill Cumb
111 a5 Howmore W Isls
80 G9 Hownam Border
52 E3 Howsham N Linc
60 C2 Howsham N York
81 J7 Howtel Nthumb
84 G10 Howwood Rens
35 K2 Hoxne Suffk
111 g3 Hoy Ork
56 E10 Hoylake Wirral
51 J1 Hoyland Nether Barns
58 H12 Hoyland Swaine Barns
24 F7 Hubberston Pembks
58 H5 Huby N York
59 M2 Huby N York
29 M5 Hucclecote Gloucs
22 G10 Hucking Kent
51 M10 Hucknall Notts
58 F10 Huddersfield Kirk
58 F9 Huddersfield Crematorium Kirk
30 C3 Huddington Worcs
65 K7 Hudswell N York
60 F3 Huggate E R Yk
20 D4 Hughenden Valley Bucks
39 K3 Hughley Shrops
2 c2 Hugh Town IoS
15 J9 Huish Devon
18 G7 Huish Wilts
16 E9 Huish Champflower Somset
17 L10 Huish Episcopi Somset
32 C12 Hulcott Bucks
6 D6 Hulham Devon
50 G10 Hulland Derbys
50 G10 Hulland Ward Derbys
18 D4 Hullavington Wilts
22 F4 Hullbridge Essex
57 Q9 Hulme Manch
50 C10 Hulme Staffs
57 L9 Hulme Warrtn
50 E8 Hulme End Staffs
49 Q3 Hulme Walfield Ches E
9 L9 Hulverstone IoW
45 P11 Hulver Street Suffk
61 J11 Humberside Airport N Linc
53 K3 Humberston NE Lin
41 N6 Humberstone C Leic
87 J9 Humbie E Loth
61 L7 Humbleton E R Yk
42 E4 Humby Lincs
80 F6 Hume Border
72 G6 Humshaugh Nthumb
110 G2 Huna Highld
41 M7 Huncote Leics
80 E9 Hundalee Border
64 H4 Hunderthwaite Dur
53 L9 Hundleby Lincs
24 G8 Hundleton Pembks
34 C7 Hundon Suffk
38 C10 Hundred House Powys
41 P6 Hungarton Leics
16 E7 Hungerford Somset
19 K7 Hungerford W Berk
19 L6 Hungerford Newtown W Berk
28 E2 Hungerstone Herefs
67 N11 Hunmanby N York
31 J1 Hunningham Warwks
31 Q3 Hunsbury Hill Nhants
21 N1 Hunsdon Herts
59 K4 Hunsingore N York
58 H7 Hunslet Leeds
71 Q7 Hunsonby Cumb
43 Q3 Hunstanton Norfk
72 G10 Hunstanworth Dur
49 M6 Hunsterson Ches E
34 F3 Hunston Suffk
10 D9 Hunston W Susx
17 P4 Hunstrete BaNES
58 F8 Hunsworth Kirk
84 C7 Hunter's Quay Ag & B
17 J10 Huntham Somset
94 H7 Hunthill Lodge Angus
33 J3 Huntingdon Cambs
35 M2 Huntingfield Suffk
59 N3 Huntington C York
49 J3 Huntington Ches W
87 J7 Huntington E Loth
38 F10 Huntington Herefs
40 C5 Huntington Staffs
29 J5 Huntley Gloucs
102 C7 Huntly Abers
22 E12 Hunton Kent
65 L8 Hunton N York
16 C7 Huntscott Somset
16 D11 Huntsham Devon
15 J7 Huntshaw Devon
17 J7 Huntspill Somset
16 H9 Huntstile Somset
17 J8 Huntworth Somset
65 L2 Hunwick Dur
44 H3 Hunworth Norfk
8 H1 Hurdcott Wilts
50 B6 Hurdsfield Ches E
20 D6 Hurley W & M
40 G8 Hurley Warwks
40 G7 Hurley Common Warwks
76 H4 Hurlford E Ayrs
8 G7 Hurn Dorset
9 M3 Hursley Hants
20 C8 Hurst Wokham
19 M10 Hurstbourne Priors Hants
19 L9 Hurstbourne Tarrant Hants
12 E5 Hurst Green E Susx
34 H12 Hurst Green Essex
57 M2 Hurst Green Lancs
21 N12 Hurst Green Surrey
11 L6 Hurstpierpoint W Susx
57 Q3 Hurstwood Lancs
111 h2 Hurtiso Ork
65 N5 Hurworth-on-Tees Darltn
65 N5 Hurworth Place Darltn
41 N10 Husbands Bosworth Leics
32 D9 Husborne Crawley C Beds
66 D11 Husthwaite N York
51 J4 Hutcliffe Wood Crematorium Sheff
51 L8 Huthwaite Notts
53 N8 Huttoft Lincs
81 J4 Hutton Border
60 H4 Hutton E R Yk
22 D4 Hutton Essex
57 J4 Hutton Lancs
17 J4 Hutton N Som
67 L10 Hutton Buscel N York
65 N11 Hutton Conyers N York
60 H4 Hutton Cranswick E R Yk
71 P7 Hutton End Cumb
65 Q1 Hutton Henry Dur
66 G9 Hutton-le-Hole N York
66 E5 Hutton Lowcross R & Cl
65 K5 Hutton Magna Dur
63 K6 Hutton Roof Cumb
71 M8 Hutton Roof Cumb
66 C6 Hutton Rudby N York
66 C11 Hutton Sessay N York
59 L4 Hutton Wandesley N York
6 C4 Huxham Devon
49 K3 Huxley Ches W
57 J10 Huyton Knows
62 C4 Hycemoor Cumb
50 C2 Hyde Tamesd
20 E4 Hyde Heath Bucks
40 B4 Hyde Lea Staffs
78 E1 Hyndford Bridge S Lans
88 C8 Hynish Ag & B
38 F4 Hyssington Powys
9 M6 Hythe Hants
13 M3 Hythe Kent
20 G8 Hythe End W & M

I

8 B6 Ibberton Dorset
50 G9 Ible Derbys
8 H5 Ibsley Hants
41 K5 Ibstock Leics
20 C5 Ibstone Bucks
19 L9 Ibthorpe Hants
67 J6 Iburndale N York
19 P9 Ibworth Hants
90 D9 Ichrachan Ag & B
44 D10 Ickburgh Norfk
20 H6 Ickenham Gt Lon
31 N11 Ickford Bucks
23 N10 Ickham Kent
32 H9 Ickleford Herts
12 G6 Icklesham E Susx
33 M7 Ickleton Cambs
34 C3 Icklingham Suffk
58 C5 Ickornshaw N York
32 G7 Ickwell Green C Beds
34 D4 Ickworth Suffk
30 G9 Icomb Gloucs
30 G9 Idbury Oxon
15 K9 Iddesleigh Devon
6 B5 Ide Devon
6 B7 Ideford Devon
21 P11 Ide Hill Kent
12 H5 Iden E Susx
12 E3 Iden Green Kent
12 F4 Iden Green Kent
58 F6 Idle C Brad
3 J6 Idless Cnwll
30 H5 Idlicote Warwks
18 H12 Idmiston Wilts
25 P6 Idole Carmth
50 H10 Idridgehay Derbys
104 E9 Idrigill Highld
19 J4 Idstone Oxon
31 M12 Iffley Oxon
11 K3 Ifield W Susx
10 G4 Ifold W Susx
8 G8 Iford Bmouth
11 N8 Iford E Susx
28 F10 Ifton Mons
49 L7 Ightfield Shrops
22 C11 Ightham Kent
50 F10 Ilam Staffs
17 M10 Ilchester Somset
81 L9 Ilderton Nthumb
21 N6 Ilford Gt Lon
17 K11 Ilford Somset
15 J3 Ilfracombe Devon
51 L11 Ilkeston Derbys
45 N11 Ilketshall St Andrew Suffk
45 M11 Ilketshall St Margaret Suffk
58 E5 Ilkley C Brad
4 G5 Illand Cnwll
40 C10 Illey Dudley
2 G7 Illogan Cnwll
41 P7 Illston on the Hill Leics
20 C3 Ilmer Bucks
30 G5 Ilmington Warwks
17 J12 Ilminster Somset
5 Q5 Ilsington Devon
26 D10 Ilston Swans
65 L11 Ilton N York
17 J11 Ilton Somset
75 N4 Imachar N Ayrs
61 K10 Immingham NE Lin
61 K10 Immingham Dock NE Lin
33 M4 Impington Cambs
57 J12 Ince Ches W
56 G8 Ince Blundell Sefton
57 L7 Ince-in-Makerfield Wigan
106 G8 Inchbae Lodge Hotel Highld
95 K8 Inchbare Angus
101 L4 Inchberry Moray
105 Q9 Incheril Highld
84 H8 Inchinnan Rens
98 B8 Inchlaggan Highld
93 J9 Inchmichael P & K
98 E6 Inchnacardoch Hotel Highld
108 E10 Inchnadamph Highld
93 K9 Inchture P & K
98 C2 Inchvuilt Highld
92 H10 Inchyra P & K
3 K4 Indian Queens Cnwll
22 D4 Ingatestone Essex
58 G11 Ingbirchworth Barns
40 C3 Ingestre Staffs
52 D6 Ingham Lincs
45 N5 Ingham Norfk
34 E3 Ingham Suffk
45 N5 Ingham Corner Norfk
41 J3 Ingleby Derbys
66 C7 Ingleby Arncliffe N York
66 C5 Ingleby Barwick S on T
66 E6 Ingleby Greenhow N York
15 K10 Ingleigh Green Devon
17 Q4 Inglesbatch BaNES
18 H2 Inglesham Swindn
70 F3 Ingleston D & G
65 L4 Ingleton Dur
63 M7 Ingleton N York
57 K2 Inglewhite Lancs
73 J6 Ingoe Nthumb
57 J3 Ingol Lancs
44 B4 Ingoldisthorpe Norfk
53 N9 Ingoldmells Lincs
42 E4 Ingoldsby Lincs
81 L10 Ingram Nthumb
22 D5 Ingrave Essex
58 D6 Ingrow C Brad
63 J3 Ings Cumb
28 G10 Ingst S Glos
42 E8 Ingthorpe Rutlnd
45 K4 Ingworth Norfk
30 D3 Inkberrow Worcs
103 J7 Inkhorn Abers
19 L7 Inkpen W Berk
110 F2 Inkstack Highld
84 C8 Innellan Ag & B
79 M2 Innerleithen Border
86 H3 Innerleven Fife
68 E6 Innermessan D & G
87 N7 Innerwick E Loth
101 K3 Innesmill Moray
102 E9 Insch Abers
99 M8 Insh Highld
57 J2 Inskip Lancs
14 H6 Instow Devon
51 K4 Intake Sheff
94 D4 Inver Abers
107 P6 Inver Highld
92 F7 Inver P & K
97 K12 Inverailort Highld
105 M10 Inveralligin Highld
103 L3 Inverallochy Abers
107 J3 Inveran Highld
84 B2 Inveraray Ag & B
96 G3 Inverarish Highld
93 M6 Inverarity Angus
91 J11 Inverarnan Stirlg
105 M5 Inverasdale Highld
84 F4 Inverbeg Ag & B
95 N7 Inverbervie Abers
102 E3 Inver-boyndie Abers
90 D7 Invercreran House Hotel Ag & B
99 N6 Inverdruie Highld
86 G7 Inveresk E Loth
90 D8 Inveresragan Ag & B
105 M6 Inverewe Garden Highld
94 B4 Inverey Abers
98 G4 Inverfarigaig Highld
90 C7 Inverfolla Ag & B
98 D8 Invergarry Highld
91 Q10 Invergeldie P & K
98 C10 Invergloy Highld
107 L8 Invergordon Highld
93 L9 Invergowrie P & K
97 K8 Inverguseran Highld
91 P5 Inverhadden P & K
91 K10 Inverherive Hotel Stirlg
97 K9 Inverie Highld
90 D11 Inverinan Ag & B
97 N5 Inverinate Highld
93 R6 Inverkeilor Angus
86 D5 Inverkeithing Fife
102 E6 Inverkeithny Abers
84 D8 Inverkip Inver
108 B10 Inverkirkaig Highld
106 C5 Inverlael Highld
98 D11 Inverlair Highld
83 N2 Inverliever Lodge Ag & B
90 G10 Inverlochy Ag & B
94 G6 Invermark Angus
98 F5 Invermoriston Highld
109 M4 Invernaver Highld
107 L12 Inverness Highld
99 J1 Inverness Crematorium Highld
107 M11 Inverness Dalcross Airport Highld
84 C4 Invernoaden Ag & B
90 H7 Inveroran Hotel Ag & B
93 M4 Inverquharity Angus
103 L6 Inverquhomery Abers
98 C11 Inverroy Highld
90 C4 Inversanda Highld
97 N6 Invershiel Highld
107 J3 Invershin Highld
110 F8 Invershore Highld
84 F2 Inversnaid Hotel Stirlg
103 M6 Inverugie Abers
84 F2 Inveruglas Ag & B
99 M8 Inveruglass Highld
102 G10 Inverurie Abers
15 K11 Inwardleigh Devon
34 E12 Inworth Essex
111 a5 Iochdar W Isls
88 G10 Iona Ag & B
10 D5 Iping W Susx
5 Q7 Ipplepen Devon
19 Q4 Ipsden Oxon
50 D10 Ipstones Staffs
35 J7 Ipswich Suffk
35 K7 Ipswich Crematorium Suffk
56 F11 Irby Wirral
53 M10 Irby in the Marsh Lincs
52 H3 Irby upon Humber NE Lin
32 D4 Irchester Nhants
71 K7 Ireby Cumb
63 M7 Ireby Lancs
62 E6 Ireleth Cumb
72 F12 Ireshopeburn Dur
57 N9 Irlam Salfd
42 E5 Irnham Lincs
29 J11 Iron Acton S Glos
39 M2 Ironbridge Wrekin
39 M2 Ironbridge Gorge Shrops
69 P4 Ironmacannie D & G
51 K9 Ironville Derbys
45 M6 Irstead Norfk
71 P4 Irthington Cumb
32 D3 Irthlingborough Nhants
67 L10 Irton N York
76 F4 Irvine N Ayrs
76 E4 Irvine Maritime Centre N Ayrs
110 A3 Isauld Highld
111 k2 Isbister Shet
111 m3 Isbister Shet
11 N6 Isfield E Susx
32 C3 Isham Nhants
10 C2 Isington Hants
82 E7 Islay Ag & B
74 D3 Islay Airport Ag & B
17 J11 Isle Abbotts Somset
17 K11 Isle Brewers Somset
33 Q2 Isleham Cambs
21 M7 Isle of Dogs Gt Lon
22 G7 Isle of Grain Medway
111 d2 Isle of Lewis W Isls
56 c4 Isle of Man IoM
56 b7 Isle of Man Ronaldsway Airport IoM
89 M8 Isle of Mull Ag & B
8 E10 Isle of Purbeck Dorset
23 J9 Isle of Sheppey Kent
96 E3 Isle of Skye Highld
23 P9 Isle of Thanet Kent
62 E8 Isle of Walney Cumb
69 L10 Isle of Whithorn D & G
9 N9 Isle of Wight IoW
9 N8 Isle of Wight Crematorium IoW
97 J7 Isleornsay Highld
2 c2 Isles of Scilly St Mary's Airport IoS
70 F2 Islesteps D & G
21 J8 Isleworth Gt Lon
41 K3 Isley Walton Leics
111 b2 Islibhig W Isls
21 L6 Islington Gt Lon
21 L5 Islington Crematorium Gt Lon
32 E2 Islip Nhants
31 M10 Islip Oxon
111 b2 Islivig W Isls
49 L11 Isombridge Wrekin
9 N2 Itchen Abbas Hants
9 P2 Itchen Stoke Hants
11 J4 Itchingfield W Susx
45 J4 Itteringham Norfk
28 F9 Itton Mons
28 F9 Itton Common Mons
71 N6 Ivegill Cumb
20 G7 Iver Bucks
20 G6 Iver Heath Bucks
73 K10 Iveston Dur
32 D12 Ivinghoe Bucks
32 D12 Ivinghoe Aston Bucks
39 J10 Ivington Herefs
5 M8 Ivybridge Devon
13 K5 Ivychurch Kent
22 C11 Ivy Hatch Kent
22 H9 Iwade Kent
8 C5 Iwerne Courtney or Shroton Dorset
8 C5 Iwerne Minster Dorset
34 F3 Ixworth Suffk
34 F3 Ixworth Thorpe Suffk

J

6 D4 Jack-in-the-Green Devon
85 K11 Jackton S Lans
4 F2 Jacobstow Cnwll
15 K10 Jacobstowe Devon
25 J8 Jameston Pembks
106 H10 Jamestown Highld
84 G6 Jamestown W Duns
110 E8 Janetstown Highld
110 G5 Janets-town Highld
78 H10 Jardine Hall D & G
73 N7 Jarrow S Tyne
34 C10 Jasper's Green Essex
85 P7 Jawcraig Falk
23 M1 Jaywick Essex
80 E9 Jedburgh Border
25 J7 Jeffreyston Pembks
107 M8 Jemimaville Highld
6 c2 Jerbourg Guern
7 a2 Jersey Airport Jersey
7 b2 Jersey Crematorium Jersey
73 M7 Jesmond N u Ty
12 C9 Jevington E Susx
20 G1 Jockey End Herts
71 N8 Johnby Cumb
56 H11 John Lennon Airport Lpool
110 H2 John o' Groats Highld
95 N8 Johnshaven Abers
24 G6 Johnston Pembks
79 L8 Johnstone D & G
84 G9 Johnstone Rens
78 H9 Johnstonebridge D & G
25 P5 Johnstown Carmth
48 F6 Johnstown Wrexhm
86 G7 Joppa C Edin
37 J7 Joppa Cerdgn
76 G7 Joppa S Ayrs
24 G3 Jordanston Pembks
21 P8 Joyden's Wood Kent
72 G8 Juniper Nthumb
86 E8 Juniper Green C Edin
82 G6 Jura Ag & B
56 c2 Jurby IoM

K

64 E5 Kaber Cumb
86 B11 Kaimend S Lans
83 P8 Kames Ag & B
77 L6 Kames E Ayrs
3 J7 Kea Cnwll
60 E10 Keadby N Linc
53 K10 Keal Cotes Lincs
57 N7 Kearsley Bolton
13 P2 Kearsney Kent
63 L6 Kearstwick Cumb
34 B7 Kedington Suffk
50 H11 Kedleston Derbys
61 K11 Keelby Lincs
49 P6 Keele Staffs
49 P6 Keele Services Staffs
58 E7 Keelham C Brad
24 F5 Keeston Pembks
18 D8 Keevil Wilts
41 L3 Kegworth Leics
2 F7 Kehelland Cnwll
102 D10 Keig Abers
58 D6 Keighley C Brad
58 D6 Keighley Crematorium C Brad
85 P4 Keilarsbrae Clacks
92 E9 Keillour P & K
94 C4 Keiloch Abers
82 G8 Keils Ag & B

17 M9 Keinton Mandeville Somset
78 E9 Keir Mill D & G
64 D3 Keisley Cumb
110 G4 Keiss Highld
101 N5 Keith Moray
93 J7 Keithick P & K
95 K8 Keithock Angus
106 I10 Keithtown Highld
58 B5 Kelbrook Lancs
42 E2 Kelby Lincs
64 F7 Keld N York
59 N6 Kelfield N York
51 Q9 Kelfield N York
71 J2 Kelhead D & G
56 H3 Kellamergh Lancs
93 M8 Kellas Angus
101 J5 Kellas Moray
5 Q11 Kellaton Devon
44 H2 Kelling Norfk
59 M8 Kellington N York
73 N12 Kelloe Dur
77 M8 Kelloholm D & G
5 J4 Kelly Devon
41 Q10 Kelmarsh Nhants
19 J2 Kelmscott Oxon
35 N4 Kelsale Suffk
49 K2 Kelsall Ches W
33 K9 Kelshall Herts
71 K5 Kelsick Cumb
80 G7 Kelso Border
51 J7 Kelstedge Derbys
53 J5 Kelstern Lincs
17 Q3 Kelston BaNES
92 B6 Keltneyburn P & K
70 G2 Kelton D & G
86 D4 Kelty Fife
34 E11 Kelvedon Essex
22 C4 Kelvedon Hatch Essex
2 B9 Kelynack Cnwll
93 M11 Kemback Fife
39 N2 Kemberton Shrops
29 P8 Kemble Gloucs
29 N2 Kemerton Worcs
28 D7 Kemeys Commander Mons
102 F11 Kemnay Abers
29 J3 Kempley Gloucs
29 J3 Kempley Green Gloucs
39 Q11 Kempsey Worcs
18 H2 Kempsford Gloucs
19 P10 Kempshott Hants
32 E7 Kempston Bed
38 G5 Kempton Shrops
11 M8 Kemp Town Br & H
22 B10 Kemsing Kent
13 J4 Kenardington Kent
38 H12 Kenchester Herefs
30 G12 Kencot Oxon
63 K4 Kendal Cumb
26 H11 Kenfig Brdgnd
40 H12 Kenilworth Warwks
21 L10 Kenley Gt Lon
39 K3 Kenley Shrops
105 L10 Kenmore Highld
92 B6 Kenmore P & K
6 C6 Kenn Devon
17 K3 Kenn N Som
83 M9 Kennacraig Ag & B
15 P10 Kennerleigh Devon
56 H8 Kennessee Green Sefton
85 Q5 Kennet Clacks
102 C9 Kennethmont Abers
34 B3 Kennett Cambs
6 C5 Kennford Devon
44 G11 Kenninghall Norfk
13 K2 Kennington Kent
19 N1 Kennington Oxon
86 G2 Kennoway Fife
17 J11 Kenny Somset
33 Q2 Kennyhill Suffk
60 D2 Kennythorpe N York
88 C7 Kenovay Ag & B
104 F11 Kensaleyre Highld
21 K7 Kensington Gt Lon
32 E12 Kensworth Common C Beds
90 D5 Kentallen Highld
12 C3 Kent and Sussex Crematorium Kent
28 E4 Kentchurch Herefs
34 B4 Kentford Suffk
23 P9 Kent International Airport Kent
6 E2 Kentisbeare Devon
15 L4 Kentisbury Devon
21 L6 Kentish Town Gt Lon
63 J2 Kentmere Cumb
6 C6 Kenton Devon
21 J6 Kenton Gt Lon
73 L7 Kenton N u Ty
35 K4 Kenton Suffk
89 N3 Kentra Highld
29 K4 Kent's Green Gloucs
9 K3 Kent's Oak Hants
3 J6 Kenwyn Cnwll
108 G3 Keoldale Highld
97 M5 Keppoch Highld
66 C8 Kepwick N York
40 H10 Keresley Covtry
89 Q10 Kerrera Ag & B
2 C9 Kerris Cnwll
38 D4 Kerry Powys
84 B10 Kerrycroy Ag & B
51 Q8 Kersall Notts
6 E6 Kersbrook Devon
34 G7 Kersey Suffk
111 d2 Kershader W Isls
6 E2 Kerswell Devon
39 Q11 Kerswell Green Worcs
35 K7 Kesgrave Suffk
45 Q11 Kessingland Suffk
3 L6 Kestle Cnwll
3 J4 Kestle Mill Cnwll
21 N9 Keston Gt Lon
71 L10 Keswick Cumb
45 K8 Keswick Norfk
32 C2 Kettering Nhants
32 C2 Kettering Crematorium Nhants
45 J9 Ketteringham Norfk
93 J7 Kettins P & K
34 F6 Kettlebaston Suffk
86 G2 Kettlebridge Fife
40 G6 Kettlebrook Staffs
35 L5 Kettleburgh Suffk
79 J12 Kettleholm D & G
50 C5 Kettleshulme Ches E
58 G3 Kettlesing N York
58 G3 Kettlesing Bottom N York
44 F4 Kettlestone Norfk
52 C8 Kettlethorpe Lincs
111 i1 Kettletoft Ork
64 H11 Kettlewell N York
42 E8 Ketton Rutlnd

21 J7 Kew Gt Lon
17 J4 Kewstoke N Som
60 C4 Kexby C York
52 C6 Kexby Lincs
50 B7 Key Green Ches E
41 P6 Keyham Leics
9 K8 Keyhaven Hants
61 L8 Keyingham E R Yk
11 L7 Keymer W Susx
17 P3 Keynsham BaNES
32 F4 Keysoe Bed
32 F5 Keysoe Row Bed
32 F2 Keyston Cambs
41 N2 Keyworth Notts
73 M9 Kibblesworth Gatesd
41 P8 Kibworth Beauchamp Leics
41 P8 Kibworth Harcourt Leics
21 N7 Kidbrooke Gt Lon
39 Q6 Kidderminster Worcs
31 L10 Kidlington Oxon
20 B7 Kidmore End Oxon
69 L10 Kidsdale D & G
49 Q5 Kidsgrove Staffs
25 P7 Kidwelly Carmth
90 C8 Kiel Crofts Ag & B
72 B3 Kielder Nthumb
82 F8 Kiells Ag & B
84 G9 Kilbarchan Rens
97 J8 Kilbeg Highld
83 K9 Kilberry Ag & B
84 E11 Kilbirnie N Ayrs
83 L7 Kilbride Ag & B
83 Q9 Kilbride Ag & B
100 G4 Kilbuiack Moray
51 J10 Kilburn Derbys
21 K6 Kilburn Gt Lon
66 D10 Kilburn N York
41 N8 Kilby Leics
83 M10 Kilchamaig Ag & B
82 E4 Kilchattan Ag & B
84 B11 Kilchattan Ag & B
89 Q8 Kilcheran Ag & B
89 K4 Kilchoan Highld
82 C9 Kilchoman Ag & B
90 E10 Kilchrenan Ag & B
87 J2 Kilconquhar Fife
29 J4 Kilcot Gloucs
107 J11 Kilcoy Highld
84 D6 Kilcreggan Ag & B
66 E5 Kildale N York
75 L8 Kildalloig Ag & B
107 M7 Kildary Highld
83 Q9 Kildavaig Ag & B
83 Q9 Kildavanan Ag & B
109 Q10 Kildonan Highld
75 Q8 Kildonan N Ayrs
109 Q10 Kildonan Lodge Highld
96 F11 Kildonnan Highld
68 E7 Kildrochet House D & G
101 N10 Kildrummy Abers
58 D5 Kildwick N York
83 P7 Kilfinan Ag & B
98 C9 Kilfinnan Highld
25 K7 Kilgetty Pembks
76 E10 Kilgrammie S Ayrs
28 F8 Kilgwrrwg Common Mons
60 H2 Kilham E R Yk
88 B7 Kilkenneth Ag & B
75 K7 Kilkenzie Ag & B
75 L8 Kilkerran Ag & B
14 E9 Kilkhampton Cnwll
51 L5 Killamarsh Derbys
26 E9 Killay Swans
85 J6 Killearn Stirlg
107 L10 Killen Highld
65 L4 Killerby Darltn
6 D3 Killerton Devon
91 M5 Killichonan P & K
98 C11 Killiechonate Highld
89 L7 Killiechronan Ag & B
92 D3 Killiecrankie P & K
97 N4 Killilan Highld
110 G4 Killimster Highld
91 N9 Killin Stirlg
58 H3 Killinghall N York
63 L8 Killington Cumb
63 L4 Killington Lake Services Cumb
73 M6 Killingworth N Tyne
87 J12 Killochyett Border
84 F8 Kilmacolm Inver
85 K2 Kilmahog Stirlg
83 L4 Kilmahumaig Ag & B
104 F7 Kilmaluag Highld
93 L10 Kilmany Fife
76 G3 Kilmarnock E Ayrs
83 M3 Kilmartin Ag & B
76 G3 Kilmaurs E Ayrs
83 M1 Kilmelford Ag & B
17 Q6 Kilmersdon Somset
9 P3 Kilmeston Hants
75 K7 Kilmichael Ag & B
83 N4 Kilmichael Glassary Ag & B
83 L6 Kilmichael of Inverlussa Ag & B
6 H4 Kilmington Devon
18 B12 Kilmington Wilts
8 B1 Kilmington Common Wilts
8 B1 Kilmington Street Wilts
106 H12 Kilmorack Highld
90 B10 Kilmore Ag & B
97 J8 Kilmore Highld
83 K7 Kilmory Ag & B
89 L3 Kilmory Highld
75 P7 Kilmory N Ayrs
104 C11 Kilmuir Highld
104 E8 Kilmuir Highld
107 L11 Kilmuir Highld
107 M7 Kilmuir Highld
84 C6 Kilmun Ag & B
82 D8 Kilnave Ag & B
77 P2 Kilncadzow S Lans
12 E3 Kilndown Kent
89 Q11 Kilninver Ag & B
61 P10 Kilnsea E R Yk
58 C1 Kilnsey N York
60 G4 Kilnwick E R Yk
82 E4 Kiloran Ag & B
75 N7 Kilpatrick N Ayrs
28 E3 Kilpeck Herefs
60 D8 Kilpin E R Yk
87 L2 Kilrenny Fife
41 M12 Kilsby Nhants
93 J9 Kilspindie P & K
68 F10 Kilstay D & G
85 M7 Kilsyth N Lans
98 G2 Kiltarlity Highld
66 F4 Kilton R & Cl
66 F4 Kilton Thorpe R & Cl
104 E8 Kilvaxter Highld
16 F7 Kilve Somset

42 B2 Kilvington Notts
76 E3 Kilwinning N Ayrs
44 H8 Kimberley Norfk
51 L11 Kimberley Notts
51 K3 Kimberworth Rothm
73 M10 Kimblesworth Dur
32 F4 Kimbolton Cambs
39 K9 Kimbolton Herefs
41 N9 Kimcote Leics
8 D10 Kimmeridge Dorset
19 J10 Kimpton Hants
32 H11 Kimpton Herts
109 Q8 Kinbrace Highld
85 N3 Kinbuck Stirlg
93 N11 Kincaple Fife
85 Q5 Kincardine Fife
107 K5 Kincardine Highld
95 K3 Kincardine O'Neil Abers
92 H7 Kinclaven P & K
95 Q2 Kincorth C Aber
100 F3 Kincorth House Moray
99 M7 Kincraig Highld
92 E6 Kincraigie P & K
92 E6 Kindallachan P & K
75 J2 Kinerarach Ag & B
30 E8 Kineton Gloucs
31 J4 Kineton Warwks
92 H10 Kinfauns P & K
84 B10 Kingarth Ag & B
47 M9 King Arthur's Labyrinth Gwynd
95 P3 Kingcausie Abers
28 E7 Kingcoed Mons
52 F5 Kingerby Lincs
30 H8 Kingham Oxon
70 F2 Kingholm Quay D & G
86 F5 Kinghorn Fife
86 E3 Kinglassie Fife
93 L5 Kingoldrum Angus
93 L9 Kingoodie P & K
5 J9 Kingsand Cnwll
93 Q12 Kingsbarns Fife
5 P10 Kingsbridge Devon
16 D8 Kingsbridge Somset
40 E4 King's Bromley Staffs
104 E10 Kingsburgh Highld
21 J5 Kingsbury Gt Lon
40 G8 Kingsbury Warwks
17 L11 Kingsbury Episcopi Somset
28 G3 King's Caple Herefs
19 N8 Kingsclere Hants
42 E10 King's Cliffe Nhants
29 L9 Kingscote Gloucs
15 J8 Kingscott Devon
30 E3 King's Coughton Warwks
75 Q6 Kingscross N Ayrs
17 M10 Kingsdon Somset
13 Q1 Kingsdown Kent
18 H3 Kingsdown Swindn
18 B7 Kingsdown Wilts
18 H3 Kingsdown Crematorium Swindn
86 D4 Kingseat Fife
20 C3 Kingsey Bucks
11 J3 Kingsfold W Susx
95 P1 Kingsford C Aber
76 H2 Kingsford E Ayrs
23 Q8 Kingsgate Kent
34 F4 Kingshall Street Suffk
40 E10 King's Heath Birm
22 D11 Kings Hill Kent
40 C8 King's Hill Wsall
90 H5 Kings House Hotel Highld
91 N11 Kingshouse Hotel Stirlg
6 B8 Kingskerswell Devon
86 G1 Kingskettle Fife
39 J9 Kingsland Herefs
54 C5 Kingsland IoA
20 H3 Kings Langley Herts
49 K1 Kingsley Ches W
10 C3 Kingsley Hants
50 D10 Kingsley Staffs
10 E4 Kingsley Green W Susx
31 Q2 Kingsley Park Nhants
45 P6 King's Lynn Norfk
64 B4 Kings Meaburn Cumb
6 b2 Kings Mills Guern
93 N6 Kingsmuir Angus
79 L2 Kings Muir Border
87 K1 Kingsmuir Fife
13 J3 Kingsnorth Kent
40 D10 King's Norton Birm
41 P7 King's Norton Leics
15 M8 King's Nympton Devon
38 H11 King's Pyon Herefs
33 J2 Kings Ripton Cambs
9 L2 King's Somborne Hants
7 Q1 King's Stag Dorset
29 L7 King's Stanley Gloucs
31 L6 King's Sutton Nhants
40 E8 Kingstanding Birm
6 B8 Kingsteignton Devon
28 F3 Kingsthorne Herefs
31 Q2 Kingsthorpe Nhants
33 K6 Kingston Cambs
4 H5 Kingston Cnwll
5 M10 Kingston Devon
7 Q2 Kingston Dorset
8 E10 Kingston Dorset
87 K6 Kingston E Loth
9 N10 Kingston IoW
23 M12 Kingston Kent
19 L2 Kingston Bagpuize Oxon
20 B4 Kingston Blount Oxon
18 C12 Kingston Deverill Wilts
28 E2 Kingstone Herefs
17 K12 Kingstone Somset
40 D2 Kingstone Staffs
19 K4 Kingston Lisle Oxon
11 N8 Kingston near Lewes E Susx
41 L2 Kingston on Soar Notts
101 L3 Kingston on Spey Moray
7 N5 Kingston Russell Dorset
16 G9 Kingston St Mary Somset
17 K3 Kingston Seymour N Som
61 J8 Kingston upon Hull C KuH
21 J9 Kingston upon Thames Gt Lon
21 J9 Kingston upon Thames Crematorium Gt Lon
32 C11 King's Walden Herts
6 B11 Kingswear Devon
95 P1 Kingswells C Aber
28 G12 Kings Weston Bristl
40 B9 Kingswinford Dudley
31 P9 Kingswood Bucks
29 K9 Kingswood Gloucs
17 P2 Kingswood S Glos
16 F8 Kingswood Somset
21 K11 Kingswood Surrey
40 F12 Kingswood Warwks
39 Q2 Kingswood Common Staffs

9 N2 Kings Worthy Hants
52 G8 Kingthorpe Lincs
38 F10 Kington Herefs
28 H10 Kington S Glos
30 C3 Kington Worcs
18 D5 Kington Langley Wilts
8 B3 Kington Magna Dorset
18 D5 Kington St Michael Wilts
99 L8 Kingussie Highld
17 M9 Kingweston Somset
103 J8 Kinharrachie Abers
70 F3 Kinharvie D & G
92 D11 Kinkell Bridge P & K
103 L7 Kinknockie Abers
68 E8 Kinleith C Edin
39 N6 Kinlet Shrops
96 E9 Kinloch Highld
108 G8 Kinloch Highld
109 K5 Kinloch Highld
92 H6 Kinloch P & K
84 H3 Kinlochard Stirlg
108 E4 Kinlochbervie Highld
90 D1 Kinlocheil Highld
105 Q9 Kinlochewe Highld
97 N8 Kinloch Hourn Highld
98 G10 Kinlochlaggan Highld
90 G4 Kinlochleven Highld
89 P2 Kinlochmoidart Highld
97 K11 Kinlochnanuagh Highld
91 P5 Kinloch Rannoch P & K
100 G3 Kinloss Moray
55 P5 Kinmel Bay Conwy
102 H10 Kinmuck Abers
103 J10 Kinmundy Abers
74 D4 Kinnabus Ag & B
103 K6 Kinnadie Abers
92 E4 Kinnaird P & K
95 N6 Kinneff Abers
78 G8 Kinnelhead D & G
93 Q5 Kinnell Angus
48 G10 Kinnerley Shrops
38 G11 Kinnersley Herefs
39 Q12 Kinnersley Worcs
38 E9 Kinnerton Powys
86 E2 Kinnesswood P & K
93 L5 Kinnordy Angus
41 P2 Kinoulton Notts
86 D2 Kinross P & K
92 H8 Kinrossie P & K
86 D2 Kinross Services P & K
38 G8 Kinsham Herefs
29 N2 Kinsham Worcs
59 K10 Kinsley Wakefd
8 F7 Kinson Bmouth
97 P6 Kintail Highld
19 L7 Kintbury W Berk
100 F4 Kintessack Moray
92 G11 Kintillo P & K
38 H7 Kinton Herefs
48 G10 Kinton Shrops
102 G11 Kintore Abers
74 F3 Kintour Ag & B
74 D3 Kintra Ag & B
88 H10 Kintra Ag & B
83 M3 Kintraw Ag & B
75 L5 Kintyre Ag & B
99 N5 Kinveachy Highld
39 Q5 Kinver Staffs
59 K7 Kippax Leeds
85 L4 Kippen Stirlg
70 D5 Kippford or Scaur D & G
12 D3 Kipping's Cross Kent
111 h2 Kirbister Ork
45 L8 Kirby Bedon Norfk
41 Q4 Kirby Bellars Leics
45 N10 Kirby Cane Norfk
35 K11 Kirby Cross Essex
41 M6 Kirby Fields Leics
60 F1 Kirby Grindalythe N York
59 K1 Kirby Hill N York
65 K6 Kirby Hill N York
66 C9 Kirby Knowle N York
35 K11 Kirby le Soken Essex
66 H10 Kirby Misperton N York
41 M6 Kirby Muxloe Leics
60 D3 Kirby Underdale E R Yk
65 P9 Kirby Wiske N York
10 G5 Kirdford W Susx
110 F4 Kirk Highld
111 k4 Kirkabister Shet
69 N9 Kirkandrews D & G
71 M4 Kirkandrews upon Eden Cumb
71 L4 Kirkbampton Cumb
70 F4 Kirkbean D & G
59 N10 Kirk Bramwith Donc
71 K4 Kirkbride Cumb
93 N7 Kirkbuddo Angus
79 L2 Kirkburn Border
60 G3 Kirkburn E R Yk
58 G10 Kirkburton Kirk
56 H8 Kirkby Knows
52 F5 Kirkby Lincs
66 D6 Kirkby N York
56 H8 Kirkby Fleetham N York
52 F11 Kirkby Green Lincs
51 L9 Kirkby in Ashfield Notts
62 E6 Kirkby-in-Furness Cumb
72 F12 Kirkby la Thorpe Lincs
63 L6 Kirkby Lonsdale Cumb
58 B3 Kirkby Malham N York
41 L7 Kirkby Mallory Leics
65 M11 Kirkby Malzeard N York
66 F9 Kirkbymoorside N York
53 J10 Kirkby on Bain Lincs
32 J4 Kirkby Overblow N York
64 E6 Kirkby Stephen Cumb
64 B3 Kirkby Thore Cumb
42 F5 Kirkby Underwood Lincs
59 L6 Kirkby Wharf N York
86 F4 Kirkcaldy Fife
86 F4 Kirkcaldy Crematorium Fife
71 Q3 Kirkcambeck Cumb
69 P8 Kirkchrist D & G
68 D5 Kirkcolm D & G
77 M8 Kirkconnel D & G
70 F2 Kirkconnell D & G
69 P8 Kirkcowan D & G
69 P8 Kirkcudbright D & G
56 G9 Kirkdale Lpool
59 K4 Kirk Deighton N York
60 H8 Kirk Ella E R Yk
77 P3 Kirkfieldbank S Lans
70 E3 Kirkgunzeon D & G
51 L11 Kirk Hallam Derbys
56 H3 Kirkham Lancs
60 C8 Kirkham N York
59 J9 Kirk Hammerton N York
72 C10 Kirkhaugh Nthumb
58 F9 Kirkheaton Kirk
72 H5 Kirkheaton Nthumb
107 J12 Kirkhill Highld
78 H12 Kirkhope S Lans

96 G6 Kirkibost Highld
93 K6 Kirkinch P & K
69 K8 Kirkinner D & G
85 L8 Kirkintilloch E Duns
50 H10 Kirk Ireton Derbys
70 H11 Kirkland Cumb
77 M8 Kirkland D & G
78 D10 Kirkland D & G
78 G10 Kirkland D & G
50 H11 Kirk Langley Derbys
66 E3 Kirkleatham R & Cl
66 B5 Kirklevington S on T
45 Q10 Kirkley Suffk
59 K10 Kirklington N York
51 P8 Kirklington Notts
71 N3 Kirklinton Cumb
86 D7 Kirkliston C Edin
69 L7 Kirkmabreck D & G
68 F10 Kirkmaiden D & G
56 C4 Kirk Michael IoM
94 B9 Kirkmichael P & K
76 F9 Kirkmichael S Ayrs
77 N3 Kirkmuirhill S Lans
81 J8 Kirknewton Nthumb
86 D8 Kirknewton W Loth
101 P8 Kirkney Abers
85 P9 Kirk of Shotts N Lans
71 Q7 Kirkoswald Cumb
76 D9 Kirkoswald S Ayrs
78 E10 Kirkpatrick D & G
70 C2 Kirkpatrick Durham D & G
71 L2 Kirkpatrick-Fleming D & G
59 N11 Kirk Sandall Donc
62 D6 Kirksanton Cumb
59 M10 Kirk Smeaton N York
58 H7 Kirkstall Leeds
52 H10 Kirkstead Lincs
102 C8 Kirkstile Abers
79 M10 Kirkstile D & G
110 G2 Kirkstyle Highld
59 J9 Kirkthorpe Wakefd
102 E9 Kirkton Abers
78 F11 Kirkton D & G
93 L10 Kirkton Fife
97 L4 Kirkton Highld
97 N2 Kirkton Highld
92 E11 Kirkton P & K
93 K2 Kirkton Manor Border
93 K5 Kirkton of Airlie Angus
93 L7 Kirkton of Auchterhouse Angus
107 N11 Kirkton of Barevan Highld
92 H8 Kirkton of Collace P & K
101 M11 Kirkton of Glenbuchat Abers
103 K8 Kirkton of Logie Buchan Abers
95 J8 Kirkton of Menmuir Angus
93 N7 Kirkton of Monikie Angus
102 F8 Kirkton of Rayne Abers
95 N1 Kirkton of Skene Abers
93 L8 Kirkton of Strathmartine Angus
93 M7 Kirkton of Tealing Angus
102 D11 Kirkton of Tough Abers
103 K3 Kirktown Abers
103 M5 Kirktown Abers
102 H4 Kirktown of Alvah Abers
102 G9 Kirktown of Bourtie Abers
95 P5 Kirktown of Fetteresso Abers
101 L7 Kirktown of Mortlach Moray
103 L9 Kirktown of Slains Abers
86 D12 Kirkurd Border
111 h2 Kirkwall Ork
111 h2 Kirkwall Airport Ork
72 H4 Kirkwhelpington Nthumb
80 H8 Kirk Yetholm Border
61 J11 Kirmington N Linc
52 H5 Kirmond le Mire Lincs
84 C7 Kirn Ag & B
93 L5 Kirriemuir Angus
45 L10 Kirstead Green Norfk
71 K2 Kirtlebridge D & G
34 B5 Kirtling Cambs
34 B5 Kirtling Green Cambs
31 L9 Kirtlington Oxon
109 N3 Kirtomy Highld
43 K3 Kirton Lincs
51 P7 Kirton Notts
35 L8 Kirton Suffk
84 G7 Kirtonhill W Duns
52 D4 Kirton in Lindsey N Linc
69 K8 Kirwaugh D & G
97 L2 Kishorn Highld
31 P3 Kislingbury Nhants
16 E10 Kittisford Somset
95 Q1 Kittybrewster C Aber
28 F3 Kivernoll Herefs
51 L4 Kiveton Park Rothm
52 B6 Knaith Lincs
8 B3 Knap Corner Dorset
20 F10 Knaphill Surrey
17 J10 Knapp Somset
59 M4 Knapton C York
67 J11 Knapton N York
45 M4 Knapton Norfk
33 K4 Knapwell Cambs
59 J3 Knaresborough N York
72 C9 Knarsdale Nthumb
103 J6 Knaven Abers
66 B9 Knayton N York
33 J11 Knebworth Herts
60 C8 Knedlington E R Yk
51 P7 Kneesall Notts
33 K7 Kneesworth Cambs
51 P10 Kneeton Notts
26 C10 Knelston Swans
50 B12 Knenhall Staffs
31 K4 Knightcote Warwks
49 P9 Knightley Staffs
41 N7 Knighton C Leic
7 N1 Knighton Dorset
38 F7 Knighton Powys
16 G7 Knighton Somset
49 N7 Knighton Staffs
49 N9 Knighton Staffs
39 L7 Knighton on Teme Worcs
39 N10 Knightwick Worcs
38 F9 Knill Herefs
42 B4 Knipton Leics
50 H10 Kniveton Derbys
64 C3 Knock Cumb
97 J7 Knock Highld
102 C5 Knock Moray
111 d2 Knock W Isls
110 D9 Knockally Highld
106 D1 Knockan Highld

101 J7 Knockando Moray
98 H1 Knockbain Highld
107 K10 Knockbain Highld
84 D9 Knock Castle N Ayrs
110 D4 Knockdee Highld
84 B8 Knockdow Ag & B
18 C3 Knockdown Wilts
76 E11 Knockeen S Ayrs
75 Q7 Knockenkelly N Ayrs
76 G4 Knockentiber E Ayrs
21 P10 Knockholt Kent
21 P10 Knockholt Pound Kent
48 G10 Knockin Shrops
76 G4 Knockinlaw E Ayrs
68 C6 Knocknain D & G
82 H8 Knockrome Ag & B
56 b4 Knocksharry IoM
69 N3 Knocksheen D & G
70 C2 Knockvennie Smithy D & G
35 N4 Knodishall Suffk
35 P5 Knodishall Common Suffk
17 L10 Knole Somset
57 P11 Knolls Green Ches E
48 H7 Knolton Wrexhm
18 D11 Knook Wilts
42 B8 Knossington Leics
62 G11 Knott End-on-Sea Lancs
32 E4 Knotting Bed
32 E4 Knotting Green Bed
59 L9 Knottingley Wakefd
56 H9 Knotty Ash Lpool
39 L7 Knowbury Shrops
69 J5 Knowe D & G
69 N2 Knowehead D & G
76 E8 Knoweside S Ayrs
17 N3 Knowle Bristl
6 D2 Knowle Devon
6 E6 Knowle Devon
15 J5 Knowle Devon
15 N10 Knowle Devon
39 L7 Knowle Shrops
40 F11 Knowle Solhll
16 C7 Knowle Somset
71 N4 Knowlefield Cumb
57 L2 Knowle Green Lancs
7 J1 Knowle St Giles Somset
20 D7 Knowl Hill W & M
56 H9 Knowsley Knows
57 J9 Knowsley Safari Park Knows
15 P7 Knowstone Devon
12 F2 Knox Bridge Kent
38 F7 Knucklas Powys
32 D4 Knuston Nhants
57 N12 Knutsford Ches E
57 N12 Knutsford Services Ches E
58 D9 Krumlin Calder
2 G11 Kuggar Cnwll
97 K4 Kyleakin Highld
97 K4 Kyle of Lochalsh Highld
97 L5 Kylerhea Highld
108 E8 Kylesku Highld
97 L10 Kylesmorar Highld
111 C3 Kyles Scalpay W Isls
108 E8 Kylestrome Highld
49 M11 Kynnersley Wrekin
39 L8 Kyrewood Worcs

L

111 d2 Lacasaigh W Isls
111 d2 Lacasdal W Isls
52 H3 Laceby NE Lin
20 D4 Lacey Green Bucks
49 N2 Lach Dennis Ches W
34 D3 Lackford Suffk
34 D3 Lackford Green Suffk
18 D7 Lacock Wilts
31 K3 Ladbroke Warwks
12 E1 Laddingford Kent
3 K5 Ladock Cnwll
111 i1 Lady Ork
93 K12 Ladybank Fife
78 F4 Ladygill S Lans
62 E5 Lady Hall Cumb
81 J5 Ladykirk Border
40 D9 Ladywood Birm
39 Q9 Ladywood Worcs
6 c1 La Fontenelle Guern
78 E10 Lag D & G
89 N4 Laga Highld
74 F4 Lagavulin Ag & B
75 P7 Lagg N Ayrs
98 D9 Laggan Highld
99 J9 Laggan Highld
99 M8 Lagganlia Highld
7 a1 La Greve de Lecq Jersey
108 H4 Laid Highld
105 N4 Laide Highld
96 F11 Laig Highld
76 H2 Laigh Clunch E Ayrs
76 H3 Laigh Fenwick E Ayrs
77 K7 Laigh Glenmuir E Ayrs
85 M11 Laighstonehall S Lans
22 D5 Laindon Essex
107 J2 Lairg Highld
58 F7 Laisterdyke C Brad
9 P10 Lake IoW
8 E8 Lake Poole
18 G11 Lake Wilts
62 E1 Lake District National Park Cumb
44 H4 Lakenheath Suffk
43 N10 Lakesend Norfk
27 J11 Laleston Brdgnd
34 E9 Lamarsh Essex
45 L5 Lamas Norfk
80 G5 Lambden Border
12 D3 Lamberhurst Kent
12 D3 Lamberhurst Down Kent
81 K3 Lamberton Border
21 L7 Lambeth Gt Lon
21 L8 Lambeth Crematorium Gt Lon
34 B6 Lambfair Green Suffk
51 N10 Lambley Notts
72 C8 Lambley Nthumb
19 K5 Lambourn Berks
21 P5 Lambourne End Essex
11 K3 Lambs Green W Susx
5 K5 Lamerton Devon
73 M8 Lamesley Gatesd
78 F3 Lamington S Lans
75 Q6 Lamlash N Ayrs
71 N8 Lamonby Cumb
2 C10 Lamorna Cnwll
3 K7 Lamorran Cnwll
37 J10 Lampeter Cerdgn
25 K6 Lampeter Velfrey Pembks
24 H8 Lamphey Pembks

70 H10 Lamplugh Cumb
41 Q11 Lamport Nhants
17 P8 Lamyatt Somset
77 P3 Lanark S Lans
63 J9 Lancaster Lancs
63 J9 Lancaster & Morecambe Crematorium Lancs
63 J10 Lancaster Services (Forton) Lancs
73 L10 Lanchester Dur
11 J8 Lancing W Susx
6 c1 L'Ancresse Guern
33 M4 Landbeach Cambs
14 H7 Landcross Devon
95 M2 Landerberry Abers
9 J4 Landford Wilts
110 E8 Land-hallow Highld
56 F10 Landican Crematorium Wirral
26 C9 Landimore Swans
15 K6 Landkey Devon
26 F9 Landore Swans
4 H7 Landrake Cnwll
2 A10 Land's End Cnwll
2 B9 Land's End Airport Cnwll
5 J7 Landulph Cnwll
3 J4 Lane Cnwll
4 F4 Laneast Cnwll
20 D5 Lane End Bucks
18 B10 Lane End Wilts
40 G1 Lane Ends Derbys
52 B8 Laneham Notts
65 K5 Lane Head Dur
72 F11 Lanehead Dur
16 H10 Langaller Somset
41 Q1 Langar Notts
84 F8 Langbank Rens
58 E4 Langbar N York
63 P8 Langcliffe N York
67 K8 Langdale End N York
9 M6 Langdown Hants
86 G2 Langdyke Fife
34 G11 Langenhoe Essex
32 H8 Langford C Beds
6 D3 Langford Devon
22 G2 Langford Essex
52 B10 Langford Notts
30 G12 Langford Oxon
16 F10 Langford Budville Somset
34 G9 Langham Essex
44 G2 Langham Norfk
42 B7 Langham Rutlnd
34 F3 Langham Suffk
57 N3 Langho Lancs
79 M11 Langholm D & G
80 C7 Langlee Border
9 M7 Langley Hants
32 H11 Langley Herts
22 F11 Langley Kent
72 E8 Langley Nthumb
20 G7 Langley Slough
16 E9 Langley Somset
30 F2 Langley Warwks
18 D6 Langley Burrell Wilts
34 E11 Langley Green Essex
16 E9 Langley Marsh Somset
73 L11 Langley Park Dur
45 N9 Langley Street Norfk
33 M9 Langley Upper Green Essex
12 D9 Langney E Susx
51 M4 Langold Notts
4 G3 Langore Cnwll
17 K10 Langport Somset
43 J1 Langrick Lincs
17 Q3 Langridge BaNES
71 J6 Langrigg Cumb
10 B5 Langrish Hants
50 G2 Langsett Barns
92 B11 Langside P & K
10 B8 Langstone Hants
65 M8 Langthorne N York
59 K1 Langthorpe N York
64 H7 Langthwaite N York
60 H2 Langtoft E R Yk
42 G7 Langtoft Lincs
65 L4 Langton Dur
52 H9 Langton Lincs
53 L9 Langton Lincs
60 D2 Langton N York
52 G7 Langton by Wragby Lincs
12 B3 Langton Green Kent
7 N6 Langton Herring Dorset
8 E10 Langton Matravers Dorset
14 H8 Langtree Devon
71 R8 Langwathby Cumb
110 D10 Langwell House Highld
51 M6 Langwith Derbys
51 L7 Langwith Junction Derbys
52 F8 Langworth Lincs
3 N3 Lanhydrock House & Gardens Cnwll
3 M3 Lanivet Cnwll
3 N4 Lanjeth Cnwll
2 G7 Lanner Cnwll
4 E8 Lanreath Cnwll
4 E9 Lansallos Cnwll
4 D4 Lanteglos Cnwll
4 E9 Lanteglos Highway Cnwll
80 E9 Lanton Border
81 K7 Lanton Nthumb
15 M9 Lapford Devon
74 E4 Laphroaig Ag & B
49 Q11 Lapley Staffs
40 F12 Lapworth Warwks
91 N6 Larachbeg Highld
85 P6 Larbert Falk
102 D8 Largie Abers
83 P6 Largiemore Ag & B
87 J1 Largoward Fife
84 D10 Largs N Ayrs
75 Q7 Largybeg N Ayrs
75 Q7 Largymore N Ayrs
84 D7 Larkfield Inver
22 E10 Larkfield Kent
77 M2 Larkhall S Lans
18 G11 Larkhill Wilts
44 G11 Larling Norfk
7 c2 La Rocque Jersey
6 H4 Lartington Dur
10 A2 Lasham Hants
86 G8 Lasswade Mdloth
66 G9 Lastingham N York
22 G4 Latchingdon Essex
3 J5 Latchley Cnwll
21 M7 Lathbury M Keyn
110 E8 Latheron Highld
110 E8 Latheronwheel Highld
87 J1 Lathones Fife
20 G4 Latimer Bucks
29 J10 Latteridge S Glos
17 Q10 Lattiford Somset

18 G2 Latton Wilts
80 C5 Lauder Border
25 M6 Laugharne Carmth
52 B8 Laughterton Lincs
11 P7 Laughton E Susx
42 F4 Laughton Leics
52 B4 Laughton Lincs
53 M4 Laughton Lincs
51 M4 Laughton-en-le-Morthen Rothm
14 E10 Launcells Cnwll
4 H4 Launceston Cnwll
31 N9 Launton Oxon
95 L7 Laurencekirk Abers
69 P6 Laurieston D & G
85 Q7 Laurieston Falk
32 D6 Lavendon M Keyn
34 F7 Lavenham Suffk
16 G3 Lavernock V Glam
71 P3 Laversdale Cumb
8 H2 Laverstock Wilts
19 N10 Laverstoke Hants
30 E7 Laverton Gloucs
65 M11 Laverton N York
18 B9 Laverton Somset
6 b2 La Villette Guern
48 G4 Lavister Wrexhm
85 N11 Law S Lans
91 Q5 Lawers P & K
34 H9 Lawford Essex
16 F8 Lawford Somset
85 N11 Law Hill S Lans
4 H4 Lawhitton Cnwll
63 P8 Lawkland N York
58 H6 Lawns Wood Crematorium Leeds
24 H7 Lawrenny Pembks
34 E6 Lawshall Suffk
111 d2 Laxay W Isls
111 d2 Laxdale W Isls
56 d4 Laxey IoM
35 L3 Laxfield Suffk
108 E6 Laxford Bridge Highld
111 k3 Laxo Shet
60 D8 Laxton E R Yk
42 D10 Laxton Nhants
51 Q7 Laxton Notts
58 D6 Laycock C Brad
34 F12 Layer Breton Essex
34 F11 Layer-de-la-Haye Essex
34 F12 Layer Marney Essex
34 G8 Layham Suffk
7 K2 Laymore Dorset
60 D6 Laytham E R Yk
71 Q7 Lazonby Cumb
51 J8 Lea Derbys
28 H4 Lea Herefs
52 B6 Lea Lincs
38 G4 Lea Shrops
18 E4 Lea Wilts
107 K12 Leachkin Highld
86 F10 Leadburn Border
52 D11 Leadenham Lincs
22 C1 Leaden Roding Essex
73 K9 Leadgate Dur
78 E6 Leadhills S Lans
30 H10 Leafield Oxon
32 F11 Leagrave Luton
53 L11 Leake Common Side Lincs
66 G6 Lealholm N York
104 G9 Lealt Highld
40 G8 Lea Marston Warwks
31 K1 Leamington Hastings Warwks
30 H2 Leamington Spa Warwks
12 C7 Leap Cross E Susx
63 J5 Leasgill Cumb
42 F1 Leasingham Lincs
65 M2 Leasingthorne Dur
21 J11 Leatherhead Surrey
58 G5 Leathley N York
49 J10 Leaton Shrops
23 J11 Leaveland Kent
34 F8 Leavenheath Suffk
60 D2 Leavening N York
21 N10 Leaves Green Gt Lon
67 M10 Lebberston N York
6 b2 Le Bourg Guern
18 H2 Lechlade on Thames Gloucs
82 D8 Lecht Gruinart Ag & B
63 M2 Leck Lancs
91 Q8 Leckbuie P & K
19 L12 Leckford Hants
31 Q6 Leckhampstead Bucks
19 M5 Leckhampstead W Berk
19 M5 Leckhampstead Thicket W Berk
29 N5 Leckhampton Gloucs
106 C4 Leckmelm Highld
60 H5 Leconfield E R Yk
90 E8 Ledaig Ag & B
32 C11 Ledburn Bucks
29 J2 Ledbury Herefs
38 H11 Ledgemoor Herefs
108 E12 Ledmore Junction Highld
59 L8 Ledsham Leeds
59 K8 Ledston Leeds
31 K8 Ledwell Oxon
14 H3 Lee Devon
21 M8 Lee Gt Lon
39 J3 Leebotwood Shrops
49 K9 Lee Brockhurst Shrops
62 E9 Leece Cumb
22 E6 Lee Chapel Essex
20 E3 Lee Clump Bucks
22 G11 Leeds Kent
58 H7 Leeds Leeds
58 G6 Leeds Bradford Airport Leeds
22 G11 Leeds Castle Kent
2 E8 Leedstown Cnwll
50 C9 Leek Staffs
30 H1 Leek Wootton Warwks
5 M8 Lee Mill Devon
65 N9 Leeming N York
65 M9 Leeming Bar N York
9 P7 Lee-on-the-Solent Hants
50 H12 Lees Derbys
58 C12 Lees Oldham
50 H12 Lees Green Derbys
51 K9 Leesthorpe Leics
48 F4 Leeswood Flints
93 J10 Leetown P & K
49 M2 Leftwich Ches W
65 K9 Legbourne Lincs
80 D5 Legerwood Border
21 M6 Legoland W & M
52 G6 Legsby Lincs
41 N6 Leicester C Leic
41 M7 Leicester Forest East Leics
41 M7 Leicester Forest East Services Leics

41 L5 Leicester (Markfield) Services Leics
7 N2 Leigh Dorset
29 M4 Leigh Gloucs
12 B2 Leigh Kent
11 K1 Leigh Surrey
57 M8 Leigh Wigan
18 F3 Leigh Wilts
39 P10 Leigh Worcs
22 F6 Leigh Beck Essex
18 C5 Leigh Delamere Wilts
18 D5 Leigh Delamere Services Wilts
12 H4 Leigh Green Kent
77 K2 Leigh Knoweglass S Lans
22 G6 Leigh-on-Sea Sthend
8 F7 Leigh Park Dorset
39 P11 Leigh Sinton Worcs
40 D7 Leighswood Wsall
29 L9 Leighterton Gloucs
38 E2 Leighton Powys
39 L2 Leighton Shrops
32 G2 Leighton Bromswold Cambs
32 D10 Leighton Buzzard C Beds
17 Q6 Leigh upon Mendip Somset
17 N2 Leigh Woods N Som
39 J8 Leinthall Earls Herefs
38 H8 Leinthall Starkes Herefs
38 H7 Leintwardine Herefs
41 M9 Leire Leics
35 P4 Leiston Suffk
86 F7 Leith C Edin
80 C5 Leitholm Border
2 E8 Lelant Cnwll
61 L7 Lelley E R Yk
80 G7 Lempitlaw Border
111 d3 Lemreway W Isls
21 K2 Lemsford Herts
30 D5 Lenchwick Worcs
68 F2 Lendalfoot S Ayrs
85 J2 Lendrick Stirlg
103 M7 Lendrum Terrace Abers
22 H11 Lenham Kent
22 H12 Lenham Heath Kent
98 G4 Lenie Highld
80 H6 Lennel Border
69 N8 Lennox Plunton D & G
85 K7 Lennoxtown E Duns
51 M11 Lenton C Nott
42 E4 Lenton Lincs
44 H6 Lenwade Norfk
85 L8 Lenzie E Duns
102 C12 Leochel-Cushnie Abers
39 J9 Leominster Herefs
29 L7 Leonard Stanley Gloucs
104 B11 Lephin Highld
58 G10 Lepton Kirk
6 B10 Lerags Ag & B
4 E8 Lerryn Cnwll
111 k4 Lerwick Shet
81 P10 Lesbury Nthumb
102 D9 Leslie Abers
86 F2 Leslie Fife
78 D2 Lesmahagow S Lans
4 E3 Lesnewth Cnwll
6 c1 Les Quartiers Guern
7 a2 Les Quennevais Jersey
45 N5 Lessingham Norfk
71 K5 Lessonhall Cumb
6 D6 Leswalt D & G
7 a1 L'Etacq Jersey
21 J4 Letchmore Heath Herts
32 H9 Letchworth Garden City Herts
19 L4 Letcombe Bassett Oxon
19 L4 Letcombe Regis Oxon
93 P6 Letham Angus
81 F11 Letham Border
85 P6 Letham Falk
93 K11 Letham Fife
93 Q6 Letham Grange Angus
92 G7 Lethendy P & K
102 D10 Lethenty Abers
102 H7 Lethenty Abers
35 L5 Letheringham Suffk
44 H3 Letheringsett Norfk
105 P7 Letterewe Highld
97 M5 Letterfearn Highld
97 C10 Letterfinlay Lodge Hotel Highld
97 K10 Lettermorar Highld
106 C5 Letters Highld
78 E5 Lettershaw S Lans
24 G3 Letterston Pembks
99 G5 Lettoch Highld
100 H8 Lettoch Highld
38 G11 Letton Herefs
21 L2 Letty Green Herts
51 M4 Letwell Rothm
93 M10 Leuchars Fife
111 d3 Leumrabhagh W Isls
111 d2 Leurbost W Isls
40 B4 Levedale Staffs
61 J5 Leven E R Yk
86 H3 Leven Fife
63 J5 Levens Cumb
33 K11 Levens Green Herts
57 Q9 Levenshulme Manch
111 k5 Levenwick Shet
111 c4 Leverburgh W Isls
43 M7 Leverington Cambs
20 H3 Leverstock Green Herts
43 L1 Leverton Lincs
6 b1 Le Villocq Guern
35 K8 Levington Suffk
67 J8 Levisham N York
32 G10 Lew Oxon
4 G4 Lewannick Cnwll
5 K3 Lewdown Devon
11 N7 Lewes E Susx
24 G4 Leweston Pembks
21 M8 Lewisham Gt Lon
21 N8 Lewisham Crematorium Gt Lon
98 G4 Lewiston Highld
27 K10 Lewistown Brdgnd
20 B4 Lewknor Oxon
23 J10 Lewson Street Kent
5 K3 Lewtrenchard Devon
34 F10 Lexden Essex
16 H8 Lexworthy Somset
22 D10 Leybourne Kent
65 K9 Leyburn N York
32 G10 Ley Hill Bucks
54 F4 Leyland Lancs
102 G11 Leylodge Abers
103 K5 Leys Abers
93 J7 Leys P & K
23 K8 Leysdown-on-Sea Kent
93 Q6 Leysmill Angus

93 L6 Leys of Cossans Angus
39 K8 Leysters Herefs
21 M6 Leyton Gt Lon
21 K6 Leytonstone Gt Lon
4 H4 Lezant Cnwll
101 K3 Lhanbryde Moray
27 L4 Libanus Powys
78 G1 Libberton S Lans
86 F8 Liberton C Edin
40 E8 Lichfield Staffs
40 C11 Lickey Worcs
40 C11 Lickey End Worcs
10 E5 Lickfold W Susx
89 Q4 Liddesdale Highld
18 H5 Liddington Swindn
34 C5 Lidgate Suffk
32 E8 Lidlington C Beds
93 L8 Liff Angus
40 D10 Lifford Birm
5 J4 Lifton Devon
4 H3 Liftondown Devon
31 J3 Lighthorne Warwks
31 J3 Lighthorne Heath Warwks
20 E10 Lightwater Surrey
41 M11 Lilbourne Nhants
49 N11 Lilleshall Wrekin
32 G10 Lilley Herts
80 C8 Lilliesleaf Border
31 P6 Lillingstone Dayrell Bucks
31 P6 Lillingstone Lovell Bucks
7 P1 Lillington Dorset
8 F9 Lilliput Poole
16 F7 Lilstock Somset
32 F11 Limbury Luton
77 M2 Limekilnburn S Lans
86 C5 Limekilns Fife
85 P8 Limerigg Falk
9 M10 Limerstone IoW
29 L3 Lime Street Worcs
17 M10 Limington Somset
77 K6 Limmerhaugh E Ayrs
45 N8 Limpenhoe Norfk
18 B8 Limpley Stoke Wilts
21 N11 Limpsfield Surrey
21 N11 Limpsfield Chart Surrey
51 M9 Linby Notts
10 D4 Linchmere W Susx
78 F12 Lincluden D & G
52 D8 Lincoln Lincs
52 E9 Lincoln Crematorium Lincs
39 P8 Lincomb Worcs
62 H6 Lindale Cumb
62 F7 Lindal in Furness Cumb
11 M5 Lindfield W Susx
10 D5 Lindford Hants
58 E9 Lindley Kirk
39 M8 Lindridge Worcs
33 Q10 Lindsell Essex
34 G7 Lindsey Suffk
34 G7 Lindsey Tye Suffk
66 F4 Lingdale R & Cl
38 G8 Lingen Herefs
11 M2 Lingfield Surrey
45 M8 Lingwood Norfk
104 E8 Linicro Highld
29 L3 Linkend Worcs
19 L8 Linkenholt Hants
4 G5 Linkinhorne Cnwll
86 F4 Linktown Fife
101 K3 Linkwood Moray
38 G4 Linley Shrops
39 M10 Linley Green Herefs
86 B6 Linlithgow W Loth
107 J3 Linsidemore Highld
32 C5 Linslade C Beds
35 M2 Linstead Parva Suffk
71 N4 Linstock Cumb
40 D11 Linthurst Worcs
58 E10 Linthwaite Kirk
87 Q9 Lintlaw Border
101 P3 Lintmill Moray
80 G8 Linton Border
33 P7 Linton Cambs
40 H4 Linton Derbys
28 H4 Linton Herefs
22 F12 Linton Kent
59 K5 Linton Leeds
58 C2 Linton N York
29 J4 Linton Hill Herefs
59 L3 Linton-on-Ouse N York
52 G6 Linwood Lincs
84 G9 Linwood Rens
111 b5 Lionacleit W Isls
111 e1 Lional W Isls
10 H4 Liphook Hants
56 F9 Liscard Wirral
15 P5 Liscombe Somset
4 F7 Liskeard Cnwll
90 B7 Lismore Ag & B
10 C5 Liss Hants
61 K3 Lissett E R Yk
52 G6 Lissington Lincs
27 P11 Lisvane Cardif
28 D10 Liswerry Newpt
44 E6 Litcham Norfk
31 N4 Litchborough Nhants
19 M9 Litchfield Hants
56 G8 Litherland Sefton
33 K8 Litlington Cambs
11 Q9 Litlington E Susx
33 N7 Little Abington Cambs
32 D3 Little Addington Nhants
69 K9 Little Airies D & G
30 F2 Little Alne Warwks
56 F7 Little Altcar Sefton
21 M2 Little Amwell Herts
40 E7 Little Aston Staffs
66 D5 Little Ayton N York
22 F2 Little Baddow Essex
18 B5 Little Badminton S Glos
71 L5 Little Bampton Cumb
33 R5 Little Bardfield Essex
32 H5 Little Barford Bed
45 J4 Little Barningham Norfk
30 G10 Little Barrington Gloucs
49 J2 Little Barrow Ches S
72 H5 Little Bavington Nthumb
19 K7 Little Bedwyn Wilts
35 J10 Little Bentley Essex
21 L2 Little Berkhamsted Herts
32 B4 Little Billing Nhants
32 D11 Little Billington C Beds
28 F3 Little Birch Herefs
34 H7 Little Blakenham Suffk
71 Q8 Little Blencow Cumb
10 C6 Little Bognor W Susx
51 K8 Little Bollington Ches E
20 H11 Little Bookham Surrey
52 B7 Littleborough Notts
58 C11 Littleborough Rochdl
23 N11 Littlebourne Kent
31 L5 Little Bourton Oxon
22 G1 Little Braxted Essex
95 J9 Little Brechin Angus

17 M9 **Keinton Mandeville** Somset
78 E9 **Keir Mill** D & G
64 D3 **Keisley** Cumb
110 G4 **Keiss** Highld
101 N5 **Keith** Moray
93 J7 **Keithick** P & K
95 K8 **Keithock** Angus
106 H10 **Keithtown** Highld
58 B5 **Kelbrook** Lancs
42 E2 **Kelby** Lincs
64 F7 **Keld** N York
59 N6 **Kelfield** N York
51 Q9 **Kelfield** N York
71 J2 **Kelham** Notts
56 H3 **Kellamergh** Lancs
93 M8 **Kellas** Angus
101 J5 **Kellas** Moray
5 Q11 **Kellaton** Devon
44 H2 **Kelling** Norfk
59 M8 **Kellington** N York
73 N12 **Kelloe** Dur
77 M8 **Kelloholm** D & G
5 J4 **Kelly** Devon
41 Q10 **Kelmarsh** Nhants
19 J2 **Kelmscott** Oxon
35 N4 **Kelsale** Suffk
49 K2 **Kelsall** Ches W
33 K9 **Kelshall** Herts
71 K5 **Kelsick** Cumb
80 G7 **Kelso** Border
51 J7 **Kelstedge** Derbys
53 J5 **Kelstern** Lincs
17 Q3 **Kelston** BaNES
92 B6 **Keltneyburn** P & K
70 G2 **Kelton** D & G
86 D4 **Kelty** Fife
34 E11 **Kelvedon** Essex
22 C4 **Kelvedon Hatch** Essex
2 B9 **Kelynack** Cnwll
93 M11 **Kemback** Fife
39 N2 **Kemberton** Shrops
29 P8 **Kemble** Gloucs
29 N2 **Kemerton** Worcs
28 D7 **Kemeys Commander** Mons
102 F11 **Kemnay** Abers
29 J3 **Kempley** Gloucs
29 J3 **Kempley Green** Gloucs
39 Q11 **Kempsey** Worcs
18 H2 **Kempsford** Gloucs
19 P10 **Kempshott** Hants
32 E7 **Kempston** Bed
38 G5 **Kempton** Shrops
11 M8 **Kemp Town** Br & H
22 B10 **Kemsing** Kent
13 J4 **Kenardington** Kent
38 H12 **Kenchester** Herefs
30 G12 **Kencot** Oxon
63 K4 **Kendal** Cumb
26 H11 **Kenfig** Brdgnd
40 H12 **Kenilworth** Warwks
21 L10 **Kenley** Gt Lon
39 K3 **Kenley** Shrops
105 L10 **Kenmore** Highld
92 B6 **Kenmore** P & K
6 C6 **Kenn** Devon
17 K3 **Kenn** N Som
83 M9 **Kennacraig** Ag & B
5 P10 **Kennerleigh** Devon
56 H8 **Kennessee Green** Sefton
85 Q5 **Kennet** Clacks
102 C9 **Kennethmont** Abers
34 B3 **Kennett** Cambs
6 C5 **Kennford** Devon
44 G11 **Kenninghall** Norfk
13 K2 **Kennington** Kent
19 N1 **Kennington** Oxon
86 G2 **Kennoway** Fife
17 J11 **Kenny** Somset
33 Q2 **Kennyhill** Suffk
60 D2 **Kennythorpe** N York
88 C7 **Kenovay** Ag & B
104 F11 **Kensaleyre** Highld
21 K7 **Kensington** Gt Lon
32 E12 **Kensworth Common** C Beds
90 D5 **Kentallen** Highld
12 C3 **Kent and Sussex Crematorium** Kent
28 E4 **Kentchurch** Herefs
34 B4 **Kentford** Suffk
23 P9 *Kent International Airport* Kent
6 E2 **Kentisbeare** Devon
15 L4 **Kentisbury** Devon
21 L6 **Kentish Town** Gt Lon
63 J2 **Kentmere** Cumb
6 C6 **Kenton** Devon
21 J6 **Kenton** Gt Lon
73 L7 **Kenton** N u Ty
35 K4 **Kenton** Suffk
89 N3 **Kentra** Highld
29 K4 **Kent's Green** Gloucs
9 K3 **Kent's Oak** Hants
3 J6 **Kenwyn** Cnwll
108 G3 **Keoldale** Highld
97 M5 **Keppoch** Highld
66 C8 **Kepwick** N York
40 H10 **Keresley** Covtry
89 Q10 **Kerrera** Ag & B
2 C9 **Kerris** Cnwll
38 D4 **Kerry** Powys
84 B10 **Kerrycroy** Ag & B
51 Q8 **Kersall** Notts
6 E6 **Kersbrook** Devon
34 G7 **Kersey** Suffk
111 d2 **Kershader** W Isls
6 E2 **Kerswell** Devon
39 Q11 **Kerswell Green** Worcs
35 K7 **Kesgrave** Suffk
45 Q11 **Kessingland** Suffk
3 L6 **Kestle** Cnwll
3 J4 **Kestle Mill** Cnwll
21 N9 **Keston** Gt Lon
71 L10 **Keswick** Cumb
45 K8 **Keswick** Norfk
32 C2 **Kettering** Nhants
32 C2 **Kettering Crematorium** Nhants
45 J9 **Ketteringham** Norfk
93 J7 **Kettins** P & K
34 F6 **Kettlebaston** Suffk
86 G2 **Kettlebridge** Fife
40 G6 **Kettlebrook** Staffs
35 L5 **Kettleburgh** Suffk
79 J12 **Kettleholm** D & G
50 C5 **Kettleshulme** Ches E
58 G3 **Kettlesing** N York
58 G3 **Kettlesing Bottom** N York
44 F4 **Kettlestone** Norfk
52 C8 **Kettlethorpe** Lincs
111 i1 **Kettletoft** Ork
64 H11 **Kettlewell** N York
42 E8 **Ketton** Rutlnd

21 J7 **Kew** Gt Lon
17 J4 **Kewstoke** N Som
60 C4 **Kexby** C York
52 C6 **Kexby** Lincs
50 B7 **Key Green** Ches E
41 P6 **Keyham** Leics
9 K8 **Keyhaven** Hants
61 J8 **Keyingham** E R Yk
11 L7 **Keymer** W Susx
17 P3 **Keynsham** BaNES
32 F4 **Keysoe** Bed
32 F5 **Keysoe Row** Bed
32 F2 **Keyston** Cambs
41 N2 **Keyworth** Notts
73 M9 **Kibblesworth** Gatesd
41 P8 **Kibworth Beauchamp** Leics
41 P8 **Kibworth Harcourt** Leics
21 N7 **Kidbrooke** Gt Lon
39 Q6 **Kidderminster** Worcs
31 L10 **Kidlington** Oxon
20 B7 **Kidmore End** Oxon
69 L10 **Kidsdale** D & G
49 Q5 **Kidsgrove** Staffs
25 P7 **Kidwelly** Carmth
90 C8 **Kiel Crofts** Ag & B
72 B3 **Kielder** Nthumb
82 F8 **Kiells** Ag & B
84 G9 **Kilbarchan** Rens
97 J8 **Kilbeg** Highld
83 K9 **Kilberry** Ag & B
84 E11 **Kilbirnie** N Ayrs
83 L7 **Kilbride** Ag & B
83 Q9 **Kilbride** Ag & B
100 G4 **Kilbuiack** Moray
51 J10 **Kilburn** Derbys
21 K6 **Kilburn** Gt Lon
66 D10 **Kilburn** N York
41 N8 **Kilby** Leics
83 M10 **Kilchamaig** Ag & B
82 E4 **Kilchattan** Ag & B
84 B11 **Kilchattan** Ag & B
89 Q8 **Kilcheran** Ag & B
89 K4 **Kilchoan** Highld
82 C9 **Kilchoman** Ag & B
90 E10 **Kilchrenan** Ag & B
87 J2 **Kilconquhar** Fife
29 J4 **Kilcot** Gloucs
107 J11 **Kilcoy** Highld
84 D6 **Kilcreggan** Ag & B
66 E5 **Kildale** N York
75 L8 **Kildalloig** Ag & B
107 M7 **Kildary** Highld
83 Q9 **Kildavaig** Ag & B
83 Q9 **Kildavanan** Ag & B
109 Q10 **Kildonan** Highld
75 Q8 **Kildonan** N Ayrs
109 Q10 **Kildonan Lodge** Highld
96 F11 **Kildonnan** Highld
68 E7 **Kildrochet House** D & G
101 N10 **Kildrummy** Abers
58 D10 **Kildwick** N York
83 P7 **Kilfinan** Ag & B
98 C9 **Kilfinnan** Highld
25 K7 **Kilgetty** Pembks
76 E10 **Kilgrammie** S Ayrs
28 F8 **Kilgwrrwg Common** Mons
60 H2 **Kilham** E R Yk
88 B7 **Kilkenneth** Ag & B
75 K7 **Kilkenzie** Ag & B
75 L8 **Kilkerran** Ag & B
14 E9 **Kilkhampton** Cnwll
51 L5 **Killamarsh** Derbys
26 E4 **Killay** Swans
85 J6 **Killearn** Stirlg
107 L10 **Killen** Highld
65 L4 **Killerby** Darltn
6 D3 **Killerton** Devon
91 M5 **Killichonan** P & K
98 C11 **Killiechonate** Highld
89 L7 **Killiechronan** Ag & B
92 D3 **Killiecrankie** P & K
97 N4 **Killilan** Highld
110 G4 **Killimster** Highld
91 N9 **Killin** Stirlg
58 H3 **Killinghall** N York
63 L5 **Killington** Cumb
63 L4 *Killington Lake Services* Cumb
73 M6 **Killingworth** N Tyne
87 J12 **Killochyett** Border
84 F8 **Kilmacolm** Inver
85 K2 **Kilmahog** Stirlg
83 L4 **Kilmahumaig** Ag & B
104 F7 **Kilmaluag** Highld
93 L10 **Kilmany** Fife
76 G3 **Kilmarnock** E Ayrs
83 M3 **Kilmartin** Ag & B
76 G3 **Kilmaurs** E Ayrs
83 M1 **Kilmelford** Ag & B
17 Q6 **Kilmersdon** Somset
9 P3 **Kilmeston** Hants
75 K7 **Kilmichael** Ag & B
83 N4 **Kilmichael Glassary** Ag & B
83 L6 **Kilmichael of Inverlussa** Ag & B
6 H4 **Kilmington** Devon
8 B12 **Kilmington** Wilts
8 B1 **Kilmington Common** Wilts
8 B1 **Kilmington Street** Wilts
106 H12 **Kilmorack** Highld
90 B10 **Kilmore** Ag & B
97 J8 **Kilmore** Highld
83 K7 **Kilmory** Ag & B
89 L3 **Kilmory** Highld
75 P7 **Kilmory** N Ayrs
104 C11 **Kilmuir** Highld
104 E8 **Kilmuir** Highld
107 L11 **Kilmuir** Highld
107 M7 **Kilmuir** Highld
84 C6 **Kilmun** Ag & B
82 D8 **Kilnave** Ag & B
77 P2 **Kilncadzow** S Lans
12 E3 **Kilndown** Kent
89 Q11 **Kilninver** Ag & B
61 P10 **Kilnsea** E R Yk
58 C1 **Kilnsey** N York
60 G4 **Kilnwick** E R Yk
82 E4 **Kiloran** Ag & B
75 N7 **Kilpatrick** N Ayrs
28 E3 **Kilpeck** Herefs
60 D8 **Kilpin** E R Yk
87 L2 **Kilrenny** Fife
41 M12 **Kilsby** Nhants
93 J9 **Kilspindie** P & K
68 F10 **Kilstay** D & G
85 M1 **Kilsyth** N Lans
98 G2 **Kiltarlity** Highld
66 F4 **Kilton** R & Cl
66 F4 **Kilton** R & Cl
66 F4 **Kilton Thorpe** R & Cl
104 E8 **Kilvaxter** Highld
16 F7 **Kilve** Somset

42 B2 **Kilvington** Notts
76 E3 **Kilwinning** N Ayrs
44 H8 **Kimberley** Norfk
51 L11 **Kimberley** Notts
51 K3 **Kimberworth** Rothm
73 M10 **Kimblesworth** Dur
32 F4 **Kimbolton** Cambs
39 K9 **Kimbolton** Herefs
41 N9 **Kimcote** Leics
8 D10 **Kimmeridge** Dorset
19 J10 **Kimpton** Hants
32 H11 **Kimpton** Herts
109 Q8 **Kinbrace** Highld
85 N3 **Kinbuck** Stirlg
93 N11 **Kincaple** Fife
85 Q5 **Kincardine** Fife
107 K5 **Kincardine** Highld
95 K3 **Kincardine O'Neil** Abers
92 H7 **Kinclaven** P & K
95 Q2 **Kincorth** C Aber
100 F3 **Kincorth House** Moray
99 M7 **Kincraig** Highld
92 E6 **Kincraigie** P & K
92 E6 **Kindallachan** P & K
75 J2 **Kinerarach** Ag & B
30 E8 **Kineton** Gloucs
31 J4 **Kineton** Warwks
92 H10 **Kinfauns** P & K
84 B10 **Kingarth** Ag & B
47 M9 **King Arthur's Labyrinth** Gwynd
95 P3 **Kingcausie** Abers
28 E7 **Kingcoed** Mons
52 F5 **Kingerby** Lincs
30 H8 **Kingham** Oxon
70 F2 **Kingholm Quay** D & G
86 F5 **Kinghorn** Fife
86 E3 **Kinglassie** Fife
93 L5 **Kingoldrum** Angus
93 L5 **Kingoodie** P & K
5 J9 **Kingsand** Cnwll
93 Q11 **Kingsbarns** Fife
5 P10 **Kingsbridge** Devon
16 D8 **Kingsbridge** Somset
40 E4 **King's Bromley** Staffs
104 E10 **Kingsburgh** Highld
21 J5 **Kingsbury** Gt Lon
40 G8 **Kingsbury** Warwks
17 L11 **Kingsbury Episcopi** Somset
28 G3 **King's Caple** Herefs
19 N8 **Kingsclere** Hants
42 H10 **King's Cliffe** Nhants
29 L9 **Kingscote** Gloucs
15 J8 **Kingscott** Devon
30 E3 **King's Coughton** Warwks
75 Q6 **Kingscross** N Ayrs
17 M10 **Kingsdon** Somset
13 Q1 **Kingsdown** Kent
18 H3 **Kingsdown** Swindn
18 B7 **Kingsdown** Wilts
18 H3 **Kingsdown Crematorium** Swindn
86 D4 **Kingseat** Fife
20 C3 **Kingsey** Bucks
11 J3 **Kingsfold** W Susx
95 P1 **Kingsford** C Aber
76 H2 **Kingsford** E Ayrs
23 M2 **Kingsgate** Kent
34 F4 **Kingshall Street** Suffk
40 E10 **King's Heath** Birm
22 D11 **King's Hill** Kent
40 C8 **King's Hill** Wsall
90 H5 **Kings House Hotel** Highld
91 N11 **Kingshouse Hotel** Stirlg
6 B8 **Kingskerswell** Devon
86 G1 **Kingskettle** Fife
39 J9 **Kingsland** Herefs
54 C5 **Kingsland** IoA
20 H3 **Kings Langley** Herts
49 L1 **Kingsley** Ches W
10 C3 **Kingsley** Hants
50 D10 **Kingsley** Staffs
10 E4 **Kingsley Green** W Susx
31 Q2 **Kingsley Park** Nhants
43 P6 **King's Lynn** Norfk
64 B4 **Kings Meaburn** Cumb
6 b2 **King's Mills** Guern
93 N6 **Kingsmuir** Angus
79 L2 **Kings Muir** Border
87 K1 **Kingsmuir** Fife
13 J3 **Kingsnorth** Kent
40 D10 **King's Norton** Birm
41 P7 **King's Norton** Leics
15 M8 **King's Nympton** Devon
38 H11 **King's Pyon** Herefs
33 J2 **Kings Ripton** Cambs
9 L2 **King's Somborne** Hants
7 Q1 **King's Stag** Dorset
29 L7 **King's Stanley** Gloucs
31 L6 **King's Sutton** Nhants
40 E8 **Kingstanding** Birm
6 B8 **Kingsteignton** Devon
28 F3 **Kingsthorne** Herefs
31 Q2 **Kingsthorpe** Nhants
33 K6 **Kingston** Cambs
4 H5 **Kingston** Cnwll
5 M10 **Kingston** Devon
7 Q2 **Kingston** Dorset
8 E10 **Kingston** Dorset
87 K6 **Kingston** E Loth
9 N10 **Kingston** IoW
23 M12 **Kingston** Kent
19 L2 **Kingston Bagpuize** Oxon
20 B4 **Kingston Blount** Oxon
18 C12 **Kingston Deverill** Wilts
28 E2 **Kingstone** Herefs
17 K12 **Kingstone** Somset
40 D2 **Kingstone** Staffs
19 K4 **Kingston Lisle** Oxon
11 N8 **Kingston near Lewes** E Susx
41 L2 **Kingston on Soar** Notts
101 L3 **Kingston on Spey** Moray
7 N5 **Kingston Russell** Dorset
16 G9 **Kingston St Mary** Somset
17 K3 **Kingston Seymour** N Som
61 J8 **Kingston upon Hull** C KuH
21 J9 **Kingston upon Thames** Gt Lon
21 J9 **Kingston upon Thames Crematorium** Gt Lon
32 G11 **King's Walden** Herts
6 B11 **Kingswear** Devon
95 P1 **Kingswells** C Aber
28 G12 **Kings Weston** Bristl
40 B9 **Kingswinford** Dudley
31 P9 **Kingswood** Bucks
29 K9 **Kingswood** Gloucs
17 P2 **Kingswood** S Glos
16 F8 **Kingswood** Somset
21 K11 **Kingswood** Surrey
40 F12 **Kingswood** Warwks
39 Q2 **Kingswood Common** Staffs

9 N2 **Kings Worthy** Hants
52 G8 **Kingthorpe** Lincs
38 F10 **Kington** Herefs
28 H10 **Kington** S Glos
30 C3 **Kington** Worcs
18 D5 **Kington Langley** Wilts
8 B3 **Kington Magna** Dorset
18 D5 **Kington St Michael** Wilts
99 L8 **Kingussie** Highld
17 M9 **Kingweston** Somset
103 J8 **Kinharrachie** Abers
70 F3 **Kinharvie** D & G
92 D11 **Kinkell Bridge** P & K
103 L7 **Kinknockie** Abers
86 E8 **Kinleith** C Edin
39 N6 **Kinlet** Shrops
96 F9 **Kinloch** Highld
108 G8 **Kinloch** Highld
109 K5 **Kinloch** Highld
92 H6 **Kinloch** P & K
92 H6 **Kinloch** P & K
97 M7 **Kinlochard** Stirlg
108 E4 **Kinlochbervie** Highld
90 D1 **Kinlocheil** Highld
105 Q9 **Kinlochewe** Highld
97 N8 **Kinloch Hourn** Highld
98 G10 **Kinlochlaggan** Highld
90 G4 **Kinlochleven** Highld
89 P2 **Kinlochmoidart** Highld
97 K11 **Kinlochnanuagh** Highld
91 P5 **Kinloch Rannoch** P & K
100 G3 **Kinloss** Moray
55 P5 **Kinmel Bay** Conwy
102 H10 **Kinmuck** Abers
103 J10 **Kinmundy** Abers
74 D4 **Kinnabus** Ag & B
103 K6 **Kinnadie** Abers
92 E6 **Kinnaird** P & K
95 N6 **Kinneff** Abers
78 G8 **Kinnelhead** D & G
93 Q5 **Kinnell** Angus
48 G10 **Kinnerley** Shrops
38 G11 **Kinnersley** Herefs
39 Q12 **Kinnersley** Worcs
38 E9 **Kinnerton** Powys
86 E2 **Kinnesswood** P & K
93 L5 **Kinnordy** Angus
41 P2 **Kinoulton** Notts
86 D2 **Kinross** P & K
92 H8 **Kinrossie** P & K
86 D2 *Kinross Services* P & K
38 G8 **Kinsham** Herefs
29 N2 **Kinsham** Worcs
59 K10 **Kinsley** Wakefd
8 F7 **Kinson** Bmouth
97 P6 **Kintail** Highld
19 L7 **Kintbury** W Berk
100 F4 **Kintessack** Moray
92 G11 **Kintillo** P & K
38 H7 **Kinton** Herefs
48 G10 **Kinton** Shrops
102 G11 **Kintore** Abers
74 F3 **Kintour** Ag & B
74 D3 **Kintra** Ag & B
88 H10 **Kintra** Ag & B
83 M3 **Kintraw** Ag & B
75 L5 **Kintyre** Ag & B
99 N5 **Kinveachy** Highld
39 Q5 **Kinver** Staffs
59 K7 **Kippax** Leeds
85 L4 **Kippen** Stirlg
70 D5 **Kippford or Scaur** D & G
12 D3 **Kipping's Cross** Kent
111 h2 **Kirbister** Ork
45 L8 **Kirby Bedon** Norfk
41 Q4 **Kirby Bellars** Leics
45 N10 **Kirby Cane** Norfk
35 K11 **Kirby Cross** Essex
41 M6 **Kirby Fields** Leics
60 F1 **Kirby Grindalythe** N York
59 K1 **Kirby Hill** N York
65 K6 **Kirby Hill** N York
66 C9 **Kirby Knowle** N York
35 K11 **Kirby le Soken** Essex
66 H10 **Kirby Misperton** N York
41 M6 **Kirby Muxloe** Leics
60 D3 **Kirby Underdale** E R Yk
65 P9 **Kirby Wiske** N York
10 G5 **Kirdford** W Susx
110 F4 **Kirk** Highld
111 k4 **Kirkabister** Shet
69 N9 **Kirkandrews** D & G
71 M4 **Kirkandrews upon Eden** Cumb
71 L4 **Kirkbampton** Cumb
70 F4 **Kirkbean** D & G
59 N10 **Kirk Bramwith** Donc
71 K4 **Kirkbride** Cumb
93 N7 **Kirkbuddo** Angus
79 L2 **Kirkburn** Border
60 G3 **Kirkburn** E R Yk
58 G10 **Kirkburton** Kirk
56 H8 **Kirkby** Knows
52 F5 **Kirkby** Lincs
66 D6 **Kirkby** N York
52 F11 **Kirkby Green** Lincs
51 K9 **Kirkby in Ashfield** Notts
62 E6 **Kirkby-in-Furness** Cumb
63 L6 **Kirkby la Thorpe** Lincs
63 L6 **Kirkby Lonsdale** Cumb
58 B3 **Kirkby Malham** N York
41 L5 **Kirkby Mallory** Leics
65 M11 **Kirkby Malzeard** N York
66 F9 **Kirkbymoorside** N York
53 J10 **Kirkby on Bain** Lincs
32 J4 **Kirkby Overblow** N York
64 E6 **Kirkby Stephen** Cumb
64 B3 **Kirkby Thore** Cumb
42 F5 **Kirkby Underwood** Lincs
43 L4 **Kirkby Wharf** N York
86 F4 **Kirkcaldy** Fife
86 F4 **Kirkcaldy Crematorium** Fife
71 Q2 **Kirkcambeck** Cumb
69 P8 **Kirkchrist** D & G
68 D5 **Kirkcolm** D & G
77 M8 **Kirkconnel** D & G
70 F2 **Kirkconnell** D & G
69 P8 **Kirkcowan** D & G
69 P8 **Kirkcudbright** D & G
56 G9 **Kirkdale** Lpool
59 N4 **Kirk Deighton** N York
60 H8 **Kirk Ella** E R Yk
77 P3 **Kirkfieldbank** S Lans
70 E3 **Kirkgunzeon** D & G
51 L11 **Kirk Hallam** Derbys
56 H3 **Kirkham** Lancs
60 C2 **Kirkham** N York
59 L3 **Kirk Hammerton** N York
58 F9 **Kirkheaton** Kirk
72 H5 **Kirkheaton** Nthumb
107 J12 **Kirkhill** Highld
78 F7 **Kirkhope** S Lans

96 G6 **Kirkibost** Highld
93 K6 **Kirkinch** P & K
69 K8 **Kirkinner** D & G
85 L8 **Kirkintilloch** E Duns
50 H10 **Kirk Ireton** Derbys
70 H11 **Kirkland** Cumb
77 M8 **Kirkland** D & G
78 D10 **Kirkland** D & G
82 G10 **Kirkland** D & G
50 H11 **Kirk Langley** Derbys
66 E3 **Kirkleatham** R & Cl
66 B5 **Kirklevington** S on T
45 Q10 **Kirkley** Suffk
65 N10 **Kirklington** N York
51 P8 **Kirklington** Notts
71 N3 **Kirklinton** Cumb
86 D7 **Kirkliston** C Edin
69 L7 **Kirkmabreck** D & G
68 F10 **Kirkmaiden** D & G
65 M2 **Kirk Merrington** Dur
56 c4 **Kirk Michael** IoM
94 B9 **Kirkmichael** P & K
76 F9 **Kirkmichael** S Ayrs
77 N3 **Kirkmuirhill** S Lans
81 J3 **Kirknewton** Nthumb
86 D8 **Kirknewton** W Loth
101 P8 **Kirkney** Abers
85 P9 **Kirk of Shotts** N Lans
71 Q7 **Kirkoswald** Cumb
76 D9 **Kirkoswald** S Ayrs
78 E10 **Kirkpatrick** D & G
70 C2 **Kirkpatrick Durham** D & G
71 L2 **Kirkpatrick-Fleming** D & G
59 N11 **Kirk Sandall** Donc
62 D6 **Kirksanton** Cumb
59 M10 **Kirk Smeaton** N York
58 H7 **Kirkstall** Leeds
53 H10 **Kirkstead** Lincs
102 C8 **Kirkstile** Abers
79 M10 **Kirkstile** D & G
110 G2 **Kirkstyle** Highld
59 J9 **Kirkthorpe** Wakefd
102 E9 **Kirkton** Abers
78 F11 **Kirkton** D & G
83 L10 **Kirkton** Fife
97 L4 **Kirkton** Highld
97 N2 **Kirkton** Highld
92 E11 **Kirkton** P & K
78 K2 **Kirkton Manor** Border
93 K5 **Kirkton of Airlie** Angus
93 L7 **Kirkton of Auchterhouse** Angus
107 N11 **Kirkton of Barevan** Highld
92 H8 **Kirkton of Collace** P & K
101 M11 **Kirkton of Glenbuchat** Abers
103 K8 **Kirkton of Logie Buchan** Abers
95 J8 **Kirkton of Menmuir** Angus
93 N7 **Kirkton of Monikie** Angus
102 F8 **Kirkton of Rayne** Abers
95 N1 **Kirkton of Skene** Abers
93 L8 **Kirkton of Strathmartine** Angus
93 M7 **Kirkton of Tealing** Angus
102 D11 **Kirkton of Tough** Abers
103 K3 **Kirktown** Abers
103 M5 **Kirktown** Abers
102 E4 **Kirktown of Alvah** Abers
102 G9 **Kirktown of Bourtie** Abers
95 P5 **Kirktown of Fetteresso** Abers
101 L7 **Kirktown of Mortlach** Moray
103 L9 **Kirktown of Slains** Abers
86 D12 **Kirkurd** Border
111 h2 **Kirkwall** Ork
111 h2 *Kirkwall Airport* Ork
72 H4 **Kirkwhelpington** Nthumb
80 H8 **Kirk Yetholm** Border
61 J11 **Kirmington** N Linc
52 H5 **Kirmond le Mire** Lincs
84 C7 **Kirn** Ag & B
93 L5 **Kirriemuir** Angus
45 L10 **Kirstead Green** Norfk
71 K2 **Kirtlebridge** D & G
34 B5 **Kirtling** Cambs
34 B5 **Kirtling Green** Cambs
31 L9 **Kirtlington** Oxon
109 N3 **Kirtomy** Highld
43 K3 **Kirton** Lincs
51 P7 **Kirton** Notts
35 L8 **Kirton** Suffk
84 C7 **Kirtonhill** W Duns
52 D4 **Kirton in Lindsey** N Linc
84 G9 **Kirwaugh** D & G
97 L2 **Kishorn** Highld
31 P3 **Kislingbury** Nhants
16 E10 **Kittisford** Somset
95 Q1 **Kittybrewster** C Aber
28 F3 **Kivernoll** Herefs
51 L4 **Kiveton Park** Rothm
52 B6 **Knaith** Lincs
8 B3 **Knap Corner** Dorset
20 F10 **Knaphill** Surrey
59 M4 **Knapp** Somset
33 K4 **Knapton** C York
67 J11 **Knapton** N York
45 M4 **Knapton** Norfk
33 K4 **Knapwell** Cambs
59 J3 **Knaresborough** N York
72 C9 **Knarsdale** Nthumb
103 J6 **Knaven** Abers
66 B9 **Knayton** N York
33 J11 **Knebworth** Herts
60 C8 **Knedlington** E R Yk
51 P7 **Kneesall** Notts
33 K7 **Kneesworth** Cambs
51 P10 **Kneeton** Notts
26 C10 **Knelston** Swans
50 B12 **Knenhall** Staffs
31 K4 **Knightcote** Warwks
49 P9 **Knightley** Staffs
41 N7 **Knighton** C Leic
7 N1 **Knighton** Dorset
38 F7 **Knighton** Powys
16 G7 **Knighton** Somset
49 M7 **Knighton** Staffs
49 N9 **Knighton** Staffs
39 L7 **Knighton on Teme** Worcs
39 N10 **Knightwick** Worcs
38 F9 **Knill** Herefs
42 B4 **Knipton** Leics
50 G10 **Kniveton** Derbys
64 C3 **Knock** Cumb
97 J7 **Knock** Highld
102 C5 **Knock** Moray
111 d2 **Knock** W Isls
110 D9 **Knockally** Highld
106 D1 **Knockan** Highld

101 J7 Knockando Moray
98 H1 Knockbain Highld
107 K10 Knockbain Highld
84 D9 Knock Castle N Ayrs
110 D4 Knockdee Highld
84 B8 Knockdow Ag & B
18 C3 Knockdown Wilts
76 E11 Knockeen S Ayrs
75 Q7 Knockenkelly N Ayrs
76 G4 Knockentiber E Ayrs
21 P10 Knockholt Kent
21 P10 Knockholt Pound Kent
48 G10 Knockin Shrops
76 G4 Knockinlaw E Ayrs
68 C6 Knocknain D & G
82 H8 Knockrome Ag & B
56 b4 Knocksharry IoM
69 N3 Knocksheen D & G
70 C2 Knockvennie Smithy D & G
35 N4 Knodishall Suffk
35 P5 Knodishall Common Suffk
17 L10 Knole Somset
57 P11 Knolls Green Ches E
48 H7 Knolton Wrexhm
18 D11 Knook Wilts
42 B8 Knossington Leics
62 G11 Knott End-on-Sea Lancs
32 E4 Knotting Bed
32 E4 Knotting Green Bed
59 L9 Knottingley Wakefd
56 H9 Knotty Ash Lpool
39 L7 Knowbury Shrops
69 J5 Knowe D & G
69 N2 Knowehead D & G
76 E8 Knoweside S Ayrs
17 N3 Knowle Bristl
6 D2 Knowle Devon
6 E6 Knowle Devon
15 J5 Knowle Devon
15 N10 Knowle Devon
39 L7 Knowle Shrops
40 F11 Knowle Solhll
16 C7 Knowle Somset
71 N4 Knowlefield Cumb
57 L2 Knowle Green Lancs
7 J1 Knowle St Giles Somset
20 D7 Knowl Hill W & M
56 H9 Knowsley Knows
57 J9 Knowsley Safari Park Knows
15 P7 Knowstone Devon
12 F2 Knox Bridge Kent
38 F7 Knucklas Powys
32 D4 Knuston Nhants
57 N12 Knutsford Ches E
57 N12 Knutsford Services Ches E
58 D9 Krumlin Calder
2 G11 Kuggar Cnwll
97 K4 Kyleakin Highld
97 K4 Kyle of Lochalsh Highld
97 L5 Kylerhea Highld
108 E8 Kylesku Highld
97 L10 Kylesmorar Highld
111 c3 Kyles Scalpay W Isls
108 E8 Kylestrome Highld
49 M11 Kynnersley Wrekin
39 L8 Kyrewood Worcs

L

111 d2 Lacasaigh W Isls
111 d2 Lacasdal W Isls
52 H3 Laceby NE Lin
20 D4 Lacey Green Bucks
49 N2 Lach Dennis Ches W
34 D3 Lackford Suffk
34 D3 Lackford Green Suffk
18 D7 Lacock Wilts
31 K3 Ladbroke Warwks
12 E1 Laddingford Kent
3 K5 Ladock Cnwll
111 i1 Lady Ork
93 K12 Ladybank Fife
78 F4 Ladygill S Lans
62 E5 Lady Hall Cumb
81 J5 Ladykirk Border
40 D9 Ladywood Birm
39 Q9 Ladywood Worcs
6 c1 La Fontenelle Guern
78 E10 Lag D & G
89 N4 Laga Highld
74 F4 Lagavulin Ag & B
75 P7 Lagg N Ayrs
98 D9 Laggan Highld
99 J9 Laggan Highld
99 M8 Lagganlia Highld
7 a1 La Greve de Lecq Jersey
108 H4 Laid Highld
105 N4 Laide Highld
96 F11 Laig Highld
76 H2 Laigh Clunch E Ayrs
76 H3 Laigh Fenwick E Ayrs
77 K7 Laigh Glenmuir E Ayrs
85 M11 Laighstonehall S Lans
22 D5 Laindon Essex
107 J2 Lairg Highld
58 F7 Laisterdyke C Brad
9 P10 Lake IoW
8 E8 Lake Poole
8 G11 Lake Wilts
62 E1 Lake District National Park Cumb
44 B12 Lakenheath Suffk
43 N10 Lakesend Norfk
27 J11 Laleston Brdgnd
34 E9 Lamarsh Essex
45 L5 Lamas Norfk
80 G5 Lambden Border
12 D3 Lamberhurst Kent
12 D3 Lamberhurst Down Kent
81 K3 Lamberton Border
21 L7 Lambeth Gt Lon
21 L8 Lambeth Crematorium Gt Lon
34 B6 Lambfair Green Suffk
51 N10 Lambley Notts
72 C8 Lambley Nthumb
19 K5 Lambourn W Berk
21 P5 Lambourne End Essex
11 K3 Lambs Green W Susx
5 K5 Lamerton Devon
73 M8 Lamesley Gatesd
78 F3 Lamington S Lans
75 Q4 Lamlash N Ayrs
71 N8 Lamonby Cumb
2 C10 Lamorna Cnwll
3 K7 Lamorran Cnwll
37 J10 Lampeter Cerdgn
25 K6 Lampeter Velfrey Pembks
24 H8 Lamphey Pembks

70 H10 Lamplugh Cumb
41 Q11 Lamport Nhants
17 P8 Lamyatt Somset
77 P3 Lanark S Lans
63 J9 Lancaster Lancs
63 J9 Lancaster & Morecambe Crematorium Lancs
63 J10 Lancaster Services (Forton) Lancs
73 L10 Lanchester Dur
11 J8 Lancing W Susx
6 c1 L'Ancresse Guern
33 M4 Landbeach Cambs
14 H7 Landcross Devon
95 M2 Landerberry Abers
9 J4 Landford Wilts
110 E8 Land-hallow Highld
56 F10 Landican Crematorium Wirral
26 C9 Landimore Swans
15 K6 Landkey Devon
26 F9 Landore Swans
4 H7 Landrake Cnwll
2 A10 Land's End Cnwll
2 B9 Land's End Airport Cnwll
5 J7 Landulph Cnwll
3 J4 Lane Cnwll
4 F4 Laneast Cnwll
20 D5 Lane End Bucks
18 B10 Lane End Wilts
40 G1 Lane Ends Derbys
52 B8 Laneham Notts
65 K5 Lane Head Dur
72 F11 Lanehead Dur
16 H10 Langaller Somset
41 Q1 Langar Notts
84 F8 Langbank Rens
58 E4 Langbar N York
63 P8 Langcliffe N York
67 K8 Langdale End N York
9 M6 Langdown Hants
86 Q2 Langdyke Fife
34 G11 Langenhoe Essex
32 H8 Langford C Beds
6 D3 Langford Devon
22 G2 Langford Essex
52 B10 Langford Notts
30 G12 Langford Oxon
16 F10 Langford Budville Somset
34 G9 Langham Essex
44 G2 Langham Norfk
42 B7 Langham Rutlnd
34 F3 Langham Suffk
57 N3 Langho Lancs
79 M11 Langholm D & G
80 C7 Langlee Border
9 M7 Langley Hants
32 H11 Langley Herts
22 F11 Langley Kent
72 E8 Langley Nthumb
20 G7 Langley Slough
16 E9 Langley Somset
10 D4 Langley W Susx
30 F2 Langley Warwks
18 D6 Langley Burrell Wilts
34 E11 Langley Green Essex
16 E9 Langley Marsh Somset
73 L11 Langley Park Dur
45 N9 Langley Street Norfk
33 M9 Langley Upper Green Essex
12 D9 Langney E Susx
51 N4 Langold Notts
4 G3 Langore Cnwll
17 K10 Langport Somset
43 J1 Langrick Lincs
17 Q3 Langridge BaNES
71 J6 Langrigg Cumb
10 B5 Langrish Hants
50 G2 Langsett Barns
92 B11 Langside P & K
10 B8 Langstone Hants
65 M8 Langthorne N York
59 K1 Langthorpe N York
64 H7 Langthwaite N York
60 H2 Langtoft E R Yk
42 G7 Langtoft Lincs
65 L4 Langton Dur
52 H9 Langton Lincs
53 L9 Langton Lincs
60 D2 Langton N York
52 G7 Langton by Wragby Lincs
12 B3 Langton Green Kent
7 N6 Langton Herring Dorset
8 E10 Langton Matravers Dorset
14 H8 Langtree Devon
71 R8 Langwathby Cumb
110 D10 Langwell House Highld
51 M6 Langwith Derbys
51 L7 Langwith Junction Derbys
52 F8 Langworth Lincs
3 N3 Lanhydrock House & Gardens Cnwll
3 M3 Lanivet Cnwll
3 N4 Lanlivery Cnwll
2 G7 Lanner Cnwll
4 E8 Lanreath Cnwll
4 E9 Lansallos Cnwll
4 D4 Lanteglos Cnwll
4 E9 Lanteglos Highway Cnwll
80 E9 Lanton Border
81 K7 Lanton Nthumb
15 M9 Lapford Devon
74 E4 Laphroaig Ag & B
49 Q11 Lapley Staffs
40 F12 Lapworth Warwks
97 N6 Larachbeg Highld
85 P6 Larbert Falk
102 D8 Largie Abers
83 P6 Largiemore Ag & B
87 J1 Largoward Fife
84 D10 Largs N Ayrs
75 Q7 Largybeg N Ayrs
75 Q7 Largymore N Ayrs
84 D7 Larkfield Inver
22 E10 Larkfield Kent
77 M2 Larkhall S Lans
18 G11 Larkhill Wilts
44 G11 Larling Norfk
7 c2 La Rocque Jersey
64 H4 Lartington Dur
10 A2 Lasham Hants
86 G8 Lasswade Mdloth
66 G9 Lastingham N York
22 G4 Latchingdon Essex
2 J5 Latchley Cnwll
32 C7 Lathbury M Keyn
110 E6 Latheron Highld
110 E6 Latheronwheel Highld
87 J1 Lathones Fife
20 G4 Latimer Bucks
29 J10 Latteridge S Glos
17 Q10 Lattiford Somset

18 G2 Latton Wilts
80 C5 Lauder Border
25 M6 Laugharne Carmth
52 B8 Laughterton Lincs
11 P7 Laughton E Susx
42 F4 Laughton Leics
51 M4 Laughton Lincs
51 M4 Laughton-en-le-Morthen Rothm
14 E10 Launcells Cnwll
4 H4 Launceston Cnwll
31 N9 Launton Oxon
95 L7 Laurencekirk Abers
69 L6 Laurieston D & G
85 Q7 Laurieston Falk
32 D6 Lavendon M Keyn
34 F7 Lavenham Suffk
16 G3 Lavernock V Glam
71 P3 Laversdale Cumb
8 H2 Laverstock Wilts
19 N10 Laverstoke Hants
30 E5 Laverton Gloucs
65 M11 Laverton N York
18 B9 Laverton Somset
6 b2 La Villette Guern
48 G4 Lavister Wrexhm
85 N11 Law S Lans
91 Q8 Lawers P & K
34 H9 Lawford Essex
16 F8 Lawford Somset
85 N11 Law Hill S Lans
4 H4 Lawhitton Cnwll
63 P8 Lawkland N York
58 H6 Lawns Wood Crematorium Leeds
24 H7 Lawrenny Pembks
34 E6 Lawshall Suffk
111 d2 Laxay W Isls
111 d2 Laxdale W Isls
56 d4 Laxey IoM
35 L3 Laxfield Suffk
108 E6 Laxford Bridge Highld
111 k3 Laxo Shet
60 D8 Laxton E R Yk
42 D10 Laxton Nhants
51 Q7 Laxton Notts
58 D6 Laycock C Brad
34 F12 Layer Breton Essex
34 F11 Layer-de-la-Haye Essex
34 F12 Layer Marney Essex
34 G8 Layham Suffk
7 K2 Laymore Dorset
60 D6 Laytham E R Yk
71 Q7 Lazonby Cumb
51 J8 Lea Derbys
28 H4 Lea Herefs
52 B6 Lea Lincs
38 G4 Lea Shrops
18 E4 Lea Wilts
107 K12 Leachkin Highld
86 F10 Leadburn Border
52 D11 Leadenham Lincs
22 C1 Leaden Roding Essex
73 K9 Leadgate Dur
78 E6 Leadhills S Lans
30 H10 Leafield Oxon
32 F11 Leagrave Luton
53 L11 Leake Common Side Lincs
66 G6 Lealholm N York
104 G9 Lealt Highld
40 G8 Lea Marston Warwks
31 K1 Leamington Hastings Warwks
30 H2 Leamington Spa Warwks
12 C7 Leap Cross E Susx
63 J3 Leasgill Cumb
42 F1 Leasingham Lincs
65 M2 Leasingthorne Dur
21 J11 Leatherhead Surrey
58 G5 Leathley N York
49 J10 Leaton Shrops
23 J11 Leaveland Kent
34 F8 Leavenheath Suffk
60 D2 Leavening N York
21 N10 Leaves Green Gt Lon
67 M10 Lebberston N York
6 b2 Le Bourg Guern
18 H2 Lechlade on Thames Gloucs
82 D8 Lecht Gruinart Ag & B
63 M6 Leck Lancs
91 Q8 Leckbuie P & K
19 L12 Leckford Hants
31 Q6 Leckhampstead Bucks
19 M5 Leckhampstead W Berk
19 M5 Leckhampstead Thicket W Berk
29 N5 Leckhampton Gloucs
106 C4 Leckmelm Highld
60 H5 Leconfield E R Yk
90 B7 Ledaig Ag & B
32 C11 Ledburn Bucks
29 J2 Ledbury Herefs
38 H11 Ledgemoor Herefs
108 E12 Ledmore Junction Highld
59 L8 Ledsham Leeds
59 K8 Ledston Leeds
31 K8 Ledwell Oxon
14 H3 Lee Devon
21 M8 Lee Gt Lon
39 J3 Leebotwood Shrops
49 K9 Lee Brockhurst Shrops
62 E8 Leece Cumb
22 C2 Lee Chapel Essex
20 E3 Lee Clump Bucks
22 G11 Leeds Kent
58 H7 Leeds Leeds
58 G6 Leeds Bradford Airport Leeds
22 G11 Leeds Castle Kent
2 E8 Leedstown Cnwll
50 C9 Leek Staffs
30 H1 Leek Wootton Warwks
5 M8 Lee Mill Devon
66 C6 Leeming N York
65 M9 Leeming Bar N York
9 P7 Lee-on-the-Solent Hants
50 H12 Lees Derbys
58 C12 Lees Oldham
50 H12 Lees Green Derbys
42 B7 Leesthorpe Leics
93 J10 Leetown P & K
49 M2 Leftwich Ches W
53 L6 Legbourne Lincs
80 D5 Legerwood Border
32 G6 Legsby Lincs
41 N6 Leicester C Leic
41 M6 Leicester Forest East Leics
41 M7 Leicester Forest East Services Leics

41 L5 Leicester (Markfield) Services Leics
7 N2 Leigh Dorset
29 M4 Leigh Gloucs
12 B2 Leigh Kent
11 K1 Leigh Surrey
57 M8 Leigh Wigan
18 F3 Leigh Wilts
39 P10 Leigh Worcs
22 F6 Leigh Beck Essex
18 C5 Leigh Delamere Wilts
18 D5 Leigh Delamere Services Wilts
12 H4 Leigh Green Kent
77 K2 Leigh Knoweglass S Lans
22 G6 Leigh-on-Sea Sthend
8 F7 Leigh Park Dorset
39 P11 Leigh Sinton Worcs
40 D7 Leighswood Wsall
29 L9 Leighterton Gloucs
38 E2 Leighton Powys
39 L2 Leighton Shrops
32 G2 Leighton Bromswold Cambs
32 D10 Leighton Buzzard C Beds
17 Q6 Leigh upon Mendip Somset
17 N2 Leigh Woods N Som
39 J8 Leinthall Earls Herefs
38 H8 Leinthall Starkes Herefs
38 H7 Leintwardine Herefs
41 M9 Leire Leics
35 P4 Leiston Suffk
86 F7 Leith C Edin
80 G5 Leitholm Border
2 E8 Lelant Cnwll
61 L7 Lelley E R Yk
80 G7 Lempitlaw Border
111 d3 Lemreway W Isls
21 K2 Lemsford Herts
30 D5 Lenchwick Worcs
68 F2 Lendalfoot S Ayrs
85 J2 Lendrick Stirlg
103 M7 Lendrum Terrace Abers
22 H11 Lenham Kent
22 H12 Lenham Heath Kent
98 G4 Lenie Highld
80 H6 Lennel Border
69 N8 Lennox Plunton D & G
85 K7 Lennoxtown E Duns
51 M11 Lenton C Nott
42 E4 Lenton Lincs
44 H6 Lenwade Norfk
85 L8 Lenzie E Duns
102 C12 Leochel-Cushnie Abers
39 J9 Leominster Herefs
29 L7 Leonard Stanley Gloucs
104 B11 Lephin Highld
60 D2 Leppington N York
58 G10 Lepton Kirk
90 B3 Lerags Ag & B
4 E8 Lerryn Cnwll
111 k4 Lerwick Shet
81 P10 Lesbury Nthumb
102 D9 Leslie Abers
86 F2 Leslie Fife
78 D2 Lesmahagow S Lans
4 E3 Lesnewth Cnwll
6 c1 Les Quartiers Guern
7 a2 Les Quennevais Jersey
45 N5 Lessingham Norfk
71 K5 Lessonhall Cumb
78 D & G Leswalt
7 a1 L'Etacq Jersey
21 J4 Letchmore Heath Herts
32 H9 Letchworth Garden City Herts
19 L4 Letcombe Bassett Oxon
19 L4 Letcombe Regis Oxon
93 P6 Letham Angus
81 P6 Letham Border
85 P6 Letham Falk
87 K11 Letham Fife
93 Q6 Letham Grange Angus
92 G7 Lethendy P & K
102 D10 Lethenty Abers
102 H7 Lethenty Abers
35 L5 Letheringham Suffk
44 H3 Letheringsett Norfk
105 P7 Letterewe Highld
97 M5 Letterfearn Highld
97 C10 Letterfinlay Lodge Hotel Highld
97 K10 Lettermorar Highld
106 C5 Letters Highld
78 E5 Lettershaw S Lans
24 G3 Letterston Pembks
99 G5 Lettoch Highld
100 H8 Lettoch Highld
38 G11 Letton Herefs
21 L2 Letty Green Herts
51 M4 Letwell Rothm
93 M10 Leuchars Fife
111 d3 Leumrabhagh W Isls
111 d2 Leurbost W Isls
40 B4 Levedale Staffs
61 J5 Leven E R Yk
86 H3 Leven Fife
63 J5 Levens Cumb
33 K11 Levens Green Herts
57 Q9 Levenshulme Manch
111 k5 Levenwick Shet
111 c4 Leverburgh W Isls
43 M7 Leverington Cambs
20 H3 Leverstock Green Herts
43 L1 Leverton Lincs
6 b1 Le Villocq Guern
35 K8 Levington Suffk
67 J8 Levisham N York
31 J11 Lew Oxon
4 G4 Lewannick Cnwll
5 K3 Lewdown Devon
11 N7 Lewes E Susx
24 G4 Leweston Pembks
21 M8 Lewisham Gt Lon
21 N8 Lewisham Crematorium Gt Lon
98 G4 Lewiston Highld
27 K10 Lewistown Brdgnd
20 B4 Lewknor Oxon
23 J10 Lewson Street Kent
5 K3 Lewtrenchard Devon
34 F10 Lexden Essex
16 H8 Lexworthy Somset
22 D10 Leybourne Kent
65 K9 Leyburn N York
32 H5 Leygreen Herts
57 K4 Ley Hill Bucks
57 K4 Leyland Lancs
102 G11 Leylodge Abers
103 K5 Leys Abers
93 J7 Leys P & K
23 K8 Leysdown-on-Sea Kent
93 Q6 Leysmill Angus

93 L6 Leys of Cossans Angus
39 K8 Leysters Herefs
21 M6 Leyton Gt Lon
21 N6 Leytonstone Gt Lon
4 H4 Lezant Cnwll
101 K3 Lhanbryde Moray
27 L4 Libanus Powys
78 G1 Liberton C Edin
86 F8 Liberton S Lans
40 E5 Lichfield Staffs
4 C11 Lickey Worcs
40 C11 Lickey End Worcs
10 E5 Lickfold W Susx
89 Q4 Liddesdale Highld
18 H5 Liddington Swindn
34 C5 Lidgate Suffk
32 E8 Lidlington C Beds
93 L8 Liff Angus
4 D10 Lifford Birm
5 J3 Lifton Devon
4 H3 Liftondown Devon
31 J3 Lighthorne Warwks
31 J3 Lighthorne Heath Warwks
20 E10 Lightwater Surrey
4 M11 Lilbourne Nhants
49 N11 Lilleshall Wrekin
32 G10 Lilley Herts
80 C8 Lilliesleaf Border
31 P6 Lillingstone Dayrell Bucks
31 P6 Lillingstone Lovell Bucks
7 P1 Lillington Dorset
8 F9 Lilliput Poole
16 F7 Lilstock Somset
32 F11 Limbury Luton
77 M2 Limekilnburn S Lans
86 C5 Limekilns Fife
85 P8 Limerigg Falk
9 M10 Limerstone IoW
29 L3 Lime Street Worcs
17 M10 Limington Somset
77 K6 Limmerhaugh E Ayrs
45 N8 Limpenhoe Norfk
18 B3 Limpley Stoke Wilts
21 N11 Limpsfield Surrey
21 N11 Limpsfield Chart Surrey
51 M9 Linby Notts
10 D4 Linchmere W Susx
78 F12 Lincluden D & G
52 D8 Lincoln Lincs
52 E9 Lincoln Crematorium Lincs
39 P8 Lincomb Worcs
62 H6 Lindale Cumb
62 F7 Lindal in Furness Cumb
11 M5 Lindfield W Susx
10 D5 Lindford Hants
39 M8 Lindridge Worcs
34 E11 Lindsell Essex
34 G7 Lindsey Suffk
34 G7 Lindsey Tye Suffk
66 F4 Lingdale R & Cl
38 G8 Lingen Herefs
11 M2 Lingfield Surrey
45 M8 Lingwood Norfk
104 E8 Linicro Highld
29 L3 Linkend Worcs
19 L8 Linkenholt Hants
4 G5 Linkinhorne Cnwll
86 F4 Linktown Fife
101 K3 Linkwood Moray
39 M10 Linley Green Herefs
86 B6 Linlithgow W Loth
107 J3 Linsidemore Highld
32 C10 Linslade C Beds
35 M2 Linstead Parva Suffk
71 N4 Linstock Cumb
40 D11 Linthurst Worcs
58 E10 Linthwaite Kirk
87 Q9 Lintlaw Border
101 P3 Lintmill Moray
80 G8 Linton Border
33 P7 Linton Cambs
40 H4 Linton Derbys
28 H4 Linton Herefs
22 F12 Linton Kent
59 K5 Linton Leeds
59 L3 Linton N York
29 J4 Linton Hill Herefs
59 L3 Linton-on-Ouse N York
52 G6 Linwood Hants
84 G9 Linwood Rens
111 b5 Lionacleit W Isls
111 e1 Lional W Isls
10 H4 Liphook Hants
56 F9 Liscard Wirral
15 P5 Liscombe Somset
4 F7 Liskeard Cnwll
90 B7 Lismore Ag & B
10 C5 Liss Hants
61 K3 Lissett E R Yk
52 G6 Lissington Lincs
27 P11 Lisvane Cardif
28 D10 Liswerry Newpt
44 E6 Litcham Norfk
31 N4 Litchborough Nhants
19 M9 Litchfield Hants
56 G8 Litherland Sefton
33 K8 Litlington Cambs
11 Q9 Litlington E Susx
33 N7 Little Abington Cambs
32 D3 Little Addington Nhants
69 K9 Little Airies D & G
30 F2 Little Alne Warwks
56 F7 Little Altcar Sefton
21 M2 Little Amwell Herts
40 E7 Little Aston Staffs
66 D5 Little Ayton N York
22 F2 Little Baddow Essex
18 B4 Little Badminton S Glos
71 L5 Little Bampton Cumb
34 B6 Little Bardfield Essex
32 H5 Little Barford Bed
45 J4 Little Barningham Norfk
30 G10 Little Barrington Gloucs
49 J2 Little Barrow Ches W
72 H5 Little Bavington Nthumb
19 K7 Little Bedwyn Wilts
35 J10 Little Bentley Essex
21 L2 Little Berkhamsted Herts
32 B4 Little Billing Nhants
32 D11 Little Billington C Beds
28 F5 Little Birch Herefs
34 D3 Little Blakenham Suffk
71 P8 Little Blencow Cumb
10 G6 Little Bognor W Susx
51 J8 Little Bollington Ches E
21 J11 Little Bookham Surrey
52 B7 Littleborough Notts
58 C10 Littleborough Rochdl
23 N11 Littlebourne Kent
31 L5 Little Bourton Oxon
33 P8 Little Braxted Essex
95 J9 Little Brechin Angus

7 N5 Littlebredy Dorset
32 C9 Little Brickhill M Keyn
31 P2 Little Brington Nhants
34 H10 Little Bromley Essex
49 L3 Little Budworth Ches W
107 K10 Littleburn Highld
22 D5 Little Burstead Essex
33 N8 Littlebury Essex
33 M8 Littlebury Green Essex
42 E6 Little Bytham Lincs
53 L6 Little Carlton Lincs
42 E8 Little Casterton Rutlnd
53 K6 Little Cawthorpe Lincs
20 F4 Little Chalfont Bucks
12 H2 Little Chart Kent
33 N8 Little Chesterford Essex
18 E9 Little Cheverell Wilts
33 L8 Little Chishill Cambs
35 J11 Little Clacton Essex
70 H9 Little Clifton Cumb
30 C5 Little Comberton Worcs
12 E8 Little Common E Susx
30 H7 Little Compton Warwks
34 E8 Little Cornard Suffk
39 L11 Little Cowarne Herefs
19 K3 Little Coxwell Oxon
65 M9 Little Crakehall N York
44 E9 Little Cressingham Norfk
56 G8 Little Crosby Sefton
50 F12 Little Cubley Derbys
41 Q5 Little Dalby Leics
29 J6 Littledean Gloucs
28 F3 Little Dewchurch Herefs
33 Q5 Little Ditton Cambs
43 N12 Little Downham Cambs
60 H3 Little Driffield E R Yk
44 E7 Little Dunham Norfk
92 F7 Little Dunkeld P & K
33 Q11 Little Dunmow Essex
8 G1 Little Durnford Wilts
33 P11 Little Easton Essex
51 J11 Little Eaton Derbys
44 G9 Little Ellingham Norfk
31 N3 Little Everdon Nhants
33 L6 Little Eversden Cambs
19 J1 Little Faringdon Oxon
65 M8 Little Fencote N York
59 M7 Little Fenton N York
44 E7 Little Fransham Norfk
20 F2 Little Gaddesden Herts
35 M5 Little Glemham Suffk
29 J4 Little Gorsley Herefs
33 J6 Little Gransden Cambs
17 Q6 Little Green Somset
33 M11 Little Hadham Herts
42 G2 Little Hale Lincs
51 L11 Little Hallam Derbys
33 N12 Little Hallingbury Essex
6 D6 Littleham Devon
14 H7 Littleham Devon
10 G9 Littlehampton W Susx
32 C3 Little Harrowden Nhants
19 Q1 Little Haseley Oxon
24 F6 Little Haven Pembks
11 J4 Littlehaven W Susx
40 E7 Little Hay Staffs
40 D3 Little Haywood Staffs
5 Q7 Littlehempston Devon
39 K8 Little Hereford Herefs
34 F9 Little Horkesley Essex
33 L10 Little Hormead Herts
11 P6 Little Horsted E Susx
58 F7 Little Horton C Brad
32 B10 Little Horwood Bucks
59 K11 Little Houghton Barns
32 B5 Little Houghton Nhants
50 F5 Little Hucklow Derbys
66 C11 Little Hutton N York
32 C4 Little Irchester Nhants
18 B10 Little Keyford Somset
20 D3 Little Kimble Bucks
31 J4 Little Kineton Warwks
20 E4 Little Kingshill Bucks
70 D4 Little Knox D & G
62 G2 Little Langdale Cumb
18 F12 Little Langford Wilts
49 M2 Little Leigh Ches W
34 C12 Little Leighs Essex
49 N1 Little Lever Bolton
32 B7 Little Linford M Keyn
17 L10 Little Load Somset
12 C6 Little London E Susx
19 L10 Little London Hants
19 Q8 Little London Hants
50 F6 Little Longstone Derbys
34 B8 Little Maplestead Essex
29 J2 Little Marcle Herefs
20 E6 Little Marlow Bucks
44 D5 Little Massingham Norfk
45 J8 Little Melton Norfk
94 E3 Littlemill Abers
100 E5 Littlemill Highld
28 C8 Little Mill Mons
19 Q1 Little Milton Oxon
20 E4 Little Missenden Bucks
31 M12 Littlemore Oxon
64 D5 Little Musgrave Cumb
48 H10 Little Ness Shrops
24 G3 Little Newcastle Pembks
65 K4 Little Newsham Dur
17 L11 Little Norton Somset
35 K10 Little Oakley Essex
42 C11 Little Oakley Nhants
71 M5 Little Orton Cumb
41 J1 Littleover C Derb
40 G9 Little Packington Warwks
32 H4 Little Paxton Cambs
3 K2 Little Petherick Cnwll
45 M7 Little Plumstead Norfk
42 D4 Little Ponton Lincs
43 P11 Littleport Cambs
31 N4 Little Preston Nhants
33 J2 Little Raveley Cambs
60 D9 Little Reedness E R Yk
59 J4 Little Ribston N York
30 F9 Little Rissington Gloucs
30 H7 Little Rollright Oxon
44 F5 Little Ryburgh Norfk
71 Q8 Little Salkeld Cumb
33 Q9 Little Sampford Essex
48 G2 Little Saughall Ches W
34 D4 Little Saxham Suffk
106 F10 Little Scatwell Highld
33 M6 Little Shelford Cambs
56 G2 Little Singleton Lancs
59 P6 Little Skipwith N York
59 M10 Little Smeaton N York
44 F4 Little Snoring Norfk
18 A4 Little Sodbury S Glos
9 L2 Little Somborne Hants
18 E4 Little Somerford Wilts
49 N9 Little Soudley Shrops
65 N4 Little Stainton Darltn
48 H1 Little Stanney Ches W
32 F4 Little Staughton Bed
53 M10 Little Steeping Lincs
40 B2 Little Stoke Staffs
13 L5 Littlestone-on-Sea Kent
35 J5 Little Stonham Suffk
41 P7 Little Stretton Leics
39 J4 Little Stretton Shrops
71 Q10 Little Strickland Cumb
32 H2 Little Stukeley Cambs
49 P8 Little Sugnall Staffs
72 G5 Little Swinburne Nthumb
70 B5 Little Sypland D & G
31 J8 Little Tew Oxon
34 E11 Little Tey Essex
33 N2 Little Thetford Cambs
73 Q11 Little Thorpe Dur
41 M7 Littlethorpe Leics
59 J1 Littlethorpe N York
34 B6 Little Thurlow Suffk
22 D7 Little Thurrock Thurr
93 L5 Littleton Angus
48 H3 Littleton Ches W
69 P7 Littleton D & G
9 M2 Littleton Hants
17 L9 Littleton Somset
20 H9 Littleton Surrey
18 C5 Littleton Drew Wilts
28 H10 Littleton-on-Severn S Glos
18 E9 Littleton Pannell Wilts
15 J8 Little Torrington Devon
73 N11 Littletown Dur
57 M2 Little Town Lancs
62 F7 Little Urswick Cumb
22 H6 Little Wakering Essex
33 N8 Little Walden Essex
34 F7 Little Waldingfield Suffk
44 F3 Little Walsingham Norfk
22 E2 Little Waltham Essex
60 G7 Little Weighton E R Yk
42 D11 Little Weldon Nhants
39 M2 Little Wenlock Wrekin
17 N10 Little Weston Somset
9 P9 Little Whitefield IoW
20 D7 Littlewick Green W & M
33 N5 Little Wilbraham Cambs
29 M6 Little Witcombe Gloucs
39 P8 Little Witley Worcs
19 P3 Little Wittenham Oxon
30 H7 Little Wolford Warwks
21 L10 Little Woodcote Gt Lon
19 K2 Littleworth Oxon
40 C3 Littleworth Staffs
30 B4 Littleworth Worcs
32 D4 Little Wymington Bed
32 H10 Little Wymondley Herts
40 D6 Little Wyrley Staffs
34 C8 Little Yeldham Essex
34 B12 Littley Green Essex
50 F6 Litton Derbys
64 G11 Litton N York
17 N5 Litton Somset
7 M5 Litton Cheney Dorset
111 d2 Liurbost W Isls
56 G10 Liverpool Lpool
58 G9 Liversedge Kirk
5 Q5 Liverton Devon
66 G4 Liverton R & Cl
86 C8 Livingston W Loth
86 C8 Livingston Village W Loth
48 D2 Lixwm Flints
2 G12 Lizard Cnwll
46 F3 Llanaelhaearn Gwynd
37 L6 Llanafan Cerdgn
37 Q9 Llanafan-Fawr Powys
54 G5 Llanallgo IoA
48 D8 Llanarmon Dyffryn Ceiriog Wrexhm
48 E4 Llanarmon-yn-Ial Denbgs
36 G8 Llanarth Cerdgn
28 D6 Llanarth Mons
26 D5 Llanarthne Carmth
56 C11 Llanasa Flints
37 K4 Llanbadarn Fawr Cerdgn
38 C6 Llanbadarn Fynydd Powys
28 D8 Llanbadoc Mons
28 D10 Llanbeder Newpt
47 J6 Llanbedr Gwynd
27 P5 Llanbedr Powys
48 D4 Llanbedr-Dyffryn-Clwyd Denbgs
54 G5 Llanbedrgoch IoA
46 E5 Llanbedrog Gwynd
55 L7 Llanbedr-y-Cennin Conwy
54 H9 Llanberis Gwynd
16 D3 Llanbethery V Glam
38 C7 Llanbister Powys
16 D2 Llanblethian V Glam
25 L4 Llanboidy Carmth
27 N10 Llanbradach Caerph
47 P10 Llanbrynmair Powys
16 D3 Llancadle V Glam
16 E3 Llancarfan V Glam
28 F5 Llancloudy Herefs
27 N12 Llandaff Cardif
47 J5 Llandanwg Gwynd
54 G7 Llanddaniel Fab IoA
26 C5 Llanddarog Carmth
37 J6 Llanddeiniol Cerdgn
54 G8 Llanddeiniolen Gwynd
47 R4 Llandderfel Gwynd
54 D5 Llanddeusant IoA
27 M3 Llanddew Powys
26 B10 Llanddewi Swans
37 L9 Llanddewi Brefi Cerdgn
28 D6 Llanddewi Rhydderch Mons
25 K5 Llanddewi Velfrey Pembks
38 C8 Llanddewi Ystradenni Powys
55 L8 Llanddoget Conwy
54 H5 Llanddona IoA
25 M6 Llanddowror Carmth
55 N6 Llanddulas Conwy
47 J6 Llanddwywe Gwynd
54 G6 Llanddyfnan IoA
27 N3 Llandefaelog-Tre'r-Graig Powys
27 M2 Llandefalle Powys
54 H6 Llandegfan IoA
48 E5 Llandegla Denbgs
38 D9 Llandegley Powys
28 D9 Llandegveth Mons
26 E4 Llandeilo Carmth
38 C12 Llandeilo Graban Powys
24 F4 Llandeloy Pembks
28 E7 Llandenny Mons
28 E10 Llandevaud Newpt
28 E10 Llandevenny Mons
38 B5 Llandinam Powys
25 K5 Llandissilio Pembks
28 F7 Llandogo Mons
16 D2 Llandough V Glam
16 F2 Llandough V Glam
26 G2 Llandovery Carmth
16 C2 Llandow V Glam
37 L11 Llandre Carmth
37 K4 Llandre Cerdgn
25 K3 Llandre Isaf Pembks
48 B7 Llandrillo Denbgs
55 M5 Llandrillo-yn-Rhos Conwy
38 C9 Llandrindod Wells Powys
48 F11 Llandrinio Powys
55 L5 Llandudno Conwy
55 L6 Llandudno Junction Conwy
37 P11 Llandulas Powys
54 F9 Llandwrog Gwynd
26 E6 Llandybie Carmth
25 P6 Llandyfaelog Carmth
36 F11 Llandyfriog Cerdgn
54 H7 Llandygai Gwynd
36 D11 Llandygwydd Cerdgn
48 C3 Llandyrnog Denbgs
38 E3 Llandyssil Powys
36 G11 Llandysul Cerdgn
27 P11 Llanedeyrn Cardif
27 M2 Llaneglwys Powys
47 K9 Llanegryn Gwynd
26 C5 Llanegwad Carmth
54 F3 Llaneilian IoA
55 M6 Llanelian-yn-Rhôs Conwy
48 C5 Llanelidan Denbgs
27 P3 Llanelieu Powys
28 C6 Llanellen Mons
26 C8 Llanelli Carmth
26 D8 Llanelli Crematorium Carmth
47 L7 Llanelltyd Gwynd
38 B10 Llanelwedd Powys
47 J6 Llanenddwyn Gwynd
46 E6 Llanengan Gwynd
54 F5 Llanerchymedd IoA
48 B12 Llanerfyl Powys
54 D5 Llanfachraeth IoA
47 M6 Llanfachreth Gwynd
54 D7 Llanfaelog IoA
46 D6 Llanfaelrhys Gwynd
54 D4 Llanfaethlu IoA
47 J5 Llanfair Gwynd
38 C2 Llanfair Caereinion Powys
37 K9 Llanfair Clydogau Cerdgn
48 D4 Llanfair Dyffryn Clwyd Denbgs
55 K6 Llanfairfechan Conwy
54 G7 Llanfair P G IoA
55 N7 Llanfair Talhaiarn Conwy
38 E6 Llanfair Waterdine Shrops
54 D4 Llanfairynghornwy IoA
54 D6 Llanfair-yn-Neubwll IoA
25 K5 Llanfallteg Carmth
25 K5 Llanfallteg West Carmth
37 J5 Llanfarian Cerdgn
48 E10 Llanfechain Powys
54 E4 Llanfechell IoA
48 E4 Llanferres Denbgs
36 G11 Llanfihangel-ar-arth Carmth
55 P10 Llanfihangel Glyn Myfyr Conwy
27 K2 Llanfihangel Nant Bran Powys
38 D8 Llanfihangel Rhydithon Powys
28 E10 Llanfihangel Rogiet Mons
37 L5 Llanfihangel-y-Creuddyn Cerdgn
48 C11 Llanfihangel-yng-Ngwynfa Powys
54 D6 Llanfihangel yn Nhowyn IoA
47 K4 Llanfihangel-y-traethau Gwynd
27 N3 Llanfilo Powys
28 C6 Llanfoist Mons
47 Q4 Llanfor Gwynd
28 C9 Llanfrechfa Torfn
27 M4 Llanfrynach Powys
48 D4 Llanfwrog Denbgs
54 D5 Llanfwrog IoA
48 D10 Llanfyllin Powys
26 D5 Llanfynydd Carmth
48 F4 Llanfynydd Flints
25 L3 Llanfyrnach Pembks
48 B12 Llangadfan Powys
26 F3 Llangadog Carmth
54 F7 Llangadwaladr IoA
54 F7 Llangaffo IoA
37 Q10 Llangammarch Wells Powys
27 K12 Llangan V Glam
28 F5 Llangarron Herefs
26 D4 Llangathen Carmth
27 P5 Llangattock Powys
28 D5 Llangattock Lingoed Mons
48 E10 Llangedwyn Powys
54 F6 Llangefni IoA
27 J10 Llangeinor Brdgnd
37 K8 Llangeitho Cerdgn
36 F11 Llangeler Carmth
47 J9 Llangelynin Gwynd
26 B6 Llangendeirne Carmth
26 D8 Llangennech Carmth
25 P9 Llangennith Swans
55 N7 Llangernyw Conwy
46 E5 Llangian Gwynd
24 F3 Llangloffan Pembks
25 L4 Llanglydwen Carmth
54 H6 Llangoed IoA
48 E7 Llangollen Denbgs
25 K4 Llangolman Pembks
27 N4 Llangors Powys
47 P5 Llangower Gwynd
36 E9 Llangranog Cerdgn
54 F6 Llangristiolus IoA
28 F5 Llangrove Herefs
38 E7 Llangunllo Powys
25 P5 Llangunnor Carmth
37 P5 Llangurig Powys
47 Q3 Llangwm Conwy
28 E8 Llangwm Mons
24 H6 Llangwm Pembks
46 D5 Llangwnnadl Gwynd
37 K6 Llangwyryfon Cerdgn
37 K9 Llangybi Cerdgn
46 G3 Llangybi Gwynd
28 D9 Llangybi Mons
48 D3 Llangynhafal Denbgs
27 N5 Llangynidr Powys
25 M5 Llangynin Carmth
25 N6 Llangynog Carmth
48 B9 Llangynog Powys
27 J10 Llangynwyd Brdgnd
27 M4 Llanhamlach Powys
27 L11 Llanharan Rhondd
27 L11 Llanharry Rhondd
28 D9 Llanhennock Mons
27 P8 Llanhilleth Blae G
37 Q4 Llanidloes Powys
46 E5 Llaniestyn Gwynd
27 P2 Llanigon Powys
37 K5 Llanilar Cerdgn
27 K11 Llanilid Rhondd
36 G8 Llanina Cerdgn
27 N11 Llanishen Cardif
28 F7 Llanishen Mons
55 J7 Llanllechid Gwynd
28 D8 Llanllowell Mons
38 C2 Llanllugan Powys
25 P5 Llanllwch Carmth
38 D4 Llanllwchaiarn Powys
36 H11 Llanllwni Carmth
54 F10 Llanllyfni Gwynd
25 Q9 Llanmadoc Swans
16 D3 Llanmaes V Glam
28 D10 Llanmartin Newpt
25 M7 Llanmiloe Carmth
55 P7 Llannefydd Conwy
26 D7 Llannon Carmth
46 F4 Llannor Gwynd
36 H7 Llanon Cerdgn
28 C7 Llanover Mons
25 P3 Llanpumsaint Carmth
48 D9 Llanrhaeadr-ym-Mochnant Powys
24 E3 Llanrhian Pembks
26 C9 Llanrhidian Swans
55 L8 Llanrhychwyn Conwy
54 D4 Llanrhyddlad IoA
37 J6 Llanrhystud Cerdgn
54 G8 Llanrug Gwynd
27 P11 Llanrumney Cardif
55 L8 Llanrwst Conwy
25 M6 Llansadurnen Carmth
26 F3 Llansadwrn Carmth
54 H6 Llansadwrn IoA
25 P7 Llansaint Carmth
26 F8 Llansamlet Swans
55 L6 Llansanffraid Glan Conwy Conwy
55 N8 Llansannan Conwy
27 N4 Llansantffraed Powys
37 Q7 Llansantffraed-Cwmdeuddwr Powys
38 C10 Llansantffraed-in-Elvel Powys
36 H7 Llansantffraid Cerdgn
48 E10 Llansantffraid-ym-Mechain Powys
26 E2 Llansawel Carmth
48 E9 Llansilin Powys
28 E8 Llansoy Mons
27 L3 Llanspyddid Powys
24 G7 Llanstadwell Pembks
25 N6 Llansteffan Carmth
28 C9 Llantarnam Torfn
25 L6 Llanteg Pembks
28 D5 Llanthewy Skirrid Mons
28 C4 Llanthony Mons
28 D6 Llantilio-Crossenny Mons
28 C5 Llantilio Pertholey Mons
28 D9 Llantrisant Mons
27 L11 Llantrisant Rhondd
16 E2 Llantrithyd V Glam
27 M10 Llantwit Fardre Rhondd
16 C3 Llantwit Major V Glam
47 P5 Llanuwchllyn Gwynd
28 E9 Llanvaches Newpt
28 E9 Llanvair Discoed Mons
28 D6 Llanvapley Mons
28 D5 Llanvetherine Mons
28 C5 Llanvihangel Crucorney Mons
48 B10 Llanwddyn Powys
36 H10 Llanwenog Cerdgn
28 D10 Llanwern Newpt
25 M4 Llanwinio Carmth
54 F9 Llanwnda Gwynd
24 G2 Llanwnda Pembks
37 J10 Llanwnnen Cerdgn
38 B4 Llanwnog Powys
26 F3 Llanwrda Carmth
47 M9 Llanwrin Powys
37 Q7 Llanwrthwl Powys
37 P10 Llanwrtyd Wells Powys
38 C2 Llanwyddelan Powys
48 E10 Llanyblodwel Shrops
25 N6 Llanybri Carmth
36 H10 Llanybydder Carmth
25 J4 Llanycefn Pembks
24 H2 Llanychaer Bridge Pembks
47 P7 Llanymawddwy Gwynd
48 F10 Llanymynech Powys
54 D5 Llanynghenedl IoA
48 C3 Llanynys Denbgs
38 B9 Llanyre Powys
46 H4 Llanystumdwy Gwynd
27 M3 Llanywern Powys
25 J5 Llawhaden Pembks
37 Q3 Llawryglyn Powys
48 G4 Llay Wrexhm
27 M7 Llechrhyd Caerph
36 D11 Llechryd Cerdgn
37 K6 Lledrod Cerdgn
46 E4 Lleyn Peninsula Gwynd
46 F3 Llithfaen Gwynd
56 D12 Lloc Flints
27 P1 Llowes Powys
27 L7 Llwydcoed Rhondd
27 L7 Llwydcoed Crematorium Rhondd
48 B11 Llwydiarth Powys
36 G8 Llwyncelyn Cerdgn
36 F9 Llwyndafydd Cerdgn
47 J9 Llwyngwril Gwynd
48 E7 Llwynmawr Wrexhm
27 L9 Llwynypia Rhondd
48 F10 Llynclys Shrops
54 E6 Llynfaes IoA
55 N6 Llysfaen Conwy
27 N2 Llyswen Powys
16 C2 Llysworney V Glam
24 H4 Llys-y-frân Pembks
27 J3 Llywel Powys
85 Q7 Loan Falk
86 F8 Loanhead Mdloth
70 F4 Loaningfoot D & G
76 F5 Loans S Ayrs
5 K3 Lobhillcross Devon
97 K12 Lochailort Highld
89 N7 Lochaline Highld
68 E7 Lochans D & G
78 G11 Locharbriggs D & G
90 C12 Lochavich Ag & B
90 F10 Lochawe Ag & B
111 b6 Loch Baghasdail W Isls
111 b6 Lochboisdale W Isls
89 M10 Lochbuie Ag & B
97 M2 Lochcarron Highld
89 P9 Lochdon Ag & B
89 P9 Lochdonhead Ag & B
83 L7 Lochead Ag & B
91 N10 Lochearnhead Stirlg
93 L8 Lochee C Dund
90 D1 Locheilside Station Highld
98 H2 Lochend Highld
111 b4 Locheport W Isls
111 b4 Loch Euphoirt W Isls
70 E2 Lochfoot D & G
83 P5 Lochgair Ag & B
86 E4 Lochgelly Fife
83 N5 Lochgilphead Ag & B
84 D3 Lochgoilhead Ag & B
93 J11 Lochieheads Fife
101 K3 Lochill Moray
100 E8 Lochindorb Lodge Highld
108 C10 Lochinver Highld
84 F5 Loch Lomond
106 F9 Lochluichart Highld
78 H11 Lochmaben D & G
111 b4 Lochmaddy W Isls
105 N8 Loch Maree Hotel Highld
111 b4 Loch nam Madadh W Isls
98 G4 Loch Ness Highld
86 E3 Lochore Fife
75 P3 Lochranza N Ayrs
95 M8 Lochside Abers
78 F12 Lochside D & G
107 N11 Lochside Highld
107 N6 Lochslin Highld
68 H3 Lochton S Ayrs
95 J9 Lochty Angus
87 K1 Lochty Fife
89 Q5 Lochuisge Highld
84 F10 Lochwinnoch Rens
78 H9 Lochwood D & G
3 M4 Lockengate Cnwll
79 J11 Lockerbie D & G
18 G7 Lockeridge Wilts
9 K3 Lockerley Hants
17 J4 Locking N Som
57 M9 Locking Stumps Warrtn
60 G5 Lockington E R Yk
49 M9 Lockleywood Shrops
21 N9 Locksbottom Gt Lon
9 N6 Locks Heath Hants
67 J9 Lockton N York
42 B9 Loddington Leics
32 B2 Loddington Nhants
5 P9 Loddiswell Devon
45 M9 Loddon Norfk
33 N4 Lode Cambs
40 F10 Lode Heath Solhll
7 L4 Loders Dorset
40 D10 Lodge Hill Crematorium Birm
10 E5 Lodsworth W Susx
59 J8 Lofthouse Leeds
65 K11 Lofthouse N York
59 J8 Lofthouse Gate Wakefd
66 G4 Loftus R & Cl
77 K7 Logan E Ayrs
86 B9 Loganlea W Loth
49 N8 Loggerheads Staffs
95 L8 Logie Angus
93 M10 Logie Fife
100 F5 Logie Moray
94 G2 Logie Coldstone Abers
102 E7 Logie Newton Abers
95 L8 Logie Pert Angus
92 E5 Logierait P & K
103 J9 Logierieve Abers
25 K4 Login Carmth
33 L4 Lolworth Cambs
105 K10 Lonbain Highld
60 E5 Londesborough E R Yk
21 L7 London Gt Lon
3 M6 London Apprentice Cnwll
21 J3 London Colney Herts
65 N9 Londonderry N York
21 K5 London Gateway Services Gt Lon
42 D3 Londonthorpe Lincs
105 M6 Londubh Highld
105 L6 Lonemore Highld
17 M3 Long Ashton N Som
39 N7 Long Bank Worcs
42 B2 Long Bennington Lincs
73 M7 Longbenton N Tyne
30 F8 Longborough Gloucs
7 N5 Long Bredy Dorset
40 D11 Longbridge Birm
18 C11 Longbridge Deverill Wilts
31 N1 Long Buckby Nhants
7 P1 Longburton Dorset
41 Q3 Long Clawson Leics
50 G9 Longcliffe Derbys
5 Q8 Longcombe Devon
49 Q10 Long Compton Staffs
30 H7 Long Compton Warwks
19 J3 Longcot Oxon
20 B2 Long Crendon Bucks
8 E5 Long Crichel Dorset
38 H2 Longden Shrops
21 J9 Long Ditton Surrey
40 E5 Longdon Staffs
29 L2 Longdon Worcs
40 E5 Longdon Green Staffs
49 L11 Longdon upon Tern Wrekin
6 B5 Longdown Devon
2 H8 Longdowns Cnwll
51 K6 Long Duckmanton Derbys
41 L2 Long Eaton Derbys
22 C9 Longfield Kent
41 J10 Longford Covtry
50 G12 Longford Derbys
29 L5 Longford Gloucs
49 M8 Longford Shrops
49 N10 Longford Wrekin
93 K9 Longforgan P & K
87 N10 Longformacus Border
73 K1 Longframlington Nthumb
49 J2 Long Green Ches W
8 F7 Longham Dorset
44 F7 Longham Norfk
31 K10 Long Hanborough Oxon
103 M7 Longhaven Abers
73 L3 Longhirst Nthumb
29 J5 Longhope Gloucs
111 g3 Longhope Ork
73 K2 Longhorsley Nthumb
81 P10 Longhoughton Nthumb
31 K2 Long Itchington Warwks
50 G12 Longlane Derbys
41 L11 Long Lawford Warwks
18 B11 Longleat Safari Park Wilts
29 L5 Longlevens Gloucs
93 K7 Longleys P & K
17 L10 Long Load Somset
102 F3 Longmanhill Abers
20 E1 Long Marston Herts

59 L4 Long Marston N York
30 F4 Long Marston Warwks
64 C3 Long Marton Cumb
34 E7 Long Melford Suffk
10 C4 Longmoor Camp Hants
101 K4 Longmorn Moray
50 B6 Longmoss Ches E
29 M9 Long Newnton Gloucs
80 D8 Longnewton Border
87 K8 Long Newton E Loth
65 P4 Longnewton S on T
29 K6 Longney Gloucs
87 J7 Longniddry E Loth
39 J3 Longnor Shrops
50 E7 Longnor Staffs
19 M10 Longparish Hants
63 Q9 Long Preston N York
57 L2 Longridge Lancs
85 Q9 Longridge W Loth
85 N8 Longriggend N Lans
61 J6 Long Riston E R Yk
2 D9 Longrock Cnwll
50 C9 Longsdon Staffs
103 L6 Longside Abers
33 L4 Longstanton Cambs
19 L12 Longstock Hants
33 K6 Longstowe Cambs
45 K10 Long Stratton Norfk
32 B7 Long Street M Keyn
18 G9 Longstreet Wilts
10 B1 Long Sutton Hants
43 L5 Long Sutton Lincs
17 L10 Long Sutton Somset
42 G9 Longthorpe C Pete
34 G3 Long Thurlow Suffk
71 N10 Longthwaite Cumb
50 B11 Longton C Stke
57 J4 Longton Lancs
71 N2 Longtown Cumb
28 C3 Longtown Herefs
7 c2 Longueville Jersey
39 K4 Longville in the Dale Shrops
49 L11 Long Waste Wrekin
41 L3 Long Whatton Leics
32 C3 Longwick Bucks
19 P3 Long Wittenham Oxon
73 L3 Longwitton Nthumb
70 B4 Longwood D & G
19 L2 Longworth Oxon
87 K8 Longyester E Loth
103 L4 Lonmay Abers
104 C12 Lonmore Highld
4 F9 Looe Cnwll
22 F11 Loose Kent
20 D4 Loosley Row Bucks
102 D5 Lootcherbrae Abers
17 K12 Lopen Somset
49 J9 Loppington Shrops
22 F10 Lords Wood Medway
92 H6 Lornty P & K
51 K10 Loscoe Derbys
101 K2 Lossiemouth Moray
3 M6 Lost Gardens of Heligan Cnwll
49 M1 Lostock Gralam Ches W
49 M2 Lostock Green Ches W
4 D8 Lostwithiel Cnwll
107 Q1 Lothbeg Highld
58 C5 Lothersdale N York
110 A12 Lothmore Highld
20 E5 Loudwater Bucks
41 M4 Loughborough Leics
41 M4 Loughborough Crematorium Leics
26 D8 Loughor Swans
21 N4 Loughton Essex
32 B8 Loughton M Keyn
42 F6 Lound Lincs
51 P4 Lound Notts
45 Q9 Lound Suffk
41 K4 Lount Leics
53 K6 Louth Lincs
10 B7 Lovedean Hants
8 H4 Lover Wilts
51 M2 Loversall Donc
22 D3 Loves Green Essex
25 J7 Loveston Pembks
17 N9 Lovington Somset
59 K10 Low Ackworth Wakefd
68 D6 Low Barbeth D & G
63 M8 Low Bentham N York
63 L6 Low Biggins Cumb
63 L3 Low Borrowbridge Cumb
50 H3 Low Bradfield Sheff
58 D5 Low Bradley N York
52 A3 Low Burnham N Linc
70 F10 Lowca Cumb
60 C4 Low Catton E R Yk
71 P4 Low Crosby Cumb
51 P10 Lowdham Notts
65 N5 Low Dinsdale Darltn
16 G8 Lower Aisholt Somset
8 B6 Lower Ansty Dorset
29 M4 Lower Apperley Gloucs
6 A6 Lower Ashton Devon
20 C6 Lower Assendon Oxon
57 J3 Lower Bartle Lancs
19 Q5 Lower Basildon W Berk
11 K5 Lower Beeding W Susx
42 E11 Lower Benefield Nhants
30 C2 Lower Bentley Worcs
31 L4 Lower Boddington Nhants
10 D2 Lower Bourne Surrey
30 H6 Lower Brailes Warwks
97 J5 Lower Breakish Highld
39 P10 Lower Broadheath Worcs
38 G10 Lower Broxwood Herefs
28 F2 Lower Bullingham Herefs
8 H4 Lower Burgate Hants
32 H7 Lower Caldecote C Beds
27 L2 Lower Chapel Powys
8 E2 Lower Chicksgrove Wilts
19 K9 Lower Chute Wilts
21 M6 Lower Clapton Gt Lon
40 B10 Lower Clent Worcs
58 G11 Lower Cumberworth Kirk
32 F3 Lower Dean Bed
105 L9 Lower Diabaig Highld
12 B7 Lower Dicker E Susx
38 G5 Lower Down Shrops
59 K2 Lower Dunsforth N York
39 L11 Lower Egleton Herefs
32 D8 Lower End M Keyn
23 P12 Lower Eythorne Kent
17 M2 Lower Failand N Som
10 B3 Lower Farringdon Hants
20 H8 Lower Feltham Gt Lon
10 C2 Lower Froyle Hants
6 C8 Lower Gabwell Devon
107 K4 Lower Gledfield Highld
17 L7 Lower Godney Somset
32 G9 Lower Gravenhurst C Beds
12 C3 Lower Green Kent
12 D2 Lower Green Kent
20 H9 Lower Halliford Surrey
22 G9 Lower Halstow Kent
8 E8 Lower Hamworthy Poole
23 M11 Lower Hardres Kent
20 C2 Lower Hartwell Bucks
38 F10 Lower Hergest Herefs
31 L8 Lower Heyford Oxon
58 F10 Lower Houses Kirk
57 N9 Lower Irlam Salfd
74 D4 Lower Killeyan Ag & B
17 L4 Lower Langford N Som
86 H2 Lower Largo Fife
40 D1 Lower Leigh Staffs
15 K5 Lower Loxhore Devon
28 G5 Lower Lydbrook Gloucs
38 H8 Lower Lye Herefs
27 P10 Lower Machen Newpt
16 G8 Lower Merridge Somset
31 L6 Lower Middleton Cheney Nhants
30 C5 Lower Moor Worcs
28 H9 Lower Morton S Glos
21 N3 Lower Nazeing Essex
16 G3 Lower Penarth V Glam
39 Q3 Lower Penn Staffs
49 N1 Lower Peover Ches E
30 F5 Lower Quinton Warwks
34 G8 Lower Raydon Suffk
16 D8 Lower Roadwater Somset
18 E5 Lower Seagry Wilts
32 E8 Lower Shelton C Beds
20 C7 Lower Shiplake Oxon
31 L2 Lower Shuckburgh Warwks
30 F9 Lower Slaughter Gloucs
13 N3 Lower Standen Kent
18 D5 Lower Stanton St Quintin Wilts
22 G8 Lower Stoke Medway
29 J9 Lower Stone Gloucs
44 F10 Lower Stow Bedon Norfk
45 L3 Lower Street Norfk
35 J6 Lower Street Suffk
9 N5 Lower Swanwick Hants
30 F8 Lower Swell Gloucs
50 D12 Lower Tean Staffs
5 P5 Lower Town Devon
24 G2 Lower Town Pembks
6 B6 Lower Upcott Devon
9 N4 Lower Upham Hants
17 K5 Lower Weare Somset
38 F11 Lower Welson Herefs
29 N2 Lower Westmancote Worcs
17 Q6 Lower Whatley Somset
57 L11 Lower Whitley Ches W
19 Q11 Lower Wield Hants
12 C9 Lower Willingdon E Susx
49 P2 Lower Withington Ches E
8 G1 Lower Woodford Wilts
7 N3 Lower Wraxhall Dorset
41 Q6 Lowesby Leics
45 Q10 Lowestoft Suffk
71 J10 Loweswater Cumb
73 M8 Low Fell Gatesd
11 L3 Lowfield Heath W Susx
84 H6 Low Gartachorrans Stirlg
65 M12 Low Grantley N York
17 L9 Low Ham Somset
58 H3 Low Harrogate N York
71 P6 Low Hesket Cumb
60 D1 Low Hutton N York
32 E1 Lowick Nhants
81 L6 Lowick Nthumb
62 F5 Lowick Green Cumb
71 J9 Low Lorton Cumb
52 B9 Low Marnham Notts
66 F8 Low Mill N York
73 N10 Low Moorsley Sundld
70 G10 Low Moresby Cumb
62 H6 Low Newton Cumb
72 B8 Low Row Cumb
64 H7 Low Row N York
68 D6 Low Salchrie D & G
60 G10 Low Santon N Linc
30 F1 Lowsonford Warwks
45 K10 Low Tharston Norfk
71 Q10 Lowther Cumb
61 J3 Lowthorpe E R Yk
16 G11 Lowton Somset
86 B5 Low Torry Fife
65 P5 Low Worsall N York
62 G2 Low Wray Cumb
16 C11 Loxbeare Devon
10 G3 Loxhill Surrey
15 K4 Loxhore Devon
30 H4 Loxley Warwks
17 K5 Loxton N Som
10 G4 Loxwood W Susx
109 L6 Loyal Lodge Highld
41 P9 Lubenham Leics
16 C7 Luccombe Somset
9 P10 Luccombe Village IoW
81 N8 Lucker Nthumb
5 J5 Luckett Cnwll
34 D9 Lucking Street Essex
18 C4 Luckington Wilts
93 M10 Lucklawhill Fife
16 B8 Luckwell Bridge Somset
38 H8 Lucton Herefs
111 b6 Ludag W Isls
53 J4 Ludborough Lincs
5 N8 Ludbrook Devon
25 K6 Ludchurch Pembks
58 D8 Luddenden Calder
58 D8 Luddenden Foot Calder
22 D9 Luddesdown Kent
60 E10 Luddington N Linc
30 F4 Luddington Warwks
42 F12 Luddington in the Brook Nhants
52 H5 Ludford Lincs
39 K7 Ludford Shrops
31 P10 Ludgershall Bucks
19 J9 Ludgershall Wilts
2 D8 Ludgvan Cnwll
45 N6 Ludham Norfk
39 K7 Ludlow Shrops
7 K1 Ludney Somset
8 D3 Ludwell Wilts
73 P11 Ludworth Dur
87 J6 Luffness E Loth
77 K7 Lugar E Ayrs
87 L7 Luggate Burn E Loth
85 M8 Luggiebank N Lans
84 G11 Lugton E Ayrs
28 G1 Lugwardine Herefs
96 G4 Luib Highld
83 L2 Luing Ag & B
28 E1 Lulham Herefs
40 G5 Lullington Derbys
18 B9 Lullington Somset
17 M3 Lulsgate Bottom N Som
39 N10 Lulsley Worcs
58 D9 Lumb Calder
59 L7 Lumby N York
85 K8 Lumloch E Duns
95 J2 Lumphanan Abers
86 E4 Lumphinnans Fife
101 N10 Lumsden Abers
95 L10 Lunan Angus
93 N5 Lunanhead Angus
92 G9 Luncarty P & K
60 G5 Lund E R Yk
59 P7 Lund N York
93 K8 Lundie Angus
86 H2 Lundin Links Fife
86 H2 Lundin Mill Fife
14 C3 Lundy Devon
83 K2 Lunga Ag & B
111 k3 Lunna Shet
22 E10 Lunsford Kent
12 E7 Lunsford's Cross E Susx
56 G8 Lunt Sefton
6 F2 Luppitt Devon
58 H9 Lupset Wakefd
63 K6 Lupton Cumb
10 F5 Lurgashall W Susx
16 C12 Lurley Devon
5 Q8 Luscombe Devon
84 F4 Luss Ag & B
83 J6 Lussagiven Ag & B
104 C10 Lusta Highld
5 Q4 Lustleigh Devon
39 J8 Luston Herefs
95 L8 Luthermuir Abers
93 K10 Luthrie Fife
6 B7 Luton Devon
6 E3 Luton Devon
32 F11 Luton Luton
22 F9 Luton Medway
32 G11 *Luton Airport* Luton
41 M9 Lutterworth Leics
5 M8 Lutton Devon
5 N7 Lutton Devon
43 M5 Lutton Lincs
42 G11 Lutton Nhants
16 D8 Luxborough Somset
3 M4 Luxulyan Cnwll
110 F8 Lybster Highld
38 G5 Lydbury North Shrops
13 K6 Lydd Kent
13 K6 *Lydd Airport* Kent
13 N2 Lydden Kent
23 Q9 Lydden Kent
42 C10 Lyddington Rutlnd
16 F9 Lydeard St Lawrence Somset
5 K3 Lydford Devon
17 N9 Lydford on Fosse Somset
58 B8 Lydgate Calder
38 G4 Lydham Shrops
18 G4 Lydiard Millicent Wilts
18 G4 Lydiard Tregoze Swindn
56 G7 Lydiate Sefton
40 C11 Lydiate Ash Worcs
17 Q12 Lydlinch Dorset
28 H7 Lydney Gloucs
25 J8 Lydstep Pembks
40 B10 Lye Dudley
11 P4 Lye Green E Susx
30 G2 Lye Green Warwks
18 B10 Lye's Green Wilts
19 L2 Lyford Oxon
13 L2 Lymbridge Green Kent
7 J4 Lyme Regis Dorset
13 M2 Lyminge Kent
9 K8 Lymington Hants
10 G8 Lyminster W Susx
57 M10 Lymm Warrtn
57 M11 Lymm Services Warrtn
13 L3 Lympne Kent
17 J5 Lympsham Somset
6 D6 Lympstone Devon
99 L8 Lynchat Highld
45 J8 Lynch Green Norfk
9 K6 Lyndhurst Hants
42 C8 Lyndon Rutlnd
79 K1 Lyne Border
20 G9 Lyne Surrey
49 J8 Lyneal Shrops
30 H9 Lyneham Oxon
18 F5 Lyneham Wilts
18 E5 *Lyneham Airport* Wilts
73 N3 Lynemouth Nthumb
102 G12 Lyne of Skene Abers
111 g3 Lyness Ork
44 H6 Lyng Norfk
17 J9 Lyng Somset
15 M3 Lynmouth Devon
22 H10 Lynsted Kent
15 M3 Lynton Devon
7 P2 Lyon's Gate Dorset
38 G10 Lyonshall Herefs
8 D8 Lytchett Matravers Dorset
8 E8 Lytchett Minster Dorset
110 F3 Lyth Highld
56 G4 Lytham Lancs
56 G4 Lytham St Anne's Lancs
67 J5 Lythe N York
110 C3 Lythmore Highld

M

2 H8 Mabe Burnthouse Cnwll
53 N6 Mablethorpe Lincs
50 B6 Macclesfield Ches E
50 B6 Macclesfield Crematorium Ches E
102 F3 Macduff Abers
75 L9 Macharioch Ag & B
27 P10 Machen Caerph
75 N5 Machrie N Ayrs
75 J8 Machrihanish Ag & B
82 E4 Machrins Ag & B
47 M10 Machynlleth Powys
26 C8 Machynys Carmth
50 H12 Mackworth Derbys
87 J7 Macmerry E Loth
92 E10 Madderty P & K
85 Q7 Maddiston Falk
49 P6 Madeley Staffs
39 M2 Madeley Wrekin
33 L5 Madingley Cambs
28 E2 Madley Herefs
39 P11 Madresfield Worcs
2 C9 Madron Cnwll
25 J4 Maenclochog Pembks
16 D2 Maendy V Glam
47 L3 Maentwrog Gwynd
36 F8 Maen-y-groes Cerdgn
49 P7 Maer Staffs
27 K8 Maerdy Rhondd
48 F10 Maesbrook Shrops
48 F9 Maesbury Shrops
48 G9 Maesbury Marsh Shrops
36 F10 Maesllyn Cerdgn
27 J10 Maesteg Brdgnd
26 D5 Maesybont Carmth
27 N9 Maesycwmmer Caerph
101 L6 Maggieknockater Moray
12 C7 Magham Down E Susx
56 G8 Maghull Sefton
41 L9 Magna Park Leics
28 E10 Magor Mons
28 E10 Magor Services Mons
11 L3 Maidenbower W Susx
18 B11 Maiden Bradley Wilts
6 C8 Maidencombe Torbay
6 H4 Maidenhayne Devon
17 N3 Maiden Head N Som
20 E7 Maidenhead W & M
7 N4 Maiden Newton Dorset
76 D9 Maidens S Ayrs
20 E8 Maiden's Green Br For
24 G8 Maiden Wells Pembks
31 N4 Maidford Nhants
31 P7 Maids Moreton Bucks
22 F11 Maidstone Kent
22 G11 Maidstone Services Kent
41 Q11 Maidwell Nhants
111 k4 Mail Shet
28 C10 Maindee Newpt
111 h2 Mainland Ork
111 k4 Mainland Shet
65 N2 Mainsforth Dur
94 H8 Mains of Balhall Angus
95 K7 Mains of Balnakettle Abers
100 H8 Mains of Dalvey Highld
95 L7 Mains of Haulkerton Abers
101 N9 Mains of Lesmoir Abers
93 P5 Mains of Melgunds Angus
70 F4 Mainsriddle D & G
38 F5 Mainstone Shrops
29 L5 Maisemore Gloucs
5 P11 Malborough Devon
22 G3 Maldon Essex
58 B2 Malham N York
104 G9 Maligar Highld
97 J9 Mallaig Highld
97 J9 Mallaigvaig Highld
86 E8 Malleny Mills C Edin
54 E7 Malltraeth IoA
47 P8 Mallwyd Gwynd
18 D4 Malmesbury Wilts
15 N3 Malmsmead Devon
49 J6 Malpas Ches W
3 J7 Malpas Cnwll
28 C10 Malpas Newpt
51 M3 Maltby Rothm
66 C5 Maltby S on T
53 M7 Maltby le Marsh Lincs
12 H2 Maltman's Hill Kent
66 H12 Malton N York
39 P12 Malvern Hills
39 P11 Malvern Link Worcs
29 K1 Malvern Wells Worcs
39 M7 Mamble Worcs
28 C7 Mamhilad Mons
2 H10 Manaccan Cnwll
38 C2 Manafon Powys
111 c3 Manais W Isls
5 P4 Manaton Devon
53 L6 Manby Lincs
40 H7 Mancetter Warwks
57 Q8 Manchester Manch
57 P11 *Manchester Airport* Manch
48 G3 Mancot Flints
98 D8 Mandally Highld
80 H4 Manderston House Border
43 M11 Manea Cambs
40 E8 Maney Birm
65 L5 Manfield N York
17 P2 Mangotsfield S Glos
111 c3 Manish W Isls
49 J2 Manley Ches W
27 P7 Manmoel Caerph
88 C8 Mannel Ag & B
18 G8 Manningford Bohune Wilts
18 G8 Manningford Bruce Wilts
58 F7 Manningham C Brad
11 K4 Manning's Heath W Susx
8 F6 Mannington Dorset
34 H9 Manningtree Essex
95 Q2 Mannofield C Aber
25 J8 Manorbier Pembks
24 H8 Manorbier Newton Pembks
80 F7 Manorhill Border
24 G2 Manorowen Pembks
21 N6 Manor Park Gt Lon
21 N6 Manor Park Crematorium Gt Lon
38 H12 Mansell Gamage Herefs
38 H11 Mansell Lacy Herefs
77 K8 Mansfield E Ayrs
51 M8 Mansfield Notts
51 M8 Mansfield & District Crematorium Notts
51 M7 Mansfield Woodhouse Notts
8 B4 Manston Dorset
23 Q9 Manston Kent
59 J7 Manston Leeds
8 E6 Manswood Dorset
42 F7 Manthorpe Lincs
52 D3 Manton N Linc
42 C8 Manton Rutlnd
18 H7 Manton Wilts
33 M10 Manuden Essex
17 P10 Maperton Somset
51 P8 Maplebeck Notts
19 R5 Mapledurham Oxon
20 B12 Mapledurwell Hants
11 J5 Maplehurst W Susx
22 C9 Maplescombe Kent
50 F10 Mapleton Derbys
51 K11 Mapperley Derbys
51 M11 Mapperley Park C Nott
7 M3 Mapperton Dorset
30 E2 Mappleborough Green Warwks
61 L5 Mappleton E R Yk
59 J11 Mapplewell Barns
7 Q2 Mappowder Dorset
2 H6 Marazanvose Cnwll
2 D9 Marazion Cnwll
49 K6 Marbury Ches E
43 L10 March Cambs
78 G6 March S Lans
19 M2 Marcham Oxon
49 L9 Marchamley Shrops
40 F2 Marchington Staffs
46 E6 Marchros Gwynd
48 G6 Marchwiel Wrexhm
9 L5 Marchwood Hants
16 C3 Marcross V Glam
39 K11 Marden Herefs
12 E2 Marden Kent
18 G8 Marden Wilts
12 F2 Marden Thorn Kent
28 C5 Mardy Mons
53 J10 Mareham le Fen Lincs
53 J9 Mareham on the Hill Lincs
10 G6 Marehill W Susx
11 P5 Maresfield E Susx
61 K8 Marfleet C KuH
48 G4 Marford Wrexhm
26 G10 Margam Neath
26 H10 Margam Crematorium Neath
8 B4 Margaret Marsh Dorset
22 D3 Margaretting Essex
22 D4 Margaretting Tye Essex
23 Q8 Margate Kent
75 Q6 Margnaheglish N Ayrs
69 N8 Margrie D & G
66 F4 Margrove Park R & Cl
44 B7 Marham Norfk
14 D10 Marhamchurch Cnwll
42 G9 Marholm C Pete
15 M7 Mariansleigh Devon
22 H8 Marine Town Kent
95 L1 Marionburgh Abers
104 G9 Marishader Highld
5 K7 Maristow Devon
78 H11 Marjoriebanks D & G
17 K6 Mark Somset
11 P2 Markbeech Kent
53 M7 Markby Lincs
12 C4 Mark Cross E Susx
51 J12 Markeaton Crematorium C Derb
41 K6 Market Bosworth Leics
42 G7 Market Deeping Lincs
49 M8 Market Drayton Shrops
41 Q9 Market Harborough Leics
18 E9 Market Lavington Wilts
42 C6 Market Overton Rutlnd
52 G5 Market Rasen Lincs
52 H7 Market Stainton Lincs
51 M7 Market Warsop Notts
60 F6 Market Weighton E R Yk
34 G2 Market Weston Suffk
41 L5 Markfield Leics
27 N8 Markham Caerph
51 Q6 Markham Moor Notts
86 G2 Markinch Fife
58 H2 Markington N York
87 L6 Markle E Loth
17 P4 Marksbury BaNES
34 E11 Marks Tey Essex
32 F12 Markyate Herts
18 H7 Marlborough Wilts
30 E4 Marlcliff Warwks
6 B9 Marldon Devon
35 M5 Marlesford Suffk
45 J8 Marlingford Norfk
24 E7 Marloes Pembks
20 D6 Marlow Bucks
20 D6 Marlow Bottom Bucks
11 N1 Marlpit Hill Kent
8 B4 Marnhull Dorset
50 C3 Marple Stockp
59 L12 Marr Donc
65 J7 Marrick N York
58 D10 Marsden Kirk
73 P7 Marsden S Tyne
21 J2 Marshalswick Herts
45 K5 Marsham Norfk
19 P2 Marsh Baldon Oxon
23 P11 Marshborough Kent
38 H4 Marshbrook Shrops
53 K4 Marshchapel Lincs
32 F10 Marsh Farm Luton
28 B11 Marshfield Newpt
18 B6 Marshfield S Glos
4 E2 Marshgate Cnwll
31 N9 Marsh Gibbon Bucks
6 E4 Marsh Green Devon
11 N2 Marsh Green Kent
43 N8 Marshland St James Norfk
51 K5 Marsh Lane Derbys
16 D7 Marsh Street Somset
7 K3 Marshwood Dorset
65 K7 Marske N York
66 E3 Marske-by-the-Sea R & Cl
38 G10 Marston Herefs
42 C2 Marston Lincs
31 M11 Marston Oxon
40 B3 Marston Staffs
18 E9 Marston Wilts
40 F9 Marston Green Solhll
17 N10 Marston Magna Somset
18 G2 Marston Meysey Wilts
50 F12 Marston Montgomery Derbys
32 E8 Marston Moretaine C Beds
40 G2 Marston on Dove Derbys
31 M6 Marston St Lawrence Nhants
41 P9 Marston Trussell Nhants
28 G5 Marstow Herefs
20 E1 Marsworth Bucks
19 K8 Marten Wilts
45 P6 Martham Norfk
8 F4 Martin Hants
13 Q1 Martin Kent
52 G10 Martin Lincs
15 L3 Martinhoe Devon
39 Q9 Martin Hussingtree Worcs
7 P5 Martinstown Dorset
35 L7 Martlesham Suffk
35 L7 Martlesham Heath Suffk
24 H6 Martletwy Pembks
39 N9 Martley Worcs
17 L11 Martock Somset
49 Q2 Marton Ches E
61 K6 Marton E R Yk
52 B7 Marton Lincs
66 D4 Marton Middsb
59 K2 Marton N York
66 G10 Marton N York
38 F2 Marton Shrops
31 K1 Marton Warwks
65 P12 Marton-le-Moor N York
9 N2 Martyr Worthy Hants
111 g2 Marwick Ork
15 J5 Marwood Devon
106 H10 Marybank Highld
107 J10 Maryburgh Highld
95 P3 Maryculter Abers
87 P9 Marygold Border
85 J8 Maryhill C Glas
95 L8 Marykirk Abers

21 L7 Marylebone Gt Lon
57 L7 Marylebone Wigan
101 J7 Marypark Moray
70 G8 Maryport Cumb
68 F11 Maryport D & G
5 J4 Marystow Devon
5 K4 Mary Tavy Devon
95 L10 Maryton Angus
95 J3 Marywell Abers
95 Q3 Marywell Abers
93 Q6 Marywell Angus
65 L10 Masham N York
63 M7 Masongill N York
76 F7 Masonhill Crematorium S Ayrs
51 L5 Mastin Moor Derbys
21 Q2 Matching Green Essex
21 P2 Matching Tye Essex
73 J6 Matfen Nthumb
12 D2 Matfield Kent
28 F9 Mathern Mons
39 N11 Mathon Herefs
24 F3 Mathry Pembks
45 J3 Matlask Norfk
50 H8 Matlock Derbys
50 H8 Matlock Bath Derbys
29 L5 Matson Gloucs
51 P3 Mattersey Notts
20 B10 Mattingley Hants
44 H7 Mattishall Norfk
44 H7 Mattishall Burgh Norfk
76 H6 Mauchline E Ayrs
103 J6 Maud Abers
7 c1 Maufant Jersey
30 G8 Maugersbury Gloucs
56 e3 Maughold IoM
98 E2 Mauld Highld
32 F8 Maulden C Beds
64 B4 Maulds Meaburn Cumb
65 N9 Maunby N York
16 E9 Maundown Somset
45 P7 Mautby Norfk
40 E4 Mavesyn Ridware Staffs
53 K9 Mavis Enderby Lincs
70 H6 Mawbray Cumb
57 J6 Mawdesley Lancs
26 H11 Mawdlam Brdgnd
2 G10 Mawgan Cnwll
3 J3 Mawgan Porth Cnwll
2 G6 Mawla Cnwll
2 H9 Mawnan Cnwll
2 H9 Mawnan Smith Cnwll
32 B2 Mawsley Nhants
42 G8 Maxey C Pete
40 G9 Maxstoke Warwks
80 E7 Maxton Border
13 P2 Maxton Kent
70 F1 Maxwell Town D & G
4 G2 Maxworthy Cnwll
49 Q6 May Bank Staffs
76 E8 Maybole S Ayrs
20 G10 Maybury Surrey
12 C5 Mayfield E Susx
86 G8 Mayfield Mdloth
50 F10 Mayfield Staffs
20 F11 Mayford Surrey
29 J5 May Hill Gloucs
22 H3 Mayland Essex
22 H3 Maylandsea Essex
12 C6 Maynard's Green E Susx
45 N10 Maypole Green Norfk
34 F5 Maypole Green Suffk
17 P5 Meadgate BaNES
20 C3 Meadle Bucks
73 M11 Meadowfield Dur
5 J4 Meadwell Devon
58 H6 Meanwood Leeds
17 L7 Meare Somset
16 H10 Meare Green Somset
17 J10 Meare Green Somset
85 J11 Mearns E Rens
32 B4 Mears Ashby Nhants
41 J5 Measham Leics
62 H6 Meathop Cumb
5 L6 Meavy Devon
42 B10 Medbourne Leics
14 E8 Meddon Devon
51 M6 Meden Vale Notts
20 D6 Medmenham Bucks
73 K9 Medomsley Dur
19 Q12 Medstead Hants
22 E10 Medway Crematorium Kent
22 G10 Medway Services Medway
50 C8 Meerbrook Staffs
33 L9 Meesden Herts
15 J9 Meeth Devon
45 M5 Meeting House Hill Norfk
25 M5 Meidrim Carmth
48 D11 Meifod Powys
93 K6 Meigle P & K
77 N8 Meikle Carco D & G
85 M11 Meikle Earnock S Lans
83 R10 Meikle Kilmory Ag & B
92 F8 Meikle Obney P & K
92 H7 Meikleour P & K
102 F8 Meikle Wartle Abers
26 B6 Meinciau Carmth
50 C11 Meir C Stke
33 L7 Melbourn Cambs
41 J3 Melbourne Derbys
60 D5 Melbourne E R Yk
8 C4 Melbury Abbas Dorset
7 N2 Melbury Bubb Dorset
7 N2 Melbury Osmond Dorset
32 E4 Melchbourne Bed
8 B6 Melcombe Bingham Dorset
5 L2 Meldon Devon
73 K4 Meldon Nthumb
33 L7 Meldreth Cambs
85 M3 Meldrum Stirlg
90 B12 Melfort Ag & B
56 C11 Meliden Denbgs
26 B6 Melin-y-wig Denbgs
71 Q9 Melkinthorpe Cumb
72 D7 Melkridge Nthumb
18 D7 Melksham Wilts
63 L7 Melling Lancs
56 H8 Melling Sefton
34 H2 Mellis Suffk
105 M4 Mellon Charles Highld
105 N3 Mellon Udrigle Highld
57 M3 Mellor Lancs
50 C3 Mellor Stockp
57 M3 Mellor Brook Lancs
17 Q6 Mells Somset
72 B12 Melmerby Cumb
65 J9 Melmerby N York
65 N11 Melmerby N York
109 K4 Melness Highld
7 L3 Melplash Dorset
80 D7 Melrose Border
111 g3 Melsetter Ork
65 L6 Melsonby N York
58 E11 Meltham Kirk
60 G8 Melton E R Yk
35 L6 Melton Suffk
44 H4 Melton Constable Norfk
41 Q4 Melton Mowbray Leics
60 H11 Melton Ross N Linc
105 L5 Melvaig Highld
48 G11 Melverley Shrops
109 Q3 Melvich Highld
6 H3 Membury Devon
19 K5 Membury Services W Berk
103 K3 Memsie Abers
93 M4 Memus Angus
54 H7 Menai Bridge IoA
45 L12 Mendham Suffk
17 M5 Mendip Hills
34 H4 Mendlesham Suffk
34 H4 Mendlesham Green Suffk
4 G7 Menheniot Cnwll
77 N9 Mennock D & G
58 F5 Menston C Brad
85 P4 Menstrie Clacks
32 C11 Mentmore Bucks
97 L11 Meoble Highld
49 J12 Meole Brace Shrops
9 Q4 Meonstoke Hants
22 D9 Meopham Kent
33 M1 Mepal Cambs
32 G9 Meppershall C Beds
57 N11 Mere Ches E
8 B2 Mere Wilts
56 H5 Mere Brow Lancs
57 Q3 Mereclough Lancs
22 D11 Mereworth Kent
40 G10 Meriden Solhll
96 D4 Merkadale Highld
8 F7 Merley Poole
24 G8 Merrion Pembks
7 L1 Merriott Somset
20 G12 Merrow Surrey
21 J5 Merry Hill Herts
40 B7 Merryhill Wolves
4 G7 Merrymeet Cnwll
23 K1 Mersea Island Essex
13 K3 Mersham Kent
21 L11 Merstham Surrey
10 E9 Merston W Susx
9 N9 Merstone IoW
27 L2 Merthyr Cynog Powys
27 J12 Merthyr Mawr Brdgnd
27 M7 Merthyr Tydfil Myr Td
27 M8 Merthyr Vale Myr Td
15 J9 Merton Devon
21 K9 Merton Gt Lon
44 E9 Merton Norfk
31 M9 Merton Oxon
15 N8 Meshaw Devon
34 E11 Messing Essex
52 C3 Messingham N Linc
35 L1 Metfield Suffk
5 J6 Metherell Cnwll
52 F10 Metheringham Lincs
86 H3 Methil Fife
86 G3 Methilhill Fife
102 H7 Methlick Abers
92 F9 Methven P & K
44 C10 Methwold Norfk
44 B10 Methwold Hythe Norfk
45 M11 Mettingham Suffk
45 K3 Metton Norfk
3 M6 Mevagissey Cnwll
51 L2 Mexborough Donc
110 F2 Mey Highld
46 D5 Meyllteyrn Gwynd
18 G1 Meysey Hampton Gloucs
111 c2 Miabhig W Isls
111 c2 Miavaig W Isls
28 F4 Michaelchurch Herefs
28 C3 Michaelchurch Escley Herefs
27 P11 Michaelstone-y-Fedw Newpt
16 F2 Michaelston-le-Pit V Glam
4 D4 Michaelstow Cnwll
29 J9 Michaelwood Services Gloucs
19 N11 Micheldever Hants
19 N11 Micheldever Station Hants
9 L3 Michelmersh Hants
35 J4 Mickfield Suffk
51 L2 Micklebring Donc
66 H5 Mickleby N York
59 K7 Micklefield Leeds
21 J11 Mickleham Surrey
40 H1 Mickleover C Derb
64 H3 Mickleton Dur
30 F5 Mickleton Gloucs
59 K8 Mickletown Leeds
49 J2 Mickle Trafford Ches W
65 M11 Mickley N York
73 J8 Mickley Square Nthumb
103 K3 Mid Ardlaw Abers
111 h1 Midbea Ork
95 K2 Mid Beltie Abers
86 C8 Mid Calder W Loth
110 F8 Mid Clyth Highld
102 E3 Mid Culbeuchly Abers
31 L8 Middle Aston Oxon
31 K8 Middle Barton Oxon
71 K1 Middlebie D & G
92 D3 Middlebridge P & K
17 L12 Middle Chinnock Somset
31 Q8 Middle Claydon Bucks
65 K9 Middleham N York
51 K5 Middle Handley Derbys
18 B7 Middlehill Wilts
39 J4 Middlehope Shrops
83 N5 Middle Kames Ag & B
30 E5 Middle Littleton Worcs
7 P2 Middlemarsh Dorset
50 F10 Middle Mayfield Staffs
52 F5 Middle Rasen Lincs
6 B8 Middle Rocombe Devon
66 C4 Middlesbrough Middsb
63 K4 Middleshaw Cumb
65 J11 Middlesmoor N York
22 G8 Middle Stoke Medway
65 M2 Middlestone Dur
58 H10 Middlestown Wakefd
80 F5 Middlethird Border
88 B7 Middleton Ag & B
50 G8 Middleton Derbys
50 H9 Middleton Derbys
34 E8 Middleton Essex
19 M11 Middleton Hants
39 K8 Middleton Herefs
58 H8 Middleton Leeds
58 E4 Middleton N York
66 H9 Middleton N York
42 B11 Middleton Nhants
43 Q6 Middleton Norfk
73 J4 Middleton Nthumb
86 D2 Middleton P & K
57 Q7 Middleton Rochdl
39 K6 Middleton Shrops
35 N3 Middleton Suffk
25 P10 Middleton Swans
40 F7 Middleton Warwks
31 L6 Middleton Cheney Nhants
58 B11 Middleton Crematorium Rochdl
64 G3 Middleton-in-Teesdale Dur
35 N4 Middleton Moor Suffk
65 P5 Middleton One Row Darltn
10 F9 Middleton-on-Sea W Susx
39 K8 Middleton on the Hill Herefs
60 G4 Middleton on the Wolds E R Yk
103 J11 Middleton Park C Aber
65 N10 Middleton Quernhow N York
65 N5 Middleton St George Darltn
39 M5 Middleton Scriven Shrops
31 M9 Middleton Stoney Oxon
65 M6 Middleton Tyas N York
2 b3 Middle Town IoS
48 F11 Middletown Powys
31 J5 Middle Tysoe Warwks
19 K12 Middle Wallop Hants
49 N3 Middlewich Ches E
9 J2 Middle Winterslow Wilts
4 G5 Middlewood Cnwll
18 G12 Middle Woodford Wilts
34 H5 Middlewood Green Suffk
77 J5 Middleyard E Ayrs
17 K9 Middlezoy Somset
18 B8 Midford BaNES
19 P7 Midgham W Berk
58 D8 Midgley Calder
58 H10 Midgley Wakefd
50 G2 Midhopestones Sheff
10 E6 Midhurst W Susx
10 D8 Mid Lavant W Susx
80 C8 Midlem Border
98 F2 Mid Mains Highld
83 Q10 Midpark Ag & B
17 P5 Midsomer Norton BaNES
109 K4 Midtown Highld
30 H3 Mid Warwickshire Crematorium Warwks
111 k2 Mid Yell Shet
94 G1 Migvie Abers
17 P11 Milborne Port Somset
8 B7 Milborne St Andrew Dorset
17 P11 Milborne Wick Somset
73 K6 Milbourne Nthumb
18 D4 Milbourne Wilts
64 C2 Milburn Cumb
29 J10 Milbury Heath S Glos
59 K1 Milby N York
31 K7 Milcombe Oxon
34 F7 Milden Suffk
34 B2 Mildenhall Suffk
18 H6 Mildenhall Wilts
44 F6 Mileham Norfk
11 K8 Mile Oak Br & H
86 C5 Milesmark Fife
57 Q8 Miles Platting Manch
22 H8 Mile Town Kent
81 K7 Milfield Nthumb
51 J10 Milford Derbys
14 E7 Milford Devon
40 C4 Milford Staffs
10 F2 Milford Surrey
24 F7 Milford Haven Pembks
9 K8 Milford on Sea Hants
28 G7 Milkwall Gloucs
10 D4 Milland W Susx
58 D9 Mill Bank Calder
103 K6 Millbreck Abers
10 D2 Millbridge Surrey
32 E8 Millbrook C Beds
9 L5 Millbrook C Sotn
5 J9 Millbrook Cnwll
7 b2 Millbrook Jersey
50 C3 Mill Brow Stockp
102 G12 Millbuie Abers
107 J11 Millbuie Highld
12 G5 Millcorner E Susx
107 L7 Millcraig Highld
50 F9 Milldale Staffs
20 C6 Mill End Bucks
33 K9 Mill End Herts
86 G8 Millerhill Mdloth
50 F6 Miller's Dale Derbys
85 K8 Millerston C Glas
33 P7 Mill Green Cambs
22 D3 Mill Green Essex
42 H5 Mill Green Lincs
34 F8 Mill Green Suffk
34 G5 Mill Green Suffk
35 J5 Mill Green Suffk
38 F11 Millhalf Herefs
77 M2 Millheugh S Lans
21 K5 Mill Hill Gt Lon
83 P8 Millhouse Ag & B
78 H10 Millhousebridge D & G
58 G12 Millhouse Green Barns
51 J4 Millhouses Sheff
84 G9 Milliken Park Rens
60 E4 Millington E R Yk
49 Q8 Millmeece Staffs
92 C11 Mill of Drummond P & K
84 G6 Mill of Haldane W Duns
62 D6 Millom Cumb
84 C11 Millport N Ayrs
34 H3 Mill Street Suffk
63 M4 Millthrop Cumb
95 P2 Milltimber C Aber
101 K12 Milltown Abers
101 N11 Milltown Abers
71 M1 Milltown D & G
15 K4 Milltown Devon
95 L2 Milltown of Campfield Abers
101 K7 Milltown of Edinvillie Moray
95 K2 Milltown of Learney Abers
86 D2 Milnathort P & K
85 J7 Milngavie E Duns
58 B10 Milnrow Rochdl
63 J6 Milnthorpe Cumb
104 B11 Milovaig Highld
39 M7 Milson Shrops
22 H10 Milstead Kent
18 H10 Milston Wilts
31 N5 Milthorpe Nhants
33 M4 Milton Cambs
71 Q4 Milton Cumb
68 G8 Milton D & G
70 D2 Milton D & G
40 H3 Milton Derbys
97 J2 Milton Highld
98 G3 Milton Highld
107 J11 Milton Highld
107 M7 Milton Highld
110 G5 Milton Highld
84 F8 Milton Inver
22 D8 Milton Kent
101 J10 Milton Moray
101 P3 Milton Moray
17 J4 Milton N Som
51 P6 Milton Notts
19 N3 Milton Oxon
31 L7 Milton Oxon
94 B9 Milton P & K
24 H8 Milton Pembks
17 L10 Milton Somset
84 H3 Milton Stirlg
84 G7 Milton W Duns
8 B7 Milton Abbas Dorset
5 J4 Milton Abbot Devon
86 F9 Milton Bridge Mdloth
32 D10 Milton Bryan C Beds
17 P8 Milton Clevedon Somset
5 K7 Milton Combe Devon
14 G9 Milton Damerel Devon
32 E5 Milton Ernest Bed
49 J4 Milton Green Ches W
19 M3 Milton Hill Oxon
32 C8 Milton Keynes M Keyn
18 H8 Milton Lilbourne Wilts
31 Q3 Milton Malsor Nhants
91 P8 Milton Morenish P & K
95 J2 Milton of Auchinhove Abers
86 G3 Milton of Balgonie Fife
84 G5 Milton of Buchanan Stirlg
85 L7 Milton of Campsie E Duns
99 K1 Milton of Leys Highld
95 P2 Milton of Murtle C Aber
94 F3 Milton of Tullich Abers
8 B2 Milton on Stour Dorset
22 H9 Milton Regis Kent
30 H9 Milton-under-Wychwood Oxon
16 F10 Milverton Somset
30 H2 Milverton Warwks
40 C2 Milwich Staffs
83 P4 Minard Ag & B
29 M8 Minchinhampton Gloucs
16 C6 Minehead Somset
48 F5 Minera Wrexhm
18 F3 Minety Wilts
47 J4 Minffordd Gwynd
89 N3 Mingarrypark Highld
53 K10 Miningsby Lincs
4 G6 Minions Cnwll
76 F8 Minishant S Ayrs
47 P8 Minllyn Gwynd
69 K6 Minnigaff D & G
102 G4 Minnonie Abers
59 K2 Minskip N York
9 K5 Minstead Hants
10 D6 Minsted W Susx
23 J8 Minster Kent
23 P9 Minster Kent
38 G2 Minsterley Shrops
30 H10 Minster Lovell Oxon
29 K5 Minsterworth Gloucs
7 P2 Minterne Magna Dorset
52 H8 Minting Lincs
103 K6 Mintlaw Abers
43 Q6 Mintlyn Crematorium Norfk
80 D9 Minto Border
38 H4 Minton Shrops
70 F11 Mirehouse Cumb
110 G4 Mireland Highld
58 G9 Mirfield Kirk
29 N7 Miserden Gloucs
27 L11 Miskin Rhondd
51 P2 Misson Notts
41 M10 Misterton Leics
51 Q2 Misterton Notts
7 L2 Misterton Somset
35 J9 Mistley Essex
21 L9 Mitcham Gt Lon
29 J5 Mitcheldean Gloucs
3 J5 Mitchell Cnwll
78 F9 Mitchellslacks D & G
28 F6 Mitchel Troy Mons
73 L4 Mitford Nthumb
2 H5 Mithian Cnwll
31 N7 Mixbury Oxon
57 P11 Mobberley Ches E
50 D11 Mobberley Staffs
38 C4 Mochdre Powys
69 J9 Mochrum D & G
12 E1 Mockbeggar Kent
70 H10 Mockerkin Cumb
5 N9 Modbury Devon
50 B12 Moddershall Staffs
54 G4 Moelfre IoA
48 E9 Moelfre Powys
78 H7 Moffat D & G
32 G6 Moggerhanger C Beds
40 H4 Moira Leics
23 K11 Molash Kent
96 E7 Mol-chlach Highld
48 E3 Mold Flints
58 F10 Moldgreen Kirk
33 P10 Molehill Green Essex
60 H6 Molescroft E R Yk
32 F2 Molesworth Cambs
15 N6 Molland Devon
48 H2 Mollington Ches W
31 K5 Mollington Oxon
85 M8 Mollinsburn N Lans
95 M6 Mondynes Abers
35 L5 Monewden Suffk
92 F9 Moneydie P & K
78 C10 Moniaive D & G
93 N8 Monifieth Angus
93 N7 Monikie Angus
93 K11 Monimail Fife
21 K4 Monken Hadley Gt Lon
59 L8 Monk Fryston N York
39 L12 Monkhide Herefs
71 M4 Monkhill Cumb
39 L4 Monkhopton Shrops
39 J10 Monkland Herefs
14 H7 Monkleigh Devon
16 C3 Monknash V Glam
15 K10 Monkokehampton Devon
73 N6 Monkseaton N Tyne
34 F7 Monks Eleigh Suffk
11 K5 Monk's Gate W Susx
49 Q1 Monks Heath Ches E
19 Q9 Monk Sherborne Hants
16 E8 Monksilver Somset
41 L10 Monks Kirby Warwks
35 K4 Monk Soham Suffk
20 D3 Monks Risborough Bucks
53 M9 Monksthorpe Lincs
33 P10 Monk Street Essex
28 D8 Monkswood Mons
6 G3 Monkton Devon
23 P9 Monkton Kent
76 F6 Monkton S Ayrs
73 N8 Monkton S Tyne
18 B8 Monkton Combe BaNES
18 C12 Monkton Deverill Wilts
18 B7 Monkton Farleigh Wilts
16 H10 Monkton Heathfield Somset
7 J4 Monkton Wyld Dorset
73 P8 Monkwearmouth Sundld
9 Q2 Monkwood Hants
40 B7 Monmore Green Wolves
28 F6 Monmouth Mons
38 G12 Monnington on Wye Herefs
69 J10 Monreith D & G
17 M11 Montacute Somset
48 H11 Montford Shrops
48 H11 Montford Bridge Shrops
102 D10 Montgarrie Abers
38 E3 Montgomery Powys
95 L9 Montrose Angus
6 b2 Mont Saint Guern
19 K11 Monxton Hants
50 F7 Monyash Derbys
102 F11 Monymusk Abers
92 C9 Monzie P & K
85 L8 Moodiesburn N Lans
93 L11 Moonzie Fife
58 H6 Moor Allerton Leeds
53 J10 Moorby Lincs
8 E6 Moor Crichel Dorset
8 G8 Moordown Bmouth
57 L11 Moore Halton
58 D8 Moor End Calder
59 P10 Moorends Donc
58 F6 Moorhead C Brad
71 M4 Moorhouse Cumb
51 Q7 Moorhouse Notts
21 N11 Moorhouse Bank Surrey
17 K8 Moorlinch Somset
59 L3 Moor Monkton N York
66 F5 Moorsholm R & Cl
8 B4 Moorside Dorset
4 F7 Moorswater Cnwll
59 L11 Moorthorpe Wakefd
58 H6 Moortown Leeds
52 F4 Moortown Lincs
107 M5 Morangie Highld
97 J10 Morar Highld
101 M3 Moray Crematorium Moray
42 G10 Morborne Cambs
15 N10 Morchard Bishop Devon
7 K4 Morcombelake Dorset
42 D9 Morcott Rutlnd
48 F9 Morda Shrops
8 D8 Morden Dorset
21 K9 Morden Gt Lon
28 G2 Mordiford Herefs
65 N3 Mordon Dur
38 G4 More Shrops
16 C10 Morebath Devon
80 G8 Morebattle Border
62 H8 Morecambe Lancs
18 G4 Moredon Swindn
106 B4 Morefield Highld
13 N3 Morehall Kent
5 P9 Moreleigh Devon
91 N8 Morenish P & K
9 N3 Morestead Hants
8 B9 Moreton Dorset
21 Q3 Moreton Essex
39 J8 Moreton Herefs
20 B3 Moreton Oxon
56 F10 Moreton Wirral
49 K10 Moreton Corbet Shrops
5 P3 Moretonhampstead Devon
30 G7 Moreton-in-Marsh Gloucs
39 L11 Moreton Jeffries Herefs
30 H3 Moreton Morrell Warwks
39 J11 Moreton on Lugg Herefs
31 M4 Moreton Pinkney Nhants
49 L8 Moreton Say Shrops
29 K6 Moreton Valence Gloucs
46 E4 Morfa Nefyn Gwynd
87 K7 Morham E Loth
64 B3 Morland Cumb
57 P11 Morley Ches E
51 K11 Morley Derbys
58 H8 Morley Leeds
57 P11 Morley Green Ches E
44 H9 Morley St Botolph Norfk
86 F7 Morningside C Edin
85 N11 Morningside N Lans
45 K10 Morningthorpe Norfk
73 L4 Morpeth Nthumb
95 L8 Morphie Abers
40 E4 Morrey Staffs
26 F8 Morriston Swans
44 G2 Morston Norfk
14 H3 Mortehoe Devon
51 L3 Morthen Rothm
19 Q7 Mortimer W Berk
19 Q7 Mortimer West End Hants
21 K8 Mortlake Gt Lon
21 K8 Mortlake Crematorium Gt Lon
71 N5 Morton Cumb
51 K8 Morton Derbys
42 F5 Morton Lincs
52 B5 Morton Lincs
51 Q9 Morton Notts
48 F9 Morton Shrops
86 F8 Mortonhall Crematorium C Edin
65 N8 Morton-on-Swale N York
45 J6 Morton on the Hill Norfk
2 B8 Morvah Cnwll
97 N5 Morvich Highld
39 M4 Morville Shrops
5 J6 Morwellham Quay Devon
14 D8 Morwenstow Cnwll
51 K5 Mosborough Sheff
76 H4 Moscow E Ayrs
40 E10 Moseley Birm
40 C7 Moseley Wolves
39 P9 Moseley Worcs
88 B7 Moss Ag & B
59 N10 Moss Donc
101 N10 Mossat Abers
111 k3 Mossbank Shet
57 K8 Moss Bank St Hel
70 G9 Mossbay Cumb
76 G6 Mossblown S Ayrs
80 F10 Mossburnford Border
69 P5 Mossdale D & G
76 H9 Mossdale E Ayrs
62 H12 Moss Edge Lancs
85 M10 Mossend N Lans
50 C1 Mossley Tamesd

79 N8 **Mosspaul Hotel** Border
100 D4 **Moss-side** Highld
101 L4 **Mosstodloch** Moray
69 M8 **Mossyard** D & G
57 K6 **Mossy Lea** Lancs
7 L2 **Mosterton** Dorset
57 Q8 **Moston** Manch
56 D11 **Mostyn** Flints
8 C3 **Motcombe** Dorset
5 M10 **Mothecombe** Devon
71 N9 **Motherby** Cumb
85 M10 **Motherwell** N Lans
21 K9 **Motspur Park** Gt Lon
21 N8 **Mottingham** Gt Lon
9 K3 **Mottisfont** Hants
9 L10 **Mottistone** IoW
50 C2 **Mottram in Longdendale** Tamesd
57 Q12 **Mottram St Andrew** Ches E
49 J2 **Mouldsworth** Ches W
92 E4 **Moulin** P & K
11 M8 **Moulsecoomb** Br & H
19 P4 **Moulsford** Oxon
32 C8 **Moulsoe** M Keyn
107 K7 **Moultavie** Highld
49 M2 **Moulton** Ches W
43 K5 **Moulton** Lincs
65 M6 **Moulton** N York
32 B4 **Moulton** Nhants
34 B4 **Moulton** Suffk
16 E3 **Moulton** V Glam
43 J6 **Moulton Chapel** Lincs
45 N8 **Moulton St Mary** Norfk
43 K5 **Moulton Seas End** Lincs
4 E6 **Mount** Cnwll
58 E7 **Mountain** C Brad
27 L8 **Mountain Ash** Rhondd
86 D11 **Mountain Cross** Border
2 G7 **Mount Ambrose** Cnwll
34 E9 **Mount Bures** Essex
12 E6 **Mountfield** E Susx
107 J9 **Mountgerald House** Highld
2 G6 **Mount Hawke** Cnwll
3 K4 **Mountjoy** Cnwll
86 F10 **Mount Lothian** Mdloth
22 D4 **Mountnessing** Essex
28 F9 **Mounton** Mons
51 J10 **Mount Pleasant** Derbys
34 C7 **Mount Pleasant** Suffk
73 L9 **Mountsett Crematorium** Dur
41 M5 **Mountsorrel** Leics
58 D8 **Mount Tabor** Calder
10 F2 **Mousehill** Surrey
2 C9 **Mousehole** Cnwll
70 H2 **Mouswald** D & G
49 Q4 **Mow Cop** Ches E
80 H9 **Mowhaugh** Border
41 N9 **Mowsley** Leics
98 F11 **Moy** Highld
99 L3 **Moy** Highld
97 M6 **Moyle** Highld
36 B10 **Moylegrove** Pembks
75 K4 **Muasdale** Ag & B
95 P4 **Muchalls** Abers
28 F3 **Much Birch** Herefs
39 L11 **Much Cowarne** Herefs
28 F3 **Much Dewchurch** Herefs
17 K10 **Muchelney** Somset
17 L10 **Muchelney Ham** Somset
33 L11 **Much Hadham** Herts
57 J4 **Much Hoole** Lancs
4 F8 **Muchlarnick** Cnwll
28 H3 **Much Marcle** Herefs
39 L3 **Much Wenlock** Shrops
89 J1 **Muck** Highld
44 H2 **Muckleburgh Collection** Norfk
49 N7 **Mucklestone** Staffs
53 L7 **Muckton** Lincs
15 K5 **Muddiford** Devon
12 B7 **Muddles Green** E Susx
8 H8 **Mudeford** Dorset
17 N11 **Mudford** Somset
17 M11 **Mudford Sock** Somset
35 J7 **Mugdock** Stirlg
96 E2 **Mugeary** Highld
50 H11 **Mugginton** Derbys
102 F5 **Muirden** Abers
93 P8 **Muirdrum** Angus
102 F5 **Muiresk** Abers
93 L8 **Muirhead** Angus
86 F2 **Muirhead** Fife
85 L8 **Muirhead** N Lans
77 L6 **Muirkirk** E Ayrs
85 M6 **Muirmill** Stirlg
102 D11 **Muir of Fowlis** Abers
101 J4 **Muir of Miltonduff** Moray
107 J11 **Muir of Ord** Highld
98 A11 **Muirshearlich** Highld
103 K7 **Muirtack** Abers
85 Q1 **Muirton** P & K
106 H10 **Muirton Mains** Highld
92 H7 **Muirton of Ardblair** P & K
64 G7 **Muker** N York
45 K9 **Mulbarton** Norfk
101 L5 **Mulben** Moray
89 M8 **Mull** Ag & B
2 G11 **Mullion** Cnwll
2 F11 **Mullion Cove** Cnwll
53 N8 **Mumby** Lincs
39 M10 **Munderfield Row** Herefs
39 M11 **Munderfield Stocks** Herefs
45 M3 **Mundesley** Norfk
44 D10 **Mundford** Norfk
45 M9 **Mundham** Norfk
22 G3 **Mundon Hill** Essex
71 M9 **Mungrisdale** Cumb
107 K10 **Munlochy** Highld
76 E2 **Munnoch** N Ayrs
29 J1 **Munsley** Herefs
39 K5 **Munslow** Shrops
5 N3 **Murchington** Devon
31 N10 **Murcott** Oxon
110 D3 **Murkle** Highld
97 P10 **Murlaggan** Highld
93 N8 **Murroes** Angus
43 L8 **Murrow** Cambs
32 B10 **Mursley** Bucks
93 N4 **Murthill** Angus
92 G7 **Murthly** P & K
59 P4 **Murton** C York
64 D3 **Murton** Cumb
73 P10 **Murton** Dur
81 K5 **Murton** Nthumb
6 H4 **Musbury** Devon
86 G7 **Musselburgh** E Loth
42 B3 **Muston** Leics
67 N10 **Muston** N York
21 L5 **Muswell Hill** Gt Lon
69 P8 **Mutehill** D & G
45 P11 **Mutford** Suffk
92 C11 **Muthill** P & K
110 D5 **Mybster** Highld
26 G3 **Myddfai** Carmth
49 J10 **Myddle** Shrops
36 G9 **Mydroilyn** Cerdgn
3 J8 **Mylor** Cnwll
3 J8 **Mylor Bridge** Cnwll
25 K3 **Mynachlog ddu** Pembks
28 F9 **Mynydd-bach** Mons
26 E8 **Mynydd-Bach** Swans
25 P7 **Mynyddgarreg** Carmth
48 F3 **Mynydd Isa** Flints
95 M3 **Myrebird** Abers
72 B2 **Myredykes** Border
20 E11 **Mytchett** Surrey
58 C8 **Mytholm** Calder
58 D8 **Mytholmroyd** Calder
59 K2 **Myton-on-Swale** N York

N

105 M6 **Naast** Highld
111 c3 **Na Buirgh** W Isls
59 N5 **Naburn** C York
58 E6 **Nab Wood Crematorium** C Brad
23 M11 **Nackington** Kent
35 K8 **Nacton** Suffk
60 H3 **Nafferton** E R Yk
16 G9 **Nailsbourne** Somset
17 L3 **Nailsea** N Som
41 K6 **Nailstone** Leics
29 L8 **Nailsworth** Gloucs
100 D4 **Nairn** Highld
48 D2 **Nannerch** Flints
41 L4 **Nanpantan** Leics
3 L5 **Nanpean** Cnwll
3 M3 **Nanstallon** Cnwll
36 F8 **Nanternis** Cerdgn
26 C5 **Nantgaredig** Carmth
55 Q8 **Nantglyn** Denbgs
38 B8 **Nantmel** Powys
47 K3 **Nantmor** Gwynd
54 H9 **Nant Peris** Gwynd
49 M5 **Nantwich** Ches E
27 P6 **Nantyglo** Blae G
27 K9 **Nant-y-moel** Brdgnd
20 D4 **Naphill** Bucks
31 L2 **Napton on the Hill** Warwks
25 J6 **Narberth** Pembks
41 M7 **Narborough** Leics
44 C7 **Narborough** Norfk
54 F10 **Nasareth** Gwynd
41 P10 **Naseby** Nhants
32 B9 **Nash** Bucks
28 D11 **Nash** Newpt
39 L7 **Nash** Shrops
42 F10 **Nassington** Nhants
64 E6 **Nateby** Cumb
63 J12 **Nateby** Lancs
40 F5 **National Memorial Arboretum** Staffs
41 N6 **National Space Science Centre** C Leic
63 K4 **Natland** Cumb
34 G7 **Naughton** Suffk
30 E9 **Naunton** Gloucs
29 M2 **Naunton** Worcs
30 C4 **Naunton Beauchamp** Worcs
52 E10 **Navenby** Lincs
21 Q4 **Navestock** Essex
22 C4 **Navestock Side** Essex
110 B11 **Navidale House Hotel** Highld
107 N8 **Navity** Highld
66 F9 **Nawton** N York
34 F9 **Nayland** Suffk
21 N3 **Nazeing** Essex
111 k4 **Neap** Shet
50 E10 **Near Cotton** Staffs
62 G3 **Near Sawrey** Cumb
21 K6 **Neasden** Gt Lon
65 N5 **Neasham** Darltn
26 G8 **Neath** Neath
10 C3 **Neatham** Hants
45 M6 **Neatishead** Norfk
37 J7 **Nebo** Cerdgn
55 M9 **Nebo** Conwy
54 F10 **Nebo** Gwynd
54 F4 **Nebo** IoA
44 E8 **Necton** Norfk
108 C8 **Nedd** Highld
34 G7 **Nedging** Suffk
34 G6 **Nedging Tye** Suffk
35 K1 **Needham** Norfk
34 H6 **Needham Market** Suffk
33 K3 **Needingworth** Cambs
39 M6 **Neen Savage** Shrops
39 M7 **Neen Sollars** Shrops
39 M5 **Neenton** Shrops
46 E4 **Nefyn** Gwynd
84 H10 **Neilston** E Rens
27 M9 **Nelson** Caerph
57 Q2 **Nelson** Lancs
77 P3 **Nemphlar** S Lans
17 M4 **Nempnett Thrubwell** BaNES
72 E11 **Nenthead** Cumb
80 F6 **Nenthorn** Border
48 E4 **Nercwys** Flints
82 C11 **Nereabolls** Ag & B
85 L10 **Nerston** S Lans
81 K7 **Nesbit** Nthumb
58 E4 **Nesfield** N York
48 F1 **Ness Botanic Gardens** Ches W
48 H10 **Nesscliffe** Shrops
56 F12 **Neston** Ches W
18 C7 **Neston** Wilts
39 L4 **Netchwood** Shrops
49 Q1 **Nether Alderley** Ches E
18 G10 **Netheravon** Wilts
80 D5 **Nether Blainslie** Border
102 G4 **Netherbrae** Abers
41 P3 **Nether Broughton** Leics
77 N2 **Netherburn** S Lans
7 L3 **Netherbury** Dorset
59 J5 **Netherby** N York
7 P3 **Nether Cerne** Dorset
79 J10 **Nethercleuch** D & G
17 N11 **Nether Compton** Dorset
102 H10 **Nether Crimond** Abers
101 M3 **Nether Dallachy** Moray
28 G8 **Netherend** Gloucs
12 E6 **Netherfield** E Susx
12 E6 **Netherfield Road** E Susx
78 F6 **Nether Fingland** S Lans
8 G2 **Netherhampton** Wilts
93 L7 **Nether Handwick** Angus
51 K2 **Nether Haugh** Rothm
7 K2 **Netherhay** Dorset
51 Q5 **Nether Headon** Notts
51 J10 **Nether Heage** Derbys
31 P3 **Nether Heyford** Nhants
78 G6 **Nether Howcleugh** S Lans
63 J8 **Nether Kellet** Lancs
103 L6 **Nether Kinmundy** Abers
51 M6 **Nether Langwith** Notts
70 C6 **Netherlaw** D & G
95 P4 **Netherley** Abers
78 G10 **Nethermill** D & G
103 J6 **Nethermuir** Abers
21 L11 **Netherne-on-the-Hill** Surrey
58 F9 **Netheroyd Hill** Kirk
50 G5 **Nether Padley** Derbys
85 J11 **Netherplace** E Rens
59 M4 **Nether Poppleton** C York
40 H5 **Netherseal** Derbys
66 C8 **Nether Silton** N York
16 G8 **Nether Stowey** Somset
58 F11 **Netherthong** Kirk
93 P4 **Netherton** Angus
6 B8 **Netherton** Devon
40 C9 **Netherton** Dudley
58 F10 **Netherton** Kirk
85 N11 **Netherton** N Lans
81 K11 **Netherton** Nthumb
92 H5 **Netherton** P & K
85 J7 **Netherton** Stirlg
58 H10 **Netherton** Wakefd
62 B1 **Nethertown** Cumb
110 G1 **Nethertown** Highld
40 E4 **Nethertown** Staffs
86 D12 **Netherurd** Border
19 K12 **Nether Wallop** Hants
62 D2 **Nether Wasdale** Cumb
30 G9 **Nether Westcote** Gloucs
40 G8 **Nether Whitacre** Warwks
78 D5 **Nether Whitecleuch** S Lans
31 Q10 **Nether Winchendon** Bucks
73 K3 **Netherwitton** Nthumb
99 Q5 **Nethy Bridge** Highld
9 M6 **Netley** Hants
9 K5 **Netley Marsh** Hants
20 B6 **Nettlebed** Oxon
17 P6 **Nettlebridge** Somset
7 M4 **Nettlecombe** Dorset
20 G2 **Nettleden** Herts
52 E8 **Nettleham** Lincs
22 D11 **Nettlestead** Kent
22 D12 **Nettlestead Green** Kent
9 Q8 **Nettlestone** IoW
73 M10 **Nettlesworth** Dur
52 G4 **Nettleton** Lincs
18 B5 **Nettleton** Wilts
18 G12 **Netton** Wilts
36 B11 **Nevern** Pembks
42 B10 **Nevill Holt** Leics
70 F3 **New Abbey** D & G
103 J3 **New Aberdour** Abers
21 M10 **New Addington** Gt Lon
58 G5 **Newall** Leeds
9 P2 **New Alresford** Hants
93 J6 **New Alyth** P & K
111 i1 **Newark** Ork
52 B11 **Newark-on-Trent** Notts
85 N10 **Newarthill** N Lans
22 C9 **New Ash Green** Kent
52 B11 **New Balderton** Notts
22 C9 **New Barn** Kent
21 L4 **New Barnet** Gt Lon
86 G8 **Newbattle** Mdloth
81 M9 **New Bewick** Nthumb
71 K3 **Newbie** D & G
64 B2 **Newbiggin** Cumb
71 P9 **Newbiggin** Cumb
71 Q6 **Newbiggin** Cumb
64 G3 **Newbiggin** Dur
64 H9 **Newbiggin** N York
73 N4 **Newbiggin-by-the-Sea** Nthumb
93 K7 **Newbigging** Angus
93 M8 **Newbigging** Angus
93 N8 **Newbigging** Angus
86 B11 **Newbigging** S Lans
63 N2 **Newbiggin-on-Lune** Cumb
41 L11 **New Bilton** Warwks
51 J6 **Newbold** Derbys
41 L11 **Newbold on Avon** Warwks
30 G5 **Newbold on Stour** Warwks
30 H3 **Newbold Pacey** Warwks
41 K6 **Newbold Verdon** Leics
53 K11 **New Bolingbroke** Lincs
42 H8 **Newborough** C Pete
54 F8 **Newborough** IoA
40 F3 **Newborough** Staffs
52 D8 **New Boultham** Lincs
35 L8 **Newbourne** Suffk
32 B8 **New Bradwell** M Keyn
51 J6 **New Brampton** Derbys
73 M11 **New Brancepeth** Dur
86 D7 **Newbridge** C Edin
27 P8 **Newbridge** Caerph
2 C9 **Newbridge** Cnwll
78 F11 **Newbridge** D & G
9 K4 **Newbridge** Hants
9 M9 **Newbridge** IoW
29 L2 **Newbridge Green** Worcs
38 B9 **Newbridge on Wye** Powys
56 F9 **New Brighton** Wirral
72 F7 **Newbrough** Nthumb
44 H11 **New Buckenham** Norfk
15 N10 **Newbuildings** Devon
103 K4 **Newburgh** Abers
103 K9 **Newburgh** Abers
93 J11 **Newburgh** Fife
57 J6 **Newburgh** Lancs
66 D11 **Newburgh Priory** N York
73 L7 **Newburn** N u Ty
17 Q6 **Newbury** Somset
19 M7 **Newbury** W Berk
21 N6 **Newbury Park** Gt Lon
64 B4 **Newby** Cumb
63 P11 **Newby** Lancs
63 N8 **Newby** N York
66 C5 **Newby** N York
62 G5 **Newby Bridge** Cumb
71 P4 **Newby East** Cumb
102 H5 **New Byth** Abers
71 M5 **Newby West** Cumb
28 E5 **Newcastle** Mons
38 F5 **Newcastle** Shrops
73 L6 **Newcastle Airport** Nthumb
36 E11 **Newcastle Emlyn** Carmth
79 P10 **Newcastleton** Border
49 Q6 **Newcastle-under-Lyme** Staffs
73 M7 **Newcastle upon Tyne** N u Ty
36 D11 **Newchapel** Pembks
11 M2 **Newchapel** Surrey
9 P9 **Newchurch** IoW
13 K4 **Newchurch** Kent
28 E8 **Newchurch** Mons
38 E11 **Newchurch** Powys
40 F3 **Newchurch** Staffs
45 K7 **New Costessey** Norfk
86 G7 **Newcraighall** C Edin
59 K10 **New Crofton** Wakefd
21 M7 **New Cross** Gt Lon
17 K11 **New Cross** Somset
77 K8 **New Cumnock** E Ayrs
103 J6 **New Deer** Abers
20 G6 **New Denham** Bucks
11 K2 **Newdigate** Surrey
31 Q2 **New Duston** Nhants
59 N3 **New Earswick** C York
51 M2 **New Edlington** Donc
101 J3 **New Elgin** Moray
61 K6 **New Ellerby** E R Yk
20 E8 **Newell Green** Br For
21 N8 **New Eltham** Gt Lon
30 D3 **New End** Worcs
12 G5 **Newenden** Kent
42 H9 **New England** C Pete
29 J4 **Newent** Gloucs
65 L2 **Newfield** Dur
107 N7 **Newfield** Highld
42 H9 **New Fletton** C Pete
9 K6 **New Forest National Park**
24 E4 **Newgale** Pembks
69 P4 **New Galloway** D & G
21 L3 **Newgate Street** Herts
87 J1 **New Gilston** Fife
2 b1 **New Grimsby** IoS
49 L6 **Newhall** Ches E
73 N5 **New Hartley** Nthumb
86 F7 **Newhaven** C Edin
11 N9 **Newhaven** E Susx
20 G10 **New Haw** Surrey
25 K8 **New Hedges** Pembks
61 J9 **New Holland** N Linc
67 J5 **Newholm** N York
51 L7 **New Houghton** Derbys
44 D5 **New Houghton** Norfk
85 N10 **Newhouse** N Lans
63 K4 **New Hutton** Cumb
11 N6 **Newick** E Susx
13 M3 **Newington** Kent
22 G9 **Newington** Kent
19 Q2 **Newington** Oxon
26 C2 **New Inn** Carmth
28 C8 **New Inn** Torfn
38 F6 **New Invention** Shrops
45 K8 **New Lakenham** Norfk
78 E1 **New Lanark** S Lans
61 J7 **Newland** C KuH
28 G6 **Newland** Gloucs
59 P8 **Newland** N York
15 P5 **Newland** Somset
39 P11 **Newland** Worcs
86 H9 **Newlandrig** Mdloth
79 Q9 **Newlands** Border
73 J9 **Newlands** Nthumb
101 L5 **Newlands of Dundurcas** Moray
79 M11 **New Langholm** D & G
53 L11 **New Leake** Lincs
103 K4 **New Leeds** Abers
59 J11 **New Lodge** Barns
57 K4 **New Longton** Lancs
68 G6 **New Luce** D & G
2 C9 **Newlyn** Cnwll
3 J5 **Newlyn East** Cnwll
103 J10 **Newmachar** Abers
85 N10 **Newmains** N Lans
21 K9 **New Malden** Gt Lon
34 E7 **Newman's Green** Suffk
33 Q4 **Newmarket** Suffk
111 d2 **Newmarket** W Isls
66 E4 **New Marske** R & Cl
31 M11 **New Marston** Oxon
95 N5 **New Mill** Abers
79 P6 **Newmill** Border
2 C8 **New Mill** Cnwll
58 F11 **New Mill** Kirk
101 N5 **Newmill** Moray
59 J10 **Newmillerdam** Wakefd
94 G9 **Newmill of Inshewan** Angus
86 E8 **Newmills** C Edin
50 D4 **New Mills** Derbys
86 B5 **Newmills** Fife
28 F7 **Newmills** Mons
38 C2 **New Mills** Powys
92 G9 **Newmiln** P & K
77 J4 **Newmilns** E Ayrs
9 J8 **New Milton** Hants
35 J9 **New Mistley** Essex
25 J4 **New Moat** Pembks
22 D3 **Newney Green** Essex
29 J6 **Newnham** Gloucs
20 B11 **Newnham** Hants
33 J8 **Newnham** Herts
23 J11 **Newnham** Kent
31 M3 **Newnham** Nhants
39 M8 **Newnham** Worcs
51 P7 **New Ollerton** Notts
103 J4 **New Pitsligo** Abers
4 H3 **Newport** Cnwll
60 E7 **Newport** E R Yk
33 N9 **Newport** Essex
29 J8 **Newport** Gloucs
110 D10 **Newport** Highld
9 N9 **Newport** IoW
28 C10 **Newport** Newpt
25 J2 **Newport** Pembks
49 N10 **Newport** Wrekin
93 M9 **Newport-on-Tay** Fife
32 C7 **Newport Pagnell** M Keyn
32 C7 **Newport Pagnell Services** M Keyn
76 F6 **New Prestwick** S Ayrs
36 F8 **New Quay** Cerdgn
3 J4 **Newquay** Cnwll
3 K3 *Newquay Airport* Cnwll
45 L7 **New Rackheath** Norfk
38 E9 **New Radnor** Powys
73 J8 **New Ridley** Nthumb
13 K5 **New Romney** Kent
51 N2 **New Rossington** Donc
85 P4 **New Sauchie** Clacks
102 F8 **Newseat** Abers
57 K2 **Newsham** Lancs
65 K5 **Newsham** N York
65 P9 **Newsham** N York
73 N5 **Newsham** Nthumb
59 J9 **New Sharlston** Wakefd
60 C8 **Newsholme** E R Yk
73 P9 **New Silksworth** Sundld
58 F10 **Newsome** Kirk
42 D3 **New Somerby** Lincs
21 L5 **New Southgate Crematorium** Gt Lon
80 D7 **Newstead** Border
51 L9 **Newstead** Notts
81 N8 **Newstead** Nthumb
85 M10 **New Stevenston** N Lans
51 L10 **Newthorpe** Notts
83 Q4 **Newton** Ag & B
80 E9 **Newton** Border
26 H12 **Newton** Brdgnd
32 H7 **Newton** C Beds
33 M6 **Newton** Cambs
43 M7 **Newton** Cambs
48 H2 **Newton** Ches W
49 J4 **Newton** Ches W
62 E7 **Newton** Cumb
51 K8 **Newton** Derbys
28 D3 **Newton** Herefs
39 K10 **Newton** Herefs
107 J11 **Newton** Highld
107 M11 **Newton** Highld
107 M8 **Newton** Highld
110 G6 **Newton** Highld
63 M11 **Newton** Lancs
42 F3 **Newton** Lincs
86 G8 **Newton** Mdloth
100 H3 **Newton** Moray
101 L3 **Newton** Moray
42 C12 **Newton** Nhants
44 D7 **Newton** Norfk
51 P11 **Newton** Notts
73 J7 **Newton** Nthumb
78 F3 **Newton** S Lans
85 L10 **Newton** S Lans
40 D3 **Newton** Staffs
34 F8 **Newton** Suffk
86 C6 **Newton** W Loth
41 M10 **Newton** Warwks
6 B8 **Newton Abbot** Devon
71 K5 **Newton Arlosh** Cumb
65 M3 **Newton Aycliffe** Dur
66 C3 **Newton Bewley** Hartpl
32 D6 **Newton Blossomville** M Keyn
32 E4 **Newton Bromswold** Nhants
41 J6 **Newton Burgoland** Leics
81 P8 **Newton-by-the-Sea** Nthumb
52 F6 **Newton by Toft** Lincs
4 H7 **Newton Ferrers** Cnwll
5 L9 **Newton Ferrers** Devon
111 b4 **Newton Ferry** W Isls
45 K9 **Newton Flotman** Norfk
86 G8 **Newtongrange** Mdloth
28 F9 **Newton Green** Mons
41 N7 **Newton Harcourt** Leics
57 Q8 **Newton Heath** Manch
95 P4 **Newtonhill** Abers
59 L5 **Newton Kyme** N York
65 L9 **Newton-le-Willows** N York
57 L9 **Newton-le-Willows** St Hel
86 G9 **Newtonloan** Mdloth
32 C9 **Newton Longville** Bucks
85 J11 **Newton Mearns** E Rens
95 K8 **Newtonmill** Angus
99 K8 **Newtonmore** Highld
65 M5 **Newton Morrell** N York
92 H12 **Newton of Balcanquhal** P & K
87 K2 **Newton of Balcormo** Fife
59 L3 **Newton on Ouse** N York
66 H9 **Newton-on-Rawcliffe** N York
81 N12 **Newton-on-the-Moor** Nthumb
52 B8 **Newton on Trent** Lincs
6 E5 **Newton Poppleford** Devon
31 N7 **Newton Purcell** Oxon
40 H6 **Newton Regis** Warwks
71 P8 **Newton Reigny** Cumb
15 Q11 **Newton St Cyres** Devon
45 K6 **Newton St Faith** Norfk
17 Q3 **Newton St Loe** BaNES
14 G9 **Newton St Petrock** Devon
40 H3 **Newton Solney** Derbys
19 M11 **Newton Stacey** Hants
69 K6 **Newton Stewart** D & G
19 J11 **Newton Tony** Wilts
15 J6 **Newton Tracey** Devon
66 D5 **Newton under Roseberry** R & Cl
60 C4 **Newton upon Derwent** E R Yk
10 B4 **Newton Valence** Hants
78 H9 **Newton Wamphray** D & G
57 J3 **Newton with Scales** Lancs
70 H6 **Newtown** Cumb
71 P3 **Newtown** Cumb
77 N8 **Newtown** D & G
6 E3 **Newtown** Devon
15 N7 **Newtown** Devon
8 D4 **New Town** Dorset
8 E4 **New Town** Dorset
11 P6 **New Town** E Susx
29 J8 **Newtown** Gloucs
9 Q5 **Newtown** Hants
29 J2 **Newtown** Herefs
39 L12 **Newtown** Herefs
98 E7 **Newtown** Highld
9 M8 **Newtown** IoW
81 L8 **Newtown** Nthumb
8 F8 **Newtown** Poole
38 C4 **Newtown** Powys
48 H10 **Newtown** Shrops
49 J8 **Newtown** Shrops
6 H1 **Newtown** Somset
50 B8 **Newtown** Staffs
57 K7 **Newtown** Wigan
39 Q10 **Newtown** Worcs
41 M5 **Newtown Linford** Leics
84 F10 **Newtown of Beltrees** Rens
80 D7 **Newtown St Boswells** Border
27 N7 **New Tredegar** Caerph
77 N4 **New Trows** S Lans
93 K7 **Newtyle** Angus
43 M8 **New Walsoken** Cambs
53 J3 **New Waltham** NE Lin
87 J7 **New Winton** E Loth
83 P2 **Newyork** Ag & B
53 J11 **New York** Lincs
24 G7 **Neyland** Pembks
16 E11 **Nicholashayne** Devon
26 C10 **Nicholaston** Swans
58 H3 **Nidd** N York
95 Q2 **Nigg** C Aber
107 N7 **Nigg** Highld
107 N8 **Nigg Ferry** Highld

72 E9 **Ninebanks** Nthumb
18 G4 **Nine Elms** Swindn
39 L8 **Nineveh** Worcs
12 E7 **Ninfield** E Susx
9 L9 **Ningwood** IoW
80 F8 **Nisbet** Border
80 H4 **Nisbet Hill** Border
9 N11 **Niton** IoW
85 J10 **Nitshill** C Glas
52 F10 **Nocton** Lincs
31 M10 **Noke** Oxon
24 F5 **Nolton** Pembks
24 F5 **Nolton Haven** Pembks
49 K6 **No Man's Heath** Ches W
40 H6 **No Man's Heath** Warwks
15 P9 **Nomansland** Devon
9 J4 **Nomansland** Wilts
49 J9 **Noneley** Shrops
23 N11 **Nonington** Kent
63 K6 **Nook** Cumb
21 K9 **Norbiton** Gt Lon
49 K6 **Norbury** Ches E
50 F11 **Norbury** Derbys
21 L9 **Norbury** Gt Lon
38 G4 **Norbury** Shrops
49 P10 **Norbury** Staffs
39 Q8 **Norchard** Worcs
43 N9 **Nordelph** Norfk
39 M3 **Nordley** Shrops
45 P8 **Norfolk Broads** Norfk
81 J5 **Norham** Nthumb
49 K2 **Norley** Ches W
9 L7 **Norleywood** Hants
52 E6 **Normanby** Lincs
60 F10 **Normanby** N Linc
66 G10 **Normanby** N York
66 D4 **Normanby** R & Cl
52 G5 **Normanby le Wold** Lincs
20 E11 **Normandy** Surrey
6 E3 **Norman's Green** Devon
41 J2 **Normanton** C Derb
42 B2 **Normanton** Leics
42 D2 **Normanton** Lincs
51 P9 **Normanton** Notts
59 J9 **Normanton** Wakefd
41 J5 **Normanton le Heath** Leics
41 L3 **Normanton on Soar** Notts
41 N2 **Normanton on the Wolds** Notts
52 B9 **Normanton on Trent** Notts
41 J4 **Norris Hill** Leics
58 G9 **Norristhorpe** Kirk
32 D11 **Northall** Bucks
65 P8 **Northallerton** N York
9 M5 **Northam** C Sotn
14 H6 **Northam** Devon
31 Q2 **Northampton** Nhants
39 Q8 **Northampton** Worcs
51 M4 **North Anston** Rothm
20 E9 **North Ascot** Br For
31 L8 **North Aston** Oxon
21 L3 **Northaw** Herts
6 H1 **Northay** Somset
9 L4 **North Baddesley** Hants
90 E4 **North Ballachulish** Highld
17 N9 **North Barrow** Somset
44 F3 **North Barsham** Norfk
22 F5 **North Benfleet** Essex
10 E9 **North Bersted** W Susx
87 K5 **North Berwick** E Loth
9 P5 **North Boarhunt** Hants
42 G8 **Northborough** C Pete
23 P11 **Northbourne** Kent
5 P4 **North Bovey** Devon
18 C9 **North Bradley** Wilts
5 K4 **North Brentor** Devon
17 Q8 **North Brewham** Somset
19 N11 **Northbrook** Hants
14 H4 **North Buckland** Devon
45 N7 **North Burlingham** Norfk
17 P10 **North Cadbury** Somset
52 D7 **North Carlton** Lincs
51 N4 **North Carlton** Notts
60 F7 **North Cave** E R Yk
30 D11 **North Cerney** Gloucs
11 N6 **North Chailey** E Susx
10 F4 **Northchapel** W Susx
8 H4 **North Charford** Hants
81 N9 **North Charlton** Nthumb
21 K9 **North Cheam** Gt Lon
17 Q10 **North Cheriton** Somset
7 K4 **North Chideock** Dorset
21 K2 **Northchurch** Herts
20 E6 **North Cliffe** E R Yk
52 B8 **North Clifton** Notts
53 L5 **North Cockerington** Lincs
90 C9 **North Connel** Ag & B
26 H11 **North Cornelly** Brdgnd
53 K4 **North Cotes** Lincs
4 H2 **Northcott** Devon
19 N2 **Northcourt** Oxon
45 P11 **North Cove** Suffk
65 M6 **North Cowton** N York
32 D7 **North Crawley** M Keyn
44 E3 **North Creake** Norfk
17 J10 **North Curry** Somset
60 F4 **North Dalton** E R Yk
59 K4 **North Deighton** N York
15 J6 **North Devon Crematorium** Devon
23 Q8 **Northdown** Kent
22 H11 **North Downs**
59 P6 **North Duffield** N York
104 F7 **North Duntulm** Highld
21 K9 **North East Surrey Crematorium** Gt Lon
44 G6 **North Elmham** Norfk
59 L10 **North Elmsall** Wakefd
9 Q7 **North End** C Port
33 Q11 **North End** Essex
8 G4 **North End** Hants
32 D3 **North End** Nhants
10 F8 **North End** W Susx
31 K4 **Northend** Warwks
57 P10 **Northenden** Manch
105 L6 **North Erradale** Highld
41 N6 **North Evington** C Leic
22 G4 **North Fambridge** Essex
60 G8 **North Ferriby** E R Yk
40 D10 **Northfield** Birm
103 J12 **Northfield** C Aber
60 H8 **Northfield** E R Yk
42 E8 **Northfields** Lincs
22 D8 **Northfleet** Kent
61 J4 **North Frodingham** E R Yk
8 H5 **North Gorley** Hants
35 M4 **North Green** Suffk
52 E8 **North Greetwell** Lincs
60 E1 **North Grimston** N York
10 B9 **North Hayling** Hants
4 G5 **North Hill** Cnwll
20 H6 **North Hillingdon** Gt Lon
31 L11 **North Hinksey Village** Oxon
11 J1 **North Holmwood** Surrey
5 P8 **North Huish** Devon
52 D9 **North Hykeham** Lincs
12 G5 **Northiam** E Susx
32 G7 **Northill** C Beds
19 P12 **Northington** Hants
52 F3 **North Kelsey** Lincs
107 L11 **North Kessock** Highld
61 K10 **North Killingholme** N Linc
65 Q9 **North Kilvington** N York
41 N10 **North Kilworth** Leics
52 G11 **North Kyme** Lincs
67 Q12 **North Landing** E R Yk
53 K11 **Northlands** Lincs
30 E10 **Northleach** Gloucs
20 D2 **North Lee** Bucks
6 G4 **Northleigh** Devon
31 K10 **North Leigh** Oxon
52 B7 **North Leverton with Habblesthorpe** Notts
15 J11 **Northlew** Devon
30 E5 **North Littleton** Worcs
44 G12 **North Lopham** Norfk
42 D9 **North Luffenham** Rutlnd
10 D6 **North Marden** W Susx
31 Q9 **North Marston** Bucks
86 G9 **North Middleton** Mdloth
102 H6 **North Millbrex** Abers
68 E8 **North Milmain** D & G
15 M6 **North Molton** Devon
31 K12 **Northmoor** Oxon
19 P3 **North Moreton** Oxon
93 L5 **Northmuir** Angus
10 E9 **North Mundham** W Susx
52 B10 **North Muskham** Notts
60 F6 **North Newbald** E R Yk
31 K6 **North Newington** Oxon
18 G8 **North Newnton** Wilts
17 J9 **North Newton** Somset
10 B8 **Northney** Hants
29 K9 **North Nibley** Gloucs
21 J6 **Northolt** Gt Lon
48 E2 **Northop** Flints
48 F2 **Northop Hall** Flints
66 D4 **North Ormesby** Middsb
53 J5 **North Ormsby** Lincs
58 G9 **Northorpe** Kirk
42 H3 **Northorpe** Lincs
52 C4 **Northorpe** Lincs
65 P9 **North Otterington** N York
52 F5 **North Owersby** Lincs
58 E8 **Northowram** Calder
7 L2 **North Perrott** Somset
16 H9 **North Petherton** Somset
4 G3 **North Petherwin** Cnwll
44 E8 **North Pickenham** Norfk
30 C3 **North Piddle** Worcs
7 M3 **North Poorton** Dorset
8 D9 **Northport** Dorset
86 D6 **North Queensferry** Fife
42 E2 **North Rauceby** Lincs
45 L3 **Northrepps** Norfk
53 L6 **North Reston** Lincs
58 H4 **North Rigton** N York
50 B7 **North Rode** Ches E
111 i1 **North Ronaldsay** Ork
111 i1 *North Ronaldsay Airport* Ork
43 Q6 **North Runcton** Norfk
52 C9 **North Scarle** Lincs
90 C7 **North Shian** Ag & B
73 N7 **North Shields** N Tyne
22 H6 **North Shoebury** Sthend
56 F2 **North Shore** Bpool
43 J9 **North Side** C Pete
53 L4 **North Somercotes** Lincs
65 M11 **North Stainley** N York
22 C7 **North Stifford** Thurr
17 Q3 **North Stoke** BaNES
19 Q4 **North Stoke** Oxon
10 G7 **North Stoke** W Susx
23 K10 **North Street** Kent
19 Q6 **North Street** W Berk
81 P7 **North Sunderland** Nthumb
14 F11 **North Tamerton** Cnwll
15 L10 **North Tawton** Devon
85 M5 **North Third** Stirlg
53 J4 **North Thoresby** Lincs
111 b3 **Northton** W Isls
15 J9 **North Town** Devon
17 N7 **North Town** Somset
20 E7 **North Town** W & M
44 G7 **North Tuddenham** Norfk
111 a4 **North Uist** W Isls
72 F1 **Northumberland National Park** Nthumb
45 L4 **North Walsham** Norfk
19 P10 **North Waltham** Hants
20 B12 **North Warnborough** Hants
21 P3 **North Weald Bassett** Essex
51 Q4 **North Wheatley** Notts
49 M2 **Northwich** Ches W
39 Q9 **Northwick** Worcs
17 N5 **North Widcombe** BaNES
52 G6 **North Willingham** Lincs
51 K7 **North Wingfield** Derbys
42 D6 **North Witham** Lincs
44 C10 **Northwold** Norfk
20 H5 **Northwood** Gt Lon
9 N8 **Northwood** IoW
49 J8 **Northwood** Shrops
29 J5 **Northwood Green** Gloucs
17 P12 **North Wootton** Dorset
43 Q5 **North Wootton** Norfk
17 N7 **North Wootton** Somset
18 B6 **North Wraxall** Wilts
66 G7 **North York Moors National Park**
59 M10 **Norton** Donc
11 P9 **Norton** E Susx
29 M4 **Norton** Gloucs
66 H12 **Norton** N York
31 N2 **Norton** Nhants
51 M6 **Norton** Notts
38 F8 **Norton** Powys
66 C3 **Norton** S on T
39 N3 **Norton** Shrops
34 F4 **Norton** Suffk
10 E8 **Norton** W Susx
18 C4 **Norton** Wilts
30 D5 **Norton** Worcs
39 Q11 **Norton** Worcs
18 D11 **Norton Bavant** Wilts
49 Q9 **Norton Bridge** Staffs
40 D6 **Norton Canes** Staffs
40 D6 *Norton Canes Services* Staffs
38 H11 **Norton Canon** Herefs
52 C10 **Norton Disney** Lincs
16 G10 **Norton Fitzwarren** Somset
9 K9 **Norton Green** IoW
17 N4 **Norton Hawkfield** BaNES
22 C3 **Norton Heath** Essex
49 N7 **Norton in Hales** Shrops
41 J6 **Norton-Juxta-Twycross** Leics
65 P12 **Norton-le-Clay** N York
30 G2 **Norton Lindsey** Warwks
34 F4 **Norton Little Green** Suffk
17 N3 **Norton Malreward** BaNES
18 B9 **Norton St Philip** Somset
45 N9 **Norton Subcourse** Norfk
17 L11 **Norton sub Hamdon** Somset
51 Q8 **Norwell** Notts
51 Q8 **Norwell Woodhouse** Notts
45 K8 **Norwich** Norfk
45 K7 *Norwich Airport* Norfk
45 K8 **Norwich Cathedral** Norfk
45 K7 **Norwich (St Faith) Crematorium** Norfk
111 m2 **Norwick** Shet
85 P4 **Norwood** Clacks
21 J7 **Norwood Green** Gt Lon
11 K2 **Norwood Hill** Surrey
41 Q7 **Noseley** Leics
5 L10 **Noss Mayo** Devon
65 M10 **Nosterfield** N York
97 M4 **Nostie** Highld
30 E9 **Notgrove** Gloucs
26 H12 **Nottage** Brdgnd
51 M11 **Nottingham** C Nott
59 J10 **Notton** Wakefd
18 D6 **Notton** Wilts
39 P8 **Noutard's Green** Worcs
19 Q4 **Nuffield** Oxon
60 E5 **Nunburnholme** E R Yk
41 J8 **Nuneaton** Warwks
21 M8 **Nunhead** Gt Lon
59 L3 **Nun Monkton** N York
17 Q7 **Nunney** Somset
66 F10 **Nunnington** N York
53 J2 **Nunsthorpe** NE Lin
59 N4 **Nunthorpe** C York
66 D5 **Nunthorpe** Middsb
66 D5 **Nunthorpe Village** Middsb
8 H3 **Nunton** Wilts
65 N11 **Nunwick** N York
9 L4 **Nursling** Hants
10 C8 **Nutbourne** W Susx
10 H6 **Nutbourne** W Susx
21 L12 **Nutfield** Surrey
51 M11 **Nuthall** Notts
33 L9 **Nuthampstead** Herts
11 J5 **Nuthurst** W Susx
11 N5 **Nutley** E Susx
57 P5 **Nuttall** Bury
110 G3 **Nybster** Highld
10 E9 **Nyetimber** W Susx
10 C6 **Nyewood** W Susx
15 M9 **Nymet Rowland** Devon
15 M11 **Nymet Tracey** Devon
29 L8 **Nympsfield** Gloucs
16 F10 **Nynehead** Somset
10 E8 **Nyton** W Susx

O

41 N7 **Oadby** Leics
22 G10 **Oad Street** Kent
50 D11 **Oakamoor** Staffs
86 C8 **Oakbank** W Loth
15 J11 **Oak Cross** Devon
27 P8 **Oakdale** Caerph
16 F10 **Oake** Somset
39 Q2 **Oaken** Staffs
63 K11 **Oakenclough** Lancs
49 M12 **Oakengates** Wrekin
73 L12 **Oakenshaw** Dur
58 F8 **Oakenshaw** Kirk
36 G8 **Oakford** Cerdgn
16 C11 **Oakford** Devon
42 C8 **Oakham** Rutlnd
10 C3 **Oakhanger** Hants
17 P6 **Oakhill** Somset
33 L4 **Oakington** Cambs
29 K5 **Oakle Street** Gloucs
32 E6 **Oakley** Bed
31 N10 **Oakley** Bucks
86 B4 **Oakley** Fife
19 P9 **Oakley** Hants
35 J2 **Oakley** Suffk
29 M7 **Oakridge** Gloucs
29 P9 **Oaksey** Wilts
40 H5 **Oakthorpe** Leics
51 J12 **Oakwood** C Derb
58 D6 **Oakworth** C Brad
23 J10 **Oare** Kent
15 N3 **Oare** Somset
18 H7 **Oare** Wilts
42 E3 **Oasby** Lincs
17 K10 **Oath** Somset
93 N4 **Oathlaw** Angus
20 H9 **Oatlands Park** Surrey
90 B9 **Oban** Ag & B
90 C8 *Oban Airport* Ag & B
38 G6 **Obley** Shrops
92 F8 **Obney** P & K
17 P11 **Oborne** Dorset
35 J3 **Occold** Suffk
110 F8 **Occumster** Highld
76 H7 **Ochiltree** E Ayrs
41 K1 **Ockbrook** Derbys
20 H11 **Ockham** Surrey
89 L3 **Ockle** Highld
11 J3 **Ockley** Surrey
39 L11 **Ocle Pychard** Herefs
17 M11 **Odcombe** Somset
17 Q4 **Odd Down** BaNES
30 B3 **Oddingley** Worcs
30 G8 **Oddington** Gloucs
31 M10 **Oddington** Oxon
32 D5 **Odell** Bed
20 C12 **Odiham** Hants
58 F8 **Odsal** C Brad
33 J8 **Odsey** Cambs
8 G3 **Odstock** Wilts
41 K6 **Odstone** Leics
31 J2 **Offchurch** Warwks
30 D5 **Offenham** Worcs
50 B3 **Offerton** Stockp
11 N7 **Offham** E Susx
22 D11 **Offham** Kent
10 G8 **Offham** W Susx
32 H4 **Offord Cluny** Cambs
32 H4 **Offord D'Arcy** Cambs
34 H6 **Offton** Suffk
6 G3 **Offwell** Devon
18 H6 **Ogbourne Maizey** Wilts
18 H6 **Ogbourne St Andrew** Wilts
18 H6 **Ogbourne St George** Wilts
73 K5 **Ogle** Nthumb
56 H11 **Oglet** Lpool
16 B2 **Ogmore** V Glam
16 B2 **Ogmore-by-Sea** V Glam
27 K10 **Ogmore Vale** Brdgnd
8 B5 **Okeford Fitzpaine** Dorset
5 M2 **Okehampton** Devon
50 H8 **Oker Side** Derbys
11 J3 **Okewood Hill** Surrey
32 B3 **Old** Nhants
95 Q1 **Old Aberdeen** C Aber
9 P1 **Old Alresford** Hants
108 C8 **Oldany** Highld
77 M11 **Old Auchenbrack** D & G
51 M11 **Old Basford** C Nott
19 Q9 **Old Basing** Hants
44 F6 **Old Beetley** Norfk
30 E2 **Oldberrow** Warwks
81 M9 **Old Bewick** Nthumb
53 K9 **Old Bolingbroke** Lincs
58 G5 **Old Bramhope** Leeds
51 J6 **Old Brampton** Derbys
70 C3 **Old Bridge of Urr** D & G
44 H10 **Old Buckenham** Norfk
19 M8 **Old Burghclere** Hants
40 C9 **Oldbury** Sandw
39 N4 **Oldbury** Shrops
40 H8 **Oldbury** Warwks
28 H9 **Oldbury-on-Severn** S Glos
18 B3 **Oldbury on the Hill** Gloucs
66 D9 **Old Byland** N York
51 N1 **Old Cantley** Donc
28 C4 **Oldcastle** Mons
45 K7 **Old Catton** Norfk
53 J2 **Old Clee** NE Lin
16 E7 **Old Cleeve** Somset
51 N7 **Old Clipstone** Notts
55 M6 **Old Colwyn** Conwy
51 N3 **Oldcotes** Notts
76 D10 **Old Dailly** S Ayrs
41 P3 **Old Dalby** Leics
103 K6 **Old Deer** Abers
51 M2 **Old Edlington** Donc
61 K6 **Old Ellerby** E R Yk
35 M9 **Old Felixstowe** Suffk
39 Q8 **Oldfield** Worcs
42 H10 **Old Fletton** C Pete
18 B10 **Oldford** Somset
28 G5 **Old Forge** Herefs
2 b1 **Old Grimsby** IoS
33 L11 **Old Hall Green** Herts
58 B12 **Oldham** Oldham
87 N7 **Oldhamstocks** E Loth
21 P2 **Old Harlow** Essex
44 B2 **Old Hunstanton** Norfk
33 J2 **Old Hurst** Cambs
63 K5 **Old Hutton** Cumb
84 H8 **Old Kilpatrick** W Duns
32 H11 **Old Knebworth** Herts
45 K8 **Old Lakenham** Norfk
17 P2 **Oldland** S Glos
57 M2 **Old Langho** Lancs
53 L12 **Old Leake** Lincs
66 H11 **Old Malton** N York
102 H9 **Oldmeldrum** Abers
4 H5 **Oldmill** Cnwll
30 H1 **Old Milverton** Warwks
17 J5 **Oldmixon** N Som
34 H4 **Old Newton** Suffk
38 F9 **Old Radnor** Powys
102 E9 **Old Rayne** Abers
13 K5 **Old Romney** Kent
11 K8 **Old Shoreham** W Susx
108 D4 **Oldshoremore** Highld
29 K11 **Old Sodbury** S Glos
42 D4 **Old Somerby** Lincs
66 D10 **Oldstead** N York
31 Q6 **Old Stratford** Nhants
92 C3 **Old Struan** P & K
40 B10 **Old Swinford** Dudley
66 B10 **Old Thirsk** N York
63 L5 **Old Town** Cumb
12 C9 **Old Town** E Susx
2 c2 **Old Town** IoS
57 P9 **Old Trafford** Traffd
71 P4 **Oldwall** Cumb
26 C9 **Oldwalls** Swans
32 G7 **Old Warden** C Beds
32 F2 **Old Weston** Cambs
110 G6 **Old Wick** Highld
20 F8 **Old Windsor** W & M
23 K11 **Old Wives Lees** Kent
20 G11 **Old Woking** Surrey
110 C5 **Olgrinmore** Highld
40 E4 **Olive Green** Staffs
9 M2 **Oliver's Battery** Hants
111 k3 **Ollaberry** Shet
96 F3 **Ollach** Highld
57 P12 **Ollerton** Ches E
51 P7 **Ollerton** Notts
49 M9 **Ollerton** Shrops
32 C6 **Olney** M Keyn
110 E3 **Olrig House** Highld
40 F10 **Olton** Solhll
28 H10 **Olveston** S Glos
39 Q8 **Ombersley** Worcs
51 P7 **Ompton** Notts
56 d5 **Onchan** IoM
50 D9 **Onecote** Staffs
39 J6 **Onibury** Shrops
90 E4 **Onich** Highld
26 H6 **Onllwyn** Neath
49 N6 **Onneley** Staffs
20 F12 **Onslow Village** Surrey
49 L1 **Onston** Ches W
105 L7 **Opinan** Highld
101 L4 **Orbliston** Moray
96 B2 **Orbost** Highld
53 M9 **Orby** Lincs
16 H10 **Orchard Portman** Somset
18 F10 **Orcheston** Wilts
28 F4 **Orcop** Herefs
28 F4 **Orcop Hill** Herefs
102 E4 **Ord** Abers
102 E12 **Ordhead** Abers
94 G2 **Ordie** Abers
101 L4 **Ordiequish** Moray
51 P5 **Ordsall** Notts
12 G7 **Ore** E Susx
35 N6 **Orford** Suffk
57 L10 **Orford** Warrtn
8 D8 **Organford** Dorset
13 J3 **Orlestone** Kent
39 J8 **Orleton** Herefs
39 M8 **Orleton** Worcs
32 C3 **Orlingbury** Nhants
66 D4 **Ormesby** R & Cl
45 P7 **Ormesby St Margaret** Norfk
45 P7 **Ormesby St Michael** Norfk
105 M4 **Ormiscaig** Highld
86 H8 **Ormiston** E Loth
89 K4 **Ormsaigmore** Highld
83 L8 **Ormsary** Ag & B
56 H7 **Ormskirk** Lancs
82 E5 **Oronsay** Ag & B
111 h2 **Orphir** Ork
21 P9 **Orpington** Gt Lon
56 G9 **Orrell** Sefton
57 K7 **Orrell** Wigan
70 C6 **Orroland** D & G
22 D7 **Orsett** Thurr
49 P11 **Orslow** Staffs
51 Q11 **Orston** Notts
63 L1 **Orton** Cumb
32 B2 **Orton** Nhants
39 Q3 **Orton** Staffs
42 G10 **Orton Longueville** C Pete
40 H6 **Orton-on-the-Hill** Leics
42 G10 **Orton Waterville** C Pete
33 K6 **Orwell** Cambs
57 M3 **Osbaldeston** Lancs
59 N4 **Osbaldwick** C York
41 K6 **Osbaston** Leics
48 G10 **Osbaston** Shrops
9 N8 **Osborne House** IoW
42 F3 **Osbournby** Lincs
49 J3 **Oscroft** Ches W
96 C2 **Ose** Highld
41 K4 **Osgathorpe** Leics
52 F5 **Osgodby** Lincs
59 N7 **Osgodby** N York
67 M9 **Osgodby** N York
96 G3 **Oskaig** Highld
89 K8 **Oskamull** Ag & B
33 Q12 **Onslow Green** Essex
50 G11 **Osmaston** Derbys
7 Q6 **Osmington** Dorset
7 Q6 **Osmington Mills** Dorset
59 J7 **Osmondthorpe** Leeds
66 C7 **Osmotherley** N York
31 L11 **Osney** Oxon
23 J10 **Ospringe** Kent
58 H9 **Ossett** Wakefd
51 Q7 **Ossington** Notts
21 J7 **Osterley** Gt Lon
66 E10 **Oswaldkirk** N York
57 N4 **Oswaldtwistle** Lancs
48 F9 **Oswestry** Shrops
21 Q10 **Otford** Kent
22 F11 **Otham** Kent
17 K9 **Othery** Somset
58 G5 **Otley** Leeds
35 K5 **Otley** Suffk
9 M3 **Otterbourne** Hants
63 Q9 **Otterburn** N York
72 F3 **Otterburn** Nthumb
83 P6 **Otter Ferry** Ag & B
4 E3 **Otterham** Cnwll
16 H7 **Otterhampton** Somset
111 b4 **Otternish** W Isls
20 G9 **Ottershaw** Surrey
111 k3 **Otterswick** Shet
6 E6 **Otterton** Devon
6 E4 **Ottery St Mary** Devon
13 M2 **Ottinge** Kent
61 M8 **Ottringham** E R Yk
71 J7 **Oughterside** Cumb
50 H3 **Oughtibridge** Sheff
57 M10 **Oughtrington** Warrtn
66 D11 **Oulston** N York
71 K5 **Oulton** Cumb
45 J4 **Oulton** Norfk
40 B1 **Oulton** Staffs
45 Q10 **Oulton** Suffk
45 Q10 **Oulton Broad** Suffk
45 J5 **Oulton Street** Norfk
42 E11 **Oundle** Nhants
39 Q4 **Ounsdale** Staffs
64 B1 **Ousby** Cumb
34 C5 **Ousden** Suffk
60 E9 **Ousefleet** E R Yk
73 M9 **Ouston** Dur
62 G3 **Outgate** Cumb
64 E7 **Outhgill** Cumb
30 E2 **Outhill** Warwks
58 E9 **Outlane** Kirk
56 H1 **Out Rawcliffe** Lancs
43 N8 **Outwell** Norfk
11 L2 **Outwood** Surrey
49 P11 **Outwoods** Staffs
59 J8 **Ouzlewell Green** Leeds
33 L3 **Over** Cambs
29 N2 **Overbury** Worcs
7 Q6 **Overcombe** Dorset
17 N11 **Over Compton** Dorset
57 M7 **Overdale Crematorium** Bolton
50 G7 **Over Haddon** Derbys
63 K8 **Over Kellet** Lancs
31 K9 **Over Kiddington** Oxon
17 L8 **Overleigh** Somset
30 H8 **Over Norton** Oxon
49 P1 **Over Peover** Ches E
56 H12 **Overpool** Ches W
108 H10 **Overscaig Hotel** Highld
40 H4 **Overseal** Derbys
66 C8 **Over Silton** N York
23 K11 **Oversland** Kent
32 B4 **Overstone** Nhants
16 G8 **Over Stowey** Somset
45 L3 **Overstrand** Norfk
17 L11 **Over Stratton** Somset
31 L6 **Overthorpe** Nhants
102 H11 **Overton** C Aber
19 N10 **Overton** Hants
62 H9 **Overton** Lancs
59 N3 **Overton** N York
39 J7 **Overton** Shrops
26 B10 **Overton** Swans
58 H10 **Overton** Wakefd
48 G7 **Overton** Wrexhm
85 N11 **Overtown** N Lans
19 K11 **Over Wallop** Hants
40 G8 **Over Whitacre** Warwks
31 K8 **Over Worton** Oxon
32 A11 **Oving** Bucks
10 E8 **Oving** W Susx
11 M8 **Ovingdean** Br & H
73 J7 **Ovingham** Nthumb
65 K5 **Ovington** Dur
34 C8 **Ovington** Essex
9 P2 **Ovington** Hants
44 F9 **Ovington** Norfk
73 J7 **Ovington** Nthumb
9 K4 **Ower** Hants
8 B9 **Owermoigne** Dorset
51 J3 **Owlerton** Sheff
20 D10 **Owlsmoor** Br For
20 C3 **Owlswick** Bucks
52 E6 **Owmby** Lincs
52 F3 **Owmby** Lincs
9 N3 **Owslebury** Hants

59 M11 Owston Donc
41 Q6 Owston Leics
52 B4 Owston Ferry N Linc
61 M7 Owstwick E R Yk
61 N8 Owthorne E R Yk
41 P2 Owthorpe Notts
66 C2 Owton Manor Hartpl
44 C9 Oxborough Norfk
53 K7 Oxcombe Lincs
63 K4 Oxenholme Cumb
58 D7 Oxenhope C Brad
62 G5 Oxen Park Cumb
17 L7 Oxenpill Somset
29 N3 Oxenton Gloucs
19 K8 Oxenwood Wilts
31 L11 Oxford Oxon
31 L10 Oxford Airport Oxon
31 M11 Oxford Crematorium Oxon
31 N12 Oxford Services Oxon
20 H4 Oxhey Herts
30 H5 Oxhill Warwks
40 B7 Oxley Wolves
22 H1 Oxley Green Essex
43 M11 Oxlode Cambs
80 F9 Oxnam Border
45 K5 Oxnead Norfk
21 J10 Oxshott Surrey
50 H1 Oxspring Barns
21 M11 Oxted Surrey
80 C4 Oxton Border
59 L5 Oxton N York
51 N9 Oxton Notts
26 C10 Oxwich Swans
26 C10 Oxwich Green Swans
106 F3 Oykel Bridge Hotel Highld
102 E9 Oyne Abers
26 E10 Oystermouth Swans

P

111 e2 Pabail W Isls
41 J5 Packington Leics
93 M5 Padanaram Angus
31 Q7 Padbury Bucks
21 L7 Paddington Gt Lon
13 M3 Paddlesworth Kent
22 D10 Paddlesworth Kent
12 D2 Paddock Wood Kent
57 P3 Padiham Lancs
58 F3 Padside N York
3 K1 Padstow Cnwll
19 Q7 Padworth W Berk
10 E9 Pagham W Susx
22 H5 Paglesham Essex
6 B10 Paignton Torbay
41 L10 Pailton Warwks
38 D11 Painscastle Powys
73 J8 Painshawfield Nthumb
60 E3 Painsthorpe E R Yk
29 M6 Painswick Gloucs
23 J10 Painter's Forstal Kent
84 H9 Paisley Rens
45 Q11 Pakefield Suffk
34 F4 Pakenham Suffk
20 E7 Paley Street W & M
40 D7 Palfrey Wsall
35 J2 Palgrave Suffk
8 B8 Pallington Dorset
76 H7 Palmerston E Ayrs
70 D4 Palnackie D & G
69 L6 Palnure D & G
51 L7 Palterton Derbys
19 Q8 Pamber End Hants
19 Q8 Pamber Green Hants
19 Q8 Pamber Heath Hants
29 N3 Pamington Gloucs
8 E7 Pamphill Dorset
33 N7 Pampisford Cambs
93 P8 Panbride Angus
14 F10 Pancrasweek Devon
28 D4 Pandy Mons
55 M8 Pandy Tudur Conwy
34 C10 Panfield Essex
19 Q5 Pangbourne W Berk
11 L7 Pangdean W Susx
58 H4 Pannal N York
58 H4 Pannal Ash N York
94 G3 Pannanich Wells Hotel Abers
48 F10 Pant Shrops
48 D1 Pantasaph Flints
27 K11 Pant-ffrwyth Brdgnd
46 H2 Pant Glas Gwynd
47 M10 Pantglas Powys
52 H7 Panton Lincs
37 R6 Pant-y-dwr Powys
48 E3 Pant-y-mwyn Flints
45 M7 Panxworth Norfk
111 h1 Papa Westray Airport Ork
70 H8 Papcastle Cumb
110 H5 Papigoe Highld
87 L7 Papple E Loth
51 M9 Papplewick Notts
33 J4 Papworth Everard Cambs
33 J4 Papworth St Agnes Cambs
3 N5 Par Cnwll
57 J6 Parbold Lancs
17 N8 Parbrook Somset
47 P5 Parc Gwynd
25 K6 Parc Gwyn Crematorium Pembks
28 E9 Parc Seymour Newpt
70 H9 Pardshaw Cumb
35 M5 Parham Suffk
78 E10 Park D & G
72 C8 Park Nthumb
20 B6 Park Corner Oxon
56 G3 Park Crematorium Lancs
28 H7 Parkend Gloucs
12 C1 Parkers Green Kent
13 J3 Park Farm Kent
56 F12 Parkgate Ches W
78 G10 Parkgate D & G
9 N6 Park Gate Hants
58 F6 Park Gate Leeds
11 K2 Parkgate Surrey
93 Q6 Parkgrove Crematorium Angus
84 H8 Parkhall W Duns
14 G7 Parkham Devon
26 D10 Parkmill Swans
21 K7 Park Royal Gt Lon
73 Q10 Parkside Dur
85 N10 Parkside N Lans
8 F8 Parkstone Poole
21 J3 Park Street Herts
58 E9 Park Wood Crematorium Calder
21 N2 Parndon Essex
21 N3 Parndon Wood Crematorium Essex
15 L3 Parracombe Devon
43 L8 Parson Drove Cambs
34 G10 Parson's Heath Essex
85 J9 Partick C Glas
57 N9 Partington Traffd
53 L9 Partney Lincs
70 F10 Parton Cumb
11 J6 Partridge Green W Susx
50 F9 Parwich Derbys
32 A8 Passenham Nhants
45 M4 Paston Norfk
11 L8 Patcham Br & H
10 H8 Patching W Susx
28 H11 Patchway S Glos
58 F2 Pateley Bridge N York
86 F4 Pathhead Fife
86 H9 Pathhead Mdloth
92 G12 Path of Condie P & K
76 G8 Patna E Ayrs
18 F8 Patney Wilts
56 b5 Patrick IoM
65 L8 Patrick Brompton N York
57 N8 Patricroft Salfd
61 M9 Patrington E R Yk
61 M9 Patrington Haven E R Yk
23 M11 Patrixbourne Kent
71 N11 Patterdale Cumb
39 P3 Pattingham Staffs
31 P4 Pattishall Nhants
34 D11 Pattiswick Green Essex
2 C9 Paul Cnwll
31 Q5 Paulerspury Nhants
61 K8 Paull E R Yk
8 G2 Paul's Dene Wilts
17 P5 Paulton BaNES
73 K2 Pauperhaugh Nthumb
32 E5 Pavenham Bed
16 H7 Pawlett Somset
30 F6 Paxford Gloucs
81 K4 Paxton Border
6 E3 Payhembury Devon
63 P10 Paythorne Lancs
11 N9 Peacehaven E Susx
50 F3 Peak District National Park
50 E5 Peak Forest Derbys
42 G8 Peakirk C Pete
17 Q5 Peasedown St John BaNES
44 H6 Peaseland Green Norfk
19 M5 Peasemore W Berk
35 M3 Peasenhall Suffk
11 L4 Pease Pottage W Susx
11 L4 Pease Pottage Services W Susx
10 H2 Peaslake Surrey
57 K9 Peasley Cross St Hel
12 H5 Peasmarsh E Susx
103 J3 Peathill Abers
87 J1 Peat Inn Fife
41 N8 Peatling Magna Leics
41 N9 Peatling Parva Leics
34 E9 Pebmarsh Essex
30 F5 Pebworth Worcs
58 C8 Pecket Well Calder
49 K4 Peckforton Ches E
21 M8 Peckham Gt Lon
41 L7 Peckleton Leics
13 L3 Pedlinge Kent
40 B10 Pedmore Dudley
17 K8 Pedwell Somset
79 L2 Peebles Border
56 b4 Peel IoM
13 M3 Peene Kent
32 G9 Pegsdon C Beds
73 M4 Pegswood Nthumb
23 Q9 Pegwell Kent
96 G3 Peinchorran Highld
104 F10 Peinlich Highld
34 G12 Peldon Essex
40 D6 Pelsall Wsall
73 M9 Pelton Dur
4 F8 Pelynt Cnwll
26 D8 Pemberton Carmth
57 K7 Pemberton Wigan
25 P8 Pembrey Carmth
38 H9 Pembridge Herefs
24 H8 Pembroke Pembks
24 G7 Pembroke Dock Pembks
24 E5 Pembrokeshire Coast National Park Pembks
12 D2 Pembury Kent
28 G3 Pen-allt Herefs
28 F6 Penallt Mons
25 K8 Penally Pembks
16 G2 Penarth V Glam
37 L4 Pen-bont Rhydybeddau Cerdgn
36 E9 Penbryn Cerdgn
25 Q2 Pencader Carmth
87 J8 Pencaitland E Loth
54 D6 Pencarnisiog IoA
37 J10 Pencarreg Carmth
27 M4 Pencelli Powys
26 D9 Penclawdd Swans
27 K11 Pencoed Brdgnd
39 L10 Pencombe Herefs
28 G5 Pencraig Herefs
48 B9 Pencraig Powys
2 B8 Pendeen Cnwll
27 K7 Penderyn Rhondd
25 L7 Pendine Carmth
57 P8 Pendlebury Salfd
57 N2 Pendleton Lancs
29 K3 Pendock Worcs
4 C4 Pendoggett Cnwll
7 M1 Pendomer Somset
16 E2 Pendoylan V Glam
47 M10 Penegoes Powys
25 J4 Pen-ffordd Pembks
27 N8 Pengam Caerph
27 P12 Pengam Cardif
21 M8 Penge Gt Lon
4 D4 Pengelly Cnwll
2 H5 Penhallow Cnwll
2 G8 Penhalvean Cnwll
18 H3 Penhill Swindn
28 E10 Penhow Newpt
86 F9 Penicuik Mdloth
96 F2 Penifiler Highld
75 L7 Peninver Ag & B
50 G1 Penistone Barns
76 D10 Penkill S Ayrs
40 B5 Penkridge Staffs
48 H7 Penley Wrexhm
16 C2 Penllyn V Glam
55 L10 Penmachno Conwy
27 P8 Penmaen Caerph
26 D10 Penmaen Swans
55 K6 Penmaenmawr Conwy
47 L7 Penmaenpool Gwynd
16 E3 Penmark V Glam
3 J6 Penmount Crematorium Cnwll
54 G6 Penmynydd IoA
20 E5 Penn Bucks
47 L10 Pennal Gwynd
102 H3 Pennan Abers
47 P10 Pennant Powys
38 G3 Pennerley Shrops
58 C7 Pennines
62 F6 Pennington Cumb
27 M4 Pennorth Powys
20 E4 Penn Street Bucks
62 F5 Penny Bridge Cumb
89 L10 Pennycross Ag & B
89 L10 Pennyghael Ag & B
76 E8 Pennyglen S Ayrs
15 P9 Pennymoor Devon
73 P9 Pennywell Sundld
36 D10 Penparc Cerdgn
28 C7 Penperlleni Mons
4 E8 Penpoll Cnwll
2 F7 Penponds Cnwll
78 D9 Penpont D & G
36 D11 Pen-rhiw Pembks
27 M8 Penrhiwceiber Rhondd
26 G6 Pen Rhiwfawr Neath
36 F11 Penrhiw-llan Cerdgn
36 F10 Penrhiw-pal Cerdgn
46 F5 Penrhos Gwynd
28 E6 Penrhos Mons
55 M5 Penrhyn Bay Conwy
54 H7 Penrhyn Castle Gwynd
47 K4 Penrhyndeudraeth Gwynd
26 C10 Penrice Swans
75 N4 Penrioch N Ayrs
71 Q9 Penrith Cumb
3 K2 Penrose Cnwll
71 N9 Penruddock Cumb
2 H8 Penryn Cnwll
55 P6 Pensarn Conwy
39 N8 Pensax Worcs
17 R9 Penselwood Somset
17 N4 Pensford BaNES
30 C5 Pensham Worcs
73 N9 Penshaw Sundld
11 Q2 Penshurst Kent
4 G6 Pensilva Cnwll
3 M6 Pentewan Cnwll
54 H8 Pentir Gwynd
2 H4 Pentire Cnwll
34 D7 Pentlow Essex
44 C7 Pentney Norfk
79 P12 Pentonbridge Cumb
19 K10 Penton Mewsey Hants
54 G6 Pentraeth IoA
28 E8 Pentre Mons
27 K9 Pentre Rhondd
48 G11 Pentre Shrops
27 M7 Pentrebach Myr Td
27 J3 Pentre-bach Powys
54 F7 Pentre Berw IoA
48 F6 Pentrebychan Crematorium Wrexhm
48 D5 Pentre-celyn Denbgs
47 P9 Pentre-celyn Powys
26 F9 Pentre-chwyth Swans
25 P2 Pentre-cwrt Carmth
48 E6 Pentredwr Denbgs
47 J4 Pentrefelin Gwynd
55 M10 Pentrefoelas Conwy
36 F9 Pentregat Cerdgn
26 E5 Pentre-Gwenlais Carmth
38 G6 Pentre Hodrey Shrops
48 C3 Pentre Llanrhaeadr Denbgs
16 C2 Pentre Meyrick V Glam
55 M8 Pentre-tafarn-y-fedw Conwy
51 J9 Pentrich Derbys
8 F4 Pentridge Dorset
28 F7 Pen-twyn Mons
27 P9 Pentwynmaur Caerph
27 M11 Pentyrch Cardif
3 M5 Penwithick Cnwll
26 E4 Penybanc Carmth
38 C8 Penybont Powys
48 E10 Pen-y-bont Powys
48 C9 Pen-y-bont-fawr Powys
36 C11 Pen-y-bryn Pembks
48 F6 Penycae Wrexhm
28 E7 Pen-y-clawdd Mons
27 M10 Pen-y-coedcae Rhondd
24 E4 Pen-y-cwn Pembks
48 D2 Pen-y-felin Flints
48 F4 Penyffordd Flints
48 C10 Pen-y-Garnedd Powys
46 C5 Pen-y-graig Gwynd
27 L10 Penygraig Rhondd
26 D6 Penygroes Carmth
54 F10 Penygroes Gwynd
26 C7 Pen-y-Mynydd Carmth
48 F3 Penymynydd Flints
54 F4 Penysarn IoA
48 E5 Pen-y-stryt Denbgs
27 K7 Penywaun Rhondd
2 D9 Penzance Cnwll
2 D9 Penzance Heliport Cnwll
30 C4 Peopleton Worcs
49 L9 Peplow Shrops
76 F4 Perceton N Ayrs
103 K3 Percyhorner Abers
19 J10 Perham Down Wilts
16 C7 Periton Somset
21 J6 Perivale Gt Lon
6 D5 Perkins Village Devon
51 N6 Perlethorpe Notts
2 H7 Perranarworthal Cnwll
2 H5 Perranporth Cnwll
2 D9 Perranuthnoe Cnwll
2 H7 Perranwell Cnwll
2 H5 Perranzabuloe Cnwll
40 E8 Perry Barr Birm
40 E8 Perry Barr Crematorium Birm
18 E3 Perry Green Wilts
49 P9 Pershall Staffs
30 C5 Pershore Worcs
32 F4 Pertenhall Bed
92 G10 Perth P & K
92 G9 Perth Crematorium P & K
48 G8 Perthy Shrops
28 H2 Perton Herefs
39 Q3 Perton Staffs
42 H9 Peterborough C Pete
42 G9 Peterborough Crematorium C Pete
42 G10 Peterborough Services Cambs
28 D2 Peterchurch Herefs
95 N2 Peterculter C Aber
103 M6 Peterhead Abers
73 Q11 Peterlee Dur
10 C5 Petersfield Hants
32 G11 Peter's Green Herts
21 J8 Petersham Gt Lon
14 H9 Peters Marland Devon
28 B11 Peterstone Wentlooge Newpt
16 E2 Peterston-super-Ely V Glam
28 G4 Peterstow Herefs
5 K5 Peter Tavy Devon
23 L12 Petham Kent
4 G3 Petherwin Gate Cnwll
15 J9 Petrockstow Devon
12 G7 Pett E Susx
35 J5 Pettaugh Suffk
93 M7 Petterden Angus
78 F1 Pettinain S Lans
35 L6 Pettistree Suffk
16 D10 Petton Devon
21 N9 Petts Wood Gt Lon
86 F5 Pettycur Fife
103 J9 Pettymuk Abers
10 F6 Petworth W Susx
12 D8 Pevensey E Susx
12 D8 Pevensey Bay E Susx
18 H8 Pewsey Wilts
30 C3 Phepson Worcs
14 E7 Philham Devon
79 N4 Philiphaugh Border
2 E7 Phillack Cnwll
3 K7 Philleigh Cnwll
86 C6 Philpstoun W Loth
20 C11 Phoenix Green Hants
99 K9 Phones Highld
17 L10 Pibsbury Somset
59 L11 Pickburn Donc
66 H10 Pickering N York
40 H10 Pickford Covtry
65 N10 Pickhill N York
38 H3 Picklescott Shrops
57 M12 Pickmere Ches E
16 G9 Pickney Somset
42 B7 Pickwell Leics
42 F4 Pickworth Lincs
42 E7 Pickworth Rutlnd
48 H2 Picton Ches W
65 P6 Picton N York
11 N9 Piddinghoe E Susx
32 B6 Piddington Nhants
31 N10 Piddington Oxon
7 Q4 Piddlehinton Dorset
7 Q3 Piddletrenthide Dorset
33 K2 Pidley Cambs
65 L4 Piercebridge Darltn
111 h1 Pierowall Ork
22 C4 Pilgrims Hatch Essex
52 C5 Pilham Lincs
4 H7 Pillaton Cnwll
30 H4 Pillerton Hersey Warwks
30 H5 Pillerton Priors Warwks
51 J1 Pilley Barns
9 K7 Pilley Hants
62 H11 Pilling Lancs
28 G10 Pilning S Glos
50 E7 Pilsbury Derbys
7 K3 Pilsdon Dorset
50 G6 Pilsley Derbys
51 K8 Pilsley Derbys
45 N7 Pilson Green Norfk
11 N5 Piltdown E Susx
15 K5 Pilton Devon
42 E12 Pilton Nhants
42 D9 Pilton Rutlnd
17 N7 Pilton Somset
8 D5 Pimperne Dorset
43 J5 Pinchbeck Lincs
33 J10 Pin Green Herts
6 C4 Pinhoe Devon
30 G2 Pinley Green Warwks
76 D11 Pinminnoch S Ayrs
76 D11 Pinmore S Ayrs
6 E5 Pinn Devon
20 H5 Pinner Gt Lon
20 H5 Pinner Green Gt Lon
30 C4 Pinvin Worcs
68 G2 Pinwherry S Ayrs
51 L9 Pinxton Derbys
39 J12 Pipe and Lyde Herefs
39 J7 Pipe Aston Herefs
49 N7 Pipe Gate Shrops
100 D5 Piperhill Highld
42 B11 Pipewell Nhants
20 F11 Pirbright Surrey
80 E8 Pirnie Border
75 N4 Pirnmill N Ayrs
32 G9 Pirton Herts
20 B5 Pishill Oxon
46 E3 Pistyll Gwynd
92 C3 Pitagowan P & K
103 K3 Pitblae Abers
92 F9 Pitcairngreen P & K
107 N7 Pitcalnie Highld
102 F9 Pitcaple Abers
94 F8 Pitcarity Angus
29 L7 Pitchcombe Gloucs
31 Q9 Pitchcott Bucks
39 K2 Pitchford Shrops
20 C3 Pitch Green Bucks
101 J7 Pitchroy Moray
17 P9 Pitcombe Somset
87 M7 Pitcox E Loth
102 E11 Pitfichie Abers
102 F6 Pitglassie Abers
107 N4 Pitgrudy Highld
86 G1 Pitlessie Fife
92 D4 Pitlochry P & K
102 E9 Pitmachie Abers
99 L8 Pitmain Highld
103 J9 Pitmedden Abers
103 J9 Pitmedden Garden Abers
16 G11 Pitminster Somset
93 P6 Pitmuies Angus
102 E11 Pitmunie Abers
17 L9 Pitney Somset
93 J10 Pitroddie P & K
93 M11 Pitscottie Fife
22 E6 Pitsea Essex
31 Q1 Pitsford Nhants
20 F1 Pitstone Bucks
95 M7 Pittarrow Abers
87 K2 Pittenweem Fife
86 F3 Pitteuchar Fife
73 N11 Pittington Dur
102 F9 Pittodrie House Hotel Abers
8 H2 Pitton Wilts
103 K2 Pittulie Abers
73 M10 Pity Me Dur
21 J12 Pixham Surrey
85 N9 Plains N Lans
39 K3 Plaish Shrops
21 N6 Plaistow Gt Lon
10 G4 Plaistow W Susx
9 J4 Plaitford Hants
22 D11 Platt Kent
73 M10 Plawsworth Dur
22 C11 Plaxtol Kent
12 H6 Playden E Susx
35 K7 Playford Suffk
20 B7 Play Hatch Oxon
3 J7 Playing Place Cnwll
29 K3 Playley Green Gloucs
38 H2 Plealey Shrops
85 P5 Plean Stirlg
93 J12 Pleasance Fife
57 M4 Pleasington Bl w D
57 M4 Pleasington Crematorium Bl w D
51 L7 Pleasley Derbys
49 J2 Plemstall Ches W
22 D1 Pleshey Essex
97 L3 Plockton Highld
38 H5 Plowden Shrops
12 H2 Pluckley Kent
12 H2 Pluckley Thorne Kent
71 J7 Plumbland Cumb
49 N1 Plumley Ches E
71 P7 Plumpton Cumb
11 M7 Plumpton E Susx
31 N5 Plumpton Nhants
11 M6 Plumpton Green E Susx
21 N7 Plumstead Gt Lon
45 J3 Plumstead Norfk
41 N2 Plumtree Notts
41 Q1 Plungar Leics
12 H3 Plurenden Kent
7 Q3 Plush Dorset
36 F9 Plwmp Cerdgn
5 K8 Plymouth C Plym
5 K7 Plymouth Airport C Plym
5 L8 Plympton C Plym
5 L9 Plymstock C Plym
6 E3 Plymtree Devon
66 F9 Pockley N York
60 D4 Pocklington E R Yk
17 M10 Podimore Somset
32 D4 Podington Bed
49 P8 Podmore Staffs
42 G4 Pointon Lincs
8 G8 Pokesdown Bmouth
105 Q1 Polbain Highld
4 H8 Polbathic Cnwll
86 B9 Polbeth W Loth
2 G9 Poldark Mine Cnwll
42 F11 Polebrook Nhants
12 C8 Polegate E Susx
40 H7 Polesworth Warwks
105 Q2 Polglass Highld
3 M5 Polgooth Cnwll
77 M9 Polgown D & G
10 G8 Poling W Susx
10 G8 Poling Corner W Susx
4 D9 Polkerris Cnwll
59 N9 Pollington E R Yk
89 Q3 Polloch Highld
85 J10 Pollokshaws C Glas
85 J9 Pollokshields C Glas
3 L6 Polmassick Cnwll
85 Q7 Polmont Falk
97 K12 Polnish Highld
4 F9 Polperro Cnwll
4 E9 Polruan Cnwll
34 G8 Polstead Suffk
83 M4 Poltalloch Ag & B
6 C4 Poltimore Devon
86 F8 Polton Mdloth
80 G4 Polwarth Border
4 G4 Polyphant Cnwll
4 B4 Polzeath Cnwll
86 F9 Pomathorn Mdloth
43 J10 Pondersbridge Cambs
21 M4 Ponders End Gt Lon
2 H8 Ponsanooth Cnwll
5 N5 Ponsworthy Devon
26 D7 Pont Abraham Services Carmth
25 Q6 Pontantwn Carmth
26 F7 Pontardawe Neath
26 D7 Pontarddulais Swans
26 C5 Pont-ar-gothi Carmth
25 Q3 Pontarsais Carmth
48 F4 Pontblyddyn Flints
59 L9 Pontefract Wakefd
59 K9 Pontefract Crematorium Wakefd
73 L6 Ponteland Nthumb
37 M4 Ponterwyd Cerdgn
38 H2 Pontesbury Shrops
38 H2 Pontesford Shrops
48 E7 Pontfadog Wrexhm
24 H3 Pontfaen Pembks
27 L3 Pont-faen Powys
36 F9 Pontgarreg Cerdgn
26 C7 Ponthenry Carmth
28 C9 Ponthir Torfn
36 D10 Ponthirwaun Cerdgn
27 P9 Pontllanfraith Caerph
26 E8 Pontlliw Swans
27 N7 Pontlottyn Caerph
54 F10 Pontlyfni Gwynd
27 J7 Pontneddfechan Neath
28 C9 Pontnewydd Torfn
37 M7 Pontrhydfendigaid Cerdgn
26 H9 Pont-rhyd-y-fen Neath
37 M6 Pontrhydygroes Cerdgn
28 D4 Pontrilas Herefs
48 C11 Pont Robert Powys
36 G10 Pontshaen Cerdgn
27 M6 Pontsticill Myr Td
36 G11 Pontwelly Carmth
26 C7 Pontyates Carmth
26 C6 Pontyberem Carmth
48 F4 Pontybodkin Flints
27 L11 Pontyclun Rhondd
27 J9 Pontycymer Brdgnd
55 L10 Pont-y-pant Conwy
28 C8 Pontypool Torfn
27 M10 Pontypridd Rhondd
27 P9 Pontywaun Caerph
2 G7 Pool Cnwll
58 G5 Pool Leeds
8 E8 Poole Poole
8 E8 Poole Crematorium Poole
18 E2 Poole Keynes Gloucs
105 M6 Poolewe Highld
71 P10 Pooley Bridge Cumb
50 B8 Poolfold Staffs
29 K3 Poolhill Gloucs
86 B3 Pool of Muckhart Clacks
34 C8 Pool Street Essex
21 M7 Poplar Gt Lon
9 M8 Porchfield IoW
45 L9 Poringland Norfk
2 G8 Porkellis Cnwll
15 Q3 Porlock Somset
15 P3 Porlock Weir Somset
83 L10 Portachoillan Ag & B
97 K4 Port-an-Eorna Highld
90 C7 Port Appin Ag & B
82 F8 Port Askaig Ag & B

83 P8 Portavadie Ag & B
84 B9 Port Bannatyne Ag & B
17 M2 Portbury N Som
71 K3 Port Carlisle Cumb
82 C10 Port Charlotte Ag & B
9 Q6 Portchester Hants
9 Q6 Portchester Crematorium Hants
83 Q8 Port Driseach Ag & B
26 C10 Port Einon Swans
74 E4 Port Ellen Ag & B
102 G10 Port Elphinstone Abers
68 D5 Portencalzie D & G
76 C2 Portencross N Ayrs
56 a6 Port Erin IoM
7 N5 Portesham Dorset
101 N3 Portessie Moray
24 G6 Portfield Gate Pembks
5 J3 Portgate Devon
4 C4 Port Gaverne Cnwll
84 F7 Port Glasgow Inver
101 M3 Portgordon Moray
110 B11 Portgower Highld
3 J4 Porth Cnwll
27 L9 Porth Rhondd
2 H10 Porthallow Cnwll
4 F9 Porthallow Cnwll
26 H12 Porthcawl Brdgnd
3 K2 Porthcothan Cnwll
2 B10 Porthcurno Cnwll
105 L7 Port Henderson Highld
24 E3 Porthgain Pembks
2 B10 Porthgwarra Cnwll
16 E3 Porthkerry V Glam
2 F9 Porthleven Cnwll
47 J4 Porthmadog Gwynd
2 H9 Porth Navas Cnwll
3 J10 Porthoustock Cnwll
3 M5 Porthpean Cnwll
2 G6 Porthtowan Cnwll
26 C5 Porthyrhyd Carmth
84 D4 Portincaple Ag & B
60 D7 Portington E R Yk
83 P2 Portinnisherrich Ag & B
71 L10 Portinscale Cumb
4 C4 Port Isaac Cnwll
17 L2 Portishead N Som
101 N2 Portknockie Moray
7 P8 Portland Dorset
95 Q3 Portlethen Abers
70 E5 Portling D & G
3 L7 Portloe Cnwll
68 E10 Port Logan D & G
107 Q5 Portmahomack Highld
47 J4 Portmeirion Gwynd
3 M7 Portmellon Cnwll
89 J1 Port Mor Highld
90 C6 Portnacroish Ag & B
111 e2 Portnaguran W Isls
74 B2 Portnahaven Ag & B
96 D3 Portnalong Highld
111 e2 Port nan Giuran W Isls
111 b4 Port nan Long W Isls
111 e1 Port Nis W Isls
86 G7 Portobello C Edin
40 C7 Portobello Wolves
85 K3 Port of Menteith Stirlg
111 e1 Port of Ness W Isls
18 H12 Porton Wilts
68 D8 Portpatrick D & G
4 B4 Port Quin Cnwll
90 B7 Port Ramsay Ag & B
2 F6 Portreath Cnwll
96 F2 Portree Highld
56 b7 Port St Mary IoM
3 K8 Portscatho Cnwll
9 Q7 Portsea C Port
109 Q3 Portskerra Highld
28 F10 Portskewett Mons
11 K8 Portslade Br & H
11 L8 Portslade-by-Sea Br & H
68 D7 Portslogan D & G
9 Q7 Portsmouth C Port
58 B8 Portsmouth Calder
56 c6 Port Soderick IoM
90 E11 Portsonachan Hotel Ag & B
102 D3 Portsoy Abers
56 G11 Port Sunlight Wirral
9 M5 Portswood C Sotn
26 G10 Port Talbot Neath
89 K3 Portuairk Highld
40 E11 Portway Worcs
74 B3 Port Wemyss Ag & B
69 J9 Port William D & G
4 H9 Portwrinkle Cnwll
69 L10 Portyerrock D & G
34 C7 Poslingford Suffk
79 K3 Posso Border
5 N4 Postbridge Devon
20 B4 Postcombe Oxon
13 M3 Postling Kent
45 L8 Postwick Norfk
95 K3 Potarch Abers
20 G2 Potten End Herts
67 L11 Potter Brompton N York
52 F9 Potterhanworth Lincs
52 F9 Potterhanworth Booths Lincs
45 N6 Potter Heigham Norfk
18 E8 Potterne Wilts
18 E8 Potterne Wick Wilts
21 K3 Potters Bar Herts
20 H3 Potters Crouch Herts
41 J10 Potters Green Covtry
41 L8 Potters Marston Leics
31 Q5 Potterspury Nhants
103 K11 Potterton Abers
66 C6 Potto N York
32 H6 Potton C Beds
50 C5 Pott Shrigley Ches E
14 D10 Poughill Cnwll
15 P9 Poughill Devon
8 H6 Poulner Hants
18 E8 Poulshot Wilts
18 G1 Poulton Gloucs
56 G2 Poulton-le-Fylde Lancs
26 D9 Poundffald Swans
11 P5 Pound Green E Susx
34 C6 Pound Green Suffk
11 L3 Pound Hill W Susx
31 N8 Poundon Bucks
5 N6 Poundsgate Devon
14 D11 Poundstock Cnwll
69 L9 Pouton D & G
11 L2 Povey Cross Surrey
81 M10 Powburn Nthumb
6 C6 Powderham Devon
7 M4 Powerstock Dorset
71 J3 Powfoot D & G
39 Q10 Powick Worcs
86 B3 Powmill P & K
7 Q6 Poxwell Dorset
20 G7 Poyle Slough
11 L7 Poynings W Susx
17 P11 Poyntington Dorset
50 B4 Poynton Ches E
49 K10 Poynton Green Wrekin
2 E9 Praa Sands Cnwll
21 P10 Pratt's Bottom Gt Lon
2 F8 Praze-an-Beeble Cnwll
49 K8 Prees Shrops
62 G11 Preesall Lancs
49 K8 Prees Green Shrops
49 K7 Prees Heath Shrops
49 K8 Prees Higher Heath Shrops
36 G10 Pren-gwyn Cerdgn
47 J3 Prenteg Gwynd
57 J9 Prescot Knows
16 E12 Prescott Devon
94 C8 Presnerb Angus
56 C11 Prestatyn Denbgs
50 B5 Prestbury Ches E
29 N4 Prestbury Gloucs
38 G8 Presteigne Powys
17 P7 Prestleigh Somset
87 P10 Preston Border
11 L8 Preston Br & H
6 B7 Preston Devon
7 Q6 Preston Dorset
61 K7 Preston E R Yk
18 F1 Preston Gloucs
32 H10 Preston Herts
23 K10 Preston Kent
23 N10 Preston Kent
57 K3 Preston Lancs
81 P8 Preston Nthumb
42 C9 Preston Rutlnd
16 E8 Preston Somset
34 F6 Preston Suffk
6 B9 Preston Torbay
18 F5 Preston Wilts
30 F2 Preston Bagot Warwks
31 P8 Preston Bissett Bucks
16 F10 Preston Bowyer Somset
49 K9 Preston Brockhurst Shrops
57 K11 Preston Brook Halton
19 Q11 Preston Candover Hants
31 M3 Preston Capes Nhants
57 L3 Preston Crematorium Lancs
30 F2 Preston Green Warwks
49 J10 Preston Gubbals Shrops
30 G4 Preston on Stour Warwks
57 K11 Preston on the Hill Halton
28 D1 Preston on Wye Herefs
86 H7 Prestonpans E Loth
63 K5 Preston Patrick Cumb
17 M11 Preston Plucknett Somset
65 J8 Preston-under-Scar N York
49 M11 Preston upon the Weald Moors Wrekin
39 K11 Preston Wynne Herefs
57 P7 Prestwich Bury
76 F6 Prestwick S Ayrs
76 F6 Prestwick Airport S Ayrs
20 E4 Prestwood Bucks
33 P1 Prickwillow Cambs
17 M6 Priddy Somset
63 K7 Priest Hutton Lancs
77 J4 Priestland E Ayrs
38 F3 Priest Weston Shrops
87 P10 Primrosehill Border
80 H8 Primsidemill Border
20 D3 Princes Risborough Bucks
41 K12 Princethorpe Warwks
5 M5 Princetown Devon
31 J3 Priors Hardwick Warwks
49 N12 Priorslee Wrekin
31 J3 Priors Marston Warwks
29 M4 Priors Norton Gloucs
18 G3 Priory Vale Swindn
17 Q4 Priston BaNES
22 G6 Prittlewell Sthend
10 B5 Privett Hants
15 J5 Prixford Devon
3 K6 Probus Cnwll
87 K6 Prora E Loth
71 J7 Prospect Cumb
2 F9 Prospidnick Cnwll
102 H3 Protstonhill Abers
73 K8 Prudhoe Nthumb
17 P4 Publow BaNES
33 L11 Puckeridge Herts
17 K11 Puckington Somset
17 Q2 Pucklechurch S Glos
48 G2 Puddington Ches W
15 P9 Puddington Devon
7 Q4 Puddletown Dorset
58 G7 Pudsey Leeds
10 G6 Pulborough W Susx
48 G4 Pulford Ches W
7 Q2 Pulham Dorset
45 K11 Pulham Market Norfk
45 K11 Pulham St Mary Norfk
32 F9 Pulloxhill C Beds
86 C8 Pumpherston W Loth
37 K11 Pumsaint Carmth
24 H3 Puncheston Pembks
7 M5 Puncknowle Dorset
12 C6 Punnett's Town E Susx
10 A8 Purbrook Hants
22 B7 Purfleet Thurr
17 J7 Puriton Somset
22 G3 Purleigh Essex
21 L10 Purley Gt Lon
19 Q5 Purley W Berk
17 Q11 Purse Caundle Dorset
7 K2 Purtington Somset
29 J7 Purton Gloucs
29 J7 Purton Gloucs
18 G4 Purton Wilts
18 G3 Purton Stoke Wilts
31 P5 Pury End Nhants
19 L2 Pusey Oxon
28 H2 Putley Herefs
28 H2 Putley Green Herefs
21 K8 Putney Gt Lon
21 K8 Putney Vale Crematorium Gt Lon
10 E1 Puttenham Surrey
31 Q6 Puxley Nhants
17 K4 Puxton N Som
26 C8 Pwll Carmth
48 C5 Pwll-glas Denbgs
27 L3 Pwllgloyw Powys
46 F4 Pwllheli Gwynd
28 F9 Pwllmeyric Mons
25 M5 Pwll Trap Carmth
26 H9 Pwll-y-glaw Neath
51 K9 Pye Bridge Derbys
11 L7 Pyecombe W Susx
26 H11 Pyle Brdgnd
16 F9 Pyleigh Somset
17 N8 Pylle Somset
43 M11 Pymoor Cambs
7 L4 Pymore Dorset
20 G10 Pyrford Surrey
20 B4 Pyrton Oxon
32 C2 Pytchley Nhants
14 F10 Pyworthy Devon

Q

42 H4 Quadring Lincs
43 J4 Quadring Eaudike Lincs
31 Q9 Quainton Bucks
16 G8 Quantock Hills Somset
111 k4 Quarff Shet
19 J11 Quarley Hants
51 J11 Quarndon Derbys
84 F9 Quarrier's Village Inver
42 F2 Quarrington Lincs
73 N12 Quarrington Hill Dur
40 B9 Quarry Bank Dudley
101 J3 Quarrywood Moray
84 D10 Quarter N Ayrs
85 M11 Quarter S Lans
39 N4 Quatford Shrops
39 N5 Quatt Shrops
73 L11 Quebec Dur
29 L6 Quedgeley Gloucs
33 P1 Queen Adelaide Cambs
22 H8 Queenborough Kent
17 N10 Queen Camel Somset
17 P3 Queen Charlton BaNES
84 H3 Queen Elizabeth Forest Park Stirlg
29 M2 Queenhill Worcs
8 B2 Queen Oak Dorset
9 P9 Queen's Bower IoW
58 E7 Queensbury C Brad
48 G2 Queensferry Flints
85 L9 Queenslie C Glas
85 L7 Queenzieburn N Lans
33 N10 Quendon Essex
41 N5 Queniborough Leics
30 F12 Quenington Gloucs
40 E8 Queslett Birm
4 G7 Quethiock Cnwll
44 G11 Quidenham Norfk
8 G2 Quidhampton Wilts
31 R4 Quinton Nhants
3 J4 Quintrell Downs Cnwll
87 P9 Quixwood Border
92 C10 Quoig P & K
41 M4 Quorn Leics
78 G2 Quothquan S Lans
111 h2 Quoyburray Ork
111 g2 Quoyloo Ork

R

96 G2 Raasay Highld
79 J3 Rachan Mill Border
55 J7 Rachub Gwynd
15 P8 Rackenford Devon
10 G7 Rackham W Susx
45 L7 Rackheath Norfk
70 G1 Racks D & G
111 g3 Rackwick Ork
40 H1 Radbourne Derbys
57 P7 Radcliffe Bury
51 N11 Radcliffe on Trent Notts
31 P7 Radclive Bucks
107 L9 Raddery Highld
87 J1 Radernie Fife
41 J10 Radford Covtry
31 J2 Radford Semele Warwks
21 J4 Radlett Herts
19 N2 Radley Oxon
22 D3 Radley Green Essex
20 C4 Radnage Bucks
17 P5 Radstock BaNES
31 N6 Radstone Nhants
31 J5 Radway Warwks
32 E5 Radwell Bed
32 H9 Radwell Herts
33 P8 Radwinter Essex
27 N11 Radyr Cardif
100 G4 Rafford Moray
41 P4 Ragdale Leics
28 E7 Raglan Mons
52 B8 Ragnall Notts
99 M4 Raigbeg Highld
39 Q10 Rainbow Hill Worcs
57 J8 Rainford St Hel
21 Q7 Rainham Gt Lon
22 F9 Rainham Medway
57 J9 Rainhill St Hel
57 J10 Rainhill Stoops St Hel
50 C6 Rainow Ches E
65 P11 Rainton N York
51 N8 Rainworth Notts
93 J9 Rait P & K
53 K6 Raithby Lincs
53 L9 Raithby Lincs
10 C5 Rake Hants
99 K9 Ralia Highld
96 A2 Ramasaig Highld
2 G8 Rame Cnwll
5 J9 Rame Cnwll
7 N3 Rampisham Dorset
62 E8 Rampside Cumb
33 L3 Rampton Cambs
52 B7 Rampton Notts
57 P5 Ramsbottom Bury
19 J6 Ramsbury Wilts
110 D9 Ramscraigs Highld
10 B5 Ramsdean Hants
19 P8 Ramsdell Hants
31 J10 Ramsden Oxon
22 E5 Ramsden Bellhouse Essex
43 J11 Ramsey Cambs
35 K10 Ramsey Essex
56 e3 Ramsey IoM
43 K11 Ramsey Forty Foot Cambs
43 J12 Ramsey Heights Cambs
23 J3 Ramsey Island Essex
24 C4 Ramsey Island Pembks
43 J11 Ramsey Mereside Cambs
43 J11 Ramsey St Mary's Cambs
23 Q9 Ramsgate Kent
65 K12 Ramsgill N York
80 G12 Ramshope Nthumb
50 E10 Ramshorn Staffs
10 F4 Ramsnest Common Surrey
52 H7 Ranby Lincs
51 P5 Ranby Notts
52 G7 Rand Lincs
21 J11 Randalls Park Crematorium Surrey
29 L7 Randwick Gloucs
84 G9 Ranfurly Rens
40 F3 Rangemore Staffs
29 J10 Rangeworthy S Glos
76 H8 Rankinston E Ayrs
91 L5 Rannoch Station P & K
16 C7 Ranscombe Somset
51 P4 Ranskill Notts
49 Q10 Ranton Staffs
49 Q10 Ranton Green Staffs
45 M7 Ranworth Norfk
85 N4 Raploch Stirlg
111 h1 Rapness Ork
70 D6 Rascarrel D & G
84 C6 Rashfield Ag & B
30 B2 Rashwood Worcs
66 C12 Raskelf N York
58 F9 Rastrick Calder
97 N6 Ratagan Highld
41 L6 Ratby Leics
41 J7 Ratcliffe Culey Leics
41 L2 Ratcliffe on Soar Notts
41 N5 Ratcliffe on the Wreake Leics
103 K3 Rathen Abers
93 L10 Rathillet Fife
63 P9 Rathmell N York
86 D7 Ratho C Edin
86 D7 Ratho Station C Edin
101 N3 Rathven Moray
31 J5 Ratley Warwks
23 N11 Ratling Kent
38 H3 Ratlinghope Shrops
110 F2 Rattar Highld
5 P7 Rattery Devon
34 F5 Rattlesden Suffk
12 C9 Ratton Village E Susx
92 H6 Rattray P & K
32 E3 Raunds Nhants
51 L2 Ravenfield Rothm
62 C3 Ravenglass Cumb
45 N10 Raveningham Norfk
67 L7 Ravenscar N York
32 F6 Ravensden Bed
51 M9 Ravenshead Notts
58 G9 Ravensthorpe Kirk
41 P12 Ravensthorpe Nhants
41 K5 Ravenstone Leics
32 C6 Ravenstone M Keyn
63 N2 Ravenstonedale Cumb
77 Q3 Ravenstruther S Lans
65 K6 Ravensworth N York
59 M4 Rawcliffe C York
59 P9 Rawcliffe E R Yk
58 G6 Rawdon Leeds
58 G6 Rawdon Crematorium Leeds
22 H10 Rawling Street Kent
51 K2 Rawmarsh Rothm
22 F5 Rawreth Essex
6 G2 Rawridge Devon
57 P4 Rawtenstall Lancs
34 H8 Raydon Suffk
22 F5 Rayleigh Essex
34 C11 Rayne Essex
21 K9 Raynes Park Gt Lon
33 P4 Reach Cambs
57 P2 Read Lancs
20 B8 Reading Readg
20 B8 Reading Crematorium Readg
20 A9 Reading Services W Berk
12 H4 Reading Street Kent
23 Q9 Reading Street Kent
64 B4 Reagill Cumb
2 F8 Realwa Cnwll
107 M4 Rearquhar Highld
41 P5 Rearsby Leics
110 A3 Reay Highld
23 N9 Reculver Kent
16 E11 Red Ball Devon
25 J7 Redberth Pembks
20 H2 Redbourn Herts
52 D4 Redbourne N Linc
28 G6 Redbrook Gloucs
49 K7 Redbrook Wrexhm
12 H3 Redbrook Street Kent
100 E6 Redburn Highld
66 E3 Redcar R & Cl
70 D3 Redcastle D & G
107 J11 Redcastle Highld
85 Q7 Redding Falk
85 Q7 Reddingmuirhead Falk
30 D1 Redditch Worcs
30 D1 Redditch Crematorium Worcs
34 D5 Rede Suffk
45 L12 Redenhall Norfk
72 F5 Redesmouth Nthumb
95 M7 Redford Abers
93 P6 Redford Angus
10 D5 Redford W Susx
79 M6 Redfordgreen Border
92 G9 Redgorton P & K
34 H2 Redgrave Suffk
95 M2 Redhill Abers
8 G8 Red Hill Bmouth
33 J9 Redhill Herts
17 M4 Redhill N Som
21 L12 Redhill Surrey
45 N12 Redisham Suffk
17 N2 Redland Bristl
111 h2 Redland Ork
35 K3 Redlingfield Suffk
35 K3 Redlingfield Green Suffk
33 B3 Red Lodge Suffk
17 Q9 Redlynch Somset
8 H3 Redlynch Wilts
39 N8 Redmarley Worcs
29 K3 Redmarley D'Abitot Gloucs
65 P4 Redmarshall S on T
42 B3 Redmile Leics
65 J8 Redmire N York
95 M6 Redmyre Abers
48 G9 Rednal Shrops
80 D7 Redpath Border
105 K8 Redpoint Highld
25 L6 Red Roses Carmth
73 M2 Red Row Nthumb
2 G7 Redruth Cnwll
92 H8 Redstone P & K
54 G5 Red Wharf Bay IoA
28 E11 Redwick Newpt
28 G10 Redwick S Glos
65 M3 Redworth Darltn
33 K9 Reed Herts
45 N9 Reedham Norfk
60 D9 Reedness E R Yk
57 P4 Reeds Holme Lancs
52 E8 Reepham Lincs
44 H5 Reepham Norfk
65 J7 Reeth N York
40 H11 Reeves Green Solhll
17 M4 Regil N Som
108 A11 Reiff Highld
21 K12 Reigate Surrey
67 N11 Reighton N York
103 J10 Reisque Abers
110 G5 Reiss Highld
2 E8 Relubbus Cnwll
100 F5 Relugas Moray
20 C6 Remenham Wokham
20 C6 Remenham Hill Wokham
41 M3 Rempstone Notts
30 D11 Rendcomb Gloucs
35 M4 Rendham Suffk
35 M6 Rendlesham Suffk
84 H9 Renfrew Rens
32 F6 Renhold Bed
51 K5 Renishaw Derbys
81 P9 Rennington Nthumb
84 G7 Renton W Duns
72 B11 Renwick Cumb
45 N6 Repps Norfk
40 H3 Repton Derbys
107 L12 Resaurie Highld
89 P4 Resipole Highld
2 F7 Reskadinnick Cnwll
107 L8 Resolis Highld
26 H8 Resolven Neath
84 D2 Rest and be thankful Ag & B
87 R9 Reston Border
93 N5 Reswallie Angus
51 P5 Retford Notts
22 F4 Rettendon Essex
53 J10 Revesby Lincs
6 C3 Rewe Devon
9 M8 Rew Street IoW
35 P2 Reydon Suffk
44 G8 Reymerston Norfk
25 J7 Reynalton Pembks
26 C10 Reynoldston Swans
4 H5 Rezare Cnwll
37 M11 Rhandirmwyn Carmth
37 Q7 Rhayader Powys
106 H11 Rheindown Highld
48 E2 Rhes-y-cae Flints
48 C4 Rhewl Denbgs
48 D6 Rhewl Denbgs
108 C10 Rhicarn Highld
108 E5 Rhiconich Highld
107 L7 Rhicullen Highld
27 K7 Rhigos Rhondd
105 Q4 Rhireavach Highld
107 N3 Rhives Highld
27 N11 Rhiwbina Cardif
28 B10 Rhiwderyn Newpt
54 H8 Rhiwlas Gwynd
12 D2 Rhoden Green Kent
13 M2 Rhodes Minnis Kent
24 D4 Rhodiad-y-brenin Pembks
70 C4 Rhonehouse D & G
16 E3 Rhoose V Glam
25 P2 Rhos Carmth
26 G8 Rhos Neath
54 C6 Rhoscolyn IoA
24 F8 Rhoscrowther Pembks
48 E2 Rhosemor Flints
38 E11 Rhosgoch Powys
36 C11 Rhoshill Pembks
46 C5 Rhoshirwaun Gwynd
47 J9 Rhoslefain Gwynd
48 F6 Rhosllanerchrugog Wrexhm
54 F6 Rhosmeirch IoA
54 D7 Rhosneigr IoA
48 G5 Rhosnesni Wrexhm
55 M5 Rhôs-on-Sea Conwy
25 P10 Rhossili Swans
54 G9 Rhostryfan Gwynd
48 F6 Rhostyllen Wrexhm
54 F4 Rhosybol IoA
47 Q4 Rhos-y-gwaliau Gwynd
48 F7 Rhosymedre Wrexhm
84 E6 Rhu Ag & B
48 C1 Rhualit Denbgs
83 Q8 Rhubodach Ag & B
55 Q6 Rhuddlan Denbgs
75 K3 Rhunahaorine Ag & B
47 K3 Rhyd Gwynd
25 Q4 Rhydargaeau Carmth
26 D2 Rhydcymerau Carmth
54 H10 Rhyd-Ddu Gwynd
36 F10 Rhydlewis Cerdgn
36 G10 Rhydowen Cerdgn
47 P4 Rhyd-uchaf Gwynd
46 E4 Rhyd-y-clafdy Gwynd
55 N6 Rhyd-y-foel Conwy
26 F7 Rhydyfro Neath
54 H8 Rhyd-y-groes Gwynd
37 K4 Rhyd-y pennau Cerdgn
55 Q5 Rhyl Denbgs
27 N7 Rhymney Caerph
92 H10 Rhynd P & K
101 P9 Rhynie Abers
107 P6 Rhynie Highld
39 P7 Ribbesford Worcs
57 K3 Ribbleton Lancs
57 M2 Ribchester Lancs
52 H3 Riby Lincs
59 N6 Riccall N York
79 Q9 Riccarton Border
76 G4 Riccarton E Ayrs
39 J8 Richards Castle Herefs
21 J8 Richmond Gt Lon
65 L7 Richmond N York
51 K4 Richmond Sheff
40 B4 Rickerscote Staffs
17 L4 Rickford N Som
5 P11 Rickham Devon
34 H2 Rickinghall Suffk
33 N10 Rickling Green Essex
20 G5 Rickmansworth Herts
80 C8 Riddell Border
15 K8 Riddlecombe Devon
58 E5 Riddlesden C Brad
8 D9 Ridge Dorset
21 K4 Ridge Herts
8 D2 Ridge Wilts
40 H8 Ridge Lane Warwks
51 K5 Ridgeway Derbys
34 C8 Ridgewell Essex
11 P6 Ridgewood E Susx
32 D9 Ridgmont C Beds
72 H8 Riding Mill Nthumb
45 M4 Ridlington Norfk
42 C9 Ridlington Rutlnd
72 G4 Ridsdale Nthumb
66 E9 Rievaulx N York
66 E9 Rievaulx Abbey N York
71 L3 Rigg D & G
85 M8 Riggend N Lans
100 D5 Righoul Highld
53 L8 Rigsby Lincs
78 E2 Rigside S Lans
57 L4 Riley Green Lancs
4 G5 Rilla Mill Cnwll
67 J11 Rillington N York
63 P11 Rimington Lancs

17 N10 Rimpton Somset
61 M8 Rimswell E R Yk
24 H4 Rinaston Pembks
39 N3 Rindleford Shrops
69 Q7 Ringford D & G
45 J7 Ringland Norfk
11 N7 Ringmer E Susx
5 N10 Ringmore Devon
6 C8 Ringmore Devon
101 K6 Ringorm Moray
45 N11 Ringsfield Suffk
45 N11 Ringsfield Corner Suffk
21 P11 Ringshall Herts
34 G6 Ringshall Suffk
34 H6 Ringshall Stocks Suffk
32 E2 Ringstead Nhants
44 B3 Ringstead Norfk
8 H6 Ringwood Hants
13 Q1 Ringwould Kent
11 P7 Ripe E Susx
51 K10 Ripley Derbys
8 H7 Ripley Hants
58 H3 Ripley N York
20 G11 Ripley Surrey
9 Q3 Riplington Hants
65 N12 Ripon N York
42 F5 Rippingale Lincs
23 Q12 Ripple Kent
29 M2 Ripple Worcs
58 D9 Ripponden Calder
74 D4 Risabus Ag & B
39 K10 Risbury Herefs
34 D4 Risby Suffk
27 P9 Risca Caerph
61 K6 Rise E R Yk
42 H4 Risegate Lincs
32 F4 Riseley Bed
20 B10 Riseley Wokham
35 J3 Rishangles Suffk
57 N3 Rishton Lancs
58 D9 Rishworth Calder
41 L1 Risley Derbys
57 M9 Risley Warrtn
58 G1 Risplith N York
13 P2 River Kent
10 F5 River W Susx
107 J10 Riverford Highld
21 P11 Riverhead Kent
57 L6 Rivington Lancs
31 Q4 Roade Nhants
77 P2 Roadmeetings S Lans
77 K7 Roadside E Ayrs
110 D4 Roadside Highld
16 D8 Roadwater Somset
96 C2 Roag Highld
76 E9 Roan of Craigoch S Ayrs
27 P12 Roath Cardif
79 N6 Roberton Border
78 F3 Roberton S Lans
12 E5 Robertsbridge E Susx
58 G9 Roberttown Kirk
25 J5 Robeston Wathen Pembks
71 L2 Robgill Tower D & G
40 E10 Robin Hood Crematorium Solhll
51 P2 Robin Hood Doncaster Sheffield Airport Donc
67 K6 Robin Hood's Bay N York
5 K7 Roborough Devon
15 K8 Roborough Devon
56 H10 Roby Knows
50 E11 Rocester Staffs
24 F5 Roch Pembks
58 B10 Rochdale Rochdl
57 Q6 Rochdale Crematorium Rochdl
3 L4 Roche Cnwll
22 E9 Rochester Medway
72 E2 Rochester Nthumb
22 G5 Rochford Essex
39 L8 Rochford Worcs
3 L1 Rock Cnwll
81 P9 Rock Nthumb
39 N7 Rock Worcs
6 D4 Rockbeare Devon
8 G4 Rockbourne Hants
71 M4 Rockcliffe Cumb
70 D5 Rockcliffe D & G
6 C9 Rockend Torbay
56 G10 Rock Ferry Wirral
107 Q6 Rockfield Highld
28 F6 Rockfield Mons
15 N3 Rockford Devon
28 H9 Rockhampton S Glos
38 F6 Rockhill Shrops
42 C10 Rockingham Nhants
44 G10 Rockland All Saints Norfk
45 M8 Rockland St Mary Norfk
44 G9 Rockland St Peter Norfk
51 Q6 Rockley Notts
84 D5 Rockville Ag & B
20 C6 Rockwell End Bucks
29 L7 Rodborough Gloucs
18 G4 Rodbourne Swindn
18 D4 Rodbourne Wilts
7 N6 Rodden Dorset
18 B9 Rode Somset
49 P4 Rode Heath Ches E
111 c4 Rodel W Isls
49 L11 Roden Wrekin
16 D8 Rodhuish Somset
49 L11 Rodington Wrekin
49 L11 Rodington Heath Wrekin
29 K6 Rodley Gloucs
29 N8 Rodmarton Gloucs
11 N8 Rodmell E Susx
22 H10 Rodmersham Kent
22 H10 Rodmersham Green Kent
17 L6 Rodney Stoke Somset
50 G11 Rodsley Derbys
59 J2 Roecliffe N York
21 K2 Roe Green Herts
33 K9 Roe Green Herts
21 K8 Roehampton Gt Lon
11 K4 Roffey W Susx
107 M2 Rogart Highld
10 D5 Rogate W Susx
28 C10 Rogerstone Newpt
111 c4 Roghadal W Isls
28 E10 Rogiet Mons
19 Q3 Roke Oxon
73 P8 Roker Sundld
45 P7 Rollesby Norfk
41 Q7 Rolleston Leics
51 Q9 Rolleston Notts
40 G3 Rolleston on Dove Staffs
61 L5 Rolston E R Yk
12 G4 Rolvenden Kent
12 G4 Rolvenden Layne Kent
64 H3 Romaldkirk Dur
17 Q3 Roman Baths & Pump Room BaNES
65 P8 Romanby N York
86 D11 Romanno Bridge Border
15 M7 Romansleigh Devon
104 E10 Romesdal Highld
8 F5 Romford Dorset
21 P5 Romford Gt Lon
50 C3 Romiley Stockp
9 L3 Romsey Hants
39 P5 Romsley Shrops
40 C10 Romsley Worcs
105 J10 Rona Highld
83 L11 Ronachan Ag & B
72 G11 Rookhope Dur
9 N9 Rookley IoW
17 K5 Rooks Bridge Somset
16 E9 Rooks Nest Somset
65 L9 Rookwith N York
61 M7 Roos E R Yk
32 F5 Roothams Green Bed
9 Q2 Ropley Hants
9 Q2 Ropley Dean Hants
42 E4 Ropsley Lincs
103 L5 Rora Abers
38 F3 Rorrington Shrops
101 M5 Rosarie Moray
2 H5 Rose Cnwll
15 N7 Rose Ash Devon
77 N2 Rosebank S Lans
25 J3 Rosebush Pembks
66 G8 Rosedale Abbey N York
34 E10 Rose Green Essex
34 F7 Rose Green Suffk
34 F8 Rose Green Suffk
10 E9 Rose Green W Susx
106 H2 Rosehall Highld
103 J2 Rosehearty Abers
57 P3 Rose Hill Lancs
100 H2 Roseisle Moray
12 C9 Roselands E Susx
24 G7 Rosemarket Pembks
107 M10 Rosemarkie Highld
16 F12 Rosemary Lane Devon
92 H7 Rosemount P & K
3 L3 Rosenannon Cnwll
86 F9 Rosewell Mdloth
65 Q3 Roseworth S on T
71 Q11 Rosgill Cumb
96 C1 Roskhill Highld
71 M6 Rosley Cumb
86 F9 Roslin Mdloth
40 G4 Rosliston Derbys
84 E6 Rosneath Ag & B
69 P9 Ross D & G
48 G4 Rossett Wrexhm
58 H4 Rossett Green N York
51 N2 Rossington Donc
84 G8 Rossland Rens
28 H4 Ross-on-Wye Herefs
110 F7 Roster Highld
57 N11 Rostherne Ches E
71 L11 Rosthwaite Cumb
50 F11 Roston Derbys
86 D5 Rosyth Fife
73 J1 Rothbury Nthumb
41 P4 Rotherby Leics
12 B4 Rotherfield E Susx
20 B7 Rotherfield Greys Oxon
20 B7 Rotherfield Peppard Oxon
51 K3 Rotherham Rothm
51 L3 Rotherham Crematorium Rothm
31 Q3 Rothersthorpe Nhants
31 Q3 Rothersthorpe Services Nhants
20 B11 Rotherwick Hants
101 K5 Rothes Moray
84 B9 Rothesay Ag & B
102 G7 Rothiebrisbane Abers
102 D5 Rothiemay Moray
99 P7 Rothiemurchus Lodge Highld
102 F7 Rothienorman Abers
41 N5 Rothley Leics
102 F8 Rothmaise Abers
59 J8 Rothwell Leeds
52 G4 Rothwell Lincs
32 B1 Rothwell Nhants
94 F7 Rottal Lodge Angus
11 M9 Rottingdean Br & H
70 F11 Rottington Cumb
78 G12 Roucan D & G
78 G12 Roucan Loch Crematorium D & G
44 D6 Rougham Norfk
34 E4 Rougham Green Suffk
23 L10 Rough Common Kent
101 L11 Roughpark Abers
53 J9 Roughton Lincs
45 K3 Roughton Norfk
39 N4 Roughton Shrops
22 C1 Roundbush Green Essex
32 F11 Round Green Luton
7 K2 Roundham Somset
59 J6 Roundhay Leeds
18 E7 Roundway Wilts
93 L5 Roundyhill Angus
111 h1 Rousay Ork
15 K5 Rousdon Devon
31 L8 Rousham Oxon
30 D4 Rous Lench Worcs
84 D10 Routenburn N Ayrs
61 J6 Routh E R Yk
63 J4 Row Cumb
79 N12 Rowanburn D & G
84 F4 Rowardennan Stirlg
50 D3 Rowarth Derbys
17 L5 Rowberrow Somset
18 E8 Rowde Wilts
55 L7 Rowen Conwy
72 C8 Rowfoot Nthumb
34 G11 Rowhedge Essex
40 G12 Rowington Warwks
50 G6 Rowland Derbys
10 B7 Rowland's Castle Hants
73 L8 Rowland's Gill Gatesd
10 D2 Rowledge Surrey
73 J10 Rowley Dur
33 P4 Rowley Mile Services Suffk
40 C9 Rowley Regis Sandw
40 C9 Rowley Regis Crematorium Sandw
28 D4 Rowlstone Herefs
10 G2 Rowly Surrey
9 P7 Rowner Hants
40 D12 Rowney Green Worcs
9 L4 Rownhams Hants
9 L4 Rownhams Services Hants
70 H10 Rowrah Cumb
32 C12 Rowsham Bucks
50 G7 Rowsley Derbys
52 F11 Rowston Lincs
49 J3 Rowton Ches W
49 L10 Rowton Wrekin
80 F7 Roxburgh Border
60 F10 Roxby N Linc
32 G6 Roxton Bed
22 D2 Roxwell Essex
21 J7 Royal Botanic Gardens Gt Lon
98 C11 Roy Bridge Highld
21 N2 Roydon Essex
34 H1 Roydon Norfk
44 B5 Roydon Norfk
21 N2 Roydon Hamlet Essex
59 J11 Royston Barns
33 K8 Royston Herts
58 B11 Royton Oldham
7 c1 Rozel Jersey
48 F6 Ruabon Wrexhm
88 D6 Ruaig Ag & B
3 K7 Ruan Lanihorne Cnwll
2 G11 Ruan Major Cnwll
2 G11 Ruan Minor Cnwll
28 H5 Ruardean Gloucs
28 H5 Ruardean Hill Gloucs
28 H5 Ruardean Woodside Gloucs
40 C11 Rubery Birm
111 b6 Rubha Ban W Isls
28 E2 Ruckhall Herefs
13 K4 Ruckinge Kent
39 K3 Ruckley Shrops
66 C6 Rudby N York
73 K7 Rudchester Nthumb
41 M2 Ruddington Notts
18 C9 Rudge Somset
28 H10 Rudgeway S Glos
10 H4 Rudgwick W Susx
49 M2 Rudheath Ches W
22 G3 Rudley Green Essex
18 C6 Rudloe Wilts
27 P10 Rudry Caerph
61 J1 Rudston E R Yk
50 C8 Rudyard Staffs
80 E9 Ruecastle Border
57 J6 Rufford Lancs
59 M4 Rufforth C York
41 L11 Rugby Warwks
40 D4 Rugeley Staffs
16 H10 Ruishton Somset
20 H6 Ruislip Gt Lon
96 D9 Rùm Highld
101 M5 Rumbach Moray
86 B3 Rumbling Bridge P & K
35 M1 Rumburgh Suffk
3 K2 Rumford Cnwll
85 Q7 Rumford Falk
27 P11 Rumney Cardif
57 K11 Runcorn Halton
10 E9 Runcton W Susx
43 P8 Runcton Holme Norfk
10 D1 Runfold Surrey
44 H8 Runhall Norfk
45 P7 Runham Norfk
16 F10 Runnington Somset
66 H4 Runswick N York
94 E8 Runtaleave Angus
22 F5 Runwell Essex
20 C8 Ruscombe Wokham
28 H2 Rushall Herefs
45 K12 Rushall Norfk
18 G9 Rushall Wilts
34 E5 Rushbrooke Suffk
39 K4 Rushbury Shrops
33 K9 Rushden Herts
32 D4 Rushden Nhants
22 H8 Rushenden Kent
34 F1 Rushford Norfk
23 M1 Rush Green Essex
21 P6 Rush Green Gt Lon
12 D6 Rushlake Green E Susx
45 P11 Rushmere Suffk
10 E3 Rushmoor Surrey
40 B12 Rushock Worcs
57 Q9 Rusholme Manch
42 B12 Rushton Nhants
50 C8 Rushton Spencer Staffs
39 P10 Rushwick Worcs
65 M2 Rushyford Dur
85 K3 Ruskie Stirlg
52 F12 Ruskington Lincs
62 G5 Rusland Cross Cumb
11 K3 Rusper W Susx
29 J6 Ruspidge Gloucs
20 B5 Russell's Water Oxon
11 K3 Russ Hill Surrey
12 C3 Rusthall Kent
10 G9 Rustington W Susx
67 K10 Ruston N York
60 H2 Ruston Parva E R Yk
67 J5 Ruswarp N York
80 E7 Rutherford Border
85 K10 Rutherglen S Lans
3 M3 Ruthernbridge Cnwll
48 D4 Ruthin Denbgs
95 Q2 Ruthrieston C Aber
101 P6 Ruthven Abers
93 K6 Ruthven Angus
99 L8 Ruthven Highld
3 K4 Ruthvoes Cnwll
70 H3 Ruthwell D & G
48 H10 Ruyton-XI-Towns Shrops
72 H6 Ryal Nthumb
7 K4 Ryall Dorset
29 M1 Ryall Worcs
22 D10 Ryarsh Kent
62 G2 Rydal Cumb
9 P8 Ryde IoW
12 H6 Rye E Susx
12 H5 Rye Foreign E Susx
29 K2 Rye Street Worcs
42 E7 Ryhall Rutlnd
59 J10 Ryhill Wakefd
73 P9 Ryhope Sundld
52 E7 Ryland Lincs
41 M1 Rylands Notts
58 C3 Rylstone N York
7 N1 Ryme Intrinseca Dorset
59 M6 Ryther N York
73 K7 Ryton Gatesd
39 N2 Ryton Shrops
41 J11 Ryton-on-Dunsmore Warwks

S

57 P2 Sabden Lancs
33 K11 Sacombe Herts
73 M10 Sacriston Dur
65 N4 Sadberge Darltn
75 L6 Saddell Ag & B
41 P8 Saddington Leics
43 P7 Saddle Bow Norfk
11 L7 Saddlescombe W Susx
33 N8 Saffron Walden Essex
25 J7 Sageston Pembks
44 E9 Saham Hills Norfk
44 E9 Saham Toney Norfk
49 J3 Saighton Ches W
81 J1 St Abbs Border
87 M9 St Agnes Border
2 G5 St Agnes Cnwll
2 b3 St Agnes IoS
21 J2 St Albans Herts
3 J5 St Allen Cnwll
6 b2 St Andrew Guern
93 N11 St Andrews Fife
93 N11 St Andrews Botanic Garden Fife
16 F2 St Andrew's Major V Glam
7 L4 St Andrews Well Dorset
56 G3 St Anne's Lancs
78 H9 St Ann's D & G
5 J6 St Ann's Chapel Cnwll
5 N10 St Ann's Chapel Devon
2 H10 St Anthony Cnwll
12 D9 St Anthony's Hill E Susx
28 F9 St Arvans Mons
48 B1 St Asaph Denbgs
16 D3 St Athan V Glam
7 b2 St Aubin Jersey
3 M5 St Austell Cnwll
70 F12 St Bees Cumb
3 N5 St Blazey Cnwll
80 D7 St Boswells Border
7 a2 St Brelade Jersey
7 a2 St Brelade's Bay Jersey
3 L2 St Breock Cnwll
4 D5 St Breward Cnwll
28 G7 St Briavels Gloucs
16 B2 St Bride's Major V Glam
27 M12 St Brides super-Ely V Glam
28 C11 St Brides Wentlooge Newpt
5 K8 St Budeaux C Plym
30 E6 Saintbury Gloucs
2 C9 St Buryan Cnwll
84 C2 St Catherines Ag & B
29 L8 St Chloe Gloucs
25 M5 St Clears Carmth
4 F6 St Cleer Cnwll
3 J7 St Clement Cnwll
7 c2 St Clement Jersey
4 F4 St Clether Cnwll
83 Q9 St Colmac Ag & B
3 K3 St Columb Major Cnwll
3 J4 St Columb Minor Cnwll
3 K4 St Columb Road Cnwll
103 L3 St Combs Abers
45 L12 St Cross South Elmham Suffk
95 M8 St Cyrus Abers
92 E10 St David's P & K
24 D4 St David's Pembks
2 G7 St Day Cnwll
3 L4 St Dennis Cnwll
36 C10 St Dogmaels Pembks
5 J6 St Dominick Cnwll
16 C3 St Donats V Glam
4 C5 St Endellion Cnwll
3 K4 St Enoder Cnwll
3 J6 St Erme Cnwll
4 H8 St Erney Cnwll
2 E8 St Erth Cnwll
2 E8 St Erth Praze Cnwll
3 K2 St Ervan Cnwll
3 K3 St Eval Cnwll
3 L6 St Ewe Cnwll
27 N12 St Fagans Cardif
27 N12 St Fagans Welsh Life Museum Cardif
103 M5 St Fergus Abers
91 Q10 St Fillans P & K
25 J8 St Florence Pembks
14 C11 St Gennys Cnwll
55 P6 St George Conwy
17 K4 St Georges N Som
16 E2 St George's V Glam
4 H8 St Germans Cnwll
15 J8 St Giles in the Wood Devon
4 H3 St Giles-on-the-Heath Devon
38 B7 St Harmon Powys
65 L3 St Helen Auckland Dur
9 Q9 St Helens IoW
57 K9 St Helens St Hel
57 J9 St Helens Crematorium St Hel
21 L9 St Helier Gt Lon
7 b2 St Helier Jersey
2 E9 St Hilary Cnwll
16 D2 St Hilary V Glam
32 H10 St Ippollitts Herts
24 E7 St Ishmael's Pembks
3 L2 St Issey Cnwll
4 G6 St Ive Cnwll
33 K3 St Ives Cambs
2 D7 St Ives Cnwll
31 Q3 St James's End Nhants
35 M1 St James South Elmham Suffk
3 L2 St Jidgey Cnwll
5 J9 St John Cnwll
7 b1 St John Jersey
56 b5 St John's IoM
21 Q11 St Johns Kent
20 F10 St Johns Surrey
39 Q10 St Johns Worcs
15 J6 St John's Chapel Devon
72 F12 St John's Chapel Dur
43 N7 St John's Fen End Norfk
78 F2 St John's Kirk S Lans
69 N3 St John's Town of Dalry D & G
21 L6 St John's Wood Gt Lon
56 d3 St Jude's IoM
2 B9 St Just Cnwll
3 J8 St Just-in-Roseland Cnwll
102 G8 St Katherines Abers
2 H10 St Keverne Cnwll
3 M1 St Kew Cnwll
3 M1 St Kew Highway Cnwll
4 F7 St Keyne Cnwll
23 J3 St Lawrence Essex
9 N11 St Lawrence IoW
7 b1 St Lawrence Jersey
23 Q9 St Lawrence Kent
20 E3 St Leonards Bucks
8 G6 St Leonards Dorset
12 F8 St Leonards E Susx
2 B10 St Levan Cnwll
16 F2 St Lythans V Glam
3 M2 St Mabyn Cnwll
92 H10 St Madoes P & K
28 D3 St Margarets Herefs
21 M2 St Margarets Herts
13 Q2 St Margaret's at Cliffe Kent
111 h3 St Margaret's Hope Ork
45 M12 St Margaret South Elmham Suffk
56 c6 St Marks IoM
2 H10 St Martin Cnwll
4 G8 St Martin Cnwll
6 b2 St Martin Guern
7 c1 St Martin Jersey
2 c1 St Martin's IoS
92 H9 St Martin's P & K
48 G8 St Martins Shrops
7 a1 St Mary Jersey
19 M10 St Mary Bourne Hants
6 C9 St Marychurch Torbay
16 D2 St Mary Church V Glam
21 P9 St Mary Cray Gt Lon
13 K5 St Mary in the Marsh Kent
21 L5 St Marylebone Crematorium Gt Lon
2 c2 St Mary's IoS
111 h2 St Mary's Ork
13 L5 St Mary's Bay Kent
22 F7 St Mary's Hoo Medway
28 F5 St Maughans Green Mons
3 J8 St Mawes Cnwll
3 K3 St Mawgan Cnwll
5 J7 St Mellion Cnwll
27 P11 St Mellons Cardif
3 K2 St Merryn Cnwll
3 L7 St Michael Caerhays Cnwll
17 J9 St Michael Church Somset
3 J7 St Michael Penkevil Cnwll
12 H3 St Michaels Kent
39 L8 St Michaels Worcs
57 J1 St Michael's on Wyre Lancs
3 L1 St Minver Cnwll
87 K2 St Monans Fife
4 E6 St Neot Cnwll
32 H5 St Neots Cambs
24 F2 St Nicholas Pembks
16 E2 St Nicholas V Glam
23 N9 St Nicholas at Wade Kent
85 N5 St Ninians Stirlg
45 P9 St Olaves Norfk
23 L1 St Osyth Essex
7 a1 St Ouen Jersey
28 G4 St Owens Cross Herefs
21 P9 St Pauls Cray Gt Lon
32 H11 St Paul's Walden Herts
7 a1 St Peter Jersey
6 c2 St Peter Port Guern
6 b2 St Peter's Guern
23 Q9 St Peter's Kent
4 F7 St Pinnock Cnwll
76 F6 St Quivox S Ayrs
6 c1 St Sampson Guern
6 b2 St Saviour Guern
7 b2 St Saviour Jersey
3 L5 St Stephen Cnwll
4 H3 St Stephens Cnwll
5 J8 St Stephens Cnwll
4 D4 St Teath Cnwll
3 N1 St Tudy Cnwll
24 G8 St Twynnells Pembks
4 E8 St Veep Cnwll
93 Q7 St Vigeans Angus
3 L3 St Wenn Cnwll
28 F4 St Weonards Herefs
5 P11 Salcombe Devon
6 F5 Salcombe Regis Devon
23 J1 Salcott-cum-Virley Essex
57 P9 Sale Traffd
53 M7 Saleby Lincs
30 B3 Sale Green Worcs
12 E5 Salehurst E Susx
37 L4 Salem Cerdgn
89 M7 Salen Ag & B
89 N4 Salen Highld
32 D8 Salford C Beds
30 H8 Salford Oxon
57 P8 Salford Salfd
30 E4 Salford Priors Warwks
11 L2 Salfords Surrey
45 M7 Salhouse Norfk
86 B4 Saline Fife
8 G2 Salisbury Wilts
8 G2 Salisbury Cathedral Wilts
8 H2 Salisbury Crematorium Wilts
18 F10 Salisbury Plain Wilts
71 Q7 Salkeld Dykes Cumb
45 J5 Salle Norfk
53 K8 Salmonby Lincs
30 E9 Salperton Gloucs
85 N9 Salsburgh N Lans
40 C2 Salt Staffs
58 F6 Saltaire C Brad
5 J8 Saltash Cnwll
107 M8 Saltburn Highld
66 F4 Saltburn-by-the-Sea R & Cl
42 C5 Saltby Leics
76 D3 Saltcoats N Ayrs
11 M9 Saltdean Br & H
70 G9 Salterbeck Cumb
58 B5 Salterforth Lancs
18 G12 Salterton Wilts
53 M5 Saltfleet Lincs
53 M5 Saltfleetby All Saints Lincs
53 M5 Saltfleetby St Clement Lincs
53 M5 Saltfleetby St Peter Lincs
17 P3 Saltford BaNES
44 H2 Salthouse Norfk
60 D8 Saltmarshe E R Yk
48 H3 Saltney Flints
66 G10 Salton N York
14 H7 Saltrens Devon
73 M8 Saltwell Crematorium Gatesd
13 M3 Saltwood Kent
10 H8 Salvington W Susx
39 Q9 Salwarpe Worcs
7 L4 Salway Ash Dorset
30 D2 Sambourne Warwks
49 N9 Sambrook Wrekin
16 F11 Sampford Arundel Somset
16 E7 Sampford Brett Somset
15 L11 Sampford Courtenay Devon
16 F11 Sampford Moor Somset
16 D12 Sampford Peverell Devon
5 L6 Sampford Spiney Devon
111 i2 Samsonlane Ork
87 J7 Samuelston E Loth
82 C8 Sanaigmore Ag & B
2 C9 Sancreed Cnwll
60 F6 Sancton E R Yk
97 K8 Sandaig Highld
59 J9 Sandal Magna Wakefd

96 F11 Sandavore Highld
111 i1 Sanday Ork
111 i1 Sanday Airport Ork
49 N4 Sandbach Ches E
49 P4 Sandbach Services Ches E
84 C6 Sandbank Ag & B
8 F9 Sandbanks Poole
102 D3 Sandend Abers
21 M10 Sanderstead Gt Lon
64 D4 Sandford Cumb
15 P10 Sandford Devon
8 D9 Sandford Dorset
8 H7 Sandford Hants
9 N10 Sandford IoW
17 K4 Sandford N Som
77 M3 Sandford S Lans
19 N1 Sandford-on-Thames Oxon
17 P11 Sandford Orcas Dorset
31 K8 Sandford St Martin Oxon
13 M3 Sandgate Kent
103 K2 Sandhaven Abers
68 E8 Sandhead D & G
59 J6 Sand Hills Leeds
31 M11 Sandhills Oxon
10 F3 Sandhills Surrey
72 H7 Sandhoe Nthumb
83 Q4 Sandhole Ag & B
60 E6 Sand Hole E R Yk
60 E7 Sandholme E R Yk
20 D10 Sandhurst Br For
29 L4 Sandhurst Gloucs
12 F4 Sandhurst Kent
59 P3 Sand Hutton N York
65 P10 Sandhutton N York
51 L12 Sandiacre Derbys
53 N7 Sandilands Lincs
8 G4 Sandleheath Hants
19 M1 Sandleigh Oxon
8 B3 Sandley Dorset
111 j4 Sandness Shet
22 E3 Sandon Essex
33 K9 Sandon Herts
40 C2 Sandon Staffs
40 C2 Sandon Bank Staffs
9 P9 Sandown IoW
4 F8 Sandplace Cnwll
21 J2 Sandridge Herts
44 B4 Sandringham Norfk
67 J5 Sandsend N York
60 D11 Sandtoft N Linc
22 H12 Sandway Kent
23 P10 Sandwich Kent
111 k5 Sandwick Shet
111 d2 Sandwick W Isls
70 F11 Sandwith Cumb
32 G7 Sandy C Beds
79 K9 Sandyford D & G
6 B7 Sandygate Devon
56 d3 Sandygate IoM
70 E5 Sandyhills D & G
62 H9 Sandylands Lancs
18 E7 Sandy Lane Wilts
5 P3 Sandy Park Devon
108 H3 Sangobeg Highld
108 H3 Sangomore Highld
39 P8 Sankyn's Green Worcs
89 K3 Sanna Bay Highld
111 d2 Sanndabhaig W Isls
75 Q4 Sannox N Ayrs
77 N8 Sanquhar D & G
62 C2 Santon Bridge Cumb
44 D11 Santon Downham Suffk
41 L8 Sapcote Leics
39 M8 Sapey Common Herefs
34 F2 Sapiston Suffk
29 N7 Sapperton Gloucs
42 E4 Sapperton Lincs
43 K5 Saracen's Head Lincs
110 G7 Sarclet Highld
9 N5 Sarisbury Hants
46 D5 Sarn Gwynd
38 E4 Sarn Powys
47 Q10 Sarn Powys
36 E9 Sarnau Cerdgn
48 E11 Sarnau Powys
27 J11 Sarn Park Services Brdgnd
26 E6 Saron Carmth
54 G8 Saron Gwynd
20 G4 Sarratt Herts
23 N9 Sarre Kent
30 H9 Sarsden Oxon
73 K11 Satley Dur
15 L7 Satterleigh Devon
62 G4 Satterthwaite Cumb
102 F11 Sauchen Abers
92 H8 Saucher P & K
95 L7 Sauchieburn Abers
29 K7 Saul Gloucs
52 B6 Saundby Notts
25 K7 Saundersfoot Pembks
20 C3 Saunderton Bucks
14 H5 Saunton Devon
53 L9 Sausthorpe Lincs
58 G9 Savile Town Kirk
31 L2 Sawbridge Warwks
21 P1 Sawbridgeworth Herts
67 K9 Sawdon N York
63 P11 Sawley Lancs
58 G1 Sawley N York
33 M7 Sawston Cambs
42 G12 Sawtry Cambs
42 B6 Saxby Leics
52 E6 Saxby Lincs
60 G10 Saxby All Saints N Linc
41 P4 Saxelbye Leics
34 H5 Saxham Street Suffk
52 C8 Saxilby Lincs
44 G3 Saxlingham Norfk
45 L10 Saxlingham Green Norfk
45 K10 Saxlingham Nethergate Norfk
45 K9 Saxlingham Thorpe Norfk
35 N4 Saxmundham Suffk
51 P11 Saxondale Notts
34 B5 Saxon Street Cambs
35 L4 Saxtead Suffk
35 L4 Saxtead Green Suffk
35 L4 Saxtead Little Green Suffk
45 J4 Saxthorpe Norfk
59 L6 Saxton N York
11 L6 Sayers Common W Susx
66 F11 Scackleton N York
62 E2 Scafell Pike Cumb
51 P3 Scaftworth Notts
67 J11 Scagglethorpe N York
82 E4 Scalasaig Ag & B
60 E8 Scalby E R Yk
67 L9 Scalby N York
41 Q11 Scaldwell Nhants
71 P3 Scaleby Cumb
71 P3 Scalebyhill Cumb
62 F7 Scales Cumb
71 M9 Scales Cumb
41 Q3 Scalford Leics
66 G5 Scaling N York
111 k4 Scalloway Shet
96 H4 Scalpay Highld
53 J7 Scamblesby Lincs
90 B2 Scamodale Highld
67 J11 Scampston N York
52 D7 Scampton Lincs
99 J2 Scaniport Highld
58 E10 Scapegoat Hill Kirk
83 K3 Scarba Ag & B
67 M9 Scarborough N York
3 K5 Scarcewater Cnwll
51 L7 Scarcliffe Derbys
59 J6 Scarcroft Leeds
110 F2 Scarfskerry Highld
88 C7 Scarinish Ag & B
56 H6 Scarisbrick Lancs
44 F7 Scarning Norfk
51 Q11 Scarrington Notts
53 J3 Scartho NE Lin
111 k3 Scatsta Airport Shet
52 D3 Scawby N Linc
59 M12 Scawsby Donc
59 M11 Scawthorpe Donc
66 D10 Scawton N York
11 M5 Scayne's Hill W Susx
27 M4 Scethrog Powys
49 Q4 Scholar Green Ches E
58 F7 Scholemoor Crematorium C Brad
58 F11 Scholes Kirk
59 J6 Scholes Leeds
51 K2 Scholes Rothm
57 L7 Scholes Wigan
58 G11 Scissett Kirk
24 G2 Scleddau Pembks
51 N5 Scofton Notts
35 J2 Scole Norfk
92 H9 Scone P & K
96 F4 Sconser Highld
86 H2 Scoonie Fife
52 F11 Scopwick Lincs
105 Q3 Scoraig Highld
60 H5 Scorborough E R Yk
2 G7 Scorrier Cnwll
63 J11 Scorton Lancs
65 M7 Scorton N York
71 P5 Scotby Cumb
65 L6 Scotch Corner N York
65 L6 Scotch Corner Services N York
63 J9 Scotforth Lancs
52 E7 Scothern Lincs
86 E2 Scotlandwell P & K
110 C5 Scotscalder Station Highld
73 J4 Scot's Gap Nthumb
102 D10 Scotsmill Abers
85 J9 Scotstoun C Glas
73 L7 Scotswood N u Ty
52 C4 Scotter Lincs
52 C3 Scotterthorpe Lincs
52 C4 Scotton Lincs
59 J3 Scotton N York
65 L8 Scotton N York
44 G9 Scoulton Norfk
108 D6 Scourie Highld
108 D7 Scourie More Highld
111 k5 Scousburgh Shet
110 C2 Scrabster Highld
80 F9 Scraesburgh Border
43 L2 Scrane End Lincs
41 P6 Scraptoft Leics
45 Q7 Scratby Norfk
60 C3 Scrayingham N York
42 F3 Scredington Lincs
53 M9 Scremby Lincs
81 L4 Scremerston Nthumb
51 Q11 Screveton Notts
59 J3 Scriven N York
51 P3 Scrooby Notts
40 G2 Scropton Derbys
52 H11 Scrub Hill Lincs
65 N8 Scruton N York
109 L4 Scullomie Highld
44 E4 Sculthorpe Norfk
60 F11 Scunthorpe N Linc
7 K2 Seaborough Dorset
13 M3 Seabrook Kent
73 P8 Seaburn Sundld
59 J7 Seacroft Leeds
96 F2 Seafield Highld
86 B8 Seafield W Loth
86 F7 Seafield Crematorium C Edin
11 P9 Seaford E Susx
56 G9 Seaforth Sefton
41 N4 Seagrave Leics
73 P10 Seaham Dur
81 P7 Seahouses Nthumb
22 B11 Seal Kent
10 E1 Seale Surrey
66 C5 Seamer N York
67 L10 Seamer N York
76 D2 Seamill N Ayrs
45 N5 Sea Palling Norfk
52 F3 Searby Lincs
23 L9 Seasalter Kent
62 B3 Seascale Cumb
62 E3 Seathwaite Cumb
71 L11 Seatoller Cumb
4 G8 Seaton Cnwll
70 G8 Seaton Cumb
6 H5 Seaton Devon
61 K5 Seaton E R Yk
23 N10 Seaton Kent
73 N5 Seaton Nthumb
42 C9 Seaton Rutlnd
66 D2 Seaton Carew Hartpl
73 N6 Seaton Delaval Nthumb
60 D6 Seaton Ross E R Yk
73 N5 Seaton Sluice Nthumb
7 K4 Seatown Dorset
66 D7 Seave Green N York
9 Q8 Seaview IoW
71 J5 Seaville Cumb
17 K12 Seavington St Mary Somset
17 K12 Seavington St Michael Somset
71 M7 Sebergham Cumb
40 H6 Seckington Warwks
63 M4 Sedbergh Cumb
28 G9 Sedbury Gloucs
64 F8 Sedbusk N York
30 D6 Sedgeberrow Worcs
42 C3 Sedgebrook Lincs
65 P2 Sedgefield Dur
44 B3 Sedgeford Norfk
8 C2 Sedgehill Wilts
17 J5 Sedgemoor Services Somset
40 B8 Sedgley Dudley
63 K5 Sedgwick Cumb
12 F6 Sedlescombe E Susx
20 C2 Sedrup Bucks
18 D8 Seend Wilts
18 D8 Seend Cleeve Wilts
20 F5 Seer Green Bucks
45 M9 Seething Norfk
56 G8 Sefton Sefton
49 Q9 Seighford Staffs
54 H8 Seion Gwynd
39 Q3 Seisdon Staffs
48 F8 Selattyn Shrops
10 C4 Selborne Hants
59 N7 Selby N York
10 E6 Selham W Susx
21 M9 Selhurst Gt Lon
79 P3 Selkirk Border
28 G4 Sellack Herefs
111 k2 Sellafirth Shet
13 L3 Sellindge Kent
23 K11 Selling Kent
18 D8 Sells Green Wilts
40 D10 Selly Oak Birm
11 P8 Selmeston E Susx
21 M10 Selsdon Gt Lon
29 L7 Selsey Gloucs
10 D10 Selsey W Susx
64 E11 Selside N York
13 N2 Selsted Kent
51 L9 Selston Notts
16 C6 Selworthy Somset
34 G7 Semer Suffk
18 D8 Semington Wilts
8 D3 Semley Wilts
20 G11 Send Surrey
27 N10 Senghenydd Caerph
2 B10 Sennen Cnwll
2 B9 Sennen Cove Cnwll
27 K3 Sennybridge Powys
66 C11 Sessay N York
43 Q7 Setchey Norfk
87 J7 Seton Mains E Loth
63 P9 Settle N York
67 J12 Settrington N York
30 D9 Sevenhampton Gloucs
18 H3 Sevenhampton Swindn
21 P6 Seven Kings Gt Lon
21 Q11 Sevenoaks Kent
21 Q12 Sevenoaks Weald Kent
26 H7 Seven Sisters Neath
34 F10 Seven Star Green Essex
28 G10 Severn Beach S Glos
39 Q12 Severn Stoke Worcs
28 G10 Severn View Services S Glos
13 K2 Sevington Kent
33 P8 Sewards End Essex
32 E11 Sewell C Beds
61 L1 Sewerby E R Yk
2 G9 Seworgan Cnwll
42 C6 Sewstern Leics
111 e1 Sgiogarstaigh W Isls
31 P11 Shabbington Bucks
41 J6 Shackerstone Leics
10 E2 Shackleford Surrey
111 d1 Shader W Isls
73 N11 Shadforth Dur
45 P12 Shadingfield Suffk
13 J3 Shadoxhurst Kent
44 F12 Shadwell Norfk
33 L8 Shaftenhoe End Herts
8 C3 Shaftesbury Dorset
59 K11 Shafton Barns
57 M8 Shakerley Wigan
19 K7 Shalbourne Wilts
10 B2 Shalden Hants
6 C8 Shaldon Devon
9 M9 Shalfleet IoW
34 C10 Shalford Essex
10 G1 Shalford Surrey
34 B10 Shalford Green Essex
23 L11 Shalmsford Street Kent
31 N6 Shalstone Bucks
10 G2 Shamley Green Surrey
94 H9 Shandford Angus
84 E6 Shandon Ag & B
107 P7 Shandwick Highld
41 Q8 Shangton Leics
9 P10 Shanklin IoW
71 Q11 Shap Cumb
111 h2 Shapinsay Ork
8 D7 Shapwick Dorset
17 K8 Shapwick Somset
41 K2 Shardlow Derbys
40 C6 Shareshill Staffs
59 K9 Sharlston Wakefd
32 E5 Sharnbrook Bed
41 L8 Sharnford Leics
57 K3 Sharoe Green Lancs
65 N12 Sharow N York
32 F10 Sharpenhoe C Beds
81 K12 Sharperton Nthumb
29 J8 Sharpness Gloucs
44 G3 Sharrington Norfk
39 P6 Shatterford Worcs
5 L7 Shaugh Prior Devon
49 M5 Shavington Ches E
58 C11 Shaw Oldham
19 N7 Shaw W Berk
18 D7 Shaw Wilts
49 M11 Shawbirch Wrekin
111 d1 Shawbost W Isls
49 K10 Shawbury Shrops
41 M10 Shawell Leics
9 M3 Shawford Hants
70 E1 Shawhead D & G
58 G2 Shaw Mills N York
77 N2 Shawsburn S Lans
70 G3 Shearington D & G
41 N8 Shearsby Leics
16 H9 Shearston Somset
14 H9 Shebbear Devon
49 N9 Shebdon Staffs
110 B3 Shebster Highld
85 J10 Sheddens E Rens
9 P5 Shedfield Hants
50 E8 Sheen Staffs
58 F9 Sheepridge Kirk
58 H7 Sheepscar Leeds
29 M6 Sheepscombe Gloucs
5 L6 Sheepstor Devon
14 H10 Sheepwash Devon
41 J7 Sheepy Magna Leics
41 J7 Sheepy Parva Leics
21 P1 Sheering Essex
22 H8 Sheerness Kent
20 G10 Sheerwater Surrey
10 C5 Sheet Hants
51 J4 Sheffield Sheff
51 J4 Sheffield City Road Crematorium Sheff
32 G8 Shefford C Beds
108 D4 Sheigra Highld
39 L2 Sheinton Shrops
38 H6 Shelderton Shrops
40 F9 Sheldon Birm
50 F7 Sheldon Derbys
6 F2 Sheldon Devon
23 K11 Sheldwich Kent
45 J12 Shelfanger Norfk
51 P11 Shelford Notts
58 G11 Shelley Kirk
34 G8 Shelley Suffk
19 K3 Shellingford Oxon
22 C2 Shellow Bowells Essex
39 N9 Shelsley Beauchamp Worcs
39 N9 Shelsley Walsh Worcs
32 E3 Shelton Bed
45 K11 Shelton Norfk
42 B2 Shelton Notts
49 P7 Shelton Under Harley Staffs
38 G3 Shelve Shrops
39 K12 Shelwick Herefs
22 C4 Shenfield Essex
31 J5 Shenington Oxon
21 J4 Shenley Herts
32 B9 Shenley Brook End M Keyn
32 B9 Shenley Church End M Keyn
28 D2 Shenmore Herefs
69 J6 Shennanton D & G
40 E6 Shenstone Staffs
39 Q7 Shenstone Worcs
41 J7 Shenton Leics
101 J8 Shenval Moray
33 J11 Shephall Herts
21 K7 Shepherd's Bush Gt Lon
13 N1 Shepherdswell Kent
58 G11 Shepley Kirk
20 H9 Shepperton Surrey
33 L7 Shepreth Cambs
41 L4 Shepshed Leics
17 K11 Shepton Beauchamp Somset
17 N7 Shepton Mallet Somset
17 P9 Shepton Montague Somset
22 F11 Shepway Kent
66 C1 Sheraton Dur
17 P11 Sherborne Dorset
30 F10 Sherborne Gloucs
17 N5 Sherborne Somset
19 Q9 Sherborne St John Hants
30 H2 Sherbourne Warwks
73 N11 Sherburn Dur
67 K11 Sherburn N York
73 N11 Sherburn Hill Dur
59 L7 Sherburn in Elmet N York
10 H1 Shere Surrey
44 E4 Shereford Norfk
9 K3 Sherfield English Hants
20 B10 Sherfield on Loddon Hants
5 Q10 Sherford Devon
49 N11 Sheriffhales Shrops
59 P2 Sheriff Hutton N York
45 J2 Sheringham Norfk
32 C7 Sherington M Keyn
44 B4 Shernborne Norfk
18 E11 Sherrington Wilts
18 C4 Sherston Wilts
51 M11 Sherwood C Nott
51 N9 Sherwood Forest Notts
51 P7 Sherwood Forest Crematorium Notts
85 L9 Shettleston C Glas
57 K7 Shevington Wigan
4 H8 Sheviock Cnwll
58 E8 Shibden Head C Brad
9 N9 Shide IoW
80 H6 Shidlaw Nthumb
97 N6 Shiel Bridge Highld
105 M10 Shieldaig Highld
78 G11 Shieldhill D & G
85 P7 Shieldhill Falk
78 G2 Shieldhill House Hotel S Lans
85 N11 Shields N Lans
89 N3 Shielfoot Highld
93 M4 Shielhill Angus
84 D8 Shielhill Inver
39 N1 Shifnal Shrops
81 P11 Shilbottle Nthumb
65 M3 Shildon Dur
84 H10 Shillford E Rens
16 D10 Shillingford Devon
19 P3 Shillingford Oxon
6 B5 Shillingford Abbot Devon
6 B5 Shillingford St George Devon
8 C5 Shillingstone Dorset
32 G9 Shillington C Beds
30 H11 Shilton Oxon
41 K9 Shilton Warwks
45 J12 Shimpling Norfk
34 E6 Shimpling Suffk
34 E6 Shimpling Street Suffk
73 N11 Shincliffe Dur
73 N9 Shiney Row Sundld
20 B9 Shinfield Wokham
109 J11 Shinness Highld
22 C11 Shipbourne Kent
44 F8 Shipdham Norfk
17 L5 Shipham Somset
6 B9 Shiphay Torbay
20 C7 Shiplake Oxon
58 F6 Shipley C Brad
11 J6 Shipley W Susx
11 L3 Shipley Bridge Surrey
45 N11 Shipmeadow Suffk
19 N2 Shippon Oxon
30 G6 Shipston on Stour Warwks
30 D9 Shipton Gloucs
59 M3 Shipton N York
39 K4 Shipton Shrops
19 J10 Shipton Bellinger Hants
7 M5 Shipton Gorge Dorset
10 C9 Shipton Green W Susx
29 M10 Shipton Moyne Gloucs
31 L10 Shipton-on-Cherwell Oxon
60 E5 Shiptonthorpe E R Yk
30 H9 Shipton-under-Wychwood Oxon
20 B4 Shirburn Oxon
56 G6 Shirdley Hill Lancs
51 M7 Shirebrook Derbys
51 J3 Shiregreen Sheff
28 G12 Shirehampton Bristl
73 N6 Shiremoor N Tyne
28 F9 Shirenewton Mons
51 M5 Shireoaks Notts
51 K8 Shirland Derbys
9 L5 Shirley C Sotn
50 G11 Shirley Derbys
21 M9 Shirley Gt Lon
40 E10 Shirley Solhll
9 P5 Shirrell Heath Hants
83 N6 Shirvan Ag & B
15 K5 Shirwell Devon
75 N6 Shiskine N Ayrs
38 H9 Shobdon Herefs
15 P11 Shobrooke Devon
41 P4 Shoby Leics
48 H5 Shocklach Ches W
22 H6 Shoeburyness Sthend
23 Q11 Sholden Kent
9 M5 Sholing C Sotn
14 E8 Shop Cnwll
21 M6 Shoreditch Gt Lon
16 H10 Shoreditch Somset
21 P10 Shoreham Kent
11 K8 Shoreham Airport W Susx
11 K8 Shoreham-by-Sea W Susx
9 P3 Shorley Hants
22 E8 Shorne Kent
11 P7 Shortgate E Susx
3 J6 Shortlanesend Cnwll
76 G4 Shortlees E Ayrs
32 F7 Shortstown Bed
9 M10 Shorwell IoW
17 Q5 Shoscombe BaNES
45 L9 Shotesham Norfk
22 F5 Shotgate Essex
35 K9 Shotley Suffk
73 J9 Shotley Bridge Dur
35 L9 Shotley Gate Suffk
35 K9 Shotley Street Suffk
23 K11 Shottenden Kent
30 F3 Shottery Warwks
31 K5 Shotteswell Warwks
35 M7 Shottisham Suffk
50 H10 Shottlegate Derbys
73 P11 Shotton Dur
48 F2 Shotton Flints
73 P11 Shotton Colliery Dur
85 P10 Shotts N Lans
48 G2 Shotwick Ches W
101 J4 Shougle Moray
44 B8 Shouldham Norfk
43 Q8 Shouldham Thorpe Norfk
39 P9 Shoulton Worcs
48 H11 Shrawardine Shrops
39 P8 Shrawley Worcs
30 G1 Shrewley Warwks
49 J11 Shrewsbury Shrops
18 F11 Shrewton Wilts
10 F9 Shripney W Susx
19 J3 Shrivenham Oxon
44 G10 Shropham Norfk
28 G1 Shucknall Herefs
33 P7 Shudy Camps Cambs
83 L2 Shuna Ag & B
29 N5 Shurdington Gloucs
20 D8 Shurlock Row W & M
110 B4 Shurrery Highld
110 B4 Shurrery Lodge Highld
16 G7 Shurton Somset
40 G8 Shustoke Warwks
6 H4 Shute Devon
15 Q11 Shute Devon
31 J6 Shutford Oxon
49 Q10 Shut Heath Staffs
29 M2 Shuthonger Gloucs
31 Q4 Shutlanger Nhants
40 G6 Shuttington Warwks
51 L6 Shuttlewood Derbys
57 P5 Shuttleworth Bury
111 d1 Siabost W Isls
111 d1 Siadar W Isls
41 P10 Sibbertoft Nhants
31 J6 Sibford Ferris Oxon
31 J6 Sibford Gower Oxon
34 C9 Sible Hedingham Essex
33 P10 Sibley's Green Essex
53 K12 Sibsey Lincs
42 F10 Sibson Cambs
41 J7 Sibson Leics
110 G5 Sibster Highld
51 Q10 Sibthorpe Notts
51 Q6 Sibthorpe Notts
35 M3 Sibton Suffk
34 E5 Sicklesmere Suffk
59 J5 Sicklinghall N York
6 F4 Sidbury Devon
39 M5 Sidbury Shrops
17 K5 Sidcot N Som
21 P8 Sidcup Gt Lon
49 Q2 Siddington Ches E
18 F2 Siddington Gloucs
45 L3 Sidestrand Norfk
6 F5 Sidford Devon
10 D9 Sidlesham W Susx
12 E8 Sidley E Susx
6 F5 Sidmouth Devon
61 K5 Sigglesthorne E R Yk
16 C2 Sigingstone V Glam
19 Q8 Silchester Hants
41 N5 Sileby Leics
62 D6 Silecroft Cumb
45 J9 Silfield Norfk
58 H11 Silkstone Barns
58 H12 Silkstone Common Barns
42 F2 Silk Willoughby Lincs
70 H5 Silloth Cumb
67 L8 Silpho N York
58 D5 Silsden C Brad
32 F9 Silsoe C Beds
8 B2 Silton Dorset
86 E9 Silverburn Mdloth
63 J7 Silverdale Lancs
49 P6 Silverdale Staffs
34 D11 Silver End Essex
102 G3 Silverford Abers
31 P5 Silverstone Nhants
6 C3 Silverton Devon
39 L6 Silvington Shrops
72 F6 Simonburn Nthumb
15 N4 Simonsbath Somset
57 P3 Simonstone Lancs
80 H5 Simprim Border
32 C9 Simpson M Keyn
24 F5 Simpson Cross Pembks
80 H4 Sinclair's Hill Border
76 H7 Sinclairston E Ayrs
65 N10 Sinderby N York
57 N10 Sinderland Green Traffd
20 C9 Sindlesham Wokham
41 J2 Sinfin C Derb
13 J2 Singleton Kent
56 H2 Singleton Lancs
10 E7 Singleton W Susx
22 D8 Singlewell Kent
101 N11 Sinnarhard Abers
66 G9 Sinnington N York
39 P9 Sinton Worcs
39 P9 Sinton Green Worcs
12 F3 Sissinghurst Kent
17 P2 Siston S Glos
2 F9 Sithney Cnwll

22 H10 Sittingbourne Kent
39 P4 Six Ashes Shrops
52 G6 Sixhills Lincs
33 P5 Six Mile Bottom Cambs
13 L2 Sixmile Cottages Kent
8 E4 Sixpenny Handley Dorset
63 J5 Sizergh Castle Cumb
111 h2 Skaill Ork
77 J7 Skares E Ayrs
95 P4 Skateraw Abers
87 N7 Skateraw E Loth
104 F11 Skeabost Highld
65 L7 Skeeby N York
41 Q7 Skeffington Leics
61 N9 Skeffling E R Yk
51 L8 Skegby Notts
52 B9 Skegby Notts
53 P10 Skegness Lincs
107 N4 Skelbo Highld
107 N4 Skelbo Street Highld
59 L10 Skelbrooke Donc
43 K3 Skeldyke Lincs
52 D8 Skellingthorpe Lincs
59 M11 Skellow Donc
58 G11 Skelmanthorpe Kirk
57 J7 Skelmersdale Lancs
84 D9 Skelmorlie N Ayrs
109 M5 Skelpick Highld
78 D10 Skelston D & G
59 M3 Skelton C York
71 N8 Skelton Cumb
60 D8 Skelton E R Yk
59 J1 Skelton N York
66 F4 Skelton R & Cl
62 G2 Skelwith Bridge Cumb
53 M9 Skendleby Lincs
102 G12 Skene House Abers
28 E5 Skenfrith Mons
60 H3 Skerne E R Yk
109 L3 Skerray Highld
108 E5 Skerricha Highld
63 J9 Skerton Lancs
41 K8 Sketchley Leics
26 E9 Sketty Swans
26 G9 Skewen Neath
66 E12 Skewsby N York
110 B3 Skiall Highld
60 H7 Skidby E R Yk
111 e1 Skigersta W Isls
16 D10 Skilgate Somset
42 C5 Skillington Lincs
71 J4 Skinburness Cumb
85 Q6 Skinflats Falk
104 C11 Skinidin Highld
83 N10 Skipness Ag & B
79 M11 Skipper's Bridge D & G
61 K3 Skipsea E R Yk
58 C4 Skipton N York
65 P10 Skipton-on-Swale N York
59 P6 Skipwith N York
61 K6 Skirlaugh E R Yk
78 H2 Skirling Border
20 C5 Skirmett Bucks
60 D3 Skirpenbeck E R Yk
64 B2 Skirwith Cumb
110 H3 Skirza Highld
24 D7 Skokholm Island Pembks
24 D7 Skomer Island Pembks
97 J5 Skulamus Highld
34 E11 Skye Green Essex
99 P4 Skye of Curr Highld
58 C8 Slack Calder
102 H6 Slacks of Cairnbanno Abers
29 M7 Slad Gloucs
15 J3 Slade Devon
21 Q7 Slade Green Gt Lon
51 M3 Slade Hooton Rothm
72 C9 Slaggyford Nthumb
63 N10 Slaidburn Lancs
58 E10 Slaithwaite Kirk
72 H8 Slaley Nthumb
85 P8 Slamannan Falk
32 D11 Slapton Bucks
5 Q10 Slapton Devon
31 N5 Slapton Nhants
11 K5 Slaugham W Susx
18 C6 Slaughterford Wilts
41 R8 Slawston Leics
10 C3 Sleaford Hants
42 F2 Sleaford Lincs
64 B4 Sleagill Cumb
49 L11 Sleapford Wrekin
107 K3 Sleasdairidh Highld
60 F2 Sledmere E R Yk
79 P12 Sleetbeck Cumb
67 J6 Sleights N York
110 F3 Slickly Highld
75 P7 Sliddery N Ayrs
96 F4 Sligachan Highld
84 C5 Sligrachan Ag & B
29 K7 Slimbridge Gloucs
49 P8 Slindon Staffs
10 F8 Slindon W Susx
10 H4 Slinfold W Susx
66 F11 Slingsby N York
32 F11 Slip End C Beds
33 J8 Slip End Herts
32 D2 Slipton Nhants
40 D4 Slitting Mill Staffs
83 M4 Slockavullin Ag & B
5 P3 Sloncombe Devon
53 M8 Sloothby Lincs
20 F7 Slough Slough
20 F7 Slough Crematorium Bucks
16 H11 Slough Green Somset
97 M2 Slumbay Highld
63 J8 Slyne Lancs
87 E7 Smailholm Border
45 M5 Smallburgh Norfk
11 K7 Small Dole W Susx
51 K11 Smalley Derbys
11 L2 Smallfield Surrey
40 E9 Small Heath Birm
12 H4 Small Hythe Kent
7 J3 Smallridge Devon
34 G1 Smallworth Norfk
19 L10 Smannell Hants
12 G2 Smarden Kent
12 G2 Smarden Bell Kent
11 Q2 Smart's Hill Kent
89 N2 Smearisary Highld
6 G1 Smeatharpe Devon
13 K3 Smeeth Kent
41 P8 Smeeton Westerby Leics
110 D8 Smerral Highld
39 Q4 Smestow Staffs
40 D9 Smethwick Sandw
41 J4 Smisby Derbys
71 P3 Smithfield Cumb
33 Q8 Smith's Green Essex
105 L6 Smithstown Highld
107 L12 Smithton Highld
108 H3 Smoo Highld
34 F11 Smythe's Green Essex
78 D10 Snade D & G
38 G2 Snailbeach Shrops
33 Q4 Snailwell Cambs
67 K10 Snainton N York
59 N9 Snaith E R Yk
65 M10 Snape N York
35 N5 Snape Suffk
35 N5 Snape Street Suffk
21 N5 Snaresbrook Gt Lon
41 J5 Snarestone Leics
52 F7 Snarford Lincs
13 J4 Snargate Kent
13 K4 Snave Kent
67 J6 Sneaton N York
52 F7 Snelland Lincs
50 F11 Snelston Derbys
44 G11 Snetterton Norfk
44 B4 Snettisham Norfk
81 L12 Snitter Nthumb
52 E5 Snitterby Lincs
30 G3 Snitterfield Warwks
39 K7 Snitton Shrops
22 E10 Snodland Kent
54 H10 Snowdon Gwynd
47 N5 Snowdonia National Park
33 L9 Snow End Herts
30 E7 Snowshill Gloucs
9 Q5 Soake Hants
96 E7 Soay Highld
9 Q4 Soberton Hants
9 P5 Soberton Heath Hants
65 N6 Sockburn Darltn
33 P3 Soham Cambs
111 b4 Solas W Isls
9 Q1 Soldridge Hants
22 D9 Sole Street Kent
23 L12 Sole Street Kent
40 F10 Solihull Solhll
38 H10 Sollers Dilwyn Herefs
28 H3 Sollers Hope Herefs
24 E4 Solva Pembks
79 L12 Solwaybank D & G
41 R5 Somerby Leics
52 F3 Somerby Lincs
51 K9 Somercotes Derbys
8 H8 Somerford Dorset
18 E2 Somerford Keynes Gloucs
10 D9 Somerley W Susx
45 P10 Somerleyton Suffk
40 F1 Somersal Herbert Derbys
53 K8 Somersby Lincs
33 K2 Somersham Cambs
34 H7 Somersham Suffk
31 L8 Somerton Oxon
17 L9 Somerton Somset
34 D6 Somerton Suffk
11 J8 Sompting W Susx
20 C8 Sonning Wokham
20 B7 Sonning Common Oxon
8 H7 Sopley Hants
18 C4 Sopworth Wilts
69 L9 Sorbie D & G
110 D4 Sordale Highld
88 G4 Sorisdale Ag & B
77 J6 Sorn E Ayrs
110 F3 Sortat Highld
52 H7 Sotby Lincs
45 P12 Sotterley Suffk
48 E3 Soughton Flints
32 C10 Soulbury Bucks
64 D5 Soulby Cumb
31 M7 Souldern Oxon
32 E4 Souldrop Bed
49 L6 Sound Ches E
101 M5 Sound Muir Moray
17 P2 Soundwell S Glos
5 L3 Sourton Devon
62 E6 Soutergate Cumb
44 D7 South Acre Norfk
13 N2 South Alkham Kent
20 H7 Southall Gt Lon
5 Q11 South Allington Devon
85 P5 South Alloa Falk
29 N4 Southam Gloucs
31 K2 Southam Warwks
10 E6 South Ambersham W Susx
9 M5 Southampton C Sotn
9 M4 Southampton Airport Hants
9 M4 Southampton Crematorium Hants
51 L4 South Anston Rothm
13 J2 South Ashford Kent
9 L7 South Baddesley Hants
90 E5 South Ballachulish Highld
59 N4 South Bank C York
17 N9 South Barrow Somset
21 L10 South Beddington Gt Lon
22 F6 South Benfleet Essex
10 F9 South Bersted W Susx
21 N9 Southborough Gt Lon
12 C2 Southborough Kent
8 G8 Southbourne Bmouth
10 C8 Southbourne W Susx
59 N11 South Bramwith Donc
5 N8 South Brent Devon
17 Q8 South Brewham Somset
17 N3 South Bristol Crematorium Bristl
73 M2 South Broomhill Nthumb
44 G8 Southburgh Norfk
45 N8 South Burlingham Norfk
60 G4 Southburn E R Yk
17 P10 South Cadbury Somset
52 D8 South Carlton Lincs
51 N4 South Carlton Notts
60 F7 South Cave E R Yk
18 F2 South Cerney Gloucs
11 N6 South Chailey E Susx
81 N9 South Charlton Nthumb
17 Q10 South Cheriton Somset
65 L2 South Church Dur
22 H6 Southchurch Sthend
60 E7 South Cliffe E R Yk
52 B9 South Clifton Notts
53 L6 South Cockerington Lincs
26 H11 South Cornelly Brdgnd
4 F2 Southcott Cnwll
5 P4 Southcott Devon
20 D2 Southcourt Bucks
35 P1 South Cove Suffk
44 E3 South Creake Norfk
41 P5 South Croxton Leics
60 G5 South Dalton E R Yk
22 C9 South Darenth Kent
11 M8 South Downs
59 P7 South Duffield N York
11 N8 Southease E Susx
53 J6 South Elkington Lincs
59 L11 South Elmsall Wakefd
75 K10 Southend Ag & B
22 G5 Southend Airport Essex
22 H6 Southend Crematorium Sthend
22 H6 Southend-on-Sea Sthend
16 B2 Southerndown V Glam
70 F5 Southerness D & G
105 L7 South Erradale Highld
6 E5 Southerton Devon
43 P10 Southery Norfk
22 C6 South Essex Crematorium Gt Lon
22 G5 South Fambridge Essex
60 G9 South Ferriby N Linc
60 H8 South Field E R Yk
85 P8 Southfield Falk
22 C8 Southfleet Kent
21 L5 Southgate Gt Lon
26 D10 Southgate Swans
8 H5 South Gorley Hants
73 M7 South Gosforth N u Ty
22 D5 South Green Essex
22 G10 South Green Kent
44 H7 South Green Norfk
86 E7 South Gyle C Edin
22 E4 South Hanningfield Essex
10 C6 South Harting W Susx
10 B9 South Hayling Hants
20 E3 South Heath Bucks
11 N9 South Heighton E Susx
73 P10 South Hetton Dur
59 K10 South Hiendley Wakefd
4 H5 South Hill Cnwll
31 L12 South Hinksey Oxon
11 J2 South Holmwood Surrey
21 P6 South Hornchurch Gt Lon
5 N11 South Huish Devon
52 D9 South Hykeham Lincs
73 P9 South Hylton Sundld
32 G8 Southill C Beds
19 N10 Southington Hants
52 E4 South Kelsey Lincs
107 L11 South Kessock Highld
61 K10 South Killingholme N Linc
65 Q10 South Kilvington N York
41 N10 South Kilworth Leics
59 K11 South Kirkby Wakefd
52 G12 South Kyme Lincs
85 L10 South Lanarkshire Crematorium S Lans
6 G4 Southleigh Devon
31 K11 South Leigh Oxon
52 A7 South Leverton Notts
30 E5 South Littleton Worcs
21 L9 South London Crematorium Gt Lon
34 G1 South Lopham Norfk
42 D9 South Luffenham Rutlnd
11 N7 South Malling E Susx
18 H3 South Marston Swindn
21 L11 South Merstham Surrey
59 L7 South Milford N York
5 N10 South Milton Devon
21 K3 South Mimms Herts
21 K4 South Mimms Services Herts
23 J4 Southminster Essex
15 M7 South Molton Devon
73 L9 South Moor Dur
19 L2 Southmoor Oxon
19 P3 South Moreton Oxon
93 L5 Southmuir Angus
10 E9 South Mundham W Susx
60 F7 South Newbald E R Yk
31 K7 South Newington Oxon
8 G1 South Newton Wilts
51 K9 South Normanton Derbys
21 M9 South Norwood Gt Lon
22 C6 South Ockendon Thurr
32 H4 Southoe Cambs
35 K3 Southolt Suffk
53 L8 South Ormsby Lincs
42 F9 Southorpe C Pete
65 P9 South Otterington N York
7 N4 Southover Dorset
52 F5 South Owersby Lincs
58 E9 Southowram Calder
11 K1 South Park Surrey
7 L2 South Perrott Dorset
17 L11 South Petherton Somset
4 G4 South Petherwin Cnwll
44 E8 South Pickenham Norfk
5 J8 South Pill Cnwll
5 Q11 South Pool Devon
7 M4 South Poorton Dorset
56 G5 Southport Sefton
56 G6 Southport Crematorium Lancs
86 D6 South Queensferry C Edin
42 E2 South Rauceby Lincs
44 E5 South Raynham Norfk
45 L3 Southrepps Norfk
53 L6 South Reston Lincs
52 G9 Southrey Lincs
111 h3 South Ronaldsay Ork
30 G12 Southrop Gloucs
19 Q10 Southrope Hants
43 Q8 South Runcton Norfk
52 B10 South Scarle Notts
9 Q7 Southsea C Port
90 C7 South Shian Ag & B
73 P7 South Shields S Tyne
73 N8 South Shields Crematorium S Tyne
56 F3 South Shore Bpool
65 K3 Southside Dur
58 H2 South Stainley N York
17 Q4 South Stoke BaNES
19 P4 South Stoke Oxon
10 G7 South Stoke W Susx
23 K10 South Street Kent
23 L9 South Street Kent
86 B10 South Tarbrax S Lans
5 N2 South Tawton Devon
2 F7 South Tehidy Cnwll
53 L7 South Thoresby Lincs
45 Q8 Southtown Norfk
111 b6 South Uist W Isls
71 P6 Southwaite Cumb
71 P6 Southwaite Services Cumb
45 M7 South Walsham Norfk
21 L7 Southwark Gt Lon
10 B1 South Warnborough Hants
11 J5 Southwater W Susx
22 C5 South Weald Essex
51 P9 Southwell Notts
20 H8 South West Middlesex Crematorium Gt Lon
20 B4 South Weston Oxon
9 Q6 Southwick Hants
42 E10 Southwick Nhants
73 P8 Southwick Sundld
11 K8 Southwick W Susx
18 C9 Southwick Wilts
17 N5 South Widcombe BaNES
41 N7 South Wigston Leics
13 K2 South Willesborough Kent
52 H6 South Willingham Lincs
51 J9 South Wingfield Derbys
42 D6 South Witham Lincs
35 Q2 Southwold Suffk
22 F4 South Woodham Ferrers Essex
43 Q5 South Wootton Norfk
18 C7 South Wraxall Wilts
5 N2 South Zeal Devon
58 D9 Sowerby Calder
66 B10 Sowerby N York
58 D9 Sowerby Bridge Calder
58 E9 Sowood Calder
5 K7 Sowton Devon
6 D4 Sowton Devon
58 D9 Soyland Town Calder
33 Q8 Spain's End Essex
43 J5 Spalding Lincs
60 D7 Spaldington E R Yk
32 G3 Spaldwick Cambs
52 B9 Spalford Notts
42 F3 Spanby Lincs
44 H6 Sparham Norfk
62 F5 Spark Bridge Cumb
17 N10 Sparkford Somset
40 E10 Sparkhill Birm
5 M8 Sparkwell Devon
50 E5 Sparrowpit Derbys
12 D4 Sparrows Green E Susx
9 M2 Sparsholt Hants
19 L4 Sparsholt Oxon
66 G9 Spaunton N York
16 G8 Spaxton Somset
98 C11 Spean Bridge Highld
9 K2 Spearywell Hants
20 D4 Speen Bucks
19 M7 Speen W Berk
67 N11 Speeton N York
56 H11 Speke Lpool
12 B2 Speldhurst Kent
33 M12 Spellbrook Herts
20 B9 Spencers Wood Wokham
49 P4 Spen Green Ches E
65 K9 Spennithorne N York
65 M2 Spennymoor Dur
30 B4 Spetchley Worcs
8 D7 Spetisbury Dorset
35 N2 Spexhall Suffk
101 L3 Spey Bay Moray
100 G9 Speybridge Highld
101 K6 Speyview Moray
53 L9 Spilsby Lincs
51 L5 Spinkhill Derbys
107 L4 Spinningdale Highld
51 N3 Spital Hill Donc
87 J6 Spittal E Loth
110 D5 Spittal Highld
81 L4 Spittal Nthumb
24 G4 Spittal Pembks
92 G7 Spittalfield P & K
94 E5 Spittal of Glenmuick Abers
94 B7 Spittal of Glenshee P & K
80 D9 Spittal-on-Rule Border
45 L7 Spixworth Norfk
15 K10 Splatt Devon
11 N5 Splayne's Green E Susx
27 P12 Splottlands Cardif
59 J4 Spofforth N York
41 K1 Spondon C Derb
44 H10 Spooner Row Norfk
44 E7 Sporle Norfk
87 M7 Spott E Loth
80 E4 Spottiswoode Border
41 Q12 Spratton Nhants
10 D2 Spreakley Surrey
15 M11 Spreyton Devon
5 L9 Spriddlestone Devon
52 E6 Spridlington Lincs
85 K8 Springburn C Glas
71 M2 Springfield D & G
22 E2 Springfield Essex
93 L12 Springfield Fife
70 D2 Springholm D & G
76 F4 Springside N Ayrs
52 C5 Springthorpe Lincs
73 M8 Springwell Sundld
56 H10 Springwood Crematorium Lpool
61 K7 Sproatley E R Yk
49 N3 Sproston Green Ches W
51 M1 Sprotbrough Donc
35 J7 Sproughton Suffk
80 G7 Sprouston Border
45 L7 Sprowston Norfk
42 C5 Sproxton Leics
66 E10 Sproxton N York
49 K4 Spurstow Ches E
7 M4 Spyway Dorset
39 N3 Stableford Shrops
50 H3 Stacey Bank Sheff
63 P8 Stackhouse N York
24 H9 Stackpole Pembks
5 K9 Staddiscombe C Plym
19 Q2 Stadhampton Oxon
111 a5 Stadhlaigearraidh W Isls
71 Q7 Staffield Cumb
104 G8 Staffin Highld
40 B3 Stafford Staffs
40 C3 Stafford Crematorium Staffs
40 B2 Stafford Services (northbound) Staffs
40 B2 Stafford Services (southbound) Staffs
32 E7 Stagsden Bed
70 G9 Stainburn Cumb
42 C5 Stainby Lincs
59 J11 Staincross Barns
65 K4 Staindrop Dur
20 G8 Staines Surrey
59 N10 Stainforth Donc
63 P8 Stainforth N York
56 G2 Staining Lancs
58 E9 Stainland Calder
67 K6 Stainsacre N York
63 K5 Stainton Cumb
71 P9 Stainton Cumb
51 M3 Stainton Donc
65 J4 Stainton Dur
66 C5 Stainton Middsb
52 F7 Stainton by Langworth Lincs
67 L7 Staintondale N York
52 H5 Stainton le Vale Lincs
62 F7 Stainton with Adgarley Cumb
76 G6 Stair E Ayrs
68 G8 Stairhaven D & G
66 H4 Staithes N York
73 M4 Stakeford Nthumb
10 B8 Stakes Hants
17 Q11 Stalbridge Dorset
17 Q11 Stalbridge Weston Dorset
45 N5 Stalham Norfk
23 J11 Stalisfield Green Kent
17 N11 Stallen Dorset
61 K11 Stallingborough NE Lin
62 G12 Stalmine Lancs
50 C2 Stalybridge Tamesd
34 C8 Stambourne Essex
34 B8 Stambourne Green Essex
42 E8 Stamford Lincs
81 P9 Stamford Nthumb
49 J3 Stamford Bridge Ches W
60 C3 Stamford Bridge E R Yk
73 J6 Stamfordham Nthumb
21 M6 Stamford Hill Gt Lon
32 D11 Stanbridge C Beds
58 D6 Stanbury C Brad
85 M8 Stand N Lans
85 Q7 Standburn Falk
40 B6 Standeford Staffs
12 G3 Standen Kent
18 B10 Standerwick Somset
10 D3 Standford Hants
70 H8 Standingstone Cumb
57 K6 Standish Wigan
31 K12 Standlake Oxon
9 M3 Standon Hants
33 L11 Standon Herts
49 P8 Standon Staffs
85 P10 Stane N Lans
44 F6 Stanfield Norfk
32 G8 Stanford C Beds
13 L3 Stanford Kent
39 M10 Stanford Bishop Herefs
39 N8 Stanford Bridge Worcs
19 P6 Stanford Dingley W Berk
19 K3 Stanford in the Vale Oxon
22 D7 Stanford le Hope Thurr
41 N10 Stanford on Avon Nhants
41 M3 Stanford on Soar Notts
39 N8 Stanford on Teme Worcs
51 L6 Stanfree Derbys
66 F4 Stanghow R & Cl
42 H10 Stanground C Pete
44 D3 Stanhoe Norfk
79 J3 Stanhope Border
72 H11 Stanhope Dur
13 J2 Stanhope Kent
42 D11 Stanion Nhants
51 K11 Stanley Derbys
73 L9 Stanley Dur
92 G8 Stanley P & K
50 B9 Stanley Staffs
73 L12 Stanley Crook Dur
30 D7 Stanley Pontlarge Gloucs
11 M7 Stanmer Br & H
21 J5 Stanmore Gt Lon
9 M2 Stanmore Hants
72 D4 Stannersburn Nthumb
34 E5 Stanningfield Suffk
73 L5 Stannington Nthumb
50 H4 Stannington Sheff
73 L5 Stannington Station Nthumb
38 G9 Stansbatch Herefs
34 D6 Stansfield Suffk
34 D7 Stanstead Suffk
21 M2 Stanstead Abbotts Herts
22 C10 Stansted Kent
33 N11 Stansted Airport Essex
33 N10 Stansted Mountfitchet Essex
30 E7 Stanton Gloucs
73 K3 Stanton Nthumb
50 E10 Stanton Staffs
34 F3 Stanton Suffk
41 J3 Stanton by Bridge Derbys
51 L12 Stanton by Dale Derbys
17 N4 Stanton Drew BaNES
18 H3 Stanton Fitzwarren Swindn
31 K11 Stanton Harcourt Oxon
50 G7 Stanton in Peak Derbys
39 J6 Stanton Lacy Shrops
50 G8 Stanton Lees Derbys
39 L4 Stanton Long Shrops
41 N2 Stanton on the Wolds Notts
17 P4 Stanton Prior BaNES
18 G8 Stanton St Bernard Wilts
31 M11 Stanton St John Oxon
18 D5 Stanton St Quintin Wilts
34 F4 Stanton Street Suffk
41 L5 Stanton under Bardon Leics
49 K10 Stanton upon Hine Heath Shrops
17 N4 Stanton Wick BaNES
34 F11 Stanway Essex
30 D7 Stanway Gloucs
20 G8 Stanwell Surrey
32 E3 Stanwick Nhants
71 N4 Stanwix Cumb
111 a5 Staoinebrig W Isls
66 H8 Stape N York
49 M5 Stapeley Ches E
40 G3 Stapenhill Staffs
23 P11 Staple Kent
16 D11 Staple Cross Devon
12 F5 Staplecross E Susx
11 L5 Staplefield W Susx
16 H11 Staple Fitzpaine Somset
33 M6 Stapleford Cambs
33 K12 Stapleford Herts
42 B6 Stapleford Leics
52 C11 Stapleford Lincs
51 L12 Stapleford Notts
18 F12 Stapleford Wilts
21 P5 Stapleford Abbotts Essex
16 G10 Staplegrove Somset
16 G10 Staplehay Somset
12 F2 Staplehurst Kent
23 K10 Staplestreet Kent
38 G8 Stapleton Herefs
41 K7 Stapleton Leics
65 M5 Stapleton N York
39 J2 Stapleton Shrops
17 L11 Stapleton Somset
16 G12 Stapley Somset
32 G5 Staploe Bed
29 J1 Staplow Herefs
86 G2 Star Fife
25 M2 Star Pembks
17 L5 Star Somset
59 J3 Starbeck N York
64 G11 Starbotton N York
6 C6 Starcross Devon
41 J12 Stareton Warwks
33 M9 Starlings Green Essex
45 K12 Starston Norfk
65 J4 Startforth Dur
18 D4 Startley Wilts

23 P11 Statenborough Kent
17 K9 Stathe Somset
41 Q2 Stathern Leics
32 G4 Staughton Green Cambs
28 G6 Staunton Gloucs
29 K3 Staunton Gloucs
38 G9 Staunton on Arrow Herefs
38 G12 Staunton on Wye Herefs
62 H5 Staveley Cumb
63 J3 Staveley Cumb
51 K6 Staveley Derbys
59 J2 Staveley N York
5 Q7 Staverton Devon
29 M4 Staverton Gloucs
31 M2 Staverton Nhants
18 C8 Staverton Wilts
17 K8 Stawell Somset
16 E10 Stawley Somset
110 H5 Staxigoe Highld
67 L10 Staxton N York
62 G12 Staynall Lancs
65 J11 Stean N York
66 E12 Stearsby N York
16 H7 Steart Somset
33 Q11 Stebbing Essex
10 D5 Stedham W Susx
86 B4 Steelend Fife
79 Q9 Steele Road Border
39 K10 Steen's Bridge Herefs
10 C5 Steep Hants
58 D9 Steep Lane Calder
22 H3 Steeple Essex
18 D9 Steeple Ashton Wilts
31 L8 Steeple Aston Oxon
34 B8 Steeple Bumpstead Essex
31 P8 Steeple Claydon Bucks
32 G1 Steeple Gidding Cambs
18 F12 Steeple Langford Wilts
33 J8 Steeple Morden Cambs
58 D5 Steeton C Brad
104 C10 Stein Highld
13 M1 Stelling Minnis Kent
17 K11 Stembridge Somset
3 M4 Stenalees Cnwll
77 N11 Stenhouse D & G
85 P6 Stenhousemuir Falk
104 F8 Stenscholl Highld
41 J2 Stenson Fields Derbys
87 M7 Stenton E Loth
111 d2 Steornabhagh W Isls
25 K7 Stepaside Pembks
78 E11 Stepford D & G
21 M7 Stepney Gt Lon
32 E9 Steppingley C Beds
85 L8 Stepps N Lans
35 N5 Sternfield Suffk
18 F8 Stert Wilts
33 Q5 Stetchworth Cambs
32 H10 Stevenage Herts
76 E3 Stevenston N Ayrs
19 P10 Steventon Hants
19 M3 Steventon Oxon
33 P8 Steventon End Essex
32 E6 Stevington Bed
32 E8 Stewartby Bed
85 K11 Stewartfield S Lans
76 G3 Stewarton E Ayrs
32 C10 Stewkley Bucks
17 J11 Stewley Somset
11 J7 Steyning W Susx
24 G7 Steynton Pembks
14 D9 Stibb Cnwll
44 G4 Stibbard Norfk
14 H8 Stibb Cross Devon
19 J8 Stibb Green Wilts
42 F9 Stibbington Cambs
80 F6 Stichill Border
3 L6 Sticker Cnwll
53 K10 Stickford Lincs
5 M2 Sticklepath Devon
53 K11 Stickney Lincs
44 F2 Stiffkey Norfk
111 a5 Stilligarry W Isls
59 N6 Stillingfleet N York
59 N1 Stillington N York
65 P3 Stillington S on T
42 G11 Stilton Cambs
29 K8 Stinchcombe Gloucs
7 Q5 Stinsford Dorset
38 G3 Stiperstones Shrops
39 M1 Stirchley Wrekin
103 M6 Stirling Abers
85 N4 Stirling Stirlg
85 N5 Stirling Services Stirlg
32 H4 Stirtloe Cambs
58 C4 Stirton N York
34 D10 Stisted Essex
2 G8 Stithians Cnwll
41 J11 Stivichall Covtry
52 H9 Stixwould Lincs
48 H2 Stoak Ches W
79 K2 Stobo Border
8 D9 Stoborough Dorset
80 C11 Stobs Castle Border
73 L2 Stobswood Nthumb
22 E4 Stock Essex
17 L4 Stock N Som
9 L1 Stockbridge Hants
77 N4 Stockbriggs S Lans
22 G10 Stockbury Kent
19 M7 Stockcross W Berk
42 B9 Stockerston Leics
30 C3 Stock Green Worcs
28 H3 Stocking Herefs
41 J8 Stockingford Warwks
33 M10 Stocking Pelham Herts
6 H2 Stockland Devon
16 H7 Stockland Bristol Somset
15 P10 Stockleigh English Devon
15 P10 Stockleigh Pomeroy Devon
18 E7 Stockley Wilts
17 K11 Stocklinch Somset
50 B3 Stockport Stockp
50 B3 Stockport Crematorium Stockp
50 H2 Stocksbridge Sheff
73 J8 Stocksfield Nthumb
39 K9 Stockton Herefs
45 N10 Stockton Norfk
39 N3 Stockton Shrops
31 K2 Stockton Warwks
18 E12 Stockton Wilts
49 P11 Stockton Wrekin
57 L10 Stockton Heath Warrtn
66 C4 Stockton-on-Tees S on T
39 N8 Stockton on Teme Worcs
59 P3 Stockton on the Forest C York
17 P3 Stockwood Bristl
7 N2 Stockwood Dorset
30 D3 Stock Wood Worcs
23 N10 Stodmarsh Kent
44 H3 Stody Norfk
108 B9 Stoer Highld
17 N12 Stoford Somset
8 F1 Stoford Wilts
16 E8 Stogumber Somset
16 G7 Stogursey Somset
41 J10 Stoke Covtry
14 E7 Stoke Devon
10 B9 Stoke Hants
19 L9 Stoke Hants
22 G8 Stoke Medway
7 L3 Stoke Abbott Dorset
42 B11 Stoke Albany Nhants
35 J3 Stoke Ash Suffk
51 N11 Stoke Bardolph Notts
39 M9 Stoke Bliss Worcs
31 Q4 Stoke Bruerne Nhants
34 C7 Stoke by Clare Suffk
34 G9 Stoke-by-Nayland Suffk
6 C3 Stoke Canon Devon
19 N11 Stoke Charity Hants
4 H5 Stoke Climsland Cnwll
39 L11 Stoke Cross Herefs
20 H10 Stoke D'Abernon Surrey
42 E11 Stoke Doyle Nhants
42 C10 Stoke Dry Rutlnd
28 H1 Stoke Edith Herefs
8 F3 Stoke Farthing Wilts
44 B9 Stoke Ferry Norfk
6 B11 Stoke Fleming Devon
8 C9 Stokeford Dorset
6 B10 Stoke Gabriel Devon
28 H11 Stoke Gifford S Glos
41 K7 Stoke Golding Leics
32 B7 Stoke Goldington M Keyn
52 A7 Stokeham Notts
32 C10 Stoke Hammond Bucks
45 K9 Stoke Holy Cross Norfk
6 C8 Stokeinteignhead Devon
39 L11 Stoke Lacy Herefs
31 M8 Stoke Lyne Oxon
20 D2 Stoke Mandeville Bucks
20 C4 Stokenchurch Bucks
21 M6 Stoke Newington Gt Lon
5 Q10 Stokenham Devon
50 B10 Stoke-on-Trent C Stke
29 M3 Stoke Orchard Gloucs
20 F6 Stoke Poges Bucks
39 K10 Stoke Prior Herefs
30 C1 Stoke Prior Worcs
15 L5 Stoke Rivers Devon
42 D5 Stoke Rochford Lincs
20 B6 Stoke Row Oxon
17 J10 Stoke St Gregory Somset
16 H10 Stoke St Mary Somset
17 P6 Stoke St Michael Somset
39 K5 Stoke St Milborough Shrops
38 H6 Stokesay Castle Shrops
45 N7 Stokesby Norfk
66 D6 Stokesley N York
17 L11 Stoke sub Hamdon Somset
20 B4 Stoke Talmage Oxon
17 Q9 Stoke Trister Somset
49 M9 Stoke upon Tern Shrops
49 Q6 Stoke-upon-Trent C Stke
16 G7 Stolford Somset
22 C4 Stondon Massey Essex
20 C2 Stone Bucks
29 J9 Stone Gloucs
12 H5 Stone Kent
51 M3 Stone Rothm
40 B1 Stone Staffs
39 Q7 Stone Worcs
17 K6 Stone Allerton Somset
17 N5 Ston Easton Somset
17 K4 Stonebridge N Som
40 G10 Stonebridge Warwks
51 K8 Stonebroom Derbys
23 P11 Stone Cross Kent
12 E4 Stonecrouch Kent
61 J7 Stoneferry C KuH
83 N8 Stonefield Castle Hotel Ag & B
12 D4 Stonegate E Susx
66 F11 Stonegrave N York
95 P5 Stonehaven Abers
18 G11 Stonehenge Wilts
5 K9 Stonehouse C Plym
29 L7 Stonehouse Gloucs
77 M3 Stonehouse S Lans
41 J11 Stoneleigh Warwks
42 B5 Stonesby Leics
31 K10 Stonesfield Oxon
35 J10 Stones Green Essex
22 C11 Stone Street Kent
35 N1 Stone Street Suffk
101 K3 Stonewells Moray
111 a5 Stoneybridge W Isls
86 B9 Stoneyburn W Loth
41 N7 Stoneygate C Leic
68 E8 Stoneykirk D & G
50 G6 Stoney Middleton Derbys
41 L8 Stoney Stanton Leics
17 Q9 Stoney Stoke Somset
17 P8 Stoney Stratton Somset
103 J11 Stoneywood C Aber
85 N6 Stoneywood Falk
35 J5 Stonham Aspal Suffk
40 E6 Stonnall Staffs
20 B6 Stonor Oxon
41 Q8 Stonton Wyville Leics
51 L7 Stony Houghton Derbys
32 B8 Stony Stratford M Keyn
15 L6 Stoodleigh Devon
16 C11 Stoodleigh Devon
13 L3 Stop 24 Services Kent
10 G6 Stopham W Susx
32 F11 Stopsley Luton
111 d2 Stornoway W Isls
111 d2 Stornoway Airport W Isls
10 H7 Storrington W Susx
63 J6 Storth Cumb
60 C5 Storwood E R Yk
101 J2 Stotfield Moray
32 H9 Stotfold C Beds
39 M5 Stottesdon Shrops
41 N7 Stoughton Leics
20 F12 Stoughton Surrey
10 C7 Stoughton W Susx
30 B4 Stoulton Worcs
40 B10 Stourbridge Dudley
40 B10 Stourbridge Crematorium Dudley
8 C5 Stourpaine Dorset
39 P7 Stourport-on-Severn Worcs
8 B3 Stour Provost Dorset
8 B3 Stour Row Dorset
39 Q5 Stourton Staffs
30 H6 Stourton Warwks
8 B1 Stourton Wilts
17 Q12 Stourton Caundle Dorset
111 k5 Stove Shet
35 P1 Stoven Suffk
87 J12 Stow Border
52 C7 Stow Lincs
43 P8 Stow Bardolph Norfk
44 F10 Stow Bedon Norfk
43 P8 Stowbridge Norfk
33 N5 Stow-cum-Quy Cambs
38 F7 Stowe Shrops
40 D3 Stowe by Chartley Staffs
17 P10 Stowell Somset
17 N4 Stowey BaNES
5 J3 Stowford Devon
34 F3 Stowlangtoft Suffk
32 G3 Stow Longa Cambs
22 G4 Stow Maries Essex
34 H5 Stowmarket Suffk
30 F8 Stow-on-the-Wold Gloucs
13 L2 Stowting Kent
13 L2 Stowting Common Kent
34 H5 Stowupland Suffk
99 P6 Straanruie Highld
95 L4 Strachan Abers
84 B3 Strachur Ag & B
35 K3 Stradbroke Suffk
34 C6 Stradishall Suffk
43 Q8 Stradsett Norfk
52 C11 Stragglethorpe Lincs
86 F8 Straiton Mdloth
76 G9 Straiton S Ayrs
102 H10 Straloch Abers
92 F3 Straloch P & K
40 E1 Stramshall Staffs
56 c5 Strang IoM
57 P8 Strangeways Salfd
28 G4 Strangford Herefs
68 E7 Stranraer D & G
19 Q7 Stratfield Mortimer W Berk
20 B10 Stratfield Saye Hants
20 B10 Stratfield Turgis Hants
21 M6 Stratford Gt Lon
35 M5 Stratford St Andrew Suffk
34 H9 Stratford St Mary Suffk
8 G3 Stratford Tony Wilts
30 G3 Stratford-upon-Avon Warwks
105 L6 Strath Highld
108 C10 Strathan Highld
109 K3 Strathan Highld
77 L3 Strathaven S Lans
85 J7 Strathblane Stirlg
106 C3 Strathcanaird Highld
97 N2 Strathcarron Highld
89 N9 Strathcoil Ag & B
101 L11 Strathdon Abers
93 M11 Strathkinness Fife
85 Q8 Strathloanhead W Loth
98 H10 Strathmashie House Highld
86 E1 Strathmiglo Fife
106 H10 Strathpeffer Highld
92 D5 Strathtay P & K
75 Q5 Strathwhillan N Ayrs
109 P3 Strathy Highld
109 P3 Strathy Inn Highld
91 N11 Strathyre Stirlg
14 E10 Stratton Cnwll
7 P4 Stratton Dorset
30 D12 Stratton Gloucs
31 N8 Stratton Audley Oxon
17 P6 Stratton-on-the-Fosse Somset
18 H4 Stratton St Margaret Swindn
45 K10 Stratton St Michael Norfk
45 K6 Stratton Strawless Norfk
11 M7 Streat E Susx
21 L8 Streatham Gt Lon
32 F10 Streatley C Beds
19 P5 Streatley W Berk
6 G5 Street Devon
17 L8 Street Somset
41 L10 Street Ashton Warwks
48 G7 Street Dinas Shrops
23 M11 Street End Kent
10 D9 Street End W Susx
40 F5 Streethay Staffs
65 N7 Streetlam N York
40 E7 Streetly Crematorium Wsall
33 P7 Streetly End Cambs
17 N8 Street on the Fosse Somset
92 H8 Strelitz P & K
51 L11 Strelley Notts
59 N3 Strensall C York
29 M1 Strensham Services (northbound) Worcs
29 M2 Strensham Services (southbound) Worcs
16 H7 Stretcholt Somset
5 R10 Strete Devon
57 P9 Stretford Traffd
33 M8 Strethall Essex
33 N2 Stretham Cambs
10 E8 Strettington W Susx
51 K8 Stretton Derbys
42 D7 Stretton Rutlnd
40 B5 Stretton Staffs
40 G3 Stretton Staffs
57 L11 Stretton Warrtn
39 L12 Stretton Grandison Herefs
41 K11 Stretton-on-Dunsmore Warwks
30 G6 Stretton on Fosse Warwks
28 E1 Stretton Sugwas Herefs
41 L10 Stretton under Fosse Warwks
39 L3 Stretton Westwood Shrops
103 K4 Strichen Abers
16 G7 Stringston Somset
32 C4 Strixton Nhants
28 G8 Stroat Gloucs
110 G1 Stroma Highld
97 M3 Stromeferry Highld
111 g2 Stromness Ork
84 G2 Stronachlachar Stirlg
83 Q6 Stronafian Ag & B
108 E11 Stronchrubie Highld
84 D6 Strone Ag & B
98 A11 Strone Highld
98 G4 Strone Highld
98 B11 Stronenaba Highld
90 F10 Stronmilchan Ag & B
111 i2 Stronsay Ork
111 i2 Stronsay Airport Ork
89 Q4 Strontian Highld
22 E9 Strood Medway
29 L7 Stroud Gloucs
10 B5 Stroud Hants
29 L7 Stroud Green Gloucs
42 C4 Stroxton Lincs
96 D3 Struan Highld
92 B3 Struan P & K
45 M8 Strumpshaw Norfk
77 M2 Strutherhill S Lans
86 H1 Struthers Fife
98 E2 Struy Highld
103 K6 Stuartfield Abers
9 P6 Stubbington Hants
57 P5 Stubbins Lancs
42 C1 Stubton Lincs
8 H5 Stuckton Hants
32 E12 Studham C Beds
8 F10 Studland Dorset
30 E2 Studley Warwks
18 E6 Studley Wilts
65 N12 Studley Roger N York
65 M12 Studley Royal N York
33 N2 Stuntney Cambs
34 B7 Sturmer Essex
8 B5 Sturminster Common Dorset
8 D7 Sturminster Marshall Dorset
8 B5 Sturminster Newton Dorset
23 M10 Sturry Kent
52 D3 Sturton N Linc
52 C7 Sturton by Stow Lincs
52 B6 Sturton le Steeple Notts
35 J2 Stuston Suffk
59 L6 Stutton N York
35 J9 Stutton Suffk
57 Q11 Styal Ches E
101 L3 Stynie Moray
51 N3 Styrrup Notts
84 E2 Succoth Ag & B
39 N10 Suckley Worcs
32 D1 Sudborough Nhants
35 N6 Sudbourne Suffk
42 D2 Sudbrook Lincs
28 F10 Sudbrook Mons
52 E8 Sudbrooke Lincs
40 F2 Sudbury Derbys
21 J6 Sudbury Gt Lon
34 E8 Sudbury Suffk
39 Q9 Suddington Worcs
67 L8 Suffield N York
45 K4 Suffield Norfk
49 P8 Sugnall Staffs
28 E1 Sugwas Pool Herefs
96 H6 Suisnish Highld
56 d3 Sulby IoM
31 M5 Sulgrave Nhants
31 M5 Sulgrave Manor Nhants
19 Q6 Sulham W Berk
19 Q7 Sulhamstead W Berk
111 k3 Sullom Shet
111 k3 Sullom Voe Shet
16 F3 Sully V Glam
111 k5 Sumburgh Airport Shet
58 G2 Summerbridge N York
3 K5 Summercourt Cnwll
44 C3 Summerfield Norfk
25 K7 Summerhill Pembks
65 L4 Summerhouse Darltn
10 D8 Summersdale W Susx
57 P6 Summerseat Bury
31 L11 Summertown Oxon
20 H9 Sunbury Surrey
78 D11 Sundaywell D & G
82 C9 Sunderland Ag & B
71 J8 Sunderland Cumb
62 H10 Sunderland Lancs
73 P9 Sunderland Sundld
73 M12 Sunderland Bridge Dur
73 P9 Sunderland Crematorium Sundld
79 M4 Sundhope Border
32 F10 Sundon Park Luton
21 P11 Sundridge Kent
20 F9 Sunningdale W & M
20 F9 Sunninghill W & M
19 N1 Sunningwell Oxon
73 K12 Sunniside Dur
73 L8 Sunniside Gatesd
41 J2 Sunnyhill C Derb
57 M4 Sunnyhurst Bl w D
85 N4 Sunnylaw Stirlg
31 L11 Sunnymead Oxon
21 J9 Surbiton Gt Lon
43 J5 Surfleet Lincs
45 M8 Surlingham Norfk
34 E11 Surrex Essex
11 L3 Surrey & Sussex Crematorium W Susx
45 K3 Sustead Norfk
52 B3 Susworth Lincs
14 F9 Sutcombe Devon
14 F9 Sutcombemill Devon
53 L8 Sutterby Lincs
43 J3 Sutterton Lincs
32 H7 Sutton C Beds
42 F9 Sutton C Pete
33 M2 Sutton Cambs
5 N10 Sutton Devon
11 P9 Sutton E Susx
21 K9 Sutton Gt Lon
23 P12 Sutton Kent
59 L8 Sutton N York
45 N5 Sutton Norfk
51 Q12 Sutton Notts
31 K11 Sutton Oxon
39 N5 Sutton Shrops
49 N10 Sutton Staffs
35 M7 Sutton Suffk
10 F7 Sutton W Susx
22 B9 Sutton at Hone Kent
41 Q9 Sutton Bassett Nhants
18 D5 Sutton Benger Wilts
41 L3 Sutton Bonington Notts
43 M6 Sutton Bridge Lincs
41 K7 Sutton Cheney Leics
40 E8 Sutton Coldfield Birm
40 F7 Sutton Coldfield Crematorium Birm
19 N2 Sutton Courtenay Oxon
51 P4 Sutton cum Lound Notts
20 G11 Sutton Green Surrey
65 N10 Sutton Howgrave N York
51 L8 Sutton in Ashfield Notts
58 D5 Sutton-in-Craven N York
39 N2 Sutton Maddock Shrops
17 K8 Sutton Mallet Somset
8 E2 Sutton Mandeville Wilts
17 P10 Sutton Montis Somset
61 J7 Sutton-on-Hull C KuH
53 N7 Sutton on Sea Lincs
59 M2 Sutton-on-the-Forest N York
40 G2 Sutton on the Hill Derbys
52 B9 Sutton on Trent Notts
43 L7 Sutton St Edmund Lincs
43 L6 Sutton St James Lincs
39 K11 Sutton St Nicholas Herefs
19 M11 Sutton Scotney Hants
19 M11 Sutton Scotney Services Hants
30 H6 Sutton-under-Brailes Warwks
66 C10 Sutton-under-Whitestonecliffe N York
60 C5 Sutton upon Derwent E R Yk
12 F1 Sutton Valence Kent
18 D11 Sutton Veny Wilts
8 C4 Sutton Waldron Dorset
57 K11 Sutton Weaver Ches W
17 N4 Sutton Wick BaNES
19 N2 Sutton Wick Oxon
53 L7 Swaby Lincs
40 H4 Swadlincote Derbys
44 D8 Swaffham Norfk
33 N4 Swaffham Bulbeck Cambs
33 P4 Swaffham Prior Cambs
45 L4 Swafield Norfk
66 C7 Swainby N York
45 K9 Swainsthorpe Norfk
18 B7 Swainswick BaNES
31 J6 Swalcliffe Oxon
23 L9 Swalecliffe Kent
52 H3 Swallow Lincs
52 D9 Swallow Beck Lincs
8 E3 Swallowcliffe Wilts
20 B9 Swallowfield Wokham
8 F10 Swanage Dorset
32 B10 Swanbourne Bucks
49 N2 Swan Green Ches W
60 G8 Swanland E R Yk
21 P9 Swanley Kent
21 Q9 Swanley Village Kent
9 P4 Swanmore Hants
41 K4 Swannington Leics
45 J6 Swannington Norfk
52 D9 Swanpool Garden Suburb Lincs
22 C8 Swanscombe Kent
26 E9 Swansea Swans
26 D9 Swansea Airport Swans
26 E8 Swansea Crematorium Swans
26 E8 Swansea West Services Swans
45 L5 Swanton Abbot Norfk
44 G6 Swanton Morley Norfk
44 G4 Swanton Novers Norfk
51 K9 Swanwick Derbys
9 N5 Swanwick Hants
42 F5 Swarby Lincs
45 K9 Swardeston Norfk
41 J2 Swarkestone Derbys
81 N12 Swarland Nthumb
19 P12 Swarraton Hants
62 F6 Swarthmoor Cumb
42 G3 Swaton Lincs
33 K3 Swavesey Cambs
9 J7 Sway Hants
42 E5 Swayfield Lincs
9 M4 Swaythling C Sotn
15 Q11 Sweetham Devon
11 P4 Sweethaws E Susx
4 E2 Sweets Cnwll
3 N4 Sweetshouse Cnwll
35 M4 Swefling Suffk
41 J5 Swepstone Leics
31 J7 Swerford Oxon
49 P3 Swettenham Ches E
35 K6 Swilland Suffk
59 J7 Swillington Leeds
15 L6 Swimbridge Devon
15 K6 Swimbridge Newland Devon
30 H10 Swinbrook Oxon
58 G3 Swincliffe N York
52 C10 Swinderby Lincs
29 N4 Swindon Gloucs
39 Q4 Swindon Staffs
18 G4 Swindon Swindn
61 K7 Swine E R Yk
60 D9 Swinefleet E R Yk
32 F4 Swineshead Bed
43 J3 Swineshead Lincs
110 E8 Swiney Highld
41 M10 Swinford Leics
13 N2 Swingfield Minnis Kent
13 N2 Swingfield Street Kent
34 F7 Swingleton Green Suffk
81 P8 Swinhoe Nthumb
65 J9 Swinithwaite N York
71 K10 Swinside Cumb
42 E5 Swinstead Lincs
80 H5 Swinton Border
65 L10 Swinton N York
66 G11 Swinton N York
51 K2 Swinton Rothm
57 P8 Swinton Salfd
41 M5 Swithland Leics
107 J8 Swordale Highld
97 L10 Swordland Highld
109 N3 Swordly Highld
49 Q8 Swynnerton Staffs
7 M5 Swyre Dorset
38 B1 Sychtyn Powys
29 N6 Syde Gloucs
21 M8 Sydenham Gt Lon
20 B3 Sydenham Oxon
5 J5 Sydenham Damerel Devon
44 D4 Syderstone Norfk
7 P3 Sydling St Nicholas Dorset
19 N8 Sydmonton Hants
51 Q10 Syerston Notts
54 H10 Sygun Copper Mine Gwynd
59 N10 Sykehouse Donc
111 k3 Symbister Shet
76 G5 Symington S Ayrs
78 G2 Symington S Lans
7 L4 Symondsbury Dorset
28 G5 Symonds Yat Herefs
109 M7 Syre Highld
30 D9 Syreford Gloucs
31 N6 Syresham Nhants
41 N5 Syston Leics
42 D2 Syston Lincs
39 Q8 Sytchampton Worcs
32 B4 Sywell Nhants

T

31 L9 Tackley Oxon
45 J10 Tacolneston Norfk
59 L5 Tadcaster N York
50 F6 Taddington Derbys
19 P8 Tadley Hants
33 J7 Tadlow Cambs
31 K6 Tadmarton Oxon

21 K11 Tadworth Surrey
27 N11 Taff's Well Rhondd
26 G10 Taibach Neath
107 M6 Tain Highld
110 E3 Tain Highld
111 c3 Tairbeart W Isls
33 P11 Takeley Essex
33 N11 Takeley Street Essex
6 E3 Talaton Devon
24 E6 Talbenny Pembks
6 E4 Taleford Devon
47 Q10 Talerddig Powys
36 G9 Talgarreg Cerdgn
37 J5 Talgarth Powys
96 D4 Talisker Highld
49 P5 Talke Staffs
71 Q4 Talkin Cumb
105 N8 Talladale Highld
79 J5 Talla Linnfoots Border
76 G10 Tallaminnock S Ayrs
49 J6 Tallarn Green Wrexhm
70 H8 Tallentire Cumb
26 E3 Talley Carmth
42 F8 Tallington Lincs
109 K3 Talmine Highld
25 N4 Talog Carmth
37 J9 Talsarn Cerdgn
47 K4 Talsarnau Gwynd
3 K3 Talskiddy Cnwll
54 G6 Talwrn IoA
37 K3 Tal-y-bont Cerdgn
55 L7 Tal-y-Bont Conwy
47 J7 Tal-y-bont Gwynd
54 H7 Tal-y-bont Gwynd
27 N4 Talybont-on-Usk Powys
55 L7 Tal-y-Cafn Conwy
28 E6 Tal-y-coed Mons
54 G10 Talysarn Gwynd
5 K7 Tamerton Foliot C Plym
40 G6 Tamworth Staffs
40 G7 Tamworth Services Warwks
21 M12 Tandridge Surrey
73 L9 Tanfield Dur
73 L9 Tanfield Lea Dur
19 K9 Tangley Hants
10 E8 Tangmere W Susx
111 a7 Tangusdale W Isls
111 h2 Tankerness Ork
51 J2 Tankersley Barns
23 L9 Tankerton Kent
110 G6 Tannach Highld
95 N5 Tannachie Abers
93 N4 Tannadice Angus
40 E11 Tanner's Green Worcs
35 L4 Tannington Suffk
85 L10 Tannochside N Lans
51 J8 Tansley Derbys
42 F11 Tansor Nhants
73 L9 Tantobie Dur
40 E12 Tanworth in Arden Warwks
36 E10 Tan-y-groes Cerdgn
111 b3 Taobh Tuath W Isls
20 E7 Taplow Bucks
75 J3 Tarbert Ag & B
83 N8 Tarbert Ag & B
111 c3 Tarbert W Isls
84 F3 Tarbet Ag & B
97 L10 Tarbet Highld
108 D6 Tarbet Highld
76 G6 Tarbolton S Ayrs
86 B10 Tarbrax S Lans
30 D1 Tardebigge Worcs
94 H6 Tarfside Angus
94 H2 Tarland Abers
57 J5 Tarleton Lancs
29 N8 Tarlton Gloucs
17 K5 Tarnock Somset
49 K3 Tarporley Ches W
8 D6 Tarrant Crawford Dorset
8 D5 Tarrant Gunville Dorset
8 D5 Tarrant Hinton Dorset
8 D6 Tarrant Keyneston Dorset
8 D5 Tarrant Launceston Dorset
8 D6 Tarrant Monkton Dorset
8 D6 Tarrant Rawston Dorset
8 D6 Tarrant Rushton Dorset
11 N8 Tarring Neville E Susx
28 H1 Tarrington Herefs
96 H7 Tarskavaig Highld
102 H8 Tarves Abers
49 J3 Tarvin Ches W
45 K10 Tasburgh Norfk
40 G3 Tatenhill Staffs
53 K6 Tathwell Lincs
21 N11 Tatsfield Surrey
49 J4 Tattenhall Ches W
44 E5 Tatterford Norfk
44 E4 Tattersett Norfk
52 H11 Tattershall Lincs
52 H10 Tattershall Thorpe Lincs
35 J8 Tattingstone Suffk
35 J8 Tattingstone White Horse Suffk
7 J2 Tatworth Somset
101 M5 Tauchers Moray
16 G10 Taunton Somset
16 G10 Taunton Deane Crematorium Somset
16 G11 Taunton Deane Services Somset
45 J7 Taverham Norfk
25 L6 Tavernspite Pembks
5 K5 Tavistock Devon
15 L11 Taw Green Devon
15 K6 Tawstock Devon
50 D5 Taxal Derbys
90 E11 Taychreggan Hotel Ag & B
92 B4 Tay Forest Park P & K
75 K4 Tayinloan Ag & B
29 J4 Taynton Gloucs
30 G10 Taynton Oxon
90 D9 Taynuilt Ag & B
93 M9 Tayport Fife
83 L5 Tayvallich Ag & B
52 G5 Tealby Lincs
93 M7 Tealing Angus
73 M8 Team Valley Gatesd
97 J7 Teangue Highld
107 K9 Teanord Highld
63 L2 Tebay Cumb
63 L2 Tebay Services Cumb
32 E10 Tebworth C Beds
5 Q2 Tedburn St Mary Devon
29 N3 Teddington Gloucs
21 J8 Teddington Gt Lon
39 M9 Tedstone Delamere Herefs
39 M9 Tedstone Wafer Herefs
66 C4 Teesside Crematorium Middsb
41 P12 Teeton Nhants
8 E2 Teffont Evias Wilts
8 E2 Teffont Magna Wilts
25 L3 Tegryn Pembks
42 C7 Teigh Rutlnd
6 B7 Teigngrace Devon
6 C8 Teignmouth Devon
79 P7 Teindside Border
39 M1 Telford Wrekin
49 N12 Telford Crematorium Wrekin
39 N1 Telford Services Shrops
18 B9 Tellisford Somset
11 N8 Telscombe E Susx
91 Q5 Tempar P & K
78 H10 Templand D & G
4 E5 Temple Cnwll
86 G9 Temple Mdloth
37 J9 Temple Bar Cerdgn
17 P5 Temple Cloud BaNES
17 Q10 Templecombe Somset
13 P2 Temple Ewell Kent
30 E3 Temple Grafton Warwks
30 E8 Temple Guiting Gloucs
59 N8 Temple Hirst N York
51 K7 Temple Normanton Derbys
95 N6 Temple of Fiddes Abers
64 B3 Temple Sowerby Cumb
15 Q9 Templeton Devon
25 K6 Templeton Pembks
73 K10 Templetown Dur
32 G6 Tempsford C Beds
39 L8 Tenbury Wells Worcs
25 K8 Tenby Pembks
35 J11 Tendring Essex
35 J10 Tendring Green Essex
35 J10 Tendring Heath Essex
43 P10 Ten Mile Bank Norfk
12 H4 Tenterden Kent
22 F1 Terling Essex
49 L8 Ternhill Shrops
78 F12 Terregles D & G
66 F12 Terrington N York
43 N6 Terrington St Clement Norfk
43 N7 Terrington St John Norfk
22 E11 Teston Kent
9 L5 Testwood Hants
29 M9 Tetbury Gloucs
48 H8 Tetchill Shrops
14 F11 Tetcott Devon
53 K8 Tetford Lincs
53 K4 Tetney Lincs
20 B3 Tetsworth Oxon
40 B7 Tettenhall Wolves
51 L8 Teversal Notts
33 M5 Teversham Cambs
79 N7 Teviothead Border
21 L1 Tewin Herts
29 M3 Tewkesbury Gloucs
23 J10 Teynham Kent
58 F6 Thackley C Brad
10 H6 Thakeham W Susx
20 B3 Thame Oxon
21 J9 Thames Ditton Surrey
21 P7 Thamesmead Gt Lon
23 Q9 Thanet Crematorium Kent
23 L11 Thanington Kent
78 F2 Thankerton S Lans
45 K10 Tharston Norfk
19 N7 Thatcham W Berk
33 P9 Thaxted Essex
65 N9 Theakston N York
60 F9 Thealby N Linc
17 L7 Theale Somset
19 Q6 Theale W Berk
61 J6 Thearne E R Yk
18 F1 The Beeches Gloucs
35 P4 Theberton Suffk
96 G3 The Braes Highld
87 M7 The Brunt E Loth
56 d4 The Bungalow IoM
39 P8 The Burf Worcs
29 M5 The Butts Gloucs
20 C4 The City Bucks
9 J2 The Common Wilts
31 Q3 The Counties Crematorium Nhants
41 P9 Theddingworth Leics
53 M6 Theddlethorpe All Saints Lincs
53 M6 Theddlethorpe St Helen Lincs
76 F2 The Den N Ayrs
28 H6 The Forest of Dean Crematorium Gloucs
13 K3 The Forstal Kent
22 H9 The Garden of England Crematorium Kent
62 D5 The Green Cumb
34 C11 The Green Essex
66 H6 The Green N York
8 C2 The Green Wilts
66 D1 The Headland Hartpl
62 D5 The Hill Cumb
20 E3 The Lee Bucks
56 d2 The Lhen IoM
85 K10 The Linn Crematorium E Rens
34 G2 Thelnetham Suffk
101 L3 The Lochs Moray
35 J1 Thelveton Norfk
57 M10 Thelwall Warrtn
57 P9 The Manchester Crematorium Manch
44 H5 Themelthorpe Norfk
12 F4 The Moor Kent
26 E10 The Mumbles Swans
85 K11 The Murray S Lans
95 M3 The Neuk Abers
31 M6 Thenford Nhants
10 E1 The Park Crematorium Hants
29 M5 The Reddings Gloucs
33 K8 Therfield Herts
51 N1 The Rose Hill Crematorium Donc
92 B10 The Ross P & K
12 H5 The Stocks Kent
18 D8 The Strand Wilts
44 E12 Thetford Norfk
44 D11 Thetford Forest Park
32 G10 The Vale Crematorium Luton
21 N4 Theydon Bois Essex
18 C6 Thickwood Wilts
53 J9 Thimbleby Lincs
66 C8 Thimbleby N York
56 F11 Thingwall Wirral
66 C10 Thirkleby N York
66 C10 Thirlby N York
80 D5 Thirlestane Border
65 L9 Thirn N York
65 Q10 Thirsk N York
56 H2 Thistleton Lancs
42 D6 Thistleton Rutlnd
33 Q2 Thistley Green Suffk
60 E3 Thixendale N York
72 G5 Thockrington Nthumb
43 L8 Tholomas Drove Cambs
59 L2 Tholthorpe N York
102 D7 Thomastown Abers
44 F10 Thompson Norfk
64 H9 Thoralby N York
52 G4 Thoresway Lincs
52 H4 Thorganby Lincs
59 P6 Thorganby N York
66 G7 Thorgill N York
35 N2 Thorington Suffk
34 G9 Thorington Street Suffk
58 C4 Thorlby N York
33 M11 Thorley Herts
9 L9 Thorley Street IoW
66 C11 Thormanby N York
66 C4 Thornaby-on-Tees S on T
44 H3 Thornage Norfk
31 Q7 Thornborough Bucks
65 N10 Thornborough N York
58 G7 Thornbury C Brad
14 G9 Thornbury Devon
39 L9 Thornbury Herefs
28 H10 Thornbury S Glos
41 P11 Thornby Nhants
50 D8 Thorncliff Staffs
62 E7 Thorncliffe Crematorium Cumb
7 K3 Thorncombe Dorset
35 J3 Thorndon Suffk
5 L2 Thorndon Cross Devon
59 P10 Thorne Donc
17 M11 Thorne Somset
59 J6 Thorner Leeds
16 E11 Thorne St Margaret Somset
43 J8 Thorney C Pete
52 C8 Thorney Notts
17 K10 Thorney Somset
8 H7 Thorney Hill Hants
10 C9 Thorney Island W Susx
16 H10 Thornfalcon Somset
17 N12 Thornford Dorset
72 E7 Thorngrafton Nthumb
61 L8 Thorngumbald E R Yk
44 C2 Thornham Norfk
34 H3 Thornham Magna Suffk
35 J3 Thornham Parva Suffk
42 F9 Thornhaugh C Pete
9 M5 Thornhill C Sotn
62 B1 Thornhill Cumb
78 E9 Thornhill D & G
50 G4 Thornhill Derbys
58 G9 Thornhill Kirk
85 L3 Thornhill Stirlg
27 N11 Thornhill Crematorium Cardif
61 J2 Thornholme E R Yk
8 C6 Thornicombe Dorset
81 J7 Thornington Nthumb
73 K12 Thornley Dur
73 P11 Thornley Dur
85 J10 Thornliebank E Rens
34 C6 Thorns Suffk
50 D4 Thornsett Derbys
71 K9 Thornthwaite Cumb
58 F3 Thornthwaite N York
93 M6 Thornton Angus
31 Q7 Thornton Bucks
58 E7 Thornton C Brad
60 D5 Thornton E R Yk
86 F3 Thornton Fife
56 G1 Thornton Lancs
41 L6 Thornton Leics
66 C5 Thornton Middsb
81 K5 Thornton Nthumb
61 J9 Thornton Curtis N Linc
56 G8 Thornton Garden of Rest Crematorium Sefton
85 K11 Thorntonhall S Lans
21 L9 Thornton Heath Gt Lon
56 F11 Thornton Hough Wirral
58 B5 Thornton-in-Craven N York
63 M7 Thornton in Lonsdale N York
65 P9 Thornton-le-Beans N York
59 P2 Thornton-le-Clay N York
67 J10 Thornton le Dale N York
52 F4 Thornton le Moor Lincs
65 P9 Thornton-le-Moor N York
48 H1 Thornton-le-Moors Ches W
65 P9 Thornton-le-Street N York
87 N7 Thorntonloch E Loth
64 G9 Thornton Rust N York
65 L9 Thornton Steward N York
65 M9 Thornton Watlass N York
80 E5 Thornydykes Border
71 N10 Thornythwaite Cumb
51 Q11 Thoroton Notts
59 K5 Thorp Arch Leeds
50 F10 Thorpe Derbys
60 G5 Thorpe E R Yk
58 D2 Thorpe N York
51 Q10 Thorpe Notts
20 G9 Thorpe Surrey
35 K2 Thorpe Abbotts Norfk
41 Q4 Thorpe Arnold Leics
59 L10 Thorpe Audlin Wakefd
67 J11 Thorpe Bassett N York
22 H6 Thorpe Bay Sthend
42 C10 Thorpe by Water Rutlnd
40 H6 Thorpe Constantine Staffs
45 L7 Thorpe End Norfk
35 J11 Thorpe Green Essex
34 F6 Thorpe Green Suffk
51 J2 Thorpe Hesley Rothm
59 N11 Thorpe in Balne Donc
41 Q8 Thorpe Langton Leics
20 G8 Thorpe Lea Surrey
35 K11 Thorpe-le-Soken Essex
60 E5 Thorpe le Street E R Yk
32 B2 Thorpe Malsor Nhants
31 M5 Thorpe Mandeville Nhants
45 L3 Thorpe Market Norfk
45 K7 Thorpe Marriot Norfk
34 F6 Thorpe Morieux Suffk
35 P5 Thorpeness Suffk
52 C9 Thorpe on the Hill Lincs
20 G9 Thorpe Park Surrey
45 L8 Thorpe St Andrew Norfk
53 M10 Thorpe St Peter Lincs
51 M5 Thorpe Salvin Rothm
41 Q5 Thorpe Satchville Leics
65 P3 Thorpe Thewles S on T
52 G11 Thorpe Tilney Lincs
59 L3 Thorpe Underwood N York
32 E1 Thorpe Waterville Nhants
59 M7 Thorpe Willoughby N York
34 H11 Thorrington Essex
6 C3 Thorverton Devon
35 J2 Thrandeston Suffk
32 E2 Thrapston Nhants
48 H6 Threapwood Ches W
50 D11 Threapwood Staffs
76 F9 Threave S Ayrs
70 C3 Threave Castle D & G
11 L3 Three Bridges W Susx
12 G3 Three Chimneys Kent
27 N2 Three Cocks Powys
34 D10 Three Counties Crematorium Essex
26 D9 Three Crosses Swans
12 D6 Three Cups Corner E Susx
42 F3 Threekingham Lincs
12 D4 Three Leg Cross E Susx
8 F6 Three Legged Cross Dorset
20 B9 Three Mile Cross Wokham
2 H6 Threemilestone Cnwll
86 C7 Three Miletown W Loth
12 G7 Three Oaks E Susx
71 M9 Threlkeld Cumb
21 P2 Threshers Bush Essex
58 C2 Threshfield N York
45 P7 Thrigby Norfk
41 K4 Thringstone Leics
65 N8 Thrintoft N York
33 M7 Thriplow Cambs
33 K10 Throcking Herts
73 K7 Throckley N u Ty
30 C4 Throckmorton Worcs
8 G8 Throop Bmouth
72 H1 Thropton Nthumb
85 P5 Throsk Stirlg
78 E11 Throughgate D & G
5 N3 Throwleigh Devon
23 J11 Throwley Forstal Kent
41 L2 Thrumpton Notts
110 G6 Thrumster Highld
53 K2 Thrunscoe NE Lin
29 M7 Thrupp Gloucs
41 P4 Thrussington Leics
19 K10 Thruxton Hants
28 E2 Thruxton Herefs
51 L2 Thrybergh Rothm
41 K2 Thulston Derbys
22 F6 Thundersley Essex
41 M5 Thurcaston Leics
51 L3 Thurcroft Rothm
45 K3 Thurgarton Norfk
51 P10 Thurgarton Notts
50 H1 Thurgoland Barns
41 L7 Thurlaston Leics
41 L12 Thurlaston Warwks
16 H11 Thurlbear Somset
42 F6 Thurlby Lincs
52 C10 Thurlby Lincs
53 M8 Thurlby Lincs
32 F5 Thurleigh Bed
5 N10 Thurlestone Devon
16 H9 Thurloxton Somset
58 G12 Thurlstone Barns
45 N9 Thurlton Norfk
41 N5 Thurmaston Leics
41 N6 Thurnby Leics
45 N7 Thurne Norfk
22 F11 Thurnham Kent
42 F12 Thurning Nhants
44 H4 Thurning Norfk
59 L11 Thurnscoe Barns
22 C7 Thurrock Services Thurr
71 M5 Thursby Cumb
44 G4 Thursford Norfk
10 E3 Thursley Surrey
110 D3 Thurso Highld
56 F11 Thurstaston Wirral
34 F4 Thurston Suffk
71 M4 Thurstonfield Cumb
58 F11 Thurstonland Kirk
45 M9 Thurton Norfk
50 G12 Thurvaston Derbys
44 G8 Thuxton Norfk
64 F7 Thwaite N York
35 J3 Thwaite Suffk
62 G4 Thwaite Head Cumb
45 M10 Thwaite St Mary Norfk
67 M12 Thwing E R Yk
92 F10 Tibbermore P & K
78 E9 Tibbers D & G
29 K4 Tibberton Gloucs
30 B3 Tibberton Worcs
49 M10 Tibberton Wrekin
79 K5 Tibbie Shiels Inn Border
45 J11 Tibenham Norfk
51 K8 Tibshelf Derbys
60 G3 Tibthorpe E R Yk
12 E4 Ticehurst E Susx
9 P2 Tichborne Hants
42 E8 Tickencote Rutlnd
17 L2 Tickenham N Som
51 N3 Tickhill Donc
39 J4 Ticklerton Shrops
41 J3 Ticknall Derbys
61 J6 Tickton E R Yk
19 K8 Tidcombe Wilts
31 P12 Tiddington Oxon
30 G3 Tiddington Warwks
12 C4 Tidebrook E Susx
4 H8 Tideford Cnwll
28 G9 Tidenham Gloucs
50 F6 Tideswell Derbys
19 Q6 Tidmarsh W Berk
30 H6 Tidmington Warwks
19 J10 Tidworth Wilts
24 F6 Tiers Cross Pembks
31 P4 Tiffield Nhants
95 J8 Tigerton Angus
111 a4 Tigh a Ghearraidh W Isls
111 a4 Tigharry W Isls
83 P8 Tighnabruaich Ag & B
5 P7 Tigley Devon
32 F3 Tilbrook Cambs
22 D8 Tilbury Thurr
40 H11 Tile Hill Covtry
19 Q6 Tilehurst Readg
10 E2 Tilford Surrey
11 L3 Tilgate W Susx
17 M8 Tilham Street Somset
85 Q4 Tillicoultry Clacks
77 N3 Tillietudlem S Lans
23 J3 Tillingham Essex
39 J12 Tillington Herefs
10 F6 Tillington W Susx
39 J11 Tillington Common Herefs
95 L1 Tillybirloch Abers
102 E11 Tillyfourie Abers
103 J10 Tillygreig Abers
86 D2 Tillyrie P & K
23 P12 Tilmanstone Kent
43 P6 Tilney All Saints Norfk
43 N6 Tilney High End Norfk
43 N7 Tilney St Lawrence Norfk
18 F10 Tilshead Wilts
49 K7 Tilstock Shrops
49 J5 Tilston Ches W
49 K4 Tilstone Fearnall Ches W
32 E11 Tilsworth C Beds
41 Q6 Tilton on the Hill Leics
29 L8 Tiltups End Gloucs
52 G10 Timberland Lincs
50 B8 Timbersbrook Ches E
16 C7 Timberscombe Somset
58 F4 Timble N York
71 M1 Timpanheck D & G
57 P10 Timperley Traffd
17 P4 Timsbury BaNES
9 L3 Timsbury Hants
111 c2 Timsgarry W Isls
111 c2 Timsgearraidh W Isls
34 E3 Timworth Suffk
34 E3 Timworth Green Suffk
8 B8 Tincleton Dorset
72 B8 Tindale Cumb
65 L3 Tindale Crescent Dur
31 P7 Tingewick Bucks
32 E9 Tingrith C Beds
111 k4 Tingwall Airport Shet
5 J3 Tinhay Devon
51 K3 Tinsley Sheff
11 L3 Tinsley Green W Susx
4 C3 Tintagel Cnwll
4 C3 Tintagel Castle Cnwll
28 G8 Tintern Abbey Mons
28 F8 Tintern Parva Mons
17 M11 Tintinhull Somset
50 D2 Tintwistle Derbys
78 G11 Tinwald D & G
42 E8 Tinwell Rutlnd
40 C8 Tipton Sandw
6 E5 Tipton St John Devon
34 E12 Tiptree Essex
22 G1 Tiptree Heath Essex
37 P11 Tirabad Powys
88 C7 Tiree Ag & B
88 C7 Tiree Airport Ag & B
83 K9 Tiretigan Ag & B
29 L3 Tirley Gloucs
27 N7 Tirphil Caerph
71 P9 Tirril Cumb
8 D2 Tisbury Wilts
50 F9 Tissington Derbys
14 E6 Titchberry Devon
9 P6 Titchfield Hants
32 E2 Titchmarsh Nhants
44 C2 Titchwell Norfk
51 P12 Tithby Notts
38 G9 Titley Herefs
21 N11 Titsey Surrey
14 E10 Titson Cnwll
49 Q7 Tittensor Staffs
44 E6 Tittleshall Norfk
39 P7 Titton Worcs
49 K4 Tiverton Ches W
6 C1 Tiverton Devon
45 K11 Tivetshall St Margaret Norfk
45 J11 Tivetshall St Mary Norfk
40 C3 Tixall Staffs
42 D9 Tixover Rutlnd
111 k5 Toab Shet
89 L5 Tobermory Ag & B
83 L2 Toberonochy Ag & B
111 a5 Tobha Mor W Isls
102 F8 Tocher Abers
101 P3 Tochieneal Moray
18 F5 Tockenham Wilts
57 M4 Tockholes Bl w D
28 H10 Tockington S Glos
59 L4 Tockwith N York
8 B4 Todber Dorset
32 E10 Toddington C Beds
30 D7 Toddington Gloucs
32 E10 Toddington Services C Beds
30 G7 Todenham Gloucs
93 M7 Todhills Angus
71 N3 Todhills Services Cumb
58 C8 Todmorden Calder
51 L4 Todwick Rothm
33 K5 Toft Cambs
42 F6 Toft Lincs
111 k3 Toft Shet
65 K2 Toft Hill Dur
45 N10 Toft Monks Norfk
52 E6 Toft next Newton Lincs
44 E5 Toftrees Norfk
73 M1 Togston Nthumb
96 H7 Tokavaig Highld
20 B7 Tokers Green Oxon
111 e1 Tolastadh W Isls
16 E9 Tolland Somset
8 D4 Tollard Royal Wilts
59 M11 Toll Bar Donc
7 N4 Toller Fratrum Dorset
7 N3 Toller Porcorum Dorset
59 L2 Tollerton N York
41 N1 Tollerton Notts
23 J2 Tollesbury Essex
22 H2 Tolleshunt D'Arcy Essex
22 H1 Tolleshunt Knights Essex
22 H2 Tolleshunt Major Essex
8 B8 Tolpuddle Dorset
111 e1 Tolsta W Isls
21 J9 Tolworth Gt Lon
99 M4 Tomatin Highld
98 C6 Tomchrasky Highld
98 B8 Tomdoun Highld
98 D4 Tomich Highld
107 J11 Tomich Highld
107 K2 Tomich Highld
107 L8 Tomich Highld
101 J10 Tomintoul Moray
98 G2 Tomnacross Highld
101 J9 Tomnavoulin Moray
12 C2 Tonbridge Kent
27 J11 Tondu Brdgnd
16 F11 Tonedale Somset
58 G7 Tong C Brad
23 J11 Tong Kent
39 P1 Tong Shrops
41 K3 Tonge Leics
10 E1 Tongham Surrey
69 Q8 Tongland D & G
39 P1 Tong Norton Shrops
109 K4 Tongue Highld
27 N11 Tongwynlais Cardif
26 H9 Tonmawr Neath
26 G8 Tonna Neath
33 K12 Tonwell Herts
27 L9 Tonypandy Rhondd
27 L10 Tonyrefail Rhondd
19 P1 Toot Baldon Oxon

21 P3 Toot Hill Essex
18 G4 Toothill Swindn
21 L8 Tooting Gt Lon
21 L8 Tooting Bec Gt Lon
65 P11 Topcliffe N York
45 L10 Topcroft Norfk
45 L10 Topcroft Street Norfk
34 C8 Toppesfield Essex
45 J9 Toprow Norfk
6 C5 Topsham Devon
75 N6 Torbeg N Ayrs
107 M3 Torboll Highld
99 J2 Torbreck Highld
5 Q6 Torbryan Devon
90 F1 Torcastle Highld
5 Q10 Torcross Devon
107 K10 Tore Highld
83 M9 Torinturk Ag & B
52 B7 Torksey Lincs
18 B5 Tormarton S Glos
75 N6 Tormore N Ayrs
107 M11 Tornagrain Highld
95 K2 Tornaveen Abers
98 H4 Torness Highld
65 L2 Toronto Dur
89 P8 Torosay Castle Ag & B
71 K7 Torpenhow Cumb
86 A7 Torphichen W Loth
95 K2 Torphins Abers
5 J8 Torpoint Cnwll
6 C9 Torquay Torbay
6 B9 Torquay Crematorium Torbay
87 J11 Torquhan Border
104 H11 Torran Highld
85 K8 Torrance E Duns
76 F3 Torranyard N Ayrs
105 N10 Torridon Highld
105 M10 Torridon House Highld
96 G5 Torrin Highld
75 M5 Torrisdale Ag & B
109 M4 Torrisdale Highld
110 A11 Torrish Highld
63 J9 Torrisholme Lancs
107 K2 Torrobull Highld
95 Q2 Torry C Aber
86 B5 Torryburn Fife
6 a2 Torteval Guern
78 G12 Torthorwald D & G
10 G8 Tortington W Susx
39 Q7 Torton Worcs
29 J9 Tortworth S Glos
96 F2 Torvaig Highld
62 F4 Torver Cumb
85 P6 Torwood Falk
79 P2 Torwoodlee Border
51 P4 Torworth Notts
97 J3 Toscaig Highld
33 J4 Toseland Cambs
63 P10 Tosside Lancs
34 F4 Tostock Suffk
104 B11 Totaig Highld
104 F11 Tote Highld
104 G9 Tote Highld
9 K9 Totland IoW
50 H5 Totley Sheff
5 Q7 Totnes Devon
41 L1 Toton Notts
88 E5 Totronald Ag & B
104 E8 Totscore Highld
21 M5 Tottenham Gt Lon
43 Q7 Tottenhill Norfk
21 K5 Totteridge Gt Lon
32 E11 Totternhoe C Beds
57 P6 Tottington Bury
9 L5 Totton Hants
16 G9 Toulton Somset
107 P6 Toulvaddie Highld
22 F11 Tovil Kent
84 C8 Toward Ag & B
84 B9 Toward Quay Ag & B
31 P4 Towcester Nhants
2 D7 Towednack Cnwll
20 B3 Towersey Oxon
101 N11 Towie Abers
73 K11 Tow Law Dur
43 L10 Town End Cambs
84 G7 Townend W Duns
50 F1 Townhead Barns
78 G10 Townhead D & G
70 C3 Townhead of Greenlaw D & G
86 D4 Townhill Fife
11 N6 Town Littleworth E Susx
19 P8 Towns End Hants
2 E8 Townshend Cnwll
44 C11 Town Street Suffk
80 H8 Town Yetholm Border
59 N3 Towthorpe C York
59 L6 Towton N York
55 P6 Towyn Conwy
56 G10 Toxteth Lpool
53 L10 Toynton All Saints Lincs
21 P12 Toy's Hill Kent
76 G7 Trabboch E Ayrs
76 H7 Trabbochburn E Ayrs
100 D4 Tradespark Highld
27 K3 Trallong Powys
51 J9 Tramway Museum Derbys
86 H7 Tranent E Loth
56 G10 Tranmere Wirral
109 Q5 Trantelbeg Highld
109 Q5 Trantlemore Highld
26 E5 Trapp Carmth
87 L7 Traprain E Loth
79 M3 Traquair Border
58 B6 Trawden Lancs
47 L4 Trawsfynydd Gwynd
27 L9 Trealaw Rhondd
56 H3 Treales Lancs
54 C6 Trearddur Bay IoA
104 E10 Treaslane Highld
4 B5 Trebetherick Cnwll
16 D8 Treborough Somset
4 H5 Trebullett Cnwll
4 H5 Treburley Cnwll
27 J3 Trecastle Powys
24 G3 Trecwn Pembks
27 L7 Trecynon Rhondd
27 N7 Tredegar Blae G
29 M3 Tredington Gloucs
30 H5 Tredington Warwks
28 D9 Tredunnock Mons
2 B10 Treen Cnwll
51 K4 Treeton Rothm
24 F2 Trefasser Pembks
27 N3 Trefecca Powys
37 Q3 Trefeglwys Powys
24 G4 Treffgarne Pembks
24 F4 Treffgarne Owen Pembks
27 M10 Trefforest Rhondd
37 J8 Trefilan Cerdgn
24 E3 Trefin Pembks
48 B2 Trefnant Denbgs
48 F9 Trefonen Shrops
46 F3 Trefor Gwynd
55 L8 Trefriw Conwy
4 G4 Tregadillett Cnwll
28 E6 Tregare Mons
37 L8 Tregaron Cerdgn
54 H7 Tregarth Gwynd
4 F3 Tregeare Cnwll
48 D8 Tregeiriog Wrexhm
54 E3 Tregele IoA
24 E3 Treglemais Pembks
3 L3 Tregonetha Cnwll
3 K6 Tregony Cnwll
3 M5 Tregorrick Cnwll
27 P2 Tregoyd Powys
36 G10 Tre-groes Cerdgn
38 C3 Tregynon Powys
25 P5 Tre-gynwr Carmth
27 L10 Trehafod Rhondd
5 J8 Trehan Cnwll
27 M9 Treharris Myr Td
27 K8 Treherbert Rhondd
4 H5 Trekenner Cnwll
4 C3 Treknow Cnwll
56 C11 Trelawnyd Flints
25 M3 Trelech Carmth
24 D3 Treleddyd-fawr Pembks
27 M9 Trelewis Myr Td
4 B4 Trelights Cnwll
4 C5 Trelill Cnwll
3 J7 Trelissick Garden Cnwll
28 F7 Trellech Mons
56 D11 Trelogan Flints
47 J4 Tremadog Gwynd
4 E3 Tremail Cnwll
36 D10 Tremain Cerdgn
4 F3 Tremaine Cnwll
4 G6 Tremar Cnwll
5 J8 Trematon Cnwll
48 C2 Tremeirchion Denbgs
3 J3 Trenance Cnwll
3 L2 Trenance Cnwll
49 M11 Trench Wrekin
2 G9 Trenear Cnwll
4 F3 Treneglos Cnwll
17 N11 Trent Dorset
49 Q7 Trentham C Stke
15 L3 Trentishoe Devon
27 K12 Treoes V Glam
27 K8 Treorchy Rhondd
3 M1 Trequite Cnwll
27 L12 Trerhyngyll V Glam
4 H8 Trerulefoot Cnwll
36 E9 Tresaith Cerdgn
2 b2 Tresco IoS
2 b2 Tresco Heliport IoS
2 E9 Trescowe Cnwll
2 H4 Tresean Cnwll
29 L9 Tresham Gloucs
88 G7 Treshnish Isles Ag & B
3 K6 Tresillian Cnwll
14 D11 Treskinnick Cross Cnwll
4 F3 Tresmeer Cnwll
4 E2 Tresparrett Cnwll
92 C4 Tressait P & K
111 k4 Tresta Shet
111 m2 Tresta Shet
52 A7 Treswell Notts
37 L3 Tre Taliesin Cerdgn
4 D3 Trethevey Cnwll
2 B10 Trethewey Cnwll
3 M5 Trethurgy Cnwll
28 F4 Tretire Herefs
27 P5 Tretower Powys
48 F4 Treuddyn Flints
4 D3 Trevalga Cnwll
48 H4 Trevalyn Wrexhm
3 J3 Trevarrian Cnwll
2 H4 Treveal Cnwll
4 D4 Treveighan Cnwll
2 H5 Trevellas Downs Cnwll
4 F7 Trevelmond Cnwll
2 H9 Treverva Cnwll
2 B10 Trevescan Cnwll
3 L5 Treviscoe Cnwll
3 K1 Trevone Cnwll
48 F7 Trevor Wrexhm
4 D4 Trewalder Cnwll
4 D3 Trewarmett Cnwll
4 F4 Trewen Cnwll
4 F4 Trewint Cnwll
3 K8 Trewithian Cnwll
3 L5 Trewoon Cnwll
10 D6 Treyford W Susx
65 P1 Trimdon Dur
65 P1 Trimdon Colliery Dur
65 P1 Trimdon Grange Dur
45 L3 Trimingham Norfk
35 L8 Trimley St Martin Suffk
35 L9 Trimley St Mary Suffk
26 B7 Trimsaran Carmth
15 J4 Trimstone Devon
91 Q4 Trinafour P & K
20 E2 Tring Herts
95 K9 Trinity Angus
7 b1 Trinity Jersey
92 E11 Trinity Gask P & K
16 F8 Triscombe Somset
90 E2 Trislaig Highld
3 J6 Trispen Cnwll
73 L3 Tritlington Nthumb
92 E7 Trochry P & K
36 E10 Troedyraur Cerdgn
27 M8 Troedyrhiw Myr Td
2 F8 Troon Cnwll
76 F5 Troon S Ayrs
59 J6 Tropical World Roundhay Park Leeds
84 H2 Trossachs Stirlg
84 H2 Trossachs Pier Stirlg
34 E3 Troston Suffk
30 B3 Trotshill Worcs
22 D10 Trottiscliffe Kent
10 D5 Trotton W Susx
62 H2 Troutbeck Cumb
62 H3 Troutbeck Bridge Cumb
51 K5 Troway Derbys
18 C8 Trowbridge Wilts
51 L11 Trowell Notts
51 L11 Trowell Services Notts
45 L8 Trowse Newton Norfk
17 Q7 Trudoxhill Somset
16 G10 Trull Somset
104 C9 Trumpan Highld
28 H2 Trumpet Herefs
33 M6 Trumpington Cambs
45 L3 Trunch Norfk
3 J6 Truro Cnwll
3 J6 Truro Cathedral Cnwll
6 B6 Trusham Devon
40 G1 Trusley Derbys
53 N6 Trusthorpe Lincs
39 Q4 Trysull Staffs
19 M2 Tubney Oxon
5 Q8 Tuckenhay Devon
39 P5 Tuckhill Shrops
2 F7 Tuckingmill Cnwll
8 D2 Tuckingmill Wilts
8 G8 Tuckton Bmouth
34 C3 Tuddenham Suffk
35 K7 Tuddenham Suffk
12 C2 Tudeley Kent
65 M1 Tudhoe Dur
46 D4 Tudweiliog Gwynd
29 L6 Tuffley Gloucs
19 M10 Tufton Hants
24 H3 Tufton Pembks
41 Q7 Tugby Leics
39 K5 Tugford Shrops
81 P8 Tughall Nthumb
85 P4 Tullibody Clacks
99 J4 Tullich Highld
107 P7 Tullich Highld
92 E5 Tulliemet P & K
102 G8 Tulloch Abers
83 P4 Tullochgorm Ag & B
98 E11 Tulloch Station Highld
92 H5 Tullymurdoch P & K
102 D10 Tullynessle Abers
21 L8 Tulse Hill Gt Lon
26 D6 Tumble Carmth
53 J10 Tumby Lincs
53 J11 Tumby Woodside Lincs
92 B4 Tummel Bridge P & K
12 C3 Tunbridge Wells Kent
79 J11 Tundergarth D & G
17 Q4 Tunley BaNES
49 Q5 Tunstall C Stke
61 M7 Tunstall E R Yk
22 H10 Tunstall Kent
63 L7 Tunstall Lancs
65 L8 Tunstall N York
45 N8 Tunstall Norfk
49 P9 Tunstall Staffs
35 M6 Tunstall Suffk
73 P9 Tunstall Sundld
50 E6 Tunstead Derbys
45 L6 Tunstead Norfk
50 D5 Tunstead Milton Derbys
20 B10 Turgis Green Hants
30 E9 Turkdean Gloucs
41 Q8 Tur Langton Leics
18 B8 Turleigh Wilts
28 D2 Turnastone Herefs
76 D9 Turnberry S Ayrs
50 H10 Turnditch Derbys
11 M3 Turner's Hill W Susx
86 D7 Turnhouse C Edin
8 B6 Turnworth Dorset
102 F5 Turriff Abers
57 N6 Turton Bottoms Bl w D
43 K10 Turves Cambs
32 D6 Turvey Bed
20 C5 Turville Bucks
31 N6 Turweston Bucks
79 L5 Tushielaw Inn Border
40 G2 Tutbury Staffs
28 G9 Tutshill Gloucs
45 K5 Tuttington Norfk
51 Q6 Tuxford Notts
111 g2 Twatt Ork
111 k4 Twatt Shet
85 L7 Twechar E Duns
80 C7 Tweedbank Border
81 L4 Tweedmouth Nthumb
78 H4 Tweedsmuir Border
2 H7 Twelveheads Cnwll
49 P2 Twemlow Green Ches E
42 G6 Twenty Lincs
17 Q4 Twerton BaNES
21 J8 Twickenham Gt Lon
29 L4 Twigworth Gloucs
11 K6 Twineham W Susx
34 E9 Twinstead Essex
15 N6 Twitchen Devon
50 H8 Two Dales Derbys
40 G7 Two Gates Staffs
41 J6 Twycross Leics
40 H6 Twycross Zoo Leics
31 P8 Twyford Bucks
9 N3 Twyford Hants
41 Q5 Twyford Leics
44 G5 Twyford Norfk
20 C8 Twyford Wokham
69 P8 Twynholm D & G
29 M2 Twyning Green Gloucs
26 G4 Twynllanan Carmth
32 D2 Twywell Nhants
28 D2 Tyberton Herefs
26 E6 Tycroes Carmth
48 C10 Tycrwyn Powys
43 M6 Tydd Gote Lincs
43 L6 Tydd St Giles Cambs
43 M6 Tydd St Mary Lincs
33 P9 Tye Green Essex
57 M8 Tyldesley Wigan
23 L10 Tyler Hill Kent
27 L9 Tylorstown Rhondd
48 B6 Ty-nant Conwy
91 J9 Tyndrum Stirlg
48 E7 Ty'n-dwr Denbgs
73 P7 Tynemouth N Tyne
73 N7 Tynemouth Crematorium N Tyne
87 L6 Tyninghame E Loth
77 N11 Tynron D & G
17 M2 Tyntesfield N Som
37 L6 Tynygraig Cerdgn
55 L7 Ty'n-y-Groes Conwy
27 M10 Tyn-y-nant Rhondd
32 C7 Tyringham M Keyn
27 J11 Tythegston Brdgnd
50 B6 Tytherington Ches E
29 J10 Tytherington S Glos
18 D11 Tytherington Wilts
7 J3 Tytherleigh Devon
18 D6 Tytherton Lucas Wilts
3 N5 Tywardreath Cnwll
47 J10 Tywyn Gwynd

U

35 M3 Ubbeston Green Suffk
17 M5 Ubley BaNES
11 P6 Uckfield E Susx
29 M2 Uckinghall Worcs
29 M4 Uckington Gloucs
85 L10 Uddingston S Lans
78 E3 Uddington S Lans
12 G6 Udimore E Susx
103 J9 Udny Green Abers
103 J9 Udny Station Abers
16 E12 Uffculme Devon
42 F8 Uffington Lincs
19 K3 Uffington Oxon
49 K11 Uffington Shrops
42 F8 Ufford C Pete
35 L6 Ufford Suffk
31 J2 Ufton Warwks
19 Q7 Ufton Nervet W Berk
75 L6 Ugadale Ag & B
5 N8 Ugborough Devon
35 P2 Uggeshall Suffk
67 J6 Ugglebarnby N York
50 G3 Ughill Sheff
33 N10 Ugley Essex
33 N10 Ugley Green Essex
66 H5 Ugthorpe N York
111 b6 Uibhist A Deas W Isls
111 a4 Uibhist A Tuath W Isls
88 E5 Uig Ag & B
104 B10 Uig Highld
104 E9 Uig Highld
111 c2 Uig W Isls
104 F12 Uigshader Highld
89 J11 Uisken Ag & B
110 G7 Ulbster Highld
53 L8 Ulceby Lincs
61 J10 Ulceby N Linc
61 J10 Ulceby Skitter N Linc
12 G1 Ulcombe Kent
71 L7 Uldale Cumb
29 K8 Uley Gloucs
73 M3 Ulgham Nthumb
106 B4 Ullapool Highld
30 E1 Ullenhall Warwks
59 M6 Ulleskelf N York
41 L9 Ullesthorpe Leics
51 L4 Ulley Rothm
39 L11 Ullingswick Herefs
96 C3 Ullinish Lodge Hotel Highld
70 H10 Ullock Cumb
71 N10 Ullswater Cumb
62 E4 Ulpha Cumb
61 K3 Ulrome E R Yk
111 k3 Ulsta Shet
89 J8 Ulva Ag & B
62 F6 Ulverston Cumb
8 F10 Ulwell Dorset
77 N9 Ulzieside D & G
15 K7 Umberleigh Devon
108 E8 Unapool Highld
63 J4 Underbarrow Cumb
79 P11 Under Burnmouth Border
58 F7 Undercliffe C Brad
49 J11 Underdale Shrops
22 B11 Under River Kent
51 L10 Underwood Notts
28 E10 Undy Mons
56 c5 Union Mills IoM
111 m2 Unst Shet
51 J5 Unstone Derbys
18 G9 Upavon Wilts
22 G9 Upchurch Kent
15 N6 Upcott Devon
6 C3 Up Exe Devon
45 J6 Upgate Norfk
7 M3 Uphall Dorset
86 C7 Uphall W Loth
15 Q9 Upham Devon
9 N4 Upham Hants
38 H9 Uphampton Herefs
39 Q8 Uphampton Worcs
17 J5 Uphill N Som
57 K7 Up Holland Lancs
84 G11 Uplawmoor E Rens
29 K4 Upleadon Gloucs
66 E4 Upleatham R & Cl
7 M4 Uploders Dorset
16 D11 Uplowman Devon
7 J4 Uplyme Devon
10 C7 Up Marden W Susx
22 C6 Upminster Gt Lon
17 N11 Up Mudford Somset
20 B11 Up Nately Hants
6 G2 Upottery Devon
39 J5 Upper Affcot Shrops
107 K5 Upper Ardchronie Highld
39 N6 Upper Arley Worcs
19 P5 Upper Basildon W Berk
11 K7 Upper Beeding W Susx
42 E11 Upper Benefield Nhants
30 C2 Upper Bentley Worcs
109 Q4 Upper Bighouse Highld
31 L4 Upper Boddington Nhants
30 H6 Upper Brailes Warwks
97 J5 Upper Breakish Highld
39 P10 Upper Broadheath Worcs
41 P3 Upper Broughton Notts
19 P7 Upper Bucklebury W Berk
8 H4 Upper Burgate Hants
71 N5 Upperby Cumb
32 G7 Upper Caldecote C Beds
27 L1 Upper Chapel Powys
8 E2 Upper Chicksgrove Wilts
19 K9 Upper Chute Wilts
21 M6 Upper Clapton Gt Lon
19 L11 Upper Clatford Hants
39 K2 Upper Cound Shrops
58 G11 Upper Cumberworth Kirk
101 M3 Upper Dallachy Moray
23 Q11 Upper Deal Kent
32 F4 Upper Dean Bed
58 G11 Upper Denby Kirk
12 B7 Upper Dicker E Susx
110 B3 Upper Dounreay Highld
35 K9 Upper Dovercourt Essex
85 L2 Upper Drumbane Stirlg
59 K2 Upper Dunsforth N York
10 F2 Upper Eashing Surrey
107 M9 Upper Eathie Highld
39 M12 Upper Egleton Herefs
50 D8 Upper Elkstone Staffs
50 E11 Upper Ellastone Staffs
10 B3 Upper Farringdon Hants
29 K6 Upper Framilode Gloucs
10 C2 Upper Froyle Hants
104 D11 Upperglen Highld
17 L7 Upper Godney Somset
32 G9 Upper Gravenhurst C Beds
19 L7 Upper Green W Berk
28 G4 Upper Grove Common Herefs
10 D1 Upper Hale Surrey
20 H9 Upper Halliford Surrey
42 C8 Upper Hambleton Rutlnd
23 L10 Upper Harbledown Kent
11 P3 Upper Hartfield E Susx
29 M5 Upper Hatherley Gloucs
58 F9 Upper Heaton Kirk
59 P3 Upper Helmsley N York
38 F10 Upper Hergest Herefs
31 P3 Upper Heyford Nhants
31 L8 Upper Heyford Oxon
39 J10 Upper Hill Herefs
58 G9 Upper Hopton Kirk
50 D8 Upper Hulme Staffs
18 H2 Upper Inglesham Swindn
26 D9 Upper Killay Swans
90 G10 Upper Kinchrackine Ag & B
19 K5 Upper Lambourn W Berk
40 C6 Upper Landywood Staffs
17 L4 Upper Langford N Som
51 L6 Upper Langwith Derbys
87 J2 Upper Largo Fife
50 D12 Upper Leigh Staffs
95 L3 Upper Lochton Abers
40 D5 Upper Longdon Staffs
32 G9 Upper & Lower Stondon C Beds
110 F8 Upper Lybster Highld
28 H6 Upper Lydbrook Gloucs
38 H8 Upper Lye Herefs
58 C11 Uppermill Oldham
39 P7 Upper Milton Worcs
18 E3 Upper Minety Wilts
101 L5 Upper Mulben Moray
39 L4 Upper Netchwood Shrops
40 D1 Upper Nobut Staffs
10 F6 Upper Norwood W Susx
59 M4 Upper Poppleton C York
9 K3 Upper Ratley Hants
30 G9 Upper Rissington Gloucs
39 L8 Upper Rochford Worcs
69 N6 Upper Ruscoe D & G
39 M8 Upper Sapey Herefs
18 D5 Upper Seagry Wilts
32 E7 Upper Shelton C Beds
45 J2 Upper Sheringham Norfk
84 D9 Upper Skelmorlie N Ayrs
30 F9 Upper Slaughter Gloucs
28 H6 Upper Soudley Gloucs
13 N3 Upper Standen Kent
45 L9 Upper Stoke Norfk
31 N3 Upper Stowe Nhants
8 H4 Upper Street Hants
45 M6 Upper Street Norfk
45 M6 Upper Street Norfk
34 C6 Upper Street Suffk
34 H6 Upper Street Suffk
32 F10 Upper Sundon C Beds
30 F8 Upper Swell Gloucs
45 K10 Upper Tasburgh Norfk
50 D11 Upper Tean Staffs
58 F11 Upperthong Kirk
10 F5 Upperton W Susx
39 L11 Upper Town Herefs
110 G1 Uppertown Highld
17 M3 Upper Town N Som
34 F4 Upper Town Suffk
26 D6 Upper Tumble Carmth
31 J5 Upper Tysoe Warwks
93 P8 Upper Victoria Angus
31 L5 Upper Wardington Oxon
29 K1 Upper Welland Worcs
11 N7 Upper Wellingham E Susx
35 K2 Upper Weybread Suffk
19 Q11 Upper Wield Hants
31 Q10 Upper Winchendon Bucks
18 G12 Upper Woodford Wilts
18 B6 Upper Wraxall Wilts
42 C9 Uppingham Rutlnd
49 L12 Uppington Shrops
66 C9 Upsall N York
81 J5 Upsettlington Border
21 N4 Upshire Essex
9 L2 Up Somborne Hants
23 N10 Upstreet Kent
31 Q10 Upton Bucks
42 G9 Upton C Pete
32 H2 Upton Cambs
48 H2 Upton Ches W
4 G6 Upton Cnwll
5 N10 Upton Devon
6 E3 Upton Devon
7 Q6 Upton Dorset
8 E8 Upton Dorset
9 L4 Upton Hants
19 L9 Upton Hants
41 J7 Upton Leics
52 C6 Upton Lincs
45 N7 Upton Norfk
51 Q5 Upton Notts
51 Q9 Upton Notts
19 N4 Upton Oxon
20 F7 Upton Slough
16 D9 Upton Somset
17 L10 Upton Somset
59 L10 Upton Wakefd
56 F10 Upton Wirral
28 H4 Upton Bishop Herefs
17 Q3 Upton Cheyney S Glos
39 M4 Upton Cressett Shrops
10 B1 Upton Grey Hants
15 P10 Upton Hellions Devon
18 D11 Upton Lovell Wilts
49 K11 Upton Magna Shrops
17 Q8 Upton Noble Somset
6 C3 Upton Pyne Devon
29 M6 Upton St Leonards Gloucs
18 C10 Upton Scudamore Wilts
30 C4 Upton Snodsbury Worcs
29 L1 Upton upon Severn Worcs
30 B1 Upton Warren Worcs
10 F7 Upwaltham W Susx
43 N9 Upwell Norfk
43 J12 Upwood Cambs
18 F8 Urchfont Wilts
57 P9 Urmston Traffd
101 K3 Urquhart Moray
66 D7 Urra N York
106 H10 Urray Highld
95 M10 Usan Angus
73 M11 Ushaw Moor Dur
28 D8 Usk Mons
52 F5 Usselby Lincs
73 N8 Usworth Sundld
49 K3 Utkinton Ches W
58 D5 Utley C Brad
15 P11 Uton Devon
53 K5 Utterby Lincs
40 E2 Uttoxeter Staffs
20 G6 Uxbridge Gt Lon
111 m2 Uyeasound Shet
24 G6 Uzmaston Pembks

V

6 c1 Vale Guern
37 L5 Vale of Rheidol Railway Cerdgn
54 D6 Valley IoA
104 G9 Valtos Highld
111 c2 Valtos W Isls
22 E6 Vange Essex
111 k2 Vatsetter Shet
96 C2 Vatten Highld
27 L6 Vaynor Myr Td

111 K4 Veensgarth Shet
27 P2 Velindre Powys
14 G9 Venngreen Devon
6 E5 Venn Ottery Devon
9 P11 Ventnor IoW
5 M8 Venton Devon
19 K9 Vernham Dean Hants
19 L8 Vernham Street Hants
8 G5 Verwood Dorset
3 K7 Veryan Cnwll
62 E8 Vickerstown Cumb
3 L4 Victoria Cnwll
111 k3 Vidlin Shet
101 K3 Viewfield Moray
85 M10 Viewpark N Lans
22 D10 Vigo Kent
6 c2 Village de Putron Guern
12 C6 Vines Cross E Susx
22 F11 Vinters Park Crematorium Kent
20 G9 Virginia Water Surrey
4 H2 Virginstow Devon
17 Q6 Vobster Somset
111 k3 Voe Shet
28 D2 Vowchurch Herefs

W

62 C4 Waberthwaite Cumb
65 K3 Wackerfield Dur
45 K10 Wacton Norfk
30 B5 Wadborough Worcs
31 Q10 Waddesdon Bucks
6 B10 Waddeton Devon
52 E4 Waddingham Lincs
63 N12 Waddington Lancs
52 D9 Waddington Lincs
3 L2 Wadebridge Cnwll
7 J1 Wadeford Somset
42 E12 Wadenhoe Nhants
33 K12 Wadesmill Herts
12 D4 Wadhurst E Susx
50 H6 Wadshelf Derbys
51 M2 Wadworth Donc
53 N10 Wainfleet All Saints Lincs
53 M10 Wainfleet St Mary Lincs
4 E2 Wainhouse Corner Cnwll
22 E8 Wainscott Medway
58 D8 Wainstalls Calder
64 D6 Waitby Cumb
53 J4 Waithe Lincs
59 J9 Wakefield Wakefd
58 H10 Wakefield Crematorium Wakefd
42 D9 Wakerley Nhants
34 E10 Wakes Colne Essex
35 P2 Walberswick Suffk
10 F8 Walberton W Susx
70 C2 Walbutt D & G
17 M6 Walcombe Somset
42 F3 Walcot Lincs
49 L11 Walcot Shrops
18 H4 Walcot Swindn
41 M10 Walcote Leics
35 J1 Walcot Green Norfk
52 G11 Walcott Lincs
45 M4 Walcott Norfk
59 M10 Walden Stubbs N York
22 F10 Walderslade Medway
10 C7 Walderton W Susx
7 L4 Walditch Dorset
73 M10 Waldridge Dur
35 L7 Waldringfield Suffk
12 B6 Waldron E Susx
51 L4 Wales Rothm
17 N10 Wales Somset
52 G5 Walesby Lincs
51 P6 Walesby Notts
28 G5 Walford Herefs
38 H7 Walford Herefs
49 J10 Walford Heath Shrops
49 M6 Walgherton Ches E
32 B3 Walgrave Nhants
57 N8 Walkden Salfd
73 M7 Walker N u Ty
79 M2 Walkerburn Border
51 Q3 Walkeringham Notts
52 B5 Walkerith Lincs
33 J10 Walkern Herts
86 F3 Walkerton Fife
8 H8 Walkford Dorset
5 L6 Walkhampton Devon
60 G6 Walkington E R Yk
51 J3 Walkley Sheff
57 Q3 Walk Mill Lancs
30 D2 Walkwood Worcs
72 G7 Wall Nthumb
40 E6 Wall Staffs
76 E10 Wallacetown S Ayrs
76 F6 Wallacetown S Ayrs
11 N7 Wallands Park E Susx
56 F9 Wallasey Wirral
19 P3 Wallingford Oxon
21 L9 Wallington Gt Lon
9 P6 Wallington Hants
33 J9 Wallington Herts
8 F8 Wallisdown Poole
111 j4 Walls Shet
73 N7 Wallsend N Tyne
86 H7 Wallyford E Loth
23 Q12 Walmer Kent
57 J4 Walmer Bridge Lancs
40 F8 Walmley Birm
35 P3 Walpole Suffk
43 N6 Walpole Cross Keys Norfk
43 N7 Walpole Highway Norfk
43 N6 Walpole St Andrew Norfk
43 N6 Walpole St Peter Norfk
40 D7 Walsall Wsall
58 C9 Walsden Calder
41 J10 Walsgrave on Sowe Covtry
34 G3 Walsham le Willows Suffk
59 K4 Walshford N York
43 M7 Walsoken Norfk
86 C12 Walston S Lans
32 H10 Walsworth Herts
20 D4 Walter's Ash Bucks
13 L1 Waltham Kent
53 J3 Waltham NE Lin
21 M4 Waltham Abbey Essex
9 P4 Waltham Chase Hants
21 M4 Waltham Cross Herts
42 B5 Waltham on the Wolds Leics
20 D7 Waltham St Lawrence W & M
21 M5 Walthamstow Gt Lon
71 Q3 Walton Cumb
51 J7 Walton Derbys
59 K5 Walton Leeds
41 N9 Walton Leics
32 C9 Walton M Keyn
38 F9 Walton Powys
17 L8 Walton Somset
35 L9 Walton Suffk
10 D8 Walton W Susx
59 J10 Walton Wakefd
49 L10 Walton Wrekin
29 M3 Walton Cardiff Gloucs
24 H4 Walton East Pembks
17 K2 Walton-in-Gordano N Som
57 L10 Walton Lea Crematorium Warrtn
57 K4 Walton-le-Dale Lancs
20 H9 Walton-on-Thames Surrey
40 C4 Walton-on-the-Hill Staffs
21 K11 Walton on the Hill Surrey
35 L11 Walton on the Naze Essex
41 N4 Walton on the Wolds Leics
40 G4 Walton-on-Trent Derbys
17 K2 Walton Park N Som
24 F6 Walton West Pembks
58 C4 Waltonwrays Crematorium N York
65 M4 Walworth Darltn
21 M7 Walworth Gt Lon
24 F6 Walwyn's Castle Pembks
6 H2 Wambrook Somset
10 E1 Wanborough Surrey
18 H4 Wanborough Swindn
21 K8 Wandsworth Gt Lon
35 P2 Wangford Suffk
41 N5 Wanlip Leics
78 E6 Wanlockhead D & G
12 C8 Wannock E Susx
42 F9 Wansford C Pete
60 H3 Wansford E R Yk
12 F2 Wanshurst Green Kent
21 N6 Wanstead Gt Lon
17 Q7 Wanstrow Somset
29 J8 Wanswell Gloucs
19 L3 Wantage Oxon
41 J12 Wappenbury Warwks
31 N5 Wappenham Nhants
12 C6 Warbleton E Susx
19 P3 Warborough Oxon
33 K2 Warboys Cambs
56 G2 Warbreck Bpool
4 F3 Warbstow Cnwll
57 M10 Warburton Traffd
64 D5 Warcop Cumb
72 G7 Warden Nthumb
31 L5 Wardington Oxon
49 L4 Wardle Ches E
58 B10 Wardle Rochdl
73 N8 Wardley Gatesd
42 B9 Wardley Rutlnd
50 F6 Wardlow Derbys
33 M1 Wardy Hill Cambs
21 M1 Ware Herts
8 D9 Wareham Dorset
13 J4 Warehorne Kent
81 N8 Warenford Nthumb
21 N1 Wareside Herts
33 J6 Waresley Cambs
20 E8 Warfield Br For
6 B11 Warfleet Devon
20 C7 Wargrave Wokham
44 F2 Warham All Saints Norfk
44 F2 Warham St Mary Norfk
72 F5 Wark Nthumb
80 H6 Wark Nthumb
15 L7 Warkleigh Devon
32 C2 Warkton Nhants
31 L6 Warkworth Nhants
81 P11 Warkworth Nthumb
65 N8 Warlaby N York
4 E6 Warleggan Cnwll
58 D8 Warley Town Calder
21 M10 Warlingham Surrey
59 J9 Warmfield Wakefd
49 N4 Warmingham Ches E
42 F11 Warmington Nhants
31 K5 Warmington Warwks
18 C10 Warminster Wilts
17 P2 Warmley S Glos
51 M1 Warmsworth Donc
7 Q5 Warmwell Dorset
9 Q3 Warnford Hants
11 J4 Warnham W Susx
10 G8 Warningcamp W Susx
11 K5 Warninglid W Susx
50 B6 Warren Ches E
24 G8 Warren Pembks
78 F2 Warrenhill S Lans
20 D7 Warren Row W & M
22 H11 Warren Street Kent
32 C6 Warrington M Keyn
57 L10 Warrington Warrtn
86 F7 Warriston C Edin
86 F7 Warriston Crematorium C Edin
9 N6 Warsash Hants
50 E8 Warslow Staffs
60 E4 Warter E R Yk
65 L10 Warthermaske N York
59 P3 Warthill N York
12 D8 Wartling E Susx
41 P3 Wartnaby Leics
56 H3 Warton Lancs
63 J7 Warton Lancs
40 H6 Warton Warwks
30 H2 Warwick Warwks
71 P4 Warwick Bridge Cumb
30 H2 Warwick Castle Warwks
31 J3 Warwick Services Warwks
111 h1 Wasbister Ork
62 E1 Wasdale Head Cumb
3 M2 Washaway Cnwll
5 Q8 Washbourne Devon
35 J8 Washbrook Suffk
16 C11 Washfield Devon
65 J7 Washfold N York
16 E7 Washford Somset
15 N9 Washford Pyne Devon
52 E8 Washingborough Lincs
73 N9 Washington Sundld
10 H7 Washington W Susx
73 M9 Washington Services Gatesd
30 H3 Wasperton Warwks
66 D10 Wass N York
16 E7 Watchet Somset
19 J3 Watchfield Oxon
63 K3 Watchgate Cumb
5 P4 Water Devon
33 M4 Waterbeach Cambs
10 E8 Waterbeach W Susx
79 L12 Waterbeck D & G
60 D6 Water End E R Yk
50 E9 Waterfall Staffs
85 J11 Waterfoot E Rens
21 L1 Waterford Herts
86 F11 Waterheads Border
50 E10 Waterhouses Staffs
22 E11 Wateringbury Kent
97 J5 Waterloo Highld
85 N11 Waterloo N Lans
92 F8 Waterloo P & K
24 G7 Waterloo Pembks
56 G8 Waterloo Sefton
10 B7 Waterlooville Hants
71 P10 Watermillock Cumb
42 G10 Water Newton Cambs
40 F8 Water Orton Warwks
31 N11 Waterperry Oxon
16 E10 Waterrow Somset
10 G6 Watersfield W Susx
57 N4 Waterside Bl w D
76 G9 Waterside E Ayrs
76 H3 Waterside E Ayrs
85 L8 Waterside E Duns
104 A11 Waterstein Highld
31 N11 Waterstock Oxon
24 G7 Waterston Pembks
31 P7 Water Stratford Bucks
49 L10 Waters Upton Wrekin
20 H4 Watford Herts
31 N1 Watford Nhants
31 N1 Watford Gap Services Nhants
58 F1 Wath N York
65 N11 Wath N York
51 K1 Wath upon Dearne Rothm
43 P7 Watlington Norfk
20 B5 Watlington Oxon
110 F5 Watten Highld
34 G2 Wattisfield Suffk
34 G6 Wattisham Suffk
7 L4 Watton Dorset
60 H4 Watton E R Yk
44 F9 Watton Norfk
33 K11 Watton-at-Stone Herts
85 N8 Wattston N Lans
27 P9 Wattsville Caerph
95 K4 Waulkmill Abers
26 E9 Waunarlwydd Swans
37 K4 Waunfawr Cerdgn
54 G9 Waunfawr Gwynd
32 C8 Wavendon M Keyn
71 K6 Waverbridge Cumb
49 J3 Waverton Ches W
71 K6 Waverton Cumb
61 J6 Wawne E R Yk
45 P5 Waxham Norfk
7 K2 Wayford Somset
7 L4 Waytown Dorset
15 Q9 Way Village Devon
16 F7 Weacombe Somset
19 K1 Weald Oxon
21 J5 Wealdstone Gt Lon
58 H5 Weardley Leeds
17 K5 Weare Somset
14 H7 Weare Giffard Devon
72 F11 Wearhead Dur
17 K9 Wearne Somset
65 M2 Wear Valley Crematorium Dur
44 E6 Weasenham All Saints Norfk
44 E5 Weasenham St Peter Norfk
57 P8 Weaste Salfd
49 L1 Weaverham Ches W
67 L12 Weaverthorpe N York
30 D2 Webheath Worcs
102 H8 Wedderlairs Abers
41 J8 Weddington Warwks
18 F8 Wedhampton Wilts
17 L6 Wedmore Somset
40 C8 Wednesbury Sandw
40 C7 Wednesfield Wolves
32 B12 Weedon Bucks
31 N3 Weedon Nhants
31 N5 Weedon Lois Nhants
40 F6 Weeford Staffs
9 M2 Weeke Hants
32 C1 Weekley Nhants
14 E11 Week St Mary Cnwll
60 H6 Weel E R Yk
35 J11 Weeley Essex
35 J11 Weeley Crematorium Essex
35 J11 Weeley Heath Essex
92 C6 Weem P & K
30 D3 Weethley Warwks
44 C11 Weeting Norfk
61 N9 Weeton E R Yk
56 H2 Weeton Lancs
58 H5 Weeton N York
58 H6 Weetwood Leeds
57 Q4 Weir Lancs
5 J7 Weir Quay Devon
111 k4 Weisdale Shet
44 H7 Welborne Norfk
52 D11 Welbourn Lincs
60 C1 Welburn N York
65 P7 Welbury N York
42 D3 Welby Lincs
14 E8 Welcombe Devon
41 N10 Welford Nhants
19 L6 Welford W Berk
30 F4 Welford-on-Avon Warwks
41 Q8 Welham Leics
51 Q5 Welham Notts
21 K3 Welham Green Herts
10 C2 Well Hants
53 M8 Well Lincs
65 M10 Well N York
29 L2 Welland Worcs
93 N8 Wellbank Angus
30 H3 Wellesbourne Warwks
32 H10 Well Head Herts
21 P8 Welling Gt Lon
32 C3 Wellingborough Nhants
44 E6 Wellingham Norfk
52 E11 Wellingore Lincs
62 C2 Wellington Cumb
39 J11 Wellington Herefs
16 F11 Wellington Somset
49 M12 Wellington Wrekin
29 J1 Wellington Heath Herefs
17 Q5 Wellow BaNES
9 L9 Wellow IoW
51 P7 Wellow Notts
17 M7 Wells Somset
44 F2 Wells-next-the-sea Norfk
33 Q11 Wellstye Green Essex
92 E10 Welltree P & K
86 C5 Wellwood Fife
43 N10 Welney Norfk
48 H8 Welshampton Shrops
48 G8 Welsh Frankton Shrops
28 F5 Welsh Newton Herefs
38 E1 Welshpool Powys
16 D2 Welsh St Donats V Glam
71 M6 Welton Cumb
60 G8 Welton E R Yk
52 E7 Welton Lincs
31 N2 Welton Nhants
53 M9 Welton le Marsh Lincs
53 J6 Welton le Wold Lincs
61 N9 Welwick E R Yk
32 H12 Welwyn Herts
21 K2 Welwyn Garden City Herts
49 K9 Wem Shrops
16 H8 Wembdon Somset
21 J6 Wembley Gt Lon
5 L9 Wembury Devon
15 L9 Wembworthy Devon
84 D8 Wemyss Bay Inver
33 N9 Wendens Ambo Essex
31 M9 Wendlebury Oxon
44 F7 Wendling Norfk
20 D2 Wendover Bucks
2 G9 Wendron Cnwll
33 K7 Wendy Cambs
35 N2 Wenhaston Suffk
33 J2 Wennington Cambs
22 B7 Wennington Gt Lon
63 L8 Wennington Lancs
50 H8 Wensley Derbys
65 J9 Wensley N York
59 L10 Wentbridge Wakefd
38 H4 Wentnor Shrops
33 M2 Wentworth Cambs
51 J2 Wentworth Rothm
16 F2 Wenvoe V Glam
38 H10 Weobley Herefs
10 G8 Wepham W Susx
44 B9 Wereham Norfk
42 G9 Werrington C Pete
4 H3 Werrington Cnwll
48 H2 Wervin Ches W
56 H3 Wesham Lancs
51 J8 Wessington Derbys
44 C7 West Acre Norfk
5 P10 West Alvington Devon
15 P6 West Anstey Devon
53 J8 West Ashby Lincs
10 D8 West Ashling W Susx
18 C9 West Ashton Wilts
65 L3 West Auckland Dur
67 L9 West Ayton N York
16 G9 West Bagborough Somset
57 K11 West Bank Halton
52 G7 West Barkwith Lincs
66 H5 West Barnby N York
87 M6 West Barns E Loth
44 E4 West Barsham Norfk
7 L5 West Bay Dorset
45 J3 West Beckham Norfk
20 H8 West Bedfont Surrey
23 M10 Westbere Kent
34 F10 West Bergholt Essex
19 P7 West Berkshire Crematorium W Berk
7 M5 West Bexington Dorset
44 B7 West Bilney Norfk
11 L8 West Blatchington Br & H
73 P8 West Boldon S Tyne
42 C2 Westborough Lincs
8 F8 Westbourne Bmouth
10 C8 Westbourne W Susx
58 F7 West Bowling C Brad
44 F8 West Bradenham Norfk
63 N12 West Bradford Lancs
17 M8 West Bradley Somset
58 H10 West Bretton Wakefd
51 N12 West Bridgford Notts
40 D8 West Bromwich Sandw
40 D8 West Bromwich Crematorium Sandw
23 Q8 Westbrook Kent
19 M6 Westbrook W Berk
15 L6 West Buckland Devon
16 G11 West Buckland Somset
64 H9 West Burton N York
31 N7 Westbury Bucks
38 G1 Westbury Shrops
18 C9 Westbury Wilts
18 C10 Westbury Leigh Wilts
29 J6 Westbury on Severn Gloucs
28 G12 Westbury-on-Trym Bristl
17 M6 Westbury-sub-Mendip Somset
52 B3 West Butterwick N Linc
56 H3 Westby Lancs
20 G10 West Byfleet Surrey
68 F11 West Cairngaan D & G
45 Q7 West Caister Norfk
86 B9 West Calder W Loth
17 N10 West Camel Somset
8 B10 West Chaldon Dorset
19 L3 West Challow Oxon
5 P10 West Charleton Devon
10 H6 West Chiltington W Susx
17 L12 West Chinnock Somset
20 G11 West Clandon Surrey
13 Q2 West Cliffe Kent
22 G6 Westcliff-on-Sea Sthend
17 M12 West Coker Somset
17 P8 Westcombe Somset
17 N7 West Compton Somset
7 N4 West Compton Abbas Dorset
30 G9 Westcote Gloucs
31 K8 Westcote Barton Oxon
31 Q10 Westcott Bucks
6 D2 Westcott Devon
11 J1 Westcott Surrey
59 P6 West Cottingwith N York
19 J8 Westcourt Wilts
59 P9 West Cowick E R Yk
26 E10 West Cross Swans
71 M6 West Curthwaite Cumb
11 Q9 Westdean E Susx
10 D7 West Dean W Susx
9 J3 West Dean Wilts
42 G8 West Deeping Lincs
56 H9 West Derby Lpool
43 Q9 West Dereham Norfk
15 J4 West Down Devon
4 C4 Westdowns Cnwll
20 G7 West Drayton Gt Lon
51 P6 West Drayton Notts
110 E2 West Dunnet Highld
60 H8 West Ella E R Yk
32 E6 West End Bed
9 M5 West End Hants
17 L3 West End N Som
45 Q7 West End Norfk
20 F10 West End Surrey
8 E3 West End Wilts
19 Q8 West End Green Hants
110 D5 Westerdale Highld
66 F6 Westerdale N York
35 K7 Westerfield Suffk
10 F8 Westergate W Susx
21 N11 Westerham Kent
73 L7 Westerhope N u Ty
6 B9 Westerland Devon
29 J11 Westerleigh S Glos
29 J12 Westerleigh Crematorium S Glos
86 B7 Wester Ochiltree W Loth
87 K2 Wester Pitkierie Fife
105 P6 Wester Ross Highld
93 R5 Westerton of Rossie Angus
111 j4 Westerwick Shet
22 E11 West Farleigh Kent
31 M4 West Farndon Nhants
48 G9 West Felton Shrops
17 P5 Westfield BaNES
70 G9 Westfield Cumb
12 F7 Westfield E Susx
110 C3 Westfield Highld
85 M8 Westfield N Lans
44 G8 Westfield Norfk
85 Q8 Westfield W Loth
92 H6 Westfields of Rattray P & K
72 G12 Westgate Dur
60 D11 Westgate N Linc
23 P8 Westgate on Sea Kent
19 J8 West Grafton Wilts
20 C11 West Green Hants
8 H3 West Grimstead Wilts
11 J5 West Grinstead W Susx
59 M8 West Haddlesey N York
41 N12 West Haddon Nhants
19 N3 West Hagbourne Oxon
40 B10 West Hagley Worcs
35 N1 Westhall Suffk
51 K11 West Hallam Derbys
60 F9 West Halton N Linc
7 P7 Westham Dorset
12 D8 Westham E Susx
21 N6 West Ham Gt Lon
17 K6 Westham Somset
10 E8 Westhampnett W Susx
51 K5 West Handley Derbys
19 L3 West Hanney Oxon
22 E4 West Hanningfield Essex
8 G2 West Harnham Wilts
17 M5 West Harptree BaNES
10 C6 West Harting W Susx
16 H11 West Hatch Somset
8 D2 West Hatch Wilts
93 P8 West Haven Angus
17 L7 Westhay Somset
40 D11 West Heath Birm
110 B11 West Helmsdale Highld
19 M3 West Hendred Oxon
20 H3 West Hertfordshire Crematorium Herts
67 K11 West Heslerton N York
17 K4 West Hewish N Som
39 L12 Westhide Herefs
95 N1 Westhill Abers
6 E4 West Hill Devon
11 M4 West Hoathly W Susx
8 C9 West Holme Dorset
39 J11 Westhope Herefs
39 J5 Westhope Shrops
22 D6 West Horndon Essex
42 H4 Westhorpe Lincs
34 H3 Westhorpe Suffk
17 N6 West Horrington Somset
20 H11 West Horsley Surrey
13 N3 West Hougham Kent
57 M7 Westhoughton Bolton
63 M7 Westhouse N York
51 K8 Westhouses Derbys
8 F8 West Howe Bmouth
21 J11 Westhumble Surrey
92 G10 West Huntingtower P & K
17 J7 West Huntspill Somset
13 L3 West Hythe Kent
19 M4 West Ilsley W Berk
10 C9 West Itchenor W Susx
18 G7 West Kennett Wilts
76 D2 West Kilbride N Ayrs
22 C10 West Kingsdown Kent
18 B5 West Kington Wilts
56 E10 West Kirby Wirral
67 J11 West Knapton N York
7 Q5 West Knighton Dorset
8 C2 West Knoyle Wilts
5 M9 Westlake Devon
17 K11 West Lambrook Somset
13 P1 West Langdon Kent
10 E6 West Lavington W Susx
18 E9 West Lavington Wilts
65 K5 West Layton N York
41 M3 West Leake Notts
14 H6 Westleigh Devon
16 E11 Westleigh Devon
16 F9 West Leigh Somset
35 P3 Westleton Suffk
44 D6 West Lexham Norfk
34 D4 Westley Suffk
33 P5 Westley Waterless Cambs
59 P2 West Lilling N York
31 Q11 Westlington Bucks
86 D10 West Linton Border
71 N3 Westlinton Cumb
18 B5 West Littleton S Glos
19 M4 West Lockinge Oxon
21 K7 West London Crematorium Gt Lon
8 B10 West Lulworth Dorset
60 F1 West Lutton N York
17 N9 West Lydford Somset
17 J9 West Lyng Somset
43 P6 West Lynn Norfk
22 D10 West Malling Kent
39 N11 West Malvern Worcs
10 C7 West Marden W Susx
51 Q6 West Markham Notts
23 P10 Westmarsh Kent
61 L11 West Marsh NE Lin
58 B4 West Marton N York
8 C4 West Melbury Dorset
9 Q3 West Meon Hants
23 J2 West Mersea Essex
11 M7 Westmeston E Susx
39 P7 West Midland Safari Park Worcs
33 K10 Westmill Herts
7 M4 West Milton Dorset
21 L7 Westminster Gt Lon
22 H8 West Minster Kent
21 J9 West Molesey Surrey
16 H9 West Monkton Somset
8 F6 West Moors Dorset
8 D8 West Morden Dorset
80 E6 West Morriston Border
17 N11 West Mudford Somset
93 L5 Westmuir Angus
66 F10 West Ness N York
71 J6 Westnewton Cumb
61 L6 West Newton E R Yk

44 B5 West Newton Norfk
16 H9 West Newton Somset
21 L8 West Norwood Gt Lon
21 L8 West Norwood Crematorium Gt Lon
73 P7 Westoe S Tyne
5 Q6 West Ogwell Devon
17 Q3 Weston BaNES
49 N5 Weston Ches E
6 F3 Weston Devon
6 F5 Weston Devon
10 B6 Weston Hants
33 J10 Weston Herts
43 J5 Weston Lincs
58 F5 Weston N York
31 N5 Weston Nhants
51 Q7 Weston Notts
39 L4 Weston Shrops
48 F9 Weston Shrops
40 C3 Weston Staffs
19 L6 Weston W Berk
28 G1 Weston Beggard Herefs
18 C3 Westonbirt Gloucs
41 Q8 Weston by Welland Nhants
33 P6 Weston Colville Cambs
10 B1 Weston Corbett Hants
50 C11 Weston Coyney C Stke
32 B4 Weston Favell Nhants
33 P6 Weston Green Cambs
49 P11 Weston Heath Shrops
32 E9 Westoning C Beds
17 L2 Weston-in-Gordano N Som
49 N10 Weston Jones Staffs
45 J7 Weston Longville Norfk
48 H9 Weston Lullingfields Shrops
5 K8 Weston Mill Crematorium C Plym
31 M9 Weston-on-the-Green Oxon
10 B1 Weston Patrick Hants
48 F8 Weston Rhyn Shrops
30 E6 Weston-sub-Edge Gloucs
17 J4 Weston-Super-Mare N Som
17 J4 Weston-super-Mare Crematorium N Som
20 D2 Weston Turville Bucks
49 P12 Weston-under-Lizard Staffs
28 H4 Weston under Penyard Herefs
49 K9 Weston-under-Redcastle Shrops
41 J12 Weston under Wetherley Warwks
50 H11 Weston Underwood Derbys
32 C6 Weston Underwood M Keyn
41 K2 Weston-upon-Trent Derbys
17 J8 Westonzoyland Somset
8 B4 West Orchard Dorset
18 G7 West Overton Wilts
60 D2 Westow N York
95 N3 West Park Abers
8 G7 West Parley Dorset
22 D11 West Peckham Kent
73 M9 West Pelton Dur
17 M8 West Pennard Somset
2 H4 West Pentire Cnwll
32 G4 West Perry Cambs
15 P3 West Porlock Somset
17 K11 Westport Somset
14 G8 West Putford Devon
16 F7 West Quantoxhead Somset
85 Q7 Westquarter Falk
73 N10 West Rainton Dur
52 F5 West Rasen Lincs
111 h1 Westray Ork
111 h1 Westray Airport Ork
44 E5 West Raynham Norfk
85 Q9 Westrigg W Loth
73 L7 West Road Crematorium N u Ty
18 H3 Westrop Swindn
65 P6 West Rounton N York
34 B2 West Row Suffk
44 D5 West Rudham Norfk
45 K2 West Runton Norfk
80 E4 Westruther Border
43 L9 Westry Cambs
87 J8 West Saltoun E Loth
15 N10 West Sandford Devon
111 k3 West Sandwick Shet
65 J10 West Scrafton N York
7 Q5 West Stafford Dorset
52 B5 West Stockwith Notts
10 D8 West Stoke W Susx
8 B3 West Stour Dorset
23 N10 West Stourmouth Kent
34 D3 West Stow Suffk
18 G8 West Stowell Wilts
34 G3 West Street Suffk
34 D4 West Suffolk Crematorium Suffk
65 M10 West Tanfield N York
4 E7 West Taphouse Cnwll
83 M9 West Tarbert Ag & B
10 H8 West Tarring W Susx
73 L2 West Thirston Nthumb
10 C9 West Thorney W Susx
41 N3 West Thorpe Notts
22 C7 West Thurrock Thurr
22 D7 West Tilbury Thurr
9 Q2 West Tisted Hants
52 G7 West Torrington Lincs
10 B9 West Town Hants
17 L3 West Town N Som
9 J2 West Tytherley Hants
43 M7 West Walton Norfk
43 M7 West Walton Highway Norfk
71 L6 Westward Cumb
14 H6 Westward Ho! Devon
13 J1 Westwell Kent
30 G11 Westwell Oxon
13 J1 Westwell Leacon Kent
9 K4 West Wellow Hants
5 L9 West Wembury Devon
86 G4 West Wemyss Fife
33 L4 Westwick Cambs
33 P6 West Wickham Cambs
21 M9 West Wickham Gt Lon
24 H7 West Williamston Pembks
18 D8 West Wiltshire Crematorium Wilts
43 Q6 West Winch Norfk
9 J2 West Winterslow Wilts
10 C9 West Wittering W Susx
65 J9 West Witton N York
6 D3 Westwood Devon
23 Q9 Westwood Kent
18 B8 Westwood Wilts
72 F4 West Woodburn Nthumb
19 L8 West Woodhay W Berk
51 Q2 Westwoodside N Linc
10 C3 West Worldham Hants
11 J9 West Worthing W Susx
33 P6 West Wratting Cambs
71 P5 Wetheral Cumb
59 K5 Wetherby Leeds
34 G4 Wetherden Suffk
35 J4 Wetheringsett Suffk
34 B9 Wethersfield Essex
35 J4 Wetherup Street Suffk
50 C10 Wetley Rocks Staffs
49 L4 Wettenhall Ches E
50 E9 Wetton Staffs
60 F3 Wetwang E R Yk
49 P8 Wetwood Staffs
19 J8 Wexcombe Wilts
45 J2 Weybourne Norfk
10 D1 Weybourne Surrey
35 L1 Weybread Suffk
35 L2 Weybread Street Suffk
20 H9 Weybridge Surrey
7 J3 Weycroft Devon
110 D3 Weydale Highld
19 K10 Weyhill Hants
7 P7 Weymouth Dorset
7 P7 Weymouth Crematorium Dorset
32 B9 Whaddon Bucks
33 K7 Whaddon Cambs
29 L6 Whaddon Gloucs
8 H3 Whaddon Wilts
18 C8 Whaddon Wilts
51 L6 Whaley Derbys
50 D5 Whaley Bridge Derbys
51 M6 Whaley Thorns Derbys
110 G7 Whaligoe Highld
57 N2 Whalley Lancs
111 m3 Whalsay Shet
73 K5 Whalton Nthumb
43 K5 Whaplode Lincs
43 K7 Whaplode Drove Lincs
31 K4 Wharf Warwks
63 P8 Wharfe N York
57 J2 Wharles Lancs
32 D7 Wharley End C Beds
50 H2 Wharncliffe Side Sheff
60 E2 Wharram-le-Street N York
39 J10 Wharton Herefs
65 K6 Whashton N York
63 K6 Whasset Cumb
30 H5 Whatcote Warwks
40 G7 Whateley Warwks
34 G7 Whatfield Suffk
7 J2 Whatley Somset
17 Q6 Whatley Somset
12 F6 Whatlington E Susx
51 Q11 Whatton Notts
69 K8 Whauphill D & G
45 P10 Wheatacre Norfk
21 J1 Wheathampstead Herts
10 C3 Wheatley Hants
31 N11 Wheatley Oxon
73 P11 Wheatley Hill Dur
59 N12 Wheatley Hills Donc
49 Q11 Wheaton Aston Staffs
16 C8 Wheddon Cross Somset
49 N4 Wheelock Ches E
57 L5 Wheelton Lancs
59 P5 Wheldrake C York
18 H2 Whelford Gloucs
20 F3 Whelpley Hill Bucks
33 K11 Whempstead Herts
66 E12 Whenby N York
34 D5 Whepstead Suffk
35 J8 Wherstead Suffk
19 L11 Wherwell Hants
50 F5 Wheston Derbys
12 D2 Whetsted Kent
41 M7 Whetstone Leics
62 D6 Whicham Cumb
30 H7 Whichford Warwks
73 L8 Whickham Gatesd
5 N2 Whiddon Down Devon
93 N6 Whigstreet Angus
31 N2 Whilton Nhants
6 E4 Whimple Devon
45 N4 Whimpwell Green Norfk
44 G8 Whinburgh Norfk
70 B5 Whinnie Liggate D & G
103 M8 Whinnyfold Abers
9 N8 Whippingham IoW
32 E12 Whipsnade C Beds
32 E12 Whipsnade Wild Animal Park C Beds
6 C4 Whipton Devon
52 C9 Whisby Lincs
42 B7 Whissendine Rutlnd
44 F5 Whissonsett Norfk
84 D4 Whistlefield Ag & B
84 C4 Whistlefield Inn Ag & B
20 C8 Whistley Green Wokham
57 J9 Whiston Knows
32 C5 Whiston Nhants
51 K3 Whiston Rothm
40 B5 Whiston Staffs
50 D10 Whiston Staffs
62 D5 Whitbeck Cumb
39 N10 Whitbourne Herefs
73 P8 Whitburn S Tyne
85 Q9 Whitburn W Loth
67 J5 Whitby N York
87 N9 Whitchester Border
17 N3 Whitchurch BaNES
32 B11 Whitchurch Bucks
27 N11 Whitchurch Cardif
5 K5 Whitchurch Devon
19 M10 Whitchurch Hants
28 G5 Whitchurch Herefs
19 Q5 Whitchurch Oxon
24 E4 Whitchurch Pembks
49 K7 Whitchurch Shrops
7 K4 Whitchurch Canonicorum Dorset
19 Q5 Whitchurch Hill Oxon
7 Q5 Whitcombe Dorset
38 H4 Whitcot Shrops
38 F5 Whitcott Keysett Shrops
40 G8 Whiteacre Heath Warwks
16 E11 White Ball Somset
98 G6 Whitebridge Highld
28 G7 Whitebrook Mons
103 J10 Whitecairns Abers
21 M7 Whitechapel Gt Lon
57 K1 White Chapel Lancs
28 G6 Whitecliffe Gloucs
34 E10 White Colne Essex
86 G8 Whitecraig E Loth
68 F7 Whitecrook D & G
2 G10 White Cross Cnwll
85 R7 Whitecross Falk
107 L5 Whiteface Highld
75 N4 Whitefarland N Ayrs
76 E8 Whitefaulds S Ayrs
57 Q7 Whitefield Bury
16 E9 Whitefield Somset
102 F9 Whiteford Abers
49 L2 Whitegate Ches W
111 i2 Whitehall Ork
70 F11 Whitehaven Cumb
10 C4 Whitehill and Bordon Hants
102 E3 Whitehills Abers
102 E11 Whitehouse Abers
83 M10 Whitehouse Ag & B
87 L6 Whitekirk E Loth
7 Q3 White Lackington Dorset
17 K11 Whitelackington Somset
30 B4 White Ladies Aston Worcs
20 D3 Whiteleaf Bucks
9 P10 Whiteley Bank IoW
100 F5 Whitemire Moray
51 M11 Whitemoor C Nott
3 L4 Whitemoor Cnwll
111 k4 Whiteness Shet
34 D11 White Notley Essex
9 J3 Whiteparish Wilts
53 L7 White Pit Lincs
102 H9 Whiterashes Abers
22 C1 White Roding Essex
110 G6 Whiterow Highld
100 F4 Whiterow Moray
29 L7 Whiteshill Gloucs
11 Q7 Whitesmith E Susx
6 H1 Whitestaunton Somset
6 B4 Whitestone Cross Devon
20 D7 White Waltham W & M
63 M11 Whitewell Lancs
13 P2 Whitfield Kent
31 N6 Whitfield Nhants
72 E8 Whitfield Nthumb
29 J9 Whitfield S Glos
6 H4 Whitford Devon
56 D12 Whitford Flints
60 E9 Whitgift E R Yk
40 B2 Whitgreave Staffs
69 L10 Whithorn D & G
75 Q7 Whiting Bay N Ayrs
59 J7 Whitkirk Leeds
25 L5 Whitland Carmth
80 C10 Whitlaw Border
76 F6 Whitletts S Ayrs
59 M9 Whitley N York
20 B8 Whitley Readg
51 J2 Whitley Sheff
18 C7 Whitley Wilts
73 N6 Whitley Bay N Tyne
73 N6 Whitley Bay Crematorium N Tyne
72 G8 Whitley Chapel Nthumb
58 G10 Whitley Lower Kirk
29 K7 Whitminster Gloucs
49 P7 Whitmore Staffs
16 D11 Whitnage Devon
31 J2 Whitnash Warwks
38 F11 Whitney-on-Wye Herefs
8 G4 Whitsbury Hants
81 J4 Whitsome Border
28 D11 Whitson Newpt
23 L9 Whitstable Kent
14 E11 Whitstone Cnwll
81 M10 Whittingham Nthumb
38 H4 Whittingslow Shrops
51 J6 Whittington Derbys
30 D9 Whittington Gloucs
63 L7 Whittington Lancs
44 B9 Whittington Norfk
48 G8 Whittington Shrops
39 Q5 Whittington Staffs
40 F6 Whittington Staffs
40 H7 Whittington Warwks
39 Q10 Whittington Worcs
31 P5 Whittlebury Nhants
57 L5 Whittle-le-Woods Lancs
43 J10 Whittlesey Cambs
33 M7 Whittlesford Cambs
60 F8 Whitton N Linc
73 J1 Whitton Nthumb
38 F8 Whitton Powys
65 P3 Whitton S on T
39 L7 Whitton Shrops
73 J9 Whittonstall Nthumb
19 M8 Whitway Hants
51 M5 Whitwell Derbys
32 H11 Whitwell Herts
9 N10 Whitwell IoW
65 M7 Whitwell N York
42 D8 Whitwell Rutlnd
60 C2 Whitwell-on-the-Hill N York
44 H6 Whitwell Street Norfk
41 K4 Whitwick Leics
58 B9 Whitworth Lancs
49 K8 Whixall Shrops
59 K3 Whixley N York
65 K5 Whorlton Dur
39 K9 Whyle Herefs
21 M10 Whyteleafe Surrey
58 F7 Wibsey C Brad
41 L9 Wibtoft Warwks
39 P9 Wichenford Worcs
22 H11 Wichling Kent
8 H8 Wick Bmouth
110 G5 Wick Highld
17 Q2 Wick S Glos
16 C2 Wick V Glam
10 G8 Wick W Susx
30 C5 Wick Worcs
110 G5 Wick Airport Highld
33 P3 Wicken Cambs
31 Q6 Wicken Nhants
33 N9 Wicken Bonhunt Essex
52 F7 Wickenby Lincs
44 D4 Wicken Green Village Norfk
51 L3 Wickersley Rothm
34 F8 Wicker Street Green Suffk
22 E5 Wickford Essex
9 P5 Wickham Hants
19 L6 Wickham W Berk
22 G2 Wickham Bishops Essex
23 N10 Wickhambreaux Kent
34 C6 Wickhambrook Suffk
30 E6 Wickhamford Worcs
34 H3 Wickham Green Suffk
35 M5 Wickham Market Suffk
45 N8 Wickhampton Norfk
34 D9 Wickham St Paul Essex
34 H3 Wickham Skeith Suffk
34 H3 Wickham Street Suffk
44 H9 Wicklewood Norfk
45 J4 Wickmere Norfk
17 K3 Wick St Lawrence N Som
29 J10 Wickwar S Glos
33 N9 Widdington Essex
73 M2 Widdrington Nthumb
73 M3 Widdrington Station Nthumb
5 P5 Widecombe in the Moor Devon
4 G8 Widegates Cnwll
14 D10 Widemouth Bay Cnwll
73 M6 Wide Open N Tyne
22 E3 Widford Essex
33 L12 Widford Herts
20 E4 Widmer End Bucks
41 N2 Widmerpool Notts
21 N9 Widmore Gt Lon
57 K11 Widnes Halton
57 K10 Widnes Crematorium Halton
6 G3 Widworthy Devon
57 L7 Wigan Wigan
57 L7 Wigan Crematorium Wigan
17 L12 Wigborough Somset
6 E4 Wiggaton Devon
43 P7 Wiggenhall St Germans Norfk
43 P7 Wiggenhall St Mary Magdalen Norfk
43 P7 Wiggenhall St Mary the Virgin Norfk
59 N3 Wigginton C York
20 F2 Wigginton Herts
31 K7 Wigginton Oxon
40 G6 Wigginton Staffs
63 P10 Wigglesworth N York
71 L5 Wiggonby Cumb
59 L5 Wighill N York
44 F3 Wighton Norfk
39 Q3 Wightwick Wolves
9 K4 Wigley Hants
38 H8 Wigmore Herefs
22 F9 Wigmore Medway
52 C9 Wigsley Notts
32 F1 Wigsthorpe Nhants
41 N7 Wigston Leics
41 L9 Wigston Parva Leics
51 N4 Wigthorpe Notts
43 J3 Wigtoft Lincs
71 L6 Wigton Cumb
69 L7 Wigtown D & G
59 J5 Wike Leeds
42 B11 Wilbarston Nhants
60 C4 Wilberfoss E R Yk
33 M2 Wilburton Cambs
32 C4 Wilby Nhants
44 G11 Wilby Norfk
35 L3 Wilby Suffk
18 G8 Wilcot Wilts
48 H10 Wilcott Shrops
50 C7 Wildboarclough Ches E
32 F6 Wilden Bed
39 P7 Wilden Worcs
85 N11 Wildmanbridge S Lans
40 C11 Wildmoor Worcs
52 B4 Wildsworth Lincs
41 M1 Wilford Hill Crematorium Notts
49 L7 Wilkesley Ches E
107 Q5 Wilkhaven Highld
86 D8 Wilkieston W Loth
6 D1 Willand Devon
49 M5 Willaston Ches E
56 G12 Willaston Ches W
32 C8 Willen M Keyn
41 J11 Willenhall Covtry
40 C7 Willenhall Wsall
60 H7 Willerby E R Yk
67 L10 Willerby N York
30 E6 Willersey Gloucs
38 G11 Willersley Herefs
13 K2 Willesborough Kent
13 K2 Willesborough Lees Kent
21 K6 Willesden Gt Lon
18 C3 Willesley Wilts
16 F9 Willett Somset
39 M3 Willey Shrops
41 L9 Willey Warwks
20 F12 Willey Green Surrey
31 L5 Williamscot Oxon
32 H9 Willian Herts
22 C2 Willingale Essex
12 C9 Willingdon E Susx
33 L3 Willingham Cambs
52 C6 Willingham by Stow Lincs
32 G6 Willington Bed
40 H2 Willington Derbys
65 L1 Willington Dur
22 F11 Willington Kent
30 H6 Willington Warwks
73 N7 Willington Quay N Tyne
60 C7 Willitoft E R Yk
16 E7 Williton Somset
53 M8 Willoughby Lincs
31 M1 Willoughby Warwks
41 N3 Willoughby-on-the-Wolds Notts
41 M8 Willoughby Waterleys Leics
52 D5 Willoughton Lincs
34 C11 Willows Green Essex
17 K10 Willtown Somset
30 F3 Wilmcote Warwks
6 G3 Wilmington Devon
12 B8 Wilmington E Susx
22 B8 Wilmington Kent
57 Q11 Wilmslow Ches E
57 M3 Wilpshire Lancs
58 E6 Wilsden C Brad
42 E2 Wilsford Lincs
18 G11 Wilsford Wilts
18 G8 Wilsford Wilts
58 E11 Wilshaw Kirk
58 F2 Wilsill N York
41 K3 Wilson Leics
85 Q11 Wilsontown S Lans
32 F7 Wilstead Bed
42 F7 Wilsthorpe Lincs
20 E1 Wilstone Herts
28 G4 Wilton Herefs
67 J10 Wilton N York
66 E4 Wilton R & Cl
8 G2 Wilton Wilts
19 J8 Wilton Wilts
80 C10 Wilton Dean Border
33 P9 Wimbish Green Essex
21 K8 Wimbledon Gt Lon
43 L10 Wimblington Cambs
49 M3 Wimboldsley Ches W
8 E7 Wimborne Minster Dorset
8 F5 Wimborne St Giles Dorset
43 P8 Wimbotsham Norfk
33 K6 Wimpole Cambs
30 G4 Wimpstone Warwks
17 Q9 Wincanton Somset
86 C7 Winchburgh W Loth
30 D8 Winchcombe Gloucs
12 H6 Winchelsea E Susx
9 N2 Winchester Hants
9 N1 Winchester Services Hants
12 E2 Winchet Hill Kent
20 C11 Winchfield Hants
20 E4 Winchmore Hill Bucks
21 L5 Winchmore Hill Gt Lon
50 C7 Wincle Ches E
51 J3 Wincobank Sheff
62 H3 Windermere Cumb
31 J6 Winderton Warwks
107 J11 Windhill Highld
20 E9 Windlesham Surrey
3 K2 Windmill Cnwll
12 D7 Windmill Hill E Susx
17 J11 Windmill Hill Somset
30 F10 Windrush Gloucs
102 D4 Windsole Abers
20 F7 Windsor W & M
20 F7 Windsor Castle W & M
29 L8 Windsoredge Gloucs
34 E6 Windsor Green Suffk
40 H12 Windy Arbour Warwks
86 G3 Windygates Fife
11 K6 Wineham W Susx
61 M8 Winestead E R Yk
45 J11 Winfarthing Norfk
9 P9 Winford IoW
17 M3 Winford N Som
38 F11 Winforton Herefs
8 B9 Winfrith Newburgh Dorset
32 C11 Wing Bucks
42 C9 Wing Rutlnd
73 P12 Wingate Dur
51 J7 Wingerworth Derbys
32 E10 Wingfield C Beds
35 K2 Wingfield Suffk
18 B9 Wingfield Wilts
23 N11 Wingham Kent
32 C11 Wingrave Bucks
51 P8 Winkburn Notts
20 E8 Winkfield Br For
20 E8 Winkfield Row Br For
50 D9 Winkhill Staffs
15 L9 Winkleigh Devon
65 M12 Winksley N York
73 L8 Winlaton Gatesd
110 G5 Winless Highld
63 J11 Winmarleigh Lancs
9 N2 Winnall Hants
20 C8 Winnersh Wokham
49 M1 Winnington Ches W
17 K5 Winscombe N Som
49 M3 Winsford Ches W
16 B8 Winsford Somset
7 K2 Winsham Somset
40 H3 Winshill Staffs
26 F9 Winshwen Swans
64 B1 Winskill Cumb
18 B8 Winsley Wilts
31 Q8 Winslow Bucks
30 E11 Winson Gloucs
9 K5 Winsor Hants
62 H4 Winster Cumb
50 G8 Winster Derbys
65 K4 Winston Dur
35 K5 Winston Suffk
29 N6 Winstone Gloucs
15 J9 Winswell Devon
7 Q5 Winterborne Came Dorset
8 C6 Winterborne Clenston Dorset
8 B6 Winterborne Houghton Dorset
8 C7 Winterborne Kingston Dorset
7 P5 Winterborne Monkton Dorset
8 C6 Winterborne Stickland Dorset
8 C7 Winterborne Whitechurch Dorset
8 D7 Winterborne Zelston Dorset
28 H11 Winterbourne S Glos
19 M6 Winterbourne W Berk
7 N5 Winterbourne Abbas Dorset
18 G6 Winterbourne Bassett Wilts
8 H1 Winterbourne Dauntsey Wilts
8 H1 Winterbourne Earls Wilts
8 H1 Winterbourne Gunner Wilts
18 G6 Winterbourne Monkton Wilts
7 P5 Winterbourne Steepleton Dorset
18 F11 Winterbourne Stoke Wilts
58 C3 Winterburn N York
60 F9 Winteringham N Linc
49 N4 Winterley Ches E
9 J2 Winterslow Wilts
60 F9 Winterton N Linc
45 P6 Winterton-on-Sea Norfk
52 B11 Winthorpe Notts
8 G8 Winton Bmouth
64 E5 Winton Cumb
67 J11 Wintringham N York
32 F1 Winwick Cambs
41 N11 Winwick Nhants
57 L9 Winwick Warrtn
50 H9 Wirksworth Derbys
56 F10 Wirral
49 K6 Wirswall Ches E
43 M8 Wisbech Cambs
43 L8 Wisbech St Mary Cambs
10 G5 Wisborough Green W Susx
25 K7 Wiseman's Bridge Pembks
51 Q3 Wiseton Notts
85 N11 Wishaw N Lans
40 F8 Wishaw Warwks
20 G10 Wisley Gardens Surrey
52 H8 Wispington Lincs
35 M2 Wissett Suffk
34 F9 Wissington Suffk
38 H5 Wistanstow Shrops
49 M9 Wistanswick Shrops
49 M5 Wistaston Ches E
24 H5 Wiston Pembks
78 F3 Wiston S Lans
11 J7 Wiston W Susx
33 J1 Wistow Cambs
59 N7 Wistow N York
57 N2 Wiswell Lancs
33 M2 Witcham Cambs
8 E6 Witchampton Dorset
33 N2 Witchford Cambs
17 L10 Witcombe Somset

22 G1 Witham Essex
17 Q7 Witham Friary Somset
42 F6 Witham on the Hill Lincs
53 J6 Withcall Lincs
11 L8 Withdean Br & H
12 D5 Witherenden Hill E Susx
15 N8 Witheridge Devon
41 J7 Witherley Leics
53 L7 Withern Lincs
61 N8 Withernsea E R Yk
61 K6 Withernwick E R Yk
35 L1 Withersdale Street Suffk
33 Q7 Withersfield Suffk
62 H5 Witherslack Cumb
3 M3 Withiel Cnwll
16 D9 Withiel Florey Somset
30 D10 Withington Gloucs
39 K12 Withington Herefs
57 Q9 Withington Manch
49 L11 Withington Shrops
40 D1 Withington Staffs
6 B1 Withleigh Devon
57 L4 Withnell Lancs
40 D11 Withybed Green Worcs
41 K10 Withybrook Warwks
16 D7 Withycombe Somset
11 P3 Withyham E Susx
15 P5 Withypool Somset
17 N3 Withywood Bristl
10 F3 Witley Surrey
35 K6 Witnesham Suffk
31 J11 Witney Oxon
42 F9 Wittering C Pete
12 H5 Wittersham Kent
40 E8 Witton Birm
45 M4 Witton Norfk
45 M8 Witton Norfk
73 M10 Witton Gilbert Dur
65 K2 Witton le Wear Dur
65 L2 Witton Park Dur
16 E9 Wiveliscombe Somset
19 R12 Wivelrod Hants
11 M6 Wivelsfield E Susx
11 M6 Wivelsfield Green E Susx
34 G11 Wivenhoe Essex
44 G2 Wiveton Norfk
35 J10 Wix Essex
30 E3 Wixford Warwks
34 C8 Wixoe Suffk
32 D9 Woburn C Beds
32 D9 Woburn Abbey C Beds
32 D9 Woburn Sands M Keyn
20 G10 Woking Surrey
20 F11 Woking Crematorium Surrey
20 D9 Wokingham Wokham
21 M11 Woldingham Surrey
67 M11 Wold Newton E R Yk
53 J4 Wold Newton NE Lin
78 G2 Wolfclyde S Lans
43 Q4 Wolferton Norfk
92 H8 Wolfhill P & K
24 G4 Wolf's Castle Pembks
24 G5 Wolfsdale Pembks
40 B9 Wollaston Dudley
32 C4 Wollaston Nhants
48 G11 Wollaston Shrops
51 M11 Wollaton C Nott
49 L9 Wollerton Shrops
40 B10 Wollescote Dudley
40 D4 Wolseley Bridge Staffs
73 J12 Wolsingham Dur
49 Q6 Wolstanton Staffs
41 K11 Wolston Warwks
31 L11 Wolvercote Oxon
40 B7 Wolverhampton Wolves
39 P4 Wolverhampton Business Airport Staffs
39 P6 Wolverley Worcs
19 P8 Wolverton Hants
32 B8 Wolverton M Keyn
30 G2 Wolverton Warwks
8 B2 Wolverton Wilts
28 E8 Wolvesnewton Mons
41 K9 Wolvey Warwks
41 K9 Wolvey Heath Warwks
66 C3 Wolviston S on T
66 F10 Wombleton N York
39 Q4 Wombourne Staffs
51 K1 Wombwell Barns
23 N12 Womenswold Kent
59 M9 Womersley N York
10 G2 Wonersh Surrey
6 C4 Wonford Devon
7 Q2 Wonston Dorset
19 M11 Wonston Hants
20 E6 Wooburn Bucks
20 E6 Wooburn Green Bucks
14 G9 Woodacott Devon
51 L5 Woodall Rothm
51 L5 Woodall Services Rothm
45 M7 Woodbastwick Norfk
30 D4 Wood Bevington Warwks
51 N10 Woodborough Notts
18 G8 Woodborough Wilts
35 L7 Woodbridge Suffk
6 D5 Woodbury Devon
6 D5 Woodbury Salterton Devon
29 L8 Woodchester Gloucs
12 H3 Woodchurch Kent
16 C6 Woodcombe Somset
21 L10 Woodcote Gt Lon
19 Q4 Woodcote Oxon
49 P11 Woodcote Wrekin
28 G9 Woodcroft Gloucs
44 H5 Wood Dalling Norfk
33 Q5 Woodditton Cambs
31 M10 Woodeaton Oxon
20 H7 Wood End Gt Lon
33 K10 Wood End Herts
89 Q4 Woodend Highld
31 N4 Woodend Nhants
85 Q8 Woodend W Loth
10 D8 Woodend W Susx
40 E11 Wood End Warwks
53 J10 Wood Enderby Lincs
8 H4 Woodfalls Wilts
14 D9 Woodford Cnwll
29 J9 Woodford Gloucs
21 N5 Woodford Gt Lon
32 D2 Woodford Nhants
50 B4 Woodford Stockp
21 N5 Woodford Bridge Gt Lon
31 M4 Woodford Halse Nhants
21 N5 Woodford Wells Gt Lon
40 D10 Woodgate Birm
16 E12 Woodgate Devon
10 F8 Woodgate W Susx
30 C2 Woodgate Worcs
21 L5 Wood Green Gt Lon
8 H4 Woodgreen Hants
64 H9 Woodhall N York
52 H10 Woodhall Spa Lincs
31 P9 Woodham Bucks

20 G10 Woodham Surrey
22 F4 Woodham Ferrers Essex
22 F3 Woodham Mortimer Essex
22 F3 Woodham Walter Essex
40 C7 Wood Hayes Wolves
102 G7 Woodhead Abers
39 N5 Woodhill Shrops
17 J10 Woodhill Somset
73 N3 Woodhorn Nthumb
58 H7 Woodhouse Leeds
41 M5 Woodhouse Leics
51 K4 Woodhouse Sheff
59 J9 Woodhouse Wakefd
41 M5 Woodhouse Eaves Leics
86 F8 Woodhouselee Mdloth
71 N1 Woodhouselees D & G
40 F4 Woodhouses Staffs
33 K2 Woodhurst Cambs
11 M8 Woodingdean Br & H
58 H8 Woodkirk Leeds
103 J9 Woodland Abers
5 M8 Woodland Devon
5 Q6 Woodland Devon
65 J3 Woodland Dur
76 C11 Woodland S Ayrs
95 N3 Woodlands Abers
59 M11 Woodlands Donc
8 F5 Woodlands Dorset
9 K5 Woodlands Hants
59 J3 Woodlands N York
40 F9 Woodlands (Coleshill) Crematorium Warwks
20 D7 Woodlands Park W & M
67 L9 Woodlands (Scarborough) Crematorium N York
60 F11 Woodlands (Scunthorpe) Crematorium N Linc
5 P9 Woodleigh Devon
20 C8 Woodley Wokham
29 K8 Woodmancote Gloucs
29 N4 Woodmancote Gloucs
30 D11 Woodmancote Gloucs
10 C8 Woodmancote W Susx
11 K7 Woodmancote W Susx
19 P11 Woodmancott Hants
60 H6 Woodmansey E R Yk
10 D5 Woodmansgreen W Susx
21 L10 Woodmansterne Surrey
6 D5 Woodmanton Devon
23 P11 Woodnesborough Kent
42 E10 Woodnewton Nhants
44 G5 Wood Norton Norfk
57 J2 Woodplumpton Lancs
44 G9 Woodrising Norfk
12 D6 Wood's Corner E Susx
49 P9 Woodseaves Staffs
51 M4 Woodsetts Rothm
8 A8 Woodsford Dorset
12 D4 Wood's Green E Susx
20 E8 Woodside Br For
86 H1 Woodside Fife
21 M9 Woodside Gt Lon
93 J7 Woodside P & K
31 K10 Woodstock Oxon
42 H10 Woodston C Pete
45 N6 Wood Street Norfk
20 F12 Wood Street Village Surrey
45 L10 Woodton Norfk
14 G7 Woodtown Devon
11 L8 Woodvale Crematorium Br & H
32 H1 Wood Walton Cambs
39 K8 Woofferton Shrops
17 M7 Wookey Somset
17 M6 Wookey Hole Somset
8 C9 Wool Dorset
14 H4 Woolacombe Devon
23 N12 Woolage Green Kent
28 G8 Woolaston Gloucs
28 G8 Woolaston Common Gloucs
17 J7 Woolavington Somset
10 E5 Woolbeding W Susx
5 F5 Woolbrook Devon
81 L8 Wooler Nthumb
14 F7 Woolfardisworthy Devon
15 P9 Woolfardisworthy Devon
86 B10 Woolfords S Lans
19 P7 Woolhampton W Berk
28 H2 Woolhope Herefs
8 B6 Woolland Dorset
17 Q3 Woolley BaNES
32 G2 Woolley Cambs
58 H10 Woolley Wakefd
58 H10 Woolley Edge Services Wakefd
30 C2 Woolmere Green Worcs
33 J11 Woolmer Green Herts
7 K2 Woolminstone Somset
34 F4 Woolpit Suffk
39 J3 Woolstaston Shrops
42 B4 Woolsthorpe Lincs
42 D5 Woolsthorpe-by-Colsterworth Lincs
9 M5 Woolston C Sotn
48 G9 Woolston Shrops
16 E8 Woolston Somset
17 P9 Woolston Somset
57 M10 Woolston Warrtn
29 N3 Woolstone Gloucs
32 C8 Woolstone M Keyn
19 K4 Woolstone Oxon
5 Q7 Woolston Green Devon
56 H10 Woolton Lpool
19 M8 Woolton Hill Hants
35 K8 Woolverstone Suffk
18 B9 Woolverton Somset
21 N7 Woolwich Gt Lon
38 G10 Woonton Herefs
45 N3 Wooton Shrops
45 K3 Wootten Green Suffk
32 E7 Wootton Bed
13 N2 Wootton Kent
61 J10 Wootton N Linc
31 Q3 Wootton Nhants
19 N1 Wootton Oxon
31 K9 Wootton Oxon
40 E10 Wootton Staffs
18 F4 Wootton Bassett Wilts
9 P8 Wootton Bridge IoW
16 C7 Wootton Courtenay Somset
7 K4 Wootton Fitzpaine Dorset
18 H8 Wootton Rivers Wilts
19 P9 Wootton St Lawrence Hants
30 F2 Wootton Wawen Warwks
30 Q10 Worcester Worcs
21 K9 Worcester Park Gt Lon
40 B9 Wordsley Dudley
39 N3 Worfield Shrops

70 G9 Workington Cumb
51 N5 Worksop Notts
60 H10 Worlaby N Linc
9 Q5 Worlds End Hants
11 L6 Worlds End W Susx
17 J4 Worle N Som
49 M4 Worleston Ches E
45 P11 Worlingham Suffk
15 N9 Worlington Devon
34 B3 Worlington Suffk
35 K3 Worlingworth Suffk
28 E3 Wormbridge Herefs
43 Q7 Wormegay Norfk
28 F3 Wormelow Tump Herefs
50 E6 Wormhill Derbys
34 F9 Wormingford Essex
31 N11 Worminghall Bucks
30 D6 Wormington Gloucs
93 M9 Wormit Fife
31 K4 Wormleighton Warwks
21 M3 Wormley Herts
10 F3 Wormley Surrey
22 G11 Wormshill Kent
38 H11 Wormsley Herefs
20 F11 Worplesdon Surrey
50 H3 Worrall Sheff
51 J1 Worsbrough Barns
59 J12 Worsbrough Bridge Barns
59 J12 Worsbrough Dale Barns
57 N8 Worsley Salfd
45 M5 Worstead Norfk
57 Q3 Worsthorne Lancs
5 M9 Worston Devon
57 P1 Worston Lancs
23 P11 Worth Kent
34 H2 Wortham Suffk
38 G2 Worthen Shrops
48 H6 Worthenbury Wrexhm
44 G6 Worthing Norfk
11 J9 Worthing W Susx
10 H8 Worthing Crematorium W Susx
41 K4 Worthington Leics
8 E11 Worth Matravers Dorset
50 H2 Wortley Barns
58 H7 Wortley Leeds
64 G9 Worton N York
18 E8 Worton Wilts
45 L12 Wortwell Norfk
29 K9 Wotton-under-Edge Gloucs
31 P10 Wotton Underwood Bucks
32 C8 Woughton on the Green M Keyn
22 E9 Wouldham Kent
35 K9 Wrabness Essex
15 J3 Wrafton Devon
52 G7 Wragby Lincs
59 K10 Wragby Wakefd
5 N8 Wrangaton Devon
53 L12 Wrangle Lincs
16 F11 Wrangway Somset
17 J10 Wrantage Somset
52 E2 Wrawby N Linc
17 L2 Wraxall N Som
17 N8 Wraxall Somset
63 L8 Wray Lancs
20 G8 Wraysbury W & M
63 L7 Wrayton Lancs
56 H3 Wrea Green Lancs
71 N6 Wreay Cumb
10 D2 Wrecclesham Surrey
73 M8 Wrekenton Gatesd
66 G9 Wrelton N York
49 L6 Wrenbury Ches E
35 J9 Wreningham Norfk
35 Q1 Wrentham Suffk
38 H2 Wrentnall Shrops
60 C7 Wressle E R Yk
52 D2 Wressle N Linc
33 J7 Wrestlingworth C Beds
44 B9 Wretton Norfk
48 G5 Wrexham Wrexhm
39 P7 Wribbenhall Worcs
49 N6 Wrinehill Staffs
17 L4 Wrington N Som
17 Q5 Writhlington BaNES
22 D3 Writtle Essex
49 L11 Wrockwardine Wrekin
60 C12 Wroot N Linc
58 F6 Wrose C Brad
22 C10 Wrotham Kent
18 G5 Wroughton Swindn
9 P10 Wroxall IoW
40 G12 Wroxall Warwks
39 K1 Wroxeter Shrops
45 L6 Wroxham Norfk
31 K6 Wroxton Oxon
50 F11 Wyaston Derbys
43 K3 Wyberton East Lincs
32 G5 Wyboston Bed
49 M5 Wybunbury Ches E
30 B2 Wychbold Worcs
40 F4 Wychnor Staffs
30 F9 Wyck Rissington Gloucs
65 K5 Wycliffe Dur
58 C6 Wycoller Lancs
58 C6 Wycomb Leics
20 E5 Wycombe Marsh Bucks
33 L9 Wyddial Herts
13 K1 Wye Kent
58 F8 Wyke C Brad
8 B3 Wyke Dorset
17 P8 Wyke Champflower Somset
67 L10 Wykeham N York
41 J10 Wyken Covtry
39 N3 Wyken Shrops
7 P7 Wyke Regis Dorset
48 H9 Wykey Shrops
73 K7 Wylam Nthumb
40 E8 Wylde Green Birm
18 E12 Wylye Wilts
41 N3 Wymeswold Leics
32 D4 Wymington Bed
42 C6 Wymondham Leics
45 J9 Wymondham Norfk
7 N4 Wynford Eagle Dorset
30 C5 Wyre Piddle Worcs
41 N3 Wysall Notts
40 E11 Wythall Worcs
31 L11 Wytham Oxon
57 P10 Wythenshawe Manch
33 J3 Wyton Cambs
61 K7 Wyton E R Yk
34 F3 Wyverstone Suffk
34 G4 Wyverstone Street Suffk